Occupied America

A History of Chicanos

Ninth Edition

Rodolfo F. Acuña
Emeritus California State University at Northridge

Portfolio Manager: *Manjula Anaskar*
Content Producer: *Sugandh Juneja*
Portfolio Manager Assistant: *Anna Austin*
Product Marketer: *Marianela Silvestri*
Art/Designer: *Pearson CSC*
Full-Service Vendor: *Pearson CSC*
Full-Service Project Manager: *Bhanuprakash Sherla, Pearson CSC*
Compositor: *Pearson CSC*
Printer/Binder: *LSC Communications, Inc.*
Cover Printer: *LSC Communications, Inc.*
Cover Design: *Lumina Datamatics, Inc.*
Cover Art: *Sergio Hernández*

Acknowledgments of third-party content appear on pages within the text.

Copyright © 2020, 2015, 2011 by Rodolfo F. Acuña, Inc. All Rights Reserved. Printed in the United States of America. This publication is protected by copyright, and permission should be obtained from the publisher prior to any prohibited reproduction, storage in a retrieval system, or transmission in any form or by any means, electronic, mechanical, photocopying, recording, or otherwise. For information regarding permissions, request forms and the appropriate contacts within the Pearson Education Global Rights & Permissions department, please visit www.pearsoned.com/permissions/.

PEARSON and ALWAYS LEARNING are exclusive trademarks owned by Pearson Education, Inc. or its affiliates, in the United States and/or other countries.

Unless otherwise indicated herein, any third-party trademarks that may appear in this work are the property of their respective owners and any references to third-party trademarks, logos, or other trade dress are for demonstrative or descriptive purposes only. Such references are not intended to imply any sponsorship, endorsement, authorization, or promotion of Pearson's products by the owners of such marks, or any relationship between the owner and Pearson Education, Inc. or its affiliates, authors, licensees, or distributors.

Cataloging-in-Publication Data is available on file at the Library of Congress.

Rental Edition
ISBN-10:   0-13-571956-9
ISBN-13: 978-0-13-571956-5

Instructor's Review Copy
ISBN-10:   0-13-521544-7
ISBN-13: 978-0-13-521544-9

Brief Contents

1 A Cradle of Civilization: Not Just Pyramids, Explorers, and Heroes 1

2 El Imperio Español 21

3 The Invasion of Mexico: Legacy of Hate 44

4 Occupied Texas: The Colonizers and their Myths 68

5 New Mexico: The American Occupation 90

6 Sonora Invaded: The Occupation of Arizona 112

7 California Lost: Image and Reality 130

8 Immigration, Labor, and Generational Change: White Lies 154

9 The 1920s: Making America Great 182

10 Mexican American Communities in the Making: The Tin Man Has No Heart 206

11 World War II: The Betrayal of Promises 240

12 "Happy Days": Mexican American Communities under Siege 267

13 Goodbye America: The Chicana/o in the 1960s 291

14 The 1970s: The Resurgence of White Nationalism 328

15 Blade Runner: Replicants are Illegal 353

16 The Millennium 380

17 The Decline of the American Empire 403

Contents

Preface ... xi

1 A Cradle of Civilization: Not Just Pyramids, Explorers, and Heroes ... 1

Europeans Did Not Discover Writing ... 1
The Cradles of Civilizations ... 2
    The Corn People: An Overview ... 2
    The Olmeca 1500 BCE–500 BCE ... 3
The Maya ... 4
    Maya Hieroglyphic Writing ... 4
    Maya Society ... 5
    The Decline of Maya Civilization ... 5
Teotihuacán ... 6
    Urbanism and Trade ... 6
    The Tolteca ... 7
Other Corn Civilizations ... 7
    The Tarasco ... 8
    The Azteca ... 8
    Los Norteños ... 10
Conclusion: The World System in 1519 ... 13
Notes ... 14

2 El Imperio Español ... 21

The Illusions ... 21
    Always Roman ... 22
    Africa Begins at the Pyrenees ... 22
The Spanish Conquest ... 23
    Faith versus Rationality ... 24
    The Spanish Invasion of the Mexica ... 24
Colonialism ... 24
    The Colonization of Indigenous Mesoamerica ... 25
    Smallpox and Other Plagues ... 25
    Race and Labor in Mesoamerica ... 25
Women in Colonial Mesoamerica ... 27
    The Changing Roles of Women ... 27
    The Assimilation of Native Women ... 28
Al Norte: God, Gold, Glory, Silver, and Slaves ... 29
    The Decimation Towards the Indigenous Population ... 29
The Changing Order ... 30
    The Bonanzas ... 30
    Forced Labor ... 31
The Northern Corridor ... 32
    The Decline of the Native Population ... 33
The Colonization of Texas ... 33
    El Paso del Norte ... 33
    The Tlaxcala and the Castas ... 34
    The Importance of San Antonio and Links to the Rio Bravo ... 34
The Occupation of Alta California: Paradise Lost ... 34
    Los Indigenas ... 35
    The Missions: Myth and Reality ... 35
Conclusion: On the Eve of the Mexican War of Independence ... 35
Notes ... 37

3 The Invasion of Mexico: Legacy of Hate ... 44

Who Started the War? ... 44
Mexican Independence from Spain ... 45
Background to the Invasion of Texas ... 45
    A Lie is a Lie! ... 46
    Follow the Money: The Land Companies and Trade ... 46
    The Re-annexation of Texas ... 47
    The Point of No Return ... 47
The Invasion of Texas ... 47
    The Pretext: Myths of the Alamo ... 48
    The Defense of the Mexican Homeland ... 48
    Texas Belonged to Native Americans ... 49
    The American Cabal was not Texan ... 50
The Invasion of Mexico ... 51
    The Manufactured War ... 51
    American Aggression ... 51
The Pretext for Conquest ... 52
    Playing Moses: God is on Our Side! ... 52
    History is Propaganda ... 52
    Blessed are the Peacemakers? ... 53
    The San Patricio Battalion ... 53
    War Crimes ... 54
    It Was Not Just a Man's War ... 54
    The War Mexico Did Not Want ... 55
The Treaty of Guadalupe Hidalgo ... 55
    The Controversy ... 55
    The Deception: A Lie is a Lie ... 56
    The Honorable Man ... 56
Conclusion: The Border Crossed Us ... 57
Notes ... 58

"...erica... Born and Bred of Empire":
...he Occupation of the Americas ... 65

4 Occupied Texas: The Colonizers and their Myths ... 68

Follow the Water ... 68
 Crossing the Northwest Texas Mexican Border ... 69
The Mexican Corridor ... 70
 Control of the Corridor ... 70
 Trade Wars and the Rise of Juan Cortina ... 71
 Enter "Cheno" Cortina ... 71
 The Civil War ... 72
The Transformation ... 73
 Hang 'em High! ... 73
 The Historian as an Agent of Social Control ... 74
 Controlling Mexicans ... 75
 Politics of Race and Gender ... 76
Resistance ... 76
 The People's Revolt ... 77
 The Ballad of Gregorio Cortez ... 77
Boss Rule ... 78
 The Railroad and the Advent of Industrial Capitalism ... 79
The Chickens Come Home to Roost ... 79
 Reform Politics and Mexicans ... 80
The Growth of the Mexican Population ... 80
 The Growth of Racist Nativism ... 80
 Mexican Resistance ... 81
Conclusion: The Marginalization of the Other ... 82
Notes ... 82

5 New Mexico: The American Occupation ... 90

On the Frontier ... 90
 The Santa Fé Trail: The Trojan Horse ... 91
 Gringo Go Home ... 92
The American Invasion ... 92
 The Myth of the Bloodless Conquest ... 92
 Inventing Whiteness ... 93
The Transition ... 94
 The Illusion of Inclusion ... 94
 Gringos and Ricos ... 95
 How New Mexico was Looted ... 95
 Corruption, Fraud, Intimidation ... 96
 The Legend of the Lincoln County War ... 97
Socialization ... 98
 The American Catholic Church ... 98
The New Mexican Diaspora ... 99
 "El Agua Es Vida" ... 99
 The Marketplace ... 99
 New Mexico in Colorado ... 100
The Resistance ... 100
 Barbed Wire, Irrigation, and the Railroad ... 100
 The Village People Defend their Land ... 101
 The American Dream ... 102
The End of the Frontier ... 102
 The Growth of Industrial Mining ... 102
 Changes in Society ... 103
 Federal Encroachment ... 103
 The Last Years of the Territory ... 103
Conclusion: Colonial Legacies ... 104
Notes ... 104

6 Sonora Invaded: The Occupation of Arizona ... 112

Forgotten People ... 112
 The American Occupation of Arizona ... 113
The Frontier ... 114
 The Gadsden Purchase ... 115
 War Hawks ... 115
 Filibustering Expeditions into Sonora ... 115
Mexicans in Early Arizona ... 116
The War of the Races ... 116
The Race Question ... 117
 Marrying Up! ... 117
 The Alliance of Elites ... 118
 The War on the Apache ... 118
 The So-called "Friendly Indian" ... 118
 The Land-Grant Grab ... 119
The Transformation of Arizona ... 119
 From Adobe to Copper ... 119
 Border Conflicts ... 120
The Pull Factors ... 120
The Industrialization of Arizona ... 120
 The Importance of Mining ... 120
 The Expansion of Capital ... 121
 The 1890s: Deskilling Mine Work ... 121
 The Impact of Industrialization on Mexicans ... 122
 Mutual-Aid Societies ... 122
 Middle-Class Mexicans ... 122
 Patriarchy ... 122
 The Emergence of Trade Unions ... 123
It's the Water ... 123
Conclusion: The Assault on the Saguara ... 124
Notes ... 124

7 California Lost: Image and Reality ... 130

Forgotten California ... 130
The Myth That Has Become Legend ... 130
 Mexican Period ... 131
 The Class and Racial Gap ... 132
 Women in the Transformation of California ... 133

The Bear Flag 133
   John C. Fremont and the Bear Flag 133
   U.S. Invasion of California 134
Gold Transforms California 134
   The Gold Rush Creates a Template 134
   Complicity of the Californios 135
   Legalized Theft: The Foreign Miners' Tax 135
Decline of the Californios 136
   The Locusts 136
   Taxation without Representation 136
   Marrying White 137
   Legalizing Racism 137
   Legitimization of Violence 137
   The Mexican Whore 138
   The American Delusion: The Lugos Trial 138
The Disillusionment 139
   El Clamor Público 139
   Class Divisions 140
Social Banditry 141
   I am Joaquin! 141
   The Social Bandit 142
Mexicans in a Changing Society 143
   Becoming a Minority 143
   Holy Mother the Church 144
   Labor 144
The Exclusion of the Other 144
   Colonias 144
Conclusion: Mexican Labor Builds California 145
Notes 146

8 Immigration, Labor, and Generational Change: White Lies 154

Time Marches On 154
Overview 157
   The Forging of America 157
   Ideas Cross Borders 158
   Justice Knows No Borders 159
   Mexican Women Precursors 159
   Industrial Bonanzas 160
   Workers Find Their Voice 160
   The Nurturing of Ideas 161
   "Mexicans Are Not Fit to Raise White Babies" 161
   The Mexican Diaspora 162
   Early Struggle to Control Working Conditions 162
   Separate is Not Equal 163
The Mexican Revolution 164
   Bullets Across the Border 164
   A Revolution on Horseback! 165
   The Revolution 165
   In Defense of the Community 166

A Changing Society 168
   Mexican Workers Under Siege 168
   The "Amazon" Protest: Story of Carmelita Torres ... 169
   The Hysteria: The Plan of San Diego 170
World War I: The Shift 170
   Shifts in Political Consciousness 170
   Mexican Responses to Industrial Transformation ... 171
   The Failure of American Brotherhood 171
The Westward Movement of King Cotton 172
Conclusion: The Color Line 172
Notes 173

9 The 1920s: Making America Great 182

Greasers Go Home 183
   Keeping America WASP 183
Americanization: A Study of Extremes 185
   Protestant Churches and Americanization of the Mexican 186
   Catholic Churches React to Americanization 186
   Nationalism versus Americanization 186
   Mexicans and Mexican Americans 187
The Influence of World War I on Becoming Mexican American 187
   The League of United Latin American Citizens 188
The Move to The Cities 189
   San Antonio's West Side 189
   Los Angeles: "Where Only the Weeds Grow" 190
   Mexicans in the Midwest and Points East 191
Mexican Labor in The 1920s 193
   Importance of the Sugar Beet Industry 193
   Mexicans in the Northwest 194
   Mexican Workers in Texas 194
   Mexican Workers in the Midwest 195
   The Growth of California Agribusiness 195
The Formation of Mexican Unions 195
   Change in Mexican Identity: The Mexican Revolution 196
Conclusion: Making America White Again 197
Notes 198

10 Mexican American Communities in the Making: The Tin Man Has No Heart 206

The Great Depression: *La Crisis* 207
   La Crisis 208
Life During The Great Depression 209
   The Importance of San Antonio 211
Nativist Deportations of The 1930s 211
   Repatriation Texas-Style 212
   The Fate of the Deportee in Mexico 212

Contents

Factories in The Fields	
Texas Farms	213
Reserve Labor Pool	213
Renting Mexicans	214
The Farmworkers' Revolt	214
The El Monte Strike	215
The Tagus Ranch	215
In Dubious Battle	215
The San Joaquín Valley Cotton Strike	216
The Imperial Valley, 1934	217
CUCOM and Mexican Strikes	218
The Congress of Industrial Organizations	218
Rural Workers in the Lone Star State	219
Colorado and the Manitos	219
The City	220
Mexican Women Garment Workers in Los Angeles	220
San Antonio Mexicana Workers	221
La Pasionaria, the Pecan Shellers' Strike, and San Antonio	221
Unionization in Los Angeles	222
Labor in the Midwest: Chicago	223
The Mexican American Miners' Revolt	224
The Mexican-Origin Community	225
The Angeleño Community	225
The Mexican American Movement	226
El Congreso de los Pueblos de Habla Español	226
Fighting Segregation	227
The Manitos	227
The Windy City: Chicago	228
Conclusion: An Embattled Community	228
Notes	229

11 World War II: The Betrayal of Promises — 240

Mexican Americans	241
World War II and the Mexican	241
Guy Gabaldón: Discrimination	242
The Story of Company E: The All-Mexican Unit	242
Racism at Home and Abroad	243
Chicanas in the Military	243
A Profile of Courage	243
Scapegoats	244
The Sleepy Lagoon Trial	245
Mutiny in the Streets of Los Angeles	246
Mexicanas Break Barriers	248
Rosita the Riveter	248
The Federal Employment Practices Commission	249
Cold War Politics of Control	250
The Communists Are Coming	251
Postwar Opportunities	251
Toward a Civil Rights Agenda	252
The American G.I. Forum	252
Controlling Mexicans	253
Farm Labor Militancy	254
Renting Mexicans	255
Conclusion: The Consequences of World War II	257
Notes	258

12 "Happy Days": Mexican American Communities under Siege — 267

Mexican Americans	268
The Cold War	269
The Korean War: Historical Amnesia	269
The Empire Strikes	270
Keeping America White	270
Militarization of the Immigration and Naturalization Service	272
The Diaspora: An American Odyssey	273
Education a National Mexican American Priority	275
New Mexico: The Illusion of Being Political Players	276
Los Angeles Politics	276
San Antonio	277
El Paso	278
Civil Rights	278
The "Salt of the Earth"	278
Toward Equality	279
California	280
National Spanish-Speaking Council	280
The Struggle to Preserve the *Barrios*	281
The FHA Mortgage Guarantee and the G.I. Bill	281
Urban Renewal: The Day of the Bulldozer	281
The Dodgers and Chávez Ravine	282
Urban Removal in the Midwest	283
The Sputnik Moment	283
Conclusion: A New Generation	283
Notes	284

13 Goodbye America: The Chicana/o in the 1960s — 291

The Early 1960s	292
In Denial: Proving Poverty	292
Harvest of Shame: The Forgotten People	293
Delusions of the Awakening of the Sleeping Giant	294
San Antonio and Texas Politics	294
Los Angeles Politics	295
Political Organizing in Chicago	295
The Building of a Civil Rights Coalition	296
Viva Johnson	296
Building the Great Society	296
The Albuquerque, New Mexico, Walkout	296
Bilingual Education	297
The Black–White Syndrome	297
A Second Coming	298

The Disillusion	298	The Media Sell Racist Nativism	339
Impact of the War on Poverty	298	Getting Away with Terror	339
Magnetization of the Border	299	In Defense of the Foreign Born	339
The Immigration Act of 1965	299	Chicanas/os For Sale	340
Mexican American Reaction to Nativism	300	A Redefinition of the Political Middle	340
The Road to Delano	300	Political Gains	340
La Casita Farms Corporation Strike of 1966 and the Aftershocks	301	Education: The Stairway to the American Dream	341
The Road to Brown Power	302	The Lack of Educational Equity	341
The Making of a Movement	304	The "Pochoization" of the Political Vocabulary	342
The Formation of Core Groups	304	The Myth of a Color-Blind Society	342
The East LA Walkout	305	Legacy Admits	343
Chicana/o Student Militancy Spreads	305	Why Progressive Organizations Fail	343
Brown Berets and White Angst	306	The Swagger Stick: The Unraveling of the Empire	343
Tlatelolco, Mexico	307	**Conclusion: The Final Year**	**344**
"Wild Tribes of . . . the Inner Mountains of Mexico"	307	**Notes**	**345**
Gringos and Tejanos	308		
No Place for Mexicans	309	**15 Blade Runner: Replicants are Illegal**	**353**
The Crusade for Justice	310	The Replicants in 1980	354
El Grito del Norte	310	The Decade of the Hispanic	355
Rubén Salazar: The Schools Failed Us	311	Immigrants Keep the Economy Going	356
Other Movement Voices	311	The Central American Wave	356
The Chicano Youth Movement Gains Steam	312	The Invasion of the Body Snatchers	357
Where Is God?	312	The Backlash	358
Gender and homophobia	313	*La Zorra Nunca Se Ve Su Cola* (The Fox Tail Never Sees His Own Tail)	359
Violence at Home	313		
Chicanas/os under Siege	314	Mexican American Labor	360
The Provocateurs	315	The Return of the Sleeping Giant:	360
Conclusion: The Chicana/o Legacy	**316**	Why Mexican Americans Fail to Organize	361
Notes	**317**	The New Breed	362
		Tear Off the Label	363
14 The 1970s: The Resurgence of White Nationalism	**328**	Sabotaging Labor	364
		Saint Ronald: The Seduction of the Political Game	365
The Baby Boomers Retire	328	Chicago	366
Distorting Racism	330	Back to the Milagro Beanfield War	367
Government Legitimizes Racism	330	Can You Smell the Refried Beans?	367
A Politics of Cynicism: Nixon's Hispanic Strategy	331	The Glass Ceiling	368
Dismantling the War on Poverty	331	Immigrant Women Workers	369
La Raza Unida Party	331	Regional Differences	369
The Last Days of *La Raza Unida*	332	Gold Fever: The Erasure of History	371
Inequality from Within: Never Letting Go	333	**Conclusion: The End Industrial Labor and Upward Mobility**	**372**
Chicana Voices	333	**Notes**	**373**
The Learning Curve	334		
The Birth of Chicana/o Studies	335	**16 The Millennium**	**380**
Sterilization: Saving Taxpayers' Money	336	The Chickens Come Home to Roost	381
The Road to Delano	336	The Erasure of Memory	381
The Farah Strike: The Breaking of Labor	337	Toward the Millennium	381
Sin Fronteras	337	The North American Free Trade Agreement	383
Nativism Is White	337	"Don't Mourn, Organize!"	384
Centro de Acción Social Autónoma–Hermandad General de Trabajadores	337	Haciendo Patria (Creating the Homeland)	384
		Making the Caravans Inevitable: Exporting Gangs	385
Criminalization of Mexicans	338	Racism is based on color: Police Brutality	386

Chicana/o Studies is a Pedagogy ... 386
The Mexican Bandito and the Mexican Whore ... 387
    Who Am I? The Fight for Identity ... 388
    Fight for the Truth ... 388
    The Renaissance in Chicana/Chicano Thought and Arts ... 389
Follow the Money ... 390
From the Heart of Texas: The Migrant Stream ... 392
War on Drugs ... 394
The Mexican Billionaires ... 395
    Mexicans Become a National Minority ... 396
Conclusion: The Problem of Becoming the Nation's Largest Minority ... 396
Notes ... 396

17 The Decline of the American Empire ... 403

The Empire is Broken ... 403
    Into the Twenty-first Century: No More Babies ... 404
    The Death of Democracy ... 404
    The Bankrupting of the Empire ... 404
    Census 2000 ... 405
    Political Roundup: 2000 ... 407
    The Death Penalty: A Symptom of Inequality or Racism ... 408
California Electoral Politics ... 410
    The Eyes of Texas Are Upon You ... 410
    The Sleeping Giant ... 411
    Mapping Mexican Americans ... 411
    The 2007 Immigration Bill ... 412
    The Presidential Election of 2004 ... 413
    The Big Apple ... 413
The Building of a Collective Historical Memory: Solidarity ... 414
    Democrats Never Learn: Presidential Elections 2008 ... 415
    The Crash of 2008 ... 415
    The Dreamers ... 416
    The Killing Fields: Words have consequences ... 417
    Communitarianism: Helping the family! ... 417
    Border Towns ... 417
    The Consequences of a Lack of a Firewall ... 418
    Squeezed out of the American Dream ... 418
    The Death of the Salesman ... 419
    A Changing Community ... 419
Education Under Attack: Fight Back ... 420
Keeping the Masses in Tow ... 421
Conclusion: Politics Begin At Home: The Rise of the Millennials ... 422
Notes ... 423

Epilogue: Peeling the Onion ... 433

Deny, Deny, Deny! ... 433
    The Disintegration of Civil Society ... 434
    Kill Zapata! ... 435
    The Aftermath of NAFTA ... 436
    Make America Great Again ... 437
Illusions and Delusions ... 438
Trump and the Last Days of the Empire ... 439
    The Blue Wave ... 439
Notes ... 440

Index ... 443

Preface

The first edition of *Occupied America* (1972) opened:

> Mexicans—Chicanos—in the United States today are an oppressed people. They are citizens, but their citizenship is second-class at best. They are exploited and manipulated by those with more power. And, sadly, many believe that the only way to get along in Anglo-America is to become "Americanized" themselves. Awareness of their history—of their contributions and struggles, of the fact that they were not the "treacherous enemy" that Anglo-American histories have said they were—can restore pride and a sense of heritage to a people who have been oppressed for so long. In short, awareness can help them to liberate themselves.[1]

The book immediately got caught up in controversy from those who claimed that I had made a mistake and should have called it *Occupied Mexico* since the land once belonged to Mexico. I responded that I was referring to the invasion of the continents that are America. Next some Chicanos objected to the internal colonial model insisting that, according to the Marxist paradigm, Chicanos were not internally colonized. I was surprised to find Chicano graduate students at the forefront of the criticism. Many of these detractors were at the time enamored with the theories of Immanuel Wallerstein's World Systems Analysis that emphasized globalization and colonialism.[2] I realized that the misunderstanding was epistemological. Most were Americanist that is they were sociologists and social scientists whose area of study was the United States. In Latin America, the internal colonial model had kicked around since the 1950s. Pablo Gonzalez Casanova and Andre Gunder Frank refer to Internal Colonialism as did other Third World intellectuals.[3]

It was not that I did not want engage in the debate, but anyone who knows me knows that teaching is my first love. I had been a public school teacher for seven years and a junior college teacher for three years. I had recently committed myself to starting the Chicano Studies Department at San Fernando Valley State and my teaching and activism prepared me to work on curriculum development. Realizing that the detractors were mostly Americanist, I chose to withdraw from the intellectual fray and concentrate on Chicana/o Studies that at the moment was more important and productive.[4]

With this edition I chose to return to the past and reintroduce the theme of colonialism from the vantage point of the colonized. In doing this I choose not to dwell on theory, rather to peel the onion a metaphor for the colonized person and his or her colonial mentality and search for the truth and unravel the myths, lies, and peel the onion that has formed us over 500 years of colonialism. This seems apropos with the demise of Europe's system of direct colonialism and the surge of who I choose to call the colonized. In doing so I touch on systematic inequality of Mexican Americans/Latinos in the policies and practices of American institutions and the lies history tells, and deal with subordination, not least of which includes cultural production and finance.

In engaging this theme I must pay tribute Franz Fanon. Fanon was a West Indian who received his doctorate in psychiatry in Paris. He went to Algeria and found that he could not practice because he did not understand the Algerian culture, he had to learn about the different layers of the onion to become a psychiatrist and a revolutionary.

In this cognitive dissonance theory, Fanon stresses attitude change and behaviors. In his book *Black Skin, White Masks*, Fanon wrote:

> Sometimes people hold a core belief that is very strong. When they are presented with evidence that works against that belief, the new evidence cannot be accepted. It would create a feeling that is extremely uncomfortable, called cognitive dissonance. And because it is so important to protect the core belief, they will rationalize, ignore and even deny anything that doesn't fit in with the core belief.[5]

Franz Fanon makes it clear that colonization is possible only with the complicity of members of the colonized. Fanon gives us a glimpse into the complexity of race.[6]

I return to the classroom and my life experiences for answers. My friend René Martínez, a former teacher in the Tucson Mexican American program, quotes an African proverb to his students: "Until the lions have their historians [storytellers], tales of the hunted will always glorify the hunter," adding that in the Mexican American program,[7] "We talk about how we come from the lion's perspective, from the story that's never told [and] which continues to be left out." An example is the story of the First Peoples of the Americas and the history of people other than those of Western European heritage. Hopefully this book will question the hunter and form a counternarrative that is closer to the truth

Occupied America is about the history of the Chicana/o or Mexican in the United States. Biases are difficult to root out—as in the case of propaganda films of World War II, the distortions are woven into the nation's historical memory and are kept alive by schools and the media. For instance, Pulitzer Prize-winning presidential biographer Jon Meacham is often a guest contributor on MSNBC; his presidential biography of Andrew Jackson, *American Lion*, won the 2009 Pulitzer Prize for biography or autobiography. From the Lion's perspective, Meacham's book celebrates Jackson and lacks a healthy skepticism that is essential in the search for the truth.[8]

Meacham, like most successful American historians, is popular; he smiles and adheres to the American paradigm and the canons of the American Historical Association and the Organization of American Historians.

In *That Noble Dream: The "Objectivity Question" and the American Historical Profession*, University of Chicago historian Peter Novick argues that "there is no such thing as 'truth in history'." Historical objectivity, according to Novick is "incoherent" and "dubious" and that "most historians generally write about their colleagues the way Arthur Schlesinger Jr., writes about the Kennedys." According to Novick, historians ignore the flaws such as "racism and ultra-patriotism" of their protagonists. Novick continues that professional, political, psychological, and cultural pressures control historians. These pressures determine their epistemological interpretation and their philosophical and professional biases.[9]

The social sciences exercise far-reaching powers over research. For many years based on the discovery of several pre-Clovis sites near Clovis, New Mexico in the 1920s and 1930s, archaeologists insisted that the Clovis people were the first humans to inhabit the hemisphere and laid the foundation for Indigenous arrivals about 13,500 years ago. The official story became that Ice Age hunters from Siberia crossed into North America. "Armed with stone weapons, called Clovis points, these hunters spread rapidly across the continent and feasted on animals" unknown before to humans.[10] The theory was almost immediately challenged; however, the Clovis hypothesis or myth persisted up until recently. Anyone challenging the model was professionally ostracized.[11] The Clovis-first paradigm was the dominant hypothesis from the early twentieth century until recently, when other antiquities forced archeologists to take another look. The preponderance of evidence is that humans arrived thousands of years before the accepted arrival date from Asia. The new school holds that other sites predated Clovis and it cast doubt on the accepted paradigm.[12]

For years archaeologists dismissed Native American social scientists accounts of the Indigenous Peoples. The great Native American historian Jack Forbes took a broadside at European perspective in his book titled *The American Discovery of Europe*.[13]

Forbes wrote:

> Most PEOPLE have probably never heard of the idea that ancient Americans might have traveled to other parts of the globe, so strong is the fixation with the "newness" of America. "Mainstream" archaeology in the twentieth century exhibited hostility toward any ideas that suggest a remote antiquity for humans in the Americas, or to the idea that Americans might have "spilled over" into Siberia and other parts of Eurasia.[14]

Forbes did not raise the question to get tangled in controversy, but to show the probabilities of the footsteps pointing the other way and how the Eurocentric bias in history limits possibilities of 100 million people being discovered.

What Is New in This Edition?

The simple proposition of the book is that a lie is a lie. This is the ninth edition and most probably my last edition of *Occupied America*. At 86 I have a strong sense of my own mortality. So this book is about language, the truth, and an effort to be more precise than in previous editions. A lie is a lie. The urgency brought about by the election of Donald Trump to the presidency and his attack on the truth and the popularization of propaganda news "alternative facts" have made it more difficult to find the truth. As will be discussed, a distortion of history is more American than apple pie, although the distortion of the truth is common among nations. The change was obvious since the end of World War II when the United States became a global power and its imperial pretensions expanded. Notions of grandeur and a distortion of the truth propped up claims of moral authority. The Eisenhower Doctrine (1950s) accelerated interventions throughout the globe and put the Monroe Doctrine on steroids.

These events and those that followed put us on the road to the election of Trump and the world of doublespeak. *Gore v. Bush* (2000) accelerated the decline of democracy and brought on Middle Eastern Wars and the great recession in 2008. They heightened the irrational and unrelenting racist nativism and came after 40 years of the decline of the American Empire. Many Americans did not understand or resented this loss in moral authority as well as were incapable of dealing with an of control inferiority complex.

By the twenty-first century many Americans came to realize that the United States got whipped by the tiny nation of Vietnam as it had by North Korea. The wars bankrupted America and the nation's infrastructure was sadly neglected. Public sector jobs declined, real wages fell and no longer could fathers sustain the family as women were *forced* to work to survive. Economist and Secretary of Labor under Bill Clinton (1993 to 1997) Robert Reich singled out for women working outside the home it was not a matter of choice, it covered up the wage gap.[15] Finally, by the twenty-first century, it was no longer possible for lower-middle-class Americans to afford to buy a home. The educational crisis of the early 1990s shut out higher education as the stairway to the middle class—it cost too much. On a positive note, the decade produced the Dream Act movement that was built on the pro–foreign-born of the Chicana/o generation. By their fathers' standards Americans were losers; this realization hit white males particularly hard. The natural outcome was scapegoating non-whites.

In the 1980s I met a young lady who had just gotten out of a mental sanatorium. A racist but loving white family had adopted her. When she grew up, they told her that she was adopted and was Mexican. She said she could cope with being Mexican, but could not cope with not being white. Today empires throughout the world are coping with the reality of not being great, not being benevolent and indeed, being exploiters. My generation of Americans grew up with the illusion that everyone loved Americans.[16] It was a lie.

The first of the Trump Years drove home the importance of being blunt and not hiding behind language. Distorted news and national biases must be challenged. A lie is a lie. Although I am no longer religious I acknowledge the importance of my early education. I recognize the importance of epistemology (the theory of knowledge) that places an emphasis on methods, validity, and scope of the question and investigates what distinguishes belief from opinion. The study of Latin and the figuring out syllogisms taught me the art of negation.

A note of caution: The book will abstain from using the term *Indian* or *Indio* unless quoting a source or within the context of an event. In the United States and Mexico, the word *Indio/Indian* has been used pejoratively. It is a product of Spanish conquest and colonialism and was constructed as a lie. Indio/Indian often means that the person is dumb or slow. In the United States, it accompanies names such as "Indian giver" or "Redskin." The First People and their descendants will be referred to as Indigenous Peoples, which is what they are.

In discussing identity, it must be remembered that America is not the name of a single nation. But for better or for worse, it is the name of two continents. More than a 100,000 people lived here and they had no say in what it was called. It was named after Amerigo Vespucci—an Italian Florentine explorer, financier, navigator, and cartographer who in 1502 drew a map of Brazil and the West Indies that showed that the colonizers were not in Asia. Columbus mistakenly called the people Indians because he thought he had reached India, so it was with the reasoning that Vespucci "discovered America." (In honor of Amerigo the name of two continents became America.)[17]

I use various terms to refer to Mexican Americans. I continue to use the term Chicana/o because that is what I call myself, but I try to limit it to a particular generation and time in history. The U.S. Census uses the terms Latinas/os or Hispanics as do most studies. As a historian I am of the opinion that this leads to a fake identity. It includes everyone from Latin America, Spain, Italy, and France.

Occupied America chooses to spell Mexican American without a hyphen. If written with a hyphen, the word Mexican becomes an adjective. The experiences of Mexican Americans within the United States make the word Mexican American a noun. A hyphen should not qualify their identity. The nationality of Mexican Americans hangs around their necks and should remind them that they are a colonized people. Mexico is part of their American national identity. Mexico is not an insignificant part of our future. As we keep repeating, it is the 10th largest nation in the world. In the United States, the Mexican American population larger than Canada and most American states. Mexico is among the top 10 global leaders in engineering and computer science graduates.[18]

The failure to communicate has produced what Stuart Chase called "The Tyranny of Words." Mexican Americans and other Latinos use the tag Hispanic. However, this term is in error. It refers to people from Spain, of a Spanish nationality. They were the people who invaded Mexico and began imposing what Stuart Chase calls a caste system *The Tyranny of Words*. The truth is that people from Spain are Hispanics, and people from Mexico are Mexicans.

The term Latino refers to anyone whose language derives from Latin—it includes Spaniards, Portuguese, French, Latin Americans, Romanians, and Italians. The name dates to the 1860s when Napoleon III of France coined the term "Latin America." Napoleon wanted to make his puppet Maximilian Emperor of Mexico. Napoleon pushed the notion of a cultural affinity between France and Latin America. In using the ethnic identification of Hispanic and Latino they may have good intentions, but they weaken the individual national identity of each Spanish-speaking group. A people without an identity are a people without a history. Mexicans, Guatemalans, Salvadorans, and others have histories.[19] Latinas/os are of different nationalities like Asian Americans. They are not one nationality and the lack of specificity leads to a distortion of history. For example, Argentinians were not at the Alamo but some people would substitute Hispanics for Mexicans rewriting history. The word Latino comes from "Latin America." It referred to a cultural kinship with France. Supporters of the term Latino argue that times have changed and national identities as we once knew them are outdated and that the term Latino is more inclusive. Others prefer Hispanic that has similar etymological problems. Hispanic refers to Spanish people. It refers to their language and culture. Hispanic is popular among professional and national organizations. In my day, to say you were Spanish was like denying that you were Mexican. It has gotten to the point that I have heard some people say that they were eating Hispanic Food. My reaction is what is wrong with the "M-word"? This challenge is getting more involved as Mexican American youth refuse to be European and are searching for an Indigenous identity.

There are 33 different nationalities in Latin America where the Spanish, Italians, and Portuguese do not use Latino—it would offend the social order. They differentiate Spaniards from Mexicans. However, in the United States we lump everyone together as if we all belonged to a single nationality. This makes it difficult to ferret out Mexican data from the Census and other reports. I try to adjust and use the terms Mexican American, Mexican/Latino, and U.S. Mexican. I feel it is important to know and respect the identity of Salvadorans, Guatemalans, Puerto Ricans, and others. It helps unravel the lie. Making them generic Latinos/Hispanics will hurt them. A lie is a lie.

Acknowledgments

I dedicate this book to my wife Guadalupe Compeán. It is because of her that I have lived this long, not only physically but intellectually. I have always had a tendency to escape into a shell; Lupe forces me to engage. I owe her an intellectual debt. Also to my daughter Angela who is always correcting my 1950s language expressions, my sons Walter and Frank, and my grandsons and granddaughters. Thanks to my family, colleagues, students, community, and those who struggle for justice and care. As you get older you think a lot about the past. I remember my father and his stories. He was a reserved man, but one story stands out. When he first came to the United States in the early 1920s he did not know a word of English and for six months the only thing he ate was ham and eggs. My father was a tailor and I remember him telling me that it was easier to make a suit from scratch than make alterations. I remembered my father's advice working through the nine editions.

Lastly, to my mother who went blind at the age of five. She never went to school and taught herself to read using a gigantic magnifying glass. When I was child, boys never did the dishes or housework. However, because of my mother's health, I washed dishes and scrubbed floors. It was an important lesson in life. My parents were immigrants who added layers to my onion and while many of the layers were positive, many of the layers had to be peeled away.

It would be remiss if I did not thank Sergio Hernández for his beautiful rendition of the Saguaro Cactus found in the Arizona and Sonoran Deserts. The giant saguaro is the symbol of resistance to Spanish and American Colonialism. Some stand 40-60 ft high. For thousands of years, people have the saguaro lived in harmony with the First People such as the Hohokam resisted Spanish and American Occupations; i.e., conquistadores, homesteaders and ranchers. Thank you Sergio.

Notes

1. Rodolfo F, Acuña, *Occupied America: The Chicano's Struggle Toward Liberation* (San Francisco: Canfield Press, 1972).
2. Immanuel Wallerstein, *The Modern World-System: Capitalist Agriculture and the Origins of the European World-Economy in the Sixteenth Century* (New York: Academic Press, 1974).
3. Pablo Gonzalez Casanova, *Sociedad plural, Colonialismo Interno y desarrollo* (UNESCO,1963). Paulo Henrique Martins, "Internal Colonialism, Postcolonial Criticism and Social Theory," *Journal du MAUSS*, http://www.journaldumauss.net/?Internal-Colonialism-Postcolonial-Criticism-and-Social-Theory.
4. Rodolfo F. Acuña, *The Making of Chicana/o Studies: In the Trenches of Academe* (New Brunswick: Rutgers University Press, 2011).
5. "Franz Fanon: "The Psychopathology of Colonization," *Internationalist 360°*, https://libya360.wordpress.com/2017/01/16/franz-fanon-the-psychopathology-of-colonization/.
6. Rodolfo F. Acuña, "The Illusive Race Question & Class: A Bacteria That Constantly Mutates," Julian Samora Center, Occasional Paper No. 59, November 2005, https://jsri.msu.edu/upload/occasional-papers/oc59.pdf.
7. "African Proverb of the Month," African Proverbs, Sayings and Stories, April, 2006, http://www.afriprov.org/african-proverb-of-the-month/32-2006proverbs/224-april-2006-proverb-quntil-the-lion-has-his-or-her-own-storyteller-the-hunter-will-always-have-the-best-part-of-the-storyq-ewe-mina-benin-ghana-and-togo-.html.
8. Jon Meacham, *American Lion: Andrew Jackson in the White House* (New York: Random House, 2009).
9. Peter Novick, *That Noble Dream: The "Objectivity Question" and the American Historical Profession* (Cambridge: Cambridge University Press, 1988), 149. Rodolfo F. Acuña, *Sometimes There is no other Side* (Notre Dame: University of Notre Dame Press, 1998).
10. "Young Americans," *Nature*, 485, 6, May 2, 2012, http://www.nature.com/nature/journal/v485/n7396/full/485006b.html?foxtrotcallback=true.
11. Heather Pringle, "What Happens When an Archaeologist Challenges Mainstream Scientific Thinking?" *Hakai Magazine*, March 8, 2017, http://www.smithsonianmag.com/science-nature/jacques-cinq-mars-bluefish-caves-scientific-progress-180962410/.
12. Alexander Ewen, "Humans Populated Americas 130,000 Years Ago? Mastodon Findings Spark Controversy," *Indian Country Today*, April 27, 2017, https://indiancountrymedianetwork.com/history/events/humans-populated-americas-130000-years-ago-mastodon-findings-controversy/. Stefan Lovgren, "Who Were The First Americans?" *National Geographic News*, September 3, 2003, http://news.nationalgeographic.com/news/2003/09/0903_030903_bajaskull.html.
13. Jack D. Forbes, *The American Discovery of Europe* (University of Illinois Press, 2011).

14 Forbes, Ibid., p. 80.
15 Robert Reich, "Inequality for All," Moyers & Company, Nov. 20, 2013, https://www.youtub.com/watch?v=O_LkMWP2Q2A.
16 Traveling through Europe in the post–World War II era, many Americans were shocked to know that Europeans did not love them. After all they had liberated them, they thought, from the Germans. Instead of trying to find the truth as to why, they would say that it was because Europeans were jealous.
17 Jessie Szalay, "Amerigo Vespucci: Facts, Biography & Naming of America," *LiveScience*, September 20, 2017, https://www.livescience.com/42510-ameri-go-vespucci.html.
18 Jared Wade, "Mexico Is a World Leader in Engineering and Computer Science Grads," *MexicoIt*, June 3, 2016. http://www.mexico-it.net/mexico-become-world-leader-engineering-computer-science-graduates/.
19 "Carta a Napoleón III sobre la influencia francesa en América," *El Clamor Público*, Los Ángeles, sábado 19 de marzo de 1859, http://www.filosofia.org/hem/185/1859c19.htm. Why did Napoleon III coin the term "Latin America?" English Language & Usage, https://english.stackexchange.com/questions/16003/why-did-napoleon-iii-coin-the-term-latin-america. Jessie Szalay, "Amerigo Vespucci: Facts, Biography & Naming of America," *LiveScience*, September 20, 2017, https://www.livescience.com/42510-ameri-go-vespucci.html.

Chapter 1
A Cradle of Civilization: Not Just Pyramids, Explorers, and Heroes

 ## Learning Objectives

1.1 Describe Mesoamerican civilization/s at the end of the Formative period.

1.2 Outline the history and development of Maya civilization.

1.3 Explain how Teotihuacán and the Tolteca influenced Mesoamerica and each other.

1.4 Describe the importance of corn in the development of civilizations of Mesoamerica and North America.

When I was preparing my classes, I previewed several documentaries on the Maya writing system. "Cracking The Maya Code" was of particular interest;[1] it was a fascinating account of how archaeologists learned to decipher ancient Maya script. The documentary, however, neglected to show how the ability to read glyphs was lost in the first place: The Spaniards burned or destroyed hundreds, if not thousands of Maya books because they believed they were works of the devil. The recovery of this knowledge required years, and thousands of hours spent deciphering the script. For me the obvious question was: Why were Maya speakers not used to interpret the Maya language until the last phases? The narrative became a saga of white people hundreds of years later saving the day instead of addressing the fact that it was Europeans—in this case, Spaniards—who destroyed a culture and vast amounts of knowledge.

The contributions of Indigenous Peoples have been purposely minimized and until recently, many scholars, for instance, erroneously said that Náhuatl books were based entirely on oral traditions denying that the Náhuatl People had a written language. Their writing was pictographic and ideographic with a significant number of logograms and syllabic signs. Náhuatl was the language of Azteca/Mexica and the Tolteca from the Central Highlands of Mexico.[2] Their books were considered sacred, and were written on cloth "on which diviners cast maize grains or beans to perform a divination."[3]

Europeans Did Not Discover Writing

A common cultural trait of Mesoamerican groups is writing. Indigenous writing systems existed centuries before the European colonization. The Olmeca, Maya, and Zapoteca/Mixteca in present-day Oaxaca developed writing systems.[4] Hundreds of years of neglect led to an incredible loss of knowledge about the Mesoamerican People. The Zapoteca, for example, developed a 365-day solar calendar (called yza) and a 260-day sacred calendar (called piye). Unlike Mixteca and Azteca scripts, Zapoteca writing was much more textual, possibly capable of representing sentences. "When the Spanish conquistadores arrived in Oaxaca in the 16th century CE, the Zapoteca script was long forgotten, although the Zapoteca language continues to be spoken to this date."[5]

The primary culture of Mexico and the Americas remains Indigenous. Many western scholars sleight the histories of the Indigenous Peoples. Mesoamerican and Andean civilizations did not need Europeans to give them civilization; they are two of the world's six cradles rivaling those in China, the Indus Valley, Mesopotamia, and the Nile River. The Mesoamerican and Andean civilizations share with them similar features and importance.[6]

The Cradles of Civilizations

1.1 Describe Mesoamerican civilization/s at the end of the Formative period.

The popular story is that most humans clustered in hunting and food gathering societies until about 12,000 years ago. Worldwide, people followed a similar pattern and began settling in sedentary farming communities around 8000 BCE. These communities formed laws based on mores and folkways. Slowly, six cradles of civilization formed independently in China, the Indus Valley, Mesopotamia, the Nile, the Andean region of South America, and Mesoamerica.[7] Food surpluses made possible specialization of labor and the development of complex social institutions such as organized religion and education. Trade and a writing system facilitated the cross fertilization of cultures.

The Time Line organizes the evolution of knowledge accumulated by Mesoamericans into time periods and shows the stages of human development.

| 40000 BCE | 8000 BCE | 2000 BCE | CE 200 | CE 900 | CE 1519 |

Stages of Evolution		
40000 BCE–8000 BCE	Paleoindian	*Hunting and gathering.* Characterized by bands of hunters and by seed and fruit gatherers.
8000 BCE–2000 BCE	Archaic	*Incipient agriculture.* Domestication of maize and other plants. Earliest corn grown in Tehuacán circa 5000 BCE.
2000 BCE–CE 200	Formative Preclassic	Intensification of farming and growth of villages. Olmeca chiefdom stands out. Reliance on maize and the spread of a religious tradition that focuses on the earth and fertility. Organizational evolution, 1200–400 BCE: numerous chiefdoms evolve through Mesoamerica. The Maya appear during this period. Monte Albán is established circa 400 BCE–CE 200. Rapid population growth, a market system, and agricultural intensification occur. Development of solar calendar. Villages grow into centers.
CE 200–900	Classic	*The Golden Age of Mesoamerica.* The evolution of state-level societies. The emergence of kings. Priests become more important. Complex irrigation, population growth, and highly stratified society. Excellent ceramics, sculpture, and murals. Building of huge pyramids. Teotihuacán had more than 150,000 people, making it the largest city outside China.
CE 900–1519	Postclassic	*Growth of City-states and Confederations.* Civil, market, and commercial elements become more important. The Azteca and Tarascan confederations emerge as dominant powers. Cyclical conquests. Use of metals, increased trade, and warfare.

SOURCES: Robert M. Carmack, Janine Gasco, and Gary H. Gossen, *The Legacy of Mesoamerica: History and Culture of a Native American Civilization* (Upper Saddle River, NJ: Prentice Hall, 1996), 48–49; also see Michael C. Meyer, William L. Sherman, and Susan M. Deeds, *The Course of Mexican History*, 6th ed. (New York: Oxford Press, 1998), 4.

The Corn People: An Overview

It is not precisely known when the first modern humans migrated to the Americas. Evidence exists that humans were present in the Americas long before 13,500 years ago. For instance, archaeologists discovered 14,550-year-old stone tools and butchered mastodon bones in Florida—1,000 years earlier than previously thought possible.[8] Currently, scientists believe that the migration to the Americas began about 20,000–30,000 years ago. According to some accounts, humans reached the New World by 15000 BCE. The probability further exists that people might have migrated back to Asia from the Americas, with the last migrations ceasing when the Bering Strait's ice bridge melted around 9000 BCE. According to linguists, the languages spoken in North America and Siberia are related,[9] but some linguists raise the notion that language spread from south to north instead of from north to south.[10]

Linguistic evidence has been uncovered during the past 25 years that points to a much earlier colonization than previously theorized. Linguists say that the sheer number of distinct language families in the Americas leads to this conclusion. They suggest a much broader diversity than does the archaeological evidence. "[T]he linguistic evidence consistently yields rates of diversification and spread that clearly imply a much greater age for the American population than the genetic, archaeological, and paleo climatological evidence suggests."[11] Direct migration was mostly to high-latitude coastal areas.[12]

According to archaeologist Robert J. Sharer, the earliest known villages in the Americas appeared along the coasts as early as 12,500 years ago.[13] But it was not until around 7000 BCE that the hunters and fruit gatherers began to farm: to alter and control their environment. In the Valley of Mexico, the climate changed, and water sources, game, and flora became scarcer. As the population grew, the people were forced to turn to agriculture or perish. The cultivation of maize (corn) made the evolution of the Valley possible. The origin probably occurred in the central Valley of Mexico as early as 9,000 years ago. Corn was the primary dietary staple throughout Mesoamerica, and then spread northward and southward.[14] Maize, beans, and squash formed the basis of their diet.

Maize unified Native American cultures. Recent studies show that people traveled with the seed to various places in the Americas. Archaeologists discovered the remains of the largest human settlement in the American Southwest dating from 760 BCE to 200 BCE; it included evidence of maize farming.[15] The widespread nature of the maize culture supports the theory that Mesoamerican farmers brought corn into the Southwest. Corn spread a way of life that extended from the present-day Southwest along what is now U.S. Highway 10 into the eastern half of the United States, eventually becoming a staple throughout much of North America.[16] The symbolic significance of maize and its role is evident in ceremony and ritual throughout Mesoamerica and the Southwest. Maize was found in modern-day Peru as early as CE 450. *Science Daily* reports that "[some] of the oldest known corncobs, husks, stalks and tassels, dating from 6,700 to 3,000 years ago were found at Paredones and Huaca Prieta, two mound sites on Peru's arid northern coast."[17]

The European invasion endangered the corn cultures to the point of extinction. This threat continues today in places like the remote mountains of Oaxaca, Mexico, where traces of genetically modified organisms (GMOs) have compromised the native corn. Mexico banned commercial planting of transgenic corn in 1998. However, it imports about 6.2 million tons of corn a year, mostly from the United States. About a quarter of the U.S. commercial corn crop contains GMOs, and after harvest it is mixed with conventional corn. Mexican corn contains low levels of GMOs. This concerns Mexicans since GMO foods and seed are an environmental threat to wild plants and species such as the monarch butterfly.[18]

The Olmeca 1500 BCE–500 BCE

Around 3000 BCE, a qualitative change took place in the life of the corn people. Agriculture surpluses and the concentration of population encouraged specialization of labor. Shamans became more important in society. Tools became more sophisticated and pottery more crafted. History shows the development of Agricultural civilization occurring at about the same time as in North Africa and Asia, where the "cradle of civilization" is traditionally believed to have been located. A dependence on maize agriculture and a growing population began to form Mesoamerican identity.[19]

Because the Olmeca civilization was so advanced, some people speculate that the Olmeca suddenly arrived from Africa—or even from outer space! Most scholars, however, agree that Olmeca, known as the mother culture of Mexico, was the product of the cross-fertilization of indigenous cultures.[20] The Olmeca built the first kingdoms establishing the worldview and political symbolism that were inherited by the Maya.[21]

The Olmeca culture was one of the world's first tropical lowland civilizations, an antecedent to Maya "Classic" culture. They created villages and cities in the Gulf Coast lowlands in present-day southeastern Veracruz and Tabasco and in northern Central America.

By 2000 BCE, the production of maize and other domesticated crops was sufficient to support whole villages. A second breakthrough occurred with the introduction of pottery throughout the region. The earliest pottery came from the Oco, who lived on the Pacific coast of Chiapas and Guatemala. Although not much is known about the Oco, their pottery is found from Veracruz to El Salvador and Honduras. The development of pottery allowed the storage of food surpluses, encouraging the Olmeca and other Mesoamericans to form small villages. Little evidence of social ranking and craft specialization exists in the early villages, which evolved from an egalitarian community into a hierarchical agrarian society of toolmakers, potters, and sculptors. As they evolved, the Olmeca became more patriarchal.

The Olmeca began to build villages on the Gulf Coast as early as 1500 BCE. By 1150 BCE they formed settlements of thousands of people, constructed large formal temples built on earthen mounds, and carved colossal nine-feet-high stone heads. An example of the splendor of the Olmeca was San Lorenzo, an urban center with public buildings, a drainage system, and a ball court.

La Venta (population 18,000), a major ceremonial site in Tabasco, eclipsed San Lorenzo (population 2,500) as the center of the Olmeca civilization in about 900 BCE.[22] Tres Zapotes (population 3,000) would eventually overtake La Venta. By the Middle Formative period, other chiefdoms emerged throughout Mesoamerica. Trade networks linked the Olmeca to contemporaries in Oaxaca and Central Mexico. In the Valley of Oaxaca, San José Mogote functioned as a primary center, as did Chalcatzingo in the present-day state of Morelos. Priestly elite dominated the primary Olmeca settlements. As time marched on, the shaman class played an ever-increasing role in the lives of the people. From these centers, they ruled dispersed populations of farmers, who periodically assembled at the ceremonial and trade sites to meet labor obligations, attend ceremonies, and patronize the marketplace. The elites had greater access to valuable trade goods and occupied larger homes than the common people. The elites were buried in larger tombs.

The Olmeca left behind archaeological evidence of their hieroglyphic script and the foundations for the complex Mayan and Zapotecan calendars. They developed three calendars: a ritual calendar with a 260-day cycle that was used for religious purposes; a solar calendar with 18 months of 20 days, plus 5 days tacked on (corresponding to our 365-day calendar); and a combination of the two calendars in which religious days determined tasks such as the naming of a newborn infant.[23]

The development of the calendar required an advanced knowledge of mathematics. There is considerable difference of opinion about whether the Olmeca or the Maya discovered the concept of the number *zero* circa 200 BCE. (The Hindus discovered the zero in the fifth century CE, and not until CE 1202 did Arab mathematicians export the concept to Europe.[24]) Before the time of Christ, the Olmeca used a more accurate calendar than the West today. Pre-Columbian astronomy, too, was far ahead of Europe's. The writing system of the Olmeca is still being deciphered. These hieroglyphic texts represent more than a history; they also constitute literature.[25] Other Olmeca legacies are the ball game and the feathered-serpent cult of Quetzalcóatl that they shared with most Mesoamerican cultures.[26]

Increased agricultural surpluses and trade gave the Olmeca the luxury of developing advanced art forms. Although they are best known for the massive carved full-rounded heads, they also crafted smaller figurines of polished jade. Religion and the natural world inspired the subject matter for Olmeca art.

The Olmeca culture also passed its organizational forms, religion, and art to the Maya, Teotihuacán, and later Azteca societies. About 300 BCE, Olmeca civilization mysteriously vanished. In truth, it continued to exist from 150 BCE to CE 450, in what scholars call the Epi-Olmeca period.[27]

The Maya

1.2 Outline the history and development of Maya civilization.

Mayan agricultural villages appeared about 1800 BCE. The Maya formed a trade network that interacted with other chiefdoms in the Gulf Coast, Oaxaca, and Central Mexico. Merchants from Teotihuacán lived in Maya centers such as Tikal at least from the first century CE.[28] They constructed raised fields, dug irrigation canals, and reclaimed wetlands. As their population increased, they built larger ceremonial centers. As in the case of other Mesoamerican societies, rulers took control of religious rituals and the belief system.

From CE 250 to 900, the Maya lived in an area roughly half the size of Texas (today the Mexican states of Yucatán, Campeche, Quintana Roo, parts of Chiapas, Tabasco, Guatemala, Belize, western Honduras, and El Salvador). The divine *ahauob*, the "divine lord," ruled millions of farmers, craftsmen, merchants, warriors, and nobles and presided over capitals studded with pyramids, temples, palaces, and vast open plazas serviced by urban populations numbering in the tens of thousands.[29] The Maya built temple-pyramids, monuments, and palaces of limestone masonry in dozens of states. Their calendars continued at the center of time science.[30]

In the ninth century CE, the Maya Classic culture sharply declined, probably due to revolts, warfare, disease, and/or crop failure. Overpopulation partially explains the internal strife as well as growing dissatisfaction with their leadership. Meanwhile, scholars look for answers. In a limestone cavern in northern Guatemala, through narrow tunnels frequented 12 centuries ago, there are black carbon images of a sacred ball game, musicians, dwarfs contemplating shells, homosexual lovers locked in embrace, and columns of intricately entwined hieroglyphs, showing an extremely complex society.

The decipherment of the glyphs raises questions. For example, little doubt exists about the presence of homosexuality; the question is how society formed attitudes toward homosexuality.[31] Research in this area is just beginning and, like past literature on the subject, it comes from highly biased sources. Richard Trexler argues that Spaniards would often feminize their enemies in warfare, calling them sodomites and pederasts. Trexler says that European notions formed much of what we know about homosexuality. In the case of the invasion and subjugation of the Mesoamericans, the Spaniards' homophobia suggested to them their own moral supremacy. Sodomy "was seen as either a sign of insufficient civilization or a sign of moral decay."[32]

Maya Hieroglyphic Writing

The decoding of hieroglyphic writing is leading to a greater understanding of the Maya culture, including the identification of dynasties of rulers and an understanding of how the various people interacted.[33] DNA evidence from bones of the ancient Maya suggests that the common people seldom lived beyond the age of 40: Many died in infancy and early childhood. Men and women in the ruling class were physically larger—as much as four inches taller. Furthermore, the evidence shows that the ruling class sometimes lived remarkably long lives. One of the greatest rulers of the ancient city of Yaxchilán, Shield Jaguar, lived almost 100 years.

Maya glyphs show that the ball game played throughout Mesoamerica was a means of communicating with the gods. It was a substitute for war.[34] Revered by both the Maya and the Azteca, the game had deep religious significance. It was played by small groups in an outdoor stone court; the objective was to pass a large rubber ball through a stone ring at opposite ends of the court.[35]

The Maya based their numerical system of counting on the fingers and toes; for example, in Quiché, a branch of Maya culture, the word for the number 20 symbolized "a whole person." This method of counting also reflects decimal divisions. The Maya used a system based on the number 20, with only three symbols: a bar for *five*, a dot for *one*, and a stylized shell for *zero*. As we have discussed, the Maya, if not the Olmeca, were probably the first people to develop the mathematical concept of zero.[36]

The astronomy of the Maya was not limited to observation of the stars and approximate predictions of the movements of the heavenly bodies. Using sophisticated numerical systems and various tabular calculations in conjunction with the hieroglyphic script, Maya astronomers calculated figures running into millions.[37]

At the time of the Spanish conquest, the Maya still wrote in glyphs—not only on stone slate but in handmade books. In 1566 in the Yucatán, Friar Diego de Landa read a great number of Maya books. According to him, because the books were about the indigenous antiquities and sciences, which he believed were based on superstitions and falsehoods of the devil, he burned them. However, not all of the Maya books were burned; some were sent to Europe as part of the booty Cortés seized from the Native Americans. The Spaniards could not decipher them, and over the years, most crumbled into dust or were thrown out as trash. In summary, most Maya codices, or books, were destroyed. Much of what we know about the Maya is speculation—the conquerors burned the Mayans' documents.

Maya Society

Like other Mesoamerican societies, the Maya lived within the matrix of the community. "Both nuclear and extended families were found among the Maya."[38] Couples would generally marry in their late teens or early twenties. The Maya organized into extended families.[39] "The Maya governance had several powerful leaders who performed the task of maintaining harmony and order. There was a proper hierarchical structure followed throughout the kingdom."[40] This structure evolved over thousands of years.

The inheritor of supreme authority was established through primogeniture, which resulted in the rule by clan elders. Kings based their legitimacy on their membership in a clan. The kings erected monuments to commemorate their victories and to record their lineage.[41]

During the Late Classic period, Tikal, a kingdom of around 500,000 people, was the largest known Maya center. It covered about 14 square miles and included more than 3,000 structures. It made alliances with other city-states but also often used force to expand their territory.[42]

The glyphs on a prominent Tikal building reveal the names of notable women such as Bird Claw, Jaguar Seat, Twelve Macaw, and the Woman of Tikal.[43] These women, although buried in honored places, were present only through a relationship with an important male. The differences between males and females changed with time. Scholars suggest that there was more equality before CE 25 than after. As in most advanced civilizations, class differences existed, and over time, one's position in society became hereditary. There was a distinct divide between high-ranking members of Tikal society and the poor that widened over time.

The glyphs reveal few actual Maya woman rulers. During the sixth and seventh centuries, two woman monarchs, Lady Kanal-Ikal and Lady Zac-Kuk, ruled in Palenque. Both were the descendants of kings and thus legitimate rulers. They inherited the throne and passed it to their children. Lady Zac-Kuk was the granddaughter of Lady Kanal-Ikal and was the mother of the Great Pacal, who built grand buildings as testimony to his mother's greatness. Indeed, Pacal inherited his legitimacy through Lady Kanal-Ikal's line of ancestry. She lived for 25 years into his reign. Pacal died in his nineties.[44]

Shifts occurred in the role of Maya women that were affected by warfare and exposure to other societies. Increasingly, they participated in rituals connecting the supernatural world and politics. History is the study of documents, but because colonizers destroyed Indigenous documents, the truth cannot be firmly established. Much of what we know is theory.

The Decline of Maya Civilization

After CE 909, the Maya built fewer new temples, and fewer cities, except in the northern Yucatán, at sites such as Chichén Itzá and Tulum. Governed by priests, Chichén Itzá was founded about CE 400. The architecture suggests a religious dominance and there are many representations of the god Chaac, the Maya rain god, on the buildings. With the arrival of the Itzá from Central Mexico about CE 850, the city was rebuilt and images of the god Kukulcán, the plumed serpent, became numerous. The Itzá were politically and commercially aggressive rulers.[45] Chichén Itzá, the dominant Maya center in the Yucatán Peninsula during the early Postclassic period, was closely linked to the Tula people in the north, and was influenced by that culture. The importance of the center declined after the late twelfth century, when a rival Maya group sacked it. Tulum and other coastal cities were important centers for sea-based commerce.[46]

Glyphs may someday partially answer questions about the Maya, who built their civilization in a hostile and fragile rain forest. It stands to reason that the most intricate details were transcribed in the Mayan books that the Spaniards destroyed. These documents could have answered questions such as, how did six million Maya coexist in this difficult environment? What we know is that for a time, these civilizations met the challenge, and they developed an advanced knowledge of astronomy and mathematics that allowed them to increase production of food and other necessities. They constructed a mosaic of sunken gardens, fruit trees, and terraces—a system that used rainfall and fertile soil, and shaped the jungle to their advantage without permanently harming it. Maya farmers dug canals and built raised fields in the swamps for intensive agriculture.[47] Until recently, archaeologists assumed the Maya used a slash-and-burn method where farmers cut and burned the jungle-planted crops for a few years and then moved on when nutrients were depleted.[48] A true slash-and-burn method would have supported only about 65 people per square mile. By CE 600, the Maya population density reached about 125 people per square mile.

After hundreds of years of relative prosperity and power, the urban infrastructure of many Maya cities broke down. The drop in the food supply increased the gap between the lower and the elite classes and between city-states. Today, Mesoamerican scholars generally agree that no single factor caused this fall. But by the Late Classic period, populations suffered from malnutrition and other chronic diseases. The environment simply could not sustain the large population indefinitely.[49]

Growing social gaps and war played roles in the decline. These factors, however, cannot be compared to the Spanish colonial class domination that included racial subjugation. In the Maya world, the common person labored in the fields, maintaining a complex agricultural network, while priests resided in empty ceremonial centers. The nobles plainly exploited the commoner—the warrior, temple builder, and farmer. The Maya organized construction crews of *corvee*, or unpaid labor, and over time the growth of this system magnified class hostilities. In addition, there was a sharp decrease in rainfall between CE 800 and 1000—one of the most severe climate changes in 10,000 years—at roughly the same time as the Maya decline in the ninth century. The drought aggravated tensions: The result was that cities, villages, and fields were burned and wars increased.[50] The absence of documents prevents specificity.

Although the cities of the Maya lowlands shared a common culture, they lacked political unity. Each region had a capital city and numerous smaller subject cities, towns, and villages. Furthermore, increased trade and competition led to warfare. The Maya civilization, however, endured for more than 1,000 years. In the Postclassic period, the Maya experienced a gradual breakdown of its social structures, marked by a decline of the priest class and the growing political and cultural influences of a rising merchant class.[51]

Until recently, scholars portrayed Maya society as peaceful. They reached this conclusion based on glyphs. However, archaeologists have recently developed another view of the Maya, based on glyphs showing the practice of human sacrifice and bloodletting.[52] The current interpretation is that the Maya believed that the gods controlled the natural elements, and that the gods demanded bloodletting.[53] Allegedly, human sacrifice was limited to prisoners, slaves, and orphaned or illegitimate children purchased for the occasion.

Generally, it was more common to sacrifice animals. This bloodletting and human sacrifice placated the gods and assured the Maya that their crops would grow and their children would be born healthy. As drought and a drop in the food supply took their toll, there was a corresponding increase in human sacrifice to appease the gods and to assure success in warfare. An analogy can be made between human sacrifice and war and the Christian Bible.

Teotihuacán

1.3 Explain how Teotihuacán and the Tolteca influenced Mesoamerica and each other.

Teotihuacán (400 BCE–CE 700), the "city of the gods," was an ancient commercial and religious center in the central Valley of Mexico. It was located in the Valley of Teotihuacán in a pocket-like extension of the Valley of Mexico, becoming the primary center of Mesoamerican civilization around 200 BCE. By the end of the Formative Preclassic period, it concentrated sufficient authority and technology to make quantitative and qualitative leaps in progress and power, and it accumulated influence throughout the region.[54] The civic–religious complex laid the foundation for the development. At its height, at the end of the sixth century CE, Teotihuacán covered about eight square miles and housed more than 150,000 inhabitants, making it the largest city in the world outside China.[55]

In the Early Classic period, the people of Teotihuacán lived in apartment compounds. There were more than 2,000 separate residential structures within the city. Commerce linked outlying villages to the core city. As with peasants in other societies, these workers contributed labor, food, and other products for urban elites and state institutions. A strong central government gave control to the elites over peasants in the city and countryside. The ruling elite forcibly moved the rural peasants into the city during the Early Classic period. A highly centralized state conquered a territory that covered most of the central Mexican highlands.

Urbanism and Trade

Teotihuacán was a major manufacturing center in the Early Classic period. The products of its craft workers spread over much of Mesoamerica, as far south as Honduras. The pottery represented Teotihuacán's highest present day achievement. Its hallmark featured a cylindrical vessel with three slab legs and a cover. Vessels shaped like modern flower vases and cream pitchers graced the city. Artifacts from other civilizations also added to the city's splendor. Teotihuacán was so revered that Azteca royalty annually made pilgrimages to the city.[56]

Teotihuacán was the hub of trade networks from Central America to today's southwestern United States.

It grew to a population of 100,000–200,000. Without trade, Mesoamerica would have remained at the chiefdom stage, instead of evolving into a sophisticated world system that stressed material production and common ideas.

Teotihuacán suffered from internal civil strife in the seventh century, and again at the beginning of the tenth century. In about CE 600–650, unknown invaders burned the civic ceremonial center of the city, marking a turning point in its history. From Teotihuacán sprang a network of societies, such as the city of Xochicalco, later associated with the Tolteca people. Teotihuacán was also a center of long-distance trade that maintained robust mercantile contact with other regions.[57] Even after its decline, Teotihuacán was a great city of 30,000 inhabitants until about CE 950. Without its dominance, Mesoamerican societies were less centralized, breaking into dozens of city-states, which competed for trade and influence.

The Tolteca

The secularization of Mesoamerica characterized the Postclassic period. Religion remained important but the roles of the civil and commercial sectors increased, leading to the expansion of market systems and long-distance exchanges. A Toltec Domain emerged in what is today Central Mexico in about the tenth century CE.[58]

The Tolteca were a dominant force during the period from about CE 900 to 1150. A subgroup of the Chichimeca, a Nahua-speaking people from the northern desert, the Tolteca controlled the Valley of Mexico.[59] Their capital was Tula (Tollan), about 40 miles north of present-day Mexico City. Founded in the ninth century, Tula incorporated part of the heritage of Teotihuacán, although it is generally associated with Tolteca culture. Tolteca refugees migrated to Teotihuacán after its fall in CE 700, adopting many of its cultural features. Topiltzin Ce Acatl Quetzalcóatl (Our Prince One-Reed Feathered Serpent) ruled Tula from CE 923 to 947. Ce Acatl is often confused with the Azteca deity Quetzalcóatl, the feathered serpent who for 1,000 years was part of Mesoamerican mythology.

The Tolteca developed a set of cosmological concepts, practiced religious rites including human sacrifice, and built grand temples to their gods. In the courtyards of Tula, supporting the roof of the great Temple of Quetzalcóatl, stood 15-foot columns in the form of stylized human figures, that is, enormous statues of warriors standing stiffly under the weight of their weapons and wearing rigid crowns of eagle feathers. Processions or military marches, and eagles and jaguars devouring human hearts are portrayed. The Plumed Serpent, formerly interpreted in Teotihuacán as the benevolent divinity of agricultural plenty, in Tula became a god of the Morning Star, the archer-god with fearsome arrows.

Tula was not at the crossroads of the international trade networks. In the mid-1100s, the Tolteca collapsed, perhaps under attack by nomadic tribes, and Tula was abandoned. By that time the Tolteca extended their sphere of influence into what is now Central America. This culture was transposed to Yucatán, where it was superimposed on Maya tradition, evolving and becoming more flexible and elegant. A hybrid art form of dazzling brilliance developed and lasted for two centuries. The Tolteca influence can be seen in a cross-cultural fusion of deities depicted in Mayan glyphs, frescos, and designs.

Tula was the axis of the Tolteca civilization. It controlled most of Central Mexico, the Yucatán Peninsula, and the Gulf Coast, and it is speculated that its interests extended to Chiapas and the Pacific coast. The Tolteca expanded trade with people as far away as Zacatecas, Veracruz, and Puebla; New Mexico and Arizona; and Costa Rica and Guatemala. They aggressively assimilated with the peoples that they had ties with, often appropriating their customs. For instance, by the end of the ninth and the beginning of the tenth century, the Mayan culture was in decline. The Itzá began to substitute their gods and architectural styles. The Tolteca built the Observatory, Kukulcán's Pyramid, the Temple of the Warriors, the Ball Court, and the Group of the Thousand Columns. The architecture and artifacts became representative of cross-fertilization between the two cultural areas.[60]

Other Corn Civilizations

1.4 Describe the importance of corn in the development of civilizations of Mesoamerica and North America.

The Zapoteca were the original occupants of the Valley of Oaxaca. About 4,000 years ago, Oaxaca's people settled in agricultural villages. Interaction with common ancestors played an important role in integrating autonomous villages. Between 500 BCE and 100 BCE, a highly centralized, urbanized state emerged, with Monte Albán as the principal center.[61] Great plazas, pyramids, a ball court, and underground passageways graced the city. The Zapoteca and the Olmeca engaged in long-distance trading that dates to the time of San Lorenzo. The Zapoteca later enjoyed good relations with the city of Teotihuacán.

Zapoteca society was religious; it held that a supreme being created everything, although not alone, and there was no beginning and no end of the universe. Like other Mesoamerican societies, the Zapoteca wrote in hieroglyphics and were obsessed with astronomical observation. Their 365- and 260-day calendars set a rhythm for their lives, with the latter serving as a religious guide and marking the birthdays of its adherents.

The Zapoteca script was the earliest known writing system in Mesoamerica that used a logo-syllabic system (the use of a single symbol for an entire word). These written symbols were the building blocks of words. It was developed around 600 BCE. Over time, however, it eroded. The importance of the writing system is that it is an archaeological record of the genesis of inequalities and marks the evolution of a society. In most cases the conquistadores wiped out written evidence in Mesoamerica preventing a full appreciation of this civilization.

"The Mexican state of Oaxaca was the heartland of one of the oldest and most enduring Mesoamerican polities."[62] Between 300 BCE and CE 700, the ancient Zapoteca state flourished. Zapoteca script spread and other groups appropriated it. It flourished for about 1,500 years, declining after the collapse of Monte Albán but eventually became the "Mixteca-Puebla" (CE 1250–1550)[63].

After CE 650, Monte Albán declined and other strong city-states emerged in the valley. Mitla, in the eastern part of the Oaxaca valley took on greater importance.[64] Mitla is the best-known Postclassical site, continuously occupied since the Early Formative period, and is thought to have been a Zapoteca religious center. Despite the growth of other societies, the Zapoteca remained a major player in the region.

Meanwhile, in the highlands, the Mixteca increased their influence, and by the eleventh century they interacted with the Zapoteca-speaking people of the valley. There was a high degree of assimilation and intermarriage between the Mixteca and the Zapoteca nobility. The Mixteca are known to have engaged in a highly ritualized form of warfare and they were known for military prowess. Despite their influence, the Mixteca, like the Zapoteca before them, were not a dominant power. They established the kingdom of Tututepec on the coast, which was important enough to extract tribute from other kingdoms. By forging strong bonds with other city-states through intermarriage and war, the Mixteca expanded their power.[65]

The Mixteca developed their own unique art style. However, they were influenced by the Zapoteca, and the two cultures created a synthesis. The creations of their goldsmiths and their manuscript illuminations are exceptional. Mixteca books or codices constitute an illustrated encyclopedia, reflecting religious beliefs and rites and the history of the aboriginal dynasties and national heroes. The style and color range of the illustrations, as well as the symbols linked to the ritual calendar, are also found in their murals.[66] The history depicted in the codices is a sacred history, showing an abundance of deities and rituals. The Mixteca also excelled in ceramics, which became highly prized ware in fourteenth- and fifteenth-century Mexico.

The Tarasco

By the twelfth century, the Tarasco people, also known as the Purépecha, ruled a vast territory in West Mexico, centered in present-day Michoacán. Where they came from is unknown. They were probably part of the Chichimeca migration. The Chichimeca were part of nomadic groups from the northern frontier that migrated to what is today Central Mexico. The Tarasco were considered uncivilized by the older tribes. The Azteca along with the Tarasco were part of Nahua migration. The Tarasco civilization was formed the political unification of some eight city-states located within the Párzcuaro basin.[67] The Tarasco occupied the region for more than 1,600 years (150 BCE–CE 1530). Their development resembled that of other Mesoamerican cultures. Ceramic artifacts link the Tarasco to the old traditions of Chupicuaro (present-day Guanajuato). Their pottery and metalwork styles are unique, although they borrowed heavily from surrounding societies. This borrowing was common. For example, ceramics found in the present-day northern Mexican states of Zacatecas and Durango bear resemblance to the Hohokam ceramic found in what is today Arizona.

The capital city of the Tarasco Tzintzuntzán was built on the shores of Lake Pátzuaro and dominated by a huge platform that supported five round temples. The Tarasco raised a well-trained army and from Tzintzuntzán forged a powerful realm. However, Tarasco military prowess did not tell the whole story. Their language and culture dominated the region, with many of the surrounding villages assimilating into it. They were excellent craftspeople, and they invaded other people for honey, cotton, feathers, copal, and deposits of salt, gold, and copper. Tarasco lords were placed in conquered lands and collected tributes in goods.

Unlike other Mesoamericans, the Tarasco were not known as renowned traders. Nevertheless, historians speculate that they engaged in long-distance trading by sea, reaching South America. Tarasco society was socially stratified between nobility, commoners, and slaves. The capital city dominated the area, although most people lived in rural settlements.

The Tarasco worshipped many deities who, among other things, were associated with animals and calendrical days. Ceremonial dances affirmed their connection with ancestral gods. Enemies of the Aztecs, the Tarasco flourished from CE 1100 to 1530. The Azteca attempted to conquer the Tarasco but failed. In CE 1478, 24,000 Azteca retreated in the face of a Tarasco army of 40,000 warriors. But because the Tarasco did not leave a written language, scholars know relatively little about them.[68]

The Azteca

The Azteca or Mexica were Náhuatl speakers. Náhuatl belongs to the Uto-Aztecan family spoken from Oregon to Panama. It is not related to most Mesoamerican languages. The Azteca belonged to diverse polities and ethnic groups. They were not a single ethnic group; they were comprised of many ethnicities that shared a like culture and shared history.

The Azteca[69] arrived from a legendary place in the north called Aztlán.[70] (Some Chicanos say that it was in what is today the southwest United States; others, in northern Mexico, in the area of Zacatecas.) A network of trade routes linked the high plateau of Central Mexico with Maya territories, reaching as far as the most remote northern districts of the realm, in what is now the southwestern United States.[71] The Azteca prospered between CE 1345 and 1521 and dominated most of northern Mesoamerica. They had a tribute system in which craftspeople could share their ware. From this was born the tributary system. At first tribute system was layered with commoners paying tribute to nobles. This system expanded after the formation of the Triple Alliance that is often referred to as the Azteca Empire. It was an alliance of three Nahua altepetl city-states of Tenochtitlán, Texcoco, and Tlacopan.[72]

Between CE 1325 and 1345, the Azteca established Tenochtitlán on an island in Lake Texcoco. The Azteca built a confederation of city-states that had more than 350,000 people. The leader of the Triple Alliance was Tenochtitlán known for its military prowess. The Azteca ruler directly controlled the Alliance although local governments remained in place. A Tributary Economic System developed where client states paid tribute to the Alliance. Although members of the Alliance shared in the tribute, the political and military power rested with the Azteca nobility and state. It reached from the Pacific to the Gulf of Mexico, from Central Mexico all the way to Guatemala, El Salvador, and Honduras. The Mexica were not culturally homogeneous, but consisted of 17 ethnic groups. Scholars have mislabeled this confederation the Azteca Empire.[73]

Rarely is the colonization process in relation to the provinces discussed or that the tributaries retained their ethnic identities. Today the notion empires are discussed in the context of a Euro centric world view thus empires are based on the concept of imperium generally references Rome. For example, sociologist George Steinmetz research on empires focuses on mechanisms such as capitalism. In most studies of an Azteca Empire the "institutional dimensions" are thin. Most models are based on European experiences. I maintain that most scholars are more infatuated with the word "empire" than its particularities.[74]

The Azteca farm surpluses underwrote the "craft-manufacturing economy". The Azteca supplied food to large cities. The growth of market systems gave the Azteca more opportunities to exchange their goods as well as providing a means to trade and accumulate tribute as well as the opportunity to spread their culture. The society was stratified, with the elites extracting tribute and the commoners paying it. Life was better in the city that the periphery. In Teotihuacán they lived in small adobe houses with stone roofs and had more access to material goods.

The Azteca benefited from their highly productive agricultural infrastructure. They farmed on raised fields, or *chinampas*, fashioned by piling earth over the natural growing surface, as a way of reclaiming swampland for cultivation.[75] They stacked flat mounds of fertile river sediment and then deepened the ditches or canals around them to create a waffle-like pattern. The advantage of raised fields was that they could be cultivated year-round, even during the dry season, because swamp water percolated up into the nutrient-rich soil. Five hundred acres of fields could have fed up to 5,200 people.[76]

The Azteca assimilated the cultural experiences of generations of native peoples. Mixteca art played an important role in Azteca artistic skill development. Azteca sculpture displayed technical perfection and powerful symbolism. The Azteca knew and appreciated the masterpieces of the civilizations that preceded them and those of contemporaries such as in Monte Albán. They developed a well-defined literature, some of which has been preserved through oral testimony. Much of this tradition was conserved in codices, which consist of a combination of pictographs and ideographs. Religious and cosmological themes dominate the codices. The Azteca did not neglect the socialization of its people. They had two kinds of schools—one for commoners, the other for nobility. In both, boys and girls were taught rhetoric, history, ritual dancing, and singing; in the Calmecac School for future leaders, the curriculum included law, architecture, arithmetic, astronomy, and agriculture. Their poets were frequently kings or military captains from satellite principalities.[77]

Although a lot is known about the work performed by women, relatively little is known about cultural attitudes toward them. Some scholars assume that Azteca society was rigidly patriarchal, and that it became increasingly so with the militarization of society. Another viewpoint is that the "prehispanic Azteca gender system appears to have combined gender parallelism (where men and women played different but parallel and equivalent roles) with gender hierarchy. Gender parallelism was rooted in the kinship structures and in religious and secular ideology. Men and women were genealogically and structurally equivalent."[78]

The lower classes, as in most societies, bore the burden of class oppression. Lower-class women did embroidering, which they often sold in the *mercado* (marketplace). Generally, a woman's caste, as in contemporary society, determined her occupation and she was schooled to play that role. Women could enter the priesthood, and although there were female goddesses, women could not become the musicians or poets who honored goddesses in public. Furthermore, they could not engage in violent activities or participate directly in mercantile caravans. Women had few options, and circumstances sometimes forced them into prostitution. The woman who worked outside the sphere of male control was suspect. According to Irene Silverblatt, "class and social standing critically shaped the social experiences of Mexica men and women."[79]

Anthropologist June Nash's "The Aztecs and the Ideology of Male Dominance"[80] describes the transformation of the Azteca society from a kinship-based society to a class-structured empire, claiming that there was a diminution of the power of women beginning in CE 830 and continuing to the fifteenth century CE. Despite this, women enjoyed equal rights under the law and could participate in the economy. According to Nash, women were active producers as well as vendors. They could hold property—but whether they did and how much depended on social class.

The Azteca were the beneficiary of Tolteca culture, and many Azteca males took Tolteca wives, which quickened the assimilation process. According to Nash, polygamy "weakened the role of women in royal families" this was because their sons were not guaranteed succession to the throne. By the late fifteenth century a division of labor based on gender was well established. The codices show men teaching boys to fish, cultivate, and work metal and women teaching girls to weave, tend babies, and cook. According to Nash, sacrificial ceremonies glorified the cult of male dominance.[81]

While Azteca society may have ignored forms of male homosexuality, lesbians were disdained as lower than prostitutes. Contradictorily, there were male transvestite performers who are said to have been bisexual, and they enjoyed access to both male and female. In short, Azteca culture appears to be highly puritanical, militaristic, and male-centered. Among men, power came with age, which brought privileges.

As with other Mesoamerican civilizations, human sacrifice and war were apparently interwoven into Azteca religious practice. The Azteca justification for human sacrifice was a cosmic view that encompassed the demands of their god Huitzilopochtli, lord of the sun and god of war.[82] The Azteca placed their faith in their priests, who revealed that the sun and the earth had been destroyed four times; the present era was known as *el quinto sol*, "the fifth sun" the final destruction of which was imminent. Only special intervention through Huitzilopochtli would save them. [It is similar to the Christian idea that the world will end during a millennial and Christ will rise to save them.][83] The coming of the fifth sun is predicted in the Aztec Calendar Stone.

The religious system legitimized the authority and the tributary rights of its leaders. Blood sacrifice was necessary to preserve the Sun, and the whole structure of the universe, from the threat of cosmic destruction. The logic was that the sacrifices appeased the Sun; it was based on the cyclical belief that the sun provided food and the sacrifices fed the sun. The need for sacrifices was made even more important after the drought of CE 1450 ravaged Central Mexico with many believing that the calamities of 1450 were because too few victims had been offered to the gods.[84] The Azteca rationalized war, which was the result of politics and trade, in much the same way as Christians, Jews, and Muslims rationalize their holy wars.

Every aspect of Azteca life, from the birth of a young warrior to a woman's continuous sweeping of dust from the house, symbolized the intricacy of war as well as their advanced society. Azteca society was well ordered and highly moralistic, treating commoners with "consideration, compassion, and mercy,"[85] while also demanding from them moral conformity. Medical treatment was on a par with Europe's, and life was less harsh than it was in Europe at the time of the arrival of the Spaniards.

Náhuatl writing was primarily written on perishable materials such as deerskin and paper. Like other books and documents, they were burned because, according to the conquistadores, they were works of the devil. Surviving documents in Náhuatl were written after the Conquest. The writing was in the form of pictographs. The codex painters were educated in the calmecacs. While mostly for nobles, some commoner children were trained as scribes. "After the Spanish conquest, codex painters worked with the priests, recording the details of Aztec life. These codices are the richest source of information we have about the Aztecs."[86]

Los Norteños

North America was not sparsely populated. There were an estimated four to six million Indigenous Americans in what is today the United States in 1492, which is probably a dramatic undercount.[87] The numbers and the evolution of these people must be put in context and must not be compared to Mesoamerica or any other people. For example, in 1500 Spain had a population of six to ten million; Portugal had about a million people.[88] Moreover, historians like to compare Mesoamerican and other civilizations. They get so involved with the architecture and neglect the story of the Southwest and the rest of the Indigenous Americans, forgetting that they were in totally different environments. In North America over thousands of years, the Indigenous People through trial and error became among the world's great botanists and environmentalists, learning to conserve water, and recognizing the properties of the Southwest's plants. Buildings alone do not define greatness.

In the Southwest cacti are not all alike—some could be eaten, some contained water, while others had medicinal properties. Some bore fruit. What white people considered weeds the Indigenous People ate, such as the Verdolagas (purslane), a vitamin powerhouse that white Americans are just discovering.[89] It grows in many Southwest backyards in the summer. It spreads like a weed after a downpour of rain. Verdolagas are high in Vitamin C. The Yaqui, or Yoeme, of present-day Sonora and the Tohono O'odham (Papago) of the Sonoran Desert dealt with the great aridity and extreme heat by selecting native flora such tepari beans that require little water to cook.[90]

The distribution of maize (corn) into the Southwest from Mesoamerica in probability began about 4,000 years ago. Maize adapted to the climatic and cultural environment of the Southwest with a drought tolerance.[91]

The choice of a trail to reach a water source and selected plants involve economy. Choices had to be made which paths were the safest, best and most direct; the trails were used for transportation. They were not exclusively used by the young, but entire families used them. Since prehistoric times, Native American families chose the best ways to get from one point to the next before they had beasts of burden; the entire family blazed the trail, carrying their household goods with them. So the choices they made were very important. The planners made sure there was water, so they followed the paths of the animals to creeks, arroyos, and rivers. They selected the paths that were the easiest to walk. They crossed rivers at the shallowest point.[92]

Thousands of years before the arrival of the Spaniards, trade thrived between what is today the Native Americans of Mexico and North America. There were no borders, there were no walls. The very first trailblazers of the Southwest were animals. The Native Americans followed the paths of the animals to find water and then made paths of their own. They mapped North America. Long before Columbus, the Native Americans traveled over trading paths or trails that crisscrossed the Southwest and what is today the United States.

> Merchants and itinerant traders linked Paquime (Casas Grandes, Chihuahua) to what archaeologist J. Charles Kelley has called the "Aztatlan Mercantile System," a vast network of trade routes and markets, which extended from the Valley of Mexico up through northern and western Mexico into the southwestern United States.[93]

When other people arrived the natives not only had knowledge of what plants were safe to eat but which were nutritious and medicinal.

The Anasazi, Mogollon, and Hohokam began farming corn in abundance as early as 2000 BCE. Corn fueled the rise of Mesoamerica and northern people. Mexico's north had varied societies, most of which lacked sufficient water to sustain large populations. Nevertheless, the Southwest, outside of Mesoamerica and northern Mexico, have a continuous history of habitation and contact. The Indigenous Populations of the Southwest shared an agricultural tradition with Mesoamericans revolving around corn and the use of ceramics. Unlike Mesoamerica, most of the Southwest with the exception of the Pueblos are believed to have lacked state-level societies and urban centers.

People arrived in what is now the Southwest between 23000 BCE and 10000 BCE.[94] (They probably got here a hundred thousand years ago, but American archaeologists quibble that they were not *Homo sapiens* but Neanderthals, which they consider a lower classification.) About 4,000 years ago, maize (corn) was first introduced into the southwestern United States from Mexico through highland corridors along the Sierra Madre Mountains. As agriculture spread some built villages similar to what is present-day northern Mexico. Many formed homes in villages or *rancherías* or remained hunters. Agriculture transformed the lives of the people and by 500 BCE, corn, squash, and beans were grown and pottery was crafted. The widespread cultivation of corn is estimated to have occurred from 1100 BCE to 500 BCE.[95] The progress of agriculture varied throughout the Southwest and the rest of what is the United States reaching advanced levels in what is Arizona and New Mexico today. This led to complex social and economic systems among the northern peoples—the Hohokam, the Mogollon, and the Anasazi. *Ranchería* populations comprised of Opata and Pima Altos lived in northern Sonora/Arizona.

Carlos Vélez-Ibañez writes, "A triad of complex agriculturally based societies that included the Hohokam of Southern Arizona and Sonora, perhaps the Mogollon of Casas Grandes, Chihuahua, Mexico, and to a lesser extent the Anasazi of Chaco Canyon and Mesa Verde who inhabited the Four Corners area of New Mexico, Arizona, Utah, and Colorado, lived in the region."[96] One of the most successful civilizations was the Hohokam, who began their transformation about 300 BCE, although, as with the Mesoamerican civilizations, the process began hundreds of years before this date. According to anthropologist Vélez-Ibáñez, the Hohokam were probably migrants from Mesoamerica.[97] For nearly 1,700 years, they flourished along the Desert Rivers before vanishing in the fifteenth century CE.[98]

During the Formative period, the Hohokam lived mainly in flask-shaped huts set in shallow pits, plastered with mud over a framework of poles and woven twigs. Early villages were loose clusters of houses separated by stretches of packed clay.[99] After about CE 1000, Hohokam villages took on a more urban aspect. Each contained several "great houses," typically three or four stories high, and numerous smaller dwellings similar to the early pit houses. One city stretched for a mile and included at least 25 compounds of buildings. A vast irrigation network consisting of more than a thousand miles of canals crisscrossed an area of some 10,000 square miles.[100]

Archaeologists estimate that at least 100,000 and possibly a million people lived in these ancient cities. They subsisted on the barren desert, making the desert productive through irrigation and by breeding a variety of drought-tolerant corn that would grow from planting to harvest on a single watering. In addition, they cultivated squash, beans, tobacco, and cotton. Acid-etched shells suggest that the Hohokam traded with tribes a thousand miles to the east.[101]

By 1450, Hohokam civilization vanished. Legend has it that raiders from the east swept down on the Hohokam, destroying homes and fields. The invaders killed or enslaved the inhabitants of the great cities. Some Hohokam escaped, but upon returning they never rebuilt the cities or canals. Some archaeological authorities believe the demise of the Hohokam came after a gradual transition. They theorized that the Hohokam never left, but abandoned most of their villages in the Salt and Gila River Valleys, around CE 1450. The theory is that Hohokam society collapsed because of internal conflicts brought about by environmental pressures and they taxed the land's capacity to feed the people. The floods during fourteenth late 14th century probably damaged the Hohokam canal systems. These disasters weakened the control and authority of the secular or theocratic elite. This did not happen overnight, but was a slow process that lasted several generations. Another theory is that the Salado, a mixture of Anasazi and Mogollon cultures, simply migrated in and took over, blending with the Hohokam and diffusing them out of existence. Further evidence suggests that the long-term effects of irrigation contributed to the Hohokam demise. River water carries dissolved minerals. As this water evaporates from irrigated fields, it leaves behind mineral residues—usually alkali salts that gradually make the soil unfit for plants.

The Anasazi (meaning "ancient ones" in the Navajo language), who neighbored the Hohokam, settled in the Four Corners region in about CE 100–1300. Ancestors of Pueblo People now living in New Mexico and Arizona, the Anasazi farmed and produced fine baskets, pottery, cloth, ornaments, and tools. Villages evolved in caves that consisted of an array of semi-subterranean houses. Houses in the open also consisted of chambers below and above ground. Pit houses, known as *kivas*, served ceremonial purposes; these were community structures with up to a 1,000 rooms.[102] Multistoried pueblos like Chaco Canyon and cliff dwellings like Betakin and Mesa Verde are examples. The Anasazi abandoned the cliff houses in the late thirteenth century, possibly because of a severe drought between CE 1276 and 1299, and because of pressure from the Navajo and the Apaches. The Anasazi were the ancestors of today's Hopis, Zunis, and Rio Grande Pueblo peoples.[103]

The Mogollon lived in the southeastern mountains of Arizona and southwestern New Mexico between 200 BCE and CE 1200. In all probability, the Mogollon made the first pottery in the Southwest. They depended on rain and stream diversions for their farming, a technique that influenced the Anasazi or Puebla culture. From about CE 700 on, the Mogollon in New Mexico were greatly influenced by the neighboring Anasazi.[104]

According to Vélez-Ibáñez, Casas Grandes, Chihuahua was, a Mogollon city.[105] Also called Paquime, it was a major trading and manufacturing center on the northern frontier within the Mesoamerican world system, from which Mesoamerican culture was dispersed. A link is made between Casas Grandes and the Mimbres culture of southwestern New Mexico, a branch of the Mogollon peoples, who produced painted pottery between CE 800 and 1150 similar to that found in the Casas Grandes area. Some scholars call Paquime an outpost for Mesoamerican traders controlling trade between the Southwest and Mesoamerica; others link it to the Anasazi.

Present-day Casas Grandes is within a vast network of ancient ruins that was once the heart of one of the Southwest's largest trading centers. The area is still being excavated, and a lot remains unknown about this center. Small villages surrounded the city of Paquime, which evolved into a sophisticated center with an irrigation system that included dams, reservoirs, and *trincheras* (stone ditches). It had warehouses, ball courts, ceremonial structures, plazas, and steam rooms. By the late thirteenth or early fourteenth century, the area began to stagnate. Climatic change, environmental degradation, sociopolitical conflict, and shifting trade patterns all took their toll on the Mogollon people.[106]

At this point, hundreds of tribes with different cultures and linguistic dialects lived in northern Mexico and the Southwest. For example, Texas Indigenous People lived in camps perhaps as early as 37,000 years ago.[107] They went through the evolutionary cycle, at first surviving primarily on wild game. In fertile East Texas, tribes built permanent villages, and had well-developed farms and political and religious systems. These tribes formed a loose federation, known as the Caddo confederacies, to preserve the peace and provide mutual protection.[108] This ancient culture originally occupied the Red River area in what is now Louisiana and Arkansas. Semi-sedentary agricultural people, these tribes grouped around ceremonial mounds that resembled temples. Some scholars speculate that these skillful potters and basket makers were linked to the Mesoamerican cultures of the South.[109]

By the latter part of the eighteenth century, thousands of miles to the west in present-day Alta California, one of the largest concentrations of Indigenous People lived. Dozens of tribes adapted to its varied climate and topography. California mostly had a mild climate and an abundance of food. Like Hawaii, it had an abundance of game, wild fruits and plants, and fish, and most tribes did not have to farm. Trade with the native people to the east and among themselves supplemented their ways of life that amounted to living off California's rich vegetation. Their habitation of central California began between 12000 and 10000 BCE, and their evolutionary cycles resembled those of other native peoples. They left artifacts, traditions, and their descendants.

Edward H. Spicer's *Cycles of Conquest* is one of the most important studies of the native peoples in northern Mexico who, at one point, were part of the Mesoamerican sphere of influence.[110] The Pima, Opata, and the Tohono O'odham did not have a border marking Mexico and the Southwest,

They used the land to its fullest, building *rancherías* and some cases small villages" or retained as such. They used the land to its fullest. Notable among the tribes were the Cáhita, who spanned northern Sinaloa to Central Sonora. Among the Cáhita were the Yaqui; they had a strong sense of identity with the Yaqui River, one of the great waterways of North America.[111] Because of the fast-flowing river, the Yaqui were able to form villages of up to 3,000 villagers, unlike other people of the desert. Their lives differed from the Tarahumara (Rarámuri) and the Conchos, who lived on the eastern slopes and to the east of the Sierra Madre. These tribes, although they numbered in the tens of thousands, traveled in bands of 30 or fewer people, farming, hunting, and gathering to survive. When the sun got blisteringly hot, they migrated to the headwaters of the sierras to farm; in the harsh winters they migrated to lower altitudes to hunt and gather.

The Indigenous People to the north did not build great cities but like other people, the corn and trade bound them together. They endured frequent droughts, often warred with each other, and they endured.

Conclusion: The World System in 1519

Mesoamerica was an interconnected world that was integrated and in which events taking place in one social unit affected those in another over an extended region. It was composed of large towns and their dependent rural communities. The rural communities consisted mostly of patri-lineal kinship groups; the nobles and other elites lived in the large centers, exercising authority over the commoners. The forms of government varied from chiefdoms to fully developed states. In the Valley of Mexico, there were about 50 city-states with rulers or joint rulers appointed by the "royal" lineage as the supreme authority. They called the supreme ruler a *tlatoani*, "he who speaks," or in the case of joint rulers, *tlatoque*. In the highlands of Guatemala, the Maya called the ruler or king *ajpop*, "he of the mat." Because he ruled sitting on a mat that symbolized a throne.[112] The Azteca Empire was a loose coalition of subject city-states that paid tribute to an imperial center.

Scholars are split on whether the Azteca attempted to impose their culture on their subject peoples. One thing is certain: There was considerable ethnic diversity among the people of Mesoamerica. The dominant cultures influenced some, while others remained segregated as distinct cultures. Mesoamerica, although influenced by the dominant world systems of the Maya, Tolteca, and other cultures, was not under the political control of a single power.

The Core Zones

Mesoamerica, meaning "Middle America"—located between North and South America—was divided into multiple core zones, of which Central Mexico was the most prominent. The exchanges between the core, periphery, and semi-periphery were important in determining the flow of luxury goods—cotton garments, jade, cacao beans, hides, feathers, and gold ornaments. The core—through conquest, tributary demands, or trade activities—often obtained the goods that in great part were a product of its demands.

The core zones were Central Mexico, West Mexico, Oaxaca, and the Maya zone. Tenochtitlán was the capital of the Central Mexico zone, inhabited by some 200,000 persons. The Azteca ruled over about 300 city-states and over another 100 or so client states throughout the Central Mexico core zone. The Azteca appointed administrators to oversee the states and in other instances cemented alliances though marriage between Azteca and other elites. Considerable cultural and linguistic diversity existed within this core.

The Tarasco held sway over the West Mexico core zone. The Tarasco zone, more centralized and militaristic than the Azteca, held a tighter grip over its city-states. But the Tarasco did not have the same impact that the Azteca did on Mesoamerica.

The Oaxaca core zone was less integrated than the previous two zones. This zone consisted of 50 small kingdoms in which the dominant languages were Zapoteca and Mixteca. However, as in the other zones, multiple languages coexisted with the dominant languages. At the time of the Spanish invasion, the Mixteca states enjoyed considerable unity, forged by intermarriage between the ruling families. Trade took place within and outside the core. Intermarriage also occurred between the Mixteca and Azteca, who had significant cultural exchange.

The Maya core zone structurally resembled that of Central Mexico. Maya language and culture dominated the zone, although there was little unity between the highland and the lowland core states. Moreover, Maya had multiple dialects and non-Maya speakers also lived within the zone. The city-states competed with one another and some, like Quiché, incorporated approximately 30 tribute-paying provinces. The smaller zones within the main core zone were densely populated, and trade and warfare existed between them. Although generally peaceful, tensions existed between many Maya and the Azteca cores often due to trade competition.

The Semi-Peripheral Zones

The semi-peripheral zones, regions that mediated between the core and the periphery, were important to the exchange network, especially when dealing among competing core states. They assimilated much of the trade and the religion of the core and the periphery. Casas Grandes, in what is now the state of Chihuahua, was one such semi-peripheral region (although it did not exist at the time the Spaniards arrived). The Mexican state of Tabasco on the Gulf Coast was also an important semi-peripheral zone. Many of these regions were port-of-trade societies, and centers such as Xicalanco were quite cosmopolitan. They organized the governing classes, comprised of merchants, into political councils, in which women could reach high positions of authority. The south Pacific coast region is less well known. The Azteca and Quiché Maya vied for control of the Xoconusco area, which ultimately became a tributary province of the Azteca. The Caribbean coast, including the Yucatán Peninsula and the Central American isthmus, was another important semi-peripheral zone. Among the most important of these semi-peripheral centers was the island of Cozumel, which was run by merchants who invested in massive temples, shrines, and palaces. These port towns bordered the Caribbean all the way to Panama.

The Mesoamerican Periphery

The zones of the Mesoamerican periphery actively participated in the economic, political, and cultural life of the Mesoamerican world. However, the people in the periphery played a subordinate role. They were unequal, and often subject provinces. The periphery should not be confused with frontier zones, from which the Azteca originally came. The periphery extended to Mexico's northwest, from Colima to Culiacán and well into Sonora. In the northeastern part of what is now Mexico, the Huaxteca played a peripheral role. Its people had no writing system, and tension existed between them and the Azteca. Southeastern Central America was also a peripheral zone, occupied mainly by people speaking Pipil, which is closely related to Náhuatl. The Lenca language was also spoken in this peripheral zone. This peripheral zone was especially rich with diverse peoples, who interacted with the Maya and were organized into simple city-states or chiefdoms.

It is important to repeat that contact also existed with what is now the U.S. Southwest. This contact varied, but was most intense with the descendants of the Hohokam and other sedentary populations. Distance played a role in how much influence the core had. Frontier people such as the Azteca were eventually integrated into the core. The main point is that the diverse peoples of Mesoamerica were unified under a vast, well-defined world system, in many ways more distinct than the European world system.

Although more research is needed, it is highly probable that a trade structure existed that further integrated the disparate regions. Exotic commodities from Mesoamerica have been found in the Southwest, and it is probable that they were circulated through local native trade networks. Turquoise was an important trade item, and long-distance trade between the Zuni and Sonora existed. There was also an intense use of turquoise in Mesoamerica. Trade contributed to the evolution of the division of labor; it led to the evolution of state systems in Mexico proper, and it was a mechanism of economic integration. The population of what is today Mexico and Central America had reached a population of between 25–38 million on the arrival of the Spanish, and because of the population explosion in what is the Mesoamerican region, it is probable that contact would have increased the quest for water. In sum, the Americas did not need Europe for its growth and survival.

Notes

1. "Cracking The Maya Code," Nova (PBS), Youtube.com, Published on June 17, 2015, https://www.youtube.com/watch?v=UHPXD_aGeSM. YouTube has a treasure trove of documentaries on Maya.
2. Aztecs, Central Mexican Writing Systems, Mexico Lore, http://www.mexicolore.co.uk/aztecs/writing/central-mexican-writing-systems.
3. Olivier, Guilhem (2004) *Tezcatlipoca. Burlas y metamórfosis de un dios azteca.* (México, Fondo de Cultura Económica), 454–455; pic 3.
4. Also an under researched area.
5. Zapotec, Ancient Scripts. http://www.ancientscripts.com/zapotec.html. Mesoamerican Writing Systems, http://www.ancientscripts.com/ma_ws.html.
6. Brendan Borrell, "What's So Hot About Chili Peppers?" *Smithsonian*, April 2009, http://www.smithsonianmag.com/science-nature/Whats-So-Hot-About-Chili-Peppers.html. The author makes the point that while chili may have originated in Bolivia, chili is generally associated with Mexico.
7. Scholars presuppose that agriculture is essential for the development of village life and the evolution

of civilizations. The following article describes the building of a massive worship center 11,000 years ago, centuries before intensive farming. This discovery upends the conventional theory that agriculture was necessary before labor could be organized in this fashion. Andrew Curry, "Gobekli Tepe: The World's First Temple?" *Smithsonian*, November 2008, http://www.smithsonianmag.com/history-archaeology/gobekli-tepe.html.

8   Erin Brodwin, "Archaeologists have uncovered genetic evidence that rewrites a fundamental aspect of American history," *Business Insider*, Aug. 11, 2016, http://www.businessinsider.com/new-archaeology-study-shows-how-the-first-people-came-to-north-america-2016-8.

9   Joseph Stromberg, "Ancient Migration Patterns to North America Are Hidden in Languages Spoken Today," *Smithsonian*, March 12, 2014, https://www.smithsonianmag.com/science-nature/ancient-migration-patterns-north-america-are-hidden-languages-spoken-today-180950053/.

10 "The First Americans," *The Economist* (February 21, 1998): 79. See also Virginia Morell, "Genes May Link Ancient Eurasians, Native Americans," *Science* 280, No. 5363 (April 24, 1998): 520. Ruben Bareiro Saguier, "The Indian Languages of Latin America," *UNESCO Courier* (July 1983): 12. "First Americans Arrived As Two Separate Migrations, According To New Genetic Evidence," *Science Daily*, January 21, 2009, http://www.sciencedaily.com/releases/2009/01/090108121618.htm. Some experts say that humans were in the Americas at least 40,000 years ago. See Patricia McBroom, "Incredible Journeys of Our Native Tongues," *Berkleyan* (March 11, 1998), http://www.berkeley.edu/news/berkeleyan/1998/0311/linguistics.html. "Bering Strait Theory," http://www.native-languages.org/bering.htm.

11 Johanna Nichols, Ibid., pp. 3–4.

12 Johanna Nichols, Michael David Frachetti, and Robert N. III Spengler, eds., "How America was colonized: Linguistic evidence." In *Mobility and Ancient Society in Asia and the Americas*, 117–126 (New York: Springe, 2015), p. 6, https://escholarship.org/uc/item/94f0g00p.

13 Robert J. Sharer, *The Ancient Mayan*, 6th ed. (Stanford, CA: Stanford University Press, 1994), 4.

14 Louis Grivetti, Jan Corlett, and Cassius Lockett, "Food in American History, Part 1: Maize: Bountiful Gifts: America On The Eve of European Colonization (Antiquity To 1565)," *Nutrition Today*, 36, No. 1 (January 2001): 20. Temma Ehrenfeld, "Prehistoric Farming (Origin of Maize)," *Newsweek International* (November 24, 2003): 59.

15 Mark Muro, "New Finds Explode Old Views of the American Southwest (Findings of a Primitive Culture)," *Science* 279, No. 5351 (January 30, 1998): 653–54. J. Brett Hill, Jeffery J. Clark, William H. Doelle, and Patrick D. Lyons, "Prehistoric Demography in the Southwest: Migration, Coalescence, and Hohokam Population Decline," *American Antiquity* 69, No. 4 (October 2004): 689–707. Paul Mirocha, "Corn's Journey to North America," Corn's Journey, http://paulmirocha.com/projects/corns-journey/.

16 Kristen J. Gremillion, "Corn and Culture in the Prehistoric New World," *American Antiquity* 60, No. 3 (July 1995): 553–54. Michael W. Diehl, "The Intensity of Maize Processing and Production in Upland Mogollon Pithouse Villages A.D. 200–1000," *American Antiquity* 61, No. 1 (January 1996): 102–15.

17 Sissel Johannessen and Christine A. Hastorf, "Corn and Culture in Central Andean Prehistory," *Science* 244, No. 4905 (May 12, 1989): 690–92. "Ancient Popcorn Discovered in Peru," *Science Daily* (January 18, 2012), http://www.sciencedaily.com/releases/2012/01/120118143624.htm states "People living along the coast of Peru were eating popcorn 1,000 years earlier than previously reported and before ceramic pottery was used there . . . " suggesting there was contact with Mesoamerica. Corn cobs have been founded suggesting the cultivation of corn much earlier.

18 Claire Hope Cummings, "Risking Corn, Risking Culture," *World Watch* 15, No. 6 (November–December 2002): 8–18ff. Elizabeth Fitting, "Importing corn, exporting labor: The neoliberal corn regime, GMOs, and the erosion of Mexican biodiversity," *Agriculture and Human Values* (2006) 23: 15–26. Mark Stevenson, "Mexicans angered by spread of genetically modified corn," Organic Consumers Organization, December 29, 2001, https://www.organicconsumers.org/old_articles/corn/spreadofGECorn.php

19 Sharer, *The Ancient Mayan*, 58. Michael C. Meyer, William L. Sherman, and Susan M. Deeds, *The Course of Mexican History*, 6th ed. (New York: Oxford University Press, 1999), 6–7. Karl Cole, "Colossal Head," *School Arts* (Sept. 1999): 29.

20 Some African American scholars say that there was African contact. They point to the massive Olmeca stone heads as proof of this. However, this is not a view held by most Mesoamerican scholars. Robert M. Carmack, Janine Gasco, and Gary H. Gossen, *The Legacy of Mesoamerica: History and Culture of a Native American Civilization* (Upper Saddle River, NJ: Prentice Hall, 1996), 26. William F. Rust and Robert J. Sharer, "Olmec Settlement Data from La Venta, Tabasco, Mexico," *Science* 242, No. 4875 (October 7, 1988): 102–03. Claims that the Olmeca were from Africa are mostly based on the facial characteristics

of the artifacts, especially the Olmeca stone heads. See The Olmec—Ancient Mexico, http://www.youtube.com/watch?v=lKo9mUeIueM. There is no scientific evidence that the Olmeca are not part of the Amerindian family. Nicholas Mott, "Let's try: New Evidence Unearthed for the Origins of the Maya. The Maya culture began differently than previously thought, study says," National Geographic News, April 26, 2013. https://news.nationalgeographic.com/news/2013/13/130425-maya-origins-olmec-pyramid-ceibal-inomata-archaeology-science/. "The mysterious civilization of the Olmecs," Ancient Origins. January 7, 2015, https://www.ancient-origins.net/news-ancient-places-americas/mysterious-civilization-olmecs-002540.

21 Linda Schele and David Freidel, *A Forest of Kings: The Untold Story of the Ancient Mayan* (New York: Quill William Morrow, 1990), 56. Carmack et al., *The Legacy*, 52. Love, M., & Kaplan, J. (2011). *The Southern Maya in the Late Preclassic: The Rise and Fall of an Early Mesoamerican Civilization*, Norman: University Press of Colorado.

22 Olmec Civilization, http://www.crystalinks.com/olmec.html. Maria del Carmen Rodríguez Martínez et al., "Oldest Writing in the New World," *Science* 15, Vol. 313 No. 5793 (September 2006):1610–1614.

23 Carmack et al., *The Legacy*, 53. Spencer, C., & Redmond, E. (2004), Primary State Formation In Mesoamerica, *Annual Review of Anthropology*, 33, 173–199.

24 Jessie Szalay, "Who Invented Zero?" *Live Science*, September 18, 2017, https://www.livescience.com/27853-who-invented-zero.html.

25 Meyer, Sherman, and Deeds, *Course of Mexican History*, 14. Schele and Freidel, *Forest of Kings*, 55.

26 Anna Blume, "Maya Concepts of Zero," *Proceedings of the American Philosophical Society*, Vol. 155, Issue 1 (March 2011): 51–88.

27 Robert N. Zeitlin, "Ancient Chalcatzingo," *Science* 241, No. 4861 (July 1, 1988): 103ff. John S. Justeson and Terrence Kaufman, "A Decipherment of epi-Olmec Hieroglyphic Writing," *Science* 259, No. 5102 (March 19, 1993): 1703ff. Scott Faber, "Signs of Civilization—epi-Olmec Hieroglyphics Deciphered—1993—The Year in Science—Column," *Discover* 15, No. 1 (January 1994): 82ff.

28 Schele and Freidel, *Forest of Kings*, 159. Tikal dates to the Middle Formative (about 800 BC), and it was occupied to about AD 900. The Ruins of Tikal, http://www.youtube.com/watch?v=lOvYZiMvZ1Y.

29 Schele and Freidel, *Forest of Kings*, 17.

30 YouTube has a comprehensive 16-part series on the Mayan Calendar Explained (Part 1 of 16)—Ian Xel Lungold, http://www.youtube.com/watch?v=jEyZFbkvJjw. "The Mayan Calendar," http://www.youtube.com/watch?v=BeE-3BBqG58. Raymond E. Crist and Louis A. Paganini, "The Rise and Fall of Maya Civilization," *The American Journal of Economics and Society* Vol. 39, No. 1 (Jan., 1980): 23–30.

31 Virginia Morell, "The Lost Language of Coba," *Science* 86, No. 7 (March 1986): 48ff. Francis Mark Mondimore, *A Natural History of Homosexuality City* (John Hopkins University Press, 1997). Louis Crompton, "'An Army of Lovers': The Sacred Band of Thebes (Homosexual Soldiers in Ancient Greece)," *History Today* 44, No. 11 (November 1994): 23ff. See Colin Spencer, *Homosexuality in History* (Harcourt Brace, 1996).

32 Pete Sigal, "Ethnohistory and Homosexual Desire: A Review of Recent Works," *Ethnohistory* 45, No. 1 (Winter 1998): 139. Sigal, Pete, The politicization of pederasty among the colonial Yucatan Maya, *Journal of the History of Sexuality*, July, 1997, Vol. 8(1), pp.1–24.

33 Norman Scribes Hammond, "Warriors and Kings: The City of Copan and the Ancient Mayan," *History Today* 43 (January 1993): 54ff. See "Maya writing," http://www.youtube.com/watch?v=u9LRbLXMzyM&feature=related.

34 See Vernon L. Scarborough and David R. Wilcox, eds. *The Mesoamerican Ballgame* (Tucson: The University of Arizona Press, 1991). Vernon L. Scarborough, "Courts in the Southern Mayan Lowlands: A Study in Pre-Hispanic Ballgame Architecture," 129–44. The following has three parts: "Mayan Ball Game," http://www.youtube.com/watch?v=zcal8GcS41I. "A brief tour of Chich'en Itza, Yucatan, México, focusing on the ball court," http://www.youtube.com/watch?v=hobmU4Y8-8I.

35 Karl A. Taube, "The Mesoamerican Ballgame," *Science* 256, No. 5059 (May 15, 1992): 1064ff. Theodore Stern, *The Mesoamerican Ballgame* (University of Arizona Press, 1991). Google lists several excellent sites on the Mesoamerican ball game.

36 Meyer, Sherman, and Deeds, *Course of Mexican History*, 361. "Mayan Numbers Lesson," http://www.youtube.com/watch?v=W-om9DkpvgA or "Mayan Counting System," http://www.youtube.com/watch?v=0Mon20Zf56U.

37 See Preface for a discussion of "Mayan prophecy for December 21, 2012–End of Time," http://www.youtube.com/watch?v=QEJ8C2qw5FM&feature=PlayList&p=B2878C04EE3C336D&playnext=1&playnext_from=PL&index=37. "2012 Mayan Prophecy End of an Age Part 1," https://www.youtube.com/watch?v=JBlXJEqEpJg. "The Actual Astronomy of 2012—Absolutely Amazing," http://www.youtube.com/watch?v=cGPcjMe6Qlw.

38 "Mayan Family Life," Ancient Mayan Civilization, https://sites.google.com/site/ancientmayancivilization/mayan-family-life.

39 "It was the Maya's fractured political structure that thwarted attempts by the Conquistadors to conquer them. Cortés could take down the entire Aztec Empire by simply toppling Tenochtitlán. But conquest of the Maya would require winning battles with hundreds of individual clans scattered throughout the Yucatan." Francisco J. Collazo, "The History of the Maya Civilization," April 26, 2005, http://www.fjcollazo.com/documents/MayaReport.htm.

40 Mayan Political Hierarchy, "Hierarchy Structure," http://www.hierarchystructure.com/mayan-political-hierarchy/.

41 Schele and Freidel, *Forest of Kings*, 84–85.

42 See "Tikal, a place of remembered voices," http://mayaruins.com/tikal.html. Also Mystery of Tikal, http://www.youtube.com/watch?v=Prtjff2ftjM. See "Maya Trade and Economy," Authentic Maya, Guatemala, Cradle of Maya Civilization, http://www.authenticmaya.com/maya_trade_and_economy.htm.

43 Schele and Freidel, *Forest of Kings*, 57. Carmack et al., *The Legacy*, 323.

44 Palenque, "Pakal's Mystery," http://www.youtube.com/watch?v=TBI-BWiatRo. Schele and Freidel, *Forest of Kings*, 221–305. "Anahuac Civilizations: A Focus on Women," http://www.youtube.com/watch?v=zBIYpRW9fgU&feature=related.

45 Palenque—Mexico, http://www.youtube.com/watch?v=Wq-yZzy-cTk.

46 "Mayan Ruins at Tulum" (YouTube Edition), http://www.youtube.com/watch?v=Y9Vy06GIVMo&feature=related.

47 Michael C. Meyer, William L. Sherman, and Susan M. Deeds, *The Course of Mexican History*, 8th ed. (Oxford, UK: Oxford University Press, 2007), 386. Thomas O'Toole, "Radar Used to Discover Mayan Irrigation Canals," *Washington Post*, June 3, 1980.

48 The use of radar technology and photographs taken by satellites has revised estimates based on newly discovered evidence. "Science/Medicine: Developments in Brief; NASA Images Aid in Mayan Research," *Los Angeles Times*, March 1, 1987.

49 Vilma Barr, "A Mayan Engineering Legacy—Coba (Includes Related Article on Acid Rain Effects)," *Mechanical Engineering-CIME* 112, No. 2 (February 1990): 66ff. Alison Bass, "Agriculture: Learning from the Past," *Technology Review* 87 (July 1984): 71ff. Carmack et al., *The Legacy*, 63.

50 Carmack et al., *The Legacy*, 61. Morell, "Lost Language of Coba," 48ff. Frank J. Greene, "Smile—You May Be on Candid Satellite," *The San Diego Union-Tribune*, May 10, 1986. "Satellite Discovers Lost Mayan Ruins," *The New York Times*, June 19, 1984. "What Killed the Mayas: War or Weather?; A Global Weakening of the Ties . . . ," *Outlook; Science & Society* 118, No. 23. *U.S. News & World Report* (June 12, 1995): 10ff.

51 Schele and Freidel, *Forest of Kings*, 321–22. Overpopulation was one of the major problems. As the population grew, it became more difficult to eke out a living. The best farmland rested under many of the newly built buildings in places like Yax-Pac, where the ball court area alone had over 1,500 structures. An estimated 3,000 people per square kilometer lived there. Deforestation also led to other problems such as erosion and it affected climate and rainfall.

52 British scholar Eric Thompson was responsible for the myth of the peaceful people. Alfredo Lopez Austin, Leonardo López Luján, and Bernard R. Ortiz De Montellano, *Mexico's Indigenous Past* (Norman: University of Oklahoma Press, 2005), 137. However, it is important to note that no empire has ever been peaceful. The Old Testament is not a peaceful story, nor is the history of the United States. Likewise, it is difficult to get beyond the sensational on YouTube or most articles, scholarly and popular.

53 Again, it is impossible without the burned documents, to put the alleged human sacrifices into context. The Old Testament is replete with examples of human dscrifices that have been sanitized over time.

54 "Pirámides de Teotihuacán, México," 1 de 5, https://www.youtube.com/watch?v=2JdcM-jCTks, "Pyramids of Teotihuacán, Outside Mexico City, Mexico," https://www.youtube.com/watch?v=qDEnFchx5ng. Teotihuacán, http://www.youtube.com/watch?v=D7nbKa5__XM. Some sources use the term empire loosely and apply it to Teotihuacan. The word "empire" is ambiguous and has meant many different things over time.

55 Rene Millon, "The Beginnings of Teotihuacán," *American Antiquity* Vol. 26, No. 1 (July 1960): 1–10.

56 Meyer, Sherman, and Deeds, *Course of Mexican History*, 11. Carmack et al., *The Legacy*, 57, 60, 77.

57 Carmack et al., *The Legacy*, 33. Kenneth Hirth, "Xochicalco: Urban Growth and State Formation in Central Mexico," *Science* 225 (August 10, 1984): 579.

58 Dana Leibsohn. *Script and Glyph: Pre-Hispanic History, Colonial Bookmaking, and the Historia Tolteca-Chichimeca* (Washington, DC: Dunbarton Oaks Research Library and Collection, 2009).

59 Carmack et al., *The Legacy*, 71. Jacques Soustelle, *Daily Life of the Aztecs on the Eve of the Spanish Conquest* (Stanford, CA: Stanford University Press, 1961).

60 The lecture about Maya Toltec History in Chichén Itzá, Mexico, http://www.youtube.com/watch?v=mror2p7qm1o. Second Life—Chichén Itzá Mexico, http://www.youtube.com/watch?v=PPI8s4JZnDg. Chichén Itzá—Wonder of the

World http://www.youtube.com/watch?v=kuSvd1T EHXo&feature=fvw.
61. Zapotec and Mixtecan Culture at Monte Albán, http://www.youtube.com/watch?v=EfJd4_LA4vg. Early Astrology at Monte Albán, http://www.youtube.com/watch?v=z2EgwqyFDDg&feature=related. Zapotec Ruins of Monte Albán http://www.youtube.com/watch?v=qBEUrd2Jbbc. Javier Urcid Serrano (2001). Zapotec Hieroglyphic Writing. Studies in Pre-Columbian Art and Archaeology, (Washington, D.C.: Dumbarton Oaks Research Library and Collection) (34), I-487. A. Robinson, Lost languages: The enigma of the world's undeciphered scripts, (Thames & Hudson; Reprint edition, 2009).
62. Zapotec, Ancient Scripts.com, http://www.ancientscripts.com/zapotec.html.
63. "Pre-Columbian Art of Mexico, Art of the Oaxaca region-The Mixteca-Puebla." ArS Artistic Adventure of Mankind, https://arsartisticadventureofmankind.wordpress.com/tag/the-mixteca-puebla/
64. Carmack et al., *The Legacy*, 71. Jacques Soustelle, *Daily Life of the Aztecs on the Eve of the Spanish Conquest* (Stanford, CA: Stanford University Press, 1961).
65. Joyce Marcus and Kent V. Flannery, *Zapotec Civilizations: How Urban Society Evolved in Mexico's Oaxaca Valley* (London: Thame and Hudson, 1996), 12, 20, 84. Carmack et al., *The Legacy*, 73, 91. Matt Krystal, "Conquest and Colonialism: The Mixtec Case," *Human Mosaic* 26, No. 1 (1992): 55. Cultura Mixteca y Zapoteca, http://www.youtube.com/watch?v=wnUmY0Ak5VA.
66. Mixtecs, http://www.latinamericanstudies.org/mixtec.htm. Maarten Jansen, "The Search for History in Mixtec Codices," *Ancient Mesoamerica* 1 (1990): 99–109.
67. Victoria Reifler Bricker, *Supplement to the Handbook of Middle American Indians, Volume 5* (University of Texas Press; 1st edition, 1992), 155–57.
68. Pollard, Helen; Haskell, David; Darras, Véronique; Hernández, Christine; Healan, Dan; Maldonado, Blanca; Hirshman, Amy; Begun, Erica, "Recent research on the emergence of the Tarascan state," *Ancient Mesoamerica*, Oct 2008, Vol. 19(2), pp. 217–318.
69. The Azteca called nomadic tribes north of Central Mexico Chichimeca. The name generally meant barbarians. They were different and varying ethnic and linguistic groups.
70. See Richard Townsend, *The Aztec* (Thames & Hudson, 1992). The concept of Aztlán is controversial among right-wing scholars and nativist groups who claim that it is an example of Chicano sentiment to retake the Southwest. If the truth be told, it just says that the Azteca came from a place called Aztlán, which has been documented to have existed. It is not a matter of faith, and it is a process of deductive reasoning, based on early maps. Journalists Roberto Rodríguez and Patrisia Gonzales have done serious research into its existence. The Azteca probably did come from the Southwest. A wider view of indigenous culture comes from an understanding of the corn culture that bonded the peoples of the Americas. What is Aztlán? Roberto Rodriquez, "Utah Said to be Historical Location of the Mythical Aztlán," http://www.aztlan.net/quest_for_aztlan.htm.
71. Peter W. Rees, "Origins of Colonial Transportation in Mexico," *Geographical Review* 65, No. 3 (July, 1975): 323–34. Spanish transportation followed the corridors established by the Azteca and other Mesoamerican merchants who established the first El Camino Reals.
72. Morehart, Christopher T., "What If the Aztec Empire Never Existed? The Prerequisites of Empire and the Politics of Plausible Alternative Histories," *American Anthropologist*, June 2012, Vol. 114(2), 267–281. Smith, M. Aztec city-state capitals (Ancient cities of the New World) (Gainesville: University Press of Florida, 2008). Michael E. Smith, *The Aztecs* (Cambridge, Mass.: Blackwell Publishers, Inc., 1996).
73. Benjamin Keen, *The Aztec Image in Western Thought* (New Brunswick, NJ: Rutgers University Press, 1990); *perpetuated the myth of the Azteca Empire of the role of Hernán Cortés*. A lot more research has to be done before labeling it an Azteca Empire and the scholars must free themselves of their eurocentrism.
74. George Steinmetz, "Empires and Colonialism," *Oxford Bibliographies*, 13 January 2014, 77, http://www.oxfordbibliographies.com/view/document/obo-9780199756384/obo-9780199756384-0090.xml.
75. Morehart, C. & Frederick, C. (2014). The chronology and collapse of pre-Aztec raised field (*chinampa*) agriculture in the northern Basin of Mexico. *Antiquity*, 88(340), 531–548.
76. Carmack et al., *The Legacy*, 77–78. Ross Hassig, *Trade, Tribute, and Transportation: The Sixteenth-Century Political Economy of the Valley of Mexico* (Norman: University of Oklahoma Press, 1985).
77. Miguel León-Portilla, *El Destino de la palabra de la oralidad y los códices mesoamericans a la escritura alfatéticos* (México, DF: Fonda de la cultura, 1996), 45. Miguel León-Portilla, *Toltecáyotl aspectos de la cultura náhuatl* (México, DF: Fondo de la Cultura, 1995). Rozanne Dunbar Ortiz, "Aboriginal People and Imperialism in the Western Hemisphere," *Monthly Review* 44, No. 4 (September 1992): 1ff.
78. Carmack et al., *The Legacy*, 324.
79. Inga Clendinnen, *Los Aztecas: Una Interpretación* (México, DF: Editorial Patria, 1998), 205–77, or *Aztecs:*

80 June Nash, "The Aztecs and the Ideology of Male Dominance," *Signs* 4, No. 2 (1978): 349–62.
81 Ibid., 355–6, 359.
82 Owen Jarus, "25 Cultures That Practiced Human Sacrifice," *Live Science*, June 16, 2017, https://www.livescience.com/59514-cultures-that-practiced-human-sacrifice.html. Mike Parker-Pearson, "The Practice of Human Sacrifice," BBC, Feb. 28, 2011, http://www.bbc.co.uk/history/ancient/british_prehistory/human_sacrifice_01.shtml. Joseph Watts; Sheehan, Oliver; Atkinson, Quentin D; Bulbulia, Joseph; Gray, Russell D, *Nature*, 14 April 2016, Vol. 532 (7598), pp. 228–31.
83 Aztec Legend of the Fifth Sun, http://www.youtube.com/watch?v=eFJKzz-eolg&translated=1. Leyenda Azteca, Tenochititlan, http://www.youtube.com/watch?v=6Ado6TVJaU8&translated=1.
84 Clendinnen, *Los Aztecas: Una Interpretacion*, 225, makes the point that it is unknown in what context the transvestite was portrayed—in a comedy or drama or perhaps a cult. Meyer, Sherman, and Deeds, *Course of Mexican History*, 64. Carmack et al., *The Legacy*, 116. Soustelle, *Daily Life of the Aztecs*, 101–02. Mark Cartwright, "Aztec Civilization," Ancient, History, February 26 2014, https://www.ancient.eu/Aztec_Civilization/.
85 Clendinnen, *Los Aztecas: Una Interpretacion*, 155–89. Meyer, Sherman, and Deeds, *Course of Mexican History*, 70.
86 "Aztec System of Writing: Pictograms," History on the Net, http://www.historyonthenet.com/aztec-system-of-writing-pictograms/
87 John D. Daniels, "The Indian Population of North America in 1492," *The William and Mary Quarterly*, Vol. 49, No. 2 (April 1992), 298–320.
88 Population of Western Europe, Tacitus Nu, http://www.tacitus.nu/historical-atlas/population/westeurope.htm.
89 Robinson, F. (2005), Power-Packed Purslane, *Mother Earth News*, (209), 55–56.
90 González de Mejía, Grajeda Cota, Celada, and Valencia (1988), Characterization of the nutritional potential of tepari bean (Phaseolus acutifolius) grown in Mexico. *Archivos Latinoamericanos De Nutricion*, 38(4), 907–24.
91 Arthur Weir Smith (Ed.), "The Medicinal Plants Of North America," Revised from the *Transactions of the American Eclectic Materia Medical Association*, https://soilandhealth.org/wp-content/uploads/04.medical.library/0401.herbalmedicine/040132.Smith-The_Medicinal_Plants_of_North_America.pdf.
92 John Upton Terrell, *Traders of the Western Morning: Aboriginal Commerce in Precolumbian North America* 1st Edition (Los Angeles: Southwest Museum; 1st edition, 1967).
93 "Paquime – Casas Grandes: The Great Puebloan Abandonments and Migrations," Desert USA, https://www.desertusa.com/ind1/ind_new/ind13.html.
94 Barry M. Pritzker, *A Native American Encyclopedia: History, Culture, and Peoples* (USA: Oxford University Press, 2000), 3.
95 Timothy A. Kohler, Matt Pier Glaude, Jean-Pierre Bocquet-Appel, and Brian M. Kemp, "The Neolithic Demographic Transition in the U.S. Southwest," *American Antiquity* 73 (4), 2008, pp. 645–669. http://libarts.wsu.edu/anthro/pdf/Kohler%20et%20al%20SW%20NDT%20AAq.pdf states that "maize reached northeastern Arizona by 1940 BCE, which is almost as early as the southern Arizona dates. More lag can be seen in its subsequent east–west spread—for example, it reached the Northern Rio Grande in New Mexico by about 1200 BCE."
96 Carlos G. Vélez-Ibáñez, *Border Visions: Mexican Cultures of the Southwestern United States* (Tucson: University of Arizona Press, 1996), 20–3, 29.
97 Carlos G. Vélez-Ibáñez, *Border Visions: Mexican Cultures of the Southwestern United States* (Tucson: University of Arizona Press, 1996), 20–3, 29. James M. Bayman, "The Hohokam of Southwest North America," *Journal of World Prehistory*, Vol. 15, No. 3, (2001): 257–311.
98 Patricia L. Crown, James W. Judge. *Chaco and Hohokam: Prehistoric Regional Systems in the American* (Santa Fe, N.M.: University of Washington Press, 1991).
99 Nearly two dozen large towns were constructed in or around what is now Phoenix. Vélez-Ibáñez, *Border Visions*, 20–55.
100 Daniel B. Adams, "Last Ditch Archeology," *Science* 83, No. 4 (December 1983): 28ff.
101 E. Haury, (1976). *The Hohokam, Desert Farmers & Craftsmen: Excavations at Snaketown*, 1964–1965 (Tucson: University of Arizona Press, 1976). A lot of the early literature was published by the University of Arizona Press.
102 David E Stuart, *Anasazi America: Seventeen Centuries on the Road from Center Place*, 2nd Edition (Albuquerque: University of New Mexico Press, 2014).
103 Thomas E. Sheridan, "The Limits of Power: The Political Ecology of the Spanish Empire in the Greater Southwest," *Antiquity* 66 (1992): 156.
104 Reid, J., & Whittlesey, S., *Prehistory, Personality, and Place: Emil W. Haury and the Mogollon Controversy* (Tucson, AZ, USA: University of Arizona Press, 2011).
105 Paul E. Minnis and Michael E. Whalen, "The Local and the Distant in the Origin of Casas Grandes, Chihuahua, Mexico," *American Antiquity* Vol: 68:2 (2003): 314–32.

106 Harold S. Colton, "Reconstruction of Anasazi History," *Proceedings of the American Philosophical Society* 86, No. 2: 264–69. Hector Neff, Daniel O. Larson, and Michael D. Glascock, "The Evolution of Anasazi Ceramic Production and Distribution: Compositional Evidence from a Pueblo III Site in South-Central Utah," *Journal of Field Archaeology* 24, No. 4 (Winter, 1997): 473–92.

107 "Texas: Early history," *Encyclopedia Britannica*, http://www.britannica.com/EBchecked/topic/589288/Texas/79043/History. Gunnar Brune, "Major And Historical Springs Of Texas," Texas Water Development Board, Report 189 (Austin: Texas Water Development Board, March 1975), 5, https://www.twdb.texas.gov/publications/reports/numbered_reports/doc/R189/R189.pdf.

108 John Wesley Arnn III, *Land of the Tejas: Native American Identity and Interaction in Texas, A.D. 1300 to 1700* (Austin: University of Texas Press, 2012).

109 Donald E. Chipman, *Spanish Texas, 1519–1821* (Austin: University of Texas, 1992).

110 Edward H. Spicer, *Cycles of Conquest: The Impact of Spain, Mexico, and the United States on Indians of the Southwest, 1533–1960* (Tucson: University of Arizona Press, 1961). Rodolfo F. Acuña, *Corridors of Migration: The Odyssey of Mexican Laborers, 1600–1933* (Tucson: University of Arizona Press, 2007).

111 Rio Yaqui, *Life and death*, http://www.youtube.com/watch?v=K0JAWRGVyyk&translated=1. Yaqui Ritual Performance Mexico, http://www.youtube.com/watch?v=hCIfVH7CskY.

112 Robert M. Carmack, Janine L. Gasco, Gary H. Gossen (eds), 2nd Edition, *The Legacy of Mesoamerica: History and Culture of a Native American Civilization* (New York: Routledge, 2007), 121.

Chapter 2
El Imperio Español

Learning Objectives

2.1 Analyze how Spain developed the historical and cultural justifications for imperialism.

2.2 Analyze Spain's justifications for the destruction of Mesoamerican Civilizations.

2.3 Describe how Spain's location and history paved the way for slavery in the Americas.

2.4 Analyze how the Spanish Caste system maintained a system of racial and gender control.

2.5 Describe role of silver in Indigenous and colonial Spanish interactions in the Mesoamerica northern New Spain.

2.6 Explain how mining bonanzas impacted life for Indigenous People as the Spanish moved into the Rio Grande region.

2.7 Describe interactions between the Pueblo people and Spanish colonizers.

2.8 Deconstruct the notion that European Colonialism did not impact the Native American because the land was uninhabited.

2.9 Characterize the notion that the missions were more a institution to colonize the people than to convert them to Christianity.

The Illusions

2.1 Analyze how Spain developed the historical and cultural justifications for imperialism.

Rome colonized Iberia for about 600 years leaving its language, culture, institutions, and pretensions. The occupation profoundly impacted the Indigenous population, assimilating most people on the peninsula into the Roman culture. Only in the north were people able to partially resist this absorption.[1]

Spain did not become an Empire by accident: globalization, racism, capitalism, and Catholicism stoked the illusion. Castile during the Reconquista (CE 711–1492) built a military machine and a war mentality. It intervened in Northern Africa and competed with Portugal. In 1402 Henry III of Castile colonized the Canary Islands. A growth in Europe's population increased the demand for sugar and led to the expansion of the sugar trade as well as a thriving African slave trade Spanish and Portuguese on the Atlantic islands of the Madeiras and São Tomé and Principe off the west-central African coast. The Canaries and the Azores, along with the Mediterranean Islands also prospered producing 80 to 90 percent of CE western European sugar market.[2]

A sugar industry began on the shores of the Mediterranean between CE 700–1600.[3] Sugar was part of the Arab Agricultural Revolution that followed the founding of Islam and the Arab occupation of Syria, Palestine, and Egypt in the first half of the seventh century. It spread throughout the Levant (eastern Mediterranean region).[4] The Arab Agricultural Revolution developed trade, organization of labor, and land that was the genesis of a colonial plantation system.

In the fourteenth century incessant warfare brought about a change in the eastern Mediterranean sugar industry as the Ottoman Turks extended their power, shifting production to the western Mediterranean.[5]

Early Arab sugar cultivation also flourished in North Africa, southern Spain, Sicily, and Morocco.[6] The Norman conquest of Sicily in the eleventh century and the Crusades brought northern Europeans into contact with the sugar-producing lands. Sugar was new to the Middle East. By the 700s, sugar was cultivated in Palestine and Egypt and by the 800s in Sicily. It was a key part of the Arab Agricultural Revolution.

Sugar was a luxury among western Europeans, who discovered it during the Crusaders in the eleventh century. The rich used it as a spice for their pastries, replacing honey.[7] The Mediterranean sugar trade and the exploration of the African coast set the stage for the colonization of Madeira, the Canaries, and the Americas.

The Black Plague killed an estimated 75 to 200 million people in Eurasia and peaking in Europe between 1346 and 1353. Its effects were monumental, resulting in a dependence on African slaves. A restructuring took place because of the decline in production of major suppliers such as Egypt and Palestine; Venice and Genoa filled the gap. The slave trade expanded in the fourteenth and fifteenth centuries, enabling an increase in sugar production in Granada, where the Genoese played an important role in the trade. The Genoese were also heavily involved in the Canaries and Madeira.[8] The colonial plantation system also emerged in the Azores and São Tomé. By the early sixteenth century, the plantation system was a tested form of colonial land use.[9]

Its rivalry with Portugal also added to the Spanish notion of empire. During the second half of the 1400s, the Portuguese explored Africa's western coast, rouning the Cape of Good Hope in 1488. Soon afterwards Spanish ships raced to build the larger navy. The rivalry raged until the two countries reached an agreement in the fifteenth century that prohibited Spanish exploration and commerce south of the Sahara.

Slavery was indispensable to Spanish expansion, in 1500 Spain only had about seven million people and there was a shortage of labor. Portugal was also sparsely populated and in Lisbon and Évora and throughout much of southern Portugal slaves were essential because of the scarcity of labor. Slaves comprised roughly 10 percent of the population by the mid-1550s. North African, eastern Mediterranean, and Morisco slaves were common in Iberia.[10]

Always Roman

It is not surprising that when Spain invaded the Americas that it called itself *el Imperio español*, it grew to be one of the largest empires in history. The empire reached its peak under the Spanish Habsburgs in the sixteenth and seventeenth centuries.[11] The empire began with the inaugural of Charles I (1500–1558) as king of Spain in 1506, who became Emperor Charles V of the Holy Roman Empire in 1519. The ascension of Charles touched off wars with other Habsburgs and European states, for which Spain's colonies paid for. During the Protestant Reformation, the Holy Roman Empire essentially meant Spain; it defended the Vatican as well as promoted the spread of Catholicism in the Americas. Charles's son Philip II inherited the Spanish Empire, including its possessions in the Netherlands and Italy.

Habsburg Spain was a superpower and the center of a global maritime empire. Trade flourished across the Atlantic and Pacific Oceans. Toppling the Azteca and Inca civilizations, Spain laid claim to vast territories in North and South America.[12] The Spanish Empire dominated the oceans; victorious in Europe, it entered a cultural golden age in the sixteenth and seventeenth centuries, paid for by silver and gold from American mines. Incessant wars with other European countries (e.g., France, England etc.) fractured hopes for a commercial empire.

Spain's occupation violently disrupted Mesoamerica's evolution. It destroyed Mesoamerican social institutions, religion, and infrastructure. Within 80 years, between 1519–1600, the Indigenous population of New Spain fell from at least 25 million to about a million. What followed was 300 years of colonial rule, making possible the political and economic exploitation of Indigenous People. Systems of control such as the categorization of people by color, and the projection of the dominant class's worldview, made this possible. The exploitation pulled Spain and, ultimately, all of Europe out of the dark ages and allowed them to buy into a world market dominated by China.

The Asian market's demand for silver in the early 1500s contributed to the growth of mining districts such as Zacatecas. In the early 1500s, the gold/silver ratio was 1:6 in China; in Europe it hovered around 1:12, in Persia 1:10, and in India 1:8. Thus, with six ounces of silver, merchants could buy a full ounce of gold in China. In Europe, the same six ounces had a purchasing power of one-half ounce of gold. This trade put a premium on silver. In 1571, the Spaniards founded the city of Manila, Philippines, and it became a global center of substantial and continuous trade across the Pacific Ocean. Through the seventeenth century, Pacific galleons transported more than 50 tons in silver annually from Acapulco to Manila, where Chinese merchants would ship the cargo to the mainland. Trade with eastern Asia pushed demand for Mexican bullion as the Chinese population zoomed from 55 million in 1500 to 231 million in 1600 and 268 million in 1650.[13] Zacatecas and the northern periphery of New Spain depended on the demand for silver in the Orient.

Africa Begins at the Pyrenees

French novelist and playwright Alexandre Dumas (1802–1870) is generally credited with the aphorism "Africa begins at the Pyrenees."[14] It was originally a disparaging remark meaning the Spanish were really not Europeans but Africans:

> It is an error of geography to have assigned Spain to Europe; it belongs to Africa: blood, manners, language, the way of life and making war, in Spain everything is African. The two nations have been mixed up for too long—the Carthaginians who came from Africa to Spain, the Vandals who left Spain for Africa, the Moors who stayed in Spain for 700 years—for such a long cohabitation not to have confused the race and customs of the two countries. If the Spaniard were Mohammedan, he would be completely African; it is religion that has kept it in Europe.[15]

In truth, Iberia (modern-day Spain and Portugal) was much more a part of the ancient world that included Phoenicia, Carthage, Greece, Rome, and the Muslim world than it was a part of western Europe. The intermingling of the races began in about 35000 BCE. By 5000 BCE, the Basque people lived in the north, in the Pyrenees region. Between 4000 and 3500 BCE, the Iberians entered from North Africa, in all probability through Gibraltar. Around 1100 BCE, Phoenician merchants from present-day Lebanon established trading posts in Cádiz and elsewhere along the Spanish Mediterranean coast. Greek merchants traded along the northeastern coast and Jewish merchants from North Africa settled on the Iberian Peninsula.[16] The Celts arrived through the Pyrenees or the Atlantic Ocean between 900 and 650 BCE, bringing knowledge of iron metallurgy. The Phoenician colony of Carthage, in what is modern-day Tunisia, was an offshoot of the Lebanese Phoenicians. Iberia came under the rule of Carthage, but following the Punic Wars (264–246 BCE) it was eclipsed by Rome laying the foundations for Spanish language and culture.[17]

The fall of the Western Roman Empire in the fifth century CE opened the way for the Visigoths, a nomadic Germanic people from central Europe, to rule Spain. In 711, the Muslims of northern Africa launched invasions across the Strait of Gibraltar, occupying most of the peninsula. The African presence lasted more than seven centuries.[18] Under Muslim rule, Spain was a center of learning and art. The Muslims preserved the writings of many Greek, Roman, and Middle-Eastern intellectuals—writings that otherwise would have been lost. Muslims brought improved irrigations methods, enabling production of cotton and foods such as rice, sugar cane, oranges, and other fruits and vegetables. The Africans also brought other breeds of animals; using stock from the Muslims and Moors, the Spaniards developed a breed of horse that was better adapted to an arid climate. They developed strategies to travel long distances, herding African cattle and churro sheep.[19]

Meanwhile, the northern Christian kingdoms gradually gained power in holy wars known as *la Reconquista*, driving the Moors southward. By the 1000s, Christians were gaining the upper hand, and by the 1200s, they had driven the Muslims into the Granada region of the Iberian Peninsula. In 1479, the marriage of Queen Isabela and King Fernando united the kingdoms of Castile and Aragón, and in 1492, they conquered the last Moorish kingdom, Granada, which occupied the eastern half of present-day Andalusia.[20] That same year they expelled between 120,000 and 150,000 Spanish Jews. These events set the stage for "Occupied America."[21]

The Spanish Conquest

2.2 Analyze Spain's justifications for the destruction of Mesoamerican Civilizations.

Who is Christopher Columbus?[22] He is claimed by Italians, Jews, Spaniards, and Catalans! In 2006, a forensic team led by Spanish geneticist José Antonio Lorente has compared DNA from bone fragments that Spain says are from the explorer—and that were buried in a cathedral in Seville—with DNA from remains that are known to be from Columbus's brother Diego, who is also buried in the southern Spanish city.[23] The DNA findings were immediately challenged by the Genovese and Jews who claim Colón. The only ethnic groups that do not claim him are Native Americans and those condemning the Indigenous genocide. The controversy continued and three years later another "study by Estelle Irizarry, based on official documents and letters of the explorer, found that Columbus came from the kingdom of Aragón and his native tongue was Catalan. Irizarry also concluded that Christopher Columbus's origins were not obscure by chance, but rather the result of the famed explorer's having purposely hid the fact he was *a converso*, a Jewish convert to Christianity."[24]

Columbus traveled to Portugal, the center of the African slave trade, before going to Spain. In all probability, Cristóbal Colón was a slave trader and took part in the African slave trade before 1492. He saw firsthand the wealth that could be accumulated by trafficking in slaves. In 1492, Columbus landed in what are now the islands of the Caribbean. "On his first day in the New World, he ordered six of the natives to be seized, writing in his journal that he believed they would be good servants. Columbus returned to Barcelona with six Taíno natives who were paraded as curiosities before King Ferdinand and Queen Isabella. Throughout his years in the New World, Columbus enacted policies of forced labor in which natives were forced to work."[25]

During Columbus's expeditions between 1493 and 1501 some 3,000 Indigenous are known to have been shipped to Europe. When the Indigenous People revolted, Columbus was brutal and ordered the dismembered bodies of the freedom fighters to be paraded through the streets.[26] On the island of Española, sometime in 1495, the Spaniards forced Indigenous People to surrender goods, including gold ore. When he could not find sufficient gold and wealth, he turned to slave trading. In 1495, he rounded up 1,500 Taínos (Arawaks), selecting 500 of the "best specimens," and set sail for Spain.[27] Only 300 natives survived the trip to Spain. By 1650, few Taíno or Caribs remained alive.[28]

As mentioned, Columbus was probably trained in the Madeira sugar trade. On his second voyage of 1493, he introduced sugar cane plants to the Caribbean. Columbus knew that sugar and slavery were inseparable and that tremendous profits could be gotten from sugar. By the early 1500s, sugar-growing plantations flourished on the Caribbean Islands, built on the model of the Mediterranean plantation system. The sugar industry thrived on Santo Domingo, then on Cuba, and soon after on Puerto Rico.[29]

Meanwhile, the pope condemned the Portuguese practice of plunder and the enslavement of human beings along the coast of Africa. However, he left a loophole. The natives could be enslaved if they were cannibals. Columbus himself justified the enslavement of the Indigenous People, claiming they were cannibals. The Spaniards used this loophole throughout the colonial period. In Central America, they captured and sold tens of thousands of natives as slaves. They shipped Nicaragua natives to Peru to work in the mines and *haciendas*, plantation-like estates.[30]

Today's racial attitudes began a long time ago. Feelings of superiority and destiny planted the idea of European superiority. Pope Alexander VI issued a papal document on May 3, 1493, "granting" to Spain—at the request of Fernando and Isabella—the right to conquer the lands that Columbus had found, as well as any lands which Spain might "discover" in the future. In 1494, the Treaty of Tordesillas gave Christian nations the right to colonize non-Christian lands under the Doctrine of Discovery, a series of papal bulls issued in the fifteenth century that absolved present and past generations for atrocities committed in the conquest of the Indigenous Peoples.[31] This absolution created a mindset of entitlement for Europeans.

Faith versus Rationality

Apologists for Columbus say that he did not invent the institution of slavery. They claim that Spain tried to control slavery, and that the crown promulgated the Laws of Burgos in 1512 that included regulations protecting Indigenous labor and ensuring their Christianization. They argue that Spaniards such as the Dominicans Antonio de Montesinos and Bartolomé de las Casas defended the rights of the Native Americans.[32] But the Laws of Burgos were almost never enforced, and the famed national debate over whether or not the natives had rational souls did not occur until six decades after the initial contact in the Caribbean and three decades after the fall of the Azteca Empire.

The debate between Bartolomé de las Casas and the renowned Spanish scholar Juan Ginés de Sepúlveda took place in 1550–1551 in Valladolid, Spain. Ginés based his arguments on Aristotle's doctrine of natural slavery: "that one part of mankind is set aside by nature to be slaves in the service of masters born for a life of virtue free of manual labor." Sepúlveda wrote a treatise justifying war against the natives. According to him, the Spaniards had the right to rule the "barbarians" because of their superiority. He compared the natives to wild beasts.[33] The judges in the debate never reached a decision as to the validity of Sepúlveda or las Casas's point of view.

The Spanish Invasion of the Mexica

The Spaniards explored the Caribbean coastline of Middle America, gathering information. By 1511, the invaders conquered Cuba, and in the late 1510s, Hernán Cortés landed on the mainland that was to become Mexico. On the island of Cozumel, Cortés encountered the Maya. In 1519, Cortés sailed to what today is Veracruz, and within two years Cortés's forces conquered the great Azteca Empire and began the colonization of what they later called New Spain.[34]

Throughout the Spanish advance to the Azteca capital of Tenochtitlán, gunpowder, horses, snarling dogs, and glistening armor helped the Spaniards. Unlike the invaders, the Indigenous warriors did not intend to kill their enemies, hoping to wound and capture them, and use them as sacrifices to the gods. Western historians often dwell on human sacrifice but overlook the brutality of the conquest and praise the achievements of Cortés and other Spanish explorers. The invaders created an empire based on the fiction of the right of discovery and conquest. They gave absolute "property rights of any European nation who claimed the land."[35] They minimized Cortés's cruelty during his march to Tenochtitlán in 1519, when Cortés and his Indigenous allies slaughtered 5,000 to 10,000 unarmed Cholulans in less than two hours. His atrocity was based on his suspicion that the Cholula were planning to ambush him.[36] Similarly, rape was justified or worse, it was such a matter of fact that it was not mentioned. It is said that as many as 240,000 Azteca died during the 80 days of the fall of the Mexica. It is reported that five to eight million people perished in a smallpox epidemic during 1519–1520.[37] The Azteca were not immune to smallpox and other European diseases, so outbreaks of these diseases had the effect of germ warfare. At a critical moment, when it seemed as if the Azteca might drive out Cortés's men, a smallpox epidemic ravaged the Indigenous population.[38]

The Azteca also stopped fighting periodically to remove their dead and wounded from the battlefield. At close range, Native Americans used wooden clubs ridged with razor-sharp obsidian—vicious weapons against other Indigenous People, but weapons that shattered against Spanish helmets.[39] The double-bladed swords of the Spaniards in close combat slashed left and right, killing or maiming. Their armament allowed them to drive directly at warriors clustered around their leaders. When the Spaniards captured or killed a local chief, the chief's warriors fell back. In the battle for Tenochtitlán, this weaponry gave the Spaniards a decisive advantage over the Azteca.[40]

Colonialism

2.3 Describe how Spain's location and history paved the way for slavery in the Americas.

Early European colonial occupations consisted of systematic massacres, ethnic cleansing, forced labor, and coerced religious conversion. The Spanish tightened control and adopted a policy of exploiting the occupied country through full or partial political control. They sent Spanish colonist to occupy the country.[41]

In the case of Latin America, colonialism amounted to total control of its political and religious structure. Colonialism relied on a caste system to govern as well as the imposition of the European god. They justified colonialism by claiming an Empire that had the right of discovery. It mattered little that the colonized were not lost. They were the original inhabitants. Colonialism also resulted in a mentality whereby the colonized people felt inferior to their colonizers, an attitude that often persisted long after independence.

The Colonization of Indigenous Mesoamerica

After the conquest of the Azteca, the Spaniards—through looting, torture, and rape—conquered the Tarasco; they executed the Cazonci, the Tarascan ruler, by dragging him through town behind a horse and burning him at the stake. Cortés's men also subdued the natives of Oaxaca, but the conquest of the Maya proved more arduous. Many Maya fled to the dense forests that remained out of the control of the Spaniards for 200 years.

Not every Maya City was abandoned, however.

> The southern lowlands were nearly deserted. But Maya splendor lived on in the Yucatán peninsula. When Spanish explorers got there in the early sixteenth century, they found cities full of people. They saw highly decorated palaces and temples raised on stepped pyramids. They found paved stone roads and busy marketplaces. They met leaders wearing jade and gold jewelry. These leaders also wore intricate headdresses, jaguar-skin skirts, and bright feathered capes. The Spanish were also met by warriors with bows, arrows, and clubs.[42]

As late as 1680, the Spanish only occupied the northwestern third of the Yucatán Peninsula. The Itzá kingdom survived in the jungles of the Maya lowlands to the south. (The occupation of what is today southern Mexico and parts of Central America was slower because of the conquistadores' preoccupation with silver and gold. As of 1700 there were only five million people in Spain proper. It did not have sufficient population to settle or hold on to their possessions.)

Smallpox and Other Plagues

The distinguishing characteristic of the subjugation of the Mesoamerican native populations was its genocidal proportion. The term *genocide* is used here because when people lose 90 percent or more of their population, millions of lives, an explanation must be forthcoming. As with a nuclear disaster, saying it was accidental is no excuse. After the conquest of Tenochtitlán, smallpox and other epidemics spread throughout the countryside, subsiding and recurring, until eventually as many as 24 million died in what is now Mexico. Certainly, the smallpox, measles, and influenza outbreaks hit urban areas hardest because of the population concentration. (These three diseases are highly communicable, being transmitted mainly by air.)[43]

Four major epidemics occurred in the first 60 years of Spanish occupation. Smallpox caused the first epidemic of 1520–1521, the second year after Spanish contact. Azteca medicine could not stop its spread, and untold thousands died. The second epidemic of smallpox (possibly combined with measles) broke out in 1531. The Azteca called it *tepiton zahuatl*, or "little leprosy." The third epidemic began in 1545 and lasted three years. The Azteca called this *cocoliztli*, or "pest," thought today to have been hemorrhagic fever. A fourth epidemic, again named cocoliztli, lasted from 1576 to 1581, and an estimated 300,000–400,000 Native Americans died of it in New Spain.[44]

Apologists argue that the Indigenous People had a predisposition to diseases that made them vulnerable to European diseases; they theorized that the native peoples were vulnerable to these diseases because their slow trek across the Bering landmass more than 15,000 years before created a biologic selector and "cold screen" that eliminated harmful bacteria and viruses from their bodies. A more plausible explanation is that the lack of larger-sized domesticated animals shielded the natives from diseases carried by animals.[45] The introduction of domestic animals, accordingly, contributed to the spread of diseases to the natives.

The Columbian Exchange refers to widespread exchange of animals; plants; culture; and human populations that included slavery, communicable disease, and ideas between Spain and the New World. Some put a positive spin on the enrichment that occurred because of the exchange. However, to do so is to forget the cost in lives, the destruction of cultures and environment, and the appropriation that took place. It ignores the Atlantic slave trade, the enslavement of Indigenous Peoples, and the diseases that killed millions of them.

The Spaniards brought gunpowder, the horse, and the Catholic Church to the Americas. The Americas' part of the exchange sent corn, the potatoes, the tomato, peppers, pumpkins, squash, pineapples, cacao beans (for chocolate), the sweet potatoes, and fowls such as turkeys. The Europeans brought livestock such as cattle, pigs, and sheep that caused disastrous environmental destruction, and grains such as wheat that condemned generations to diabetes. They brought the onion, citrus fruits, bananas, coffee beans[46], olives, grapes, rice, and sugar cane from other parts of the world. But they also brought smallpox, influenza, malaria, measles, typhus, and syphilis.[47] The exchange wiped out the Indigenous religions, submerged their languages, and tried to blank out their history. They introduced a European construct of race that lasts to this day.[48]

Race and Labor in Mesoamerica

The conquerors practiced a "scorched-earth" strategy that caused widespread environmental destruction and social disorganization. Large numbers of displaced, disoriented, and depressed refugees roamed the countryside, suffering severe nutritional deficiency and often starving to death.

Illness often prevented many natives from caring for their crops or from processing corn into tortillas. The acute food shortage resulted in starvation, and contaminated food and water spread disease. Meanwhile, the Spaniards forcefully herded natives into new farming schemes. Alcoholism took an additional toll with the distilling of native drinks. Before the invasion, *pique*, which was low in alcoholic content and rich in vitamins, was used for religious purposes. It resembled beer rather than hard liquor. When the Spaniards introduced distilled alcohol, it provided an escape from the destruction of society, and addiction became common.[49] Urban resettlement plans only reinforced substantial crowding and lack of hygiene, and native centers became breeding grounds for epidemics.

INDIGENOUS LABOR A "Viceroy," or vice-king, governed New Spain, ruling the colonial government that was subdivided into smaller administrative units. The crown gave former *conquistadors*[*] (meaning "leaders of the crusades") *encomiendas*, large tracts of land with native subjects, an institution that was established in Spain during the Reconquista and also used in the Caribbean Islands. The *encomendero* received tribute from a village along with Indigenous labor. In principle, encomenderos would protect the natives under their care and supervise their conversion to Catholicism.[50] In reality the conquerors often mistreated and abused the natives, keeping them in a state of serfdom. Critics correctly say it was a system to control and regulate Indigenous labor and behavior.[51] The encomienda was a fiction that allowed the crown to circumvent ideological biases against slavery.

THEORY VERSUS PRACTICE Throughout the colonial period, Spain passed legislation supposedly to protect the natives. In theory, the Laws of Burgos, passed in 1512 as *Recopilación de las Leyes de los Reynos de las Indias* (Recopilation of the Royal Law of the Indies), protected the natives. Spain strengthened the laws in 1542, eliminating the right of encomenderos to unlimited use of Indigenous labor. Occasionally, the natives successfully sued; some used the laws to protect their lands or personal labor. However, there was a difference between what the law said and how it was enforced. Justice rarely went beyond an occasional victory in the courts.[52]

The Spanish crown abolished Indigenous slavery and the *encomienda* in the 1550s. Yet, they flourished on the peripheries and frontiers of New Spain well into the nineteenth century. The *repartimiento*, requiring a native community to provide labor for public projects, agriculture, mines, and as carriers of goods was practiced into the eighteenth-century. Although the system mandated wages for the natives, employers often ignored the decree.[53] The repartimiento was not limited to labor; it also included the requirement that natives purchase goods from Spanish authorities. The generous grants of land and labor favored the crown because it made it easier to confiscate the grants as well giving the conquistadores an incentive to conquer and develop regions in New Spain. Moreover, the crown did not have to directly finance this expansion. Lastly, "The Crown also endeavored to convert the natives to Catholicism. Even if life on earth was not pleasant, a converted Indigena could look forward to an afterlife in heaven. A miserable Christian, the Crown reasoned, was much better off than a free 'heathen.' Encomenderos were required to instruct the natives in the faith and enforce attendance at Mass on Sundays. Slave owners could have carried out similar responsibilities."[54]

STRUCTURAL CONTROLS The native communities endured the catastrophes of the invasion and colonization of Mesoamerica, but not before Spaniards dramatically changed them. In order to control them, colonial authorities grouped native communities into *municipios*, townships. The largest town of the municipios was the *cabecera*, or head community. While this structure led to the survival of the native community, it strengthened colonial control of the native village. Its purpose was to isolate natives in order for them to identify with the local village rather than forming class or ethnic identities. This division made it difficult for the different communities to unite against Spanish rule, destroying intercommunity regional networks and the pre-invasion world system. This concentrated power in the hands of Indigenous *caciques*, chiefs, who ran the local system, and were loyal to the Spaniards.

The Spaniards allowed the Indigenous Peoples to keep their languages, but Spanish was the official language. All official government business was conducted in Spanish. If the native or the *casta*, of mixed race, spoke Spanish, he or she was considered superior to those who did not. The Catholic Church was the state religion, and the Christian god supplanted the Indigenous gods.[55] The paternalism of the Spanish friars was an expression of racism, in that they saw the natives as being childlike. They believed that the natives lacked the spiritual and mental capacity to understand Catholicism. During the early colonial period, the Spanish crown did not allow natives to become priests or nuns.[56]

Spain administered the religious conquest from Iberia most members of the hierarchy were from the upper classes. The monarchy and the Church were one with the crown appointing the bishops—a right generally reserved for the pope. The Spanish Reconquista influenced the colonizers: They were intolerant and hostile toward any person who was non-Catholic. To hold office or be a noble in Spain, the nominee was required to prove a *limpieza de sangre* (purity

---

[*] The name *conquistador* expresses the similarity of conquests in the New World and the conquest of the Moors in Spain. It is similar to a knight who participated in the crusades or the *Reconquista*.

of blood); that they were not of Jewish or Moorish blood.[57] The intolerance extended to Spain's colonies. As previously mentioned, to consolidate its power, Spain imposed a caste system based on race that designated an individual's rank according to color. Spanish priests listed racial classification on baptismal certificates. There were four main racial categories: the "peninsular" or Spaniard born in Spain; the "criollo/a," a person of Spanish descent born in Mesoamerica; the "indio/ia," or native; and the "negro/a," of African slave descent. Innumerable subcategories of hybrids developed over time.[58] This complex system, used for social control, lasted in various forms throughout the colonial period, although it became more difficult to keep track of one's class position as the castas (those of mixed race), moved north. Distance allowed them to fudge on their race. The advantage of moving up in race is obvious: The more Spanish one looked and claimed to be, the more privileges the person enjoyed.[59]

Women in Colonial Mesoamerica

2.4 Analyze how the Spanish Caste system maintained a system of racial and gender control.

Class, status, and gender shaped one's role in society.[60] There was considerable violence against Indigenous women; however, they resisted. Maya women used the courts to bring complaints against priests and other officials for sexual harassment. However, the priest's or official's family connections often predetermined the outcome. In these cases, the Indigenous women were at a disadvantage compared with Indigenous men.[61] "Whereas native men, *hijosdel pueblo,* were assured rights to community land women's entitlements were much more precarious. Women enjoyed independent access to land in central Mexico before the Spanish conquest and they were able to extend their holdings in the mid-sixteenth century, when the decline in native population rendered land abundant."[62]

The Changing Roles of Women

During the colonization, women were the victims of rape, which is considered to be part of the colonization strategy. It is the ultimate symbol of subordination and conquest.[63] Structurally, under colonialism, women were at the bottom of their castes. The new economy, however, opened limited opportunities for women. In Yucatán, the introduction of sheep led to the commercial production of wool. Women were generally responsible for making woolen goods, thus enabling their participation in the wool trade.[64] Yet this was not entirely positive, since the repetitive motions in textile work resulted in physical ailments.

In Azteca society, women were recognized as adults. They had rights before the law and society; this status varied greatly according to their class. Under Spanish rule, their standing was weakened. Spanish law allowed them to litigate inheritance and land rights in court. Nahua women took advantage of these rights, and they actively litigated and testified on their own behalf in the colonial courts. This activity became less frequent in the seventeenth century, as Nahua husbands and fathers increasingly represented the women in court. Native women were not always recognized as *hijas del pueblo*, daughters or citizens of the town, with communal land rights. Women's rights to property narrowed under colonialism, and their participation changed as commercial agriculture pressured *los de abajo* (the poor and powerless) to abandon or sell their land.[65]

PATRIARCHY Gender roles were strongly influenced by the Catholic Church and resulted in deep divisions between the genders. Patriarchy was not only a form of social control but part of a managerial or caste system. Patriarchy resembles the organization of the Catholic Church where the hierarchy is male. The nuclear family was similarly engineered through patriarchy. "Because environments, Indigenous languages, patterns of political, economic, and spiritual organization, ways of structuring family life, varieties of cultural expression, and forms of interrelationships with Spaniards varied so much, Indigenous People did not experience a single New Spain. Instead, a multiplicity . . . emerged."[66] The Catholic Church saw the nuclear family as essential to converting the Indigenous People to Christianity.[67]

The colonizers strengthened their colonial control. Marriage and family was strictly controlled via the casta system.[68] Before the arrival of the Spaniards, women generally married when they were about 20 years of age. After the arrival of the Spaniards, however, Church friars encouraged females to marry at 12 or 14. Early reproduction often resulted in health disorders, including anemia. Society was patriarchal, and men received preferential treatment in nutrition.[69] Even in death, men were favored, as they were more likely than women to be buried within the church courtyard. In sum, colonization worsened the status of women and increased violence toward them.

The family structure changed during the colonial period. For a time, the native nobility kept much of their prestige. But the colonization led to the breakdown of the traditional Indigenous family framework, which was based on an extended family (clan) rather than the highly patriarchal nuclear family that the Spaniards favored. According to Carmack and his colleagues, "Colonial authorities believed that the Indigenous would be easier to supervise and control if divided into small nuclear households," which not only reduced the authority of the elders but also removed the support network for women within the clan.

Early marriage also influenced gender relations and increased the power of the male within the nuclear family, reducing the authority of native women within the clan. The age difference between male and female spouses favored the male. A 20-year-old male who married a 14-year-old girl held much more power than he would have if both were 20 years old.[70]

Finally, the designation of a natural (illegitimate) child that was written into baptismal certificates served as a form of control.

> Illegitimacy was, as other expressions of social behavior, closely linked with race and environment. Urban Indios showed a much higher rate than rural Indios, getting close to rates shown by Españoles and Castas. In Valladolid, for example, between 1760 and 1790, the rates stood at 17% for mestizos, 19% for Indios, 29% for Españoles, and 29% for mulattos. In the countryside, rates for Indios ranged from 2 to 10% in Zacatelco, Acatzingo, Tula or San Luis de la Paz, lower, often by as much as one half, than the rates found for other groups.[71]

The term "Castas" was generally applied only to non-white that were not clearly Indigenous. Whites were considered legitimate. However, the Castas were suspected of "illegitimacy or slavery in their lineage."[72] Illegitimacy could only in part be forgiven by the father acknowledging fatherhood. Being a natural child could bar a person from becoming a member of the clergy or a civil servant.

The Assimilation of Native Women

Native women, according to some sources, experienced a diminished participation in traditional social domains. The Catholic Church promoted rigid attitudes toward women, making women the scapegoats for its failures in converting the natives. Priests blamed Indigenous mothers for not socializing their children, although little attention was paid to educating them. There were few religious schools for women in colonial society. By contrast, during the preconquest period, women worked as marketers, doctors, artisans, and priests, and perhaps, occasionally, as rulers. The opportunities for life outside the home were based on class: native noblewomen who married the conquerors and brought a dowry were more readily assimilated and acculturated than the poor.[73]

THE MYTH OF PASSIVITY Indigenous women were anything but passive or invisible, however. By the end of the eighteenth century, they accounted for one-third of the Tenochitilán, or Mexico City, workforce. (Tenochitilán had become the capital of New Spain and was renamed "Mexico City.") A sizeable number of native, African, and mixed-race women worked outside the home. In Mexico City, 46 percent of native women and 36 percent of women from *las castas* (mixed races) engaged in work outside the home, whereas only 13 percent of the Spanish or criollos worked outside the home in the labor force. Most women found employment as domestic servants. We can deduce that native women and women las castas performed the menial work while middle-class women pursued some education.[74]

As mentioned, native women also were far from docile; legal documents show many examples of resistance. Take the case of Josefa María Francisca, a *cacica*, or noblewoman, who for some 30 years played a leading role in Tepoztlán, near Cuernavaca. Francisca did not know how to read or write and probably was unable to speak Spanish; nevertheless, her fiery temperament made her a respected ally and a feared opponent.[75] What angered Francisca was the repartimiento, which forcefully took the village's men to the hated mines of Taxco. In 1725, when authorities arrested repartimiento workers, she led an assault on the jail and freed them. In September a group of 100 women broke into the sacristy, liberated the ornaments and vestments, and sold them to pay for litigation. Angelina María Francisco, the wife of Miguel Francisco, Francisca's lover for 30 years, led the revolt and authorities sentenced her to one year in an *obraje*—a sweatshop—and six months at the *hospital de indios*. They later commuted her sentence.

In the winter of 1797–1798, as typhus ravaged the Maya village of Ixil, the women feared that the royal administrators would tax the village based on its pre-epidemic population. In addition, Spanish authorities violated the tradition of burying local Maya within the church compound and ordered that typhus victims be buried outside the church boundaries, which infuriated the women. They locked the doctor and the priest in the church and made their release contingent on proper interment of the deceased.[76]

Throughout the colonial period, women lodged complaints against clergy for sexual improprieties. This was no small feat considering they were appealing to a patriarchal structure.

ICON OF SOCIAL CONTROL OR LIBERATOR? For many Mexicans today, the appearance of the *Virgén de Guadalupe* to an Indigenous person is proof of the Church's benevolence. For others Guadalupe is the symbol of Spanish social control, representing a passive female role model, subservient to male authority. According to critics, the supposed appearance of the Virgin Mother to Juan Diego[77] at Tepeyac in 1531 is an example of church authorities' substitution of the Virgin of Guadalupe for the Indigenous goddess Tonantzin, mother of gods. The story of the Virgin of Guadalupe may be the product of "the invention of tradition" rather than historical fact. Today, however, the Virgén de Guadalupe has become a Chicana cultural expression that gives strength to women and unifies and defines Mexican culture. For many, she has become a liberator, a symbol of hope and liberation for her community. Sandra

Cisneros and Gloria Anzaldúa have underscored the Indigenous roots of the Virgin and her symbol as a source of inspiration.[78]

Vincentian Father Stafford Poole, C.M., in *Our Lady of Guadalupe*, traces the making of the Mexican tradition of Guadalupe based on documents produced in the colonial period. According to Poole's evidence, most authorities and priests did not know about the Tepeyac shrine representing the Virgin's appearance for some 20 years after the Virgin supposedly appeared to Juan Diego. Spaniards confused her with the medieval Spanish Lady of Guadalupe shrine (in Extremadura, Spain), and venerated the Virgin. Not until the seventeenth century, when the criollo population began to celebrate her, did she become popular among native populations. From conquest to seventeenth century Indigenous Peoples had identified with local religious symbols, which had played a central role in the development of their own religious practices. Consequently, by the mid-1600s, the Church was able to baptize most natives in Central Mexico.[79]

During the sixteenth and seventeenth centuries, Guadalupe was more a symbol of criollo nationalism than an Indigenous icon, according to Poole. He argues that even the story of the apparition appears to have changed during the colonial era as did the tradition itself, until Father Miguel Hidalgo used her as a symbol of Mexican independence in 1810. Notwithstanding, today the Virgén de Guadalupe has taken on different dimensions, symbolizing for many Mexicans and Latin Americans a "renewal and rebirth as a people. Guadalupe stands for both transformation and continuity in Mexican religious and national life."[80]

Al Norte: God, Gold, Glory, Silver, and Slaves

2.5 Describe role of silver in Indigenous and colonial Spanish interactions in the Mesoamerica northern New Spain.

The Spaniards sent expeditions in every direction searching for riches. A Cuban-based expedition in 1565 planted one of the oldest European colonies in the United States near present-day St. Augustine, Florida. Meanwhile, the viceroy sent scouting expeditions from Central Mexico to investigate rumors of another Tenochitlán to the north. In 1533 Diego de Guzmán, a slave trader, penetrated as far as Yaqui Valley, in what today is Sonora, Mexico. In 1540 Francisco Vázquez de Coronado, in search of Cibola, the legendary city of gold, led an army of mostly Native Americans and five Franciscan friars as far as the Grand Canyon and across the central plains to Kansas before retreating to Mexico without finding a trace of gold.[81]

Unlike the Azteca and the natives of central New Spain, many natives of the north did not live in concentrated areas. Some lacked the complex social and political organization of the towns of south-central New Spain. Nevertheless, the northern tribes resisted the Spanish encroachments, and the Spaniards called them *indios bárbaros,* or barbaric Indigenous People. In short, the conquistadores felt entitled and were offended that the Indigenous did not meet them with open arms.

Meanwhile, the Spanish named the colonial administrative region in western Colonial Mexico "Nueva Galicia"; it made up of roughly the present states of Jalisco, Nayarit, and southern Sinaloa. Guadalajara was its administrative capital and base of operations for expeditions into the northwestern frontier. Governor Nuño de Guzmán led an expedition that left a trail of depredations, enslavement, and mistreatment of natives as the Spaniards explored and secured the area as far north as Sinaloa. Among the largest were those of the Tepeque and Zacatecas at Tepechitlán.

Bonanzas, or large mining strikes, energized the pull north. They made possible the exploitation of river valleys and the establishment of haciendas, missions, and settlements. The northward movement was not easy, as the northern tribes resisted the encroachment. It was not until after the 1541 Mixtón Rebellion that the Spanish were able to open the mines of Zacatecas, which, at their height, produced one-third of Mexico's silver and employed 5,000 workers. The bonanza drew prospectors and Christian natives to the mines. It generated institutions such as the hacienda and the mission. Bonanzas in Guanajuato (1548) and Real del Monte (1552) followed Zacatecas. The Chichimeca, sometimes called Otomí or Zacatecas, and their allies fought the advance of the Spaniards throughout the 1560s and 1570s, with Spanish settlements forming a large triangle between Guadalajara, Saltillo, and Querétero.[82]

The Decimation Towards the Indigenous Population

The Spaniards' arrival on the northern frontier, accompanied by natives from the interior and domesticated animals, devastated the native ecology and intensified competition for rivers and valleys pushing the native peoples off their lands.[83] The Spanish authorities responded to native resistance by organizing *presidios*, forts, which became an integral part of the invasion after the Chichimeca War of the 1560s. As with the Mesoamerican civilizations, the numbers of natives fell drastically during the Spanish occupation. The Greater Southwest, according to Thomas Sheridan, encompassed "that vast arid convulsion of deserts and mountains north of Mesoamerica," with an estimated population of around 1,700,000 in 1519, plummeting to 165,000 by 1800.[84]

THE LIVING PATTERNS OF THE NORTHERN CORN PEOPLE Most natives lived in *rancherías*, semi-fixed farming settlements. Three-quarters of all Indigenous ranchería natives were Uto-Aztecan. But they varied greatly as to their population density, mode of living, and organization, depending on rainfall and the flow of rivers. For example, at the time of the arrival of the Spaniards, fixed villages did not exist in Chihuahua; instead, natives moved in search of water. In the spring they would travel to the headwaters in the sierras, farm, and live there for the summer, and then migrate east to the deserts during the winter where they would subsist on desert vegetation. This pattern of migration meant that the size of the ranchería was smaller than a traditional native village, numbering between 30 and 50.

The Tarahumara people of modern Chihuahua/Durango lived over a large area; they would come together at *tesgüinadas*, festivals during which the Tarahumara practiced rituals that included imbibing corn beer. In Sonora, the Pima and the Yaqui lived in areas that were more compact. Their rivers, such as the Great Rio Bravo or Grande, gave life to villages of thousands and complex social and political systems. The Pueblo people, found mostly in what is today New Mexico, Colorado, Arizona, and Texas, also lived in villages. In comparison, the nomadic people were still in the process of migration when the Spanish arrived.[85]

The Changing Order

2.6 Explain how mining bonanzas impacted life for Indigenous People as the Spanish moved into the Rio Grande region.

The mining city of Zacatecas was a melting pot of varied races and people. Near the mines, *haciendas* for cattle raising sprang up, which caused tensions with the native populations in these valleys as the newcomers usurped the best land and believed themselves entitled to native labor. As in the south, the Spanish elites considered themselves conquistadores entitled to encomiendas of natives.

Slowly, the Spanish imperial system moved up the Pacific coast to Culiacán, and, simultaneously, up the Zacatecas trail to Durango and Chihuahua. The Spaniards established presidios, missions, haciendas, and pueblos (Indigenous villages or towns). Because of the lack of population and capital, Catholic missions played an essential role in extending and holding the empire's borders and congregating, forging a native workforce and religious presence on the frontier. The demands on native labor occurred both inside and outside the mission orbit: The growth of the mining industry increased the need for food production, forcing the natives to work longer hours, while the mines and the haciendas pressured the missionaries to provide more native workers. These demands, along with the frequent droughts and epidemics that depopulated the region, made the natives restless. Their frequent uprisings made the Franciscan and Jesuit missionaries, as well as the outside settlers, increasingly dependent on the presidios to maintain order by force.[86]

Meanwhile, the missions profoundly changed the lives of Indigenous People. For example, while life had always been harsh for women, often subjected to the raiding and enslavement due to intertribal warfare, they always held strong roles in their communities. Females and males seem to have inherited wealth equally, and women were involved in the trade of weaving and pottery. Both men and women could marry multiple times before they found the ideal mate.[87] A native woman had the choice of abortion, and women participated in ceremonies, although their religious roles were subordinate to those of males. Pre-conquest women shared these cultural memories and religious values; however, the missions ended these choices, as they imposed the attitudes and values of Spanish society on the natives. A hierarchical structure made clear distinctions between the male and female spheres. Meanwhile, Spanish institutions such as the repartimiento shifted women to work that men had previously done.

The Bonanzas

Mining bonanzas forged the *Camino Real* (Royal Road) from Mexico City to Zacatecas, then through today's Durango to Chihuahua, and then to New Mexico. Natives from Central Mexico as well as Africans, Spaniards, mestizos, and castas were drawn over this road to the mines. The conquerors uprooted Native Americans from their villages and destroyed their institutions. Consequently, natives caught in a work-or-starve situation formed a large sector of the wage earners. Dozens of small and large ore strikes brought these workers through Durango to Santa Bárbara and then to Parral in 1631.[88]

By the turn of the sixteenth century, Spain attempted to expand its dominion into present-day New Mexico, where it anticipated another bonanza. In 1598 Don Juan de Oñate, whom the viceroy had appointed governor of the territory of New Mexico, set out with a party of some 500 colonists, including 10 Franciscans and hispanicized Tlazcala and Tarasco natives, many of whom were from Central Mexico, to establish a colony. Juan de Oñate's father was a prominent mine owner, one of the founders of Zacatecas. The younger Oñate, married to a granddaughter of Cortés and a great-granddaughter of Moctezuma, financed the operation. When Oñate and his party failed to find gold or silver, he returned to Mexico City in disgrace.[89] Most narratives about the conquistadores in the Southwest forget that they were invaders. In what is today eastern New Mexico, a few miles south of the city of Clovis, an archeologist found the Clovis spear tips, which were for a long time reputed to be the oldest known spear tips in the Americas. Clovis type spears changed the people from primarily foragers into big game hunters.

The Indigenous People lived in different places during the changing seasons. They moved with the animals and the availability of plants and fruit bearing trees. Over thousands of years they became farmers gradually digging canals to extend the area of farming, constantly gaining more control over their own food. They were no longer collectors but food producers. They were constantly learning: weavers of baskets, sandals, mats, string, and ropes.

"The Mogollon people grew food in small gardens. They also planted crops on mesas. They depended on mountain rains to water their gardens and crops."[90] Most villages were made pit houses. They were built on the side of the mountain that received the most rain. These were the ancestors of the pueblos that were built with stone, brick, and clay. They built multi-room apartment houses, often three stories high.

New Mexico was hardly a wasteland at the time Oñate and his men arrived. It had a future with the mighty Rio Grande running through its middle and the spread of pueblos as its population grew. At Zuni and Acoma and along the Rio Grande and its tributaries, the Spanish encountered people who lived in multistoried cities and cultivated the land. Further into the interior of this vast unknown frontier, they encountered nomadic societies that followed the migration of immense herds of strange cattle-like beasts with enormous humps. On August 18, 1598, the new settlers began work, and by early September they were ready to dedicate the pueblo. For this occasion, they invited the Indigenous chiefs, opening the festivities by thanking god, and proceeding with a tournament and a great fiesta. The settlers fought mock battles, and participated in jousting contests and horse shows. Toward sunset, the colonists took time out to act in a play written by Captain Marcos de Farfán, recounting the epic story of the opening of New Mexico. It was the first known European play written in the American Southwest.

From the European point of view, the Oñate expedition had a romantic flavor. However, the reality was that Indigenous People suffered extreme hardships under the colonizers. These Spaniards, like other conquistadores, imposed themselves and their civilization on the conquered. The native New Mexicans who resisted were severely punished. When the Acoma resisted colonization, Oñate retaliated and sent a small force against its pueblo, destroying Acoma, and killing 800 men, women, and children. Oñate ordered one foot cut off all the male captives older than 25.

Not everyone is enamored with the Oñate legacy. The Pueblo Revolt of 1680 spread throughout New Mexico and northern Mexico and lasted until 1692. The Indigenous pueblo people rose up against the Spanish colonizers in Santa Fé, New Mexico. Other Indigenous Peoples such as the Apache joined the pueblos and drove the Spanish colonists out of New Mexico. The revolt affected Chihuahua and Sonora where Indigenous People supported the pueblos. After the 1680 Revolt the crown built presidios from Sonora to Texas. When the Spanish settlers returned in the 1690s, many New Mexican families remained in Sonora and Chihuahua.

In 1998 a 12-foot high statue of Oñate's statue erected was stationed a few miles north of Española.[91] Vandals cut off its right foot with an electric saw, leaving the message, "We took the liberty of removing Oñate's right foot on behalf of our brothers and sisters of Acoma Pueblo. We see no glory in celebrating Oñate's fourth centennial, and we do not want our faces rubbed in it."[92]

For most of the seventeenth century, New Mexico was an outpost. The land between Santa Bárbara/Parral and New Mexico had few villages. Continuous small mining strikes filled this century. However, the northern expansion did not come without cost as the Indigenous People resisted the encroachment as well as enslavement and other forms of forced labor. Due to war and epidemics, the Indigenous populations of Chihuahua and New Mexico dwindled radically.

The native population in New Mexico numbered more than 60,000 at the time of the Spanish arrival. By 1800 the population fell to 9,000. Throughout the frontier, from 1560 to 1650 the population declined by 50 percent. The population fell 90–95 percent by 1678. Frequent smallpox epidemics brought heightened competition for farm labor in the north; those in 1639–1640, the 1640s, and 1650s were especially severe. In the 1690s, yet another epidemic of measles broke out.[93] Droughts and labor shortages affected the supply of food. Due to these tensions, frequent revolts spread throughout northwestern New Spain during the 1600s.

Forced Labor

Coercion was part of the colonial process. Government officials in collusion with the agricultural establishment perceived the Indigenous populations as key to production.[94] Landowners and miners could avoid restrictions on forced labor due to their distance from central government. They sought arrangements that bound natives without being required to pay wages or credit advances. The repartimiento was the optimal form of labor control because it improved reliability. The types of labor varied in the mines, and haciendas used mixed crews of wage laborers of all races who worked alongside African and Indigenous slaves.

Periodic bonanzas increased demand for labor. Mine owners and *hacendados* pressured the missions for workers. The mission congregation almost invariably followed the establishment of Spanish mining camps and estates.

The earliest encomiendas drew workers from the native rancherías; encomenderos competed with the missions and Indigenous villages for workers. The encomenderos were in full control of the native population under their charge, often abusing their "trust" by renting the natives to mine owners and other hacendados. Colonial elites also relied on native caciques to furnish them with workers, further stressing the native population.

The repartimiento, although primarily used for agricultural labor, was sometimes used for the mines. The repartimiento as an institution continued long after "free" wage labor was employed in the mines and hacienda. The forced labor draft was crucial to agriculture. In addition, repartimientos were used for maintaining public works. An overlapping progression from slavery to encomienda, to repartimiento, to free labor operated often simultaneously. In this scheme, the missions were training schools, often supplying the haciendas and mines with skilled workers.[95]

The Northern Corridor

2.7 Describe interactions between the Pueblo people and Spanish colonizers.

Nueva Vizcaya was the "heartland" of the northern frontier for some 250 years. It encompassed the area north of Zacatecas and included most of the modern Mexican states of Chihuahua and Durango, and, at different times, parts of Sinaloa, Sonora, and Coahuila. The capital of the province was Durango. Exploratory and missionary expeditions launched from Nueva Vizcaya resulted in the settlement of New Mexico, Parras and Saltillo, and Sonora and Sinaloa.

The first colony settled north of Nueva Vizcaya in what is today the United States was Nuevo México where, as mentioned, the Spaniards hoped to find gold or silver. However, its existence and prosperity rested on the waters of the Rio Grande that ran from the Rocky Mountains down through the center of the province. Because of large numbers of sedentary natives, there was also a ready supply of labor that made possible the development of large haciendas and trade with various other Indigenous People.

In New Mexico, the Spanish settlers repeated the patterns of exploitation described in Nueva Vizcaya and Sonora. The use of bonded servants was widespread. New Mexican colonists used fictions such as indios *de depósito* to forcibly place natives in Christian households under the pretense that they would receive a Christian education. Forced Indigenous labor was so widespread in New Mexico that the colonists had no need to import expensive black slaves. Indeed, New Mexico was a net exporter of slaves to the mines of Parral and elsewhere.[96]

The Pueblo People lived in this region since at least CE 1 AND shared the traditional Indigenous perceptions of the world of nature, differing only in language. The Pueblo also shared a theocratic lifestyle that interrelated their kinships and religious groups with the world of nature. The members of each village organized themselves to cope with their particular environment. Survival disciplined them to note even the minutest variations in climate and topography—the amount and seasonal rhythm of precipitation, the form of a flood plain, or the erosion of a temporary stream.

The Pueblo's social grouping was matrilineal, that is, they grouped kinship around the core of blood-related women. The Pueblo conceived kinship as timeless, extending back into the remote past and extending forward through generations of unborn. Thus, they related the kinship system symbolically beyond the human community into the world of nature, using animals and plants as symbols for different clans.

The colonists established Santa Fé as the capital of the province in 1610. During these early years, the hispanicized population of the province increased from a few hundred to a few thousand who were dispersed in isolated farms, ranches, and hamlets.[97] Spanish settlers and their livestock encroached on native fields. Although tensions existed, there is evidence that the newcomers commingled with the natives and often intermarried.

However, tensions mounted as encroachment on native lands, forced labor, a prolonged drought in the region, and Apache raids contributed to the Pueblo Revolt of 1680. Popé of the San Juan Pueblo led the rebellion, joined by some mestizos and half-African persons. The natives drove the colonists from New Mexico, the bulk of whom did not return until the 1690s.[98]

The 1680 Revolt affected the whole of Nueva Vizcaya and Sonora; it became known as the "Great Northern Revolt." In New Mexico, the revolt had millenarian trappings. The natives washed off the stains of baptism, annulled Catholic marriages, and destroyed churches. The New Mexicans wanted the Spaniards and their god out of their space and wanted to return to the old ways.[99]

According to Ramón Gutiérrez, "Within New Mexican households slave treatment ran the gamut from the kind neglect of some to the utter sadism of others."[100] At the time of the revolt, 426 slaves were dispersed among the Hispanic households. Some 56 percent of the households had one or more slaves. In this system, female slaves were worth more than males and were sold openly at fairs, as females were valued as household servants and for bearing children, who would also be born into this class. The Spanish merchants also marched New Mexican slaves to Parral to work in the silver mines. Some ended up in the plantations of Veracruz and, after 1800, in Havana, Cuba, and Yucatán. When the Spanish army put down the rebellion, military authorities tried the rebels in Spanish courts and sentenced them to hanging, whipping, dismemberment of hands or feet, or slavery.

The Decline of the Native Population

Constant warfare reduced the Pueblo population from 17,000 in 1680 to 14,000 in 1700. Many Pueblo went into exile with the Apache, Navajo, and Hopi. After the colonists returned to New Mexico, the repartimiento replaced encomienda system. The excessive use of the repartimiento system had a devastating impact on Indigenous People, depriving the native communities of labor for their own crops, which caused a shortage of food, and ultimately malnutrition.[101]

By the end of the eighteenth century, only 68 of some 16,000 persons was born outside New Mexico, with two born in Spain. The landed peasants, mostly mestizos, lived above Santa Fé in areas they called *Rio Arriba* and *Rio Abajo*. Until the mid-eighteenth century, land grants were largely private grants. After this point, colonial authorities parceled out community grants—that is, community land grants that included common pasture lands and common rights for using land—to buttress the haciendas of the elite in the south of Rio Abajo from native attacks. Most of the mestizo colonists were of humble birth, although they fashioned themselves Spaniards and tried to distance themselves from the *indios* and other lower castas.

The Rio Arriba and Abajo villages were self-sufficient. As a group, the villagers were distinct from the hacendados. Both the Pueblo and the villagers were at a disadvantage compared with the hacendados. However, according to Roxanne Dunbar-Ortiz, "Though Pueblos and Hispano villages had no political or economic power during the eighteenth century, the elite, on the other hand, never gained the necessary economic prosperity to affect the predominant village life of the province nor to change land tenure patterns radically during the colonial period."[102] Still, considerable tension existed between the Pueblo population and the colonial administration; as late as 1793, the governor jailed the caciques of various Tewa Pueblos for holding "seditious" meetings.[103]

The Colonization of Texas

2.8 Deconstruct the notion that European Colonialism did not impact the Native American because the land was uninhabited.

Texas natives lived in camps perhaps as early as 13,500 years ago and subsisted primarily on wild game.[104] Because of the vastness and remote location of what eventually became Texas, it took the Viceroyalty of New Spain hundreds of years to occupy it. While on the periphery of the Viceroyalty, it had been fully explored. But unlike other parts of the Viceroyalty, there was no evidence of mineral wealth to attract expeditions and adventurers from the south. Its occupation came from three directions. El Paso del Norte belonged to New Mexico and was a corridor to Chihuahua and Sonora. East of El Paso, where the Rio Grande joined the Conchos River at La Junta de los Ríos, the Spanish founded missions in Nueva Vizcaya. The Conchos River was a corridor into West Texas and the area along the Rio Grande. The coastal region from the Nueces River to the Rio Grande and upstream to Laredo was settled from the province of Nuevo Santander after 1749. The movement into Texas was from these areas.

By the eighteenth century, Spain entered a period of declining revenues and defense of its territories. Spain was a declining power and the expenses of the missions and presidios drained the royal treasury. Hence, the crown encouraged the establishment of self-sufficient Pueblos, consisting of castas and a sprinkling of Spanish peasants. Unlike Nueva Vizcaya and Sonora, where mining drew settlers, the occupation of Texas was more a matter of holding onto frontier territory.

The Rio Grande played a key role, seen by many as the answer to the development of New Mexico and much of northern Mexico. The river had the potential of an all-water route to the Gulf of Mexico. Plans to exploit the river and navigate it never fully developed—Spain just did not have the resources. But the importance of the Rio Bravo did not escape the early colonists, who recognized the interdependence of the frontier colonies in what today is called the American Southwest and northern Mexico.[105]

El Paso del Norte

The oldest Spanish settlement in Texas was in the El Paso area. The first Spanish entry into the El Paso area took place in 1581 with the Rodríguez-Sánchez expedition, consisting primarily of natives from Mexico. They passed through two mountain ranges rising out of the desert with a deep gap between them at the crossing of the Rio Bravo (Grande), which they named El Paso del Norte. (El Paso refers not to a passage through the mountains but rather to the crossing of the river.) Oñate's expedition also passed through there, near today's San Elizario in 1598, when Oñate claimed the entire territory drained by the Rio Bravo. It was not until 1659 that Fray García de San Francisco founded Nuestra Señora de Guadalupe Mission. The Pueblo Indigenous Revolt of 1680 drove Spanish colonists, Franciscan missionaries, and Pueblo and Tigua natives from northern New Mexico (which sided with the Spaniards) to El Paso del Norte. South of the river, some 12 miles from today's downtown El Paso, the refugees settled at Santisimo Sacramento, later known as Ysleta del Sur. Two years later, construction of a mission began there and was completed in 1692.

By 1682, the Spanish crown had founded the missions and settlement of El Paso del Norte, San Lorenzo, Senecú, Ysleta, and Socorro, all south of the river. This cluster of settlements became a trade and farm center on the Camino Real. Throughout the colonial period, this area was more properly part of New Mexico, Chihuahua, and the northwest Mexican territory than of Texas, with some elite families from other provinces moving there.[106]

The Tlaxcala and the Castas

As with New Mexico, natives from Central Mexico played an important role in the colonizing of Texas proper. According to Carlos Vélez-Ibáñez, the Tlaxcala initially served as scouts and auxiliary soldiers on various expeditions. In 1688, the Tlaxcala participated in the building of the presidio of San Juan Bautista near today's Eagle Pass. In response to French exploration along the Mississippi River Valley, Spanish friars established six missions along New Spain's eastern frontier in 1690. The missions' isolation—a three-month journey away from the capital in Mexico City—left the missions vulnerable.

Spanish friars established Mission San Antonio de Valero, now known as the Alamo, as a way station on the San Antonio River in 1718. The following year the French that were active in present-day northwest Louisiana forced the Spaniards to abandon the East Texas missions, and the missionaries took refuge at Mission San Antonio. By 1731, a chain of five missions (three of which had moved from East Texas), populated by Indigenous recruits from Texas, operated along the San Antonio River. Mission San José, founded in 1720, quickly grew prosperous and became the largest of the Texas missions. An *acequia*, an irrigation ditch, boosted agricultural production, and the mission sold the surplus to the growing settlements around the military presidio and the villa of San Antonio. The mission's holdings included El Rancho Atascoso, about 30 miles to the south, where native *vaqueros*, or cowboys, tended 1,500 cattle, 5,000 sheep and goats, and herds of mules and horses.[107]

The Importance of San Antonio and Links to the Rio Bravo

The area that is today San Antonio was vital to the future of this frontier. In the early 1730s, a contingent of 55 peasants arrived from the Canary Islands. The colonists revived the villa of San Antonio. The Canarians joined the descendants of the first colonists and friars to form a community, depending on the local garrison for trade and outside merchandise. The population increased slowly but began to prosper somewhat by the 1770s when the community developed new markets in Louisiana and in the El Paso area.[108]

Spain chose to colonize the rich valleys of the upper Rio Grande and the mining districts of Nuevo León and Coahuila to prevent French encroachment into this area. The incentive for this expansion was the need for more pasturage for their herds and the growing demand for cattle and their by-products by the mines. The colony of Nuevo Santander included the Mexican state of Tamaulipas and South Texas. Tomás Sánchez and other hacendados established the colony of Laredo in 1755, downstream from Sánchez's *Hacienda de Dolores*, where some 30 families lived.[109] As in other areas, the natives resisted Spanish encroachments.

By 1767, Laredo numbered 186 persons. The 1789 census listed 45.3 percent of Laredo's residents as *españoles*, 17.2 percent as mestizos, 17.2 percent as mixed blacks, and 15.6 percent as indios. Only 6.7 percent of the married persons said they were intermarried. Illegitimacy was the highest between the mixed blacks and the Indigenous. Tejano historian Gilberto Hinojosa writes that the Spanish population increased to 57.2 percent of the population by 1820 and that the non-Spanish population seemed to have fallen by 23.9 percent. He speculates that the indios may have moved back to their ranchería settlements. A more plausible explanation is that colonists self-identified themselves as Spanish.[110] The population grew to 2,052 in 1828. In 1824, Laredo had 700 sheep; four years later, it had 3,223. Wool became Laredo's chief export traded with Mexican merchants from the interior. Racial divisions that existed in 1789 persisted in the 1835 census.

Meanwhile, the population of Nuevo Santander grew from 31,000 in 1794 to 56,937 in 1810. (In 1519 the Native American population of Nuevo Santander was estimated at 190,000. By 1800 the population fell to 3,000.) By 1820, despite the turmoil of the Mexican War of Independence from Spain, the colony had grown to 67,434. The combined population of Reynosa, Camargo, Mier, Revilla, Laredo, and Matamoros, on both sides of the Rio Bravo, numbered 1,479 in 1749; by 1829, it had increased to 24,686. The administrative structure of the colony was stratified into large landholders, high government officials, and merchants. The rancheros made up a middle group along with artisans, while the natives and servants lingered at the bottom of the social ladder. Seventeen haciendas and 437 ranchos dotted Nuevo Santander by 1794. As in other provinces, the presidio played an important role in the order and brought in government revenue. Ranching and commerce became the main economic pursuits in the Lower Rio Grande.[111]

The Occupation of Alta California: Paradise Lost

2.9 Characterize notion that the missions were more a institution to colonize the people than to convert them to Christianity.

The colonization of *Alta*, or Upper, California began in 1769. Upper California had been one of the most densely populated regions in what is now the United States, with a native population of nearly half a million. The population fell to half that number during the Spanish colonial period. The Franciscans led the colonization of Alta California, where they established 21 missions. At the height of their influence, the missions had 20,000 natives living under their control.

Los Indigenas

From south to north the missions housed the Diegueño, Juaneño, Gabrieliño, Chumash, and Costanoan peoples. Inhabiting the coastland, these tribes were skilled artisans who fashioned sea vessels out of soapstone and used clamshell-bead currency. These tribes bore the brunt of missionary activity.

The Spaniards never missionized the Yokut, who lived in settlements that ran the length of the San Joaquín Valley and the western foothills of the Sierra Madre just south of present-day Fresno. They were divided into as many as 50 tribelets, each with their own dialect. The Yokut, also known as Mariposan, spoke a Penutian language. Master hunters and food gatherers, the Yokut lived in communal houses inhabited by as many as 10 persons. Chiefs or co-chiefs headed the tribes; these were hereditary positions that women could inherit. The women also had a wealth of knowledge about religious questions.

The Yokut carried on extensive trade with other California natives. They harbored runaway mission natives, and thus tension existed between them and Spanish authorities. Like native peoples elsewhere, a large number, 75 percent, of the Yokut died because of epidemics, the most devastating of which occurred in 1833.[112]

The Missions: Myth and Reality

In principle, the missions were supposed to prepare the natives for self-rule. This did not happen in the Spanish or Mexican periods. Because of the friars' puritanism and harsh treatment, they drove the Indigenous populations to rebellion.[113] Critics point to the falling birthrate among the Indigenous People during the mission period. Furthermore, work was associated with a complex system of punishments and rewards. The Indigenous People in California were not used to the type of confined physical labor found in the missions.

The missions, presidios, and pueblos consolidated Spanish rule. Mostly mixed-race colonists from Sonora and Sinaloa settled in the pueblos. Spanish officials granted land, known as *ranchos*, to many former presidio soldiers where they raised cattle and sheep. Some received larger grants for haciendas. The California natives did most of the labor, usually trained by the missions to be vaqueros, soap makers, tanners, shoemakers, carpenters, blacksmiths, bakers, cooks, servants, pages, fishermen, farmers, and carpenters, as well as a host of other occupations.

Tension existed between military and ecclesiastical authorities over the soldiers' mistreatment of the Indigenous women; historian Antonia I. Castañeda says that we can assume that this was the case in other provinces of New Spain as well. Father Junípero Serra, himself a severe taskmaster, often complained about soldier misconduct, saying that the Indigenous People resisted conversion and sometimes became warlike and hostile "because of the soldiers' repeated outrages against the women." Serra lamented, "Even the children who came to the mission were not safe from their baseness."[114] Evidence suggests that offenses against women were not remedied; rape and even murder went unpunished. Military officials assumed a "boys-will-be-boys" attitude, although the official policy prohibited such abuses.

In 1785, natives from eight rancherías united and attacked Mission San Gabriel, killing all the Spanish settlers. Toypurina, a 24-year-old medicine woman, persuaded six of the eight villages to join the rebellion. The soldiers captured and punished her along with three other leaders.

Conclusion: On the Eve of the Mexican War of Independence

By the eve of the Mexican War of Independence, a complex society evolved on the northern frontier of New Spain. Although they were isolated, there was considerable interaction between the different regions in northern New Spain. The non-Indigenous settlers tapped into a network of routes used before their arrival by the natives. The Chihuahua Trail, part of the Camino Real, was the trade route linking Santa Fé to Chihuahua and Mexico City. After Taos, New Mexico, was founded in the 1790s, they extended this trail to its plaza. A major part of the trail within New Mexico was a river road, following the Rio Grande. Caravans traveled this road and brought imported goods and luxuries to the settlements of the Rio Grande as they had to the mining camps of Nueva Vizcaya. Exchanges would include ore, slaves, and other goods. There were also well-established routes connecting Alta California, Sonora, New Mexico, and Texas.[115]

We should not romanticize this society as egalitarian or idyllic. Though most of the inhabitants were non-European, the elites in these societies were recently immigrated Spaniards and/or their criollo children. The vast numbers of subjects were Castas, those of mixed race, which had limited access to land. Indeed, the 1793 census shows the dynamic race mixture that was taking place in

New Spain. A word of caution is that although there was diversity, race established privilege, and the more Spanish the subjects appeared the more privileges they had.

By the nineteenth century, race was based more on sight than on the rigid categories of the sixteenth century. What would become the Mexican (and Central American) was a conglomerate of people whose racial identity could change from generation to generation—it went beyond the mestizo paradigm popularly portrayed. For instance, the 1810 census suggests that more than 10 percent of the population were Afromestizos, a classification that generally meant they looked mixed black, or more African than Spanish.[116] Over generations, those who were originally African or native looked *or wanted to look* more like Spaniards.

As has been mentioned throughout the chapter, forced labor, the wars, the enslavement of the natives, and droughts and plagues had taken their toll on the native population. Either they had become hispanicized, or they perished or were forced into exile. In some cases, like that of the Tarahumara, a large portion of them retreated further into the Sierra Madre. The Yaqui, who had warred with the Spaniards, were later drawn into battle with the Mexicans in the 1920s in defense of their homeland. The Mexicans' justification was that they were *gente de razón* (people of reason), or better still, Christians, and those who opposed them were *indios bárbaros*.

On the eve of the Mexican Revolution, Mexico did not yet have a set national identity. As the reader can deduct from the chart following, the new nation was racially diverse. The population was predominantly Indigenous, and Africans were at least 10 percent of the population. Given the 300-year tradition of lying about race in order to gain racial status, it can be speculated that as many as 20 percent of the population had some African blood and fewer than stated were full-blooded Spaniards.[117] The colonial mentality and racial ambivalence are a factor even today among the Mexican people. Yet it is clear from current population data that most racial mixing took place after Independence with the mestizo population going from 10 percent in 1810 to about 60 percent today; on the downside the Indigenous population fell from 60 percent to 30 percent.

Three hundred years of mercantilism left New Spain without its own commercial or manufacturing infrastructure. Spanish capital fled the country and the mainstays of its economy—agriculture, ranching, and mining—went bankrupt. The Spanish tightly ruled New Spain because it was Spain's most valuable commodity, giving the castas little experience in self-rule. Indeed, mixed bloods would continue to be excluded from the governance of the republic after independence. Most Mexicans lacked experience in self-government and they lacked a professional civil service bureaucracy. In addition, Mexico experienced a long war of independence (1810–1821), losing an estimated 10 percent of its population, worsening Mexico's serious underpopulation that resulted from the mass migrations to the northern frontier.[118] Colonialism had seriously retarded Mexico's development.

On the positive side, influenced by the Enlightenment and representative constitutionalism, many of Mexico's new leaders wanted a modern society based on reason rather than theology. However, Mexicans had to overcome 300 years of Spanish colonialism, which was no small order. On the negative side, secularization and modernization meant not only the privatization of property belonging to the Catholic Church, but elimination of the feudalism that meant the privatization of Indigenous land. To build their own nation, Mexicans had to create a new identity for themselves. A crucial part of creating a new identity and nation building was replacing the old saints with new, secular heroes—heroes who would call on the people to celebrate Mexico and everything it meant to be Mexican.[119] Within this was interwoven the acceptance of the Indigenous heritage, a process that really did not begin until a 100 years later with the Second Mexican Revolution.[120]

The Spanish colonization annihilated a universal Mexican identity. It created a tension within the Mexican that grew over time as the culture and identity of the colonizer has created schizophrenia among many Mexican Americans as they learn their history. Parts of their identity once thought to have been wiped out clash with their colonial mentality. The colonized begins to question phrases such a "inferior races" and the colonized understand their birthright.[121]

Population of Mexico in 1810

Racial Category	Number	Percentage
Indigenous	3,676,281	60
Europeans (peninsulares)	15,000	0.3
Criollos (Euromestizos)	1,092,397	18
Mestizos (Indiomestizos)	704,245	11
Mixed Africans and zambos (Afromestizos)	624,461	10
Blacks	10,000	0.2

SOURCES: *Austín Cue Cánovas, Historia social y económica de México (1521–1854)* (Mexico, 1972), p. 134, adapted in Meyer and Sherman, p. 218.

Notes

1. Frances M. Lopez-Morillas and Julian Marias, *Understanding Spain* (Ann Arbor: University of Michigan Press, 1991).
2. J. H. Galloway, "The Mediterranean Sugar Industry," *Geographical Review*, Vol. 67, No. 2 (April, 1977), 177–194.
3. J. H. Galloway, *The Sugar Cane Industry: An Historical Geography from Its Origins to 1914* (Cambridge: Cambridge University Press, 1989), 31–36.
4. Ibid., 33.
5. Faruk Tabak, *The Waning of the Mediterranean, 1550–1870: A Geohistorical Approach* (Baltimore: Johns Hopkins University Press, 2010), 1–10.
6. J. H. Galloway, "The Mediterranean Sugar Industry," *Geographical Review*, Vol. 67, No. 2 (April, 1977), 177–1. http://www.rogerlouismartinez.com/wp-content/uploads/2015/01/mediterreanean-sugar.pdf.
7. "How Sugar is Made - the History," http://www.sucrose.com/lhist.html. Rich Cohen, "Sugar," *National Geographic*, August 2013, http://ngm.nationalgeographic.com/2013/08/sugar/cohen-text. Kristy Mucci, "The Illustrated History of How Sugar Conquered the World," *Saveur*, January 9, 2017, https://www.saveur.com/sugar-history-of-the-world.
8. Darra Goldstein, ed., *The Oxford Companion to Sugar and Sweets* (New York: Oxford University Press, 2015), 695.
9. Candice Goucher, Charles LeGuin, and Linda Walton, "Commerce and Change: The Creation of a Global Economy and the Expansion of Europe," *In the Balance: Themes in Global History* (Boston: McGraw-Hill, 1998), 491–508. Philip D, Curtin, *The Rise and Fall of the Plantation System*, 2nd ed. (Cambridge: Cambridge University Press, 1998), pp. 19–22.
10. David Wheat, "Iberian Roots of the Transatlantic Slave Trade, 1440–1640," *History Now*, https://www.gilderlehrman.org/history-by-era/origins-slavery/essays/iberian-roots-transatlantic-slave-trade-1440%E2%80%931640.
11. William S. Maltby, *The rise and fall of the Spanish Empire* (New York: Palgrave Macmillan, 2009). Thomas H. Holloway, *A Companion to Latin American History* (London: John Wiley & Sons, 2011).
12. Tomás J. Gasch. "Globalisation, Market Formation and Commoditisation in The Spanish Empire. Consumer Demand for Asian Goods In Mexico City and Seville, c. 1571–1630," *Revista de Historia Económica / Journal of Iberian and Latin American Economic History*, 2014, Vol. 32(2), 189–221.
13. Dennis O. Flynn and Arturo Giráldez, "Cycles of Silver: Global Economic Unity through the Mid-Eighteenth Century," *Journal of World History* 13, No. 2 (2002), 391–427. This chapter is discussed in the first chapter of Rodolfo F. Acuña, *Corridors of Migration: The Odyssey of Mexican Laborers, 1600–1933* (Tucson, AZ: University of Arizona Press, 2007) in greater detail.
14. Blog, "Africa begins at the Pyrenees," London's Singing Organ-Grinder, May 2, 2010, http://elorganillero.com/blog/2010/05/02/the-true-origins-of-africa-begins-at-the-pyrenees/.
15. Ibid., M. de Pradt (Dominique Georges Frédéric), *Mémoires historiques sur la révolution d'Espagne* (Paris: Various editions, 1816), 48 or 68.
16. Jane S. Gerber, *The Jews of Spain: A History of the Sephardic Experience* (New York: Free Press, 1992), 3. The Jews lived not as isolated individuals but as organized communities in Spain.
17. Punic Wars, http://www.youtube.com/watch?v=ARF2r3Ol80Y&feature=related.
18. Gerber, *The Jews of Spain*, 18–19.
19. W. Montgomery Watt and Pierre Cachia, *A History of Islamic Spain* (Garden City, NY: Anchor Books, 1967), 40.
20. Ibid., Islamic Spain: A Golden Age? http://www.youtube.com/watch?v=o8rGNBHdmdQ, Ibid., (2/2), http://www.youtube.com/watch?v=hahOI9LKw2Y.
21. Many—not all—of the YouTube clips are in Spanish; in most cases a translation to English can be obtained from the YouTube site. *Reconquista Española*, http://www.youtube.com/watch?v=ci2jTnI2qqk&feature=channel. When the Moors Ruled in Spain (1 of 11), http://www.youtube.com/watch?v=wBsDDGCIFLQ&feature=related. S. Alfassa Marks, "The Jews in Islamic Spain: Al Andalus," *Foundation for the Advancement of Sephardic Studies and Culture*, http://www.sephardicstudies.org/islam.html.
22. Christopher Columbus and William Bigelow, "Once upon a Genocide: Christopher Columbus in Children's Literature," *Language Arts* Vol. 69, Issue 2 (1992), 112–120. David E. Stannard, "Columbus's Legacy: Genocide in the Americas," *The Nation*, Vol. 255, Issue 12 (19 October 1992), 430–433.
23. "DNA Tests on Christopher Columbus's bones, on his relatives and on Genoese and Catalan claimants," http://www.christopher-columbus.eu/dna-tests.htm. Harmon, Amy, "Columbus's Origins, With a Swab" (National Desk)(THE DNA AGE)(Christopher Columbus), *The New York Times*, Oct 8, 2007, http://www.nytimes.com/2007/10/08/us/08columbus.html.
24. "Columbus was Catalan, possibly Jewish, Georgetown professor says," *Jerusalem Post*, November 3, 2009,

http://www.jpost.com/Jewish-World/Columbus-was-Catalan-possibly-Jewish-Georgetown-professor-says.

25 Quoted in "Columbus Controversy," *History*, http://www.history.com/topics/exploration/columbus-controversy. Jack Weatherford, "'Explorer' Columbus originated slave trade," *Toronto Star*, (1989, October 13), A25.

26 Nicholas Walton, *Genoa, "La Superba": The Rise and Fall of a Merchant Pirate Superpower* (London: Hurst & Co, 2015), 108–110.

27 Edmund S. Morgan, "Columbus' Confusion About the New World. The European discovery of America opened possibilities for those with eyes to see. But Columbus was not one of them," *Smithsonian Magazine*, October 2009, http://www.smithsonianmag.com/travel/columbus-confusion-about-the-new-world-140132422/.

28 Jalil Sued-Badillo, "Christopher Columbus and the Enslavement of the Amerindians in the Caribbean; Columbus and the New World Order 1492–1992," *Monthly Review* 44, No. 3 (July 1992), 71ff. This article shows the involvement of the Genoese in the spread of sugar production and slavery and their involvement in the Azores and other islands of the Atlantic coast including the Canary Islands, where they experimented with mercantile capitalism. John H. Elliot, *Imperial Spain 1469–1716* (New York: A Mentor Book, 1966), 56–57. Robert M. Carmack, Janine Gasco, and Gary H. Gossen, *The Legacy of Mesoamerica: History and Culture of a Native American Civilization* (Upper Saddle River, NJ: Prentice Hall, 1996), 131. Peter Muilenburg, "The Savage Sea the Indians Who Gave Their Name to the Caribbean Stopped at Nothing to Satisfy Their Appetite for Adventure—and Human Flesh," *Sun-Sentinel* (Fort Lauderdale, April 25, 1993), an example of a popular article repeating myths about the Caribs. Claudius Fergus, "Why an Atlantic Slave Trade?" *Journal of Caribbean History*, Vol. 42, Issue 1 (2008): 1–22.

29 Sued-Badillo, "Columbus and the enslavement," 71ff. From 1494 to the turn of the century about 2,000 slaves were taken to Castile. Kirkpatrick Sale, "What Columbus Discovered," *The Nation* 251, No. 13 (October 22, 1990), 444–446. Vincent Villanueva Mayer, Jr., "The Black Slave On New Spain's Northern Frontier: San Jose De Parral 1632–76," (PhD Dissertation, University of Utah, Utah, 1975). The Spaniards imported slaves from China, Cambodia, Java, Siam, Bengal, Persia, and the Philippines who entered through Acapulco on the yearly Manila galleon. These slaves were designated as *chinos* and *esclavos de la India de Portugal*. Helen Nader, "Desperate Men, Questionable Acts: The Moral Dilemma of Italian Merchants in the Spanish Slave Trade," *The Sixteenth Century Journal* Vol. 33, No. 2 (Summer, 2002), 402–422.

30 Slave traders transported at least 10 million Africans to the Americas during the colonial period. They sold over 5 million to the Guianas and the Caribbean Islands, almost 4 million to Brazil, some 600,000 to mainland Spanish holdings, and the remaining 900,000 to the British colonies in North America and to Europe in roughly equal shares. Sued-Badillo, "Christopher Columbus and the Enslavement of the Amerindians in the Caribbean; Columbus and the New World Order 1492–1992," 71. The Spaniards also sold Indigenous persons in the slave markets of Havana, Mexico City, and even Manila.

31 Steven Newcomb, *Pagans in the Promised Land: Decoding the Doctrine of Christian Discovery* (Golden, Colorado: Fulcrum Publishing, 2008). Watson, Blake A. *The doctrine of discovery and the elusive definition of Indian title* (The Future of International Law in Indigenous Affairs: *The Doctrine of Discovery, the United Nations, and the Organization of American States*), *Lewis & Clark Law Review*, Winter, 2011, Vol. 15(4), 995–1024.

32 Digital Story—Bartolomé de las Casas, http://www.youtube.com/watch?v=kAkY0u6aH20. United Methodist Women, "Reformations: 1453–1800." "The Bible: The Book That Bridges the Millennia," http://gbgm-umc.org/umw/bible/ref.stm.

33 Carmack et al., *The Legacy of Mesoamerica*, 132–36. Lewis Hanke, *Aristotle and the American Indians: A Study in Race Prejudice in the Modern World* (Chicago, IL: Henry Regnery Company, 1959), 13, 33, 45.

34 H. Cortés and J. Bayard Morris, *Five Letters 1519–1526* (Hoboken: Taylor and Francis, 2014). The letters are found in e-Book form.

35 Ronald A. Barnett, "New Spain: The right of conquest," *Mexconnect*, http://www.mexconnect.com/articles/3357-new-spain-the-right-of-conquest.

36 Karen Vieira Powers, *Women in the Crucible of Conquest: The Gendered Genesis of Spanish American Society 1500–1600* (Albuquerque: University of New Mexico Press, 2005). G.A. Henty, By *right of conquest; or, With Cortez in Mexico* (London: Latimer House, 1957). William Hickling Prescott, George Ticknor, William Robertson, *The Works of William H. Prescott: History of the conquest of Mexico*, Vol. 2 (London: JB Lippincott, 1904), 210.

37 Rodolfo Acuña-Soto, David W. Stahle, Malcolm K. Cleaveland, and Matthew D. Therrell, "Megadrought and Megadeath in 16th Century Mexico," *Historical Review*, Vol. 8, No. 4 (April 2002), https://wwwnc.cdc.gov/eid/article/8/4/01-0175_article.

38 "Tenochtitlán," http://www.youtube.com/watch?v=F3QA2J9UxJE. "La Noche Triste," http://www

.youtube.com/watch?v=lJA_tYOIBaY&feature=related.

39 Charles L. Mee Jr., "That Fateful Moment When Two Civilizations Came Face to Face; Spaniards and Aztecs," *Smithsonian* 23, No. 7 (October 1992), 56ff.

40 David Martinez, "Is it true that not one street in Mexico is named after that Spanish 'hero' Hernan Cortes?" Quora, https://www.quora.com/Is-it-true-that-not-one-street-in-Mexico-is-named-after-that-Spanish-hero-Hernan-Cortes.

41 Kalevi Jaakko Holsti, *Taming the Sovereigns: Institutional Change in International Politics* (New York: Cambridge Press, 2004), p. 227.

42 "The Spanish Conquest and the Decline of the Maya," Kids Discover, https://online.kidsdiscover.com/unit/the-maya/topic/the-spanish-conquest-and-the-decline-of-the-maya. Grant D. Jones, *The Conquest of the Last Maya Kingdom* 1st ed. (Stanford: Stanford University Press, 1998). Elizabeth Graham, Scott E. Simmons, and Christine D. White, "The Spanish conquest and the Maya," *World Archaeology*, Vol. 45(1): 161–185, http://discovery.ucl.ac.uk/1396311/1/10.1080-00438243.2013.770962.pdf.

43 Noble David Cook, *Born To Die: Disease and New World Conquest* (New York: Cambridge University Press, 1998), 206. Francis J. Brooks, "Revising the Conquest of Mexico: Smallpox, Sources, and Populations," *Journal of Interdisciplinary History* 24, No. 1 (Summer 1993): 1–29. David Henige, *Numbers from Nowhere: The American Indian Contact Population Debate* (Norman, OK: University of Oklahoma Press, 1998).

44 Susan Kellogg, "Hegemony Out of Conquest: The First Two Centuries of Spanish Rule in Central Mexico," *Radical History Review* 53 (1991): 32. Gunter B. Risse, "What Columbus's Voyages Wrought; Editorial," *The Western Journal of Medicine* 160, No. 6 (June 1994): 577ff.

45 Kellogg, "Hegemony Out of Conquest," 29. Alfred W. Crosby, Jr., *The Columbian Exchange: Biological and Cultural Consequences of 1492* (Westport, CT: Greenwood Press, 1972), 48–58. See Cook, 132, 139, 140, 168, 170, 193, for table summaries of epidemics in Mexico and Guatemala. Michael H. Crawford, *The Origins of Native Americans: Evidence from Anthropological Genetics* (Cambridge: Cambridge University Press, 2001), 51–2.

46 "Coffee originated in Ethiopia during the thirteenth century and spread to Egypt and Yemen." Tish Lewis, "Coffee in the Columbian Exchange," Prezi, September 25, 2012, https://prezi.com/q3nbpsm6_ysl/coffe-in-the-columbian-exchange/.

47 Sources claim that syphilis was an American disease; however, many critics said it traveled the other way around. "Diseases," http://public.gettysburg.edu/~tshannon/hist106web/site19/diseases.htm. However, there is evidence that it came from Europe. Charles Q. Choi, "Case Closed? Columbus Introduced Syphilis to Europe," *LiveScience*, December 27, 2011, https://www.scientificamerican.com/article/case-closed-columbus/.

48 Nathan Nunn and Nancy Qian, "The Columbian Exchange: A History of Disease, Food, and Ideas," *Journal of Economic Perspectives* Vol. 24, No. 2 (Spring 2010), 163–188.

49 Neil Robert Kasiak, "Fermenting Identities: Race and Pulque Politics in Mexico City between 1519 and 1754" (Master of Arts Thesis, Eastern Kentucky University, 2012).

50 Michael C. Meyer, William L. Sherman, and Susan M. Deeds, *The Course of Mexican History*, 6th ed. (New York: Oxford University Press, 1999), 130–2. Jason Edward Lemon, "The *encomienda* in early New Spain" (PhD Dissertation, Emory University, 2000).

51 Lesley Byrd Simpson, *The encomienda in New Spain: The beginning of Spanish Mexico* (Rev. and enl. ed., History e-book project) (Berkeley: University of California Press, 1950). Silvio Zavala, *New viewpoints on the Spanish colonization of America* (New York: Russell & Russell, 1968). Ronald Batchelder and Sanchez, Nicolas, "The *encomienda* and the optimizing imperialist: an interpretation of Spanish imperialism in the Americas," *Public Choice*, 2013, Vol. 156(1), 45–6.

52 Hanns J. Prem, "Spanish Colonization and Indian Property in Central Mexico, 1521–1620." *Annals of the Association of American Geographers* 82, No. 3 (September 1992), 446.

53 Andre Gundar Frank, *Mexican agriculture, 1521–1630: Transformation of the mode of production* (Cambridge, New York: Cambridge University Press, 1979).

54 Timothy J. Yaeger, "Encomienda or Slavery? The Spanish Crown's Choice of Labor Organization in Sixteenth-Century Spanish America," *The Journal of Economic History*, Vol. 55, No. 4 (Dec. 1995), 844.

55 C. Haring, *The Spanish Empire in America* (New York: Harcourt, Brace & World, Inc., 1963). Carmack et al., *The Legacy of Mesoamerica*, 166: "[N]ative people had no concept of a 'religion' or a 'faith' as such a clearly defined entity separable from the rest of culture, and they did not comprehend what it was they were supposed to be giving up and taking on."

56 James Lockhart, *The Nahuas After the Conquest: Social and Cultural History of the Indians of Central Mexico, Sixteenth Through Eighteenth Centuries* (Stanford, CA: Stanford University Press, 1992), 14–58, 62, 428, argues that many aspects of the Azteca system remained intact, especially during the first 50 years

after the invasion. His account, based on Nahuatl sources, is intriguing, if not always persuasive.

57 María Elena Martínez, *Genealogical Fictions: Limpieza de Sangre, Religion, and Gender in Colonial Mexico* (Stanford: Stanford University Press, 2011). Patricia Lopes Don, "Franciscans, Indian Sorcerers, and the Inquisition in New Spain, 1536–1543," *Journal of World History* Vol. 17, No. 1 (March, 2006): 27–49.

58 Marcela Tostado Gutiérrez, *El álbum de la mujer de las mexicanas. Volumén II/Época colonial* (México, DF: Instituto Nacional de Antropología é Historia, 1991), 109. Most racial designations were not used after the sixteenth century. The mixed races were referred to as castas. *Diccionario Porrúa: Historia, Biografía y Geografía De México* Quinta Edición (México DF: Editorial Porrúa, S. A., 1986), 535 lists the categories. Adrian Bustamante, "The Matter Was Never Resolved: The Casta System in Colonial New Mexico, 1693–1823," *New Mexico Historical Review* 66, No. 2 (April 1991), 143–63; page 144 presents another variation. Castas, http://faculty.smu.edu/bakewell/BAKEWELL/thinksheets/castas.html.

59 Pinturas de Castas, Painting of Castas, http://www.youtube.com/watch?v=ZMjO2Ckc1iE. D. A. Brading, "Source," *The Hispanic American Historical Review* 53, No. 3 (August 1973), 389–414. Stafford Poole, "Church Law on the Ordination of Indians and Castas in New Spain," *The Hispanic American Historical Review* Vol. 61, No. 4 (Nov, 1981): 637–650. Magali Marie Carrera, *Imagining identity in New Spain: race, lineage, and the colonial body in portraiture and casta paintings* (Austin: University of Texas Press, 2003). Remnants of the casta system persist to this day. Paul Smith and Jesús Lozano, *Crónica de castas* (Chronicle of castes), and *Sangre Bárbara* (Barbarous blood). *Film Quarterly*, Lxviii (4) (2015), 59–62.

60 Matthew Restall, Lisa Sousa, and Kevin Terraciano (eds.), *Mesoamerican Voices: Native Language Writings from Colonial Mexico, Oaxaca, Yucatan, and Guatemala* (Cambridge: Cambridge University Press, 2005), 128. Ann M. Pescatello, *Power and Pawn: The Female in Iberian Families, Societies and Cultures* (Westport, CT: Greenwood Press, 1976). Karen Vieira Powers, *Women in the Crucible of Conquest: The Gendered Genesis of Spanish American Society, 1500–1600* (Albuquerque: University of New Mexico Press, 2005). Socolow, Susan Migden, *The Women of Colonial Latin America* (New York: Cambridge University Press, 2000).

61 Matthew Restall, Lisa Sousa and Kevin Terraciano, *Mesoamerican Voices: Native Language Writings from Colonial Mexico, Yucatan* . . . Ibid., 167. Catherine Komisaruk, "Rape Narratives, Rape Silences: Sexual Violence and Judicial Testimony in Colonial Guatemala," *University of Hawaii Press*, Vol. 31, No. 3, Summer 2008, 369–396.

62 Irene Silverblatt, "Lessons of Gender and Ethnohistory in Mesoamerica," *Ethnohistory* Vol. 42, No. 4, *Women, Power, and Resistance in Colonial Mesoamerica* (Autumn, 1995), 639–650.

63 John Kunat "Play me false: Rape, Race, and Conquest in The Tempest," *Shakespeare Quarterly*, 65(3) (2014), 307–327. Jonathan Saha, "The male state," *The Indian Economic and Social History Review*, 2010, Vol.47(3), 343–376.

64 Patricia Greenfield, "Implications of Commerce and Urbanization for the Learning Environments of Everyday Life: A Zinacantec Maya Family Across Time and Space," UCLA Center for the Study of Women, 2012, http://escholarship.org/uc/item/3kp816bz#page-2.

65 Silverblatt, "Lessons of Gender and Ethnohistory," 183–84. Juliana Barr, "From Captives to Slaves: Commodifying Indian Women in the Borderlands," *The Journal of American History* Vol. 92, No. 1 (Jun, 2005): 18–46.

66 Susan Kellogg, "The Colonial Mosaic of Indigenous New Spain, 1519–1821" *Oxford Research Encyclopedias*, June 2016, http://latinamericanhistory.oxfordre.com/view/10.1093/acrefore/9780199366439.001.0001/acrefore-9780199366439-e-29.

67 Cheryl English Martin, *Governance and Society in Colonial Mexico: Chihuahua in the Eighteenth Century* (Stanford: Stanford University Press, 1996), 150.

68 Robert McCaa, "Calidad, Clase, and Marriage in Colonial Mexico: The Case of Parral, 1788–90," *The Hispanic American Historical Review*, Vol. 64, No. 3 (Aug, 1984), 477–501, https://www.jstor.org/stable/2514936?seq=1#page_scan_tab_contents.

69 Marie Elaine Danforth, Keith Jacobi, and Mark Nathan Cohen, "Gender and Health Among the Colonial Mayan of Tipu, Belize," *Ancient Mesoamerica* 8, No. 1 (Spring 1997): 1, 15.

70 Carmack et al., *The Legacy of Mesoamerica*, 181–83. Linda Schele and David Freidel, *A Forest of Kings: The Untold Story of the Ancient Mayan* (New York: Quill William Morrow, 1990), 40–41.

71 Claude Morin, "Age at Marriage and Female Employment in Colonial Mexico," Paper read at the International Conference "Women's Employment, Marriage-Age and Population Change," University of Delhi, Developing Countries Research Center, March 3–5, 1997, https://www.webdepot.umontreal.ca/Usagers/morinc/MonDepotPublic/pub/CIDHInd97.htm.

72 Ibid.

73 Louise Burkhart, "Mexica Women on the Home Front: Housework and Religion in Aztec Mexico," in Susan Schroeder, Stephanie Wood, and Robert Haskett, eds., *Indian Women of Early Mexico* (Norman, OK: University of Oklahoma Press, 1997), 25–27. Susan Kellogg, "From Parallel and Equivalent to Separate but Unequal: Tenocha Mexica Women, 1500–1700," in Susan Schroeder et al., *Indian Women of Early Mexico*, 123–37. Pedro Carrasco, "Indian-Spanish Marriages in the First Century of the Colony," in Susan Schroeder, et al., 87–89, 93, 97.

74 Carmack et al., *The Legacy of Mesoamerica*, 330.

75 Robert Haskett, "Activist or Adulteress: The Life and Struggle of Doña Josefa María of Tepoztlán," in Susan Schroeder, Stephanie Wood, and Robert Haskett, eds., *Indian Women of Early Mexico* (Norman, OK: University of Oklahoma Press, 1997), 147–53.

76 Silverblatt, "Lessons of Gender and Ethnohistory," 641, 645–46. Javier Pérez Escohotado, *Sexo e Inquisición en España* (Madrid: Ediciones Termas Hoy, 1998), 173–90, deals with the Inquisition in Spain and homosexuality. Laura A. Lewis, "The 'Weakness' of Women and the Feminization of the Indian in Colonial Mexico," *Colonial Latin American Review* Vol. 5, Issue 1 (Jun, 1996), 73–95. Douglas Richmond, "The Legacy of African Slavery in Colonial Mexico, 1519–1810," *The Journal of Popular Culture* Vol. 35, Issue 2 (Fall 2001), 1–16.

77 Juan Diego was canonized in 2002.

78 Eric Hobsbawm and Terence Ranger, eds., *The Invention of Tradition* (London: Cambridge University Press, 1983), http://www.ic.arizona.edu/~ws5001/virgin.html. Sandra Cisneros, "Guadalupe as the Sex Goddess," in Ana Castillo, ed., *Goddess of the Americas: Writing on the Virgin of Guadalupe* (New York: Riverhead Books, 1996), 49–50. Gloria Anzaldúa, *Borderlands/La Frontera: The New Mestiza* (San Francisco, CA: Aunt Lute Books, 1987), 27. C. M. Stafford Poole, *Our Lady of Guadalupe: The Origins and Sources of a Mexican National Symbol, 1531–1797* (Tucson, AZ: University of Arizona Press, 1995). Carmack et al., *The Legacy of Mesoamerica*, 191–92. Timothy Matovina, "A Response to Stafford Poole," *The Catholic Historical Review*, Vol. 100, No. 2, Spring 2014, 284–291.

79 Poole, *Our Lady of Guadalupe*. Carmack et al., *The Legacy of Mesoamerica*, 191–92.

80 Poole, *Our Lady of Guadalupe*, 5.

81 Map of Spanish Exploration and Early Colonization Activities in North America, 1513–1607, http://www.artifacts.org/conquest.htm.

82 Thomas P. Moore, "A brief history of early: silver mining in Spanish America," *The Mineralogical Record*. 39.6 (November–December 2008), 5–21.

83 Raymond Pierotti, *Indigenous Knowledge, Ecology, and Evolutionary Biology* (New York: Routledge, 2011), 45.

84 Thomas E. Sheridan, "The limits of power: the political ecology of the Spanish Empire in the Greater Southwest," *Antiquity* 66 (1992): 153, 164, 167.

85 Thomas E Sheridan and Thomas H. Naylor, *Rarámuri, a Tarahumara colonial chronicle, 1607–1791*, 1st ed. (Flagstaff, Ariz: Northland Press, 1979).

86 David J. Weber, *The Spanish Frontier in North America* (New Haven: Yale University Press, 1992), 94, 118. Kellogg, "Hegemony Out of Conquest," 29. See Chapter 1 in Acuña, *Corridors of Migration*, especially the footnotes and bibliography.

87 Susan M. Deeds, "Double Jeopardy: Indian Women in Jesuit Missions of Nueva Vizcaya," in Susan Schroeder, Stephanie Wood, and Robert Haskett, eds., *Indian Women of Early Mexico* (Norman, OK: University of Oklahoma Press, 1997), 255–59, 263. Catholic divorce or annulment was practically unavailable to Indigenous women.

88 Florence C. Lister and Robert H. Lister, *Chihuahua: Storehouse of Storms* (Albuquerque, NM: University of New Mexico Press, 1966), 15–20. Carmack et al., *The Legacy of Mesoamerica*, 5. Acuña, *Corridors of Migration*, 12–14.

89 Tina Griego, "A Foot Note to History; Amputation of N.M. Statue Underlines 400-Year-Old Grudge," *The Denver Rocky Mountain News* (Denver, CO, June 21, 1998). Just prior to the 400th anniversary, the *Cuarto Centenario* of Oñate's conquest of New Mexico, someone expertly cut the right foot off a bronze statue of Oñate. During Oñate's conquest of New Mexico, the people of Acoma Pueblo resisted the invasion and Oñate punished the people by condemning 24 Acoma men to the amputation of a foot and banished their women and children into slavery.

90 Native Peoples of North America: "Agricultural Societies In Pre-European Times: Southwestern U.S. and Northwestern Mexico," https://www.cabrillo.edu/~crsmith/southwest.html.

91 James Brooke, "Oñate's Missing Foot," 1998, http://pages.ucsd.edu/~rfrank/class_web/ES-112A/Onate.html.

92 "Statue of Juan De Oñate," New Mexico, United States. Date of incident: 01/1998, http://samdurant.net/defaced_monuments/Pages/NewMex/newmex.html.

93 See Susan M. Deeds, "Rural Work in Nueva Vizcaya: Forms of Labor Coercion on the Periphery," *The Hispanic American Historical Review* 69, No. 3 (August 1, 1989), 425–49.

94 Deeds, "Rural Work," 435. Acuña, *Corridors of Migration*, 13–14, 37, 71. Estevan Rael-Galvez, "Identifying

captivity and capturing identity: Narratives of American Indian slavery. Colorado and New Mexico, 1776–1934" (PhD Dissertation, University of Michigan, 2002).

95 Jeremy Baskes, "Coerced or Voluntary? The Repartimiento and Market Participation of Peasants in Late Colonial Oaxaca," *Journal of Latin American Studies*, Vol. 28, No. 1 (Feb, 1996), 1–28.

96 Weber, *The Spanish Frontier in North America*, 128.

97 Angelina F. Veyna, "Women in Early New Mexico: A Preliminary View," in Teresa Córova et al., eds., *Chicana Voices: Intersections of Class, Race, and Gender* (Austin, TX: Center for Mexican American Studies, 1986), 120–35.

98 "The Pueblo Revolt of 1680," *Native Peoples Magazine*, http://worldhistoryproject.org/1680/8/21/pueblo-indians-capture-santa-fe-from-the-spanish. Jack D. Forbes, *Apache, Navaho and Spaniard* (Norman, OK: University of Oklahoma Press, 1960), 200–24. Luis Aboites Aguilar, *Breve Historia de Chihuahua* (Mexico City: Fondo de Cultura Economica, 1994), 42–44; Susan M. Deeds, *Defiance and Deference in Mexico's Colonial North: Indians under Spanish Rule in Nueva Vizcaya* (Austin, TX: University of Texas Press, 2003), 87.

99 The 1680 Revolt inspired Indigenous Revolts throughout present-day Chihuahua, Durango, and Sonora. Acuña, *Corridors of Migration*, 4–17. Earlier drafts in Acuña Collection, CSUN, have more extensive treatments.

100 Ramón A. Gutiérrez, *When Jesus Came, the Corn Mothers Went Away: Marriage, Sexuality, and Power in New Mexico, 1500–1846* (Stanford, CA: Stanford University Press, 1991), 171. Roxanne Amanda Dunbar, "Land Tenure in Northern New Mexico: An Historical Perspective" (PhD Dissertation, University of California, Los Angeles, 1974), 6. Jonathan Hass, "Warfare among the Pueblos: Myth, History, and Ethnography," *Ethnohistory* 44, No. 2 (Spring 1997): 235–61. Also see Jonathan Haas, "Warfare and the Evolution of Tribal Politics in the Prehistoric Southwest," in Jonathan Haas, ed., *Anthropology of War* (New York: Cambridge University Press, 1990), 171–89, quote 182. Weber, *The Spanish Frontier in North America*, 122.

101 Gutiérrez, *When Jesus Came, the Corn Mothers Went Away*, 159, 174. Angelina F. Veyna "A Look at Colonial Nueva Mexicanas through Their Testaments," in Adela de la Torre and Beatríz M. Pesquera, eds., *Building with Our Hands: New Directions in Chicana Studies* (Berkeley, CA: University of California Press, 1993), 91–108. Weber, *The Spanish Frontier in North America*, 125. Also see Bustamante, 1991, 145–47, which points out that many of the census and parish records were destroyed during the 1680 Pueblo Revolt.

102 Roxanne Dunbar-Ortiz, "Land Tenure and Resistance in New Mexico," *Counterpunch*, September 22, 2007, https://www.counterpunch.org/2007/09/22/land-tenure-and-resistance-in-new-mexico/. For a more recent work see Roxanne, Dunbar-Ortiz, *An Indigenous Peoples' History of the United States* (Boston: Beacon Press, 2012).

103 Dunbar, "Land Tenure in Northern New Mexico," 15–17, 97, 107, quote, 133. Guitiérrez, *When Jesus Came, the Corn Mothers Went Away*, 150, 162.

104 Donald E. Chipman, *Spanish Texas, 1519–1821* (Austin, TX: University of Texas, 1992). *Handbook of Texas Online*, Spanish Texas, http://www.tshaonline.org/handbook/online/articles/nps01. "Old Records and Archeological Remains: Making Sense of the Evidence," *Texas Beyond History*, University of Texas, http://www.texasbeyondhistory.net/plateaus/peoples/records.html.

105 Jesús E. De La Teja, *San Antonio De Béxar, A Community on New Spain's Northern Frontier* (Albuquerque, NM: University of New Mexico Press, 1995), 3–5.

106 For example, Francisco Elías González de Zayas, the founder of the Elías family of Sonora, was a presidio captain, rancher, and miner; he had arrived at Alamos, Sonora, from La Rioja, Spain, in 1729. He was Captain of the Presidio of Terrenate in 1768, lived in Arizpe, which was founded by his family, and died in Paso del Norte, Chihuahua, Mexico, in 1790 as a merchant.

107 Carlos Vélez-Ibáñez, *Border Visions: Mexican Cultures of The Southwest United States* (Tucson, AZ: University of Arizona Press, 1996), 47–48. Weber, *The Spanish Frontier in North America*, 179.

108 Weber, *The Spanish Frontier in North America*, 193–95.

109 Gilberto Miguel Hinojosa, *A Borderlands Town in Transition: Laredo, 1755–1870* (College Station, TX: Texas A&M University Press, 1983), 3. Armando C. Alonzo, *Tejano Legacy: Ranchers and Settlers in South Texas, 1734–1900* (Albuquerque, NM: University of New Mexico Press, 1998), 31. An often overlooked book is Reynaldo Ayala Vallejo, *Geografía Histórica De Parras: El Hombre Cambia a la Tierra* (Saltillo, Coahuila: Sandra de la Cruz González, 1996), 52–55. Tlaxcaláns were very important in the colonization of the area as were black slaves who were brought into the area by the hacendados, missionaries, and mine owners. From 1 to 30 percent of the population was either black or mixed black.

110 Hinojosa, *A Borderlands Town in Transition*, 18, 33.

111 Sheridan, "The Limits of Power," 167. Alonzo, *Tejano Legacy*, 67, 160–61.

112 Brooke S. Arkush, "Yokuts Trade Networks and Native Culture Change in Central and Eastern California," *Ethnohistory* 40, No. 4 (Fall 1993), 619–40.

113 Sherburne F. Cook, *The Conflict Between the California Indian and White Civilization*, Vol. I (Berkeley, CA: University of California Press, 1943), 11–157.

114 Antonia I. Castañeda, "Sexual Violence in the Politics and Policies of Conquest: Amerindian Women and the Spanish Conquest of Alta California," in Adela de la Torre and Beatríz M. Pesquera, eds., *Building with Our Hands: New Directions in Chicana Studies* (Berkeley, CA: University of California Press, 1993), 15–33.

115 David J. Weber, *The Mexican Frontier 1821–1846: The American Southwest Under Mexico* (Albuquerque, NM: University of New Mexico Press, 1982), 1. Armando Miguélez, "La trémula luz del relámpago: Lenguaje metafórico en El Clamor Público," Trabajo presentado en la conferencia El Clamor Público: 150 Years of Latino Newspapers in Southern California, the Huntington Library, San Marino, California, October 28, 2005. Rodolfo F. Acuña, "El Clamor Público: The Sonora Connection (rough draft)," Paper presented at the conference *El Clamor Público*: 150 Years of Latino Newspapers in Southern California, the Huntington Library, San Marino, California, October 28, 2005.

116 Note that Chihuahuans, like New Mexicans, took great pride in so-called racial purity. See examination of censuses for Santa Bárbara, Chihuahua, Padrón de Santa Bárbara, Chihuahua 1778 (AGI indiferente 102), Padrones de Cusiguriachic 1778 (Archivo General de Indias), and various others. Compiled by Sylvia Magdaleno of *La Familia* Ancestral Research Association. The compilation explodes the myth of racial purity. The various *castas* are represented in different censuses. "The El Paso Del Norte: Nuestra Señora de Guadalupe Marriage and Death Records, 1728–1775." Extracted by Aaron Magdaleno, of *La Familia* Ancestral Research Association, January 1998 also shows that although race is not designated in every case, there is substantial mixing.

117 In 1560, blacks and mulattos outnumbered Spaniards in Mexico City; Africans came to Mexico in greater numbers than whites until the 1700s.

118 *Diccionario Porrúa: De Historia, Biografía y Geografía* Quinta Edición, Vol. I (México DF: Editorial Porrúa 1986), 876–77; has an interesting summary of demographic patterns in Mexico.

119 The Mexican census of 1921 shines a bright light on the question of identity. See John P. Schmal, "Racial Makeup of Native-Born Mexicans (from the 1921 Census)," *The Hispanic Experience*, http://www.houstonculture.org/hispanic/censustable.html and Schmal, "Indigenous Identity In The Mexican Census," *The Hispanic Experience*, http://www.houstonculture.org/hispanic/census.html.

120 Readers are encouraged to explore the following archive. Wallace L. McKeehan, "Mexican Independence," Sons of Dewitt Colony Texas, http://www.tamu.edu/ccbn/dewitt/dewitt.htm. See Pilar Gonzalbo. "La familia en México colonial: Una historia de conflictos cotidianos," *Mexican Studies/Estudios Mexicanos* 14, No. 2 (Summer 1998), 389–406.

121 Frantz Fanon, *The Wretched of the Earth* (New York: Grove, 1968).

Chapter 3
The Invasion of Mexico: Legacy of Hate

Learning Objectives

3.1 Explain the relationship between slavery and U.S aggression toward Mexico.

3.2 Describe the Mexican Revolution and the Mexican state in the early 1800s.

3.3 Characterize the behaviors of the U.S. and American immigrants in Texas.

3.4 Compare ways that different populations experienced and described the U.S. invasion of Texas.

3.5 Describe the justification of Americans for the seizure of Texas.

3.6 Describe the reasons for individual American opposition to the Mexican American War.

3.7 Analyze the political and cultural ramifications of the Treaty of Guadalupe Hidalgo.

The late historian Howard Zinn points out in *A People's History of the United States*, that history is a weapon.¹ Zinn puts forth the thesis that the United States was driven by the notion of empire much the same as in Spain and Europe, writing.

> Expansion overseas was not a new idea. Even before the war against Mexico carried the United States to the Pacific, the Monroe Doctrine looked southward into and beyond the Caribbean. Issued in 1823 when the countries of Latin America were winning independence from Spanish control, it made plain to European nations that the United States considered Latin America its sphere of influence. Not long after, some Americans began thinking into the Pacific: of Hawaii, Japan, and the great markets of China.²

Like Spain and Portugal, the United States built a navy that fed its global ambitions. The new country was driven by the profit system and because of "its natural tendency for expansion, had already begun to look overseas."³ The invasion of Mexico's northern territory fed this obsession. Like the Spaniards and the ancient Israelites, their god provided the justification that, like Moses at the Battle of Rephidim against the Amalekites, the slaughter was said to be in the name of god.⁴ According to Zinn, "the profit system, with its natural tendency for expansion, had already begun to look overseas."⁵ It gave them a sense of exceptionalism and entitlement and they felt that is if it was god's will to slaughter the Indigenous People.

The Puritan Bible gave the early colonials a sense of destiny. The God of the Old Testament, they believed, predestined them to own the Americas. Only god knew their fate and it was the will of god that they slaughter the Indigenous People. This narrative began as early as 1613 with declarations such as that of the theologian Alexander Whitaker, who said that god brought the Virginia colonists to the Americas. Whitaker was known as "The Apostle of Virginia."⁶ Seven years later the Puritans founded Massachusetts Bay Colony, and its first governor John Winthrop said that "God hath opened this passage unto us."⁷ In 1767 Benjamin Franklin spoke of the entitlement of British colonists; in 1776 Franklin and Thomas Jefferson wanted to include an image of the Promised Land on the Great Seal of the new nation.⁸ Testimonials about being the chosen people can be plotted on a timeline leading up to the invasions of Texas in 1836 and Mexico in 1847.

Who Started the War?

3.1 Explain the relationship between slavery and U.S aggression toward Mexico.

The Louisiana Purchase in 1803 doubled the size of the United States and put it on the border of New Spain. In 1821 parts of it, including Texas, New Mexico, Utah, Nevada, Arizona, California, and part of Colorado, became part of

Mexico. Texas was the first to fall. It was a land with many rivers and ports on the Gulf of Mexico. It was ideal for plantations because land was cheap; most recent arrivals from the United States. were from the nearby southern slaveholding states, and some of them owned slaves. It mattered little to slave owners that slavery in Mexico was in the process of being outlawed. The slave issue was an important motivating factor in the illusion of an Empire: They felt entitled to Texas, they felt it was part of their Zion (Jerusalem). God meant them to be rich.

U.S. President Ulysses S. Grant (1822–1885), recognized the truth that the United States was an aggressor in these wars. Grant wrote, "For myself, I was bitterly opposed to the measure, and to this day regard the war (with Mexico) ... one of the most unjust ever waged by a stronger against a weaker nation. It was an instance of a republic following the bad example of European monarchies, in not considering justice in their desire to acquire additional territory."

Grant added,

"Texas was originally a state belonging to the republic of Mexico.... [The American] colonists paid very little attention to the supreme government, and introduced slavery into the state almost from the start, though the constitution of Mexico did not, nor does it now, sanction that institution." Of the annexation of Texas, Grant said, "The occupation, separation and annexation were, from the inception of the movement to its final consummation, a conspiracy to acquire territory out of which slave states might be formed for the American Union." Grant concluded, "Even if the annexation itself could be justified, the manner in which the subsequent war was forced upon Mexico cannot."⁹

Colonel Ethan Allen Hitchcock wrote in his diary of Gen. Zachary Taylor who once denounced the annexation of Texas:

He seems to have lost all respect for Mexican rights and is willing to be an instrument of Mr. Polk for pushing our boundary as far west as possible. When I told him that, if he suggested a movement (which he told me he intended), Mr. Polk would seize upon it and throw the responsibility on him, he at once said he would take it, and added that if the President instructed him to use his discretion, he would ask no orders, but would go upon the Rio Grande as soon as he could get transportation. I think the General wants an additional brevet, and would strain a point to get it.¹⁰

Illinois Congressman Abraham Lincoln shared this point of view and said of Polk's motives:

I am now through the whole of the President's evidence; and it is a singular fact, that if anyone should declare the President sent the army into the midst of a settlement of Mexican people, who had never submitted, by consent or by force, to the authority of Texas or of the United States, and that there, and thereby, the first blood of the war was shed, there is not one word in all the President has said, which would either admit or deny the declaration.¹¹

Mexican Independence from Spain

3.2 Describe the Mexican Revolution and the early Mexican state in the early 1800s.

On September 16, 1810, Father Miguel Hidalgo y Costilla, with an army made up of *los de abajo*, the underdogs, sparked a social revolution. Under the banner of the Virgén de Guadalupe, the movement's ranks swelled to some 80,000. Despite the fervor, the revolutionary army was ill-prepared, and in early 1811, the Spanish royal troops captured and executed Hidalgo. José María Morelos y Pavón, an Indigenous priest with African blood, took up the banner and led a better-organized army, with a wider social base. The largely native army also recruited African Americans and mulattos from the sugar plantations. After the death of Morelos in 1815, revolutionary bands formed smaller forces under leaders like Guadalupe Victoria and Vicente Guerrero, a mixture of Indigenous and African, who waged guerrilla warfare against the Spaniards.¹²

Guerrero joined Agustín de Iturbide, the commander of the Royalist forces and drew up the Plan of Iguala, which offered guarantees of religion, independence, and union. The Plan called for respect for the church, and equality between Mexicans and peninsulars. It won the support of many criollos, Spaniards, and even former rebels. In 1822, Iturbide became Agustín I, emperor of Mexico. A year later, Guadalupe Victoria overthrew Iturbide. Most of Central America broke from Mexico, catapulting Antonio López de Santa Anna to the center stage of Mexican politics.¹³

Colonialism ravaged Mexico. The Mexican state was bankrupt, with little chance for stability. The challenge was to form a nation-state that would integrate the new nation's varied population and regions and create an overriding identity.¹⁴ The nation was 60 percent Indigena, 30 percent mestizo, and 10 percent criollo and other. The long and arduous process of state building proved chaotic, and the state formation was not completed until the 1890s.¹⁵ Unlike the newly born United States, the Mexican nation was made up of different races, making nation building harder. Unlike the United States, the Indigenous People were in the mix. The Texas (1836) and Mexican (1845–1848) Wars were devastating and added to the delay of state formation.

Background to the Invasion of Texas

3.3 Characterize the behaviors of the U.S. and American immigrants in Texas.

The word *filibuster* refers primarily to the U.S. Senate, where senators use it to delay debate or block legislation. The word originally referred to the buccaneers, the pirates infesting the high seas. For Latin Americans and Mexicans, filibuster has a more sinister meaning. *Filibuster refers to an adventurer who preys on a foreign country with a private military.* Thus, Mexicans call the Stephen Austins and Sam Houstons of this world filibusters. Filibustering or freebooting was quite common in the nineteenth century when many Americans were trying to be Sam Adams, a leader of the American Revolution. The wannabes staked out foreign territories for U.S. expansion. The most popular was William Walker who in the 1850s invaded Lower California, Sonora, and Nicaragua.

Florida set the pattern for the Texas filibusters. In 1818, U.S. troops seized several posts in east Florida, an act that was never officially condemned by the United States. In the Adams-Onis, or Transcontinental, Treaty (1819), Spain ceded Florida to the United States and the United States in turn, renounced its claim to Texas, a part of Coahuila. Notwithstanding this agreement, many North Americans still argued that Texas belonged to the United States, repeating Jefferson's claim that Texas's boundary extended to the Rio Grande and that it was part of the Louisiana Purchase. Americans made forays into Texas similar to those they had made into Florida. In 1819, James Long led an abortive invasion to establish the "Republic of Texas." Believing that Texas belonged to the United States, Long maintained that "the Congress of the United States did not have the right or power to sell Texas."[16]

Inexplicably, the Mexican government opened Texas to American colonization. Spain had given Moses Austin permission to settle in Texas. After he died Mexico gave his son Stephen permission to settle in Texas, and in December 1821, Stephen Austin founded the colony of San Felipe de Austin. Large numbers of colonists from the United States entered Texas in the 1820s as a result of the Depression of 1819. By 1830, about 20,000 colonists were settled in Texas, along with some 2,000 slaves.[17]

A Lie is a Lie!

The preponderance of evidence shows that the early American settlers intended to obey Mexican laws just so long as the laws did not interfere with their property rights—which meant the right to own slaves, and they reacted adversely to Mexico's attempts to enforce its laws.[18] American colonists had agreed to obey the conditions set by the Mexican government that all immigrants to Texas become Catholics and that they take an oath of allegiance to Mexico. However, the newcomers became resentful when Mexico tried to enforce the agreements. Mexico, in turn, grew increasingly alarmed at the flood of immigrants from the United States.[19]

Americans considered the Native Mexicans the intruders. The Hayden Edwards affair is a case in point: Edwards arbitrarily attempted to evict colonists from his land grant before Mexican authorities had the opportunity to resolve conflicting claims. As a result, the Mexican government nullified his contract and ordered him out of the territory. On December 21, 1826, Edwards and his followers seized the town of Nacogdoches, declaring it the "Republic of Fredonia." Mexicans suppressed the Edwards Revolt with the support of Stephen Austin. A number of U.S. newspapers portrayed the rebellion as "200 Men Against a Nation!" and described Edwards and his followers as "apostles of democracy crushed by an alien civilization."[20]

Events in the United States encouraged the American colonists' arrogance in Texas. In 1823, President James Monroe announced that European powers were not permitted to colonize the Americas or interfere with the affairs of its sovereign nations.[21] Critics say that this proclamation suggested that the "Americas" were for the United States of America only. A year later, Secretary of State John Quincy Adams pressured Mexico to readjust its borders. The United States was not satisfied with the Sabine River as the boundary and wanted to push the boundary to the Rio Grande.[22] Two years later Adams, now president, offered to buy Texas for $1 million. When Mexican authorities refused the offer, the United States launched an aggressive diplomatic campaign designed to coerce Mexico into selling Texas.

Slavery gave North Americans a huge economic advantage, helping to create a privileged class of plantation owners. North Americans in Texas protected this privilege. When on September 15, 1829 Mexico abolished slavery, slave owners circumvented the law by "freeing" their slaves and then signing them to lifelong contracts as indentured servants. North Americans resented the Mexican order and considered the abolishment of slavery an infringement on their personal liberties. In 1830, Mexico prohibited further North American immigration. Meanwhile, Andrew Jackson increased tensions by attempting to purchase Texas for as much as $5 million. Mexican authorities reacted by moving troop reinforcements into Coahuila; Americans viewed this defensive measure as a provocation.[23]

Follow the Money: The Land Companies and Trade

United States–based land companies strained relations between the United States and Mexico by lobbying for Washington, D.C., to intervene.[24] In the rush to occupy Texas, the land companies feverishly issued land scrip that entitled them to land in Texas. According to Mexican-American historian Dr. Carlos Castañeda:

> The activities of the "Land Companies" after 1834 cannot be ignored. Their widespread promotion of cheap land and indiscriminate sale of "landscrip" sent hundreds, perhaps thousands, to Texas under the impression that they had legitimate title to lands equal to the amount of scrip bought. The Galveston Bay and Texas Land Company, which bought the contracts of David S. Burnet, Joseph

Vahlein, and Lorenzo de Zavala, and the Nashville Company, which acquired the contract of Robert Leftwich, are the two best known. They first sold scrip at from one to ten cents an acre, calling for a total of seven and one-half million acres. The company was selling only its permit to acquire a given amount of land in Texas, but since an empresario contract was nontransferable, the scrip was, in fact, worthless.[25] That is, the scrip was worthless as long as Texas belonged to Mexico.

The North Americans saw the separation of Texas from Mexico and eventual union with the United States as the most profitable political arrangement. Castañeda notes that "Trade with New Orleans and other American ports had increased steadily." This strengthened strong economic ties with the United States rather than with Mexico. Castañeda continues, "Juan H. Almonte in his 1834 report, estimated the total foreign trade of Texas—chiefly with the United States—at more than 1,000,000 pesos, of which imports constituted 630,000 and exports, 500,000." The exportation of cotton by the colonists reached approximately 2,000 bales in 1833.[26] Colonel Almonte's report recommended concessions to the dissidents but also urged that Mexico be prepared.

The Re-annexation of Texas

The die was cast by 1830 and the Mexican government was taking measures to tighten control of Texas—and the response was harsh.[27] The colonists refused to pay customs to Mexico, abetting smuggling activities. When the "war party" rioted at Anáhuac in December 1831, it had the popular support among white colonists. One of its leaders, Sam Houston, according to historian Eugene C. Barker, "was a known protégé of Andrew Jackson, now president of the United States . . . Houston's motivation was to bring Texas into the United States."[28] The next summer, Mexican troops routed a group of Americans who attacked a garrison. Relations deteriorated when the colonists convened at San Felipe in October 1832 and drafted resolutions calling for more autonomy for Texas. They sent the demands to the Mexican government and to the state of Coahuila. The secessionists held a second convention in January 1833. Not one Mexican Pueblo supported either convention, branding the act seditious. The war party had achieved its purpose. The members elected Houston to lead the army and appointed Austin to take their grievances and resolutions to Mexico City.[29]

The Point of No Return

In Mexico City, Austin pressed for lifting restrictions on American immigration and for separate statehood. The slave issue also burned in his mind. Austin wrote, anything but conciliatory, to a friend, "If our application is refused . . . I shall be in favor of organizing *without it.*

I see no other way of saving the country from total anarchy and ruin. I am totally done with conciliatory measures and, for the future, shall be uncompromising as to Texas."[30]

On October 2, 1833, Austin wrote to the San Antonio *ayuntamiento* (municipal government), urging it to declare Texas a separate state. Austin later said that he had done so "in a moment of irritation and impatience"; yet, his actions were not those of a moderate. Contents of the note fell into the hands of Mexican authorities, who questioned Austin's good faith and imprisoned him. Meanwhile, the U.S. minister to Mexico, Anthony Butler, attempted to bribe Mexican officials into selling Texas to the United States. Butler offered one Mexican official $200,000 to "play ball."[31]

On July 13, 1835, a general amnesty released Austin from prison. While en route to Texas, he wrote to a cousin from New Orleans that Texas should be Americanized, saying that Texas would one day come under the American flag. Austin called for a massive immigration of Americans to Texas, "each man with his rifle," who he hoped would come with "passports or no passports, *anyhow.*" He continued, "For fourteen years I have had a hard time of it, but nothing shall daunt my courage or abate my . . . object . . . to *Americanize* Texas."[32]

On September 19, 1835, Austin concluded, "War is our only recourse. There is no other remedy."[33] Americans enjoyed huge advantages. They were defending terrain that they were familiar with, and they were receiving arms from the United States. The overwhelming majority of the 5,000 Mexicans living in Texas stayed loyal to Mexico, but the American population totally eclipsed the Mexican population, their number having swelled to almost 30,000. Politically, Mexico was divided; Mexico's independence was just over a dozen years old, and Mexico City was thousands of miles from the center of Texas.

The Invasion of Texas

3.4 Compare ways that different populations experienced and described the U.S. invasion of Texas.

A favorite ploy of historians to obscure culpability is to talk about causes as if they were objective and immutable. It also gives the implication that things could not have been changed or made different in any way. The other side was always at fault. It deflects attention from who was the aggressor and prevents a realistic evaluation of the events. The reader must ask, to what country did Texas belong? In the United States, many opposed the war and saw the Texas Revolution as a disgraceful act promoted by slaveholders and land speculators. U.S. historians such as Eugene Barker blame Mexico, arguing that the immediate cause of the war was Antonio López de Santa Anna's overthrow of "the nominal republic and the substitution of centralized oligarchy." Barker ignores or denies that slavery was a prime issue.

Instead, Barker draws parallels between the Texas filibuster and the American Revolution, arguing that the general cause of revolts was "sudden effort to extend imperial authority at the expense of local privilege." Barker posits that "Texans saw themselves in danger of becoming the alien subjects of a people to whom they deliberately believed themselves morally, intellectually, and politically superior."[34] Barker claims that the Mexicans also mistrusted the Americans on racial grounds. According to Barker, when Mexican authorities took drastic measures to keep the American colonists in line, the American Texans believed that their liberty was endangered and they revolted.[35] But what Barker forgets is that most of the leaders and their followers in the revolt were outsiders. None of them had been born in Texas.

The Pretext: Myths of the Alamo

Historical myths are a combination of fiction and half-truth, justifying the actions of the actors. Myths are common in history, and often become legends. In the case of the Texas filibuster, a score of popular books have been written about Mexican cruelty at the Alamo and about the heroics of the doomed men, producing the Alamo myth, which justifies the Texas insurrection. Like so many myths, the story of the Alamo is a distortion of reality, with its exaggeration of 187 filibusters standing against the barbarians at the gates of civilization. The "defenders" allegedly barricaded themselves in the Alamo in defiance of Santa Anna's force, which, according to Mexican sources, numbered 1,400, and the Mexicans eventually triumphed.[36]

Many U.S. historians have riddled the myths of the Alamo with dramatic half-truths, portraying those in the mission as selfless heroes who sacrificed their lives to buy more time for their comrades-in-arms. Walter Lord, in an article entitled "Myths and Realities of the Alamo," broke with the Texas story, which portrays the defenders of the Alamo as freedom-loving Texans who were protecting their homes.[37] Actually, two-thirds of the self-proclaimed defenders had recently arrived from the United States, and only a half dozen had been in Texas for more than six years. The filibusters were adventurers who were spoiling for a fight.

As Howard Zinn has pointed out, "History is a Weapon," and the Alamo has been used in this fashion and trotted out every time the United States wants to appeal to jingoism. Movies such as the Alamo reinforce popular culture as witness in World War II popular movies. The Alamo has been used in this fashion and every time there is a question about American exceptionalism a new version comes out.

1911	The Immortal Alamo
1914	Siege and Fall of the Alamo
1915	The Martyrs of the Alamo or the Birth of Texas
1926	Davy Crockett at the fall of the Alamo
1937	Heroes of the Alamo
1938	Fall of the Alamo
1953	The Man from the Alamo
1955	Davy Crockett, King of the Wild Frontier
1955	The Last Command
1960	The Alamo
1969	Viva Max
1987	The Alamo: Thirteen Days to Glory
1987	Alamo: The Price of Freedom
1995	Texas
2004	The Alamo

SOURCE: The Alamo, Frank Thompson, "The Alamo," *Texas Monthly* Jul 1991, p. 108.

The story is additionally obscured by the blurring of fact and fiction.

The Defense of the Mexican Homeland

Santa Anna led an army of about 6,000 soldiers into Texas. Mexicans were defending the homeland—of which Texas was a part. Many of Santa Anna's soldiers were forcefully conscripted into the army and then marched hundreds of miles over hot, arid desert land. They were largely poorly equipped Maya natives who did not speak Spanish. In February 1836, the main contingent arrived in Texas sick and ill-prepared to fight. In San Antonio, the filibusters prepared to defend themselves in a former mission, the Alamo. The siege began in the first week of March. In the days that followed, the defenders inflicted heavy casualties on the Mexican forces, but the Mexicans eventually won.

Those inside the Alamo were hardly the stuff that legends are made. William Barrett Travis fled to Texas after killing a man and abandoning his wife and unborn child; he "renounced the paternity of his yet unborn child."[38] James Bowie, an infamous brawler, had made a fortune hunting down runaway slaves and wandered into Texas searching for lost mines and money opportunities. The aging Davy Crockett fought for the sake of fighting. Most of the filibusters came to Texas for riches and glory, and not as peaceful colonists protecting their homes.

As the story goes, William Barrett Travis told his men that they were doomed and drew a line in the sand with his sword, saying that all who crossed it would elect to remain and fight to the last. Supposedly, all the men valiantly stepped across the line, with an old man in a cot begging to be carried across the line. Countless Hollywood movies have continued to perpetuate the myth of the bravery of the defenders.[39]

In reality, the Alamo had little strategic value, in fact it was the best-protected fort west of the Mississippi, and the men fully expected help. The defenders commanded 21 cannons to the Mexicans' 8 or 10, and were expert shots equipped with rifles with a range of 200 yards, while the inadequately trained Mexicans were armed with smoothbore muskets with a range of only 70 yards. The walls of the mission protected the Americans, while the Mexicans advanced in the open and fired at concealed targets. In short, ill-prepared, ill-equipped, and ill-fed Mexicans attacked well-armed, professional and well-protected soldiers. Moreover, from all reliable sources, it is doubtful whether Travis ever drew a line in the sand. San Antonio survivors, females and non-combatants, did not tell the story until many years later, when the story gained currency and the myth became legend. Probably the most widely circulated story was that of the last stand of the aging Davy Crockett, who fell "fighting like a tiger," killing Mexicans with his bare hands. The truth is that seven of the defenders surrendered; Crockett was among them. The Mexican force executed them; only one man, Louis Rose, escaped.[40]

Travis's stand delayed Santa Anna's timetable by only four days, San Antonio fell on March 6, 1836. At first, the stand at the Alamo did not even have propaganda value. Afterward, Houston's army dwindled, with many volunteers rushing home to help their families flee from the advancing Mexican army. Most Americans realized that they lost at the Alamo. Nevertheless, the Alamo battle and the Mexican victory at Goliad resulted in massive aid from the United States as volunteers, weapons, and money entered Texas. The cry "Remember the Alamo" became a call to arms for Americans in both Texas and the United States.

Texas Belonged to Native Americans

As mentioned in Chapter 2, The Indigenous History of Texas did not begin with the arrival of Spanish explorers in the 1500s. Indigenous People lived in Texas as early as 13,500 years ago.

They farmed and built permanent villages. As many as 25 separate Caddo groups linked by language and customs settled mostly in East Texas. By CE 900 the Caddo had developed a distinctive life in the present states of Arkansas and Louisiana. By the late seventeenth century, the Caddo lived on the Red River and in East Texas. After the Louisiana Purchase of 1803, white settlements further pressured them to move to Spanish territory where larger numbers of Caddo lived in the 1820s, only to be displaced to Oklahoma in the 30s.[41] In East Texas, they formed the Caddo confederacies.

The eastern U.S. Indigenous Nations in Texas expanded dramatically in the 1830s as they migrated into Texas to escape American colonial expansion. By 1836, Texas was far from uninhabited. Aside from the Caddo, other nations were uprooted and relocated to the area. The Alabama and Coushatta were pushed out of what became Alabama,

The original inhabitants of the area that is now Texas included:

- Apache
- Bidai
- Coahuiltecan and Carrizo tribes
- Caddo
- Comanche
- Jumano, Suma, Piro, and other Eastern Pueblos
- Karankawa
- Kiowa
- Kitsai
- Tawakoni
- Tonkawa
- Wichita

Nations driven into Texas after Europeans arrived included:

- Alabama
- Cherokee
- Coushatta
- Kickapoo
- Tigua Pueblo

SOURCE: Native American Tribes of Texas, http://www.native-languages.org/texas.htm.

Mississippi, and Georgia; they eventually settled in the Big Thicket area of southeast Texas. The Coushatta Tribe first arrived in 1807, settling on the Trinity River in 1807. Soon thereafter, the Alabama Tribe made the move from Louisiana to Texas, settling on the Neches River.

The Apache controlled almost all of West Texas, an area that included Arkansas, Arizona, and northern Mexico. In 1757, the Spanish established Mission Santa Cruz de San Sabá north of San Antonio for the Lipan Apache. The missionaries hoped to missionize the Lipans, promising to protect the Apache from the Comanche and other enemies. The Apache belonged to the Athabascan branch originally from Alaska, western Canada, and the American Southwest.[42] As the 1700s wore on, they were increasingly raided by Comanche who ruled the Great Plains. The Comancheria encompassed eastern New Mexico, southeastern Colorado, and southwestern Kansas.

Over 125,000 Native Americans lived on millions of acres of land in Georgia, Tennessee, Alabama, North Carolina, and Florida. The Cherokee were one of the main Texas Indigenous Nations in 1836. They had migrated to Missouri, Arkansas, and Texas to preserve their traditional way of life. In Texas, the Cherokee settled near the Red River. They were pressed further south by American colonial expansion. In 1820, about 60 families under Chief Bowl (Duwali) settled in Rusk County near the Caddo, where they lived in peace. The Cherokee were later forcibly removed to "Indian" Territory (Oklahoma) during the cruel "Trail of Tears" that began in the late 1830s.

The process was accelerated by the Indian Removal Act of 1830, signed by U.S. President Andrew Jackson that cleared the land for white settlement. By the end of the decade, few Indigenous People remained anywhere in the southeastern United States. Again, the government cleared the Indigenous People's land in response to the demands of white cotton growers. This pernicious death march is known as the Trail of Tears.

Like the Cherokee, the Chickasaw migrated to Texas. They were originally from present-day Kentucky, Tennessee, Mississippi, and Alabama. They lived in sophisticated town sites and had a highly developed ruling system, complete with laws and religion. After years of resisting American pressure to move, in the mid-1830s the Chickasaws, along with the Cherokee, Choctaw, Creek, and Seminole, were forcibly removed to Oklahoma.

In 1790, the Indigenous population in Texas numbered about 2,510, while in New Mexico it exceeded 20,000. The period 1821–1835 brought many settlers into Texas. The Indigenous population was dominant, however. By 1830 the total population in Texas was about 20,000; the area was huge and sparsely settled. In 1834 Juan N. Almonte, after a visit to Texas, placed the population at 24,700, including slaves.[43] The *Handbook of Texas History* estimates that in 1836 there were probably 5,000 Blacks, 30,000 white Americans, 3,470 Mexicans, and 14,200 native people in Texas.[44] By 1836 there were probably 5,000 Blacks, 30,000 white Americans, 3,470 Hispanics, and 14,200 Indigenous People in Texas.[45]

Indigenous relations were crucial to both sides. Filibusters such as Sam Houston, for all of their faults, knew how to count. If the Indigenous People joined the Mexican cause, the result for the Texas Revolt could be disastrous. In February 1836, the provisional government entered into a treaty promising to respect Indigenous neutrality and to respect the Indigenous land rights in East Texas, setting clear and legal boundaries with the Indigenous Nations. The government also appointed three commissioners to the Indigenous Nations.

White Texans almost immediately broke their promises and at the Convention of 1836 failed to ratify the treaty. David G. Burnet, who served as interim president of the Republic of Texas from March to October 1836, attempted to negotiate a peace treaty with the Shawnee, Delaware, and Kickapoo in northeastern Texas.[46] Meanwhile, the U.S. command under General Edmund Pendleton Gaines had his troops waiting to send them to the Louisiana-Texas frontier to guard against hypothetical threats from the Cherokee, Caddo, and other East Texas Tribes.

Neither side was successful in establishing lasting relations with the Indigenous Nations. Spain granted citizenship to the Indigenous Peoples of Mexico in 1820 (including residents of the Southwest). Both Spanish colonialism and white American attitudes of racial superiority and entitlement interfered with the forging of lasting relations. Meanwhile, the election of Mirabeau B. Lamar as president of the Republic in 1838 worsened relations between the races and Lamar openly advocated the expulsion of all Indigenous Peoples from the Lone Star Republic. President Mirabeau B. Lamar summarized his feelings in an address to the Texas Congress said: "The white man and the red man cannot dwell in harmony together. Nature forbids it." He added that the policy of the Lone Star State "is to push a rigorous war against them to their hiding places without mitigation or compassion."[47]

The Texas Indigenous People were mistreated under Spanish colonial rule. However, the Spanish settlements were too small to threaten them. After independence, the Indigenous Peoples technically became Mexican citizens; that meant that they were subject to Mexican law. Under Spanish and Mexican rule, the Spanish-speaking population was small and felt threatened by the Indigenous People. The Spanish and the Mexican colonials were heavily dependent on the military and they called Indigenous resistance depredations.

Meanwhile, Texas joined the United States on the condition that Texas was for Texans: Indians were not welcome in the new state. The U.S. federal government was to assume responsibility for the Indians, while the new state of Texas reserved all rights to "public" lands (those lands which had been Indian lands). Indians were to be removed to Oklahoma.[48]

The American Cabal Was not Texan

During the early morning hours of October 9, 1835, white Texans attacked Mexican soldiers at a fort near Goliad. For several months afterward the two sides skirmished. During this period, Stephen Austin was in contact with Mexican liberals and tried to get their support. In New Orleans George Fisher and José Antonio Mexía led a revolt against the Mexican government and on October 13, 1835 attacked Tampico in an attempt to instigate a rebellion in the eastern states of Mexico.

At Goliad on March 20, 1836, southeast of San Antonio, José de Urrea defeated troops under the command of James W. Fannin. On March 27, on the orders of Santa Anna, the Mexican army executed 342 prisoners at Goliad, an act most Mexican commanders disapproved of. Goliad gave the filibusters a cause and cries went up to "Remember Goliad."[49] As brutal as the act was it must be kept in the context that the Texans were not Texans and were engaged in a seditious plot to overthrow the government.[50]

The Mexican army ran Sam Houston out of the territory northwest of the San Jacinto River. Meanwhile, Houston positioned about 1,100 men near San Jacinto. On April 20, 1836 the two armies skirmished. Santa Anna, however, failed to follow up his advantage. Predicting that Houston would attack on April 22, Santa Anna and his troops settled down and rested for the anticipated battle. The filibusters attacked during the siesta hour on April 21. Santa Anna was negligent; he knew that Houston led an army of 1,000, and let the surprise attack catch him totally off guard. Shouts of "Remember the Alamo! Remember Goliad!" filled the air. Houston's men captured Santa Anna, who signed Mexican territory away. The Mexican Congress rejected the treaty; however, Mexico did not have the resources to pursue its claim and sending additional troops to Texas would have brought the full force of the U.S. Army into the war. In this void, Houston was elected president of the Republic of Texas.[51]

Houston's men took few Mexican prisoners at San Jacinto. Those who surrendered "were clubbed and stabbed, some on their knees. The slaughter . . . became methodical: the Texan riflemen knelt and poured a steady fire into the packed, jostling ranks." The final death count was 630 Mexicans but only 2 Texans.[52]

The victory was a prelude to the Mexican–American War. Officially, the United States did not take sides, but it poured men, money, and supplies into Texas to aid fellow Americans. United States citizens participated in the invasion of Texas with the open support of their government. According to Lota M. Spell, Mexico's minister to the United States, Manuel Eduardo Gorostiza, protested the "arming and shipment of troops and supplies to territory that was part of Mexico, and the dispatch of United States troops into territory clearly defined by treaty as Mexican territory." President Andrew Jackson sent General Edmund P. Gaines, Southwest commander, into western Louisiana on January 23, 1836; shortly thereafter he crossed into Texas, which Mexicans interpreted as U.S. support for the filibusters. In and out of Texas, U.S. citizens loudly applauded Jackson's actions. The Mexican minister resigned in protest.[53]

The Invasion of Mexico

3.5 **Describe the justification of Americans for the seizure of Texas.**

Another myth is that the United States won the war in a fair fight—and, therefore, has no culpability. The reality is that in the mid-1840s, the U.S. population of 17 million people of European Americans and 3 million slaves was much larger than Mexico's 7 million, of which 4 million were Indigenous, and 3 million mestizo, Afro-mestizo, and European. The United States acted arrogantly in foreign affairs, partly because it had a homogenous people who believed they were culturally and racially superior. They felt entitled to what belong to others. While the United States received British and Scottish investment, Mexico had financial problems, internal ethnic conflicts, and poor leadership. Anarchy plagued Mexico and retarded the nation's development.[54]

The war pushed the borders further south crossing people, rivers, and other resources. The U.S. admission of Texas on March 1, 1845, was a provocation for war. Even if Mexico would have accepted the loss of Texas, there was the question of the location of the border. Mexico claimed the Nueces River (Rio Grande) that was 150 miles north of the Rio Bravo as Mexican. Using the Treaty of Velasco of 1836 as its authority, the United States claimed the Rio Grande as the boundary. The war cost Mexico more than 500,000 square miles of territory.

The Manufactured War

By 1845 war with Mexico was a matter of time. James K. Polk, who encouraged the annexation of Texas won the presidency by a small margin. He interpreted his election as a mandate for national expansion. Outgoing President Tyler called upon Congress to annex Texas by joint resolution. Congress passed the measure a few days before the inauguration of Polk who, upon becoming president, approved the annexation, and in December 1845, Texas became a state. Mexico promptly broke off diplomatic relations with the United States, and Polk ordered General Zachary Taylor into Texas to "protect" the border, whose location both sides disputed.[55]

In November 1845, Polk sent John Slidell on a secret mission to Mexico to negotiate. The presence of American troops in the disputed territory and the annexation of Texas made negotiations a charade. The Mexican government refused to accept Polk's minister's credentials, although they did offer to give him ad hoc status.[56] Slidell declined anything less than full recognition and returned to Washington in March 1846, convinced that Mexico had to be "chastised" before it would negotiate. By March 28, Polk ordered Taylor and an army of 4,000 to the Rio Grande. Polk was incensed at Mexico's refusal to meet with Slidell on his terms and at General Mariano Paredes's reaffirmation of claims to all of Texas. When the president learned of the Mexican attack on Taylor's troops in the disputed territory, he began to draft a declaration of war, claiming that Mexico attacked the United States and "shed American blood upon the American soil." On May 13, 1846, Congress declared war and authorized the recruitment and supplying of 50,000 troops.[57]

American Aggression

General Ulysses S. Grant wrote to his fiancée Julia Dent that President Polk provoked the war and that the annexation of Texas was, in fact, an act of aggression. Grant agonized, "I had a horror of the Mexican War . . . only I had not moral courage enough to resign . . . I considered my supreme duty was to my flag."[58] Grant was not alone in his opposition to the war. When Congress declared war on

Mexico in May 1846, northern Whigs feared victory would add more slave states to United States. Sixty-seven Whig representatives along with Lincoln voted against mobilization and appropriations for a war, and Ohio Senator Tom Corwin accused Polk of involving the United States in a war of aggression.[59] Intellectuals such as Ralph Waldo Emerson bitterly opposed any move toward annexation of Texas; Henry David Thoreau committed civil disobedience.

The Pretext for Conquest

3.6 Describe the reasons for individual American opposition to the Mexican American War.

There is no doubt that Polk sent General Zachary Taylor to the contested region to provoke the Mexican army. Polk planned to ask Congress for a declaration before the American public knew of the Mexican soldiers' gunfire. The words of Polk's war message of May 11, 1846, laid out his pretext for the war:

> The strong desire to establish peace with Mexico on liberal and honorable terms, and the readiness of this Government to regulate and adjust our boundary and other causes of difference with that power on such fair and equitable principles as would lead to permanent relations of the most friendly nature, induced me in September last to seek reopening of diplomatic relations between the two countries.

The United States, Polk continued, had not wanted to provoke Mexico, but the Mexican government refused to receive the U.S. minister. Polk concluded,

> As war exists, and notwithstanding all our efforts to avoid it, exists by the act of Mexico herself, we are called upon by every consideration of duty and patriotism to vindicate with decision the honor, the rights, and the interests of our country.[60]

Playing Moses: God is on Our Side!

American poet Walt Whitman in his *Leaves of Grass*, 1855, sets the sentiment for the war. A romantic, Whitman sang about the greatness and superiority of the American nation. Whitman praised the uniqueness (exceptionalism) of the American people in "Song of Myself." Whitman saw *America* as the prime mover of human history—a belief that most Americans shared at the time.[61]

This feeling of exceptionalism carried with it feelings of moral superiority. In his *Origins of the War with Mexico: The Polk-Stockton Intrigue*, Glenn W. Price wrote, "Americans have found it rather more difficult than other peoples to deal rationally with their wars. We have thought of ourselves as unique, and of this society as specially planned and created to avoid the errors of all other nations."[62]

Many U.S. historians dismiss the war as simply a "bad war" that took place during the era of Manifest Destiny, blaming it on "youthful indiscretions." The roots of Manifest Destiny are in Puritan doctrines that continue to this day to influence U.S. policy.[63] Accordingly, the United States is the embodiment of the City of God and the European race was chosen for salvation. They believe that god predestined them to spread his word to the "New World."[64]

Despite the doublespeak, most Americans knew that the theft of Mexican land was the principle motive for the war. Some feared that the acquisition would tip the balance of power in favor of the northern states and would result in larger numbers of non-whites. U.S. Senator John C. Calhoun (Democrat, South Carolina) advocated the annexation of Texas in 1836. However, he grew suspicious of President James K. Polk's intrigues and feared that the acquisition would hurt the slave states. He argued, "To incorporate Mexico, would be the very first instance of the kind of incorporating an Indian race for more than half of the Mexicans are Indians, and the other is composed chiefly of mixed tribes. I protest against such a union as that! Ours, sir, is the Government of a white race."[65]

History is Propaganda

In 1920, Justin H. Smith received the Pulitzer Prize in history for a work blaming the war on Mexico. What is amazing is that Smith allegedly examined more than 100,000 manuscripts, 120,000 books and pamphlets, and 200 or more periodicals to come to this conclusion. He was rewarded for relieving the American conscience. Smith, in his two-volume "study," *The War with Mexico*, argues:

> At the beginning of her independent existence, our people felt earnestly and enthusiastically anxious to maintain cordial relations with our sister republic, and many crossed the line of absurd sentimentality in the cause. Friction was inevitable, however. The Americans were direct, positive, brusque, angular and pushing; and they would not understand their neighbors in the south. The Mexicans were equally unable to fathom our goodwill, sincerity, patriotism, resoluteness and courage; and certain features of their character and national condition made it far from easy to get on with them.[66]

Smith's self-righteous attitude was reflected in the attitudes of government officials and the North American public who believed that Mexicans should be grateful that they were given the benefits of democracy and were liberated from a tyrannical past. This in their eyes justified the war.

Anti-Catholicism and racism went a long way in fanning the war fever. General Zachary Taylor's artillery leveled the Mexican city of Matamoros, killing hundreds of innocent civilians with *la bomba* (the bomb). Many Mexicans jumped into the Rio Grande, into a watery grave.[67] The occupation that followed was even more terrorizing. Taylor was unable to control his volunteers:

> The regulars regarded the volunteers, of whom about two thousand had reached Matamoros by the end of May, with impatience and contempt.... They robbed Mexicans of their cattle and corn, stole their fences for firewood, got drunk, and killed several inoffensive inhabitants of the town in the streets.[68]

On July 25, 1846, Grant wrote to Julia Dent:

> Since we have been in Matamoros a great many murders have been committed, and what is strange there seems [sic] to be very week [sic] means made use of to prevent frequent repetitions. Some of the volunteers and about all the Texans seem to think it perfectly right to impose on the people of a conquered City to any extent, and even to murder them where the act can be covered by dark. And how much they seem to enjoy acts of violence too! I would not pretend to guess the number of murders that have been committed upon the persons of poor Mexicans and our soldiers, since we have been here, but the number would startle you.[69]

On July 9, 1846, George Gordon Meade, who, like Grant, was later a general during the U.S. Civil War, wrote,

> They [the volunteers] have killed five or six innocent people walking in the street, for no other object than their own amusement.... They rob and steal the cattle and corn of the poor farmers, and in fact act more like a body of hostile Indians than civilized Whites. Their officers have no command or control over them.[70]

Grant acknowledged that Taylor failed to restrain his men. In a letter to his superiors, Taylor admitted "there is scarcely a form of crime that has not been reported to me as committed by them."[71] Taylor requested that they send no further troops from the state of Texas to him.

The cannons from U.S. naval ships destroyed much of the civilian sector of Veracruz, leveling a hospital, churches, and homes. U.S. troops destroyed almost every city they invaded and plundered. American volunteers showed little respect, desecrating churches and abusing priests and nuns.

Blessed are the Peacemakers?

For Mexicans, the U.S. invasion and occupation left a legacy of bitterness. Mexico was politically divided and militarily unprepared. U.S. President James K. Polk believed the United States had the right to spread across the continent to the Pacific Ocean. The war reinforced Mexican mistrust of Americans while the easy victory of the United States confirmed Americans perceptions of Mexicans as weak. However, some Americans condemned the aggression, accusing U.S. leaders of being insolent, arrogant, and land-hungry, and for manufacturing the war. Among the critics was Abiel Abbot Livermore who in *The War with Mexico Reviewed* wrote:

> Again, the pride of race has swollen to still greater insolence the pride of country, always quite active enough for the due observance of the claims of universal brotherhood. The Anglo-Saxons have been apparently persuaded to think themselves the chosen people, anointed race of the Lord, commissioned to drive out the heathen, and plant their religion and institutions in every Canaan they could subjugate.... Our treatment both of the red man and the black man has habituated us to feel our power and forget right.... The god Terminus is an unknown deity in America. Like the hunger of the pauper boy of fiction, the cry had been, "more, more, give us more."[72]

Livermore's work, published in 1850, won the American Peace Society prize for "the best review of the Mexican War and the principles of Christianity, and an enlightened statesmanship."

Lincoln accused Polk of wanting to seize Texas, California, and other Southwest land areas. Polk knowingly took the nation into a war against Mexico to support the South's expansionist ambitions of the slave states. God had nothing to do with the war—American greed did.[73]

The San Patricio Battalion

A number of Irish immigrants and other Americans, deserted to the Mexican side, forming the San Patricio Battalion. Many Irish Catholics resented the Protestants' ill-treatment of Catholic priests, nuns, churches, and other institutions. The American army captured Irish soldiers; executing them and hanging some Mexican civilians for cooperating with the guerrillas. As many as 260 Americans fought on the Mexican side at Churubusco alone in 1847:

> Some eighty appear to have been captured.... A number were found not guilty of deserting and were released. About fifteen, who had deserted before the declaration of war, were merely branded with a "D," and fifty of those taken at Churubusco were executed.[74]

Other captives received 200 lashes and were forced to the dig graves of their executed comrades.[75]

The acts were similar to those George Meade described in Monterrey on December 2, 1846:

> They plunder the poor inhabitants of everything they can lay their hands on, and shoot them when they remonstrate; and if one of their number happens to get into a drunken brawl and is killed, they run over the country, killing all the poor innocent people they find in their way to avenge, as they say, the murder of their brother.[76]

Meade was certainly not a compromised source. Meade in that same December 2 letter writes,

> The volunteers have been creating disturbances, which have at last aroused the old General so much that he has ordered one regiment, the First Kentucky foot, to march to the rear, as they have disgraced themselves and their State . . . [Taylor] impressed upon the officers the necessity of controlling the men and putting a stop to these outrages, which would inevitably end in the massacre of many innocent persons . . . [The Kentuckians] vowing their intention of killing Mexicans, to revenge their murdered comrades, and the same day one man, a Mexican, was shot within a hundred yards of the camp, and a little boy of twelve years of age, who was cutting cornstalks to bring to the camp for sale, was shot in the field and his leg broken. This poor little fellow, all bleeding and crying, was brought by his relatives and laid down in front of the General's tent, and he called out to look at him.[77]

As General Winfield Scott's army left Monterrey, soldiers under his command shot Mexican prisoners of war.[78]

War Crimes

Americans wrote memoires, diaries, and news accounts describing a reign of terror. Samuel E. Chamberlain's *My Confessions* records American racism and destruction. Chamberlain was only 17 when he enlisted in the army to fight the "greasers." At the Mexican city of Parras, he wrote,

> We found the patrol had been guilty of many outrages. . . . They had ridden into the church of San José during Mass, the place crowded with kneeling women and children, and with oaths and ribald jest had arrested soldiers who had permission to be present.[79]

On another occasion, Chamberlain described a massacre by volunteers, mostly from Yell's Cavalry, at a cave:

> On reaching the place we found a "greaser" shot and scalped, but still breathing; the poor fellow held in his hands a Rosary and a medal of the "Virgin of Guadalupe," only his feeble motions kept the fierce harpies from falling on him while yet alive. A Sabre thrust was given him in mercy, and on we went at a run. Soon shouts and curses, cries of women and children reached our ears, coming apparently from a cave at the end of the ravine. Climbing over the rocks we reached the entrance, and as soon as we could see in the comparative darkness a horrid sight was before us. The cave was full of our volunteers yelling like fiends, while on the rocky floor lay over twenty Mexicans, dead and dying in pools of blood. Women and children were clinging to the knees of the murderers shrieking for mercy. . . . Most of the butchered Mexicans had been scalped; only three men were found unharmed. A rough crucifix was fastened to a rock, and some irreverent wretch had crowned the image with a bloody scalp. A sickening smell filled the place. The surviving women and children sent up loud screams on seeing us, thinking we had returned to finish the work! . . . No one was punished for this outrage.[80]

Chamberlain accused General Taylor of forcefully collecting more than $1 million (from the Mexican people), and letting "loose on the country packs of human bloodhounds called Texas Rangers," who committed wanton acts of cruelty.[81]

It Was Not Just a Man's War

During the Mexican–American War rape was common. The invaders were not benefactors. "Mexican women . . . were drawn into the conflict, and some found themselves thrust suddenly into combat roles."[82] The Mexican army traveled with a large contingent of *soldaderas*, the female camp followers, wives, daughters, or lovers, who marched with the soldiers and carried their packs. At the Battle of Bracito, north of El Paso, in March 1847, Colonel Alexander W. Doniphan's men observed Mexican women fighting beside the male soldiers, attending the Mexican cannon. That same spring, after the Battle of Cerro Gordo, northwest of Veracruz, women were among the casualties. They were also prominent in the defense of Mexico City and Monterrey where they were engaged in street fighting.[83]

There is the story of Dos Amades, as Mexicans know her, who commanded a company of lancers. Dos Amades donned a captain's lancers uniform and swore that she would not yield until the Mexicans drove the "Northern barbarians" from Mexico. Dos Amades survived the war and returned to her home, never to be heard of again. In Monterrey María Josefa Zozaya was killed carrying food to the soldiers and tending to their wounds.[84]

Americans told countless other stories.

> "Coexisting with the racism of the period was an exalted view of Mexican womanhood that fueled the heroic fantasies of U.S. troops . . . ." Some viewed them as "damsels in distress, eager to be rescued by virile Anglo Americans." This sexualized view was popularized reinforced by dime store novels that the Americans as saviors where "Mexican women fell in love with American soldiers, thereby presenting the war as an allegory of sexual conquest."[85]

The fact is American commanders did not control their troops: "The dynamic changed when volunteers moved into the area and immediately began raiding the local farms. As the boredom of garrison duty began to set in, plundering, personal assaults, rape, and other crimes against Mexicans quickly multiplied. During the first month after the volunteers arrived, some twenty murders occurred."[86] President Donald Trump's characterization in 2016 of Mexicans as rapists opens up the study of rapes during the Mexican–American War and other U.S. occupations.

The War Mexico Did Not Want

The poorly equipped and poorly led Mexican army stood little chance against the expansion-minded Americans. Even before the war, President Polk planned the campaign in stages: (1) Mexicans would be cleared out of Texas; (2) the United States would occupy California and New Mexico; and (3) U.S. forces would march to Mexico City to force the beaten government to make peace on Polk's terms.[87] In the end, at a relatively small cost in men and money, the war netted the United States huge territorial gains. In all, the United States took over a half million square miles from Mexico.[88]

The U.S. 1850 Census reported a population of 23,191,867 Americans. Mexico in that year had 7.5 million. Mexico did not have the factories or the money to pay for professional navy or even good uniforms. In addition, Mexico did not fight a strategic war. Part of the problem was its commander Santa Anna, who had returned to Mexico from exile and recruited an army of more than 20,000 men whom he hardly trained; the result was the loss of several major battles. The most that can be said of the Mexican army was that it did not give up. In turn, the United States had a professional navy that allowed the largest amphibious landing in history up to that time—General Scott and his 12,000 men landed at Veracruz. The Mexicans were successful only when they conducted guerrilla operations, but Santa Anna infrequently used that tactic. He learned very little from Mexico's War of Independence when the ragamuffin rebels had not beaten the Spaniards but had worn them down.

By late August 1847, the war was almost at an end. Scott's defeat of Santa Anna at the hard-fought battle at Churubusco put U.S. troops at the gates of Mexico City. Santa Anna made overtures for an armistice that broke down after two weeks, and the war resumed. On September 13, 1847, Scott marched into the city. Although Mexicans fought valiantly, the battle left 4,000 dead, with another 3,000 taken prisoner. On September 13, before the occupation of Mexico City began, *Los Niños Heroes* (The Boy Heroes) leaped to their deaths from Chapultepec Hill in Mexico City rather than surrender. Teenage cadets—Francisco Márquez, Agustín Melgar, Juan Escutia, Fernando Montes de Oca, Vicente Suárez, and Juan de la Barrera—became "a symbol and image of this unrighteous war."[89] Francisco Márquez, the youngest, was 13 and the squadron leader, Juan de la Barrera, the oldest, was 20.

The Mexicans continued fighting. Manuel de la Peña, the presiding justice of the Supreme Court, assumed the presidency. De la Peña knew Mexico had lost and he wanted to salvage as much as possible, as U.S. troops took control of much of Mexico. Meanwhile, the United States lost 13,780 men and many more were wounded. Mexico lost at least double that number.[90]

The Treaty of Guadalupe Hidalgo

3.7 Analyze the political and cultural ramifications of the Treaty of Guadalupe Hidalgo.

On May 6, 1847, peace commissioner Nicholas Trist arrived in Veracruz. A controversy with General Scott over Trist's authority delayed an armistice and hostilities continued. After the fall of Mexico City, Secretary of State James Buchanan ordered Trist to break off negotiations and return home.[91] President Polk wanted more land from Mexico than originally planned, and he wanted to replace Trist with a tougher negotiator. Trist, however, with the support of General Winfield Scott, ignored Polk's order and began negotiations on January 2, 1848, on the original terms. Mexico, badly beaten, her government in turmoil, had no choice but to agree to the U.S. proposals. The negotiations were difficult for Trist. He was aware of the Mexicans' humiliation and felt a sense of embarrassment. Trist himself knew that the war had been a pretext to seize Mexican land.[92]

On February 2, 1848, the Mexican Congress ratified the Treaty of Guadalupe Hidalgo, with Mexico accepting the Rio Grande as the Texas border and ceding almost half of its territory (which incorporated the present-day states of California, New Mexico, Nevada, and parts of Colorado, Arizona, Utah, and even Oklahoma) to the United States in return for $15 million.[93]

A furious Polk considered Trist "contemptibly base" for having ignored his orders. Yet, he had no choice but to submit the treaty to the Senate. With the exception of Article X, which concerned the rights of Mexicans in ceded territory, the Senate ratified the treaty on March 10, 1848, by a vote of 28 to 14. To insist on more territory would have meant more fighting, and both Polk and the Senate realized that the war was already unpopular in many circles. The United States sent the treaty to the Mexican Congress for ratification. The Congress had difficulty forming a quorum, barely ratifying the treaty by a 52-to-35 vote on May 19.[94] Hostilities between the two nations officially ended. Polk, disappointed with the settlement, branded Trist as a "scoundrel," however. In fact, there had been considerable support in the United States for acquisition of all Mexico.[95]

The Controversy

During the talks Mexican negotiators expressed great reservations about Mexicans living in the lost territory being forced to "merge or blend" into American culture. Mexican negotiators protested the exclusion of provisions that protected Mexican citizens' rights, land titles, and religion.[96] They wanted a treaty to protect their rights.

Articles VIII, IX, and X specifically referred to the rights of Mexicans in the occupied territory. Under the treaty, Mexicans were given a year to choose whether to return to Mexico or remain in "occupied Mexico." About 2,000 elected to leave; most remained in what they considered *their* land.

Article IX of the treaty guaranteed Mexicans "the enjoyment of all the rights of citizens of the United States according to the principles of the Constitution; and in the meantime shall be maintained and protected in the free enjoyment of their liberty and property, and secured in the free exercise of their religion without restriction."[97] Lynn I. Perrigo, in *The American Southwest*, summarizes the guarantees of Articles VIII and IX: "In other words, besides the rights and duties of American citizenship, they [the Mexicans] would have special privileges derived from their previous customs in language, law, and religion."[98]

The Deception: A Lie is a Lie

The omitted Article X gave comprehensive guarantees protecting "all prior and pending titles to property of every description." When the U.S. Senate deleted Article X, Mexican officials protested. Emissaries from the United States reassured them by drafting a Statement of Protocol on May 26, 1848:

> The American government by suppressing the Xth article of the Treaty of Guadalupe Hidalgo did not in any way intend to annul the grants of lands made by Mexico in the ceded territories. These grants . . . preserve the legal value which they may possess, and the grantees may cause their legitimate (titles) to be acknowledged before the American tribunals.
>
> Conformable to the law of the United States, legitimate titles to every description of property, personal and real, existing in the ceded territories, are those which were legitimate titles under the Mexican law of California and New Mexico up to the 13th of May, 1846, and in Texas up on the 2nd of March, 1836.[99]

Considering the Mexican opposition to the treaty, it is doubtful whether the Mexican Congress would have ratified the treaty without this clarification. The vote was close—it passed by only one vote.

The importance of the Statement of Protocol was that it proved the bad faith of Polk and U.S. authorities. Even as they were selling the statement to Mexican authorities, they called it worthless in the United States because Trist did not have the authority to sign the treaty. What is amazing is that Polk's diary clearly shows that he considered the treaty valid. The fact was that Article X depended on the good faith of the United States—without good faith, the letter of protocol was meaningless. Armando Rendón in *Chicano Manifesto* writes that the omission of Article X resulted in the federal government's seizing millions of acres of land from the states, impacting the descendants of the Mexicans and Native Americans left behind. In New Mexico alone the federal government seized 1.7 million acres of communal land.[100]

A letter of protocol assured that the omission of Article X would not affect the validity of most land titles protected by the words, "the legal value which they *may* possess."[101] It threw Mexicans at the mercy of U.S. courts. In practice, they ignored the treaty, and during the nineteenth century most Mexicans in the United States were considered as a class apart from the dominant race.[102] The United States violated nearly every one of the duties discussed above, confirming the prophecy of Mexican diplomat Manuel Crescion Rejón, who, at the time the treaty was signed, commented:

> Our race, our unfortunate people will have to wander in search of hospitality in a strange land, only to be ejected later. Descendants of the Indians that we are, the North Americans hate us, their spokesmen depreciate us, even if they recognize the justice of our cause, and they consider us unworthy to form with them one nation and one society, they clearly manifest that their future expansion begins with the territory that they take from us and pushing [sic] aside our citizens who inhabit the land.[103]

The Honorable Man

Upon returning to the United States, Trist wrote in detail about his experience. In a letter to a friend of the family he wrote:

> If those Mexicans . . . had been able to look into my heart at that moment, they would have found that the sincere shame I felt as a North American was stronger than theirs as Mexicans. Although I was unable to say it at the time, it was something that any North American should be ashamed of. . . .

Following the Texas and Mexican–American Wars and the U.S. aggressions, the occupation of conquered territory began. In material terms, in exchange for 12,000 lives and more than $100 million, the United States got a colony two and a half times as large as France, containing rich farmlands and natural resources such as gold, silver, zinc, copper, oil, and uranium, which would make possible its unprecedented industrial boom.[104] It got ports on the Pacific that generated further economic expansion across that ocean. The two Mexican wars gave U.S. commerce, industry, mining, agriculture, and stock raising a tremendous stimulus. "The truth is that [by the 1840s] the Pacific Coast belonged to the commercial empire that the United States was already building in that ocean."[105] Mexico was left with its shrunken resources to face the continued advances of the United States. In the next century, it would be severely hindered in its ability to build a strong economic infrastructure to keep up with the population growth that began to approach pre-conquest levels.

Conclusion: The Border Crossed Us

Not counting the wars against Indigenous Americans, the Texas and Mexican–American Wars were among the United States' first imperial wars.

> Americans were reaching out beyond their border. Advancements in transportation and communications technologies were dissolving the nation's geographic and cultural isolation. Commerce expanded and travel increased as interest in exploration carried Americans around the globe. The war was a "window" through which Americans saw a strange and exotic land of alien manners, customs, and attitudes. Many were convinced that America would never be the same.[106]

Americans got their first taste of blood. "[M]ore than 5,800 Americans were killed or wounded in battle, and 11,000 soldiers died from diseases, in addition to others who succumbed from their war injuries soon after being mustered out of service. The enormous financial cost, estimated at more than $75 million, was another negative factor."[107] However, it was a small price to pay for the "exhilarating effect of a string of military victories and the acquisition of half a million miles of territory. The discovery of rich gold and silver deposits in California and Nevada was an unexpected bonanza that greatly contributed to the national economy and to the westward movement of the population."[108]

Not counting Texas, Mexico lost 525,000 square miles to U.S. territory, including all or parts of Arizona, California, Colorado, Nevada, New Mexico, Utah and Wyoming. The appropriation of Texas was about 261,914 sq. miles. Apart from the impact of the loss of over half of Mexico's territory, the Mexicans lost a measure of dignity. Moreover, the wars left a legacy of hate and in order to absolve themselves from the stigma of being known as a pariah, Americans justified their actions by becoming more aggressively racist.

To this day, the lack of enforcement of the Treaty of Guadalupe Hidalgo remains an issue between Americans and Chicanos, although with time the Mexican government opportunistically made adjustments, such as making enforcement of the treaty a moot issue. The reality is Mexican officials treat their history as a political commodity that the Mexican government barters for trade and other concessions. For example, after the passage of the North American Fair Trade Agreement (NAFTA) in late 1993, it became expedient for Mexico to rewrite its history and downplay the war and the theft of half of Mexico's territory. Not too surprisingly, the treaty is an expendable item of history.

The consequences of the wars went far beyond the immediate losses, still impacting the lives of Mexicans today. The oil of Texas and California alone would have made Mexico a major power. Moreover, Mexico lost major rivers such as the Rio Grande, and the Gila and Colorado Rivers. Even if the boundary had been the Nueces, the Rio Grande would have run through the center of Mexico. The lack of arable land and resources forces the migration of millions of Mexicans and Central Americans north in search of survival. The treaty itself is symbolic of the illusive relations between Mexican Americans and Americans. The treaty gives the illusion that it protects Mexican Americans while the courts interpret the treaty in favor of special interests. Getting justice from the courts is nearly impossible.

Caution should, however, be taken not to romanticize the treaty, which is after all a document that the ruling elites of two nation-states negotiated and signed. There are troubling aspects about the Treaty of Guadalupe Hidalgo. For instance, the treaty recognizes the Spanish and Mexican governments' right of prior conquest. The treaty also imposes on the United States the duty to control by force *los indios barbaros*. The treaty pretended to protect the land rights of Mexicans and Native Americans left behind (most Indigenous Peoples were considered Mexican citizens). In reality, the treaty reduced the rights of some native tribes, penalizing tribes that had suffered multiple conquests—first by Spain and Mexico, and later by the United States. They lost rights to which they might otherwise be entitled under federal Indian policy. This breach should certainly be considered in any discussion of the treaty.

University of Texas anthropologist Martha Menchaca makes a persuasive argument that the United States' violation of the treaty racialized the status of Mexicans and Native Americans.[109] She argues that because the treaty "was broken and they did not give Mexicans the political rights of White citizens a legacy of racial discrimination followed." Instead of a template for interracial harmony, Menchaca cites a history of segregation of public facilities, housing, poll taxes, and other instances of unequal access, which to her and others shows that the Treaty of Guadalupe was and continues to be violated and the legacy of hate the wars left continues to impact our lives.

Notes

1. Howard Zinn, *A People's History of the United States* Reissue Edition (New York: Harper Perennial Modern Classics, 2015). For the convenience of the reader I have cited the digitized version in "History is a Weapon," http://www.historyisaweapon.com/zinnapeopleshistory.html, specifically Chapter 12.
2. Zinn, Chapter 12, Ibid.
3. Howard Zinn, Kathy Emery and Ellen Reeves, *A People's History of the United States Revised and Updated* (New York: The New Press, 2003), p. 219.
4. Exodus 17:12
5. Howard Zinn, Kathy Emery and Ellen Reeves. *A People's History of the United States Revised and Updated* (New York: The New Press, 2003), p. 219
6. Alexander Whitaker, "Good Newes from Virginia," In Conrad Cherry (ed.), *God's New Israel: Religious Interpretations of American Destiny* (Chapel Hill: University of North Carolina Press 1998), pp. 30–36.
7. John Winthrop, "Model of Christian Charity," in Cherry, 43. Document also in the Hanover Historical Texts Project, http://history.hanover.edu/texts/winthmod.html.
8. Frederic Cople Jaher, *A Scapegoat in the New Wilderness: The Origins and Rise of Anti-Semitism in America* (Cambridge, MA: Harvard University Press, 1996), 100. "People & Ideas: The Puritans," God in the Americas, PBS SoCal, http://www.pbs.org/godinamerica/people/puritans.html.
9. Ulysses S. Grant, *Personal Memoirs of U.S. Grant* (New York: Charles L. Webster & Co., 1885): 22–24, quoted in http://www.sewanee.edu/faculty/Willis/Civil_War/documents/Grant.html. Ibid., http://www.bartleby.com/1011/.
10. Zinn, p. 150; Peter M. Karsten, *Military in America* (New York: Free Press, 1986), Chapter 12: Ethan Allen Hitchcock, "A Crisis of Conscience."
11. "Abraham Lincoln on War with Mexico," *To the Moon*, November 30, 2008, https://markcole.wordpress.com/2008/11/30/abraham-lincoln-on-war-with-mexico/. Printed Resolution and Preamble on Mexican War: "Spot Resolutions," *The Abraham Lincoln Papers at the Library of Congress*, http://memory.loc.gov/cgi-bin/query/r?ammem/mal:@field(DOCID+@lit(d0007000). Rodolfo F. Acuña and Guadalupe Compeán, eds. *Voices of the U.S. Latino Experience, I* (Westport: Greenwood Books, 2008), 89–90.
12. Josefina Zoraida Vázquez, "The Mexican Declaration of Independence," *The Journal of American History* Vol. 85, No. 4 (Mar., 1999): 1362–1369. Beau D.J. Gaitors, "The Afro-Mexican presence in Guadalajara at the dawn of independence," Master of Arts Thesis, Purdue University, 2010.
13. An excellent source of primary documents translated into English can be found in the papers of the Sons of DeWitt Colony Texas, http://www.tamu.edu/ccbn/dewitt/mexicanrev.htm. Rodolfo F Acuña and Guadalupe Compeán, eds., *Voices of the U.S. Latino Experience*, 3 Vols. (Westport, CT: Greenwood, 2008): 11–13. In E-Book form.
14. For general discussions see David Held, *Political Theory and the Modern State: Essays on State, Power, and Democracy* (Stanford, CA: Stanford University Press, 1989), and Models of Democracy (Stanford, CA: Stanford University Press, 1987). Michael Mann, *Sources of Social Power, Vol. II: The Rise of Classes and Nation-States, 1760–1914* (Cambridge: Cambridge University Press, 1993). Nora Hamilton, *Modern Mexico, State, Economy, and Social Conflict* (Thousand Oaks, CA: Sage Publications, 1986).
15. Andrés Reséndez, "National Identity on a Shifting Border: Texas and New Mexico in the Age of Transition, 1821–1848," in *Rethinking History and the Nation-State: Mexico and the United States*, Journal of American History, http://www.journalofamericanhistory.org/issues/862/. Marina Iris Mercado-Mont, "Origins of state formation in Mexico" (PhD Dissertation, New School for Social Research, 1988).
16. Richard W. Van Alstyne, *The Rising American Empire* (New York: Norton, 1974), 101. T. R. Fehrenbach, *Lone Star: A History of Texas and the Texans* (New York: Macmillan, 1968), 128. *Castañeda*, Vol. 6, 160–62.
17. See Andrés Tijerina, *Texanos Under the Mexican Flag, 1821–1836* (College Station: Texas A&M University Press, 1994), 3–24. Lester G. Bugbee, "Slavery In Early Texas," *Political Science Quarterly* Vol: XIII, Issue 3 (1898), http://www.tamu.edu/faculty/ccbn/dewitt/slaverybugbee.htm. Fane Downs, "The History of Mexicans in Texas, 1820–1845" (PhD dissertation, Texas Tech University, 1970), 1, 5–6. Tina Laurel Meacham, "The population of Spanish and Mexican Texas, 1716—1836" (PhD Dissertation, The University of Texas at Austin, 2000), vii.
18. Stephen F. Austin; This is a true copy of the letter, rec'd from S. F. Austin. Received from Mrs. Bell and I presume was addressed to her husband Josiah H Bell. (Guy M. Bryan), Sons of DeWitt Colony Texas, http://www.tamu.edu/ccbn/dewitt/slaveryletters.htm.

Petition Concerning Slavery, June 10, 1824, Sons of DeWitt Colony Texas, http://www.tamu.edu/ccbn/dewitt/slaveryletters.htm#petitioncongress. Bugbee, Ibid. Sons of DeWitt Colony Texas, http://www.tamu.edu/faculty/ccbn/dewitt/slaverybugbee.htm. Index of Correspondence regarding Slavery in Texas, http://www.tamu.edu/faculty/ccbn/dewitt/slaveryletters.htm. Acuña and Compeán, 25–41. Linda Myers Purcell, "Slavery In The Republic Of Texas" (Master of Arts Thesis, North Texas State, Denton, 1982). Abigail Curlee, "The History of a Texas Slave Plantation," *Southwestern historical quarterly* Vol. 26, Issue 1 (July 1922–April 1923), 79–127.

19 Walter Prescott Webb, *The Texas Rangers: A Century of Frontier Defense* (Austin: University of Texas Press, 1965), 21–22. Tijerina, *Tejanos under the Mexican Flag*, 25–45. Letter from Gen. Manuel de Mier y Terán to Lucás Alamán, "En qué parará Texas? En lo que Dios quiera." ("What is to become of Texas? Whatever God wills."), July 2, 1832, Sons of DeWitt Colony Texas, http://www.tamu.edu/ccbn/dewitt/teranmanuel.htm.

20 Fehrenbach, *Lone Star*, 163–64. Hayden Edwards and The Fredonian Rebellion, 1826–1827, http://www.tamu.edu/ccbn/dewitt/fredonian.htm.

21 The Monroe Doctrine, December 2, 1823, http://avalon.law.yale.edu/19th_century/monroe.asp.

22 Van Alstyne, *The Rising American Empire*, 101.

23 Tijerina, *Tejanos under the Mexican Flag*, 65–78. Laws of Coahuila y Texas 1825, http://www.tamu.edu/ccbn/dewitt/cololaws.htm#coahuila. Colonization Law of 1832, http://www.tamu.edu/ccbn/dewitt/lundy5.htm#cololaw1832. Andrew Jonathan Torget, "Cotton empire: Slavery and the Texas borderlands, 1820–1837" (PhD Dissertation, University of Virginia, 2009), 195, 197.

24 Nathaniel W. Stephenson, *Texas and the Mexican War: A Chronicle of the Winning of the Southwest* (New York: United States Publishing, 1921), 52. The Galveston Bay and Texas Land Company of New York, Anthony Butler, lobbied for U.S. support. Francis W. Wilson and Dorcas Baumgartner, The Tennessee-Texas Land Company, http://www.tamu.edu/ccbn/dewitt/tenntexland.htm. Colony Expansion: The Burkets, Kents, and Zumwalts, http://www.tamu.edu/ccbn/dewitt/expansion.htm#titles. DeWitt Land Grants, 1825–1832, http://www.tamu.edu/ccbn/dewitt/landgrants.htm.

25 *Castañeda*, Vol. 6, 217–18.

26 *Castañeda*, Vol. 6, 240–41. Fehrenbach, *Lone Star*, 180. Juan Nepomuceno Almonte 1803–1869, http://www.tamu.edu/ccbn/dewitt/almontejn.htm. Juan Almonte's Report on Texas Spring/Summer 1834 (Published January 1835), http://www.tamu.edu/ccbn/dewitt/almonterep.htm.

27 "Bustamante's Decree of 1830," http://www.tamu.edu/ccbn/dewitt/consultframe.htm. San Felipe de Austin, October 4, 1832, "To the Federal Congress of Mexico," http://www.tamu.edu/ccbn/dewitt/consultframe.htm. See DeWitt Papers. "Archivo Digital de Documentos Sobre la Guerra de Texas, 1835, y la Guerra Mexico-Estados Unidos, 1846–1848," http://www.sre.gob.mx/acervo/index.php?option=com_content&view=article&id=65&Itemid=343. http://forchicanachicanostudies.wikispaces.com/Archival+Research.

28 Eugene C. Barker, *Mexico and Texas, 1821–1835* (New York: Russell & Russell, 1965), 52, 74–80, 80–82. David J. Weber, ed. *Foreigners in Their Native Land* (Albuquerque: University of New Mexico Press, 1973), 89. Quoted in Fehrenbach, *Lone Star*, 182. Leroy Graf "The Economic History of the Lower Rio Grande, 1820–1870" (PhD Dissertation, Harvard University, Cambridge, 1942), 91. Sam Houston Letter to Andrew Jackson, Natchitoches, Louisiana, February 13, 1833, http://www.sonofthesouth.net/texas/sam-houston-letters-jackson.htm. "Cotton Empire," 203–06, ff 4; dissects Barker's argument that slavery played no part in the rebellion.

29 *Castañeda*, Vol. 6, 252–53. Fehrenbach, *Lone Star*, 181. Tijerina, *Tejanos under the Mexican Flag*, 113, shed light on these politics. See Stephen F. Austin, Texas State Library & Archives Commission. Eugene C. Barker, "Minutes of the Ayuntamiento of San Felipe de Austin, 1828–1832," *The Southwestern Historical Quarterly* Vol. 21, No. 3 (Jan., 1918), 299–326.

30 Stephenson, *Texas and the Mexican War*, 51. Graf, "The Economic History of the Lower Rio Grande, 1820–1870," 111. Austin was involved in opening this trade to non-Mexican vessels. Ironically, there was little trade between the valley and Central and Northern Texas. Torget, "Cotton Empire," 207. Austin actively played the cotton market.

31 Stephenson, *Texas and the Mexican War*, 52. Barker, *Mexico and Texas, 1821–1835*, 128. Castañeda, in Vol. 6, 234. Gene M. Brack, *Mexico Views Manifest*.

32 Fehrenbach, *Lone Star*, 188. Hutchinson, 6. Address of the Honorable S. F. Austin, Louisville, Kentucky, March 7, 1836, The Avalon Project, http://avalon.law.yale.edu/19th_century/texind01.asp. Also in J. C. Edmondson, *Alamo Story: From Early History to Current Conflicts* (Lanham: The Republic of Texas Press, 2000), 225.

33 Fehrenbach, *Lone Star*, 189. See "The Texas Revolution: Part A" (September–October 1835), http://www.tshaonline.org/lshl/texhisdocs04a.html. Austin, September 19, 1835 letter, http://www.tsl.state.tx.us/treasures/giants/austin/austin-safety-1.html.

34 Also in Robert D. Morritt, *The Lure of Texas* (London: Cambridge Scholars, 2011), 389.

35 Barker, *Mexico and Texas, 1821–1835*, 146, 147, 162. Barker, on Stephen Austin, http://www.tamu.edu/ccbn/dewitt/austinbio.htm.

36 The DeWitt Colony Alamo Defenders Index, http://www.tamu.edu/ccbn/dewitt/gonreliefframe.htm; http://www.tamu.edu/ccbn/dewitt/dewitt.htm. The DeWitt Papers function as genealogy pointing the reader to the genealogy of those inside the Alamo; only the Mexicans were from Texas. Mary Ann Cooper, "Remember the Alamo? Maybe Not," *The Hispanic Outlook in Higher Education* 15, 2 (Oct 18, 2004), 9.

37 Walter Lord, *A Time to Stand: The Epic of the Alamo* (Lincoln, NE: Bison Books, 1978), 213–20. Jeff Long's *Duel of Eagles: The Mexican and U.S. Fight for the Alamo* (New York: William Morrow and Co, Inc., 1990). Lord, "Myths and Realities of the Alamo," *The American West* 3 (May 1964), 18–25. Stephen Hardin's, *Texian Iliad: A Military History of the Texas Revolution* (Austin: University of Texas Press, 1996). Tijerina's *Tejanos Under the Mexican Flag, 1821–1836*. Timothy M. Matovina, *The Alamo Remembered: Tejano Accounts and Perspectives* (Austin: University of Texas Press, 1995).

38 Archie P. McDonald, "William Barret Travis 1809–1836," http://www.sonsofdewittcolony.org/adp/history/bios/travis/travis.html. "The story has been told that Travis suspected his wife of infidelity, doubted his parenthood of her unborn child, and killed a man because of it. The story is probably correct, given its persistence, but hard evidence of it is lacking." *Biography: Col. William Barrett Travis August 9, 1809 – Hero of the Alamo* by Donna R Causey.

39 Archie P. McDonald, "William Barret Travis 1809–1836," http://www.tamu.edu/ccbn/dewitt/adp/history/bios/travis/travis.html. William Barret Travis's Letter from the Alamo, "Alabama Pioneerism," http://www.alabamapioneers.com/biography-col-william-barrett-travis-born-1809-hero-alamo/.

40 Lord, "Myths and Realities of the Alamo," 18, 20, 24. Ramón Martínez Caro, "A True Account of the First Texas Campaign," in Carlos E. Castañeda, ed., *The Mexican Side of the Texas Revolution* (Dallas, TX: L. Turner Co., 1928), 103.

41 Caddo Tribe, https://www.warpaths2peacepipes.com/indian-tribes/caddo-tribe.htm.

42 *Handbook of Texas Online*, Jeffrey D. Carlisle, "Apache Indians," accessed November 4, 2017, http://www.tshaonline.org/handbook/online/articles/bma33. Uploaded on June 9, 2010. Modified on July 1, 2016. Published by the Texas State Historical Association. Odie B. Faulk, *The Last Years of Spanish Texas, 1778–1821* (The Hague: Mouton, 1964).

43 David La Vere, *The Texas Indians* (Texas A & M Press, 2004), 170.

44 Handbook of Texas Online, "Census and Census Records," accessed November 4, 2017, http://www.tshaonline.org/handbook/online/articles/ulc01.

45 Ibid.

46 "Indians and the Texas Revolution," Native American Relations in Texas, Texas State Library, https://www.tsl.texas.gov/exhibits/indian/early/page1.html.

47 Ojibwa, "The Republic of Texas and the Cherokee Indians," Native American Netroots, March 25, 2010, http://nativeamericannetroots.net/diary/429.

48 Ojibwa, "The Republic of Texas and the Cherokee Indians," Native American Netroots, March 25, 2010, http://nativeamericannetroots.net/diary/429.

49 Fannin's Fight and The Massacre at La Bahia (Goliad), http://www.tamu.edu/ccbn/dewitt/goliadmassacre.htm, Goliad Region January–March 27, 1836. Johnson & Grant & Colonel James Fannin's Command, http://www.tamu.edu/ccbn/dewitt/goliadmenframe.htm. Archival Communications Fannin and Goliad August 1835–March 1836, http://www.tamu.edu/ccbn/dewitt/goliadofficial.htm. M. B. Lamar, S. Whiting, and J. W. J. Niles, "No. 746 Oak Grove June 16, 1838," in Charles Adams Gulick, Jr., and Katherine Elliott, eds., *The Papers of Mirabeau Buonaparte Lamar*, Vol. II (Austin: A. C. Ialdwin A Sop Printer, 1922), 167–68.

50 Cecilia Ballí, "The Second Battle of Goliad," *Texas Monthly*, May 2001, https://www.texasmonthly.com/the-culture/the-second-battle-of-goliad/.

51 Explore documents such as Santa Anna's account. Victory at San Jacinto, Sons of the DeWitt Colony, http://www.tamu.edu/ccbn/dewitt/dewitt.htm. José Enrique de la Peña, *With Santa Anna in Texas: A Personal Narrative of the Revolution*, trans. Carmen Perry (College Station: Texas A&M University, 1997), 53.

52 Carlos Castañeda, *Our Catholic Heritage in Texas, 1519–1933*, Vol. 7; *The Church in Texas Since Independence, 1836–1950*, 5. Sam Houston's Copy of His Official Report of the Battle of San Jacinto.

53. Quote in Lota M. Spell, "Gorostiza and Texas," *Hispanic American Historical Review* 37, No. 4 (November 1957), 446. Brack, *Mexico Views Manifest*, 74–75. Burl Noggle, "Anglo Observers of the Southwest Borderlands, 1825–1890: The Rise of a Concept," *Arizona and the West* 1, No. 2 (Summer 1959): 122. Treaty of Velasco, May 14, 1836, Courtesy of the Yale University Law School Library. The Avalon Project, http://avalon.law.yale.edu/19th_century/velasco.asp. The Treaty of Velasco was negotiated between officials of the interim government of the Republic of Texas and General Antonio López de Santa Anna (1794–1876) about three weeks after his capture on April 22, 1836. Santa Anna did not have the authority to negotiate the treaty that gave Texas to the United States.

54. Medina Castro, *El Gran Dispojo*, 74. Charles A. Hale, *Mexican Liberalism in the Age of Mora, 1821–1853* (New Haven, CT: Yale University Press, 1968), 11–12, 16.

55. On March 1, 1845, Congress passed the joint resolution, but it was not until July 1845 that a convention in Texas voted to accept annexation to the United States. The political maneuverings behind annexation in the U.S. Congress document the economic motive underlying it. Van Alstyne, *The Rising American Empire*, 104. José María Roa Barcena, *Recuerdos de la Invasión Norte Americana (1846–1848)*, in I. Antonio Castro Leal, ed. (México, DF: Editorial Porrúa, 1947), 25–27. For the Mexican reaction see José Joaquín de Herrera, "A Proclamation Denouncing the United States' Intention to Annex Texas," June 4, 1845, in Steven R. Butler, ed., *A Documentary History of the Mexican War* (Richardson, TX: Descendants of Mexican War Veterans, 1995), 5, http://www.dmwv.org/mexwar/documents/herrera.htm.

56. Albert C. Ramsey, ed. and trans., *The Old Side or Notes for the History of the War Between Mexico and the United States*, reprinted (New York: Burt Franklin, 1970), 28–29. Ramón Alcaraz et al., *Apuntes para la Historia de la Guerra Entre México y los Estados Unidos* (México, DF: Tipografía de Manuel Payno, Hiho, 1848), 27–28. For an excellent account of Slidell's mission, see Dennis Eugene Berge, "Mexican Response to United States Expansion, 1841–1848" (PhD Dissertation, University of California, Los Angeles, 1965).

57. James. D. Richardson, *A Compilation of the Messages and Papers of the Presidents*, 10 Vols. (Washington, DC: Government Printing Office, 1905), 4, 428–42, quoted in Arvin Rappaport, ed., *The War with Mexico: Why Did It Happen?* (Skokie, IL: Rand McNally, 1964), 16. President James Polk's State of the Union Address, December 2, 1845. Joint Session of Congress, State of the Union Address, 29th Congress, First Session, December 2, 1845, http://www.presidentialrhetoric.com/historicspeeches/polk/stateoftheunion1845.html. James K. Polk, Message on War with Mexico, May 11, 1846, http://www.pbs.org/weta/thewest/resources/archives/two/mexdec.htm.

58. Grady McWhiney and Sue McWhiney, eds., *To Mexico with Taylor and Scott, 1845–1847* (Waltham, MA: Praisell, 1969), 3. Letter from Ulysses S. Grant to Fiancée Julia Dent, July 25, 1846. John Y. Simon, *The Papers of Ulysses S. Grant*, Vol. 1 (London: Feffer & Simons, 1967), 102. Also see Gilbert King, "General Grant in Love and War: The officer who gained glory as a warrior in the Civil War also had a domestic side," smithsonian.com, February 14, 2012, https://www.smithsonianmag.com/history/general-grant-in-love-and-war-94609512/.

59. Abraham Lincoln's "Spot Resolutions: Resolution and Preamble on Mexican War," *The Abraham Lincoln Papers at the Library of Congress*, December 22, 1847, http://quod.lib.umich.edu/cgi/t/text/text-idx?c=lincoln;rgn=div1;view=text;idno=lincoln1;node=lincoln1%3A434.

60. Rappaport, *The War with Mexico*, 16.

61. Walt Whitman, *Leaves of Grass* (Brooklyn, NY: Gabriel Harrison daguerreotype, 1855), iii, iv, xi. I.

62. Glenn W. Price, *Origins of the War with Mexico: The Polk-Stockton Intrigue* (Austin: University of Texas Press, 1967), 7.

63. As noted, the belief that Americans are the chosen people is part of the formation of the American image of themselves. The term *Manifest Destiny* was written by John O'Sullivan in 1839. "The Great Nation of Futurity," *The United States Democratic Review* 6, No. 23 (November 1839): 426–30. Cornell University Library, http://cdl.library.cornell.edu/cgi-bin/moa/sgml/moa-idx?notisid=AGD1642-0006-46; http://www.mtholyoke.edu/acad/intrel/osulliva.htm.

64. For a good discussion of Calvinist Europe, see Richard van Dulmen, *Los Inicios De La Europa Moderna 1550–1680* (México: Siglo XXI, 1990), 246–63.

65. John C. Calhoun, *Conquest of Mexico*. TeachingAmericanHistory.org, http://teachingamericanhistory.org/library/document/conquest-of-mexico/. Daniel Alejandro Garza, "So easily misunderstood: U.S.-Mexican War soldiers' motivation, experience, and memory, (1846-1890)" (Master of Arts Thesis, Southern Methodist University, 2010).

66. Justin H. Smith, *The War with Mexico*, Vol. 2 (Gloucester, MA: Peter Smith, 1963), 310.

67. T. B. Thorpe, *Our Army on the Rio Grande*, quoted in Abiel Abbot Livermore, *The War with Mexico Reviewed* (Boston, MA: American Peace Society, 1850), 126. A reviewer questioned claims of the incessant bombing of Matamoros. The following memo appears to support this event. Congratulatory Orders. 151. HEAD-QUARTERS, ARMY OF OCCUPATION, Resaca de la Palma, May 11, 1846. By order of Brigadier-General Taylor. "While the main body of the army has been thus actively employed, the garrison left opposite Matamoros has rendered no less distinguished service, by sustaining a severe cannonade and bombardment for many successive days." In Nathan Covington Brooks, *Complete History of the Mexican War: Its Causes, Conduct, and Consequences: Comprising an Account of the Various Military and Naval Operations, from Its Commencement to the Treaty of Peace* (Philadelphia: Grigg, Elliot & Co., 1849), 151.
68. Alfred Hoyt Bill, *Rehearsal for Conflict* (New York: Knopf, 1947), 122.
69. John Y. Simon, *The Papers of Ulysses S. Grant*, Vol. 1 (London and Amsterdam: Feffer & Simons, 1967), 102.
70. William Starr Meyers, ed., *The Mexican War Diary of General B. Clellan*, Vol. 1 (Princeton, NJ: Princeton University Press, 1917), 109–10.
71. Quoted in Livermore, *The War with Mexico Reviewed*, 148–9.
72. Livermore, *The War with Mexico Reviewed*, 8, 11, 12.
73. Abraham Lincoln's Speech to Congress against Seizing Mexican Territory, January 12, 1848, U.S. House of Representatives. *The Abraham Lincoln Papers at the Library of Congress.* Series 1. General Correspondence. 1833–1916. Library of Congress, http://memory.loc.gov/cgi-bin/query/r?ammem/mal:@field(DOCID+@lit(d0007400)). In January 1848 he opposed seizing Mexican territory and laid out the causes for the war. Acuña and Compeán, *Voices of U.S. Latino*, 95–100. Shelley Streeby, "American Sensations: Empire, Amnesia, and the US-Mexican War," *American Literary History* Vol. 13, No. 1, (Spring, 2001): 1–40.
74. Smith, *The War with Mexico*, 385, No. 18. Smith, *The War with Mexico*, Vol. 1, 550, No. 6. The Saint Patrick's Battalion (Batallón de San Patricio), http://www.youtube.com/watch?v=WiogUx5h28c. Batalla de Monterrey 1846, http://www.youtube.com/watch?v=5-KYgBW_RBA.
75. Livermore, *War with Mexico Reviewed*, 160. Mark R. Day, "Los San Patricios: La Tragica Historia del Batallón de San Patricio" (Vista, CA: San Patricio Productions, 1997), is a video documentary on the San Patricios. The video is also available in English. Clips of the movie can be found on YouTube.
76. Meyers, *The Mexican War Diary of General B. Clellan*, Vol. 1, 161–62.
77. George Gordon Meade, MONTERREY, December 2, 1846, George Gordon Meade, *The life and letters of George Gordon Meade: Major-general United States Army*, Vol. 1 (New York: Charles Scribner's Sons, 1913), 160–61.
78. Winfield Scott, *Memoirs of Lieut.-General Scott*, Vol. 2 (New York: Sheldon, 1864), 392. Timothy A Garvin, "'An Immortal Band of Rouges': Immigrant Disaffection and the San Patricio Battalion in the United States-Mexican War, 1846–848" (Master of Arts Thesis, California State University, Long Beach, 2004).
79. Samuel E. Chamberlain, *My Confessions* (New York: Harper & Row, 1956), 75.
80. Chamberlain, *My Confessions*, 87, 88.
81. Stephen B. Oates, "*Los Diablos Tejanos*: Texas Rangers," in Odie B. Faulk and Joseph A. Stout, Jr., eds., *The Mexican War: Changing Interpretations* (Chicago, IL: Sage, 1973), 121. Paul Foos, *Short, Offhand, Killing Affair: Soldiers and Social Conflict During the Mexican-American War* (New York: Scholarly Books, 2002). Foos uses soldiers' diaries and letters. He relies largely on U.S. sources to document American atrocities against Mexican civilians. Foos raises the question of widespread discontent within the Euro-American forces. Depredations against Mexicans were based on feelings of racial superiority. Judah Swann, "The Texas Rangers in the Mexican War" (Master of Arts Thesis, California State University, Dominguez Hills, 2000).
82. Johannsen, *To the Halls of the Montezumas*, 137. Elizabeth Salas, *Soldaderas in the Mexican Military: Myth and History* (Austin: University of Texas Press, 1990). Peggy Mullarkey Cashion, "Women and the Mexican War, 1846–1848" (Master of Art Thesis, University of Texas Arlington, 1990).
83. Johannsen, *To the Halls of the Montezumas*, 137.
84. Pablo Ramos Benitez y Ahmed Valtier, "Maria Josefa Zozaya, La Heroina de la Batalla de Monterrey," *Revista Atisbo* No. 10 Diciembre del 2007, Miercoles, 6 de Febrero de 2008. Daniel Walker Howe, *What Hath God Wrought: The Transformation of America, 1815–1848* (New York: Oxford University Press, 2007), 778–79. Christopher Conway,

"Sisters at War: Mexican Women's Poetry and the U.S.-Mexican War," *Latin American Research Review* Vol. 47, No. 1, (2012): 3–13.

85 "Mexican Women and the War," The U.S.–Mexican War, University of Texas, Austin, http://library.uta.edu/usmexicowar/topic.php?topic_id=29.

86 Stephen A. Carney, *The Occupation of Mexico, May 1846–July 1848* (U.S. Army Center of Military History, May 23, 2006), 17, https://history.army.mil/brochures/Occupation/Occupation.htm. Ron Briley, "Occupation Blues: Let's Not Forget the Mexican War," *Washington Post*, Dec. 10, 2006, http://historynewsnetwork.org/article/32495.

87 Peter J. Michel, "No Mere Holiday Affair: The Capture of Santa Fe in the Mexican-American War," *Gateway Heritage Quarterly* 9, No. 4 (Spring 1989): 12–25. Joseph G. Dawson III, "'Zealous for Annexation': Volunteer Soldiering, Military Government, and the Service of Colonel Alexander Doniphan in the Mexican-American War," *The Journal of Strategic Studies* 19, No. 4 (December 1, 1996), 10–36. Randy L. Yoder, "Rackensackers and Rangers: Brutality in the Conquest of Northern Mexico, 1846–1848" (Master of Arts Thesis, Oklahoma State University, 2006).

88 Brack, *Mexico Views Manifest*, 2.

89 David S. Heidler and Jeanne T. Heidler, *The Mexican War* (Westport, CT: Greenwood Press, 2006), 75.

90 George Lockhart Rives, *The United States and Mexico: A History of the Relations Between the Two Countries from the Independence of Mexico to the Close of the War with the United States*, Vol. II (New York: Charles Scribner's Sons, 1913), 584–86. Los Niños Heroes: Mexico City's Boy Heroes, http://www.youtube.com/watch?v=x5yAeE1MuMo). Los Niños Héroes, http://www.youtube.com/watch?v=xP6PLFG_b8Y.

91 Dexter Perkins and Glyndon G. Van Deusen, *The American Democracy: Its Rise to Power* (New York: Macmillan, 1964), 273.

92 Alejandro Sobarzo, *Deber y consciences: Nicolás Trist, el negociador norteamericano en la Guerra del 47* (México: Fondo de Cultura Económica, 1996), 283–85.

93 The treaty drew the boundary between the United States and Mexico at the Rio Grande and the Gila River, for a payment of $15,000,000. The United States received more than 525,000 square miles (1,360,000 square kilometer) of land (now Arizona, California, western Colorado, Nevada, New Mexico, Texas, and Utah). In return it agreed to settle the more than $3,000,000 in claims made by U.S. citizens against Mexico. The treaty was a cause of Civil War in both Mexico and the United States. The expansion of slavery in the United States supposedly had been settled by the Missouri Compromise (1820). The addition of the vast Mexican tract as new U.S. territory reopened the question. Attempts to settle it led to the uneasy Compromise of 1850.

94 Robert Self Henry, *The Story of the Mexican War* (New York: Ungar, 1950), 390. Treaty of Guadalupe Hidalgo, 1848, February 2, 1848. The Avalon Project at Yale Law School, http://avalon.law.yale.edu/19th_century/guadhida.asp.

95 See John D. Fuller, *The Movement for the Acquisition of All Mexico* (New York: DaCapo Press, 1969). Netzahualcoyotl Avelar, "A Critical Analysis of the 1848 Treaty of Guadalupe Hidalgo Between the United States of America and the Republic of Mexico: Educational Implications" (Doctor of Education, University of San Francisco, 1993).

96 Letter from Commissioner Trist to Secretary Buchanan, Mexico, January 25, 1848, *Senate Executive Documents*, No. 52, 283.

97 Wayne Moquin et al., eds., *A Documentary History of the Mexican American* (New York: Praeger, 1971), 185. Irving W Levinson, "The causes, course, and settlement of the Mexican-American War" (Master of Arts, University of Houston, 1997).

98 Lynn I. Perrigo, *The American Southwest* (New York: Holt, Rinehart and Winston, 1971), 176.

99 *Compilation of Treaties in Force* (Washington, DC: Government Printing Office, 1899), 402, quoted in Perrigo, *The American Southwest*, 176. The Querétaro Protocol, May 26, 1848, Protocol of Querétaro In Rodolfo F. Acuña and Guadalupe Compeán, eds., *Voices of the U.S. Latino Experience [Three Volumes]*. (Westport: Greenwood, 2008), 113–4. Article X shows Polk's duplicity President James K. Polk (1795–1849) on Article X of the Treaty of Guadalupe Hidalgo, February 22, 1848, U.S. Senate, 30th Cong., 1st Sess., Executive Order 68, *Congressional Record*.

100 Armando B. Rendón, *Chicano Manifesto* (New York: Collier Books, 1970), 75–78. Deleted Article X from the Treaty of Guadalupe Hidalgo, 1848, http://www.loc.gov/rr/hispanic/ghtreaty/. President James K. Polk (1795–1849) on Article X of the Treaty of Guadalupe Hidalgo, February 22, 1848, U.S. Senate, 30th Cong., 1st Sess., Executive Order 68, *Congressional Record*.

101 Rendón, *Chicano Manifesto*, 78.

102 Weber, *Foreigners in Their Native Land*, 14, states that the Supreme Court in *McKinney v. Saviego*, 1855, found that the treaty did not apply to Texas.

103 Antonio de la Peña y Reyes, *Algunos Documentos Sobre el Tratado de Guadalupe-Hidalgo* (México, DF: Sec de Rel. Ext., 1930), 159, quoted in Richard Gonzales, "Commentary on the Treaty of Guadalupe Hidalgo," in Feliciano Rivera, ed., *A Mexican American Source Book* (Menlo Park, CA: Educational Consulting Associates, 1970), 185.
104 Leroy B. Hafen and Carl Coke Rister, *Western America*, 2nd ed. (Englewood Cliffs, NJ: Prentice-Hall, 1950), 312.
105 Van Alstyne, *The Rising American Empire*, 106.
106 Robert Ryal Miller, "The War Between the United States and Mexico," U.S.–Mexican War, PBS, http://www.pbs.org/kera/usmexicanwar/aftermath/war.html.
107 Ibid.
108 Ibid.
109 Martha Menchaca, "A History of Colonization and Mexican American Education," Paper Presented for a Conference, *Harvard Educational Review*, March 9, 1998, at the University of California, Irvine.

"America . . . Born and Bred of Empire": The Occupation of the Americas

The first edition of *Occupied America* (1972) began:

> Mexicans – Chicanos – in the United States today are an oppressed people. They are citizens, but their citizenship is second-class at best. They are exploited and manipulated by those with more power. And, sadly, many believe that the only way to get along in Anglo-America is to become "Americanized" themselves. Awareness of their history—of their contributions and struggles, of the fact that they were not the "treacherous enemy" that Anglo-American histories have said they were—can restore pride and a sense of heritage to a people who have been oppressed for so long. In short, awareness can help them to liberate themselves."[1]

Although I abandoned the internal colonial model due to other priorities, the idea never left me and in subsequent editions I added research. I recently contemplated condensing Chapters 4 through 7 on the occupied territory immediately following the war. Colleagues, however, cautioned me, pointing out that this would weaken the thesis of *Occupied America*. It is those chapters that set the tone for the occupation.

William Appleman Williams, in the aftermath of Vietnam, reminds us that,

> "America[2] was born and bred of empire. That does not mean that we are unique; indeed, just the opposite. We are part and parcel of the imperial outreach of Western Europe that came to dominate the world. But therein lies the irreducible cause of our present predicament. We have from the beginning defined and viewed ourselves as unique. The differences between ourselves and other nations are not incidental but they are irrelevant to the fundamental issue. We are different only because we acquired the empire at a very low cost, because the rewards have been enormous and because until now we have masked our imperial truth with the rhetoric of freedom."[3]

During the mid-20th century, Williams was among the nation's most influential historians. His work put a bright light on American foreign policy and went a long way in explaining the contradictions of the Vietnam War. He paved the way for William J. Fulbright's *The Arrogance of Power* and other treatises of the era.[4] Williams popularized the thesis that the American Empire began long before the Spanish American War. He reminded us that there were 26 original British colonies in America in 1776. Britain occupied colonies in the Caribbean—Jamaica, Barbados, the Leeward Islands, Grenada and Tobago, St. Vincent; and Dominica. The island colonies developed close social and trade ties with the mainland. Most North American British colonists lived less than 200 miles inland and the ocean often acted as a highway.[5] The islands' plantation system resembled that of the South. However, they shared more in common with England and, like the planter class on the mainland, identified as British. The revolution divided mainlanders and islanders; with the islanders mostly wanted to be part of the British Empire.

American historians used euphemisms such as "The Winning of the West," to rationalize the Making of the American Empire and justify the genocide of Indigenous Americans. They use phrases such as "American Expansion," and the "Westward Movement" giving the impression that these acts were natural phenomena. Indeed, most Americans until recently paid little attention to the dark passages of American history.[6]

The U.S.–Mexico border is the battleground where most U.S.'s aggression begins. Historians differ as to the causes of tension between people the north and south of this 2,000-mile border. Napoleon Bonaparte once said "What is history, but a fable agreed upon?" and that in turn inspired the quote "history is written by victors." In the 20th century, Winston Churchill—or maybe Hermann Göring—popularized this sentiment. Knowing the political importance of history American historians have standardized the official historical narrative from elementary school through higher education. Thus a majority of students of all ages do not know that the Texas and Mexican American Wars ever happened.[7]

Why Mexicans and Americans see wars differently. The United States from the beginning justified its aggression as part of God's will and had the attitude it was doing the Indigenous People and the Mexicans a favor by spreading democracy. Americans saw and see themselves as a just and benevolent people. Indiana University historian Peter Guardino, makes the point that American soldiers during the American invasion of Mexico "saw guerrilla warfare not as proof of Mexican nationalism but instead that many Mexicans were violent and treacherous racial inferiors."[8] In turn, Mexicans vividly remember the atrocities of American soldiers and the nation's loss while most Americans prefer to forget or rewrite the truth.

Frederick Jackson Turner's *The Significance of the Frontier in American History* (1893) is the most influential historical work on American exceptionality:

> The American frontier is sharply distinguished from the European frontier—a fortified boundary line running through dense populations. The most significant thing about the American frontier is that it lies at the hither edge of free land. In the census reports it is treated as the margin of that settlement which has a density of two or more to the square mile. The term is an elastic one, and for our purposes does not need sharp definition. We shall consider the whole frontier belt including the Indian country and the outer margin of the "settled area" of the census reports. This paper will make no attempt to treat the subject exhaustively; its aim is simply to call attention to the frontier as a fertile field for investigation, and to suggest some of the problems which arise in connection with it.[9]

The Turner Thesis and the belief in American exceptionalism—on what makes Americans unique—has nursed countless generations of graduate students and historians.

Despite a history of expansion, some Americans take offense at the notion of an American Empire. They are reluctant to accept that the United States was an aggressor nation and deny U.S. invasion of Mexico, and the theft of half of its territory. They offer a counterargument that Mexican Americans are plotting a Reconquista, the reconquest of the stolen land. Mexicans to this day use of words such as *intervention*, if they are polite, or *the American Invasion of Mexico* if they are blunt. Amidst all this, many theorists insist they empire.

Was the U.S. invasion of Mexico an "imperialist war?" Was the United States, as Americans claim, spreading democracy to Mexico? Was the conquest based on altruistic motives? Were the intentions in 1836 or 1847 any different from those in 1898—or the present when, according to some American leaders, the purpose of U.S. intervention is to preserve democracy throughout the world?

> During the years between the Mexican-American War and the Civil War, the United States became increasingly involved in Central America and the Caribbean. While U.S. Government officials attempted to acquire territorial possessions in that region, private citizens (known as "filibusters") also organized armed expeditions to various places in Mexico, Central America, and Cuba. Filibustering and official U.S. diplomacy were equally unsuccessful in acquiring permanent and significant territorial gains, and also tended to incite local antagonism against U.S. actions in the region.[10]

American interest in Latin American countries did not begin or end with the acquisition of Florida and the Mexican cession. The events merely abetted the notion of empire. Even before the "Mexican adventure," Americans sought to secure their interests in the Caribbean and Central America believing that they were ripe for American "re-annexation," and, according to expansionists, the territories were necessary to the construction of a "U.S." inter-ocean canal and defense of U.S. interests in the region.

Meanwhile, the question remained as to whether the U.S. should re-annex Cuba. It was heatedly debated in Congress and in the media during the 1850s when slave interests pressed for a repetition of Texas.[11] After the signing of the Treaty of Guadalupe Hidalgo, some American politicos were dissatisfied with the border: Texas claimed the Rio Grande as its western boundary that included half of New Mexico; expansionists wanted the re-annex more Mexican land insisting that it was their land anyway.[12] Almost immediately the North and the South sought to further their interests in the newly acquired territory. The South wanted slavery legalized, but the North wanted the opposite. Before the American invasion of Mexico, Congress passed the Wilmot Proviso (1846) as an amendment to a House of Representatives bill. It prohibited slavery in territory acquired from Mexico. Once the war was over, however, slave interests agitated a crisis similar to that of the Missouri Compromise of 1820.[13] A small vocal group claimed that the border was further south.[14] Meanwhile, the border was referred to as the Mexican border rather than the American border.

Actually, the border meant little to people who lived along it. A person would have been hard pressed to distinguish between the Lower Rio Grande Valley and Mexico. As commercial agriculture on the U.S. side spread and African Americans were freed, thousands of Mexican laborers and their families crossed the boundary.

The next four chapters of this book discuss the unfolding events in four states—Texas, New Mexico, Arizona, and California—that formed the center of Mexican life in the United States. To assist the reader to better understand the topics discussed, the following wheel model has been developed, which are helpful to connect the events and data to timelines.

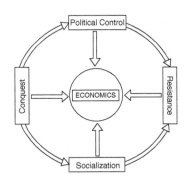

The above wheel resembles a outline. At the hub of the wheel is, *Economics* it is the central reason for the conquest. Profit makes the wheel go round, and determines the motive for each of the other variables. The word *Conquest* does not exist in a vacuum; in each of the four states or territories there were distinct motives for conquest. Once the land and other resources were taken, the people were *Politically Controlled* through police powers, government, courts, and so forth. Laws set norms essential to social control. Administrators or judges were appointed by the conquering people or elected by the conquerors. The courts interpret the law, which is backed by "legitimate" force.

People are not easily controlled; violence and police powers only go so far toward keeping them in line. They have to believe that the system is fair and that it serves and protects them. They are socialized to believe the system is fair through the schools. The media, and religion, to accept the legitimacy and common codes of conduct of the ruling elite. In colonial situations, as in every other situation, people resist when government becomes tyrannical. This *Resistance* is manifested in the form of social banditry and mob rebellions, and in milder forms such as opposition newspapers and other media.

History does not stand still. New memories are constantly added and older ones revised. Individuals and groups adapt to the changes in the modes of economic production. The modes of production evolved from subsistence level farming to mercantile and finally in 1880, railroad lines connected the Southwest to the more densely populated eastern United States, and large-scale commercial agriculture and mining produced massive quantities that affected the economy of the entire nation. Industrialization demanded large amounts of capital and human labor. These changes in the mode of production determined how people made their living, what the relations were between people and their work, and the relations between social classes and how they organized to bring about change. The formation of slavery and the wars with the Native Americans and the Mexicans hardened the nation's notion of race that was formed by the American Empire.

The U.S. after Spain was the second European Empire to colonize the Southwest. This section of *Occupied America* focuses mainly on the American invasion It makes clear that the final challenge is the decolonization of both American and Spanish Imperialism. They form the many layers of the onion that have to be peeled back before the heart of the onion can be revealed as sweet heart or rotten at the core. Like in psychoanalysis, it is a search for the truth.

Chapter 4
Occupied Texas: The Colonizers and their Myths

Learning Objectives

4.1 Analyze how Spanish Colonialism affected the relations between the colonizers and the colonized.

4.2 Explain how trade and racism influenced Mexico–Texas relations from the mid-1800s through the U.S. Civil War.

4.3 Describe how Caste system affected life in Texas after the U.S. Civil War.

4.4 Describe post–Civil War resistance movements in Texas.

4.5 Characterize boss rule in Texas.

4.6 Explain how commercial agriculture changed Texas in the 1880s.

4.7 Explain the role of Mexican Labor in the growth of Texas.

Follow the Water

4.1 **Analyze how Spanish Colonialism affected the relations between the colonizers and the colonized.**

The thirst for an Empire motivated the expansion of the United States. Aside from water, land, and harbors for cotton production and trade, the purpose of the invasion and conquest of Texas was to control the Rio Grande as well as the trade of northern Mexico. Americans were as obsessed with controlling the mighty Rio Grande as they had been in controlling the mouth of the Mississippi River and establishing control over the entire Mississippi delta. (Both these rivers emptied into the Gulf of Mexico.) Thus, not surprisingly, Texas pressed a nebulous claim to the entire length of the river—1,885 miles, from southern Colorado to the Gulf of Mexico. South Texas was the base of operations for this land grab.[15]

It did not take a genius to recognize the strategic and economic importance of the Rio Grande. It was known to the Spaniards and the Mexicans. According to David Montejano,

> The commercial importance of the Rio Grande did not lie simply with the distant Santa Fe trade. What is usually overlooked but proved to be critical and more directly related to the outbreak of hostilities was the port trade of Matamoros on the lower end of the Rio Grande. In the late 1820s, silver bullion, lead, wool, hides, and beef tallow from Monterey, Saltillo, and San Luis Potosí were all passing through Matamoros, with silver constituting 90 percent or more of the value of the exports.[16]

Border towns sprang up on the north side of the Rio Grande and linked northern Mexico to San Antonio. The Alamo City was a Tejano (Texas Mexican) city; between 1836 and the Civil War, Mexicans made up most of its population. Numbers gave Tejanos the illusion that they were part of the governance process and would be part of its future. The occupation brought about a decline in the number of Tejano office holders; in 1837, 41 Spanish-surnamed candidates ran for office in San Antonio; a decade later the number dwindled to five. The aldermanic council included only one or two Mexicans between 1848 and 1866. The loss of symbolic power accompanied the erosion of the peaceful accommodation that characterized relations between Mexican and American elites. Racism united white Americans and gave them an advantage. At the same time, racial divisions divided Mexicans in reducing the Tejano elites' influence.[17]

Color played a huge role in the relations between the two races. Acceptance depended on whether Mexicans looked Caucasian or "colored." University of Texas professor Neil Foley writes that although the new republic adopted liberal land policies, only white heads of household were eligible to receive land, which meant Texas whites and "Spanish" Mexicans who aided in the Texas Revolt.[18] Whiteness, according to Foley, increasingly became the litmus test for acceptance. By the 1840s, racist policies forced at least 200 old "Spanish" families in San Antonio to move to Mexico. "Juan Seguin, captain in the

Texas army, hero of San Jacinto, and [until recently] the last Mexican mayor of San Antonio . . . " was forced to flee to Mexico in 1842.[19]

Most American immigrants came from southern states and over time their racist attitudes became the accepted norm. The antipathy toward Mexicans was irrational—by the 1850s they were barely over 2 percent of the population. While visiting San Antonio, American landscape architect Frederick Law Olmsted observed that a Mexican caught attempting to steal a horse would have been lynched if it had not been for the intercession of an outraged Mexican public. Trying to take advantage of the crisis, the sheriff raised a posse of 500 men to drive Mexicans out of the area.[20]

Memories of the war fanned hatreds. Each incoming wave of U.S. colonists internalized the war and the myth of the Alamo became part of white Texas lore. Tensions remained high as Mexico refused to recognize the Republic of Texas. Mexican prisoners of war were subjected to untold indignities that included confinement in cages with many dying of starvation. In the years prior to annexation, the Texan wannabes warred on Native Americans and stepped up their diplomatic front against Mexico.[21] An estimated population of 35,000 Americans in the fall of 1835 grew to more than 100,000 by 1845. They considered themselves pioneers, entitled to push the old *Tejano* families aside—after all, according to them, "Americans" paid for Texas with their blood. Not surprisingly, many Mexicans resented their inferior status.[22]

Towns continued to grow on both sides of the Rio Grande and Mexican American and American merchants developed commercial ties with Mexican merchants, drawn to the border from the Mexican Border States and Mexico's interior. Capitalizing on economic and political favoritism, U.S. merchants monopolized a disproportionate amount of land and resources.[23]

Professor Armando Villarreal y Talamantes writes that between "1837 and 1842, 14 upper class Mexicans bought a total of 278,769 acres from 67 Mexican landowners. During the same period, American buyers purchased 1,368,574 acres from 358 Mexicans, four times the amount purchased by their Mexican counterparts."[24] Many Mexicans who sold their land repatriated to Mexico in search of better opportunities.

The Comanche and Lipan Apache raids resumed during the 1830s. The *ranchos* (ranches), especially around Laredo, bore the brunt of these raids that sharply cut the number of livestock in the valley. Ranching continued as the principal occupation of Mexican settlers. At this point, farming was precarious because of the lack extensive irrigation projects.[25]

The Republic of Texas's Georgia-born President Mirabeau Buonaparte Lamar immigrated to Texas in 1835 where he fought in the so-called revolt. In 1839 Lamar became governor and pressed for a settlement of the boundary, offering Mexico a $5 million bribe to accept the Rio Grande (Bravo) as the border. This theft would have given Texas half of New Mexico. In 1841, Lamar worsened tensions by dispatching the ill-fated Santa Fé Expedition to New Mexico.[26]

Crossing the Northwest Texas Mexican Border

For all their pretentious Mexican gentry accommodated to the new order while the largely poor and dark Mexican population suffered blatant discrimination and exploitation. Discontent was widespread. Along the northeastern border, a line separated Spanish-speaking from the French, and later, Mexico from the United States. Competition over trade fanned border tensions. The French and later Americans used Nacogdoches as a gateway for their smuggling operations. In the early 1820s, tension increased between the Mexican old timers and white Americans who were pushing them aside. According to Janice Elaine Watkins, "Nowhere would the lack of respect for and noncompliance to authority be more apparent than in Nacogdoches. Distance enabled the Nacogdoches land men to ignore orders and conduct their land schemes without interference, and their actions and reactions affected the subsequent Texas revolution."[27]

By the end of the 1830s, an estimated 1,000 Americans per month entered Texas by way of Brazos River. Divisions increased along racial lines.[28] In 1835, Vicente Córdova, a native-born Texan, was the *alcalde* (mayor) of Nacogdoches. However, within a year a white alcalde replaced Córdova as the white population overwhelmed Mexicans. Córdova was then appointed Captain of the Military District[*].

When hostilities broke out, Córdova was pressured to take sides and he refused. After the Texas War, the Republic sought revenge on those who had not supported the filibusters. Some Native Americans with long-standing friendships with Mexicans joined Córdova and against the Lone Star Republic.[29] According to oral tradition, when his employer asked Guillermo Cruz why Mexicans were revolting, he replied, "they were going to fight for their rights, they had been dogs long enough." Córdova expected help from Mexico, but it was not forthcoming. Against all odds, the Mexicans fought the Republic of Texas until 1839, when the revolutionary band dwindled to fewer than 75 Tejanos, Blacks, and Native Americans. Wounded, Córdova retreated to Matamoros, and the families of other surviving East Texas Mexicans sought refuge in the woods. Texas authorities tried 33 Tejanos for treason. They found only one, Antonio Menchaca guilty and sentenced him to be hanged. President Mirabeau B. Lamar of the Texas Republic

---

[*] Military districts are military regions of a state's armed forces designating an area for which the army is responsible for.

intervened and commuted Menchaca's sentence, banishing Menchaca and his family from Texas. Authorities used the revolt as a justification to remove the Cherokee, Delaware, Shawnee, and other tribes from Texas in the Trail of Tears. In Mexico, Córdova continued to war against the Republic of Texas, attracting native, Mexican, Black, and white followers.[30]

The Mexican Corridor

4.2 Explain how trade and racism influenced Mexico–Texas relations from the mid-1800s through the U.S. Civil War.

Mexico's harboring of runaway slaves before and after the Civil War enraged slave owners. By 1855, some 4,000 fugitive slaves escaped to northern Mexico.[31] Texas authorities estimated plantation owners lost $3.2 million and alleged that Mexican authorities encouraged slaves to run away. When slave owners demanded their return, Mexican officials refused. White Texans led several expeditions to recover runaways, greatly increasing border tensions. White Texans suspected all Mexicans of aiding Blacks.[32] In 1853, the federal government stationed 2,176 soldiers in the state of Texas (the United States had a standing army of 10,417). The next year, the town of Seguín passed an ordinance forbidding Mexicans from entering the county or associating with Blacks. According to James Marten, Mexicans were suspected of not only disloyalty but inciting slaves. Vigilantism increased, and in 1854 "a vigilance committee in Austin expelled at least twenty Mexican families, and Austin businessmen pledged not to hire Mexican laborers . . ." claiming that they gave African slaves a "false notion of freedom . . . ."[33] In East Texas, a vigilante group called the Moderators harassed the Mexican population.

Not all Mexicans sympathized with the escaped slaves. Some supported the slave plutocracy and they considered themselves different from the slaves and the darker-skinned Mexicans. For example, José Antonio Navarro of San Antonio matriculated his son Angel at Harvard University. Navarro was a representative to the state constitutional convention, and helped secure the Mexican vote. In the 1850s, Navarro also fought the Know-Nothing Party. However, he sided with pro-slavery interests and his sons fought for the concederacy. Navarro led white supremacists during post–Civil War Reconstruction.[34]

Control of the Corridor

Charles Stillman (1810–1875) arrived in the Lower Rio Grande Vallein 1846, starting out in Matamoros as a merchant; anticipating the American occupation, Stillman and other merchants bought property on the U.S. side of the river. In 1848 Stillman, established a trading post in a cotton field across the river from Matamoros. Within four years, a lucrative trade with Mexico developed with the town of Brownsville. The boom inflated land prices and attracted more Americans.[35]

A large number of white merchants were camp followers or former soldiers who came to Texas during the American War. In 1850, white Americans composed slightly over half of Brownsville's population. They controlled the government, and set the rules; racism led them to believe that their authority came from the natural law. White Americans occupied 80 percent of the professional, mercantile, and government positions. Upriver, Laredo, Eagle Pass, and Del Rio were trade centers where merchants made fortunes from commercial links with Mexico. In turn, the merchants monopolized the land purchased or stolen from Mexican landowners. By manipulating government officials, lawyers enabled the process.

The cabal's control of the political and social processes gave white Americans an economic edge. The clique feared that the state of Texas would protect Mexican land claims, so they flirted with the idea of seceding South Texas. They enlisted powerful congressmen such as U.S Senator, Henry Clay and Secretary of State, William Seward. The other leaders were Richard King, James O'Donnell, Captain Mifflin Kenedy, and Sam Belden who in turn recruited Mexicans. When the conspiracy failed, Stillman turned to a more familiar practice of acquiring land—he stole it.[36]

Stillman's trading post stood on the *Espíritu Santo* grant, belonging to the descendants of Francisco Cavazos. Stillman moved squatters onto the Cavazoses' land, confusing the title and then purchased the squatters' claims and challenged Cavazos's ownership. Although a magistrate ruled in the Cavazoses' favor, Stillman threatened to appeal, forcing the Cavazoses to accept $33,000 for the grant; it was valued at $214,000.[37] Stillman's attorneys negotiated the agreement. The lawyers promptly transferred the title to Stillman and declared bankruptcy without paying the Cavazoses a cent.

Richard King (1825–1885) was born in New York City in 1824 to poor Irish immigrant parents, ran away to sea and became a pilot on a steamboat mastered by Mifflin–Kenedy. During the Mexican American War King and Kennedy were on the Rio Grande, after which the war; King ran a flophouse at Boca del Rio and later bought a vessel from the U.S. government and went into the freighting business. During his early career, he smuggled merchandises to the Mexican ranchers and miners in northern Mexico.[38]

In 1850, Stillman, King, and Kenedy formed a business partnership that controlled the waterborne trade of northern Mexico. In 1852, King purchased the 15,500 acre-*Santa Gertrudis* grant for less than 2 cents an acre. During the Civil War, King, a Confederate sympathizer, made a fortune in war profiteering; selling cattle, horses, and mules to Confederate troops; and running cotton to Mexican markets.

Flying the Mexican flag, he ran Union blockades. In 1866, Stillman left the border, and King and Kenedy took over his operations.

Richard King amassed over 600,000 acres of land during his lifetime; his widow increased the family holdings to more than one million acres. The King Ranch Corporation hired author and artist Tom Lea to write a two-volume work entitled *The King Ranch*. Lea portrayed King as a tough-minded, two-fisted Horatio Alger who brought prosperity to South Texas. King was as pure as the driven snow, according to Lea, and never harmed anyone, except in self-defense. Lea ignores or denies the allegations that King evicted small Mexican ranchers. When referring to Mexican resentment toward Americans like King, Lea dismisses it as jealousy.

Trade Wars and the Rise of Juan Cortina

Competition for trade transformed the borderlands into a battleground; in 1855 U.S. merchants lynched 11 Mexicans along the Nueces River. In Helena, in August 1857, 40 masked white American freighters attacked 17 carts transporting goods from the Texas coast to San Antonio, brutally murdering 65-year-old Antonio Delgado. Vigilantes in Goliad ran Mexican cart men out of the San Antonio area, with the freighters murdering at least 75 more. In the same year, Uvalde County passed a resolution prohibiting Mexicans from traveling through Uvalde unless they had a passport. At Goliad, the townspeople killed several Mexicans when the cart men used public roads. The Cart War took place almost simultaneously with the rise of the Know-Nothing Party and the national hysteria over the foreign-born; the vigilantes resented the economic competition.[39]

Although the Alamo City did not have access to the U.S. and world markets comparable to that of Houston and Galveston, San Antonio merchants profited handsomely from smuggling. After the U.S. invasion, San Antonio prospered as a service and distribution center. By 1850, the population of San Antonio jumped to nearly 3,500 residents and by the eve of the Civil War more than 8,000. In 1850, the first Texas federal census reported over 14,000 Mexican residents compared to 54,034 whites, 397 free Blacks, and 58,161 slaves.[40]

In 1858, Tamaulipas Governor Ramón Guerra created *La Zona Libre*, a free trade zone that protected Mexican merchants from federal tariffs, where they could pay only small municipal taxes and an administrative fee. The purpose of *La Zona* was to control American smuggling. The law exempted Matamoros, Reynosa, Camargo, Mier, Guerrero, and Nuevo Laredo from taxes. In 1861, Mexico extended the zone from the Gulf of Mexico to the Pacific within 12.5 miles of the U.S. border. U.S. merchants claimed that trade advantages cost them $2 million to $6 million annually. Brownsville business leaders pressured the U.S. government to intervene and to invade Mexico to force it to get rid of *La Zona Libre*.[41]

According to William D. Carrigan and Clive Webb, between 1848 and 1928, mobs lynched at least 597 Mexicans in the United States. The Mexican population suffered fewer lynchings than African Americans overall; however, according to Carrigan and Webb the number of Mexicans lynched was proportionately higher. Between 1848 and 1879, "Mexicans were lynched at a rate of 473 per 100,000 of population. The magnitude can be gauged by the extraordinarily high number of Blacks lynched in Mississippi during this same period that was 52.8 victims per 100,000 of population."[42] The purpose and effect of lynching is obvious. According to Judith L. Stephens it was a form of white supremacy and violence that was fostered by racism. It was designed to keep people of color in their place. In the case of the Mexicans, it began immediately after the occupation and flourished into the 1930s. The purpose was to institutionalize white supremacy throughout Texas. No doubt that emancipation of Black slaves added to this urgency.[43]

Enter "Cheno" Cortina

Juan "Cheno" Cortina was born on May 16, 1822, in Camargo, on the Mexican side of the river. His parents were landowners; his mother owned a land grant near Brownsville, where the family moved during the American War.[44] Cortina fought to defend northern Mexico from the American encroachments. U.S. historians portray Cortina as an outlaw, originally from a good family, but an illiterate rogue who "turned bad." Lyman Woodman, a retired military officer, described him as a "soldier, bandit, murderer, cattle thief, mail robber, civil and military governor of the State of Tamaulipas, and general in the Mexican army" who hated gringos.

After 1848, Cortina supported the filibustering expeditions of 1851, led by José María Carbajal (?–1874). White merchants and ranchers led by King and Kenedy wanted to form the Republic of the Sierra Madre. In partnership with the nefarious German, Adolphus Glavecke, Cortina rustled cattle belonging to Mexicans. However, by 1859, this alliance ended, and Glavecke and Cortina became bitter enemies. Glavecke played a major role in building the image of Cortina as a dangerous bandit.

Cortina's career as a revolutionary began accidentally on a hot July morning in 1859. Returning to his mother's ranch, Cheno encountered Marshal Bob Spears pistol-whipping an apparently drunk Mexican.[45] The victim had worked for Cheno's mother, so Cortina offered to take responsibility for the prisoner. But Spears replied, "What is it to you, you damned Mexican?" Cortina first fired a warning shot and then shot the marshal in the shoulder, riding off with the victim.

Knowing a fair trial was impossible, Cheno prepared to leave for Mexico. Before his departure he rounded up 50–60 followers and rode into Brownsville where he raised the Mexican flag. Cortina's detractors claim that he plundered the city—a charge that his supporters deny. According to Cortina's advocates, his men only attacked whites who blatantly mistreated Mexicans, killing the jailer and four other men, two of whom were guilty of murdering innocent Mexicans.[46]

Cortina originally did not plan to lead a revolution. He published a manifesto citing the injustices suffered by the Mexican people. He appealed to the U.S. government to stop protecting the "oppressors of the Mexicans" and to bring them to justice. Upon issuing his statement, Cortina prepared to immigrate to Mexico.[47]

However, instead Cortina's war accelerated after the citizens of Brownsville took Tomás Cabrera prisoner, a man of advanced age and a friend of Cortina. Cortina recruited an army of about 1,200 men and demanded Cabrera's release, threatening to burn Brownsville. The Brownsville Tigers (the local militia) and the Mexican army at Matamoros attacked Cortina. He defeated them; but they lynched Cabrera.[48]

The events radicalized Cortina who called for the liberation of Mexicans and the extermination of the "tyrants," calling them "flocks of vampires, in guise of men."

> My part is taken; the voice of revelation whispers to me that to me is entrusted the work of breaking the chains of your slavery, and that the Lord will enable me, with powerful arm, to fight against our enemies.[49]

A state commissioner wrote to Governor Sam Houston, "The Mexicans are arming everything that can carry a gun, and I anticipate much trouble here. I believe that a general war is inevitable.... New arms have been distributed to all the *rancheros*, so I apprehend trouble." Houston asked the federal government for assistance and wrote to the secretary of war for help. Meanwhile, state and national press sensationalized the myth of the Cortina menace.

In February 1860, President James Buchanan sent Robert E. Lee (1807–1870) to Texas to find the elusive Cortina. Mexican authorities cooperated with Lee. However, till the end of March, Lee could not catch Cortina and began referring to "that myth Cortina."

By May, Lee believed that Cortina had abandoned Texas. But Cortina merely shifted his base of operations. "Even after the outbreak of the Civil War, unrest and insecurity prevailed along the Rio Grande, and we can only speculate how long it would have been before another showdown would have come had it not been for the prosperity the war brought, even to the poorest."[50]

A reign of terror followed that is difficult to assess because of the press's sensationalism and outright lies. Merchants and business elites used Cortina as a pretext for violence against Mexicans and a reason to attract government contracts and troops. Governor Houston sent Commissioner Robert Taylor to investigate conditions on the border, who filed a confidential report: "I am sorry to say a good many ... who have been Burning and Hanging and shooting Mexicans without authority by law are more dreaded than Cortina."[51] Cortina went to Tamaulipas, where, from 1861 to 1867, he defended the state against the French intervention. Cortina became for a time its military governor as well as a general in the Mexican army. From his Mexican base, Cortina led raids against Americans who in many cases had stolen them from Mexican ranchers.[52]

The Civil War

The Mexican elite often mediated for the new American ruling elite and helped control the Mexican masses. They were vital in maintaining the illusion of democracy. In Brownsville, Francisco Ytúrria (1830–1912), Jeremiah Galván, and the Spaniard José San Román (1822–1895) amassed fortunes by allying with Charles Stillman. Texas historian David Montejano writes, "In the Lower Valley, the conservative upper class, fearful of outright confiscation of their property, was divided in the response to the Anglo presence."[53] In San Antonio, the Canary Islanders lived apart, harboring illusions of their racial purity. Like the Mexican elites they benefited from the new regime.

By 1860, a handful of white Americans dominated the Texas economy. A census taken that year showed that 263 Texans—presumably mostly male—owned more than $100,000 apiece in real property. Fifty-seven of them were wealthy individuals who lived in southeast Texas; only two were of Mexican, with their holdings in Cameron County. In Bexar County, out of seven wealthy Texans, not one was Mexican. The real property value and the personal worth of the 261 Texans were roughly in balance, while the two Mexicans' personal worth was far below their real wealth.[54] Despite the racism, a number of Mexicans continued to own large- and medium-size ranches and commercial houses.

Texas Ranger "Rip" Ford estimated that as much as $10 million to $14 million passed through the Rio Grande annually. ($100 in 1869 was equivalent to $1672.96 in 2015.) During the Civil War, merchants amassed fortunes running cotton through Mexico, making possible the expansion of the cotton industry as well as the commercial houses.[55] The population of Matamoros mushroomed to 50,000 by the end of 1862. The town conducted an estimated weekly trade of $2 million throughout the 1850s. Merchants on both sides of La Linea vied for the trade, and the Mexican government feared the dominance of U.S. merchants who by smuggling and underselling Mexican merchants avoided paying import taxes.

Not all of the elite Tejanos and whites favored the Confederacy, James Marten writes that "despite family and social pressures, hundreds of Texans, including a large number of Mexican Americans, signed on with the Union army. . . ."⁵⁶ Americans comprised 46.3 percent, Germans 13.1 percent, and Mexicans 40.6 percent of the Texas Union Regiment. Proportionately, the Mexican share was much higher than their part of the state's population.

Col. Santos Benavides fought for the Confederacy. Benavides, a wealthy Mexican-born rancher and merchant, was a power broker in the valley. Santos came to the Nueces Valley during the American invasion; when the Americans occupied the strip. Benavides became a U.S. citizen and in 1863 he led troops against the Union army and Juan Cortina.⁵⁷

The story of Adrián J. Vidal is interesting. Some say he was the son of a Mexican woman and a white merchant. In fact, Vidal was the stepson of Mifflin Kenedy. Born in Monterrey, Nuevo León, Mexico in 1840 to Col. Luis Vidal and Petra Vela, after the death of his father, the family moved to Mier, where Petra met Kenedy, and then moved to Brownsville, where Adrián Vidal learned about steamboats and the geographical region. Vidal enlisted as a private in the Confederate army and within a year, he was promoted to captain because of his knowledge of the border. In 1863 he killed two Confederate couriers. Speculation was it was because of a remark made about his race that implied that he was a half-breed. Vidal then deserted, taking 89 men with him. He went over to the Union side that then occupied the Valley, but he again deserted, crossing the border to fight against Emperor Maximilian and the French. The French Imperialists captured and executed him.⁵⁸

Throughout the war, the Union sought to shut down the Mexican corridor. However, with the support of Santos Benavides and Mexican merchant allies on both sides of the border, the Confederacy successfully kept it open. After the Civil War, Kenedy and King returned with full pardons, resuming trade with the Mexican merchants and seeking to gain special privileges. Other changes took place as Americans, Germans, and French outnumbered the Tejano in San Antonio. The Mexican elite's power fell with the decline in the Mexican population, and the newcomers monopolized the banks and commercial houses. Racial and social segregation also increased. After this three factors contributed to the dramatic worsening of Texas and white Mexican relations: barbed wire, irrigation and the railroad. Simultaneously by 1877, the railroad linked San Antonio and the rest of Texas to the U.S. markets.⁵⁹

The Transformation

4.3 Describe how Caste system affected life in Texas after the U.S. Civil War.

The Reconstruction Era pitted the different races against each other. Texas escaped the economic ravages of the war, but that did not prevent the white Americans there from acting more Confederate than those in the Deep South. Losing the war increased the bravado and racism of many white Texans. The loss made them more chauvinistic and insecure. The large presence of Mexicans posed a threat to Southern institutions and their whiteness.

In every sense Mexicans were a minority and although the Lone Star's Mexican population grew to 20,000 in 1860, it remained small relative to 600,000 Americans and 182,000 Blacks. Before the Civil War, slave labor lessened the need for Mexican workers, and Americans were able to limit them largely in South Texas. Emancipation changed this dynamic and heating up of the Texas economy created a demand for Mexicans who were imported in large numbers to create a larger surplus labor pool. By the 1870s, Mexicans worked alongside Blacks in the Brazos area. More efficient transportation also increased the availability of beef and increased demand in domestic and world markets. As a consequence, western stock-raising expanded, increasing the demand for Mexican labor. By the 1880s, cotton production also reached an all-time high. The emancipation of the slaves led to a shortage of captive workers and the reduction of the African American labor force dramatically increased the pull of Mexican laborers to the Lone Star State.⁶⁰

As mentioned the loss of slave labor forced Texas agriculture to restructure. By 1870, sharecropping was common. In this arrangement, an owner lends land to tenants, who usually give the landlord one-half to two-thirds of the crop. Railroad expansion also quickened land speculation and a flood of whites into Texas, with the number of white people in some border counties equaling the number of Mexicans.⁶¹ By 1890, the open range gave way to mechanization and irrigation, again changing methods of production and further increasing the demand for Mexican labor.

Competition between Mexicans and African Americans also increased tensions. Growers inflamed antagonism between the races. In August 1894, African Americans attacked Mexicans at Beeville, Texas. The growers had brought Mexicans into Beeville to beat down wages of Blacks. African Americans blamed Mexicans rather than the growers for their low standard of living and raided the Mexican quarter. Meanwhile, the federal government stationed Black soldiers in Mexican areas to control the Mexicans. At Fort McIntosh in Laredo, the Tenth Cavalry, an all-Black unit, policed the Mexican population.⁶²

Hang 'em High!

U.S. merchants accumulated fortunes supplying military installations on the frontier. Meanwhile, they and the townspeople lived in fear of the removal of the forts often exaggerating the threat of Mexican bandits and/or the "savages" in order to justify a large number of troops stationed on the border. Forts meant soldiers, horses, and government contracts. The soldiers' spending was a bonanza for the merchants and cattle dealers. Fewer troops would mean economic hardships for merchants and ranchers so they ensured their presence at all cost.[63]

King and Kenedy alleged they lost 200,000 heads of cattle and 5,300 horses from 1869 to 1872. They blamed Cortina. According to Texas Ranger John Salmon "Rip" Ford, "Cortina hates Americans, particularly Texans. . . . He has an old and deep-seated grudge against Brownsville."[64] While using Cortina as a pretext whites attacked and killed innocent Mexicans, while merchants called for more federal troops and demanded that the United States invade northern Mexico. This began the second Cortina War, known as the "Skinning Wars" that was brought on by the fall of beef prices to 62.5 cents a cow, and hides sold for $4.50—increasing competition and disputes over ownership of cattle. Naturally Mexicans were blamed and white Americans formed minute companies and vigilance committees. Corpus Christi cowboys raided Mexicans, driving small Mexican operators out of business. This greed touched off increased fencing of ranches.[65]

Meanwhile, it became a war zone as both sides raided the other. An estimated three million cattle in the open range of the "Nueces Strip." The Cortina hysteria led to the passage of the Frontier Protection Act of 1874 that reestablished the Rangers, funding 6 mounted battalions of 75 men each.[66] By the spring and summer of 1874, a full-scale race war raged.[67] The following year, due to pressure from American authorities, Mexican officials exiled Cortina to Mexico City and jailed him on charges of cattle rustling. Cortina did not return to the border until the spring of 1890; when he visited the area for a brief time, received a hero's welcome. Cortina's career had transformed him from a social bandit to a revolutionary hero.

Meanwhile, in 1874 in Goliad County a mob lynched Juan Moya and his two sons for allegedly killing a white family. Authorities later apprehended the real killers, whom they did not prosecute. In April 1877 Andrés Martínez and José María Cordena were arrested in Collins County, Texas, and charged with horse stealing. Instead of receiving a trial, 10 masked men seized and hanged them. In July of that same year, whites in Nueces County, Texas, slaughtered as many as 40 Mexicans, allegedly to avenge the death of one of their white friends.

In the 1870s, a Mexican Boundary Commission claimed that Mexicans raided the Nueces area to retrieve their stolen cattle. Richard King had branded calves "that belonged to his neighbors' cows."[68] The Commission's report charged that King employed known cattle rustlers, such as Tomás Vásquez and Fernando López, to steal cattle and horses from Mexican ranchers. Other prominent Texans, such as Thaddeus Rhodes, a justice of the peace in Hidalgo County and a former Ranger, were also implicated in cattle rustling making huge profits from this illicit trade.[69] They based the report on extensive interviews and public records.

The Boundary Commission accused King's cabal of funding separatists such as José María Cabajal in 1851, in his war to form the Republic of the Sierra Madre.[70]

King became president of the Stock Raisers Association of Western Texas that ranchers formed to protect the "interests" of the big ranchers. The Association organized a private militia, called "minute companies," to wage war on the so-called Mexican bandits. When the minute companies disbanded, Ranger Captain Leander McNeely continued the war on Mexicans and ignored a federal order prohibiting him from entering Mexican territory. He led a troop of Rangers across the border and tortured and murdered four innocent Mexicans. King rewarded McNeely's men with a $500 bonus.[71]

In March 1881, Rangers arrested Onofrio Baca in Mexico and charged him with murder. He was illegally returned to Texas where a mob lynched him on the crossbeams of the gate of the courthouse. In August 1883, Captain Juan Cárdenas led a protest march in San Antonio to San Pedro Park. They protested the actions of Fred Kerble, the lessee, who on the orders of the town council, prohibited Mexicans from using the dance floor. The following year Mexicans were run out of the Fort Davis area.[72]

The Historian as an Agent of Social Control

In researching the history of the Texas Rangers, it always puzzles me why Mexican Americans do not react more vigorously to the naming of a major league team after the Texas Rangers (Arlington, Texas). One wonders, what would the reaction of the Jewish community be if a team were called the Hitler All Stars? Part of the explanation is that the historian's job is often to socialize with the public and distort the truth. The other is that state violence is a form of social control.

Historians have played a major role in masking this violence, calling men "founders of American industry" in order to clean up their image as robber barons. Critics, on the other hand, saw them as unscrupulous highwaymen and blamed them for the misery and poverty of the masses. In the early twentieth century, concerned with this image, industrialists funded philanthropic ventures. They funded revisionist historians who wrote books arguing that the robber barons were essential to building a world power. Yet at the same time, the illusion of the American Dream was wiping out memories and converting the colonized into colonizers. In rooting for the Rangers, even for a moment, their fans become part of this illusion.

Racism, racial stereotypes, and fear are important in social control. The Spaniards disciplined the disparate populations through racial categorization (see Chapter 2 in this text). In the United States, race limits access to political and economic power and justifies inequality. National and state laws are designed to institutionalize racism and perpetuate white rule.[73] At each stage of the country's development, whiteness was the standard of goodness and was rewarded by privileges. In the United States, there are stricter categorizations applying a Black–white standard; in Mexico and the rest of Latin America, racial categories form a continuum.

Controlling Mexicans

From multiple accounts and documents, the Texas Rangers were paid assassins. So how did they become the nice guys? Walter Prescott Webb, a professor of the history faculty at the University of Texas at Austin and past president of the American Historical Association, memorialized the Rangers in his books such as *The Texas Rangers*, *The Great Plains*, and *Divided We Stand*, portraying them as bringing civilization to the frontier.[74] The irony is that Webb admitted that the Rangers' actions were often excessive and brutal. After he published an article, "The Bandits of Las Cuevas," in *True West* in October 1962, he received a letter from Enrique Mendiola of Alice, Texas, whose grandfather owned the ranch that the Rangers, under McNeely, mistakenly attacked. Mendiola stated,

> Most historians have classified these men as cattle thieves, bandits, etc. This might be true of some of the crowd, but most of them, including General Juan Flores, were trying to recover their own cattle that had been taken away from them when they were driven out of their little ranches in South Texas. They were driven out by such men as Mifflin Kenedy, Richard King and [the] Armstrongs.[75]

Webb's reply to Mendiola was revealing:

> To get a balanced account, one would need the records from the south side of the river, and these are simply not available. . . . The unfortunate fact is that the Mexicans were not as good at keeping records as were the people on this side. . . . I have often wished that the Mexicans, or someone who had their confidence, would have gone among them and got their stories of the raids and counter raids. I am sure that these stories would take on a different color and tone.[76]

Mexicans recorded their story in *corridos* (ballads) that celebrated the deeds of men who stood up to the oppressors. These corridos are still sung in the Rio Grande Valley and elsewhere in the Southwest. Many corridos were dedicated to Juan Cortina because Cortina resisted the gringos from the 1850s through mid-1870s. The corridos document the Mexicans' struggle against racism and injustice.[77] They portray the Rangers as assassins; they view the Rangers in much the same way as Jews see the Gestapo.

Like all history, there are two sides. Rip Ford, a Ranger himself, expressed the American view, writing, "A Texas Ranger can ride like a Mexican, trail like an Indian, shoot like a Tennessean, and fight like the very devil!"[78] Not surprisingly, most contemporary studies of the Rangers mimic Webb, who wrote,

> When we see him at his daily task of maintaining law, restoring order, and promoting peace—even though his methods be vigorous—we see him in the proper setting, a man standing alone between a society and its enemies.[79]

Webb continued:,

> Without disparagement it may be said that there is a cruel streak in the Mexican nature, or so the history of Texas would lead one to believe. This cruelty may be a heritage from the Spanish of the Inquisition; it may, and doubtless should, be attributed partly to the Indian blood.[80]

Webb's influence on historians and the public cannot be overstated—even today hundreds of thousands cheer for the Texas Rangers baseball team without knowing or caring about the atrocities of their team's namesake.

Américo Paredes calls the Rangers puppets of white ranchers and merchants who controlled the Rio Grande Valley. They kept order for a white oligarchy. Violence was sanctioned by Texas capitalists. The members of the oligarchy were mostly white and who purposely kept Mexicans out of power. It was a closed social structure that excluded Mexicans and other racial minorities. They recruited gunslingers who hated Mexicans, shooting first and asking questions afterward. Paredes writes, "That the Rangers stirred up more trouble than they put down is an opinion that has been expressed by less partisan sources."[81]

Paredes's research was based on oral traditions and documents, and his findings refute Webb's version of reality. For example, concerning the murder of the Cerdas, a prominent family near Brownsville in 1902, Paredes wrote,

> The Cerdas were prosperous ranchers near Brownsville, but it was their misfortune to live next to one of the "cattle barons" who was not through expanding yet. One day three Texas Rangers came down from Austin and "executed" the elder Cerda and one of his sons as cattle rustlers. The youngest son fled across the river, and thus the Cerda ranch was vacated. Five months later the remaining son, Alfredo Cerda, crossed over to Brownsville. He died the same day, shot down by a Ranger's gun.[82]

Paredes uses official documents and eyewitness accounts. Marcelo Garza, Sr. of Brownsville, a respected businessman, told Paredes that a Ranger shot the unarmed Alfredo, "stalking him like a wild animal."

In contrast, Webb's version was based exclusively on Ranger sources. According to Webb, Baker, a Ranger, surprised Ramón De La Cerda branding a calf that belonged to the King Ranch. De La Cerda shot at Baker, and the Ranger shot back, killing Ramón in self-defense. The Ranger was cleared at an inquest. Nevertheless, Mexicans, not accepting this verdict, disinterred De La Cerda's body and conducted their own inquest. They found "evidence" [quotes are Webb's] . . . to the effect that De La Cerda had been dragged and otherwise maltreated. Public sentiment was sharply divided. . . . The findings of the secret inquest, together with wild rumors growing out of it, only served to inflame the minds of De La Cerda's supporters.

Webb ignored the fact that the Cerdas were a respected family whose land the Kings coveted. "Captain Brooks reported that Baker made bail in the sum of ten thousand dollars, and that he was supported by such people as the Kings, Major John Armstrong—McNeely's lieutenant— and the Lyman Brothers."[83] Further, Webb did not question the financial support of the Kings for the Rangers and especially for Baker. The Cerda affair exposed both the use of violence taking over land and legalizing murder through the court system. It was not an isolated incident; it represented the activities of Rangers throughout the century.

Politics of Race and Gender

When the Spaniards conquered Mexico, Cortés commanded his officers to marry the daughters of the Azteca nobles, thus consolidating his control of the conquered people. Americans followed the same pattern in Texas and intermarriage between the native aristocracy and the white ruling elite was common. The process was helped because of a lack of white women. Intermarriage also gave the colonizers access to old money and family networks that helped control the native population. Captain Mifflin Kenedy's marriage to the wealthy widow Petra Vela de Vidal has already been discussed.[84]

When convenient, the whites identified designated Mexican women as white. During the nineteenth century, it was popular to speak about the "dark-eyed *señoritas*." Occasionally, they compared Mexican women with the ideal southern belle, and they especially praised *Las Güeras* (the blondes). American males described these light-skinned Mexicans as being of pure northern Spanish descent with "faultlessly white" flesh and blue eyes. It must be remembered that, in general, intermarriage among different ranks suggested a weakening of ethnic identities and allegiances. As more white women moved into the area, Americans' infatuation with the whitest of Mexican women cooled, intermarriage dropped, and racially mixed couples became subject to social disapproval and, eventually, persecution.[85]

> 906 Mexican women wed Mexican men, while only 88 chose to marry Anglo-Americans. But of those Anglo-Mexican unions almost half, or 42, involved women from high status families. The significance of those interracial marriages goes far beyond their numbers, since at least one daughter from every rico family in San Antonio married an Anglo.[86]

Scholars documented only five unions between Mexican males and American females.

As in the case of Spanish colonialism, skin color determined social, political, and economic status. In a letter to his cousin John Donelson Coffee, Jr., dated January 20, 1855, R. W. Brahan, Jr., referred to contacts with women of Castilian blood whose "parents avowed their determination to have them wed to genuine Americans."[87] Brahan dwelt on Mexican women's color and said, "Their complexion is very fair," but distinguished poorer Mexican women as "styled greasers." Brahan concluded, "many of these 'greasers,' of fine figures & good features, the color of a mulatto, are kept by votaries of sensuality." As with the Blacks in the South, the dominant society fabricated sexual myths about Mexicans such as those "suggesting that, if Mexican women easily lapsed from propriety, they especially coveted the company (and intimacy) of white men."[88]

In turn, intermarriage enhanced the racial and class pretensions of elite Mexican families. Through intermarriage, Mexican elites got a son-in-law whose skin looked white. The Mexican family also received a measure of legal protection and freedom from the stigma of disloyalty, while the American got a wife and her property. Under the law, daughters inherited property on an equal share with their brothers. Intermarriage accelerated "civilization," and although youngsters maintained strong Mexican influences "during their early childhood," they strongly identified with the father's ethnic group. For instance, the daughters of Antonio Navarro became Methodists, which is itself an indication of assimilation, and affiliation of mixed couples with English-speaking Roman Catholic parishes was common.

This is not to say that the ricos escaped discrimination; even rich Tejanos were victims of racism. Most of San Antonio's Mexicans during the nineteenth century, even if Americanized, were not treated as equals. "Only the women and children with Anglo surnames, light skins, and wealth had a reasonable chance to escape the stigma attached to their Mexican ancestry."[89] Even in the choice of intermarriage, the male head of the family made the decision based on class interests.

Resistance

4.4 Describe post–Civil War resistance movements in Texas.

Rebellions were frequent and often took the form of so-called bandit activity. However, when divisions exist between people due to unequal power relations, bandit activity can assume the form of primitive rebellion. The British historian E. J. Hobsbawm, in *Primitive Rebels*, makes the point that in colonial situations dissidents are commonly labeled bandits; the British called George Washington a bandit. Hobsbawm wrote, "in one sense [banditry was] . . . a primitive form of organized social protest, perhaps the most primitive we know."[90] Social bandits rebel against an injustice, and the people of their race or class often support them even if covertly. These primitive rebels did not intend to transform or level society; they simply had enough. Social bandits differ from revolutionaries, who have the trajectory to change power relationships.

The People's Revolt

Salt, like water, is essential for life in arid environments. But while the Southwest is replete with stories of range wars over water, there are few recorded stories of the usurpation of the Mexican settlers' access to necessary minerals, rangeland, or the forests. Salt protects one's health by helping the body to retain fluids; in the nineteenth century, it was used as a preservative in the absence of refrigeration.

In the late 1860s, a power struggle erupted over control of the salt deposits in the Guadalupe Mountains 110 miles east of El Paso. Mexicans visited the area in search of free salt that they either used or sold. The salt beds supplied all of western Texas, southern New Mexico, and Mexico. The competition between W. W. Mills, Albert J. Fountain, and Louis Cardis to acquire title to the salt beds grew into bitter struggle and led to bloody battles in the 1870s. The Salt Ring was comprised of influential American politicos. There were two factions that vied for control of the salt beds. The competition deteriorated into a race war.

Hostilities centered in the small town of San Elizario, near present-day El Paso, Texas, in 1877. One faction was led by the Salt Ring, and the other by Father Antonio Borrajo and Cardis, a local politico. Charles Howard, a Missouri lawyer and former Confederate officer, at first supported the Borrajo–Cardis faction. In 1872, the fighting broke out as Cardis and Howard tried to break the Republican machine's control of the Salt Ring. This alliance fell apart when Howard betrayed Cardis and took control of the salt flats in 1877. The sides further polarized when Howard shot and killed Cardis. This enraged Borrajo, who agitated Mexican parishioners. Howard, a former Texas Ranger, enlisted the support of the Rangers, and a troop of 20 Texas Rangers rode into San Elizario. Governor Richard B. Hubbard ordered Major John B. Jones of the Texas Rangers to El Paso to put down the rebellion. When the Rangers sided with Howard, Borrajo told the Mexican people, "Shoot the *gringo* [Howard] and I will absolve you."[91]

Ysleta farmer Francisco "Chico" Barela organized a group of 18 Mexicans and shot Howard. Several days of fighting ensued and the Rangers and vigilantes indiscriminately attacked Mexican townspeople. Governor Hubbard sent to Silver City for 30 hired gunmen, who, under Sheriff Charles Kerner, committed "rapes, homicides, and other crimes." Mexican families fled to Mexico where many did not.[92]

A Report by W. M. Dunn found that:

> The outbreak [of the Salt War] was, it is believed, the result of a desire for revenge for the murder of [Louis] Cardis, a crime which had no justification, which was deliberate and brutal, and which exasperated the people beyond control. [Charles] Howard was brought before a justice of the peace for the murder, but was released at once on bail, in violation of law, and as not long before he had caused the arrest and imprisonment of two men for the mere offense of saying that they meant to get salt from the ponds, law or no law, the Spanish–American populace naturally thought they saw that there was no equality of justice, and felt compelled to take the law into their own hands.[93]

A letter from Colonel John H. King to the Bureau of Military Justice found that "No evidence taken substantiates the report heretofore prevalent, that the people coming from Mexico and taking part in these criminal proceedings were an organized body previously drilled and disciplined by officers of the Mexican Army."[94]

The Ballad of Gregorio Cortez

Social banditry is a natural phenomenon. People rebel when unpopular governments impose unfair laws on them. Many common folks vicariously cope with their grievances through the rebellion of the bandit who functions outside the law. Support of the social bandit becomes a form of social protest. In the case of the Mexicans in Texas and elsewhere, the deeds of the social bandit are memorialized by corridos.

Racism and brutality was statewide. Texas banditry was an excuse to demonize a population and use state violence against them. In 1897, a group called the "white caps," believing Mexicans were depressing wages, sent warnings to farmers not to employ Mexicans or Blacks. A vigilante group in Gonzalez sent out a flyer in 1898 warning: "Hell, Texas, Feb. 16. Notice to the Mexicans: You all have got ten days to leave in. Mr. May Renfro and brother get your Mexicans all off your place. If not, you will get the same that they do. Signed: Whitecaps."[95] In central and northern Texas, vigilantism revolved around labor competition whereas in South Texas it was more about property and jealousy that Mexicans owned land; lynching was used to take property away from Mexicans. An example was the hanging of seven of Toribio Lozano's sheepherders in 1873. Lozano owned a large ranch in the Mexican state of Nuevo León and regularly grazed sheep on the U.S. side of the border. In Texas, Lozano led a torturous fight for compensation for the sheepherders' dependents, enlisting the support of Mexican diplomats.[96]

Because of injustices like these, dozens of Mexican bandits operated in Texas. As in other places, the bandit was often idolized. The fact that the Texas Rangers and local enforcement authorities refused to help prosecute perpetrators heightened a sense of injustice. As discussed, Juan Cortina was not in strict sense a social bandit; he had a political plan. A better example of a social bandit is Gregorio Cortez, who Mexicans considered a hero; whites called him a "sheriff killer." Cortez was a border Mexican who worked on ranches in Gonzales and Karnes Counties, and on the surrounding areas.

On June 12, 1901, Karnes County Sheriff, W. T. "Brack" Morris went to the Cortez farm to investigate a horse theft. Deputy Boone Choate, acting as interpreter, misunderstood Cortez's answers to Sheriff Morris' questions as to whether he recently acquired a *caballo*, which means stallion in Spanish. Cortez answered that he had bought a *yegua*, a mare.[97] Believing that Cortez was lying, Morris drew his gun and shot Cortez's brother, provoking Cortez to shoot the sheriff. The incident made Cortez an outlaw, and he was hunted by several possess comprised of hundreds of men. The Mexican population in Karnes County and throughout Texas supported Cortez, who became a border hero. For 10 days, this army chased Cortez over 500 miles; during this pursuit, the dreaded cowboys hounded his supporters and his family members.

A posse surrounded the home of Refugia Robledo, where Cortez was hiding, driving her husband, sons, and Cortez out of the house, while Refugia were trapped inside with three children. A deputy entered the house, shooting down young Ramón Rodríguez, as Refugia shielded the other two children with her body. The posse arrested Refugia, her two sons, and the wounded Ramón, charging her with the murder of the sheriff, who had been killed in the shootout. She was released only after she said that Cortez killed the sheriff.[98]

Betrayed by a friend, Cortez was captured on June 22, 1901, after which he faced numerous trials. Cortez was finally convicted and sentenced to 50 years' imprisonment for second-degree murder. While on appeal, a mob of 300 white men threatened to lynch him. A Texas Court of Criminal Appeals reversed the verdict, and Cortez was retried; he was again convicted. In 1913, Cortez was pardoned. Meanwhile, countless corridos memorialized Cortez and his war with the gringos.

Boss Rule

4.5 Characterize boss rule in Texas.

The post–Civil War period saw the rise of boss rule in Texas that involved a cabal of powerful white leaders in collusion with local Mexican elites who manipulated the votes of Mexican majorities. They resembled Eastern machines like Tammany Hall of New York City. Often the machines shielded Mexican immigrants with unofficial welfare services and gave them the illusion that they had palanca[99] or influence with those in power. These machines controlled the patronage system and secured jobs and favors from local and state governments thus centralizing their power.

In South Texas the machines engaged in graft, and played all sides—often selling out the welfare of their constituents. As in other places in the Southwest, the leadership was composed of attorneys who represented the interests of the landed elites. The bosses lobbied on behalf of the Texas Rangers, which they used to control or subjugate Mexicans. On the other hand, although the bosses found the Rangers useful, they also restrained them when they went too far. The bosses catered to land speculators, developers, bankers, and merchants and promoted development. There was often a paternalistic arrangement, and many bosses acted like modern-day hacendados and would go to baptisms, marriages, and funerals.

By the mid-1880s, Bryan V. Callaghan, Jr., political boss, county judge, and mayor of San Antonio, whose mother was from an elite Mexican family and spoke fluent Spanish, organized a political machine in San Antonio. Callaghan's power was based on his control of the Mexican wards that supported the machine because it gave the residents a measure of protection, patronage, and the illusion of political participation. The machine handed out patronage—city jobs, contracts, franchises, and public utilities. The bosses won elections by turning out the Mexican vote. In the border towns, the machines also controlled the customhouses.

Characteristically, the poor were left with few options, and the *ricos* (the rich Mexicans) rarely sided with the Mexican masses. They often displayed attitudes and interests that favored their class and racial category. Many members of old Mexican families openly sympathized with the Ku Klux Klan; in San Antonio Alejo Ruiz, Vicente Martínez, John Barrera, Rafael Ytúrris, and José Antonio Navarro allied themselves with ultraconservative factions. After the Civil War, they even campaigned for white supremacist southern Democrats. Through all this, Mexican elites seemed oblivious to the persecution of their fellow Mexicans. By avoiding an advocacy role, Mexican merchants profited and they maintained valuable business contacts.

Attorneys made fortunes representing Mexicans. Stephen Powers of Brownsville, an expert on Spanish and Mexican land grant law, defended some Mexican elites, giving him entrance to that community. Powers accumulated 44,000 acres and built vast political power. When Powers died, his junior associate James B. Wells inherited his law practice and his connections, and "a substantial number of Tejano land holdings in much of the Lower Valley. . . . "[100]

From 1882 to 1920, the machine controlled several counties; they transported Mexican voters to the polls and marked their ballots for them. Arnold De León states that in the border areas whites employed Mexicans to cross into Mexico to recruit people whom the bosses paid to vote for selected candidates. Hundreds of Mexicans were marched to the county clerk's office and naturalized for the modest sum of 25 cents.[101]

Wells's political power rested on delivering the Mexican vote. He was a godfather to the Mexican people. Wells shared power with the Klebergs, who owned the King Ranch, and had satellite rings headed by Ed Vela from Hidalgo and the Guerra family of Starr County. The Guerras, along with the Yzaguirre and Ramírez families, owned most of Starr County. Manuel Guerra, a banker and rancher, became Jim Wells's right arm and was the political boss of the Democratic Party in Starr County.[102]

The Guerras' control of Starr County reached into the 1940s, an arrangement that remained undisturbed by state authorities. Even Judge J. T. Canales of Brownsville, a maverick, often cooperated with the machine, serving in the state legislature from 1909 to 1911, in 1917, and in 1919. He was a county judge in 1914. (In Texas, the county judge was, and still is, the most powerful local official.) Along with Alonso Perales, Manuel González, Ben Garza, and Andrés de Luna.[103]

In *Boss Rule in South Texas* Evan Anders attributes machine politics, in part, to the history of the Spanish patron–peon relationship. However, Anders oversimplifies the phenomenon, since "boss rule" in South Texas resembled political machines in eastern U.S. cities. An important difference between bossism in South Texas and the East was that the Texas machine had fewer constitutional restraints. Moreover, Tejanos had limited access to organizational alternatives such as trade unions.

In 1890, North American reformers blamed Mexicans for corrupt political machines and attempted to end bossism by disenfranchising Mexicans. They passed a constitutional amendment requiring foreigners "to file for citizenship six months before the election." Then, in 1902, the reformers passed a poll tax to further discourage the Mexican vote. Both these measures failed to limit the power of the bosses. The Jim Wells machine remained intact until the 1920s, and its end in part can be attributed to Wells's failure to check the extreme violence of the Texas Rangers in South Texas in 1915 and 1917.[104]

By 1900, Tejanos had settled in all three sections. They formed a minority in Central Texas and a majority in South Texas; they held a demographic advantage along the border counties of West Texas, but whites outnumbered them in the interior.[105]

The Railroad and the Advent of Industrial Capitalism

The most important railroad built during these early years was the Mexican Central Railway (Ferrocarril Central Mexicano). From 1880 to 1884, an aggressive railroad-building program brought this railroad up the Central Valley of Mexico, providing a direct link between Mexico City and the northern border. By April 1884, this route consisted of 1,969 kilometers (1,224 miles) of rails that ran from Mexico City through Aguascalientes, Zacatecas, and Chihuahua to the border towns of Paso del Norte, Chihuahua and El Paso, Texas.[106]

Similarly, by the 1880s, railroads crisscrossed Texas, making possible the commercialization of agriculture and further incorporating the state into world markets. Mexicans constituted most of the workers on the Texas and Mexican Railroad as well as on other lines. In addition to the arrival of the railroad, the expansion of the agriculture industry was made possible by the expansion of banking and speculation in the area. Credit became increasingly necessary as producers had to purchase land, sink wells, build miles of fences of plank and wire, and finance stock improvement programs to compete. The 1890s saw the arrival of eastern, British, and Scottish syndicates in much the same way in Arizona and other western states, to exploit mining and agriculture. Meanwhile, Kenedy sold his 242,000-acre plantation for $1.1 million.

Between 1865 and 1885, San Antonio's population increased by 208 percent to 37,000. The railroad played an essential role in the rapid development of San Antonio and South Texas after the Civil War. In the 1870s, San Antonio merchants and business leaders financed a line between their city and Galveston. By 1885, two additional lines passed through the city connecting it with north Texas and Mexico. Along with the development of the railroads was the growth of the cattle trade in South Texas and the tourist trade in San Antonio.

Four million head of cattle were driven north to market between 1866 and 1880. Land companies planted barbed wire fences, ending the open range, displacing small cattlemen and cowboys. Racism increased as ranchers segregated Mexican and white cowhands in Central and South Texas. Most small Mexican operators went out of business because these new operations required large amounts of capital. Adding to the problems of small cattlemen during the 1880s were overproduction in the cattle industry, overgrazing, droughts, quarantine laws, and closing of the cattle trails.[107]

The Chickens Come Home to Roost

4.6 Explain how commercial agriculture changed Texas in the 1880s.

The development of commercial agriculture broke up the provincial cattle-based economy, favoring the expansion of cotton and vegetable production. The new labor market demanded armies of migrant workers. In the 1880s, the

United States controlled some 40 percent of Mexico's export trade; by the turn of the century it controlled over 70 percent of this trade, eclipsing British interests. The railroad also made it easier for Mexicans in the Border States to reach U.S. markets than the interior of Mexico. The growth of the Mexican population and the inability of the Mexican economic infrastructure to absorb this growth heightened tensions, and Mexican migration to the United States increased.

During the 1880s, the commercialization of Mexican cotton production in places like Coahuila and eastern Durango also contributed to this population shift. The Laguna district of western Coahuila attracted an industrial labor force of an estimated 30,000 workers from the interior of Mexico. After the harvest season, they would migrate to Texas to pick cotton. The exchange contributed to a transfers of ideas and labor strategies.

Commercial agriculture brought the deterioration of the old way of life and changed the mode of production. While farmers were relatively prosperous during 1860–1890, the mechanization of agriculture needed heavy outlays of capital. The changes created factory farms that drove small producers out of business. The Mexicans' cotton industry and migrant workers were a symptom of this change, not the cause. However, small farmers and workers scapegoated Mexicans for the decline or in some cases the end of small farms, the loss of year-round jobs, and the lowering of wages.[108] In this new world order, labor organizations ignored or excluded Mexicans.

The abandoned Mexican laborers turned to their own devices. The proliferation of *mutualistas*, or mutual aid societies, began in the 1870s. These societies, popular in Mexico since the 1860s, promoted identity and provided death benefits, loans, and financial assistance.[109] They were organized to soften the shock of urbanization and industrialization on artisans and other workers, and were important in uniting Mexican people and maintaining Mexican culture. The middle class furnished the leadership of many of these groups, and thus the political orientation of these groups greatly depended on the ideology of their leaders, which was sometimes radical and sometimes quite conservative. At first the Mexican government sponsored the mutualistas since their self-help philosophy released the emerging capitalist class from furnishing social benefits. However, this changed as radicals used the societies to criticize and organize against the state. South Texas became a center of radical opposition to the Díaz Regime.

Reform Politics and Mexicans

By the late 1880s, both Populists and Republicans pushed for the disenfranchisement of all Mexicans. The Populist, or People's Party, while fighting the spread of agribusiness and demanding reforms in government, scapegoated Mexicans, blaming them for the decline of small farms and the demise of rural America. Mexicans fought back. In San Antonio, A. L. Montalvo vowed to fight for civil rights and condemned the Populists for attempting to reduce the Texas Mexicans "to the category of pack animals, who may be good enough to work, but not good enough to exercise their civil rights."[110]

Although many of the People's Party's interests were compatible with those of the Mexican workers, the party regarded them as its enemy. The Texas Populists forged alliances with Black workers, while attacking Mexicans and threatening to deport them. The Populists used the pretext that the Democratic Party manipulated their vote. Instead of organizing progressive elements within the Mexican community and attempting to check the machines, the Populists made Mexicans their scapegoats, popularizing crass racist arguments.[111]

The Growth of the Mexican Population

4.7 Explain the role of Mexican Labor in the growth of Texas.

The 1880 Census counted about 43,000 Mexicans in Texas. Most lived in the southern part of the state, where they remained the overwhelming majority until the arrival of large numbers of white Americans in the 1890s. The white newcomers formed their own neighborhoods, strictly segregating Mexicans to the older parts of town. Increased numbers of white Americans strengthened their control of the political, social, and economic institutions. Mexicans as a community were often too poor to support independent political movements and depended on their Mexican bosses for whatever influence they had.

By 1900, the total population of Texas reached 3,048,710; there were 620,722 African Americans. The Mexican population was not officially counted in the census. Texas Mexicans lived largely in rural areas and numbered an estimated 70,000 statewide; unofficially there were closer to 165,000. Mexicans, however, were less than 5 percent of the population in Texas—Blacks were the state's largest minority.[112] Demographic changes in the last two decades of the nineteenth century, along with the spread of cotton and commercial agriculture, led to the modernization of the Texas economy in the next century. Land companies and irrigation projects put enormous tracts of land into production, increasing the demand for Mexican labor. The majority of Mexicans continued to live in *jacales* (shacks).

The Growth of Racist Nativism

American nativists saw Mexicans, whether born in the United States or Mexico, as aliens. Through the courts, nativists attempted to exclude them from citizenship. By inference, the Treaty of Guadalupe Hidalgo (1848) made

Mexicans white, without being white they could not exercise or immigrate to the United States. In 1897, Richard Rodríguez, who was born in Mexico, applied for citizenship but it was denied because immigration authorities said he was Native American. Rodríguez had lived in Texas for 10 years. Federal attorneys argued against his eligibility on the grounds that Rodríguez was "not a white person, not an African, nor of African descent." U.S. District Judge Thomas Maxey held that because Rodríguez knew "nothing of the Aztecs or Toltecs," he was not an Indian and thus had the right to become a naturalized citizen. This issue would continue to plague Mexican Americans throughout the twentieth century.

Racism's uglier side went beyond denial of citizenship, however. In 1895, a mob lynched Cotula jailer Florentino Suaste.[113] In January 1896, authorities found the mutilated body of Aureliano Castellón in San Antonio. He had made the mistake of courting Emma Stanfield, a white girl, over the objections of her brothers. He was shot eight times and his body was burned. On June 30, 1896, the *San Antonio Express* published a note entitled "Slaughter the Gringo," signed by 25 Mexicans. The signers allegedly threatened to kill only gringos and Germans, exempting Blacks, Italians, and Cubans.[114]

Two years later, the Spanish–American War spread fear among Americans, who believed that Mexicans would ally with Spain and begin border raids. In places such as San Diego, Texas, Americans formed Minuteman companies to "protect" themselves. Although they soon learned that Mexicans had little empathy with Spain and the uprisings never took place, the situation gave racists an excuse to persecute all Mexicans.

The White Cap movement of South Texas in the late 1890s aggravated conditions. (Texas White Caps should not be confused with the Mexican *Gorras Blancas*, White Caps of New Mexico; see Chapter 5.) Texas White Caps were a vigilante group that demanded that white planters refuse to rent to Blacks and Mexicans and that they fire Mexican field hands. White Cap activity centered in Wilson, Gonzales, and DeWitt Counties, where its members terrorized Mexicans. "Astonishing numbers of Mexicans in the nineteenth century fell victim to lynch law and cold-blooded deaths at the hands of whites who thought nothing of killing Mexicans."[115] Social attitudes reinforced by violence froze Mexicans into a caste system that facilitated exploitation of their labor in the twentieth century.

Mexican Resistance

Despite discrimination, Mexicans were active in politics. By 1900, Mexicans numbered 24,033, or 55.5 percent of the population of El Paso County.[116] Victor L. Ochoa in April 1891 gave a speech calling on Mexicans to organize and promote self-help. He wanted them to pressure government not to award public works contracts to firms that hired workers directly from Mexico and lobbied to create an office of a superintendent of public works who would hire Mexicans from El Paso. Ochoa advocated equal pay for Mexican American police and other Mexican American public employees, who were then paid less than whites.[117]

Ochoa, along with revolutionary and spiritualist Lauro Aguirre, was among those participating in the plots against Mexican dictator Porfirio Díaz. They had contact with Mexican revolutionaries in the Guerrero, Chihuahua. Guerrero was a transition zone between ranching country and Sierra, the location of native villages, mine settlements, and logging camps. The arrival of the Mexican Central Railroad in 1884, the telegraph, and the elimination of the Apache had fanned tensions in Chihuahua and the situation was ripe for a revolution. El Paso Mexican leaders formed ties with the Mexican dissidents. In 1892 Ochoa and his circle condemned federal troops for the slaughter of innocent people at Tomochic and Santo Tomás in 1892.

In November 1893, the *revoltosos* (revolutionaries) attacked the border town of Palomas. The *El Paso Evening Tribune* reported that 3,000 rebels were marching on Guerrero, which was defended by 800 Mexican soldiers. At Palomas, the rebels under the command of Valente García and Ochoa, then only 23 and editor of *The Hispano Americano*, occupied the customhouse. Only three rebels, including Ochoa, made it back to the United States. Ochoa was charged with violating the U.S. Neutrality Laws.[118]

On January 15, 1894 the rebels made another abortive strike. Ochoa escaped, dressed in the clothes of a Mexican soldier, made his way to El Paso, and was arrested in October for filibustering. The U.S. government had no difficulty in proving its case. At the insistence of the Mexican government, the sheriff held him at Fort Stockton and attempted to extradite him. They intended to kidnap him and take him to Mexico. Ochoa was convicted and sent to the Kings County Penitentiary.[119] After his release from prison, Ochoa continued his anti-Díaz activities. In October 1915, Ochoa, along with José Orozco and E. L. Holmdahl, was again convicted of conspiring to violate neutrality laws and was sentenced to 18 months in Leavenworth.[120]

Meanwhile, in the United States some Mexicans became increasingly politically conscious. In the 1870s and 1880s, Texas Spanish-language newspapers catered to the Mexican populace. After the 1880s, there was a constant immigration of political exiles from Mexico, especially in San Antonio, El Paso, and along the Rio Grande. The exiles gave leadership to workers, and they integrated themselves into the Tejano society via the mutualistas and other institutions. In 1885, Catarino Garza, a journalist, traveling salesman, and former Mexican consul at St. Louis, Missouri, organized mutualistas in the valley and exhorted Mexicans to unite and fight racism. Garza accused a U.S. customs inspector, Victor Sebree, of assassinating Mexican prisoners who opposed Díaz; in 1888, on the streets of Rio Grande City, Sebree shot and wounded Garza.

Garza soon became a leader of the anti-Díaz movement. Garza recruited adherents through *La Sociedad Mexicana*, which was founded by Dr. Ignacio Martínez, who like Garza was once a supporter of the Mexican president. Journalist Paulino Martínez also supported Garza as did powerful generals in Mexico, including Sostenes Rocha, Francisco Naranjo, Sebastian Villareal, Francisco Estrada, Luis E. Torres, and Luis Terrazas.

In the early morning on Mexican Independence Day of 1891, Catarino Garza and a small band of his armed supporters crossed the Rio Grande near Mier, Tamaulipas, and proclaimed a revolution to overthrow the government of President Porfirio Diaz. For the next couple of years Garza and his followers evaded capture by the Texas Rangers, the U.S. Army, and Mexican military forces, and occasionally raided towns on the Mexican side of the border.[121]

Garza and his associates plotted the overthrow of the Díaz regime. They had wanted to incite a popular revolt. On three other occasions that year, Garza crossed into Mexico only to be chased out of Mexico by the U.S. cavalry, sheriffs, and marshals as well as Mexican forces. U.S. military authorities asked for an additional 10,000 troops to put down the revolt, claiming that Garza cost the Mexican government $2 million. Sensational newspaper accounts raised concerns that Mexicans would arm themselves, rekindling old fears of a Mexican revolt. Also rumored was that General Juan Cortina would soon return to Texas from Mexico City to lead the revolution. The pursuit forced Garza to flee to Key West, Florida, where he helped Cuban exiles fight for their independence. He then went to Central America, where he fought for liberal causes.[122] Garza died in 1895, killed by Colombian troops after joining Colombian rebels. By 1896 Lauro Aguirre resided in El Paso, where he allied with other dissidents Victor Ochoa, Pedro García de Lama, Manuel Flora Chapa, and Teresa (Teresita) Urrea. The cabal led several abortive forays into Mexico.[123]

Conclusion: The Marginalization of the Other

By 1900, mass migration from Mexico to Texas although relatively small intensified racism despite the fact that there was a booming economy. Meanwhile, the number of farms swelled from 12,000 in 1850, to 340,000 by 1900. One-third of the Mexican population was employed in agriculture. Their wages declined an estimated 30 percent, while urban wages increased, contributing to a flight to the cities. Moreover, child labor was more common in agriculture, further encouraging migration to urban areas.[124]

The foreign-born Mexican population went from 47.1 percent in 1850 to 61.2 percent in 1900; the white foreign-born population dipped from 44.8 percent to 24.3 percent among workers in Central Texas, the Lower Rio Grande Valley, and the El Paso region. By 1900, 85 percent of the South Texas population was of Mexican extraction. Significantly, literacy declined among Mexicans from 25.1 percent to 13.0 percent, while among whites it increased from 86.6 percent to 92.2 percent.[125] Historian Trinidad Gonzales, in a groundbreaking work, shows how the attitude among Valley Mexicans changed. According to Gonzales, in 1900 Mexicans considered the area "Occupied Mexico, but that within two decades they recognized it as American territory. They held on to the Mexican culture, *lo mexicano*, with a Tejano identity emerging."[126]

Notes

1. Rodolfo Acuña, *Occupied America: The Chicano's Struggle Toward Liberation* (San Francisco: Canfield Press, 1972), 1.
2. Unlike many colleagues I will not fight for the ownership of the name America. It is the invention of the Italian cartographer Amerigo Vespucci and has no particular significance for me.
3. William Appleman Williams, "Empire as a Way of Life," *The Nation*, August 29, 1980, 104–107.
4. J. William Fulbright, *The Arrogance of Power* (New York: Random House, 1967).
5. Andrew Jackson O'Shaughnessy, *An Empire Divided: The American Revolution and the British Caribbean* (University of Pennsylvania Press, 2000).
6. Howard Zinn, "A People's History of American Empire," 2008, https://www.youtube.com/watch?v=Arn3lF5XSUg.
7. A university-wide committee at the University of California at Santa Barbara overturned my appointment to Chicana/o Studies because the members said I lied because I said that the U.S. invaded Mexico. Much for the same reason Occupied Mexico was banned in Arizona. No documentation to the contrary was proposed, just supposition. Rodolfo F. Acuña, "Truth and Objectivity and Chicano History Occasional Paper No. 9," Julian Samora Institute, Occasional Paper No. 9, December 1997, https://jsri.msu.edu/upload/occasional-papers/oc09.pdf.

8 Peter Guardino, *The Dead March: A History of the Mexican-American War* (Cambridge: Harvard University Press, 2017). Jesús Velasco-Márquez, "A Mexican Viewpoint on the War With the United States," PBS SOCAL, http://www.pbs.org/kera/usmexicanwar/prelude/md_a_mexican_viewpoint.html.

9 A paper read at the meeting of the American Historical Association in Chicago, July 12, 1893. Report of the American Historical Association for 1893, 199–227, http://xroads.virginia.edu/~hyper/turner/chapter1.html.

10 "Territorial Expansion, Filibustering, and U.S. Interest in Central America and Cuba, 1849–1861," Office of the Historian, https://history.state.gov/milestones/1830-1860/territorial-expansion.

11 Rodolfo F. Acuña and Guadalupe Compeán, eds., *Voices of the U.S. Latino Experience*, 3 vols. (Westport, CT: Greenwood, 2008), 215–71. *The United States Magazine and Democratic Review* 25, No. cxxxv (September 1849): 197, 198, 200, 203, 205. Letter from U.S. Secretary of State James Buchanan to R. M. Saunders, June 17, 1848, 193–204, http://cdl.library.cornell.edu/cgi-bin/moa/moa-cgi?notisid=AGD1642-0025&byte=226352056. Clayton-Bulwer Treaty, 1850, http://avalon.law.yale.edu/19th_century/br1850.asp. Ostend Manifesto, October 18, 1854, http://xroads.virginia.edu/~HYPER/HNS/OSTEND/ostend.html. Speech Given by William Walker in New Orleans, May 30, 1857, "Filibusterism," *New York Daily Times* (June 8, 1857), 2. The *New York Times* is full of articles on the Cuban Question during the 1850s.

12 Greg Niemann, "The Filibuster of 1890 – Plotting to Annex Baja," Baja Bound.com, https://www.bajabound.com/bajaadventures/bajafever/annexbaja.php. There is continuing interest in the question why the United States did not just annex Baja California.

13 Compromise of 1850, January 29, 1850, http://www.loc.gov/rr/program/bib/ourdocs/Compromise1850.html.

14 Governor William Carr Lane's Manifesto Regarding the Drawing of the Boundary Between Mexico and the United States, *New York Daily Times* (June 20, 1853), 3. Commissioner James Bartlett's Reply to William Carr Lane, "The Mesilla Valley," *New York Daily Times* (May 5, 1853), 6.

15 By 1826 Americans dominated commerce along Lower Rio Grande, changing the economic face of the region. Andres Reséndez, "National Identity on a Shifting Border: Texas and New Mexico in the Age of Transition, 1821–1848," *The Journal of American History* 86, No. 2 (September 1999), 679, 681, 683.

16 David Montejano, *Anglos and Mexicans in the Making of Texas, 1836–1986* (Austin: University of Texas Press, 1987), 16. See Memoirs of Antonio Menchaca, Yanaguana Society, San Antonio, 1937. Courtesy of Wallace L. McKeehan, Sons of DeWitt Colony Texas, http://www.tamu.edu/ccbn/dewitt/menchacamem.htm. José María Salomé Rodríguez, *The Memoirs of Early Texas*, 1913, Sons of DeWitt Colony Texas, http://www.tamu.edu/ccbn/dewitt/rodmemoirs.htm. José Antonio Navarro's Letter to the Editor of the San Antonio *Ledger* (October 30, 1853), http://www.tamu.edu/ccbn/dewitt/navarromem1.htm. Armando Villarreal y Talamantes, "Intervention and Conflict in the Trans-Nueces, 1755–1850" (Master's Thesis, University of Texas at Arlington, 2003), 7.

17 David R. Johnson, John A. Booth, and Richard J. Harris, eds., *The Politics of San Antonio* (Lincoln: University of Nebraska Press, 1983), 5. Montejano, *Anglos and Mexicans in the Making of Texas, 1836–1986*, 26–27. Gilberto Miguel Hinojosa, *A Borderland Town in Transition: Laredo, 1755–1870* (College Station: Texas A&M University Press, 1983), 35. Raúl A. Ramos, *Beyond the Alamo: Forging Mexican Ethnicity in San Antonio, 1821–1861* (Chapel Hill: The University of North Carolina Press, 2008), 171, 174.

18 Neil Foley, *The White Scourge: Mexicans, Blacks, and Poor Whites in Texas Cotton Culture* (Berkeley: University of California Press, 1997), 19–20.

19 Montejano, *Anglos and Mexicans in the Making of Texas, 1836–1986*, 26–27. Hinojosa, *A Borderland Town in Transition*, 59. Juan Seguín's Address to the Texas Senate, February 1840, The Seguin Family Historical Society, "The Original and Official Seguín Family Organization and Web Site," http://www.seguinfamilyhistory.com/index.html#address. Ramos, *Beyond the Alamo*, 167–68, 177–78. As tensions with Mexico increased, the Tejanos were looked at as a suspect class.

20 Frederick Law Olmsted, *Journey Through Texas* (New York: Dix, Edwards & Co., 1857), 164–165.

21 T. R. Fehrenbach, *Lone Star: A History of Texas and the Texans* (New York: Macmillan, 1968), 245. Donald E. Chipman, *Spanish Texas, 1519–1821* (Austin: University of Texas Press, 1992). Andrés Tijerina, *Tejanos & Texas Under the Mexican Flag, 1821–1836* (College Station: Texas A&M University Press, 1994), 137–44. Michael Paul Rogin, *Fathers and Children: Andrew Jackson and the Subjugation of the American Indian* (Edison, NJ: Transaction Press, 1991), 306. James Alan Marten, *Texas Divided: Loyalty and Dissent in the Lone Star State, 1856–1874* (Lexington: University Press of Kentucky, 1990), 12, 19, 29.

22 Allison Brownell Tirres, "American Law Comes to the Border: Law and Colonization on the U.S./Mexico Divide, 1848–1890," (PhD Dissertation, Harvard

University, Cambridge, 2008), 8–9; concentrates on El Paso. The other is J. Edward Townes, "Invisible Lines: The Life and Death of a Borderland," (PhD Dissertation, Texas Christian University, Fort Worth, 2008).

23 Arnold De León, *The Tejano Community, 1836–1900* (Albuquerque: University of New Mexico Press, 1982), 20. Montejano, *Anglos and Mexicans in the Making of Texas, 1836–1986*, 31. Hinojosa, *A Borderland Town in Transition*, 65–6. Stephen L. Moore, *Savage Frontier: 1840–1841: Rangers, Riflemen, and Indian Wars in Texas*, Vol. 3 (Denton: University of North Texas Press, 2007), 289.

24 Villarreal y Talamantes, "Intervention and Conflict in the Trans-Nueces, 1755–1850," 33.

25 Armando Alonzo, *Tejano Legacy: Rancheros and Settlers in South Texas 1734–1900* (Albuquerque: University of New Mexico Press, 1998), 85–6, 93.

26 Letter from Texas President Mirabeau B. Lamar to the People of Santa Fé, April 14, 1840, Courtesy of Sons of DeWitt Colony Texas and President M.B. Lamar Address to the People of Santa Fé, June 5, 1841, http://www.tamu.edu/ccbn/dewitt/santafeexped.htm. Mirabeau B. Lamar to James Webb, February 23, 1842, http://www.tsl.state.tx.us/treasures/giants/lamar/lamar-webb-1.html. Moore, *Savage Frontier*, 275. Glen Sample Ely, "Gone from Texas and Trading with the Enemy: New Perspectives on Civil War West Texas," *Southwestern Historical Quarterly* CX, No. 4 (April 2007), 439, 440. Rodolfo F. Acuña, *Corridors of Migration: The Odyssey of Mexican Laborers, 1600–1933* (Tucson: University of Arizona Press, 2007), 87, 207.

27 Janice Elaine Watkins, "Nacogdoches land men and the Texas Revolution" (Master of Arts Thesis, Stephen F. Austin State University, 2009), 1, 5, 34–37.

28 Ibid., 46.

29 Townes, "Invisible Lines," 208, 214–7.

30 Paul D. Lack, "The Córdova Revolt," in Gerald R. Poyo, ed., *Tejano Journey, 1770–1850* (Austin: University of Texas Press, 1996), 89–109. Letter from Vicente Córdova to Manuel Flores, July 19, 1838, Texas Indian Papers, Vol. 1, No. 2. Archives and Manuscripts, Texas State Library and Archives Commission, www.tsl.state.tx.us/exhibits/indian/early/cordova-1838.html. John Henry Brown, "Vicente Córdova and the Córdova Rebellion," *From History of Texas*, http://www.tamu.edu/ccbn/dewitt/cordovavicente.htm#brown. J. W. Wilbarger, *The Córdova Fight, From Indian Depredations in Texas*. Wilbarger, "The Flores Fight and Archival Correspondence," http://www.tamu.edu/faculty/ccbn/dewitt/cordovavicente2.htm. Mike Coppock, "The forced expulsion of the Texas Cherokees: Houston supported them but not Lamar," *Wild West* 21.2 (Aug. 2008), 22–23.

31 Testimonies of fugitive slaves can be found at "Fugitive Slave Cases, 1862," May 15–19, 1862; Transcribed from National Archives Microfilm Publication M433 "Records of the United States District Court for the District of Columbia Relating to Slaves, 1851–1863, Roll 3." Christine's Genealogy Website, http://ccharity.com/contents/fugitive-slave-cases-1862-may-15-19-1862/fugitive-slave-cases-1862-may-15-19-1862-0/.

32 Jack C. Vowell, "Politics at El Paso: 1850–1920" (Master's Thesis, Texas Western College, El Paso, 1952), 145. De León, *The Tejano Community, 1836–1900*, xvi. José Antonio Navarro, 1795–1871, biography, autobiography, and letter to Stephen Austin, Sons of DeWitt Colony Texas, http://www.tamu.edu/ccbn/dewitt/Navarro.htm.

33 Ronnie G. Tyler, "The Callahan Expedition of 1855: Indians or Negroes?" *Southwest Historical Quarterly* 70, No. 4 (April 1967): 575, 582. Arnoldo De León, "White Racial Attitudes Toward Mexicanos in Texas, 1821–1920" (PhD Dissertation, Texas Christian University, Fort Worth, 1974), 141.

34 Marten, *Texas Divided*, 13. Alberto Rodríguez, "Ethnic Conflict in South Texas: 1860–1930" (Master of Arts, The University of Texas Pan American, Edinburg, 2005), 2–5, 8, 21, 30, 36.

35 Vowell, "Politics at El Paso." De León, *The Tejano Community, 1836–1900*, xvi. José Antonio Navarro, 1795–1871.

36 LeRoy P. Graf, "The Economic History of the Lower Río Grande Valley, 1820–1875" (PhD Dissertation, Harvard University, Cambridge, Massachusetts, 1942), 212, 236. Montejano, *Anglos and Mexicans in the Making of Texas, 1836–1986*, 41–3.

37 Hinojosa, *A Borderland Town in Transition*, 65. Alonzo, *Tejano Legacy*, 99. Montejano, *Anglos and Mexicans in the Making of Texas, 1836–1986*, 42–3. Graf, "The Economic History of the Lower Río Grande Valley, 1820–1875," 212. Clarence C. Clendenen, *Blood on the Border: The United States Army and the Mexican Irregulars* (New York: Macmillan, 1969), 18.

38 Alonzo, *Tejano Legacy*, 146–52. "Investigating Commission of the Northern Frontier," in Carlos E. Cortés, ed., *The Mexican Experience in Texas* (New York: Arno Press, 1976). Charles W. Goldfinch, *Juan Cortina, 1824–1892: A Re-Appraisal* (Brownsville, TX: Bishop's Print Shop, 1950), 21, 31.

39 Tom Lea, *The King Ranch*, 2 Vols., Vol. 1 (Boston, MA: Little, Brown, 1957), 457. Graf, "The Economic History of the Lower Río Grande Valley, 1820–1875," 192. James Arthur Irby, "Line of the Rio Grande: War and Trade on the Confederate Frontier, 1861–1865" (PhD Dissertation, University of Georgia, Athens, 1969), v, xi. William D. Carrigan, Clive Webb, *Forgotten Dead: Mob*

Violence Against Mexicans in the United States, 1848–1928 (New York: Oxford University Press, 2013), 64–66. During the Cart War Texas Governor Elisha Pease got the state legislature to pay for militia to protect Mexican teamsters. However, Mexican cart men had already bypassed Goliad. John Salmon Ford in Stephen B. Oates, ed., *Rip Ford's Texas* (Austin: University of Texas Press, 1963), 467. Frank H. Dugan, "The 1850 Affair of the Brownsville Separatists," *Southwestern Historical Quarterly* 61, No. 2 (October 1957), 270–3. Marten, Texas Divided, 30; *Report of the Mexican Commission on the Northern Frontier*, Investigating Commission of the Northern Frontier (New York: Baker & Godwin Printer, 1875), 130–2, condemned the atrocities.

40 *Handbook of Texas Online*, Arnoldo De León, "Mexican Americans," accessed November 11, 2017, http://www.tshaonline.org/handbook/online/articles/pqmue.

41 Edward H. Moseley, "The Texas Threat, 1855–1860," *Journal of Mexican American History* 3 (1973), 89–90. De León, "White Racial Attitudes Toward Mexicanos in Texas, 1821–1920," 7, 147. David J. Weber, ed., *Foreigners in Their Native Land* (Albuquerque: University of New Mexico Press, 1973), 155–6. Jerry Thompson, *Cortina: Defending the Mexican Name in Texas* (College Station: Texas A & M Press, 2007), 9, 12; his father Trinidad Cortina was the alcalde of Camargo.

42 William D. Carrigan, Clive Webb, "The Lynching of Persons of Mexican Origin or Descent in the United States, 1848 to 1928," *Journal of Social History*, Vol. 37, No. 2 (Winter 2003), 411–438. This excellent article has been expanded to a book, Carrigan, Webb, *Forgotten Dead*, 7.

43 Judith L. Stephens, "Racial Violence and Representation: Performance Strategies in Lynching Dramas of the 1920s," *African American Review*, December 1, 1999, Vol. 33, pp. 655–671.

44 Michael Gordon Webster, "Texan Manifest Destiny and Mexican Border Conflict, 1865–1880" (PhD Dissertation, Indiana University, Bloomington, 1972), 30, 74–76. Graf, "The Economic History of the Lower Rio Grande Valley, 1820–1875," 664–665; the full impact of the Free Zone was not felt in the valley during the first years because of internal disorders and the relatively insecure status of the zone. *Report of the Mexican Commission on the Northern Frontier*, 208. Moore, *Savage Frontier*, 293.

45 Goldfinch, *Juan Cortina, 1824–1892*, 1–3, 17. José T. Canales, *Juan N. Cortina Presents His Motion for a New Trial* (San Antonio, TX: Artes Gráficas, 1951), 6.

46 Graf, "The Economic History of the Lower Río Grande Valley, 1820–1875," 375–401.

47 Juan Nepomuceno Cortina to the inhabitants of the state of Texas, and especially to those of the city of Brownsville (September 30, 1859). To the Mexican inhabitants of the state of Texas: Proclamation (November 23, 1859). (TEXT: U.S. Congress, House, Difficulties on the Southwestern Frontier, 36th Congress; 1st Session, 1860, H. Exec. Doc. 52, 70–82), http://www.pbs.org/weta/thewest/resources/archives/four/cortinas.htm#0959.

48 Walter Prescott Webb, *The Texas Rangers: A Century of Frontier Defense* (Austin: University of Texas Press, 1965), 176. Lyman Woodman, *Cortina: Rogue of the Rio Grande* (San Antonio, TX: Naylor, 1950), 8. Graf, "The Economic History of the Lower Río Grande Valley, 1820–1875," 320–2. James LeRoy Evans, "The Indian Savage, the Mexican Bandit, the Chinese Heathen: Three Popular Stereotypes" (PhD Dissertation, University of Texas, El Paso, 1967), 107, 118. *Report of the Mexican Commission on the Northern Frontier*, 28–9.

49 Webb, *The Texas Rangers*, 178. Goldfinch, *Juan Cortina, 1824–1892*, 44–5. Webster, "Texan Manifest Destiny and Mexican Border Conflict, 1865–1880," 18. Evans, "The Indian Savage, the Mexican Bandit, the Chinese Heathen," 107, 121. *Report of the Mexican Commission on the Northern Frontier*, 137–9.

50 Wayne Moquin et al., eds., *A Documentary History of the Mexican American* (New York: Praeger, 1971), 207–9. For the complete text of the speech, delivered on November 23, 1859, see *Report of the Mexican Commission on the Northern Frontier*, 133, No. 62.

51 Graf, "The Economic History of the Lower Río Grande Valley, 1820–1875," 397. See Angel Navarro to Houston (January 26, 1860). Texas State Library and Archives Commission, http://www.tsl.state.tx.us/governors/earlystate/houston-navarro-1.html.

52 Evans, "The Indian Savage, the Mexican Bandit, the Chinese Heathen," 127.

53 Montejano, *Anglos and Mexicans in the Making of Texas, 1836–1986*, 36. Woodman, *Cortina*, 53, 55, 59, 98–9. Evans, "The Indian Savage, the Mexican Bandit, the Chinese Heathen," 105, 111, 113, 308–9. Report of Major Samuel P. Heintzelman to Colonel Robert E. Lee (March 1, 1860). In "Troubles on Texas Frontier," House of Representatives, 36th Congress, 1st Session, Ex. Doc. No. 81, Letter from the Secretary of War, 2–14.

54 Montejano, *Anglos and Mexicans in the Making of Texas, 1836–1986*, 36. Ford, *Rip Ford's Texas*, 467.

55 Ralph Wooster, "Wealthy Texans," *Southwestern Historical Quarterly* (October 1967), 163, 173. Irby, "Line of the Rio Grande," 3, 13, 63. Kenedy in 1860 listed his real estate holdings at $50,000 and his personal estate at $50,000. José San Ramón, another merchant, listed his real estate holdings at $50,000 and personal

estate at $200,000. Stillman had a modest $13,000 in real estate and $600 in personal holdings.

56 James Marten, *Texas Divided: Loyalty and Dissent in the Lone Star State, 1856–1874* (Lexington, Kentucky: University of Kentucky Press, 1990), 77.

57 Jeffrey William Hunt, *The Last Battle of the Civil War: Palmetto Ranch* (Austin: University of Texas Press, 2002), 17–20. Mary Margaret McAllen Amberson, "The Politics of Commerce: Merchants' and Military Officials' Machinations to Prolong Civil War Turmoil Along the Lower Rio Grande, 1865–1867" (Master's Thesis, University of Texas, San Antonio, 2007), 3.

58 Marten, *Texas Divided*, 93, 32, 77, 123, 125. Irby, "Line of the Rio Grande," 34, 142. Ranger Rip Ford had relations with many of the elite Mexican families in the valley. For instance, he refused to extradite his friend Juan María Carbajal to Mexico. Captain Santos Benavides aided the American campaigns against Juan Cortina, a bitter enemy of Ford. Col. Santo Benavides, http://www.37thtexas.org/html/Santosbio.html. Confederates in Mexico, http://www.youtube.com/watch?v=QQQ5S33XUCM. Mexican Confederates, http://www.youtube.com/watch?v=X79xmf7B7pg. Mexican Texans in the Civil War, http://www.tshaonline.org/handbook/online/articles/pom02. Jerry D. Thompson ed., *Tejanos In Gray: Civil War Letters of Captains Joseph Rafael de la Garza and Manuel Yturri* (College Station, Texas: Texas A&M University Press, 2011).

59 Marten, *Texas Divided*, 126. Brewster Hudspeth, "The Short but Eventful Life of Adrián J. Vidal 1840–1865," http://www.texasescapes.com/FallingBehind/Short-but-Eventful-life-of-Adrian-J-Vidal.htm. Richard Nelson Current, *Lincoln's Loyalists: Union Soldiers from the Confederacy* (Boston, MA: Northeastern University Press, 1992), 99–102, 137. "Nearly three times as many Mexican-Texans served the Rebels as served the Yankees." Jane Clements Monday and Frances Brannen Vick, *Petra's Legacy: The South Texas Ranching Empire of Petra Vela and Mifflin Kenedy*, 1st ed. (College Station: Texas A&M University Press, October 30, 2007).

60 Tina N. Cannon, "Bordering on Trouble: Conflict between Tejanos and Anglos in South Texas, 1880–1920," (Master of Arts, Baylor University, Waco, College Station, 2001), 28, 32, 33, 36. Introduction of barbed wire placed Mexicans and Texans at odds by reducing payrolls and long drives. Railroads brought an end to long drives. Barbed wire, irrigation, and railroads encouraged immigration to South Texas. Railroads took off in the 1870s; in 1881 Texas and Pacific gained a charter from the state. Amberson, "The Politics of Commerce," 4, 6, 13, 18, 21. Alberto Rodriguez, "Ethnic conflict in South Texas: 1860–1930," (Master of Arts Thesis, Pan American University, 2005), 5; the Black population went from 58,161 in 1850 to over 82,000 in 1860. King Cotton dominated the economy. Jesse Dorsett, "Blacks in Reconstruction Texas, 1865–1877," (PhD dissertation, Abilene, Texas, Texas Christian University, 1981)

61 De León, *The Tejano Community, 1836–1900*, 63. Alonzo, *Tejano Legacy*, 169.

62 Fehrenbach, *Lone Star*, 678–9. Weber, *Foreigners in Their Native Land*, 146, states that 11,212 Mexicans lived in Texas in 1850, constituting only 5 percent of the population. John R. Scotford, *Within These Borders* (New York: Friendship Press, 1953), 35. Montejano, *Anglos and Mexicans in the Making of Texas, 1836–1986*, 172–6. John Solomon Otto, *The Final Frontiers, 1880–1930: Settling the Southern Bottomlands* (Portsmouth, NH: Greenwood Press, 199), 101. "World of the Tenant Farmer," Texas Beyond History, University of Texas, http://www.texasbeyondhistory.net/osborn/world.html.

63 De León, "White Racial Attitudes Toward Mexicanos in Texas, 1821–1920," 140, 238, 239.

64 Ford, *Rip Ford's Texas*, 371. Webster, "Texan Manifest Destiny and Mexican Border Conflict, 1865–1880," 76. James LeRoy Evans, "The Indian Savage, the Mexican Bandit, the Chinese Heathen," vii. Alonzo, *Tejano Legacy*, 163–5.

65 Ford, *Rip Ford's Texas*, 371.

66 *Report of the Mexican Commission on the Northern Frontier*, 154–5. Webster, "Texan Manifest Destiny and Mexican Border Conflict, 1865–1880," 79–80. Montejano, *Anglos and Mexicans in the Making of Texas, 1836–1986*, 53.

67 An Act to Provide for the Protection of the Frontier, 1874. Texas Ranger Research Center, http://www.texasranger.org/ReCenter/org1874.htm.

68 Leonard Morris, "The Mexican Raid of 1875 on Corpus Christi," *Texas Historical Association Quarterly* 55, No. 2 (October 1900), 128.

69 Lea, *The King Ranch*, 2 vols., 275.

70 *Report of the Mexican Commission on the Northern Frontier*. This report is an indictment of U.S. merchants and ranchers.

71 Graf, "The Economic History of the Lower Río Grande Valley, 1820–1875," 320–2.

72 *Report of the Mexican Commission on the Northern Frontier*, 29–30, 62, 105. Alonzo, *Tejano Legacy*, 142. Montejano, *Anglos and Mexicans in the Making of Texas, 1836–1986*, 38. Moore, *Savage Frontier*, 289, 293.

73 Jacob S. Hacker and Paul Piersonnov, "Robbing Blue States to Pay Red," *New York Times*, Nov. 13, 2017, https://www.nytimes.com/2017/11/13/opinion/tax-plan-states-gop.html.

74 De León, "White Racial Attitudes," 159–61, 172, 239. De León, *The Tejano Community, 1836–1900*, 18–19, 33–34. William D. Carrigan and Clive Webb, "The Lynching of Persons of Mexican Origin or Descent in the United States, 1848 to 1928," *Journal of Social History* 37, No. 2 (2003): 413–14, 416–418, 425. There were Mexicans in the Rangers, http://www.texasranger.org/ReCenter/hispanic_indian_rangers.htm. "A Little Standing Army in Himself": N. A. Jennings Tells of the Texas Rangers, 1875, http://historymatters.gmu.edu/d/6534.

75 Larry McMurtry, *In a Narrow Grave* (Austin, TX: Encino Press, 1968), 40, underscores the inconsistencies of Webb's description of the Rangers' role in the siege of Mexico City.

76 Llerena B. Friend, "W. Webb's Texas Rangers," *Southwestern Historical Quarterly* 74, No. 3 (January 1971), 321.

77 Ibid.

78 Editorial by John Salmon Ford in the *Texas Democrat*, September 9, 1846; quoted in Fehrenbach, *Lone Star*, 465. [Contextual] Américo Paredes, *With a Pistol in His Hand* (Austin: University of Texas Press, 1958). Alonzo, *Tejano Legacy*, 75–6.

79 Editorial by John Salmon Ford in the *Texas Democrat* (September 9, 1846) quoted in Fehrenbach, *Lone Star*, 465.

80 Webb, *The Texas Rangers*, xv.

81 Ibid.

82 Paredes, *With a Pistol in His Hand*, 31. Julian Samora, Joe Bernal, and Albert Peña, *Gun Powder Justice: A Reassessment of the Texas Rangers* (Notre Dame: University of Notre Dame Press, 1979), 56–7. "De La" means "of the." Paredes uses just Cerda, while Webb uses "De La." It is the same family. It was probably used interchangeably. Samora et al., use it the same way as I do.

83 Paredes, *With a Pistol in His Hand*, 29.

84 Webb, *The Texas Rangers*, 463–64.

85 Quote in Paredes, *With a Pistol in His Hand*, 31. [contextual] The revisionism is evident in the biography of Monday and Vick, *Petra's Legacy*, 250–1, writing how King memorialized McNeely. Teresa Palomo Acosta and Ruthe Winegarten, *Las Tejanas: 300 Years of History* (Austin: University of Texas Press, 2003), 45–68.

86 [quote] De León, "White Racial Attitudes," 126. [contextual] E. Larry Dickens, "Mestizaje in 19th Century Texas," *Journal of Mexican American History* 2, No. 2 (Spring 1972), 63.

87 Jane Dysart, "Mexican Women in San Antonio, 1830–1860: The Assimilation Process," *Western Historical Quarterly* 7, No. 4 (October 1976), 370.

88 Quoted in Aaron M. Boom, ed., "Texas in the 1850's as Viewed by a Recent Arrival," *Southwestern Historical Quarterly* 70, No. 2 (October 1966), 282–5.

89 De León, "White Racial Attitudes," 126.

90 Dysart, "Mexican Women," quote on 375, 370–4.

91 Eric J. Hobsbawm, *Primitive Rebels: Studies in Archaic Forms of Social Movement in the 19th and 20th Centuries* (New York: Norton, 1965), 13.

92 Webb, *The Texas Rangers*, 360–1. Vowell, "Politics at El Paso," 69–70. "A Little War on the Border," *The New York Times* (October 22, 1877), 4. Congressional Record. Letter from Colonel John H. King, Secretary of War, House of Representatives, to the Bureau of Military Justice (April 19, 1878), "El Paso Troubles in Texas," 13–8.

93 W. M. Dunn's Report to War Department, Bureau of Military Justice (April 19, 1878). "El Paso Troubles in Texas," Letter from the Secretary of War, House of Representatives, 45th Cong., 2d. Sess., Ex. Doc. No. 93 (May 28, 1878), 3–5.

94 Leon Metz, "Atrocities, Plunder Mark End of El Paso Salt War," *El Paso Times* (March 17, 1974). Webster, "Texan Manifest Destiny and Mexican Border Conflict, 1865–1880," 238. "Salt Trade, Trails, and Wars," http://www.texasbeyondhistory.net/trans-p/images/he3.html. Vowell, "Politics at El Paso," 65–6, 69, 72–3. Fehrenbach, *Lone Star*, 289. Carey McWilliams, *North from Mexico* (New York: Greenwood Press, 1968), 110. Webster, "Texan Manifest Destiny and Mexican Border Conflict, 1865–1880," 234. Webb, *The Texas Rangers*, 350.

95 William D. Carrigan and Clive Webb, *Forgotten Dead: Mob Violence against Mexicans in the United States, 1848–1928* (New York: Oxford University res, 2013), 49.

96 Carrigan and Webb, *Forgotten Dead*, 26–29, 67, 86–89 (Manuscript). William D. Carrigan and Clive Webb, "When Americans Lynched Mexicans," *New York Times*, Feb. 20, 2015, https://www.nytimes.com/2015/02/20/opinion/when-americans-lynched-mexicans.html. New book: William D. Carrigan and Clive Webb, *Forgotten Dead: Mob Violence against Mexicans in the United States, 1848–1928* (Cambridge: Oxford University Press; Reprint edition, 2017).

97 W. M. Dunn's Report to War Department, Bureau of Military Justice (April 19, 1878). Letter from Colonel John H. King, Secretary of War, "El Paso Troubles in Texas," 45th Cong., 2d. Sess., Ex. Doc. No 93 (May 28, 1878), 13–8.

98 *The Ballad of Gregorio Cortez* [the movie], http://www.youtube.com/watch?v=FsApt0st_u4. "Los Alegres De Teran—Gregorio Cortez," http://www.youtube.com/watch?v=jj4-6ZCc7i4.

99 Robert J. Rosenbaum, *Mexicano Resistance in the Southwest* (Austin: University of Texas Press, 1981), 55.
100 Armando C. Alonzo, Tejano Legacy: Rancheros and Settlers in South Texas, 1734–1900 (Albuquerque: University of New Mexico Press, 1998), 276.
101 Alonzo, *Tejano Legacy*, 161. Montejano, *Anglos and Mexicans in the Making of Texas, 1836–1986*, 43–4.
102 O. Douglas Weeks, "The Texas-Mexican and the Politics of South Texas," *American Political and Social Science Review* 24 (August 1930), 611–3. De León, "White Racial Attitudes," 164.
103 Edgar Greer Shelton, Jr., "Political Conditions among Texas Mexicans Along the Rio Grande" (Master's Thesis, University of Texas, Austin, 1946), 26–8, 32–6. By the early 1920s, Wells had lost control, but the machine stayed intact, with power divided among his lieutenants. He died in 1922. The patriarch was José Alejandro Guerra, a surveyor for the Spanish crown in 1767. He had received *porciones* in the valley, which his heir Manuel Guerra inherited. Manuel started a mercantile house in Roma, Texas, in 1856. He married Virginia Cox, daughter of a Kentuckian father and Mexican mother.
104 Shelton, "Political Conditions," 36–7, 90, 98, 123. At one point Canales quarreled with the Guerras in Starr County, and in 1933 he organized a new party to oppose them.
105 Handbook of Texas Online, Arnoldo De León, "Mexican Americans," accessed November 12, 2017, http://www.tshaonline.org/handbook/online/articles/pqmue.
106 Donna S. Morales and John P. Schmal, "How We Got Here: The Roads We Took To America," Houston Institute for Culture, http://www.houstonculture.org/hispanic/roads.html.
107 Evan Anders, *Boss Rule in South Texas* (Austin: University of Texas Press, 1982), 283.
108 De León, *The Tejano Community, 1836–1900*, 90. Montejano, *Anglos and Mexicans in the Making of Texas, 1836–1986*, 62–3. Hector R. Pérez, "The Parrs: Patrones of Duval County, Texas, 1905–1975" (Master of Arts Thesis, Texas A&M University, Kingsville, 2003), 1.
109 Emilio Zamora, *The World of the Mexican Worker in Texas* (College Station: Texas A&M Press, 1993), 16, 34.
110 Ibid., 92–93.
111 De León, "White Racial Attitudes," 166, 168. Robert Miller Worth, "Building a Progressive Coalition in Texas: The Populist-Reform Democrat Rapprochement, 1900-1907," *The Journal of Southern History*, Vol. 52, No. 2 (May, 1986), 163–182. The Populists were not progressive when it came to immigrants.
112 Fehrenbach, *Lone Star*, 627. Rupert N. Richardson, *Texas: The Lone Star State*, 2nd ed. (Englewood Cliffs, NJ: Prentice-Hall, 1958), 271, 274.
113 De León, *The Tejano Community, 1836–1900*, 20–2. Donald W. Meinig, *Imperial Texas* (Austin: University of Texas Press, 1969), 65.
114 William D. Carrigan and Clive Webb, "The Lynching of Persons of Mexican Origin."
115 De León, "White Racial Attitudes," 186–7, 226–7, 232.
116 Ibid., 192–3, 267–8.
117 De León, *The Tejano Community, 1836–1900*, 43.
118 "Ochoa, once with a $50,000 price on his head," *Smithsonian*, http://www.smithsonianeducation.org/scitech/impacto/graphic/victor/revolutionary_arrested.html.
119 "Mexican Revolt," *El Paso Evening Tribune* (April 18, 1893). "More Fighting," *El Paso Evening Tribune* (April 19, 1993). "All Quiet on Potomac," *El Paso Evening Tribune* (April 20, 1893). "The Chihuahuan Troubles," *El Paso Evening Tribune* (April 24., 1893). "Alarma Infundada," *El Norte*, Vol. iii, No. 130, Chihuahua, Chi (November 13, 1893). "Rebelion de Palomas y El Manzano, Anos de 1893 y 1894," *AGN MGR*, Vol. 8. "El Robo a La Aduna De Palomas," *El Norte: Bisenanario de Información* Año III, No. 129, Chihuahua, Chi (November 19, 1893). "Rebelión de Palomas y el Manzano, 1893–1894," *AGN MGR*, Vol. 8. "Rebels Again Take Palomas," *El Paso Times* (November 16, 1893). "Perez Issues Manifesto," *El Paso Times* (December 3, 1893). Santana Pérez, a rebel leader in western Chihuahua, calls Díaz a traitor. "Rebels Hang Federal General," *El Paso Times* (December 13, 1893). "Charged with Aiding Rebels; Mexican Vice Consul Causes the Arrest of an American Citizen," *The New York Times* (December 1, 1893). "Los Sucesos de Tomochic," Vol. 7, Ramo Gobernación, Paquete # 590, Exp 13. This section has all of the primary documents on the siege of Tomóchic, Vol. 8, El Estado de Chihuahua, XVII, # 320 (February 3, 1894). "Rebelion de Palomas y El Manzo: Anos de 1893 y 1894," Periodico Oficial, 11 bandidos in District of Bravo, march on rebels. "Fighting Near Colonia Juarez," *El Paso Times* (December 14, 1893); 100 rebels, 17 hours of fighting.
120 "To Mexico for Revenge," *The New York Times* (August 17, 1895). Almada, *Diccionario Historia Geografia y Biografia Chihuahuenses*, 33. "Something Wrong," *Los Angeles Times* (January 20, 1894). A dispatch from the mayor of Juárez said revolutionists attacked west side of town. Federal garrison responded. Masses of people were in sympathy with Santana Perez. "Charged With Aiding Rebels," *The New York Times* (December 1, 1893). "Simón Analla [sic] reported dead," *El Paso Times* (May 2, 1893).

121 Elliot Young, "Remembering Catarino Garza's 1891 revolution: An aborted border insurrection," *Mexican Studies*, Summer 1996, Vol.12(2), p. 231.
122 "Sentence Carranza Agents," *The New York Times* (October 21, 1915).
123 De León, *The Tejano Community, 1836–1900*, 30, 45, 48. De León, "White Racial Attitudes," 234–5, 263–4. Emilio Zamora, "Mexican Labor Activity in South Texas, 1900–1920" (PhD Dissertation, The University of Texas, Austin, 1983), 86–7. Celso Garza Guajardo, *En busca de Catarino Garza, 1859–1895* (Nuevo León: Atonoma de Nuevo León, 1989), contains his memoirs. "Another Fight in Texas," *The New York Times* (January 4, 1892). M. Romero, "The Garza Raid and Its Lessons," *North American Review* (Spring 1892): 327.
124 Paul J. Vanderwood, *The Power of God*, 291–2. Ochoa in 1890 organized *la Union-Occidental Mexicana*. De León, *The Tejano Community, 1836–1900*, 130, 196.
125 Kenneth L. Stewart and Arnold De León, *Not Room Enough: Mexicans, Anglos, and Socio-economic Change in Texas, 1859–1900* (Albuquerque: University of New Mexico Press, 1993), 21, 23, 26, 29, 33, 35–6. De León, *The Tejano Community, 1836–1900*, 73, 107. Alonzo, *Tejano Legacy*, 110. David M. Vigness and Mark Odintz, "Rio Grande Valley," *Handbook of Texas Online*, The Texas State Historical Association. "The Valley" encompasses Starr, Cameron, Hidalgo, and Willacy.
126 Trinidad Gonzales, "The World of Mexico Texanos, Mexicanos and Mexico Americanos: Transnational and National Identities In the Lower Rio Grande Valley During the Last Phase of United States Colonization, 1900–1930" (PhD Dissertation, University of Houston, 2008), 5–6. Rodolfo F. Acuña, *Corridors of Migration: The Odyssey of Mexican Laborers, 1600–1933* (Tucson: University of Arizona Press, 2007). Rodolfo F. Acuña, *Anything But Mexican: Chicanos in Contemporary Los Angeles* (London: Verso, 1996).

Chapter 5
New Mexico: The American Occupation

Learning Objectives

5.1 Characterize the role of the Indigenous People in New Mexico before and after the creation of the Santa Fé Trail.

5.2 Explain how the actions of the colonizing peoples of New Mexico reflected their racism and exceptionalism.

5.3 Describe the operations of the Santa Fé Ring designed in maintaining the caste system.

5.4 Explain how the split in the Catholic Church reflected social divisions in New Mexico.

5.5 Explain how the market economy changed the relationship of New Mexicans to the land and widened the gaps aning the different peoples.

5.6 Outline the history of resistance to enclosure and railroad power in New Mexico.

5.7 Characterize social and political realities in New Mexico during its last years as a territory.

On the Frontier

5.1 Characterize the role of the Indigenous People in New Mexico before and after the creation of the Santa Fé Trail.

At the time of the Spanish conquest, New Mexico was heavily populated. The Indigenous Nations included the Apache, Comanche, Jemez, Kiowa, Manso, Navaho, Pecos, Ute, Pueblo, and Zuni. The conquest brought a wide range of diseases that devastated the native people. Taxes, forced labor, and enslavement also took a toll and contributed to a crash 100 years after the first contact. Dramatic ecological disasters included an increase in forest fires as well as diseases and deportations.[1] Thus, once thriving villages fell into disarray.

As mentioned in Chapter 2, the Spanish colonization did not go smoothly, and in 1680 the Pueblo and other Indigenous Nations throughout the Southwest and northern Mexico revolted. The Spanish colonizers only succeeded in regaining a foothold after the revolt because of organization and sense of mission. The 700 years' war against the Muslims professionalized Spain's military and they developed superior weapons and—more importantly—they knew how to use them. A common religion forged unity and purpose and gave the Spaniards a sense of invincibility.[2] Driven by religious fervor notions of altruism did not limit them. Moreover, in New Mexico, the establishment of presidios enabled the colonists to control the Rio Grande and thus the people.

The Spanish occupation of New Mexico began in 1598 and after years of clashes and adjustments the original settlement grew. In 1600, about 700 Spanish colonials and 80,000 Pueblos lived there.[3] By 1796 there were 23,648 Spanish colonists and 10,557 Native Americans living in the province. Twenty-four years later, New Mexico's population was estimated at about 28,436 Hispanos and 9,923 Pueblos. By the 1820s, El Paso, Santa Fé, and Albuquerque grew to towns of several thousand dwellers.[4] During the Spanish period, a safe zone was formed in Rio Abajo, with its center in Albuquerque.[5] When the Spanish settlers arrived, Rio Abajo was heavily settled by Pueblo people that they displaced. Over time large estates, haciendas, squeezed the villagers and displaced the natives.

The Indigenous People throughout northern Mexico joined the 1680 war against the Spanish colonists, driving them out of the province. Indigenous People also revolted and many New Mexican colonists retreated to Chihuahua and Sonora.[6] The uprisings encouraged the Apache to rebel.

In response to the threat, the Spanish crown built presidios (forts) from Sonora to Texas.

When the Spaniards returned to New Mexico in the 1690s, many New Mexican families remained in Sonora and Chihuahua. Slowly the returnees reconquered the province and fortified Rio Abajo. In 1720, the Spanish crown disseminated new kinds of grants whose purpose was to encourage the Spanish settlement of the northern frontier in Rio Arriba. Town ownership grants, community grants, and ranch grants were given to encourage colonization.[7] As in other parts of northern Mexico, some Rio Arriba families earned their livelihood by grazing livestock on common lands and engaging in small farming.[8] An increase in population crowded the Pueblo and nomadic peoples, causing them to rebel. In response to the Indigenous hostilities, the Spaniards set up colonies in Rio Arriba that served as a buffer between the hacendados (owners of large haciendas), the Rio Abajo colonists, and the natives. Communal grants encouraged populating the frontier. Throughout the province, poor shepherds depended on *partido* contracts—raising sheep for large owners and taking half the increase in stock. While the Spanish elites ran large sheep- and cattle-ranching operations, the poor survived through subsistence farming supplemented by the grazing of sheep.

A few northern New Mexican villagers coexisted with the Pueblo people—trading and occasionally intermarrying. Denise Holladay Damico writes, "'Hispanos' grew the same crops as Puebloan and, like the people of the Pueblos, used irrigation ditches.[9] Foreign trappers and traders periodically intruded on the isolated province. Mexican Independence accelerated the decline of this way of life."[10] Increased population and privatization of resources strained the infrastructure. All the while trade caravans traveled along the Camino Real that linked New Mexico to Chihuahua and the rest of Mexico. By 1804, exports to Chihuahua reached 60,000 pesos per annum.

Land and water were New Mexico's prime resources; they were at the heart of the Puebloan grievances against the Spaniards, many of whom, according to Roxanne Dunbar-Ortiz, attempted to "build large hereditary estates using Pueblo lands and labor."[11] The Rio Grande that began its 1,800-mile trek in mountains of Colorado bound the people together.[12] The Rio Grande furnished a good part of the water that enabled farm communities to form along the Rio and its tributaries.

Josiah Gregg wrote in the early 1840s about New Mexico's irrigation system:

> One acequia madre (mother ditch) suffices generally to convey water for the irrigation of an entire valley. Or at least for all the fields of one town or settlement... Where there is not a superabundance of water, which is the case on the smaller streams, each farmer has his day, or portion of a day allotted to him for irrigation; and at no other time is he permitted to extend water from the acequia madre.[13]

The Santa Fé Trail: The Trojan Horse

During the seventeenth century, the Spanish colonizers traded with the Comanche and Utes for elk, buffalo, beaver, and other hides. This trade increased after the Louisiana Purchase of 1803 and after Mexican independence in 1821. North Americans secretly traded with New Mexicans after the Louisiana Purchase. By 1821, the Santa Fé Trail ran between Independence, Missouri with Santa Fé, New Mexico with annual caravans trekking from Missouri to Santa Fé.[14] This opening connected merchants to the Camino Real that ran from Mexico City to Santa Fé. Meanwhile, North American commercial interests operated out of Taos where Charles Bent, the leader of the area's Americans, built Bent's Fort. Bent married a prominent Mexican woman, establishing ties with New Mexican merchants and elites.[15]

According to Deena González, "In the 1820s, as many as one hundred American merchants resided in Santa Fé [alone] and by the 1830s, another hundred had arrived."[16] In the late 1840s, Santa Fé was a town of 2,000–6,000 inhabitants. El Paso del Norte, established in 1659 on the south side of the river, by 1805 had a population of over 6,000 (shortly afterward, El Paso was no longer counted as part of New Mexico).[17]

At first, Mexican merchant/s straded almost exclusively with the Indigenous Peoples. The control changed after Bent monopolized the traffic. Nevertheless, economic self-interest forced alliances between North American Hispanos, and by the 1840s, Mexican merchants sent their children to parochial schools in St. Louis and to business houses (as apprentices).[18]

Before the opening of the Santa Fé Trail, New Mexicans traded extensively with Chihuahua, whose merchants controlled the inter province commerce. New Mexico's and Chihuahua's histories were interdependent, jointly warring against the Apache. Indigenous prisoners of wars were sold in the slave market of Parral, Chihuahua where many labored in the mines. The Apache slave trade enriched New Mexican governors such as Luis de Rosas.[19] Trade between the two provinces led to the growth of the El Paso del Norte area where merchants from Sonora and Chihuahua migrated. After 1826, New Mexicans organized caravans to Chihuahua. U.S. economic infiltration set a pattern, paving the way for the invasion of New Mexico. They followed the old Camino Real that ran from Chihuahua to Santa Fé, where it linked to St. Louis via the Santa Fé Trail. American merchants operated over this route before the U.S. military entered Santa Fé in 1846.[20]

The opening of the Santa Fé Trail proved disruptive to the self-sufficient northern villages. It strengthened the capitalist class, and it increased the gap between *los ricos* and the poor villagers. By the 1830s, New Mexicans worked in mercantile activities such as the sale of livestock, trade with native communities, and commercial stores. Trade allowed them to expand their property holdings at the expense of subsistence farmers. Ten years after the American initial presence they began to control property in Santa Fé.

Meanwhile, the Santa Fé Trail trade increased from $15,000 in 1822 to $90,000 four years later to a quarter of a million annually by the early 1830s. In 1846, the Santa Fé Trail transported a million dollars' worth of merchandise. Although North Americans monopolized a major share of the profits, a handful of New Mexicans profited handsomely. Even before the American invasion, wealthy New York merchant Edwin Norris and Prussian born trader German Albert Speyer conducted business directly with New Mexicans.[21]

Gringo Go Home

Americans' racist and monopolistic tendencies in Texas did not go unnoticed. Many locals resented the governor's grants to the newcomers—prominent among the critics was Fray Antonio José Martínez.[22] In addition, they resented the partnerships of Americans and influential New Mexicans. Many were imperial designs of the Texas Republic, which claimed as its western boundary the Rio Grande.

In 1841, General Hugh McLeod's expedition of about 300 Texans into New Mexico increased New Mexican angst. Governor Manuel Armijo sounded the alarm; Armijo tricked the Texans into believing he had a large army, bluffing them into surrendering. McLeod claimed it was a trading expedition. Conspiracy was rife and New Mexicans blamed Bent and his associates for the invasion and imprisoned him in Santa Fé. A mob attacked the house of U.S. consul Manuel Alvárez, who they accused of complicity with the Texans; Alvárez was a close ally of Charles Bent.

White Americans retaliated, and a guerrilla war with racial overtones followed. Through 1842 and 1843, clashes were more frequent. New Mexicans temporarily banished Bent, accusing him of smuggling, theft, and collusion with the Texans, harboring thieves, and selling firearms to natives. In 1843, Colonel Jacob Snively attacked a New Mexican caravan, wounding 23 Mexicans. Padre Antonio José Martínez, leader of the anti-American party, wrote to Antonio López de Santa Anna, warning him of U.S. encroachments and their construction of forts on the Arkansas and Platte Rivers.[23]

The American Invasion

5.2 Explain how the actions of the colonizing peoples of New Mexico reflected their racism and exceptionalism.

In June 1846, Colonel Stephen Watts Kearny led the Army of the West into New Mexico. As Kearny approached New Mexico, he sent the well-known merchant James W. Magoffin to Governor Armijo with an ultimatum. U.S. authorities would not bother them if they surrendered; if they did not, they would suffer the consequences.[24]

By August Kearny captured Las Vegas, New Mexico, and prepared to attack Santa Fé. Armijo fled south without firing a shot, allowing the Army of the West to enter the capital without resistance. In all probability negotiators bribed Armijo. On August 22, Kearny issued a proclamation to the people of New Mexico, announcing his intention of occupying the province as a permanent possession of the United States. This was the first statement that revealed the true purpose of the war. Believing that New Mexican resistance was broken, Kearny left for California on September 25; in mid-December, Colonel Alexander W. Doniphan was sent south to conquer Chihuahua. Doniphan wrote, "A people conquered but yesterday could have no friendly feeling for their conquerors, who have taken possession of their country, changed its laws and appointed new officers, principally foreigners."[25]

The Myth of the Bloodless Conquest

As with most societies, those who are colonized change. Some remain in the past with imperial pretensions of their own exceptionalism. Many elite New Mexicans were unhappy with Mexican rule and sided with the Americans. At the same time, the harshness of the U.S. occupation had been unexpected and it drove many influential New Mexicans to conspire against the American occupying army; among the rebels were Tomás Ortiz, Colonel Diego Archuleta, Padre Antonio José Martínez, and Reverend Juan Felipe Ortiz, vicar general of the diocese. They planned to ambush U.S. authorities during the Christmas season. However, Governor Bent's spies uncovered the plot.[26]

Soon afterward, on January 19, 1847, Pablo Montoya, a Mexican peasant, and Tomasito Romero, a Pueblo, led an attack on the Americans, killing Governor Bent and five other important members of the American bloc.[27] Nearly every village in Rio Arriba supported the revolt. The rebel army numbered over 1,000. The role of Padre Martínez is unclear; his brother Pascual allegedly was part of the revolt.[28] Padre Martínez apparently attempted to restrain the rebels; a realist, he knew that an unorganized revolt would fail and that the consequences would be disastrous.

U.S. Colonel Sterling Price and his army retaliated and attacked some 4,500 Mexicans and Pueblo natives. The army slaughtered the rebels on the snow-covered ground outside the insurgent capital of Taos. Meanwhile, Rio Abajo elites supported Price, shedding light on Simone de Beauvoir's statement in *The Ethics of Ambiguity* that "the oppressor would not be so strong if he did not have accomplices among the oppressed themselves; mystification is one of the forms of oppression."[29] The rebels retreated to the Pueblo's church, defending themselves from intense artillery fire. During the brutal attack the U.S. troops killed about 150 Mexicans. Although a declaration of war between the United States and Mexico had been issued on May 13, 1846 the surviving resistors were tried for treason.

According to historian Hubert Howe Bancroft, "The Taos Trial was controversial from the beginning. First, a state of war existed and there was a question as to whether the defendants could be tried for treason. Moreover, the judges and jurors were not impartial; close friends and relatives of the slain occupiers served as judge and jury: for example, a close friend of the slain governor served as a judge, and relatives of other occupiers also served. The brother of the slain governor was foreman of the grand jury. Another juror was a relative of the dead sheriff. One American eyewitness reported hearing a French juror who did not speak English asked the American jury foreman what he should do: 'Why, hang them, of course; what did you come here for?' Jurors were quoted as saying they had come to hang the defendants."[30] The tribunal sentenced 15 rebels to death—one for high treason.[31]

The termination of the Taos Revolt did not end tensions. Colonel Price's despotic occupation percolated the resentment, and Manuel Cortés, a fugitive of the Taos rebellion, led a group in guerrilla warfare. The military occupation of New Mexico continued to 1851. Even afterward the new governor, James S. Calhoun acknowledged that "treason is rife."[32]

In order to live with the memory of the repression, some New Mexicans invented the myth of the "bloodless conquest of New Mexico" that New Mexicans welcomed the North American troops as liberators. This myth survives to this day despite the fact that most of the 60,000 people living in New Mexico were not enthusiastic about the U.S. invasion; considerable anti-American feeling existed because of white American attitudes of racial superiority.

This form of rationalization or colonial mentality is not uncommon in times of colonial conquests. Oppressed groups within society separate themselves believing that one is better than the other, as in the case of social castes. Conquered people internalize a colonial mentality, not wanting to associate with their own people lest their low status rub off on them. Attitudes of ethnic or cultural inferiority are internalized and many conquered societies take on the belief that the cultural values of the colonizer are inherently superior. The British, American, and Spanish conquests shared the colonizers' racial and cultural attitudes. According to New Mexico Professor of Law Laura Gómez, during the invasion of New Mexico, racist feelings ran deep and many white American soldiers believed that New Mexicans belonged to a mongrel nation whose women would contaminate the soldiers upon contact.[33]

Inventing Whiteness

Most of New Mexico's early colonizers were descendants of people recruited from the interior of Mexico and Zacatecas, and were related to Mexican families in Chihuahua and Sonora. They did not immigrate to New Mexico directly from Spain. Yet many New Mexicans chose to call themselves *Hispanos*, or Spanish Americans, rather than Mexicans. It was a self-deception that they were descendants of the original settlers and related to Spanish conquistadors.[34] According to them, New Mexico was isolated from the rest of the Southwest and Mexico during the colonial era, so New Mexicans remained racially pure and were Europeans, in contrast to the mestizo (half-breed) Mexicans.[35] This is historically incorrect, and in addition it can be seen that New Mexican colonials bore striking similarities to colonials in Chihuahua and Sonora.

For most of their history, many New Mexicans perpetuated the illusion that they could distance themselves from the intense racism and hatred toward Mexicans, allowing them to better their economic and, sometimes, their social status by separating themselves from the Mexicans. Most New Mexicans are not descendants of the colonials who arrived with Oñate in 1598. Over the years, many mixed with the Pueblo and with Mexican Indigenous People who settled there. New Mexican scholar Nancie González writes that it was not until the twentieth century that New Mexicans denied their Mexican identity.

During the 1910s and 1920s, an influx of Mexican laborers entered New Mexico, along with white Texans, Oklahomans, and other southerners settled in the eastern plains. The latter brought their prejudices of color, intensifying discrimination against Mexicans. According to González, some New Mexicans did what was expedient and pleaded with Americans, "You don't like Mexicans, and we don't like them either, but we are Spanish-Americans, not Mexicans." By this simple denial of their ethnicity, New Mexicans thought they could escape discrimination and qualify for higher-paying jobs, which in most cases did not happen. Some were white but a different shade of white.

The *manitos*, a nickname for Mexicans from New Mexico, (from *hermanitos*, or "little brothers") state of mind cannot solely be attributed to U.S. racism. New Mexicans' racial prejudices were deeply rooted in the Spanish conquest and colonization. "Thinking white" was encouraged by the Spanish colonial pecking order (see Chapter 2). Thinking white was a state of mind, which facilitated the exploitation of the castas. Color determined purity and was a sign of prominence and/or insignificance. That is why, between Mexicans and people of color overall, a bleaching-out took place, a phenomenon that occurs consciously or unconsciously, encouraging individuals to supposedly marry "up"—that is, marry someone lighter than they are.[36]

New Mexicans felt like strangers in their own land; consequently many returned to their Mexican homeland. According to Samuel E. Sisneros,

> Beginning in 1849, more than 150 families from central and southern Texas, a small group from California, close to 4,000 people from Nuevo México, along with approximately seven hundred people from the present El Paso Lower Valley (Socorro, Ysleta and San Elizario), chose to retain their Mexican citizenship and emigrate. They followed the receding and consequently redrawn border dividing México and the United States and crossed over to the Republic of México.[37]

The Mexican government actively recruited Mexican citizens to return to the homeland, and, according to a Mexican commissioner, many New Mexicans agreed to return. Undoubtedly, more would have returned if New Mexican authorities had not placed obstacles in their way, violating the terms of the Treaty of Guadalupe Hidalgo.[38] Later in the decade, New Mexican officials retaliated against those who surrendered their American citizenship and would not allow them to reverse their decisions nor would they let them hold public office. For example, in 1855 Miguel A. Otero successfully challenged the election of Father José Manuel Gallegos to the assembly; Gallegos had kept his Mexican citizenship and allegedly was sympathetic to the Taos Revolt of 1847.

The joint boundary commission's drawing of the border got off to a bumpy start. John Russell Bartlett and the Mexican commissioners met in the El Paso, Texas, to resolve the location of the southern boundary of New Mexico. Several serious discrepancies were found in the official Disturnell Treaty map used by the framers of the Treaty of Guadalupe Hidalgo to set the boundaries. Bartlett and the Mexican Commissioner General Pedro García Conde reached a compromise in the spring of 1851. The ink was not dry before federal, state, and local representatives from New Mexico and the rest of the country accused Bartlett of giving "their" land to Mexico. This angered Mexican authorities in Chihuahua who accused the United States of wanting to provoke Mexico into another war in order to seize more land. The rhetoric got so heated that Mexican troops were put on alert. The dispute remained an issue until the United States pressured Mexico into signing the Gadsden Treaty of 1853.[39]

The Transition

5.3 Describe the operations of the Santa Fé Ring designed in maintaining the caste system.

According to New Mexican historian Rubén Sálaz Márquez, in 1846 about 6,000 persons, 10 percent of New Mexican families, lived on small land claims without titles. An estimated 3,000 persons, or 1 out of every 26 New Mexicans, were small farmers. They overwhelmingly lived on community grants; they held residential and agricultural lands sharing the common lands. The water, pasture, and forests were communal. Under the new order, water and open space such as forests and pastures were private property and their value was determined by the marketplace.[40]

Compared to most American western territories, New Mexico's population was dense. Many New Mexicans favored statehood since it would allow them to vote for the governor and judges. A small percentage, mostly New Mexican elites, favored a territorial form of government because they could circumvent electoral process and directly lobby and influence the selection of public officials. Under the territorial form of government, the president of the United States appointed the governor, and the governor appointed the judges and other territorial officials. The president designated the land surveyor. Hence, under the territorial system the people were limited to voting for the territorial assembly and local offices.

During the 1850s horses and mules increased from 13,733 to 21,357; head of cattle from 32,977 to 88,729; and sheep from 377,271 to 830,116. The demand for beef, wool, and transportation animals increased during the California Gold Rush. Wagons and mules carried freight, charging between 9 and 10 cents a pound to ship goods to St. Louis or Chihuahua. Trade fairs were popular throughout the territory. The profits from this trade encouraged the ricos to expand their holdings, putting further stress on the Pueblos and the villagers, as cattle and sheep owners encroached on their land, pushing many villagers out of their river valleys. In the 1860s, settlers from the northern villages moved from the Rio Arriba area to the northwest and from the Chama Valley to the San Juan area. By the 1870s, wealthy and powerful cattlemen expanded their holdings in Rio Arriba, squeezing out many small farmers. The new order forced small farmers to rely solely on sheep.[41]

The Illusion of Inclusion

On June 2, 1851, the first New Mexican territorial assembly convened. It was dominated by the Hispano elite. It did publish the proceedings in Spanish and English. Rio Abajo hacendados, land speculators, the Catholic Church hierarchy, and merchants controlled the assembly. In 1850, 25,085 adults could not read or write in the territory, with that number increasing to 32,785 a decade later. New Mexico had only 17 public schools with 33 teachers throughout the territory.

Although the territorial legislature required public education, it was up to local taxpayers to support the schools. Voters more often did not approve school funding. Better off New Mexicans who could afford an education sent their children to Catholic boarding schools. Later in the 1800s, Protestant missionaries introduced inexpensive education at mission schools, but the Catholic Church opposed these schools and made deals with legislators to keep Catholic control of education. Access to schooling depended not only on wealth but also on color. Mexicans were more limited than their white counterparts, and by 1913 only 7 of 87 students graduating from New Mexico's public schools were of Mexican origin.

According to Sarah Deutsch, "At the time of the Emancipation Proclamation there were some six hundred Indian slaves in the territory. The territorial legislature was not thinking only of Negroes when, in 1859, it passed an act 'for the protection of slave property in the territory.'"[42] Hispano legislators refused to abolish debt-peonage or Native American slavery until the U.S. Congress did so in 1867. As mentioned, they did not fund public education, favoring a parochial school system that exclusively served the rich. It was not until 1891 that the legislators approved an education funding bill, and this occurred because Congress was about to pass one. Statehood was inevitable, and compulsory education was a prerequisite for statehood.

Gringos and Ricos

By the Civil War (1861–1865), the alliance with American elites was sealed. The ricos controlled the New Mexican peasant and village vote. Through the legislature, they could block policies that did not serve their interests. The arrangement continued until a more aggressive and educated white American entered the territory following the Civil War. These cabals used their political influence in Washington, D.C., to get the appointment of the governor and friendly bureaucrats.[43]

The Santa Fé Ring manipulated territorial politics through smaller satellite rings. In the two decades following the Civil War, ring members grabbed an estimated 80 percent of the New Mexico land grants. The U.S. government approved 48 of 212 grants before 1891. The 212 grants were a fraction of the approximately 1,000 grants that Spain and the Mexican government granted. Out of the 8.5 million acres confirmed, the Court of Private Claims reduced that amount to 2 million acres. The excessive cost of litigation discouraged many Mexican grantees from filing their claims. The Santa Fé Ring monopolized the territorial bureaucracy. Money and influence centralized control of the territory. Lawyers and speculators, through intimidation, bribery, and fraud, wielded enormous power and made huge profits.[44]

In 1850, there were 1,578 Americans; by 1900 there were 50,000. Meanwhile, the number of people of Mexican origin was about 55,000 and Pueblo about 5,000 in 1850. The number increased to just over 93,000 of Mexican origin in 1900, and the Pueblo increased to just over 8,000.[45] The battle was in the "Communities [that] were located on running rivers or streams, often in mountain valleys. The valleys contained the best land for crop cultivation. Each individual family received a 'long-lot' of this agricultural land, near or on the river."[46] Monopolization and privatization of these resources would uproot them.

How New Mexico was Looted

As mentioned, the Santa Fé Ring began operating after the Civil War. In 1848, private and communal land grants encompassed 15 million square acres. Congress established a surveyor's office with broad powers that put the burden on the grantees to prove ownership. The land could not be sold until titles were confirmed. By 1863 only 25 private and town grants and 17 Pueblo grants were filed. New Mexico was a territory, so Washington, D.C. appointed its lackeys as governors. A small cabal controlled the police—local, state, and federal; through violence it intimidated its foes. The ring further tightened its control through its members' banks that gave them access to capital. Meanwhile, merchants and bankers charged excessive interest rates, forcing New Mexicans to borrow money at extremely high rates. They used their land as collateral, enabling banks to foreclose when the Mexican landowners were unable to meet payments.[47]

After the Civil War, the capitalist-friendly U.S. government subsidized corporate agriculturalists by supplying them with large quantities of water at government expense. Reclamation projects changed the balance of nature on the Rio Grande with some areas receiving to much or too little water. The people did not have a say as to where the government built dams. Yet New Mexican farmers paid for "improvements" through taxes whether they wanted them or not; when they could not pay the increased taxes, their land was foreclosed. Mechanization gave farm corporations an edge in the production of cash crops such as cotton. Small farmers could not compete, because they did not have the capital to mechanize.

Further, the federal government granted large concessions of land to railroad corporations and to institutions of higher learning. Conservationists, concerned by the industry's rape of timber and recreation land, pressed the federal government to create national forests. The custodial conservationists would not allow shepherds to graze their flocks on national forest lands without permits that increasingly went to the large operators. New Mexicans lost 2 million acres of public land and 1.7 million acres of communal land. Since community and communal holdings were more common than individual grants and farmers had less money, they were more vulnerable. More than 80 percent of the grant holders lost their lands. The slowness of litigation fell hardest on small farmers and herders; they did not have the means to survive the process. Historian Deena González writes that within "ten years of the signing of the treaty ending the war, ninety percent of New Mexicans had lost their lands."[48]

Corruption, Fraud, Intimidation

The Santa Fé Ring comprised mostly of lawyers who used government contacts to corner real estate markets. Its leaders, Thomas B. Catron, Stephen B. Elkins, and LeBaron Bradford Prince were mostly Republicans, but there was no shortage of Democrats or elite Mexicans. Most officeholders were in one way or another associated with the ring. This included Max Frost, editor of *The New Mexican*, the territory's most influential newspaper.

Catron, the ring's leader, arrived in New Mexico in the late 1860s and eventually became U.S. attorney general for the territory. Through litigation, purchases, and fraud, Catron acquired more than one million acres of land. Stephen Elkins, a close friend of Catron, arrived in 1863. Eight years later, he was president of the First National Bank of Santa Fé, and represented the ring's interests in Washington. He became a delegate to the U.S. Congress, later serving as President Benjamin Harrison's secretary of war.[49] In 1884, Elkins chaired the executive committee of the National Republican Committee. LeBaron Bradford Prince was from New York, where he participated in machine politics. President Chester A. Arthur offered him the governorship of New Mexico, but he declined and instead became the chief justice of New Mexico in 1879. In the 1890s, he became the governor of the territory. The cabal formed joint stock companies and private investment pools. Speculators and numerous smaller rings were active in land deals, railroads, mills, farming, small-scale manufacturing, and shipping.[50] The ring's most nefarious caper was its takeover of the Maxwell Land Grant: Charles Beaubien and Guadalupe Miranda received the grant in 1841. Fray Martínez, the leader of the Mexican clergy, objected to the grant because it was, according to Martínez, part of the Taos community grant, and he said that the grant was being given to the North American clique that at the time was becoming more numerous in New Mexico. Over the next few years, Beaubien, Native Americans, Mexican tenant farmers, Mexican villagers, and American squatters contested parts of the Maxwell Grant.

In 1858, Lucien Maxwell, the son-in-law of Beaubien, bought out Miranda's share, as well as his father-in-law's interests in the land grant. Years later, after the death of his father-in-law, Maxwell purchased other shares, for a total outlay of no more than $50,000. In 1869, Maxwell sold his grant to a British combine, which included members of the Santa Fé Ring, for $1.5 million. After the combine took control of the Maxwell Land Grant, it encountered problems with tenant farmers.

Meanwhile, in 1866 gold was discovered on the property, attracting prospectors. The title to the land became even murkier when the federal government claimed part of the grant for a reservation and park. Taking a cue from these challenges, Mexican and white American squatters occupied the land, believing it would become public domain. If it did, they would be entitled to between 20 and 50 acres of irrigated land. Thus far the government had not surveyed the grant.

Lucien Maxwell estimated the grant as measuring between 32,000 and 97,424 acres. However, by the time the ring reconfigured it, the grant was 1,714,765 acres. The Mexican Colonization Act limited grants of this category to 22 leagues (97,000 acres). A consequence was that the altered Maxwell Grant threatened land titles in Colfax County. Colfax residents prepared to defend their property rights. On September 14, 1875, T. J. Tolby, a Methodist minister and an opposition leader, was murdered. Vigilantes accused Cruz Vega, the Mexican constable of the Cimarron precinct, of the homicide; he denied any involvement but they lynched him anyway. The hanging set off a bloody war between the Maxwell Land Grant Company and the white squatters. An alliance between the white squatters and the Mexicanos would have given them a clear advantage. But, because of the racism of the squatters, it did not happen, and Mexicans remained neutral during the decade of the 70s.[51]

It was not until the 1880s that more New Mexicans contested the ownership of the Maxwell Land Grant. In 1881, squatters formed the Squatters Club to raise money for litigation; however, only one New Mexican was a member. Slowly alliances developed, and by 1887 the Mexican and American squatters rode together. Meanwhile, the combine brought legal proceedings against the squatters. M. P. Pels, the company agent, promised cash settlements if they would abandon their claims. On July 23, 1888, 75 armed Mexicans and Americans prevented the sheriff and the company from evicting them. Jacinto Santistevan and his son Julian were among the resistance leaders. The unity was short-lived, as divisions arose between the two races. The failure of the white farmers to support Mexican farmers when the company agent evicted them from Vermejo Park angered the Mexicans, who vowed never to help the gringos again.

On February 21, 1891, after the rebels killed its business agent, the company retaliated by organizing a 23-man posse to track down the killers. Mexican rebels burned crops, cut fences, destroyed buildings, and slaughtered cattle. As the spring wore on, armed outbreaks became more common. In responding to the stiff resistance, the company changed its tactics and began to give Mexicans preferential treatment, hoping to turn U.S. farmers against them. By 1893, litigation took its toll and Santistevan left the area. After this point, many farmers capitulated. A Dutch combine placed the management of the grant in the hands of the Maxwell Land and Railway Company.

Throughout the violence, the Santa Fé group shamelessly manipulated the legal system. The territorial legislature passed laws authorizing the courts to partition grants when even the smallest owner of the property requested a partition. This meant that the ring could buy out a minority holder and force the sale of the entire grant. The territorial legislature passed a law in January 1876 that annexed Colfax County to Taos County. This development was significant since the Taos judges were controlled by the ring, and hence they sided with the ring's interests in dispossessing small farmers. Because the ring controlled the appointment of the governor, the governor refused to intervene in the ring's wars or fraudulent deals. The appointment of John T. Elkins, brother of Stephen B. Elkins, to survey the Maxwell Grant put the final nail in the coffin. The Maxwell holdings included millions of acres in southern Colorado and northern New Mexico,[52] stolen by land grabbers and their brokers by using the state and federal governments. Today, the federal government owns 34.9 percent of the land in New Mexico. The state government owns 12 percent, while federal Indigenous reservations own 6.8 percent. Thus the state and federal governments together own 53.7 percent of New Mexico, with the U.S. Forest Service controlling one-third of the state's land.[53]

The Legend of the Lincoln County War

World events affected happenings in New Mexico. In the 1870s, increased demand for beef and mutton in the United Kingdom and in the eastern United States led to the growth of the beef industry and intensified competition for the open range in New Mexico, leading to range wars and land speculation. The land grabs greatly affected the small subsistence farmers and sheepherders.

The arrival of large numbers of Americans seeking to profit by running cattle on the open rangeland in places like Lincoln County pushed Mexicans off the land. The cowboys clashed with the Mexican sheepherders on the range, and invented the fiction that sheep and cattle could not graze on the same land. In the early 1870s, ring member Lawrence Gustave Murphy Gustave Murphy enjoyed a near-monopoly, supplying the government with beef for forts and reservations, and shutting out other cattlemen from the county. John H. Chisum, owner of the largest herds in the territory, challenged Murphy with the support of the local Mexican population. The outcome was the Lincoln County War.[54]

The Murphy clan hired outlaws to steal cattle for their beef-supply enterprise. Many Texans, renowned for their hatred of Mexicans, joined the Murphy gang. By January 27, 1874, the Santa Fé *New Mexican* editorialized that Lincoln County had exploded into an "unfortunate war between the Texans and the Mexicans."[55] The newspaper intentionally distracted the public's attention by focusing on racial conflicts instead of the economic causes of the conflict. The war broke down along racial and political lines. The Murphy group controlled Republican Party politics, while Chisum represented the Democrats.

Juan Patrón was the Mexican leader in Lincoln. North American outlaws had killed his father. Born in 1855 in La Placita, he attended parochial schools in New Mexico, eventually graduating from the University of Notre Dame in Indiana. Friends described him as honest, studious, and industrious. In 1878, as a delegate to the territorial House of Representatives, he was elected Speaker. Patrón also served without pay as Lincoln County's sole schoolteacher.

The Lincoln County War began in the spring of 1877 when Englishman John H. Tunstall opened a mercantile store that competed with the Murphy establishment. Alexander McSween, a lawyer, and John Chisum were Tunstall's principal allies. The Chisum–Tunstall group opened a bank that competed with the First National Bank, controlled by Stephen Elkins and Catron. Most Mexicans joined Juan Patrón and backed the Tunstall group. Frequent shootouts followed. The ring hired the Jesse Evans gang to launch a reign of terror. The ring murdered Tunstall, whereupon his supporters—among whom was the notorious William Bonnie, better known as Billy the Kid—sought revenge. The ring attacked Patrón in the newspaper *New Mexican*, charging that he was the leader of the county's lawless Mexican element.[56]

Governor Samuel B. Axtell refused to intervene. The murders of Reverend Tolby in Colfax and of Tunstall, a British subject, attracted national and international attention. Catron and Elkins supported the ring and lobbied on its behalf in Washington. On September 4, 1878, U.S. President Rutherford B. Hayes appointed General Lew Wallace governor. Hayes told Wallace to clean up the mess in Lincoln County. Upon arriving in New Mexico, Wallace formed a local militia, led by Juan Patrón, and order restored in 1879.

Because of harassment, Patrón moved to Puerto de Luna, several hundred miles away from Lincoln County. A cowboy named Mitch Maney murdered Patrón while he was having a drink in a saloon with a friend. Although Maney was a penniless cowboy, one of the most prestigious territorial legal firms represented him. The prosecutor was none other than Thomas Catron. The trial resulted in a hung jury, and Maney was never retried.

Mexican shepherds and Texas cowboys continued to fight over land and water; by the 1880s, the cattle raisers eliminated the Mexican as a competitor. During the decade, the conflict degenerated into a race war. With railroads linking Lincoln County to national and international markets, time favored white Americans. During the same period, railroads made wool more accessible to the world market; soon nearly three million head of sheep roamed the territory, most belonging to white Americans.[57]

Socialization

5.4 Explain how the split in the Catholic Church reflected social divisions in New Mexico.

Historian Deena González writes, "Conquest and colonization impoverished most of the residents of Santa Fé and perhaps much of the New Mexican north. It disempowered women, who had previously exercised certain rights guaranteed by Spanish law. And it made most Spanish-Mexicans dependent on wages earned in jobs controlled by Americans."[58] The new merchant capitalists displayed racial and cultural prejudices toward the resident population throughout the territory—more evident in places like Santa Fé because of the large numbers of Americans. The first thing they noticed was the New Mexican women's dark skin. One soldier wrote, "Instead of the black-eyed Spanish women, we found ourselves amongst a swarthy, copper-colored, half-Indian race."[59] Professor González reminds us that 75 percent of the female adult population (over the age of 15) labored as domestics, laundresses, or seamstresses in 1860. This number increased during the American "liberation." The already marginalized extended family networks, held together by rich and poor women alike, were destroyed. However, there was a difference between rich and poor: Women with powerful family ties were better able to negotiate their space.

Intermarriage continued between Americans and New Mexican elites. In the overall scheme, the number was relatively small if one considers that only 239 Americans lived in Santa Fé versus 4,000 New Mexicans.[60] As in Texas, intermarriage became less popular with the passage of time and the arrival of white women.

The American Catholic Church

The Catholic Church split into a Mexican and a American Catholic Church. The leader of the Mexican clergy was Father Antonio José Martínez, known as "the priest of Taos." Born in Abiquiú in Rio Arriba County, on January 7, 1793, Martínez married, but his wife and daughter died and he became a priest. In 1824, Martínez was the pastor of a parish in Taos, where after two years he established a seminary. Through his graduates, Martínez's ideas spread throughout New Mexico. From 1830 to 1836, Martínez served in the New Mexico's departmental assembly, and in 1835, he published a newspaper called *El Creúsculo (The Dawn)*. Martínez frequently criticized the Church for allowing priests to charge excessive fees. He also opposed the granting of large land grants, insisting that the land should go to the people. Under white rule he served in the legislature from 1851 to 1853.

In 1851, the new vicar general, Fray J. B. Lamy, arrived in New Mexico. French by birth, Lamy worked in the Baltimore diocese and in the mid-1850s became a bishop. Lamy's partisans claim that Lamy revitalized religion in New Mexico by founding schools, building churches, and increasing the number of priests from 10 to 37. Through alliances with government officials, Lamy kept control of education. His critics allege that Lamy made his reforms on the backs of the poor, and they condemn him for his failure to speak out against the injustices suffered by the people.

Lamy was a product of post–revolutionary France and he viewed liberalism as anti-Catholic. Lamy began almost immediately to pattern New Mexican churches after French models based on orthodoxy. The controversy over the separation of Church and state profoundly influenced him as did the debate over the infallibility of the pope.[61] To strengthen the New Mexican Church and insulate it from the challenge of the Protestant sects that by 1890 were 5 percent of the population, Lamy taxed the poor and collected church fees for baptism, marriage, and other rites, which is a criticism that could be directed at the institution itself. There is also some sentiment that Mexican priests had been more lenient in their collection.[62]

Lamy purged the Holy Brotherhood of Penitentes, an association popular among the poor of northern New Mexico. (Indeed, confraternities were a part of the culture of the Spanish and then Mexican churches.) Descended from the Third Order of St. Francis of Assisi, it practiced public flagellation and, during Holy Week, imitated the ordeals of Christ. It was a secret society, to which prominent leaders such as Antonio José Martínez belonged. Established Mexicans like Miguel A. Otero disdained the Brotherhood, seeing it as backward and ignorant. Lamy and his successors persecuted members, denying them the sacraments.[63]

Soon after Lamy's arrival, a power struggle developed between him and the Mexican clergy, many of whom were Martínez's former students. Critics attacked Martínez and his followers for not being celibate (which may or may not have been true). Defenders say that the real reason was the involvement of the Mexican clergy in temporal matters, especially their role as advocates for the people. Martínez avoided an open rift with Lamy, keeping quiet even when Lamy excommunicated Martínez's close friends. When Lamy sent a letter to all the parishes insisting that priests collect tithes and first fruits and instructing them to withhold the sacraments from those who did not comply, Martínez rebelled. Lamy excommunicated Martínez.

Lamy set the pattern for church-state cooperation and the church's almost unconditional support of the state. Writing in his later years, Lamy wrote, "Our Mexican population has quite a sad future. Very few of them will be able to follow modern progress. They cannot be compared to the Americans in the way of intellectual liveliness, ordinary skills, and industry; they will thus be scorned and considered an inferior race."[64]

The New Mexican Diaspora

5.5 Explain how the market economy changed the relationship of New Mexicans to the land.

The Civil War brought further demand for beef. Within 25 years newcomers flocked to New Mexico with the arrival of the railroad bringing big capital: railroads, lumber mills, coal mines, and commercial agriculture and stock enterprises. Paying jobs momentarily gave Mexican males opportunity, but for many it changed their relationship to the land.

In the villages, farmers owned a small plot of land, a house, and some farmland. Most holdings in Rio Arriba allowed villagers to use pastures and the forests in common. In the new economy men became seasonal migrants or they migrated to the mines of southern Colorado. Meanwhile, women often plowed, harrowed, hoed, harvested, and threshed. Women also herded and sheared sheep collectively. Subsistence farming was further marginalized, and seasonal wage labor became a necessity for families to survive.[65]

The merchants of northern New Mexico and southern Colorado were not as powerful as the hacendados of Rio Abajo or the cattlemen on the territorial ranges—they were wealthy, however. As time went by, more families barely survived on what they grew or raised. The villages became overcrowded, the land overused, and the pasture depleted. In Rio Arriba County, sheepmen grazed 21 sheep per square mile; by 1900, this number increased to about 120.[66]

"El Agua Es Vida"

New Mexico's "acequia culture" is not unique—it is a product of the Spanish conquest and Pueblo cultures. As Denise Holladay Damico points out, it was part of the Spanish Imperial project of the colonization in New Spain's far northern frontier. The acequia was often the only local form of government that villagers had daily contact with. This was the same whether the villager lived in northern New Mexico, Chihuahua, or Sonora. Communities were settled along running rivers or streams, as well as mountain valleys.

After plots were allocated, the villagers dug the acequia to irrigate their agricultural lots. An intensification of the market economy began in the late eighteenth century. Forces such mining provided markets. In the nineteenth century the opening of the Santa Fé Trail in 1821 and the Treaty of Guadalupe Hidalgo in 1848 led to increased commercialization. In New Mexico the latter two events were a boon to locations such as Taos where competition for land caused tensions between locals and incoming Americans. The resultant tension drew a line under the interconnections between land and water disputes.[67]

This same process occurred in Chihuahua where acequias were dug in the nineteenth century. Disputes over water were common. Disputants often physically diverted the water into their ditch, or sabotaged their foe's canal. They sued in order to resolve water conflicts. Frequently commercial farmers encroached on mission and Indigenous lands or bought out other villagers. The land was almost worthless without water and irrigated land had a much higher value. Disputes grew ugly during drought seasons or when an upriver community diverted too much water. Litigation was expensive in New Mexico and Chihuahua, placing added burdens on the litigants who were generally cash-strapped. Meanwhile, the land grant grabs threatened the Pueblo and the villagers. In the late nineteenth century, in northern Mexico and New Mexico, the railroads added pressure to privatize land and water.[68]

The railroad increased agricultural production and encroachments. On November 26, 1884, the Atlantic and Pacific Railroad ran tracks through Acoma Pueblo, taking ownership of the land along those tracks.

In the 1880s, railroads spread like a prairie fire coming down into New Mexico from Colorado, to Las Vegas, and then to Albuquerque, areas with plentiful water and standing populations. The tracks followed the old Spanish trail. In 1887, a state law was passed that allowed the incorporation of for-profit companies to privatize the sale of water. The law explicitly linked the supplying of water to "colonization" and "improvement" of lands. Water was brought in via pipeline or canal. The railroads played an active role. by attracting large numbers of workers and settlers. Because they contributed to the rapid-populating of the area.[69]

The Marketplace

In the new market economy, the land base was inadequate to support the needs of the villagers; by the turn of the century, at least 50 percent of them had partido contracts. "The seasonal nature of agricultural, livestock, and even wage income in the area resulted in the extension of so much credit that some 70 to 80 percent of the trade was of this nature," forcing the small merchants out of the market. In addition, New Mexicans were increasingly forced out of grazing land, because either they could not afford or they did not have the political connections to obtain grazing permits.

Women worked outside the home as midwives, took in boarders, and often contributed to the survival of the family through family gardens. "As the loss of land led to a decline in livestock, the garden grew in significance." Often the family sold the women's surplus *chili* for cash or goat's milk. (Chili was one of the principal cash crops.) "Picking the peppers from the plant, sorting, and stringing them supplied many of the women and some of the men living on small farms with a supplemental income." The gardens saved the family from buying outside goods. However, the transformation changed the sphere of so-called women's work. The women had been involved in plastering their homes for years, but by the twentieth century, many were doing this work for other villagers. Women also made money by weaving and mattress making.[70]

New Mexico in Colorado

By 1881 cattle and sheep replaced the buffalo herds on Colorado's plains, and steel was produced in Pueblo. The growth of coal mining in southern Colorado changed the landscape of Mexican Pueblos. Their plazas greatly resembled those in northern New Mexico with mining camps surrounding the villages. Over 11,000 New Mexicans migrated to southern Colorado during the first decade of the 1900s, but thousands of working-class Europeans also moved to southern Colorado during this period, making the Mexicans a minority. Discrimination was rampant; in 1880, suffragist Susan B. Anthony blamed the failure of her Colorado tour on the "Mexican greasers." Research on the Western Federation of *Miners' magazine*, from its inception to about 1920, clearly shows the organizers and the rank and file marginalization of Mexican miners.

Depressions and droughts occurred in the early 1890s, forcing ranchers to migrate to Colorado in search of wage work. Migrancy affected the entire family—women, men, and children all suffered. However, for many northern New Mexicans, migrancy became a way of life and they were able to earn enough money to help their families subsist and return home to plant or harvest their crops.[71]

In the next decade, the Dingley Tariff of 1897 increased sugar beet production in northern Colorado, attracting New Mexican migrant farm labor. Again, it increased the burden on the women and the family; since they all became migrants, family farm plots became neglected. By the end of the century, whole villages worked for others as farm laborers, shepherds, or railroad workers. They had to adjust to the changes, such as race and wage discrimination.

The Resistance

5.6 Outline the history of resistance to enclosure and railroad power in New Mexico.

San Miguel County is located in northern New Mexico, a mountainous land with the town of Las Vegas at its center. The tract of land that came to be known as the Las Vegas grant contained 500,000 acres of fine timber, agricultural, and grazing lands—the meadows of Las Vegas are especially rich.

The Spanish crown and then the Mexican government awarded grants to individuals in northern New Mexico because of indigenous attacks. However, most of the grantees failed to settle on their lands. By 1841, 131 families lived around Las Vegas. "On June 21, 1860, Congress confirmed 496,446 acres as belonging to the town of Las Vegas."[72] A large sector of the population of Las Vegas subsisted by grazing sheep and farming. According to Mexican law and traditions, the people held the land in common and could not sell it.

After the Civil War, the arrival of Americans threatened the New Mexican way of life. Whites had a tradition of squatting on public land. They had little knowledge or respect for village lands or the open range. In the 1880s, merchants and farmers with capital began to buy tracts from New Mexicans even though, according to Mexican law, the settlers, as users of the land, did not have the right to sell the land if such a sale conflicted with communal interests.

By 1875 whites owned nearly all the businesses. The arrival of the railroad concentrated wealth and within five years 84 percent of the merchants were white American. Women of all colors were peripheral; Mexican women worked as waitresses and in menial jobs. The American of both sexes stereotyped Mexican women as backward, superstitious, morally lax, and poor due to their Catholic faith and sought to "Americanize" them. The town of Las Vegas looked especially like a brickyard, according to one white wife.[73]

Barbed Wire, Irrigation, and the Railroad

Land grabbers fenced their claims, enclosing as many as 10,000 acres. The fencing denied Mexicans access to common lands for timber, water, and grazing. *Las Gorras Blancas* (the White Caps) led the opposition to enclosure. The controversy became embroiled in the conflicts over public education and land grant cases. *Millhiser v. Padilla* (1887) was about the control of public lands that the Santa Fé Ring and the colonizers wanted to privatize. In San Miguel County, on August 20, 1887, a wealthy rancher, Phillip Millhiser, and others attempted to claim private legal ownership to portions of the Las Vegas community land grant. They filed a test case challenging the accepted Mexican Law that protected communal grants and access to common lands.

Millhiser and other white owners claimed that they bought the land from the original owner and therefore had absolute title and a proportionate interest in common lands. They contested claims by José Padilla and the other defendants that the land was not awarded to individuals and the right to use common lands was a collective right. Passions ran high and unexpectedly the local court found in favor of the defendants, Padilla et al.[74]

The decision touched off a three-hour demonstration. An intense struggle began as the lower court's decision was appealed and Governor Prince, bombarded by white ranchers, appealed to Washington to do something about

Las Gorras Blancas. After considerable arm twisting, the courts ruled in favor of Millhiser; it was a victory for the Santa Fé Ring and the colonizers.[75] Once again the courts, through the pressure of the colonizers, violated the rights of the colonized. The colonizers controlled the political process and the army.[76]

The land grabs continued and in 1899 Las Gorras rode again, and between 1899–1891 land wars raged. The Gorras' leaders were taken to court but the charges were dismissed. The controversy lasts to this day and many New Mexicans claim that the common lands are protected by the Treaty of Guadalupe Hidalgo.

The Village People Defend their Land

Mexicans suffered racially motivated lynching. In 1882, near Bloomfield, in the northeastern part of the territory, a mob lynched Sheriff Guadalupe Archuleta because he shot and killed a white man in the line of duty. That same year, in Lincoln County, a mob broke into the jail and kidnapped a Mexican accused of stealing horses; he was never found. Another mob broke into a jail in northern New Mexico at Los Lunas and hanged Mexicans accused of murdering a saloon keeper.[77]

The 1880s saw increased resistance to the enclosure movement. The railroad intensified tensions, as private contractors stripped the timber from the mountainsides. Competition strained an already bad economic situation; and inequalities in pay between white American and Mexican workers widened. By the middle of the decade, Mexicans organized the Association of the Brotherhood for the Protection of the Rights and Privileges of the People of New Mexico, whose stated purpose was to liberate New Mexico from corrupt politicians and monopolies—symbolized by the railroads and fences. A leading figure in the struggle against the encroachers, Juan José Herrera, formed Las Gorras Blancas around 1887. Herrera functioned as a district organizer for the Knights of Labor, a national trade union founded in 1869 by garment workers. In response to the railroads, workers organized Knights in San Miguel County in 1884; within three years, it had three assemblies in the city of Las Vegas, New Mexico. In 1887 the union formed the Las Vegas Grant Association to give the townspeople legal aid to defend themselves against land speculators.[78]

On November 1, 1889, "[a]rmed with rifles and pistols, draped in long black coats and slickers, their faces hidden behind white masks,"[79] 66 Mexican horsemen rode into Las Vegas. They converged on the jail, asking for Sheriff Lorenzo López, and then rode on to the home of Miguel Salazar, the prosecuting attorney. The presence of the night riders climaxed a year of fence cutting, but this time they damaged no property. Authorities blamed "criminal" behavior on Las Gorras Blancas and indicted several Mexicans. On November 25, county officials brought 26 indictments against 47 suspects, among whom were Juan José and Pablo Herrera.

The White Caps enjoyed public support and claimed 1,500 members. On December 16, the townspeople marched through the city to demand the release of suspected White Caps. On March 11, 1890, Las Gorras toured East Las Vegas, distributing copies of their platform, which in part read,

> Nuestra Plataforma
>
> Our purpose is to protect the rights and interests of the people in general and especially those of the helpless classes.
>
> We want the Las Vegas Grant settled to the benefit of all concerned, and this we hold is the entire community within the Grant.
>
> We want no "land grabbers" or obstructionists of any sort to interfere. We will watch them.
>
> We are not down on lawyers as a class, but the usual knavery and unfair treatment of the people must be stopped.
>
> Our judiciary hereafter must understand that we will sustain it only when "justice" is its watchword.[80]

White Americans and established Mexicans condemned the platform as anti-American and radical. Miguel A. Otero described the White Caps as "a criminal organization."[81] *The Optic*, the town newspaper, portrayed them as a destructive influence in the community. Nevertheless, by 1890, the White Cap raids had spread to Santa Fé County.

Las Gorras continued to cut fences and destroy property; they attacked the railroad because of the high-handed manner in which it appropriated land for rights-of-way. Meanwhile, the government stepped up operations against the fence cutters. Governor LeBaron Prince threatened to send troops into the area if local authorities did not stop Las Gorras. The governor proposed that one or two companies of federal troops be stationed in San Miguel to protect railroad property and that detectives be hired to infiltrate Las Gorras. Prince was not able to carry out his plans because the secretary of the interior would not cooperate. When Prince finally visited Las Vegas, he learned to his dismay that four-fifths of the citizens whom he met sympathized with Las Gorras.

Meanwhile, Terence Powderly, president of the Knights of Labor, became concerned about Las Gorras' militancy and the group's link to the union through the Juan Herrera and his family. Even local members worried about the infiltration of Las Gorras and "the large number of 'Mexican people' of the lower classes who were being admitted to their union."[82] The Knights also resented the night riders' meddling in labor politics—on April 3, 1890, for instance, Las Gorras posted wage rates in which they told the workers what to demand for cutting and hauling railroad ties. The previous month, 300 armed men destroyed approximately 9,000 ties belonging to the Santa Fé Railway. Las

Gorras harassed workers who did not support the rate standard. Ultimately, however, the railroad undercut Las Gorras by announcing that it would no longer purchase ties in San Miguel County. This reprisal cost the county $100,000 annually, worsening unemployment. Hungry workers blamed Las Gorras instead of the railroad. Powderly and the Knights' leadership disavowed any connection with White Cap leader Juan José Herrera.

The Herreras' involvement in the People's Party also annoyed the national Knights' leadership. The People's Party challenged the boss-ridden Republicans and attracted many disillusioned members of both parties. By 1890, many party loyalists boasted that most San Miguel voters supported their organization. The Herreras represented the militants and Félix Martínez and Nestor Montoya, who published *La Voz del Pueblo*, led the moderates. Although not condoning fence cutting, *La Voz* did explain the reasons for it. When the party nominated Pablo Herrera for the territorial House of Representatives, the moderates charged that the Herreras were extremists.[83] But the fact remains that white vigilantes perpetuated most of the mob violence that continued to 1928, when a mob broke into a hospital and hanged Rafael Benavides, a sheepherder, in Farmington, New Mexico.

The American Dream

Political participation often gives the illusion that change is possible through the ballot box. This illusion discourages direct action like fence cutting, and a shift away from more assertive tactics took place. Initially, the People's Party in 1890 swept the county elections, and the party's candidates won four seats in the assembly. Yet, it was one thing to win elections, but another to pass reform legislation to regulate railroad rates or to protect the Las Vegas grant. Soon after his election, Assemblyman Pablo Herrera announced his disillusionment. Speaking before the legislature in February 1891, he said,

> Gentlemen . . . I have served several years' time in the penitentiary but only sixty days in the legislature . . . I have watched the proceedings here carefully. I would like to say that the time I spent in the penitentiary was more enjoyable than the time I spent here. There is more honesty in . . . prison than . . . [in] the legislature. I would prefer another term in prison than another election in the house.[84]

Pablo Herrera returned to San Miguel and attempted to revive Las Gorras Blancas. Meanwhile, Knights of Labor expelled him. Moderates isolated him and he became a fugitive after killing a man in Las Vegas. Felipe López, a deputy sheriff, eventually killed Herrera.

Meanwhile, Juan José Herrera was elected probate judge. The poor who distrusted the conservative and moderate factions supported him. During 1889 and 1890, under the leadership of Juan José, the White Caps stemmed land speculation; however, after this point, like Pablo Herrera, Juan José put his energies into the People's Party, struggling to keep it from ripping itself apart. Cutting fences gave way to long-drawn-out litigation that often weakened the people's initial enthusiasm and hope. Government infiltration and provocateuring took its toll. Pinkerton agent Charles A. Siringo, the infamous Spanish-speaking spy, infiltrated the party ranks. Stiringo regularly reported on the activities of the Herreras. For these and other reasons, by 1896, the party faded.[85]

By this time, Mexican representation in the legislature was limited to 26 families who served the interests of only 5 percent of Mexican Americans. Collusion served the ricos well, and their flocks went under taxed while the poor stockowners paid their full share. This inequity contributed to alienation between ricos and *pobres*—nationalism went only so far.

In 1894, the U.S. Court of Private Land Claims ruled that the San Miguel claim was a community grant, but the court limited its decision to house lots and garden plots, excluding common pasturage. Although *los hombres pobres* continued to cut fences as late as 1926 (and later in other parts of New Mexico), they failed to stop the influx of Americans and capital that symbolized the changes taking place.[86]

The End of the Frontier

5.7 Characterize social and political realities in Mexico during its last years as a territory.

The Santa Fé Ring's heyday, years of government corruption, warfare, and political favoritism, lasted from 1865 to 1885. The death of the Santa Fé Ring did not end machine politics. They simply became more professional—with merchant capitalists becoming bankers and investing their profits in mining, cattle, and land. The arrival of the Atchison, Topeka and Santa Fé Railway in 1879 quickened the changes that ended New Mexico's isolation. Within two years, this railroad joined the Southern Pacific at Deming, New Mexico, to give the territory its first transcontinental link.

The Growth of Industrial Mining

Intensive mining exploration took place in southwest New Mexico and eastern Arizona since the 1870s. However, its development was limited, since the ore had to be freighted out by mule. At this stage, merchant capitalists financed mining, and its development attracted commercial farms to supply the new mining camps, and to establish a string of settlements in the Mesilla Valley and elsewhere in New Mexico. Villages attracted a large army of migrant workers from Mexico. Southern New Mexico was at the crossroads of this activity, with miners from Chihuahua and points south also passing through the Mesilla corridor en route to the mines of Arizona and the sugar beet fields and mines of Colorado. Towns such as Las Cruces, Silver City, and Gallup grew as the result of the mixture of mines and railroad links.

By the 1880s, these enterprises expanded beyond the capabilities of the merchant and a more capital-intense society replaced the monopoly of the merchants and their network of village stores. A cash-and-carry economy increased dependency on the partido system that was similar to farm sharecropping.[87] Meanwhile, the reduction of the band tribes and the dispatch of Comanche to reservations eliminated a source of trade and further depressed the financial state of the subsistence farmers.[88]

Changes in Society

The territory's population jumped from 119,000 in 1880 to 195,000 in 1900. Property values rose from $41 million in the 1880s to $231 million by the start of the 1890s. In the 1880s, the number of sheep grew from 347,000 to over 1.5 million. By 1890, 210,000 head of cattle roamed New Mexico, compared with 14,000 in 1870. The railroad brought the mass marketing of the territory's resources. In this whirl of change, the influence of the Santa Fé Ring lessened as many young merchants and lawyers resented the monopoly and privileges of ring members. Hence, they challenged its power. At issue were the machine's control of the Mexican vote and the manipulation of elections. Yet the ring's decline did not end violence, which continued into the 1890s. Modernization changed many subsistence farmers into wage earners—a large number of them worked on the railroads, in the mines, and on commercial farms. Industrialization promoted "urbanism, capital-intensive production, and a mass labor force of individual wage earners that rapidly overwhelmed local society, no matter how collectivized."[89]

During these years, social and political controls tightened. Although warfare still raged on over the Maxwell Land Grant and in San Miguel County in the 1890s, by 1896 only Stonewall County was in open rebellion. Improved transportation ended isolation and eased the quick deployment of various law enforcement agencies. For example, the governor's control of the militia helped frustrate the development of a militant trade union movement in the territory.

Meanwhile, New Mexicans organized mutualistas—mutual aid societies—in Las Vegas, Santa Fé, Española, Albuquerque, Roswell, and Las Cruces. Between 1885 and 1912, New Mexican railroad track workers founded eight branches of the Colorado *La Sociedad Protecciòn Mutua de Trabajadores Unidos*. Like other mutualistas it developed insurance programs, but it was also used to mobilize Mexicans against the growing incidence of discrimination.[90] After the turn of the century, the *Alianza Hispano-Americana* organized chapters throughout the territory.

Federal Encroachment

After the turn of the century, the federal government through the construction of dams further stimulated large farming operations. Small farmers hung on by their fingernails and could not compete with large commercial farms. Although agribusinesses represented a small portion of the population, they controlled more than half the territory's grazing land.[91] The 1900s brought another wave of encroachers. The U.S. Congress, concerned that Mexicans owned most of the small independent farms, refused to admit New Mexico to statehood in 1903. This snub encouraged new methods to control the villagers' access to land. Agribusiness also wanted ownership of land that the federal and territorial governments held—the public domain. The privatization of this land would open it up to homesteading and would attract more white Americans. But even this was an insidious tactic since although homesteaders would have access to the public lands, the lack of water made it impossible to survive. Large agribusiness interests already owned most the land irrigated by federal water projects. When the homesteaders failed, the monopolists would purchase their land.

In all, the federal government distributed 30 million acres to homesteaders—7 million in 1909 alone. The system affected New Mexican subsistence farmers, who grazed small flocks of sheep on government land to supplement their farming. To survive, many New Mexicans ran sheep on shares for larger companies; others had to look for day work; others migrated. These changes altered the gender division of labor, and women assumed additional responsibilities, irrigating their holdings and caring for the animals, while their husbands traveled to look for work at the mines, at the railroads, and in the cities.

Until the 1930s, machine politics and the Catholic Church mediated conflicts between North Americans and Mexicans. Appointments of "safe" Mexicans such as Miguel Otero as territorial governor in 1897 proved meaningless to the situation of Mexicanos, since he merely strengthened his own political machine. During Otero's administration, the spoils system sank government to its lowest depths.[92]

The Last Years of the Territory

The blatant opportunism of "Spanish American" brokers delayed the statehood of New Mexico. For them, statehood represented the loss of their power as local bosses. Statehood "meant Anglo-American rule, taxes, public schools, anti-Church policies, and the acquisition of their remaining lands."[93] The "Spanish American" elites also strongly opposed public education, rationalizing their opposition on religious grounds. They thought *Educar un muchacho es perder un buen pastor*—"To educate a boy is to lose a good shepherd"—and statehood would mean paying taxes to educate the poor. At the time, the average villager in New Mexico, out of 109,505 inhabitants, 57,156 did not know how to read or write by the end of the territorial period and the overwhelming majority of these illiterate were Mexicans. Of 44,000 children, only 12,000 Mexican youngsters attended schools.

At the Constitutional Convention, Mexican-born Octaviano A. Larrazolo raised the issue of equality of Mexicans. Although some North Americans objected to his using race to make a point, a coalition of Mexicans and Americans passed a measure making certain that Mexicans could vote, hold office, and could not be denied the right to sit on a jury because of "religion, race, language or color, or inability to speak, read or write the English or Spanish languages—giving the illusion of equality. However, the race question was far from resolved. New Mexico, despite the participation of Spanish American politicos in the system, continued to be one of the poorest states in the United States.[94]

Conclusion: Colonial Legacies

Care must be taken not to overgeneralize about identity or the loss of traditional culture, beliefs, and values. Too often the colonized become the colonizers; at the same time both change according to their life experiences and economic class. Post-colonialism is a "continuing process of resistance and reconstruction."[95] Identities are not forever; they change and our attitudes as the colonized or the colonizers change. As Chris Kortright puts it, "Colonization . . . begins with a forced, involuntary entry . . . destroys the indigenous culture; . . . the colonized group tends to be governed by representatives of the dominate group; and . . . the system of dominant-subordinate relationship is buttressed by a racist ideology."[96] In the case of New Mexico and the other occupied territories it must be remembered that these lands had also been occupied by Spain adding to the cultural conflict and the Europeanization of the people.

Ultimately, there are those who accept or resist colonialism and an identity as one of the colonizers. To this day some accept the fables about Juan de Oñate's greatness and the uniqueness of the colonizers and those who question these narratives. However, with the march of time, there are fewer Mexican Americans who accepted these colonial identities and today reject whiteness. As they become more conscious of history they are identifying as Indigenous it bears noting that this trend is most prevalent among Mexican American youth (in other words, they are peeling the onion).[97] Cultural Imperialism dies slowly and it has left its mark on Mexico, Latin America, and many places in the United States where the colonial caste system still lives.[98]

Notes

1 Malcolm Ebright, et al. *Four Square Leagues: Pueblo Indian Land in New Mexico* (University of New Mexico Press, 2014). Lizzie Wade, "New Mexico's American Indian population crashed 100 years after Europeans arrived," *Science*, Jan. 25, 2016, http://www.sciencemag.org/news/2016/01/new-mexicos-american-indian-population-crashed-100-years-after-europeans-arrived.

2 Robert Sydney Smith, *Warfare & Diplomacy in Precolonial West Africa* 2nd ed. (Madison: University of Wisconsin Press, 1976), 64–73.

3 "Historical Maps of New Mexico," http://alabamamaps.ua.edu/historicalmaps/us_states/newmexico/index.html. Perry-Castañeda Library Map Collection: New Mexico Maps, University of Texas Austin, http://www.lib.utexas.edu/maps/new_mexico.html. David J. Weber, *The Mexican Frontier, 1821–1846: The American Southwest Under Mexico* (Albuquerque: University of New Mexico Press, 1982), 226–28. Don D. Fowler, *A Laboratory for Anthropology* (Albuquerque: University of New Mexico Press, 2000).

4 Ralph Emerson, *The Leading Facts of New Mexican History*, Vol. I (Horn and Wallace, 1911), FN506, 474.

5 Robert Hixson Julyan, *The Place Names of New Mexico*, revised ed. (Albuquerque: University of New Mexico Press, 1996), 292. Raymond Ortiz and Lauren Reichelt, "The History of Rio Arriba," http://www.rio-arriba.org/places_to_see,_things_to_do/local_history/index.html. Philip Colee, "Rio Abajo Population Movements: 1670–1750," *JSTOR: Ethnohistory*, Vol. 18, No. 4 (Autumn 1974), 353–360.

6 Luis Aboites, *Breve historia de Chihuahua* (México D.F.: Fondo De Cultura Economica, 1994), 56–57. William B. Griffen, *Apaches at War and Peace: The Janos Presidio,*

1750–1858 (Norman: University of Oklahoma Press, 1988), viii–ix, 11.

7 Donald R. Lavash, *A Journey Through New Mexico History* (Albuquerque, NM: Sunstone Press, Updated and Revised, 2006), 111. Weber, *Spanish Frontier*, 148–149. Luis Aboites, *Breve historia de Chihuahua* (México D.F.: Fondo De Cultura Economica, 1994), 56–57.

8 Phillip B. Gonzales, "Struggle for Survival: The Hispanic Land Grants of New Mexico, 1848–2001," *Agricultural History* 77, No. 2 (Spring 2003), 296–27. Deena J. González, *Refusing The Favor: The Spanish-Mexican Women of Santa Fe, 1820–1880* (New York: Oxford University Press, 2001). Oakah L. Jones, *Los Paisanos: Spanish Settlers on the Northern Frontier of New Spain* (Norman: University of Oklahoma Press, 1996). Max L. Moorhead, *New Mexico's Royal Road: Trade and Travel on the Chihuahua Trail* (Norman: University of Oklahoma Press, 1995), 7, 40. "The Concept of Common Lands Defines Community Land Grants," U.S. Government Accountability Office, http://www.gao.gov/guadalupe/commland.htm. "Land grant documents contain no direct reference to 'community land grants' nor do Spanish and Mexican laws define or use this term. Scholars, land grant literature, and popular terminology use the phrase 'community land grants' to denote land grants that set aside common lands for the use of the entire community . . . Under Spanish and Mexican law, common lands set aside as part of an original grant belonged to the entire community and could not be sold." Tom Sharpe, "New book explores Spanish conquest brutality," *The New Mexican*, March 11, 2010, http://www.santafenewmexican.com/LocalNews/New-book-explores-Spanish-conquest-brutality#.UIrNEYbs9nU.

9 Damico, "El Agua Es La Vida (Water is Life): Water, Conflict and Conquest in Nineteenth Century New Mexico" (PhD dissertation, Brandeis University, 2008), 8. Tracy Brown, "Tradition and Change in Eighteenth-Century Pueblo Indian Communities," *Journal of the Southwest* Vol. 46, No. 3 (Autumn, 2004), 463–500.

10 Weber, *The Mexican Frontier, 1821–1846*, 102, 126, 130, 135–37. Richard L. Nostrand, *The Hispano Homeland* (Norman: University of Oklahoma Press, 1996), 20, 80, 302 in Southwest. U.S. Bureau of Census, Schedules of Seventh Census, 1850, showed Hispanos 54,394, Mexican Americans 394, Pueblo Indians 3,324, Nomads 164, Anglos 1,578, Homeland 59,830. Russell Steele Saxton, "Ethnocentrism in the Historical Literature of Territorial New Mexico," (PhD Dissertation, University of New Mexico, 1980), 2, estimates 60,000 Hispanos, 9,000 Pueblos, 15,000 nomadic natives, and fewer than 2000 Euro-Americans.

11 Roxanne Dunbar-Ortiz, *Roots of Resistance: Land Tenure in New Mexico, 1680–1980* (Los Angeles, CA: Chicano Studies Research Center Publications, U.C.L.A., 1980), 41, 62. Rodolfo F. Acuña, *Corridors of Migration: The Odyssey of Mexican Laborers, 1600–1933* (Tucson: University of Arizona, 2007), Chapters 1 and 2 for similar water questions in Chihuahua, Mexico.

12 Kenneth M. Orona, "River of Culture, River of Power: Identity, Modernism, and Contest in the Middle Rio Grande Valley, 1848–1947" (New Haven, CT: Yale University, 1998), vii.

13 Orona, "River of Culture, River of Power," 55. Josiah Gregg, *Commerce of the Prairies: Life on the Great Plains in the 1830's and 1840's*, 2nd ed. (Crabtree, OR: The Narrative Press, 2001), 107.

14 Max L. Moorhead, *New Mexico's Royal Road: Trade and Travel on the Chihuahua Trail* (Norman: University of Oklahoma Press, 1995), 28–33, 52–55.

15 Carlos Vélez-Ibáñez, *Border Visions: Mexican Cultures of the Southwest United States* (Tucson: University of Arizona Press, 1996), 58. Roxanne Amanda Dunbar, "Land Tenure in Northern New Mexico: An Historical Perspective" (PhD Dissertation, UCLA, 1974), 146, 147. Bent married into the Jaramillo family. Kit Carson married into the same family. By 1831 there were American traders and trappers, tailors, carpenters, blacksmiths, shoemakers, gunsmiths, and other craftspeople in New Mexican towns. Charles Bent, The Mexico Office of the State Historian, http://www.newmexicohistory.org/filedetails.php?fileID=548.

16 González, *Refusing the Favor*, 87.

17 George B. Anderson, *History of New Mexico: Its Resources and People* (Los Angeles, CA: Pacific States Publishing Co., 1907), 81. The population was probably closer to 6,000. Jones, *Los Paisanos*, 122. David A. Sandoval, "The American Invasion of New Mexico and Mexican Merchants," *Journal of Popular Culture*, Vol. 35, Issue 2 (Fall, 2001), 61–70.

18 A American interpretation of Bent's Fort, http://www.youtube.com/watch?v=fEyF1VtV4a4. George William Beattie, "Reopening the Anza Road," *The Pacific Historical Review* 2, No. 1 (March 1933), 52. Juan Bautista de Anza opened The Old Spanish Trail from Sonora to California in 1774. In 1829 Antonio Armijo with 60 men left Abiquiú, New Mexico, for California, arriving 86 days later. This opened the floodgates to other trade expeditions the following year. These openings continued and multiplied during the 1830s and 1840s. Many New Mexicans that settled in California left their footprints, such as Julian Chávez, who the famous Chavez Ravine was

19 Acuña, *Corridors of Migration*, 13–14, 22. See Jack D. Forbes, *Apache, Navaho and Spaniard* (Norman: University of Oklahoma Press, 1960); this is a classic. Apaches were also sold in Havana and Manila, and about 100,000 Filipinos were transported to Mexico.

20 Dunbar Ortiz, "Land Tenure in Northern New Mexico," 141, 144. Dunbar Ortiz, *Roots of Resistance*, 66. Camino Real de Tierra Adentro National Historic Trail, National Park Service, Department of the Interior, http://www.nps.gov/elca/. Marc Simmons, *New Mexico!*, 3rd ed. (Albuquerque: University of New Mexico, 2004), 132–38. Santa Fé Trail, http://www.youtube.com/watch?v=g8AnAy2DdK4.

21 Eastern and European capital was arriving even before the arrival of the railroad. Dunbar, "Land Tenure in Northern New Mexico," 141, 142, 144, 150. Ortiz, *Roots of Resistance*, 66. González, *Refusing the Favor*, 41, 115–16. Robert Luthe Duffus, *The Santa Fe Trail* (Albuquerque: University of New Mexico Press, 1972), 156. Stella M. Drumm, ed., *Down the Santa Fe Trail and into Mexico: The Diary of Susan Shelby Magoffin, 1846–1847* (Lincoln, NE: Bison Books, 1982); her husband was Samuel Magoffin, a veteran Santa Fé trader; she has graphic descriptions of the people along the trail.

22 Vicente M. Martínez, *The Progeny of Padre Martinez of Taos, Fundación Presbítero Antonio*. Damico, "El Agua Es La Vida," 35–39.

23 Ward Alan Minge, *Frontier Problems in New Mexico Preceding the Mexican War, 1840–1846* (Albuquerque: University of New Mexico Press, 1965), 41, 44, 304–06. Howard R. Lamar, *The Far Southwest, 1846–1912: A Territorial History* (New York: Norton, 1970), 53. Hubert Howe Bancroft, *History of Arizona and New Mexico, 1530–1888*, Vol. XVII (San Francisco, CA: The History Company, Publishers, 1889), 320–29. Benjamin M. Read, *Illustrated History of New Mexico* (New York: Arno Press, 1976), 407–08. Thomas M. Murray, *A Study of the Resolution of the Texas-New Mexico Boundary Conflict: The Compromise of 1850* (Master of Arts Thesis, Waco, Texas: Baylor University, 1995), 31, 34–47. Twitchell, *The History of the Military Occupation of the Territory of New Mexico* (New York: Arno Press, 1976), 203–05.

24 Magoffin arrived in the region in 1828 and was married to María Gertrudes Váldez. He met with U.S. President Polk before the march, giving him a considerable amount of information about New Mexico. Stella M. Drumm, ed., *Down the Santa Fe Trail and into New Mexico* (New Haven, CT: Yale University Press, 1962), xxiv. William Aloysius Keleher, *Turmoil in New Mexico* (Santa Fé, NM: Rydal Press, 1951), 29–35. 63rd Congress, Senate, Doc. Number 608 (Washington, D.C.: Government Printing Office). John Taylor Hughes, *Doniphan's Expedition: Containing an Account of the Conquest of New Mexico* (Whitefish, MT: Kessinger Publishing, LLC, 2006).

25 Warren A. Beck, *New Mexico: A History of Four Centuries* (Norman: University of Oklahoma Press, 1962), 134. Lynn I. Perrigo, *The American Southwest* (New York: Holt, Rinehart and Winston, 1971), 164. Ralph Emerson Twitchell, *The Conquest of Santa Fe 1846* (Española, NM: Tate Gallery Publications, 1967), 52. Carolyn Zeleny, "Relations Between the Spanish-Americans and Anglo-Americans in New Mexico: A Study of Conflict and Accommodation in a Dual Ethnic Situation" (PhD Dissertation, Yale University, New Haven, 1944), 137.

26 González, *Refusing the Favor*, 73. Alvin R. Sunseri, "New Mexico in the Aftermath of the Anglo-American Conquest," (PhD Dissertation, Louisiana State University and Agricultural and Mechanical College, Baton Rouge, 1973), 131. Eric Foner on the Taos Revolt, http://www.youtube.com/watch?v=E9cX2W91fCk&playnext=1&list=PLOUTliemF1U4YXkM0sd4fBfmDJ7nBgw_z&feature=results_main.

27 Twitchell, *The History of the Military Occupation of the Territory of New Mexico*, 125. Lamar, *The Far Southwest, 1846–1912*, 70. There were also widespread acts of resistance in Arroyo. Fundación Presbítero Don Antonio José Martínez, Inc., http://padremartinez.org/index.php.

28 Dunbar Ortiz, "Land Tenure in Northern New Mexico," 191. Twitchell, *The Conquest of Santa Fe*, 133. "New Mexico Massacre: The Taos Rebellion," February 8, 2012, http://adamjamesjones.wordpress.com/2012/02/08/new-mexico-massacre-the-taos-revolt/.

29 Simone de Beauvoir, *The Ethics of Ambiguity*, 1947; excerpted at https://www.marxists.org/reference/subject/ethics/de-beauvoir/ambiguity/ch03.htm.

30 Hubert Howe Bancroft, *History of Arizona and New Mexico, 1530–1888*, Vol. XVII (San Francisco, CA: The History Company, Publishers, 1889), 320–29.

31 Laura E. Gómez, *Manifest Destinies: The Making of the Mexican American Race* (New York: New York University Press, 2007), 15–16, 34, 35. Six executions are criticized because the United States did not have political sovereignty: Bancroft, *History of Arizona and New Mexico, 1530–1888*, 436. Carey McWilliams, *North from Mexico* (New York: Greenwood Press, 1968), 118. Zeleny, "Relations between the Spanish-Americans and Anglo-Americans," 118. (Sister Mary) Loyola, *The American Occupation of New Mexico, 1821–1852* (New York: Arno Press, 1976), 71.

32 Sunseri, "New Mexico in the Aftermath of the Anglo-American Conquest," 143. Larry Dagwood Ball, "The Office of the United States Marshall in Arizona and the New Mexico Territory, 1851–1912" (PhD Dissertation, University of Colorado, Boulder, 1970), 23.

33 According to Bancroft, *History of Arizona and New Mexico, 1530–1888*, 642, the U.S. Census of 1850 listed a population of 61,547, exclusive of the Indian population; in 1860 the figure was 80,853, of whom 3,859 were native to New Mexico. D. W. Meinig, *Southwest: Three Peoples in Geographical Change, 1600–1970* (New York: Oxford University Press, 1971), 31. Lamar, *The Far Southwest, 1846–1912*, 30. Gómez, *Manifest Destinies*, 25, 27.

34 Elinore M. Barrett, *The Spanish Colonial Settlement Landscapes of New Mexico, 1598–1680* (Albuquerque, New Mexico, 2012).

35 Pem Davidson Buck, "Whither Whiteness? Empire, State, and the Re-Ordering of Whiteness," *Transforming Anthropology* Vol. 20, Issue 2 (October 2012), 103; argues "Acting for elite interests by shedding blood and enforcing labor exploitation has historically whitened and may again whiten some who are seen as a threat to White supremacy and the racially defined mythical nation."

36 Nancie González, *The Spanish-Americans of New Mexico: A Heritage of Pride* (Albuquerque: University of New Mexico Press, 1967), 205. New Mexico's racial identification resembles that of other northern Mexican states. The 1793 Census of Sonora found that out of 40,249 inhabitants, less than 0.3 percent was white, 42 percent mestizo, and 58 percent Indian. Acuña, *Corridors of Migration*, 70. However, despite Mexico being a mestizo and Indian nation (90 percent), 41.85 percent of Sonorans identified as white in 1921. In Chihuahua 36.33 percent identified as white in that census although in 1810 most identified as Indigenous and mestizo with 10 percent identified as mulatto. John P. Schmal, "Indigenous Identity In The Mexican Census," Houston Institute for Culture, http://www.houstonculture.org/hispanic/census.html.

37 Samuel E. Sisneros, "Los Emigrantes Nuevomexicanos: The 1849 Repatriation to Guadalupe and San Ignacio, Chihuahua, Mexico" (Master's Thesis, University of Texas at El Paso, 2001), 1.

38 Bancroft, *History of Arizona and New Mexico, 1530–1888*, 468, 472.

39 "Governor William Carr Lane's Manifesto Regarding the Drawing of the Boundary between Mexico and the United States, 1853," *New York Daily Times* (June 20, 1853), 3. Commissioner James Bartlett's Reply to William Carr Lane, 1853, "The Mesilla Valley," *New York Daily Times* (May 5, 1853), 6. John Disturnell to the *New York Daily Times* on the Drawing of the New-Mexican Boundary (May 6, 1853), *New York Daily Times* (May 7, 1853), 3. Acuña, *Corridors of Migration*, 32. Gadsden Purchase Treaty, December 30, 1853, The Avalon Project, Yale University Law School, http://avalon.law.yale.edu/19th_century/mx1853.asp, http://atlas.nmhum.org/pdfs/Gray1851NewMexico.pdf.

40 Rubén D Sálaz, Land Grant History, 1999, http://www.historynothype.com/landgrants.htm. Malcolm Ebright, *Land Grants and Lawsuits in Northern New Mexico* (Albuquerque: University of New Mexico Press, 1994); excellent synthesis of land grant process. Rubén Sálaz Márquez, *New Mexico: A Brief Multi-History* (Albuquerque, NM: Cosmic House, 2007).

41 Bancroft, *History of Arizona and New Mexico, 1530–1888*, 632–33. Erna Fergusson, *New Mexico: A Pageant of Three Peoples*, 2nd ed. (Albuquerque: University of New Mexico Press, 1973), 316. Dunbar, "Land Tenure in Northern New Mexico," 227. González, *Refusing the Favor*, 30. Joseph Franklin Sexton, "New Mexico: Intellectual and Cultural Developments 1885–1825. Conflict Among Ideas and Institutions" (PhD Dissertation, The University of Oklahoma, Norman, 1982), 6. The period 1850–1880 was a period of transition as Americans constructed their hegemony. Susan A. Roberts, *New Mexico* (Albuquerque: University of New Mexico Press, 2006), 107–08.

42 Sarah Deutsch, *No Separate Refuge: Culture, Class, and Gender on an Anglo-Hispanic Frontier in the American Southwest, 1880–1940* (New York: Oxford University Press, 1987), 27–28, 66. Fergusson, *New Mexico*, 270. Roberts, *New Mexico*, 108–11. Benjamin M. Reed, *A History of Education in New Mexico* (Santa Fé: New Mexico Printing Co, 1911), 16–18, http://www.archive.org/stream/historyofeducati00reediala. Rael-Galvez, Estevan, "Identifying Captivity and Capturing Identity: Narratives of American Indian Slavery in Colorado and New Mexico, 1776–1934," *American Quarterly*, 55.4 (2003), 817.

43 Robert Johnson Rosenbaum, "Mexicano Versus Americano: A Study of Hispanic-American Resistance to Anglo-American Control in New Mexico Territory, 1870–1900" (PhD Dissertation, University of Texas, Arlington, 1972), 5. Meinig, *Southwest*, 63–64.

44 Dunbar Ortiz, "Land Tenure in Northern New Mexico," 207. Deutsch, *No Separate Refuge*, 20. Ortiz, *Roots of Resistance*, 94. Robert J. Rosenbaum, *Mexicano Resistance in the Southwest* (Austin: University of Texas Press, 1981), 23. The import of the Treaty of Guadalupe Hidalgo can be surmised by reading

the excluded Article X. See Treaty of Guadalupe Hidalgo, February 2, 1848. The Avalon Project at Yale Law School, http://avalon.law.yale.edu/19th_century/guadhida.asp. The Querétaro Protocol, May 26, 1848, Protocol of Querétaro in La Prensa de San Diego, http://laprensa-sandiego.org/archieve/september21/treaty.htm. President James K. Polk (1795–1849) on Article X of the Treaty of Guadalupe Hidalgo, February 22, 1848, U.S. Senate, 30th Cong., 1st Sess., Executive Order 68. *Congressional Record*; cited in Rodolfo F. Acuña and Guadalupe Compeán, eds., *Voices of the U.S. Latino Experience*, 3 Vols. (Westport, CT: Greenwood, 2008), 113.

45 Denise Holladay Damico, "El Agua Es la Vida (Water is Life): Water Conflict and Conquest in Nineteenth Century New Mexico" (PhD dissertation, Brandeis University, 2008), 10, 14, 17. Nostrand, *The Hispano Homeland*, 20.

46 Nostrand, *Hispano Homeland*, 11. Denise Holladay Damico, "El Agua Es la Vida," 14.

47 Gordon Morris Bakken, ed., *Law in Western United States* (Norman: University of Oklahoma Press, 2000), 534.

48 González, *Refusing the Favor*, 140. David J. Weber, ed., *Foreigners in Their Native Land: Historical Roots of the Mexican Americans* (Albuquerque: University of New Mexico Press, 1973), 157. González, *The Spanish-Americans of New Mexico*, 52–53.

49 McWilliams, *North from Mexico*, 122. Robert W. Larson, *New Mexico's Quest for Statehood, 1846–1912* (Albuquerque: University of New Mexico Press, 1968), 143. William A. Keleher, *The Maxwell Grant* (Santa Fé: Rydal Press, 1942), 152. Howard R. Lamar, *The Far Southwest, 1846–1919* (New Haven, CT: Yale University Press, 1966), 150. Miguel Antonio Otero, *The Real Billy the Kid: With New Light on the Lincoln County War* (Houston, TX: Arte Público Press, 1998), xxx–xxxiii, 45. Robert J. Torres, *Myth of the Hanging Tree: Stories of Crime and Punishment in Territorial New Mexico* (Albuquerque: University of New Mexico Press, 2008), 68–69, based heavily on the Catron Papers.

50 Herbert O. Brayer, *William Blackmore: The Spanish-Mexican Land Grants of New Mexico and Colorado, 1863–1878* (Denver, CO: Bradford-Robinson, 1949), reprinted in Carlos E. Cortés, ed., *Spanish and Mexican Land Grants* (New York: Arno Press, 1974), 173.

51 Keleher, *The Maxwell Grant*, 29, 150. Rosenbaum, "Mexicano Versus Americano," 42, 61, 64, 71, 75–79. Lamar, *The Far Southwest, 1846–1912*, 142. F. Stanley, *The Grant That Maxwell Bought* (Denver, CO: World Press, 1953), in William H. Wroth, "Maxwell Land Grant," New Mexico Office of the State Historian, http://www.newmexicohistory.org/filedetails.php?fileID=512; has original documents and maps.

52 Rosenbaum, "Mexicano Versus Americano," 80, 86–93, 95–96, 98–99. Keleher, *The Maxwell Grant*, 109–10. Larson, *New Mexico's Quest for Statehood*, 138. Sexton, "New Mexico: Intellectual and Cultural," 67–68, 114–16. Maria Elaine Montoya, "Disposed People: Settler Resistance on the Maxwell Land Grant, 1860–1901" (PhD Dissertation, Yale University, New Haven, 1993), 1, 11, 87; excellent synthesis.

53 Stan Steiner, *La Raza: The Mexican Americans* (New York: Harper & Row, 1969), 8.

54 Otero, *The Real Billy the Kid*, 43. Dunbar, "Land Tenure in Northern New Mexico," 221. Charles L. Kenner, *A History of New Mexican-Plains Indian Relations* (Norman: University of Oklahoma Press, 1969), 41. Brayer, *William Blackmore*, 244–45. Beck, *New Mexico*, 255, 260. Maurice G. Fulton, *History of the Lincoln County War* (Tucson: University of Arizona Press, 1968), 8.

55 Rosenbaum, "Mexicano Versus Americano," 116.

56 Otero, *The Real Billy*, 5–6. Elego Baca, New Mexico, American Memory, Library of Congress, http://lcweb2.loc.gov/wpa/20040209.html.

57 Fulton, *History of the Lincoln County War*, 45–47, 291–92, 405–09. Rosenbaum, "Mexicano Versus Americano," 119, 340. Perrigo, *The American Southwest*, 279. Fergusson, *New Mexico*, 275–76. Otero, *The Real Billy*, 61.

58 González, *Refusing the Favor*, 9. Carol Archer, "Surviving the Transition: Women's Property Rights and Inheritance in New Mexico, 1848–1912" (Master of Arts Thesis, University of Calgary, Alberta, 2006), 19, 30; makes the point that New Mexican women lost property rights under American law. A significant number of American males married Mexican women, acquiring their property rights. Doña Ana County had the highest percentage of intermarriages at 27.5 percent. Jason Pierce, "Making the White Man's West: Whiteness and the Creation of the American West," (PhD Dissertation, University of Arkansas, Fayetteville, 2008), 2; Pierce makes the point that whiteness has been narrowly defined since colonial times.

59 Janet Lecompte, "The Independent Women of Hispanic New Mexico, 1821–1846," *The Western Historical Quarterly* 12, No. 1 (January 1981), quote on 18. The article gives a clear portrait of the women's lives.

60 González, *Refusing the Favor*, 41–55, 168, 215–16. Rodolfo F. Acuña, *Assault on Mexican American Collective Memory, 2010–2015: Swimming with Sharks* (New York: Lexington, 2017), 210.

61 During the nineteenth Century the pope frequently intervened in the internal affairs of France and Italy. The pope saw the rise of secular governments as a threat to the Church's hegemony and moved to extend his power by stacking the College of Cardinals and passing the doctrine of papal infallibility during Vatican Council I in 1870. Lamy was brought up during this era. In 1869, Lamy was one of the 600 specially elevated by the Pope at the Vatican Council. Paul Horgan, *Lamy of Santa Fe* (Wesleyan University Press, 1975), 362. On page 365 Horgan goes into the jurisdictional controversy between the Mexican and American clergy.

62 Pedro Sánchez, *Memorias Sobre la Vida del Presbitero Don Antonio José Antonio Martínez* (Santa Fé: Compania Impresora del Nuevo Mexicano, 1903), reprinted in David Weber, ed., *Northern Mexico on the Eve of the North American Invasion* (New York: Arno Press, 1976), 11. William A. Keleher, *Turmoil in New Mexico, 1846–1868* (Santa Fé, NM: Rydal Press, 1952), No. 71, 132. Keleher, *The Maxwell Grant*, 15, 133. Fergusson, *New Mexico*, 260–61. Zeleny, "Relations between the Spanish-Americans and Anglo-Americans," 257–58. Larson, *New Mexico's Quest for Statehood*, 82. Perrigo, *The American Southwest*, 219–20. Loyola, *The American Occupation of New Mexico, 1821–1852*, 35. Paul Horgan, *Lamy of Santa Fe: His Life and Times* (New York: Farrar, Straus & Giroux, 1975). For an excellent discussion of the Church in New Mexico, see González, *Refusing the Favor*, 64, 199–214. Ray John De Aragón, *Padre Martínez and Bishop Lamy* (Las Vegas, NV: Pan-American Publishing, 1978), 98. Shirley Jean Sands, "Religious Art: Reflectors of Change In the Catholic Church of New Mexico, 1830–1910" (PhD Dissertation, Louisiana State University, Baton Rouge, 1999), 2–3, 48–49, 59, 175. The clash between the Mexican clergy was both with the Americans and the French; before the coming of the foreign church, New Mexico had been administered by the Bishop of Durango.

63 Alex M. Darley, *The Passionist of the Southwest or the Holy Brotherhood* (1893), reprinted in Carlos E. Cortés, ed., *The Penitentes of New Mexico* (New York: Arno Press, 1974), 5. Francis Leon Swadesh, *Los Primeros Pobladores* (Notre Dame: University of Notre Dame Press, 1974), 78. Miguel Antonio Otero, *Otero: An Autobiographical Trilogy*, Vol. 2 (New York: Arno Press, 1974), 46. Los Hermanos Penitentes, *Société Périllos*, http://www.perillos.com/penitentes.html (accessed April 30, 2009).

64 Quoted in De Aragón, *Padre Martínez and Bishop Lamy*, 105. Horgan, *Lamy of Santa Fe*, 229. On 353 Horgan makes the point that Martínez died one of the richest men in New Mexico.

65 Deutsch, *No Separate Refuge*, 13, 14. Marta Weigle, *Hispanic Villages of Northern New Mexico: A Reprint of Volume II of the 1935 Tewa Basin Study, with Supplementary Materials* (Santa Fé, NM: The Lightning Tree, 1975), 35. González, *Refusing the Favor*, 80.

66 Deutsch, *No Separate Refuge*, 15–17, 21.

67 The Colegio de Mexico in Mexico City has excellent acequia schools. Luis Aboites, *Breve historia de Chihuahua* (México D.F.: Fondo De Cultura Economica, 1994).

68 Rodolfo F. Acuña, *Corridors of Migration: The Odyssey of Mexican Laborers, 1600–1933* (Tucson, AZ: University of Arizona Press, 2007).

69 Mexican sources place greater emphasis on the importance of water to the land. See Damico, "El Agua Es La Vida," 12, 14, 20, 36–39, 90, 98, 106, 112, 118. Luis Aboites Aguilar, *La Irrigación Revolucionaria: Historia Del Sistema Nacional De Riego Del Río Conchos, Chihuahua, 1927–1938* (México, D.F.: Centro de Investigaciones y Estudios Superiores en Antropologia Social, 1987), 59. Rocio Castañeda González, *Irrigacion y reforma agraria: las comunidades de riego del valle de Santa Rosalía, Chihuahua 1920–1945* (México, D.F.: Centro de Investigaciones y Estudios Superiores en Antropologia Social, 1995), 21–22. Acuña, *Corridors of Migration*, Chapters 1 and 2. See extensive archival material in Rodolfo F. Acuña Archives, Special Collection, Oviatt Library, California State University Northridge.

70 Weigle, *Hispanic Villages of Northern New Mexico*, 120, 151, 229. Deutsch, *No Separate Refuge*, 50–51, 101, 87–106. Prepared by the SOFA Team and Cheryl Doss, "The Role of Women in Agriculture," Agricultural Development Economics Division of the Food and Agriculture Organization of the United Nations. ESA Working Paper No. 11-02 (March 2011), http://www.fao.org/docrep/013/am307e/am307e00.pdf.

71 Deutsch, *No Separate Refuge*, 87–106. Weigle, *Hispanic Villages of Northern New Mexico*, 151.

72 Andrew Bancroft Schlesinger, "Las Gorras Blancas, 1889–1891," *Journal of Mexican American History* 1 (Spring 1971), 93, 44. Herrera, a native of New Mexico, had lived in Santa Fé and San Miguel counties until 1866, when he left the territory. Meeting the Knights in Colorado, he reputedly became acquainted in 1883 with the philosophy of Joseph Buchanan, founder of the anarchist Red International. Four years later Herrera returned to Las Vegas. Meanwhile, a rift occurred within the Knights between its president, Terence Powderly, and union militants. Juan José Herrera, joined by his two brothers, Pablo and Nicanor, identified with the militants.

73. Kate Horsley Parker, "I Brought With Me Many Eastern Ways: American Income-Earning Women in New Mexico, 1850–1880" (PhD Dissertation, University of New Mexico, Albuquerque, 1984), 10. Cheryl J. Foote, *Women of the New Mexico Frontier, 1846–1912*, 2nd ed. (Albuquerque: University of New Mexico Press, 2005), xx, 32, 74.

74. Alfredo Mirandé, Gringo Justice: *Catholicism in American Culture* (Notre Dame: University of Notre Dame, 1990), Chapter 3. Mary Romero, "Class struggle and resistance against the transformation of land ownership and usage in northern New Mexico: The case of las gorras blancas," *Chicana/o-Latina/o Law Review*, 26 Chicana/o-Latina/o L. Rev. 8 (Spring, 2006), 87–94.

75. Howard Roberts Lamar, *Charlie Siringo's West: An Interpretive Biography* (Albuquerque: University of New Mexico Press, 2005), 162.

76. Rosenbaum, "Mexicano Versus Americano," 148, 198. William Aloysius Keleher, *The Fabulous Frontier* (Albuquerque: University of New Mexico Press, 1982), xxi, 6, 185, 280. *New Mexico: Its Resources And People Illustrated*, Vol. I (Los Angeles, CA: Pacific States Publishing Co, 1907), 314.

77. William Carrigan and Clive Webb, *Forgotten Dead: Mob Violence Against Mexicans in the United States, 1848-1928* (New York: Oxford University Press, 2013), 69, 127 (Final Manuscript). The authors make the point that the fact that Mexicans were in the majority put a firewall between them and vigilantes, and set it apart from the other former Mexican provinces.

78. Robert W. Larson, "The Knights of Labor and Native Protest in New Mexico," in Robert Kern, ed., *Labor in New Mexico: Union, Strikes and Social History Since 1881* (Albuquerque: University of New Mexico Press, 1983), 4, 36. Rosenbaum, "Mexicano Versus Americano," 132–33, 139–40. Schlesinger, "Las Gorras Blancas, 1889–1891," 87–143. David Correia, "Retribution Will Be Their Reward: New Mexico's Las Gorras Blancas and the Fight for the Las Vegas Land Grant Commons," *Radical History Review* Issue 108 (Fall 2010): 49–72; well-illustrated.

79. Acuña, *Corridors*, 51.

80. *The Optic*, March 12, 1890, quoted in Schlesinger, *Las Gorras Blancas*, 107–08. Las Gorras Blancas, New Mexico Office of the State Historian, http://www.newmexicohistory.org/filedetails.php?fileID=375.

81. Otero, *Otero*, Vol. 2, 166.

82. Rosenbaum, "Mexicano Versus Americano," 156, 171, 200. Larson, "The Knights of Labor and Native Protest in New Mexico," 39.

83. Schlesinger, "Las Gorras Blancas," 121, 122. Rosenbaum, "Mexicano Versus Americano," 201, 225, 229, 235. Sheriff Lorenzo López represented conservatives within the partido. Already a *jefé político* (political boss), he joined because of a rift with his brother-in-law Eugenio Romero, the boss of San Miguel's Republican Party.

84. Schlesinger, "Las Gorras Blancas," 123.

85. David Correia, "Las Gorras Blancas of San Miguel County," New Mexico History, http://newmexicohistory.org/people/las-gorras-blancas-of-san-miguel-county.

86. Deutsch, *No Separate Refuge*, 29. Rosenbaum, "Mexicano Versus Americano," 247, 261, 324. Between 1891 and 1904, the Court of Private Land Claims heard cases involving 235,491,020 acres, allowing 2,051,526 acres to remain intact. Weber, *Foreigners in Their Native Land*, 157, writes, "In New Mexico, for example, more than 80 percent of the grant builders lost their land. There, since community grants and communal holdings were more common than individual grants, the slowness of litigation had its greatest impact on small farmers and herders." James W. Fraser, *A History of Hope When Americans Have Dared to Dream of a Better Future* (Hampshire: Palgrave Macmillan, 2003), 60–65.

87. Jon M. Wallace, "Livestock, Land, and Dollars: The Sheep Industry of Territorial New Mexico" (MA Thesis, Albuquerque: University of New Mexico, December 2013), http://citeseerx.ist.psu.edu/viewdoc/download?doi=10.1.1.840.4513&rep=rep1&type=pdf

88. Roxanne Dunbar-Ortiz, "Land Tenure and Resistance in New Mexico," counterpunch, September 22, 2007. https://www.counterpunch.org/2007/09/22/land-tenure-and-resistance-in-new-mexico/

89. Kern, *Labor in New Mexico*, 4. Dunbar, "Land Tenure in Northern New Mexico," 220. Lamar, *The Far Southwest, 1846–1912*, 172–201.

90. Deutsch, *No Separate Refuge*, 26. Michael Leon Trujillo, "The Land of Disenchantment: Transformation, Continuity, and Negation in the Greater Española Valley, New Mexico," (PhD Dissertation, The University of Texas at Austin, 2005), 5–6. The Greater Española Valley is largely located within Rio Arriba County and is situated at the center of the Rio Arriba region of northern New Mexico and southern Colorado. This region has long maintained a concentrated and long-term resident Hispanic population.

91. Zeleny, "Relations Between the Spanish-Americans and Anglo-Americans," 176–77.

92. Joan Jensen, "New Mexico Farm Women, 1900–1940," in Kern, ed., *Labor in New Mexico: Strikes, Unions and Social History since 1881* (Albuquerque: University of New Mexico Press, 1983), 63. Zeleny, "Relations Between the Spanish-Americans and Anglo-Americans," 179, 187, 190, 192–93, 200–01, 216, 217.

93 Lamar, *The Far Southwest, 1846–1912*, 190.
94 Ibid.
95 Zandra Kambysellis, "Post-colonialism: The Unconscious Changing of a Culture," '01, English 27, Autumn 1997, http://www.postcolonialweb.org/poldiscourse/kz1.html.
96 Chris Kortright, "Colonization and Identity," The Anarchist Library, January 1, 2003. https://theanarchistlibrary.org/library/chris-kortright-colonization-and-identity.
97 Geoffrey Decker, "Hispanics Identifying Themselves as Indians," *New York Times*, July 3, 2011, https://www.nytimes.com/2011/07/04/nyregion/more-hispanics-in-us-calling-themselves-indian.html.
98 Roberto Rodriguez, "Mexico's Color Line and the Cultural Imperialism of Light-Skin Preference," Truthout, May 26, 2018, http://www.truth-out.org/opinion/item/44493-mexico-s-color-line-and-the-cultural-imperialism-of-light-skin-preference.

Chapter 6
Sonora Invaded: The Occupation of Arizona

 ## Learning Objectives

6.1 Contrast the image of Arizona as uninhabitable desert before the American Invasion to realty.

6.2 Describe the ways Mexicans and Euro-Americans land grabbed in the Sonora and the layer they put on the onion.

6.3 Describe how the social order and social rankings changed in the new order.

6.4 Describe the role of lynching in the maintenance of the caste

6.5 Analyze the ways that wealth and racism influenced life on the Arizona frontier.

6.6 Describe the economic transformation and racial polarization of Arizona in the late 1800s.

6.7 Explain the relationship between copper mining and population movement in Arizona and how it affected the social order.

6.8 Describe ways that Arizona populations were impacted by and responded to industrialization.

6.9 Describe the impact of water conservation on commercial farming and the pull of Mexicans into Arizona.

Forgotten People

6.1 Contrast the image of Arizona as uninhabitable desert before the American Invasion to realty.

Arizona was settled at least 12,000 years ago before the Spanish and then the American occupations. It has dozens of tribal settlements. Today, it still has one of the highest percentages of Native Americans in the United States. The Navajo Nation lives in what is the largest U.S. Native American reservation, extending through Utah, Arizona, and New Mexico, covering over 27,000 square miles. The Diné Bikéyah, or Navajoland, covers an area larger than 10 of the 50 American states.

The second-largest Arizona Indigenous Nation is the Tohono O'odham. They are grouped with the Akimel O'odham (the River People), known as Pima, who live in what is now central and southern Arizona. The Pima Nation lived along the Gila, Salt, Yaqui, and Sonora Rivers. According to legend, the original Pima Tribe was in the Salt River Valley and extended into the Gila River Valley. Remnants can be found in the Casa Grande Ruins National Monument. They also built numerous Pueblo villages in the Gila and Salt River Valleys.

The Cochise culture of eastern Arizona and western New Mexico dates back an estimated 9,000 to 2,000 years. Archeological sites found in southern Arizona and northern Sonora are thought to be that of the ancestors of Mogollon and Hohokam. The Mogollon culture were prehistoric North American Indigenous Peoples who lived in the Arizona area from approximately CE 200–1450. They resided in the mountainous region of what became southeastern Arizona and southwestern New Mexico. The Anasazi, or "Ancestral Pueblo," inhabited the Colorado Plateau in southern Utah and Colorado and northern Arizona and New Mexico since before the time of Jesus.

The Chiricahua Apache best-known chiefs were Cochise, Victorio, Loco, Chato, Nahche, Bonito, and Geronimo. Other branches of the Apache Nation thrived in Arizona. Native people also lived on the Colorado River, the deserts, and the mountains. The Hopi today live in the Four Corners area where Arizona, Colorado, New Mexico, and Utah meet. Indigenous reservations comprise more than a quarter of Arizona and house about 22 Indigenous nations. This fact has not been lost on developers and the waste dumping industry who, with the support of state and federal agencies, has encroached on Indigenous lands.[1] Privatization perpetually threatens Indigenous Peoples.[2]

The American Occupation of Arizona

In 1848 a Boundary Commission was convened by the United States and Mexico to adjust the border in accordance with the terms of the Treaty of Guadalupe Hidalgo. Before the ink was dry on the agreement, in 1854 New Mexico Territorial Governor William Carr Lane claimed that the area known as la Mesilla belonged to New Mexico, and that the United States gave la Mesilla to Mexico illegally—la Mesilla belonged to the Territory of New Mexico[3]. The governor alleged that the Boundary Commission intended to claim la Mesilla but that Congress prevented the Commission from making the transfer. The controversy wore on with many local and national politicians supporting Lane.[4]

The Treaty of Guadalupe Hidalgo (1848) ceded the northern part of Arizona to the United States. Not satisfied with the agreement, the United States aggressively pursued the Gadsden Purchase, also known as the Treaty of La Mesilla that in 1853 became part of the United States as a result of diplomatic pressure. The pretext of the American emissaries was that the United States wanted la Mesilla as a route for a projected railroad to the Pacific. The United States used threats to pressure Mexico to sell. James Gadsden, a former military officer and aide to General Andrew Jackson, was sent to Mexico as an ambassador. He reportedly ordered Mexican officials to sell or the United States would take it. The Gadsden Purchase encompassed a 29,670-square-mile strip of land in southern Arizona and southwestern New Mexico. The Gadsden Treaty, while adjusting the boundaries between the two nations, was controversial. The bordering states had historical ties with Arizona and New Mexico. With this so-called acquisition completed the empire consolidated its national space.

La Mesilla linked Arizona's mining centers to those in adjoining Chihuahua and Sonora. Mining was the principal reason Americans first moved to Arizona. The mining industry intensified operations during the 1849 California Gold Rush, with American prospectors traveling through the region to California. From the beginning, tension existed between the colonizers and the colonized, and gold fever only increased it. For example, in 1863, American prospectors working the Colorado River above Yuma discovered gold at La Paz; the strike attracted 5,000 prospectors within the year. White miners attempted to ban Mexicans from mining camps.

As the American Empire integrated the southwest, its worldview expanded, intensifiing feelings of entitlement, with Americans viewing Indigenous People and the Mexicans as foreigners. The empire revealed its imperial intentions as economic pressure to defend financial holdings increased and the merchant class and cotton interests sought financial advantages.

American Expansion 1783–1867		
1783	U.S. Independence	892,135 sq miles
1803	Louisiana Purchase	827,987 sq miles
1821	Florida Purchase	72,101 sq miles
1845	Texas	389,166 sq miles
1846	Oregon Purchase	286,541 sq miles
1848	Mexican Cession	529,189 sq miles
1853	Gadsden Purchase	29,670 sq miles
1867	Alaska	591,000 sq miles
1867	Midway Islands	2 sq miles

Excerpted: "U.S. Territorial Acquisitions," United States History, http://www.u-s-history.com/pages/h1049.html.

Americans found it necessary to justify the expansion of its empire. As mentioned, part of the rhetoric promoting the so-called Gadsden Purchase was that it was necessary for a railroad—it was worthless for mining or agriculture. In reality, la Mesilla was part of modern Sonora–Arizona and was known to have vast mineral resources long before the Purchase. Mining bonanzas attracted prospectors from other provinces of Mexico. Eventually a railroad was constructed through la Mesilla; however, it was to serve the copper mines, not the continental railroad.

The arrival of white American prospectors brought warfare and diseases and led to the death of large numbers of Indigenous People. It also brought another variant of colonialism to Arizona and the Southwest. Despite the similarities, American and Spanish colonialism differed. Both brutalized the Indigenous Peoples. Both were self-interested and in both cases religion played a role in justifying imperialism.

In both cases, the conquerors attempted to control the narrative by portraying themselves as benevolent overlords and claiming that god was on their side. In the case of Spain it was bringing salvation to the Natives, basing its legitimacy on the authority of the Catholic Church. In the case of the American Empire, the conquest was rooted in the Old Testament. Exodus 17:11 (King James 2000 Bible), when the Israelis came upon the Amalek, god ordered Moses to slaughter them. When Moses arms were held up, Israel prevailed. It was god who slaughtered the infidels not the Israelis. British/American colonialism and its Old Testament underpinnings justified and made inevitable the annihilation of the infidels. In various forms it was part of a white supremacy ideology. This partially explains race relations in Arizona where what is Indigenous is being annihilated.

Spanish America was part of the world market. New Spain (Mexico) and Peru were world producers of silver, which was a primary medium of exchange in the Asiatic trade. In order maintain production, labor was necessary: Indigenous, African, and in some cases Filipinos. Spain in

1500 had a population of 8.5 million. It needed Indigenous labor to sustain its bureaucracy as wekk as to fight costly European wars. The colonial control was based on color Spanish colonialism integrated the colonized into a caste (casta) where their rights and duties were based on color.

While much of Sonora is arid and mountainous, it has more water resources than most other northern Mexican states. Sonora is on the west side of the Sierra Madre Occidental, and the mountains capture the moisture of the winds blowing off the ocean, producing running rivers such as the mighty Rio Yaqui,[5] and other smaller rivers such as the Mayo, Sonora, Gila, and Colorado. The availability of a constant flow of water facilitated the concentration of populations along its rivers. Meanwhile, the camps of small bands became grew into village villages. On the Colorado, Gila, Salt, and Santa Cruz Rivers.[6] An abundance of mountains—mountains meant water and minerals. More than half of Arizona consists of mountains and plateau regions. In the north, Humphreys Peak rises to 12,633 feet near Flagstaff.

By 1848 Mexican rancheros cultivated wheat and raised cattle on the northern frontier. All was not perfect the criollo hierarchy controlled the mines as well as the settlements around them. Sonoran elite continued to segregate themselves from the mixed-blood population.[7]

Many of mixed-blood ancestry insisted that Sonora was a criollo province. Censuses vary greatly but suggest considerable mixing, and in all probability the criollo myth came about to ensure self-identification and to qualify for colonial necessities that were granted only to some populations. A 1793 northern Sonora census listed 128 Europeans, only two of whom were women. Euromestizo males numbered 4,216, and Euro mestizo females, 5,899. The same census lists 1,630 Afro mestizo males and 1,385 Afromestizo females, and 1,932 Indo mestizo males and 1,870 Indio mestizo females. The Indigenous People constituted the majority, numbering 12,569 native males and 10,620 native females.[8] Over the years identity became confused and some priests used to note the colonial baptismal certificates, "dicen que es español."[9]

As in other parts of Nueva Vizcaya, the Sonorenses practiced slavery. African and Indigenous slaves labored at the mines and haciendas. Spain inherited the practice of slavery from the Romans and sank to lower depths in their conquests in the Americas, Africa, and Asia. They imported large numbers of Africans to meet their insatiable demand for labor, which made the exploitation of the land and its minerals profitable. Although the crown forbade the enslavement of Indigenous Peoples, mine owners, hacendados, and other colonists used legal loopholes to force the Native Americans to work in the mines, haciendas, and public projects. For instance, it was permissible to enslave Indigenous People taken in open and just warfare, those who were cannibals, or those who renounced Jesus. Spanish slave-hunters invaded the Sonoran frontier and took slaves from northern Pima villages.

The enslavement of the Apache was common since the seventeenth century. In 1734 the local pastor, Fray Joseph Manuel de Equia y Leronbe, of Nambe, an Indigenous village north of Santa Fé, wrote, "They claim that by selling Apache into slavery they will be redeemed from their lives as infidels. What benefit is it to condemn them so that they do not live as infidels? Enslave them so that they do not have freedom?"[10] The enslavement of Indigenous People was profitable: It cost up to five times more to buy an African slave than an Indigenous slave. Consequently, because Indigenous People were worth less money, they were expendable and were used in the most hazardous work.[11]

The Frontier

6.2 **Describe the ways Mexicans and Euro-Americans land grabbed in the Sonora and the layer they put on the onion.**

The Sonoran Desert, including southern Arizona, had been inhabited for at least 10 millennia. Extensive canal irrigation took place in the Tucson area during the first millennium BCE. However, it disappeared shortly before the Spaniards arrived in the New World. Hohokam occupation of the Phoenix Basin flourished between CE 500 and CE 1400; the area was irrigated by the Salt and Gila Rivers. The area sustained large urban centers and trading systems and an infrastructure that supported 225 ball courts. The sudden disappearance of the Hohokam remains a mystery. Scholars speculate that the Pima and the Tohono O'odham, who to this day are excellent farmers, are descendants of the Hohokam.[12]

The Tucson presidio was a staging area for the colonization of Arizona. In the 1830s, a presidio defended the tiny Tucson settlement, defending it from nomadic tribes. It had 465 Mexicans and about 486 Apache Mansos who were mostly farmers. By 1821 the secularization of the missions was underway and, Sonoran elites land grants in southeast Arizona and around Tucson, the new settlers drove the Pima off their farms along Santa Cruz River. The granting of land grants pressured the Apache and other native people to attack land-grant holders. Between 1790 and 1810, Sonora and Chihuahua brought the Apache under control by bribing them with goods. When the Mexican government discontinued this practice shortly after independence, the Apache once again attacked them. By the 1830s the Apache and the Sonorans were at war, and in the 1840s the Apache drove the settlers from their land grants.[13]

The Gadsden Purchase

Large numbers of white Americans became acquainted with la Mesilla, or southern Arizona, during the California Gold Rush of 1848–1850 when thousands of white Americans and more than 10,000 Sonorans passed through it to get to the California gold fields. Americans coveted the legendary mineral wealth of Sonora and hence worried about the growing influence of the French in Sonora and their attempts to establish French colonies there. Many American politicos urged Washington, D.C., to invoke the Monroe Doctrine and to take Sonora so the French could not get it. In 1853, President Franklin Pierce appointed James Gadsden—a soldier, diplomat, and railroad president—as U.S. minister to Mexico, with instructions to purchase as much of northern Mexico as possible. Gadsden proposed the purchase of five northern Mexican states and Baja California. When Mexican officials refused the deal, the United States sent 2,000 troops to the New Mexico border "to preserve order." Mexico would not sell Sonora, so Gadsden settled for the Mesilla, threatening Mexican ministers that, if Mexico did not sell southern Arizona and parts of New Mexico, "we shall take it."[14]

As mentioned the United States claimed that it wanted the land for a railroad route from El Paso to the California coast. Mexican sources contended that what the United States wanted was the port of Guaymas, Sonora.[15] This was a reasonable assumption, since vast deserts separated the Arizona mines from California ports, and Guaymas was one of the premier ports on the Pacific coast. Sonora also had a pool of experienced miners and manual laborers as well as urban centers. Historian Hubert Howe Bancroft wrote, "the northern republic could afford to pay for a railroad route through a country said to be rich in mines." In 1854, Charles Poston and Sylvester Mowry operated mines in the newly acquired land with the backing of Eastern capital; however, the military did not take possession of la Mesilla until two years later.[16]

War Hawks

Sonorans accused Americans of inciting the Apache to raid Sonora. West Point graduate, politician, miner, and land speculator Sylvester Mowry, in an address to the Geographical Society in New York on February 3, 1859, cynically stated that:

> The Apache Indian is preparing Sonora for the rule of a higher civilization than the Mexican. In the past half century the Mexican element has disappeared from that which is now called Arizona, before the devastating career of the Apache. It is every day retreating further south, leaving to us (when the time is ripe for our own possession) the territory without the population.[17]

Little doubt remains that Arizona miners and ranchers struck bargains with the Apache, guaranteeing them sanctuary in return for not raiding; Poston, owner of the Sonora Exploring and Mining Company and the so-called "Father of Arizona," made deals with the Apache. In return for sanctuary and arms, the Apache agreed not to steal from Poston, nor to kill his men. Moreover, Captain R. S. Ewell, the commanding officer at Fort Buchanan, who was supposed to be keeping the peace, was too busy working on his Patagonia mine to deal with military and civil matters.

The *Weekly Arizonian*, on April 28, 1859, condemned the use of the Apache to annihilate Sonorans as piracy. Miner and soldier Herman Ehrenberg wrote, "If we hate Mexicans, or if we want to take their country, we want no bloodthirsty savages to do the work for us, or to injure them."[18] It was not altruism on Ehrenberg's part; he knew that Mexican labor and trade with Sonora were essential to the growth of Arizona, and condemned the policy of making separate treaties with the Apache.

Filibustering Expeditions into Sonora

Filibustering expeditions continued throughout the 1850s. In 1857 Henry Crabb, a southerner and former member of the California legislature, led a 100 Californians into Sonora on what some American sources described as a peaceful colonizing expedition. The Mexicans ordered Crabb to leave the state. When he did not leave, the Sonorans ambushed his army and executed Crabb, cutting off his head and preserving it in alcohol. President James Buchanan condemned the Mexican "brutality" and attempted to use the incident as an excuse to invade Mexico.[19]

In the Senate, Sam Houston sponsored a resolution proposing that Mexico be made a protectorate of the United States. Two decades later, Poston confirmed that President Buchanan and his cabinet, prodded by powerful New York and New England capitalists, planned to first occupy northern Sonora and submit the matter to Congress afterward. Thus, in 1859 Buchanan sent the USS *St. Mary* to Guaymas for the purpose of provoking a war. The pretext was Governor Ignacio Pesqueira's refusal to allow Charles P. Stone to survey Sonora's public lands. The Mexican government had signed a contract with the Jecker-Torre Company and a group of U.S. investors, giving them rights over one-third of the public lands they surveyed, with an option to buy another third of the surveyed lands. However, when he arrived, Stone was obnoxious and arrogant, so Pesqueira refused to honor the agreement and ordered him out of the state. Stone responded by lobbying American authorities for government intervention.

William Porter captain of the *St. Mary* in 1859 demanded Pesqueira permit Stone to continue his survey and in November, threatened to bombard Guaymas. Pesqueira responded that if one shell fell on Guaymas, he would not guarantee the safety of American lives or property in Sonora. The *St. Mary* left, but tensions mounted as Buchanan inflamed passions, claiming that Mexicans expelled peaceful

Americans, violating their personal and real property rights. He requested that Congress approve the occupation of Sonora as well as Chihuahua. However, the impending Civil War prevented Buchanan from another unjust war.[20]

Mexicans in Early Arizona

6.3 Describe how the social order and social rankings changed in the new order.

During the initial years of the American intrusion, mining was the sole economic enterprise, and Eastern companies invested considerable capital in its silver mines. Lobbying of Washington, D.C. officials undoubtedly promoted these efforts to station soldiers in Arizona, allegedly to protect the mines against the Apache. In 1859, the population of la Mesilla was estimated at 7,695 residents, 7,125 of whom were Mexicans. Approximately 5,000–10,000 Pima and Tohono O'odhams also lived in la Mesilla.

In 1860, just over 70 percent of Tucson's population was Mexican. Most freight traveled to and from Guaymas, Sonora. The trip took 16 days and the cargo cost about $80 a ton to transport to San Francisco by ship. Over land, it took four months and cost $350–$400 a ton.[21] During the 1850s and 1860s, there was brisk trade between Guaymas and San Francisco. Arizona remained in the Sonoran orbit, using Mexican pesos as its currency. During this period, political turmoil in Sonora strengthened and weakened the ties between Mexico and the United States. The years 1861–1865 saw France invade Mexico and the crowning of an Austrian (1864–1867) as an emperor of Mexico. This triggered a civil war, causing a flood of political refugees to pour into Tucson.[22]

In 1863 Congress divided Arizona and New Mexico, creating the Arizona territory.[23] As with Texas and New Mexico, a political elite controlled government patronage. The new territorial government replaced the Santa Fé appointees. During the Civil War, most Americans in the territory were pro-Southern, and Arizona became a Confederate state in March 1861. This changed in June 1862, when the California Volunteers, under Major General James Henry Carleton, drove the Confederate forces out of Arizona. Carleton who had been born in Massachusetts commanded the 1st California Infantry in the District of Southern California. The Californians remained and defended Arizona from sedition, warded off the possibility of a French intervention in Sonora, and supposedly from the Apache. Meanwhile, the white population increased, with white farmers settling along the rivers in the center of Arizona, concentrating in the Santa Cruz Valley (the location of Tucson and Tubac), the lower reaches of the Gila and Colorado Rivers, and central Arizona.[24]

Territorial status brought public education to Arizona. In 1863 the Arizona legislature allocated $500 for Tucson public schools with the stipulation that English would be part of the curriculum. Americanization was very much on the mind of the legislators. Augustus Brichta was the town's first school teacher. However, owing to a lack of funds, the public school got off to a shaky start. In 1870 the sisters of St. Joseph established a school for girls; San Agustín remained the school for boys. In 1872 the Arizona territorial legislature passed the first public school law, and by the end of the 1870s, with the support of the Mexican community, public education became a reality. Nevertheless, the Mexican community preferred parochial schools because they allowed the teaching of Spanish and religion. Moreover, many opposed coeducation, which was mandatory in the public schools.[25]

The War of the Races

6.4 Describe the role of lynching in the maintenance of the caste

At times, a war of races seemed imminent. Mexican authorities often refused to extradite Mexicans accused of crimes committed in the United States For instance, on December 24, 1870, Mexicans killed three white Americans, Charles Reed, James Little, and Thomas Oliver, and wounded Reed's wife in a dispute over the alleged theft of furniture and five horses. After the shooting, one of the suspects fled to Sonora, and Arizona authorities demanded his extradition. The suspects claimed that the employer severely abused one of them and that they acted in self-defense. On the U.S. side, vigilantes rode to the ranch of Francisco Gándara, brother of the former governor of Sonora, shot him in front of his wife and children, and stole his valuables. An act of racism, with no proof, they had accused Gándara of stealing a mule and killing a white American.[26]

William Carrigan and Clive Webb list seven victims of mob violence even before the shooting of Gándara whose murder Arizona historians ignored. Carrigan and Webb write that on May 9, 1859, using the murder of a white man as a pretext, white colonials shot and killed four Mexicans in the Sonoita Valley as part of a plan to run Mexicans out of the valley. On August 3, 1859 Rafael Polaco was hanged in Tucson. On October 15 an unknown Mexican was shot and his ears cut off near Tubac; Mateo García was hanged in Arizona City in 1860. Ramón Cordova was hanged in Phoenix in 1872. 1873 was especially violent: Domingo García was clubbed to death near Tucson in 1873. Mariano Tisnado was hanged in Phoenix in 1873, and vigilantes hanged nine Mexicans in Phoenix in that same year and vigilantes hanged nine Mexicans in Phoenix in the same year in July. Leonard Cordova, Clemente López, and Jesús Saguaripa were hanged in Tucson August 8, 1873. On the August 31 of the same month Lúcas Lugas was shot in back the head at Kenyon Station by a posse, and in early September of that year a mob hanged Manuel Subiate in Yuma City.[27]

At Tombstone, founded in 1879, cowboy gangs raided defenseless Mexican villages. Racial tensions worsened with the arrival of the "cowboys," generally Texans. They precipitated much of the racial tension between Mexicans and white Americans. The worst type of Texas outlaws were drawn to the town, escalating racism as owners of businesses and mines refused to hire Mexicans for fear of antagonizing the cowboys. The Texans showed little respect for women or children.[28] Race relations would have gotten even worse if it had not been for the fact that Americans feared the Apache.

The Race Question

6.5 Analyze the ways that wealth and racism influenced life on the Arizona frontier.

Adhering to the caste system whites demonstrated generalized racism, whereas elite whites were more selective about their prejudices. Opportunistic considerations, such as their need for marital connections, defense, and/or business contacts dictated their actions. Sonora was right next door, and trade was essential to Arizona's prosperity. The Mexican elites failed to take advantage of this vulnerability and some even colluded with the white elite. A partial explanation was that some of them were descendants of criollos who arrived in Sonora and Chihuahua during the eighteenth century, and considered themselves superior to poor whites and the darker-skinned Mexicans. Moreover, many elites cultivated contacts with white power brokers. As in New Mexico, a number of Arizona Mexicans prospered under U.S. colonial rule.

Examples include Felipe Amabisca and Antonio Contreras, who reached Arizona City in 1858 and opened a mercantile store and a freighting business. Estevánn Ochoa from Chihuahua, educated in Independence, Missouri, and formerly from New Mexico's la Mesilla, moved to Tucson and started a freighting business with Pinckney Randolph Tully. M. G. Samaniego, born in Sonora and raised in Chihuahua, ran successful businesses in Chihuahua and la Mesilla before arriving in Tucson. Samaniego was a graduate of St. Louis University. He was conservative, and sympathized with Confederacy during the Civil War. These men had the necessary educational and financial capital to succeed.

As in New Mexico, a clique of Americans and their Mexican collaborators ran the territorial government after the Civil War. Federal appointees in Tucson, along with business leaders and voters, lobbied Congress for appropriations to subsidize military operations, highways, Indigenous reservations, and the railroad. Freighters like Tully and Ochoa profited handsomely from government contracts procured through their political acquaintances.[29] By contrast, the overwhelming Mexican population labored for subsistence wages.

Marrying Up!

What Americans thought of Mexican women greatly depended on the hue of the woman's skin and social class. American suitors often described these women as independent and skilled in riding horses; they occasionally described higher-class Sonoran women as intelligent and white. Not much was written about the poor women. What we know is that all classes of Mexicans migrated to Arizona in family units. Even with its harshness, the frontier gave Mexican women better access to traditionally male-dominated occupations. The better-off Mexican women inherited land and mercantile houses from their fathers or husbands.

Often marriage was a business arrangement, and rich Mexican fathers received a measure of protection from having a white son-in-law. However, not all the marriages were between prominent Mexican women and white males. According to Salvador Acosta, "working-class Mexican women accounted for a large percentage of the wives of white men in nineteenth-century Tucson, most of who were also of working-class origins."[30] Poor women did not take financial capital to their marriages but they did much more, performing menial chores, caring for the animals, working in farms, and contributing to the defense of the community. In cases of interracial relationships, poor women lacked the protection of a powerful family, however.[31]

The 1860 Arizona Census showed that women in Tucson were concentrated in jobs such as seamstress or washerwoman, work that could be done from home. Mexican males worked in blue-collar occupations; nearly half of them were unskilled. Mexicans made up 58 percent of Tucson's laborers, and only seven Mexicans out of a total Mexican population of 653 persons, worked as merchants, traders, or shopkeepers. Tucson listed 168 Americans, 160 of whom were male. That same census listed 1,716 Mexicans and 871 non-Mexicans in southern Arizona. By the 1870s, 62 percent of the mixed marriages in Pima County were between American males and Mexican females. According to historian Salvador Acosta, Mexicans were technically white so the territory's anti-miscegenation laws did not apply to them.[32] The ambiguity of the Mexicans' race worked to the advantage of the white population because without Mexicans the territory would have had only 600 white residents. Arizona's first legislature (1864) passed an anti-miscegenation law that remained in effect until 1962. Indeed, Arizona was one of the first legislatures "to adopt strict definitions of whiteness in its miscegenation law."[33]

Between 1872 and 1899, intermarriage rates between white men and Mexican females remained high, constituting 148 of 784, or 19 percent of all marriages; during the same period only six marriages involved Mexican men and American women. Acosta concluded that "Between 1860 and 1900, Mexican women accounted for 30 percent of all unions involving white men. The percentage break down is as follows: 67 percent in 1860, 91 percent in 1864, 79 percent in 1870, 40 percent in 1880, and 16 percent in 1900." Intermarriages among people of mixed ancestry almost always had white American surnames. After this point unions between Mexican males and white women became more widespread, although the frequency of intermarriages overall did not approach those of the nineteenth century. In 1946, only 3 percent of the marriages were between American men and Mexican women, and only 1 percent between Mexican men and white females.[34]

Intermarriages were an opportunity for the newcomers to inherit property from their Mexican fathers-in-law or to go into business with their wives' families. Mexican women also held the key to participation in the social life of the Pueblo and access to extended families. As time passed, intermarriage became less of an advantage: The railroad ended Arizona's isolation and American women arrived in larger numbers in the 1800s, making Mexican women less desireable to gringos. The railroad also ended the Apache threat by accelerating the transportation of troops and dramatically increasing the territory's population.[35]

Some Mexican women were housewives, domestics, or worked in *cantinas* (bars); a few operated businesses and subsistence farms. Eulalia Elías (1788–1860) ran the first major cattle ranch in Arizona. She was admitted to the Arizona Women's Hall of Fame in the 1980s. Though unusual, it was not completely surprising because Eulalia belonged to a wealthy and powerful founding family. Such opportunities were not open to poor Mexicans of either gender. The highest job a Mexican woman could aspire to was a schoolteacher, like Rosa Ortiz, who in the 1870s ran a Mexican private school where the medium of instruction was Spanish.[36]

The Alliance of Elites

By the 1870s, Tucson and the rest of Arizona were starting to become culturally "American." The population of Tucson mushroomed to 8,007, which included a large number of Americans. Most new "American" immigrants settled in the northern part of the territory, necessitating moving the state capital from Tucson to Prescott in 1877. A year later Arizona's population grew to 40,000. The number of elected Mexican officials declined, and fewer Spanish surnames appeared in the social columns of Tucson English-language newspapers. Still, the Mexican population kept a social and cultural presence in the Pueblo. Spanish-language newspapers such as *Las dos Repúblicas*, *El Fronterizo*, and later, *El Tucsonense*, which began publishing in the mid-1870s, covered local news as well as that of Sonora and the rest of Latin America. *El Tucsonense* protested the negative stereotypes of Mexicans and championed their rights.

By the late 1870s, upward social and economic mobility among Mexicans slowed as businesses became capital-intensive and Mexican access to capital tightened.

As Tucson's history was recorded by Americans, Mexicans were excluded from Tucson's historical past. For example, in 1884 when Samaniego became a member of the Society of Arizona Pioneers, consisting of those who arrived in Arizona before 1870, fewer than 10 percent of its members were Mexican American.[37]

The War on the Apache

The Mexican cooperation with white colonials in fighting the Apache was not admirable. For example, in 1871, 6 white Americans, 48 Mexicans, and 94 Tohono O'odhams attacked a defenseless Apache camp near Camp Grant, massacring more than 100 Apache women and children. Army officials attributed it to freighters and government contractors, who allegedly provoked the incident to keep the forts stocked to allay locals' fears. Arizona historian Thomas Sheridan argues that this is an oversimplification, since passions ran deep and the Apache had warred with Tohono O'odhams and Mexicans for decades. "Both sides murdered adults and carried off children whenever they found them. Both sought vengeance for their dead. . . . Bloody as it was, the Camp Grant Massacre was no aberration. On the contrary, it was," according to Sheridan, "the culmination of two centuries of conflict on the Arizona frontier."[38] Though this may be partly true, to excuse the massacre is to ignore the impact of the American and Spanish colonialism that institutionalized this kind of behavior. The military and the so-called citizens' militias pursued the Apache throughout the 1870s, capturing and shipping hundreds to Florida and the other so-called reservations. The Apaches were not the only natives to suffer. Colonists also relentlessly pursued the Navajo in Arizona and New Mexico.[39]

The So-called "Friendly Indian"

Before the 1870s, the Pima and the Tohono O'odhams, who were generally considered "friendly Indigenous" People did much of farming. The Homestead Act of 1862 encouraged the in-migration of white colonists, intensifying competition for land and water. American farmers trickled into Arizona in the 1860s, but by the 1870s, irrigation projects were initiated in the Salt River Valley. By the middle of the decade, white farmers cultivated hay and cotton. Commercial agriculture worsened mutual relations among the Mexicans, the natives, and white Americans.

The end of the Apache threat, due to the influx of Americans and the proximity of troops via the railroad, opened more space for white colonials and encouraged further encroachment on Pima land. By the 1870s, the Pima, former allies of the Spanish colonists, who fed American and Mexican argonauts during the California Gold Rush, were producing three million pounds of wheat a year. A decade earlier, Mexican farmers dug irrigation canals upriver from the Pima around Florence, diverting water. When the Pima complained in 1873 to Washington officials, authorities suggested that they move to Indigenous Territory in Oklahoma. Over time, the Pima's lands were bled dry, and they were eventually reduced to accepting a small ration of water.[40]

The Land-Grant Grab

Mexicans in Arizona fought the land-grant battle, although on a smaller scale. Congress in 1870 authorized the surveyor general of Arizona "to ascertain and report" upon claims. The surveys were purposely slow, dragging into the 1880s and thus encouraging squatters to occupy the land. The nonfeasance and the malfeasance of the courts encouraged the filing of fraudulent claims and schemes to invalidate Mexican titles. The law gave landowners little or no protection against squatters. Because Mexicans could not work their land, they could not pay their taxes, which resulted in losing title to their land.[41] The railroad land grants also took their bite. Meanwhile, the New Mexico and Arizona Land Co. acquired land and uranium ore deposits throughout Arizona, Texas, New Mexico, and Colorado.[42]

The Transformation of Arizona

6.6 Describe the economic transformation and racial polarization of Arizona in the late 1800s.

The number of cattle in Arizona was small because of Apache raids; most cattle raisers were small operators. The railroads and the 1877 Desert Land Act changed this, accelerating the industrialization of Arizona. Mining also stimulated cattle and farming enterprises to feed the miners, attracting large numbers of Texas cowboys, who, according to professor Raquel Rubio-Goldsmith, brought "their English language and dislike of Mexicans." The *New York Times* announced the availability of homestead land in Arizona, announcing on June 4, 1880, "This Territory is largely populated by ignorant and non-English speaking Mexicans and 'greasers,' and has been much harried by Indigenous wars." The *New York Times* wrote that the main attraction was mining and livestock grazing and that there was no reason to fear the Indigenous People any longer.[43]

Cattlemen flocked to Arizona during the 1880s, overgrazing the range, damaging water supplies, and causing severe ecological damage. Commercial sheep stock-raising increased, with the number of commercially raised sheep catapulting from 76,524 in 1880 to 698,404 in 1890. Stock-raising enterprises expanded with Arizona's dependence on national and international markets. The last decades of the nineteenth century saw rapid agricultural and commercial expansion, though this reliance led to hardships during times of economic fluctuation and droughts.

From Adobe to Copper

Tucson continued as a center of Mexican life. In 1879, The *New York Times* described Tucson as having some 10,000 souls "living in the low adobe houses, lining irregular and narrow streets, deserted in the heat of the day," but coming to life during the evening hours. The *NY Times* referred to the Mexicans as "greasers," saying that few "Americans" lived there and fewer were "blessed" with wives of their color. According to the *NY Times*, "jealous" Mexicans stood guard over their female property.

During the first years of American occupation, travelers stopped in Tucson en route to California, and it became the overland gateway to Sonora and California. Trade with Sonora increased, and Tucson was perfectly placed to be the center of that trade. Tucson merchants catered to the military posts, the mines, and the farms within their orbits.

The importance of Tucson dimmed as irrigation projects opened larger agricultural areas north of the Gila River, and eclipsed those of Guaymas. More and more government contractors used the road through Yuma to ship their army supplies, a more northern route that followed the Gila River, almost completely bypassing Tucson. The new route contributed to the growth of Pumpkinville—population of 300—that grew to become Phoenix in 1871. Phoenix's population increased owing to the growth of commercial agriculture in the Salt River Valley and its use as army trade route. These population changes boosted the political influence of Phoenix at the expense of Tucson. This change affected the fortunes of the Mexican elite, many of whom were centered in Tucson, and it marked the decline of the popularity of the Mexican peso, the "doby dollar" (*adobe dollar*), as a medium of exchange.[44]

The decline of the Tucson elite did not reduce the presence of Mexicans; nor did it mean that Tucson was no longer a commercial center, however. In the 1880s, railroads bound Sonora to the United States. Nogales remained the main port of entry from Sonora. However, Nogales did not have the distinctiveness or historical importance of El Paso. Tucson was 70 miles north of La Linea and older than Nogales, so it remained the commercial center of the Sonora–Arizona border area; it was a hub city for the copper mines of northern Sonora and eastern Arizona. As the city grew, Mexican laborers were attracted to Tucson and Sonoran notables sent their sons and daughters there for schooling. In Tucson, the more prominent families lived in north Tucson, while laborers were clustered in the southern part of the city, close to the old plaza, and isolated from whites.

Spanish-language newspapers regularly reported the separate literary and social life of Mexicans. Mexicans celebrated *las fiestas patrias* and San Juan's (St. John the Baptist's) Day on June 24—dancing, picnicking, and swimming in the Santa Cruz River. Many Mexicans traveled to Magdalena, Sonora, for the feast of San Francisco in early October. Tucson's Mexican population patronized traveling Sonoran troupes rather than American entertainments. Culturally, Mexicans and Americans grew even further apart as the twentieth century approached.[45]

Border Conflicts

As the territory's population grew, polarization between the two races increased as the caste became more rigid. The arrival of new colonials, mostly farmers, from Utah, Colorado, and points east worsened the racial divide. These new settlers were "peace-loving and God-fearing"—that is, they were racist, rationalizing that the Mexicans were the intruders because they believed the land was their privilege as Americans. Even the saloons were segregated; in 1880, for instance, Jesús Carrillo entered the Tip Top saloon in Prescott where white miners assaulted him. They put a noose around his neck and dragged him around town for daring to enter "their" saloon.

Few women lived in the mining camps, and the majority who did were Mexican. They were the targets of stereotypes, sexual harassment, and assault. This tension response to what was occurring at the border, where cattle rustling and murders erupted on both sides; fights often broke out over women. Tombstone remained a refuge for drunken white laborers who publicly tried to take women away from their Mexican partners. Conflict between so-called American authorities and Mexicans did not abate during this decade even as commercial relations increased between the two people.[46]

Meanwhile, the policy of annihilation of the Indigenous People continued.

The Pull Factors

6.7 Explain the relationship between copper mining and population movement in Arizona and how it affected the social order.

Beginning in the 1880s, copper mining attracted huge numbers of skilled and non-skilled laborers from Mexico. Up to this point the greatest in-migration was from Sonora, but with the growth of copper mining, larger numbers arrived from New Mexico, Chihuahua, and other Mexican states. Mexicans continued their tradition of working plots of land and, in the off season, working in nearby mines for cash and goods. Reminiscent of the colonial period, mining bonanzas lured large numbers of people. Mining generated ripples of economic activity in agriculture and livestock operations that fed the miners.

By the turn of the century, these two corridors were heavily traveled, as thousands of workers passed back and forth across the border to and from the mines. The first eastern Arizona mine owners were merchants and prospectors from the Las Cruces and Silver City areas, who recruited Mexican miners and their families from El Paso.[47] Besides the recruits from El Paso-Juárez, Mexican workers migrated to eastern Arizona from New Mexico and Sonora. Many Mexican miners had previously been small farmers, and only worked seasonally in mining. Some continued this practice, often returning home to harvest their crops.

The Industrialization of Arizona

6.8 Describe ways that Arizona populations were impacted by and responded to industrialization.

The Southern Pacific Railroad reached Tucson in 1880, and 10 years later 1,000 miles of line had been laid in the territory, in addition to 700 miles of canals. Arizona, like the rest of the Southwest, was underdeveloped in terms of capitalist enterprises. Before the introduction of the railroad that made possible the large-scale exploitation of the territory's resources and its integration into the American Empire. Improved transportation brought industrialization and more white Americans and, along with them, eastern and foreign capital. The railroad incorporated Arizona into the rest of the country, dramatically transforming its economy. The Southern Pacific, for example, could haul goods from Yuma to Tucson for 1½ cents a pound in one day, whereas freighters charged 5½–14 cents per pound, and took up to 20 days to deliver their cargo. The railroad led to the era of the "Three C's"—cattle, copper, and cotton—and impacted the Mexican identity, as fewer Mexicans controlled production.[48]

The Importance of Mining

Mining predated the railroad; Mexicans worked as prospectors and laborers in camps around the Gila and Colorado Rivers. Mexican miners were usually the first to enter the camps and remained even after the camps were abandoned. They founded the mining strikes at Black Canyon, Bradshaw district, and Walnut Grove. Despite intense discrimination, Mexicans endured and pushed the frontier back.

The Walker diggings at Lynx Creek typify American–Mexican clashes in these camps. In 1863–1864, the town of Walker passed a law that "no Mexicans shall have the right to buy, take up, or preempt a claim on this river [the Hassayampa] or in this district for the term of six months." Although the town did not allow Mexicans to own claims, the townspeople did "permit" them to work for wages. The white miners nicknamed Walker "Greaserville."[49]

Nikola Tesla, a former employee of Thomas Edison, developed the alternating current (AC) system of electricity in 1887. This system made possible long-distance transmission of electricity that used copper as the conductor. George Westinghouse, a major competitor of Edison, bought the rights. The most efficient conduit for the AC was copper.[50] Gold and silver were important, but copper was King.

By the turn of the century Arizona was a major world producer of copper ore, attracting large armies of Mexican workers. Development had begun in the 1870s when merchant capitalists funded mining enterprises. Arizona in the early twentieth century became the second-largest and then the largest copper producer in the world. Clifton-Morenci-Metcalf, the Copper Queen of Bisbee, and copper mining camps of Jerome, Globe, and Miami housed legendary mining companies that were built by the blood and sweat of Mexicans.

Monopolization in the industry increased and, by the end of the 1880s, large Scottish combines, along with eastern capital, controlled Arizona copper. Railroads linked Arizona mines with the copper mines of Cananea and Nacozari, Sonora, and the smelters of El Paso. These enterprises attracted thousands of Mexican laborers. The copper mining industry fueled a second American industrial revolution, as copper wiring became the mainstay of electricity distribution, motors, and other products needed by the growing nation. Mammoth copper production required mammoth amounts of labor—and in Arizona that meant Mexicans.[51]

The Expansion of Capital

Arizona's population expanded rapidly and the number of people engaging in commercial enterprises jumped from 591 in 1870 to 3,252 in 1880. A decade before, Arizona had no banks merchants provided banking services—thus the territory had a weak financial infrastructure. The Bank of Arizona was chartered in Prescott in 1877 to serve 3,000 miners in the nearby Bradshaw Mountains. As the Arizona market expanded, San Francisco and New York bankers moved into the territory and established monopolies.

The railroads, new technology, and engineering drove the mining boom of the 1880s. Telegraph and electrical wires required copper, and the copper mines of southern Arizona lured investors from San Francisco and eastern United States, as well as foreign capital. Financed by California capitalists and Louis Zeckendorf, the Copper Queen Mining Company opened in Bisbee. The mine was later acquired by the Phelps–Dodge Company, which became the largest copper producer in the territory.

New industries received federal protection, which meant army forts, which in turn meant government contracts. The army herded Native Americans into reservations, bringing even more government contracts to the territory. The demand for large quantities of wood for the mineshafts spread the economic boom to the forests of northern Arizona. The territory's population increased from 40,000 in 1880 to 90,000 seven years later, with Americans finally outnumbering Mexicans. Arizona boomed and the market value of property increased to $26 million.[52]

The 1890s: Deskilling Mine Work

In the 1890s, Sonoran workers met most of Arizona's labor needs, but the Mexicans continued to endure racism. By the 1890s, the high-grade copper mines were depleted. This changed the mode of production as technology made possible the mining of lower-grade ores of copper. Deskilled mining operations required massive of amounts of dirt to be taken out of the earth from which the ore was concentrated, leached out, and refined.[53] This production required armies of unskilled miners with picks and shovels. The need for non-skilled labor led to the importation of large numbers of Mexican workers from Chihuahua and the other Mexican Border States and New Mexico.

The arrival of the railroad also opened up opportunities for skilled labor, specifically those with access to capital and education. For the most part, small Mexican businesses could not compete in this new market. Even the merchant capitalists who initially financed the copper mines often were unable to afford upgrades required by the new technology. For example, in the early 1880s, the Longfellow Mining Co. built a 36-inch narrow-gauge railway between Clifton, Arizona, and Lordsburg, New Mexico, at a cost of $1,542,275 for 71 miles—a fortune at the time.[54] Mine owners were required to construct dozens of small inclines and spurs in the Clifton-Morenci-Metcalf area alone. Not all were able to keep up.

The burro- and horse-drawn mills and hand pulverization processes gave way to larger and more sophisticated smelters and concentrators for processing the ore. Mechanization quickly restructured the industry, as unskilled miners replaced the skilled hard-rock miners, who blamed Mexicans for the changes. Even in good times, workers were vulnerable, with frequent economic depressions creating havoc. Economic safety nets were few and unemployment meant starvation. Worsening the plight of the miners was the lack of workers' compensation for those injured on the job. Moreover, the mine managers manipulated racial tensions between the Mexican and the American miners to divide and conquer for their own economic benefit, promoting segregated communities and even segregated dressing areas for miners. At home, the workers lived in hovels with their wives, who were expended physically with—among other chores—washing their work clothes. Mexican hovels lacked plumbing, and the women walked miles for water, which they hauled back to their homes and heated.

The Impact of Industrialization on Mexicans

In 1870, Arizona numbered 9,658 persons; 30 years later, the population grew to 122,931, of which 14,171 Mexicans were born in Mexico and 29,000 in the United States. By 1880, Tucson had 7,007 residents; 4,469 were of Mexican origin. Tucson, however, grew only marginally in the next 20 years, to only 7,531 during which time the Mexican population fell to 4,122. Tucson no longer housed the largest concentration of Mexicans; by 1900 the mining towns and commercial-agriculture areas along the uppermost western part of the Gila River had a majority of Mexican workers. However, because the Mexican population in the mining camps was highly transitory, Tucson continued as the organizational and social capital of Mexicans in the territory despite this shift. Tucson was the gateway to Sonora, where many of the miners kept homes. Miners from camps throughout Arizona would travel to Tucson for shopping and fiestas.[55]

Mutual-Aid Societies

Mexicans formed organizations throughout the 1860s and 1870s. With the growing alienation of Mexican workers, the decline of labor guilds, and the isolation of the Mexican population, new forms of self-help societies and fraternal organizations sprang up among the workers and the middle class. *Mutualistas*, or mutual-aid societies, were the most popular self-help organizations. Mexican immigrants were familiar with multualistas in Mexico where they were organized during the late nineteenth century as skilled tradesmen struggled to cope with economic fluctuations. During this period, *juntas patrióticas* were formed on both sides of the border to celebrate Mexican heroes and other historical events. These organizations flourished during the French Intervention (Dec. 8, 1861–June 21, 1867) and were active in the United States.

As with the Irish, these societies and organizations helped Mexican workers integrate into the immigrant community. When migrating to different camps, miners found support in local chapters of the *mutualista*. This sense of *mutualismo* grew out of shared race, religion, national origin, or some combination of these. A sense of unity and ethnicity, and the desire to share in and strengthen that sense, was at the heart of mutual-aid efforts and fraternal associations. The *mutualistas* differed according to the work environment; in the mines, for example, they often served as forums for labor activities. Socialists, for the most part, criticized *mutualistas*, alleging that they relieved capitalism of the duty of paying for the social costs of production.[56]

On January 14, 1894, *Tucsonenses* formed *La Alianza Hispano Americana* in response to the anti-immigrant assaults, which had worsened during the Depression of 1893. The American Protective Association harbored white nativists and was aggressively anti-Mexican. Ignacio Calvillo, a founder of *La Alianza*, remembered, "In those days the English and Spanish-speaking had a hard time getting along. The element opposed to the Spanish-American people in the Southwest had organized itself into the American Protective Association."

La Alianza, initially a local organization, held its first national convention in 1897. By 1910, it grew to more than 3,000 members and had chapters in Arizona, Texas, New Mexico, California, and Mexico. *La Alianza* was popular in the mining camps of Arizona. Its prime mover was Carlos I. Velasco, who was a member of the Sonoran legislature (ca. 1869) before he immigrated to Arizona. He worked as a clerk in a store in 1870. Starting in 1878, Velasco became the editor of the Tucson newspaper *El Fronterizo*, and was a founding member of the *La Alianza*. He served as its Supreme President from 1894–1896.[57]

Middle-Class Mexicans

Tucson's Mexican middle class represented the interests of its caste and culture. Some were descendants of the criollo notables who founded Sonora, joined by a smattering of Mexicans from Border States such as Chihuahua. Family connections were important socially and economically, as Féderico José María Ronstadt recalled. At the age of 14, Ronstadt went to Tucson from Magdalena, Sonora, to serve as an apprentice to his mother's brother-in-law, and lived with his aunt. Ronstadt was related to many of the old families of Sonora that maintained links with elites in Tucson.[58]

Settled families supported other family members in business interests with relatives, immigrating later, and quickly integrating them into the social life of Consensuses circle of clubs. As a class they were not liberal; on the contrary, most were quite conservative and their organizations more often opposed organized labor. As early as 1878, *Las Dos Repúblicas* condemned workers' societies, alleging that they were made up of "idle and depraved people" who wanted "a repetition of the 1792 Revolution in France."[59]

Although housing and commercial segregation was common and racial slurs frequent, few middle-class leaders made the connection between racism and exploitation. They internalized colonial mentalities and considered themselves white and superior to Americans and were thus somewhat surprised and offended that someone would consider them "colored."

Patriarchy

Women played a subservient role in Tucson society; changes were, however, taking place. In 1880 women headed a quarter of the households; by 1900 this number climbed to a third. Widows headed most of these households. In some cases, women adapted their roles to the demands of the workplace. For example, after the turn of the century, in Douglas, where U.S. stores relied on trade from northern Sonora for survival, "young women who could speak both Spanish and English were critical intermediaries. Women [however] were restricted to clerk positions, but there was little open discrimination because they were in demand.... Mexican American women with less education or English worked as maids and cooks."[60]

The Emergence of Trade Unions

In 1871, Arizona produced only 1 percent of copper produced nationwide; by 1885, its share had risen to 15 percent. During the early decades, hard-rock miners did most of the mining. But the deskilling of the industry caused the number of workers to multiply. Laborers organized to challenge the giant corporations that controlled the mines. However, these unions were racist and excluded Mexicans from the brotherhoods. Even the Western Federation of Miners (WFM), supposedly led by radicals, did not recruit Mexicans because of the hostility of white miners toward them. They branded Mexican workers as "cheap labor" and moved to exclude them from the camps.

The WFM encouraged the labeling of Globe as a white man's camp and Clifton-Morenci-Metcalf as Mexican camps where wages and housing were dismal. The WFM worked to limit the number of Mexicans living in the mining camps. The lack of working-class unity and the pretensions to superiority of the white miners allowed employers to use a double-wage standard that paid Mexicans less than white Americans. Mexicans resented getting paid less for equal work as well as the other forms of discrimination (i.e., segregated housing and so on). In 1901, the Arizona legislature created the Arizona Rangers, who closely resembled the Texas Rangers, to keep Mexicans in their place. Although politicos claimed that the Rangers were formed to stop cattle rustling, they were more often used as strikebreakers.[61]

It's the Water

6.9 Describe the impact of water conservation on commercial farming and the pull of Mexicans into Arizona.

Commercial farming lagged a decade or two behind mining but similarly it jumped from small to huge, with absentee owners and managers' agribusiness managing estates. Commercial farmers and ranchers drove small farmers out of business by diverting waterways and monopolizing water resources. Small Mexican farmers operated near the mining camps, but they had to follow the water. Water was at a premium in Arizona, and irrigation cost money. The lack of capital drove many Mexican, Native American, and small white farmers out of farming.

The greening of the Salt River and Imperial Valley attracted armies of Mexican workers and their families to Arizona's and eastern California's deserts. As a consequence of the Reclamation Act of 1902, farmers in the Salt River Valley received federal assistance to construct irrigation projects on the Salt River and later on the Verde River.[62]

Between 1905 and 1911, financed by the Federal Reclamation Act, the Roosevelt Dam was constructed. It had the potential to irrigate large fields in the desert for about two years "even if no rain" fell. The Roosevelt Dam made huge cotton plantations possible. Although the Reclamation Act was supposed to create a class of small farmers, big planters monopolized the land and the water, and some 1,000 American families acquired 200,000 acres of well-watered land. The expansion of the plantation farms drove the growth of Phoenix and cleared the way for the damming of the Colorado River.[63]

Phoenix's Mexican community had lived there since the beginning of the town's existence. In 1870 the valley had 240 residents, 124 of them Mexican. Many of the workers employed on irrigation projects or the Phoenix town site were laid-off miners or laborers who alternated between mining and agriculture. According to Bradford Luckingham, "The labor and expertise of Mexicans proved essential to the success of early irrigation operations in the valley."[64]

As elsewhere in the Southwest, development depended on railroads that linked the fields to a core city. The railroads also brought in more Mexicans to labor in the fields and in other industries. The Southern Pacific was a major player, acquiring land not far from Phoenix, which became the Territorial Capital, attracting equipment, investors, and Mexicans. Massive water projects not only expanded commercial farming but also generated energy. Pacific Gas and Electric Company, a Phoenix–Los Angeles Corporation, held a monopoly on hydroelectric power generation. The government spent $61 million reclaiming the land, which farmers claimed would be repaid—but never was.[65]

Meanwhile, Los Angeles capitalists flocked to the Salt River area, which was as important to Los Angeles as was the Imperial Valley. In the Phoenix area, L.A. capitalists speculated heavily in real estate and farming. Arizona tourists also spent $1 million to $2 million annually in Los Angeles. By 1912, the reclaimed land was producing and marketing more than 450 bales of Egyptian cotton annually, which was the newly developed Pima cotton. (Pima cotton was an extra-long staple and it was thus grown in the Southwest United States starting about 1910.) The longer staple length made Pima a premium cotton fiber and ideal for tire building. The dramatic jump in the production of cotton meant a need for more seasonal workers, drawn from the mines, Sonora, and the interior of Mexico. The growth in population also meant more pick-and-shovel work, which meant more Mexicans.[66]

In 1915, the completion of the Roosevelt Reservoir gave new life to Salt River Valley. Wheat, cantaloupe, and watermelon crops were taking off, keeping many pickers and their families in the area year round. That year, six carloads of Thompson seedless grapes were shipped east. In 1916, cotton prices increased by 10 cents, reaching 40 cents a pound, and planters made a $70-an-acre profit. Meanwhile, as tire production multiplied, there was an increasing demand for Pima cotton. By 1918, Texans arrived to lease land and to pick cotton, which in turn meant an increase of racial discrimination toward the Mexicans.[67]

Conclusion: The Assault on the Saguara

In less than 50 years, Arizona passed from a subsistence farming economy to mercantile capitalism, to become one of the most industrialized places in the American Empire. The railroad and subsequent killing and herding of the Apache and other Indigenous Peoples into reservations made this possible. The mining boom created cities and racism in the mining camps sowed divisions. The political process was used to control the workers as wealth increasingly was concentrated in the hands of new elites and absentee owners of mines and farms. Mexican elites survived by maintaining cordial relations with the white ruling establishment.

In this environment a culture of whiteness thrived. The annihilation of the Indigenous Peoples continued with their isolation insured by their concentration in so-called reservations, and in recent years the privatization of those spaces. Mexicans have been relegated to a lower caste with color limiting their mentalities.

Notes

1. History of Native Americans, https://www.warpaths2peacepipes.com/history-of-native-americans/. Antonio Campa Soza Arizona Pictorial Biography has digital maps. See http://parentseyes.arizona.edu/booksbyedwardsoza/azpictorialbiography/foreword.htm.
2. Lydia Millet, "Selling Off Apache Holy Land," *New York Times*, May 29, 2015, https://www.nytimes.com/2015/05/29/opinion/selling-off-apache-holy-land.html; 12/03/2014 05:35 pm ET Updated. Michael McAuliff, "Congress Raids Ancestral Native American Lands With Defense Bill," *Huffingtonpost*, Dec. 12, 2014. https://www.huffingtonpost.com/2014/12/03/ndaa-land-deals_n_6264362.html.
3. Robert W. Larson. New Mexico's Quest for Statehood, 1846-1912 (Albuquerque: University of New Mexico Press, 1968), p. 322.
4. "The Gadsden Treaty," *New York Daily Times*, Mar. 17, 1854.
5. "Yaqui River," http://www.youtube.com/watch?v=lPnaQP7jJpk. Rio Yaqui - vida y muerte, http://www.youtube.com/watch?v=K0JAWRGVyyk.
6. "Arizona Lakes, Rivers and Water Resources," Geology.Com, https://geology.com/lakes-rivers-water/arizona.shtml.
7. Henry F. Dobyns, *Spanish Colonial Tucson: A Demographic History* (Tucson: University of Arizona Press, 1976). Thomas E. Sheridan, *Los Tucsonenses: The Mexican Community in Tucson, 1854–1941* (Tucson: University of Arizona Press, 1986). Miguel Tinker Salas, *In the Shadow of the Eagles: Sonora and the Transformation of the Border During the Porfiriato* (Berkeley: University of California Press, 1997), 4, 7, 27.
8. Robert H. Jackson, *Indian Population Decline: The Missions of Northwestern New Spain, 1687–1840* (Albuquerque: University of New Mexico Press, 1994), 195, ff 48, says, it is difficult to establish with precision the racial–ethnic origins of the Sonoran population. Parish priests, as in Chihuahua, exercised wide discretion. Moreover, the parish rolls of selected northern Sonora Parish Polls in the years 1796–1814 show that it was quite common to see the listing of coyote, mulatto, pardo, and mestizo. Gonzalo Aguirre Beltrán, *La población negra de México* (México, DF: Colección Firme, 1972), 228, 234–37. Horacio Sobarzo, *Vocabulario Sonorense* (México, DF: Editorial Porrua, S/S., 1966), 153. Oakah L. Jones, *Los Paisanos: Spanish Settlers on the Northern Frontier of New Spain* (Norman: University of Oklahoma Press, 1996), 184, infers different figures: A census in the early nineteenth century reported a population of 135,385, which included 38,640 Spaniards, 35,766 mixed-bloods, and 60,855 village-dwelling Christianized natives. Both figures seem exaggerated, especially the Spaniard category.
9. Rhonda M. Gonzales, "The African Presence In New Spain, c. 1528–1700," Prairie View University, http://www.pvamu.edu/tiphc/research-projects/afro-mexicans-afromestizos/the-african-presence-in-new-spain-c-1528-1700/.

10 Comment on Indian Slavery-1734: Archivo General de la Nacion (Mexico City, Mexico), Inquisicion 1734, 854. Quoted in Ramón A. Gutiérrez, *When Jesus Came, the Corn Mothers Went Away: Marriage, Sexuality, and Power in New Mexico, 1500–1846* (Stanford: Stanford University Press, 1991), 199.

11 Henry F. Dobyns, "Tubac Through Four Centuries: An Historical Resume and Analysis; Through Our Parent's Eyes," The Arizona State Parks Board (March 15, 1959), Chapter 4, http://parentseyes.arizona.edu/tubac/ (accessed October 27, 2009). Rodolfo F. Acuña, *Corridors of Migration: The Odyssey of Mexican Laborers, 1600–1933* (Tucson: University of Arizona, 2007), 2, 4–5, 7, 13–14, 17–34. "Comment on Indian Slavery," New Mexico Office of the State Historian, http://www.newmexicohistory.org/searchbytime.php?CategoryLevel_1=127&CategoryLevel_2=134. Also in the Archivo General de la Nacion (Mexico City, Mexico), Inquisicion 1734, 854.

12 Robert C. Hunt, David Guillet, David R. Abbott, James Bayman, Paul Fish, Suzanne Fish, Keith Kintigh, and James A. Neely, "Plausible Ethnographic Analogies for the Social Organization of Hohokam Canal Irrigation," *American Antiquity* 70, No. 3 (July 2005), 433. Donald M. Bahr, "Who Were the Hohokam? The Evidence from Pima-Papago Myths," *Ethnohistory* 18, No. 3 (Summer 1971), 246. Julian D. Hayden, "Of Hohokam Origins and Other Matters," *American Antiquity* 35, No. 1 (January 1970), 87. "Prehistoric and Hohokam history in Tucson Area," http://tucsonarizonahistory.tripod.com/hokoham_p1.htm.

13 Thomas E. Sheridan, *Arizona: A History* (Tucson: University of Arizona, 1995), 47. Sheridan, *Los Tucsonenses*, 17. See Ramón Eduardo Ruiz, *On the Rim of Mexico: Encounters of the Rich and Poor* (Boulder, CO: Westview Press, 1998). "Archaeological and Historical Research at Presidio San Agustín del Tucson," Center for Desert Archaeology, http://www.cdarc.org/pages/what/past/rio_nuevo/arch/tp/presidio.php. "Apache Camp," http://www.sonofthesouth.net/american-indians/apache-camp.htm.

14 Jack A. Dabbs, *The French Army in Mexico, 1861–1867* (The Hague: Mouton, 1963), 14, 65, 241, 283. Don Francisco Xavier de Gamboa, *Commentaries on the Mining Ordinances of Spain*, Vol. 2, trans. Richard Heathfield (London: Longman, Rees, Orme, Brown, and Green, 1830), 333. "The French in Sonora and Dominica—The Monroe Declaration," *New York Daily Times* (December 16, 1852). "Sonora; History of the Late French Expedition," *New York Daily Times* (January 14, 1853). Sheridan, *Los Tucsonenses*, 29. John Hosmer and the Ninth and Tenth Grade Classes of Green Fields Country Day School and University High School, Tucson, eds., "From The Santa Cruz to the Gila in 1850: An Excerpt from the Overland Journal of William Huff," *The Journal of Arizona History* 32, No. 1 (Spring 1991): 41–110. J. Fred Rippy, "A Ray of Light on the Gadsden Treaty," *Southwestern Historical Quarterly* 24 (January 1921): 241. Gadsden Purchase Treaty: December 30, 1853, Avalon Project, Yale University, http://avalon.law.yale.edu/19th_century/mx1853.asp. Desert Diary, "History/Gadsden Purchase," http://museum2.utep.edu/archive/history/DDgadsden.htm. Richard Cavendish, "The Gadsden Purchase" *History Today* Vol. 53, Issue 12 (Dec 2003), 55–56.

15 Guaymas, https://www.lomadelmarsancarlos.com/Loma-del-Mar-San-Carlos-maps.html.

16 James Neff Garber, *The Gadsden Treaty* (Gloucester, MA: Peter Smith, 1959). Hubert Howe Bancroft, *History of Arizona and New Mexico, 1530–1888*, Vol. XVII (San Francisco, CA: The History Company, Publishers, 1889), 493, 496, 498, 579. Howard R. Lamar, *The Far Southwest, 1846–1912: A Territorial History* (New York: Norton, 1970), 417–18. John B. Brebner, *Explorers of North America, 1492–1806* (Cleveland, OH: World Publishing, 1966), 407. Francisco R. Almada, *Diccionario de historia, geografía y biografía sonorenses* (Chihuahua: n.p., 1952), 140–44. Fernando Pesqueira, "Documentos Para la Historia de Sonora," 2nd series, Vol. 3, Manuscript in the University of Sonora Library, Hermosillo, Sonora. Within Sonora, there was harsh and bitter criticism of the loss of the state's patrimony. "Charles D. Poston, Arizona Pioneer," http://www.discoverseaz.com/History/Poston.html.

17 Sylvester Mowry, *Arizona and Sonora* (New York: Harper & Row, 1864), 35. Laureano Calvo Berber, *Nociones de Historia de Sonora* (México, DF: Libería de Manuel Porrúa, 1958), 50. "The Mowry Mine, originally the Patagonia Mine," http://www.discoverseaz.com/History/Mowry_Mine.html.

18 Charles D. Poston, "Building a State in Apache Land," *Overland Monthly* 24 (August 1894), 204. G. Hamlin, ed., *The Making of a Soldier: Letters of General B. S. Ewell* (Richmond, VA: Whittel & Shepperson, 1935). Clement W. Eaton, "Frontier Life in Southern Arizona, 1858–1861," *Southwestern Historical Quarterly* 36 (January 1933). Quoted in Joseph F. Park, "The History of Mexican Labor in Arizona During the Territorial Period" (Master's Thesis, University of Arizona, 1961), 20. Newspapers are important in documenting history. See Arizona Newspaper Project, Arizona State Library Archives and Public Records, http://adnp.azlibrary.gov/cdm4/colln_dir.php.

19 Diana Lindsay, ed., "Henry A. Crabb, Filibuster, and the *San Diego Herald*," *The Journal of San Diego History*

19, No. 1 (Winter 1973), http://www.sandiegohistory.org/journal/73winter/crabb.htm. Rufus Kay Wyllys, "Henry A. Crabb: A Tragedy of the Sonora Frontier," *Arizona and the West* Vol. 9, No. 2 (Jun., 1940), 183–194, a seminal article.

20. "Invasion of Sonora," *New York Daily Times* (May 21, 1857). Bancroft, *History of Arizona and New Mexico, 1530–1888*, 503. *Arizona Weekly Star*, quoted in Park, "The History of Mexican Labor," 29. Stone to Lewis Cass, Guaymas December 23, 1858, dispatches from U.S. consuls in Guaymas. "From Arizona, Indian Dependations—Outrages by Mexicans—Business," *New York Times* (September 9, 1859). "From Arizona: Mexican and American Affairs on the Frontier," *New York Times* (November 26, 1859). "The Stone Land Grant," *New York Times* (January 13, 1860). Edward Conner to Cass, Mazatlán, México, May 26, 1859, dispatches from U.S. consuls in Mazatlán, Mexico, GRDS, RG 59. *La Estrella de Occidente* (November 18, 1859). Alden to Cass, Guaymas, November 18, 21, 1859. Thomas Robinson to Alden, Guaymas, November 20, 1859, dispatches from U.S. consuls in Guaymas. Rodolfo F. Acuña, "Ignacio Pesqueira: Sonoran Caudillo," *Arizona and the West* 12, No. 2 (Summer 1970), 152–54. Rodolfo F. Acuña, *Sonoran Strongman: Ignacio Pesqueira and His Times* (Tucson: University of Arizona Press, 1974), 52–64.

21. *Cuentos de Nuestros Padres* (Stories of Our Fathers), Our Mexican American Community, University of Arizona, http://parentseyes.arizona.edu/community_mexBio.php.

22. "Arizona and Sonora—no. iv, Silver Mines," *New York Times* (January 11, 1859). "Arizona and Sonora—no. vii; The Apaches—Military Garrisons and Indian Agencies—Petition from Citizens of Arizona—Mistaken Action of the Government—The Military Becoming Interested in Mines," *New York Times* (January 26, 1859). Ed Dunbar, "Arizona and Sonora—no. ix; Population of Arizona—Fort Yuma—Cost of Transportation in Arizona—Cost of Transportation in Sonora—Difference in Favor of Sonora—Military—Difficulties and Dangers Attending Settlers—Murders by Apaches—Abandoned Trading Posts," *New York Times* (February 10, 1859). William Henry Robinson, *The Story of Arizona* (Phoenix: The Berryhill Company, 1919), 244. French Intervention and the Second Mexican Empire 1864–1867, MexicanHistory.org, http://mexicanhistory.org/French.htm.

23. An Act to provide temporary government for the Territory of Arizona, 1863, http://www.archives.gov/legislative/features/nm-az-statehood/hr357.html.

24. Edited by Konrad F. Schreier, Jr., "The California Column in The Civil War, Hazen's Civil War Diary," *The Journal of San Diego History* 26, No. 2 (Spring 1976), http://www.sandiegohistory.org/journal/76spring/civilwar.htm. "The Civil War in Arizona/New Mexico Territory," http://www.discoverseaz.com/History/Civil_War.html. 1864 federal census for the First Judicial District, Arizona Territory, http://www.rootsweb.ancestry.com/~cenfiles/az/1864/jd1/dist1-pt03.txt. (The various censuses to 1940 can be obtained through www.ancestry.com.)

25. Elise DuBord, "Mexican Elites and Language Policy in Tucson's First Public Schools," *Divergencias: Revistas de estudios linguisticos y literarios* 1 (octoño 2003), 3–17. Laura K Munoz, "Desert dreams: Mexican American education in Arizona, 1870–1930," (PhD Dissertation, Tempe, AZ: Arizona State University, 2006), 1–2, 24. Munoz makes the point that Mexican parents were active throughout the territory in the education of their children citing the work in Apache County.

26. Bancroft, *History of Arizona and New Mexico, 1530–1888*, 503, 575. Editorial, *La Estrella e Occidente* (April 12, 1872). "La Prensa de Arizona y los Horrores Perpetados en el Río Gila," *La Estrella de Occidente* (March 22, 1872). "Asesinator en el Gila," *La Estrella de Occidente* (March 22, 1872). "Trouble Ahead," *Arizona Citizen* (June 24, 1871). "Mexican Raids in Arizona; Recent Outrages Several Families Murdered, Correspondence Between the Governor of Arizona and the State Department," *New York Times* (February 5, 1872). Tinker Salas, *In the Shadow of the Eagles*.

27. William Carrigan and Clive Webb, *Forgotten Dead: Mob Violence Against Mexicans In the United States, 1848–1928* (New York: Oxford University Press), Appendix A, 319–343.

28. Douglas D. Martin, *Tombstone's Epitaph* (Albuquerque: University of New Mexico Press, 1951), 139–65.

29. Sheridan, *Los Tucsonenses*, 2, 41–54, 108. Manuel G. Gonzales, "Mariano G. Samaniego," *The Arizona Journal of Arizona History* 31, No. 2 (Summer 1990), 141–60. Manuel G. Gonzales, *Mexicanos: A History of Mexicans in the United States* (Bloomington: Indiana University Press, 1999), 94–96.

30. Salvador Acosta, "Crossing Borders, Erasing Boundaries: Interethnic Marriages in Tucson, 1854–1930" (Dissertation, Tucson: University of Arizona, 2010), 20.

31. Tinker Salas, *In the Shadow of Eagles*, 27–28, 63, 191–92, points out that in the 1890 Census, women in Sonora controlled 31 commercial establishments, including several saloons and bordellos. Women played a prominent role in mining camps. Katherine A. Benton, "What About Women in The White Man's Camp?: Gender, Nation, and the Redefinition of Race in Cochise County, Arizona, 1853–1941" (PhD Dissertation, University of Wisconsin, 2002), 33; puts forth

that the status of women depended a great deal on the hue of their skin, their family backup, and where they lived. Tucson had a support network and ties to Sonoran families, whereas in the mining camps all Mexican women were vulnerable and subject to prejudices.

32 Salvador Acosta, "Crossing Borders, Erasing Boundaries: Interethnic Marriages in Tucson, 1854–1930" (PhD Dissertation, Tucson: University of Arizona, 2010), 12–13. Acosta's dissertation improved many of my previous citations.

33 Ibid., 40, 42, 44. The 1865 Arizona legislature called "for the removal of friendly Natives and the pacification and even extermination of tribes."

34 Ibid., 20, 31, 181. Marriages between Mexican-Chinese were also common.

35 Sheridan, *Los Tucsonenses*, 38–39, 47. Jay J. Wagoner, *Arizona Territory 1863–1912: A Political History* (Tucson: University of Arizona Press, 1970), 70. Sheridan, *Arizona*, 109. Kay Lysen Briegel, "Alianza Hispano-Americana, 1894–1965: A Mexican American Fraternal Insurance Society" (PhD Dissertation, University of Southern California, 1974), 27. Marcy Gail Goldstein, "Americanization and Mexicanization: The Mexican Elite and Anglo-Americans in the Gadsden Purchase Lands, 1853–1880" (PhD Dissertation, Case Western Reserve University, 1977). Carlos G. Vélez-Ibáñez, *Border Visions: Mexican Cultures of the Southwest United States* (Tucson: The University of Arizona Press, 1996), 13–19, 95. Harry T. Getty, "Interethnic Relationships in the Community of Tucson" (PhD Dissertation, University of Chicago, 1950), 208–09, 10, 20, 48, 177. "Arizona's miscegenation law (1864–1962) prohibited the marriages of whites with Blacks, Chinese, and Indians—and eventually those with Asian Indians and Filipinos". Mexicans, legally white, could intermarry with whites, but the anti-Mexican rhetoric of manifest destiny suggests that these unions represented social transgressions.

36 "Eulalia Elías 1788–1865," Arizona Women's Hall of Fame, Arizona State Library, Archives and Public Records Carnegie Center, http://www.lib.az.us/awhof/women/elias.cfm.

37 Gonzales, "Mariano G. Samaniego," 152. "Pioneer Families of the Presidio De San Agustin," Tucson's Origins, Center for Desert Archaeology, http://www.cdarc.org/pages/what/past/rio_nuevo/people/families.php. Excellent site that includes biographies of original families.

38 Thomas E. Sheridan, *Arizona: A History*, Revised Edition (Tucson: University of Arizona, 2012), 89.

39 Report of Lt. Royal E. Whitman, "The Camp Grant Massacre; Lieut. Whitman's Report a Fearful Tale—Women and Children Butchered," *New York Times*, July 20, 1871, http://query.nytimes.com/gst/abstract.html?res=9A04E0D7103EEE34BC4851DFB166838A669FDE. Sheridan, *Arizona*, 79–81. Sheridan, *Los Tucsonenses*, 69–70. In a very interesting article, "Inter-Ethnic Fighting in Arizona: Counting the Cost of Conquest," *The Journal of Arizona History* 35, No. 2 (Summer 1994), 163–89. Henry F. Dobyns estimated that 6,443 persons were killed in Arizona's interethnic conflict between 1680 and 1890, 89.4 percent of whom (5,759) were Native Americans.

40 Sheridan, *Arizona*, 98. See Allen Broussard, "Law, Order, and Water Policy on the Arizona Frontier," *The Journal of Arizona History* 34, No. 2 (Summer 1993): 155–76. Peter L. Reich, "The 'Hispanic' Roots of Prior Appropriation in Arizona," *Arizona State Law Journal* 27, No. 2 (Summer 1995): 649–62.

41 Wagoner, *Arizona Territory 1863–1912*, 164. Bancroft, *History of Arizona and New Mexico, 1530–1888*, 599–600. "Claim for 50,000,000 Acres," *New York Times* (Jul 2, 1897), 1. There were cases of fraud: "The Baron of Arizona," http://www.miningswindles.com/html/the_baron_of_arizona.html. James H. McClintock, *Arizona: Prehistoric, Aboriginal Pioneer, Modern: The Nation's Youngest Commonwealth Within a Land of Ancient Culture*, Vol. 2 (Chicago, IL: S. J. Clarke Publishing Co., 1916), 529–37.

42 Stephanie Balzer, "N.M.-Arizona Land Acquires RRH Financial," *The Business Journal* (1997), 4.

43 Raquel Rubio-Goldsmith, "Hispanics in Arizona and Their Experiences with the Humanities," in F. Arturo Francisco Rosales and David William Foster, eds., *Hispanics and the Humanities in the Southwest: A Directory of Resources* (Tempe: Center for Latin American Studies, Arizona State University, 1983), 14. Sheridan, *Arizona*, 137. "Farms in the Great West; Opportunities for Settlers upon the Public Lands," *New York Times* (June 4, 1880). "The Indigenous People in Arizona; Settlers and Miners Have Little Reason to Fear Them," *New York Times* (June 4, 1880).

44 "Tucson's Valuable Site; a Typical Mexican Town in Arizona. Dreary by Day and Full of Excitement at Night; The Business of Which It Is the Centre"; "The Rivalry of the Southern Pacific and the Atchison, Topeka, and Santa Fe Roads," *New York Times* (July 13, 1879). C. L. Sonnichsen, *Tucson: The Life and Times of an American City* (Norman: University of Oklahoma Press, 1982), 91. Lamar, *The Far Southwest*, 453–54. Linda Gordon, *The Great Arizona Orphan Abduction* (Cambridge, MA: Harvard University Press, 1999), 23. "El Ferrocaril de Guaymas," *El Fronterizo* (February 8, 1880). *El Fronterizo* (February 22, 1880).

45 Patricia Preciado Martin, *Images and Conversations: Mexican Americans Recall a Southwestern Past* (Tucson: University of Arizona Press, 1983). Also see Heather

S. Hatch, "Fiestas Patrias and Uncle Sam: A Photographic Glimpse of Arizona Patriotism," *The Journal of Arizona History* 35, No. 4 (Winter 1994), 427–35.

46 Sheridan, *Arizona*, 151. "War on the Borders. Mexicans Massacre Five Americans in Arizona," *New York Times* (August 19, 1881). "Riddled with Bullets," *New York Times* (March 24, 1882). "Mexican killed at Tombstone"; "Mexicans and Americans Fighting," *New York Times* (May 25, 1882). "Feeling Against the Mexican," *New York Times* (February 23, 1886). "Dangerous Mexican Soldiers," *New York Times* (March 18, 1887). "Warning to Mexican Officers," *New York Times* (May 12, 1888).

47 The 1870 U.S. Federal Census, Apache Press, Pima Territory, found at www.Ancestry.com. The 1870 Census is important; it lists the state in Mexico that the workers came from. The first two listed on the census were Joaquin Salazar, 27, laborer, Sonora M593_46 Page: 10 Image: 19 Year: 1870 and Tomas Quiros, 26, Laborer, Sonora Tucson Roll: M593_46 Page: 10 Image: 19 Year: 1870. In the 1880 U.S. Census the following Subias were listed: Luis Subia, 25, Clifton Copper Mine, Apache, Arizona, single.(U.S. Census, 1880; Census Place: Clifton Copper Mine, Apache, Arizona; Roll: T9_36; Family History Film: 1254036; Page: 9B; Enumeration District: 35; Image: 0025); Delfina Subia, 38, Faustina Subia, 38, Francisco Subia, 35, from El Paso and all single.

48 Lamar, *The Far Southwest*, 475. Sheridan, *Arizona*, 104. Jacqueline Jo Ann Taylor, "Ethnic Identity and Upward Mobility of Mexican Americans in Tucson" (PhD Dissertation, University of Arizona, 1973), 16.

49 Robert L. Sprude in "The Walker-Weaver Digging and the Mexican Placero, 1863–1864," *Journal of the West* (October 1975): 64–74.

50 Bancroft, *History of Arizona and New Mexico, 1530–1888*, 602. Lamar, *The Far Southwest*, 454. Larry Schweikart, *History of Banking in Arizona* (Tucson: University of Arizona Press, 1982), 1. Sheridan, *Arizona*, 49, 123. Frank J. Tuck, "Fifty Years of Mining in the State of Arizona, 1912–1962" M 91, Arizona Historical Society. "Mining in Arizona," http://jeff.scott.tripod.com/miningaz.html. "Nikola Tesla," http://en.wikipedia.org/wiki/Nikola_Tesla.

51 See Acuña, *Corridors of Migration*. James Colquhoun, "The Early History of the Clifton-Morenci District," reprinted in Carlos E. Cortés, ed., *The Mexican Experience in Arizona* (New York: Arno Press, 1976). "Mining ~ Minería" Chicana/o Collection, Arizona State University Library, http://www.asu.edu/lib/archives/website/mining.htm.

52 Lamar, *The Far Southwest*, 475. David J. Weber, ed., *Foreigners in Their Native Land* (Albuquerque: University of New Mexican Press, 1973), 211.

53 "Morenci Copper Mine, Arizona, USA," Mining-Technology.com, http://www.mining-technology.com/projects/morenci/. "A History of Mining in AZ," http://www.azmining.com/mining-in-az/mining-history-.

54 Ramón Eduardo Ruiz, *The People of Sonora and Yankee Capitalists* (Tucson: University of Arizona Press, 1988). Mark C. Vinson, "Vanished Clifton-Morenci: An Architect's Perspective," *The Journal of Arizona History* 33, No. 2 (Summer 1992), 183–206. It has excellent descriptions and photos of Clifton-Morenci. "According to the Bureau of Labor Statistics, the dollar experienced an average inflation rate of 2.33% per year. Prices in 2014 are 2098.7% higher than prices in 1880." See http://www.in2013dollars.com/1880-dollars-in-2014.

55 Sheridan, *Los Tucsonenses*, 3.

56 Sheridan, *Los Tucsonense*, 103–09. Josiah Heyman, "Oral History of the Mexican American Community of Douglas, Arizona, 1901–1942," *Journal of the Southwest* 35, No. 2 (Summer 1993), 197–201. David T. Beito, "Poor Before Welfare: Fraternal Societies and Mutual Aid Societies Kept the Poor Afloat Long Before the Welfare State," *National Review* 48, No. 8 (May 6, 1996): 42ff. "For the People: Mutual Aid Societies/Para la Gente: Sociedades de Ayuda Mútua," http://www.asu.edu/lib/archives/website/organiza.htm (accessed October 27, 2009).

57 Briegel, "Alianza Hispano-Americana, 1894–1965," 34–38, 51, 64. Manuel Servín, "The Role of Mexican Americans in the Development of Early Arizona," in Manuel Servín, ed., *An Awakening Minority: The Mexican American*, 2nd ed. (Beverly Hills, CA: Glencoe Press, 1974), 28. Sheridan, *Los Tucsonense*, 111–30. http://azmemory.lib.az.us/cdm4/item_viewer.php?CISOROOT=/ahstuc&CISOPTR=112&CISOBOX=1&REC=3.

58 Edward F. Ronstadt, *Borderman: The Memoirs of Federico José María Ronstadt* (Tucson: University of Arizona Press, 1993), http://parentseyes.arizona.edu/borderman/index.html. Sheridan, *Los Tucsonenses*, 94–95. Ronstadt was born in Las Delicias, Sonora, in 1868. After working as a carriage maker apprentice, Ronstadt worked for Southern Pacific as a blacksmith. Eventually, he started his own carriage business. His father was a German engineer. The importance of these family connections cannot be underestimated.

59 Sheridan, *Los Tucsonenses*, 85.

60 Heyman, "Oral History of the Mexican American Community of Douglas, Arizona, 1901–1942," 192.

61 James W. Byrkit, *Forging the Copper Collar: Arizona's Labor-Management War of 1901–1921* (Tucson: The University of Arizona Press, 1982), 26. For a history

of the WFM, see Philip J. Mellinger, *Race and Labor in Western Copper: The Fight for Equality, 1896–1918* (Tucson: University of Arizona Press, 1995), 17–32. Carl M. Rathbun, "Keeping the Peace Along the Mexican Border," *Harper's Weekly* 50 (November 17, 1906): 16–32.

62 Adam M. Sowards, "Reclamation, Ranching, and Reservation: Environmental, Cultural, and Governmental Rivalries in Transitional Arizona," *Journal of the Southwest* 40, No. 3 (Autumn 1998), 333.

63 Bradford Luckingham, *Minorities in Phoenix: A Profile of Mexican American, Chinese American, and African American Communities, 1860–1992* (Tucson: University of Arizona Press, 1994). Bradford Luckingham, *Phoenix: The History of a Southwestern Metropolis*, reissue ed. (Tucson: University of Arizona Press, 1995), 8. "The Great Roosevelt Dam," *Los Angeles Times* (May 6, 1906). Robert Conway Stevens, "A History of Chandler, Arizona," *Social Science Bulletin No. 25, University of Arizona Bulletin Series* XXV, No. 4 (October 1954), 5–7, 14, 20–25. Sowards, "A 'Wasteland' Transformed: Reclamation," 301. David Brown, "Early Inhabitants and Their Canals Pave Way for Newcomers," *Arizona History* 65, No. 1 (January 2003), 14. Paul S. Taylor, "Mexicans North of the Rio Grande," *The Survey* LXVI, No. 3 (May 1, 1931), 135–36. Peter W. van der Pas, ed., "The Imperial Valley in 1904: An Account by Hugo de Vries," *The Journal of San Diego History* 22, No. 1 (Winter 1976), http://www.sandiegohistory.org/journal/76winter/imperial.htm. "Government Is Buying Canals; Which Pass into Control of Reclamation Service," *Los Angeles Times* (February 28, 1907). "Indians Thirsty for Revenge," *Los Angeles Times* (May 16, 1906). The bulk of the labor was done by Native Americans.

64 Luckingham, *Minorities in Phoenix*, 17. Interviewer: Scott Solliday. Narrator: Joe Soto. Tempe Oral History, Barrios Oral History Project. Date of Interview: January 25, 1994. Number: OH–139.

65 "Railroad Yards in Expansion; Southern Pacific Buys Land near Phoenix," *Los Angeles Times* (September 24, 1907). "Land Hold-up Big by Yuma; Scores of Entries Now in Abeyance There," *Los Angeles Times* (October 4, 1907). "Follow after Aztecs"; "The Government's Irrigation Ditches in Arizona Follow Prehistoric Canals," *Los Angeles Times* (December 25, 1907). Railroads of Arizona (2002), http://www.azrymuseum.org/Information/Arizona_Railroad_Map_2002.pdf.

66 "Angelenos Are Heavy Buyers of Lots in Parker Townsite," *Los Angeles Times* (May 17, 1910). "Phoenix Has Boom, Epoch," *Los Angeles Times* (October 8, 1909). "Los Angeles Pledges a Hundred Thousand," *Los Angeles Times* (September 18, 1912). "Cotton Crop Is Marketed," *Los Angeles Times* (November 29, 1912). "Settlers Push Verde Project," *Los Angeles Times* (September 12, 1913). "Valley Cotton of High Grade," *Los Angeles Times* (November 27, 1913). "Cotton Harvest in Full Swing," *Los Angeles Times* (October 11, 1914).

67 "Happenings on the Pacific Slope," *Los Angeles Times* (August 1, 1915). "Cotton Prices up One Dime," *Los Angeles Times* (October 31, 1916). "Arizona Cotton Brings Top Price," *Los Angeles Times* (March 26, 1917). "Arizona Cotton Crop Big of Good Quality," *Los Angeles Times* (November 1, 1918).

Chapter 7
California Lost: Image and Reality

Learning Objectives

7.1 Explain the impact of Spanish and American colonialism on California's Indigenous population from 1700–1900.

7.2 Characterize the mission system as an instrument of Spanish Colonialism during change in the Mexican and Spanish period of Alta California.

7.3 Describe early American aggression in Alta California and efforts to impose their version of history.

7.4 Summarize the ways that the Gold Rush changed life in Alta California.

7.5 Explain why and how the Californios lost their land and power.

7.6 Describe how presses like *El Clamor Público* reacted to white supremacy and the declining power of the Californios.

7.7 Contextualize social banditry in California in the context of colonialism.

7.8 Characterize the Mexican community in California at the end of the 1800s.

7.9 Where did the Native American and the Chinese rank in the Social Order.

The 1849 Gold Rush brought a huge infusion of capital and people almost overnight, California went from a mercantile economy to highly capitalized one, heavily dependent on state and national markets. The Indigenous and Mexican settlements along the coast were the most affected. Many of these settlements were built on the foundations of the missions, presidios, and pueblos. New settlements also sprang up around mining camps, similar to those of northern Mexico, where mines created makeshift towns that grew in the midst of haciendas, ranchos, and missions.

Forgotten California

7.1 Explain the impact of Spanish and American colonialism on California's Indigenous population from 1700–1900.

California before the Spanish conquest was the most densely populated area in what is today the United States. In the late 1700s, it was home to more than 300,000 native people who were organized into more than 200 tribes. It was blessed with an abundance of vegetation, wild fruit, game, and fish; there was so much vegetation that many did not have to farm. Native Californians spoke over 300 dialects with approximately 100 distinct languages.[1] This came to an abrupt end with the coming of their "saviors."[2] Spanish smallpox, influenza, dysentery, malaria, measles, and syphilis killed thousands of Indigenous People.[3]

By 1848, more than two-thirds of California's Indigenous population was reduced to about 30,000; by 1900 the number fell to 20,000. Colonialism wiped out memories that dated back at least 19,000 years (recent evidence suggests that California was inhabited at least as long as 130,000 years ago).[4] Forgotten is that during the California Gold Rush between 1849 and 1870 miners killed about 4,500 Indigenous People.[5]

The Myth That Has Become Legend

7.2 Characterize the mission system as an instrument of Spanish Colonialism during change in the Mexican and Spanish period of Alta California.

John Steven McGroarty in his book *Mission Memories* (1929) wrote,

California was the happiest land the world had ever known. There was peace and plenty, and hospitality became a religion. Song and laughter filled the sunny mornings. There was feasting and music, the strum of guitars and the click of castanets under the low hanging mofons . . . Nothing like it ever existed before, nor has any approach to it existed since.[6]

This mythical picture is capsulized by the play *Ramona*, based on a novel by Helen Hunt Jackson. The play popularized the illusion that California was Eden where Spanish rancheros roamed their ranchos helped by happy peons, much like the myth of the American South and happy slaves.[7] The book, *Ramona* was critical of the treatment of the California's native people.[8] Instead of elaborating on this injustice, the play created the illusion that Carey McWilliams in *North from Mexico* called the "Fantasy Heritage"—a heritage that never existed. Another example of this illusion is Don Mitchell's description of the Joads in Steinbeck's *Grapes of Wrath* reaching the summit of Tehachapi Pass and looking down at the California Eden, where everything appeared perfect.[9] The landscape is a metaphor for how people saw the California Eden, and it perpetuated the myth of the Spaniards bringing civilization to California. But, as the Joads got closer to Eden they saw the reality of the suffering workers.[10]

The Golden State was inhabited by the Chumash, Paiute, the Shasta, and other nations. The Spanish colonization was a continuation of the colonization of Baja California, a venture that the Jesuits began in 1697. By 1769 the Franciscans moved to conquer Alta California. The first Spanish colonizers were Africans, Indigenous Mexicans, mestizos and other mixed-race people called castas. Full-blooded Spaniards were the exceptions. Baja and, later, Alta California were on the frontier of Sonora Spaniards were not attracted to frontiers preferring urban areas, especially those where they could get rich fast, such as mining districts.

During the Spanish Colonial Period California became a refuge for the unwanted. In the interior of New Spain, California was known as a convict colony. Fray Junípero Serra complained that Spanish authorities used California as a dumping ground. As late as 1829, the Mexican government shipped convicts to California—an act that was condemned by the Californios, who by this time had pretensions of being *hidalgos*, or minor nobility.[11]

Presidios (forts) supported the missions' expansion, and soldiers regularly hunted down runaway natives. The natives resented the occupiers' mistreatment by the colonists, missionaries, and soldiers, and in 1785 the Indigenous People at Mission San Gabriel near present-day Los Angeles rebelled, incited by Toypurina, an unbaptized woman, and Nicolás José, a Mission Native, both of whom harbored grievances against the Franciscan friars and the mission as a whole. Mission San Gabriel was the jewel of the mission system; it was one of the largest in the string of 21 missions, and some called it the breadbasket of the colony. By 1785 the mission flourished, and its missionaries baptized well over 1,200 Indigenous People. Toypurina became a heroine and the symbol of Gabrielino resistance to colonialism.[12]

In 1812, rebels killed Padre Andrés Quintana at Mission Santa Cruz in response to his beatings of mission subjects. After the death of Father Quintana, Padre Ramón Olbés, the Franciscan caretaker between 1818–1821, became more oppressive. On one occasion when a woman could not conceive, Olbés tried to examine her vagina; the infuriated woman bit Olbés. She was given 50 lashes and was shackled and ordered to walk around holding a wooden doll.[13] The cumulative indignities led to the great Chumash rebellion of 1824, which encompassed Santa Inés, La Purisima Concepción, and Santa Barbara missions. The immediate cause of the revolt was the unfair punishment of a mission Native American; the injustice outraged his friends. The Chumash disarmed the soldiers and retreated to the presidio.

When the soldiers attacked, the rebels abandoned Santa Barbara and retreated to the hills. The rebellion came to an end when Spanish authorities unconditionally pardoned the rebels. It was the largest organized revolt in the history of the California missions and was brutally suppressed by military force. Throughout the Spanish and Mexican periods, Native American women not only took part in revolts but, as in the interior of Mexico and elsewhere in Spanish America, when they could use the Spanish legal system to challenge the friars, the abusive soldiers, and the despotic officials.[14]

Excessive backbreaking labor and poor nutrition increased the natives' susceptibility to disease. As many as 60 percent of the mission subjects died of European diseases. The epidemics eroded whatever little faith Native Americans had in the new order, and many escaped and returned to their native shamans. Soldiers and, in some cases priests, sexually abused the Native Californians.[15] The reality beneath the missions' facade was that life for the Indigenous People changed for the worse.[16]

Mexican Period

In 1821 California became part of the Mexican Republic, opening the province to outside trade. Mexico's liberalization of trade and immigration regulations encouraged foreigners to enter and live in California. Mercantile capitalism transformed missions into thriving enterprises, and they became the envy of the growing ranchos, when they pushed for the physical privatization of the missions. Improved transportation and increasing opportunities attracted hundreds of non-Mexicans who arrived and stayed; and, as in Texas and New Mexico, the white newcomers played the role of Trojan horse, opening the door for the later U.S. invasion of California.[17]

By 1821, 20 missions and 30 Spanish land grants had been distributed in Alta California. The Native Californian was treated as a class apart—as a colonized people. The Franciscan missions forced a religious and sexual discipline and eradicated the native culture, including practices related to sexuality, intimacy, and biological and social reproduction. The mission friars rationalized their intrusion with the chauvinistic belief that Native Californians were like children being given the privilege of the Spanish culture, the protection of its laws, and salvation through Jesus Christ. This could only be rationalized because the colonists thought of the Native Californian as chattel, both culturally and racially inferior.

The Class and Racial Gap

The missions thrived in the 1820s—by 1827 the missions possessed 210,000 branded cattle, and an estimated 100,000 unbranded cows. This wealth did not go unnoticed by the small emerging ranchero class that would most benefit from the secularization of the missions in 1834.[18] The rancheros slaughtered 60,000 cows annually, and sold 30,000–40,000 hides at two pesos apiece. The system was maintained by Indigenous labor. The growth overlapped with the Industrial Revolution in England and in other parts of Europe, as well as in the United States—the main markets for products such as leather (for footwear) and tallow (for candles).

Consequent to secularization, restraints on the use of native labor lessened and the encroachment on their land increased. Theoretically, Native Americans owned half the secularized property. But the Native Californians never received its rewards. Secularization forced the natives to work for wages as *vaqueros* (cowboys) in the expanding rancho system or as laborers in pueblos (towns). It did not free the Native Californians. It was a system where lower-class mestizos and mulattos competed in the labor pool with the natives.[19] Secularization also meant the abandonment of the presidios. Few hacendados (large landowners) could financially support a small standing army and pay soldiers.

Mercantile capitalism widened the gap between landholders and the landless. The Californios justified their privileged status by claiming racial superiority. They asserted the natives were not intelligent enough to develop the land. Like most nineteenth-century liberals, Californios favored local control over government, and they believed that they had the right to control and exploit native labor. Violence was an integral part of the system; the excesses provoked Native American revolts throughout the Mexican period.[20]

Meanwhile, the secularization of the missions uprooted mission natives, disorienting their lives and increasing their vulnerability to exploitation. Landless, wracked by disease and afflicted by alcoholism, many former mission natives wandered the countryside. The Californios treated them as wards of the government.[21]

Secularization also impacted pueblos such as Los Angeles that were forced to absorb large numbers of homeless natives. "[P]ueblos thus began to see homeless Indians, hungry, cold, and begging—no longer subservient to the missionaries."[22] The pueblos became the centers for artisan workers and day laborers, as well as merchants. Ultimately the large influx of Native American labor flooded the pueblos' infrastructure. In 1836, the census reported 252 natives in Los Angeles; eight years later, there were 650. Many Native Americans were given no choice but to join the military. As early as the late 1810s, natives served in the cavalry against their own people. Militarization of the natives further divided the Indigenous population.[23]

The secularization of the missions led to the transformation to capitalism; ironically, the pretext of the rancheros for ending the mission system was that missionaries enslaved the natives.[24] After secularization, the land passed to private ranch owners who conveniently overlooked that Native Californians legally owned half of the secularized property.[25] Secularization also meant the abandonment of the presidios, leaving the Spanish settlements vulnerable to attacks. Of the new hacendados, only Mariano Vallejo could afford a small standing army and pay soldiers to control Indigenous workers.

California experienced other changes during the 1830s. Californio rancheros no longer produced solely for local consumption, but entered the mercantile capitalist cycle. They maintained their pretensions of being hidalgos. As University of California Santa Cruz historian Lisbeth Haas wrote, "Californios used Spanish colonial ideas to define their territorial government's right to control the land of mission captives."[26]

A small group of rancheros took over the profitable hide and tallow trade after the secularization of the missions. Ranchos and haciendas were carved out of former mission holdings along the coast. Landless Native Californians either wandered the countryside or were literally forcibly bound to the land. They had few options since their institutions were destroyed and the mission system was dismantled.[27] Meanwhile, the surviving missionaries "leased out" former mission natives to rancheros, reinforcing the notion that native people were chattels.[28]

Generational differences existed among the Californios. The second—generation Californios considered themselves entitled, as the native sons of California—the real proprietors of the land, with more right to the land than the Indigenous People. They viewed Mexican immigrants who came to California during the Mexican period as foreigners—a mindset that was deepened by a paranoia that Mexicans from the interior were coming to California to steal what belonged to the "native sons."

The truth is that most Californios were not descendants of elite Mexican families—very few were criollos. Pío de Jesús Pico, a typical example, belonged to a mixed race of Spanish, African, Italian, and Native American ethnicities. His parents migrated to the San Gabriel mission from Sinaloa with the famous overland Juan Bautista de Anza expedition of 1775.[29] Pico was born in the San Gabriel mission in 1801. He lived a conspicuous lifestyle, squandering wealth in a manner appropriate to a hidalgo.

Pico became governor in 1832 and again in 1845, something that would have been improbable anywhere else in New Spain. His upward mobility was not based on democratic principles or merit but rather on pretensions of superiority based on his wealth. Even his race was an illusion, and the delusion of his racial purity was maintained through family connections among Californios who were also largely of mixed races. As mentioned, race mattered little compared to wealth, family connections, and political power.[30]

Women in the Transformation of California

When the colonization began, mission fathers relied on native women from Baja California, Sonora, and Sinaloa to socialize Californian Indigenous women. Life was harsh for Native Californian women. The missionaries selected the highest-ranking native women as brides for Spanish-Mexican male colonists to forge a mestizo culture, a culture closer to the criollo ideal. Through women, the priests passed on religious tradition and the custom of protecting their daughters' chastity until marriage. Some women did achieve a measure of power, or better still, influence. In the 1830s, Doña Apolinaria Lorenzana claimed and administered—but lost—Rancho Santa Clara de Jamacha.[31] Her mother brought her to Alta California, but abandoned her after her (the mother's) marriage. Apolinaria taught herself to read, and managed a school on an estate where she taught girls reading, catechism, and sewing. She later worked as a *curandera* (healer). Like Fermina Espinosa, owner of the Santa Rita Rancho, Lorenzana rode horses and roped steers.

Women could also inherit ranchos and other property; they worked as shopkeepers and midwives. Juana Briones de Miranda was born in 1802 in what is now Santa Cruz. Juana was of mixed Spanish, African, and Indigenous ancestry. Despite a brutal marriage, she bought property in what is today San Francisco, built a cattle ranch and a dairy business in the San José area, defending her property before the U.S. Land Commission Hearings. However, these were exceptions: Californio families were patriarchal and according to Antonia Castañeda, sexual violence, rape and incest, and family violence were common.[32]

Even so Mexican women were better off legally than their American counterparts. They could own property and use the courts to defend their property interests. The status of women in Spanish and, later, in Mexican California differed subtly from those in other parts of Mexico. It was isolated and provincial unlike, for example, mining centers where gender and class lines often broke down. Groundbreaking work is being done by scholars such as Castañeda and Virginia Marie Bouvier, who are discovering the footprints that piece together the tribulations of native and mixed-blood women in California. They have opened a treasure trove of documents that include the testimonies of women like Eulalia Pérez, a caretaker of Mission San Gabriel Arcángel and owner of Rancho del Rincón de San Pascual in the present-day Los Angeles area.[33]

The Bear Flag

7.3 Describe early American aggression in Alta California.

During the Mexican period, white Americans arrived mostly by sea. Those who stayed formed strong ties with the Mexican rancheros and hacendados, often intermarrying. By 1841, the few foreigners in California consisted of ex-sailors, commercial agents, and businessmen, many of who assimilated into Mexican society. Between 1843 and 1846 this changed, as about 1,500 Americans arrived in California, traveling overland from the Midwest with their wives and families. The new wave of immigrants mixed less with the natives than did their predecessors, resulting in less intermarriage. The newcomers settled in the inland areas—uninhabited, according to them, since only natives lived there. This migration followed the pattern of previous migrations of Americans who migrated west after going bankrupt and losing their lands in the Panics of 1819 and 1837.

John C. Fremont and the Bear Flag

John C. Fremont's third expedition stands out in the rush to California. The expedition left St. Louis in May 1845, reaching California at the end of May; Fremont immediately marched to Monterey to purchase supplies. There he met with Thomas O. Larkin, a prominent merchant who arrived in California in 1832 and served as the U.S. consul. Larkin's letters to the U.S. State Department supplied the government with critical information about California. The Mexican governor gave Fremont permission to camp as long as he stayed away from coastal settlements. More white American reinforcements arrived and in March 1846, Fremont raised the U.S. flag at Hawk's Peak, about 25 miles from Monterey. Fremont was ordered to leave California immediately. Just as the expedition was about to depart, Marine Lieutenan Archibald H. Gillespie reached Fremont and delivered personal letters to him, along with verbal instructions from President James K. Polk.[34] The communiqué instructed Fremont that war with Mexico was imminent, and encouraged him to return to the Sacramento Valley. Instead, white Americans rallied behind Fremont's California Bear Flag and declared war on Mexico. White merchants convinced some Mexican ranch owners that it was in their best interest to support the invasion; the poor, on the other hand, remained loyal to Mexico and opposed the gringos. Meanwhile, the behavior of the "Bear Flaggers" alienated a few potential friends. In June 1846, Fremont's soldiers took Mexican General Mariano Vallejo prisoner at his ranch in Sonoma. Vallejo and his brother were sent to Sutter's Fort and harassed, despite the fact that Vallejo was sympathetic to Americans. Fremont further estranged rich merchants and landowners by initiating a policy of forced loans and confiscation of land and property.[35]

Bear Flaggers rustled cattle and horses, looted homes, and wounded and murdered innocent people. On one occasion, a scouting party under Kit Carson's command came upon José de los Reyes Berreyesa and his twin nephews, Francisco and Ramón de Haro. Though they were unarmed, the Americans shot them anyway. They killed Ramón, and his brother Francisco "threw himself upon his brother's body." One of the assassins then shouted, "Kill the other son of a bitch!" Upon seeing his two nephews murdered, the old man—José—called out to the Americans, "Is it possible that you kill these young men for no reason at all? It is better that you kill me who am old too!" The Bear Flaggers killed him as well.[36] The Berreyesa murders served no military purpose and their assassinations ushered in a period of the wanton murder of Mexicans, mostly by lynching. William Carrigan and Clive Webb confirm that at least 143 individuals were victims of mob violence. California ranked second to Texas, which had 232 confirmed victims.[37]

U.S. Invasion of California

In July, Commodore John Drake Sloat landed 250 Marines at Monterey and raised the U.S. flag. Later, Commodore Robert F. Stockton, a known expansionist, replaced Sloat. Fremont, promoted to the rank of major, was placed in command of the California Battalion of Volunteers. Naval forces entered Los Angeles harbor, with Captain Archibald Gillespie in charge of occupying the area. Meanwhile, José María Flores led the resistance in Los Angeles. Although the Californios were poorly armed, they defeated Gillespie and forced him to surrender. During the battle, large numbers of Angeleños watched and cheered Flores's men.[38]

In response, Colonel Stephen Kearny, leader of the Army of the West, arrived from New Mexico. On December 5, 1846, a force of 65 Mexicans met the invading army at San Pasqual Pass, northeast of San Diego. Led by Andrés Pico, the Mexicans killed 18 white Americans and wounded Kearny and many of his men; the Mexicans suffered no losses. However, a well-armed cavalry soon arrived, overwhelming the Mexican defenders. Kearny's army entered Los Angeles on January 10, 1847, and Andrés Pico surrendered at the Cahuenga Pass and signed the Treaty of Cahuenga.[39]

Gold Transforms California

7.4 Summarize the ways that the Gold Rush changed life in Alta California.

The old order came to an end with the Gold Rush of 1849. The world had known for some time that there was gold in California. Francisco López found gold six years before the crucial discovery at Sutter's Mill, in Placerita Canyon, just north of the San Fernando Valley.[40] From 1842 to 1847, Mexican miners culled some 1,300 pounds of gold from the site. On January 24, 1848, James Wilson Marshall found gold on John Sutter's Mill. Thousands of colonizers flooded into California to find gold, overwhelming the Mexican population, and ending any hope they had of participating in the governance of California.[41]

The Gold Rush in the northern part of the state instantly turned Mexicans into a minority. Chileans, Peruvians, and other Latin Americans joined them, prospecting on the northern riverbanks. In 1848, about 1,300 Mexicans and 4,000 Yankees worked in the gold fields. By mid-1849, nearly 100,000 miners panned for gold—80,000 were white, 8,000 were Mexicans, 5,000 were South Americans, and several thousands were Europeans.[42]

The Gold Rush Creates a Template

The Gold Rush set the template for North American–Mexican relations. The 1850 Census showed that 50 percent of California residents worked in gold mining; in 1852, a peak year, gold mines produced $80 million. According to the 1860 Census, 38 percent of Californians still worked in gold mining. By 1865, Californians had mined three-quarters of a billion dollars in gold. Large amounts of capital from gold mining were concentrated in the hands of a few, solidifying the monopolization of California politics: Gold belonged to those who could afford to finance the stamp mills, smelters, and foundries.

Within a few years of the arrival of the miners, houses of prostitution flourished; these houses were restricted to the non-white residential areas. Although the overwhelming majority of northern California's inhabitants were white, three-quarters of the prostitutes were non-white.

Gold mining introduced a banking system to California. Saloon keepers, express and stage operators, and mercantile capitalists—especially those who owned wholesale and retail warehouses—functioned as the first bankers. Merchants bought and sold gold, transporting the bullion to the East or holding the ore for safekeeping, and charging 5 percent per month for their services. In 1854, investors founded the Bank of California; by the following year, 19 banks and 9 insurance companies operated in California. The accumulation of capital enabled bankers to expand their operations. California financiers invested heavily in the Virginia City, Nevada Comstock Strike of 1859. The new capitalist class also bankrolled iron works, flourmills, and sugar beet refineries; San Francisco capitalists underwrote ventures throughout the Southwest. By 1862, capitalists founded the San Francisco Stock and Exchange Board, facilitating even more rapid growth of the economy.[43]

Complicity of the Californios

By 1849, California's population grew to more than 200,000 people—100,000 of whom were Native Californians; 13,000 were Mexicans. In the new social order the Californios rejected their Mexicanness and cultivated the pretensions of being *dons*.[44] The large white population guaranteed the territory would gain statehood, and a constitutional convention was held in August of that year at Monterey. Eight of the 48 delegates to the convention were Californios. The Californios failed to protect the interests of Mexicans, taking for granted that they would share in the governance and bounties of the new order. After all, Californios considered themselves different from Mexicans); they rationalized that they had more in common with the lighter-skinned Americans. Instead of voting as a bloc, Californios voted for their own individual self-interests. Of the eight Spanish-speaking delegates, only José A. Carrillo voted for the free admission of Negroes into California. Carrillo, however, cast his vote out of political opportunism, because he felt this stance would better California's chances for early statehood. Another criticism of the convention was that Mexican delegates were more interested in having fun and were largely silent during the proceedings while many white delegates (who were in large part lawyers) dominated the proceedings.[45]

The Californios could have voted to split the territory into north and south, giving Mexicans control of the southern half. Again, Californios voted their self-interest; many delegates belonged to the propertied class and believed that northern commerce rather than land interests would pay the bulk of the taxes. Californios won minor victories: suffrage was not limited to white males; the state would print laws in Spanish and English; and so on. Nevertheless, Californios accepted the California Bear, the symbol of the conquest, as the state seal. Tragically, "the constitution was the only document of importance the Mexican Californians participated in drafting".[46]

Even more disturbing is that the Mexican delegates did not protect the native people. They concurred in the belief that the Native Americans were brutish. Less than a year after the delegates voted to make California a "free state," the legislature passed the California 1850 Act for the Government and Protection of Indians. Commercial agriculturists led the fight for its passage; this social class was comprised of Americans and Californios who owned California's Spanish and Mexican land grants. The Act kept intact the Mexican rancho labor system that relegated the Indigenous People to peonage. Michael Magliari, in an excellent article, dissects the California Act, writing that Section 3 . . .

> . . . allowed employers to obtain custody of Native American children and to keep them until they reached the age of majority, which the law defined as eighteen years for males and fifteen for females. The section led to a flourishing trade in Indian children kidnapped from their parents or seized as the spoils of war by California militiamen who campaigned throughout the state during the 1850s and 1860s.

Section 3, using the guise of apprenticeship, made Indigenous minors into indentured servants. Those determined by the courts to be vagrants could be put in apprenticeships in which they worked without pay. The Indian Act sanctioned the leasing of Native Californian convicts and indentured servitude, and legalized hunting down those attempting to escape.[47]

Legalized Theft: The Foreign Miners' Tax

Gold brought a get-rich-quick-at-any-price mentality. Most argonauts wanted to strike it rich and go home; few planned to remain in California. For many speculators, however, hopes for instant fortune seldom materialized. The frustration of shattered dreams drove men to invent rationalizations for their failures and to find scapegoats. Mexicans became the scapegoats for American miners' failures, and American merchants resented the success of Mexican peddlers and mule dealers. In 1849, General Persifor F. Smith published a circular labeling non-citizens trespassers and advocating fines and imprisonment for them.

White miners applauded the Smith "doctrine"; they believed that if they allowed foreigners to mine, these outsiders would take all the gold out of the United States and strengthen another nation at the expense of white America. The Mexican minister to Washington, D.C., referring to the Treaty of Guadalupe Hidalgo, sent an official protest condemning violent treatment of Mexicans in California.

In Sacramento, California state legislator G. B. Tingley[48] warned of a foreign invasion, describing Mexicans as "devoid of intelligence." Thomas Jefferson Green—Texan, hater of Mexicans, expansionist, and white supremacist—proposed a compromise bill: Foreigners would be taxed $20 per month. The legislators rationalized that taxing foreigners would prevent violence: If foreigners paid for the right to mine, they would be more acceptable to white miners. On April 13, 1850, the California state legislature passed its first foreign miners' tax. Legislators repealed the tax less than a year after it had passed, not because the legislators cared about Mexicans or other foreigners, but because the merchants pressured Sacramento.

The racist rhetoric about the Mexicans and Chinese stealing their gold persisted among whites. Coya Brownrigg writes:

> Significantly, the lynching of Hispanos was tied to a larger pattern of displacement from land and economic resources. Lynching punished not only individual Hispanos but were often accompanied by attacks on Hispanos en masse, as the discourse of Hispano criminality combined with the urgency of an immediate and local threat was used to justify the rounding up and running out of all local Hispanos, whose land, property, or mining claims would then be appropriated by Anglo residents.[49]

According to historians Carrigan and Webb, "Gold Rush California was critically important in the national dissemination of this defense of vigilantism," and its justification. The Gold Rush was also why California led the nation in mob violence during the 1850s, and according to scholars, set the template for today's violence against immigrants.[50]

Decline of the Californios

7.5 Explain why and how the Californios lost their land and power.

Even before the Gold Rush ended, the Yankees turned their attention to securing more land for themselves. In 1851 the U.S. Congress passed a law that encouraged squatters to challenge Spanish and Mexican land grants by requiring all owners to prove title and establishing a land court to facilitate the theft. The California Land Act of 1851 clearly violated the Treaty of Guadalupe Hidalgo. Americans, believing that they had special privileges by right of conquest, thought it "undemocratic" for 200 Mexican families to own 14 million acres of land, even though the Treaty of Guadalupe Hidalgo and its Statement of Protocol gave Mexicans specific guarantees as to these grants. The author of the Land Act, Senator William Gwinn, later admitted that the law was designed to encourage squatters to invade Mexican ranchos and force owners off their land.[51]

The California Land Act established a Board of Land Commissioners to review claims set the colonial transfer of power. Judgments could be appealed to the U.S. district court and even the Supreme Court. The process was costly—of 813 claims, 549 were appealed as many as six times each. Litigation dragged on. The delay encouraged white Americans to move onto ranches that had legal title and squat on them. They were given a legal footing equal to that of the landowners, who had the burden of proof and were forced to pay exorbitant legal fees to defend titles to land that was already theirs. Judges, juries, and land commissioners were biased and were easily bribed. Hearings were held in English, which put Spanish-speaking grantees at an additional disadvantage. The result was that the commission heard 813 cases and approved only 520 of the grantees' claims, rejecting 273, with 20 not making it through the process.[52]

The Locusts

In 1858, 200 squatters and 1,000 "gun-carrying settlers" ambushed surveyors and held landowner Domingo Peralta hostage. Another landowner, Salvador Vallejo, rather than lose everything, sold his Napa ranch for $160,000; he had paid $80,000 in legal fees to secure his title to the land. By 1853, squatters moved onto every rancho around San Francisco.[53] The Land Act cast doubt on the legality of Mexican land titles. It sent a message to land-hungry whites that there was a chance the Californios did not own the land, that their land was part of the public domain, which gave Americans a right to homestead it. They knew that local authorities would not or could not do anything about it. Hence, they invaded and swarmed the land like locusts, harassing and intimidating many landowners. Simultaneously, claimants insidiously bled the Californios by pressing expensive litigation that challenged their grants in federal court.

Taxation without Representation

Forced out of northern California, Mexicans retained influence only in the southern half of the state, which was cattle country and highly vulnerable to swings of the economy and the natural environment. The rancheros experienced a brief boom in the early 1850s, when they drove 55,000 head of cattle to San Francisco annually at $50–$60 a head; but by 1855, the price of cattle had fallen. In 1850, the state legislature initiated a tax on land, shifting the tax burden from northern to southern California. In 1852, six southern California cattle counties had a population of 6,000 (mostly Mexican) and paid $42,000 in property taxes and $4,000 in poll taxes.

By contrast, northern California—with 120,000 persons—paid only $21,000 in property taxes and $3,500 in poll taxes. Simultaneously, rancheros had to pay county taxes, road tolls, and other special taxes. Between 1850 and 1856, the tax rate doubled on land, while mines were exempted. All in all, rancheros were unable to cope with fluctuations in the economy and increasing taxes. Californios, inexperienced in the new economic order, speculated and heavily mortgaged their property during the early 1850s. Thus, when the price of cattle fell, they could not meet their mortgage payments.

Some historians speculate that the size of Spanish-Mexican land grants determined the gigantic size of California's agribusiness holdings; this isn't so. From the beginning of their conquests, capitalists played the game of monopoly, and the results would most likely have been the same whether or not there had been large ranchos and haciendas. The Southern Pacific Railroad alone accumulated 11,588,000 acres—an area equivalent to one-fifth of privately owned land today in California, and larger than the 8,850,000 acres once owned by the Californios.

Richard Griswold del Castillo disproves the thesis that only rich Californios lost their land. According to Castillo, only 3 percent of the 10,000 Mexican Californios owned large ranchos, compared with 61 percent owning small parcels of land worth more than $100 in 1850. Ten years later the proportion fell to 29 percent, and by 1870 it was only 21 percent. The Indigenous population of California fell from 150,000 in 1845 to fewer than 30,000 in 1870.[54] By contrast, European ownership rose from 25 to 51 percent, and American ownership increased from 6 to 36 percent.[55] White monopolization was similar throughout California. The Homestead Act of 1862 opened up millions of acres as encouragement for the squatter movement.[56] Meanwhile, economic recessions encouraged the growth of the Know-Nothing Party throughout the United States.

Marrying White

Marrying daughters of the ricos was profitable; for the ricos it was a way to preserve their power. Horace Bell describes white males in such marriages as "matrimonial sharks" marrying "unsophisticated pastoral provincials." He wrote, "Marrying a daughter of one of the big landowners was in some respects a quicker way to clean her family of its assets than to lend money to the 'old man'."

Dara Orenstein wrote:

> Whites benefited from marrying Mexicans. White-Mexican marriages facilitated the exchange of property from an elite in "decline" to its successor elite, typically uniting white male settlers with Mexican women from established families. While historians have debated the frequency of these marriages, and feminist historians have read them as complex emotional affairs rather than simply as economic transfers, most agree they greatly determined California's distribution of wealth. In addition, by pitting "Spanish Californios" against "dirty" and "law-less" cholos and by fueling the racialization of class differences among Mexicans, these marriages enabled white settlers to avert mutiny in a society in which whites were vastly outnumbered. What is more, these marriages even aided settlers discursively.[57]

Stephen C. Foster married Antonio María Lugo's daughter, a widow and a wealthy woman, based on interests in her father's holdings. Two granddaughters of Antonio Lugo, the daughters of Isaac Williams, married Americans. One of them, John Rains, inherited the Chino ranch. All of the granddaughters of General Mariano Vallejo of Sonoma married white Americans; Vallejo obviously forgot or forgave that "his liberators" once called him a greaser. According to Bell, "Mostly the native daughters married good-looking and outwardly virile but really lazy, worthless, dissolute vagabond Americans whose object of marriage was to get rich without work." Many of them brought the women they married to ruin.

As in other southwestern states, there is little to suggest that any significant number of Mexican men, whether rich or poor, married white women. There was a scarcity of white women, and the game of supply and demand ruled. Thus, the conquerors monopolized the available supply of women, whom they reduced to commodities. As Bell explained, the heads of Mexican families often "felt that the future was in the hands of the invading race" and that the marriage of the daughter to a gringo was a form of protection. Bell also thought "the girls felt that they acquired prestige by marrying into the dominant race." To marry a gringo was to be accepted as white; to marry a gringo was to associate oneself with privilege, and it went a long way in alleviating the Californios' sense of inferiority.[58]

Legalizing Racism

While the degree of racism differed across class lines, los ricos were not spared. To repeat, most Californios were not pure-blooded Castilians, but descendants of the frontier people, who were mixtures of Native American, African American, and Spanish castas. As more Americans poured into the territory, racism increased, and to the new majority a greaser was a greaser. Most had not read the Treaty of Guadalupe Hidalgo, nor did they care to.

Section 394 of the Civil Practice Act of 1850 prohibited Chinese and Native Americans from testifying against whites. In *People v. Hall* (1854), a judge reversed the conviction of George Hall because it was based on the testimony of a Chinese. The courts also applied this section to Mexicans.[59] In 1855, the state legislature refused to allocate funds for translation of state laws into Spanish despite the Treaty of Guadalupe Hidalgo and the state constitution. That same year the legislature passed the Greaser Act that defined vagrants as "all persons who [were] commonly known as 'Greasers' or the issue of Spanish or Indian blood." In April 1857 in *People v. Elyea* a court denied Manuel Domínguez, a signer of the first California Constitution, a wealthy landowner, and a county supervisor, the right to testify because of his Native American blood.[60]

Legitimization of Violence

The term *vigilante* comes from the Committees of Vigilance. These groups proliferated in the days following the California Gold Rush.[61] Some historical accounts have romanticized the vigilantes as local citizens banding together to fight crime, and claim that they brought down the crime rate in places like San Francisco. In reality, vigilantes played to the fears and racism of their supporters.

On June 15, 1849, a "benevolent, self-protective and relief society" called *the Hounds* attacked a Chilean barrio in San Francisco. The drunken mob killed one woman, raped two more, looted, and plundered.

On July 10, 1850, four Yaqui were charged with the murder of four Americans near Sonora, California.[62] Although Justice of the Peace R. C. Barry believed that the men were innocent and attempted to forestall violence, a mob hanged the four men. In 1851, when the state passed the foreign miners' tax, Antonio Coronel, a schoolteacher, came upon a mob that was about to lynch five foreigners accused of stealing 5 pounds of gold. Although Coronel offered to pay them the cost of gold for the release of the prisoners, the miners refused. They then whipped three of the men and hanged the other two.

Public whippings and brandings were common, and it did not matter if the victims were citizens or not. Spanish speakers were lumped together as "interlopers" and "greasers." Some historians have portrayed vigilantism as an expression of democracy in action. They rationalize that the mob championed law and order, which meant taking "an eye for an eye." Accordingly, Mexicans had a criminal nature that must be controlled, and to North Americans every Mexican was a potential outlaw. Vigilantes used outlaw activity as an excuse to rob and murder peaceful Mexicans.

As mentioned, an estimated 547 Mexicans were victims of mob lynchings in the United States between 1848 and 1928. Many were hanged, or mobs summarily executed them. The foreign miners' tax fueled ethnic conflict and at least 143 Mexicans were victims in California between 1848 and 1860. These summary executions continued throughout the century.[63]

The Mexican Whore

The most flagrant act of vigilantism happened at Downieville in 1851, when, after a kangaroo trial, a mob lynched a Mexican woman they called Juanita.[64] Only 26 years old, she was the *first* woman hanged in California. Popular lore held that Juanita (aka Josefa Segovia) was a prostitute who was married to a gambler, Manuel José Loaiza. On July 4, 1851, in a drunken rage, Fred Cannon, a miner, broke down the door of Josefa's home and tried to elicit sexual favors from her. She chased him off and the next day Josefa and her husband demanded that Cannon pay for the broken door. Cannon became belligerent and called her a whore. Standing on the doorway, Josefa challenged, "This is no place to call me bad names, come into my house and call me that." As Cannon forcibly entered the house, still calling her vile names, Josefa avenged her honor by killing him with a knife.[65]

Although the miners wanted to lynch Josefa and José on the spot, they went through the motions of a trial. With Cannon's body on display in a tent, dressed in a red flannel shirt, unbuttoned to display the wound, Josefa was convicted. No matter that she was pregnant; she was hanged from a bridge, while over 2,000 men lined the river to watch. After this, lynching became commonplace in California. Among Mexicans, American democracy came to be known as *Linchocracia* (Lynchocracy).[66] In 1875, José María Loaiza filed a claim for Josefa's lynching and his banishment by a mob in 1852 in Downieville, California. The commissioner dismissed the claim.[67]

The American Delusion: The Lugos Trial

For early merchants such as Abel Stearns, racism was a matter of grape picking: They would select which Mexicans were acceptable and which were not. Stearns married Arcadia Bandini, member of an elite rancher family and said to be the most beautiful woman in all of California.[68] However, racism increased as lower-class white Americans became numerous. To them a greaser was a greaser, and they did not distinguish between rich and poor Mexicans. This generalization bothered the Californio elite who fashioned themselves as white or near white. As the Californios lost their land and their political clout, fewer Americans bothered to make distinctions.

Mexicans were still a majority in the southern counties. For a time, they were able to hold on to local offices, but the massive increase in the American population was nudging them out of government statewide. By 1851, all California-born Mexicans were excluded from the State Senate; by the 1860s, only a few Mexicans remained in the assembly; and by the 1880s, few people with Spanish surnames could be found in public offices. During these years, Mexican bosses such as Tomás Sánchez and Antonio Coronel delivered the Mexican vote in Los Angeles. However, there were chasms within the Mexican community itself—especially between the Californios and the new arrivals from Sonora and Mexico. Ex-Mexican governor Juan Bautista Alvarado called Native Californians "backward," saying they were indolent, ignorant, and lazy people.

Racial tensions polarized the Mexican and American communities. This was true especially in Los Angeles, where, although the Mexican elite actively cooperated with the new order, they often became victims of mob violence. A celebrated case involved the Lugo brothers—Francisco, 16, and Benito, 18—accused of killing a white man and his Native American companion. The brothers were the grandsons of Antonio María Lugo, head of one of the richest and most powerful Californio families. Joseph Lancaster Brent, a Los Angeles attorney with strong Southern sympathies, who later served as a general in the confederate army, defended the Lugos. Brent cultivated alliances with the ranchero elite. A Catholic from Maryland, he won over many wealthy Mexican families and in the process made a fortune representing them in court.

In January 1851, the Lugos were charged with murdering Patrick McSwiggin and his Creek companion. At the time, only about 75 "Americans" lived permanently in Los Angeles, and they lived in perpetual fear of a Californio revolt. Hearing about the murders, they began to arm themselves. Allegedly there was an eyewitness to the shooting, but *vaqueros* riding with the Lugos contradicted his testimony; they swore that the brothers had never left the camp and that the murders were not committed by them.

During the trial, Captain John "Red" Irving and about 25 men approached Brent and demanded $10,000 to ensure the safety of the Lugos. When the family refused the offer, Irving vowed to kill the brothers. With the help of Brent, about 60 armed Californios showed up, followed by U.S. troops, whose presence prevented a confrontation. The Californios escorted the Lugos to the judge, who released them on bail; further, they escorted the Lugos to their ranch.

A month later, Red Irving and his men set out for the Lugo ranch to kill the brothers. Cahuilla allies of the Lugos set a trap and killed all the gang members except one. The court finally dismissed the case in October 1852. Rumor had it that Brent collected a fee of $20,000, a measure of the price paid for justice. This was one of the few instances where the Californios showed unity, and it was based on class rather than race.[69]

The Disillusionment

7.6 **Describe how presses like *El Clamor Público* reacted to white supremacy and the declining power of the Californios.**

At the beginning of the U.S. occupation, some Mexicans were optimistic about their future. Disillusionment soon set in, and many chose to repatriate to Mexico. Many of those who remained saw their status denigrate and injustices proliferate. A division occurred between the Californios along ideological lines, with the more conservative aligning themselves with proslavery Americans. The more progressive Californios were critical of the system and opposed southern racism. The latter maintained contact with Latin America and supported the social and political movements in those countries. These progressives criticized the fate Mexicans suffered in California. This minority within a minority did not have the resources of the Picos and other Californios, who often squandered their fortunes and generally refused to fund liberal causes. In turn, the progressives started small newspapers that often enjoyed short runs because they lacked financial backing. For example, the *Clamor Público* in Los Angeles lasted four years and its readership was about 100 subscribers.[70]

El Clamor Público

Francisco Ramírez had very little formal schooling and, like many Californios and literate people throughout the world, was home-schooled. His grandfather was from Tepic and migrated to the Mission Santa Barbara. The family moved to Los Angeles in the late 1820s, where Francisco was born. At the age of 18, Ramírez, a former compositor of the Spanish page of the *Los Angeles Star*, began to publish *El Clamor Público* in Los Angeles in 1855. Four years later, the newspaper went out of business because of lack of funds. Ramírez migrated to Sonora, where he edited the state newspaper. After a short period, he returned to California and held jobs as a printer, as postmaster, and as the official translator for the state. He tried a comeback in 1872 as editor of *La Crónica* in Los Angeles.

Ramírez incorporated the best of Latin American newspapers in *El Clamor*. Not only did he report the news but also printed poetry, essays, and short stories of the time. Along with *La Crónica*, *El Eco del Pacífico*, *El Nuevo Mundo de San Francisco*, and others. *El Clamor* reflected the intellectual curiosity of Spanish-speaking Californians and the liberal-rationalist thought of the mid-nineteenth century. Many contributors were local. Ramírez exposed the barbarity of white Americans who had come to California to allegedly civilize the Mexican.[71]

Professor José Luis Benavides makes the point that many Spanish-language newspapers, such as the *Santa Barbara Gazette* (1855–1858), acted as agents of social control. Californios—or, to be more specific, California-born Mexicans along with recently arrived Mexicans—composed 95 percent of the population of the Los Angeles area. Americans established the *Gazette* with a Spanish-language section, *La Gaceta*, that introduced a American worldview; it was a translation of what the 5 percent wanted to hear. *La Gaceta* lasted six months. On the other hand, *El Clamor* proactively reported the interests of the larger audience. Ramírez's editorials reflected the Mexicanos' growing disappointments with American justice.

On June 19, 1855, in an editorial, Ramírez called for justice within the system and the recognition by California's Mexicans that the state was now part of the United States. Ramírez asked the Californios for financial support, writing that a free press was their best guarantee of liberty in the new order. Ramírez's editorials became more strident. About the filibuster William Walker,[72] Ramírez wrote, "World history tells us that the Anglo-Saxons were in the beginning thieves and pirates, the same as other nations in their infancy . . . [but] the pirate instinct of old Anglo-Saxons is still active."[73] Through the newspaper's four-year run, Walker was the prototype of the other "pirates"—the politicians and filibusters who had designs on Mexico or Latin America. In September 1855 Ramírez reprinted an article that began "Who is the foreigner in California?" and continued, "The North Americans pretend to give us lessons in humanity and to bring to our people the doctrine of salvation so we can govern ourselves, to respect the laws and conserve order. Are these the ones who treat us worse than slaves?"[74] As early as October 1855, Ramírez encouraged Mexicans and Chileans to join Jesús Isla's *Junta Colonizadora de Sonora* and return to Mexico. Ramírez editorialized, "California has fallen into the hands of the ambitious sons of North America who will not stop until they have satisfied their passions, by driving the first occupants of the land out of the country, vilifying their religion and disfiguring their customs."

A reader objected to Ramírez's "return to Mexico" campaign by responding, "California has always been the asylum of Sonorans, and the place where they have found good wages, hospitality, and happiness." Ramírez caustically wrote that the letter did not merit comment but asked, "Are the Californios as happy today as when they belonged to the Republic of Mexico, in spite of all of its revolutions and changes in government?"[75]

El Clamor's coverage of lynchings distinguished its coverage. On March 28, 1857, it reprinted a *San Francisco Daily Herald* letter by José S. Berreyesa, who recounted the Bear Flaggers' assassination of the elder Berreyesa and his two nephews. It went on to report that in July 1854 the body of a American was found on the San Vicente ranch, which belonged to the Berreyesa family. Suspecting that Encarnación Berreyesa had murdered the man, Americans dragged him out of the house as his wife and children looked on, and suspended him from a tree. When Encarnación did not confess to the killings, vigilantes left him half dead and instead hanged his brother Nemesio. Encarnación was later charged with the murder of an American in Santa Clara and lynched by vigilantes.[76] After six years of such assassinations, the Californios began arming themselves to protect their families. Soon after, on July 26, 1856, Francisco Ramírez wrote in *El Clamor Público* that conditions for Californios had never been as bad.

Ramírez continued to speak out against the rampant murder of Mexicanos. The murder of Antonio Ruiz was the straw that broke the camel's back. Deputy Marshal William W. Jenkins, alleged that Antonio Ruiz interfered with him when he tried to take repossession of a guitar in payment of a debt. An argument ensued between the deputy and Ruiz and the sheriff shot Ruiz, a respected member of the community. Friends streamed by Ruiz's deathbed to bid him a tearful goodbye. At Jenkins's trial, the defense badgered the witnesses. It took the all-white jury only 15 minutes to reach a verdict of not guilty. Soon afterward, Jenkins returned to the task of maintaining "law and order" in Los Angeles. The murder of Antonio Ruiz divided Mexicans across class lines, with the lower classes harboring deep-seated grievances against Americans.[77]

Class Divisions

Many Californios pandered to the white minority that was among the worst of U.S. society. A case in point was their support of the El Monte gang, who were located in El Monte, California, east of the Los Angeles plaza. El Monte was infested by Texans, some of whom were former Rangers. The El Monte crowd postured as defenders of white supremacy.

During 1856 and 1857, the El Monte boys used the pretext of the Juan Flores gang to commit atrocities against the Mexican community. Twenty-one-year-old Juan Flores had escaped from San Quentin prison and formed a band of almost 50 Mexicanos, including Pancho Daniel. In a shootout, the rebels killed the sheriff. Rumors spread that Flores intended to kill all whites.

Without any legal authority or evidence, the El Monte gang arrested Diego Navarro, who was seen riding away from the gun battle. Navarro admitted that he saw the gunfight, but left knowing that all Mexicans were suspect. The mob threw hot tar on Navarro's family home and broke into the house. They dragged him out and executed him, along with two other Mexicans accused of being members of the Flores gang.

Numerous ricos backed the gringos in hunting down the rebels; *los de abajo* (the underdogs) supported Flores. In a January 31, 1857 editorial, even the normally progressive Ramírez called for Californios to help enforce the laws. He praised Tomás Sánchez, the Democratic Party *cacique* (boss), and Andrés Pico for riding with the El Monte gringos.

The El Monte gang captured Flores and Daniel, who soon escaped. To make sure this did not happen again, they hanged their next nine captives immediately. Meanwhile, Andrés Pico and California Native Americans tracked Flores. Pico caught up with two members of the Flores gang and hanged them. Operating independently, the Pico posse and the El Monte people broke into houses in the middle of the night and herded suspects to jail. Fifty-two men were crammed into the jails. All except Daniel were captured. A kangaroo court convicted Flores on February 14, 1857, and hanged him.[78] *El Clamor Público* praised Andrés Pico in a February 7 editorial, saying that the Californios had vindicated the Californios' honor. Not everyone agreed with Ramírez's assessment, though, and as Historian Leonard Pitt notes, "Sánchez and Pico, who gladly rode with Texans to track down 'their own kind,' thereby won the gringos' everlasting gratitude." They were rewarded: Sánchez became a sheriff, and Pico became a brigadier in the California militia and was elected to the State Assembly. Many Mexicanos did not share the enthusiasm of *El Clamor Público* and the ricos, and condemned their participation in suppressing the Flores–Daniel rebellion. The poor could not ignore the racial and ethnic divide between "American" citizens.[79]

It is out of character that Ramírez supported this injustice, since the Picos and other Californios did not financially support his newspaper. Sánchez and others supported the Democrats, who were, among other things, proslavery. Ramírez acquiesced in the hanging of Flores; but when Daniel was caught and lynched, he called the execution "barbaric and diabolic" and wrote,

> And you, imbecile Californios! You are to blame for the lamentations that we are witnessing. We are tired of saying: open your eyes, and it is time that we demand our rights and interests. It is with shame that we say, and difficult to confess it: you are the sarcasm of humanity!

Ramírez scolded readers for not voting and for putting up with indignities, calling them "cowards and stupid." Ramírez warned Californios that until they cared, they could never cast off the "yoke of slavery."[80]

However, we should be cautious with our criticism. Paul Bryan Gray calls him "a brilliant and astonishingly precocious 18-year-old named Francisco P. Ramírez who presented his journal as a champion of the Mexican people," and that "Ramírez had embraced the principles of nineteenth century liberalism, especially the variety prevalent in Mexico. He probably read the work of Mexicans like José María Luis Mora, Ignacio Ramírez 'El Nigromante,' and other ideologues of the liberal movement headed by Benito Juárez."[81] Gray also takes the Picos and other elites to task for not financially supporting Ramírez.

Most of Gray's observations are accurate. However, some statements must be qualified; for example, the word liberal did not mean what it does today. The liberals worshiped the marketplace; they were not champions of the people, and in Mexico they pushed immigration policies that would have Europeanized Mexico. It was also liberals who harbored the deepest anti-Native American biases. They encroached on Indigenous land, and launched wars against the Yaqui and others. As for lack of support from the Picos and company, why should they have been expected to support Ramírez? Surely, his progressive white buddies did not support him. The truth was that most of the wealthy Californios were Democrats with a tradition of being proslavery. Andrés Pico was a financial backer of the newspaper *Southern Californian*, started in July 1854 by C. N. Richards and William Butts. Pico sank $10,000 into the company, which he sold to Colonel J. J. Warner in 1856. By 1855, Andrés and his brother Pío Pico owned 532,000 acres of land between them. But they had no interest in democracy or equality—they were more interested in lavish lifestyles. They had frequent guests and provided them with trayfuls of coins, so the guests would not have to spend their own money. It is not surprising that visitors often stayed for weeks at a time.[82]

These criticisms do not minimize Ramírez's contributions. However, he should be placed in the context of professor Benavides's excellent treatise on *El Clamor Público*.

Ramírez had, in fact, challenged the ideology of white supremacy in pointing out injustices committed against Blacks and Chinese. Furthermore, he opposed slavery and efforts to exclude free African Americans from exercising their rights. As Benavides points out, *El Clamor* also "reproduced stereotypes about Blacks and Native Americans, did not defend the rights of Native Californians to equal treatment, and justified the mass killings of Indigenous people as a 'war'." Despite his progressive pretensions, Ramírez found comments that equated Mexicans, Blacks, and Native Californians as demeaning to Californios.[83]

Social Banditry

7.7 Contextualize social banditry in California in the context of colonialism.

Hollywood has made at least four movies based on the life and times of Joaquin Murieta.[84] Both Chileans and Mexicans claim Murieta, who is undoubtedly the best-known "bandit" in California history. Despite the myths that surround his origins, considerable documentation attests that Murieta and his family came to California during the Gold Rush from Villa San Rafael de los Alamitos in Sonora, Mexico. Land-claim-jumpers twice invaded his land, and lynched his older brother. The gang raped his wife, and left Joaquin for dead. Unable to get justice from the system, Murieta sought his own justice and stole from the gringo thieves. He became so notorious that at least 41 Mexican bandits were identified as Joaquin Murieta. In 1853, the California legislature hired Captain Harry Love, a former Texas Ranger, to hunt down Joaquin. Love allegedly caught and killed Murieta and his band. The question is, was it really Murieta?

I am Joaquin!

Joaquin Murieta (the way his name is spelled varies according to source) has fascinated Hollywood. Even the great Chilean poet Pablo Neruda (1904–1973) claims Joaquin as a Chilean. The movie *Zorro* was fashioned on his legend. The story is simple. Murieta was attacked by Americans who raped his wife and killed his family members. Jill L. Cossley-Batt, describing the alleged death of Murieta, wrote,

> The bandits were armed exclusively with six-shooters, whereas the Rangers, being fitted out with rifles, revolvers, and shot-guns, had the advantage, and soon made short work of the swarthy desperadoes. Twelve were killed outright and two were taken prisoners. The Rangers were uninjured, but Captain Love had experienced a "close shave"....[85]

In order to prove that they killed Joaquin, Love severed Murieta's head and his associate Three-Fingered Jack's hand, and pickled them in vinegar.

Horace Bell, a Los Angeles attorney who rode in a posse looking for Joaquin, wrote in his autobiography that although he chased Murieta and other so-called Mexican bandits, he attributed much of the tension to white American racism and mistreatment of Mexicans.

> His acts were so bold and daring, and attended with such remarkable success, that he drew to him all the Mexican outlaws, cut-throats and thieves that infested the country extending from San Diego to Stockton. No one will deny the assertion that Joaquín in his organizations, and the successful ramifications of his various bands, his eluding capture, the secret intelligence conveyed from points remote from each other, manifested a degree of executive ability and genius that well fitted him for a more honorable position than that of chief of a band of robbers. In any country in America except the United States, the bold defiance of the power of the government, a half year's successful resistance, a continuous conflict with the military and civil authorities and the armed populace—the writer repeats that in any other country in America other than the United States—the operations of Joaquín Murietta would have been dignified by the title. . . . there is little doubt in the writer's mind that Joaquin's aims were higher than that of mere revenge and pillage. Educated in the school of revolution in his own country, where the line of demarcation between rebel and robber, pillager and patriot, was dimly defined, it is easy to perceive that Joaquín felt himself to be more the champion of his countrymen than an outlaw and an enemy to the human race. . . . [86]

The Social Bandit

When people cannot earn a living within the system or when they are degraded, they strike out. Rebellion against the system can take the form of organized resistance, as in the case of Juan Cortina in Texas, or it can express itself in bandit activity.

Tiburcio Vásquez was born in Monterey on August 11, 1835. His parents were of a good reputation, and Vásquez had an above-average education for the times. Vásquez never married. In about 1852, during a fiesta he was involved in the shooting of a constable and fled to the hills.[87] At the end of his career, Vásquez explained the incident and his reasons for turning *bandido*:

> My career grew out of the circumstances by which I was surrounded. As I grew to manhood I was in the habit of attending balls and parties given by the native Californians, into which the Americans, then beginning to become numerous, would force themselves and shove the native born men aside, monopolizing the dance and the women. This was about 1852. A spirit of hatred and revenge took possession of me. I had numerous fights in defense of my countrymen. The officers were continually in pursuit of me. I believed we were unjustly and wrongfully deprived of the social rights that belonged to us.[88]

By the middle of the 1850s California "was experiencing an economic depression. Money was short, the great flood of gold was nearly played out, land and cattle prices were down, and banditry was rampant."[89] Vásquez attracted a large following and his popularity grew among the poor. Although the ricos were afraid that he wanted to incite an uprising or revolution against the "Yankee invaders" of California, the rural poor supported and shielded him.[90] The *Los Angeles Express* of May 16, 1874 quoted Vásquez as claiming, "Given $60,000 I would be able to recruit enough arms and men to revolutionize Southern California."

In the fall of 1871, Vásquez and his men robbed the Visalia stage. His reputation as a *desperado* grew, and soon he was being blamed for crimes that he had not committed. The magnitude of the manhunts increased. Authorities offered money to informers in an effort to locate Vásquez. Throughout 1871, Vásquez continued his activities and evaded arrest. The Mexican populace aided him, for "to some, Vásquez must have seemed a hero dealing out his own particular brand of justice. Certainly his reputation was growing fast."[91]

On August 16, 1873, the Vásquez gang robbed Snyder's store in Tres Pinos of $1,200. This daring raid escalated him to statewide prominence. Newspapers sensationalized Vásquez's raids and wanted posters circulated. Vásquez prudently shifted doings to southern California.

During the next year the newspapers played up his exploits, and Sheriff Harry Morse quickened the chase, covering 2,720 miles in 61 days searching for Vásquez. Authorities learned that Vásquez was hiding out at the ranch of George Allen, better known as Greek George, and surrounded the ranch. Vásquez was captured. An all-American jury found him guilty, and he was sentenced to hang.

George A. Beers, a special correspondent for the *San Francisco Chronicle*, offered a partial explanation of why Vásquez captured the imagination of the Mexican populace:

> Vásquez turned to the life of a bandido because of the bitter animosity then existing, and which still exists, between the white settlers and the native or Mexican portion of the population. The native Californians, especially the lower classes, never took kindly to the stars and stripes. Their youth were taught from the very cradle to look upon the American government as that of a foreign nation.
>
> This feeling was greatly intensified by the rough, brutal conduct of the worst class of American settlers, who never missed an opportunity to openly exhibit their contempt for the native Californian or Mexican population—designating them as "d—d Greasers," and treating them like dogs. Add to this the fact that these helpless people were cheated out of their lands and possessions by every subterfuge—in many instances their property being actually wrested from them by force, and their women debauched whenever practicable—and we can understand very clearly some of the causes which have given to Joaquin (Murietta), Vasquez, and others of their stripe,

the power to call around them at any time all the followers they required, and which secured to them aid and comfort from the Mexican settlers everywhere.[92]

Vásquez's execution deepened racial animosity. Two weeks after the hanging, a man named Romo killed two Americans who had participated in Vásquez's capture; Romo was captured and lynched. Groups of Mexicanos met secretly, and the ricos feared a race war that would entangle them. Tiburcio Vásquez's death ended the era of intense Mexican rebellion.

Mexicans in a Changing Society

7.8 Characterize the Mexican community in California at the end of the 1800s.

Natural disasters of the 1860s accelerated the decline of Mexicano elite. In 1862, a flood devastated California ranches. Two years of drought, the loss of most of southern California's large cattle herds, and falling cattle prices forced ranch owners to mortgage their property at outlandish interest rates, resulting in foreclosures. With the loss of land came a loss of political power: Mexicans without money were just greasers. Piece by piece, they sold their land to pay mortgages. Within a decade, the Californios were relatively landless in California.

Meanwhile, the Mexican community grew throughout California. They formed enclaves called *barrios* or *colonias* throughout the state. The French Intervention (1861–1868) in Mexico brought exiles to California, who were recruited by the various factions. David Hayes-Bautista and his team of researchers are currently documenting the California *Juntas Patrióticas*, patriotic committees that often worked with the Mexican consulate, which flourished during this period (and still do). The French Intervention sharpened Mexican nationalism and the importance of holidays such as the Cinco de Mayo. Through the presence of the recent exiles, areas of support for Benito Juárez and the liberal cause can be documented; their absence in certain regions such as Santa Barbara and San Diego suggests the existence of conservative strongholds there. The nationalism of the newcomers further separated the Californios and the masses.[93]

Mexicans attempted to deal with problems within their own community. They formed self-help associations—such as *La Sociedad Hispanoamericana de Beneficio Mutua*, founded in Los Angeles in 1875, and the Sisters of Charity hospital for indigents, founded in 1887—to raise money for hospitals and charitable causes.[94] Organizations reflected the Mexicans' isolation and in turn they became increasingly nationalistic, celebrating the Mexican patriotic holidays (such as the Mexican independence on September 16 and the Battle of Puebla on May 5 commemorating the Mexicans' defeat of the French Army in the 1860s) and sponsoring parades, speeches, and other festivities.

The transcontinental railroad completed its link to California in 1869, and over the next decade the railroad spread throughout the state. As elsewhere in the Southwest, the "iron horse" transformed social relations. It ended the isolation of southern California, accelerating its eventual transformation into a region of large-scale agriculture. The railroad brought 70,000 newcomers a year to California, and the Mexican isolation of the 1850s and 1860s abruptly ended. After the arrival of large numbers of Americans, Mexicans played the role of a small and politically insignificant minority. Southern California had entered the era of industrialized capitalism: The Panic of 1873 put the lid on the coffin, and the arrival of the Southern Pacific Railroad in 1876 drove in the nails.[95]

Becoming a Minority

The Mexican population of Los Angeles increased only slightly from 1,331 in 1850 to 2,231 in 1880, whereas the American population rose from under 300 to some 8,000 during this same period. By 1890, the city's population had grown to 50,395 (the county's, to 101,454); again the Mexican population had increased only slightly. Los Angeles underwent other changes as well. In 1850, it had one factory employing two men; in 1880, it had 172 factories and 700 workers. Total property values in this period increased from $2,282,949 to $20,916,835. The white population expanded from 18 percent of the total population in 1850 to 80 percent in 1880.

The 1880s transformed Los Angeles into a modern city. However, Mexicans were not part of this new prosperity; their status changed little. For instance, 65 percent of Mexicans were employed as manual laborers, in contrast to the 26 percent of Americans employed as laborers. The economic order froze Mexicans into a lower class, and occupational mobility was limited among all workers; race and a historical tradition of oppression caused continued subjugation.

Though Los Angeles' isolation was ending, segregation became more common. In southern California, Americans were the majority in the 1870s. By 1873, the participation of Mexicans on juries became less frequent, as did their involvement in any other activity of governance. Mexican political bosses declined in power; by the 1880s, they had little to broker. Consequently, city officials ignored problems of health and urbanization in the barrios (known as "Sonoratown").[96] Between 1877 and 1888, infant mortality was double that of white Americans; the death rate among Mexicans between ages 5 and 20 was also double, with smallpox being a leading killer. The cost of medical care was prohibitive; doctors charged for house calls according to how far away the patient lived. Since most doctors did not live close to the Mexican colonias, the usual fee was $10—a week's salary for most Mexicans.[97]

Holy Mother the Church

The Catholic Church methodically destroyed nationalist movements among the Mexican populace. Soon after the American takeover, New York Bishop John Hughes contacted José Noriega de la Guerra to seek his advice on whom he should support to be the next Bishop of California. De La Guerra advised that it should be a Spanish-born bishop since most of the Californios were Spanish, a piece of advice that Hughes followed.[98] In 1850, Fr. Joseph Sadoc Alemany was appointed Archbishop of San Francisco, the first archbishop in California. Alemany was a Catalan and a member of the Order of St. Dominic. Evidence suggests that he did not confront the impoverished state of the masses of Mexicans and the natives. His passion was to recover control of the Pious Fund, a large fund collected during the Spanish colonial period for the benefit of the missions. That Alemany was a Dominican friar was significant: The order was at the forefront of Catholic orthodoxy and led the opposition to separation of church and state. The Spanish province of Catalan was a battleground, and the scene of violent clashes, in this controversy. As such, Alemany probably sided with the church party in Mexico and opposed liberalism, which the Dominicans and the church saw as work of the Antichrist.[99]

In 1853 Vincentian Father Thaddeus Amat was appointed Bishop of Monterey, which later became part of the Diocese of Monterey–Los Angeles. Like Alemany, he too was a Catalan. Amat summed up the priority of the church in 1870, stating that the church was "the main support of society and order, which imperatively demands respect for legitimate authority and subjugation to legitimate law."[100] The construction of new churches further segregated the Mexican poor. St. Viviana's Cathedral, built in 1876, served an American parish, as did St. Vincent's (1886), St. Andrew's (1886), and Sacred Heart (1887). St. Joseph's, built in 1888, also catered to Americans. The construction of the churches in the 1880s coincided with the mass arrival of thousands of Americans, who found sanctuary for their racism in these segregated houses of worship. The Mexicans continued to attend the *placita* (the plaza church).[101]

Labor

Unlike Arizona, Mexican labor did not dominate the California labor force during the nineteenth century. The laborers of choice were Chinese immigrants (supplemented by Indigenous Californians); for a period, the Chinese outnumbered Mexicans in the state. The new order, like the old order, treated Native Americans shamefully. They continued to be captured, sold, and raped. In 1886, the California Supreme Court, in *Thompson v. Doaksum*, ruled that land held by Indigenous People during the Mexican period and not claimed by the Land Law of 1851 was public domain. In *Botiller v. Dominguez* (1889), the highest court in the land ruled that indigenous claims by title or occupancy were invalid if they had not been legally confirmed previously. These laws were intended to legally segregate and enslave Native Americans. California vagrancy law allowed the jail keepers to sell the labor of Native Americans to private contractors who would in turn pay their fines. From 1852 to 1867, Mexicans and Americans were involved in slave trafficking, kidnapping, and the selling of more than 4,000 Native American children to Mexican rancheros and American colonists.[102]

The Exclusion of the Other

7.9 Where did the Native American and the Chinese rank in the Social Order.

The demand for Mexican labor was directly related to the decline in population of Chinese workers and Native Californians. The Chinese Exclusion Act of 1882 almost entirely stopped Chinese immigration to the United States. This, along with the dying off of the California natives, created a shortage of manual laborers and a demand for Mexican workers. Mexicans moved from pastoral occupations to menial-wage work. They took jobs at the lowest rung of the economic and social ladder. Increasingly, they became wage earners, driven from subsistence farming by the sale of common lands. At the same time, thousands of Mexicans migrated to California from Mexico and elsewhere in the Southwest.

Much of this labor was segregated. Thirteen miles south of San José, the Almaden mercury mines, active since the Mexican period, employed mostly Mexicans. Fifteen hundred miners worked at the Quicksilver Mine Company.[103] Using ancient methods, they hauled ore out of the underground mines with 200-pound sacks strapped to their foreheads and resting on their backs. Miners produced 220,000 pounds of ore per month. The company kept tight control of its workers. It segregated them not only by race, but also by occupation. The Cornish miners, for example, lived separately from the Mexican miners, who were condemned to a distinctively lower standard of living, and neither Mexican workers nor their families were allowed contact with English adults or children, who attended separate schools and churches.[104]

Colonias

An interesting account of the various colonias along the Southern Pacific rail route in northern California appeared in the San Francisco *El Cronista* in April 1885. In "Ferrocarril del Sur," Sóstenes Betancourt talks about the nationalism of the Mexican people and their genuine love for the homeland, of merchants such as Estolano F. Larios of Tres Pinos, and about the presence of Mexican ranchers. One gets a definite sense of community in Tres Pinos, which had a population of 250, 50 of whom were Mexicans. Throughout his trip, Betancourt came across Argentines and Chileans who had integrated into the Mexican population.

Betancourt writes about the miracles attributed to Joaquin Murieta's alleged wife, Mariana. In the valleys, Betancourt recounts, people spoke of the adventures of the legendary Joaquin Murieta as if they were still happening. Mariana, who had disappeared, returned to the *valle de Santa Cruz* in the company of a Frenchman and several assistants to preach about the sainthood of Franciscan Padre Magín Catalán, known as "the holy man of Santa Clara," the first missionary of the mission of that name. They claimed they were sent by *el santo padre Magín*, and on his behalf met with thousands of persons, who could "communicate" with the saint through Mariana. Apparently, the cult collected large sums of money. Mariana and her cabal then disappeared once more, with about $8,000. Betancourt suggests that millenarian motives inspired the people's fascination for Mariana, who they believed would liberate them.[105]

Conclusion: Mexican Labor Builds California

Between 1880 and 1920 California built an agricultural empire, mostly utilizing Chinese labor, whose dominance helped in the transition from peonage. The Southern Pacific Railroad alone owned more land than all the rancheros combined. It was the state's largest employer. The company advertised throughout the East and Europe to sell its land. It even established an employment agency for the new settlers.

Industrial growth meant a heavy demand for cheap labor. By the 1890s, agriculture had become intensive, and California was becoming a major exporter of grains, fruits, and vegetables.[106] After the Chinese Exclusion Act (1882), other groups filled the labor vacuum. Meanwhile, the reclamation programs of the early 1900s caused a revolution in agriculture that forced California capitalists to look to the most logical and available source of labor—Mexico. The discovery of oil and the opening of the Panama Canal would bring about further changes in the 1900s. The isolation of California and Los Angeles had completely ended. Beginning in the 1880s, Los Angeles was in the firm grip of the ruling elite, led by the *Los Angeles Times* and a cabal of white land speculators, bankers, and developers who ran the city and county for personal profit.

Discrimination toward Mexicans in the wage-labor market increased; a dual-wage system persisted, with Mexicans and Chinese paid less compared to Americans. This arbitrary treatment of Mexicans often led to confrontations. In 1889, for instance, Modesta Avila placed a sign on the tracks of the Santa Fé Railroad that read, "This land belongs to me. And if the railroad wants to run here, they will have to pay me ten thousand dollars." The sign was some 15 feet from the doorstep of her home on the former San Juan Capistrano mission. Local authorities had told Avila not to do this, to which she replied, "If they pay me for my land, they can go by." Avila was hauled before the Orange County Superior Court and sentenced to three years in jail. She died in San Quentin; she was in her mid-20s at the time of her death.[107]

In another example of the inequality, in August 1892 a mob broke into the Santa Ana jail and hanged Francisco Torres, a native of Colima, Mexico. Torres worked at the Modjeska ranch for a wage of $9 for a six-day week. The ranch foreman, William McKelvey, withheld money for a road poll tax from Torres's wages, but not from any of the other workers' pay. Torres refused his wages, demanding full payment, and in the ensuing argument, Torres in self-defense killed McKelvey with a knife. Torres stated that he did not have a gun and that he had taken a club away from the larger man; then, fearing that the foreman would use his gun, he stabbed him.

Before Torres could be tried, a mob broke into the jail and executed him, hanging a sign around his neck that read, "Change of venue." The *Santa Ana Standard* wrote that Torres was of a low type of Mexican race, emphasizing his Indigenous features. By contrast, *Las Dos Repúblicas* wrote that Torres was only guilty of being a Mexican. The execution went unpunished.[108]

By 1900, the railroad linked California to the nation's marketplace. California made the complete transition from a Mexican province to a North American state. Its population, overwhelmingly white in color and culture, numbered 1.5 million. By then, the Native Californian population dropped to about 15,000; Mexicans numbered between 10,000 and 17,000. The African American population totaled 11,045. The unprecedented economic transformation of the next century would dramatically change these proportions.[109]

Who are the Mexican Americans?

Today California remains a trendsetter. The Los Angeles Metropolitan area has more people than 40 American states. Numbers give the Mexican American community considerable influence in Mexican American popular culture and politics. In many regards, what comes out of LA influences Mexican American thought in the rest of the country. For example, it popularized the Indigenous danzantes and many Mexican Americans self-identify themselves as Indigenous. While there is evidence that 90 percent of Mexican Americans have Native Mexican blood, there is a word of caution. By self-identifying as Indigenous we ignore the effects of colonialism and absolve the racial mixtures that came about by the building of the Empire. Although it seems as if everyone today is taking DNA tests that supposedly prove they have Native American blood, this should be looked at cautiously. According to the *CIA World Fact Book*, the United States is "white 72.4%, black 12.6%, Asian 4.8%, Amerindian and Alaska native 0.9%, native Hawaiian and other Pacific islander 0.2%, other 6.2%, two or more races 2.9% (2010 estimate)."[110]

The same source reports that Mexico's population is "mestizo (Amerindian-Spanish) 62%, predominantly Amerindian 21%, Amerindian 7%, other 10% (mostly European)."[111] This suggests that 90 percent of Mexicans have Indigenous DNA—more if the growing presence of forgotten Africans is included. However, racial identification is more than saying you are one race or another. The effects of Spanish Empire are evident today in the higher echelons of the Mexican state as well as in its upper and middle classes. We are all going to have to come to grips with the Empire and not DNA tests that are available for $100 or less.

Notes

1. Barry Pritzker, *A Native American Encyclopedia: History, Culture, and Peoples* (Cambridge: Oxford University Press, 2000), 112.
2. Calisphere, "California Cultures: Native Americans," University of California, https://calisphere.org/exhibitions/t1/native-americans/. Robert F. Heizer and Mary Anne Whipple. *The California Indians: A Source Book*. 2nd ed., Rev. and Enl. ed. (Berkeley: University of California Press, 1971). Robert F. Heizer, *The Destruction of California Indians: A Collection of Documents from the Period 1847 to 1865 in Which Are Described Some of the Things That Happened to Some of the Indians of California* (Lincoln: University of Nebraska Press, 1993).
3. Charles Q. Choi, "Case Closed? Columbus Introduced Syphilis to Europe," *Live Science*, December 27, 2011, https://www.livescience.com/17643-columbus-introduced-syphilis-europe.html. David Lawler, "Christopher Columbus in the clear: research suggests he did not bring syphilis to Europe," Nov. 23, 2015, http://www.telegraph.co.uk/news/worldnews/northamerica/usa/12012903/Christopher-Columbus-in-the-clear-research-suggests-he-did-not-bring-syphilis-to-Europe.html.
4. Carl Zimmer, "Humans Lived in North America 130,000 Years Ago, Study Claims," *Science*, April 26, 2017, https://www.nytimes.com/2017/04/26/science/prehistoric-humans-north-america-california-nature-study.html. Glassow, Michael A. "Measurement of Population Growth and Decline During California Prehistory," *Journal of California and Great Basin Anthropology*, 1 January 1999, Vol.21(1), 45–66. Charles C. Mann, "The Clovis Point and the Discovery of America's First Culture," *Smithsonian Magazine*, November 2013, https://www.smithsonianmag.com/history/the-clovis-point-and-the-discovery-of-americas-first-culture-3825828/.
5. Barry M. Pritzker, *A Native American Encyclopedia: History, Culture, and Peoples* (Oxford: Oxford University Press, 2000), 114. Albert L. Hurtado, *Indian Survival on the California Frontier*, Yale Western Americana series (New Haven: Yale University Press, 1988).
6. John Steven McGroarty, *Mission Memories* (Los Angeles, CA: Neuner Corporation, 1929), 7. Also quoted in Lisa Riggin-Walden, "Spanish Missions: The Death and Resurrection of a California Institution" (PhD Dissertation, University of California Riverside, 2006), 1.
7. "Old Southern Documents Give Lie to Theory of Happy Slaves," *New York Times*, June 12, 1994, http://www.nytimes.com/1994/06/12/us/old-southern-documents-give-lie-to-theory-of-happy-slaves.html. "Frederick Douglass's 'Narrative': Myth of the Happy Slave," *National Endowment for the Humanities*, October 8, 2014, https://edsitement.neh.gov/lesson-plan/frederick-douglasss-narrative-myth-happy-slave.
8. Helen Hunt Jackson, *Ramona* (Boston, MA: Little, Brown, and Company, 1900). The novel tells the tragic love story of a mestiza (unknown to her) falling in love with an Indian male. It exposed the brutal treatment of the Californian Indian. The novel was romanticized in a play called *Ramona* that created the myth of "American apotheosis." Janice Albert, "Helen Hunt Jackson (1830–1885)," California Teachers of English, http://www.cateweb.org/CA_Authors/Jackson.html.
9. Don Mitchell, *The Lie of the Land: Migrant Workers and the California Landscape* (St. Paul: University of Minnesota Press, 1996), 9, 13.

10 Carey McWilliams, *North from Mexico: The Spanish-Speaking People of the United States* (New York: J. B. Lippincott Co., 1948), 35. It can also explain how the Dreamers who want to become Americans look at the United States.

11 Douglas Monroy, *Thrown Among Strangers: The Making of Mexican Culture in Frontier California* (Berkeley: University of California Press, 1990), 101. Gabriel Gutiérrez, "Bell Towers, Crucifixes, and Cañones Violentos: State and Identity Formation in Pre-industrial Alta California," (PhD Dissertation, University of California, Santa Barbara, 1997), 63–72. "The Royal Presidio of San Diego 1769–1835," California History and Culture Conservancy, http://historyandculture.com/chcc/presidio1.html. Greg Pabst, "To Have But Not to Hold: The Bernals of Early San Francisco and Their Lost Corner of the City," http://gregnoevly.home.mindspring.com/Bernal.html. See map of Sonora and California.

12 Steven W. Hackel, "Sources of Rebellion: Indian Testimony and the Mission San Gabriel Uprising of 1785," *Ethnohistory* 50, No. 4 (Fall 2003), 643–49, 651, 655, 657. "The Holy Woman Toypurina Attempts to Liberate the 'Indios' at San Gabriel Mission," http://www.suppressedhistories.net/articles/toypurina.html. Edward D. Castillo, "An Indian Account of the Decline and Collapse of Mexico's Hegemony over the Missionized Indians of California," *American Indian Quarterly* 13, No. 4 (Autumn 1989), 393. Duke Helfand, "Tragic Side of Mission Era Being Told" *Los Angeles Times*, September 12, 1997, A, 1:3. Sandy Banks, "Native Americans Resurrect Heritage; Ancestry: The missions' assimilation of tribes into Spanish culture left many with no knowledge of their roots" [Valley Edition], *Los Angeles Times*, September 3, 1997, 1.

13 Castillo, "An Indian Account," 393. Kent G. Lightfoot, *Indians, Missionaries, and Merchants: The Legacy of Colonial Encounters on the California Frontiers* (Berkeley: University of California Press, 2004), 89–90. James A. Sandos, *Converting California: Indians and Franciscans in the Missions* (New Haven, CT: Yale University Press, 2004), 125.

14 Rose Marie Beebe and Robert M. Senkewicz, "The End of the 1824 Chumash Revolt in Alta California: Father Vicente Sarría's Account," *The Americas* 53, No. 2 (October 1996): 273–75. Thomas Blackburn, "The Chumash Revolt of 1824: A Native Account," *The Journal of California Anthropology* 2, No. 2 (1975): 223–27, http://repositories.cdlib.org/cgi/viewcontent.cgi?article=1079&context=ucmercedlibrary/jca. Brian T. McCormack, "Conjugal Violence, Sex, Sin, and Murder in the Mission Communities of Alta California," *Journal of the History of Sexuality* 16, No. 3 (September 2007), 410. Rose Marie Beebe and Robert M. Senkewicz, "The End of the 1824 Chumash Revolt in Alta California: Father Vicente Sarría's Account," *The Americas* Vol. 53, No. 2 (Oct., 1996), 273–283. P. Nabokov, "Reconstituting the Chumash: a review essay," *American Indian Quarterly* 13.4 (1989), 535–543.

15 Quincy Newell, "'The Indians Generally Love Their Wives and Children': Native American Marriage and Sexual Practices in Missions San Francisco, Santa Clara, and San Jose," *The Catholic Historical Review* 91, No. 1 (January 2005), 60–82ff. Sandos, *Converting California*, 182–84. Efforts to canonize Serra unleashed a torrent of criticism from those claiming that the mission captives were abused. "California Genocide, Indian Country Diaries," http://www.pbs.org/indiancountry/history/calif.html. Diana G. Tumminia, "California Indian Memorial," http://www.csus.edu/indiv/t/tumminia/MEMORIAL.HTM. This is a virtual memorial to all the California natives who died in the many years of genocide.

16 Erika Perez, "Colonial intimacies: Interethnic kinship, sexuality, and marriage in southern California, 1769-1885" (PhD Dissertation, Los Angeles: University of California, 2010), 3, 18–20, 28–32, 34–41, 290. She builds her narrative around excellent use of oral testimonies.

17 M. Kat Anderson, Michael G. Barbour, and Valerie Whitworth, "A World of Balance and Plenty: Land, Plants, Animals, and Humans in a Pre-European California," in Ramón Gutiérrez and Richard L. Orsi, eds., *Contested Eden: California Before the Gold Rush* (Berkeley: University of California Press, 1998), 12–47. Monroy, *Thrown Among Strangers*, 101. Doyce B. Nunis, Jr., "Alta California's Trojan Horse: Foreign Immigration," in Gutiérrez and Orsi, eds., *Contested Eden*, 299–330. David J. Weber. *The Mexican Frontier, 1821–1846: The American Southwest Under Mexico* (Albuquerque: University of New Mexico Press, 1982), 136.

18 Monroy, *Thrown Among Strangers*, 66–67. Gabriel Gutiérrez, in "Bell Towers," 62.

19 Steven W. Hackel, "Land, Labor, and Production," *California History* 76 (Summer and Fall, 1997), 134. Rosaura Sánchez, *Telling Identities: The Californio Testimonios* (St. Paul: University of Minnesota Press, 1995), 82–83, 86. José Bandini, *A Description of California in 1828* (Berkeley, CA: Friends of the Bancroft Library, 1951), vi, 11. Don Thomas Coulter, *Notes on Upper California: A Journey from Monterey to the Colorado River in 1832* (Los Angeles, CA: Glen Dawson, 1951), 23. Robert F. Heizer and Allan F. Almquist, *The Other Californians* (Berkeley: University of California Press, 1971), 120.

20. Cris Pérez, "Extracts from Grants of Land in California Made by Spanish or Mexican Authorities," Ranchos of California, University of California Berkeley Library, http://www.lib.berkeley.edu/EART/rancho.html. William H. Dusenberry, *The Mexican Mesta: The Administration of Ranching in Colonial Mexico* (Urbana: University of Illinois Press, 1963), 181.
21. Lizbeth Haas, *Conquests and Historical Identities in California, 1769–1936* (Berkeley: University of California Press, 1996), 42, 58. Michael J. González, "'The Child of the Wilderness Weeps for the Father of Our Country': The Indian and the Politics of Church and State in Provincial California," in Gutiérrez and Orsi, eds., *Contested Eden*, 147–72. Monroy, *Thrown Among Strangers*, 59, 127.
22. Sánchez, *Telling Identities*, 168.
23. Hackel, "Land, Labor, and Production," 135–36. Sánchez, *Telling Identities*, 168. Gutiérrez, "Bell Towers," 152–58. Heather Valdez Singleton, "Surviving Urbanization: The Gabrieleño, 1850–1928," *Wicazo Sa Review* 19, No. 2 (2004), 49–50.
24. Hackel, "Land, Labor, and Production," 134. Gutiérrez, "Bell Towers," 60–62.
25. José Bandini, *A Description of California in 1828* (Berkeley, CA: Friends of the Bancroft Library 1951), reprinted in Carlos E. Cortés, ed., *Mexican California* (New York: Arno Press, 1976), vi, 11. Don Thomas Coulter, *Notes on Upper California: A Journey from Monterey to the Colorado River in 1832* (Los Angeles, CA: Glen Dawson, 1951), 23. Heizer and Almquist, *The Other Californians*, 120.
26. Haas, *Conquests and Historical Identities*, 3–4, 81. Monroy, *Thrown Among Strangers*, 81. James A. Sandos, "Between Crucifix and Lance: Indian-White Relations in California, 1769–1848," in Gutiérrez and Orsi, eds., *Contested Eden*, 196–229. Sandos makes an educated assumption that many natives died as a result of syphilis. However, death by syphilis is almost impossible to diagnose.
27. Monroy, *Thrown Among Strangers*, 127; aside from disease and alcoholism, the natives were disoriented by the loss of population and the destruction of their family network.
28. Sánchez, *Telling Identities*, 161.
29. "Juan Bautista de Anza," National Park Service, http://www.nps.gov/juba/index.htm. "Welcome to Web de Anza," http://anza.uoregon.edu/.
30. Carlos Manuel Salomon, "California son: The life of Pio Pico," (PhD Dissertation, Albuquerque: University of New Mexico, 2002), v, 5, 10, 24, 25. The authors could have been more critical. Pico was involved in over 100 legal cases. During the final one, *Pico v. Cohn*, his struggle to save Rancho Margarita finally broke him. Pico's father was listed as Spanish but the family was listed as mulatto, as was his mother. Salomon does an excellent job of tracing connections between Californio families.
31. Apolinaria Lorenzana memorias: Sta. Barbara, Calif.: ms., 1878 Mar. ana memorias: Sta. Barbara, Calif: ms., 1878 Mar. Online Archive of California, http://content.cdlib.org/ark:/13030/hb9j49p4ms/?&brand=oac.
32. Virginia Marie Bouvier, *Women and the Conquest of California, 1542–1840: Codes of Silence* (Tucson: University of Arizona Press, 2001), 85. Sánchez, *Telling Identities*, 15. Antonia I. Castañeda, "Engendering the History of Alta California, 1769–1848: Gender, Sexuality, and the Family" in Gutiérrez and Orsi, eds., *Contested Eden*, 251. Jeanne Farr McDonnell, *Juana Briones of Nineteenth-Century California* (Tucson: University of Arizona Press, 2008). "Juana Briones Heritage," http://www.brioneshouse.org/juanas_life.htm.
33. Miroslava Chávez-García. *Negotiating Conquest: Gender and Power in California, 1770s to 1880s* (Tucson: University of Arizona Press, 2004). Rodolfo F. Acuña, *Corridors of Migration: The Odyssey of Mexican Laborers, 1600–1933* (Tucson: University of Arizona Press, 2008), 12–14. See Cheryl English Martin, *Governance and Society in Colonial Mexico: Chihuahua in the Eighteenth Century* (Stanford, CA: Stanford University Press, 1996), for excellent accounts of women fighting back in colonial Chihuahua. For testimony of Eulalia Pérez, see Nancy F. Cott, Jeanne Boydson, Ann Braude, Lori D. Ginzberg, Molly Ladd-Taylor, eds., *Root of Bitterness: Documents of the Social History of American Women* (Boston, MA: Northeastern, 1996), 185–92. Eulalia Pérez de Guillén Mariné (1766–1878), http://en.wikipedia.org/wiki/Eulalia_P%C3%A9rez_de_Guill%C3%A9n_Marin%C3%A9.
34. Josiah Royce, *California* (Santa Barbara, CA: Peregrine Publishers, Inc., 1970), 31–32. Leonard Pitt, *The Decline of the Californios* (Berkeley and Los Angeles: University of California Press, 1966), 26. George Winston Smith and Charles Judah, *Chronicles of the Gringos* (Albuquerque: University of New Mexico Press, 1968), 141, 149. John Bidwell (Pioneer of '41), "Frémont in the Conquest of California," Virtual Museum of the City of San Francisco, http://www.sfmuseum.org/hist6/fremont.html.
35. Oscar Lewis, ed., *California in 1846* (San Francisco, CA: Grabhorn Press, 1934); reprinted in Carlos E. Cortés, ed., *Mexicans in the U.S. Conquest of California* (New York: Arno Press, 1976), 31. Pitt, *Decline of Californios*, 27. Richard Griswold del Castillo, "La Raza Hispano-Americana: The Emergence of an Urban Culture Among the Spanish Speaking of Los Angeles,

1850–1880" (PhD Dissertation, University of California at Los Angeles, California, 1974), 49. Genaro M. Padilla, *My History, Not Yours: The Formation of Mexican American Autobiography* (Madison, WI: University of Wisconsin Press, 1993), 42–73, 77–108.

36 Pitt, *Decline of Californios*, 30.

37 William D. Carrigan and Clive Webb, *Forgotten Dead: Mob Violence Against Mexicans in the United States, 1848–1928*, (New York: Oxford University Press, 2013), 332–357, Table 0.1.

38 D. J. Waldie, "Angelino, Angeleno, and Angeleño," KCET, January 10, 2011, https://www.kcet.org/shows/lost-la/angelino-angeleno-and-angeleno.

39 Walter Colton, *Three Years in California* (New York: A.S. Barnes, 1850), 2. Mark J. Denger, "The Mexican War and California: The Treaty of Campo de Cahuenga," California State Military Department, The California State Military Museum, A United States Army Museum Activity, Preserving California's Military Heritage, http://www.militarymuseum.org/Cahuenga.html (accessed October 21, 2009). Hubert Howe Bancroft, *History of California Vol V. 1846–1848* (San Francisco, CA: The History Company, Publishers, 1890), 422–24.

40 Leon Worden, "California's REAL First Gold," *COINage magazine* (October 2005), http://www.scvhistory.com/scvhistory/signal/coins/worden-coinage1005.htm.

41 Donald J. Pisani, "Squatter Law in California, 1850–1858," *The Western Historical Quarterly* Vol. 25, No. 3 (Autumn, 1994), 278; prior to the finding of gold, the Mexican governor had awarded Sutter 49,000 acres of land. Sutter had a made-up title but in California was treated as royalty.

42 Tomás Almaguer, *Racial Fault Lines: The Historical Origins of White Supremacy in California* (Berkeley: University of California Press, 1994), 26–27. By 1860 there were 146,528 foreign-born in California: 34,935 were Chinese, 33,247 Irish, 21,646 German, 12,227 English, and only 9,150 Mexican-born immigrants. Heizer and Almquist, *The Other Californians*, 144. "Gold Fever!" http://www.museumca.org/goldrush/fever01.html.

43 Katherine H. Chandler, "San Francisco at Statehood," Virtual Museum of the City of San Francisco, http://www.sfmuseum.com/hist5/oldsf.html.

44 David S. Torres-Rouff, "Making Los Angeles: Race, Space, and Municipal Power, 1822–1890" (PhD Dissertation, University of California, Santa Barbara, 2006), 73.

45 "California Constitutional Convention of 1849," http://www.militarymuseum.org/Constitution.htm. Susan Patricia Taylor, "Pride versus prejudice: The disparate delegates to the California Constitutional Convention of 1849, and the moderate Constitution that they fashioned" (California State University, Dominguez Hills, Master of Arts, 2010), 4.

46 Almaguer, *Racial Fault Lines*, 9. Heizer and Almquist, *The Other Californians*, 149. Stephen Clark Foster, "El Quachero: How I Want to Help Make the Constitution of California—Stirring Historical Incidents," in Carlos E. Cortés, ed., *Mexicans in California After the U.S. Conquest* (New York: Arno Press, 1976). Foster was a delegate to the Constitutional Convention of 1849. John Ross Browne, *Report of the Debates in the Convention of California on the Formation of the State Constitution, in Sept. & Oct. 1849* (Manchester, NH: Ayer Co Pub, 1973).

47 Michael Magliari, "Free Soil, Unfree Labor: Cave Johnson Courts and the Binding of Indian Workers in California, 1850–1867," *The Pacific Historical Review* 73, No. 3 (August 2004), 349, 351, 352–57. "A History of American Indians in California: 1849–1879," National Park Service, http://www.nps.gov/history/history/online_books/5views/5views1c.htm. Michael Woodiwiss, *Organized Crime and American Power: A History* (Toronto: University of Toronto Press, 2001), 50–51. James J Rawls, *Indians of California: The Changing Image* (Norman: University of Oklahoma Press, 1986), 20–21. David J. Weber, *The Mexican Frontier, 1821–1846* (Albuquerque: University of New Mexico, 1982), 211–12. Albert L. Hurtado, *Indian Survival on the California Frontier* (New Haven, CT: Yale University Press, 1990), 3–4. An Act for the Government and Protection of Indians, Chapter 133, *Statutes of California* (April 22, 1850), http://www.indiancanyon.org/ACTof1850.html.

48 Malvin Lane Miranda, *A History of Hispanics in Southern Nevada* (Reno: University of Nevada Press, 1997), 36.

49 Coya Paz Brownrigg, "Linchocracia: Performing 'America' in El Clamor Público," *California History* 84.2 (2006), https://escholarship.org/content/qt4mz2g99j/qt4mz2g99j.pdf. Coya Brownrigg, "A changing lynchocracy: Lynching and the performance of American identity in Gold Rush California, 1848—1858" (PhD Dissertation, Evanston, Illinois: University of Illinois, 2010), 4, 10, 17.

50 Heizer and Almquist, *The Other Californians*, 143, 144, 155. Leonard Pitt, "The Foreign Miner's Tax of 1850: A Study of Nativism and Anti-Nativism in Gold Rush California" (Master's Thesis, University of California at Los Angeles, 1955), 9. David J. Weber, ed., *Foreigners in Their Native Land* (Albuquerque: University of New Mexico Press, 1973), 151. Richard Morefield, "Mexicans in the California Mines, 1848–1853," *California Historical Quarterly* 24 (March 1956), 38, 43. *Daily Pacific News* (19 October 1850). Carrigan and Webb, *Forgotten Dead*, 35. Ibid. 4, 10, 17.

51 Van Hastings Garner, "The Treaty of Guadalupe Hidalgo and the California Indians," *Indian Historian* (1976), 10–13. Natalia Molina, "In a Race All Their Own: The Quest to Make Mexicans Ineligible for U.S. Citizenship," *Pacific Historical Review* Vol. 79, Issue 2 (May 2010), 167–201. Arturo Romero Nunez, "Freedom's Journal *and El Clamor Publico*: African American and Mexican American Cultural Fronts in Nineteenth-Century Newsprint," UC Berkeley Electronic Theses and Dissertations Nineteenth-Century Newsprint, Permalink, Publication 2010 https://escholarship.org/uc/item/4mz2g99j.

52 Charles Hughes, "The Decline of the Californios: The Case of San Diego, 1846–1856," in Cortés, ed., *Mexicans in California*, 17. Haas, *Conquests and Historical Identities*, 58–60, 63, 64. Mario T. García, "Merchants and Dons: San Diego's Attempt at Modernization, 1850–1860," in Cortés, *Mexicans in California*, 70. Pitt, in *Decline of the Californios*, 118, says that 813 titles were reviewed and 3 rejected. Walton Bean, *California*, 2nd ed. (New York: McGraw-Hill, 1973), 157, says that more than 800 cases were heard, of which 604 were confirmed and 209 rejected.

53 Hughes, *The Case of San Diego*, 17. Heizer and Almquist, *The Other Californians*, 150. Pisani, "Squatter Law in California, 1850–1858," 277–310.

54 "Historical Sketch of the California Indians," Digital Desert, http://mojavedesert.net/california-indian-history/04.html. Resource 6-1a: "California Population by Ethnic Groups, 1790–1880," http://explore.museumca.org/goldrush/curriculum/1stcalifornians/resourcesix.htm.

55 Richard Griswold del Castillo, *Los Angeles Barrio, 1850–1890: A Social History* (Berkeley: University of California Press, 1979), 31, 46–51. Griswold del Castillo, "La Raza Hispano-Americana," 76. John W. Caughey, *California: A Remarkable State's Life History*, 3rd ed. (Englewood Cliffs, NJ: Prentice-Hall, 1970), 219. Hughes, *The Case of San Diego*, 18. Haas, *Conquests and Historical Identities*, 67. Pisani, "Squatter Law in California," 280, 287, 295. Squatters were like locusts and Sutter wanted the governor to send the militia to Sacramento.

56 Hannah L. Anderson, "That Settles It: The Debate and Consequences of the Homestead Act of 1862," *History Teacher*, (2011), 45(1), 117–137. Bill Vlake, "Fighting for the homestead: the Homestead Act of 1862 opened the frontier door for many people, but clashes over free public lands continued until there was enough law and order out West to make a house on 160 acres a safe home," *Wild West*, Feb 2012, Vol. 24(5), 26(10).

57 Dara Orenstein, "Void for Vagueness: Mexicans and the Collapse of Miscegenation Law in California," *The Pacific Historical Review* 74, No. 3 (August 2005), 376. Horace Bell, *On the Old West Coast* (New York: Morrow, 1930), 255–57. Haas, *Conquests and Historical Identities*, 73–75. Monroy, *Thrown Among Strangers*, 159. Carlos Salomon, "California Son: The Life of Pío Pico" (PhD Dissertation, University of New Mexico, 2002), 25.

58 Bell, *On the Old West*, 255–57. Almaguer, *Racial Fault Lines*, 58.

59 *People v. Hall* (1854), http://www.cetel.org/1854_hall.html (accessed October 21, 2009). David S. Goldstein and Audrey B. Thacker, eds., *Complicating Constructions: Race, Ethnicity, and Hybridity in American Texts* (Seattle: University of Washington Press, 2008), 6–7. Edlie Wong, " Comparative racialization, immigration law, and James Williams's life and adventures," *American Literature*, 2012, Vol. 84(4), 797.

60 Heizer and Almquist, *The Other Californians*, 128–29, 131, 151. Almaguer, *Racial Fault Lines*, 13. Stephen B. Oates, *The Approaching Fury: Voices of the Storm, 1820–1861* (New York: Harper Collins, 1998).

61 Mary Floyd Williams, *Committee of Vigilance of 1851: A Study of Social Control on the California Frontier in the Days of the Gold Rush* (Berkeley: University Of California Press, 1921).

62 Clare V. McKanna, "Enclaves of Violence in Nineteenth-Century California," *The Pacific Historical Review* 73, No. 3 (August 2004), 402–03. Sonora became an "instant city" in 1850 with a population of 4,000, while Columbia exploded to 8,151. These gold camps were 95 percent male from Chile, Peru, Mexico, Australia, France, China, and the United States. Alcohol played a huge role in homicides; 65 percent of the killers and 59.5 percent of the victims had been drinking.

63 Pitt, *Decline of Californios*, 50–53, 61–63. William D. Carrigan and Clive Webb, "The Lynching of Persons of Mexican Origin or Descent in the United States, 1848 to 1928," *Journal of Social History* 37, No. 2 (2003), 415. Coya Paz Brownrigg, "Linchocracia: Performing 'America' in *El Clamor Público*," *California History* 84, No. 2 (Winter 2006–2007), 40–53. See also Coya Paz Brownrigg, "Linchocracia: Performing 'America,'" Paper presented at the conference *El Clamor Público*, University of Southern California Digital Library http://digitallibrary.usc.edu/search/controller/simplesearch.htm.

64 There was and is a tendency to stereotype all Mexican women as "Rosa," "María," or "Juanita."

65 Maythee Rojas, "Re-Membering Josefa: Reading the Mexican Female Body in California Gold Rush Chronicles," *Women's Studies Quarterly* Vol. 35, No. ½ (Spring/Summer 2007): 126–148.

66 William B. Secrest, *Juanita: The Only Woman Lynched in the Gold Rush Days* (Fresno, CA: Sage-West, 1967), 8–29. Readings on the Internet can greatly enrich our knowledge of Mexican Americans in California. Roberto Carrillo Gantz, who is a vocational instructor for Sacramento County ROP and a historian and a screenwriter, has done quite a bit of research on the subject. Moved by a PBS TV program about the California Gold Rush and about the lynching of Josefa, he went to the California State Library in Sacramento, researching the injustice for a screenplay. While browsing microfiche on the U.S. Mexican Claims Commission, he came across a claim made by Josefa's husband, José María Loaiza, filed against the U.S. government for "the lynching of his wife and the banishment of himself by a mob . . . July 4, 1852 . . . Downieville, California." [The date was inaccurate but further research verified that it was Josefa's husband.] Josefa and José Maréa Loaiza were from Sonora. "Schedule of Mexican Claims against the United States," Senate Executive Document 31, 44th Congress 2nd Session. Docket Number 904. The claim was made on June 11, 1875; it was dismissed by the commissioner. *El Clámor Público* (4 and 16 April 1857). Ken Gonzales-Day, *Lynching in the West: 1850–1935* (Durham, NC: Duke University Press, 2006), 185–89. Alton Pryor, *Fascinating Women in California History* (Roseville, CA: Stagecoach Publishers, 2003), 43–46. "Lynch Law of the Mother Lode," http://www.genealogyimagesofhistory.com/images/Lynchlaw.jpg.

67 Ibid.

68 Torres-Rouff, "Making Los Angeles," 82, 87. By 1840 racial categories hardened with the Californios casting themselves as white. Portrait of a drawing of Abel Stearns, ca. 1840–1860, USC Digital Archive, http://digarc.usc.edu/search/controller/view/chs-m15210.html.

69 W. W. Robinson, *People Versus Lugo: Story of a Famous Los Angeles Murder Case and Its Aftermath* (Los Angeles, CA: Dawson's Book Shop, 1962), 6. Joseph Lancaster Brent, *The Lugo Case: A Personal Experience* (New Orleans, LA: Searcy & Pfaff, 1926), 4, 17, 19–3, reprinted in Cortés, *Mexicans in California*, 12–13. Robinson, *People Versus Lugo*, 1–5, 10–11, 17–18, 21–22, 26–27, 33–37, 40. Paul Bryan Gray, "Biographical Sketch of Francisco Ramírez," Paper presented at the conference *El Clamor Público* (October 28, 2005).

70 Nicolás Kanellos, "*El Clamor Público* and Its Place in American Journalism," Keynote speech given at the conference *El Clamor Público* (October 28, 2005). *El Clamor Público* has been digitalized for home viewing. University of Southern California Library, http://digarc.usc.edu/search/controller/simplesearch.htm?page=1&keyword=parents:clamor-m235.

71 José Luis Benavides, "Caught in the Middle: How *El Clamor Público* Portrayed Communities of Color," Paper presented at the conference *El Clamor Público* (October 28, 2005). Armando Miguélez, "La trémula luz del relámpago: Lenguaje metafórico en *El Clamor Público*," Trabajo presentado en la conferencia *El Clamor Público* (October 28, 2005). Pitt, *Decline of Californios*, chapter 17. Paul Bryan Gray, "A Biographical Sketch of Francisco Ramírez," Paper presented at the conference *El Clamor Público* (October 28, 2005).

72 T. J. Stiles, "The Filibuster King: The Strange Career of William Walker, the Most Dangerous International Criminal of the Nineteenth Century," *History Now*, https://www.gilderlehrman.org/history-by-era/jackson-lincoln/essays/filibuster-king-strange-career-william-walker-most-dangerous-i. A. Greenberg, "Agent of Empire: William Walker and the Imperial Self in American Literature (review)," *Civil War History* (2005), 51(4), 436–438.

73 *El Clamor Público* (June 19, 1855). See Monroy, *Thrown Among Strangers*, 219–22, for general treatment. Quote in *El Clamor Público* (August 20, 1855).

74 *El Clamor Público* (18 September 1855).

75 *El Clamor Público* (May 10, 1856). *El Clamor Público* (May 17, 1856).

76 Brownrigg, "A changing lynchocracy," 11–12.

77 Veronica Torrejon, "A 'Mexican Window' into the City's Past; Los Angeles' first Spanish-language newspaper, *El Clamor Público*, was founded 150 years ago by an 18-year-old printer," Center for Law in the Public Interest, June 23, 2005, http://www.cityprojectca.org/blog/archives/115.

78 Bell, *Old West Coast*, 72. Hubert Howe Bancroft, *Popular Tribunals*, Vol. 1 (San Francisco, CA: History Company, 1887), 501–03.

79 Pitt, *Decline of Californios*, 174.

80 *El Clamor Público* (December 18, 1858).

81 Paul Bryan Gray, "A Biographical Sketch of Francisco Ramérez," Paper presented at the conference *El Clamor Público* (October 28, 2005).

82 J. M. Scanland. "The Newspapers of Los Angeles; Their Trials and Tragedies," *Los Angeles Times* (September 4, 1932).

83 José Luis Benavides, "Caught in the Middle: How El Clamor Público Portrayed Communities of Color," Paper presented at the conference *El Clamor Público* (October 28, 2005).

84 "Joaquin Murrieta," http://www.youtube.com/watch?v=gyLasg-zfd0.

85 Cossley-Batt, *The Last of the California Rangers* (New York: Funk & Wagnall's, 1928), http://www.yosemite.ca.us/library/california_rangers/

joaquin_murieta.html. A descendant of Joaquin states that he died in Sonora, Mexico. Interview with Antonio Rivera Murieta, Phoenix AZ (December 15, 2001) from David Bacon, *Communities Without Borders* (Ithaca, NY: Cornell/ILR Press, 2006), http://dbacon.igc.org/TWC/mm02_Murrieta.htm. "Joaquin Murrieta—Patriot or Desperado?" California Legends, http://www.legendsofamerica.com/CA-Murieta.html. Through the tireless work of Alfredo Figueroa, a composer and Chicano activist from Blythe, California, we know that the California Rangers got the wrong man, and the real Joaquin Murieta died of old age in Sonora, Mexico.

86 Major Horace Bell, *Reminiscences of a Ranger; or, Early Times in Southern California* (Los Angeles, CA: Yarnell, Caystile & Mathes, Printers, 1881), 23–29, 72, 108, http://memory.loc.gov/cgi-bin/query/r?ammem/calbk:%20@field%28DOCID+@lit%28calbk103%29%29.

87 Ernest May, "Tiburcio Vásquez," *Historical Society of Southern California Quarterly* 24 (1947), 123–24, places the time of the shootout in the spring of 1851. Griswold del Castillo, "La Raza Hispano-Americana," 198, states that Vásquez began his career by escaping from a lynch mob. Monroy, *Thrown Among Strangers*, 215–19.

88 Interview of Tiburcio Vásquez, *The Los Angeles Star* (May 16, 1874). Robert Greenwood, *The California Outlaw: Tiburcio Vásquez* (Los Gatos, CA: Talisman Press, 1960), 12.

89 Heizer and Almquist, *The Other Californians*, 150–51.

90 May, "Tiburcio Vásquez," 124. Greenwood, *The California Outlaw*, 13. Griswold del Castillo, "La Raza Hispano-Americana," 199. Cecile Page Vargo, "El Bandito, Vasquez," Explore Historic California, http://www.explorehistoricalif.com/bandito2.html.

91 Greenwood, *The California Outlaw*, 23–24. Griswold del Castillo, *Los Angeles Barrio*, 114–15. *La Crónica* (May 2, 1874).

92 Greenwood, *The California Outlaw*, 75. Will H. Thrall, "The Haunts and Hideouts of Tiburcio Vasquez," *Historical Society of Southern California The Quarterly* 30, No. 2. (June 1948), http://www.scvhistory.com/scvhistory/vasquez-thrall.htm. High school students in Acton, California, named their high school after Tiburcio Vásquez.

93 David E. Hayes-Bautista et al., "Empowerment, expansion, and engagement: las juntas patrioticas in California, 1848–1869," *California History* 85.1 (Winter 2007), 4–23.

94 David E. Hayes-Bautista, "The Latino Social Context of *El Clamor Público*: Indications from las Juntas Patrióticas," *El Clamor Público* (October 28, 2005). Griswold del Castillo, "La Raza Hispano-Americana," 227. Griswold del Castillo, "Health and the Mexican Americans in Los Angeles, 1850–1867," *Journal of Mexican History* 4 (1974): 22.

95 Monroy, *Thrown Among Strangers*, 234–37. Albert Michael Camarillo, "The Making of a Chicano Community: A History of the Chicanos in Santa Barbara, California, 1850–1930" (PhD Dissertation, University of California at Los Angeles, 1975), 116.

96 "Birdseye View of Sonora Town from Fort Hill, Los Angeles, ca. 1885," USC Digital Archive, http://digarc.usc.edu/search/controller/view/chs-m4932.html. Historic Buildings And Sites, "El Pueblo de Los Angeles," http://www.lasangelitas.org/buildings.htm.

97 Richard Griswold del Castillo, "Health and the Mexican Americans," 22. Caughey, *California*, 349–50.

98 Roberto Ramon Lint Sagarena, "Inheriting the Land: Defining Place in Southern California from the Mexican American War to the Plan Espiritual de Aztlán" (PhD Dissertation, Princeton University, 2000), 38–39, 47.

99 Holy Cross Cemetery/Archbishop Joseph Sadoc Alemany, O.P., http://www.nps.gov/history/history/online_books/5views/5views5h41.htm.

100 Quoted in Griswold del Castillo, "La Raza Hispano-Americana," 271.

101 Monroy, *Thrown Among Strangers*, 165.

102 Almaguer, *Racial Fault Lines*, 120, 133, 149. *Thompson v. Doaksum*, No. 9546, Supreme Court of California, 68 Cal. 593, 10 P. 199 (1886) Cal. LEXIS 498, February 25, 1886. *Botiller v. Dominguez*, No. 1370, Supreme Court of the United States, 130 U.S. 238, 9 S. Ct. 525, 32 L. Ed. 926 (1889) U.S. LEXIS 1744. Submitted January 7, 1889; Decided April 1, 1889. Monroy, *Thrown Among Strangers*, 190–94.

103 "The Legacy of the Mercury Mines," http://oaklandmuseumofcalifornia.com/creeks/z-mercurymines.html.

104 Albert Michael Camarillo, *Chicanos in California* (San Francisco, CA: Boyd & Foster, 1984), 24–25.

105 Sóstenes Betancourt. "Ferrocarril del Sur (Sección del Norte) (Impresiones de viaje)," *El Cronista*, San Francisco, año II, no. 62, sábado, abril 18, 1885, furnished by Armando Miguelez. Stephen J. Pitti, *The Devil in Silicon Valley: Northern California, Race and Mexican Americans* (Princeton: Princeton University Press, 2003) is an excellent history of the evolution of San José, Santa Clara, and northern California enclaves.

106 Caughey, *California*, 344–45. Almaguer, *Racial Fault Lines*, 75–104 describes the transformation of Ventura County agriculture, showing how the small-scale farmers were driven out of the market. Keith William Cox, "Conflicts of Interest: Race, Class, Mexicanidad and the Negotiation of Rule in U.S. Occupied Mexico,

1846–1848" (PhD Dissertation, University of California Riverside, 2007), 40.

107 Quoted in Haas, *Conquests and Historical Identities*, 1. "First Felon Was Railroaded—Story of Modesta Avila," Capistrano, http://www.sanjuancapistrano.net/history/avila.html.

108 Jean F. Riss, "The Lynching of Francisco Torres," *Journal of Mexican American History* (Spring 1972): 90–111. Griswold del Castillo, "La Raza Hispano-Americana," 193. Also see Richard Griswold del Castillo, "Myth and Reality: Chicano Economic Mobility in Los Angeles, 1850–1890," *Aztlán* 6, No. 2 (Summer 1975), 151–71. "Torres Taken," *Los Angeles Times* (August 11, 1892). "Lynch Law at Santa Ana," *Los Angeles Times* (August 21, 1892), 14. Larry Welborn, "Searching for the most notorious criminal case in Orange County history," The Orange County Register, Oct. 31, 2009, http://www.ocregister.com/articles/gibson-217191-county-case.html.

109 Almaguer, *Racial Fault Lines*, 29.

110 United States, *CIA World Fact Book*, https://www.cia.gov/library/publications/the-world-factbook/geos/us.html.

111 Mexico, *CIA World Fact Book*, https://www.cia.gov/library/publications/the-world-factbook/geos/mx.html.

Chapter 8
Immigration, Labor, and Generational Change: White Lies

  Learning Objectives

- 8.1 Identify the ideologies behind U.S. imperialism.
- 8.2 Analyze how Mexican movements for worker rights and social justice confronted U.S. imperialism and xenophobia.
- 8.3 Describe ways that the Mexican Revolution affected life in Mexico and the U.S.
- 8.4 Explain how Mexican life in the U.S. changed from 1900–1920.
- 8.5 Summarize the ways in which World War I affected Mexicans in the United States.
- 8.6 Describe how commercial cotton agriculture drove demand for Mexican labor.

Time Marches On

8.1 Identify the ideologies behind U.S. imperialism.

In 1899, British poet Rudyard Kipling wrote a poem entitled "The White Man's Burden: The United States and The Philippine Islands." He urged the U.S. to take up the "burden" of empire, which Britain and other European nations carried. The poem was written during a period of imperial expansion and sang the praises of "white supremacy".[1] America as Europe had done before them was no subjugating other nations; it was just being merciful adopting them for their good. Underlying this charge was the belief of the U.S. and northern Europe in white supremacy, Americans denied this motive and limited view of history, shrouding it in altruism claiming Americans were somehow different from their European forefathers, They were not imperialist, according to them they had struggled against European empires and unlike these empires were uniquely democratic.[2] Americans acknowledged U.S. wars with Mexico (1847), Spain (1898), and the Philippines but claim they took these lands to civilize the people and give them the gift of democracy, Underlying this historical amnesia was that "the vast majority of Americans considered [the conquered people] biologically and culturally inferior, alien, and unassimilable"[3] both at home and abroad and at home.[4] The cruel irony was that this racism stopped further territorial expansion because of racist opposition to adding more racially inferior and unassimilable people to the empire.

America's war with Mexico had a racial aspect. An "all Mexico" movement failed because of American racism and "the policies of exclusion and oppression—based on race, ethnicity, nationality, religion, and ideology"[5] prevalent in the American Immigration debates—after 1877. Well implanted in the American psyche was that the United States was a white nation and that it was the duty of its government to pursue a domestic and foreign policy that benefited white citizens. Expansionism formed a social order."[6] President James Garfield (1881–1881) told the House of Representatives, "I trust that we have seen the last of our annexations." His point was clear that such lands were in the hot zone. The Hawaiian islands and Mexico "are inhabited by people of the Latin races strangely degenerated by their mixture with native races—a population occupying a territory that naturally enfeebles man, . . . and a territory that I earnestly hope may never be made an integral part of the United States.[7]

As mentioned, the United States acquired more than 500,000 square miles of Mexican territory and killed or wounded more than 25,000 Mexicans. Fifty years later, the Treaty of Paris gave Cuba and Puerto Rico independence from Spain, and United States stole the victory from the *independistas*, denying them independence. Also forgotten is the "Philippine-American War [that] lasted three years [1899–1902] and resulted in the deaths of over 4,200 Americans and over 20,000 Filipinos.... As many as 200,000 Filipino civilians died from violence, famine, and disease."[8] Historians said that the US was not an aggressor nation, Europe had old elitist ideas and institutions whereas the U,S. The Turner This said that our "winning of the west" made us more rugged and individualistic. In other words we are unique. Naturally the slaughter of the Native Americans was not relevant to white Americans.[9]

Prior to 1848, American Caribbean foreign policy was focused on Cuba. Coveted by slaveholders, it was the largest island in the region, and only 90 miles from Florida. After the American War, American territorial spread through the entire Caribbean to the Isthmus of Panama, which Americans saw as vital to their security. Using the Monroe Doctrine as its authority, the U.S. Navy and filibusterers ravaged the Caribbean and Central America. The justification was that in order to become an empire the United States had to have a world-class navy and that meant ports to refuel.[10]

Cubans and Puerto Ricans fought for five decades to break the bonds of Spanish Imperialism. Manuel de Quesada, a Cuban patriot born in Puerto Rico, was exiled to Mexico in 1853.[11] Quesada joined Mexican President Benito Juárez and fought the French from 1861 to 1868. He became a brigadier general and the governor of Coahuila and Durango, Mexico. Quesada led the first popular Cuban insurrection in 1886. Quesada—like many precursors of Cuban and Puerto Rican independence—begged the United States for support.[12]

In 1898, after years of playing possum, the United States suddenly appeared to support the Cuban independence movement. Without consulting the revolutionaries, separately signed the Treaty of Paris (1898) with Spain. The freedom fighters were cut out of the negotiations.[13] The Treaty agreed to the U.S. occupation of Cuba and enabled the Platt Amendment (1902) that sanctioned the United States' right to militarily intervene in Cuba on any occasion the independence of Cuba was threatened and leased A treaty signed in 1934 leased Guantanamo to the United States in perpetuity. Guantanamo Bay to the U.S. for a naval base in perpetuity. Spain also ceded the islands of Puerto Rico, the other West Indies, and the island of Guam in Mariana Islands (Ladrones) to the United States.

That year the United States annexed the Hawaiian Islands and began the occupation of the Philippines. This expansion increased the pressure to build the trans-isthmian canal that Yes, it was projected through multiple sites. Among other places it was going to be built through Nicaragua was completed during the years 1903–1914, ushering in a century of U.S. armed intervention in Latin America.[14]

U.S. Intervention in Latin America

Location	Period	Type of Force	Comments on U.S. Role
Argentina	1890	Troops	Buenos Aires interests protected
Chile	1891	Troops	Marines clash with nationalist rebels
Haiti	1891	Troops	Black workers revolt on U.S.-claimed Navassa Island defeated
Nicaragua	1894	Troops	Month-long occupation of Bluefields
Panama	1895	Naval, troops	Marines land in Colombian province
Nicaragua	1896	Troops	Marines land in port of Corinto
Cuba	1898–	Naval, troops	Seized from Spain, U.S. still holds Navy base at Guantanamo
Puerto Rico	1898–	Naval, troops	Seized from Spain, occupation continues
Nicaragua	1898	Troops	Marines land at port of San Juan del Sur
Nicaragua	1899	Troops	Marines land at port of Bluefields
Honduras	1903	Troops	Marines intervene in revolution
Dominican Republic	1903–04	Troops	U.S. interests protected in Revolution
Cuba	1906–09	Troops	Marines land in democratic election
Nicaragua	1907	Troops	"Dollar Diplomacy" protectorate set up
Honduras	1907	Troops	Marines land during war with Nicaragua
Panama	1908	Troops	Marines intervene in election contest
Nicaragua	1910	Troops	Marines land in Bluefields and Corinto
Honduras	1911	Troops	U.S. interests protected in civil war
Cuba	1912	Troops	U.S. interests protected in Havana
Panama	1912	Troops	Marines land during heated election
Honduras	1912	Troops	Marines protect U.S. economic interests

(Continued)

Location	Period	Type of Force	Comments on U.S. Role
Nicaragua	1912–33	Troops, bombing	20-year occupation, fought guerrillas
Mexico	1913	Naval	Americans evacuated during revolution
Dominican Republic	1914	Naval	Fight with rebels over Santo Domingo
Mexico	1914–18	Naval, troops	Series of interventions against nationalists
Haiti	1914–34	Troops, bombing	19-year occupation after revolts
Dominican Republic	1916–24	Troops	8-year Marine occupation
Cuba	1917–33	Troops	Military occupation, economic protectorate
Panama	1918–20	Troops	"Police duty" during unrest after elections
Honduras	1919	Troops	Marines land during election campaign
Guatemala	1920	Troops	2-week intervention against unionists
Costa Rica	1921	Troops	
Panama	1921	Troops	
Honduras	1924–25	Troops	Landed twice during election strife
Panama	1925	Troops	Marines suppress general strike
El Salvador	1932	Naval	Warships sent during Farabundo Marti revolt
Uruguay	1947	Nuclear threat	Bombers deployed as show of strength
Puerto Rico	1950	Command operation	Independence rebellion crushed in Ponce
Guatemala	1954–?	Command operation, bombing, nuclear threat	CIA directs exile invasion and coup d'état after newly elected government nationalizes unused U.S.'s United Fruit Company lands; bombers based in Nicaragua; long-term result: 200,000 murdered
Panama	1958	Troops	Flag protests erupt into confrontation
Cuba	1961	Command operation	CIA-directed exile invasion fails
Cuba	1962	Nuclear threat, naval	Blockade during missile crisis; near-war with Soviet Union
Panama	1964	Troops	Panamanians shot for urging canal's return
Dominican Republic	1965–66	Troops, bombing	Marines land during election campaign
Guatemala	1966–67	Command operation	Green Berets intervene against rebels
Chile	1973	Command operation	CIA-backed coup ousts democratically elected Marxist president
El Salvador	1981–92	Command operation, troops	Advisors, overflights aid anti-rebel war, soldiers briefly involved in hostage clash; long-term result: 75,000 murdered and destruction of popular movement
Nicaragua	1981–90	Command operation, naval	CIA directs exile (Contra) invasions, plants harbor mines against revolution; result: 50,000 murdered
Honduras	1982–90	Troops	Maneuvers help build bases near borders
Grenada	1983–84	Troops, bombing	Invasion four years after revolution
Bolivia	1987	Troops	Army assists raids on cocaine region
Panama	1989	Troops, bombing	Nationalist government ousted by 27,000 soldiers, leaders arrested, 2,000 plus killed
Haiti	1994–95	Troops, naval	Blockade against military government; troops restore President Aristide to office three years after coup
Venezuela	2002	Command operation	Failed coup attempt to remove left-populist president Hugo Chavez
Haiti	2004–	Troops	Removal of democratically elected President Aristide; troops occupy country
Honduras	2009	Command operation	Support for coup that removed president Manuel Zelaya

SOURCE: Marc Becker's Homepage, https://www.yachana.org/teaching/resources/interventions.html.

The occupation of Mexican territory and the Spanish–American War fed the illusions of U.S. entitlement at home and abroad. It reawakened the debate as to whether the United States should strive to be an imperial power.[15] U.S. Senator Albert Beveridge (Republican, Indiana) was a fervent apostle of American imperialism and U.S. control of territories outside its borders. Beveridge argued that the United States should be an imperial power and that the Philippines was theirs forever— it was "territory belonging to the United States"—adding:

> It is a noble land that God has given us; a land that can feed and clothe the world; a land whose coastlines would inclose [sic] half the countries of Europe; a land set like a sentinel between the two imperial oceans of the globe, a greater

England with a nobler destiny.... We cannot fly from our world duties; it is ours to execute the purpose of a fate that has driven us to be greater than our small intentions. We cannot retreat from any soil where Providence has unfurled our banner; it is ours to save that soil for liberty and civilization....[16]

The next year, Rudyard Kipling, a British novelist and poet, wrote "The White Man's Burden: The United States and The Philippine Islands":

THE WHITE MAN'S BURDEN
Take up the White Man's burden—
Send forth the best ye breed—
Go send your sons to exile
To serve your captives' need
To wait in heavy harness
On fluttered folk and wild—
Your new-caught, sullen peoples,
Half devil and half child....[17]

This sense of "burden" gave Americans the illusion that they had an obligation to take care of their little brown brothers, justifying frequent interventions into the affairs of Latin America. They rationalized that were doing it for the peoples' own good;[18] they were bringing salvation to the infidels.

The Caribbean and Central America became inseparable in the American mind. The completion of the 51-mile Panama Canal linking the Atlantic and Pacific oceans was the lynchpin, essential to the defense of the American Empire. The Canal, was viewed as a natural extension of the United States. The American heavy-handedness bred bitterness and resentment toward the United States that has lasted until now. It unified Latin Americans in their hatred and distrust of the Colossus of the North.

Overview

8.2 Analyze how Mexican movements for worker rights and social justice confronted U.S. imperialism and xenophobia.

In 1880 America was a white man's country. Although the country was not racially or culturally integrated, an imperialist worldview developed based on the economic and political consolidation of U.S. borders (1781–1880). White Anglo-Saxon Protestants (WASPs) controlled the United States in 1880, and their hegemony lasted until the beginning/end of the twenty-first century. The WASP control of institutions such as the U.S. State Department lasted until 1997.[19] WASPs controlled the banks, industry, politics, and the law. They were the core of American nativists that that mobilized against immigration that became viral by 1880, with immigration of Chinese and then Japanese.[20] From, Americans reacted violently to any threat to their whiteness.

The United States is a mutation of the British Empire, pretentious and unaccepting of other people. Originally, the Irish were not considered WASPs; they were Catholic and somehow not "white" or "Christian."[21] Gradually the definition of WASP expanded to include people from northern Europe, British, Irish, Germans, and Scandinavians. The Irish remained outside the orbit until recent times when they decided to collaborate and become WASPs.[22]

The Forging of America

By the 1880s, an intercontinental railroad tied the United States and Mexico together and supported the expansion of trade in both countries. Privatization uprooted peasants from their farms. Big investors monopolized mining and commercial agriculture expanded. This intensified push-pull factors and the number of Mexicans migrating to the United States accelerated before the turn of the century. The railroad facilitated the movement of thousands of more Mexican[23]

During this period, "1881–1890: 5,246,613 immigrants arrived in the U.S." In the next decade, from "1891–1900: 3,687,564 immigrants arrived in the U.S."[24]

In comparison, Mexican migration during these same decades was relatively small:

"from 1880 to 1900 the Mexican-born population [in the] border states increased from 66,312 to 99,969—a gain of 33,657 in twenty years.[25]

The railroad linked the Mexican interior to U.S. markets and to the mines of northern Mexico as well. Commercial agriculture in Mexico created push factors that uprooted thousands of Mexican laborers and their families. Initially, they migrated to urban centers near their villages; some went to work on railroads; some sought employment in the mines of northern Mexico; and others fled to the Southwest. They went north, following the jobs. The railroads integrated and industrialized the U.S. economy and created jobs at the bottom level of the labor market.[26] Mexicans filled low-end jobs in factories, mines, railroads, farms, and ranches.

The two nations shared a 2,000-mile border and parts of the United States were only 700 miles from Mexico City. At first Mexicans migrated mainly from the border states; by the turn of the century, the railroad shrunk distances between the interior and northern reaches of Mexico, and people from the interior traveled in large numbers to the north. Not all Mexican migrants were uprooted peasants. Many political refugees fled the tyranny of Porfirio Díaz; some were skilled workers; others came for short periods and returned; and still others were pushed north because of natural disasters such as droughts.[27]

During the *Porfiriato*, investors financed 15,000 miles of railroad that, as mentioned, accelerated the privatization of the land and resources of the country benefiting the rich and the foreign investors, and accelerated the uprooting and migration of Mexican laborers. In the 1840s, Mexico's population stood at about 7 million; it reached 9.5 million in 1875, and 12.6 million by 1895. The *Porfiriato* ended in 1910, as the Mexican census of that year counted about 15 million people. Small family farms no longer supported large Mexican families.[28] By 1910, twenty-two Mexican cities had 20,000–50,000 people; five cities housed 50,000–100,000; and two cities had populations of more than 100,000. Mexico had a small industrial proletariat; 16.3 percent of its labor force worked in manufacturing while 68 percent labored in agriculture.[29]

An unprecedented industrial growth took place in the United States after the Civil War period (1861–1865), which until this point was mostly a nation of small farms and towns outside the South. Factories and urban centers dominated the eastern seaboard as European immigrants flocked to them for jobs. Expansion of the railroad system accelerated the commercialization of the West, where machines slowly replaced animals. The railroads created a demand for iron and steel, a demand for rails and locomotives, a demand for capital, a demand for workers, and a demand for food. The arrival of more immigrants evoked angst among the American population, which cried for limiting immigration.

Wherever the Chinese went, resentment followed them, catalyzed by the fears of native white workers who reacted mostly with suspicion to their strange and unfamiliar culture, language, and "heathen" religion, but with hostility to their low standard of living and minuscule wages.[30]

White nationalists fanned fears of the Chinese "coolie".[31]

The Chinese Exclusion Acts of 1882, 1892, and 1902, and the Gentlemen's Agreements with Japan of 1900 and 1907 severely reduced and then eliminated the number of Chinese and Japanese immigrating to the United States. This caused a shortage of labor, increasing the need for and pull of Mexican workers. By 1900 California, which had depended on Native American and then Chinese labor, could not employ enough Native Americans as their numbers fell to just 17,500. With the decline in the number of available Chinese and Native American workers, the solution was to import more Mexicans.

Such as the Laguna in the northern Mexican states of Durango and Coahuila. Once the harvest was over, many workers migrated to other agricultural areas in Mexico and the United States, following the crops. Other Mexican laborers migrated to the mines and the cities of northern Mexico and the United States. The border became a revolving door, with Mexican labor moving in and out of the United States. These workers were vital to the development of the American Southwest.[32]

More than a million Mexicans arrived in the United States between 1900–1920. The 1900 Census estimated that there were 330,000 U.S.-born Mexicans—more than three times the Mexican-born immigrant population. About 8,100 Mexican-born residents lived in California, which housed about 33,000 U.S.-born Mexicans; Arizona that had just over 14,000 Mexican-born and 29,000 U.S.-born Mexicans. New Mexico counted 6,650 Mexican immigrants and 122,000 U.S.-born Mexicans. By far the largest numbers lived in Texas, with 71,060 immigrants and 131,000 U.S.-born Mexicans. The fewest were in Colorado—274 immigrants and 15,000 U.S.-born Mexicans.[33]

By the 1920s, Mexicans accounted for more than 10 percent of all immigrants in the United States; a majority of Mexicans were U.S.-born. They remained strangers and were never accepted in the land that had been stolen from them.[34] How much racism they suffered depended on where they lived, what work they did, and the hue of their skin. The wave in which they arrived marked further differences. Middle-class Mexicans arriving before the Mexican Revolution were more apt to be liberal and differed from the post-1910 exiles who were often politically conservative. There were also variations within generations. For example, many rural migrants continued to use Spanish as their primary language—more so in smaller towns than in the cities—whereas Mexicans in urban areas tended to adopt English more quickly, especially the second generation.

Ideas Cross Borders

In 1910 the U.S. consul in Mexico, Luther E. Ellsworth, who sometimes spied for the government of Mexican dictator Porfirio Díaz, wrote:

> I have the honor to report increasing activity of the very intelligent class of Mexican exiles in the Cities and Towns along the Mexican-American Border line, between the Gulf and the Pacific Ocean . . . [They] are busily engaged [in] writing and publishing inflammatory articles intended to educate up to date, in new revolutionary ideas, the thousands of Mexicans now on the American side of the Border line, and as many as possible of those on the Mexican side.[35]

A number of Mexican migrants were political refugees and came to the United States to organize and rally workers support the overthrow of Díaz, whom they accused of subverting the Constitution of 1857. They established newspapers and were involved in civic and labor union/community organizing.

Throughout the nineteenth century, a number of Mexicans read the works of European economic and political theorists in an effort to understand government, democracy, and modernization. Because of the dramatic transformations taking place, different ideologies materialized to explain the changes in the new industrial society and the disorder they caused. The anarchist philosophy of Joseph Proudhon and Mikhail Bakunin was one of the most popular among Mexicans, partially because their works were more readily available in Spanish and Italian than were Marxist books. Urbanization led to the formation of *mutualistas* (mutual aid societies) that were used to organize workers for self-help and even strikes. In 1879, Carmén Huerta, a Mexicana, was elected president of the anarchist *El Gran Círculo de Obreros de México* (The Great Circle of the Workers of Mexico).[36] "These organizations espoused mutual aid, workers' defense, and a wide range of radical and conservative ideologies."[37]

During the *Porfiriato*, worker resentment increased as the foreign presence increased. U.S. investment was ubiquitous, and white U.S. workers enjoyed privileges and wages denied to Mexicans in their own country. Díaz jailed the dissidents, or forced them to go into exile, where they planned revolts against the regime.[38] One of the first worker revolts occurred on September 26, 1881, when a Mexican Central Railroad foreman cut workers' wages by 25 percent, from 2 pesos to 1.50 pesos. The workers went on strike; but, like most of the strikes of the period, it was short-lived.

The first miners' strike occurred in Pinos Altos, in the Municipio de Ocampo, Chihuahua, on January 21, 1883. The British mining company *Compañía Minera de Pinos Altos* required that miners spend half their wages at the company store; the workers refused and occupied the store. Local authorities sided with the management, deputizing a dozen men to put down the strike. When the mine manager attempted to address the workers, workers shot and killed him, whereupon the president of the town council arrived with 25 men and put the mining strike and placed the camp under martial law. He arrested and executed the strike leaders Blas Venegas, Cruz Baca, Ramón Mena, Francisco Campos, and Juan Valenzuela— this happened three years before the famous Haymarket Square Riot in Chicago on May 4, 1886, (which the Labor Day on May 1 commemorates), in which seven policemen and four protesters were killed and four anarchists later executed.[39]

Internal opposition to Díaz grew and crystallized in 1906 as strikes erupted in mining, railroad, and textile industries. In July 1906, mechanics on the Mexican Central Railroad in Chihuahua struck. Workers shut down repair shops from the border to Mexico City; by mid-August, the strike involved 1,500 mechanics and 3,000 other railroad employees. Díaz ordered the workers to return to work and backed his order with a show of force. The modernization of communication helped spread the news of worker discontent to urban centers and rural areas on both sides of border.[40]

Justice Knows No Borders

Before the turn of the century radicals such as Catarino Garza, Victor Ochoa, and Lauro Aguirre[41] planned and carried out unsuccessful revolutionary activities against Diaz and his successors. El Paso was a gathering point for revolutionaries; Teresa Urrea, also called *La Santa de Cabora*, made it her base of operations for a time. A millenarian figure, Urrea empowered the disenfranchised villagers of Chihuahua where the Indigenous People prayed for deliverance from the Díaz dictatorship.

The next wave of revolutionaries arrived after the turn nineteenth-century and was led by the followers of Ricardo Flores Magón, who spent more than 20 years in the United States, leading the *Partido Liberal Mexicano* (PLM) and writing not only about tyranny in Mexico but also about economic, political, and social discrimination suffered by Mexicans in "Utopia"—the United States.

Born in Oaxaca in 1873, Ricardo Flores Magón accompanied by his brother, Enrique and followers crossed the border in 1904 and started the newspaper, *Regeneración*, to educate Mexicans and Americans about repression in Mexico and the United States. While in the United States, they planned and led invasions of Mexican territory.[42] Along with Librado Rivera and Antonio I. Villarreal, Ricardo was arrested in August 1907 and held in the Los Angeles County Jail for several months. They were tried and convicted in Tombstone, Arizona for conspiracy to violate the neutrality laws and sentenced to 18 months in the territorial prison. In March 1918, the PLM issued a manifesto calling for a world anarchist revolution. The courts sentenced Flores Magón to 20 years, and his comrade Librado Rivera to 15 years in prison, for violation of U.S. neutrality acts. In November 1922, Flores Magón was found "mysteriously" dead in his cell—he was suspected to have been murdered[43]

Mexican Women Precursors

By 1880, there was a nucleus of educated women in Mexico who recognized the injustices of the system and began criticizing them. Gradually they formed a network. In 1870, Mexican poet and educator Rita Cetina Gutiérrez organized a collective, comprised mostly of schoolteachers, called *La Siempreviva* in Mérida, Yucatán; their emphasis was educating the poor and establishing a secondary school for girls. The group published a newspaper and strongly supported women's rights, advocating collective action against the regime. Yucatán became the center for feminist activity, and later a feminist league was named after Rita Cetina Gutiérrez. Three years later, in 1873 women textile workers in the Federal District of Mexico City founded the *Las Hijas de Anáhuac*. These groups set the tone for the establishment of feminist groups and newspapers that later shared the goals of the PLM and other oppositional groups. Meanwhile, the regime became more rigid and their adherents saw revolution as a vehicle for social change. Middle- and upper-class women became writers and journalists; they organized feminist and women's magazines and newspapers in which they argued for reform and gender equality. With time, their readership expanded.[44]

Feminist critiques of the Porfirian society proliferated. In 1904, schoolteacher Dolores Correa de Zapata, Laura Méndez de Cuenca, and Murgía Manteana founded the feminist magazine *La Mujer Mexicana* that was published monthly until 1908. María Sándoval de Zarco, who became Mexico's first female attorney in 1898, and Dr. Columba Rivera, the country's second practicing female physician, wrote for the magazine. In Laredo, Texas, Sara Estela Ramírez (1881–1910) edited *La Corregidora* and *Aurora*. A friend and supporter of Flores Magón, Ramírez worked for the Federal Labor Union and *La Sociedad de Obreros Igualdad y Progreso*, a mutual aid society formed in the mid-1880s. Another activist, Juana Gutiérrez de Méndoza, writing for *El Diario del Hogar*, criticized mining conditions inher writings as early as the 1890s. She served three months in jail for her anti-Díaz activities. A committed anarchist, Gutiérrez translated the works of Peter Kropotkin, Mikhail Bakunin, and Pierre-Joseph Proudhon. By 1901, she published *Vésper: Justicia y Libertad* (Dawn: Justice and Liberty) but soon broke with Ricardo Flores Magón over what she termed "matters of principle." Juana died in Mexico City in 1942, poor and forgotten.[45]

Teresa Villarreal founded *El Obrero* in San Antonio, Texas, in 1910. The organization targeted the proletariat, both men and women. From 1913 to 1915, Blanca de Moncaleano published *Pluma Roja* in Los Angeles, which, according to Clara Lomas, "placed the emancipation of women at the center of its anarchist agenda, adding a new dimension to the politics of the revolutionary struggle."[46]

Exceptional activists and thinkers, these women spread revolutionary ideas. The growth of cities and newspapers facilitated the dissemination of their ideas. Before 1910, the dissemination of information was cumbersome because both Mexico and the United States were rural. Urbanization allowed a more fluid spread of ideas as factories concentrated workers and provided year-round employment. Increased literacy also gave newspapers a reader base.

Noteworthy was the work of Elisa Acuña Rossetti (1887–1946), a Mexican anarchist and educator, feminist, journalist, revolutionary, and leader of the Mexican Cultural Missions against illiteracy. She was from Mineral del Monte, Hidalgo. Early in the 1900s, she joined *El Club Liberal Ponciano Arriaga*, founded by Camilo Arriaga. In 1901, Elisa participated in the first Congreso de Clubes Liberales. Acuña was a passionate and combative writer. In 1908, she founded *Socialismo Mexicano* and collaborated with numerous newspapers. While in exile in San Antonio, Texas, she edited the newspaper *Vesper* until 1935.

Industrial Bonanzas

During the colonial era, mining bonanzas drove the northward movement: silver and gold strikes attracted large numbers of workers who hoped to strike it rich. There would be periods of expansion and then contraction, as the workers moved on to yet another bonanza, with the hope of bettering their lives. Industrialization functions much the same way; it creates gigantic pools of jobs that attract huge numbers of Mexican laborers. Copper created these bonanzas.

After the U.S. Civil War, transportation costs dropped dramatically, encouraging the investment of capital to exploit copper. Copper became the best and the least expensive conductor in long-distance transmission of electricity. Railroads rendered giant copper camps profitable, and the "electric age" created an insatiable market for copper. Arizona became global leader in the production of copper and its copper mines employed tens of thousands of laborers. Clifton, Globe, Bisbee, and Jerome opened copper mines in the 1870s and 1880s. (See Chapter 6.) In time, each of these four districts produced more than 5 billion pounds of copper, Simultaneously, American copper barons exploited the great Mexican copper mines of Cananea, Nacozari, and other parts of Sonora.[47]

Workers Find Their Voice

As mentioned, these copper mines attracted thousands of Mexican miners. Along with them came the struggle against racism, bad working conditions, and low wages. On January 19, 1903, the Arizona legislature passed a law prohibiting miners from working more than eight hours per day underground. The eight-hour law was a major victory for the union. However, It is opined that the true purpose of the law was not worker safety but to eliminate foreign-born Mexicans, who were forced to work 10–12 hours a day to make ends meet with their lower wage scale. The cut in hours meant that Mexican miners would take even less money home: Mine owners had already cut workers' daily wages at Clifton-Morenci-Metcalf by 10 percent. On the morning of June 3, miners walked off the job, shutting down the smelters and mills, beginning what Jeanne Parks Ringgold, granddaughter of then-sheriff Jim Parks of Clifton, called the "bloodiest battle in the history of mining in Arizona." Around 1,200–1,500 miners participated, of whom 80–90 percent were Mexican, who were frustrated by the mine owners stonewalling them. The miners armed themselves, took control of the mines and shut them down.[48]

The *Bisbee Daily Review* of June 3, 1903, reported, "The Mexicans belong to numerous societies and through these they can exert some sort of organization to stand together." Initially, there was cooperation among the Mexicans, Italians and Spanish miners. Abraham Salcido, the president of a *mutualista*; Frank Colombo, an Italian; Weneslado H.

Laustaunau, a Mexican miner; and A. C. Cruz, another Mexican worker, led the strike. Two days later, the *Bisbee Daily Review* observed, "the strike is now composed almost entirely of Mexicans. Quite a number of Americans have left." Among the demands of the strikers were free hospitalization, paid life insurance for miners, locker rooms, fair prices at the company store, hiring only of men who were members of the society, and protection against being fired without cause.[49] The governor ordered the Arizona Rangers into Clifton-Morenci, and on June 9, 1903, workers staged a demonstration of solidarity. In direct defiance of the Rangers, 2,000 Mexicans marched through the streets of Morenci in torrential rains. A clash seemed imminent, but the storm dispersed the strikers; floods drowned almost 50 people and damaged some $100,000 worth of property.

Mine owners employed Mexican consul Arturo Elías, a representative of Porfirio Díaz, "to talk some sense to the Mexicans." Workers accused Elías of selling them out to the owners.[50] Meanwhile, Salcido, Colombo, Laustaunau, and Cruz were convicted for inciting a riot. Authorities sentenced them to Yuma State Penitentiary, where Laustaunau died—some believe he was murdered. The mining camps of the region would remain centers of discontent where revolutionary leaders would recruit supporters in large numbers.

Upon his release from prison in 1906, Salcido delivered a fiery speech to 2,000 people in Metcalf, denouncing Mexican President Porfirio Díaz and calling him a "traitor," "tyrant," and a "thief." U.S. authorities and the Mexican consul pressured local authorities to expel Salcido, whereupon he went to the border town of Douglas, where he joined the PLM. U.S. authorities arrested Salcido and others in September 1906 for a conspiracy to invade Mexico. Salcido was deported and sent to the dreaded San Juan de Ulúa prison near Veracruz, Mexico.[51]

This and other strikes of the decade were organized by *mutualistas*. These associations varied greatly in their political ideology, ranging from apolitical to reformist to radical. Mutual aid societies met the immigrants' need for "fellowship, security, and recreation" and were a form of collective and voluntary self-help and self-defense. Their motto—*Patria, Unión y Beneficencia* (country, unity, and benevolence)—became a common unifying symbol throughout the Southwest and eventually throughout the Midwest as well. Shut out of mainstream unions, Mexicans often used *mutualistas* as a front for union activities.[52]

Meanwhile, in May 1906, Mexican workers in neighboring Cananea, Sonora, demanded that the Consolidated Copper Company treat them the same way it did white miners. On the evening of May 31, Mexican workers at the Oversight Mine walked off the job, demanding 5 pesos for an eight-hour day. Sonoran Governor Rafael Izábal ordered the state militia to support mine owner Colonel William C. Greene. Tempers rose, and a company employee killed three demonstrators. Mexican workers responded by burning the lumberyard. Arizona Rangers crossed the international line into Mexico to help Greene; Mexican federal troops poured into Cananea. The military commander issued an ultimatum to miners—either go back to work or get drafted into the army and fight the Yaqui.[53]

The Nurturing of Ideas

Teresa Urrea, or *La Santa de Cabora*, contributed to the making of the Mexican Revolution. One of the many millenarian figures of the 1890s, she brought public attention to the suffering of the poor. Inspired by Teresa, the Yaqui in Sonora revolted, invoking her name as their patron. Mexican authorities targeted her and she fled to the United States with her father Tomás and the revolutionary journalist Lauro Aguirre. Fleeing to Via Nogales and then to El Paso, Teresa finally settled in Clifton. While Teresa is not linked to revolutionary cells, her father and stepmother were politically active.[54] The Clifton, Arizona home of her stepmother, Gabriela Cantúa, was the headquarters of the PLM, and Mexican consular records suggest that Cantúa was under constant surveillance in the years before the 1910 Mexican Revolution. The great revolutionary Práxedis Guerrero, a member of the PLM's junta, also lived and organized miners in the Clifton-Morenci-Metcalf mining camps.[55]

"Mexicans Are Not Fit to Raise White Babies"

Memories of racist experiences also contributed to forming a Mexican historical memory. In October 1904, some 16 months after the 1903 mining strike, three New York City nuns, four nurses, and forty Irish orphans arrived in the Arizona mining town of Clifton to place the orphans in respectable Catholic homes. Father Constant Mandin, the local priest, had requested to adopt the orphans, and they were closely screened the adoptive parents. The priest spoke limited English and Spanish.[56] Upon hearing that Mexicans were adopting white babies, a posse of white males armed with Winchester rifles marched to the Mexican quarter of North Clifton, to "rescue" the 40 blond babies. White men with guns broke down the doors of Mexican homes with the butts of their rifles and seized the white orphans. The pseudo posse abducted 16 of the foundlings and took them to the local church. The male posse, incited by their wives, threatened the priest, the nuns, and their agent, and forced them to surrender control of some of the children to white foster families, who were neither Catholic nor properly screened.

At the trial, the Mexican adoptive mothers were portrayed as prostitutes despite the fact they were married women of good reputation. White women testified that they felt it was their duty to save the children from the

Mexicans. The court accepted the abductors' narrative that the Mexicans were

> ... wholly unfit to be entrusted with them; that they were, with possibly one or two exceptions, of the lowest class of half-breed Mexican Indians; that they were impecunious, illiterate, unacquainted with the English language, vicious, and, in several instances, prostitutes and persons of notoriously bad character; that their homes were of the crudest sort, being for the most part built of adobe, with dirt floors and roofs; that many of them had children of their own, whom they were unable properly to support.

Charles E. Mills, the superintendent of Phelps Dodge, which employed the Mexicans and owned the housing, sided with the vigilantes, claiming that the homes were unfit for white children. In the end, the law found that Mexicans were unfit to raise white children.[57]

The Mexican Diaspora

In 1908 Victor Clark, in a U.S. government study titled *Report of the Immigration Commission*, stated,

> As recently as 1900, immigrant Mexicans were seldom found more than one hundred miles from the border. Now they are working as unskilled laborers and as section hands as far east as Chicago and as far north as Iowa, Wyoming, and San Francisco.[58]

Mexican laborers and their families migrated constantly, following job opportunities. The industrialization of agriculture and the growth of cities required huge armies of labor. Expansion and contraction of these industries constantly attracted and uprooted these workers, who searched for stability and control over their lives. Clark estimated that before 1908 about 60,000 workers and their families entered the United States annually, with most Mexicans remaining for only brief periods. Officially, 103,000 immigrants entered the United States by 1900, but the actual number was much higher. Likewise, the official figure of 222,000 for 1910 is probably low; experts estimate that the number may have been as high as 500,000.[59]

Dingley Tariff of 1897 that raised the tax on imported sugar accelerated the Mexican diaspora. It dramatically expanded the cultivation of sugar beets in the Southwest and Midwest. The number of sugar beet companies in Colorado, Kansas, and California quadrupled between 1900 and 1907. Firms such as the Holly Sugar Company and the American Sugar Beet Company recruited and transported large numbers of Mexicans to farms throughout the Southwest, Northwest, and Midwest. By 1912, a Mexican colonia formed on the west side of St. Paul, Minnesota, where Mexican sugar beet workers migrated during winter.[60] In Colorado in 1909, the Great Western Company employed 2,600 Mexican sugar beet workers and the numbers climbed.

Meanwhile, in the Rio Grande Valley, Mexican workers cleared brush and planted cotton and winter vegetables. During this period, the open range disappeared, and wire fencing sectioned off the land. At the turn of the century, the population of South Texas was 79,934; the 1920 Census counted 159,822; and in 1930, the number was 322,845. During the same period, the population of the Winter Garden area of Texas grew from 8,401 to 36,816. These numbers show that "Texas Mexican and white frontier settlers were overrun by *fuereños* (outsiders) from the interior [of Mexico] and newcomers from the Midwest and South." However, because of the heavy demand for labor, "South Texas remained basically Mexican"—with Mexicans moving out and other Mexicans moving in.[61]

Texas growers depended on the heavy migration of Mexicans, knowing that the development of the area depended on Mexican labor. Continual migration changed long-established Mexican communities such as Corpus Christi, Laredo, and Brownsville, where recently arrived Mexicans outnumbered the older Texas Mexican residents. Outside South Texas, cities such as Austin, Houston, Dallas, and Lubbock also saw the formation of Mexican enclaves. At the turn of the nineteenth century, Houston had only a few hundred Mexicans; 30 years later, that number had climbed to more than 15,000. Cotton was the main cash crop and the pull factor attracted large numbers of Mexicans until the late 1920s, after which spinach and other vegetables acquired a greater share of the market. Mexicans moved from ranchos to colonias, from where contractors recruited them to work as farmhands in California, Colorado, and Michigan.[62]

The growth of agribusiness increased the number of Mexicans in Arizona and California. The transformation in the latter state began in the 1890s, and it accelerated in the first decade of the twentieth century in response to the huge reclamation projects in western Arizona and in the Imperial Valley of California. By the turn of the nineteenth century, the annual value of intensive crops in California rose to $52 million—up from a mere $2.8 million 20 years earlier. In 1907, *California Fruit Grower* magazine noted that Mexicans were "plentiful, generally peaceable, and are satisfied with very low social conditions." The next year, farmers reaped the first commercial cotton harvest in the Imperial Valley of California. From 1907 to 1920, orange and lemon production in California quadrupled; between 1917 and 1922, cantaloupe production doubled, grapes tripled, and lettuce quadrupled. Such unprecedented production intensified the demand for Mexican labor in California agriculture, which became nothing short of a bonanza for them.[63]

Early Struggle to Control Working Conditions

The first wave of Mexicans came to the United States before the turn of the nineteenth century and mostly worked on the railroads, on farms, and in mines. Some also migrated to commercial centers such as Tucson, San Antonio, and then Los Angeles. Although they had greater opportunities than those in the migrant stream, their social and economic mobility was limited by a racist ceiling that assumed they were unequal and deserved less pay than white people. As a white mechanic conceded,

> They will never pay a Mexican what he's really worth compared with a white man. I know a Mexican that's the best blacksmith I ever knew. He has made some of the best tools I ever used. But they pay him $1.50 a day as a helper, working under an American blacksmith who gets $7 a day.[64]

As a consequence of this exploitation and discrimination there was a wave of strikes; Mexican workers demanded democracy in the workplace. In 1901, 200 Mexican construction workers went on strike at the El Paso Electric Streetcar Company, demanding higher wages and better working conditions. In 1907, 150 workers at another El Paso smelter struck. Throughout the decade and into the next, there were many incidents of smelter workers organizing and striking to better their lives. The concentration of workers at the various smelters, refineries, and railroads would draw labor organizations such as the Western Federation of Miners (WFM) and the Industrial Workers of the World (IWW) to the Gateway City that had a history of labor militancy.[65]

In 1903 in Oxnard, California, Japanese and Mexican workers protested the practices of the Western Agricultural Contracting Company (WACC) for withholding some of the workers' salaries until the end of the contract; 500 Japanese and 200 Mexican members of the Japanese–Mexican Labor Association (JMLA) called a strike. On March 23, two Mexican and two Japanese laborers were wounded, and 21-year-old Luis Vásquez was killed. The WACC conceded to most of the laborers' demands.[66]

After the strike, the workers formed the Sugar Beet and Farm Laborers' Union of Oxnard and petitioned the American Federation of Labor (AFL) for affiliation. Samuel Gompers, president of the AFL, turned down the request and denied affiliation unless the membership guaranteed that Chinese and Japanese workers would not be admitted. Mexican workers refused to abandon their Japanese comrades. They issued a statement in a letter to the AFL president:

> We refuse any other kind of charter, except one which will wipe out race prejudices and recognize our fellow workers as being as good as ourselves. I am ordered by the Mexican union to write this letter to you and they fully approve its words.[67]

That same year, Mexican workers at the Johnston Fruit Company in Santa Barbara, California, struck for higher wages and shorter hours. Lemon pickers and graders demanded the lowering of the 10-hour workday to 9 hours. The demand came at the height of the season, and workers got their 9-hour day and overtime.[68]

In the spring of 1903, Henry E. Huntington's Pacific Electric Railway laborers struck. Huntington was Los Angeles's largest employer and developed a "no concession to labor" policy, formed by his experiences during the Pullman Strike in 1894. Mexican track workers formed *La Unión Federal Mexicana* (the Mexican Federal Union), with A. N. Nieto elected as executive secretary. It had 900 members and a bank account of $600, and was headquartered in Sonoratown (the Los Angeles Mexican barrio). Mexicans demanded a raise from 17.5¢ to 20¢ an hour, 30¢ an hour for evenings, and 40¢ an hour for Sundays. The Los Angeles Merchants and Manufacturers' Association and the Citizens' Alliance joined with Huntington to fight trade unions and to keep Los Angeles an open-shop city. "The PE retaliated by firing the strikers and replacing them with Japanese, black, and white laborers whom it paid twenty-two and a half cents per hour. Again, Huntington received police protection for strikebreakers. The strike quickly collapsed . . . ." Although these organizational efforts failed, it did not mitigate worker discontent, and another unsuccessful strike against Pacific Electric took place in 1910.[69]

Separate is Not Equal

San Angelo was a Texas community of about 10,000 inhabitants including 1,500 Mexicans, about 200 of whom were Mexican children who attended segregated schools staffed primarily by ill-prepared white teachers. Throughout the United States, segregated schools were and are maintained for control. The pretexts for excluding Mexicans from white schools were that Mexicans were ill-clad, unclean, and immoral; interracial contact would lead to other relationships; Mexican children were not intelligent and learned slowly; and so forth. In reality, they segregated schools to maintain a caste system and keep Mexicans uneducated, limiting their opportunities, and preventing them from forging collective historical memories. It reinforced the caste system and their separate and unequal status. From very early on it sent a message to both Mexican and white students.

In 1910, in San Angelo, the town built new school buildings for white children, and the school board assigned the old buildings to Mexicans. Mexican parents boycotted the school—they wanted their children to share the new buildings with the white children or at least have all the buildings on the same grounds. The board refused to meet their demands. During the boycott, many parents sent their children to the Immaculate Conception Academy, a Catholic school that segregated Mexican students into a "Mexican room"; the Catholic school also refused their request to integrate. Two years later, the Presbyterian Church set up a Mexicans-only mission school that taught writing in English and Spanish languages, and subjects such as mathematics, geography, and physiology. The boycott of the public schools continued for several years until attrition ended it around 1915.[70]

American xenophobia and racist attitudes were part of American culture and have plagued each new wave of

Mexican immigrants. A 1910 *Report of the Immigration Commission* stated that Mexicans were the lowest paid of any laborers and that the majority worked as transient and migratory labor, did not settle, and returned to Mexico after only a few months. The report went on to say that, "The assimilative qualities of the Mexicans are slight because of the backward educational facilities in their native land and a constitutional prejudice on the part of the peons toward school attendance."[71] According to the report, Mexicans regarded public relief as a "pension"; the only saving grace was that they would return to Mexico within a few months.[72] What the report did not say that most immigrant groups lacked education and hence remained illiterate.

The Mexican Revolution that began in the same year the Immigration Report was published. The mass migration of Mexicans to the United States fed economic growth in the United States and brought about one of the largest population shifts in North American history and abruptly increased the presence of brown-skinned people in the United States. White xenophobia encouraged the spread of stereotypes and exaggerated them based on unfounded fears.

The Mexican Revolution

8.3 Describe ways that the Mexican Revolution affected life in Mexico and the U.S.

By 1910, the population of Mexico reached 15.16 million, and at least 382,000 persons of Mexican nativity lived in the United States. This figure does not include U.S.-born Mexicans.[73] The Mexican Revolution (1910–1920), which began that year, had a huge impact on the Mexicans and area along the 2,000 miles of U.S.–Mexico border that separated four U.S. and six Mexican states. The Revolution gave rise to hundreds of historical icons emerged: Francisco Madero, Ricardo Flores Magón, Pancho Villa, Emiliano Zapata, and Las Adelitas—Mexican women who along with Mexican soldiers risked their lives in the violent civil war.[74]

The Revolution struck an irrational fear in many white Americans who panicked and committed violent racist acts against their long-time scapegoats. For example, in Rocksprings, Texas, in November 1910, a mob killed Antonio Rodríguez, 20, while he awaited trial for the alleged shooting and killing of Mrs. Lem Henderson at her ranch home near Rocksprings on November 2, 1910. Vigilantes broke into the jail and dragged Rodríguez out of his cell, tied him to a stake, and burned him alive. Rodríguez's murder so enraged Mexicans south of the Rio Bravo that citizens throughout Mexico revolted against Díaz—days before November 20, 1910, when the Mexican Revolution officially began. The following June, Antonio Gómez, 14, was asked to leave a place of business in Thorndale, Texas. When Gómez refused, a fight broke out and the storekeeper was killed; Gómez was jailed for killing a Texas-born German. An killed mob dragging Gómez from the jail and killing him, dragged his body around town tied to the back of a buggy.[75]

In July 1911, local authorities arrested León Cárdenas Martínez, age 15, for the murder of Emma Brown in Saragosa, Texas. Cárdenas Martínez signed a confession after local police held a carbine to his head. The judge sentenced Cárdenas to death; later the courts reduced the sentence to 30 years in jail. Upon learning this, the townspeople then broke up Cárdenas's support meetings, chased his lawyer and the Cárdenas family out of town, and lynched the prisoner.[76]

Bullets Across the Border

Some of the heaviest fighting along the U.S.–Mexican border took place in Chihuahua and to a lesser extent in Sonora. These were two highly industrialized states with customhouses that made them attractive to the rebels and the *federales*. Sonora housed giant copper mining centers in its northeastern region, only 25 miles from Douglas, Arizona, and connected by a railroad system. Even a decade before the 1910 Revolution, rebels recruited heavily in Arizona mining camps. Miners as a rule owned rifles and ammunition. Because they lived at close quarters and because of the nature of their work, miners were more militant than other workers. Further, the frequent economic recessions and depressions made them restless and willing recruits by the revolutionizes for the Mexican Revolution. Tensions built up as U.S. troops, marshals, and officers of every description massed on the border. When Sonoran rebels captured El Tigre Mining Camp in March 1911 and secured over 100 high-powered rifles, U.S. authorities expressed alarm.[77]

The *Porfiriato* changed Chihuahua. As El Colegio de México professor Luis Aboites points out, "Part of this population was originally from Durango, Zacatecas and other places in the interior of the nation."[78] The commercialization of agriculture and the construction of water projects increased the number of ranchos and attracted workers from within and outside the state. In Guerrero and Benito Juárez (Cusihuiriáchic) alone, the number of Chihuahuan ranches increased from 79 in 1893 to 297 by 1908. The serranos, or people who originated in the sierras (mountains), were isolated and resembled the villagers of Rio Arriba in New Mexico, while places like Camargo were waystations for the south to north migration. Chihuahua was more industrialized than other states in Mexico; according to historian Michael Meyer, it had "a relatively large middle class of merchants, artisans, coachmen, railroad men, and clerks," which socialized migrants and residents alike. At the same time, it was more provincial and residents resented the gringos and federal government encroachments. During the first two years of the Revolution, they helped overthrow Díaz and then Victoriano Huerta. Nevertheless, factionalism existed within the ranks of the revolutionists that led to the Pascual Orozco Revolt.[79]

A Revolution on Horseback!

After 1913, Francisco "Pancho" Villa emerged as the most charismatic revolutionary in Chihuahua and throughout much of Mexico. The Mexican Revolution was a milestone in the lives of Mexicans and pivotal in forming the stereotype of the Mexican as a bandit. From the start, the North American press whipped up anti-Mexican sentiments that intensified discrimination against Mexican immigrants and perpetuated many negative images of them.

From the beginning of the 1910 Revolution, U.S. corporations, individuals doing business in Mexico, and the Catholic Church called for military intervention. Many business leaders supported Porfirio Díaz because he protected their interests. Twice, the United States violated Mexican sovereignty. The first was when it bombarded Veracruz in March 1914, claiming more than 300 Mexican lives. The excuse was that the United States was stopping a shipment of German arms to the *huertistas*—followers of the reactionary Mexican President Victoriano Huerta. The second was when when the American army crossed the border and chased Pancho Villa around Chihuahua. From March 16, 1916, to February 14, 1917, Brigadier General John J. "Black Jack" Pershing and an expeditionary force of more than 14,000 regular army troops chased Pancho Villa around Chihuahua—a chase that cost over $100 million.

President Woodrow Wilson called up 140,000 army and National Guard troops to patrol the 2,000-mile border between Mexico and the United States. The size of the force was huge; especially if we consider that the U.S. population at the time was 91,641,195. The total number of military personnel mobilized for this attack approached the populations of Arizona, 204,354; New Mexico, 327,299; California, 2.3 million; and Texas, 3.8 million. The army size was larger than the population of either Nevada (81,875) or Wyoming (145,965). This mobilization certainly prepared the people for a war with Mexico and conditioned the soldiers and their families to fear and hate Mexicans. The Hearst newspapers and the Chandlers, who owned the *Los Angeles Times*, were strident, perpetuating the myth that Mexican Americans were on the verge of revolution and blamed the PLM and other organizations like the PLM for border tensions. Meanwhile, there was a revival of industrial activity throughout the Southwest, creating a demand for unskilled labor and, temporarily, the nativism towards Mexicans to subsided.[80]

The Villa hysteria reached hysterical levels in places like Los Angeles, where the Mexican population swelled after 1910. On November 18, 1913, the Los Angeles police assigned several officers to investigate a subversive plot by Mexican "reds" and *cholos* (half-breeds). According to the *Los Angeles Times*, at least 10 percent of the city's 35,000 Mexicans were "known to the police to be rabid sympathizers of the outlaw [Pancho] Villa." Two days after Villa's raid on Columbus, New Mexico in March 1916, Los Angeles County supervisors requested federal action to deport "*cholos* likely to become public charges." When 200 Mexican laborers for the Pacific Sewer Pipe Company struck in 1918, authorities labeled the strike "German-made" to further stigmatize Mexicans by aligning them with the archenemy of the United States.[81]

The Revolution

Porfirio Díaz—at a terrible human price—brought law and order to Mexico. The hardships fell heaviest on the Indigenous People. Mexican liberalism included massive privatization projects that widened the gap between classes. The confiscation of Indigenous lands drove many into peonage. Díaz's *Rurales* brutally put down Native Mexicans who tried to defend their lands. The Sonora Yaqui were attacked during the 1880s, and the Sonoran ruling elite clubbed them into submission. Subsequently, they sold Yaqui men, women, and children to the plantations of Quintana Roo for 75 pesos a head—like cattle on the hoof.

One man or woman does not create the conditions for a revolution; it is a result of the system's excesses. At the beginning of the fall of Porfirio Díaz in 1910, Mexico was firmly under his control. Coahuilan Governor Francisco Madero, a wealthy criollo, sparked the "prairie fire" that drove Díaz from office. In 1908, Madero wrote a book, *The Presidential Succession of 1910*,[82] which called for the popular election of the vice-president. Since there was no question about Díaz being elected president, Madero reasoned that the people should at least choose the vice-president. This book made him an instant national figure.

In 1910, an anti-reelection convention nominated Madero for the presidency. At first, Díaz did not take Madero's candidacy seriously, and publicly joked about it. It was soon evident, however, that Madero had widespread support, so Díaz jailed him. Revolts sprang up throughout Mexico. Díaz, then 80 years old, refused to give up power and manipulated the vote in his own favor, "winning" the reelection.

The Revolution quickly took on major proportions, raging for some 10 years. It was the first social revolution in the Americas and brought about extensive changes in political, social and economic opportunities. The American Revolution of 1776 and the Mexican Revolution of 1910 overthrew the existing political systems, but they did not fundamentally change the economic or social order. Pancho Villa (1878–1923) defied the Mexican and American governments, and popularized the revolution in Chihuahua. He was often portrayed riding in front of his men. The Adelitas, women who fought alongside the revolutionary army, also popularized the revolution. They, along with other figures, were extremely important in garnering mass support for the Revoultion.

The Díaz regime threatened the emerging middle class of activists and many of them began to speak out against the injustices and spread ideas about social justice social justice. A historical conscience had developed, especially among the youth, who became more vocal. Some were journalists and attracted followings. Many women were schoolteachers politicized by the poverty and living conditions of their students. This new class was well read and conversant with European radical theorists who wrote about the overcrowded European cities and social inequality. They wanted solutions. Their writings influenced a minority of Mexicans to think about what kind of people they wanted to be. They also saw the injustices toward Indigenous Peoples in a clearer light. They were the precursors to the "Storm that Swept Mexico" beginning in 1910.

> "Among the numerous failures of the Porfirio Díaz government was the lack of education in rural Mexico. Statistics reveal only a fraction of the problem. In 1910, there were 11,750,996 illiterates in the population of 15,103,542, or a total of only 3,352,546 who could read or write. Illiteracy may have been even more rampant than these figures indicate. Most of Mexico was rural, and most of the effective educational efforts were in urban areas."[83]

It is not as if Díaz was not aware of the ineffectiveness of the Mexican school system; the problem was that he did not prioritize education. As Travis Evans put it, "Although Díaz showed little whole-hearted commitment to social welfare and the betterment of society, he did still contribute much in terms of welfare institutions, religious tolerance, the promotion of education, and a strong emphasis on law and order as the backbone of a successful Mexican society."[84] There were contending views on education ranging from the Díaz administration, and to labor groups, and to the Catholic Church that vied for public support. Education under Díaz was a priority "of Minister of Education Justo Sierra, who worked toward a solution. As early as 1891 Sierra proposed a dual school program for Mexico."[85] Díaz sought to address the lack of education in rural areas; however, the efforts never got off the ground.[86] Upon the formation of the Partido Liberal Mexicano on July 1, 1906, the PLM brought new energy to the debate and emphasized education.

As mentioned, the United States served as a staging ground for Mexican political exiles. Later that year, El Ingeniero Camilo Arriaga initiated a call to organize the PLM. Partisans raised funds, printed their propaganda in the United States, and sent it to Mexico. The exiles influenced Mexican Americans, who were encouraged to take sides.

The PLM was important not only because of its activism, but also for of its ability to attract other intellectuals and disseminate ideas.[87] The Magón brothers were anarchists and they influenced thought in Mexico and the United States. *Regeneración* was a model for a flurry of newspapers and magazines that critiqued the *Porfiriato* and issues of "justice and right." They attacked the Church for its antiliberal views.[88] The PLM's *Programa* (founding principles) emphasized the importance of primary education.[89] While there was no debate on the need for education, there was considerable controversy over the form it should take.

The migration during the Revolution differed from former Mexican movements into the Southwest. While most of the previous immigrants from Mexico to the United States were peasants, many of the new arrivals belonged to the middle and upper classes. These Mexicans settled in the cities of the Southwest, merging with the Mexican population already present there. Poor Mexicans arrived simultaneously and formed *barrios*, Mexican urban neighborhoods.

Among this group, Práxedis Guerrero (1882–1910) was an early martyr. He came from a well-to-do family, and decided to bring about change and to overthrow Porfirio Díaz. He joined the anarchist movement, and then led in part by Ricardo Flores Magón. Guerrero was well-versed in the teachings of Jean-Jacques Rousseau, Pierre-Joseph Proudhon, and William Godwin, and the theories of Mikhail Bakunin and Pyotr Kropotkin. Guerrero wrote incendiary essays for *Revolucion*, *Regeneración*, and *Punto Rojo* and had an audience on both sides of the border.[90]

As a journalist, Guerrero wrote about injustices in the mining camps and elsewhere in the United States. Guerrero agitated Mexicans in the United States to take action, writing that "the exploitation of and discrimination against Mexicans in the United States was directly related to conditions in Mexico." Mexicans accepted the insults from a racist society because the economic opportunities fed their families, which was impossible in Mexico. Guerrero chronicled racist encounters in Texas, Oklahoma, Arizona, and other southwestern states. He wrote, "The migrants left misery and hunger in Mexico and now [faced] shame, humiliation and hunger . . . the universal companions of the impotent." Guerrero was killed in a guerrilla encounter with federal forces at Janos, Chihuahua in 1910.[91]

In Defense of the Community

Meanwhile, the United States prospered as the result of the pre-World War I affluence that increased the demand for Mexican labor to fill the more undesirable vacancies in the railroad, sugar beet, and similar industries. The demand for Mexican labor increased with the declaration of war. Agents flooded Mexico to contract labor. Often they illegally contracted to smuggle workers into the United States.

Nicasio Idar, publisher of the Texas-based *La Cronica* newspaper, condemned racism toward Mexicans.[92] During late 1910 and early 1911, Idar, under the headline "The Mexican Children of Texas," condemned separate schools and neighborhoods for Mexican Americans, who by linguistic segregation were "isolated and kept ignorant."[93] Under Idar's leadership, *El Primer Congreso Mexicanista* (the First Mexican Congress) convened on September 11, 1911, to discuss deteriorating Texas-Mexican economic conditions, the loss of Mexican culture and Spanish language, widespread social discrimination, educational discrimination, and lynching. Men and women discussed the issues at workshops. Delegates protested the insult to State Representative J. T. Canales, whom a white politico called "the greaser from Brownsville." The *Congreso* created *La Liga Femenil Mexicanista* (the Mexican Feminist League); its first president was Jovita Idar. The women's contingent was largely composed of schoolteachers, who raised educational issues.[94]

Mexican Americans were active organizationally. In 1911, they formed *La Agrupación Protectora Mexicana* (Mexican Protective Association) in San Antonio; its purpose was to defend the human rights of Mexicans. Although *La Agrupación* supported union organizing, its primary focus was on police brutality and lynching. La Agrupación's members campaigned for the release of prisoner Gregorio Cortez. La Agrupación functioned until 1914, before internecine problems split the organization. The *Alianza Hispano-Americana* was founded on January 14, 1894, in Tucson, Arizona, as a fraternal benefit society. It offered life insurance at low rates and fostered social activities for Mexican Americans. Some say it was organized in response to hostile attitudes against Tucson Mexican Americans. By 1913, it allowed immigrants and women to join AHA and spread to other states. By 1939, the *Alianza* had 17,366 members. It focused on defending civil rights of Mexicans throughout Arizona and the Southwest.[95]

La Liga Protectora Latina was organized as a mutual aid society in Phoenix in 1915 and grew to 30 lodges by 1917 to protect the rights of the foreign-born. It opposed the Arizona Claypool–Kinney Bill, which forced the mines to employ 80 percent U.S. citizens. It had chapters in Phoenix and other mining towns throughout the state, the Southwest, and even Mexico. Much of its leadership came from the middle class and belonged to the *Alianza Hispano-Americana* and other patriotic societies and *mutualistas*. Besides sponsoring social activities, the leaders of these organizations were very much involved in politics.

Much of *La Liga's* leadership was middle class, and belonged to the Mexican wave of immigrants who arrived after 1910. In general, they were supporters of Porfirio Díaz and opposed the Mexican Revolution. Articles from *El Tucsonense* during the 1910s made it clear that the newspaper's leadership supported U.S. policy toward Mexico and favored Republican candidates. The members maintained good relations with corporate leaders of the Southern Pacific Railroad and Phelps Dodge. For most part, they were nationalistic, conservative, and anti–labor union. However, they did fight against racism and nativist immigration laws.

In perspective, some of the middle-class Mexican organizations' anti-union sentiment was a response to the unions' refusal to admit Mexicans or promote their interests. For example, "As early as 1904, Bernabé Brichta spoke out against the Locomotive Stokers Union, the Locomotive Engineers Union, and the Machinist Union because they refused to admit Mexicans, Blacks, or Chinese as members."[96] The railroad, arguably Tucson's most important industry, reserved its skilled trades for Americans. Brichta demanded an end to the unions' discrimination against Mexicans, but he also argued that they should not lump Mexicans with African Americans and Chinese. The antiunion stance of the Tucsonense middle class prevented them from supporting strikes even when Mexican workers were involved. According to Carlos Vélez-Ibañez, "proving and gaining class legitimacy was a major effort" among this class, in which one's family name and color still played a major role.[97]

The extent of the pro-immigrant struggle, warts and all, forged an impressive organizational network of middle-class Mexicans in the United States. In 1914, a group of prominent Mexicans middle-class leaders met to organize La Liga which was chartered the following year. By May 1915, *La Liga's* Tempe lodge, with 80 members, had established a bureau to provide employment referral and financial assistance. *La Liga* also supported striking miners at Ray, Arizona, but that appears to have been an aberration: Their support was more concerned with education and the protection of Mexicans' political and social rights. By 1917, it had 30 lodges; through political and legal action, it sought to protect the rights of Mexicans, increase mutual aid for *Liga* members, and improve education. Despite its support for the miners, *La Liga's* leadership resented labor militancy and often opposed the union leadership during strikes. Admittedly, the opposition of some members stemmed from nationalism and class interests.

To this end, *La Liga* shared strong ties to the Republican Party. The leadership courted the Republicans because the Democrats favored trade unions and pushed a nativist agenda. Elite leaders of *La Liga* believed that they could get political concessions because its members were well educated and, hence, would be listened to. Leadership met with Republican Governor Tom Campbell, especially in mining areas. Although Campbell was anti-labor, *La Liga* supported his candidacy because Democrats were attempting to revive the 80 percent Claypool–Kinney Bill.

At its third annual convention, *La Liga* members established a commission headed by Amado Cota Robles to lobby the state legislature for bilingual education at the primary level. Under Cota Robles's leadership, *La Liga* initiated night classes in Spanish language, arithmetic, geometry, geography, and Mexican history. Emphasis was placed on learning and reading in English. By 1919, the organization had 3,752 members and lodges in Arizona, California, New Mexico, and Philadelphia, and the group began the publication of a journal, *La Justicia*. However, in 1920 the organization started to decline. When *La Liga* raised the membership subscription to a $3 initiation fee and $1.25 a month, poor members protested, and a division developed along class lines. The isolation of Mexicans in Arizona—and in other areas of the United States—would continue.[98]

A Changing Society

8.4 Explain how Mexican life in the U.S. changed from 1900–1920.

In 1900, most Mexicans worked in agriculture and were the least urbanized immigrant group in the United States. By 1920, however, 47 percent of the Mexicans who were born in Mexico lived in urban areas; the percentage would have probably been higher if U.S.-born Mexicans had been included in the count. Many second-generation Mexicans, along with political refugees, became merchants or took middle-level jobs.[99] What happened during the intervening 20 years? Mexicans adapted to the American society in stages. Each generation included U.S.-born children, some took immigrant spouses while others took U.S.-born spouses. There were subtle differences between the disparate generations, as well as within generations, depending on the hue of their skin and where they lived.

Racism was worse in Texas, a former Confederate state, than in other southwestern states; an influx of Midwesterners into Texas worsened racial tensions. The white newcomers often resented Mexicans because they saw them as the base of the political machines that ran South Texas, and thus were part of the political problem. By the 1910s, Mexicans were caught in the middle of these contending groups.

The Midwestern faction started winning and overthrew the political bosses. In theory, this was a victory for democracy; in reality, the decline of the political machines removed arrangements that had cushioned racism toward Mexicans. It is said that the new political order came with new ways of excluding Mexicans, such as the "White Man's Primary," which was instituted to prevent Mexicans from voting in primaries and to ensure their control by the white farmers. The decline of political bosses marked the beginning of an era that saw not only the transformation of the economy of South Texas but also the increased migrancy of Mexican laborers.[100]

Mexican Workers Under Siege

Mexican workers and their families were considered expendable. Repatriations of Mexican families occurred in 1913, 1919, and 1921. The employers and Mexican consulates assumed the costs for these repatriations. Government agencies and charities disowned the starving families. When recessions hit, most employers abandoned Mexican laborers and their families, leaving them starving and homeless. As the economy improved, railroads and steel mills employed more Mexican laborers, and again the cycle of exploitation was renewed. The treatment of the reserve labor pool became more brutal with the passage of time. White American nationalism increased, and an anti-foreign and anti-radical hysteria gripped the country. White nationalism in the 1920s was led by America-Firsters who began efforts to racially engineer the color and culture of America.

These were not the finest hours for American labor organizations. Given the discriminatory exclusion of Mexicans from trade unions, throughout the 1910s *mutualistas* continued as Mexicans' most popular form of association. Occasionally, organizations such as the IWW actively organized casual workers (the Wobblies) in mining and agriculture. The Wobblies included people of color within their "one big union." One of the most dramatic strikes involving the IWW was the Wheatland Hop Field Riot of August 3, 1913, at the Ralph Durst Ranch in Wheatland, California. A crisis developed when a hops grower advertised for 1,000 picking jobs and some 2,800 people showed up. Working and living conditions at the ranch were horrendous, and wages were less than those advertised. An impasse occurred workers struck. The state actively intervened on the side of the growers to rid the fields of the IWW militants, resulting in the killing of four men and the wounding of a dozen others.[101]

The Ludlow Massacre took place in 1913 in Ludlow, Colorado. The Colorado Fuel and Iron Company—owned in its majority by the Rockefellers, John D. Sr. and John Jr.—evicted miners from company housing. As the cold winter approached, tensions grew; the governor ordered the National Guard into Ludlow. The Baldwin–Felts Detective Agency hunted down and killed the strike leaders. On April 20, 1914, the Guard occupied a hill overlooking the camp, mounted a machine gun, and exploded two bombs into the camp. The miners armed themselves, and the Guard attacked the tent colony, killing 18 people, including 9 Mexicans, 5 of whom were children. In total, 50 workers and their family members were killed.[102]

As dramatic as Ludlow was, the killing fields of Arizona ranked far higher in the annals of labor history; yet little is written about them. Race wars raged between Mexican and white American miners, largely coordinated by mine owners. Ray, Arizona, was clustered in the mountains alongside the colonias of Sonora and Barcelona, about 80 miles southeast of Phoenix; the Ray Consolidated Copper Company owned all of the area's mining operations. Mexican workers and their families migrated there in larger numbers, and by 1907, they established the colonia of Sonora, which grew to about 5,000 members in 1914–1915. "Barcelona," a Spanish colonia, developed next to Sonora with about 1,000 residents. Ray itself had 1,000 residents, mostly white and Irish.[103] Ray Consolidated employed 1,400 men; most were Mexican nationals segregated by race, not only physically, but also by a dual-wage system.

The WFM enabled Ray Consolidated's racial policies by not organizing across racial lines. Ray became a hotbed of Mexican activism, and revolutionary organizers constantly visited it, looking for volunteers, arms, and money. In 1914, the Arizona Alien Labor Law requiring companies to employ at least 80 percent white American labor went into effect, increasing tensions between Mexican and white American miners.[104] Violence broke out in the summer when whites chased Peter Smith, a "half-breed" Mexican, after he allegedly stole a horse in Ray and took to the hills. Smith and two (or more) of his companions ambushed the posse.[105] In retaliation, someone stabbed a Mexican boss of an all-Mexican mine crew to death while he was asleep. Several more shootings occurred, and a race war followed.

Regeneración reported on "A War of Races in Arizona." According to the PLM newspaper, white scabs attacked 19 Mexican workers in Ray, Arizona. Sheriff Brown was killed, along with two Mexicans, in the Devil's Canyon near Ray. That night a second confrontation took place and another Mexican was killed. Mobs of whites, descending into the Mexican barrio, entered Mexican homes and committed atrocities like beating, robbing and killing Mexicans. They went into the hills looking for Mexicans. "The American working class is the most mentally retarded class," (as originally written) Ricardo Flores Magón wrote in *Regeneración*, "not knowing its interests as workers." The *Los Angeles Times* on August 20, 1914, also wrote, "Race War in Arizona—Death List Is Sixteen." Four Americans and 12 Mexicans had been left dead in the bloody riot.[106] Thus began the reign of terror, which was abetted by the management of Ray Consolidated.

Due to competition from the IWW, the WFM reconsidered its policy of excluding Mexicans. By 1914, the copper barons escalated their campaign of intimidation, subversion, libel, and slander against labor. By this time, a core of Mexican union leaders emerged, with the backing of a minority of white American organizers who wanted to include Mexicans as members. As a result of this cooperation, in 1915 the union launched a strike at the Clifton-Morenci-Metcalf mining camps, which drew a bevy of inclusionist WFM and Mexican organizers, such as Lazaro Gutiérrez de Lara. The strike lasted five months. Although the strike was bitter, violence was averted because of the intervention of Arizona Governor George W. P. Hunt and local Sheriff James Cash, who were determined to prevent another Ludlow Massacre. The workers won some concessions, although management refused to recognize the WFM. Strikes continued to take place at the Miami, Globe, Ray, Ajo, Jerome, and Warren mines, where Mexican miners were at the vanguard.

After this, led by Phelps Dodge's Walter Douglas, mine owners went on the offensive and fueled nativist sentiments among white Americans. They cited exaggerated fears that Pancho Villa intended to invade the United States in order to avenge the firing of some 1,200 Mexican miners at Ajo in 1916, when workers requested a raise and a grievance committee.[107] In 1917, locals 80, 84, and 86 in Clifton-Morenci-Metcalf had a membership of some 5,000 Mexican miners. Yet the copper barons refused to negotiate with Mexican miners. Worker opposition to the copper barons was labeled anti-American. At the time, there were 14,000 Mexican miners in Arizona alone. Mine conditions were horrible: In the neighboring state of New Mexico, in the town of Dawson, 600 miners died in mine disasters in 1913, 1920, and 1923. Despite these horrible conditions, AFL president Samuel Gompers refused to organize Mexican miners. Gompers became increasingly fearful that Mexicans would filter into urban factories and compete with white workers.[108]

By 1917, the war between the workers and the copper barons came to a head. On June 24, the union struck at Bisbee and Jerome, where a large number of Mexican miners worked. The Cochise County sheriff immediately declared the strike subversive and announced his intention to deport any members of the IWW. With the aid of a vigilante committee, a posse deported 67 miners from Jerome and some 1,200 from Bisbee. The sheriff seized the telegraph and telephone office, and did not permit news dispatches. Local authorities, along with racist nativists, loaded strikers into boxcars and shipped them to the outskirts of Columbus, New Mexico, where state police authorities dumped them in the open desert without food or water. Because President Woodrow Wilson had strong ties to Phelps Dodge, no one was punished for the gross constitutional and human rights violations. A presidential commission was sent to study the problem; in the end, the copper barons had their way. They purged the mines of militant Mexicans and repatriated thousands, with thousands more going into agriculture, to the cities, or to the ranks of the Mexican Revolutionary army.[109]

The "Amazon" Protest: Story of Carmelita Torres

The story of Carmelita Torres, age 17, is one of exceptional heroism. She traveled from Juárez to El Paso daily to work as a maid. In 1917, she refused to take a gasoline bath when she entered the United States from Juárez. In El Paso, Texas and elsewhere along the border, Mexicans were routinely forced to undergo strip searches and were fumigated with toxic gases. The pretext for administering the baths was that Mexicans spread typhoid or that they had lice or that they were bringing diseases into the country. The soldiers would stare at the disrobed women as they took DDT or gasoline baths. The previous year, while Mexican prisoners in El Paso were given a gasoline bath, they were burned to death when a fire broke out and ignited the gas.

Carmelita persuaded the other trolley passengers not to take it. Thirty trolley passengers joined the protest, touching off two days of uprisings. The *El Paso Times* labeled the women "the Amazons." An hour later, more than 200 Mexican women blocked traffic entering the city, lying in front of the tracks. Within four hours, several thousand had joined the demonstration. Troops from Fort Bliss were joined by the *Carrancista el escuadrón de la muerte* (the death squad). When protester José María Sánchez shouted "Viva Villa!" he was escorted to the Juárez cemetery and shot. The resistance lasted for several days—more shots were fired—and the Mexican women were finally driven back across the bridge.[110]

The Hysteria: The Plan of San Diego

The harshness of the repression of Mexicans on the U.S. side of the border produced a variety of reactions. For example, in 1915 Texas authorities used the "Plan of San Diego" as an excuse to step up a reign of terror along the border. The plan, found on the person of rebel leader Basilio Ramos, called for a general uprising of Mexicans and other minorities starting February 20. The supporters were to execute all white males over age 16—Blacks, Asians, and Native Americans were to be spared. The Southwest was to become a Chicano nation, and Blacks and Native Americans were to form independent countries. Most Mexicans found the plan extreme and felt that it took focus away from legitimate grievances. Flores Magón, in *Regeneración*, never acknowledged or supported the plan, except for stating once that Texas authorities wanted "to make it appear as if the Mexican uprising in that section of the United States is part of the Plan of San Diego" in order to justify its reign of terror.

Clearly, the call for the murder all adult white males over 16 was extreme. The statement, simply put, overshadowed and confused all the legitimate reasons for an uprising. At first, officials did not take the plan seriously, viewing rebels' raids as banditry and rustling. But, by July 1915, the rebels issued a new plan, which was followed by a series of raids in the lower Rio Grande Valley. The supporters of the plan seemed to be either *huertistas*, followers of Huerta, or *carrancistas*, followers of the Mexican President Venustiano Carranza; most of them had roots in the United States. Luis de la Rosa, who was in command of the rebels, was a former deputy sheriff in Cameron County. Ancieta Pizaña, second in command, was a *carrancista*. In all, they had a force of 50 men. Between July 1915 and July 1916, this small band of rebels carried out a total of 30 raids in Texas.[111]

White Americans' perception of these raids as revolutionary incitement led to the killing of hundreds of Mexicans. In the end, U.S. authorities admitted shooting, hanging, or beating to death 300 "suspected" Mexicans, while the rebels killed 21 Americans during this period. George Marvin wrote in *World's Work* magazine in 1917 that it was "open season" on Mexicans. Walter Prescott Webb justified the "Reign of Terror" by blaming the Mexican Revolution and the border incidents, Pancho Villa, the San Diego Plan, Prohibition, and/or the Germans.[112]

World War I: The Shift

8.5 Summarize the ways in which World War I affected Mexicans in the United States.

World War I produced labor shortages, and the U.S. government, fearing that Mexicans would flee the country, enlisted Catholic bishops to assure Mexicans that they would not be drafted. Further contributing to the labor shortage, the Literacy Law of the Immigration Act of 1917 severely restricted the number of Europeans allowed to enter the country, and it also slowed down the flow of Mexicans. However, profit motive trumped racism and border security in this instance, and soon afterward, to ease the labor crisis, U.S. officials allowed exemptions for illiterate contract workers from Mexico to enter the United States—after requiring that they pay an $8 head tax, which was later waived owing to pressure from U.S. farmers.

Despite the United States' entry into World War I, it markedly relaxed efforts to control immigration. In the interests of profit, the military turned the other away as thousands of Mexicans passed freely across the river. In the four years the exemptions were in force (1917–1921), 72,862 Mexicans entered the United States with documents, and hundreds of thousands more crossed the border without documents.[113]

World War I accelerated industrialization and urbanization in California. The war industries attracted many Mexicans and African Americans, and the large numbers of Mexicans settling in Los Angeles created new social and economic pressures. Mexicans' choices as to where they would settle were determined by factors such as language and availability of transportation. In Los Angeles, the largest concentration of Mexicans was in and around the Central Plaza district, where 40 percent of the Mexican workers surveyed worked for the Southern Pacific Railroad. In an area of less than 5,000 square feet of living space, 20 needy families were forced to live in dilapidated houses. By 1919, Mexicans comprised 5 percent of Los Angeles's population of over a million. Twenty-eight percent of Mexicans lived in houses with no sinks, 32 percent had no lavatories, and 79 percent had no baths. The infant mortality rate for Americans was 54 out of 1,000; the rate for Mexicans was 152 out of 1,000. In 1914, Mexicans constituted 11.1 percent of the deaths in Los Angeles. White Americans blamed the blight around the Central Plaza on the Mexicans, saying that these foreigners contributed to a rapid disintegration of traditional "American values."[114]

Shifts in Political Consciousness

World War I was a crucial juncture in the assimilation of Mexicans.[115] The longer Mexicans remained in the United States, the more they felt entitled to constitutional protections. This attitude was more noticeable with each succeeding generation. Accordingly, many Mexicans in the United States were beginning to feel more American, and the war accelerated their assimilation but also magnified existing inequalities. Some Tejanos (Mexicans born in Texas) and Mexicans did not know how to read or write English and were supposedly exempt from conscription, yet local boards drafted them into the army; Mexicans, or other poor people, were often the only ones called upon to serve.

Mexican war casualties were high. Unacknowledged acts of bravery burned in the memories of many veterans such as J. Luz Sáenz, who recorded his recollections in his book *Los méxico-americanos en la gran guerra y su contingente en pró de la democracia, la humanidad y justicia*.[116] Sáenz had university training and taught for eight years in Texas schools and later at the League of United Latin American Citizens, but was denied officer training. Marcelino Serna, a Mexican immigrant from El Paso, single-handedly captured 24 German prisoners and prevented another soldier from shooting them. He was awarded the Distinguished Service Cross, two Purple Hearts, France's Croix de Guerre and Military Medal, Italy's Cross of Merit, and Britain's Medal of Bravery—but not the Medal of Honor, in all probability because he could not read or write English. The military also discriminated against Mexican American soldiers in other ways. El Paso veterans, most of whom were Mexican immigrants, complained that they were gassed in France but received no government disability benefits.[117]

Mexican Responses to Industrial Transformation

In the spring of 1917, several farm strikes hit the Corona, Riverside, Colton, Redlands, and San Bernardino areas of California. The cost of living rose dramatically because of World War I, but workers' wages remained the same. On March 5, Mexican workers went on strike at the Corona Lemon Company. White workers refused to join the action, and local authorities arrested Juan Peña and other leaders on unspecified charges. On March 27, 300 Mexican and Japanese orange pickers in Riverside, California joined the strike, which the growers violently suppressed by importing large numbers of strikebreakers from El Paso. Significantly, many of the participants had worked in mining and had previously experienced labor strife.[118]

European immigration slowed, and Mexican workers began to filter in greater numbers into the Midwest. During the 1919 steel strike in the Chicago-Calumet area, the steel companies imported Mexicans, who worked under guard. Throughout the history of the U.S. labor movement, companies have exploited the most recently arrived immigrants as strikebreakers. This has been true for Mexicans, Poles, Italians, and any other nationality. Mexicans employed in the steel industry before the strike supported collective bargaining efforts. However, white workers viewed Mexicans as scabs, when in reality they were only a minority of the strikebreakers, recruited from those most recently arrived. A report by Homestead Steel Works, Howard Axle Works, and Carrie Furnaces on October 8, 1919, showed that out of the 14,687 workers employed by these mills, only 130 were Mexican—that is, Mexicans comprised less than 1 percent of the workforce.[119]

Meanwhile, sugar beet companies relentlessly recruited for Mexican labor. By 1919, 98 U.S. factories produced almost 1 million tons of sugar annually. The leading sugar beet–producing states were Michigan, Ohio, and Wisconsin in the Midwest; Colorado, Utah, and Idaho in the mountain region; and California in the Far West. A constant increase in production and, in turn, a heavy reliance on Mexican labor prompted farm journals in 1920 to refer to the sugar beet crop as a "Mexican Harvest."[120]

Urbanization of Mexicans stepped up significant space for women workers of all colors. Hearings conducted in El Paso in November 1919 by the Texas Industrial Welfare Commission found that Mexican women were "the lowest-paid and most vulnerable workers in the city."[121] El Paso laundries employed large numbers of Mexicanas at unskilled jobs, whereas white American women took the skilled jobs. Mexicanas earned $8 a week compared to $16.55 earned by white American women. The work areas were segregated. In department stores white women generally worked on the main floor, whereas Mexicanas worked in the rear or basement. White American women earned as much as $40 a week compared to Mexican clerks, who were paid $10–$20 a week. Mexicanas also comprised the overwhelming majority of workers in the El Paso garment industry. White women workers in a union shop were reported to average between $18 and $20 a week for piecework, and the owner of one factory conceded that Mexicanas averaged $9.50. The pretext for the double standard was that Mexican women had fewer needs than did whites and thus required less money.[122]

Mexican women workers at El Paso's Acme Laundry called a strike because the laundry fired two workers for union activity. Almost 500 women walked out of six other laundries. The Central Labor Union (CLU) leadership undermined worker solidarity by assigning the Mexican women to the minor role of dissuading scabs from breaking the picket line. The CLU portrayed Mexican woman as passive. The newspapers, too, depicted a negative image of the emotional Mexican. However, the women strikers soon broke the stereotype as they positioned themselves at the international bridge to prevent the entry of scabs. The CLU became increasingly conservative, with many of its members entering into an alliance with a Ku Klux Klan–dominated, good-government movement. In the end, the union deserted the Mexican women. However, their political consciousness had been awakened and enhanced, and it advanced the notion of equality between Mexican women and white women in the workplace.[123]

The Failure of American Brotherhood

The Arizona mining strikes demonstrated that Mexicans wanted to be part of labor solidarity, and their participation exceeded that of white workers. However, AFL head Samuel Gompers sent contradictory messages: While Gompers and the AFL advocated "Pan-Americanism" and paid lip service to organizing Mexicans, they allowed racism to flourish among the rank and file locals that excluded Mexicans. For example, the 1916 AFL Constitution stated that unions should organize Mexicans in the United States and assist in the organization of workers in Mexico. Los Angeles alone had 15,000 Mexican workers, and there were thousands more in mining communities in Arizona and Colorado.

However, the locals were permitted to discriminate against Mexicans by supporting legislation that excluded them from the country. As mentioned, Gompers feared Mexicans would move to the cities and take the jobs from whites. On the other hand, many white workers were just plain racist.

At the first Pan-American Conference in 1918, a debate broke out between Mexican and American delegates. Mexicans demanded full union membership and accused white Americans of discriminating against them. They also attacked U.S. border authorities for their harsh treatment of Mexicans. Even though he was an organizer in the 1917 mining strikes, H. S. McCluskey of the Mine, Mill & Smelter Workers Union (UMM&S) criticized Mexican immigrant workers for their failure to organize or support AFL unions, thus perpetuating the myth of the Mexican strikebreaker. In McCluskey's case, it was not a matter of not knowing better. The Mexican representatives reacted immediately, reminding McCluskey of the AFL's attitude toward Mexican workers. A Mexican delegate admitted that there was some truth in what McCluskey said; but he objected to the the racist attitude of political candidates and pointed out that a certain candidate for the post of the governor of Arizona called for the death penalty for "Mexicans and niggers." In the 1920s, as the country became more nativist, calls for exclusion and deportation of Mexicans heightened, with American labor rewriting history minus the significant Mexican labor force participation that had existed in reality.[124]

The Westward Movement of King Cotton

8.6 Describe how commercial cotton agriculture drove demand for Mexican labor.

As early as 1913, the PLM tracked the movement of Mexican workers into cotton plantations. Cotton was important because it attracted huge armies of pickers and their families, determining where Mexicans settled. Between 1918 and 1921, the Arizona Cotton Growers Association imported more than 30,000 Mexicans at a cost of $300,000. Because of the proximity to the border, Arizona cotton growers had an ample supply of pickers. In 1916, only 7,600 acres were dedicated to cotton in Arizona; a decade later, cotton was produced on 210,000 acres, of which 186,000 acres were in the Salt River Valley. On November 3, 1919, the *Los Angeles Times* reported, "Flood of Mexican Aliens a Problem," pointing out that the Mexican pickers came with their families and picked as a unit. In 1919, Goodyear Tire and Rubber Company announced a projected 20-million-dollar factory to be built in Los Angeles. The Goodyear Company had ranches in Arizona, which supplied cotton to the; factory, but they bought additional cotton from other ranches as well.[125]

Meanwhile, the production of cotton in the Imperial Valley spread to the San Joaquin Valley. The cultivation of cotton and other crops formed a land bridge to Los Angeles, from where Mexican workers followed the crops north, south, east, and west. Many of the Mexican workers' families remained in Los Angeles. The buildup of the Mexican population was enabled by irrigated farming and land reclamation projects that resulted in the construction of massive dams and the cultivation of hundreds of thousands of acres of land.

Similar developments were taking place in Texas, which had become a leading agricultural state. Cotton was important in driving the demand for Mexican labor. San Antonio, like Los Angeles, was a distribution center for Mexican labor and a favored destination for Mexican families. The Lone Star State was a reserve labor pool for the Midwest, where Mexican agricultural workers were replacing European immigrants as the 1917 Literacy Act excluded them.

Conclusion: The Color Line

In 1881, Frederick Douglass published an article in the *North American Review* titled "The Color Line."[126] Douglass used the term "color line" in reference to racial segregation. Through the years, however, it has taken on new meaning, referring to American immigrants and the narrowing of the WASP mentality. Recent scholarly work has incorporated this notion color line and American myths such as the "melting pot" and the "salad bowl." Americans have never molted, melted, or mixed; they have surrendered.[127]

Nancy Foner's book on immigration to New York City is especially insightful; it reassesses the myths around earlier Jewish and Italian immigration and the color line's impact on Asian, Latin American, and Caribbean arrivals.[128] Foner writes that today some Jews and Italians are seen as whites but at the "turn-of-the-century scholars believed they were members of different, alien races." Not much has changed since Madison Grant's *The Passing of the Great Race* in which Grant warned that "American stock would be mongrelized by inferior Europeans such as the Alpines from central Europe, Mediterranean and, worst of all, Jews. People of inferior breeding, Grant believed, were overrunning the country, intermarrying and diminishing the quality of American blood."[129] The truth is that to many the word "American" is white and this is what has *Made America Great*. They forget that white America was never colonized and that they were the colonizers.

Notes

1 Eric T. L. Love. Race over Empire: Racism and U.S. Imperialism, 1865–1900, The University of North Carolina Press, 2004. ProQuest Ebook Central, p. xi, http://ebookcentral.proquest.com/lib/csun/detail.action?docID=413346.

2 U.S. Department of State,. "Expansion and empire, 1867–1914," Outline of U.S. History, North Carolina Digital History, http://www.learnnc.org/lp/editions/nchist-newsouth/5488,. Ewen Green, ed., *The Ideals of Empire: Political and Economic Thought, 1903–1913* (London: London: Routledge/Thoemmes, 1998).

3 Love, Ibid.

4 Rodolfo Acuña, "Truth and Objectivity in Chicano History," Occasional Paper No. 9 *Latino Studies Series*, Julian Samora Center, Michigan State University, December 1997, https://jsri.msu.edu/upload/occasional-papers/oc09.pdf.

5 Love, Ibid., xiii

6 Love, Ibid. I use Love extensively because of the his synthesis of other prominent historians because of his focus on race.

7 Love, Ibid., 108.

8 PBS, "Crucible of Empire: The Spanish–American War," YouTube.com, Published on Jan. 14, 2014, https://www.youtube.com/watch?v=8g8NpQsmxj4. Office of the Historian, "The Philippine-American War, 1899–1902," https://history.state.gov/milestones/1899-1913/war. Timothy Russ, "'I Feel Sorry For These People': African American Soldiers In The Philippine-American War, 1899–1902," *The Journal of African American History*, Summer 2014, Vol. 99(3), 197–22. Paul A. Kramer, "Race-Making and Colonial Violence in the U.S. Empire: The Philippine-American War as Race War," *Diplomatic History*, April 2006, Vol. 30(2), 169–210.

9 "Ambivalent Empire," American History: From Revolution to Reconstruction and Beyond, http://www.let.rug.nl/usa/outlines/history-2005/growth-and-transformation/ambivalent-empire.php.

10 A. T. Mahan, *The Influence of Sea Power upon History, 1660–1783* (Dover Publications; Revised ed. November 1, 1987). It was one of the most influential books of the time. Admiral Mahan argues the importance of sea power in national supremacy and stressed the interdependence of the military and commercial control of the sea.

11 M. Quesada, *Address of Cuba to the United States* (New York: Comes, Lawrence & Co., Stationers and Printers, 1873), 1–40. Library of Congress, http://memory.loc.gov/cgi-bin/query/r?ammem/murray:@field(DOCID+@lit(lcrbmrpt2502div2)).

12 Rodolfo F. Acuña, ed., Guadalupe Compeán, eds., *Voices of the U.S. Latino Experience* (Santa Barbara: ABC-CLIO E-Book, 2008), 275–306: documents surrounding the lead-up to the Spanish–American War.

13 "The World of 1898: The Spanish-American War," Hispanic Division of Library of Congress, http://www.loc.gov/rr/hispanic/1898/intro.html. Treaty of Paris, Text of the Treaty Ending the Spanish–American War, Home of Heroes, http://www.homeofheroes.com/wallofhonor/spanish_am/18_treaty.html.

14 Acuña and Compeán, eds., *Voices of U.S. Latino*, 307–336.

15 "The Age of Imperialism," An Online History of the United States, Small Planet Communications, http://www.smplanet.com/imperialism/toc.html.

16 Albert Beveridge, "The March of the Flag," Fordham University's Online Modern History Sourcebook, http://www.fordham.edu/halsall/mod/1898beveridge.html.

17 Rudyard Kipling, "The White Man's Burden," *McClure's Magazine* 12 (February 1899), available at http://www.fordham.edu/halsall/mod/Kipling.html.

18 U.S. Interventions in Latin America, http://www.zompist.com/latam.html.

19 Alan Greenblatt, "The End Of WASP-Dominated Politics," NPR, September 19, 2012, https://www.npr.org/sections/itsallpolitics/2012/09/17/161295588/the-end-of-wasp-dominated-politics.

20 "The Open Door policy and immigration to 1928," BBC, https://www.bbc.co.uk/education/guides/zkng87h/revision/1. Eric P. Kaufmann, *The Rise and Fall of Anglo-America* (Cambridge: Harvard University Press, 2004).

21 Leonard Tennenhouse, *The Importance of Feeling English: American Literature and the British* (Princeton University Press, 2009), 80.

22 Art McDonald, "How the Irish Became White," https://www.pitt.edu/~hirtle/uujec/white.html

23 Daniel Cox, Robert P. Jones, "America's Changing Religious Identity," PRRI, 2017, http://www.pewforum.org/religious-landscape-study/christians/christian/racial-and-ethnic-composition/.

24 Jaime Gilbert Jue, "Interregional trade and market integration: California and the transcontinental railroad, 1860–1900" (PhD Dissertation, University of California, Berkeley, 1999), 5. The railroad contributes to the integration of markets.

25. "US Immigration Trends 1880–1900," http://www.emmigration.info/us-immigration-trends-1880-1900.htm.
26. Samuel Bryan, "Mexican Americans and Southwestern Growth," *Digital History* ID 597, 1912, http://www.digitalhistory.uh.edu/disp_textbook.cfm?smtID=3&psid=597.
27. Teresa M. Van Hoy, "La Marcha Violenta? Railroads and Land in 19th-Century Mexico," *Bulletin of Latin American Research* Vol. 19, No. 1, (Jan., 2000), 32–33; the 1882 Mexican Land Act allowed the expropriation of public lands and permitted "the expropriation of buildings, materials and water as well as land for the construction of roads, canals, telegraphs, rechanneling of rivers, customs houses, dikes, lighthouses as well as railroads and other works of public lands." for public works. The purpose of the law was to force and facilitate railroad development. This was disastrous for Indigenous People such as the Yaqui. Also see John Coatsworth, "Indispensable Railroads in a Backward Economy: The Case of Mexico," *The Journal of Economic History* Vol. 39, Issue 4 (1979), 939–960.
28. Rodolfo F. Acuña, *Corridors of Migration: The Odyssey of Mexican Laborers, 1600–1933* (Tucson: University of Arizona, 2007).
29. George J. Sánchez, *Becoming Mexican American: Ethnicity, Culture, and Identity in Chicano Los Angeles, 1900–1945* (New York: Oxford University Press, 1993), 41. James D. Cockcroft, *Intellectual Precursors of the Mexican Revolution, 1900–1913* (Austin: University of Texas Press, 1968), 14. Charles C. Cumberland, *Mexico: The Struggle for Modernity* (New York: Oxford University Press, 1968), 216. James Cockcroft, *Mexico* (New York: Monthly Review Press, 1983), 81. Lawrence Anthony Cardoso, "Mexican Emigration to the United States, 1900–1930: An Analysis of Socio-Economic Causes" (PhD Dissertation, University of Connecticut, 1974), 23, 34–35, 43–59. John Mason Hart, *Empire and Revolution: The Americans in Mexico Since the Civil War* (Berkeley: University of California Press, 2002), 122.
30. Eric Wolf, *Sons of the Shaking Earth* (Chicago: University of Chicago Press, 1959), 247. Rodney D. Anderson, *Outcasts in Their Own Land: Mexican Workers, 1906–1911* (De Kalb: Northern Illinois Press, 1978), 38, 43. Hudson Stroude, *Timeless Mexico* (New York: Harcourt Brace Jovanovich, 1944), 210.
31. Love, Ibid., 11.
32. Ibid.
33. Emilio Zamora, *The World of the Mexican Worker in Texas* (College Station: Texas A&M University Press, 1993), 15–16, 19. George C. Kiser, "Mexican American Labor Before World War II," *Journal of Mexican American History* (Spring 1972), 123. Tomás Almaguer, *Racial Fault Lines: The Historical Origins of White Supremacy in California* (Berkeley: University of California Press, 1994), 29. Mario T. García, *Desert Immigrants: The Mexicans of El Paso, 1880–1920* (New Haven, CT: Yale University Press, 1981), 17–19.
34. Neil Foley, *The White Scourge: Mexicans, Blacks, and Poor Whites in Texas Cotton Culture* (Berkeley: University of California Press, 1997), 118–40. Matt S. Meier and Feliciano Rivera, *Dictionary of Mexican American History* (Westport, CT: Greenwood Press, 1981), 287. David G. Gutiérrez, *Walls and Mirrors: Mexican Americans, Mexican Immigrants, and the Politics of Ethnicity* (Berkeley: University of California Press, 1995), 44–48. Frank D. Bean and Marta Tienda, *The Hispanic Population of the United States* (New York: Russell Sage Foundation, 1988), 16–20.
35. John Higham, *Strangers in the Land: Patterns of American Nativism, 1860–1925* (New Brunswick, NJ: Rutgers University Press, 2002).
36. Luther E. Ellsworth, "Informe al Secretario de Estado, Fechado el 12 de Octubre de 1910 en Ciudad Porfirio Díaz, México," in Gene Z. Hanrahan, ed., *Documents on the Mexican Revolution* (Salisbury, NC: Documentary Publications, 1976); quoted in Clara Lomas, "Transborder Discourse: The Articulation of Gender in the Borderlands in the Early Twentieth Century," *Frontiers* 24, Nos. 2 & 3 (2003), 52.
37. Manuel Díaz Ramírez, *Apuntes Sobre El Movimiento Obrero Campesino de México* (México, DF: Ediciones de Cultura Popular, 1974), 66, 67–68, 70, 83. John Mason Hart, *Anarchism and the Mexican Working Class* (Austin: University of Texas Press, 1978), 32–41. Anderson, *Outcasts in Their Own Land*, 81. "Los obreros en México," 1875–1925, http://www.monografias.com/trabajos10/obre/obre.shtml.
38. Cockcroft, *Mexico*, 82.
39. Michael J. Gonzales, *The Mexican Revolution, 1910–1940* (Albuquerque: University of New Mexico Press, 2002), 5–26. David W. Walker, "Porfirian Labor Politics: Working Class Organizations in Mexico City and Porfirio Díaz, 1876–1902," *The Americas* 37, No. 3 (January 1981), 257–89.
40. Luis Aboites Aguilar, *Breve Historia de Chihuahua* (Mexico, DF: Fondo de Cultura Economica, 1994), 117. Francisco R. Almada, *Resumén de historia del estado de Chihuahua* (Mexico City: Libros Mexicanos, 1955), 330. "Huelga de Pinos Altos, 1883," 1–11, in Manuel González Ramírez, AGN v. 4. Anderson, *Outcasts in Their Own Land*, 87–88. Francisco R. Almada, *Diccionario de historia, geografía y biografía chihuahuenses*, 2d Edicion (Ciudad Juarez: Universidad de Chihuahua, 1968), 257. Acuña, *Corridors of Migration*. 40. "The Dramas of Haymarket," Chicago Historical Society, http://www.chicagohistory.org/dramas/.

41 Aboites Aguilar, *Breve Historia*, 117. Francisco R. Almada, *Resumén del estado de Chihuahua* (Mexico, DF: Libros Mexicanos, 1955), 330. Manuel Díaz Ramírez, *Apuntes Sobre El Movimiento Obrero Y Campesinos de México*, 66, 67–68, 70, 83. Douglas Kevin Bryson, "Chihuahua, the United States and the origins of a revolution," (PhD Dissertation, Houston: University of Houston, 2006), 112. By 1902 U.S. capital had invested half billion dollars in Mexican railroads.

42 "Garza, Catarino Erasmo (1859–1895)," The *Handbook of Texas Online*, http://www.tshaonline.org/handbook/online/articles/GG/fga38.html. Victor Ochoa, http://www.smithsonianeducation.org/scitech/impacto/graphic/victor/index.html. "Mexican Revolutionists Caught"; "Aguirre and Chapa Had Planned to Start a Paper Urging the People to Revolt Against Government," *New York Times* (March 12, 1896), 1, http://query.nytimes.com/mem/archive-free/pdf?res=9E01E5DC123EE333A25751C1A9659C94679ED7CF.

43 Juan Gómez-Quiñones, *Sembradores: Ricardo Flores Magón y el Partido Liberal Mexicano: A Eulogy and Critique* (Los Angeles, CA: Aztlán, 1973), 23. Cockcroft, *Intellectual Precursors*, 124. Zamora, *The World of the Mexican Worker*, 133–61. "Teresa Urrea Slide Show," http://vimeo.com/41589009. "Ricardo Flores Magón," http://flag.blackened.net/revolt/ws98/ws53_magon.html.

44 Cockcroft, *Intellectual Precursors*, 231. "Ricardo Flores Magón," History, http://dwardmac.pitzer.edu/Anarchist_Archives/bright/magon/history/index.html.

45 Julia Tuñón Pablos, *Women in Mexico: A Past Unveiled* (Austin: University of Texas Press, 1999), 80–81. Francesca Miller, *Latin American Women and the Search for Social Justice* (Lebanon, NH: University Press of New England, 1991), 71–72. Asunción Lavrin, *Latin American Women Historical Perspectives* (Westport, CT: Greenwood Press, 1978), 291–92. Marysa Navarro, Virginia Sánchez Korrol, and Kecia Ali, *Women in Latin America and the Caribbean: Restoring Women to History* (Indianapolis: University of Indiana, 1999), 87, 91. Mtra. Ma. de Lourdes Alvarado. (CESU-UNAM) Con la colaboración de Elizabeth Becerril Guzmán. "Mujeres y educación superior en el México del siglo XIX," http://biblioweb.tic.unam.mx/diccionario/htm/articulos/sec_10.htm.

46 "Sara Estela Ramírez," *Handbook of Texas Online*, http://www.tshaonline.org/handbook/online/articles/RR/fra60.html. "Juana Belén Gutiérrez de Méndoza," http://www.immortaltechnique.co.uk/Thread-Anarchists-Juana-Bel%C3%A9n-Guti%C3%A9rrez-de-Mendoza. Shirlene Soto, *Emergence of the Modern Mexican Woman: Her Participation in Revolution and Struggle for Equality, 1910–1940* (Denver, CO: Arden Press, 1990), 11–12, 15, 21–23. Emma M. Pérez, "'A La Mujer': A Critique of the Partido Liberal Mexicano's Gender Ideology on Women," in Adelaida R. Del Castillo, ed., *Between Borders: Essays on Mexicana/Chicana History* (Los Angeles, CA: Floricanto Press, 1990), 459–82, 459, 461. Gómez-Quiñones, *Sembradores*, 46. *Regeneración* (January 14, 1911). Emilio Zamora, "Chicano Socialist Labor Activity in Texas, 1900–1920," *Aztlán* 6, No. 2 (Summer 1975), 235. Lucy Eldine Gonzales from Johnson County, Texas, was married to Albert Parsons, who was executed by the state of Illinois as an alleged conspirator in the Haymarket Riot of 1886. Gonzales, an avowed anarchist, published newspapers, pamphlets, and books; traveled and lectured extensively; and led many demonstrations for worker equality. In the 1870s Gonzales was a charter member of the Chicago Working Women's Union, and in 1905 she was among the founding members of the Industrial Workers of the World (IWW). Carolyn Asbaugh, *Lucy Parsons: American Revolutionary* (Chicago: Herr, 1976), 267–68.

47 Lomas, "Transborder Discourse," 54. Daniel Levy and Gabriel Székely, *México: Paradoxes of Stability and Change* (Boulder, CO: Westview Press, 1987), 26–27. Tereza Jandura, "Revolutionary Mexican Women," University of Arizona, http://www.ic.arizona.edu/ic/mcbride/ws200/mex-jand.htm. Elena Poniatowska and David Dorado Romo, *Las Soldaderas: Women of the Mexican Revolution* (El Paso, TX: Cinco Puntos Press, 2006).

48 Richard A. Bideaux and Terry C. Wallace, "Arizona Copper," *Rocks & Minerals* 72 (January/February 1997), 10–26. A dispute exists as to whether copper or gold was the first metal used by man. Copper has played an important role in human society for at least 7,500 years. Charles S. Sargent, "Copper Star of the Arizona Urban Firmament," in Carlos A. Schwantes, ed., *Bisbee: Urban Outpost on the Frontier* (Tucson: University of Arizona Press, 1992), 30–31. By 1880, copper was mined by Globe, which brought stress to the San Carlos Reservation. Clifton and Morenci had been removed from the reservation jurisdiction earlier. George H. Hildebrand and Garth L. Mangum, *Capital and Labor in American Copper, 1845–1990: Linkages Between Product and Labor Markets* (Cambridge, MA: Harvard University Press, 1991), 1, 30, 43, 50. In 1906, open-pit mining was pioneered at Bingham Canyon in Utah. Carlos A. Schwantes, "Introduction," in Schwantes, ed., *Bisbee*, 21.

49 Joseph F. Park, "The 1903 'Mexican Affair' at Clifton," *Journal of Arizona History* 18 (Summer 1977), 119–48, http://www.library.arizona.edu/exhibits/

bisbee/docs/jahpark.html. "Mining," http://www.asu.edu/lib/archives/website/mining.htm.
50 Acuña, *Corridors of Migration*, 112–18. Jay J. Wagoner, *Arizona Territory 1863–1912: A Political History* (Tucson: University of Arizona Press, 1970), 386. *Bisbee Daily Review* (June 5, 1903), quoted in Park, "Mexican Affair," 257. "Ghosts of the Yuma Territorial Prison," Ghosts of the Prairie, History & Hauntings of America, Haunted Arizona, http://www.prairieghosts.com/yuma.html. Yuma Territorial Prison Cemetery, Yuma, Yuma County, Arizona, http://www.interment.net/data/us/az/yuma/prison/prison.htm.
51 Acuña, *Corridors of Migration*, 116.
52 James H. McClintock, *Arizona: The Youngest State*, Vol. 2 (Chicago: Clarke, 1916), 424. Park, "Mexican Affair," 258. Philip J. Mellinger, *Race and Labor in Western Copper: The Fight for Equality, 1896–1918* (Tucson: University of Arizona Press, 1995), 55. Acuña, *Corridors of Migration*, 130–33.
53 Carl Wittke, *We Built America*, rev. ed. (Cleveland, OH: Case Western Reserve University, 1967), 466. Kaye Lyon Briegel, "Alianza Hispano-Americana, 1894–1965: A Mexican Fraternal Insurance Society" (PhD Dissertation, University of Southern California, 1974), 12–15. Victor S. Clark, *Mexican Labor in the United States*, U.S. Department of Commerce Bulletin No. 78 (Washington, D.C.: Government Printing Office, 1908), 485, 492–93. Kiser, "Mexican American Labor," 125, 492–93. Zamora, "Chicano Socialist Labor," 221. Manuel G. Gonzales, *Mexicanos: A History of Mexicans in the United States* (Indianapolis: University of Indiana Press, 1999), 151. "Sociedades Mutualistas," Handbook of Texas Online, http://www.tshaonline.org/handbook/online/articles/SS/ves1.html.
54 Hart, *Anarchism*, 32–41. Anderson, *Outcasts*, 8, 88, 92. Cockcroft, *Intellectual Precursors*, 82. Juan Gómez-Quiñones, "The First Steps: Chicano Labor Conflict and Organizing, 1900–1920," *Aztlán* 3, No. 1 (1973), 18, 20. Charles C. Cumberland, *Mexican Revolution: Genesis Under Madero* (Austin: University of Texas Press, 1952), 16. Laureano Clavo Berber, *Nociones de Historia de Sonora* (México, DF: Publicaciones del Gobierno del Estado de Sonora, 1958), 277. Antonio G. Rivera, *La Revolución en Sonora* (México, DF: n.p., 1969), 139, 159. "Cananea: A Century of Internationalist Class Struggle," *The Internationalist*, http://www.internationalist.org/cananeastrike1906.html. Samuel Truett, *Fugitive Landscapes: The Forgotten History of the U.S.-Mexico Borderlands* (New Haven, CT: Yale University Press, 2006), 157. Acuña, *Corridors of Migration*, 124–32.
55 An interesting recent article is Robert McKee Irwin, "Santa Teresa de Cabora (and Her Villainous Sister Jovita): A Shape-Shifting Icon of Mexico's Northwest Borderlands," *Bilingual Review*, 2008, Vol. 29, Issue 2/3, 89–100.
56 Acuña, *Corridors of Migration*, 109, 112, 137. The the Urreas family as well as Abraham Salcido and others can be traced through the 1900 and 1910 Censuses; see www.ancestry.com. D. Martín & Ebooks Corporation, 2013, *Borderlands saints: Secular sanctity in Chicano/a and Mexican culture* (Latinidad). Ward S. Albro, P. Guerrero, Paul Avrich Collection, & Guerrero, G. Práxedis, *To die on your feet: The life, times, and writings of Práxedis G. Guerrero* (Fort Worth: Texas Christian University Press, 1996). Rey Devis, "Práxedis Guerrero: Early revolutionary; revolution is beautiful" (Mexico, 1985) *Monthly Review*, 37, 41.
57 Linda Gordon, *The Great Arizona Orphan Abduction* (Cambridge, MA: Harvard University Press, 1999), 1–2.
58 Gordon, *The Great Arizona Orphan Abduction*, 37–43, 118, 119–20, 154, 200–205. *New York Foundling Hospital v. William Norton*, in the Custody of John C. Gatti, Respondent Criminal No. 209, Supreme Court of Arizona, 9 Ariz. 105 (1905); 1905 Ariz. LEXIS 83, January 21, 1905, Filed. *New York Foundling Hospital v. Gatti*. No. 21. Supreme Court of the United States. 203 U.S. 429, 27 S. Ct. 53, 51 L. Ed. 254 (1906); 1906 U.S. LEXIS 1906. Argued April 26, 1906. Decided December 3, 1906. Acuña, *Corridors of Migration*, 119–24. As with other parts of *Corridors*, I traced the orphans through the *New York Times* and *Los Angeles Times*; this established a template. The censuses were also invaluable. Margaret Regan, "The Irish Orphan Abduction: A Tale of Race, Religion and Lawlessness in Turn-of-the-Century Southern Arizona," *Tucson Weekly* (March 15, 2007), http://www.tucsonweekly.com/tucson/the-irish-orphan-abduction/Content?oid=1087070.
59 Clark, *Mexican Labor in the United States*.
60 Clark, *Mexican Labor in the United States*. Paul S. Taylor, *An American-Mexican Frontier: Nueces County, Texas* (New York: Russell and Russell, 1971), 173. Larry García y Griego, "*Los Primeros Pasos al Norte*: Mexican Migration to the United States" (Bachelor's Thesis, Princeton University, 1973). Jorge A. Bustamante, "Mexican Immigration and the Social Relations of Capitalism" (PhD Dissertation, University of Notre Dame, Indiana, 1975), 50. Cardoso, "Mexican Emigration," 60.
61 Robert N. McLean and Charles A. Thomson, *Spanish and Mexicans in Colorado: A Survey of the Spanish Americans and Mexican in the State of Colorado* (New York: Board of National Missions of the Presbyterian Church in the U.S.A., 1924), 34. Dennis Nodín Valdés, *Mexicans in Minnesota* (Minneapolis:

Minnesota Historical Society Press, 2005), 1–5. Beet Sugar Industry, Local History Archive, Fort Collins Colorado, http://library.ci.fort-collins.co.us/local_history/topics/Ethnic/mex-beet.htm, http://history.fcgov.com/cdm4/item_viewer.php?CISOROOT=/wp2&CISOPTR=72&CISOBOX=1&REC=1.

62 David Montejano, *Anglos and Mexicans in the Making of Texas, 1836–1986* (Austin: University of Texas Press, 1987), 104, 109–10. Camilo Amado Martinez Jr, "The Mexican and Mexican-American laborers in the lower Rio Grande Valley of Texas, 1870–1930," (PhD Dissertation, Texas A&M University, 1987), 31; sugar was also grown in the valley.

63 Zamora, *The World of the Mexican Worker*, 12. Taylor, *An American-Mexican Frontier*, 85–89, 131. Montejano, *Anglos and Mexicans*, 20, 24, 31. Douglas E. Foley, Clarice Mora, Donald E. Post, and Ignacio Lozano, *From Peones to Politicos: Ethnic Relations in a South Texas Town, 1900–1977* (Austin: University of Texas Press, Center for Mexican American Studies, 1977), 6–7, 70–71, 85.

64 Almaguer, *Racial Fault Lines*, 90–104. Gilbert G. González, *Labor and Community: Mexican Citrus Worker Villages in a Southern California County, 1900–1950* (Urbana: University of Illinois Press, 1994), 20. Mark Reisler, "Passing Through Our Egypt: Mexican Labor in the United States, 1900–1940" (PhD Dissertation, Cornell University, 1974), 8–9, 13, 15.

65 Clark, *Mexican Labor in the United States*, 494, 507, 511. Sánchez, *Becoming Mexican American*, 71.

66 García, *Desert Immigrants*, 107. Acuña, *Corridors of Migration*, 176. D. Berman, *Radicalism in the mountain West, 1890–1920: Socialists, populists, miners, and Wobblies* (Boulder: University Press of Colorado, 2007). P. Mellinger, *Race and labor in western copper: The fight for equality, 1896–1918* (Tucson: University of Arizona Press, 1995).

67 Street, Richard Steven, "The 1903 Oxnard sugar beet strike: a new ending," *Labor History*, May, 1998, Vol. 39(2), 193(7).

68 Quoted in Almaguer, *Racial Fault Lines*, 202. Louie Moreno, "Labor, migration, and activism: A history of Mexican workers on the Oxnard Plain 1930–1980" (PhD Dissertation, Michigan State University, 2012).

69 "Oxnard, California Japantowns," http://www.californiajapantowns.org/oxnard.html. Gómez-Quiñones, "The First Steps," 26. Sam Kushner, *Long Road to Delano* (New York: International Publishers, 1975), 20. Almaguer, *Racial Fault Lines*, 200. Alberto M. Camarillo, "Chicano Urban History: A Study of Compton's Barrio, 1936–1970," *Aztlán* 2, No. 2 (Fall 1971), 79–106. Also see Alberto Camarillo, *Chicano in a Changing Society: From Mexican Pueblos to American Barrios in Santa Barbara and Southern California, 1848–1930* (Cambridge: Harvard University Press, 1979). "'A Foretaste of the Orient': John Murray Criticizes the AFL," http://historymatters.gmu.edu/d/5564/. "A History of Mexican Americans in California: Historic Sites," National Park Service, http://www.nps.gov/history/history/online_books/5views/5views5h21.htm.

70 Quoted in William B. Friedricks, *Henry E. Huntington and the Creation of Southern California*, E-book Format (Columbus: Ohio State University Press, 1992), 140, http://www.ohiostatepress.org/Books/Complete%20PDFs/Friedricks%20Henry/Friedricks%20Henry.htm. Charles Wollenberg, "Working on El Traque," in Norris Hundley Jr., ed., *The Chicano* (Santa Barbara, CA: Clio Books, 1975), 96–98, 102–05. Louis B. Perry and Richard S. Perry, *A History of the Los Angeles Labor Movement, 1911–1941* (Los Angeles: University of California Press, 1963), 71. "Picture Gallery of Los Angeles History," http://www.lanopalera.net/LAHistory/LAHistoryGally.html.

71 B. A. Hodges, *A History of the Mexican Mission Work* (1931), reprinted in Carlos E. Cortés, ed., *Church Views of the Mexican American* (New York: Arno Press, 1974), 5–7. Arnoldo De León, "Blowout 1910 Style: A Chicano School Boycott in West Texas," *Texana* 12, No. 2 (November 1974), 124, 129.

72 U.S. Congress, Report of the Immigration Commission, 61st Cong., 3d Sess. (1910–1911), I: 682–91 quoted in Job West Neal, "The Policy of the United States Toward Immigration from Mexico" (Master's Thesis, University of Texas at Austin, 1941), 58–59.

73 Ibid., U.S. Department of Labor, "Report of the Commissioner General of Immigration," *Report of the Department of Labor* (Washington, D.C.: Government Printing Office, 1913), 337.

74 Elizabeth Broadbent, "The Distribution of Mexican Population in the United States" (PhD Dissertation, University of Chicago, 1941), 3, 33. Clark, *Mexican Labor in the United States*, 471, 496.

75 Robert McCaa, "Missing Millions: The Human Cost of the Mexican Revolution," University of Minnesota Population Center (2001), http://www.hist.umn.edu/~rmccaa/missmill/index.htm. John Hardman, "Postcards of the Mexican Revolution," Mex Rev PC, http://www.netdotcom.com/revmexpc/default.htm. "Mexican Revolution Photos," Fotki, http://public.fotki.com/Mudhooks/my_stuff/illustrations/propaganda_posters/mexican_war_photos/. Diana Suet and Raquel Macias, "Borderlands: Soldaderas Played Important Roles in Revolution," El Paso

76 "Blancos, blancos," *Regeneración* (November 19, 1910). "Impundidad Para Los Linchadores," *Regeneración* (December 24, 1910). *Regeneración* (August 5, 1911). "La Víctima de los 'Civilizados'," *Regeneración* (August 26, 1911). Ricardo Flores Magón, "A Salvar a un Inocente," *Regeneración* (September 9, 1911). "En defensa de los Mexicanos," *Regeneración* (August 17, 1912). "Draws Lesson from Lynching," *Los Angeles Times* (November 16, 1910). *Graham Guardian* (November 18, 1910). "Americans Protests Against Insult," *Copper Era* (November 18, 1910). W. Dirk Raat, *Revoltosos: Mexico's Rebels in the United States, 1903–1923* (College Station: Texas A&M Press, 1981), 28. Florence C. Lister and Robert H. Lister, *Chihuahua: Storehouse of Storms* (Albuquerque: University of New Mexico Press, 1966), 212.

77 RFM, "La Barbarie En Los Estados Unidos," *Regeneración* (August 5, 1911). "La Víctima de los 'Civilizados'," *Regeneración* (August 26, 1911). Ricardo Flores Magón, "A Salvar a un Inocente," *Regeneración* (September 9, 1911). RFM, "Quemaron vivo a un hombre," *Regeneración* (December 9, 1911).

78 Acuña, *Corridors of Migration*, 142–54. Luther T. Ellsworth, American Consul, San Antonio, to Secretary of States (March 4, 1911), in Hanrahan, ed., *Documents on the Mexican Revolution*, Vol. I, pt 1, 203–208. Luther T. Ellsworth, Eagle Pass, Texas, to Secretary of States (December 23, 1910), in Hanrahan, ed., *Documents on the Mexican Revolution*, Vol. I, pt 1, 100. Ellsworth to Secretary of States (February 18, 1911) in *Hanrahan Documents on the Mexican Revolution*, Vol. I, pt 1, 165. Linda B. Hall and Don M. Coerver, *Revolution on the Border: The United States and Mexico, 1910–1920* (Albuquerque: University of New Mexico Press, 1988), 16–27. "Sonora Mines Again Active," *Copper Era* (January 13, 1910).

79 Aboites Aguilar, *Breve Historia*, 121. D. W. Meinig, *The Shaping of America: A Geographical Perspective on 500 Years of History* (New Haven, CT: Yale University Press, 2000), 153–55. See map on page 154.

80 Michael C. Meyer, *Mexican Rebel: Pascual Orozco and the Mexican Revolution, 1910–1915* (Lincoln: University of Nebraska Press, 1967), 9, 19. Mark Wasserman, *Capitalists, Caciques, and Revolution: Native Elite and Foreign Enterprise in Chihuahua, Mexico, 1854–1911* (Chapel Hill: University of North Carolina Press, 1984), 144. Orozco Vazquez was one of the first Mexican revolutionary leaders who joined Francisco I. Madero in late 1910 to depose Porfirio Díaz. A schism broke out between Madero and Orozco. Michael C. Meyer, *Mexican Rebel: Pascual Orozco and the Mexican Revolution, 1910–1915* (Lincoln: University of Nebraska Press, 1967). "Orozco, Pascual, Jr.," Texas State Historical Association, https://tshaonline.org/handbook/online/articles/for08.

81 Ricardo Romo, "Responses to Mexican Immigration, 1910–1930," *Aztlán* 6, No. 2 (Summer 1975), 109, 116, 117–18, 122. United States Historical Census Data Browser, http://fisher.lib.virginia.edu/census (accessed October 22, 2009). John S. D. Eisenhower, *Intervention! The United States and the Mexican Revolution: 1913–1917* (Baltimore, MD: Johns Hopkins University Press 1995), 103, 105, 231. Hall and Coerver, *Revolution on the Border*, 57–77. *Regeneración* (February 4 and 18, 1911).

82 Ricardo Romo, *East Los Angeles: A History of a Barrio* (Austin: University of Texas, 1983), 103, 108. U.S. Department of Labor, "Report of the Commissioner General of Immigration," 397.

83 "The Presidential Succession of 1910: The National Democratic Party," Library of Congress, https://www.wdl.org/en/item/7785/.

84 James Presley, "Mexican Views on Rural Education, 1900–1910," *The Americas*, Vol. 20, No. 1 (Jul., 1963), 64.

85 Travis Evens, "The Porfiriato: The stability and growth Mexico needed," SURG, Vol. 5, No. 2 (2012), https://journal.lib.uoguelph.ca/index.php/surg/article/view/1776/2415. John M. Hart, *Revolutionary Mexico: The Coming and Process of the Mexican Revolution* (Berkeley: University of California Press, 1987).

86 Ibid., p. 65.

87 Ibid., p. 66.

88 Ibid., p. 67.

89 "Liberal" did not have the same meaning then as it does today. Moreover, the definition changed during the nineteenth century. What it meant then was political and economic liberty and the secularization of society. Although the secularization was at first aimed at the Church, the definition widened to include communal property. Its primary objective was to make Mexico a capitalist nation and open public resources to the private sector.

90 Ibid., p. 67. "Programa y manifiesto del partido liberal mexicano," from Ricardo y Jesús Flores Magon, BatallPr a 14 dictadura (Mexico, 1948), 127.

91 Ward S, Albro, *To Die on Your Feet: The Life, Times, and Writings of Práxedis G. Guerrero* (Texas Christian University Press Fort Worth, 1996).

92 Ibid., p. 122.

93 "Idar, Nicasio (1855–1914)," *Handbook of Texas Online*, https://tshaonline.org/handbook/online/articles/fid02.

94 Teresa Palomo Acosta, "Idar, Nicasio," Texas State Historical Association, https://tshaonline.org/handbook/online/articles/fid02.

95 "Jovita Idar, Journalist and Activist, 1885–1946," University of Texas Austin, http://www.utexas.edu/gtw/idar.php (accessed October 22, 2009). Zamora, *The World of the Mexican Worker*, 61–65, 98. Vicki Ruiz, *From Out of the Shadows: Mexican Women in Twentieth Century America* (New York: Oxford University Press, 1998), 99. José E. Limón, "El Primer Congreso Mexicanista de 1911: A Precursor to Contemporary Chicanismo," *Aztlán* 5, No. 1–2 (Spring and Fall 1974), 80, 88, 89. "Teresa Palomo Acosta, El Primer Congreso Mexicanista," *Handbook of Texas Online*, http://www.tshaonline.org/handbook/online/articles/CC/vecyk.html. Benjamin Heber Johnson, *Revolution in Texas: How a Forgotten Rebellion and Its Bloody Suppression Turned Mexicans into Americans* (New Haven, CT: Yale University Press, 2005), 52–53, 85–88.

96 F. Arturo Rosales, *Dictionary of Latino Civil Rights History* (Houston, TX: Arte Publico Press, 2007), 4. "Sociedades Mutualistas," *Handbook of Texas Online*, http://www.tshaonline.org/handbook/online/articles/SS/ves1.html.

97 Thomas E. Sheridan, *Tucsonense: The Mexican Community in Tucson 1854-1941* (Tucson: University of Arizona, 1986), 179.

98 Carlos G. Vélez-Ibañez, *Border Visions: Mexican Cultures of the Southwest United States* (Tucson: University of Arizona, 1996), 69.

99 James D. McBride, "The *Liga Protectora Latina*: A Mexican American Benevolent Society in Arizona," *Journal of the West* 14, No. 4 (October 1975), 83, 85–87. "Organizations ~ Organizaciones," Arizona State University Library, http://www.asu.edu/lib/archives/website/organiza.htm. Eric V. Meeks, *Border Citizens: The Making of Indians, Mexicans, and Anglos in Arizona* (Austin: University of Texas, 2007), 93–96.

100 Leo Grebler, Joan W. Moore, and Ralph C. Guzmán, *The Mexican-American People: The Nation's Second Largest Minority* (New York: Free Press, 1970), 84. Zamora, *The World of the Mexican Worker*, 21. New Mexico and Arizona had the largest concentration of foreign-born, with many working in the mines.

101 Montejano, *Anglos and Mexicans*, 131–33, 143–46, 162. Zamora, *The World of the Mexican Worker*, 40.

102 Don Mitchell, *The Lie of the Land: Migrant Workers and the California Landscape* (Minneapolis: University of Minnesota Press, 1996), 40. Philip Taft, *Labor Politics American Style: California Federation of Labor* (Cambridge: Harvard University, 1968), 38–39. "Labor—and a Whole Lot More: The Legacy of Wheatland," http://www.dickmeister.com/id113.html. "1913: Wheatland Hop Riot," libcom.org, http://libcom.org/history/1913-wheatland-hop-riot.

103 Samuel Yellen, *American Labor Struggles* (New York: Russell, 1936), 205–06. Walter Fink, *The Ludlow Massacre* (Denver, CO: Williamson-Haffner, printers, 1914) and George West, *Report on the Colorado Strike* (Washington, D.C.: U.S. Commission on Industrial Relations, 1915), reprinted in Leon Stein and Philip Taft, eds., *Massacre at Ludlow: Four Reports* (New York: Arno Press, 1971), 15–16, 31. Carey McWilliams, *Factories in Fields: The Story of Migratory Labor in California* (Santa Barbara, CA, and Salt Lake City, UT: Peregrine Publishers, 1971), 89. Stuart Jamieson, *Labor Unionism in American Agriculture* (New York: Arno Press, 1976), 236–39. Colorado Coalfield War Project, http://www.du.edu/ludlow/index.html. "The Ludlow Massacre," American Experience, PBS, http://www.pbs.org/wgbh/amex/rockefellers/sfeature/sf_8.html.

104 Acuña, *Corridors of Migration*, 177–78. "Western Miners Threaten to Tie Up Smelters," *Copper Era* (June 13, 1913). "Mining Men Have Meeting and Organize," *Copper Era* (March 19, 1914). Andrea Yvette Huginnie, "'strikitos': race, class, and work in the Arizona copper industry, 1870–1920" (PhD Dissertation, Yale University, 1991), 109, 172. Wilma Gray Sain, "A History of the Miami area, Arizona" (Master's Thesis, University of Arizona, Tucson, 1944), 134.

105 Rodolfo F. Acuña, *Corridors of Migration* (Tucson: University of Arizona Press, 2007), 178.

106 Acuña, *Corridors of Migration*, 179–83. James R. Kluger, *The Clifton-Morenci Strike; Labor Difficulty in Arizona, 1915–1916* (Tucson: University of Arizona Press, 1970), 26. "Eighty Per Cent Law Changes," *Copper Era* (July 31, 1914). "The Flag and Eighty Per Cent," *Copper Era* (September 4, 1914). "Eighty Per Cent Case Before Court," *Copper Era* (October 22, 1915). "80 Per Cent Law Invalid Says Court," *Copper Era* (November 5, 1915). "Conflict with Personal Liberties and Treaties," *Graham Guardian* (January 8, 1915). "80 Percent Law Declared Unconstitutional by Federal Tribunal in San Francisco," *The Miners Magazine* (November 6, 1913), 10. "The Convention of the Arizona States Federation of Labor" second annual convention at Bisbee on October 27 endorsed 80-percent-American goal. "Foreigners To Be Barred Out," *Los Angeles Times* (February 20, 1912). The Western Federation of Miners, http://www.law.umkc.edu/faculty/projects/ftrials/haywood/HAY_WFM.HTM.

107 "Guerra de razas en Arizona," *Regeneración* (August 22, 1914). "Race War in Arizona; Death List Is Sixteen," *Los Angeles Times* (August 20, 1914).

108 Michael E. Parrish, *Mexican Workers, Progressives and Copper: The Failure of Industrial Democracy in Arizona During the Wilson Years* (La Jolla, CA: Chicano Research Publication, 1979), 32. To follow the events that were happening in Sonora and Mexico, see Acuña, *Corridors of Migration*, 150–69.

109 Robert Kern, ed., *Labor in New Mexico: Unions, Strikes, and Social History Since 1881* (Albuquerque: University of New Mexico Press, 1983), 6–7. R. Romo, "Responses to Mexican Immigration," 186–87.

110 Ralph Guzmán, *The Political Socialization of the Mexican American People* (New York: Arno Press, 1976), 65–66. Acuña, *Corridors of Migration*, 199–209. "The Bisbee Deportation of 1917," The University of Arizona Web Exhibit, http://www.library.arizona.edu/exhibits/bisbee/. Report of the Bisbee Deportations, University of Arizona Web Exhibit, http://www.library.arizona.edu/exhibits/bisbee/primarysources/reports/president/index.php.

111 *Los Angeles Times* (January 31, 1917), I5. *Los Angeles Times* (January 29, 1917), I1. "Indignity on the Border," http://www.youtube.com/watch?v=3Nz-253RaQo. Community, "Indignity on the Border," http://forchicanachicanostudies.wikispaces.com/Community. David Dorado Romo, *Ringside Seat to a Revolution, An Underground Cultural History of El Paso and Juarez: 1893–1923* (El Paso, TX: Cinco Puntos Press, 2005), 223–27. "'Viva Villa' Shouted in Riots at Juarez," *The Los Angeles Times* (January 29, 1917). "Mexicans Given Baths," *Los Angeles Times* (January 31, 1917). The practice was continued until a "compromise" was reached in the late 1950s whereby Mexicans got the bath in Juárez, where they received a certificate. Allen Morrison, "The Tramways of Ciudad Juárez," http://www.tramz.com/mx/cj/cj.html.

112 Montejano, *Anglos and Mexicans*, 125. William M. Hager, "The Plan of San Diego: Unrest on the Texas Border in 1915," *Arizona and the West* 5, No. 4 (Winter 1963), 330–36. Walter Prescott Webb, *The Texas Rangers*, 2nd ed. (Austin: University of Texas Press, 1965), 478–79, 484–85. Juan Gómez-Quiñones, *Plan de San Diego Reviewed*, *Aztlán* 1, No. 1 (Spring 1970), 125–26. Charles C. Cumberland, "Border Raids in the Lower Rio Grande Valley—1915," *Southwestern Historical Quarterly* 57 (January 1954), 290–94. *Regeneración* (October 2, 1915). Don M. Coerver and Linda B. Hall, *Texas and the Mexican Revolution: A Study in State and National Policy, 1910–1920* (San Antonio, TX: Trinity University Press, 1984), 85–108. "Mexico Repudiates Plan Of San Diego . . . " *New York Times*, http://query.nytimes.com/gst/abstract.html?res=9C06E2D61F30E033A25750C1A9649D946896D6CF. "Plan of San Diego," *Handbook of Texas Online*, http://www.tshaonline.org/handbook/online/articles/PP/ngp4.html.

113 Johnson, *Revolution in Texas*, 79–85. Edwin Larry Dickens, "The Political Role of Mexican-Americans in San Antonio" (PhD Dissertation, Texas Tech University, 1969), 38. George Marvin, "The Quick and the Dead on the Border," *The World's Word* (January 1917), 295. Webb, *The Texas Rangers*, 474, 475, 478. The 1919 Ranger Investigation Reports, http://www.tsl.state.tx.us/treasures/law/index.html. Transcripts of the three-volume investigation can be downloaded.

114 Cardoso, "Mexican Emigration," 83–87. Neal, "The Policy," 81, 100. Mark Reisler, *By the Sweat of Their Brow: Mexican Immigrant Labor in the United States, 1900–1940* (Westport, CT: Greenwood Press, 1976), 38.

115 Ricardo Romo, "Mexican Workers in the City: Los Angeles, 1915–1930" (PhD Dissertation, University of California at Los Angeles, 1975), 56–57, 81–83, 104, 106–7, 109–11, 123. R. Romo, *East Los Angeles*, 76–78. Sánchez, *Becoming Mexican American*, 81. William David Estrada, *The Los Angeles Plaza Sacred and Contested Space* (Austin: University of Texas Press, 2008), 133–59.

116 Carole E. Christian, "Joining the American Mainstream: Texas's Mexican Americans During World War I," *Southwestern Historical Quarterly* 92, No. 4 (April 1, 1989), 559–95. A classic work on World War I and the Mexican American presence is J. Luz Sáenz, *Los méxico-americanos en la gran guerra y su contingente en pró de democracia, la humanidad y la justicia* (San Antonio, TX: Artes Gráficas, 1933). Lee Stacy, ed., *Mexico and the United States* (Tarrytown, NY: Marshall Cavendish, 2003), 409.

117 Johnson, *Revolution in Texas*, 60–62. J. Luz Sáenz (Author), Emilio Zamora (Editor), Ben Maya (Translator), *The World War I Diary of José de la Luz Sáenz* (College Station: Texas A&M University Press; annotated edition, 2014); excellent addition to historiography.

118 Elena Gómez, "Borderlands: Marcelino Serna Became World War I Hero," El Paso Community College, http://epcc.libguides.com/content.php?pid=309255&sid=2603468. "Congressional Medal of Honor Award Private Marcelino Serna U.S. Army WW I," League of United Latin American Citizens, http://www.lulac.net/advocacy/resolutions/2007/mil3.html. Julie Leininger Pryciorw, "*La Raza* organizes: Mexican American Life in San

Antonio, 1915–1930, As Reflected in *Mutualista* Activities" (PhD Dissertation, University of Notre Dame, 1979), 83, 97–98, 105.

119 Jeffrey M. Garcilazo, "Mexican Strike Activity in the Riverside and San Bernardino Areas, 1917," Paper presented at the Annual National Association for Chicano Studies Conference, West Sacramento, California, March 23, 1985.

120 Paul S. Taylor, *Mexican Labor in the United States*, Vol. 2 (New York: Anro Press, 1970), 114–17. R. Romo, "Responses to Mexican Immigration," 187–90.

121 McLean and Thomson, *Spanish and Mexicans in Colorado*, 29–30, 34. Ruben Donato, *Mexicans and Hispanos in Colorado Schools and Communities, 1920–1960* (Albany: State University of New York Press, 2007), 65–75.

122 Mario T. García, *Desert Immigrants: The Mexicans of El Paso, 1880–1920* (New Haven: Yale University Press, 1981), 91.

123 Teresa Palomo Acosta and Ruthe Winegarten, *Las Tejanas: 300 years of history* (Austin: University of Texas, 2003), 131–34. Mario T. García, "Racial Dualism in the El Paso Labor Market, 1880–1920," *Aztlán* 6, No. 2 (Summer 1975), 197–218. Mario T. García, "Obreros: The Mexican Workers of El Paso, 1900–1920" (PhD Dissertation, University of California at San Diego, 1975), 199, 201–5.

124 Irene Ledesma, "Texas Newspapers and Chicana Workers' Activism, 1919–1974," *The Western Historical Quarterly* 26, No. 3 (Fall 1995), 309–31.

125 "I.W.W. Activities in Arizona," *The Miners' Magazine*, newspaper format (March 1917). Pan-American *Labor Press* (November 13, 1918). Pan American Federation of Labor, Record Group 63, Records of the Committee on Public Information, Selected Items to the American Federation of Labor—GSA, National Archives and Records Service, Washington, 1959, *John Murray Collection*. Sinclair Snow, "Samuel Gompers and the Pan-American Federation of Labor" (PhD Dissertation, University of Virginia, 1960), 1–3, 162, 164–66. Charles Toth, "Bulwark for Freedom: Samuel Gompers' Pan American Federation of Labor," *Pan-American Labor Press/Obrero Pan-Americano* (Fall 1979), 460, 461. A letter from Antonio I. Villarreal, Pan American Labor Press/Obrero Pan-Americano, September 18, 1918. "Border Mexicans Treated Badly by Americans Safe," *Pan-American Labor Press* (San Antonio, October 2, 1918). "Latins Ask Gompers Why A.F.L. Harpoons Their Workers," *New York Call* (July 8, 1919). "Pan Am Feels Weight of Rule by Gompers, Re-elects Him," *New York Call* (July 10, 1919).

126 "Twenty-million-dollar Tire Factory Coming to Los Angeles Soon," *Los Angeles Times* (June 29, 1919).

127 Frederick Douglass, "The Color Line," *North American Review*, June 1, 1881, 567–577.

128 L. Hao, *Color Lines, Country Lines: Race, Immigration, and Wealth Stratification in America* (New York: Russell Sage Foundation, 2010). Nancy Foner, *From Ellis Island to JFK: New York's two great waves of immigration* (New op. cit., New York: Yale University Press, 2000).

129 Foner, Ibid, 3–4,

130 Foner, op. cit., 144. Madison Grant, *The Passing of the Great Race* (Charles Scribner Sons, 1916), 2, 6–12, 13, 33, 34.

CHAPTER 9
The 1920s: Making America Great

Learning Objectives

9.1 Explain how white supremacy was enforced in the United States in the 1920s and how it was similar to the caste system.

9.2 Discuss how Americanization was a method of social control.

9.3 Describe the ways that Mexican Americans distanced themselves from Mexicans.

9.4 Analyze regional issues associated with Mexican urbanization.

9.5 Characterize the social and economic life of Mexican workers in the 1920s.

9.6 Relate labor organization to the Mexican worker experience in the United States.

The Gilded Age was a period of expansionism, nationalism, gross materialism and blatant political corruption. Similar periods have followed every war since the Civil War. The oligarchy by Congress and local officials lead to laissez-faire and deregulation of corporations, widening the wealth gap between the workers and the oligarchs and setting up the nation for a great fall. Witness the Panics of 1873 and 1893. The aftermath of World War I (1914–1918) saw economic prosperity, strengthening of capital, and the ascendancy of the Republican Party. In reality, the prosperity was the result of advances in technology such as aviation, automobiles, telephones, motion pictures, radio, and electric appliances; fat government contracts also made their contribution.

Imperialism gave a new meaning to being white.[1] The euphoria of global Empire kindled nationalism and xenophobia and a belief that America would be number one—as long as it remained white.[2] America has never been fond of those they considered outsiders. In 1798, Congress passed the Alien and Sedition Acts directed at enemy aliens and radical ideas.[3] The year 1898 marked the end of the Spanish–American War and popularized the notion of an American Empire; the year 1910 witnessed the Mexican Revolution that challenged U.S. economic and political hegemony in Mexico; in October 1917 the Bolshevik rose to power giving further rise to white American xenophobia. Meanwhile, the Russian Revolution of 1917 drove many Americans over the edge to the point of irrationality as they linked Communism to the immigration of millions of Europeans to the United States. They feared losing control of "their" nation. Nativists proposed nationalism as a remedy to cure the "foreign disease."

The reality was that Mexicans were doing America a favor:

> The first U.S. government-approved recruitment of Mexican workers occurred in 1917, when the U.S. Department of Labor suspended the head tax and the literacy test on Mexican workers coming to the U.S. "for the purpose of accepting employment in agricultural pursuits." The 81,000 Mexican workers admitted legally between 1917 and 1921 were required to work for the employer with whom they had up to a one-year contract or face deportation. Mexican immigration rose sharply, from 17,900 in 1917 to over 52,000 in 1920, although the U.S. recession of 1921 led to the repatriation of an estimated 150,000 Mexicans.[4]

During the 1910 Revolution, Mexicans left rural areas in search of year-round employment; by the beginning of the 1920s over 40 percent lived in urban areas. By the end of the decade over 50 percent lived in these urban spaces, numbers close to that of the U.S. urban population at large, 56 percent of which lived in cities. The increased visibility of Mexicans set off racist nativism among white Americans. At the same time, differences based on generations, classes, birthplaces, and assimilation pattern emerged within the Mexican community; these differences influenced how Mexicans responded to the majority society.[5]

The shift of the Mexican-origin population to the city put them in harm's way making them targets for racist nativists. As in all postwar periods, American capital moved to grab more control of the nation's resources and its governance. Capital popularized the philosophy of laissez-faire and the myth that the markets always know best market place. Accordingly, government should not regulate or otherwise interfere with business. The outcome was that lawmakers slashed government regulation and antitrust enforcement.

Republican Party or economic policies were intertwined with the nationalism. In the early twentieth century, big businesses used the Red Scare to attack and destroy unions, and to brand members radicals. During the 1920s, they claimed that to criticize business was un-American, and that it promoted class warfare and restrained progress. To create a smokescreen for their greed, the oligarchs attacked immigrants, calling for total assimilation, intentionally creating social tensions that distracted white Americans from the reality of growing economic, political, and social inequality. Nativists and oligarchs were incredibly successful until everything tumbled down in 1929.

Greasers Go Home

9.1 Explain how white supremacy was enforced in the United States in the 1920s and how it was similar to the caste system.

In early 1921, the bottom fell out of the economy and a recession caused heavy unemployment. Sarah Deutsch estimates that some 150,000 Mexicans were repatriated during the crisis. Although as a matter of policy the Mexican government welcomed repatriates back, the sudden return of so many to the homeland caught the government off guard. The Mexican government simply could not afford the expense of the repatriation.[6] Mexico was offended by the affront to its citizens and the callousness with which deportations were carried out—it was an insult to the nation's revolutionary nationalism. Many Mexicans were literally cheated out of their wages and dumped across the border. *El Universal* of Mexico City on March 5, 1921, reported, "When they arrived at Phoenix a party of Mexican workers were taken to Tempe and introduced to a concentration camp that looks like a dung-heap." According to this source, the men were chained and put into work gangs. Similar abuses were exposed in Kansas City, Chicago, and Colorado.[7]

In Fort Worth, Texas, 90 percent of 12,000 Mexicans were unemployed; however, whites threatened to burn out the Mexicans and Mexicans' homes and rid the city of "cheap Mexican labor." Police authorities escorted truckloads of Mexicans to Texas chain gangs. In Ranger, Texas, terrorists dragged a 100 Mexican men, women, and children from their tents and makeshift homes, beat them, and ordered them to clear out of town. In Chicago, employment of Mexicans shrank by two-thirds between 1920 and 1921. Police made frequent raids and strictly enforced vagrancy laws in the Windy City. Chicago Mayor William Hall Thompson scapegoated Mexicans for the economic downturn allocated funds to ship several hundred Mexican families back to the border. A *Denver Post* headline claimed, "Denver Safety Is Menaced by 3,500 Starving Mexicans"; authorities shipped Mexican workers en masse from the Denver area to the border. Although U.S. corporations and farmers had recruited these workers to the United States in the first place, neither they nor the U.S. government did much to relieve their suffering. The Mexican government, in contrast, spent $2.5 million to aid stranded Mexicans.[8] Many workers would have starved to death had it not been for the financial assistance advanced by Mexican President Alvaro Obregón.

Keeping America WASP

From the beginning, Americans considered even Native Americans as intruders and agreed with John Wayne's statement: "I don't feel we did wrong in taking this great country away from [Indians]. Our so-called stealing of this country from them was just a matter of survival. There were great numbers of people who needed new land, and the Indians were selfishly trying to keep it for themselves."[9] Most Americans today share this sentiment and regard Texas and the Southwest as being white man's country.

White Americans were obsessed with keeping America white; by ensuring a Nordic look. After years of debate advocating racial purity, Congress passed the Emergency Quota Act of 1921, which limited immigrant groups to the number of immigrants entering from any country to 3 percent of the number of persons from that country counted in 1910 Census. The total number admitted under the 1921 Census quota was 357,802 people. Of that number, just over half was allocated to northern and western Europeans and the remainder were eastern and southern Europeans. The Immigration Act of 1924, known as the National Origins Act or the Johnson–Reed Act, limited the number of immigrants from any country to 2 percent of the total number of persons from that country living in the United States in 1890. The law further restricted southern and eastern Europeans, limiting their number to 164,000 annually. The Act excluded East Asians and Asian Indians entirely. President Calvin Coolidge, when signing the bill into law, said, "America must be kept American,"[10] (meaning America must be kept white) and the law ushered in generations of racial engineering. The quotas drastically reduced the flow of immigrants from southeastern Europe since they were a relatively small percentage of new arrivals in the United States in the late 1800s. However, because of political pressure from the western growers, the act set no limits on immigrants from Latin America. The bottom line was that Mexicans were necessary to the functioning of Southwest's economy.

The 1924 Act touched off a battle with the restrictionists, who wanted to keep the country WASP (White Anglo-Saxon Protestant). They felt that there were too many foreigners who would subvert the 'American way of life,' and capitalists, who set aside prejudices toward Mexicans because they needed cheap labor. Many growers recalled that the 1917 Act restricted the flow of Mexican immigrants, creating a severe labor shortage that hurt growers financially; thus, the western growers opposed any restrictions on the free flow of Mexicans into the United States. In 1923, the commissioner of immigration turned his attention more fully to Mexicans, writing, "It is difficult, in fact impossible, to measure the illegal influx of Mexicans crossing the border."[11] By 1923, the economy sufficiently recovered entice Mexican workers to the United States in large numbers again.

In 1924, Congress again debated putting Mexicans on the quota. Albert Johnson of Washington, chair of the House Immigration and Naturalization Committee and sponsor of the bill, bluntly stated that the committee did not restrict the Mexicans because it did not want to hinder the passage of the 1924 Immigration Act.[12] Johnson promised the committee would sponsor another bill to create a border patrol to enforce existing laws, and claimed that a quota alone would not be effective. Anti-restrictionists argued that enforcing such a quota would be difficult, that Mexicans stayed only temporarily anyway, that they did the work white men would not, and that an economic burden would result. In order to compensate, border officials strictly applied the $8 head tax, plus the $10 visa fee. However, Mexicans continued to enter the States with and without documents. Meanwhile, Johnson's committee began hearings on the "Mexican problem."

In 1926, the commissioner wrote that 855,898 Mexicans entered with documents and predicted, "It is safe to say that over a million Mexicans are in the United States at the present time [including undocumented], and under present laws this number may be added to practically without limit."[13] U.S. Representative John Calvin Box (Democrat–Texas) introduced a bill that would apply quota provisions to the whole of the Western Hemisphere. Rep. Robert L. Bacon of New York sought to limit the extension of the quota system only to Mexico. Western representatives opposed any attempt to restrict Mexicans. S. Parker Frieselle of California stated that while he did not want Mexicans to become part of the race stock of California, Mexican labor was necessary, and for him there was simply no other alternative available.[14]

Meanwhile, Secretary of Labor James J. Davis demanded a quota for the Western Hemisphere. Secretary Davis arranged meetings with Samuel Gompers, head of the AFL, to plan a strategy to remove this "menace." Representative Martin Madden of Chicago, chairman of the House Appropriations Committee, stated,

> The bill opens the doors for perhaps the worst element that comes into the United States—the Mexican peon. . . . [It] opens the door wide and unrestricted to the most undesirable people who come under the flag.[15]

In the U.S. Senate, Frank B. Willis of Ohio echoed white nationalist sentiment: "Many of [them] . . . now coming in are, unfortunately, practically without education, and largely without experience in self-government, and in most cases not at all qualified for present citizenship or for assimilation into this country." Senator Matthew M. Neeley of West Virginia bellowed, "On the basis of merit, Mexico is the last country we should grant a special favor or extend a peculiar privilege. . . . The immigrants from many of the countries of Europe have more in common with us than the Mexicanos have."[16] On the other hand, Representative John Nance Garner of Texas emphasized that Mexicans did not pose a problem because they returned home after every picking season:

> All they want is a month's labor in the United States, and that is enough to support them in Mexico for six months. . . . In our country they do not cause any trouble, unless they stay there a long time and become Americanized; but they are a docile people. They can be imposed on; the sheriff can go out and make them do anything.[17]

Democrat Calvin Box accused opponents of his bill of attempting to attract "floating Mexican *peons*" in order to exploit them, claiming, "They are objectionable as citizens and as residents."[18] During committee hearings, Box asked a farmer whether what he really wanted was a subservient class of Mexican workers "who do not want to own land, who can be directed by men in the upper stratum of society." The farmer answered, "I believe that is about it." Box then asked, "Now, do you believe that is good Americanism?" The farmer replied, "I think it is necessary Americanism to preserve Americanism."[19] The quota act had drastically reduced the available labor pool, and agricultural and industrial interests committed themselves to keeping the Mexican border unrestricted.

In 1928, a clear split occurred between the Department of Labor that favored putting Mexicans on a quota system, and the Department of State that opposed it. The State Department knew that the quota system would seriously weaken its negotiations with Latin America and endanger trade treaties and privileges that furthered U.S. interests. Latin Americans were sensitive to American racism. The State Department joined Southwestern industrialists to kill restrictionist proposals. However, many congressmen were not satisfied and pushed for quantitative restrictions. American labor supported the restrictionists, asking, "Do you want a mongrel population, consisting largely of Mexicans?"[20]

In sum, the intent of the 1921 and 1924 Acts was to keep America white. The primary targets were Italians. "After 1924, for example, arrivals from Germany had an annual quota of over 51,000 and those from Great Britain just over 34,000, while Italy had a quota of less than 4,000, and nations such as Greece, Turkey, and Syria had the minimum of 100 annual 'legal' arrivals."[21] From the passage of the National Origins Act to the present, Mexicans replaced Italians as the favorite scapegoats of white nationalists.

Americanization: A Study of Extremes

9.2 Discuss how Americanization was a method of social control.

Between 1900 and 1910, almost 1 million immigrants entered the United States annually. The new immigrants differed from the earlier immigrant arrivals from the British Isles and Northern Europe, who dominated immigration and maintained a steady flow before and through the Civil War (1861–1865). Most of the newcomers were southern and central Europeans who were physically and culturally different. The older WASP population considered themselves the "real Americans," and panicked and initiated a campaign based on fear to put a brake on immigration. Simultaneously, the xenophobes set out to Americanize those who were already in the country. In the Southwest, the post–World War I era ushered in intense campaigns to "Americanize" Mexican families. Americans established English-only schools and set out to alter the family life patterns and dietary and health habits of the Mexican community.[22] It was a program to annihilate the Mexican identity.

As early as 1892, in towns such as Corpus Christi, Texas Mexican children (i.e., all children of Mexican descent) were denied admittance to white schools. In 1919, the Santa Ana, California, school district solicited an opinion from the state attorney general on whether segregating Mexicans to meet their "special needs" was permissible. The growing xenophobia of the 1920s saw many public school districts require that the students recite the Pledge of Allegiance to the flag. The words "my flag" were replaced with "the flag of the United States," to prevent immigrants and others from swearing allegiance to a foreign flag while facing the American flag. The American Legion and the Daughters of the American Revolution pushed the new wording at the first National Flag Conference in Washington, D.C., on June 14, 1923.[23] Americanization programs encouraged the de facto segregation of Mexican children. The reasoning was that Mexicans were "dirty, shiftless, lazy, irresponsible, unambitious, thriftless, fatalistic, selfish, promiscuous, and prone to drinking, violence, and criminal behavior" (as originally written) the nativists saw it as their mission to eliminate these evils by indoctrinating Mexican children, making sure that they had an appreciation of the institutions of this country. The continuing popularity and use of Spanish language was considered a "very real educational barrier" to the Americanization of children.[24] The Los Angeles City schools offered adult sessions in evening school and at industrial work sites, day classes for mothers, and naturalization classes.[25]

From 1915 to 1929, the home teacher—usually a single, middle-class, WASP woman—was the medium of Americanization efforts aimed at the Mexican family—Teach Mexican women to speak English; learn the "American way." When women did not respond, they blamed it on the patriarchal Mexican family. Religious missions and grower exchanges (or associations) also promoted campaigns to Americanize workers.

IQ testing played a major role in justifying programs that trained Mexicans for subordinate roles in American society. The IQ test was the reason alleged by American educators for not educating Mexicans; the test proved to them that intellectual performance was biologically determined and that Mexicans were not capable of learning. Thus, why waste tax money in trying to educate them? Mexican American educators such as Dr. George I. Sánchez, then a young graduate student, countered this pseudoscience by emphasizing that environmental factors were extremely influential in determining test results. Sánchez exploded the myth popularized by U.S. social scientists that the reason Mexicans were not assimilating quickly was a lack of intelligence. The standardized tests were in English and dealt with things strangely "Anglo" to Mexicans. Throughout his life, Sánchez battled against standardized tests, segregation based on not being proficient in English, and other forms of racism. It did not dawn on them to give white students IQ tests in Spanish.[26]

Based on racial stereotypes, school boards funneled Mexican students into vocational education programs. School districts rationalized that intellectually weaker students should be removed from the "normal" student population and tracked separately. Hence, a high percentage of Mexican students ended up in classes for slow learners or the mentally retarded as racist school boards abused these programs.[27]

Before the 1920s, Mexican children were not usually segregated. However, segregation became widespread during the 1920s, aided by the "No Spanish Rule"—the rule prohibiting Mexican children from speaking Spanish in school. By the end of the decade, about half of Mexican students attended segregated schools. In Texas, the number of special Mexican school districts doubled from 20 in 1922 to 40 in 1932. School authorities required Mexicans to attend Mexican schools, while not restricting white children by neighborhood or even by county.[28]

The heavy influx of Mexican children continued, and strategies to isolate them became more popular. By 1928, Mexicans comprised 13 percent of the Texas school population (African Americans made up 16.8 percent). In 1920, 11,000 Mexican students attended San Antonio elementary schools, with only 250 enrolled in high school.

In 1928, in the entire state of Texas, only 250 Mexicans attended college. The excuse that Mexican Americans were slow learners was refuted by the fact that in 1925, Mexican students in San Antonio scored 70 percent higher on IQ tests administered in Spanish than in tests given in English. Meanwhile, the district profited from Mexican schools because it spent less on educating Mexican students. It did not care if Mexicans dropped out of school because it could then spend more on the education of white students. One of the first successful legal challenges was brought in Tempe, Arizona, an eastern suburb of Phoenix, in 1925; a Mexican American rancher named Adolpho "Babe" Romo Sr. successfully sued the Tempe Elementary School District for denying admission to his four children in the newly opened Tenth Street School. Because the suit was not a class action suit, the impact was limited, and only Romo's children were admitted to the white school.[29]

Protestant Churches and Americanization of the Mexican

The Catholic Church often interpreted Americanization as being synonymous with Protestantism and resisted the Americanization programs because Church leaders saw Mexicans as exclusively Catholic—though, generally, as unequal members. While most Protestant churches considered Mexicans primitive, there were exceptions. For instance, some Protestant churches recruited Spanish-speaking ministers, many of whom were Latinos and Mexicans, a tradition that dated back to the Protestant missionary work in the nineteenth century in Mexico.[30] One of the most popular methods of converting Mexicans was through youth programs such as the Young Men's Christian Association (YMCA) that conducted surveys and published valuable studies on Mexican American communities.

The Rev. Robert N. McLean, an associate director of the Presbyterian Board of Missions in the United States, was from a family of ministers. The U.S. Presbyterian Church was heavily invested in missionary work worldwide, especially in countries such as China, Ireland, Puerto Rico, and Mexico. Mexicans in the United States were seen as an extension of those in Mexico, where many Mexican ministers were trained and schools established. McLean belonged to the more progressive arm of the Presbyterian Church that often advocated for the material well-being of Mexicans; church people like McLean were among the few pro-immigrant voices of the period.[31]

The work of the Protestant churches cannot be overstated. There were 60 Mexican Protestant churches in Texas as well as a network in Mexico. The Methodist Episcopal Church denomination established the Frances Pauw Industrial School for Girls in Los Angeles, the Harwood Industrial School for Girls in Albuquerque, another school for girls in Tucson, and a settlement house in El Paso. The jewel in the crown was the Spanish American Institute located in Gardena, California, which was a boarding house and school for boys. The Institute, opened in 1913, was shut down in 1971 due to a lack of funds and stricter immigration laws. It focused on vocational education, and, according to McLean, these boys were the bridge between the churches in Latin America, Mexico, and the United States since some students were recruited from families in Mexico. Many of the leaders of the Mexican American movements in the 1930s and 1940s were educated at this school.[32]

Catholic Churches React to Americanization

The response of the Catholic Church depended on what proportion of a diocese was Mexican, and its response in San Antonio where the parishioners were overwhelmingly Mexican, differed markedly from that in Los Angeles. Wherever Mexicans were in the minority, non-Mexican parishioners often opposed programs to integrate Mexican American families. In LA, Protestants evangelizing among Mexicans nudged Los Angeles Bishop John J. Cantwell to organize—with opposition from within—the Immigrant Welfare Department. He then appointed Father Robert E. Lucey as the head of the diocesan Bureau of Catholic Charities. Lucey later became Archbishop of San Antonio. In LA, Lucey launched a major campaign to include Mexicans in Church affairs, and even established a free health clinic within the Santa Rita Settlement House. The Church distributed religious books written in Spanish to Mexican Catholics, and organized the Confraternity of Christian Doctrine (CCD) to serve public school children. Cantwell hid the costs of these programs from white parishioners. *The Tidings*, the official diocesan newspaper, claimed that the Catholic Church should not promote social justice.[33]

Nationalism versus Americanization

Racist nativism generalized all social and economic classes of Mexicans. In reaction to this, Mexican consulates sponsored honorary societies that promoted, among other things, Mexican nationalism. In California, the Mexican government sponsored *escuelitas* (private schools) throughout the state. These efforts, however, were grossly inadequate and unable to serve the increasing numbers of immigrants. In Los Angeles, the *escuelitas* served a mere 200 students out of an estimated total of 80,000 Mexican and Mexican American children.[34] In Texas and Arizona too the immigrant population became more nationalistic and attempted to preserve their Mexican identity by organizing *escuelitas*. The Phoenix

Mexican consul in 1923 set up literacy classes for Mexican children. Five years later the Mexican Ministry of Education sent representatives to assist in setting up *escuelitas*. Meanwhile, a subtle division was taking form between first and second generations.[35]

Mexicans and Mexican Americans

The Mexican community was not monolithic. David G. Gutiérrez, in *Walls and Mirrors*, argues that a massive immigration of Mexicans in the 1920s caused increased tensions between Mexican Americans and the new arrivals. This is not surprising since it follows a pattern similar to that of northern and southern Italians, German Jews and Slavic Jews, and the long-time residents and the recent arrivals from Europe. Mexican newcomers competed for space with Mexican Americans, some of whose families had lived in the United States for generations. However, the large presence of Mexican-born immigrants had a positive impact on Mexican Americans, they enriched Mexican culture and the Spanish language, and influenced the cultural identity of those born in the United States.

Mexico still suffered from the effects of Spanish colonialism and as such struggling to find an identity. Most of the recent arrivals were poor, and from the interior of Mexico. They tended to be darker skin tone than Mexicans from the Border States who once made up the bulk of the Mexican immigrants. Class differences within the Mexican-origin community splintered it into middle-class immigrants and middle-class Mexican Americans, and then into rich and poor. Many Mexican political refugees who fled the Mexican Revolution in 1913 considered themselves culturally and even racially superior to poor Mexican immigrants and middle-class Mexican Americans.[36]

The massive influx of Mexican immigrants posed a challenge to working-class Mexican Americans who competed with them for jobs and housing. Resentment also existed among middle-class Mexican Americans toward better-off Mexicans. As small as it was, the Mexican middle class was better educated than the Mexican American middle class. Moreover, conditioned by history, the Mexican American middle class in general was conscious of the darker hue of the recently arrived working class. Meanwhile, the pretensions of newly arrived middle- and upper-class Mexican political refugees made the working class uneasy. The Mexican elites' disdain for the *pocho*[37] (a pejorative term for Mexican Americans who have become Americanized) and the perceived inferiority of "American" culture also unsettled many Mexican Americans. Despite the tensions, with time the different groups adjusted to each other. Ironically, American racism played an important role in this adjustment. White racism did not distinguish between the Mexican-born and the Mexican American—they were all considered "greasers."[38]

The Influence of World War I on Becoming Mexican American

9.3 Describe ways that Mexican Americans distanced themselves from Mexicans.

Returning from World War, many of the Mexican American veterans became more involved in politics. Texas also had the largest second generation and older Mexican generations. Many had never seen Mexico. They had a sense of place and began organizations that were more concerned with members acquiring U.S. citizenship and becoming Mexican American than they were with maintaining Mexican culture. New leaders such as J. Luz Sáenz, a World War I veteran who, in the early 1930s, wrote *Los México-Americanos en la Gran Guerra* (Mexican Americans in the Great War) emerged. In general, the *veteranos* (veterans) pursued their political rights more aggressively than did the first generation. The new organizations were concerned with negative stereotyping of Mexicans in the movies, and in 1922–1923, Mexicans protested what they called the Ku Klux Klan–Texas Ranger alliance.[39]

By the 1920s, Mexican Americans accepted the fact that they would not be returning to Mexico and began distinguishing themselves from Mexicans. This was especially true of U.S.-born children. This sort of identification changed with time. Americans never let Mexicans forget that they were different. Incidents such as reparations and racism bred resentment. David Barkley, the first person of Mexican descent to win a Congressional Medal of Honor, hid his Mexican identity. When Barkley enlisted in the U.S. Army, he did not reveal that his mother was Mexican out of fear of being segregated.[40] Born in Laredo, Texas, and raised by his mother Antonia Cantú, David Barkley died in action in World War I, 1918 and was posthumously awarded the Medal of Honor; it was not until 71 years later that his Mexican lineage became known. Although not all Mexican Americans were war veterans, the veterans' presence influenced the development of a community identity. They contributed to a growing sense that Mexican Americans were citizens and equals and that they were different.[41]

Organizational differences between Mexicans and Mexican Americans became noticeable during the 1920s and there was less emphasis on the Mexican *mutualistas*. In 1921, professor Sáenz, Santiago Tafolla, a lawyer, and other Mexican American World War I veterans and professionals formed *La Orden de Hijos de América* (the Order of the Sons of America). Although the organization did not insist on U.S. citizenship as a condition for membership, it emphasized the betterment of Mexican Americans in the United States. Within two years, *Los Hijos de América* had 250 members and three branches in South Texas.

By 1922, *Los Hijos de América* split, and a dissident group, *Los Hijos de Texas* (the Sons of Texas), was formed. Led by police officer Feliciano G. Flores and attorney Alonso S. Perales, it worked for the interests of Americans of Mexican extraction. In 1927, they formed *La Orden de Caballeros* (the Order of Knights). Some of the leaders of these groups also held offices in the various *mutualistas*, and *Los Hijos de América* was a member of the San Antonio Alliance of Mutualista Societies. However, leaders such as Perales and Sáenz never joined *mutualistas*, and they typified the post–World War I leadership among Mexican Americans.[42]

The League of United Latin American Citizens

The progression to an exclusively Mexican American organization was completed with the formation of the League of United Latin American Citizens (LULAC). For many years, Tejanos had discussed the need for a statewide organization that had the potential to become national. In 1927, Alonso Perales called together leaders of various organizations from South Texas to explore the possibility of merging into a single organization. Two years later, on February 17, 1929, in Corpus Christi, *Los Caballeros de América* of San Antonio, *Los Hijos de América* of Corpus Christi, and the League of Latin American Citizens of South Texas merged to form LULAC.[43] The founding members represented both the educated elite and the lower and middle class. Fluent in English and highly urbanized, they worked on civil rights such as the betterment of schools and voter registration drives, much in the same tradition as other racial and ethnic groups. For them, political and social equality was synonymous with being American. They wanted economic, social, and racial/gender equality, although women did not become voting members until 1933. The formation of LULAC marked a milestone in Chicano civil rights history.[44]

LULAC was also a new direction in the organizational history of the Mexican American. Before LULAC was formed, the Mexican-origin community was more concerned with the Mexican Revolution and whether or not the United States would intervene. Now, Mexican American community leaders acted on their own behalf as Americans struggling against discrimination and inequality. The leadership demanded their rights as U.S. citizens. The formation of LULAC also represented a symbolic break with the Mexican consular leadership.

This change was apparent in the readership of Spanish-language newspapers that mostly catered to immigrants. During the nineteenth century, 136 Spanish-language newspapers were published in the Southwest, 38 of them in Texas. Spanish-language newspapers ranked third among the foreign-language media in the United States at the close of the nineteenth century. The readership multiplied as immigrants streamed into the Southwest.

In Texas, Spanish-language newspapers addressing Mexican American issues increased after the war. They represented a separate worldview, different from that of the immigrant press. *La Prensa* of San Antonio catered to the Mexican exiles, and *Evolución* and *El Demócrata* of Laredo catered to the local population. During World War I, *La Prensa* often covered the war from a French point of view, translating French coverage of the war into Spanish. It focused on pride in Mexican nationality. *Evolución* urged its readers to be patriotic Americans. It gave a pro-American coverage of the war. "For *La Prensa*, these dough boys exemplify the fighting ideals of *la raza*; in contrast, *La Evolución* presents Mexican American servicemen as patriotic American citizens."[45]

The self-identity of the new immigrants sometimes varied from the attitudes of the Mexican Americans. Often it was based on the latter's jealousy and/or the snobbery of the Mexican intelligentsia. This division at times was reflected in the content of the newspapers. *La Prensa* betrayed the elitist notion of a Spanish cultural heritage, while other Mexican papers downplayed the Spanish past and exalted the Mexicans' Indigenous past.[46]

LULAC expressed the viewpoint of the middle-class Mexican American generation when it excluded noncitizens. This exclusion was labeled by critics as racist and anti-Mexican. But, in fairness to LULAC founders, they were expressing the common sense of the civil rights movement of the time. Many of its goals and political strategies paralleled those of the National Association for the Advancement of Colored People (NAACP). W. E. B. DuBois, NAACP founder, constantly spoke and wrote about an "educated elite" that, according to him, "would lead the masses with appropriate goals and lift them to civilization."[47] Most labor organizations in the 1920s also believed this, and most civil rights leaders belonged to the middle or upper class.[48]

Although LULAC leadership stated that it did not want to offend Mexican nationals, it distinguished between "Americans of Latin extraction" and Mexican nationals, whom it viewed as the "peon class." Alonso S. Perales, who in 1928 served in a Department of State diplomatic post in Nicaragua, was a proponent of Americanization. Writing to a fellow Tejano leader about the poverty and the "filthy and backward towns and cities" in Nicaragua, Perales asked what Mexican Americans were going to do about similar situations back home: "Are we going to continue our backward state of the past, or are we going to get out of the rut, forge ahead and keep abreast of the hardworking Anglo-Saxon?"[49]

LULAC leader Judge J. T. Canales played a key role in the exclusion of Mexican nationals. His rationale was that Mexicans were not skillful enough to work in the political arena, and, therefore, only American citizens of Mexican origin should form the new organization. According to the Spanish-language newspaper *El Comercio*, Canales said, "This organization should be integrated by Mexican

Americans exclusively, since Mexicans from MEXICO are a PITIFUL LOT who come to this country in great caravans to retard the Mexican Americans' work for unity that should be at the Anglo-Saxon's level."[50]

The Move to The Cities

9.4 Analyze regional issues associated with Mexican urbanization.

The first wave of Mexican immigrants was largely composed of single males. Mexican immigrants in general were apt to return home at some point—either to bring their wives and families or, in the case of single Mexican males, to marry Mexican-born females and return to the States with them. The influx of women accelerated the forging of a community within the United States—that is, the bonding of Mexicans with others of the same race within a specific space. The early arrival of the family distinguished Mexicans from the European immigrant communities, where the ratio of men to women was always much higher. By 1920, 50 percent of all Mexican immigrants were comprised of women and children.[51]

San Antonio's West Side

By 1920, San Antonio grew to 161,379 residents, of whom about 60,000 were of Mexican origin. At the end of the decade, about 70,000 of the city's 232,542 residents were of Mexican extraction. Some of these were Mexican religious refugees—that is those fleeing the so-called religious persecution in Mexico. (The 1920s was at the height of the Cristero movement. The Catholic Church mainly in the Mexican state of Jalisco resisted the reforms of the 1917 Mexican Constitution and a civil war broke out.) The Mexican population of San Antonio was mostly laborers in 1926; only 21 percent were skilled workers. Opportunities for women were limited; they usually filled lower-status jobs and only occasionally worked in Mexican-run businesses as clerks. As with their counterparts, the women's skin color determined their level of equality.[52]

This movement to the cities came at a cost. The existing housing and the labor market could not absorb the flood of Mexicans into San Antonio. Two-thirds of Mexicans lived in shacks on the West Side; hovels that filled the empty spaces between the warehouses and the rails, and were surrounded by a red-light district. Crowded courts—a series of one- and two-room units sharing a common toilet and a water spigot—barely met the housing needs of the poor. Mexicans also lived in long one-story *corrales* extending 100 yards with overcrowded stalls resembling stables. The workers put up with these unsanitary living conditions and all other miseries to earn a wage of 90¢ to $1.25 a week. The blight worsened with the heavy influx of farmworkers during the off-season.[53]

Powerless and too poor to pay the poll tax, Mexican Americans voted when different interest groups or political parties paid the cost. The Commission Ring, as they called it, ran the city for the interests of elites, giving free land to the military to attract bases. In the 1920s, the $38 million spent annually by military personnel in San Antonio contributed to the merchants' prosperity. However, little money was available for civic improvements because the trading installations were not taxed. There were few recreation clubs to serve the poor Mexicans, who congregated at Milam Park, waiting to be picked up as day laborers—in the city and as migrant workers.

Despite difficulties, San Antonio's Mexican population was stable and self-help organizations flourished. Between 1915 and 1930, 10,000 Mexicans joined 19 *mutualistas* and 6 *mutualista* labor unions in San Antonio; the largest was *La Sociedad de la Unión*, with more than 1,100 members in 1920. A woman, Luisa M. De González, headed at least one *mutualista*. *Mutualistas* appealed more to families than to young single males or females. The 1920s also brought an expansion of the social life of the West Side. Wealthy Mexicans frequented separate social clubs and, as a rule, did not join the *mutualistas*.[54]

La Prensa covered a variety of events; Beatriz Blanca de Hinojosa, the wife of the editor, wrote a regular column. Along with Aurora Herrera de Nobregas of *La Epoca*, Blanca de Hinojosa advocated the end of the double standard for women. Although some Mexican women expressed feminist ideas, the majority did not. An exception was *La Prensa* columnist Arianda who wrote that feminism was simply the "realization that women are not inferior to men." She implored women to become active against alcoholism, militarism, child labor, and the "degradation of women." María Luisa Garza, editor of *La Epoca*, attended the 1922 Pan-American Women's Conference in Baltimore. She later resigned to found *Alma Femenina*.

The status of women in the *mutualistas* varied; most groups admitted women and allowed them to hold office. Contrary to the popular myth, not all Mexican women remained at home; 16 percent of Mexican women worked outside the home, compared to 17 percent of all women in Texas.[55]

Mutualistas raised funds and petitioned authorities on behalf of fellow compatriots charged with crimes. Agustín Sánchez was sentenced to death for a murder in San Antonio. Convinced that he had acted in self-defense, the community formed a committee to seek a stay of execution. As a rule, *mutualistas* did not allow any political discussions at their meetings. However, members rationalized that the protection of their civil rights was not a political issue so it was proper to discuss them. *Mutualistas* allowed groups such as *La Liga Pro-Mexicana* (1927), a civil rights organization, to use their facilities for free; they also lent the facilities to labor associations. San Antonio *mutualistas* avoided radical organizations such as the Industrial Workers of the World (IWW). Their members closed ranks in cases of discrimination. For the most part, the *mutualistas* maintained close ties with the Mexican consul and frequently attended consular functions.[56]

Los Angeles: "Where Only the Weeds Grow"

In the 1920s, Los Angeles surpassed San Antonio as the U.S. city with the largest Mexican population. The Guadalajara–Nogales–Los Angeles railroad, completed in 1927, facilitated the movement of Mexicans to the West Coast. The expansion of Los Angeles led Ignacio Lozano, the publisher of *La Prensa*, to move west where he founded *La Opinión*. Los Angeles was surpassing San Antonio as the new Mexican mecca in the United Sates.[57]

Los Angeles housed an economically and socially diverse Mexican-origin population. In 1917 in Los Angeles, 91.5 percent of Mexicans were blue-collar workers, compared with 53 percent of the white population; 68 percent were engaged in manual labor such as pick-and-shovel work, compared with 6 percent of the white Angeleños.[58] As in San Antonio, a sizeable number of middle-class refugees moved to Los Angeles. Mexican Angeleños differed from those in the Alamo City because not all Mexicans lived on the east side; Some/a large number of Mexicans in San Antonio were grouped on the West Side. A number of LA Mexicans lived in racially integrated neighborhoods. The social life of many middle-class Mexicans differed from that of those in the *barrio*; in fact, there was often minimal contact among the disparate social classes. Events such as *bailes blanco y negro* (black and white dances) did not refer to race, but to a dance in which men wore black tuxedos and women wore white gowns.[59]

Mexican landowners, bankers, and business and professional men gathered at the *Centro Hispano Americano* in West Adams, where they held weekly formal balls. According to the *Los Angeles Times*, "the Mexican señorita" was changing for the better and becoming "the modern girl" who spoke perfect English and benefited from the "independent qualities borrowed from the American girl." Pretentious Mexicans also gathered at Café Cuba on Main Street. Immigrants, day laborers, truck drivers, and railroad trackwalkers frequented the plaza. According to historian Robin Scott, upper-class Mexicans in Los Angeles "extolled virtues of Mexican culture and heritage ...."[60]

The Mexican working class joined a mixture of races in Sonoratown near the *plaza*—town square—that served as a sort of community center for single males. Because of Sonoratown's proximity to the Civic Center, the land was much sought after as population density increased and city, county and state government office grew. As the value of this downtown land escalated, government buildings impinged on Mexican living space, and eventually Sonoratown was bulldozed. As a result, much of the plaza population moved east of the Los Angeles River.[61]

By the late 1920s, five "little Mexicos" formed in Belvedere Park, Maravilla Park, Boyle Heights, Palo Verde, and Lincoln Heights—with fierce competition between the Protestant and Catholic churches for Mexican souls. The urban poor in Los Angeles, as in San Antonio and other urban centers, put up with atrocious living conditions. Los Angeles's downtown white elite controlled city and county government and promoted an unregulated land boom that attracted industry and developed the agricultural resources of the region. It also brought hundreds of thousands of Americans, crowding the Mexican population who lived in makeshift housing around the plaza. In 1912, a contemporary observer described Sonoratown as a place populated by shacks, tents, and "nondescript barn-tenements of one and two rooms" often jammed with two or more families. The families occupying the housing shared the same toilet and water faucet in the rear of the courtyard. The city tore down many housing courts between 1906 and 1913, when the city council gave the Los Angeles Housing Commission the power of eminent domain.[62]

In the early 1920s, many Mexicans moved to the Belvedere–Maravilla area, about four miles east of the Civic Center, in the unincorporated area of the county. About 30,000 Mexicans lived barrio the end of the 1920s; in fact, Maravilla Park was almost 100 percent Mexican. Mexicans also occupied the crevices of Boyle Heights—once the home of a fashionable "American" community—between Sonoratown and Belvedere–Maravilla.[63]

Considerable intermarriage occurred between Mexican immigrants, Mexican Americans, and Americans despite racial tensions. Historian George J. Sánchez says that four-fifths of the Mexican immigrant men who intermarried arrived in this country before age 20. "Immigrants born in Mexico City were particularly likely to intermarry. In fact, the sample revealed that more immigrants from the Mexican capital married Anglo Americans in Los Angeles (38%) than married other Mexican immigrants (24%)." Intermarried couples were more likely to live outside the *barrio*. The number of children per family also varied according to class among families of Mexican descent: Mexican immigrant families averaged 3.17 children; Mexican/Mexican American, 2.71; and Mexican/Anglo, 1.3.[64]

The city changed the traditional husband–wife relations. Although it was uncommon, many Mexican women were working outside the home. The practical reason behind this trend was that during the 1920s many skilled workers could afford housing in places like Brooklyn Heights or Lincoln Heights, but only with the added income of their wives, or in some cases with family members pooling their all resources. Significantly, Mexican-born women were more likely to be employed than were U.S.-born Chicanas. It was also common for a woman to work outside the home to make up for her husband's lost job or to improve the family's living conditions.

Poor housing and sanitation contributed to health problems. In Los Angeles, infant mortality among Mexicans was two-and-a-half times higher than that among whites. Although Mexicans comprised one-tenth of the population, they accounted for one-fourth of the tuberculosis (TB) cases at city clinics in the 1920s. TB was one of the most dreaded diseases of the time. In 1924–1925 plague hit Sonoratown, even though the city had exterminated over hundred thousand rats in the downtown *barrio*. Thirty Mexicans died of pneumonic plague and five of bubonic plague.

The organizational life of Mexicans in Los Angeles resembled that of San Antonio, but it also differed. *Mutualistas*, as in San Antonio, met the immigrant families' "basic needs," such as maintaining their culture and when possible defending their civil rights. However, the *mutualistas* did not play the central role they did in San Antonio, partly because the Mexican-origin population of Los Angeles was widely scattered; also, proportionately, San Antonio had a larger Mexican American population than did Los Angeles. The Mexican consul in Los Angeles played an influential role in establishing *mutualista*-like organizations, such as *La Cruz Azul* (the Blue Cross, Mexican government self-help group) for women and *La Comisión Honorífica* (the Honor Commission) for men. These organizations were engaged in charitable work under the consul's auspices.[65]

Many women's organizations were active during the 1920s. *La Sociedad de Madres Mexicanas* was organized in Los Angeles in 1926 to help raise funds for the civil or criminal defense of Mexicans. *Las Madres* (The Mothers), or *Madrecitas* (Little Mothers), as they were called, supported cases that others ignored. One of their most noteworthy cases was that of Juan Reyna of Los Angeles. Police officers had called him a "dirty Mexican" and "you filthy Mexican" while dragging him off to jail. The officers' anger was provoked because Reyna disarmed the officers in a scuffle, shot and killed one officer, and wounded another before being subdued. Reyna was unrepentant and said he wished he had killed all three for their racist insults. Reyna went through sensational trials, which the Mexican public attended, before he mysteriously died in prison. *Corridos* (folk ballads) immortalized him as a defender of his dignity.[66]

Another case was that of Aurelio Pompa, a Mexican immigrant, convicted for killing an American in self-defense in 1923. Pompa's boss berated him daily and called him a dirty Mexican. When his boss badly beat him, an enraged Pompa went home, got a gun, and returned to shoot him. The defense committee hired Mexican American attorney Frank Domínguez to defend Pompa. *Mutualistas*, including *La Sociedad Melchor Ocampo* and other civic groups, supported Pompa, and they pressured the Mexican consul to support him as well. Juan de Heras, editor of *El Heraldo*, led the movement to free Pompa. Supporters handed a petition with 12,915 signatures to Governor F. W. Richardson. Mexican President Alvaro Obregón petitioned Richardson to save Pompa's life. Despite public pressure the state executed Pompa. Years later, and throughout my childhood, his father and grandfather would tell and retell the story of Aurelio Pompa, whose body was repatriated to his native Sonora. As the story went, the train taking the coffin to its destination stopped in Los Angeles for several hours as thousands of Mexicans held vigil.[67]

Mexicans became mass consumers. The automobile changed adolescents and youth overall. It enabled them to leave the confines of the *barrio* and to visit the downtown commercial center, and indulge in window-shopping, which became a favorite pastime. Youth became more fashion-conscious, going in for the latest in dresses. American entertainment, especially the movies, tremendously influenced Mexicans. Colin Gunckel in *Mexico On Main Street* posits that Main Street was the heart of Los Angeles's Mexican immigrant community. By the 1920s the movie industry was in full swing as the Mexican population tripled from 35,000 to about 100,000.[68] One-third of the Mexican households owned a radio, which exposed them to American pop music. However, Spanish-language entertainment remained popular, and had its place alongside American movies and music.[69]

Carpas (tent theaters) were the main entertainment providers throughout the nineteenth and into the twentieth century. Many troupes came from Mexico City, enacting classic as well as popular plays. These theaters kept alive the oral traditions of the people. Immigrants and the native-born were seated according to their class, with admission prices determining the seating arrangement of the audience. The *Teatro Calderón* and the *Teatro Progreso* were the most popular theaters in the Los Angeles area. There were smaller theaters as well, which were less expensive. The *California–El Teatro Digno de la Raza* was one of 15 theaters that operated in or around Los Angeles. Plays were often based on current events—like the lynching of Francisco Torres in Santa Ana in 1891.[70] These theaters kept alive the cultural consciousness of the Spanish-speaking community. As a small child, in the 1930s, I often accompanied my grandmother, and at other times his parents, to the California, the Orpheum, and the Million Dollar movie houses, where the *variedades* (variety shows) and the movies played side by side. Popcorn, ice cream, tacos, hot dogs, and drinks also competed with the *variedades* and the movies for attention.

Mexicans in the Midwest and Points East

By the late 1920s, an estimated 58,000 Mexicans, about 4 percent of the Mexican population in the United States, lived in the Midwest. Chicago was the Midwestern Mexican capital—it was a wintering quarter with service industries, stockyards, and factories. The 1910 Census showed 672 Mexicans in Illinois; 10 years later 1,224 Mexicans lived in Chicago, and at the end of the decade, almost 20,000 lived in the Windy City. Eighty-two percent of Mexicans in Chicago worked at unskilled jobs.[71]

The bitter cold in winter made life in Chicago more severe than in the Southwest. As in other cities, in Chicago Mexicans clustered in barrios close to their workplace. They suffered the litany of abuses experienced by the poor elsewhere: overcrowded housing, low-paying jobs, inadequate schooling, police harassment, and little hope for the future. Racism, too, was a problem to contend with. They competed for limited housing: Mexicans paid $27 a month in rent, but an Irish family paid $21 for the same accommodation.

In East Chicago, two theater owners limited Mexicans to the African American section; and in Gary, Indiana, a section of the municipal cemetery was reserved for Mexicans. The criminal justice system had little tolerance for Mexicans. In the mid-1920s, at least seven Mexicans were tried for first-degree murder in the Midwest, where the arrest rate of Mexicans was higher than that in the Southwest. California, with a much larger Mexican population, had four Mexicans sentenced to die in San Quentin in 1926.[72]

In Davenport, Iowa, *El Trabajo* reported support for José Ortiz Esquivel of Illinois, sentenced to die on June 12, 1925, for murdering his sweetheart. The Mexican community raised donations and successfully moved the court to postpone the execution date to June 24. Ortiz would have been the first Illinois man in 15 years to be executed. *El Trabajo* implored its readers to fight against the double standard of justice for Mexicans and whites. The newspaper equated the Ortiz case with Mexican deaths in the Southwest. Apparently, efforts of the Midwestern Mexican community were successful; the Illinois Supreme Court granted Ortiz a new trial.[73]

When Americans complained that the rights of U.S. citizens were being violated in Mexico, *El Correo Mexicano*, a Chicago newspaper, on September 30, 1926, replied, "The *Chicago Tribune* and other North American papers, like the *Boston Transcript*, should not be scandalized when an American citizen in Mexico is attacked, not by the authorities, as here, but by bandits and highwaymen."[74] It pointed out that police in Chicago and other cities victimized Mexicans on a daily basis. The *Correo* ridiculed Americans for calling for immediate justice in Mexico.

In Chicago, police regularly arrested Mexicans for disorderly conduct; in 1928–1929, this charge comprised almost 79 percent of all misdemeanor offenses. The most common charge in Chicago and in the rural Midwest was vagrancy. Polish police officers were especially brutal toward Mexicans and Mexican Americans. They looked upon Mexicans as competitors. A desk sergeant in 1925 readily admitted that he hated Mexicans, and that he told officers at another station not to take chances with Mexicans: "[they] are quick on the knife and are hot tempered."

Many arrests used "dragnet" methods—that is, police made sweeps of streets and places like pool halls, arresting Mexicans for carrying a jackknife or on the usual charge of disorderly conduct. Poverty among Mexicans was an obstacle in getting justice, since over three-quarters "did not have the money to hire a lawyer to defend them when they found themselves in trouble." The quality of the defense attorney—when they could hire one—was generally poor, and the their inability to speak English handicapped the defendant even further.

Chicago's Hull House and other settlement houses were popular centers where Mexican families sought help in the form of educational and recreational services. These houses served as intermediaries between Mexicans and the municipal apparatus, including police, and public health and welfare agencies. Protestant missionaries made inroads into the Chicago Mexican community; by the early 1930s, 23 percent of the active churchgoing Mexicans in the city were Protestants. The success of Protestants at converting Mexicans was attributed to the their offering social services, legal aid, medical assistance, classes in English, and other forms of assistance. The Masons also sponsored three Mexican lodges. In addition, Mexican Americans established societies to aid their poor. In 1924 in St. Paul, Minnesota, Luis Garzán and friends formed the *Anahuac* society to sponsor dances to raise money for the needy.[75]

Though church attendance among Mexican Catholics was low, it is impossible to overestimate the importance of the Catholic Church for Mexicans. For instance, in South Chicago the congregating center for Mexican Catholics was Our Lady of Guadalupe Chapel, built for Mexican workers by the Inland Steel Company. Apart from providing religious space, the Catholic Church gave Mexicans important social space. However, many Catholic parishes were racist and discouraged Mexicans from attending their services. In the Back of the Yards, Poles and Irish discouraged Mexicans from attending their churches. In 1928 in the Near West Side of Chicago (not too far from Back of the Yards), after the parishioners excluded Mexicans from Polish and Slavic Catholic parishes, Mexicans took over the Italian parish of St. Francis and made it the center for Mexican Catholics. Nevertheless, the Church's importance grew during this decade as more married couples put down roots in Chicago.[76]

Life for Mexican women was that of a minority within a minority, and their employment opportunities outside the home were limited due to the surplus of female labor. In 1924, they made up less than a third of the Mexican population; 11 years later, they comprised more than 50 percent, which suggests formation of permanent communities. During the 1920s, Mexican women in Chicago and other cities of the Midwest relied heavily on their own institutions, such as midwives to deliver children. They supplemented their family's income with most working as domestics; a large number also took in lodgers. The cold winters added to their burden: warm clothing and heating were expensive, and respiratory diseases were common. Life was precarious; the fact that there were few women made them targets for unwanted sexual advances, and vulnerable to abuse. They lacked support networks that cushioned the effects of spousal abuse and alcoholism, which were much too common within immigrant communities.

Mexican workers in South Chicago formed *La Sociedad Mutualista de Obreros Libres Mexicanos* (Mutual Aid Society of Independent Mexican Workers), which, among other it sponsored and funded a Mexican band to play popular Mexican music. Mexican workers were exposed to militant trade union tactics and ideas. As with the Irish, the Church hierarchy opposed militant unionism for Mexicans. The U.S. Catholic Church grew more conservative during the 1920s because of the religious war in Mexico over the separation of the Catholic Church and the Mexican state conditioned by the Cristero revolt.

Mexicans also moved to Detroit as early as 1918, when Henry Ford imported them to work in his auto plants. More than 16,000 Mexicans migrated to that city during the 1920s. In 1923, Bethlehem Steel imported 948 Mexicans to Pennsylvania to work in its mills. To help the impoverished and the ill, Mexicans organized three beneficent associations. In 1927, they founded *La Unión Protectora* (the Protective Union), which was later disbanded because Mexicans believed that non-citizens were not permitted to organize a union. *La Sociedad Azteca Mexicana* (the Mexican Aztec Society), organized in 1928, had 130 members by 1930. The organization owned and operated a community hall.[77]

Mexican Labor in The 1920s

9.5 Characterize the social and economic life of Mexican workers in the 1920s.

Where Mexicans moved and what type of work they did was determined by the economic and political changes of previous years. Improved transportation brought the increased industrialization of the Southwest—and, in turn, the growth of the region's cities and the mega growth of commercial agriculture. The Literacy Act of 1917 also slowed European immigration, as did World War I, thus increasing the dependence on Mexican labor as demand for pick-and-shovel work grew.

Although many moved to the cities, agriculture was still a major employer of Mexicans. The increased demand for Mexican labor also encouraged Mexican Americans from New Mexico, Texas, and elsewhere in the Southwest to migrate to other regions. During the nineteenth and the early-twentieth centuries, Mexicans frequently settled in enclaves that previously housed large numbers of European immigrants. This often led to clashes with the European ethnic groups, who saw Mexicans as competitors in workplace and housing. The city offered positive experiences. Older workers socialized the more recent arrivals and contributed to building their political vocabulary. Mexican immigrants often participated in workers' strike actions. Cities also provided Mexican-origin children more opportunity to attend school.

With the spread of factory farms and the mega production of crops such as cotton, demand for migrant labor soared; between 1918 and 1921, the Arizona Cotton Growers Association (ACGA) imported over 30,000 Mexicans. Meanwhile, mine owners displaced many Mexican miners, some of whom then became farmworkers. Displaced miners brought collective memories of militant mining strikes that occurred during the first two decades of the century.

Although highly industrialized, the factory farms resembled the old haciendas, where forced labor systems such as the *repartimiento* delivered Native Mexicans to the *mayordomo*. Under the new system, contractors delivered Mexicans to growers. Abuse was rampant. In 1919, *La Liga Protectora Latina* of Arizona filed charges against Rafael Estrada, a labor contractor for cotton growers in Arizona, accusing him of bullying and abusing Mexican workers. The Arizona Federation of Labor organized cotton pickers in the Salt River Valley. Growers combatted these organizational drives by deporting Mexicans as soon as they complained of low wages and breaches of contract. This caused hardships: Apolino Cruz was picked up for deportation, and his 8-year-old son was left on a ditch bank. Friends later took the boy to Tempe, and the ACGA sent him unescorted to Mexico.[78]

The farming operations were huge. In the Salt River Valley, temperatures often reached well above 100 degrees. Some 12,000–15,000 Mexicans could be found, housed in tents. This population was larger than that of the mining camps—and had even worse facilities. Mexican workers were often deported before they were paid. The U.S. Justice Department and local authorities routinely sided with the ACGA in these employer–worker disputes. The Arizona State Federation of Labor attempted, mostly in Maricopa County, to organize farmworkers but with limited success. Despite the barriers, by 1921 the federation formed 14 federal unions, averaging 300–400 members per local. However, during the recession of 1920–1921, the bottom fell out of the market and thousands of Mexicans were stranded in the desert, and within a year the locals fell apart.[79]

Importance of the Sugar Beet Industry

Reclamation projects stimulated the growth of sugar beet and cotton production. These crops, valued at $28,043,322 in 1928, represented 34.6 percent of all crops produced in the Southwest; Mexicans comprised 65 percent of the common labor. Most of the sugar beet workers came by way of Texas, spreading to the rest of the Southwestern fields and then throughout the Midwest. The seasonal nature of the work encouraged dispersion and urbanization, as many workers migrated to cities in search of work or shelter during the winter months.[80] Labor contractors further reduced the already low wages by oversupplying growers with workers.

Whites planted, irrigated, and cultivated, while Mexicans performed the heavier stoop work of weeding, hoeing, thinning, and topping. In turn, company stores charged workers exorbitant prices. Sugar beet workers formed small *mutualistas* to help cope with these inequities. Best known among them was *La Sociedad de Obreros Libres* (Free Workers Society) of Gilcrest, Colorado. A chapter of the *Alianza Hispano-Americana* (Hispano American Alliance) was organized in the beet fields around Brighton, Colorado, and Cheyenne, Wyoming. The IWW organized in 1905 by 1917 the Agricultural Workers Industrial Union; it had limited success because Colorado authorities intimidated workers, and state troopers were sent to the fields to discourage strike activity. Beet workers demanded improved housing, clean drinking water, good sanitary facilities, and guaranteed wage plan. Although management agreed that the demands were reasonable, they did nothing to improve the conditions. The local Knights of Columbus labeled the workers' actions as "red socialist menace." These strike actions added to the Mexican workers' collective historical memory, which they passed on to future generations.

Colorado refined one-fourth of all sugar processed in the United States. Until World War I, East-Central European immigrants did most of the manual labor associated with sugar beet production; however, the 1921 and 1924 Immigration Acts limited access to European labor. The Great Western Sugar Company of northern Colorado relentlessly recruited laborers from Mexico and New Mexico and, after the passage of the 1917 Literacy Act, they considered Mexican labor essential to their prosperity. The New Mexican villages had contributed workers to Colorado since the turn of the century and served as a reserve labor pool for the sugar companies that were able to cut their labor costs because of their proximity to New Mexico. Employment agents recruited Mexicans (and New Mexicans) to do the backbreaking work. The railroads also hired an estimated 5,000 Mexicans who labored on the maintenance crews within Colorado. Mines and other industries requiring cheap labor also hired Mexicans.[81]

In Colorado, Mexicans often lived in small, isolated clusters of two to eight families. Some moved to the cities, where their increased numbers triggered nativism—for instance, Ku Klux Klan was active at Walensburg.[82] As the Mexican and New Mexican communities became more socialized by the workplace, they campaigned for equal treatment of Mexicans.

In 1925, almost two-thirds of the Chicana/o children were three years behind white students in grade level. The Mexican and New Mexican community protested school segregation, but with little success. In 1927, Mexicans filed a civil rights case against restaurant proprietors in Greeley for denying them service. That same year, Chicanos called successful boycotts in Greeley and Johnstown, demanding that pejorative window signs be taken down. "White Trade Only" signs were common, and Americans spoke about the "Mexican invasion." The Mexicans fought back and protested against increased Ku Klux Klan activity.

For women, the loss of their family network resulted in a life of isolation and loneliness. Villagers migrated to southern Colorado, seeking seasonal employment, and returned home in time to harvest their crops. The histories of the two states are intertwined. Back home, New Mexican women maintained their homes and a small garden, and took care of their farms as well. The New Mexican families could not withstand competition from commercial farmers and stock raisers, and many of them were forced to sell or lose their holdings. Thus, families soon followed their menfolk to Colorado, where the men worked in the sugar beet industry, mining, and railroad work. Over half of the newly arrived women went to work in the sugar beet fields.[83]

Mexicans in the Northwest

At the beginning of the 1920s, 1,200 Mexicans lived in Utah; 10 years later the number grew to more than 4,000. Juan Ramón Martínez, a native of New Mexico, founded the Provisional Lamanite Branch of the Church of the Latter-Day Saints (Mormons) in 1921. The mid-1920s saw the formation of the usual *mutualistas*, along with Mexican protective associations such as *La Cruz Azul*. Mexicans also regularly celebrated *Cinco de Mayo* (Fifth of May) and other Mexican holidays. By 1930, Mexicans established Our Lady of Guadalupe Church as a mission in Utah.

Small numbers of Mexicans also lived in Idaho, Washington, and Oregon in the 1920s. Mexicans had individually moved to these states before World War I. After the war, sugar beet companies imported Mexicans to Idaho. By the 1920s, families made up a significant portion of the immigration; men, however, still comprised 65–70 percent of immigrants—even though women may have joined the males by entering without documents to avoid crossing fees. By the late 1920s, Mexicans worked on railroad maintenance crews in the region. As agriculture became more labor intensive, more Mexicans were attracted to Oregon and Washington.[84]

Mexican Workers in Texas

Differentials in pay rates played a large part in geographic dispersion. For instance, in Texas a cotton picker averaged

$1.75 a day; in Arizona, $2.75; in California, $3.25; and in Arkansas, Louisiana, and Mississippi, $4. One reason Texas growers kept wages low was their belief that lower wages would limit the resources of the Mexicans, make it more difficult for them to leave. Texas growers shared the obsession of California and Arizona growers with creating and controlling a large surplus labor pool. Texas relied heavily on migrant labor, majority of which it recruited directly from Mexico.[85]

Because Texas Mexicans were mostly landless and dependent on wages, they were especially vulnerable to exploitation. A form of debt peonage existed: Local sheriffs arrested Mexicans by enforcing vagrancy laws and then contracted the arrested workers to local farmers. Law enforcement officials intimidated Mexicans into believing that they would face imprisonment if they left without paying commissary debts. Cotton growers also tried to hold on to Mexican workers by restraining recruitment drives of northern sugar beet companies. Labor contractors from Michigan and northern Ohio alone hired about 10,000 Texas Mexicans annually. The Texas legislature passed a law that was in effect until the 1940s that limited the ability of labor contractors to recruit Mexican workers in the Lone Star State.[86]

Mexican Workers in the Midwest

Better pay and opportunities made migration from Texas into the Midwest attractive. Labor contractors recruited many of the migrants to this region. Initially, many Mexicans worked on the railroads and farms before jumping off into the cities. In the 1920s, Mexicans comprised 40 percent of the total railroad maintenance crews of Chicago. The railroads paid Mexicans the lowest industrial salaries: 35¢–39¢ an hour. Packinghouses paid workers 45¢–47¢ an hour, while steel factories paid them 45¢–50¢ an hour for 8-hour or 44¢ an hour for 10-hour workdays. These salaries were much higher than those in the Southwest. More importantly, they offered year-round employment in the city. However, even with higher pay, two-thirds of Mexicans in Chicago earned less than $100 a month, which was considered below the poverty line.

Not one steel plant in the Midwest employed a Mexican supervisor. Unions excluded Chicanos from building trades, which generally citizenship for union membership. The American Federation of Railroad Workers did not have a single Mexican tradesman. Organized labor continued to stereotype Mexicans as scabs and wage cutters. Other ethnic groups as well were also antagonistic toward Mexicans. Factory tensions carried over into the streets, and many neighborhoods would not rent houses to Mexicans.

The Mexican population suffered a temporary setback in 1920–1921; as in the Southwest, many Mexicans were repatriated because of a deep economic recession. The situation improved as the railroads and steel mills employed more Mexican workers. As agriculture recovered, the number of Mexican farmworkers swelled the population during the picking season. The labor bonanza of the sugar beet industry drew thousands of migrants. The Mexican community in Ohio, Indiana, Michigan, Wisconsin, and Illinois the Mexican community grew from 7,583 in 1920 to 58,317 10 years later. By the end of the decade, Midwest Mexicans were more urbanized, rising from just under 70 percent to some 88 percent. Nationwide, by 1930, 40.5 percent of the Mexican males were employed in agriculture, 26 percent in manufacturing, and 16.3 percent in transportation.[87]

The Growth of California Agribusiness

California housed "farm factories"; its climate allowed year-round production. In many places, the federal government made available water at below-cost levels, facilitating the irrigation of vast areas, and the state could boast of 118 different types of farms producing 214 different agricultural crops. Growers created exchanges that recruited an oversupply of labor and concentrated production and distribution. They formed organizations such as the Valley Fruit Growers of San Joaquin County, the Sun-Maid Raisin Growers Association (which included 75–90 percent of the raisin farmers), the Western Growers Protective Association, and the California Growers Exchange, to name a few. The San Joaquin Valley Agriculture Labor Bureau was founded in 1925. The organization consisted of six county farm bureaus, six county chambers of commerce, and countless raisin, fresh fruit, and cotton operations. Its job was to maximize profit by developing a pool of surplus labor that could be hired at the lowest possible rate.

Mechanization displaced many year-round farmworkers and increased the dependence on temporary migrant labor (read *Mexicans*), since more production meant a demand for larger labor pools at harvest time. U.S. farms were mechanizing at an unprecedented rate. Mechanization made it possible to cultivate more land. From 1920 to 1930, the number of Mexicans in agriculture tripled, increasing from 121,176 to 368,013. Also, as machines displaced animals, growers could convert land used for feed to produce cash crops, further increasing the demand for labor.[88]

The Formation of Mexican Unions

9.6 Relate labor organization to the Mexican worker experience in the United States

In 1928, agricultural economist Paul S. Taylor wrote,

> One-third of Imperial Valley is Mexican. Changing rapidly from desert in 1900 to an area of intensive agriculture, the valley has met its expanding labor needs largely with immigrants from across our southern border. . . . In this valley, a world to itself, isolated, yet an integral part of the

agricultural Southwest, the Mexican is now inextricably a part of the social and economic life of the community.[89]

The earliest Mexican workers came as track laborers. By 1910, there were Mexican colonies in the Valley and El Centro. As the demand for workers grew in cantaloupe, lettuce, and cotton farms, so did the demand for Mexicans. Meanwhile, driven largely by cotton, the influx of southern whites and blacks continued. By 1916, this "southern help" was migrating to the San Joaquin Valley, which coincided with the growth of cotton production there. Growers had turned more seriously to Mexico after 1917, when sugar beet growers began to recruit large numbers of Mexicans. By the turn of the decade, Mexicans dominated the work force and their concentration depended on the crops. At harvest time, they composed 90 percent of field workers in the Imperial Valley.

The presence of corporate farms led to the development of gigantic labor pools, which enabled many workers to stay in the same place for longer than was possible earlier, and they often became permanent residents. The involvement of Mexicans in mining before World War I expanded the corps of proletariat workers. In Arizona, Mexicans comprised nearly half of the miners in the state, and participated in the militant strikes of the 1910s. These strikes gave a core of Mexican workers organizational experience. The Mexican Revolution and the formation of national labor organizations such as *La Confederación Regional Obrera Mexicana* (CROM; Federation of Regional Mexican Workers) also offered some direction. Despite the Mexicans' history of collectively confronting capitalist inequities, American labor unions refused to accept them as brothers.[90]

This is not to say that the American Federation of Labor (AFL) was very oblivious to the needs of Mexican workers. In 1927, it sent Clemente N. Idar to organize beet workers. In the next two-and-a-half years, Idar traveled to Colorado, Nebraska, and Wyoming. In 1929, he was able to put together a labor front consisting of the AFL, the IWW, the communists, and the various Mexican unions. Under Idar's leadership, the Beet Workers Association stayed together. However, when Idar took ill and had to leave, the association fell apart.[91]

California farmworkers' organizing efforts faced overwhelming opposition by agribusiness owners. Undoubtedly, many small Mexican labor unions existed; however, they were short-lived because of the Mexicans' vulnerability to deportation and the willingness of U.S. capitalists to do anything to disorganize labor—even making membership in the IWW illegal. In times of labor tensions, agribusiness owners used immigration authorities to comb Mexican colonias: Mexicans were vulnerable because some 80 percent had no documents. The most powerful growers' association, the American Farm Bureau Federation (AFBF), united farmers nationally. It also had local and state chapters that were linked to chambers of commerce; the American Legion; the National Association of Manufacturers; and local, state, and federal elected officials and law enforcement.[92]

Labor contractors managed work crews and controlled the lives of workers. Growers paid the contractors, who in turn paid workers after subtracting their fee from each worker's earnings. Contractors withheld the first week's wages until the end of the harvest. Many workers complained that contractors often absconded with their money.[93]

In November 1927, the Federation of Mexican Societies, mostly *mutualistas*, met in Los Angeles with the express purpose of encouraging members to support trade unionism by financing their organizational efforts. In March, they formed *La Confederación de Uniónes de Campesinos y Obreras Mexicanas* (CUCOM; Federation of Mexican Workers Unions), which had a minority of communist and IWW sympathizers. With the assistance of the Mexican consul, *mutualista* leaders formed *La Unión de Trabajadores del Valle Imperial* (the Imperial Valley Workers Union).

In early May 1928, the newly formed union sent cantaloupe growers and the chambers of commerce in Brawley and El Centro letters requesting that wages be increased to 15¢ per standard crate of cantaloupes, or 75¢ an hour; that growers supply free picking sacks and ice; and that growers, not the contractors, be responsible for paying workers' wages. The growers refused. On May 7 workers at the Sears Brothers Ranch walked out. Soon, 2,000–3,000 workers joined the strike. On May 10, Sheriff Charles L. Gillett shut down the union's offices, outlawed all future strikes, and arrested more than 60 union activists. Local newspapers, public opinion, and local politicos supported the get-tough tactics of Sheriff Gillett.[94]

Change in Mexican Identity: The Mexican Revolution

The Mexican Constitution of 1917 was the most important accomplishment of the Mexican Revolution. It sought to remedy social, political, and economic grievances. On paper, Mexico regained control over its natural resources. The Constitution recognized social and labor rights; the separation of church and state; and granted universal manhood suffrage. Article 3 secularized public educations and paved the way for José Vasconcelos's school reforms in the 1920s. Article 3 also forbade censorship or prohibition of books, and guaranteed free, mandatory, and lay education. This document addressed many historical grievances.

The Mexican Constitution of 1917 was the first world Constitution that protected social rights. Article 27 vested the nation with the direct ownership of all natural resources, that is, all minerals and water. Arguably, this was the most controversial section and asserts that the subsoil, or natural resources, belong to the nation. Only Mexicans had the right to own land, water, and minerals or to acquire concessions for exploitation. Article 28 prohibited monopolies of any kind. Article 123 empowered the labor sector.

Aside from the Constitution, the Revolution's greatest legacy was its institutional memory that stories, literature, music, and art have kept alive. The passion generated from the upheaval produced a large body of literature that formed the memories of modern Mexicans. The Mexican Revolution inspired novels such as Laura Esquivel's *Como Agua Para Chocolate* (*Like Water for Chocolate*, 1989). The most celebrated of the contemporary Mexican authors were Carlos Fuentes, who wrote *The Death of Artemio Cruz* (1962); Juan Rulfo, who wrote *Pedro Páramo* (1961); and Octavio Paz, author of *El laberinto de la soledad* (1950). All take inspiration from Mariano Azuela González (1873–1952). His work *Los de Abajo* is the prototype of the Novel of the Mexican Revolution. *The Underdogs* (1915) was his masterwork. Azuela was a prolific writer of novels, works for theater, and literary criticism. He wrote about every facet of the Revolution.

The Constitution and the blood of over a million Mexicans paved the way for José Vasconselos's school reforms, the normalistas, and the spread of literacy to almost every corner of Mexico. The corridos spread the stories of Pancho Villa, Emiliano Zapata, and the Adelitas, among others. They were extremely important in telling Mexicans about their history. Out of nearly 15 million Mexicans, fewer than 12 million knew how to read or write; only 3.6 million could. For them, the folk ballad defined the Revolution's goals and its heroes. It was a living history and is as popular and vivid today as it was in 1920.[95]

Between 1920 and 1924, Vasconcelos established more than 1,000 rural schools and commissioned Mexican muralists to memorialize the Mexican Revolution as the Maya had memorialized its society by adorning the walls of the pyramids with their history. Since then murals have been used to tell the history of the Mexican Revolution as well as the Chicana/o movement. These muralists follow in the footsteps of David Siqueiros (1898–1974) and Diego Rivera (1886–1957), who wore two holstered guns while painting. José Clemente Orozco (1883–1949) is considered the best of the three great Mexican artists, possessing great force and an intense sense of form. He is famous for his cartoons of the Revolution that graphically document the emergence of Mexico after the Revolution.

As a consequence, Mexicans became Mexicans; that identity took on the cult of the mestizo. Mestizaje was addressed by Manuel Gamio who is often considered as the father of Mexican anthropological studies in Mexico. Because of this he was considered a leader in the Indigenismo Movement. Gamio, however, stopped short of advocating full sovereignty for Indigenous communities, arguing for self-governing organizations instead.[96] In 1916, Gamio wrote *Forjando Patria (Forging a Nation)*. The question of who or what is a Mexican remains unresolved to this day as Mexico and the United States are being torn apart by racial and social divisions. Critics attribute the failure to address the Indigenista Question on the Mexican Revolution that generated Mexican nationalism. Had positive results but failed to resolve questions and actions raised by nineteenth-century Mexican nationalism and put Mexico on the path of decolonizing its institutions, not least of which was the history of racism and the erasure of the History of the Indigenous History.[97]

Conclusion: Making America White Again

The 1920 U.S. Census listed Mexicans as white: "Enumerators were to enter 'W' for White, 'B' for Black, 'Mu' for mulatto, 'Ch' for Chinese, 'Jp' for Japanese, 'In' for American Indian, or 'Ot' for other races."[98] Ten years later, census takers listed the Mexican's race as Mex for Mexican, which, according to the standards of the settled times, demarcated Mexicans even more from white Americans and categorizing their social and racial caste. This loss in status would not go unnoticed by Mexican Americans. Other subtle changes occurred, such as listing the same person as "Pedro" in 1920 and "Pete" in 1930, and changing "Francisco" to "Frank" and "Miguel" to "Mike." Such changes, though not universal, were frequent enough to be noted. By the end of the decade, according to the new census, there were 1.3 million Mexicans in the United States which according to many scholars was not a reliable figure.[99]

Americanization heavily impacted the second generation; it confused more Mexican students about their identity. However, the city and its bright lights and material symbols caused the greatest changes. Like the ceremonial and trade centers of pre-Columbian times, the urban centers integrated the surrounding enclaves. Increasingly, Mexicans, like other residents of the country, traveled to the downtown areas where many would seek an escape from the drudgery of work. It was not only the radio, the music, and the silent films that intruded into their lives, subtly Americanizing them; downtown was a place where even the penniless could walk and admire the window displays of the department stores that featured material goods such as clothing and household items. The subliminal message was that the goods were available to anyone, *if* they became American (white).

Deregulation, nationalism, and greed brought on the Wall Street Crash of 1929, ending the Roaring Twenties and their prosperity, ushering in a Great Depression that brought years of suffering, while the Empire popularized the illusion that America was once great and would be great again when it became white again.[100]

Notes

1. Robert A Huttenback, *Racism and Empire: white settlers and colored immigrants in the British self-governing colonies, 1830–1910* (Ithaca: Cornell University Press, 1976). John Darwin, *The empire project: the rise and fall of the British world-system, 1830–1970* (Cambridge, UK; New York: Cambridge University Press, 2009).

2. Radhika Mohanram, *Imperial White: Race, Diaspora, and the British Empire Imperial White* (University of Minnesota Press, 2007).

3. The Alien and Sedition Acts of 1798 from Folwell's "Laws of the U.S.," Archiving Early America, http://www.earlyamerica.com/earlyamerica/milestones/sedition/.

4. Agustín Escobar Latapí, Philip Martin, Gustavo López Castro, and Katharine Donato, "Factors that Influence Migration," Portland State University, 179–180, http://citeseerx.ist.psu.edu/viewdoc/download?doi=10.1.1.554.9487&rep=rep1&type=pdf.

5. Chapter vii, "War and Repression 1900–1930," Social History Station, http://www.boisestate.edu/socwork/dhuff/us/chapters/CHAPTER%207.htm. "Historical Census Statistics on the Foreign-Born Population of the United States: 1850 to 1990," http://www.census.gov/population/www/documentation/twps0029/twps0029.html. Trinidad Gonzales, "The world of Mexico Texanos, Mexicanos and Mexico Americanos: Transnational and National Identities In the Lower Rio Grande River Valley, During the Last Phase of United States Colonization, 1900–1930" (Houston: PhD Dissertation, University of Houston, 2008), does a good job tracing generational changes in this small confined area.

6. Jaime Aguila, "Mexican/U.S. Immigration Policy prior to the Great Depression," *Diplomatic history*, Vol. 31, Issue 2 (2007), 216. He quotes Moisés González Navarro, *Los Extranjeros en México y los Mexicanos en el Extranjero, 1821–1970* (Mexico City: Colegio de México, Centro de Estudios Históricos, 1994), III: 242. "During his first eighteen months in office, he [Alvaro Obregón] helped repatriate over 150,000 Mexicans . . . ." Obregón, a native son of the northern state of Sonora, which borders Arizona, acted out of personal concern for his compatriots abroad. Quoting Moisés González Navarro he writes: "With wagons full of people, like cattle cars, which the enganchadores [smugglers] come to steal from our nation, taking advantage of this economic urgency for those unemployed, and I have seen many of those men return a few days later to the international boundary, begging for a plate of food, and for a ticket to return to their home."

7. Deutsch, *No Separate Refuge*, 124–25. Balderama and Rodríguez, *Decade of Betrayal*, 129–32.

8. Lawrence A. Cardoso, *Mexican Emigration to the United States, 1897–1931: Socio-Economic Patterns* (Tucson: University of Arizona Press, 1980), 97. Reisler, *By the Sweat of Their Brow*, 39, 50–51, 53. Morgan and Mayer, "Spanish-Speaking Population," 8, 39. *El Universal* quoted in Peterson, "Twentieth-Century Search for Cibola," 127–28.

9. "10 Outrageous (and Mostly True) Quotes on Native Americans by Famous People," *Indian Country Today*, https://indiancountrymedianetwork.com/culture/arts-entertainment/10-outrageous-and-mostly-true-quotes-on-native-americans-by-famous-people/. ICMN Staff, September 29, 2014

10. Calvin Coolidge, "We're All in the Same Boat Now: Coolidge on Immigration, Coolidge Foundation," February 19, 2016. https://www.coolidgefoundation.org/blog/were-all-in-the-same-boat-now-coolidge-on-immigration/

11. Lawrence Anthony Cardoso, "Mexican Emigration to the United States: An Analysis of Socio-Economic Causes" (PhD Dissertation, University of Connecticut, 1974), 60.

12. Richard Delgado, Jean Stefancic, eds., *The Latino/a Condition: A Critical Reader* 2nd ed. (New York: New York University Press, 2011), 87. See earlier editions for further citations. Also see Congressional Reports in following footnotes.

13. U.S. Department of Labor, *Annual Report of the Commissioner General of Immigration* (Washington, D.C.: Government Printing Office, 1926), 10. "Naturalization Bill Alters Women's Status," *New York Times* (January 6, 1921), 6. Immigration Act of 1921, Historical Documents, http://www.u-s-history.com/pages/h1398.html. The 1921 Act, http://www.memoriesfromhamblin.org/actof1921.html. The National Origins Immigration Act of 1924, *The Statutes at Large of the United States of America, from December 1923 to March 1925*, Vol. XLII, Part 1 (Washington, D.C.: Government Printing Office, 1925), 153–69. The 1924 Act, http://www-personal.umd.umich.edu/~ppennock/doc-immigAct.htm.

14. U.S. Congress, House Committee on Immigration and Naturalization, Seasonal Agricultural Laborers from Mexico: Hearing No. 69.1.7 on H.R. 6741, H.R. 7559, H.R. 9036, 69th Cong., 1st Sess. (1926), 24. Who Was Shut Out?: Immigration Quotas, 1925–1927, History Matters, http://historymatters.gmu.edu/d/5078. Maldwyn Allen Jones, *American Immigration*, 2d ed. (Chicago: University of Chicago

Press, 1992), 237–39. "National Origins," *Time Magazine* (Monday, March 11, 1929), http://www.time.com/time/magazine/article/0,9171,846255,00.html.

15 U.S. Department of Labor, *Annual Report of the Commissioner General of Immigration* (Washington, D.C.: Government Printing Office, 1923), 16. Reisler, *By the Sweat of Their Brow*, 55, 66–69. Job West Neal, "The Policy of the United States toward Immigration from Mexico" (Master's Thesis, University of Texas at Austin, 1941), 106, 107–8.

16 Quoted in Neal, "The Policy," 112, 113.

17 U.S. Congress, 190.

18 Ibid., 325.

19 Ibid., 112.

20 Quoted in Robert J. Lipshultz, "American Attitudes Toward Mexican Immigration, 1924–1952" (Master's Thesis, University of Chicago, 1962), 61.

21 Ben Railton, "DACA, The 1924 Immigration Act And American Exclusion," *HuffPost*, Sep. 07, 2017, https://www.huffingtonpost.com/entry/daca-the-1924-immigration-act-and-american-exclusion_us_59b1650ee4b0bef3378cde32. Mae M. Ngai, "The strange career of the illegal alien: Immigration restriction and deportation policy in the United States, 1921–1965," *Law and History Review*, Spring, 2003, Vol. 21(1), 69–107.

22 George J. Sánchez, *Becoming Mexican American: Ethnicity, Culture and Identity in Chicano Los Angeles, 1900–1945* (New York: Oxford University Press, 1993), 91, 97, 99, 101, 102, 155. Frederick C. Millett, "Americanization," http://uscourse.wikispaces.com/How+the+USA+influences+the+world. The models for Americanization were the earlier efforts to remake the Native American. See "Americanization (of Native Americans)," BookRags.Com, http://www.bookrags.com/studyguide-native-roots/chapanal005.html. Theodore Roosevelt, "True Americanism," *The Forum* (April 1894), http://www.theodore-roosevelt.com/images/research/speeches/trta.pdf. Rodolfo F. Acuña and Guadalupe Compeán, eds., *Voices of the U.S. Latino Experience*, Vol. 2 (Westport, CT: Greenwood, 2008), 468–75. M. Glancy, "Temporary American citizens? British audiences, Hollywood films and the threat of Americanization in the 1920s," *Historical Journal of Film, Radio and Television*, Vol. 26, Issue 4 (2006), 461–484.

23 R. G. Price, "Fascism Part II: The Rise of American Fascism" (May 15, 2004), http://rationalrevolution.net/articles/rise_of_american_fascism.htm. The article points out the extremes that the Americanization programs went to.

24 Antonia Darder, Rodolfo D. Torres, eds., *Latinos and Education: A Critical Reader* (New York: Routledge, 1997), 167.

25 G. González, *Chicano Education in the Era of Segregation*, 13, 20–21, 36, 41, 46, 67, 77. Gilbert G. González, "Chicano Education History: A Legacy of Inequality," *Humboldt Journal of Social Relations* 22, No. 1 (1996), 43–56. Gilbert G. González, *Labor and Community, Mexican Citrus Worker Villages in a Southern California County, 1900–1950* (Urbana: University of Illinois Press, 1994), 99–134.

26 "Sánchez, George Isidore (1906–1972)," *Handbook of Texas Online*, http://www.tshaonline.org/handbook/online/articles/SS/fsa20.html. "George Isidore Sánchez Papers," http://www.lib.utexas.edu/photodraw/sanchez/. Carlos Kevin Blanton and George I. Sánchez, *The Long Fight for Mexican American Integration* (New Haven: Yale University Press, 2015).

27 Still a classic on how Mexican stereotypes are embedded in the American consciousness: Cecil Robinson, *With the ears of strangers: the Mexican in American literature* (Tucson: University of Arizona Press, 1963). Norman D. Smith, "Mexican Stereotypes on Fictional Battlefields: or Dime Novel Romances of the Mexican War," *Journal of Popular Culture*, March 1980, Vol. 13(3), 526–540.

28 Erin Blakemore, "The Brutal History of Anti-Latino Discrimination in America: School segregation, lynchings and mass deportations of Spanish-speaking U.S. citizens are just some of the injustices Latinos have faced," *History*, Sep. 27, 2017, https://www.history.com/news/the-brutal-history-of-anti-latino-discrimination-in-america. Gilbert G. González, "Segregation of Mexican Children in a Southern California City: The Legacy of Expansionism and the American Southwest," *Western Historical Quarterly*, Vol. 16, No. 1 (Jan, 1985), 55–76.

29 Richard R. Valencia, *Chicano Students and the Courts: The Mexican American Legal Struggle for Educational Equality* (New York: New York University Press, 2008), 14–15. Meyer Weinberg, *A Chance to Learn: A History of Race and Education in the United States* (New York: Cambridge University Press, 1977), 145–65. An excellent article on the abuse of testing is Miroslava Chávez-García, "Intelligence Testing at Whittier School, 1890–1920," *Pacific Historical Review* 76, No. 2 (May 2007), 193–228. Laura K. Muñoz, "Separate But Equal? A Case Study of *Romo v. Laird* and Mexican American Education," http://www.slideshare.net/greenje/mexican-americans-presentation.

30 Juan Francisco Martínez, *Sea la Luz: The Making of Mexican Protestantism in the American Southwest, 1829–1900* (Denton: University of North Texas Press, 2006).

31 Sánchez, *Becoming Mexican American*, 255. Ernestine M. Alvarado, "A Plea for Mutual Understanding between Mexican Immigrants and Native Americans," 1920 annual session of the National

Conference of Social Work (1920), 264–66 (Protestant sponsored). Lina E. Bresette, *Mexicans in the United States: A Report of a Brief Survey* (Washington, D.C.: Social Action Department, National Catholic Welfare Conference, 1929), iii, 16, 17, 19. Robert N. McLean and Charles A. Thompson, *Spanish and Mexican in Colorado: A Survey of the Spanish Americans and Mexicans in the State of Colorado* (New York: Board of National Missions, Presbyterian Church in the U.S.A., 1924), vii–x, reprinted in Carlos E. Cortés, ed., *Church Views of the Mexican American* (New York: Arno Press, 1974), ix, x, 17. Ernesto Galarza, "Life in the United States for Mexican People: Out of the Experience of a Mexican," Proceedings of the National Conference of Social Work, 56th Annual Session, University of Chicago Press, 1929, excerpts in Digital History, http://www.digitalhistory.uh.edu/disp_textbook.cfm?smtID=3&psid=592. Paul Barton, *Hispanic Methodists, Presbyterians, and Baptists in Texas* (Austin: University of Texas Press, 2006), 12–14, 47 points out that members of Pancho Villa's family attended the Baptist Church in San Antonio.

32 Robert McLean and Grace Petrie Williams, *Old Spain in New America* (New York: Council of Women for Home Missions, 1916), 155–56. Guadalupe San Miguel Jr., "Culture and Education in the American Southwest: Towards an Explanation of Chicano School Attendance," *Journal of American Ethnic History*, 7, No. 2 (Spring, 1988), 6, 9. "Spanish American Institute, 1913–1971 Service to Boys," Distributed as pamphlet on May 30, 1971, Courtesy of Professor Everto Ruiz, California State University, Northridge.

33 Sánchez, *Becoming Mexican American*, 151–69. Anthony M. Stevens-Arroyo, "Pious Colonialism: Assessing the Church Paradigm for Chicano Identity," in Gastón Espinosa and Mario T. García, eds., *Mexican American Religions: Spirituality, Activism, and Culture* (Durham, NC: Duke University Press, 2008), 71–71. "Lucey, Robert Emmet (1891–1977)," *Handbook of Texas Online*, http://www.tshaonline.org/handbook/online/articles/LL/flu14.html.

34 Sánchez, *Becoming Mexican American*, 114–20. Unfortunately, much of the curriculum was nationalist in content, and the method followed had the positivist bent of the Porfiriato and continued with a *científico* (scientist) positivist view of Mexico. "Bilingual Education," *Handbook of Texas Online*, http://www.tshaonline.org/handbook/online/articles/BB/khb2.html. Francisco Arturo Rosales, *Chicano!: The History of the Mexican American Civil Rights Movement*, Revised ed. (Houston, TX: Arte Público Press, 1997), 81.

35 Lee Stacy, *Mexico and the United States* (Tarrytown, NY: Marshall Cavendish Corporation, 2002), 48–49.

36 David G. Gutiérrez, *Walls and Mirrors: Mexican Americans, Mexican Immigrants and the Politics of Ethnicity* (Berkeley: University of California Press, 1995). Many of the political exiles had been supporters of Porfirio Díaz; they allied themselves with the Catholic Church and lobbied for U.S. intervention in Mexico. The Cristero Movement in central-western Mexico (1926–1929) motivated yet another migration to *el norte*. Many of its adherents came to the United States and carried on anti-Mexican government activities there. "A Growing Community," Immigration, The Library of Congress, http://www.loc.gov/teachers/classroommaterials/presentationsandactivities/presentations/immigration/alt/mexican4.html. "Cristero Rebellion (1926–1929)," *Latin American Studies*, www.latinamericanstudies.org/cristero.htm.

37 *Pocho* literally means "Mexican Americans who do not speak Spanish, or mix it with English." Also refers to those who have adopted American customs and clothing.

38 Steven Bender, *Greasers and gringos: Latinos, Law, and the American Imagination* (New York: New York University Press, 2003), xiii–xiv. Arnoldo De León, *They Called Them Greasers: Anglo Attitudes Toward Mexicans in Texas, 1821–1900* (Austin: University of Texas Press, 1983), Preface.

39 Julie Leininger Pryciror, "*La Raza* Organizes: Mexican American Life in San Antonio, 1915–1930, as Reflected in Mutualista Activities" (PhD Dissertation, University of Notre Dame, 1979), 83, 97–98, 105. "José de la Luz Sáenz Papers, 1908–1998," Texas Archival Resources Online, http://www.lib.utexas.edu/taro/utlac/00072/lac-00072.html. J. Luz Saenz, *Los mexico-americanos en la Gran Guerra: y su contingente en pró de la democracia, la humanidad y la justicia* (San Antonio, TX: Artes Gráficas, 1933). Benjamin Heber Johnson, *Revolution in Texas: How a Forgotten Rebellion and Its Bloody Suppression Turned Mexicans into Americans* (New Haven: Yale University Press, 2005), 178–82.

40 It was not uncommon for Mexicans to pass to avoid discrimination. Take the case of Ted Williams, a baseball superstar who did not hide being half Mexican but just avoided mentioning it. Roxanne Moore Saucier, "Ted Williams' Hispanic heritage still a surprise to many," *Bangor Daily News* (January 12, 2014), https://bangordailynews.com/2014/01/12/living/ted-williams-hispanic-heritage-still-a-surprise-to-many/.

41 Orozco, "LULAC," 27–32, 123–24, 131. Guide to the Collections of the League of United Latin American Citizens (LULAC) Archives, http://www.lib.utexas.edu/benson/lulac/lulacindex.html. David Bennes Barkley, Texas State Cemetery, http://www.cemetery.state.tx.us/pub/user_form.asp?step=1&pers_

id=11240. Hispanic-American Medal of Honor Recipients, http://www.buffalosoldier.net/Hispanic-AmericanMedalofHonorRecipients.htm.

42 Alonso S. Perales, "Defending Mexican Americans," in Josh Gottheimer, ed., *Ripples of Hope: Great American Civil Rights Speeches* (New York: Basic Civitas Books, 2003), 160–62. "Perales, Alonso S. (1898–1960)," *Handbook of Texas Online*, http://www.tshaonline.org/handbook/online/articles/PP/fpe56.html. Order of the Sons of America (Council 5) Records, 1927, Abstract Minutes and financial records from 1927 for the Alice, Texas organization that was a precursor of the League of United Latin American Citizens (LULAC). Accession No. BENSON-MS ORDER SONS OF AMERICA, Texas Archival Resources, http://www.lib.utexas.edu/taro/utlac/00246/lac-00246.html. "Latino Civil Rights Timeline, 1903 to 2006," Teaching Tolerance, Southern Poverty Law Center, http://www.tolerance.org/latino-civil-rights-timeline.

43 Adela Sloss Vento, *Alonso S. Perales: His Struggle for the Rights of Mexican-Americans* (San Antonio, TX: Artes Gráficas, 1977), vii. Alonso S. Perales (1898–1960), "In Defense of My People," University of Houston Libraries, http://info.lib.uh.edu/about/campus-libraries-collections/special-collections/library-exhibits/defense-my-people-alonso-s-p. Index for Alonso Perales Microfilm Collection, Latinoteca, http://www.latinoteca.com/recovery/indexes/alonso-perales-microfilm-collection.

44 Cynthia E. Orozco, *No Mexicans, Women, or Dogs Allowed: The Rise of the Mexican American Civil Rights Movement* (University of Texas Press, 2009).

45 Carole E. Christian, "Joining the American Mainstream: Texas's Mexican Americans During World War I," *Southwestern Historical Quarterly* 92, No. 4 (April 1, 1989), 559–95. Roberto R. Treviño, "Prensa y patria: The Spanish-Language Press and the Biculturation of the Tejano Middle Class, 1920–1940," *Western Historical Quarterly* 22, No. 4 (November 1, 1991), 451–72. *La Prensa*, *Handbook of Texas Online*, http://www.tshaonline.org/handbook/online/articles/LL/eel3.html. John Maynard, "First Spanish-Language Newspaper Founded 200 Years Ago," Newseum, Washington D.C., September 15, 2008, http://www.newseum.org/news/2008/09/first-spanish-language-newspaper-founded-200-years-ago.html. Nicolás Kanellos, "A Brief History of Hispanic Periodicals in the United States," Hispanic Periodicals, http://docs.newsbank.com/bibs/KanellosNicolas/Hispanic_history.pdf.

46 Treviño, "Prensa y patria," 453, 457.

47 W. E. B. DuBois, "The Talented Tenth," Teaching AmericanHistory.org, September 1903, http://teachingamericanhistory.org/library/document/the-talented-tenth/.

48 Gutiérrez, *Walls and Mirrors*, 77. Orozco, "LULAC," 302. Rutledge M. Dennis, "Du Bois and the Role of the Educated Elite," *The Journal of Negro Education*, Vol. 46, No. 4 (Autumn, 1977), 388–402.

49 Quoted in Gutiérrez, *Walls and Mirrors*, 81–83.

50 Quoted in Orozco, "LULAC," 232–33. Lupe S. Salinas, "Legally White, Socially Brown: Alonso S. Perales and His Crusade for Justice for La Raza," University of Houston, http://www.latinoteca.com/recovery/recovery-content/papers-perales-conference/LegallyWhiteSociallyBrown_Salinas.pdf. Despite the damaging Canales quote, he was a trailblazer in the Civil Rights History of Texas. Canales was tireless in his crusade against the Texas Rangers. Also see Joseph Orbock Medina, "Trials of Unity: Rethinking the Mexican American Generation in Texas, 1948–1955," University of California at Berkeley, November 2011, http://www.latinoteca.com/recovery/recovery-content/papers-perales-conference/TrialsofUnityOrbockMedinaspaper.pdf.

51 Sánchez, *Becoming Mexican American*, 131–33. Neil Foley, *The White Scourge: Mexicans, Blacks, and Poor Whites in Texas Cotton Culture* (Berkeley: University of California Press, 1997), 43.

52 Emilio Zamora, *The World of Mexican Workers in Texas* (College Station: Texas A&M Press, 1993), 24–28. 1920 United States Federal Census, www.ancestry.com, http://content.ancestry.com/Browse/list.aspx?dbid=6061&path=texas.Bexar.San+Antonio+Ward+1. Adriana Ayala, "Negotiating Race Relations Through Activism: Women Activists and Women's Organizations in San Antonio, Texas during the 1920s" (PhD Dissertation, The University of Texas at Austin, 2005), iii; Mexican women active in varied organizations such as the Cruz Azul, Young Women's Christian Association (YWCA), the Pan-American Round Table of San Antonio, the San Antonio Mission Home and Training School, the Mexican Christian Institute, the House of Neighborly Service, the Wesley Community Center, and the Catholic Community Center. Julia G. Young, "Ristero Diaspora: Mexican Immigrants, The U.S. Catholic Church, And Mexico's Cristero War, 1926-29," The Catholic Historical Review, Vol. 98, No. 2 (April, 2012), pp. 271–300.

53 Prycior, *La Raza Organize*, 15–17. Frances Jerome Woods, *Mexican Ethnic Leadership in San Antonio* (Washington, D.C.: Catholic University Press, 1949), 20. Emilio Zamora, "Mexican Labor Activity in South

Texas, 1900–1920" (PhD Dissertation, University of Texas, Austin, 1983), 160. Julia Kirk Blackwelder, *Women of the Depression: Caste and Culture in San Antonio, 1929–1939* (College Station: Texas A&M Press, 1984), 18. George Isidro Sánchez Papers, Digitalized Photos, http://www.lib.utexas.edu/photodraw/sanchez/. For digital photos see University of Texas at San Antonio, http://digital.utsa.edu/cdm/search/searchterm/gebhardt!Box%2003,%20folder%2005/field/all!all/mode/all!exact/conn/or!or/cosuppress/. Also browse the Library of Congress, http://www.loc.gov/pictures/.

54 Orozco, "LULAC," 156. *Mutualistas* thrived throughout the Southwest and Midwest. For a more complete background, see James B. Lane and Edward J. Escobar, eds., *Forging a Community: The Latino Experience in Northwest Indiana, 1919–1975* (Chicago, IL: Cattails Press, 1987). The largest association, La Unión, had 1,540 members, mostly skilled workers and some *jornaleros* (day laborers). For *mutualista* activity in Texas, see Zamora, *The World of Mexican Workers in Texas*, 71–81. David Montejano, *Anglos and Mexicans in the Making of Texas, 1836–1986* (Austin: University of Texas Press, 1987), 204.

55 Kathleen González, "The Mexican Family in San Antonio" (Master's Thesis, University of Texas at Austin, 1928), 5–6. Pryor, *La Raza Organizes*, 77. Orozco, "LULAC," 41–46.

56 Sánchez, *Becoming Mexican American*, 69–70.

57 Drawn Southern Pacific Railway Advertisement with the Heading, "The West Coast of Mexico," ca. 1930, http://digarc.usc.edu/search/controller/view/chs-m12027.html.

58 The title of this section is taken from Guadalupe Compeán, "Where Only the Weeds Grow: An Ecological Study of Mexican Housing in Boyle Heights, 1910–1940" (Unpublished paper, School of Architecture and Urban Planning, University of California Los Angeles, December 1984). Ricardo Romo, *East Los Angeles: History of a Barrio* (Austin: University of Texas Press, 1983), 102. Pedro Castillo, "The Making of a Mexican Barrio: Los Angeles, 1890–1920" (PhD Dissertation, University of California Santa Barbara, 1979). Gregory Rodriguez, "The Emerging Latino Middle Class Explanation of Findings," Pepperdine University Institute for Public Policy and AT&T, October 1996, https://publicpolicy.pepperdine.edu/davenport-institute/content/reports/latino.pdf.

59 Group photo of the Circulo Cosmopolita, 1st Anniversary, Los Angeles Public Library. See "Two Los Angeles'," http://forchicanachicanostudies.wikispaces.com/Community.

60 "Mexican Señoritas Now Adorn Local Society," *Los Angeles Times* (October 22, 1922). "Sonoratown, Backwater in Swirling Life of City," *Los Angeles Times* (September 9, 1923). Robin Fitzgerald Scott, "The Mexican-American in the Los Angeles Area, 1920–1950: From Acquiescence to Activity" (PhD Dissertation, University of Southern California, 1971), 32–33.

61 "Sonora Town," University of Southern California Digital, http://digitallibrary.usc.edu/search/controller/simplesearch.htm, http://digitallibrary.usc.edu/search/controller/view/chs-m4929.html?x=1352074189141; follow the link, and on the Search Bar type in "Sonora Town."

62 Cloyd V. Gustavson, "An Ecological Analysis of the Hollenbeck Area of Los Angeles" (Master's Thesis, University of Southern California, 1940), 43. Elizabeth Fuller, "The Mexican Housing Problem in Los Angeles," in Carlos E. Cortés, ed., *Perspectives on Mexican-American Life* (New York: Arno Press, 1974), 6. In her 1920 study Elizabeth Fuller found that 92 percent of the homes she visited did not have gas, and 72 percent had no electricity. "Los Angeles at Work 1920–1939," Belvedere, USC Library Digital Archive, http://digitallibrary.usc.edu/search/controller/simplesearch.htm. View from Boyle Heights of a bridge leading into Los Angeles, ca. 1930–1939, USC Library Digital Archive, http://digarc.usc.edu/search/controller/view/chs-m2875.html.

63 View of Whittier Boulevard in Whittier, showing a milk truck, ca.1924, USC Library Digital Archive, http://digarc.usc.edu/search/controller/view/chs-m6804.html?x=1242327858186 (accessed November 3, 2009).

64 Sánchez, *Becoming Mexican American*, 138–39, 147–48. Kevin Starr, *Material Dreams: Southern California through the 1920s* (New York: Oxford University Press, 1990), 147–49. William Deverell, "My America or Yours? Americanization and the Battle for the Youth of Los Angeles," in Tom Sitton and William Deverell, eds., *Metropolis in the Making: Los Angeles in the 1920s* (Berkeley: University of California Press, 2001), 277–99. Edward J. Escobar, *Race, Police, and the Making of a Political Identity: Mexican Americans and the Los Angeles Police Department, 1900–1945* (Berkeley: University of California Press, 1999), 78–81.

65 Cynthia Orozco, "Comisión Honorífica Mexicana," The *Handbook of Texas Online*, http://www.tshaonline.org/handbook/online/articles/CC/pqc1.html.

66 Francisco E. Balderama and Raymond Rodríguez, *Decade of Betrayal: Mexican Repatriation in the 1930s* (Albuquerque: University of New Mexico Press, 1995), 42–43. Emma Pérez, *The Decolonial Imaginary: Writing Chicanas into History* (Bloomington: University of Indiana Press, 1999), 97–98. "Latinas," Area Studies Collection, Library of Congress, http://memory.loc.gov/ammem/awhhtml/awas12/latinas.html.

67 Francisco Arturo Rosales, *Testimonio: A Documentary History of the Mexican-American Struggle for Civil Rights* (Houston, TX: Arte Publico Press, 2000), 123–25. Stuart Banner, *The Death Penalty: An American History* (Cambridge: Harvard University Press, 2002), 173. Newspaper Archives, 248 Aurelio Pompa Documents, Genealogy Bank, http://www.genealogybank.com/gbnk/newspapers/?sort=_rank_%3AD&lname=pompa+&fname=aurelio&kwinc=&kwexc=&formDate=&processingtime=&group=.

68 Colin Gunckel, *Mexico on Main Street: Transnational Film Culture in Los Angeles before World War II* (Rutgers University Press, 2015).

69 Sánchez, *Becoming Mexican American*, 171–87. Mark Reisler, "Always the Laborer, Never the Citizen: Anglo Perceptions of the Mexican Immigrant During the 1920s," in David G. Gutiérrez, ed., *Between Two Worlds: Mexican Immigrants in the United States* (Lanham, MD: Rowan & Littlefield, 1977), 23.

70 Haas, *Conquests*, 138–64. Nicolas Kanellos, *Hispanic Literature of the United States: A Comprehensive Reference* (Westport, CT: Greenwood Press, 2003), 252–58. Yolanda Broyles-González, *El Teatro Campesino Theater in the Chicano Movement* (Austin: University of Texas, 1994), 52. "Las Carpas," Latinos in 60 Seconds, Public Broadcast System, http://video.pbs.org/program/1247309894/.

71 Juan R. García, *Mexicans in the Midwest, 1900–1932* (Tucson: University of Arizona Press, 1996). Zaragosa Vargas, *Proletarians of the North: A History of Mexican Industrial Workers in Detroit and the Midwest, 1917–1933* (Berkeley: University of California Press, 1993). Dennis Váldes, *Al Norte: Agricultural Workers in the Great Lakes Region* (Austin: University of Texas Press, 1991). Mark Reisler, *By the Sweat of Their Brow: Mexican Immigrant Labor in the United States, 1900–1921* (Westport, CN: Greenwood Press, 1976), 99–102. Ricardo Parra, "Latinos in the Midwest: Civil Rights and Community Organization," in Gilberto Cardenas, ed., *La Causa: Civil Rights, Social Justice and the Struggle for Equality in the Midwest* (Houston, TX: Arte Público Press, 2004), 4–6. Gabriela F. Arredondo, "Mexicanas in Chicago," Northern Illinois University, http://www.lib.niu.edu/2003/iht1020357.html.

72 Paul S. Taylor, "Crime and the Foreign Born: The Problem of the Mexican," in Carlos E. Cortés, ed., *The Mexican-American and the Law* (New York: Arno Press, 1974), 232. Rosales, *Chicano*, 66. Rosales, *Testimonios*, 105.

73 *El Trabajo* (April 18, May 16 and 23, June 11, 14, and 26, and July 31, 1925).

74 Quoted in Taylor, "Crime and the Foreign Born," 232.

75 Gabriela F. Arredondo, "Mexicanas in Chicago," http://www.lib.niu.edu/2003/iht1020357.html. Louise A. Kerr, "Mexicans in Chicago," http://www.lib.niu.edu/1999/iht629962.html.

76 Our Lady of Guadalupe Church (Chicago), http://www.neiu.edu/~reseller/cultinstp15.htm.

77 Paul Livingston Warnshuis, "Crime and Criminal Justice Among Mexicans of Illinois," in Cortés, ed., *The Mexican-American and the Law*, 282–84, 287, 320. Louise Año Nuevo Kerr, "The Chicano Experience in Chicago: 1920–1970" (PhD Dissertation, University of Illinois at Chicago Circle, 1976), 36, 39, 47, 49, 50, 52, 53. Reisler, *By the Sweat of Their Brow*, 141–42. John R. Scotford, *Within These Borders* (New York: Friendship Press, 1953), 105. John J. Betancur, "The Settlement Experience of Latinos in Chicago: Segregation, Speculation, and the Ecology Model," *Social Forces* 74, No. 4 (June 1996), 1299–324. Anita Edgar Jones, "Mexican Colonies in Chicago," *The Social Service Review* 2, No. 4 (December 1928), 579–97.

78 Herbert B. Peterson, "Twentieth-Century Search for Cibola: Post—World War I Mexican Labor Exploitation in Arizona," in Manuel Servín, ed., *An Awakening Minority: The Mexican American*, 2nd ed. (Beverly Hills, CA: Glencoe Press, 1974), 117, 119–21. Carey McWilliams, *Ill Fares the Land: Migrants and Migratory Labor in the United States* (New York: Arno Press, 1976), 79. "The Chicana Chicano Experience in Agriculture," http://www.asu.edu/lib/archives/website/agricult.htm. "For the People: Mutual Aid Societies/Para la Gente: Sociedades de Ayuda Mútua," http://www.asu.edu/lib/archives/website/organiza.htm. Arizona Cotton Growers Association Collection, Arizona Historical Foundation, http://www.ahfweb.org/download/Cotton_MSS_30.pdf.

79 Peterson, "Twentieth-Century Search for Cibola," 117, 119–21. Rodolfo F. Acuña, *Corridors of Migration: The Odyssey of Mexican Laborers, 1600–1933* (Tucson, University of Arizona Press: 2007), 215–19.

80 Reisler, *By the Sweat of Their Brow*, 102. George Hinman, "Report of the Commission on International and Interracial Factors in the Problems of Mexicans in the United States," National Conference Concerning Mexican and Spanish Americans in the United States (Austin, TX: University of Texas, 1926), 14, 27, 29. Paul S. Taylor, *Mexican Labor in the United States: Chicago and the Calumet Region* (Berkeley: University of California Press, 1932), 2, 111–12, 119–20, 222, 229. Immigration Committee, "Mexican Immigration," Chamber of Commerce of the United States, Washington, D.C., July 1930 (draft in the Bancroft Library), 21, 27. Selden C. Menefee, "Mexican Migratory

Workers of South Texas," reprinted in Carlos E. Cortés, ed., *Mexican Labor in the United States* (Washington, D.C.: Works Progress Administration, 1941), 17–26, 41..

81 Sara Deutsch, *No Separate Refuge: Culture, Class, and Gender on an Anglo-Hispanic Frontier in the American Southwest, 1880–1940* (New York: Oxford University Press, 1987), 137. "Late 1910s Sugar Beets and Migrant Labor," http://events.mnhs.org/timepieces/Preview.cfm?EventID=216.

82 McLean and Thomson, *Spanish and Mexicans in Colorado*, in Cortés, ed., *Church Views*, ix, x, 17. Frederic J. Athearn, "Hard Times: 1920–1940," *Land of Contrast: A History of Southeast Colorado*, Cultural Resources Series, Number 17 (Colorado: Bureau of Land Management, Colorado, 1985), chapter 11, http://www.nps.gov/history/history/online_books/blm/co/17/chap12.htm.

83 Deutsch, *No Separate Refuge*, 107–61. In 1920 there were 11,037 Mexican-born residents in Colorado and 10,272 in New Mexico. Barbara Hawthorne, Mexican American Cultural History, http://history.fcgov.com/archive/ethnic/Mexican.php.

84 Paul Morgan and Vince Mayer, "The Spanish-Speaking Population of Utah: From 1900 to 1935," Working Papers Toward a History of the Spanish-Speaking People of Utah (American West Center, Mexican-American Documentation Project, University of Utah, 1973), 32–34, 41, 46–47, 50–52. Pierrete Hondagneu-Sotelo, *Gendered Transitions: Mexican Experiences of Immigration* (Berkeley: University of California Press, 1994), 21–22. Erasmo Gamboa, "Chicanos in the Northwest: An Historical Perspective," *El Grito* 6, No. 4 (Summer 1973), 58–59, 60–62. Richard W. Slatta, "Chicanos in the Pacific Northwest: An Historical Overview of Oregon's Chicanos," *Aztlán* 6, No. 3 (Fall 1975), 328–29. Erasmo Gamboa, *Mexican Labor and World War II: Braceros in the Pacific Northwest, 1942–1947* (Seattle: University of Washington Press, 1999), 8, 27. *Mexican Americans in the Columbia Basin: Historical Overview*, http://www.vancouver.wsu.edu/crbeha/ma/ma.htm#intro. Carlos Arnaldo Schwantes, *The Pacific Northwest: An Interpretive History*, Revised and Enlarged ed. (Omaha: University of Nebraska Press, 1996), 228–32. Jerry García, "History of Latinos in the Northwest," Latino Hispanic Assessment Report, State of Washington, 2009–2010, http://www.k12.wa.us/CISL/pubdocs/historylatinopacificnorthwest.pdf.

85 Montejano, *Anglos and Mexicans*, 159, 207–11. Sana Loue and Beth E. Quill, eds., *Handbook of Rural Health* (New York: Springer, 2001), 104.

86 Montejano, *Anglos and Mexicans*, 164, 204, 207, 213. Paul S. Taylor, *An American-Mexican Frontier* (New York: Russell & Russell, 1971), 150. George Otis Coalson, *The Development of the Migratory Farm Labor System in Texas, 1900–1954* (San Francisco, CA: R and E Research Associates, 1977), 26. McWilliams, *Ill Fares the Land*, 264.

87 Daniel Rothenberg, *With These Hands: The Hidden World of Migrant Farmworkers Today* (Berkeley: University of California, 2000), 10, 274. Richard L. Nostrand, *Hispano Homeland* (Norman: University of Oklahoma, 1996), 164. Louise Año Nuevo Kerr, "Chicano Settlements in Chicago," in Manuel G. Gonzales and Cynthia M. Gonzales, eds., *En Aquel Entonces: Readings in Mexican-American History* (Bloomington: University of Indiana, 2000), 109–16. Zaragosa Vargas, "Armies in the Fields and Factories: The Mexican Working Classes in the Midwest in the 1920s," *Mexican Studies/Estudios Mexicanos* 7, No. 1 (Winter 1991), 47–71. Taylor, *Mexican Labor in the United States*, 50, 73–77, 98. Vargas, *Proletarians of the North*, 10, 59, 90. Dionicio Nodín Valdés, *Barrios Norteños: St. Paul and Midwestern Mexican Communities in the Twentieth Century* (Austin: University of Texas, 2000), 25, 32, 102.

88 Royce D. Delmatier, Clarence F. McIntosh, and Earl G. Waters, eds., *The Rumble of California Politics, 1848–1970* (New York: Wiley, 1970), 212, 216–17. Carey McWilliams, *Factories in Fields: The Story of Migratory Labor in California* (Santa Barbara and Salt Lake City: Peregrine Publishers, 1971), 185, 188. Stuart Jamieson, *Labor Unionism in American Agriculture* (New York: Arno Press, 1976), 71–72. Reisler, *By the Sweat of Their Brow*, 77–78. "Revolution to Depression: 1900–1940, Five Views: An Ethnic Historic Site Survey for California," http://www.nps.gov/history/history/online_books/5views/5views5c.htm.

89 Paul S. Taylor, "Mexican Labor in the United States: Imperial Valley," in *Mexican Labor in the United States* (New York: Arno Press, 1970), 2, 7–8, 17. Mark Reisler, "Mexican unionization in California agriculture, 1927–1936: A History of Mexican Americans in California," *Labor History* 14, No. 4 (Autumn 1973), 562–79.

90 Sinclair Snow, "Samuel Gompers and the Pan-American Federation of Labor" (PhD Dissertation, University of Virginia, 1960), 203. Gilbert G. González, "Company Unions, the Mexican Consulate, and the Imperial Valley Agricultural Strikes, 1928–1934," *The Western Historical Quarterly* 27, No. 1 (Spring 1996), 53–73.

91 Coalson, *The Development of the Migratory Farm Labor*, 36. Reisler, *By the Sweat of Their Brow*, 88. Mark Erenberg, "A Study of the Political Relocation of Texas-Mexican Migratory Farm Workers to Wisconsin" (PhD Dissertation, University of Wisconsin, 1969), 11.

Immigration Committee, "Mexican Immigration," 11. McWilliams, *Factories in Fields*, 89. Kay Lysen Briegel, "Alianza Hispano-Americana, 1894–1965: A Mexican American Fraternal Insurance Society" (PhD Dissertation, University of Southern California, 1974), 94. Taylor, *Mexican Labor in the United States*, 184. Manuel Gamio, *Mexican Immigration to the United States: A Study of Human Migration and Adjustment* (New York: Dover Publications, 1971), 86. Jamieson, *Labor Unionism*, 236–39.

92 Clark A. Chambers, *California Farm Organizations* (Berkeley: University of California Press, 1952), 22. Grant McConnell, *The Decline of Agrarian Democracy* (Berkeley: University of California Press, 1957), 160. Devra Weber, *Dark Sweat, White Gold: California Farm Workers, Cotton, and the New Deal* (Berkeley: University of California Press, 1994), 18–24, 84. Acuña, *Corridors of Migration*, 226. "We Have Fed You All for a Thousand Years," http://www.farmworkers.org/strugcal.html.

93 Jamieson, *Labor Unionism*, 75–76. Report of Governor C. C. Young's Fact Finding Committee in California, October 1930, Reprint (San Francisco: R&E Research Associates, 1970), 123, 126. George T. Edson, "Mexicans in the Beet Fields of Northeastern Colorado," August 27, 1924, in the Bancroft Library (Berkeley, CA), 5–10. Norman Lowenstein, "Strikes and Strike Tactics in California Agriculture," (Master's Thesis, University of California, Berkeley, 1940), 25. Scott, "The Mexican-American," 25–26. Charles Wollenberg, "Huelga, 1928 Style: The Imperial Valley Cantaloupe Worker's Strike," *Pacific Historical Review* 38 (February 1969), 48. G. González, "Company Unions," 53–73.

94 G. González, in "Company Unions," 54, points out that the consul's role was generally to intervene in favor of management. Attempts were made as early as 1917 to organize Imperial Valley farmworkers.

95 James Presley, "Mexican Views on Rural Education, 1900–1910," *The Americas*, Vol. 20, No. 1 (Jul., 1963), 64–71. Lee Stacy (ed.), *Mexico and the United States* (Marshall Cavendish Corp, 2002), 466.

96 David A. Brading, "Manuel Gamio and Official Indigenismo in Mexico," *Bulletin of Latin American Research*, Vol. 7, No. 1 (1988), 75–89. Guillermo Zermeno P., Maria Pilar Valles Ezquerra, Ishita Banerjee Dube Nepantla, "Between Anthropology and History: Manuel Gamio and Mexican Anthropological Modernity (1916–1935): Views from South," Duke University Press, Volume 3, Issue 2, 2002, 315–331.

97 Manuel Gamio, *The Mexican Immigrant: His Life-Story* (Chicago: The University of Chicago Press, 1931). This popular study was for U.S. audience and in many ways a synthesis to the (more) scientific study. Manuel Gamio, *Mexican immigration to the United States*; a study of human migration and adjustment (Chicago, Ill., University of Chicago Press, 1930). Guillermo Zermeno P., Maria Pilar Valles Ezquerra, Ishita Banerjee Dube Nepantla, "Between Anthropology and History: Manuel Gamio and Mexican Anthropological Modernity (1916–1935): Views from South," Duke University Press Volume 3, Issue 2, 2002, pp. 315–331.

98 "1920," The U.S. Census, https://www.census.gov/history/www/through_the_decades/index_of_questions/1920_1.html.

99 Brian Gratton and Emily Merchant, "La Raza: Mexicans in the United States Census," *Journal of Policy History*, 2016, Vol. 28(4), 537–567; The article shifts the blame of the "Mex" category to Mexicans who, it is said, considered themselves a race apart.

100 Douglas Monroy, *Rebirth: Mexican Los Angeles from the Great Migration to the Great Depression* (Berkeley: University of California Press, 1999)

Chapter 10
Mexican American Communities in the Making: The Tin Man Has No Heart[1]

 Learning Objectives

10.1 Contextualize the Great Depression for Mexican Americans.

10.2 Differentiate how Mexicans experienced the Great Depression by region, age, and gender.

10.3 Analyze the 1930s repatriation movement and its consequences.

10.4 Explain how conditions for U.S. farms and farmworkers changed during the New Deal.

10.5 Compare regional approaches to the farmworkers' struggle for labor rights.

10.6 Characterize urban unionization by Mexican communities in the 1930s.

10.7 Describe the struggle for labor rights in Mexican American mining communities.

10.8 Evaluate the different ways that Mexican Americans supported their communities in the 1930s.

> Once California belonged to Mexico and its land to Mexicans; and a horde of tattered feverish Americans poured in. And such was their hunger for land that they took the land, stole Sutter's land, Guerrero's land, took the grants and broke them up and growled and quarreled over them, those frantic hungry men; and they guarded with guns the land they had stolen. They put up houses and barns, they turned the earth and planted crops. And these things were possession, and possession was ownership.
>
> The Mexicans were weak and fled. They could not resist, because they wanted nothing in the world as frantically as the Americans wanted land.[2]

Most Mexican-origin people in the United States live in places that were once part of their homeland. This is important to remember when comparing Mexicans to other immigrants. The saying "the borders crossed us" has a special meaning to them. Look at a map and you will see a 2,000-mile border separating Mexico and the United States. A few physical regions of Texas are further south and closer to Mexico City than Tijuana, Hermosillo, and Chihuahua City. Then look at the names of towns and cities on the U.S. side of the border and compare them to those on the eastern seaboard.[3] Consider the impacts British, American, and Spanish colonialism had on the region and you will realize that in most cases Eurocentric ideologies have annihilated the Indigenous People.[4]

The Great Depression of the 1930s was not a correction of the economy. Mexicans taking jobs away from Americans did not cause it, American corporate greed did.[5] Although the Mexican-origin population was small and nativists scapegoated them for unemployment and demanded their deportation, despite the fact that the causes of the Great Depression were far too complex for the Mexicans, or any group other than Wall Street, to be responsible. Moreover, most Americans had never seen a Mexican.

The immediate causes can be found in World War I, when federal spending grew at a rate three times the growth rate of tax collections. The government cut back spending in 1920 to balance the budget, and a severe economic collapse resulted. When the nation rebounded from the slump, a decade of uncontrolled corporate growth and greed took place; mergers, takeovers, and cutthroat business practices went unregulated. The crash was caused by inequality in wages and a lack of regulation. By 1929, the richest 1 percent of the population owned 40 percent of the nation's wealth, while the bottom 93 percent experienced a 4 percent drop in per capita income.[6]

Between 1929 and 1932, more than 13 million Americans lost their jobs. As with every recession, nativists made the foreign-born scapegoats. They were a convenient target: They did not vote and were far enough down the caste that they could be pecked down by all. The so-called repatriation programs sprang up throughout the country, and the thin line between deportation and repatriation was crossed. Deportation is forced, while repatriation is supposedly voluntary. Before the 1930s, large numbers of Mexicans had been repatriated from Texas, New Mexico, Arizona, and elsewhere in the United States. What distinguished the 1930s repatriation was its massiveness, that it was managed by the federal and local governments, and that it was used as an excuse to deport between 600,000 and a million Mexicans for no other reason than their ethnicity. This reduction in population impacted the Mexican community for generations to come.[7] (The economy was an excuse and the primary motive was either elimination or annihilation of the Mexicans)

> The expulsion of the Mexicans did not come by surprise. The ugly debates surrounding the Passage of the 1921 and 1924 Immigration Acts were a warning of what was to come. White nationalism reared its ugly head, opposed only by Chambers of Commerce, economic development groups, and state farm bureaus. The American Federation of Labor agitated to put Mexicans on an immigration quota. When the Crash of 1929 occurred, Mexicans were seen as the cause. Get rid of the Mexican and America's problems would go away.[8]

Mexicans and Mexican Americans were only considered minimally when planning the economic recovery. Many elected officials sought to defend a corrupt system by blaming immigrants. President Franklin D. Roosevelt recognized that the American economy had to be revamped, but he did not take immigrants into account in planning the recovery. Indeed, non-citizens were mostly barred from participating.

During the Depression, massive unemployment caused due to job loss in the Southwest accelerated the migration of larger numbers of Mexicans to the Midwest and other regions of the country to find work. Many had papers or were long time residents. Americans had to blame someone for the collapse of the U.S. economy and the failure of capitalism. The result was the repatriation of Mexican Americans, which was a prelude to " . . . the forced relocation in 1942 of 112,000 Japanese Americans from the West Coast to internment camps."[9]

The migration of large numbers of Mexicans to the Midwest and elsewhere continued as they scampered for seasonal farm work. These workers did come on their own, they were heavily recruited by growers and other employers who hired contractors. The steel and auto factories had actively recruited Mexican workers after the passage of the 1917 Literacy Act. Mexicans were initially allowed to do farm work, and the exemption was later extended to railroads and other industries. By the 1930s, there was a sizable Mexican population in places such as Chicago, Detroit, Gary, and other Midwestern industrial centers. Migrancy deprived farmworker children of the opportunity to attend school and/or learn English. On the upside, the cities opened newer opportunities for many Mexicans and Mexican Americans who resettled there. Greater numbers of Mexican women and men joined the urban workforce, unions, and other organizations. This involvement increased social interaction.[10]

President Roosevelt's New Deal offered minimal assistance to Mexican nationals and other immigrants. Local public assistance was unreliable, and as a rule noncitizens were barred from receiving public aid. However, some Mexicans and Mexican Americans benefited from programs such as the Farm Security Administration that established camps for migrant farmworkers in California and elsewhere.[11] Mexican Americans joined the Civilian Conservation Corps (CCC) and Works Progress Administration (WPA) that provided relief jobs to unemployed Mexican Americans. But access was not even, and many Mexican Americans, although citizens, did not qualify for relief assistance because either they did not meet residency requirements or they were farmworkers who, as a class, were excluded from New Deal programs such as workers' compensation, Social Security, and the National Labor Relations Act.[12]

The Great Depression: *La Crisis*

10.1 Contextualize the Great Depression for Mexican Americans.

The Great Depression brought a sharp drop in Mexico's national income. The lack of money impacted its ability to meet its constitutional mandate to promote social equity. For all intents and purposes, the Mexican Revolution was dead. "Mexican foreign policy also experienced a marked change during this decade. In particular, the nation's relationship to the United States made a 180-degree turn towards friendship, in contrast to the open hostility that prevailed in the 1920s."[13] The only silver lining was that President Lázaro Cárdenas's nationalization of the foreign-owned oil industry in Mexico in 1938 energized agrarian reform, encouraged the creation of national industrial unions, and promoted socialist public education.[14] Among the Mexican elites, however, there was increased interest in Mexico's GDP and the impact that the Depression was having on exports, resulting in forced readjustments and the rise of conservative Mexican politics.

Mexico was a rural nation with most people living on small farms or in small towns and villages. The Depression—or

La Crisis (the Crisis)—profoundly affected Mexicans on the American side of *la linea*. The Mexican population in the United States was estimated at 2 to 3 million, but was probably higher. Mexicans as a whole were economically vulnerable; they worked at menial jobs that the Depression impacted hardest. The 1930 Census showed that 56.6 percent of the 1,422,533 Mexicans listed were native-born U.S. citizens. Migration to the cities quickened during the next decade, as opportunities in agriculture dried up, with farmers preferring to white over brown in California. In Texas, the state legislature refused to appropriate general revenue funds for relief or allow bonds to raise revenue for local relief agencies. The gap between city and rural wages widened.[15] Nationally, unemployment rose to 15 million by 1933; unemployment for all workers peaked at 41.6 percent in Los Angeles that year.[16] Unemployed white Americans began to look for any kind of work, even "Mexican work," which they once shunned. Some felt that Mexicans were taking away their job opportunities—and, with this notion, they revived the racism of the 1920s, when nativists feared the loss of "their" America to non-white foreigners. Against the backdrop of this jingoism, the California legislature passed the 1931 Alien Labor Law, which forbade contractors from hiring alien workers for highway construction, school and government office buildings, and other public projects.[17] The so-called Americans used the pretext of taking care of their own people to displace Mexicans from the labor market. American nativism was predicated on racism. "Arrivals from Mexico rose steadily after 1900, increased sharply after 1910, and peaked in the mid-1920s,"[18] There were no massive numbers of Mexicans waiting to invade the United States.

The search for white votes and a reassertion of exceptionalism led to the demonization of Mexicans. In 1931, Assemblyman George R. Bliss of Carpinteria, California, introduced a bill that would have legalized the segregation of Mexican and Mexican American students.[19] As a Carpinteria school board member, Bliss successfully segregated Mexican children, labeling their school an "Indian School." Under the California School Code, school districts were given "the power to establish separate schools for Indigenous children and children of Chinese, Japanese, and Mongolian ancestry"[20] under which category some districts included Mexicans. The Bliss Bill was defeated, but it raised the issue of disparate treatment among minorities. Native American, Chinese, and Japanese children were already segregated; however, similar categorization of Mexicans was problematic as they were classified as white based on the Treaty of Guadalupe Hidalgo. The 1930 Census shifted the battlefield by classifying Mexicans as a separate race. This shift had been taking place throughout the 1920s as "Mexican Schools" had proliferated under the pretext of Americanization. Mexico City's *Excelsior* blasted the Bliss Bill, writing, "The measure which it is intended to carry into effect with respect to Mexican children is degrading, ignoble and devoid of justice, and it has raised waves of indignation." The Mexican newspaper concluded that the bill victimized Mexican children.[21]

Taking a cue from attempted legislation such as the Bliss Bill, January 1931, Jerome T. Green, principal of the Lemon Grove Grammar School, on instructions from the school trustees, announced that Mexican children would attend a newly constructed school that Mexicans labeled the barnyard. The parents led a boycott and filed suit—*Roberto Alvarez v. the Board of Trustees of the Lemon Grove School District*. Moreover, during the 1920s, segregation of Mexican children had been institutionalized. As Roberto Alvárez underscores, "The segregation of Mexican-American children became widespread in California and Texas. In 1928, the enrollment of sixty-four schools in eight California counties was 90–100% Mexican-American." However, San Diego Judge Claude Chambers ruled in favor of the plaintiffs and ordered that the Mexican American students be reinstated.[22]

Meanwhile, cities throughout the Southwest and Midwest attracted Mexicans and Mexican Americans. Because only 27,900 Mexicans entered the United States with permanent visas in the 1930s, most of the migration was interstate, primarily to California, where Los Angeles's population tripled between 1920 and 1930 and continued to grow.[23] City life greatly impacted the Mexican-origin community. Meanwhile, at least 600,000 Mexicans were repatriated, dramatically changing the life of the Mexican community in the United States many of whose members lived in fear.

La Crisis

Though Los Angeles was hit hard during the Great Depression, it offered better opportunities since it was one of the largest agricultural counties and a leading industrial state in the United States. In contrast, *La Crisis* hit Tucson, a railroad hub, hard. The Southern Pacific Railroad transferred its jobs to El Paso, Los Angeles, and Phoenix.[24] Moreover, the availability of medical care drew Mexicans to Los Angeles where they competed for entry-level jobs. In Los Angeles, Mexicans suffered the highest incidence of tuberculosis, more than twice the proportion for African Americans and five times that of white Americans. Since the mid-1920s, the Los Angeles County Department of Health and its director, John L. Pomeroy, used these statistics for restricting Mexicans from entering the United States. He used the cover of preventing the spread of TB to call for the deportation of Mexicans. As a rule, Mexicans were treated at segregated medical facilities. Pomeroy justified the segregation, claiming Mexicans' and whites' needs were different. Throughout *La Crisis*, the department played on the whites' fears and prejudices. This was again an example of racism, since Los Angeles was one of the largest cities in the country and its medical care was, for the most part, better than it was elsewhere.[25] It is safe to say, the hysteria over TB was similar to the panic caused by HIV and AIDS during the 1980s.

Life was harder elsewhere. In Tucson, for example, the out-migration of industries and the in-migration of displaced miners and farmworkers stressed facilities. Historian Thomas Sheridan tells the story of Teresa García Coronado, who, along with her husband, fled to the United States during Mexican Revolution. Her husband labored in the Arizona mines, before the Depression, and when the mines closed during the Depression, the family migrated to the cotton fields. Teresa's daughter, Concepción, was stricken with an unknown disease that resulted in paralysis, and her husband stole eggs from neighbors' barns to feed their sick daughter. Teresa pulled the family through hard times by scavenging in the garbage dumps.[26] In the Mexican community families played a large role in surviving the Great Depression. It was common for three and even four generations to live together as a household.

Life During The Great Depression

10.2 Differentiate how Mexicans experienced the Great Depression by region, age, and gender.

Regional tensions continued to persist within the Mexican American community. Though intermixing of families in the colonias lessened the friction between native-born and immigrants some divisions still continued. For example, some northern Mexicans considered themselves superior to Mexicans from the interior because of their lighter complexion; New Mexicans were generally lighter skinned and believed that they were "Spanish" rather than Mexican. Despite these differences, the Mexican community as a whole shared the Spanish language, more or less similar skin color, and, for the most part, Catholicism. Changes were taking place: Numerous Protestant churches flourished, even deep in the heart of the West Side of San Antonio and East Los Angeles. Many Mexicans turned to the Protestant churches for assistance during *La Crisis* and, upon receiving help, joined them.[27] Catholics not too fondly called Protestants *aleluyas* (amens).

Tradition and cultural involvement helped families weather the economic turmoil. Sunday was always a big day when everyone dressed up for mass, wearing their Sunday best. Afterward, there was the Sunday meal—at home, or at the house of a relative or a friend. Those who traveled never worried about where to spend their vacations; they always had friends or relatives across the country who would add more water to the *frijoles* (beans) when the guests got there.

Popularity of movies was on the rise in most Mexican *barrios*. *Mexico On Main Street* by Colin Gunckel posits that Main Street was the heart of Los Angeles's Mexican immigrant community. The book reconstructs the Mexican immigrant community during the early stages of the American film industry that was in full swing by the 1920s. The Mexican population tripled from 35,000 to about 100,000 by the 1930s. During the decade, the Yellow Streetcars (Los Angeles Railway) took Mexicans to Broadway for entertainment and shopping. Families strolled down the Placita (Our Lady Queen of Angels) Church that was on Main Street. The surrounding neighborhood had small businesses, barbershops and La Luz del Día, and family businesses.[28]

Corridos (folk ballads) and the *ranchera* (ranch music) gave way to a dance craze that filled the nightclubs, with live bands playing Latin American music.[29] Going down to the local theater to see a *variedad* (variety show) was a treat for many families. Mexicans loved sports, and boxing remained a favorite. In Los Angeles, many Mexican boxing fans compared the new boxers with the all-time favorite Bert Colima. They also played baseball and handball.[30] The YMCA and Catholic Church sponsored leagues. The Church organized the Catholic Youth Organization (CYO) in response to the Protestant challenge.[31]

In Texas, local businesses sponsored the Mexican Baseball League, which toured the Rio Grande Valley. José Alamillo writes that in Southern California employers sponsored clubs for Mexican employees to Americanize and control Mexican workers. However, the popularity of the sport evolved into community-based semi-pro teams, such as "the Corona Athletics Baseball Club, which boasted a lineup of Mexican American male ballplayers that claimed several championship pennants and earned a reputation for producing major league players. In the face of racial discrimination and limited economic opportunities that afflicted the Mexican population in this agricultural-industrial town, baseball took on a symbolic and real social significance."[32] Alamillo adds, "Mexican Americans used baseball clubs to promote ethnic consciousness, build community solidarity, display masculine behavior, and sharpen their organizing and leadership skills." The popularity of baseball spread beyond the male universe and Mexican women clubs were formed. "Some examples of team names included: 'Los Tomboys' (Orange, CA) 'Las Debs' (Corona, CA), 'Mexico Libre' and 'Four Star Eagles' (Los Angeles, CA)."[33]

The second generation often preferred American forms of entertainment, was English-speaking. The younger generation became created a hybrid culture and "their tastes redefined the community's cultural practices and future directions of cultural adaptation."[34] Cultural assimilation of Mexican American youth did little to prevent ongoing racism. The city's white nativists, the English-only contingent, harassed local radio stations about broadcasting

Spanish-language programs. They, along with District Attorney Buron Fitts, insisted that Mexicans should listen only to English on radio. This forced radio stations to move much of the Spanish-language broadcasting to the Mexican side of the border.[35]

Los Angeles offered better employment opportunities than did California rural areas that had higher unemployment. During the Depression, large numbers of Mexicans moved out of highly seasonal agriculture and railroad work into factories in the city. The agriculture industry employed the majority of Mexicans through the 1920s, but by 1930, only 45 percent of Mexican males worked in agriculture, 24 percent worked in manufacturing, 13 percent in transportation, and only 1 percent were professionals. Of Mexican females working outside the home, 38 percent were in the service sector, 25 percent worked in blue-collar occupations, 21 percent in agriculture, and 10 percent in clerical or sales; only 3 percent were professionals.[36]

The 1930 Census showed that 18.6 percent of Mexicans in Los Angeles owned homes. In places such as Belvedere, the rate was higher, with 44.8 percent owning homes. Although home ownership did not necessarily mean moving up the economic ladder, it did suggest a degree of permanency. It seemed as if the dream of every Mexican was to own a home, and even a second one for retirement; owning a property gave Mexican families a sense of stability. Land has always been important to Mexicans. I remember my grandfather putting dirt in his mouth and tasting it, saying that he felt like the land on which the family lived was theirs (and the bank's).

Many Mexicans owned homes in the city, alternating between factory work and agriculture. They often fared better in agriculture than in the factory where the father was the sole breadwinner, whereas in farming all family members joined in. Urban-based migrant families followed the crops and returned to their homes when the harvests ended.

Permanency came at a cost to women; they often worked out of the home to help the family buy a home or a car or to supplement the family income, in addition to being homemakers and mothers. Studies show that women worked at seasonal industries such as fruit packaging and food processing. In Los Angeles, food processing and packaging industry employed more Mexican women than did any other local industry. By 1930, some 25 percent of Mexican (and Mexican American) women were in some kind of industrial employment.[37] As in earlier decades, sometimes a family would take in boarders, often members of the extended family. Older children also worked and contributed a portion of their salaries to the family finances.

Historian Juan R. García writes that in the Midwest, "Like their mothers, working daughters were subjected to exploitative wage practices. Although they required sons to contribute only part of their paychecks to their families, daughters had to give all of their earnings to their parents," adding that "Despite the long hours, unhealthy conditions, and poor wages, many young women preferred working to staying at home [where they also worked]."[38] The workplace socialized Mexican women, and the mere act of drawing pay lessened their dependence—they no longer relied on "his" money.

Self-help groups for women flourished during the Depression. María Olazábal in 1931 organized the Cooperative Society of Unemployed Mexican Ladies. Olazábal experienced hardships, such as the gas and electric companies shutting off power in her home in East Los Angeles. Members of the Cooperative sold tamales at a cost to the unemployed, being careful not to hurt their feelings—for only the most desperate would take any kind of charity. Although many Mexican families teetered on the brink of starvation, they considered taking welfare shameful.

As in Los Angeles and the rest of the Southwest, self-help groups played a big role in Tucson's survival. The Club Latino, formed in the spring of 1930, held dance programs and donated the funds to the Ochoa School to provide free lunch to students. Dora Munguía formed a chapter of the Mexican Blue Cross. Mexican organizations also fought discrimination; when S. H. Kress & Co. dismissed several Mexican female employees on racial grounds and replaced them with Americans, the Mexican community organizations pressured Kress to get the Mexicanas reinstated.[39]

Family culture was not always positive. Older children often missed school to care for younger ones and acted as official interpreters for their parents. The Mexican schools persisted through the decade. The quality of Mexican schools was universally poor, with schools described as "barns" or "chicken coops." In California, Mexican schoolteachers were a rarity. In response to pressure by a local YMCA administrator, the Placentia Board of Education hired Bert Valádez as a teacher in 1937. A year afterward, the board hired Mary Ann González. The Fullerton Union High School in 1932 voted to end the Department of Americanization.[40]

Popular culture and movies influenced Mexican youth. As "outsiders," many related to *Mafiosi* as cult heroes, since they were immigrants with power. Movies such as the *Dead-End Kids* glorified gangs, as did their young actors, and their defiance impressed disempowered youth.[41] By the 1930s, there were distinctive *barrios* across the Southwest. Sociologist Joan W. Moore describes the Macy Street and Dogtown *barrios* that established distinct identities and the local industry. These were poor areas. Often the father's inability to provide for the family eroded the children's respect for him, and Chicano gangs based on territoriality began to emerge with the decline of parental authority. One of the first gangs in Los Angeles was from Maravilla, a *barrio* that included the poorest of the poor.

Many families used the *barrio* as a home base while working in agriculture throughout the region; most spoke

Spanish. Mexicans were overrepresented in *las escuelas de burro* (schools that segregate low-achieving students), where schoolwork was easy and students could coast. "By the end of the 1930s some children were learning how to 'qualify' for these schools—how to flunk tests and act dumb to Anglo teachers."[42] El Hoyo Maravilla gang—like other Maravilla gangs—evolved in the 1930s. Racism, the Depression, and the social circumstances of Mexicans all contributed to their gang identities.[43]

The Importance of San Antonio

San Antonio was a reception depot where people would stop off, recover economically, and move on or settle in. Geography favored San Antonio which was not far from population centers of Mexico and South Texas. Mexicans lived for the most part on San Antonio's West Side. Many houses were floorless shacks without plumbing, sewer connections, or electricity. San Antonio also had a more diversified economy than places like Tucson or Santa Fé. Besides having military bases, it had dozens of smaller industries and served as a major center for farm-labor recruiting. Many newcomers arrived with little or no urban-life experience. City agencies refused them relief, and only a few churches and a small number of middle- and upper-class Mexican organizations provided some help, handing out food and clothing. Within the Mexican community the usual divisions existed between Mexico- and U.S.-born Mexicans. U.S.-born Mexicans generally fared better than the new immigrants who often occupied the bottommost rung of the economic and social ladder.[44]

An exception was Fr. Carmelo Tranchese, an Italian-born Jesuit priest whom the Catholic Church assigned to Our Lady of Guadalupe Church in 1932; otherwise, the Catholic Church was largely uninvolved. Fr. Tranchese supported workers' causes and promoted social justice.[45] He endorsed the West Side School Improvement League, which advocated reform of the public schools. Tranchese lobbied for federally funded public housing projects on the West Side, and was surprised at Mexican middle-class resistance to the project. In 1935, Tranchese started the newsletter *La Voz de la Parroquia* (The Parish Voice). Two years later, the archbishop took over *La Voz*, making it less political.

Although competition from Protestants forced the Catholic Church to make concessions, such as recruiting bilingual clergy, Mexican parishes lagged behind American parishes, which sometimes incorporated programs to attract the foreign-born. However, changes were gradually taking place, and by the mid-1930s, some parishes on the North Side, such as Our Lady of Sorrows, preached sermons in both English and Spanish.

San Antonio was the only major city in the United States that refused to provide public aid to starving residents. Thus, the charitable programs of the Catholic and Protestant churches were essential. State and federal agencies doled out what little welfare there although the WPA and other federal programs routinely excluded non-citizens. Consequently, San Antonio had a large labor pool of Mexicans who were willing to work for almost nothing.[46]

Death and disease stalked the West Side throughout the 1930s. Tuberculosis rates were five times as high for Mexicans as to whites, and infant mortality rates were much higher. Desperate people sought desperate solutions; in 1938, 28-year-old Antonia Mena, a married woman, was found dead in the living room of an abortionist.[47]

Nativist Deportations of The 1930s

10.3 Analyze the 1930s repatriation movement and its consequences.

As in every economic downturn in U.S. history, racist nativism reared its ugly head. The repatriation programs deported at least one-third of the Mexican community. The usual excuse for deportation was illegal entry into the country. Especially insidious was the emptying of prisons: giving prisoners reprieves or commuting sentences in return for voluntary "repatriation."[48]

The hysteria over uncontrolled Mexican migration was drummed up since the 1920s. President Herbert Hoover carried on with the policies of the Calvin Coolidge administration to control immigration. The U.S. consulate in Mexico City restricted visas; in 1924 Congress passed the Labor Appropriation Act, officially establishing the U.S. Border Patrol, supposedly to secure the border between inspection stations. With politicos and the press inflaming anti-Mexican fears, most Americans felt that the government did not go far enough to contain Mexicans.

Provoked by the press, the public, organizations—from the American Federation of Labor (AFL) to the American Legion to the American Eugenics Society—joined the lynch mob. Rep. John Box (Democrat–Texas) dug out his failed bill that removed Mexicans from being exempted from immigration quota laws on racial grounds. Box's racist agenda was backed by authorities such as Vanderbilt University eugenics professor Roy L. Garis, who attested to the Mexicans' moral and physical inferiority. The U.S. Senate in May 1930 passed the Mexican-quota bill by a voice vote of 51–16. The bill was referred to the House, where it was placed on the calendar. However, by August 1930 the bill was moot; the Depression reduced the number of Mexicans entering the country to a few hundreds, giving western growers the space to forestall a vote.[49]

"President Herbert Hoover ordered the deportation of ALL illegal aliens in order to make jobs available to American citizens that desperately needed work."[50] Mexican baiting is not an aberration in America and is based more on racism. Mexicans were the main target of the round-up. The accepted estimate of the number of Mexicans and their U.S.-born children who were repatriated between 1929 and 1939 was 500,000–600,000. Some scholars have revised these figures to as many as 2 million—U.S.-born children made up 60–75 percent. The repatriation was mostly carried on locally with politicos taking their cue from President Herbert Hoover who blamed undocumented workers for the Depression. Secretary of Labor William N. Doak bellowed, "My conviction is that by strict limitation and a wise selection of immigration, we can make America stronger in every way, hastening the day when our population shall be more homogeneous." On January 6, 1931, Doak requested that Congress appropriate funds for the deportation of illegal Mexicans from the United States; he alleged that an investigation revealed that 400,000 aliens had evaded immigration laws. The California Senate proposed a bill to prohibit "illegal aliens from engaging in business or seeking employment, and making it a misdemeanor to have such an alien as a partner."[51]

Los Angeles newspapers ran inflammatory headlines such as "U.S. and City Join in Drive on L.A. Aliens." According to them, the aliens were responsible for shootings, fights, and rapes. The strategy was to inflame whites and scare Mexicans out of the city, and local authorities conducted a well-orchestrated campaign of intimidation and fear. C. P. Visel, the Los Angeles local coordinator for unemployment relief, telegraphed Washington that conditions in Los Angeles were desperate and that local citizens needed the jobs the undocumented Mexicans were taking. Visel circulated leaflets that did not differentiate between illegal Mexicans and local citizens of Mexican. They were lumped together as "Mexicans". Visel warned, "20,000 deportable aliens [are] in the Los Angeles area."[52]

Meanwhile, in nearby Pacoima and San Fernando, federal immigration agents went door to door demanding the residents' official identification. At 3 p.m. on February 26, 1931, aided by a dozen police, immigration authorities surrounded the Los Angeles plaza, detaining more than 400 people for over an hour, and arresting 11 Mexicans and 9 Chinese. Authorities pressured even naturalized U.S. citizens to repatriate.[53] Meanwhile, the California Department of Unemployment pressured Mexican clients to return to Mexico. Carey McWilliams posits that the repatriation was largely motivated by racism. However, the popular rhetoric included the greed factor. Politicos dwelled on the rationale that "It cost the County of Los Angeles $77,249.29 to repatriate one train load, but the savings in relief amounted to $347,468.41"—a net savings of $270,219.12.[54]

The states of Illinois, Michigan, Indiana, and Ohio also pressured Mexicans to leave, withdrawing food rations and making them feel unwelcome. As in the Southwest, local authorities became less zealous when they learned that funds from the Reconstruction Finance Corporation (RFC) could no longer be used for the transportation of repatriates. The *Excelsior* on May 11, 1931, called U.S. behavior "shameful from the legal and humanitarian point of view."[55]

Repatriation Texas-Style

The Texas repatriation program was the harshest, beginning in the Lower Rio Grande Valley and fanning out. Authorities often did not permit deportees to sell their property or collect their wages first; counties shipped the healthy and the sick alike; and families were often separated. Most of the repatriates were from the Lower Rio Grande Valley and were employed as laborers on large truck farms; some worked in packing plants and other agribusinesses. The next wave of repatriates was from South Texas, where Mexicans worked in cotton plantations as tenant farmers and laborers. Then came those from rural communities and small towns throughout Central Texas, and, last, the Mexicans from southwest Texas, where they worked as cattlemen, sheepherders, and farmworkers.[56]

One of the stories of abominable abuses that took place in Texas was that of Mrs. Angeles Hernández de Sánchez, who had lived in the United States for 14 years. In 1931, after she returned from a long visit to Chihuahua, authorities detained her for "medical reasons" and proof of residence. Although an examination proved that Hernández de Sánchez did not have venereal disease, the doctor stated that he "suspected" she had syphilis. The Department of Labor ordered Mrs. Hernández and her children deported. After working in Juárez as a servant, she again applied for reentry in 1938, but authorities denied her petition because they had deported her. The fate of Hernández and her two U.S.-born children remains unknown.[57]

In July 1931, federal Judge F. M. Kennerly heard evidence in 83 cases, 70 of which he violated immigration statutes. In one 6-hour session, Kennerly found all of the immigration defendants guilty. The court deported 49 of them and jailed the rest. In Laredo that same year, the same judge heard 98 cases in three hours and convicted all the defendants, deporting 72 and jailing 26. Sixty percent of the Mexican residents of Austin were reportedly returned to Mexico by January 1931.[58]

The Fate of the Deportee in Mexico

Often, deported women were forced to travel to the homeland alone with small children. Adela S. Delgado traveled from Pueblo, Colorado, to the environs of Chihuahua City, Chihuahua in an old Dodge accompanied by her three daughters, ages 13, 12, and 9. Many women rode in packed trucks to remote parts of Mexico from where they walked to reach their villages. In addition to petty jealousies caused by the illusion that the Mexican government gave preferential treatment to the newly arrived *repartiados*, the returnees suffered from culture shock. It was especially difficult for women to adjust. They did not have the spatial freedom they enjoyed in the United States, and many villages lacked material amenities such as plumbing and inside stoves. In addition, the Mexican government did not have the resources to make good on its promises of free land to the repatriates. In 1932, the repatriates formed *La Unión de Repartiados Mexicanos* (the Union of Mexican Repatriates) to pressure the Mexican government to live up to its promises. The *Unión* sent word back to the United States about the Mexican government's non-compliance, and it publicized the repatriates' destitute condition. These reports dampened the enthusiasm many Mexicans had for returning home.[59]

The repatriados were not the only losers; the Mexican American community as a whole suffered losses because of their departure. Some of the repatriates might have lived in poverty, yet their contribution to the *barrio* economy had been significant. Their exodus worried merchants, who feared a negative impact on their business. Indeed, many businesses failed because of the loss of capital and human resources. Banks also suffered as Mexican clients, in anticipation of being repatriated, withdrew funds. In Los Angeles alone, banks deposits were depleted by more than 7 million dollars.[60]

Factories in The Fields

10.4 Explain how conditions for U.S. farms and farmworkers changed during the New Deal.

As the Depression took its course, in California labor surpluses and the migrant pool expanded from 119,800 in 1920 to 190,000 in 1930 and to nearly 350,000 in 1939. By the mid-1930s, white Americans outnumbered Mexicans in the California fields. Meanwhile, the prices of crops fell by more than 50 percent while electricity, water, fertilizer, and transportation costs remained the same. Seeking to make up the difference growers lowered workers' wages by more than 50 percent, making it almost impossible for farmworkers to survive. These difficulties contributed to labor unrest throughout the 1930s.

The situation in California and Arizona farms was distinct. Carey McWilliams wrote that, "farming [in California] has always resembled mining. The soil is really mined, not farmed." The concentration of farmland had accelerated during the 1920s, with rapid expansion in labor-intensive crops like cotton, fruit, nuts, and vegetables, so that, to the farmer, a large supply of labor meant economic progress. Employer–employee relations became more distant, resembling urban industrial relations. Industrialization of agriculture forged a class system similar to that in the urban areas, with a political, economic, and social chasm between growers at the top and migrant labor at the bottom.[61]

Texas Farms

In 1930, 35 percent of Texas Mexicans worked as farm laborers and 15 percent as tenant farmers. Texas farms underwent dramatic changes and were depressed throughout the 1920s. As a consequence, the condition of these workers worsened during the 1930s. The Texas farm economy was heavily dependent on a single crop—cotton—although the number of truck farms rapidly increased. The restructuring of Texas agriculture produced multiple contradictions. The Depression hit cotton production hard and when the New Deal and state laws took acreage out of production, they worsened the plight of tenants and fieldworkers. Technological innovations, such as increased use of tractors and cotton sleds, also reduced the need for labor. Natural disasters—droughts, hurricanes, and floods—also took their toll and devastated thousands of tenants and farmworkers. In 1930, the number of sharecroppers was 205,122; it declined to 76,468 in 1935 and reached a low of 39,821 in 1940.[62]

The New Deal reduced cotton acreage, increasing the size of farms while lessening the demand for tenants and sharecroppers. It was similar to the case of the feudal farm landowners in Central Europe that uprooted tenant farmers and farmworkers. Thus, the New Deal helped the "politically powerful land owning farmers at the expense of ginners, shippers, tenants, and sharecroppers . . . ."[63] It forced workers off the farm and drove them into the cities. Migrant labor took on added importance during the 1930s, a transitional period: "farm tenancy had increased in every census from 1880 to 1930, and then decreased markedly beginning with the 1940 decennial census." There was a mass displacement of white and black sharecroppers as the number of Mexican migrants increased.[64]

Reserve Labor Pool

Colonized workers are largely immigrants. These workers have historically been used as a pool of labor. They work in downgraded and disposable jobs that are not part of the regular labor force. They have fewer political rights and racism keeps them outside the mainstream and the moral consciousness of the public. In the case of Mexicans, the attitude of many Americans has been that they are not white, are culturally deprived, and not deserving of a livable wage or housing. Their low wages subsidize the economy and lack of documents makes them vulnerable to exploitation.[65] Consequently, they are trapped.

A classic example of a reserve labor pool is South Texas. It was the cradle of the Texas diaspora. This cradle was formed after 1900 when thousands of Mexican immigrants poured into the region. "These settlements became collection and recruitment areas for migrant farmworkers in Texas and eventually the rest of the nation."[66] They joined the annual "big swing," the movement of migrants following the crops, which subsidized growers and industries in the south, the Midwest, Northwest, and California. The formation of the migratory workforce catered to American agribusiness needs and government policy. Mexico had nothing to do with creating the reserve pool of cheap labor, but state and federal policies that favored large farmers did.[67]

Renting Mexicans

Agriculture, mining, railroads, and other industries, including construction companies and the garment trade, used labor contractors. The contractors, usually Mexican Americans or Mexicans, spoke English and could talk and deal with both the growers and the workers. Many of the 66,100 Mexicans who annually left Texas for other parts of the country worked through contractors who found them jobs and arranged transportation to the farms. Contractors recruited most of the 3,000–4,000 workers who migrated each year to sugar beet fields in Minnesota, Kansas, and Missouri. Another 10,000 migrated to the sugar beet fields of Michigan and northern Ohio, where contractors recruited 85 percent of the labor force—some 57 percent of whom were from Texas.[68] By the end of the decade,

> As the northern beet fields lured over fifteen thousand migrants annually, South Texas growers noticed that migrants were also travelling to Louisiana, Arkansas, and Mississippi for higher wages. Mississippi Valley cotton planters, like farm managers in California and the Great Lakes, began importing Mexicans from Texas in order to lower production expenses and avoid the economic burdens of the southern sharecropping system.[69]
>
> Some labor contractors did well. Frank Cortez of San Antonio was able to accumulate several stores, cafes, and a funeral parlor.[70]

Cortez shipped 6,000 workers annually to Michigan at $1 per head. Growers advanced Cortez this fee, which they later withdrew from the workers' pay. Cortez had no overhead costs, recruiting right outside his funeral parlor. He sent workers to the Midwest by railroad, truck, and passenger cars; frequently, 60–65 Mexicans were crammed into a truck. Passengers often stood all the way, stopping only for eating, gas and oil, and other necessities. Upon delivery, growers paid Cortez's agent $10 for each worker.

Most labor contractors did not transport the volumes that Cortez did. Many traveled with their crews, acting as "straw bosses" (crew leaders). Some Mexican workers would work for as many as three employers a day. Employers and contractors charged workers for everything from cigarettes to transportation. Employers often paid contractors directly, and contractors, in turn, paid workers. In the sugar beet industry, contractors recruited workers, handled their wages, and ran camps. Pickers sometimes received pay in tickets that they redeemed at local stores for a discount. To employers, contractors were indispensable, since they delivered a crew on the day promised. The system was wrought with abuses such as child labor, short weighing of the pickers' crops, and gross violations of human rights.[71]

The contractors made the system possible—they kept the supply of Mexicans rolling in as employers struggled to maintain a labor surplus. By the end of the 1930s, interracial labor organizations such as the Southern Tenant Farmers Union and the United Cannery, Agricultural, Packing, and Allied Workers of American (UCAPAWA-CIO) struggled to organize small farmers and workers throughout the South and Southwest.[72]

The Farmworkers' Revolt

10.5 Compare regional approaches to the farmworkers' struggle for labor rights.

In California, farmwork wages plummeted from 35¢–50¢ an hour in 1931 to 15¢–16¢ an hour by mid-1933. Workers became increasingly restless and because agribusiness attracted large armies of pickers, a series of huge strikes resulted throughout the state. The center of unrest was the Imperial Valley that experienced a strike in 1928 and where there were a core of activists and unresolved issues. In January 1933, 5,000 Imperial Valley workers, led by the Mexican Mutual Aid Association, struck. Growers quickly settled with white packers and trimmers, most of whom resided in the area. They did not settle with the harvesters, and the workers prepared to strike the planters who were vulnerable during the spring cantaloupe harvest. But an internecine conflict between radicals and moderates weakened the Mexican union, as did the Mexican consul's collusion with the Western Growers Protective Association and immigration authorities.

Meanwhile, a power struggle broke out between the Mexican union and the Agricultural Workers Industrial League (AWIL) that was led by the Communist Party, which had dropped its "boring from within" strategy and formed the Trade Union Unity League (TUUL a federation of Communist trade unions) to organize workers. Although Communist organizers initially joined the efforts of the Mexican union, soon afterward Communist Party organizers accused the Mexican leadership of selling out and/or being reformist. Mexican merchants and tradespeople who controlled the *mutualistas* felt threatened by the radicalism of the pushy gringos. These divisions weakened worker solidarity. The presence of Communist organizers in the Valley gave Sheriff Charles L. Gillett license to conduct wholesale raids—making 103 arrests in April 1933 alone. Meanwhile, the district attorney brought indictments against eight union leaders for criminal syndicalism. They received sentences of 2–28 years.[73]

California Mexicans took part in strikes throughout 1930, 1931, and 1932. In July 1931, the AWIL changed its name to the Cannery and Agricultural Workers Industrial Union (C&AWIU). The failure of Mexican unions to gain concessions from employers opened the field to the Communist union. During its first years of operations, the C&AWIU joined strikes after they had started. It was not until November 1932, at Vacaville, California, that the union took the lead. In 1933, 37 strikes involving some 47,575 farmworkers broke out in California. The C&AWIU participated in 25 of these strikes, involving 32,800 workers. Most strikes ended in partial victories.[74]

The El Monte Strike

The Los Angeles area's mix of agricultural and industrial production encouraged the movement of workers to the city. In the mid-1930s, there were 13,549 farms in the county, with 619,769 acres involved in agriculture. In Los Angeles, farming was a $76 million industry, surpassing the $23 million produced in the Imperial Valley. Thousands of Mexican workers and their families either passed through Los Angeles or lived there during the off-season. Farm labor strikes in the county agitated militancy among urban workers, and vice versa.[75]

El Monte, a town of 4,000 in the eastern half of the county, served as a trade area and housed 12,000 residents—75 percent were Americans, 20 percent Mexicans, and 5 percent Japanese. The Chicano *barrio*, known as Hicks Camp, was a shack town located across a dry river gulch from El Monte proper. Many of its 1,100 Mexicans were migratory workers, forming the bulk of the town's cheap labor force and earning an average of 15¢–20¢ an hour.

In May 1933, Mexican, Japanese, and American workers of El Monte demanded higher wages in advance of the berry-harvesting season. When farmers refused, the Mexican workers formed a strike committee. The strike began on June 1, and shortly afterward, the C&AWIU joined in, at first cooperating with the Mexican union. Because berries were highly perishable, the growers were vulnerable. The sheriff initially left the strikers alone; however, he became more proactive as the harvest season neared its end.

The Los Angeles Chamber of Commerce became concerned about the prolonged strike and contacted the U.S. Department of Labor to urge the growers to compromise. They offered the strikers an inadequate pay raise, which they rejected. After this point, the strike grew ugly; growers portrayed strike leaders as outside agitators and red-baited them (*red-baiting* is indiscriminately calling anyone on the left of the political spectrum a Communist, with the intention of discrediting him or her). The split between the factions led by the Mexican consul and that led by the C&AWIU weakened worker solidarity. The Mexican vice-consul cooperated with police authorities to purge Communist leaders who gained a substantial following among the strikers. By the time the growers finally made an offer, the peak of the harvest season passed and the growers proposed a rate lower than the one originally rejected by the union—and the union, again, turned it down. The El Monte strike failed miserably.[76]

The Tagus Ranch

After the El Monte berry strike, worker militancy increased as strike veterans exported their collective memories to other parts of California. As the workers became desperate, the C&AWIU became more attractive to the rank and file. A series of strikes launched in August 1933 infused workers with a tremendous unifying spirit. The most important of the August strikes took place at the Tagus Ranch in the San Joaquín Valley. C&AWIU organizer Pat Chambers led the strike that encompassed seven counties.[77]

Deputies and ranch guards declared war, as growers armed themselves and conducted raids on union headquarters, resulting in mass arrests and deportations of strikers. During the strike, union organizers noticed the vulnerability of strikers who resided on company property; they devised new strategies, such as setting up private camps and roving pickets. They tried to divide the small farmers from the large planters, signing separate contracts, but met with limited success. After the bitter strike, strikers got a 25¢-an-hour settlement. The Tagus victory motivated pickers in other counties to rally for the 25¢ rate. This partial victory fueled worker militancy, but growers were also bitter and more resolved to destroy the worker movement once and for all. Thus, the Tagus Ranch strike set the stage for the San Joaquín cotton strike of October 1933.[78]

In Dubious Battle

"Three-quarters of workers in *Dubious Battle* were Mexicans. . . ."[79] Reading John Steinbeck and other authors, the reader got the impression that white Oklahomans fueled the strikes.[80] It is astonishing since he wrote many novels about Mexico and Mexicans in the United States such as *Tortilla Flat* (1935), *In Dubious Battle* (1936), *Cannery Row* (1945), *and The Pearl* (1947) and made many trips to Mexico. It must be kept in mind that while Steinbeck was a political man who loved Mexican history and Mexico, he was also an author who wanted to sell books and, above all, sell a message. Steinbeck wrote *Grapes of Wrath* with a motion picture in mind and in all probability feared that white readers would not relate to Mexican protagonists. Steinbeck was also an American and shared many of the attitudes of his generation on race.

The protagonist *In Dubious Battle* was modeled after Pat Chambers, the lead communist organizer at the Tagus and San Joaquín Cotton Strikes. Chambers was a short man—one of the most sincere and dedicated men that I have interviewed.[81] However, Chambers and Carolyn Decker, like most organizers, could not remember the names of Mexican strikers or leaders. They recognized that Mexican and Filipino strikers were there in the majority and took leadership roles but they could not remember their names.

The Tagus Ranch strike raged throughout most of September. Authorities arrested C&AWIU organizers and charged them with violating the criminal syndicalism laws. Newspapers mentioned M. Esparzo, Y. López, and John García as ringleaders. G. S. Herrera, José Cota, and Willie De la Hoya were charged with criminal syndicalism. By mid-September, the strike was over.[82]

Michael Denning writes, "the 'grapes of wrath' narrative gained much of its popularity because it was told as a story of white Protestant 'plain people'."[83] He singles out a pamphlet written by Steinbeck titled "Their Blood is Strong," demonstrating the complexity of the race question even among progressive whites of the time. In it, Steinbeck wrote of the Okie:

> They are here because we need them. Before the white American migrants were here, it was the custom in California to import great numbers of Mexicans, Filipinos, Japanese, to keep them segregated, to herd them about like animals, and, if there were any complaints, to deport or imprison the leaders. This system of labor was a dream of heaven to such employers as those who now fear foreign agitators so much. But then the dust and the tractors began displacing the sharecroppers of Oklahoma, Texas, Kansas and Arkansas. Families who had lived for many years on the little "croppers' lands" were dispossessed because the land was in the hands of the banks and the finance companies and because these owners found that one man with a tractor could do the work of ten sharecroppers' families.[84]

Denning criticizes Steinbeck for his use of phrases such "foreign people labor"; the use of the title of the pamphlet "Their Blood is Strong"; and his adding "They are of the best American stock." Denning concedes that it is a political pamphlet.[85] But Steinbeck goes on, "The earlier foreign migrants have invariably been drawn from a peon class. This is not the case with the new migrants."[86] And about the Okies, "They are resourceful intelligent Americans."[87] This narrative is uncomfortable, but words matter. Words are important because they influence historical interpretation.

The San Joaquín Valley Cotton Strike

A stereotype is that most strikers were peasants who were in need of leadership. However, by the 1930s, many of the Mexican farmworkers had worked in mining and then as agricultural workers when the mines shut down. The Mexican Revolution had raised the social consciousness of others while others worked other industries. Moreover, a sizeable number had experience in other strikes. They were hardly in need of leadership, although they needed resources.[88]

In the spring of 1933, San Joaquín cotton growers signed contracts with ginning and banking companies such as the Bank of America, the San Joaquín Ginning Company, and the local ginning operations of the Anderson Clayton Company. The contracts set the price of picked cotton at 40¢ per hundredweight (cwt.). The workers wanted $1 per cwt. The strike, which began on October 2, involved 10,000–12,000 workers—18,000 by some accounts. Eighty percent were Mexican; many were women.[89]

Business leaders, newspapers, chambers of commerce, farm bureaus, elected officials, and local city and county police authorities all supported the growers. The sheriffs arrested strikers, confining workers in bullpens. Cotton growers pressured authorities to cut relief payments of Los Angeles residents to swell the labor force and pressure strikers to work in the fields. Growers even mobilized local schoolchildren, declaring school holidays and pouring them into the fields. Meanwhile, federal authorities backed the growers and ordered the deportation of strikers charged with picketing.[90]

As expected, on October 4, growers began evicting strikers and their families. Union organizers had rented five campsites at Corcoran, McFarland, Porterville, Tulare, and Wasco. Strikers and their families moved into the camps. Each camp was given complete autonomy, and this self-control contributed to a spirit of unity and class-consciousness among Mexicans. Mexican wives had their own networks that did much of the organizing within these communities; they knew each other from other camps or through kinship. Union organizers made it clear that if any of the camp committees voted to break the strike, they would end strike activities—the strike's success depended on the unity among the strikers in the camps. Therefore, it was essential for the strikers to maintain top security, and for organizers to keep grower propaganda from reaching the camps.[91]

The Corcoran camp housed 3,780 strikers who outnumbered the 2,000 townspeople. An elected committee laid out streets, arranged toilet facilities, maintained sanitation and clean drinking water, settled disputes, and guarded the camp. Barbed wire enclosed the camp, and strike leaders posted guards at the entrance and exit. The camp committee established a tent school for about 70 children and an assembly space for meetings presided over by the mayor of the camp, Lino Sánchez. Strikers also held nightly performances that the residents dubbed an "Aztec Circus."[92]

The tendency of Mexicans to migrate in larger groupings gave them wider social networks than most American farm migrants enjoyed. According to Devra Weber, "Because women migrated with their families, they had sisters, mothers, aunts, cousins and friends from their home areas to rely on. Women who migrated without other women and were not yet part of ranch life often felt isolated."[93] These networks reinforced solidarity among the Mexicans. Women had common experiences, of migrating and shouldering more than their share of responsibilities. Some stayed in the camps and cared for children; while others joined the men on the picket lines. During the strike, besides running the camps, which were the backbone of the strike, women played the role of agitators, pushing the strikers and taunting the enemy.[94]

Violence broke the strike on October 10. At Pixley, an unarmed gathering of strikers were listening to Pat Chambers speak, when a dozen cars belonging to the growers surrounded the group and opened fire; the strikers scurried back to the union hall. Two strikers were killed and 11 wounded. The assassinated strikers included Dolores Hernández, 52, and Defino D'Avila, 55. It was evident that the California Highway Patrol (CHP) was in collusion with the growers. B. H. Olivas of Madera stated that, "ranchers told our patrolmen that beginning today they would beat to hell every striker who so much as laid a hand on the fences on their properties."[95] Meanwhile, the justice system tried eight ranchers for the murders and acquitted them.

Almost simultaneously, on the morning of October 10, in nearby Arvin, growers and picketers were engaged in an exchange of words—30 armed guards and about 200 picketers faced each other. About three o'clock, fighting broke out and a prominent grower shot into the crowd, killing Pedro Subia, age 57, and wounding several strikers. Witnesses testified that all the shots came from the growers' side and that the strikers did not have guns. Eyewitnesses also identified the man who shot Subia, but authorities refused to charge the killer. Instead, they booked seven picketers for Subia's murder.

After the shootings, growers became even more aggressive. With the complicity of local authorities, they implemented a strategy to starve out hungry strikers and their families. But, when the state temporarily offered relief, even though the strikers were desperate, many refused to sign the return-to-work forms in exchange for relief, or to accept milk for their children upon condition that they sign waivers. At least nine infants died of malnutrition at the Corcoran camp alone. Top San Joaquín Valley industrialists such as J. G. Boswell encouraged this lawless behavior.

Clarence "Cockeye" Salyer, one of the largest plantation owners in the valley, told his son Fred after the Pixley shooting that he had come home with his "hands covered with blood." Fred helped his father melt down the Colt 38 Special with which, he said he had fired at the strikers. Clarence was not sure whether his bullet killed Dolores Hernández, but he was not taking any chances.[96]

The growers eventually settled the strike because of state intervention. In effect, the federal government promised the growers money to settle the strike, rewarding their vigilantism. On October 23, the governor's fact-finding committee recommended a compromise, raising the rate for cotton to 75¢ per cwt. The committee also found gross violations of human rights. Growers agreed to the terms, but many workers held out for 80¢. The governor then ordered a halt to relief payments, which the workers had just begun drawing to avoid starvation.[97]

The Imperial Valley, 1934

The C&AWIU moved to capitalize on worker goodwill gained in the 1933 strikes. In December, the union once again entered the Imperial Valley, calling for more militant tactics. Many Mexicans joined the C&AWIU; others retained their membership in the Mexican union. In January, the C&AWIU sent two well-known Communist organizers, Dorothy Ray Healy and Stanley Hancock, to the Valley. According to Pat Chambers, while the presence of Healy and Hancock generated excitement, it also drew time away from organizing efforts since Healy and Hancock had to hide from the police and were constantly on the move.

On January 12, 1934, over aggressive police attacked a union meeting and killed two people, including a child. Vigilantes assaulted and tear-gassed the strikers at will, and, on January 23, they kidnapped American Civil Liberties Union (ACLU) lawyer H. L. Wirin. On February 19, local law enforcement officers literally crushed the strike by burning the workers' shacks and evicting all 2,000 of them. By then, even state authorities were shocked at the blatant disregard for human life; they forced the growers to arbitrate the pea strike at the northern end of the Imperial Valley.

Meanwhile, divisions among the workers widened. Mexican consul Joaquín Terrazas helped form *La Asociación Mexicana del Valle Imperial* (the Mexican Association of the Imperial Valley). The C&AWIU immediately branded the association a "company union." Initially, during the cantaloupe strike of April 1934, the Mexican union worked alongside the C&AWIU, but the C&AWIU soon co-opted the strike and seized control. Although both groups claimed limited victories, the growers kept control of the Imperial Valley. On March 28, 1934, California growers, the California Chamber of Commerce, and the Farm Bureau formed the Associated Farmers of California, as what had become routine. The Associated Farmers also sent photos of labor agitators to Frank J. Palomares of the San Joaquín Labor Bureau (SJLB), an organization funded by growers, sugar companies, oil companies, railroads, and utilities.[98]

On July 20, 1934, police raided Communist headquarters in Sacramento and, based on numerous confiscated pamphlets and papers, indicted 17 alleged Communists and prosecuted 15, on charges of criminal syndicalism. The state convicted 8 of the 15, among whom were Pat Chambers and Caroline Decker who spent two years in jail before a higher court overturned their sentences. These arrests and convictions ended the four-year career of the C&AWIU.[99]

CUCOM and Mexican Strikes

Consequent to the collapse of the C&AWIU, Mexican workers formed many independent unions; some of its organizers shifted to *La Confederación de Uniónes de Campesinos y Obreros Mexicanos* (CUCOM). Mexicans took the leadership in 6 of the 18 strikes during 1935. As Mexican workers became more politically conscious following each strike, the number of union members grew.

In January 1936, CUCOM helped organize the Federation of Agricultural Workers of America, which included 11 multiracial locals of Filipinos, Japanese, and other nationalities. During the spring of 1936 in Los Angeles County, CUCOM led a walkout of 2,600 celery workers. The Los Angeles "red squads" tear-gassed parades and picket lines, beating and arresting union members.[100] A favorite grower tactic in breaking a strike was to pressure various California counties to withdraw relief, making places like Los Angeles their personal reserve labor pools.

In Orange County, 2,500–3,000 citrus-fruit pickers and packers went on strike on June 15, 1936. Workers averaged 22¢ an hour; they demanded an increase to 27.5¢, transportation, and union recognition. The activism in the county is dated from the time of the *Confederación de Uniónes Mexicanas* (the Federation of Mexican Unions, 1928), which had 15 Orange County locals. In 1935, vegetable workers organized a major walkout that set the stage for the citrus strike. Community members, the Mexican consul, and union leaders led the strike. On the other side, led by the Associated Farmers, growers recruited 400 special guards. The CHP harassed picketers along roads, and police authorities arrested some 200, herding them into stockades. Local newspapers described the situation as a civil war and blamed the Communists. The strike failed when growers would not concede to a single strike demand and state and grower violence increased.[101]

The Congress of Industrial Organizations

The National Labor Relations Act of 1935 encouraged labor to expand and organize. The passage of the so-called Wagner Act coincided with actions by John L. Lewis of the United Mine Workers and other union leaders in establishing a committee of industrial unions to launch a vast organizing campaign. When the craft-oriented AFL refused to support the Committee of Industrial Organizations, led by Lewis, industrial unionists broke with the AFL and formed the Congress of Industrial Organizations (CIO) in 1937. The CIO was more receptive to organizing farmworkers and including people of color within the various locals. Similar to the Industrial Workers of the World (IWW) in the 1910s, the CIO put pressure on the AFL to organize Mexicans and African Americans. The CIO was a training ground for many militant Chicano organizers in the Southwest and in the Chicago area.[102]

Mexican-origin migrants and white migrants competed with each other in many places, such as the Yakima Valley in Washington State; they traveled south during the winter to work and live in California, Texas, Arizona, Florida, or other states. The National Labor Relations Act (the Wagner Act), which guaranteed urban workers the right to organize, to engage in collective bargaining, and to strike, pointedly excluded farmworkers, making conditions even more desperate for them. Consequently, during 1937 and 1938, conditions in agriculture in the Southwest verged on class warfare.

By the second half of the decade, urban unions paid more attention to the plight of workers, fearing that conditions in the countryside might endanger their gains in the cities. Simultaneously, Mexican and Filipino unions realized that they were too small and isolated. Thus, during 1936 and 1937, CUCOM negotiated with other ethnic labor unions to form alliances. In July 1937, CUCOM sent delegates to Denver and joined the newly formed United Cannery, Agricultural, Packing, and Allied Workers of America (UCAPAWA), which promised to organize immigrant workers. UCAPAWA hired charismatic Latino leaders such as Luisa Moreno, who was the first Latina to serve on the executive committee of UCAPAWA. Born a wealthy Guatemalan, Moreno gave up her inheritance. Working in New York's garment industry before joining UCAPAWA, Moreno organized for the AFL. Historian David Gutiérrez writes, "UCAPAWA's immediate influence in the agricultural labor force was short-lived, however, due to the union's decision in 1938 to focus its energies on organizing packing-shed and cannery workers rather than workers in the fields."[103]

As the militancy among Mexicans increased, the planters used ever more repressive tactics to break them. Mexican locals and independent unions agitated throughout the 1930s. Growers and local authorities viciously attacked the strikes, determined to drive the Mexican workers from the fields; "Okies" (from Oklahoma) and "Arkies" (from Arkansas) were employed in large numbers to replace the strikers. By the end of the decade, Mexican farmworkers were a lesser presence in the agricultural workforce.

The Arizona farm struggle resembled California with ownership and control of land more concentrated in the hands of the few. During the Depression years, Arizona became a highway for Dust Bowl refugees enroute to California, with over 100,000 crossing the Arizona border in 1937 alone. During the 1920s and 1930s, the AFL organized there, making early gains among cotton pickers. Organizational efforts met the same fate as they did in California, and the independent unions there eventually consolidated into the UCAPAWA.[104]

Rural Workers in the Lone Star State

We can assume that Texas was more difficult to organize than California: Agribusiness was not as large and it was more dispersed. Thus, workers were not as concentrated and were more difficult to reach. The Rio Grande Valley and San Antonio literally dipped deep into the heart of Mexico, and the distance from Laredo to Mexico City is about 698 miles versus 2,000 miles for Los Angeles. There was always a sizable presence of Mexicans in Texas, and even during the Depression years, it was only a matter of walking across the border. The better-paying fields of the Midwest offered a safety net for many Tex-Mexicans who owned or rented homes in the Valley. In addition, the progressive American cores in Texas were not nearly as large or as strong as those in other states; for example, throughout the bloody agricultural strikes in California, white students from Stanford and Berkeley made their pilgrimage from San Francisco to support the strikers. Lastly, Texas was more rural and it could get away with an incredible amount of institutional violence.

The sheer size of Texas was an obstacle to union organizing of farmworkers. Despite this impediment, Mexicans organized. Eighty-five percent of the state's migrant labor force was Mexican. In 1933 in Laredo, Texas, Mexicans organized an independent union, *La Asociación de Jornaleros* (Association of Laborers), which included hat makers, painters, carpenters, construction workers, miners, and farm laborers. The next year, agent provocateurs disrupted union activity, and in the spring of 1935 near Laredo, the union led a strike of more than 1,200 onion workers. The strike failed, partly because of the organizers' inexperience and partly because of harassment by Texas Rangers, who arrested 56 strikers. The union had refused to sign with individual growers and had held out for an industry-wide contract, but its members were persuaded to return to work by a federal mediation agreement. Growers, however, broke the agreement when the federal mediators left. Meanwhile, in West Texas about 750 members of the Sheep Shearers Union (SSU) agitated, making certain demands, for which 42 SSU members were arrested.

Throughout the 1930s, the Southern Tenant Farmers' Union (STFU), founded in Arkansas by 27 white and African American sharecroppers, organized in Texas. Although Mexicans were heavily involved in cotton, no major cotton strike happened in Texas during this decade. Tenants increasingly fled to the cities or to the migrant trail. The STFU organized 328 locals and more than 16,000 members in Arkansas, but only 8 locals with fewer than 500 members in Texas. Meanwhile, wages remained pegged at 40¢ per cwt. of cotton. In 1937, Mexican cotton pickers from the Laguna district in Mexico attended the STFU conference in Muskogee, Oklahoma. Still, the STFU was unsuccessful at building a biracial movement in Texas. Part of the problem was that the STFU did not view sharecroppers and farmworkers as industrial workers, which discouraged a permanent alliance with UCAPAWA. In addition, the STFU leadership was reluctant to work with the UCAPAWA because there were prominent Communists within the newly formed industrial union.

In January 1937, the Texas Federation of Labor formed the Texas Agriculture Organizing Committee (TAOC), which participated in a series of small strikes in late June and early July. However, growers and state authorities countered the TAOC's efforts by controlling the labor pool. The Texas State Employment Service, formed in 1935, recruited workers for the different crops; in 1939 alone, the service placed 550,047 farmworkers. Texas's surplus labor pool was simply too large to allow for effective organization. In the summer of 1937, UCAPAWA absorbed the committee, and eventually recruited 5,000 dues-paying members.[105]

Colorado and the Manitos

The magnitude of the Colorado sugar beet operations attracted large numbers of Mexican sugar beet laborers. It also attracted Communist organizers who formed AWIL locals in Greeley, Fort Lupton, Fort Collins, and Denver. In February 1932, various factions formed the United Front Committee of Agricultural Workers Unions, which became active in Colorado, Nebraska, and Wyoming. In May, the United Front called a strike, which the Great Western Sugar Company easily broke with cooperation from public agencies and law enforcement officials. The more radical factions blamed the Front's failure on "conservative" or "reformist organizations" such as the Spanish-American Citizens Association of Fort Collins; but the fact was that the strike was poorly planned. Mass arrests and the deportation of militant Mexican members marked the end of the United Front. Mexican workers formed the Spanish-Speaking Workers' League in Denver as a vehicle to hold more radical workers together after the 1932 strike.[106]

Mexican workers also joined TUUL and "unemployed councils" of beet workers to agitate for adequate relief; the groups later merged with the Colorado State Federation of Labor (CFL). Membership in the council was free, but when members found jobs, they had to forfeit their membership cards. The CFL reportedly had 25,000 unemployed members. A few of the councils struck against work relief projects to improve conditions and took part in small agricultural strikes.[107]

The Beet Workers Association claimed a membership of 35,000 in Colorado, Wyoming, Nebraska, and Montana. The Jones–Costigan Act of 1934 protected the growers, giving them subsidies averaging $17.15 per acre, if they did not employ child labor. It also guaranteed workers a livable wage based on which workers demanded $23 an acre.

However, the U.S. Department of Agriculture in Colorado set a rate of $19.50 per acre for northern Colorado and $17.50 for the southern section. In Blissfield, Michigan This drove Mexicans and others to unite and form the Agriculture Workers Union (AWU). In 1935, 500 members struck near Blissfield and won a raise and union recognition. In 1936, however, the U.S. Supreme Court declared the Jones–Costigan Act unconstitutional, and growers again employed child labor and imported WPA workers from the cities to break the union. In this war against labor, local authorities deputized more than 400 vigilantes.

The Sugar Act of 1937 subsidized farmers and authorized the secretary of agriculture to set a minimum wage for beet workers. The Sugar Act was the only labor legislation that directly benefited Mexican farm labor during the decade. In the 1920s, 7,000–10,000 New Mexicans migrated to Colorado annually; by the early 1930s, the number dwindled to only 2,000. Colorado authorities repatriated some 20,000 Mexicans between 1930 and 1935. Returning to New Mexico was not a homecoming. The infrastructures of Mexican villages were flooded, and were not capable of absorbing or caring for the needs of their prodigal sons and daughters. The return of so many compatriots worsened conditions, and the small villages were further impacted by the 1931–32 drought.[108]

Away from their ancestral lands, New Mexicans in Colorado suffered intense racism. The Ku Klux Klan paraded in sugar beet towns, distributing handbills reading, "All Mexicans and all other aliens to leave the state of Colorado at once by orders of Colorado state vigilantes". "White Americans" also resented Mexicans getting any type of federal relief, including work projects employment. They chided the Mexicans because of their inability to "speak American." Life in Colorado was even more unequal in New Mexico, where women continued to hold a wide variety of positions and authority. As women moved away from the villages, they lost their base of power.[109]

The City

10.6 Characterize urban unionization by Mexican communities in the 1930s.

Los Angeles offered opportunities for politicizing the entire family—opportunities that were not available to people on the move. Besides giving Mexican families more permanency, the city gave them opportunities for education and interaction with others. The Depression added to this politicization; it challenged Mexican cultural patterns, for instance, more women had to work outside the home. In turn, factories offered more opportunities for socialization: earning paychecks, interacting with other women, and the sharing of grievances—all empowered women.

Mexican Women Garment Workers in Los Angeles

By the 1930s, Mexican women comprised a majority of the garment factory labor pool of the Southwest. Los Angeles had an estimated 150 dress factories that employed about 2,000 workers. Seventy-five percent were Mexican females; the rest were Italians, Russians, Jews, and Americans. The Depression rendered these poorly paid workers even more vulnerable. In the summer of 1933, the Los Angeles garment industry began to revive its production, and the demand for workers increased. Employers, wanting to maximize their profits, hired Mexican women at substandard wages.

The National Recovery Act (NRA) code stipulated a pay rate of $15 a week for garment workers; however, employers violated the code and paid 40 percent of the women less than $5 a week. If women protested, they lost their jobs, or worse, were deported. Rosa Pesotta, a union organizer for the International Ladies' Garment Workers Union (ILGWU), was an anarchist and a Jewish immigrant, who broke with the conventional wisdom of her union that Mexican women could not be organized. Pesotta realized that women were vulnerable: They were the victims of racism, many had unemployed husbands at home, and many were the sole providers of their families. "Poorly paid and hard driven, many of these agricultural workers, seeking to leave their thankless labors, naturally gravitated to the principal California cities, where compatriots had preceded them. Thus hundreds of Mexican women and girls, traditionally skillful with needle and eager to get away from family domination, had found their way into the garment industry in Los Angeles." Pesotta further elaborates that they lived on the outskirts of towns, "at the end of the car-lines, in rickety old shacks, unpainted, unheated, usually without baths and with outside toilets . . ." adding that "We get them . . . because we are the only *Americanos* who take them in as equals. They may well become the backbone of our union on the West Coast."[110] In 1933, the ILGWU began to recruit heavily among these Mexican women, who had nothing to lose. On October 12, 1933, the new members of ILGWU—without any previous organization experience—effected a closedown of the Los Angeles garment industry. When the local radio station stopped broadcasting ILGWU news, they used Tijuana's *El Eco de México* to broadcast union messages to Los Angeles. Strikers defied a court injunction prohibiting picketing by assembling 1,000 people in front of the Paramount Dress Company. Captain William Hynes and the "red squad" were powerless to disperse such a large gathering. Even so, the police harassed the picketers, forcing them to march two abreast, and forbidding them to holler "Scab!" Police arrested five strikers for disorderly conduct.

As their organizational experiences expanded their political vocabulary, the Mexican workers demanded more power in the union, arguing that although Mexicans composed most of Local 96, only 6 of the 19 union board members were Mexican. By 1936, the ILGWU had signed contracts for 2,650 workers in 56 firms. The gender bias was portrayed through contracts that paid women $28 and men $35, weekly. The next year, the local became part of the CIO and its membership climbed to 3,000.[111]

San Antonio Mexicana Workers

San Antonio's garment industry employed 6,000–7,000 persons—mostly piecework Mexican laborers. The city's pecan-shelling industry hired 12,000–15,000 Mexicans during peak season. Gender inequality in the workplace was common: Employers paid women even less than the rates paid to Mexican males, who were not paid on par with their white colleagues. The pretext was that women did not need much money since they were more apt to be single and live with their parents. White women monopolized the white-collar clerical and sales occupations; 91 percent of African American women worked as domestics or in service jobs. Seventy-nine percent of Mexican women worked in industrial occupations.

In August 1933, a 100 cigar rollers and tobacco strippers walked out of the Finck Cigar Company after the employer announced that workers would be fined three good cigars' worth of wages for every bad one. Led by Mrs. W. H. Ernst, a Mexican woman, Mexicanas organized an independent union. Authorities cracked down, arresting Mrs. Ernst. Federal and local authorities sided with Finck and the NRA's board signed an agreement with him, giving strippers 17.5¢ an hour and rollers 22.5¢, well below the 30¢ minimum set by the NRA. Finck blatantly violated the agreement, firing all union leaders. Again, in early 1934, the Mexicanas briefly walked out, this time affiliating with the San Antonio Trades Council. The NRA's regional board found working conditions at Finck's intolerable—that is, leaky pipes, unsanitary grounds, and inadequate toilet facilities. When the regional board ruled in favor of the workers, Finck appealed the findings, and retaliated by red-baiting the union and raising penalties for bad cigars to four to one.

The following year, members walked out again. The strike grew ugly as strikers attacked scabs, tearing off their clothes. Police Chief Owen Kilday once more arrested Mrs. Ernst, and mass arrests followed. Supported by elected officials and the Chambers of Commerce, Finck imported replacement workers from Mexico and broke the strike.[112]

San Antonio was a major garment-manufacturing center. Garment workers earned $3–$5 a week (6¢–11¢ an hour) and worked 45 hours a week. In March 1934, the ILGWU chartered two locals in the city: the Infants and Children's Wear Workers Union Local 180 and the Ladies' Garment Workers Union Local 123. The ILGWU called a strike at the A. B. Frank plant in 1936; workers closed down the plant. After six months of being picketed by Local 123, the Dorothy Frocks Company, a clothing manufacturer, moved to Dallas, where a local continued the strike until the company signed a contract in November 1936.[113]

In 1936, during President Franklin Delano Roosevelt's car caravan through the city, some 50 strikers publicly disrobed company scabs. Chief Kilday conducted mass arrests, citing strikers for unlawful assembly and obstructing the sidewalk. In the spring of 1937, Local 180 called a strike against the Shirlee Frock Company. With a judge limiting picketing to no more than three persons and prohibiting the displaying of banners, Kilday arrested 50 picketers. But the strike was successful; employers were forced to recognize the ILGWU and workers received the minimum wage of 20¢ an hour.

The ILGWU limited success in other Texas cities. Some blame must be assigned to the union's national leadership, which never attempted to hire or develop Mexican organizers. The union hired Rebecca Taylor, a white woman, as the educational director of its San Antonio office. Taylor, a schoolteacher, took the job because union organizing paid better than teaching. Taylor's sole qualifications were that she spoke Spanish and had a college degree. Taylor was born in Mexico to a middle-class Arkansas–Oklahoma–Texas religious colony established in the 1890s, which revolutionaries later broke up. During Taylor's tenure with the union, she opposed anything involving radicalism and militancy, including the more progressive Chicana/o leadership that surfaced during the pecan shellers' strike of 1938. In the 1950s, Taylor quit the union and went to work for Tex-Son, one of the ILGWU's principal adversaries.[114]

La Pasionaria, the Pecan Shellers' Strike, and San Antonio

The pecan industry of San Antonio employed 5,000–12,000 Mexicans. Gustave Duerler, a Swiss candy manufacturer, began the industry during the Civil War. He bought pecans from the Native Americans and hired Mexicans to crack open the pecans and extract the meat. By the 1880s, Duerler was shipping pecans east. In 1914, Duerler mechanized the cracking phase of his operation, but continued to use Mexican women to extract the meat by hand. In 1926, he formed the Southern Pecan Shelling Company. Ten years later, the shelling company's gross annual revenue climbed to $3 million. The company then demechanized because hiring Chicanos was cheaper than buying and maintaining machines.[115]

The pecan industry used agribusiness employment practices. Contractors furnished crackers and pickers. Often, contractors employed workers to shell pecans in their own homes. Frequently, as many as 100 pickers were packed into unventilated rooms without toilets or running water. The shellers averaged less than $2 per week in 1934. The rate increased only slightly by 1936. Management justified the low wages, saying that the workers ate pecans while on the job. The owners claimed that the workers were satisfied because they had a warm place to work in company of their friends. Moreover, they said, the shellers would not work the required hours if the shelling company paid them more; they would earn 75¢ and go home, whether it was 3 p.m. or 6 p.m. Their justification for lower wages even went to the extent that if Mexicans earned more, they would just spend their wages "on tequila and on worthless trinkets in the dime stores."

In 1933, the Mexicanas, led by labor organizer Emma Tenayuca, formed the largest of the pecan workers' unions, which claimed a membership of 4,000 by 1936. San Antonians called her La Pasionaria (passionflower, which had symbolic value to the Communists), after Dolores Ibárruri the fiery heroine of the Spanish Civil War that was taking place about the same time. When management cut rates by 1¢ a pound, thousands of shellers walked off their jobs at the peak of the pecan-shelling season on February 1, 1938. Workers walked out of 130 plants throughout the West Side, affiliating with the CIO's UCAPAWA. Local law authorities backed the management and arrested more than 1,000 picketers on various charges, including blocking sidewalks, disturbing the peace, and unlawful assembly. City officials invoked an obscure city ordinance to prevent sign-carrying picketers from using public space.

Before completing high school, Emma Tenayuca walked the picket lines with cigar strikers at the Finck Cigar Company. Tenayuca had been an organizer for the Workers Alliance, and had led demonstrations attracting tens of thousands of participants. Police Chief Kilday made Tenayuca his favorite scapegoat.[116]

At the start of the strike, *La Prensa* supported Tenayuca. Almost immediately, a power struggle over control of the strike developed between Tenayuca and the UCAPAWA leaders. Tenayuca was apparently forced, on the second day of the strike, to resign her leadership role to counteract charges of Communist influence. However, the workers voted Tenayuca the honorary strike leader.[117]

Tenayuca left San Antonio in 1939. Along with her husband, Homer Brooks, Tenayuca wrote one of the few works about the Mexican question in the Southwest that was published by the Communist Party. The thesis was that society should respect the Mexicans' cultural integrity, shifting the responsibility of assimilation from the immigrants to the majority society. The treatise argued that Mexicans were part of the U.S. working class and should struggle within the American nation instead of within the Mexican (Mexico's) working class. Tenayuca later broke with the party because of its paternalism.

On August 25, 1938, Tenayuca planned a rally at the municipal auditorium. At 8 p.m, some 6,000–7,000 people, including ranchers, veterans, housewives, and schoolchildren, collected outside the auditorium and screamed at the small group inside the venue. The rednecks yelled, "Kill the dirty reds!" and broke into the auditorium while the audience skirted out of the hall. At that point, Tenayuca quit political work. We can only speculate on her reasons: nervous exhaustion, conflicts within the party, the chauvinism of many of its white members, and, to a degree, her removal as head of the pecan shellers' struggle.[118]

The Mexican Chamber of Commerce, the League of United Latin American Citizens (LULAC), Catholic Church authorities, refused to support the pecan strike. These groups rarely opposed the Kilday machine, and the archbishop went as far as to congratulate the police for rooting out "Communistic influences." Archbishop Arthur Jerome Drossaerts did urge pecan owners to pay higher wages, because in his view lower wages bred Communism. Although federal authorities and the governor criticized Kilday's tactics, the chief flagrantly violated worker rights and closed down a soup kitchen that was dispensing free food to strikers, alleging that it violated city health ordinances.

After a prolonged struggle that lasted 37 days, the shellers won the dispute—"sort of." The shellers agreed to submit their grievances to arbitration. The board recognized Local 172 as the sole bargaining agent; it required owners to comply with the Fair Labor Standards Act, which Congress had passed on June 25, 1938, and pay the minimum wage of 25¢ an hour. The victory was short-lived, however: owners replaced workers with machines. In 1938, the average income of the 521 pecan shellers' families in San Antonio, averaging 4.6 persons per family, was $251. This sum included earnings from work and the value of food and other commodities received from charities.[119]

Unionization in Los Angeles

The growth of industries expanded the ranks of the Mexican proletariat in the city. Even before World War II, heavy industry moved to Los Angeles. Eastern corporations, enticed by cheap land, reduced fuel costs, and cheap labor, looked West. Corporations also looked to the huge local markets for automobile-related products. Ford (1930), Willys-Overland (1929), Chrysler (1931), and General Motors (1936) all established plants in Los Angeles. Goodyear, Goodrich, Firestone, and U.S. Rubber soon followed. In 1936, Los Angeles ranked second only to Detroit in auto assembly and second only to Akron in tire and rubber manufacturing. The budding aircraft industry also housed itself in Los Angeles.[120]

Officially, just fewer than 100,000 Mexicans lived in the city and 167,024 in the county in 1930; unofficially, there were more. Mexicans were the largest minority, followed by 46,000 African Americans and 35,000 Japanese. Mexicans, concentrated in limited industries, made up most of the casual labor in construction, dominating the hod-carriers' (laborers') unions. The CIO's secession from the AFL created increased competition between the two internationals—and suddenly Mexicans became attractive brothers and, in some cases, sisters. By 1940, the United Brick and Clay Workers Union, part of the AFL, had 2,000 Mexican members. The CIO had organized 15,000 Mexican workers in Los Angeles by the early 1940s.

The International Longshore and Warehouse Union (ILWU), founded on August 11, 1937, joined the CIO. Local 1–26 broke away from the AFL and became affiliated to the ILWU. The local had about 600 members then; one year after the affiliation to the CIO, membership increased to 1,300. Volunteer recruiters Bert Corona, William Trujillo, and other Chicanas/os conducted drives to enlist workers in the drug warehouse industry and in milling, paper, and hardware. By 1939, Local 1–26 had about 1,500 members. Similar organizing was done in other industries—furniture, garment, rubber, and automotive—which were multiracial and included a large contingent of women. Often the CIO and AFL fought for control of locals or set up parallel organizations. Chicanos were involved on both sides, divided by the industrial–craft debate. Meanwhile, the CIO attracted larger numbers of Mexican-origin workers than did the AFL, because of its non-discrimination policies.[121]

Labor in the Midwest: Chicago

In Chicago in the 1930s, 66 percent of the Mexican population was unskilled, versus 53 percent for African Americans, 35 percent for foreign-born whites, and 33 percent for native whites. These figures were significant, because in 1935, 83 percent of Chicagoans on relief were unskilled workers. Mexicans had a lower median of education (in number of years) than the other groups: 3.2 years versus a median of 4.7 for African Americans and 5.3 for European whites. More than 30 percent of the Mexican workforce was unemployed; access to employment and relief was contingent on citizenship. Nativism increased and authorities even pressured Mexicans to produce documents proving legal residence or a willingness to become naturalized citizens.

During that period, to counter the effects of the Depression, Mexicans actively joined a variety of labor clubs, unions, and workers' organizations, for both the employed and the unemployed, much as they had in Los Angeles and San Antonio. *Mutualistas*, working with the goal of providing economic and social support for their members, remained the organizational form of choice. However, political ideology—both radical and conservative—also influenced their choice of membership. A chapter of *El Frente Popular Mexicano* (The Mexican Popular Front) sponsored meetings, discussions, and lectures; *El Frente*, led by Refugio Martínez, was housed at the University of Chicago Settlement House in the Back of the Yards neighborhood.[122] It defended Mexican workers, but also championed other causes such as protesting the despotism of Spain's fascist leader Francisco Franco. Another organization was *El Ideal Católico Mexicano* (the Mexican Catholic Ideal) formed in 1935 to counteract the radical appeal of *El Frente* and to crusade against Marxist ideas.[123]

Group membership also depended on locale and occupation. For example, the *Sociedad de Obreros Libres Mexicanos de Sud Chicago* (Society of Free Mexican Workers of South Chicago) consisted of steel and foundry workers of the South Chicago steel mills. Chicanos also participated in the Illinois Workers Alliance, which attracted a multi-ethnic membership of both employed and unemployed workers. As early as 1933, the Alliance had two locals with 50 Mexican members.

Unions like the Brotherhood of Railroad and Maintenance Workers discriminated against Mexicans. However, after the passage of the Wagner Act (1935) and the split between the AFL and CIO, steel and meatpacking industrial unions increasingly opened their membership to Mexicans. In four months during 1936, the Steel Workers Organizing Committee (SWOC) recruited 150–200 Mexican workers who were particularly active in Local 65 at U.S. Steel South Works in Chicago. By 1936, although they composed only 5 percent of the South Works employees, Mexicans comprised 11 percent of the union membership; furthermore, only 54 percent of the general membership voted, versus 88 percent of the Chicano membership. Following U.S. Steel's recognition of the union, workers elected "Alfredo de Avila, a Mexican steelworker-turned-labor-organizer, along with the popular-front organization El Frente Popular Mexicano, helped to ameliorate the suffering of Mexicans who remained in South Chicago. Some of the male leaders emerged from organized sports and recreational activities during the economic crisis."[124]

On May 30, 1937, Mexicans and their families joined other workers striking the Republic Steel Company, the Youngstown Sheet and Tube Company, and several other steel mills. It was called the "Little Steel Strike" because these were the smaller of the steel corporations. Republic Steel refused to follow the lead of U.S. Steel (big steel) by signing a union contract. The Steel Workers Organizing Committee (SWOC) of the CIO called the strike. On Memorial Day 1937, thousands of steel workers and their families rallied in front of the Republic Steel mill in South Chicago. Amid the demonstrators were Max Guzmán and [Mrs.] Guadalupe (Lupe) Marshall who were among a contingent of Mexican strikers. "Marshall was one of the two hundred women who took part in the march on the plant,"[125] Many Mexican women had their children with them. Unexpectedly, Republic Steel representatives attacked the demonstrators, and police shot and killed 10 demonstrators.[126]

The Mexican American Miners' Revolt

10.7 Describe the struggle for labor rights in Mexican American mining communities.

During the first two decades of the twentieth century, open warfare raged in western mines. In Arizona, with the mass deportation of Mexican miners, the copper barons eliminated the trade union movement by the early 1920s. In the 1930s, these unions began to rebuild through militant worker struggles in which Mexicans played a leading role. The industry players remained the same: Phelps Dodge, Anaconda, American Smelting and Refining (AS&R), and Nevada Consolidated. Mexicans composed 50–60 percent of the Southwest's industrial mine labor. Segregated, the Mexicans worked substandard jobs and were paid less in comparison with white miners. In Arizona, the mine owners controlled the state government and the company towns where workers lived. Slowly, as World War II heated up in Europe, the demand for copper and other ores heightened.

Meanwhile, during the Depression, production continued in Gallup, New Mexico, but owners reduced the force of 2,000 miners to a two-to-three-day workweek. As in other parts of the country, the United Mine Workers of America (UMWA) and the Communist-led National Miners Union (NMU) fought for the hearts and minds of the workers. The NMU unsuccessfully led strikes in Pennsylvania and Ohio, and in the bloody Harlan County, Kentucky.

Dissatisfied with the UMWA, the largely Mexican workforce turned to the NMU, which was more militant and preached interracial solidarity. As the strike commenced in 1933, the governor mobilized the National Guard, placing McKinley County under martial law. Management red-baited the NMU and made racial slurs against the Mexicans. The controversy was mediated in favor of the owners, and, despite promises to the contrary, management retaliated against union members. In response, the Communist Party organized an Unemployed Council and a chapter of the International Labor Defense (ILD).

Without notice, the Gallup American Mining Co. sold its *Chihuahuita* property—where many of the blacklisted miners lived—to State Senator Clarence F. Vogel who told the workers to buy the land on his terms or get out. The first evictions began in April 1935, with authorities targeting the home of Victor Campos. Workers defied the notice by returning Campos's furnishings to the house. Complaints were filed against Campos and other activists. The Unemployed Council immediately organized supporters who picketed the justice's office. An altercation erupted and deputies fired a tear gas bomb on the demonstrators, resulting in the death of the sheriff and two miners.

Led by the American Legion and the Veterans of Foreign Wars, vigilantes rounded up the so-called radicals. Fourteen miners and supporters were charged with first-degree murder. Authorities handed at least five of the seven acquitted defendants to immigration authorities. Juan Ochoa, Manuel Avitia, and Leandro Velarde were found guilty of second-degree murder. The judge delivered a speech on Communism and Bolshevism before sentencing the defendants to 46–60 years. The court of appeals reversed the Velarde conviction; in 1939, the governor pardoned Ochoa and Avitia.[127]

The coming of World War II increased demand for minerals, while open-pit mining transformed copper production. In Eastern Arizona, an open pit swallowed the entire town of Metcalf. Militancy flourished with the return of prosperity and the corresponding rise in demand for cheap labor. At Silver City, New Mexico, resentful of social and economic conditions, miners began to organize. In Laredo, Texas, smelter workers, led by Juan Peña, rebuilt their union. Urban centers such as El Paso also saw the revival of AS&R Company and the revitalization of workers' movement. One outspoken worker, Nicaraguan Humberto Silex, complained about the racism that kept Latinos as assistants. The managers made an example of Silex and fired him. The National Labor Relations Board (NLRB) later ruled that Silex and 40 members of the blacklisted Bisbee Miners Union had been discriminated against.

During World War II, rebuilding of unions continued. The Phelps Dodge and AS&R refineries in Douglas–Bisbee and Laredo were unionized. In Morenci, the United Mine, Mill & Smelter Workers' (UMM&SW) union—known as Mine-Mill—represented 2,000 workers, most of them Mexican. By the war's end, Mine-Mill represented three-quarters of the copper production workers in the Southwest, with 3,000 members along the border alone. Unlike the Western Federation of Labor, Mine-Mill espoused a policy of ethnic and racial equality, and was destined to be the most progressive trade union in the Mexican American community.

In 1937, an SWOC local was formed in Los Angeles; within two years, the union established itself. At Utility Steel, workers elected a Chicano as lodge president, while the committee made gains at Bethlehem Steel and Continental Can. During these drives, a clear division existed between skilled and non-skilled Mexican workers. Mine-Mill, active in Southern California, unionized in the foundries, smelters, and extraction plants. During World War II, as Chicanos trickled into these industries, white workers drifted to the war plants.[128]

The Mexican-Origin Community

10.8 Evaluate the different ways that Mexican Americans supported their communities in the 1930s.

The Texas-Mexican experience differed from that in California only in degree. Chicanos generally suffered more from segregation and racial barriers in the Lone Star State. It was a southern state with all the social, political, and intellectual limitations of the Confederate belt. Racism inculcated cohesiveness among Tejanos—or Tex-Mexicans, as they often called themselves. Without a doubt, the LULAC was the premier Tejano organization of this period. Although LULAC at first failed to incorporate women, it eventually bred woman activists. Women generally shared the goals of the organization, and formed the LULAC Ladies' Councils in 1934. In almost every chapter, there were women leaders—many either held college degrees or worked in white-collar occupations. In 1937, Alicía Dickerson Montemayor of Laredo served as the first Chicana elected to the office of second vice president general of LULAC.

LULAC also produced intellectuals, such as professors George I. Sánchez, Arthur L. Campa, and Carlos Castañeda. The various councils were vigilant in the protection of civil rights, and although later some Chicano scholars would criticize the intellectuals for ideological flaws, it is striking that Chicano intellectuals were involved at a time when political repression was at its height, and they suffered discrimination for their involvement. For instance, during the 1930s, when white American educators and social scientists perpetuated myths about the nonachieving Mexicans, educators George I. Sánchez and H. T. Manuel attacked culturally biased IQ tests. Sánchez and other Mexican American educators emphasized the role of environment in education, raising the issue of identity—that Mexican Americans were robbed of their historical heritage by American scholar who dominated the analysis and interpretation of history. These early pioneers called for bilingual education and an end to *de jure* and *de facto* segregation.[129]

LULAC was at the forefront of the fight to desegregate the schools, and its leadership posited that "separate but equal" was a lie and segregation meant inequality. By 1930, 90 percent of South Texas schools were segregated—an essential feature in the organizing and disciplining of workers. Segregation produced a culture of "race-thinking which was in great part socially constructed by land developers and their model towns." San Antonio school districts in the early 1930s had 12,334 students in Mexican schools and 12,224 in non-Mexican schools; however, Mexicans had 11 schools compared with Americans' 28. The disparity was even wider: Despite Mexican and American school children being nearly equal in number, Mexican schools occupied 23 acres in total versus 82 acres for American schools; 286 Mexican American teachers were employed versus 339 white teachers; and the school board spent $24.50 a year per Mexican student versus $35.96 per white.[130]

In the mid-1930s, LULAC took on public leadership by forming *La Liga Pro-Defensa Escolar* (the School Improvement League), which eventually represented 70 organizations with 75,000 members. Aware that being white carried privileges, in 1936, the San Angelo, Texas, LULAC council successfully sued the Social Security Administration regarding a requirement that Mexicans designate themselves as "Mexican" and not "white." While LULAC and middle-class leaders sought equal access to public institutions, members did not want to use LULAC as a political organization. The LULAC constitution stipulated that it remain non-political. Members, however, did use fronts such as the *Club Democrático* and the League of Loyal Americans for their political activities. They believed they could achieve their goal—which was to become capitalists—in a dignified manner, like "decent" people. Their method was to work within the system and not in the streets.

LULAC sought to improve the status of Mexican Americans through the strengthening of the family, church, education, and voting rights. Members represented a new generation that wanted to do it in their own way. Throughout the 1930s, they fought for better education and for equality. LULAC members, along with other members of the Mexican American middle class, the Mexican Chamber of Commerce, and the Catholic Church, were disturbed and often outraged by militants, whom they viewed as encroaching on their turf. LULAC members believed that they earned the right to represent the Mexican community, and that radicalism threatened their interests. This is not to suggest, however, that the Mexican American middle class was politically homogeneous.[131]

The Angeleño Community

The Mexican community in Los Angeles continued to grow. Mexicans formed numerous enclaves throughout the city in what historian Ernesto Galarza called "doughnut communities"—the Mexican *barrio* was the hole and the American neighborhoods formed the dough. Not all Mexicans were poor, though. Better-off Mexicans often lived in affluent districts such as West Adams, Los Féliz, and San Marino. They sponsored social functions such as the *bailes blanco y negro* (a white-gown, black-tie dance).

Activities of the lower middle class and the poor differed from those of the upwardly mobile middle class. A few joined the Young Democrats; some participated in the Unemployed Councils and the Worker Alliance. In 1930, the Federation of Spanish-Speaking Voters attempted to unite all Mexican societies, and some scholars speculate that it was the first political group to organize in Los Angeles. Meanwhile, the Young Men's Christian Association (YMCA) worked among Mexicans, as did the Catholic Church, which was conscious of the inroads made by the Protestant competition. To attract youth, the Catholic Church formed the CYO and the Catholic settlement houses.

The Communist Party was active among Chicanas/os in Los Angeles. Reportedly, 10 percent of their local recruits were Mexican in 1936–1937. It formed *La Nueva Vida Club* (The New Life), and its *No Pasarán* (They Shall Not Pass) branch of the Young Communist League (YCL) publicized the Spanish Civil War. The Workers Alliance, which included capable organizers such as Lupe Méndoza and Guillermo Taylor, reached out to WPA workers and people on relief. The Workers Alliance had close ties to UCAPAWA, through which Luisa Moreno and Frank López had organized Chicanos.[132]

The Mexican American Movement

The Mexican American Movement (MAM) was an outgrowth of the YMCA's Older Boys' Conference in San Pedro in 1934. It sponsored annual conferences that later took the name Mexican Youth Congress. Through the years, the functions of the Youth Conference broadened, and it formed a steering committee. In 1938, MAM started a newspaper, *The Mexican Voice*. The next year, MAM set up a leadership institute and held its first regional conference at Santa Barbara. By the beginning of the next decade, MAM had sponsored a Mexican American Girls' Conference and a Mexican American Teachers' Association, and had established contacts with similar organizations in Arizona and Texas.

MAM's mission was to promote Chicano leadership in education, social work, business, and other professions. Its credo was "Progress Through Education"; its members—which included both men and women—struggled for better schools and family relations, fighting against discrimination and juvenile delinquency. Critics charge that MAM favored assimilation and—like its benefactor, the YMCA—favored Americanization. It probably did. However, we should remember that the YMCA also played a role in politically stimulating and educating Ernesto Galarza—the premier Chicano activist-scholar of the time. And, MAM members criticized Mexicans who attempted to pass off as Spanish. Leaders generally spoke about building pride in their race. On the other hand, MAM leaders told their members to think of themselves as American first and Mexican second.

Judging the organization by today's standards would be simplistic. Mexicans of Protestant backgrounds were over-represented among MAM leaders, and their interpretation of Americanization differed from that of many American missionaries, although they adopted aspects of the "Protestant ethic." They fought against the "Mexican school segregation". World War II curtailed some of MAM's activities, but it survived until about 1949. *The Mexican Voice* became *The Forward* in 1945 and reported on its members' progress in the armed forces.[133]

El Congreso de los Pueblos de Habla Español

In 1938, *El Congreso de los Pueblos de Habla Español* (the Congress of Spanish-Speaking People) of California held the first Conference of Spanish-Speaking People in Los Angeles. It scheduled the First National Congress for March 1939 in Albuquerque. Because of red-baiting, organizers moved *El Congreso* to Los Angeles, and George I. Sánchez and Arthur L. Campa, professors at the University of New Mexico, were forced to resign. The principal organizers of the national congress were Luisa Moreno, a national organizer and later vice president for UCAPAWA;[134] Josefina Fierro de Bright, its 18-year-old executive secretary; and Eduardo Quevedo, its first president and founder of the New Mexico–Arizona Club. Moreno traveled throughout the United States and generated considerable interest in the conference later held in Los Angeles.

Fierro de Bright's mother was a partisan of Ricardo Flores Magón, and Fierro had come to Los Angeles to attend the University of California at Los Angeles. While singing in a nightclub, Fierro met John Bright, a Hollywood screenwriter, whom she later married. Through Fierro de Bright, *El Congreso* raised money from movie stars and other organizations. Eduardo Quevedo was an old-line politico, who later became active in the Sleepy Lagoon case (see Chapter 11). Quevedo was the moving force behind the Mexican American Political Association in 1959.

Representatives from all over the United States came to the First National Conference: Spanish and Cuban cigar makers from Tampa, Florida; Puerto Ricans from Harlem, New York; steelworkers from Pennsylvania, Illinois, and Indiana; meat packers, miners, and farmworkers from many localities; and elected officials from New Mexico. Delegates included workers, politicians, educators, and youth.

El Congreso proposed organizing workers and publishing a newspaper and a newsletter. It set legislative priorities and took stands against oppressive laws, immigration officials, vigilantes, and police brutality. Members pushed the right of farmworkers to organize and demanded the extension of the benefits of the National Labor Relations Act to farmworkers. *El Congreso* claimed a membership of more than 6,000 during 1938–1940.[135] Neither *El Congreso* nor the Chicano community had many friends in the media or in positions of power. Newspapers and local elected officials labeled it a "subversive gathering." Because of its radical stands, *El Congreso* opened itself to intense red-baiting, and the FBI harassed its members. After 1940, its effectiveness waned rapidly, though it continued to function in the post-War period.

El Congreso was important because it provided a forum for activists such as Luisa Moreno. On March 3, 1940, Moreno addressed a Panel on Deportation and Right of Asylum of the Fourth Annual Conference of the American Committee for the Protection of the Foreign Born, in Washington, D.C. She entitled her speech "Caravan of Sorrow":

> Long before the "Grapes of Wrath" had ripened in California's vineyards a people lived on highways, under trees or tents, in shacks or railroad sections, picking crops—cotton, fruits, vegetables, cultivating sugar beets, building railroads and dams, making barren land fertile for new crops and greater riches.[136]

Moreno continued that Mexicans had been brought "by the fruit exchanges, railroad companies and cotton interests in great need of underpaid labor during the early postwar period." She condemned the repatriations and the sufferings caused by them, charging that "today the Latin Americans of the United States are alarmed by an 'antialien' drive." Moreno concluded,

> These people are not aliens. They have contributed their endurance, sacrificed youth and labor to the Southwest. Indirectly, they have paid more taxes than all the stockholders of California's industrialized agriculture, the sugar companies and the large cotton interests, that operate or have operated with the labor of Mexican workers.

Moreno put *El Congreso de Los Pueblos de Habla Español* on record as opposing anti-alien legislation.

Fighting Segregation

During the 1930s, the segregation of schools and public facilities was a major issue. Newspapers such as *El Espectador*, published by Ignacio López in Upland, California, played a role in fighting segregation. In February 1939, two Chicanos entered a movie theater and looked for seats near the center. They were told that Mexicans sat in the first 15 rows. The youths went to López, who wrote a stinging editorial calling for a mass meeting, which more than a hundred community folk attended. The Mexican community boycotted the theater, forcing it to change its policy. López also exposed the fact that Chaffey Junior College segregated its swimming pool facilities during the summer. Chicanos could use the pool only on Mondays. Another boycott was called for, and the college reversed its policy. Shortly afterward, Mexicans sued the City of San Bernardino, and the court enjoined the city from excluding Mexicans from its pools.[137]

In an editorial entitled *Quién Es El Culpable?* (Who Is to Blame?), López reprimanded the Mexican American community for permitting segregation. He crusaded against police brutality and housing segregation, and emphasized the need for political integration. López like Bert Corona, Ernesto Galarza, and George I. Sánchez was a Protestant.[138]

The Manitos

Many New Mexican *Hispanos* were under the illusion that they were players in the state's political and social life. But, even after World War II, out of 1,093 entries, *Who's Who in New Mexico* listed only 57 Mexicans. In eastern New Mexico, authorities barred Mexicans from "better" barbershops, cafes, hotels, and recreation centers. In Roswell, Mexicans could not use the public pool. In the late 1930s, the illiteracy rate in counties in which Mexicans were the majority was 16.6 percent, versus 3.1 percent in predominately white counties. During the 1930s, white city councils segregated the public schools, and Mexican schools were obviously inferior to all-white schools. For instance, the percentage of public school teachers with degrees in American counties was 82.2, versus 46.6 in Mexican counties.

New Mexicans point to the fact that Congressman Dennis Chávez was elected to Congress at a time when there were no Chicano representatives in other states. However, in New Mexico, the Chicano population was proportionately larger and more concentrated than in other states. Chávez was appointed to the Senate after U.S. Senator Bronson Cutting was killed in an airplane accident. However, this appointment did not translate itself into power for the people. Concha Ortiz y Pino from Galisteo, New Mexico, was elected to the state legislature in 1936. Her voting record was spotty; she voted against the ratification of a constitutional amendment that prohibited child labor and regulated the number of hours women could work. Ortiz y Pino also condemned the welfare offices. Yet she introduced the first bill allowing women to serve on jury panels, which in the eyes of some historians absolves her.

Jesús Pallares migrated to the United States as a teenager. Pallares had worked as a miner in Gallup and Madrid, New Mexico. Fired and blacklisted for union activities, in 1934 Pallares became an organizer for *La Liga Obrera de Habla Española* (the League of Spanish-Speaking Workers). A year later, the *Liga* had 8,000 members, who militantly defended the rights of the poor. With the cooperation of the liberal U.S. Secretary of Labor Frances Perkins, state authorities had Pallares deported.

Another New Mexican activist from this period was Isabel Malagram Gonzales, who worked in New Mexico and Colorado. In the late 1920s, Gonzales led a strike of pea workers, and in 1930, she moved to Denver, where she worked for the Colorado Tuberculosis Society. In the 1940s, she wrote for *Challenge*, a progressive newspaper, was active in politics, and ran for the city council. In 1946, the War Food Administration denied Gonzales the right to testify before it. In the late 1940s, she worked as a political activist in northern New Mexico. She died in Denver in 1949.[139]

The Windy City: Chicago

By the late 1930s, more women and children lived in the *barrios* of Chicago compared to their numbers in the previous decade, an indication that Mexicans were forging communities. In addition, fewer Mexican families shared apartments, and the "boardinghouse" was disappearing. Official attitudes were slow to change, and state relief agencies still counted Chicanos as foreign-born. Chicanos concentrated in South Chicago, the Near West Side, and Back of the Yards, with each community evolving its own individual character. According to historian Louise Kerr, the Chicano Chicagoans were "less concerned with politics than with jobs, relief, education, and accommodation to the urban environment." They joined a variety of clubs, unions, and workers' associations to meet these needs. Local Spanish-language newspapers such as *La Defensa del Ideal Católico Mexicano* (the Defense of the Mexican Catholic Ideal), *La Voz de México* (the Voice of Mexico), and *La Alianza* (The Alliance) delineated community issues and divisions.

The pool hall, no longer the center of activity, gave ground to U.S. sports such as basketball. Mexican club teams, such as Los Aztecas, Los Mexicanos, and Los Reyes, played in leagues. As in other immigrant groups, youth gangs emerged in the Chicano community. According to Kerr, "social workers felt that participation in youth gangs was a form of adaptation to the local community," a form of assimilation "learned" by Mexican youths "from the Italians and Poles who preceded them." There was an increase in Mexican-run small businesses, and school attendance by Mexican youth improved. English classes for adults also became more popular.

Hull House on the Near West Side met the needs of Chicanos. But, as Hull House devoted more time to research, its advocacy role suffered. In the late 1930s, Frank Pax organized the Mexican Youth Party, which met at Hull House. Some Mexicans preferred the smaller Mexican Social Center, established in the early 1930s. In South Chicago, some Chicanos went to the Byrd Memorial Center staffed by the Congregational Church, whose employees looked on Mexicans as backward and undependable. Meanwhile, many Catholic parishes prohibited Chicanos from belonging to their communities.

Through the work of its long-time director Mary McDowell, the University of Chicago Settlement House (in Back of the Yards) had involvement with the Mexican community at a more personal level. McDowell worked toward interethnic cooperation and actively trained women to take leadership roles under the auspices of the Mexican Mothers' Club. The groups established by McDowell continued to function after her death. In 1937, the Mexican Mothers' Club sponsored a series of discussions on local Chicago issues, and interethnic cooperation remained better in this area than in other sections of the city.[140]

Conclusion: An Embattled Community

As the U.S. Mexican community approached the 1940s, the Mexican-origin population was becoming more visible. In the *Los Angeles Times* of October 15, 1939, Timothy G. Turner published an article titled, "Unique Fusion of Races Taking Place in El Paso; Anglo-Saxons, Americans and Indo-Spanish Mexicans Double Population in 25 Years." Turner reported that the U.S. population doubled in El Paso during the previous 25 years; two-thirds of the increase was Mexican in race and culture. This migration expanded the Mexican American middle class, but, according to Turner, the migration of poor Mexicans depressed wages. Turner suggested that it was not the presence of poor Mexicans that annoyed white Texans but the increase of the middle-class Mexican population. Attempting to be generous, Turner wrote, "There is a biologically inferior Mexican stock, no doubt, but many of the newcomers here [in El Paso] are of good northern Mexican ranch stock, light mestizos (that is Spanish Indian blood), and here they have had a break." The problem, he thought, was as Mexicans moved into white-collar occupations that white people thought belonged to them, there was friction. The interaction described by Turner was played out throughout the Southwest and Midwest. It was emblematic of a greater problem. As long as Mexicans remained in their places and out of sight, most Americans could ignore them. However, when Mexicans moved up and took something Americans believed belonged to them, it was time for the Mexicans leave the country.[141]

Notes

1. Harriet Hyman Alonso, *Yip Harburg: Legendary Lyricist and Human Rights Activist* (Middletown, Connecticut: Wesleyan University Press, 2012), 54, 75–80, 82.
2. John Steinbeck, *The Grapes of Wrath* (New York: Penguin Books, 2006), 231–32.
3. "U.S.-Mexican Border," *Business Week* (May 12, 1997), http://www.businessweek.com/1997/19/b35263.htm. "Mexico," WorldAtlas.com, http://www.graphicmaps.com/webimage/countrys/namerica/mx.htm. Stephen R. Niblo, *Mexico in the 1940s: Modernity, Politics and Corruption* (Wilmington, Delaware: Scholarly Resources, 1999), 1; Mexico in 1940 had a population of under the age of 20. It was sparsely populated.
4. Lianne Mulder, "Frantz Fanon, Internalized Oppression and the Decolonization of Education Lianne Mulder, MPhil student at the University of the West Indies, Barbados (PDF) Frantz Fanon, "Internalized Oppression and the Decolonization of Education," available from: https://www.researchgate.net/publication/308773706 (accessed Nov 13 2018).
5. Robert S. McElvaine, "Post Everything Perspective: I'm a Depression historian. The GOP tax bill is straight out of 1929," *Washington Post*, November 30, 2017, https://www.washingtonpost.com/news/posteverything/wp/2017/11/30/im-a-depression-historian-the-gop-tax-bill-is-straight-out-of-1929/?utm_term=.846dc3106f65.
6. The Crash of 1929, American Experience, Public Broadcasting System, http://www.pbs.org/wgbh/americanexperience/crash/. "Photographs of the Great Depression," About.com: 20th Century History, http://history1900s.about.com/library/photos/blyindexdepression.htm. "The Great Depression," 42 explore, http://www.42explore2.com/depresn.htm.
7. "Picture this: Depression Era: 1930s," Oakland Museum of California, http://www.museumca.org/picturethis/3_2.html. Brian Gratton, Emily Merchant, "Immigration, Repatriation, and Deportation: The Mexican-Origin Population in the United States, 1920–1950," *IMR* Vol. 47, No. 4 (Winter 2013); see table 1, p. 948 and table 2, p. 950 for estimates of repatriates. On other occasions, I have heard Balderrama estimates up to two million. He is a careful scholar.
8. Steven Mintz, "Historical Context: Mexican Americans and the Great Depression," History Now, https://www.gilderlehrman.org/content/historical-context-mexican-americans-and-great-depression.
9. Steven Mintz, Ibid. The student at Occidental was later identified as Ernesto Galarza.
10. "East Grand Forks, Minnesota Mexicans," Office of War Information Photograph Collection (Library of Congress), 1937, http://www.loc.gov/pictures/search/?q=mexican%20workers%20minnesota. Bruce Johansen and Roberto Maestas, *El Pueblo: The Gallegos Family's American Journey, 1503–1980* (New York: Monthly Review Press, 1983), 72, 74, 75, 78, 80. Leonardo Macias, "Mexican immigration and repatriation during the Great Depression," (Tempe: Master's Thesis, Arizona State University, 1992), 11–14. Jaime Aguila, "Mexican/U.S. Immigration Policy prior to the Great Depression," *Diplomatic History*, Vol. 31, Issue 2 (2007): 213.
11. The camps also provided an unexpected benefit. In bringing together so many individual farm families, they increased ties within the community. Many residents began organizing their fellow workers around labor issues, and helped pave the way for the farm labor movements that emerged later in the century. This interview with a leader of the FSA camp in El Rio, California describes some of the day-to-day issues that the camp residents dealt with. "Depression and the Struggle for Survival," Library of Congress, https://www.loc.gov/teachers/classroommaterials/presentationsandactivities/presentations/immigration/alt/mexican6.html.
12. "Mexican-Americans," Franklin Delano Roosevelt Front Page, Miller Center, University of Virginia, http://millercenter.org/president/fdroosevelt/essays/biography/8. Phyllis McKenzie, *The Mexican Texans* (College Station: Texas A&M University Press, 2004), 84. Ned Duran, "Conversations with Ed Duran," transcript of an oral history interview conducted on November 5, 2002, by David Washburn; Regional Oral History Office, The Bancroft Library, University of California, Berkeley, 2002, in Rodolfo F. Acuña and Guadalupe Compeán, eds., *Voices of the U.S. Latino Experience*, Vol. 2 (Westport, CT: Greenwood Books, 2008), 563–68.
13. "Mexico, Great Depression in Encyclopedia of the Great Depression," The Gale Group Inc., 2004, http://www.encyclopedia.com/economics/encyclopedias-almanacs-transcripts-and-maps/mexico-great-depression.
14. Ibid.
15. Clara E. Rodriguez, *Changing Race: Latinos, the Census and the History of Ethnicity* (New York: New York University Press, 2000), 101–4. Leo Grebler, Joan W. Moore, and Ralph C. Guzmán, *The Mexican-American People: The Nation's Second Largest Majority* (New York: Free Press, 1970), 84. Elizabeth Broadbent,

"The Distribution of Mexican Population in the United States" (PhD Dissertation, University of Chicago, 1941), 33. David Hendricks and Amy Patterson, "Genealogy Notes: The 1930 Census in Perspective," *Prologue Magazine* 34, No. 2 (Summer 2002), The National Archives, http://www.archives.gov/publications/prologue/2002/summer/.

16. David G. Gutierrez, *Walls and Mirrors: Mexican Americans, Mexican Immigrants, and the Politics of Ethnicity* (Berkeley: University of California, 1995), 71–74. Macias, "Mexican immigration and repatriation," 29.

17. George J. Sánchez, *Becoming Mexican American: Ethnicity, Culture and Identity in Chicano Los Angeles, 1900–1945* (New York: Oxford University Press, 1993), 211. Mario T. García, *Mexican Americans: Leadership, Ideology, & Identity, 1930–1960* (New Haven, CT: Yale University Press, 1989), 15.

18. Brian Gratton, " Immigration, Repatriation, and Deportation: The Mexican-Origin Population in the United States, 1920-1950," *International Migration Review*, Vol. 47, No. 4 (Winter 2013), 944.

19. Edward S. Casey, Mary Watkins, *Up Against the Wall: Re-Imagining the U.S.-Mexico Border* (Austin: University of Texas Press, 2014), 139.

20. Rodolfo F, Acuña, *Corridors of Migration: Odyssey of Mexican Laborers, 1600-1933* (Tucson: University of Arizona Press, 2007), 228.

21. "New Protests on Bliss Bill," *Los Angeles Times* (April 5, 1933). Guadalupe T. Luna, "Beyond/Between Colors: On the Complexities of Race: The Treaty of Guadalupe Hidalgo and *Dred Scott v. Sandford*," *University of Miami Law Review* 53 (July 1999), 691–716. "Teacher Raps Race Division," *Los Angeles Times* (April 6, 1931). "'Excelsior' Fiercely Attacks Bliss Bill," *Los Angeles Times* (April 5, 1931). Sánchez, *Becoming Mexican American*, 211–12. Paula Rothenberg, *White Privilege* 3rd ed. (New York: Worth Publishers, 2007), 60–62.

22. Robert R. Alvárez, Jr., "The Lemon Grove Incident: The Nation's First Successful Desegregation Court Case," *The Journal of San Diego History* 32, No. 2 (Spring 1986), http://www.sandiegohistory.org/journal/86spring/lemongrove.htm. The documentary, http://www.youtube.com/watch?v=Uu9dxMMLGyU. E. Michael Madrid, "The Unheralded History of the Lemon Grove Desegregation Case," *Multicultural Education*, Vol. 15, Issue 3 (November 30, 2007), 15–19. Peter Y. Hong, "Roberto Alvarez, 84; Businessman Made History in 1931 With Landmark School Integration Suit," *Los Angeles Times* (February 26, 2003).

23. Vicki L. Ruiz, *Cannery Women, Cannery Lives: Mexican Women, Unionization, and the California Food Processing Industry, 1930–1950* (Albuquerque: University of New Mexico Press, 1987), 5. Bianca Barragan, "An amazing new look at Great Depression-era Los Angeles," *Curbed Los Angeles* (Oct 12, 2016), Author Interviews. "America's Forgotten History Of Mexican-American 'Repatriation'," NPR, September 10, 2015, https://www.npr.org/2015/09/10/439114563/americas-forgotten-history-of-mexican-american-repatriation.

24. Leonardo Macias, "Mexican immigration and repatriation during the Great Depression" (Master's Thesis, Tempe: Arizona State University, 1992).

25. Natalia Molina. *Fit To Be Citizens? Public Health and Race in Los Angeles, 1879–1939* (Berkeley and Los Angeles: University of California Press, 2006), 2740. Emily K. Abel, "Only the Best Class of Immigration: Public Health Policy Toward Mexicans and Filipinos in Los Angeles, 1910–1940: Public Health Then and Now," *American Journal of Public Health* 94, No. 6 (June 2004), 933–36. Thomas E. Sheridan, *Los Tucsonenses: The Mexican Community in Tucson, 1854–1941* (Tucson: University of Arizona Press, 1986), 208. Richard A. García, *Rise of the Mexican American Middle Class: San Antonio, 1929–1941* (College Station: Texas A&M University Press, 1991), 39, 223–33.

26. Sheridan, *Los Tucsonenses*, 211–12. Francisco E. Balderama and Raymond Rodríguez, *Decade of Betrayal: Mexican Repatriation in the 1930s* (Albuquerque: University of New Mexico Press, 1995). For excellent oral interviews of miners and families in Morenci, Arizona, see Elena Diaz Bjorkist, "In the Shadow of the Smokestack: An Oral History of Mexican Americans in Morenci, Arizona." Unfortunately the site is defunct; write to the author for transcripts of interviews. See Elena Diaz Bjorkist, *Suffer Smoke* (Houston: Arte Público Press, 1996). Thomas E. Sheridan, "La Crisis," in Oscar J. Martínez, ed., *U.S.-Mexico Borderlands: Historical and Contemporary Perspectives* (Lanham, MD: Rowan & Littlefied, 1996), 162–68. Macias, "Mexican immigration and repatriation," 35.

27. Gloria E. Miranda, "The Mexican Immigrant Family: Economic and Cultural Survival in Los Angeles, 1900–1945," in Norman M. Klein and Martin Schiesl, eds., *20th Century Los Angeles: Power, Promotion, and Social Conflict* (Claremont, CA: Regina Books, 1990), 42. R. García, *San Antonio*, 156–63. Donna Morales Guerra, "The Westside of San Antonio, 1930s–1950s: A Glimpse into Catholic Social Action and Community," http://www.amormeus.org/en/wp-content/uploads/2016/10/TheWestSideofSanAntonio.pdf. Rodolfo Acuña, *The Making of Chicana/o Studies: In the Trenches of Academe* (New Brunswick: Rutgers University Press, Rutgers University Press. 2011), 218.

28. Colin Gunckel, *Mexico on Main Street: Transnational Film Culture in Los Angeles before World War* (New Brunswick, NJ: Rutgers University Press, 2015).
29. The radio was popular. A favorite in Los Angeles was Pedro J. González & Los Madrugadores, *Los Hermanos Sanchez y Linares, Chicho y Chencho: 1931–1937*, http://music.yahoo.com/madrugadores/albums/hermanos-sanchez-y-linares-chicho-y-chencho-1931-1937-28392112. Written by the late California State Senator Jack B. Tenney, the state's anti-Communist crusader and a bigot, *Mexicali Rose* was a classic played throughout the 1920s and 1930s. *A movie starring Barbara Stanwyck; Trailer came out in 1929.* Gene Autry, The Singing Cowboy, *Mexicali Rose*, http://www.youtube.com/watch?v=TjoQAaBcXpo&feature=related.
30. Francisco E. Balderrama and Richard A. Santillan, *Mexican American Baseball in Los Angeles* (Arcadia Publishing, 2011).
31. Gilbert G. González, *Labor and Community: Mexican Citrus Worker Villages in a Southern California County, 1900–1950* (Urbana: University of Illinois Press, 1994), 95. R. García, San Antonio, 93. M. García, Mexican Americans, 25. Bert Colima, Archive Photo, ca. 1924, BoxingTreasures.com, http://www.boxingtreasures.com/becoarphc192.html.
32. Jorge Iber and Samuel O. Regalado, eds., *Mexican Americans and Sports: A Reader on Athletics and Barrio Life* (Texas A&M Press, 2006), 51.
33. José M. Alamillo, "Peloteros in Paradise: Mexican American Baseball and Oppositional Politics in Southern California, 1930–1950," *The Western Historical Quarterly* Vol. 34, No. 2 (Summer, 2003), 192–195. Noe Torres, *Baseball's First Mexican-American Star, The Amazing Story of Leo Najo, Ghost Leagues of South Texas* (Roswellbooks.com, 2008).
34. Quote by Sánchez, Becoming Mexican American, 186.
35. Sánchez, *Becoming Mexican American*, 185. Cecilia Rasmussen, "D.A. Fitts Was Good Match for Scandalous '30s," *Los Angeles Times*, September 19, 1999, http://articles.latimes.com/1999/sep/19/local/me-12084.
36. Sánchez, *Becoming Mexican American*, 186. Vicki L. Ruiz, *From out of the Shadows: Mexican Women in Twentieth-Century America* (New York: Oxford University Press, 1998), 9. Karen Anderson, *Changing Woman: A History of Racial Ethnic Women in Modern America* (Cambridge, MA: Oxford University Press, 1997), 102–14. Christopher Tudico, "Before We Were Chicanas/os: The Mexican American Experience In California Higher Education, 1848–1945" (PhD Dissertation, University of Pennsylvania, 2010).
37. Sánchez, *Becoming Mexican American*, 198, 200–02. Miranda, "Mexican Immigrant Family," 44. Ruiz, *Cannery Women*, 9, 14. For context, see "Latinas," Area Studies Collections, http://memory.loc.gov/ammem/awhhtml/awas12/latinas.html.
38. Juan R. García, *Mexicans in the Midwest, 1900–1932* (Tucson: University of Arizona, 1996), 92–93. Ruth Hutchinson Crocker, "Gary Mexicans and 'Christian Americanization': A Study in Cultural Conflict," in James B. Lane and Edward J. Escobar, eds., *Forging a Community: The Latino Experience in Northwest Indiana, 1919–1975* (Chicago, IL: Cattails Press, 1987). Also in Lane and Escobar; see Juan R. García, "El Círculo de Obreros Católicos, San José, 1925–1930," 115–34, for a view of the organization life of this area south of Chicago.
39. Sánchez, *Becoming Mexican American*, 209, 213. Sheridan, *Los Tucsonenses*, 216.
40. G. González, *Labor and Community*, 103–4, 107, 134.
41. Dead End 1937 pt2, http://www.youtube.com/watch?v=RD4v5Sxoy3Y&playnext=1&list=PL50403B55 5CFD0546&feature=results_main. "Organized crime in Los Angeles in 1930s," http://www.youtube.com/watch?v=UOv5PWKPUh8&feature=related.
42. Joan W. Moore, *Homeboys: Gangs, Drugs, and Prison in the Barrios of Los Angeles* (Philadelphia, PA: Temple University Press, 1978), 56–57. See Mario T. García, *Memories of Chicano History: The Life and Narrative of Bert Corona* (Berkeley: University of California Press, 1995), 103–05, on gangs. Miranda, "Mexican Immigrant Family," 56. Gunckel, Ibid.
43. Gangster movies were often a "poor boy makes good" rendition of life. The gangster gets the car and the blonde. "Scarface" [1932] Part[1], http://www.youtube.com/watch?v=tutdm85GekM. Also "Bordertown—Original Trailer 1935," http://www.tcm.com/mediaroom/video/34920/Bordertown-Re-issue-Trailer-.html.
44. R. García, *San Antonio*, 29, 35–36, 39. Julia Kirk Blackwelder, *Women of the Depression: Caste and Culture in San Antonio, 1929–1939* (College Station: Texas A&M Press, 1984), 9. "Mexican lunch wagon serving tortillas and fried beans to workers," Farm Security Administration—Office of War Information Photograph Collection (Library of Congress), 1939, http://memory.loc.gov/ammem/browse/index.html; to view this photograph follow the link and in the Search Bar type in the title reproduced above in quotes.
45. "Tranchese, Carmelo Antonio (1880–1956)," http://www.tshaonline.org/handbook/online/articles/TT/ftr20.html.
46. R. García, *San Antonio*, 165. David A. Badillo, "Between Alienation and Ethnicity: The Evolution of Mexican-American Catholicism in San Antonio, 1910–1940," *Journal of American Ethnic History* 16, No. 4 (Summer 1997), 62ff.

47 Collage: "Chicanas/os Struggle, Community," http://forchicanachicanostudies.wikispaces.com/Community.

48 "Mexican Repatriation: A Generation Between Two Borders," http://public.csusm.edu/frame004/images.html. Rosa Prieto, Veronica Smith, Rosa Moreno, Jonatán Jaimes, Adri Alatorre, and Ruth Vise, "Mexican Repatriation in 1930s is Little Known Story," *Borderlands,* El Paso Community College, http://epcc.libguides.com/content.php?pid=309255&sid=2573137. Michigan Repatriation, http://www.umich.edu/~ac213/student_projects07/repatriados/history/detroithist.html.

49 Sánchez, *Becoming Mexican American*, 184. Camille Guérin-Gonzales, *Mexican Workers & American Dreams: Immigration, Repatriation, and California Farm Labor, 1900–1939* (New Brunswick, NJ: Rutgers University Press, 1994). Balderama and Rodríguez, *Decade of Betrayal*, 50–51. George C. Kiser and Martha Woody Kiser, eds., *Mexican Workers in the United States: Historical and Political Perspectives* (Albuquerque: University of New Mexico Press, 1979), 47. Job West Neal, "The Policy of the United States Toward Immigration from Mexico" (Master's Thesis, University of Texas at Austin, 1941), 172, 194. U.S. Congress, House Committee on Immigration and Naturalization, *Western Hemisphere Immigration, H.R. 8523, H.R. 8530, H.R. 8702*, 71st Cong., 2d Sess. (1930), 436. James Hoffman Batten, "New Features of Mexican Immigration" (address before the National Conference of Social Work, Boston, June 9, 1930), 960.

50 Brooks Jackson, "Hoover, Truman & Ike: Mass Deporters?" A Project of The Annenberg Public Policy Center, July 9, 2010, http://www.factcheck.org/2010/07/hoover-truman-ike-mass-deporters/. Alex Wagner, "America's Forgotten History of Illegal Deportations," *The Atlantic*, Mar. 6, 2017, https://www.theatlantic.com/politics/archive/2017/03/americas-brutal-forgotten-history-of-illegal-deportations/517971/.

51 Balderama and Rodríguez's, *Decade of Betrayal* is the best book available on the topic. R. Reynolds McKay, "Texas Mexican Repatriation During the Great Depression" (PhD Dissertation, University of Oklahoma, 1982), 556. M. García, *Bert Corona*, 59–61. Ronald W. López, *Los Repatriados* (Seminar paper, History Department, University of California at Los Angeles, 1968), 63. Gregory Ochoa, "Some Aspects of the Repatriation of Mexican Aliens in Los Angeles County, 1931–1938" (Seminar paper, History Department, San Fernando Valley State College, 1966). Clements Papers, Special Collections Library, University of California at Los Angeles. Abraham Hoffman, *Unwanted Mexican Americans in the Great Depression* (Tucson: University of Arizona Press, 1974). Peter Neal Kirstein, "Anglo over Bracero: A History of the Mexican Worker in the United States from Roosevelt to Nixon" (PhD Dissertation, Saint Louis University, 1973). Abraham Hoffman, "Stimulus to Repatriation: The 1931 Federal Deportation Drive and the Los Angeles Mexican Community," in Norris Hundley, ed., *The Chicano* (Santa Barbara, CA: Clio, 1975), 110.

52 C.P. Visel in Clements Collection, January correspondence, Clements Collection, box 80 Special Collections, Research Library, University of California, Los Angeles. Camille Guerin-Gonzales, *Mexican Workers and American Dreams: Immigration, Repatriation, and California Farm Labor, 1900–1939* (New Brunswick, New Jersey, Rutgers University Press, 1994).

53 Quoted in Hoffman, *Unwanted Mexican Americans*, 52, 55, 113, 116, 118. López, *Los Repatriados*, 43, 55, 58. Balderama and Rodríguez, *Decade of Betrayal*, 55–57, 63. Emory S. Bogardus, "Repatriation and Readjustment," in Manuel Servín, ed., *The Mexican-Americans: An Awakening Minority* (Beverly Hills, CA: Glencoe Press, 1970), 92–93. Norman D. Humphrey, "Mexican Repatriation from Michigan: Public Assistance in Historical Perspective," *Social Service Review* 15 (September 1941), 505.

54 Carey McWilliams, *North from Mexico* (New York: Greenwood Press, 1968), 193. Robert N. McLean, "Good-bye Vincente," *Survey* 66 (May 1931), 195.

55 Hoffman, *Unwanted Mexican Americans*, 120. Neil Betten and Raymond A. Mohl, "From Discrimination to Repatriation: Mexican Life in Gary, Indiana, During the Great Depression," in Hundley, ed., *The Chicano*, 125, 138, 139. George Kiser and David Silverman, "The Mexican Repatriation During the Great Depression," *Journal of Mexican American History* 3 (1973), 153. Ochoa, "Some Aspects of the Repatriation," 65–66. Kiser and Kiser, *Mexican Workers*, 36–37.

56 McKay, "Texas Mexican Repatriation," 17, 19. "Mexican Americans and Repatriation," *Handbook of Texas Online*, http://www.tshaonline.org/handbook/online/articles/MM/pqmyk.html. Edna Ewing Kelley, "The Mexicans Go Home," *Southwest Review* XVII, No. 3 (April 1932), 303–11. "Although substantial Mexican repatriation from Texas occurred at that time, no published study has examined Mexican departures between 1836 and 1930. Mexican repatriation during the Great Depression has received more attention." Robert R. McKay, "Mexican Americans and Repatriation," *Handbook of Texas Online*, accessed December 10, 2017, http://www.tshaonline.org/handbook/online/articles/pqmyk, Uploaded on June 15, 2010. Published by the Texas State Historical Association.

57 McKay, "Texas Mexican Repatriation," 98–100.
58 Ibid., 131, 289–90. "Repatriation in San Antonio," http://colfa.utsa.edu/users/jreynolds/Ybarra/part5.htm. John Weber, *From South Texas to the Nation: The Exploitation of Mexican Labor in the Twentieth Century* (Chapel Hill, NC: The University of North Carolina Press, 2015), 137. Brian Gratton, Emily Merchant, "Immigration, Repatriation, and Deportation: The Mexican-Origin Population in the United States, 1920–1950," *IMR* Vol. 47 No. 4 (Winter 2013), 944–975.
59 Aguila, "Mexican/U.S. Immigration Policy," 209–210. Lee Stacy, ed., *Mexico and the United States* (Marshall Cavendish Corp, 2002), 267–69.
60 Balderama and Rodríguez, *Decade of Betrayal*, 107–09, 117. Valerie Orleans, "1930s Mexican Deportation," March 17, 2005, http://calstate.fullerton.edu/news/2005/valenciana.html. Susan Valot, "Locals Recall 1930s Mexican Repatriation," 89.3 KPCC, May 16, 2007, http://origin-www.scpr.org/news/stories/2007/05/16/08_mexican_repatriation.html. Ben Fox, "Mexican Deportees Seek to Correct Old Wrongs," *Orange County Register* (September 12, 2004), http://www.highbeam.com/doc/1P1-99048145.html.
61 Carey McWilliams, *California: The Great Exception* (Berkeley: University of California, 1999), 136. Stuart Jamieson, *Labor Unionism in American Agriculture* (New York: Arno Press, 1976), 7. Ernesto Galarza, *Farmworkers and Agribusiness in California, 1947–1960* (Notre Dame: University of Notre Dame Press, 1977), 25. Ronald B. Taylor, *Chavez and the Farm Workers* (Boston, MA: Beacon Press, 1975), 39. Ellen L. Halcomb, "Efforts to Organize the Migrant Workers by the Cannery and Agricultural Workers Industrial Union in the 1930's" (Master's Thesis, Chico State College, 1963), 1–2. Walter Goldschmidt, *As You Sow* (New York: Harcourt Brace Jovanovich, 1947), 248. Don Mitchell, *The Lie of the Land: Migrant Workers and the California Landscape* (Minneapolis: University of Minnesota Press, 1996), 110.
62 Neil Foley, *The White Scourge: Mexicans, Blacks, and Poor Whites in Texas Cotton Culture* (Berkeley: University of California Press, 1997), 65. Foley points out that the percentage of tenancy in Texas was 60.9 in 1930, falling to 48.9 in 1940. Daniel D. Arreola, *Tejano South Texas: A Mexican American Cultural Province* (Austin: University of Texas Press, 2002), 50–53. "Mexican carrot worker with son, Edinburg, Texas," Farm Security Administration—Office of War Information Photograph Collection (Library of Congress), 1939, http://www.loc.gov/index.html. "Mexican women leaving truck which brought them to the spinach field, La Pryor, Texas," Farm Security Administration—Office of War Information Photograph Collection (Library of Congress), 1939, http://totallyfreeimages.com/417571/Mexican-women-leaving-truck-which-brought-them-to-the-spinach-fi.
63 Reviewer(s): Johnson, Ryan. Keith J. Volanto, *Texas, Cotton, and the New Deal* (College Station, TX: Texas A&M University Press, 2005), xv. "The Marketplace of Christianity," http://eh.net/page/78/?s=how+much+is+that.
64 Keith J. Volanto, "Leaving the Land: Tenant and Sharecropper Displacement in Texas during the New Deal," *Social Science History*, December 1, 1996, Vol. 20(4), 534, 535. Keith Joseph Volanto, *Texas, Cotton, And The New Deal* (College Station: Texas A & M, 2005), 5–6, 126.
65 Barbara Rose And Stephen Franklin, "Illegal immigrants establish a labor pool vital to the U.S. economy," *Chicago Tribune*, April 29, 2006.
66 Marc Simon Rodriguez, *The Tejano Diaspora: Mexican Americanism and Ethnic Politics in Texas and Wisconsin* (Chapel Hill: The University of North Carolina Press; Reprint edition, February 1, 2014), 4.
67 Marc S. Rodriguez, ed., *Repositioning North American Migration History: New Directions in Modern Continental Migration, Citizenship, and Community* (Rochester, NY: University of Rochester Press, 2005), 207–11.
68 "Housing for Mexican sugar beet workers. Saginaw Farms, Michigan," Farm Security Administration—Office of War Information Photograph Collection (Library of Congress), 1941, http://www.ancientfaces.com/photo/housing-for-mexican-sugar-beet-workers-saginaw-far/760494. John Weber, *From South Texas to the Nation: The Exploitation of Mexican Labor in the Twentieth Century* (Chapel Hill: University of North Carolina Press, 2005), 55, 138; makes point that Mexico during the 1920s encouraged Mexicans to migrate. This is an informative book.
69 Charles D. Chamberlain, *Victory at Home: Manpower and Race in the American South During World War II* (University of Georgia Press, 2003), 74
70 Ibid.
71 Philip S. Foner, *History of the Labor Movement, Vol. 10: The TUEL, 1925–1929* (New York: International Publishers, 1991), 240–42. David Montejano, *Anglos and Mexicans in the Making of Texas, 1836–1986* (Austin: University of Texas Press, 1987), 9, 162–78. Lloyd Horace Fisher, *The Harvest Labor Market in California* (Cambridge: Harvard University Press, 1953), 22, 42. Carey McWilliams, *Ill Fares the Land: Migrants and Migratory Labor in the United States* (New York: Arno Press, 1976), 141, 257, 259–60, 264–66. George O. Coalson, *The Development of the Migratory Farm Labor System in Texas, 1900–1954* (San Francisco, CA: R&E Research Associates, 1977), 28. Mary G. Luck, "Labor Contractors," in Emily H.

Huntington, ed., *Doors to Jobs* (Berkeley: University of California Press, 1942), 314, 317, 338–42. Farm Security Administration—Office of War Information Photograph Collection (Library of Congress), 1939, http://www.loc.gov/pictures/item/fsa1997024941/PP/. Ralph F. Grajeda, "Mexicans in Nebraska," Nebraska State Historical Society, http://www.nebraskahistory.org/lib-arch/whadoin/mexampub/mexicans.htm.

72 Ibid., p. 78.

73 Sam Kushner, *Long Road to Delano* (New York: International Publishers, 1975), 58. Jamieson, *Labor Unionism*, 80–81, 83. Gilbert G. González, "Company Unions, the Mexican Consulate, and the Imperial Valley Agricultural Strikes, 1928–1934," *Western Historical Quarterly* 27, No. 1 (Spring 1996), 53–73. "Strike Agitators Named," *Los Angeles Times* (May 1, 1930). Sixteen leaders were taken in relation to Imperial Valley cantaloupe strike. "El Centro Convicts Nine Reds," *Los Angeles Times* (June 14, 1930). Emilio Alonzo was also listed as an inmate in the 1930 Census, Year: 1930; Census Place: El Centro, Imperial, California; Roll: 119; Enumeration District: 23; Image: 307.0. He was born in Mexico and was 24 years of age. Interviews on the C&AWIU in the 1930s, Phonotape 49:3, 3056 C1, Bancroft Library, George Ewart, Interviewer, "Interviews on the organization of the Cannery and Agricultural Workers' Industrial Union in California in the 1930s."

74 Pat Chambers, Interview, California State University at Northridge (April 14, 1978). Jamieson, *Labor Unionism*, 83, 84–85. Kushner, *Long Road*, 28, 63. Joan London and Henry Anderson, *So Shall Ye Reap* (New York: Crowell, 1971), 28, 29. Devra Anne Weber, "The Organizing of Mexicano Agricultural Workers: Imperial Valley and Los Angeles, 1928–1934: An Oral History Approach," *Aztlán* 3, No. 2 (1972), 321. "Syndicalism and 'Sedition' Laws in 35 States and in Philippine Islands Must Be Smashed!" in the Paul S. Taylor Collection of the Bancroft Library. See Mitchell, *The Lie of the Land*, 124–29. "What were the Imperial Valley Strikes?" Chapter 7: La Lucha: The Beginnings of the Struggle, 1920–1930s, *San Diego Mexican & Chicano History*, http://www-rohan.sdsu.edu/dept/mas/chicanohistory/chapter07/c07s01.html. Raymond P. Barry, ed., "The California Cotton Pickers Strike-1933" (Oakland, California: Federal Writers Project, 1938), http://content.cdlib.org/view?docId=hb88700929&chunk.id=div00022&br.

75 Stephanie Lewthwaite, "Race, Paternalism, and 'California Pastoral': Rural Rehabilitation and Mexican Labor in Greater Los Angeles," *Agricultural History* Vol. 81, Issue 1 (2007), 1–35.

76 Douglas Monroy, *Thrown Among Strangers: The Making of Mexican Culture in Frontier California* (Berkeley: University of California Press, 1990), 65. Selden C. Menefee and Orin C. Cassmore, *The Pecan Shellers of San Antonio: The Problem of Underpaid and Unemployed Mexican Labor* (Washington D.C.: Works Progress Administration, 1940), reprinted in Carlos E. Cortés, ed., *Mexican Labor in the United States* (New York: Arno Press, 1974), 24. See Don Mitchell, "The Disintegration of Landscape: The Workers' Revolt of 1933," in Mitchell, *The Lie of the Land*, 130–55. Sánchez, *Becoming Mexican American*, 236–38. Rodolfo F. Acuña, *Corridors of Migration: The Odyssey of Mexican Laborers, 1600–1933* (Tucson, University of Arizona Press: 2007), 226, 231–32.

77 Marc Grossman, "Chavez, Steinbeck: The ties that bind," *The Sacramento Bee*, Oct. 20, 2002, http://ufw.org/research/history/chavez-steinbeck-ties-bind-ufw-spokesman-longtime-cesar-chavez-press-secretary-marc-grossman/. Armando Ibarra and Rodolfo Torres, Ernesto Galarza, Man of Fire: Selected Writings (Urbana: University of Illinois Press, 2013), 190.

78 Halcomb, "Efforts to Organize," 9. Jamieson, *Labor Unionism*, 94, 95–96. Pat Chambers, Interview, April 13, 1978. Guérin-Gonzáles, *Mexican Workers*, 119–22. "Fruit Peace Hopes Rise," *Los Angeles Times* (August 17, 1933). "Strike Set May Be State-Wide," *Los Angeles Times* (August 19, 1933). "Ranch-Strike Injunction Case May Be Called Off," *Los Angeles Times* (August 22, 1933). "Fruit Workers Talk of Strike," *Los Angeles Times* (August 25, 1933). *Visalia Times Delta* (September 16, 1933). "Twenty Thousand California Legionnaires Will Parade at Pasadena Today," *Los Angeles Times* (August 14, 1933). "Strike Plot Laid to Reds," *Los Angeles Times* (August 17, 1933). Acuña, *Corridors of Migration*, 233–36.

79 Michael Denning, *The Cultural Front: The Laboring of American Culture in the Twentieth Century New Edition* (London: Verso; New Edition, 2011), 266, 67.

80 Carolyn Kellogg. "John Steinbeck's migrant workers," *Los Angeles Times* (August 19, 2008), http://latimesblogs.latimes.com/jacketcopy/2008/08/john-steinbeck.html.

81 Anne Loftis, *Witnesses to the Struggle: Imaging the 1930s California Labor Movement* (Las Vegas: University of Nevada Press, 1998), 2, 45–65. Jamieson, *Labor Unionism*, 15, 19–21, 36, 93. Pat Chambers interview, April 19, 1978—the latter is available in my papers in special collections (CSUN). Cletus Daniel, *Bitter Harvest: A History of California Farmworkers, 1980–1941* (Ithaca, NY: Cornell University Press, 1981), 156–58. Jackson Benson and Anne Loftis, "John Steinbeck and Farm Labor Unionization: the background In Dubious Battle," *American Literature* 52, No. 2 (May 1980), 156–58. Pat Chambers interview, April 19, 1978.

82 Rodolfo Acuña. *Corridors of Migration*, 123–24. Michael Denning, Ibid.
83 Ibid.
84 John Steinbeck, *Their Blood Is Strong*, Originally published by the Simon J. Lubin Society (San Francisco) in April, 1938. John Steinbeck, "The Harvest Gypsies", Spring 1938, *San Francisco News* (October 5–12, 1936), https://www.scribd.com/doc/127985836/John-Steinbeck-The-Harvest-Gypsies#download&from_embed.
85 Denning, Ibid., p. 266.
86 Steinbeck, "Harvest," p. 5.
87 John Steinbeck, "The Harvest Gypsies", Spring 1938, *San Francisco News* (October 5–12, 1936), https://www.scribd.com/doc/127985836/John-Steinbeck-The-Harvest-Gypsies#download&from_embed.
88 Rodolfo F. Acuña, *Corridors of Migration*, see Chapter 11. The use of genealogical records shows that many of the strikers were former miners and city dwellers.
89 Mitchell, *Lie of the Land*, 113–15. Clark A. Chambers, *California Farm Organizations* (Berkeley: University of California Press, 1952), 18, 66. Hearings Before a Subcommittee on Education and Labor, U.S. Senate, 76th Cong., (Washington, D.C.: Government Printing Office, 1940), part 51, 18579 (hereafter called *La Follette Hearings*). Paul S. Taylor and Clark Kerr, "San Joaquín Valley Strike, 1933. Violations of Free Speech and Rights of Labor," Hearings before a Subcommittee on Education and Labor, U.S. Senate, 77th Cong., pursuant to S. Res. 266, 74th Cong., part 54, *Agricultural Labor in California* (Washington, D.C.: Government Printing Office, 1940), 19947, 19949. *The Bakersfield Californian* (October 25, 1933), stated that the Southern California Edison Company registered a profit of $8,498,703 in the first nine months of 1933. Porter M. Chaffee, "A History of the Cannery and Agricultural Workers Industrial Workers Union," Unpublished Manuscript, Federal Writers Project Collection, Bancroft Library, University of California, Berkeley, Carton 35 (1938), 8. Pat Chambers, Interview (April 13, 1978). Jamieson, *Labor Unionism*, 101. Acuña, *Corridors of Migration*, 237–73.
90 *Visalia Times Delta* (September 19, 1933). Taylor and Kerr, "San Joaquin Valley Strike," 1992. "Caravan of striking cotton pickers south of Tulare, California," Farm Security Administration—Office of War Information Photograph Collection, 1933, http://www.ancientfaces.com/photo/caravan-of-striking-cotton-pickers-south-of-tulare/725860; also in http://www.loc.gov.
91 John W. Webb, *Transient Unemployed*, Monograph III (Washington, D.C.: Works Progress Administration, Division of Social Research, 1935), 1–5. Caroline Decker, Interview, August 8, 1973. Halcomb, "Efforts to Organize," 5. Jamieson, *Labor Unionism*, 102–04.
92 "Camp site of striking Mexican workers. Corcoran, California," Farm Security Administration—Office of War Information Photograph Collection, 1933, http://www.ancientfaces.com/photo/camp-site-of-striking-mexican-workers-corcoran-cal/1008762. Also see http://www.loc.gov.
93 Devra Anne Weber, Dark Sweat, White Gold: California Farm Workers, Cotton, and the New Deal (Berkeley: University of California Press, 1994), 66.
94 Ibid., pp.11, 66, 94–95.
95 *Bakersfield Californian* (October 9, 1933). Taylor and Kerr, "San Joaquin Valley Strike," 19963. Chaffee, "A History of the Cannery," 49. O. W. Bryan, a local hardware store owner at the time of the strike, was interviewed on June 22, 1973. R. Taylor, *Chavez and the Farm Workers*, 54. Dr. Ira Cross to Raymond Cato, head of the CHP, Interview, February 20, 1934, Taylor Collection, Bancroft Library. *Pixley Enterprise* (January 12, 1934; February 2, 1934). *Visalia Times-Delta* (October 11, 1933). Acuña, *Corridors of Migration*, 245–47.
96 Mark Arax and Rick Wartzman, *The King of California: J. G. Boswell and the Making of a Secret American Empire* (New York: Public Affairs, 2003), 153–54. Taylor and Kerr, "San Joaquin Valley Strike," 19958, 19975–76, 19981, 19984. Pat Chambers, Interviews August 24, 1973; October 4, 1973; November 6, 1973. Halcomb in "Efforts to Organize," 75–76, reports 12 dead, 4 hurt, 113 jailed, and 9 children dead of malnutrition in the cotton camps. According to "Report on Cotton Strikers, Kings County," in the Taylor Collection, relief did not start until October 14, 1933. Chaffee, "A History of the Cannery," 35, 49.
97 In an interview with Paul Taylor on November 17, 1933, Taylor Collection, Bancroft Library, Kern County undersheriff Tom Carter stated that growers were well prepared for the strike. They had two machine guns and had bought $1,000 worth of tear gas. *Bakersfield Californian* (October 11, 1933). Pedro Subia, 4717, Coroner's Inquest, County of Kern, State of California, October 14, 1933. Wofford B. Camp, *Cotton, Irrigation and the AAA: An Interview Conducted by Willa Lug Baum*, Regional Oral History Office, University of California, Bancroft Library, Berkeley (1971), 21. Louis Block, California State Emergency Relief Administration, C-R, f.4, Taylor Collection, Bancroft Library. Local authorities called for the state to send 1,000 CHP officers to Corcoran. The local sheriffs disbanded the camps. Corcoran was the last camp to disband. The growers burned the camp after the strikers left. The *Bakersfield Californian* (October 28, 1933) blared, "Growers to Import 1000

L.A. Workers." On January 13, 1934, the *Bakersfield Californian* reported "Cotton Men's Income Twice That of 1932." On February 6, it reported that the Agricultural Adjustment Agency paid Kern County growers $1,015,000 for plowing under 20–40 percent of their crop.

98 Norman Lowenstein, "Strikes and Strike Tactics in California Agriculture: A History" (Master's Thesis, University of California at Berkeley, 1940), 94. Jamieson, *Labor Unionism*, 106–08. *La Follette Hearings*, part 55, 20140, 20180. Weber, *Dark Sweat*, 321, 323. Guillermo Martínez, Interview, Los Angeles, June 23, 1978. Pat Chambers, Interview, June 26, 1978. In February 1934, David Martínez, R. Salazar, and F. Bustamante were sentenced to eight months for disturbing the peace. Chaffee, "A History of the Cannery," section entitled "Imperial Valley in 1934," 34. See also Jamieson, *Labor Unionism*, 108–09. See C. B. Hutchison, W. C. Jacobson, and John Phillips, *Imperial Valley Farm Situation*, Report of the Special Investigating Committee Appointed at the Request of the California State Board of Agriculture, the California Farm Bureau Federation and the Agricultural Department of the California State Chamber of Commerce (April 16, 1934), 19, 24. The Agricultural Labor Bureau of the San Joaquin Valley was established in 1926 by the Farm Bureau Federation and the Chamber of Commerce. Palomares, along with the growers, fixed wages. See Mitchell, "Disintegration," 115. Herbert Klein and Carey McWilliams, "Cold Terror in California," *The Nation* 141, No. 3655 (July 24, 1934), 97, http://newdeal.feri.org/nation/na3497.htm.

99 Robert Justin Goldstein, *Political Repression in Modern America: From 1870 to 1976* (Urbana: University of Illinois Press, 2001), 222–23. McWilliams, *California*, 148–49. Anne Loftis, *Witnesses to the Struggle: Imaging the 1930s California Labor Movement* (Las Vegas: University of Nevada Press, 1998), 17–26.

100 Jamieson, *Labor Unionism*, 119, 122–25, 128–34. Weber, *Dark Sweat*, 330–31. Lowenstein, "Strikes and Strike Tactics," 29. Theodore Johns, "Field Workers in California Cotton" (Master's Thesis, University of California at Berkeley, 1948), 86–92. Lucas Lucio was the leader of the *Comisión*. Most Mexican unions could not afford to affiliate with the AFL in this period.

101 Jamieson, *Labor Unionism*, 126–27. G. González, *Labor and Community*, 135–60. Lizbeth Haas, *Conquests and Historical Identities in California, 1769–1936* (Berkeley: University of California Press, 1995), 206–8.

102 Gutiérrez, *Walls and Mirrors*, 147–48.

103 Ibid., 110. Victoria Cepeda, "Latino Civil Rights Figures: Luisa Moreno," *News Taco*, http://www.newstaco.com/2011/08/11/latino-civil-rights-figures-luisa-moreno/. Heidi Moore, *Luisa Moreno* (London: Heinemann Educational Books, 2005). "Luisa Moreno," http://www.youtube.com/watch?v=7upHqNX6654.

104 Ronald B. Taylor, *Sweatshops in the Sun: Child Labor on the Farms* (Boston, MA: Beacon Press, 1973), 6–7. Peter Mattiessen, *Sal Si Puedes: César Chávez and the New American Revolution* (New York: Random House, 1969), 9. Carey McWilliams, *Factories in the Fields: The Story of Migratory Labor in California* (Santa Barbara and Salt Lake City: Peregrine Publishers, 1971), 196. Ruiz, *Cannery Women*, 43, 45, 53–55. Vicky L. Ruiz, "UCAPAWA, Chicanas, and the California Food Processing Industry, 1937–1950" (PhD Dissertation, Stanford University, 1982), 127.

105 Foley, *White Scourge*, 183–201. Jamieson, *Labor Unionism*, 57, 270–73, 275–78. Selden C. Menefee, "Mexican Migratory Workers of South Texas" (Washington, D.C.: Works Progress Administration, 1941), reprinted in Carlos E. Cortés, ed., *Mexican Labor*, 52.

106 Coalson, in *Migratory Farm Labor System*, 40–42, reviews labor conditions in the sugar beet industry in Michigan, Ohio, and Wisconsin. McWilliams, in *Ill Fares the Land*, 257–58, states that 66,100 Mexicans left Texas annually for seasonal work. Many went to the beet fields. Jamieson, *Labor Unionism*, 233–35, 238–41.

107 Sarah Deutsch, *No Separate Refuge: Culture, Class, and Gender on the Anglo-Hispanic Frontier in the American Southwest, 1880–1940* (New York: Oxford University Press, 1987), 163–64.

108 Jamieson, *Labor Unionism*, 242–55. Menefee, "Mexican Migratory Workers," 24. Mark Reisler, *By the Sweat of Their Brow: Mexican Immigrant Labor in the United States, 1900–1940* (Westport, CT: Greenwood Press, 1976), 248–49; McWilliams, *Ill Fares the Land*, 125; Pauline Kibbe, *Latin Americans in Texas* (New York: Arno Press, 1974), 201.

109 Deutsch, *No Separate Refuge*, 174–75, 205. "[Mrs. Juan Valdes]," American Life Histories: Manuscripts from the Federal Writers' Project, 1936–1940, 1939, Library of Congress, http://newmexicowanderings.com/launio11.htm.

110 Rosa Pesotta, *Bread upon the Water* (New York: Dodd, Mead, 1944), 19, 22, 23, 27–28, 40, 43, 50, 54–59. See "Rosa Pesotta," Anarchist Library, http://theanarchistlibrary.org/library/rose-pesotta-bread-upon-the-waters h.

111 Sánchez, *Becoming Mexican American*, 227–41. John Lasslett and Mary Tyler, *The ILGWU In Los Angeles, 1907–1988* (Inglewood, CA: Ten Star Press, 1989), 26–44. Pesotta, in *Bread upon the Water*, 75, states that Mary Gonzáles and Beatrice López were union organizers in the sweatshops of San Francisco's Chinatown.

112 Blackwelder, *Women of the Depression*, 31–32, 76–77, 131–35.

113 "International Ladies' Garment Workers' Union," *Handbook of Texas Online*, http://www.tshaonline.org/handbook/online/articles/II/oci2.html.

114 R. García, *San Antonio*, 62. George N. Green, "The ILGWU in Texas, 1930–1970," *Journal of Mexican American History* 1, No. 2 (Spring 1971), 144–45, 154, 158. Martha Cotera, *Profile of the Mexican American Woman* (Austin, TX: National Educational Laboratory Publishers, 1976), 86–87. Zaragosa Vargas, "Tejana radical: Emma Tenayuca and the San Antonio labor movement during the great depression," *Pacific Historical Review*, Nov 1997, Vol. LXVI(4), 553–580.

115 "Mexican women pecan shellers at work. Union plant. San Antonio, Texas," Farm Security Administration–Office of War Information Photograph Collection (Library of Congress), 1939, http://www.ancientfaces.com/photo/mexican-women-pecan-shellers-at-work-union-plant-s/740401.

116 "Altar for Emma Tenayuca," Houston Institute for Culture, http://www.houstonculture.org/mexico/altaremma.html. "Development of Labor Unions in San Antonio, 1930s: Emma Tenayuca," 1916, Institute of Texas Cultures, http://www.teachingtexas.org/node/827.

117 Harold Arthur Shapiro, "Workers of San Antonio, Texas, 1900–1940" (PhD Dissertation, University of Texas, 1952), 117, 119, 125, 126. Kenneth Walker, "The Pecan Shellers of San Antonio and Mechanization," *Southwestern Historical Quarterly* 69 (July 1965), 44–58. R. García, *San Antonio*, 62–64. Menefee and Cassmore, *Pecan Shellers*, 4–5. Green Peyton, *San Antonio: City in the Sun* (New York: McGraw-Hill, 1946), 169. Ruiz, *Out of the Shadows*, 80; three of the shellers at the bargaining table in 1942 were officers in UCAPAWA Local No. 172: Lydia Domínguez, president, Margarita Rendón, vice-president, and Maizie Támez, secretary treasurer. Blackwelder, *Women of the Depression*, 145–53. Roberto Calderón and Emilio Zamora, "Manuela Solis and Emma Tenayuca: A Tribute," in *Between Borders: Essays on Mexicana/Chicana History* (Encino, CA: Floricanto Press, 1990), 269–79. Irene Ledesma, "Texas Newspapers and Chicana Workers' Activism, 1919–1974," *Western Historical Quarterly* 26, No. 3 (Fall 1995), 317–21. Zaragoas Vargas, "Tejana Radical: Emma Tenayuca and the San Antonio Labor Movement during the Great Depression," *Pacific Historical Review* 66, No. 4 (November 1997), 553–80.

118 Gabriela González, "Carolina Munguia and Emma Tenayuca: The Politics of Benevolence and Radical Reform," *Frontiers: Journal of Women Studies* Vol. 24, Nos. 2 & 3 (2003), https://muse.jhu.edu/login?auth=0&type=summary&url=/journals/frontiers/v024/24.2gonzalez_g.html. Allan Turner, "A Night That Changed San Antonio/Woman Recalls Leading Labor Riot in 1939," *Houston Chronicle*, 2 Star ed. (December 14, 1986) reports that the incident happened in 1939.

119 Emma Tenayuca and Homer Brooks, "The Mexican Question in the Southwest," *Communist* 18 (May 1939), 257–68. Gutiérrez, *Walls and Mirrors*, 107–09. Peyton, *City in the Sun*, 172–74. Shapiro, "Workers of San Antonio," 130–32. Menefee and Cassmore, *Pecan Shellers*, 24. Audrey Granneberg, "Maury Maverick's San Antonio," *Survey Graphic* 28, No.7 (July 1939), 421, http://newdeal.feri.org/survey/39a07.htm.

120 Robert M. Fogelson, *The Fragmented Metropolis: Los Angeles, 1850–1930* (Berkeley: University of California Press, 1993), 132–34.

121 Luis Leobardo Arroyo, "Chicano Participation in Organized Labor: CIO in Los Angeles, 1938–1950: An Extended Research Note," *Aztlán* 6, No. 2 (Summer 1975), 277. Monroy, *Thrown Among Strangers*, 70, 99.

122 Kathryn Close, "Back of the Yards: Packingtown's Latest Drama: Civic Unity," *Survey Graphic* 29, No.12 (December 1, 1940), 612, http://newdeal.feri.org/search_details.cfm?link=http://newdeal.feri.org/survey/40c22.htm. Dominic A. Pacyga, *Polish Immigrants and Industrial Chicago: Workers on the South Side, 1880–1922* (Chicago: University of Chicago Press, 2003), 159.

123 Gabriela F. Arredondo, "Mexicanas in Chicago," *Illinois Periodicals Online*, Northern Illinois University Libraries, http://www.lib.niu.edu/2003/iht1020357.html. Louise A. N. Kerr, "Mexicans in Chicago," http://www.lib.niu.edu/1999/iht629962.html (accessed November 3, 2009). Lizabeth Cohen, *Making a New Deal: Industrial Workers in Chicago, 1919–1939* (Cambridge: Cambridge University Press, 1991), 337–38. "[Jesse Perez], Chicago," American Life Histories: Manuscripts from the Federal Writers' Project, 1936–1940, 1939, http://memory.loc.gov/ammem/index.html. "Another Case of Racial Prejudice," *Chicago Defender* (October 17, 1936), 16.

124 Louise Kerr, "The Chicano Experience in Chicago, 1920–1970" (PhD Dissertation, University of Illinois at Chicago Circle, 1976), 69–70, 72–78. The Chicago Mexican population had fallen from 20,000 in 1930 to 14,000 in 1933 and to 12,500 in 1934. See also Francisco A. Rosales and Daniel T. Simon, "Chicano Steelworkers and Unionism in the Midwest, 1919–1945," *Aztlán* No. 6 (Summer 1975), 267. Zaragosa Vargas, *Labor Rights Are Civil Rights: Mexican American Workers in Twentieth-Century America* (Princeton, NJ: Princeton University Press, 2005), 271–72.

125 Vargas, Zaragosa, "Introduction," *In Labor Rights Are Civil Rights: Mexican American Workers in Twentieth-Century America*, (Princeton University Press, 2005), 1–15, http://www.jstor.org/stable/j.ctt4cgbmf.5.

126 U.S. Congress, Senate, Committee on Education and Labor, *Violations of Free Speech and Rights of Labor: Hearings Before a Subcommittee of the Committee on Education and Labor*, 75th Cong., 1st session, June 30–July 2, 1937, Part 14, "The Chicago Memorial Day Incident," pp. 4941–4949. In F. Arturo Rosales, ed., *Testimonio: A Documentary History of the Mexican American Struggle for Civil Rights* (Houston, TX: Arte Público Press–University of Houston, 2000), 249–56. "Little Steel Strike of 1937," Ohio History Central, http://www.ohiohistorycentral.org/entry.php?rec=513. "Memorial Day massacre of 1937," http://en.wikipedia.org/wiki/Memorial_Day_massacre_of_1937.

127 Irving Bernstein, *History of the American Workers 1920–1933: The Lean Years* (Boston, MA: Houghton-Mifflin, 1960). Harry R. Rubenstein, "Political Regression in New Mexico: The Destruction of the National Miners' Union in Gallup," in Robert Kern, ed., *Labor in New Mexico: Unions, Strikers, and Social History Since 1881* (Albuquerque: University of New Mexico Press, 1983), 93–95. See *State v. Ochoa et al.*, 41 N.M. 589; 72 2d 609; 1937 N.M. Lexis 70. Francisco A. Rosales, *Chicano! The History of the Mexican American Civil Rights Movement*, 2nd Revised ed. (Houston, TX: Arte Publico Press, 1997), 122.

128 D. W. Dinwoodie, "The Rise of the Mine-Mill Union in Southwestern Copper," in James C. Foster, ed., *American Labor in the Southwest* (Tucson: University of Arizona Press, 1982), 46–48. Monroy, *Thrown Among Strangers*, 126–31. "Texas State Industrial Union Council," *Handbook of Texas Online*, http://www.tshaonline.org/handbook/online/articles/octbg.

129 "George I. Sánchez Charter School," http://www.aama.org/Sanchez-Charter-High-School/. Carlos K. Blanton, "George I. Sánchez, Ideology, and Whiteness in the Making of the Mexican American Civil Rights Movement, 1930–1960," *Journal of Southern History* 72, No. 3 (August 2006), 569–604.

130 M. García. *Mexican Americans*, 66–67.

131 "League of United Latin American Citizens," *Handbook of Texas Online*, http://www.tshaonline.org/handbook/online/articles/LL/wel1.html. Gutiérrez, *Walls and Mirrors*, 87, 89–90. M. García, *Mexican Americans*, 3, 26–40, 62–83, 175–203, 232–51, 273–90. R. García, *San Antonio*, 278. Montejano, *Anglos and Mexicans*, 160–61. Daniel D. Arreola, "Mexican Origins of South Texas Mexican Americans, 1930," *Journal of Historical Geography* 19, No. 1 (January 1993), 48–63. Peyton, *City in the Sun*, 156–59.

132 Robin Fitzgerald Scott, "The Mexican-American in the Los Angeles Area, 1920–1950: From Acquiescence to Activity" (PhD Dissertation, University of Southern California, 1971), 148–49. Monroy, *Thrown Among Strangers*, 109, 195–96.

133 Ruiz, *Out of the Shadows*, 36–50. M. García, *Bert Corona*, 30. Carlos Muñoz, Jr., *Youth, Identity, Power: The Chicano Movement* (London: Verso, 1989), 25. On March 6, 1979, Manuel Banda stated that Tom García, 33, the secretary of the YMCA, had the idea for the MAM. For more data on the MAM, see "Mexican-American Movement: Its Origins and Personnel," in the Angel Cano papers at California State University, Northridge/Chicano Studies, July 12, 1944, 3–4. (This collection is referred to hereafter as the Cano papers.) In CSUN Library, http://digital-library.csun.edu/LatArch/. See also Albert R. Lozano, "Progress Through Education," Cano papers. *Forward* (October 28, 1945 and February 24, 1949). "Félix Gutiérrez, Prominent Youth Worker, Dies at 37," *Lincoln Heights Bulletin-News* (December 1, 1955). *Forum News Bulletin* (August 7, 1949). José Rodríguez, "The Value of Education," *The Mexican Voice* (July 1938), quoted in C. Muñoz, *Youth, Identity, and Power*, 31. Rebecca Muñoz, "Horizons," *The Mexican Voice* (July 1939), quoted in C. Muñoz, *Youth, Identity, Power*, 34. C. Muñoz, *Youth, Identity, Power*, 19–42. "Supreme Council of the Mexican American Movement Papers," in Latino Archives collection, California State Northridge Urban Archives, http://digital-library.csun.edu/LatArch/.

134 Victoria Cepeda, "Luisa Moreno Founder of The Spanish-Speaking Peoples Congressm Pa'lante," August 11, 2011, https://palantelatino.com/2011/08/11/luisa-moreno-founder-of-the-spanish-speaking-peoples-congress/. Heidi Moore, *Luisa Moreno* (Heinemann-Raintree, 2005).

135 Kevin Allen Leonard, *The Battle for Los Angeles: Racial Ideology and World War II* (Albuquerque: University of New Mexico Press, 2006), 27–28. Ruiz, *Cannery Women*, 99. M. García, *Mexican Americans*, 145–74. M. García, in *Mexican Americans*, 157, suggests that Quevedo might have been cooperating with the FBI during the time that he served as an officer in the Congress. Miguel Tirado, "Mexican American Community Political Organization: The Key to Chicano Political Power," in F. Chris García, ed., *La Causa Politica: A Chicano Politics Reader* (Notre Dame, IN: University of Notre Dame Press, 1974). F. Chris García, "Manitos and Chicanos in New Mexico Politics," in F. C. García, ed., *La Causa Politica*.

Scott, "The Mexican-American," 147, 149. Gutiérrez, *Walls and Mirrors*, 111–14.

136 Luisa Moreno, "Non-citizen Americans of the Southwest: Caravan of Sorrow," Cano papers, California Sate University at Northridge, March 3, 1940, Quoted in M. García, *Mexican Americans*, 164. M. García, *Bert Corona*, 108–26.

137 Matt Garcia, "Cain contra Abel: Courtship, Masculinities, and Citizenship in Southern California Farming Communities, 1942–1964," in James T. Campbell, Matthew Pratt Guterl, and Robert G. Lee, eds., *Race, Nation, and Empire in American History* (Chapel Hill, NC: University of North Carolina Press, 2007), 180–200. Agustín Gurza, "Remembering El Espectador," *LatinoLA*, June 17, 2009, http://latinola.com/story.php?story=7568 (accessed November 3, 2009). Kaye Lyon Briegel, "*Alianza Hispano-Americana* and Some Mexican-American Civil Rights Cases in the 1950s," in Manuel Servín, ed., *An Awakening Minority: The Mexican-Americans*, 2nd ed. (Beverly Hills, CA: Glencoe Press, 1974), 176. M. García, *Mexican Americans*, 84–112. M. García, *Bert Corona*, 32. Richard Griswold de Castillo, ed., *World War II and Mexican American Civil Rights* (Austin: University of Texas Press, 2008), 87–89. Rosales, *Chicano!*, 99. Joe Blackstock, "Crusading editor led Latinos in battle against discrimination," *Daily Bulletin* (July 6, 2015).

138 Mexican ministers were sent to the United States to work with Mexicans and Puerto Ricans. Alberto Báez, a New York Methodist minister, worked with Puerto Ricans. He wrote to President Roosevelt about the needs of the Puerto Rican people and the role that English played. Alberto Báez, the grandfather of folk singer Joan Báez, was from Monterey, Mexico, and had worked with Puerto Ricans for almost 20 years. Letter from Pastor Alberto Báez to President Franklin D. Roosevelt's Administration, Franklin Delano Roosevelt Library, President's Personal File, Entry 21, Box 22, October 11, 1935, http://newdeal.feri.org/clergy/cl013.htm.

139 John R. Chávez, *The Lost Land: The Chicano Image of the Southwest* (Albuquerque: University of New Mexico Press, 1984), 97–98. Ruiz, *Out of the Shadows*, 93–94. D. H. Dinwoodie, "Deportation: The Immigration Service and the Chicano Labor Movement in the 1930s," in Antonio Rios Bustamante, ed., *Immigration and Public Policy: Human Rights for Undocumented Workers and Their Families* (Los Angeles, CA: Chicano Studies Center Publications, 1977), 163–74. Philip Stevenson, "Deporting Jesús," *The Nation* 143 (July 18, 1936), 67–69. Deutsch, *No Separate Refuge*, 173. Cotera, *Mexican American Woman*, 93–96.

140 Kerr, "Chicano Experience in Chicago," 69–74, 76–80, 83, 95–96, 99, 101–04. David Maciel, *El Mexico olvidado: La historia del pueblo chicano* (El Paso: University of Texas at El Paso, 1996), 372–75.

141 William S. Taylor, "Some Observations of Marginal Man in the United States," *The Journal of Negro Education*, 9, No. 4 (October 1940), 606–08.

Chapter 11
World War II: The Betrayal of Promises

Learning Objectives

11.1 Analyze the importance of global caste system to American and European Empires, on the eve of World War II.

11.2 Describe the impact of the growth of second generation on the Mexican struggle for political and socioeconomic righrs.

Until recently any criticism of the United States' role in World War II was said to detract from war atrocities of the Nazis and the contributions of American families. The official story was that Germany and Japan were imperial powers intent on ruling the world. Only until recently has the official story been challenged and a more balanced narrative has emerged that the blame for the war at the feet of empires intent upon expanding their realms.[1]

In 1993, Pulitzer Prize winning historian John Dower wrote:

> Even while denouncing Nazi theories of "Aryan" supremacy, the U.S. government presided over a society where blacks were subjected to demeaning Jim Crow laws, segregation was imposed even in the military establishment, racial discrimination extended to the defense industries, and immigration policy was severely biased against all nonwhites. In the wake of Pearl Harbor, these anti-"colored" biases were dramatically displayed in yet another way: the summary incarceration of over 110,000 Japanese-Americans.[2]

Works such as Dowers impacted a small number of Americans because it was ignored by public education a lack of exposure prevented a counter narrative from forming. The context for the war was ignored. Forgotten was that the war followed the racist deportation of Mexicans during the 1930s, as well as a history a history of lynching Black and brown[3] people, and the genocidal European colonial occupations in India, Asia, and Africa. It is no surprise that Americans would not remember this even after confronted with the fact that 44 percent [of British subjects] were proud of Britain's" history of colonialism, with 21 percent regretting it happened and 23 percent holding neither view."[4]

Most Americans believe that World War II began in 1941 when Japan attacked Pearl Harbor. A minority believe the war began in 1939 in Europe. The more informed believe it began in 1919 when the punitive terms of the Treaty of Versailles led to the rise of Adolph Hitler. They forget that the causes of any major historical event, including World War II, are more complex than a single episode. The tensions between the U.S. and Japan began long before the attack on Pearl Harbor and it was the culmination of a chain of events with roots in the U.S. encroachment of the Japanese sphere of influence.

When English colonials subjugated the Indigenous People, they made claims of "cultural legitimacy, property rights, and Indian savagery."[5] As shown in previous chapters, from the beginning, the rhetoric was of "the legitimacy of the conquest." Colonists based this legitimacy on the rule of law such as Papal Bulls.[6] Until recently the right of conquest was recognized in international relations as a justification. It was so from the early sixteenth century almost to this century. The right of conquest was was based on a European world view and it received legitimacy from The Doctrine of Discovery that legitimized the colonization of lands outside of Europe. It gave European nations the right to seize the Indigenous Peoples' lands. When conquered, the previous owners quite simply lost any claims to their land.[7] The Treaty of Tordesillas (1494) stipulated that only non-Christian lands could be legitimately colonized, based on the authority of Pope Alexander VI's 1493 Papal Bull that sanctioned the Spanish conquest of the New World. The document supported Spain's exclusive right to the lands discovered by Columbus.[8]

These justifications, along with the religious doctrine of predestination (Manifest Destiny) are important to the creation and maintenance of an empire. The justifications for Imperialism were, the whims of the conquerors. British critic social scientist J.A. Hobson, has succinctly put it, Imperialism exists for the sake of "forced labour."[9] Rooted in the history of expansion the moral dilemma is: Does a nation or people have the right to invade another nation and use its people's labor and resources as if they were their own?

Mexican Americans

11.1 **Analyze the importance of global caste system to American and European Empires, on the eve of World War II.**

On the eve of World War II, Mexican Americans suffered a grinding poverty stemming from hostile and indifferent public attitudes and institutionalized racism. There were few signs that these conditions would soon change: within months of the onset of hostilities, government officials felt obliged to acknowledge the community's existence and address its complaints. Authorities began to speak of a "Spanish-speaking," "Hispanic," or "Latin American" community—in effect constructing, for political purposes, an ethnic group from diverse elements of Mexican and Latin American origin.[10]

Some 60 percent of Mexican Americans lived in cities; 10 years later 70 percent did. The war years dramatically accelerated urbanization, greatly affecting the identity of the Mexican-origin population. Because of pressure from Mexican American organizations, the U.S. Census again listed Mexicans as "white" in 1940 as it had in 1920—that is, unless they looked Indigenous or of another color. The Census counted 132,165,129 residents in the United States, of which, according to the best estimate, 5.6 percent were Latinos—overwhelmingly of Mexican-origin people. Most Mexicans lived in the Southwest; however, some moved to the Midwest and Pacific Northwest as well. Repatriation and deportation of 600,000 to 1 million Mexicans tipped the balance to the second- and third-generation Mexicans. A slowing down of Mexican immigration to the United States during the Depression years affected this movement. This change was more noticeable in the Midwestern states of Indiana, Illinois, and Michigan, which saw a decline of 72 percent, 52 percent, and 62 percent, respectively, in the Mexican population—California, Texas, Arizona, and New Mexico lost 33 percent, 40 percent, 49 percent, and 45 percent, respectively, during the Great Depression.[11]

As with most wars, the poor paid a disproportionate cost. According to Robin Scott, during the war, 375,000–500,000 Mexican Americans served in the armed forces. In Los Angeles, Mexicans composed an estimated one-tenth of the population, yet accounted for one-fifth of the war casualties.[12]

World War II caused the reformation of the Mexican family system. More women worked outside the home, and the departure of soldier fathers and husbands made them more independent. Not all the changes were positive. The removal of male role models encouraged youth vagrancy that—when combined with poverty—led to a lessening of social control; these changes and the pressures of urban life proliferated the number of gangs, a made-in-the-USA institution phenomenon. Within this racially charged environment, most Mexican Americans wanted to retain their identity as Mexicans—a gut-level response to the racism of the white-dominated society that physically isolated the group.[13]

World War II and the Mexican

Steven Spielberg filmed *Saving Private Ryan* in 1998, and Tom Brokaw published *The Greatest Generation* that same year. Ken Burns in 2007 produced an award-winning documentary, *The War*. What these works had in common was that they ignored the contributions of the Mexicans and Mexican American soldiers despite the fact that the ratio of Mexicans among buck privates serving in combat was one of the highest. Raúl Morín, in *Among the Valiant*, wrote that 25 percent of the U.S. military personnel on the infamous Bataan "Death March" were Mexican Americans. Forced to march 85 miles, 6,000 of the 16,000 soldiers perished. Twelve Mexican Americans won Medals of Honor during World War II; proportionately, this number was higher than that for any other ethnic group. José M. López of Brownsville, Texas, received the Medal of Honor for bravely holding off the advancing Germans until his company was able to retreat.[14]

Many Los Angeles Mexicans were ambivalent about the war when they heard that the United States had declared war on Japan on December 8, 1941: "*Ya estuvo* (This is it)," said one. "Now we can look for the authorities to round up all the Mexicans and deport them to Mexico—bad security risks." At first, some Mexican American soldiers dissociated themselves from the war, saying that their loyalty was to Mexico, not to the United States, but in the end they went into the service. Many Mexican Americans witnessed the repatriation and the discrimination and second-class citizenship experienced by the community and were bitter.[15]

Most Mexican American soldiers were 17–21 years old, and some were even younger—like my cousin Rubén Villa, who lied about his age and enlisted in the Navy at 16. Apart from the soldiers' machismo of having to prove themselves, pressure to prove the statement "I will prove that my race knows how to die anywhere" represents the injustice of sending people with unequal rights and opportunities to war. Educational and economic status, race, and gender all play a role in determining equality.

The song *El Soldado Raso* (the buck private or peon) became a rallying cry for Mexican Americans in World War II. They often sang it before going into combat. It was an expression of the racial and communal pride of Mexican Americans who endured American racism and were at the bottom of the barrel. The underlying message was the illusion that he was proving himself to his people, and to his mother, and that he would be a good American by shedding his blood. The popularity of *El Soldado Raso* carried over to the Vietnam War. A disproportionate number of Mexican Americans who sung this haunting song were teens.[16]

Guy Gabaldón: Discrimination

Guy Gabaldón, who served in the Western Pacific, captured hundreds of Japanese prisoners. His Navy Cross citation read, "Working alone in front of the lines, he daringly entered enemy caves, pillboxes, buildings and jungle brush, frequently in the face of hostile fire, and succeeded in not only obtaining vital military information but in capturing well over 1,000 civilians and troops." Gabaldón learned the Japanese language as a child in East Los Angeles, where two Japanese American brothers befriended him. Gabaldón visited their home and eventually moved in with them. When he turned 17, he joined the Marine Corps. After the war, Gabaldón harbored resentment toward the U.S. Marines' decision to award him the Silver Star instead of the Medal of Honor. The Navy upgraded his citation to the Navy Cross after the release of the film *Hell to Eternity* (1960), which documented Guy's war experiences. The movie, however, did not mention that Gabaldón was a Mexican, and a blonde, blue-eyed actor played his character.[17]

Gabaldón accused the Marines of racism toward Mexican Americans, pointing out that he captured more prisoners than the legendary World War I Sgt. Alvin York, who received the Medal of Honor after killing 25 German soldiers and capturing 132 in France in 1918. He ridiculed the Corps' response that another recipient of the Medal was Hispanic: "Although Gabaldón deserved the medal, the Marine's father was of Portuguese descent and his mother was Hawaiian."[18]

The Story of Company E: The All-Mexican Unit

Raúl Morín, when he began writing *Among the Valiant*, was semiliterate and had little research skill; nevertheless, he wanted to tell the neglected story of the Mexican American military contribution to World War II. One of his most dramatic stories was that of Company E of the 2nd Battalion, 141st Infantry Regiment of the 36th Infantry Division, which consisted of men who had grown up in El Paso together, and has served and trained in the Texas National Guard together. Company E was an all-Chicano company that had a high *esprit-de-corps*, and was selected during basic training to receive Ranger training. Many of its members were related: three brothers, Juan, Andrés, and Antonio Saucedo served in Company E. Many attended Bowie High School.

Company E fought in North Africa and took part in the opening of the Italian Campaign. When the Company reached Italy's Rapido River near Monte Cassino monastery, 5th Army Commander General Mark Clark needed a diversionary attack to prevent the Germans from attacking the main Allied invasion force landing at Anzio. Units of the 36th infantry division were deployed and in less than 48 hours, the division lost more than 1,700 men—more than half its number. After the Rapido River assault, Company E regrouped and received replacements for the badly depleted squads. The unit fought in the Cassino area and then at Anzio, helped liberate Rome from the Germans, and landed in southern France to take pressure off allied forces preparing for the invasion of Normandy in France (the backdrop of the famous Sgt. Ryan movie).[19]

Morín wrote about the little-known incident that was a prelude to the Rapido massacre: The 5th Army command had ordered a platoon from Company E on a suicide mission to scout the Rapido Crossing. The patrol was led by Sgt. Gabriel Navarrete and was composed almost entirely of Mexican Americans. The Germans seriously wounded Navarrete, and killed or captured most of his patrol. Navarrete, knowing that the Company would lead the assault, reported his findings and pleaded that "his boys" not be again sent on a suicide mission. Navarrete closely identified with the men, who were mostly from El Paso *barrios*. The commander ordered the badly wounded Navarrete to the battalion hospital. Still, Navarrete insisted that Company E not be sent back across the river; he cautioned Battalion Commander Major Landley that if Company E was sent across, disaster was certain. Landley responded that the U.S. Army was not taking orders from an "incompetent" lieutenant "who was badly wounded and talked incoherently." Navarrete reportedly told Landley, "I will stand court martial as I am not worried for myself. But remember this, Major, if the plans are not changed and you sacrifice my E Company, you are going to answer to me personally; I will be looking for you and I will be armed." On January 21, 1944, Company E again spearheaded the crossing of the Rapido River. The crossing was a complete fiasco. Morín argues, among other things, that Gen. Clark picked Company E, the all-Mexican company, for the most dangerous jobs.

When Navarrete learned of the tragedy, he jumped from his cot and went gunning for the major. The high command immediately transferred the major out of the unit and ordered Navarrete—elevated to the rank of captain—back to the United States. "The Army brass tried to hush up the incident." Meanwhile, the army rewarded Gen. Clark with another star, over the 36th Division Association objection. The involvement of Company E and the disaster was kept under wraps, and Navarrete was ordered to keep quiet. Navarrete earned a Distinguished Service Cross, a Bronze Star, two Silver Stars, and seven Purple Hearts, told the story to Morín. In a way, Navarretes detracts from the extraordinary exploits of the all-Mexican Company E. However, his bravery and that of the rest of the men of Company E cannot be doubted.[20]

Racism at Home and Abroad

Leo Avila of Oakdale, California, a stateside instructor in the Army Air Corps B-29 Program, said, "I view the service and World War II, for me and many others, as the event that opened new doors. I was from a farm family. When I went into the Air Corps and I found I could compete with Anglo people effectively, even those with a couple of years of college, at some point along the way I realized I didn't want to go back to the farm."

Throughout the war, many white Americans treated Mexicans as second-class citizens. For example, Sergeant Macario García from Sugar Land, Texas—a recipient of the Congressional Medal of Honor—could not buy a cup of coffee in a restaurant in Richmond, California. "An Anglo-American chased him out with a baseball bat." And the García incident was not an isolated occurrence. Louis Téllez of Albuquerque was the only Mexican American in his platoon: "I'll never forget the first time I heard [a racial slur], it really hurt me. You can't do anything about it because you are all alone."

A more subtle form of racism persists to this day; for example, the exclusion of Chicanos and Chicanas from the war narrative. As mentioned, Ken Burn's PBS documentary, *The War* (2007), leaves out the Chicano/a participation in World War II.[21] Movies are important and many have been produced about white American families about more than one white family member in the war; however, white Americans were not the only ones making sacrifices. This was pretty much the rule in many Mexican American households. Rosaura Moralez from Anthony, New Mexico, prayed that her five boys would return safely. She was fortunate they all came back alive—even though the odds did not favor Raul, Armando, Catarino, Ricardo, and Esequiel Moralez's safe return. Rita Sánchez tells the story of the five Sánchez brothers from Bernalillo, New Mexico. Four served in the armed forces, and the oldest Leo, 40, tried to enlist but was rejected because of age and medical reasons. Counting the Sánchez's extended family, dozens of kin served in the armed forces, fighting in Europe and in the Pacific. The Sánchez family was not as fortunate as the Moralez family, Severo was killed during heavy fighting on the Island of Leyte.

Lita De Los Santos's eight brothers served in the war: Charlie, the eldest brother, was killed on Omaha Beach during the invasion of Normandy. Another De los Santos brother was shot down in France and taken as a prisoner of war in Germany. Another, Cano, served in Italy, where a piece of shrapnel got lodged in his heart. Ray was wounded in France, and Jesse and Pete were in combat in New Guinea and the Philippines, respectively. It is incredible that the so-called historians such as Ken Burns missed these sacrifices in their narratives.[22]

Chicanas in the Military

The song *El Soldado Razo* also dramatizes mothers' role during the war. If a family had a serviceman, they would hang a blue star in their window.[23] For every family member killed in the war, the household hung a flag with gold star. The sea of blue turned gold in the Mexican districts during the war. Sara Castro Vara had six sons who went into combat. Rudy Vara fought with Gen. George Patton and was in the first wave of soldiers of the first soldiers to help liberate the Nazi concentration camps. The Téllez family of Albuquerque sent six young men and two young women to the service.

Mexican women joined the Women's Army Auxiliary Corps (WAAC) as well as, the Women Accepted for Volunteer Emergency Service (WAVES) (also known as the U.S. Navy's women reserve) and Women's Airforce Service Pilots (WASP) units. Women went overseas as nurses and accepted other opportunities that the war opened to them. For example, Anna Torres Vásquez of East Chicago, Indiana, volunteered for the WAAC, serving as an air-traffic controller at a Florida flight school. Rafaela Muñoz Esquivel, from San Antonio, was the second oldest in a family of 15 children; as a child, Rafaela worked in the pecan-shelling industry in San Antonio. During World War II, she was an army nurse in the United States and then served in France, supporting the 82nd Airborne Division, and was stationed in Germany near Coblenz, about 5 miles from George Patton's 3rd Army. Three children in the Muñiz family served overseas during the war.[24]

A Profile of Courage

Not all sacrifices were made by soldiers. Ralph Lazo epitomized such a profile in courage. Lazo was raised among Asian Americans in the Temple–Beaudry neighborhood of Los Angeles, which included whites, Jews, Japanese, Filipino, Korean, Mexican, and Chinese residents. Ralph attended Central Junior High and Belmont High School, where he interacted with students of all races. He played basketball on a Filipino Community Church team and learned Japanese at his friends' homes; he also took Japanese language classes. His father, John Houston Lazo, a house painter and muralist, was a widower and raised Ralph and his sister, Virginia by himself.

In February 1942, President Franklin D. Roosevelt signed Executive Order 9066, sending 110,000 Japanese Americans to internment (concentration) camps on the West Coast. Ralph Lazo, 16, joined his Los Angeles Japanese American friends and was taken with them to the Manzanar internment camp. Lazo was the only non-Japanese in any of the internment camps. A local newspaper caustically wrote, "Mexican American passes for Japanese." Lazo's father, respecting his son's decision, made no effort to bring him home. The young man graduated from Manzanar High School and was drafted into the Army in August 1944. Lazo served in the South Pacific, was among the troops that liberated the Philippines, and was awarded a Bronze Star for heroism in combat.

Lazo maintained close ties to the Japanese American community until his death in 1992. He was one of 10 donors contributing $1,000 or more to the class action lawsuit against the U.S. government, which was filed to financially compensate Japanese Americans who were interned in concentration camps. At a Manzanar High School reunion years later, his classmates paid tribute to Ralph, saying, "When 140 million Americans turned their backs on us and excluded us into remote, desolate prison camps, the separation was absolute—almost. Ralph Lazo's presence among us said, No, not everyone."[25]

Scapegoats

With the Japanese gone, Mexicans became the most convenient scapegoats; further American casualties of war (even though many of them were of Mexican origin) fueled public hatred against foreigners. Despite the fact that most Mexican Americans were U.S. citizens, they were considered "aliens." Their color was their Star of David (the religious symbol Jews were forced to wear in Germany to identify them).

In Los Angeles, segregation was common, and many recreational facilities excluded Mexican Americans.[26] They could not use public swimming pools in East Los Angeles and in other Southland communities. Often, Mexicans and Blacks could swim only on Wednesdays—the day the county drained the water. In movie houses in places like San Fernando, Mexicans sat in the balcony.

A minority of Mexican youth between the ages of 13 and 17 belonged to barrio clubs that carried the names of their neighborhoods—White Fence, Alpine Street, *El Hoyo*, Happy Valley. The fad among zoot-suiters (gang members), or *pachucos* as they were called, was to tattoo the left hand, between the thumb and index finger, with a small cross with three dots or dashes above it. When they dressed up, many pachucos wore the so-called zoot suit, popular among low-income youths at that time. Pachucos spoke Spanish, but also used *Chuco* among their companions. *Chuco* was the barrio slang—a mixture of Spanish, English, old Spanish, and words adapted by the border Mexicans. Many experts suggest that the language originated around El Paso among Mexicans, who brought it to Los Angeles in the 1930s.

Before the 1943 Zoot Suit riots there was little knowledge about the pachuco. Mexican poet Octavio Paz wrote in *The Labyrinth of Solitude: Life and Thought in Mexico*:

> The pachucos are youths, for the most of Mexican origin, "who form gangs in Southern cities; they can be identified by their language and behavior as well as by the clothing they affect. They are instinctive rebels, and North American racism has vented its wrath on them more than once. But the pachucos do not attempt to vindicate their race or the nationality of their forebears. Their attitude reveals an obstinate, almost fanatical will-to-be, but this will affirm nothing specific except their determination—it is an ambiguous one, as we will see—not to be like those around them. The pachuco does not want to become a Mexican again; at the same time, he does not want to blend into the life of North America."[27]

Octavio Paz was a poet, playwright, essayist, editor, and diplomat. He was awarded a Nobel Prize in literature. In the above quote, Paz comments on Mexicans on life "north from Mexico." His observations, while beautifully written are too general and lack knowledge of the forces in American society that produced the pachuco. His remarks appear profound, but they are uninformed. The pachuco, a product of racism and a reflection on American society that was common among the so-called gente decente, comprised a sizeable number of second-generation Mexican Americans in the barrios of the 1940s gente decente.[28]

Many first generation Mexicans had an obsession with being civil and well behaved they fit into the caste. Social control in the second generation broke down and the second generation rebelled against their immigrant parents' conformity. Their fathers and mothers worked. By white standards, their fathers were failures; they spoke little English and their jobs were menial. The young Mexican peers replaced the role of the father. They joined gangs that took the name of local barrios. Feeling security in numbers, many youths wore a uniform—the zoot suit. Trousers were called drapes, and were worn high above the waist, the knees wide, pegged to 12 or 14 inches at the cuff. The jacket had padded shoulders, and was worn very long, with the hem reaching below the fingertips. Disaffected Blacks and Filipinos also wore the uniform. It represented a badge of resistance.

White authorities saw it as defiant and a challenge to their power—a manifestation of rebellion and moved to put Mexicans in their place. Many white Americans saw it as unpatriotic and fretted over the large amount of material the pachucos wasted in making the zoot suit. They said that white Americans were sacrificing for the war effort and cutting off their pant cuffs to save material for the war effort. The zoot suit was just plain un-American and soldiers would go without a uniform as a consequence. Many also resented the new car culture that brought Mexicans into white American spaces.

Discrimination against the Mexican American reached a crescendo. The first-generation Mexicans accepted a secondary status because they were concerned with earning a living for their families and not making waves. The feeling among many first-generation Mexicans was that they would save money and return to Mexico. The second generation felt less attached to the old country, and were willing to express their feelings of rejection.

World War II and the mass media further alienated the youth. The majority society became more defensively aggressive about their white institutions and what seemed to them a lessening of its social control. The pachuco did not fit the all-American mold and their growing presence challenged U.S. hegemony. During 1942 and early 1943, insecurity and fear about the war's outcome gripped many Americans.

It mattered little that white gangs existed in white neighborhoods. Indeed Americans celebrated white boy gangs in the mid- and late-30s with movies such as *The Dead End* (1937), *Angels with Dirty Faces* (1938), *Hell's Kitchen* (1939), and *They Made Me a Criminal* (1939) and in the mid-40s with the spinoff *The Bowery Boys*.[29] White Angeleños called gangs a Mexican problem, ignoring that urbanization, poverty, and Americanization caused the gang phenomenon. The *Los Angeles Times*, not known for its analytic content, reinforced this stereotype and influenced the public with stories about "Mexican hoodlums." Sociologist Joan Moore attributes the growth of gangs in Los Angeles to many condition including poverty and war. The White Fence clique evolved into a gang as role models such as fathers and older sons went off to war. Other than the territorial nature of the gangs, their most distinctive feature was their individuality. Location and the class background of the gang members played a role. For example, during the war the White Fence gang emerged in Boyle Heights, developing around La Purissima Catholic Church. In the Heights, residents were skilled workers in the brickyards, railroads, packinghouses, and other industries. Unlike Maravilla, Boyle Heights was racially integrated. In 1936, the Lorena Street School was only 22 percent Mexican; the Euclid Street School was 70 percent Mexican.[30]

Forgotten in this historical narrative was the voice of Mexican American females whom the press and the public ravaged. Catherine Sue Ramírez has resurrected documents of the painful memories of how Mexican girls were stereotyped as being as bad as the males. The press characterized them as "girl hoodlums" and "Black Widows" who were infected with venereal disease. Young Mexican girls were offended, and they protested the allegations. The press scapegoated Mexican parents; the use of Spanish and their low standard of living were held to be at fault and were contrasted with the self-perceived "wholesome" American. Mexican women were portrayed as passive, as violent, and as having loose morals, all at the same time.[31]

The Sleepy Lagoon Trial

The name "Sleepy Lagoon" was from a popular melody played by bandleader Harry James. Unable to use public pools, Mexican youth used the name of the tune to romanticize a gravel pit they frequently used for recreational purposes. On the evening of August 1, 1942, members of the 38th Street Club in South Central Los Angeles were jumped by another gang. When the 38th street members returned later with more of their friends, the rival gang was not there. Noticing a party in progress at the nearby Williams Ranch, the 38th street gang crashed in, and a fight followed. The next morning José Díaz, a guest at the party, was found dead on a dirt road near the house. Díaz had no wounds and could have been killed by a hit-and-run driver. Authorities suspected that some [i don't know, they blamed the gang and by inference all Mexicans] members of the 38th Street Club beat him to death, and the police immediately jailed the entire gang. The press portrayed the Sleepy Lagoon defendants as Mexican hoodlums, sensationalized the story. The police flagrantly violated the rights of the suspects, and authorities charged 22 members of the 38th Street boys with criminal conspiracy. Two others demanded a separate trial and the court dropped charges against them.[32]

Shortly after Díaz's death, a special committee of the grand jury accepted the report of Lieutenant Ed Durán Ayres, head of the Foreign Relations Bureau of the Los Angeles Sheriff's Department. The report attempted to justify the gross violations of the defendants' human rights. Although the report admitted that admitting that there was discrimination against Mexicans in employment, education, schooling, recreation, and labor unions was common, it concluded that Mexicans were inherently criminal and violent. According to Ayres, Mexicans were "Indians," who in turn were "Orientals," who had an utter disregard for life. Therefore, Mexicans were genetically violent. The report also stated that Mexican Americans were descendants of the Aztecs who it said sacrificed 30,000 victims a day.

Ayres wrote that "Indians" considered leniency a sign of weakness, pointing to the Mexican government's treatment of the "Indians," which he maintained was quick and severe. He urged that the courts imprison all gang members and that all Mexican youth over the age of 18 be given the option of working or enlisting in the armed forces. Mexicans, according to Ayres, could not change their spots; they had an innate desire to use a knife and let blood, and this inborn cruelty was detonated by liquor and jealousy.³³ The Ayres report, which represented official law enforcement views, goes a long way in explaining the events that subsequently took place around Sleepy Lagoon.

Henry Leyvas and the 38th Street gang were charged with Díaz's murder. Most of the defendants lived in what today is South Central Los Angeles, and many of them had attended McKinley Junior High and Jefferson High Schools—which were predominately African American. Their life experiences differed from those of Mexican Americans elsewhere in Los Angeles. The African American population was more aware of its rights, and influenced their Mexican neighbors. Mexicans students saw African Americans challenge unjust teachers—"talk back" as they called it—and this attitude influenced many Mexican American students to question unfairness as well.

The Honorable Charles W. Fricke abetted numerous irregularities during the trial. The defendants were not allowed to cut their hair or change their clothes for the duration of the proceedings. Fricke denied them the right to consult counsel and seated them in a separate section of the courtroom. Despite all these irregularities, the prosecution failed to prove that the 38th Street Club was a gang, that any criminal agreement or conspiracy existed, or that the accused had murdered Díaz. Seventeen of 22 accused were found guilty. Witnesses testified that considerable drinking had taken place at the party *before* the 38th Street members arrived. If the conspiracy theory had been applied logically, all the defendants would have received equal verdicts. However, on January 12, 1943, the court passed sentences, three defendants were guilty of first-degree murder; nine, of second-degree murder; five, of assault; and five were found not guilty.³⁴

The recent repatriation of hundreds of Mexicans and the disproportionate number of heads of households inducted into the armed forces weakened the Mexican community. Mainstream Mexican American organizations such as the League of United Latin American Citizens (LULAC) and the *mutualistas* remained silent.³⁵

Under the leadership of LaRue McCormick, supporters formed the Sleepy Lagoon Defense Committee. Carey McWilliams, a noted journalist and lawyer, chaired the committee. The parents of the defendants, especially the mothers, helped raise funds through tamale sales and by holding dances. Hollywood notables Anthony Quinn, Rita Hayworth, Orson Welles, and many other actors and actresses contributed money. African American leaders such as Carlotta Bass, editor of the *California Eagle* newspaper, condemned the injustice fearful of another Scottsboro case, in which nine Black men, ages 14–21, were tried without competent counsel for the alleged rape of two white women in Alabama in March 1931 they were hastily convicted.

Meanwhile, the press and police harassed the committee, red-baiting McWilliams and the members. Police raided their meetings, and threatened to take away the First Unitarian Church of Los Angeles's tax exemption if it allowed meetings to be held there. The California Committee on Un-American Activities, headed by State Senator Jack Tenney, investigated the Sleepy Lagoon committee, charging that it was a Communist-front organization and that Carey McWilliams had "Communist leanings," because he opposed segregation and favored miscegenation. The FBI also viewed the committee as a Communist front, stating that it "opposed all types of discrimination against Mexicans."³⁶

On October 4, 1944, the Second District Court of Appeals reversed the verdict of the lower court in a unanimous decision, holding that Judge Fricke conducted a biased trial, and that he violated the constitutional rights of the defendants. The court also found no evidence of a conspiracy to commit murder or assaults with intent to commit murder, nor any evidence tying the defendants to José Díaz. By not allowing the defendants to challenge coerced statements made at the time of arrest the upper court held that Fricke had erred. He also erred in refusing the defendants the right to consult with counsel. The court found that Fricke's conduct was biased and unfair and that he had admitted prejudicial evidence. Incredulously, the appellate court concluded that there was no evidence of racism. The sentences were reversed; however, the individuals were not retried and, hence, did not have the opportunity to prove their innocence. The ordeal emotionally scarred the Sleepy Lagoon appellants and many returned to prison for other offenses.

Compounding the travesty was the imprisonment of five of the female friends of the Sleepy Lagoon defendants, Bertha Aguilar, Dora Barrios, Lorena Encinas, Josephine Gonzales, Juanita Gonzales, Frances Silva, Lupe Ynostroza, and Betty Zeiss who were charged with rioting, and made wards of the state under the Department of Health and Human Services. Even more outrageous were the actions of the California Youth Authority who persuaded the parents of five girls to commit their daughters to the Ventura School for Girls, which according to Alice McGrath (aka Alice Greenfield in Luís Váldez's film *Zoot Suit*), had a worse reputation than San Quentin at the time, though San Quentin was a maximum-security facility that housed California's death row. The judicial system had not convicted of them any crime; their only crime was guilt by association. They remained institutionalized until the age of 21.³⁷

Mutiny in the Streets of Los Angeles

In the spring of 1943, several minor altercations broke out in Los Angeles. In April, marines and sailors invaded the Mexican barrio and black ghetto in Oakland, assaulted the people, and "depantsed" zoot-suiters. Skirmishes continued through the month of May. The "sailor riots" began on June 3, 1943. Allegedly, Mexicans attacked a group of sailors for attempting to pick up some Chicanas. The details are vague; police did not try to get the Mexicans' side of the story, but took the sailors' report at face value. Fourteen off-duty police officers, led by a detective lieutenant, went looking for the "criminals." They found no actual evidence, but made certain that the press covered the story.

That same night, sailors went on a rampage. They broke into the Carmen Theater, tore zoot suits off Mexicans, and beat up the youths. Police again arrested the victims. Word spread that pachucos were fair game, and that military personnel could assault them without fear of arrest. Sailors returned the next evening with some 200 allies. In 20 hired cabs, they cruised Whittier Boulevard, in the heart of the East Los Angeles barrio, jumping out of the cars to gang up on neighborhood youths. Police and the sheriff maintained they could not find the sailors. Finally, they arrested nine sailors but released them immediately without filing charges. The press, portraying the sailors as heroes and the youth as delinquents, slanted the news stories and headlines so as to arouse racial hatred.

Encouraged by the press and the "responsible" elements of Los Angeles, sailors, assembled on the night of June 5 and marched four abreast down the streets, warning Mexicans to shed their zoot suits or they would be stripped. On that night and the next, servicemen broke into bars and other establishments and beat up Mexicans. Police continued to abet the lawlessness, arriving only after damage had been done and the servicemen had left. Even though sailors destroyed private property. When members of the Mexican community attempted to defend themselves, police arrested them.

Events climaxed on the evening of June 7, as thousands of soldiers, sailors, and civilians surged down Main Street and Broadway in search of pachucos. The mob crashed into bars and broke the legs off stools using them as clubs. The press reported 500 zoot-suiters ready for battle. By this time, Filipinos and Blacks had also became targets. Mexicans, beaten up and their clothes ripped off, were left bleeding on the streets. The mob surged into movie theaters, turning on the lights, marching down the aisles, and pulling zoot-suit-clad youngsters out of their seats. Police arrested more than 600 Mexican youths without cause and labeled the arrests "preventive action." Seventeen-year-old Enrico Herrera, after being beaten and arrested, spent three hours at a police station, where his mother found him, still naked and bleeding. A 12-year-old boy's jaw was broken. Through all this, many Los Angeles whites cheered the servicemen and their civilian allies.[38]

At the height of the turmoil, servicemen pulled a Black man off a streetcar and gouged out his eye with a knife. Military authorities, realizing that the Los Angeles law enforcement agencies would not stop the brutality, intervened and declared downtown Los Angeles off limits for military personnel. Classified naval documents prove that the Navy believed it had a mutiny on its hands. The military shore patrols quashed the rioting—something the Los Angeles police could not or would not do.

For the next few days, police ordered mass arrests, and raided a Catholic welfare center to arrest some of its occupants. The press and city officials continued to agitate residents. An editorial by Manchester Boddy in the June 9 *Los Angeles Daily News* urged the city to clamp down on the "terrorists."[39] During the assaults, the *Los Angeles Daily News* and the *Los Angeles Times* cheered servicemen on, with headlines such as "Zoot Suit Chiefs Girding for War on Navy" and "Zoot Suiters Learn Lesson in Fight with Servicemen." Three other major newspapers ran similar headlines that poisoned the environment and generated a mass hysteria about zoot-suit violence. Radio broadcasts also inflamed the frenzy.

On June 16, 1943, the *Los Angeles Times* ran a story from Mexico City, headlined "Mexican Government Expects Damages for Zoot Suit Riot Victims." The article stated, "the Mexican government took a mildly firm stand on the rights of its nationals, emphasizing its conviction that American justice would grant 'innocent victims' their proper retribution." Federal authorities expressed concern, and Mayor Fletcher Bowron assured Washington, D.C., that no racism was involved. Soon afterward, Bowron told the Los Angeles police to stop using "cream-puff techniques on the Mexican youths," while simultaneously ordering the formation of a committee to "study the problem." City officials and the Los Angeles press became exceedingly touchy about charges of racism. When Eleanor Roosevelt commented in her nationally syndicated newspaper column that "longstanding discrimination against the Mexicans in the Southwest" caused the riots, the June 18 *Los Angeles Times* responded with the headline "Mrs. Roosevelt Blindly Stirs Race Discord." The article denied that racial discrimination had been a factor in the riots and charged that Mrs. Roosevelt's statement resembled propaganda used by the Communists; it stated that servicemen looked for "costumes and not races." The article went on that Angeleños were proud of their missions and Olvera Street, "a bit of old Mexico," and concluded, "We like Mexicans and think they like us."

Governor Earl Warren formed a committee to investigate the riots. Participating on the committee was Attorney General Robert W. Kenny; Catholic Bishop Joseph T. McGucken, who served as chair; Walter A. Gordon, Berkeley attorney; Leo Carrillo, screen actor; and Karl Holton, director of the California Youth Authority. The committee's report recommended punishment of all persons responsible for the riots—military and civilian alike. It took a slap at the press, recommending that newspapers limit the use of names and photos of juveniles. Moreover, it called for better-educated and better-trained police officers to work with Spanish-speaking youth.[40]

Mexicanas Break Barriers

Throughout the nation, Mexican American women—like other Americans—supported the war effort, making sacrifices and writing to their boyfriends, husbands, and fathers in the armed forces. They formed support groups throughout United States. In March 1944, Mr. Rosalio Ronquillo established the Spanish-American Mothers and Wives Association. Unlike other women's and men's organizations, the association was open to all women regardless of their socioeconomic class. Some 300 women—mothers, wives, daughters, sisters, and fiancées—and a handful of men, joined the organization. Rose Rodríguez edited its newsletter, *Chatter*, which the association sent to servicemen. Members wrote letters to their loved ones, bought war bonds, rolled bandages, and raised money for a postwar veterans' center. Although women ran the organization, they made what seemed to be strategic concessions to males.

Ronquillo acted as the association's permanent director. Women held the offices of president, vice president, treasurer, and secretary. The *Chatter* newsletter, originally called *Chismes*, was a lifeline to the soldiers. Although a male chaired the organization, according to Julie A. Campbell, the structure of the association encouraged women to get out of the house, get involved in planning events, and be networked with other women. The organization also acted as a support group when the members' husbands or sons were wounded or killed in action. The women also got the support of leading businessmen, receiving economic assistance from merchants and a no-fare ride to meetings in *los buses de Laos* (referring to buses of the Old Pueblo Transit Company, founded in 1924 by Roy Laos Sr., primarily serving the Mexican community (the south and west sides). The association also networked with other organizations for fund-raising or co-sponsoring events. Although the group planned to stay together after the war and raise money for a community social center, the association faded after the war ended.[41]

Elizabeth Rachel Escobedo wrote that the Depression and war changed many aspects of the Chicanas and hastened their acculturation. The push to assimilate was more intense among the second generation. The war gave them economic opportunities and weakened the institutions of social control. During the Depression, many lived under fear of deportation, and during the war, labor shortages increased the demand for workers temporarily breaking down racial barriers. Escobedo theorizes that the Sleepy Lagoon females challenged their jailers for violating their civil rights by resisting efforts to make them conform. One detention authority said that the young ladies were "very clannish" with other Mexican girls, continuing to speak Spanish "in spite of repeated requests not to do so." Escobedo writes,: "Ultimately the *pachuca* became both part and a symbol of the changing ethnic and gender landscape of World War II."[42]

Changes also took place as women came into contact with other races in the workplace. Andrea Pérez, a Mexican American, and Sylvester Davis, an African American, met while working at Lockheed in Burbank, California Owing to biases of both families, it was at first a clandestine relationship. After the war they applied for a marriage license; the County Clerk of Los Angeles turned them down citing that Pérez listed her race as "white," and Davis identified himself as "Negro." California law listed people of Mexican origin "Mexican," unless it was convenient for public officials to list them as white. The denial of the application was based on California Civil Code Section 60: "All marriages of white persons with Negroes, Mongolians, members of the Malay race, or mulattoes are illegal and void . . . ." Pérez petitioned the California Supreme Court for an original Writ of Mandate to compel the issuance of the license. Pérez and Davis were Catholics; they argued that the Church was willing to marry them, that the state's anti-miscegenation law infringed on their right to participate fully in the sacraments, and that they were being denied the fundamental right of marriage and thus were subjected to the violation of the Fourteenth Amendment. The California State Supreme Court sided with the plaintiffs in a narrow 4–3 decision, making California the first state in the twentieth century to hold an anti-miscegenation law unconstitutional. Pérez and Davis enjoyed a long and happy marriage; she later worked as an elementary schoolteacher in San Fernando, California.[43]

Rosita the Riveter[44]

Even before World War II, Mexican American women began to question the notion that a woman's place was in the home. Mexican American women were involved in the traditional roles of volunteering, wrapping bandages, and writing letters but with time, it changed. During the war, women in greater numbers worked for the male-dominated Southern Pacific Railroad. Pressured by the shortage of male workers, the railroad hired women to do maintenance and even to fire up locomotive engines. The *Susanas del SP* was the Mexican version of "Rosie the Riveter." Women also became miners in mining camps such as Morenci, Arizona, where they were often harassed and labeled "prostitutes." Other women went to work in the defense plants and toiled in what was until then considered men's work.

In recognition of these contributions, The University of Texas at Austin runs an oral history project called "U.S. Latinos and Latinas & World War II," which is preserving this narrative. The collective stories of Chicanas paints a mixed picture as to the impact the war had on the lives of Mexican women. For example, Josephine Ledesma—age

24, from Austin, Texas, and mother of a small child—was trained as an airplane mechanic. This training improved her earning power; before the war, Josephine had trouble finding a job in a department store. However, the war did little to improve race relations. At the height of the war, Josephine and her husband were asked to leave a restaurant in Big Spring, Texas; the proprietor would not serve Mexicans. "Big Spring was absolutely terrible with Mexican Americans and Blacks," according to Josephine.

The war improved the prospects of Henrietta López Rivas of San Antonio. At the age of 15, she dropped out of the ninth grade, and joined her family as migrant farmworkers. They worked in the tomato and wheat fields of Ohio and Michigan. Upon returning to San Antonio, Henrietta took up cleaning jobs at houses and barnyards, earning $1.50 a week. In 1941, Henrietta found employment with the Civil Service Department as a Spanish-speaking interpreter; her income jumped from $1.50 a week to $90 a month. Later she was offered a better civil service job at Duncan (now Kelly) Air Force Base.

Elisa Rodríguez, 21, of Waco, developed strong opinions about her country and discrimination. While working at a local department store, Elisa attended night school and learned shorthand, typing, and other clerical skills. After graduation, she applied for a job at Blackland Airfield, which turned her down because she was Mexican. After Elisa got a lawyer friend to call the company and remind the owner that the company received defense contracts, the boss said, "send her over." Having a defense contract meant that the employer was required to follow federal anti-discrimination laws. Soon afterward, she got a job at Blackland, earning about $2,000 a year; she was the only Latina at the base, and she routinely experienced discrimination. Eventually, Elisa became the equal employment opportunity coordinator. Nevertheless, she paid the price; she was never promoted.[45]

The Federal Employment Practices Commission

The war cast a bright spotlight on inequality. Executive Order 8802 forbade discrimination of workers in defense industry. President Roosevelt established the Fair Employment Practices Commission (FEPC) in response to pressure from African American and Mexican American organizations and individuals. New Mexico Senator Dennis Chávez played a leadership role in the Senate subcommittee hearings on the FEPC, with the commission hearing cases from the Southwest to the Midwest and Pacific Northwest.[46]

However, the law is one thing and getting people to comply is another, as is apparent in the testimony of Los Angeles attorney Manuel Ruiz. Proving poverty, discrimination and inequality was, and still is, an expensive proposition. Ruiz knew that discrimination existed, but there was a lack of data about Mexican Americans. Even the Census was deficient of hard data on U.S. Mexicans, and this had become more complicated with their designation as white. When Ruiz testified before the commission, he could not cite specific statistics proving discrimination toward Mexicans. Any reasonable person could walk out the door and witness discrimination and inequality, but there were few studies that proved it. Indeed, outside Texas, few scholars researched the Mexican American population. The citing of data was critical to making a case for equal treatment. Without solid evidence, the FEPC could avoid enforcing the presidential executive order.[47]

Besides the collusion of governors and local officials, the State Department also evaded the executive order by obstructing the collection of data; when the FEPC planned hearings at El Paso, the State Department pressured the agency to call off the hearings. The State Department held that admitting racism existed was bad for the U.S. image. The President participated in the charade, subordinating the FEPC to the War Manpower Commission (WMC). Overall, the administration had little respect for the concerns of U.S. Mexican leaders. Employees of the FEPC told historian Dr. Carlos E. Castañeda, a field investigator for the agency, that when the war "was over the Mexican American would be put in his place."[48]

Despite the lack of enforcement of non-discrimination laws, Mexican miners continued to organize under the auspices of the Congress of Industrial Organization (CIO) locals. CIO hearings showed that Mexican Americans were at the lowest end of the pay scale, and that white workers often refused to work alongside Mexicans; yet the copper barons refused to acknowledge there was discrimination against Mexicans.

In Arizona, FEPC hearings confirmed what everyone else knew—that the copper barons in Arizona *did* discriminate against Mexicans. The Mine, Mill, and Smelter Workers Union supported a policy of non-discrimination. However, mining companies such as Phelps Dodge set the tone by officially condemning discrimination, while doing nothing to stop it. Complaints of discrimination toward Mexicans registered by individual Mexican miners and by the union kept rolling in. Nevertheless, Castañeda's efforts to get the FEPC and other agencies to respond to discrimination were futile. Unable to decide whether to enforce the law or not, the Roosevelt administration did nothing. This charade cast doubt on the FEPC's and the government's commitment to equal employment.[49]

Defense factories hired few Mexicans and even fewer rose to supervisory positions. Alonso S. Perales testified before the Senate Fair Employment Practices Act hearings in San Antonio in 1944 that Kelly Air Force Base in that city employed 10,000 people, and not one Mexican held a position above that of a laborer or mechanic's helper. According to Perales's testimony, 150 towns and cities in Texas had public facilities that refused to serve Mexicans—including servicemen.

At the same hearings Frank Paz, president of the Spanish-Speaking People's Council of Chicago, testified that 45,000 Mexicans worked in and around Chicago, mostly in railroads, steel mills, and packinghouses. The overwhelming majority worked as railroad section hands. The railroad companies refused to promote Mexican Americans. In fact, they imported temporary workers (*braceros*) from Mexico to do skilled work as electricians, pipe fitters, steamfitters, millwrights, and so forth. According to Paz, between 1943 and 1945 the railroads imported 15,000 *braceros*. The Railroad Brotherhood refused membership to Mexicans and Blacks who worked in track repair and maintenance. The Operating Brotherhoods of the Southern Pacific never consciously admitted Mexicans to the union until the early 1960s—making them ineligible for skilled jobs and promotions.

Paz verified the discrimination against steelworker Ramón Martínez, a 20-year veteran, who was placed in charge of a section of Spanish-speaking workers. When he learned that he was being paid $50 a month less than the other foremen, Martínez complained. The reasons given for the wage differential were that he was not a citizen and that he did not have a high school education. Martínez attended night school and received a diploma, but the railroad company still refused to pay him wages on par with other foremen.[50]

Castañeda offered in evidence that in Arizona, Mexicans comprised 8,000–10,000 of the 15,000–16,000 miners in the state, but that the copper barons restricted them to menial labor. According to Castañeda, Mexicans throughout the United States were paid less than Americans for equal work. In California, in 1940, Mexicans numbered about 457,900 out of a total population of 6,907,387; Los Angeles housed 315,000 Mexicans. As of the summer of 1942, only 5,000 Mexicans worked in the basic industries of that city. Further, Los Angeles County employed about 16,000 workers, only 400 of whom were Mexicans.[51] FBI records provide data on the underrepresentation of Mexican Americans in the defense economy. A confidential report of January 14, 1944, titled "Racial Conditions (Spanish-Mexican Activities in Los Angeles Field Division)," claimed that only a couple of thousand Mexican Americans worked in the Los Angeles war plants. The same account reported that the Los Angeles Police Department employed 22 Mexican American officers out of a force of 2,547; the Los Angeles Sheriff's Department had 30 Spanish-surnamed deputies out of 821. The probation department employed three officers of Mexican extraction. Sadly, Mexicans were better represented in combat units, recruited to fight in a war ostensibly to ensure human rights abroad, something that they themselves were denied at home.[52]

Elizabeth Escobedo sheds more light on the topic. Though the FEPC brought attention to the question of equality and institutional racism, it did little to correct the problems. For instance, it did not address gender inequality in the workplace. After the war, Mexican American women were driven from the workplace, and the better-paying jobs went to returning white male veterans. Nevertheless, reports show that women during the war years were very active in using the due process of law to protect their rights, which implies that they were the object of disparaging and rude remarks by fellow workers. According to Escobedo, FEPC complaints filed in the Los Angeles area by Mexican Americans far outnumbered those of all other national-origin groups; in December 1944 alone they filed some 93 cases. Employers admitted to hiring only lighter-skinned Mexicans. Escobedo recorded a trove of case studies such as that of Guadalupe Cordero, who complained about Mexicans being replaced by inexperienced American "girls."[53]

Cold War Politics of Control

During the Cold War years that followed World War II, U.S. corporations consolidated huge fortunes made from war profiteering.[54] In 1945, the United States was an Empire and controlled more than an estimated 40 percent of the world's wealth and power. In comparison, the British Empire, at its peak, controlled 25 percent. Its global strategy for the war gave the United States a more global viewpoint of the world, which continued during the postwar years when the United States played a decisive role in "military, political, and economic questions in all regions of the world." The preeminence of the United States gave the military and the citizenry the mindset of seeing the whole world as "our" oceans, "our" skies, and "our" empire.[55] Most capitalists left behind the memories of and the lessons from the Great Depression, forgetting that the New Deal saved their system, and that war made them richer by trillions of dollars. These capitalists felt that the "free world" needed a coherent ideology to successfully resist the Communist and waged a "Cold War" both internationally and nationally, and free-market capitalism suited their worldview perfectly. "After 1945 the major corporations in America grew larger."[56]

During the war, wages were frozen, while profits went unbridled. After the war, organized labor adopted a confrontational and militant posture; many industrialists blamed the unions—especially the CIO—for work stoppages. The captains of industry acted as if *they* won the war and equated worker demands with Communism, extending the Cold War to unions. Through generous contributions to politicians' campaigns, the industrialists pressured many locals to drop radical organizers, accusing them of being Communist or at best fellow travelers. Their main target was to stop the CIO, which gave workers, control over the workplace.

In 1947, Congress passed the Taft–Hartley Act, which neutered the Wagner Act of 1935 and its National Labor Relations Board (NLRB). It gave the states authority to pass right-to-work laws. No longer did workers have to abide by the will of the majority of workers if they wanted a union.

It gave anti-union forces the power to petition for another election. Further, the U.S. president could enjoin a strike, if he thought the walkouts imperiled national security. It empowered the courts to fine strikers for alleged violations of the injunction and to establish a 60-day cooling-off period. It prohibited the use of union dues for political contributions and required all labor leaders to take a loyalty oath swearing that they were not Communists. If labor leaders refused to take the oath, the law denied their union the services of the NLRB. Thus, Taft–Hartley empowered employers and weakened the collective bargaining.[57] Its purpose was to destroy labor unions and take control of government, and return to the Gilded Age, the late 1800s to the 1920s, when business leaders accumulated titanic fortunes.[58]

These measures came at a time when Mexican Americans were just beginning to make gains in industrial unions. Luisa Moreno, elected vice president of the United Cannery, Agricultural, Packing, and Allied Workers of America (UCAPAWA), was in charge of organizing food processing in Southern California. Mexican American women in increasing numbers became members of negotiating teams; more Latinas found their way in as shop stewards, and many became union officials as did their male counterparts. This increased involvement of Mexican Americans leadership roles led to the organization of more Chicano workers and CIO locals. Because of the growing influence of the CIO among Mexican American workers, the Teamsters Union, encouraged by the AFL, launched a jurisdictional fight with UCAPAWA, which had become the Food, Tobacco, Agricultural, and Allied Workers of America (FTA).[59]

Red-baiting and thuggery characterized the Teamsters' campaign. The state and the Catholic Church joined the campaign to clean out the Reds. The California Committee on Un-American Activities (better known as the Tenney Committee) called hearings and charged the leadership of progressive unions with being Communists. By 1947, Luisa Moreno retired to private life, and by the end of the decade, only three FTA locals survived. The Loyalty Oath, Taft–Hartley, and mechanization all took their toll. Soon afterward, immigration authorities deported Moreno because of her activism.[60]

The state also hounded Josefina Fierro de Bright. Josefina was involved in social activism at the age of 18, while a student at UCLA; her mother and grandmother were Magonistas. She married screenwriter John Bright, a founder of the Screen Actors Guild, and soon became a community organizer. By 1939, she was an organizer for *El Congreso del Pueblo de Habla Española* (Spanish-speaking congress). Through her Hollywood connections, she was able to raise money for Mexican American causes. While active in *El Congreso,* she was involved in the defense of the Sleepy Lagoon defendants, and continued her association with Luisa Moreno. Under the leadership of Josefina, the *Congreso* attacked the Sinarquistas (The National Synarchist Union), a Mexican fascist group. She also criticized the schools for the treatment of Mexican children. In 1951 she unsuccessfully ran for Congress, supported by *la Asociacion Nacional Mexico-Americana*, which was founded the year before; soon afterward she left for Mexico.[61]

The Communists Are Coming

Mexican Americans earned their rights with their blood during the war. Their patriotism—like that of Japanese Americans—and their loyalty were questioned.[62] If they did not agree with the government and the excesses of capitalism, they were assumed to be disloyal. The G.I. Forum, LULAC, and most Mexican American organizations protested these charges. Yet they were under suspicion by default. Political scientist José Angel Gutiérrez is pioneering research in police surveillance. Under the Freedom of Information Act, he obtained documents proving that the FBI had spied on LULAC and on the G.I. Forum. In 1941, the FBI's Denver Office reported on a Colorado chapter of LULAC. Its officers included a county judge and a town marshal. The FBI also investigated leaders such as George I. Sánchez and Alonso Perales, reporting that Sánchez earned the distrust of the Mexican community when he converted to Reformed Methodism.

In May 1946, the FBI infiltrated a Los Angeles meeting of LULAC. An informant claimed without proof that participants had a long history of Communist activity. Again in the early 1950s, the FBI investigated LULAC. It was under suspicion because it had demanded racial integration.

FBI files show that it also conducted extensive surveillance of Los Angeles Mexican Americans during the Sleepy Lagoon Case and the so-called Zoot Suit Riots. The Bureau, highly critical of the Sleepy Lagoon Defense Committee, red-baiting its members, and singling out Eduardo Quevedo, chair of the Coordinating Council for Latin American Youth, and M. J. Avila, secretary of the Hollywood Bar Association. (The FBI contradicted reports of police malfeasance and praised local police who the FBI claimed bent over backward to get along with Mexicans.) The FBI also targeted the "Hispanic Movement" within the Catholic Church.[63]

Postwar Opportunities

11.2 Describe the impact of the growth of second generation on the Mexican struggle for political and socioeconomic rights.

Opportunities ended for most women at the end of the war as the government embarked on a policy of removing women from the workforce so that they would make room for returning veterans and have more babies. From 1946 to 1963, the U.S. birthrate showed a marked upswing—a phenomenon that social scientists labeled the "Baby Boom." For many Mexican American males, the war became a leveler—many became leaders in combat. They had great expectations, but the dominant U.S. society was not ready to accept them as equals. Hence, they became much more demanding and exercised their vote; how active depended on where they lived. For example, in Boyle Heights, California, Mexicans lived within proximity to Jewish Americans during an era when Jews were leading the fight against racism and for civil liberties. At the time, Boyle Heights housed a sizeable Jewish American community, and many of its more liberal members played a role in politicizing the Mexican American community. In 1948, many in the Boyle Heights community campaigned for the Independent Progressive Party (IPP), which supported Henry Wallace for president. The IPP recruited many Mexicans to its ranks.[64]

Though male job and education upward mobility, the ability to take advantage of these openings depended on their education and/or financial status. For instance, Californians received large windfalls of money from both the federal and state governments and benefits such as the G.I. Bill as well as establishment of the California State College System, which improved educational opportunity. In 1940, the white adults in California attained 9.8 years of schooling on average; the number rose to 11 by 1960. By contrast, Blacks achieved 8.1 grades in 1940, rising to 9.4 in 1960. Latinos had a median of 5.6 in 1940 and 7.7 in 1960. White American college graduates increased from 7.2 percent in 1940 to 10.4 in 1960 and to 21.2 in 1980, whereas the number of Black graduates grew from 2.6 percent in 1940 to 3.6 in 1960 and to 11.2 in 1980. The Latino graduates (mostly of Mexican origin) sputtered from 1.6 to 3.2 and to 5.4 percent in the respective years.[65]

In education, Texas was a disaster: The median number of years of education was 3.5 for Mexican Americans in 1950—half that of California—compared with 10.3 for whites and 7.0 for non-whites. In San Antonio, the median number of years of education for Mexican Americans was 4.5, half that of the general population of the city. Cities like Tucson mirrored California where "By 1940, nearly 75 percent of the Mexican work force was still in blue-collar occupations [in Tucson], compared with only 36 percent of Anglo workers," who held 96.5 percent of the white-collar and professional positions. Mexicans made up 54.5 percent of the unskilled labor, although they comprised only 30 percent of the city's workforce. Tucson in 1950 mirrored the rest of the Southwest: The median number of school years completed by Mexican Americans in the city was 6.5. Many returning Mexican American veterans felt that their community simply did not have the educational human capital to take advantage of the new opportunities.[66]

The positive trend was that the upward growth in population proved that numbers mattered. The U.S. Census reported that in 1940 Mexicans numbered 1,346,000 or 0.9 percent; in 1950, they numbered 1,736,000 or 1.0 percent; and the 1960 Census counted 3,464,999 Spanish-surnamed persons. By 1970, Mexican origin population was estimated to be under 5 million. That number grew to 8,740,000 or 3.9 percent in 1980.[67] These figures are flawed and represent a serious undercount; at the same time, they suggest the power of numbers making the point that the numbers become more accurate with the growth of power of a particular group.

Toward a Civil Rights Agenda

In 1946, Judge Paul J. McCormick, in the U.S. District Court in Southern California, heard the *Méndez v. Westminster School District* case and ruled the segregation of Mexican children unconstitutional. Gonzalo, a Mexican American, and Felicitas Méndez, a Puerto Rican, took the leadership in filing the case. On April 14, 1947, the U.S. Court of Appeals for the Ninth Circuit affirmed the lower court decision, holding that Mexicans and other children were entitled to "the equal protection of the laws," and that neither language nor race could be used as a reason to segregate them. In response to the *Méndez* case, the Associated Farmers of Orange County launched a bitter red-baiting campaign against the Mexican communities.[68]

On June 15, 1948, in another segregation case, Judge Ben H. Rice Jr., U.S. District Court, Western District of Texas, found in *Delgado v. Bastrop Independent School District* that the school district had violated the Fourteenth Amendment's equal protection rights of the Mexican children. The Mendez and the Delgado ruling set precedents for the historic *Brown v. Board of Education* case in 1954. They also set precedent for the U.S. Supreme Court decision in *Hernandez v. Texas* (1954), which held that the Fourteenth Amendment protected Mexican Americans. Yet the court found that Mexican Americans was not an identifiable ethnic minority.[69]

Considerable interaction existed between LULAC and the National Association for the Advancement of Colored People (NAACP) during the 1940s and 1950s. In November 1946, in Orange County, California, LULAC, with the assistance of Fred Ross (who later helped launch the Community Service Organization), initiated a campaign supporting Proposition 11 of the Fair Employment Practices Act, which prohibited discrimination in employment. LULAC chapters went door to door registering people to vote. This organizational work was crucial in ensuring the civil rights that Mexican Americans and other Latinos take for granted today. The downside was that in 1947 the district attorney pressured LULAC to get rid of Ross, red-baiting him; Ross left for Los Angeles.[70]

The American G.I. Forum

Returning Mexican American war veterans were denied many services because of their race. For instance, the American Legion and Veterans of Foreign Wars chapters refused to admit Mexicans as members. Recognizing the lack of service for Mexican American veterans, Dr. Hector

Pérez García founded the American G.I. Forum in Corpus Christi, in response to the refusal of a funeral home in Three rivers, Texas to bury Pvt. Felix Longoria, who had died in the Philippines during World War II. This outrageously racist act attracted thousands of new members to the G.I. Forum, all demanding justice; the incident was very important in politicizing new generation of activists. Senator Lyndon B. Johnson intervened and, with the cooperation of the Longoria family, had Longoria's remains buried in Arlington National Cemetery with full honors.[71]

Forum members insisted Longoria should be buried with full honors in his hometown, and the compromise of burying him in Arlington Cemetery was wrong. Tejanos vowed that never again would they accept second-class citizenship. Meanwhile, Texas officials claimed that they never denied Longoria a proper burial and accused the Forum of exploiting the controversy. At hearings of the state Good Neighbor Commission, Dr. García and the Forum's attorney, Gus García, did a brilliant job of proving the Forum's case by presenting evidence of "Mexican" and "white" cemeteries and racist burial practices in Texas. However, the all-white commission found that there had been no discrimination. The blatant bias of the commissioners further strained race relations, and from that point on the Forum became more proactive. "Unlike LULAC, whose policy was not to involve itself directly in electoral politics, the Forum openly advocated getting out the vote and endorsing candidates."[72] The Forum did not limit membership to the middle class and those fluent in English, like LULAC did. It was less accommodating to the feelings of Americans.[73]

Like most of the other Mexican American organizations of the time, the Forum stressed the importance of education. The G.I. Forum's motto was, "Education is our freedom, and freedom should be everybody's business." This new aggressiveness of Mexican Americans in Texas and elsewhere signaled a new intensity of involvement in civil rights (see Chapter 12).

Controlling Mexicans

During the 1940s in California, Mexican American Movement (MAM) membership dropped as it evolved from a student organization into a professional association. After the war, Mexican Americans looked beyond single issues, and veterans became more involved in local politics. By the 1950s, Mexican Americans were also increasingly involved in national politics, as a response to the expanding powers of the federal government. Certainly the fact that there was more opportunity in California to assimilate may also have played a role in the declining membership of MAM. A more probable explanation for the decline of MAM is that the youth of the 1930s were now older and also veterans, and integrated themselves in national organizations such as LULAC, the G.I. Forum, and emerging organizations such as the Community Service Organization. Influenced by leaders such as Saul Alinsky and Fred Ross, more Mexican Americans began to think of community organizing as a path toward political power.[74]

Changes in Mexican American community went unnoticed by the rest of the society, which continued to perceive them as foreigners. Americans ignored the number of lives sacrificed by the Mexican Americans during World War II, which were disproportionate to their numbers. Although the Mexican American leadership continued to claim they were white in order to qualify for equal rights under the constitution, racism remained an issue. The war did not end racism; the Mexican American youth were still targeted.

As large numbers of U.S. Mexicans moved into the cities, police harassment increased. Many police officers resented the use of Spanish language and what they perceived as the "cocky demeanor" of second-generation Mexican youth. Lupe Leyvas, the sister of Henry Leyvas, recalled an incident that marked a change in her attitude towards her rights. She and her family would sit on the porch of their South Central home, and every time a police car cruised the neighborhood, her mother would order everyone inside the house until one day Lupe rebelled and said, "Why should we go inside, we are not doing anything wrong."

The stigma of the pachuco continued into the postwar era—law enforcement officers treated all Mexican youth as delinquents and wanted them to look down when spoken to. In July 1946, a sheriff's deputy in Monterey Park, California, shot Eugene Montenegro in the back; the 13-year-old was seen climbing out of a window of a private residence and did not stop when the deputy ordered him to. Eugene was 5'3," unarmed, and an honors student at St. Alphonse parochial school. The press, covering the incident, portrayed Eugene's mother as irrational because she confronted the deputy who had mortally wounded her son.

In September 1947 Bruno Cano, a member of the United Furniture Workers of America Local 576, was brutally beaten by the police in East Los Angeles. Cano attempted to stop police from assaulting three Mexican youths at a tavern. Local 576, the Civil Rights Congress (CRC),[75] and the American Veterans Committee (Belvedere Chapter) protested Cano's beating. One of the officers, William Keyes, had a history of brutality; earlier in 1947, he shot two Mexicans in the back. Keyes faced no disciplinary action either in those shootings or in Cano's beating.

In March 1948, Keyes and his partner E. R. Sánchez shot down 17-year-old Agustino Salcido. According to Keyes and Sánchez, Salcido offered to sell them stolen watches. Instead of taking Salcido to the police station, they escorted him to "an empty, locked building," and shot him. At the coroner's inquest, Keyes claimed that unarmed Salcido had attempted to escape during interrogation. Witnesses contradicted Keyes, but the inquest exonerated him.[76]

The Los Angeles CIO Council and community organizations held a "people's trial" attended by nearly 600 Mexicans. Film star Margo Albert (María Marguerita Guadalupe Teresa

Estela Bolado), who acted in the film *Lost Horizon*, and was married to actor Eddie Albert, played a leadership role with the CRC. The mock trial found Keyes guilty. On top of Keyes's notoriety, pressure mounted on Judge Stanley Moffatt to accept the complaint. Meanwhile, Guillermo Gallegos, a witness to the shooting, was harassed and his life was threatened, and Judge Moffatt was red-baited by defense attorney Joseph Scott. The *Hollywood Citizen-News* accused Moffatt of being a Communist because he ran for Congress on the Henry Wallace ticket. The jury was deadlocked—seven for acquittal and five for conviction.[77]

In a new trial, Keyes appeared before a law-and-order judge. Keyes waived a jury trial and was acquitted because the judge found insufficient evidence to convict him. Yet the prosecution had proved that Keyes and Sánchez pumped bullets into Salcido, that Gallegos saw him fire the gun at Salcido, and that Keyes's gun killed Salcido. Between 1947 and 1956, the L.A. Community Service Organization conducted 35 investigations of police misconduct.[78] Enrique Buelna makes connections between the Salcido case, the *Amigos de Wallace* (Friends of [Henry] Wallace) and the pivotal role the case played in bringing together the activist community of the time. Besides the Salcido case, the battles over the FEPC, the Taft–Hartley bill, the Wallace Presidential Campaign in 1948, and the formation of *la Asociación Nacional México Americana* (ANMA) in 1949 gave rise to a new current of activism among Mexican Americans, which included activists such as the Luna sisters, Julia Mount and Celia Rodríguez, Luisa Moreno, and Josefina Fierro de Bright. In addition to this radical core, returning veterans joined the Community Service Organization, which was pursuing a political agenda.[79]

Texas housed an estimated one million Mexican Americans. During the postwar era, Mexican American organizations sponsored anti–poll tax drives, pressured local and state officials to investigate cases of police brutality, challenged segregation, and struggled to eliminate inequality in the education system. Mexican Americans would often challenge the refusal of local barbers to offer their services to them and many suffered savage beatings in return. LULAC and the G.I. Forum used the judicial process to effect changes, with the view of achieving equal protection under the law.

Alonso Perales documented dozens of cases of segregation and police malfeasance. In his book, *Are We Good Neighbors?* Perales lays out his case. Discrimination demoralized the U.S. Mexican community. For example, in February 1945, Reginaldo Romo was playing dice in a saloon after-hours. August Zimmerman, a peace officer in Ugalde, pistol-whipped him. In San Angelo, Texas, Pvt. Ben García Aguirre, 20, was beaten unconscious by about 15 Americans in September 1945. Authorities apprehended none of the assailants. In February 1946, Felipe Guarjado, Antonio Hinojosa, and Pascual Ortega were driving from San Antonio to Laredo. In Devine, Texas, they entered the Monte Carlos Inn, where Americans beat and robbed them. They filed a complaint, but the Justice of the Peace instead filing charges against the perpetrators filed charges against them. In another instance of police brutality, in March 1946, Sheriff E. E. Pond of Zavala County and two of his officers beat Manuel Delgado, 22. Delgado asked Pond not to push him, whereupon the sheriff ripped off his shirt. The other officers beat and arrested Delgado, whom the court fined $63.[80]

Colonel Homer Garrison Jr. was appointed the new director of the Department of Public Safety, which gave a boost to the Texas Rangers. Garrison appointed Rangers as plainclothesmen, detectives, and Highway Patrol officers. In World War II, they rounded up "enemy aliens" to protect the "homeland." *Los Rinches* (a pejorative reference to Texas Rangers) were the symbol of American control—especially after World War II, when they ensured Mexicans and labor were kept in their place in the caste social order. The *Rinches* made certain that labor organizing did not survive in the Valley. Despite this obstacle, unionization continued in Texas; in 1953, the combined membership of the Texas State Federation of Labor (TSFL) and the CIO reached 375,000.

The war extended occupational opportunities beyond agriculture to Mexicans. After 1940, there was a massive relocation of Mexicans to the city. In the Fort Worth area, Mexicans moved into service jobs such as busboys, elevator operators, and other service workers. Still, the better-paying corporations such as Consolidated Fort Worth and North American Aircraft of Dallas were out of reach and hired only a limited number of Mexican American workers. In the postwar era, rapid unionization of industries had a limited impact on Mexican workers because unions relied on the seniority system and few Mexicans qualified for membership in trade unions; thus, fewer were promoted.

Farm Labor Militancy

On November 18, 1948, Bill Dredge wrote an article in the *Los Angeles Times* titled "Machines and Men Bringing in Cotton." San Joaquin Valley planters were starting to use robots to pick cotton. Nevertheless, during the transition, 100,000 farm laborers were still needed to pick the cotton crop. Although Filipinos and other ethnics were involved, by 1948 it was still a Mexican affair. Yet as important as the Mexicans were, they were still considered "standby." Farmworkers had fewer opportunities. Agribusiness was very successful in lobbying government for subsidies and exemptions from worker protection regulations under the National Labor Relations.[81]

In the face of the awesome power of agribusiness, and despite its ability to create huge labor pools, and the use of the *bracero* to depress wages and break strikes, farmworkers continued to organize. In October 1947, at the Di Giorgio Fruit Corporation at Arvin, California, workers picketed the

Di Giorgio farm. The National Farm Labor Union (NFLU) Local 218 led the strike. Joseph Di Giorgio was a power house, refused the union's demands. *Fortune* magazine dubbed him the "Kublai Khan of Kern County"; in 1946, Di Giorgio earned $18 million in sales. When Di Giorgio refused the union demands, the the union struck.

As with other agricultural strikes, local government, the chambers of commerce, the American Legion, the Boy Scouts, the Associated Farmers, and the Farm Bureaus, lined up in support of Di Giorgio. Hugh M. Burns of the California Senate Committee on Un-American Activities and the reactionary State Senator Jack Tenney held hearings investigating Communist involvement, but they failed to uncover any evidence. Through the media, Di Giorgio controlled the narrative. In November 1949, a subcommittee of the House Committee on Education and Labor held hearings at Bakersfield, California. Representative Cleveland M. Bailey (West Virginia) presided, and Representatives Richard M. Nixon (California) and Tom Steed (Oklahoma) joined him. The two other members of the subcommittee, Thurston B. Morton (Kentucky) and Leonard Irving (Missouri), did not attend the hearings. The proceedings took two days, hardly enough time to conduct an in-depth investigation. The Di Giorgio Corporation filed a $2 million libel suit against the union and the Hollywood Film Council, for the controversial film *Poverty in the Land of Plenty*, produced in the spring of 1948 Di Giorgio wanted the subcommittee to prove the documentary libeled him. In the 1947 Arvin strike case, the subcommittee found nothing, so Congressman Bailey made no move to file an official report on the strike. Nor did he mention the controversy between the union and Di Giorgio in the report that the subcommittee eventually made to the committee.

In March 1949, Di Giorgio—still intent on an official condemnation of the union—commissioned Representative Thomas H. Werdel from Kern County to file a damaging report, signed by Steed, Morton, and Nixon, in the appendix of the *Congressional Record*. The appendix serves no official function other than giving members of Congress a forum to publish material sent them by constituents. The report, "Agricultural Labor at Di Giorgio Farms, California," claimed that the strike was "solely one for the purpose of organization" and that workers had no grievances, for "wages, hours, working conditions, and living conditions have never been a real issue in the Di Giorgio strike," and concluded that *Poverty in the Land of Plenty* was libelous.

The phony report dealt a deathblow to the NFLU. The California Federation of Labor (CFL) leadership ordered Local 218 to settle the libel suit (the CFL would not pay defense costs) and demanded that the strike be ended. Di Giorgio agreed to settle the suit for $1 on the conditions that the NFLU plead guilty to the judgment, admitting libel; that they remove the film from circulation and recall all prints; that they reimburse the corporation for attorney fees; and that they call off the strike. Werdel, Steed, Morton, and Nixon all knew that the report had no official status and was, at best, an opinion. They knowingly deceived the public in order to break the strike.[82]

From this point on, the NFLU was powerless. Every time workers stopped production, growers used *braceros* and undocumented workers to break the strike. The departments of Labor, Agriculture, Justice, and State acted as the planters' personal agents. Even liberal Democratic administrations favored the growers, with little difference existing between Republican Governor Goodwin Knight and Democratic Governor Edmund G. Brown, Sr.

Renting Mexicans

After placing the Japanese Americans in concentration camps, the United States had two alternatives: simply open the border and allow Mexican workers to enter the United States unencumbered, or negotiate with Mexico for an agreed-upon number of Mexican *braceros*. The Mexican government, however, would not permit this practice, insisting on a contract that protected the rights of its workers. In 1942, the two governments agreed to the Emergency Labor Program, under which both governments would supervise the recruitment of *braceros*. The program was literally an emergency program and no one complained.[83]

The *bracero* contract stipulated that Mexican workers would not displace domestic workers, exempted *braceros* from military service, and obligated the U.S. government to prevent discrimination against these Mexican workers. The contract also regulated transportation, housing, and wages of the *braceros*. Under this agreement, about 220,000 *braceros* were imported into the United States from 1942 to 1947.

At first, many farmers opposed the *bracero* agreement, preferring the World War I arrangement under which farmers recruited directly in Mexico with no government interference. Texas growers in particular wanted the government to open the border. During the first year, only a handful of U.S. growers participated in the program. States like Texas always had all the undocumented workers they needed, and they wanted to continue controlling the "free market." They did not want the federal government to regulate the Mexican workers' wages and housing. Growers disliked the 30¢ an hour minimum wage, claiming that this was the first step in federal farm-labor legislation that would inflate wages. Texas growers thus boycotted the program in 1942 and moved to avoid the agreement.

The executive branch did not receive congressional approval for the *bracero* program until 1943, when Congress passed Public Law 45. This law began the "administered migration" of Mexicans into the United States. Initially, the Farm Security Administration (FSA) oversaw the program; later, due to grower pressure, the president transferred supervisory responsibilities to the War Food Administration.

Under section 5(g), the commissioner of immigration could lift the statutory limitations, if such an action was vital to the war effort. Almost immediately, farmers pressured the commissioner to use the escape clause, and to leave the border unilaterally open and unregulated.

Mexicans flooded into border areas, where farmers eagerly employed them. The Mexican government protested this violation of the agreement. However, Mexican authorities were persuaded to allow the workers who had already entered outside the contract agreement to remain for one year; but it was made clear that, in the future, Mexico would not tolerate uncontrolled migration.

In the summer of 1943, Texas growers finally agreed to recruit *braceros*. But the Mexican government refused to issue permits for Texas because of racism and brutal transgressions against Mexican workers. Governor Coke Stevenson, in an attempt to placate the Mexican government, induced the Texas legislature to pass the so-called Caucasian Race Resolution, which affirmed the rights of all Caucasians to equal treatment within Texas. Since most Texans did not consider Mexicans as Caucasians, the law was not relevant. Governor Stevenson attempted to relieve tensions by publicly condemning racism. The Mexican government seemed on the verge of relenting when they learned of more racist incidents in Texas. On September 4, 1943, Stevenson established the Good Neighbor Commission of Texas, financed by federal funds, supposedly to end discrimination toward Mexicans through better understanding.

Not all *braceros* worked on farms; by August 1945, 67,704 *braceros* held jobs with U.S. railroads. The work was physically demanding and often hazardous. Records show deaths resulting from railroad accidents, sunstroke, and heat prostration. Abuses of the contract agreement were also frequent. Employers did not pay many of the *braceros* their wages, or when paid, involuntary deductions were made—for example, for unsolicited meals. Some growers worked the *braceros* for 12 hours while paying them only for eight. In December 1943, the *braceros* went on strike at the Southern Pacific at Live Oaks, California, protesting the dismissal of three of their comrades.

From 1943 to 1947, Texas growers continued to press for the importation of more *braceros*; the Mexican government refused because the Texas growers continued to mistreat them. Finally, in October 1947, the Mexican government relented and agreed to issue permits to Texas. Meanwhile, U.S. authorities had shipped some 46,972 *braceros* to Washington, Oregon, and Idaho during the first four years of the program. Mexican workers often were ill-prepared for the cold winters of the Yakima Valley and the Northwest; and managers at the prison-like camps did not speak Spanish. Food-poisoning incidents also occurred frequently. Townspeople, overtly racist, posted "No Mexicans, White Trade Only" signs in beer parlors and pool halls. *Braceros* frequently revolted and, throughout World War II, they struggled to improve these conditions. By 1945, the demand for Mexican *braceros* decreased as Mexican Americans began infiltrating the Northwest from Texas.

Labor shortages ceased after the war, but the *bracero* program continued. The U.S. government acted as a labor contractor at taxpayers' expense. It assured nativists that workers would return to Mexico once they finished picking the crops. Growers did not have to worry about labor disputes and always had a large supply of rented workers. Government authorities, in collusion with the growers, glutted the labor market with *braceros* to depress wages and to break strikes. Border enforcement was often slackened to allow more workers to enter. This was done by limiting government allocations to the Immigration and Naturalization Service (INS), thus controlling the number of border patrol officers. This ensured an open border to permit a constant flow of undocumented laborers into the United States.

After the war Mexico lost control of the process; when negotiations began to renew the contract, Mexico did not have the same leverage it did during the war. Its economy was dependent on the money brought back by the workers. The United States, now in a stronger negotiating position, pressured Mexico to continue the program on U.S. terms, with less emphasis on wages and working conditions. The 1947 agreement allowed U.S. growers to recruit their own workers. The Mexican government bargained for recruitment from the interior of Mexico and wanted more guarantees for its citizens. Few of its demands were met. Meanwhile, the U.S. government permitted growers to hire undocumented workers and to certify them on the spot.

In October 1948, Mexican officials finally took a hard line, refusing to sign *bracero* contracts if Texas farmers did not pay workers $3 per hundredweight (cwt) for picked cotton instead of the $2 per cwt offered by growers in other states. The Mexican government, still concerned about racism in Texas, continued to press for recruitment from the interior rather than at the border. Border recruitment compounded hardships on border towns, with workers frequently traveling thousands of miles and then not getting selected as *braceros*. Border towns grew in population by more than 1,000 percent since 1920. Unemployment rates remained extremely high, and the border towns continued to function as employment centers for U.S. industry.

The Truman administration sided with the ranchers. During a presidential whistle-stop tour in October 1948, El Paso farm agents, sugar company officials, and immigration agents apprised Truman of their problems with Mexican authorities. Shortly after Truman left, the INS allowed Mexicans to pour across the bridge into the United States, with or without Mexico's approval. Farmers waited with trucks, and a Great Western Sugar Company representative had a special train ready for the *braceros*. The United States' unilateral opening of the border destroyed Mexico's bargaining position. It could only accept official "regrets" from the United States and continue negotiations. A new agreement reaffirmed the growers' right to recruit *braceros* directly on either side of the border.

From January 23 to February 5, 1954, the United States again unilaterally opened the border. There was nothing Mexico could do to prevent the flood of unemployed, hungry workers into the United States. Left with little choice, Mexico signed a contract favorable to the United States. The gunboat diplomacy of U.S. authorities flagrantly violated international law and caused bitter resentment in Latin America at the United States' reliance on the "big stick" policy and Mexico's obvious humiliation over its failure to control its border and its citizens. Opening the border ended the labor shortage, and served notice to Mexico that it should negotiate because the United States had the power to get all the workers it wanted from Mexico—agreement or no agreement. The United States would act unilaterally, and it completely controlled the *bracero* program. In fact, many members of Congress suggested that the government abandon the pretense of the *bracero* program and simply open the border.

The steady decline of *braceros* beginning in the 1960s marks a convergence of several factors working against the program: resentment of the Mexican government, grievances of the *braceros*, increased opposition by domestic labor, and—probably the most important—changes in agricultural labor-saving techniques and in the U.S. economy. It was clear that the farmers' claim that they could not find sufficient domestic labor was a pretext. The 1958 recession intensified organized labor's opposition to the *bracero* program, and the election of a Democratic president in 1960 moved the executive branch and Congress toward a pro-labor position. The AFL–CIO also put pressure on Democrats to end the *bracero* program. Congress and the Administration, confronted with massive lobbying from labor and from Mexican organizations, allowed the *bracero* contract to lapse on December 31, 1964.[84]

Conclusion: The Consequences of World War II

Historian Dennis Nodín Valdés writes, "Stimulated by World War II, corporate agriculture in the Midwest established an increasingly sophisticated mechanism to recruit, hire and employ workers to meet expanding production and offset the tighter labor market."[85] As a consequence, Texas Mexicans moved in larger numbers to the Midwest. Housing and medical care was primitive, and entire families, including children, worked. Many of the agricultural interests were huge. For instance, in 1950, Michigan Field Crops, Inc., organized during World War II, included as members 8,767 beet growers, 6,800 pickle growers, and an estimated 3,300 growers of miscellaneous crops. That year alone they imported 5,300 Texas Mexican farmworkers. The corridor leading from Texas had been worn even before the war, as contractors transported Mexicans laborers north. Once they got the hang of it, large numbers migrated on their own. The war did little to improve opportunity for Texas Mexicans in the Midwest, with many depending on seasonal work as pickers in cherry, cucumber, tomato, and the familiar sugar beet farms. The grower associations used the reserve army of *braceros* to discipline domestic labor.

Concurrently, Texas Mexicans migrated in larger numbers to the Pacific Northwest. The war helped forge the corridor to the Yakima Valley in southern Washington and other farm areas, spilling over to urban areas as well. By the 1940s, Chicano communities in the Yakima Valley were formed, and by the end of the decade this region supported a Spanish-language radio. Erasmo Gamboa points out that over 20 percent of the 220,640 *braceros* shipped to the United States between 1943 and 1947, a total of 46,954, were sent to the Pacific Northwest to work in Washington, Idaho, and Oregon.[86] By contrast, in the late 1940s California received 8 percent of the *bracero* contract labor, and Texas, 56 percent. Many Texas Mexican workers were pushed out by cotton growers who abused the *bracero* program and created surplus labor. This led to a lowering of cotton wages in Texas by 11 percent, accelerating the Mexican-origin migration to the Midwest and the Northwest.[87]

Besides taking Mexicans north, labor contractors hauled workers throughout the state of Texas. They followed the migrant stream, picking cotton along the coast, throughout Central Texas, and into West Texas. Many migrants, whether they went north or remained in Texas, returned for the winter to their base town where many owned small shacks. They would work at casual jobs until the trek began again. By the postwar era, these South Texas towns were interwoven by a network of contractors who furnished cheap labor to growers. Organized labor and Mexican American organizations in Texas frantically attempted to stop the manipulation of the *bracero* and undocumented worker by grower interests as the number of *braceros* contracted in Texas increased from 42,218 in 1949 to 158,704 five years later.[88] Thus, the escalation of the *bracero* program and World War II contributed to the geographic dispersal of Mexican-origin laborers. By the late 1940s, significant numbers were moving out of the Southwest.

In all of their new locations, Mexican Americans deeply rooted their communities, changing the cultural landscapes of their new homes.

Fighting for Education as a Right

A disturbing statistic was the low education achievement of most Mexican Americans that in turn limited the cumulative benefits that the community was entitled to as a consequence of its service to the country during World War II (1941–1945) and the Korean War (1950–1953). The G.I Bill or Servicemen's Readjustment Act of 1944 gave educational benefits to mostly white male veterans but capped them for those with less than a high school education. Discrimination and a lack of access to these entitlements gave rise to the American G.I. Forum (1948).[89]

"As recently as 1950, 34 percent of the total population 25 or older had completed four years of more of high school...."[90] This problem was addressed, and by the year 2000 80 percent of Americans achieved a high school education. It did not escape Mexican American leaders that the end of the war brought new opportunities to white citizens that were denied to African Americans and Latinos and Latinas. For instance, the G.I. Bill and the development of the California State College System gave millions of Americans the means to go to college.

> In California, white people had achieved a median education of the eleventh grade, qualifying just under half its population for higher education—blacks achieved a median of 9.4 grades in 1960 and Latinos had a median of 7.7 in 1960. Texas was even worse: the median number of years of education for Latinos was 3.5 in 1950—half that of California—compared with 10.3 for whites and 7.0 for nonwhites. In San Antonio, the median number of years was 4.5 for Latinos, half that of the general population of the city. Cities like Tucson, Arizona, mirrored California. In 1950, the median number of school years that Mexican Americans completed in the city was 6.5. Many returning Mexican American veterans felt that their community simply did not have the educational human capital to take advantage of the new opportunities.[91]

Mexican Americans recognized that a lack of educational attainment was a barrier to their equality so the postwar period saw a proliferation of national education conferences. The First Regional Conference on Education of the Spanish-Speaking People in the Southwest took place at the University of Texas at Austin on December 13–15, 1945, focusing on school segregation and bilingual education. George I. Sánchez, Carlos E. Castañeda of the University of Texas at Austin, A. L. Campa of the University of New Mexico, and San Antonio attorney Alonso S. Perales took the lead. Delegates from the five southwestern states attended. The *Santa Fe New Mexican* reported that Sánchez chaired a New Mexico conference that dealt "specifically with fundamental problems in the education of Spanish-speaking people." Carey McWilliams keynoted the event. In the next two decades, Sánchez helped define Mexican American education and other civil rights issues. Education became the prime goal of the Mexican American or the GI generation. They were in large part second-generation the survivors of the repatriation and World War 2.

Notes

1 Werner Gruhl, *Imperial Japan's World War Two: 1931–1945* (London: Routledge. 2010). Interesting study on culpability.

2 John W Dower, *War without mercy: race and power in the pacific war* (New York: Pantheon Books, 1993), 4–5. John W. Dower, "A Rejoinder," *Pacific Historical Review*, Vol. 57, No. 2 (May, 1988), pp. 202–209.

3 William D. Carrigan and Clive Webb, *Forgotten Dead: Mob Violence against Mexicans in the United States, 1848–1928* (New York: Oxford University Press, 2013). Nicholas Villanueva Jr., *Lynching of Mexicans in the Texas Borderlands* (Albuquerque, NM: University of New Mexico Press, 2017). Ralph Ginzburg, *100 Years of Lynchings* (Black Classic Press; Reprint edition, 1996).

4 Samuel Osborne, "5 of the worst atrocities carried out by the British Empire," *Independent* (January 19, 2016), http://www.independent.co.uk/news/uk/home-news/worst-atrocities-british-empire-amritsar-boer-war-concentration-camp-mau-mau-a6821756.html. Rakhi Chakraborty, "The Bengal Famine: How the British engineered the worst genocide in human history for profit," *Our History*, August 15, 2014, https://yourstory.com/2014/08/bengal-famine-genocide/.

5 Amy E. Den Ouden, *Beyond Conquest: Native Peoples and the Struggle for History in New England* (University of Nebraska Press, 2005), 39. Paul Keal, *European Conquest and the Rights of Indigenous Peoples: The Moral Backwardness of International Society* (Cambridge: Cambridge University Press, 2003), 39.

6 "Spanish Intellectual Thought," http://www.umich.edu/~ece/student_projects/conquest/intellectual-2.html.

7 Sharon Korman, *The Right of Conquest: The Acquisition of Territory by Force in International Law and Practice* (Oxford: Clarendon Press, 1996), 7–17.

8 "The Doctrine of Discovery, 1493. A Spotlight on a Primary Source by Pope Alexander VI," *History Now*, The Gilder Lehrman Institute, https://www.gilderlehrman.org/content/doctrine-discovery-1493. "The Doctrine of Discovery, Manifest Destiny, and American Exceptionalism," *Challenging Christian Hegemony*, Jul 21, 2015, http://christianhegemony.org/the-doctrine-of-discovery-manifest-destiny-and-american-exceptionalism. Steve Newcomb, "Five Hundred Years of Injustice: The Legacy of Fifteenth Century Religious Prejudice," http://ili.nativeweb.org/sdrm_art.html. Steven T. Newcomb,

"A Movement Toward Restoration and Healing," Indigenous Law Institute, http://ili.nativeweb.org/index.html.

9. J.A. Hobson, *Imperialism: a study* (Ann Arbor: University of Michigan, 1972), 253.

10. Richard Steele, " The Federal Government Discovers Mexican Americans," in Richard Griswold del Castillo (ed.), *World War II and Mexican American Civil Rights* (Austin: University of Texas Press, 2008), 19–20, https://muse.jhu.edu/book/13909.

11. Leo Grebler, Joan W. Moore, and Ralph C. Guzmán, *The Mexican-American People: The Nation's Second Largest Minority* (New York: Free Press, 1970), 206–18. U.S. Department of Commerce, Bureau of the Census, Fifteenth and Sixteenth Censuses of the United States: 1930–1940 Population. David Hendricks and Amy Patterson, "The 1930 Census in Perspective: The Historical Census," *Prologue Magazine* 34, No. 2 (Summer 2002), http://www.archives.gov/publications/prologue/2002/summer/1930-census-perspective.html. Clara E. Rodriguez, *Changing Race: Latinos, the Census and the History of Ethnicity* (New York: New York University Press, 2000), 101–04. Gloria Sandrino-Glasser, "Los Confundidos: Deconflating Latinos/Latinas Race and Ethnicity," in Kevin R. Johnson, ed., *Mixed Race America and the Law: A Reader* (New York: New York University Press, 2003), 221–22. Gerald D. Nash, *The American West Transformed: The Impact of the Second World War* (Lincoln: University of Nebraska Press, 1990), 107–11.

12. Raúl Morín, *Among the Valiant: Mexican Americans in WWII and Korea* (Alhambra, CA: Borden Publishing Co., 1966), 16. Robin Fitzgerald Scott, "The Mexican-American in the Los Angeles Area, 1920–1950: From Acquiescence to Activity" (PhD Dissertation, University of Southern California, 1971), 156, 195, 256, 261. Thanks are due to Dr. Russell Bartley of the history department at the University of Wisconsin Milwaukee, and a student who had been provided access under the Freedom of Information Act, for allowing me to review the FBI files on the zoot-suit riots, 1943–1945. FBI files provided to Russell Bartley, History Department, University of Wisconsin Milwaukee, under Freedom of Information Act; copies in Rodolfo F. Acuña Papers, Special Collections, California State University at Northridge.

13. David G. Gutiérrez, *Walls and Mirrors: Mexican Americans, Mexican Immigrants, and the Politics of Ethnicity* (Berkeley: University of California Press, 1995), 120–22. See U.S. Latino & Latina World War II, Oral History Project, University of Texas Austin, http://lib.utexas.edu/ww2latinos/ or http://lib.utexas.edu/ww2latinos/browse-index.html. It has the most extensive online collection of Mexican American and Latina/o veteran interviews.

14. Lynn Marie Getz, "Lost Momentum: World War II and the Education of Hispanos in New Mexico," in Maggie Rivas-Rodriguez, ed., *Mexican Americans and World War II* (Austin: University of Texas Press, 2005), 93, 108. Morín, *Among the Valiant*, 34–42, 166–71. Tom Brokaw, *The Greatest Generation* (New York: Random House, 1998). Refugio I. Rochin and Lionel Fernández, "U.S. Latino Patriots: From the American Revolution to Afghanistan, An Overview," Pew Hispanic Center, http://www.pewhispanic.org/files/reports/17.3.pdf. Ken Burns and Lynn Novick, *The War*, WETA and American Lives II Film Project, LLC (Washington, D.C.: Public Broadcasting System, 2007), http://www.pbs.org/thewar/.

15. Morín, *Among the Valiant*, 15.

16. "Soldados Razos: Issues of Race in Vietnam War Drama," *Vietnam Generation*: Vol. 1: No. 2, Article 5, 38-54, http://digitalcommons.lasalle.edu/vietnamgeneration/vol1/iss2/5

17. Rubén G. Rumbaut, "The Making of a People," in Marta Tienda and Faith Mitchell, *Hispanics and the Future of America* (Washington, D.C.: The National Academic Press, 2003), 24, FN8, http://books.nap.edu/openbook.php?record_id=11539&page=16. The racism at the time cannot be minimized. Ted Williams's mother was Mexican American and he was raised with her family. In his autobiography, Ted Williams (2001) wrote that " . . . if I had had my mother's name, there is no doubt I would have run into problems in those days, [with] the prejudices people had in Southern California." Williams was arguably baseball's greatest hitter. Ted Williams with John Underwood, *My Turn At Bat: The Story of my Life* (New York: Simon and Schuster, 1988), 28–30.

18. David Reyes, "California and the West; A Marine Who Wielded the Power of Persuasion; World War II: Effort Builds to Gain Medal of Honor for Storied Mexican American Veteran Who Talked More Than 1,000 Japanese into surrendering," *Los Angeles Times* (August 31, 1998). Ted Williams with John Underwood, *My Turn At Bat*, 28–30. Gabaldón also prevented some of his fellow soldiers from shooting the captured Japanese. Ruchika Joshi, "Guy Gabaldon," Oral History Project, U.S. Latino and Latina World War II, University of Texas, http://www.lib.utexas.edu/ww2latinos/template-stories-indiv.html?work_urn=urn%3Autlol%3Awwlatin.034&work_title=Gabaldon%2C+Guy.

19. Jorge Rodriguez, "A History of El Paso's Company E in World War II" (Master's Thesis, The University of Texas at El Paso, 2010), 1, 26, 41, 42, 50–55.

20. Morín, *Among the Valiant*, 67–74. Leigh E. Smith, Jr., "El Paso's Company E Survivors Remember Rapido

River Assault," *Borderlands: El Paso Community College* 13 (Spring 1995): 6–7. Leigh E. Smith Jr., "Company E Survivor Recalls Days as Prisoner of War," *EPCC Local History Project*, http://epcc.libguides.com/content.php?pid=309255&sid=2621916. "Co. 'E' Vets," June 4, 2008, http://elpasotimes.typepad.com/morgue/2008/06/co-e-vets.html. Rodriguez, "Company E," 45, 55–59, 60, 76, 82–96. Samuel S. Ortega, Arnulfo Hernandez, Jr., *The Men of Company E Toughest Chicano Soldiers of World War II: Toughest Chicano Soldiers of World War II* (El Paso, TX: CreateSpace Independent Publishing Platform; 1 edition, 2015).

21 Ken Burns's documentary on World War II drew nationwide protests from Latino groups because he distorted history by not acknowledging the presence of Mexican Americans and Puerto Ricans in WW II. Roberto Lovato, "Saving Private Ramos: Ken Burns' World War II Documentary Continues to Incite Latino Protest," *New America Media*, http://news.newamericamedia.org/news/view_article.html?article_id=74ce20bca4b84e4a5c35736d73a90d28.

22 Figueroa, "G.I. José," 22. Alonso S. Perales, ed., *Are We Good Neighbors?* (New York: Arno Press, 1974), 79. Adrianna Alatorre, "Anthony Family Had Five Sons in World War II," *Borderlands*, El Paso Community College, http://epcc.libguides.com/content.php?pid=309255&sid=2559970. Rita Sanchez, "The Five Sanchez Brothers in World War II," in Rivas-Rodriguez, ed., *Mexican Americans & World War II*, 1–38. Brooke N. Miller, "Angelita De Los Santos," Latinos and Latinas & World War II, University of Texas, http://www.lib.utexas.edu/ww2latinos/template-stories-indiv.html?work_urn=urn%3Autlol%3Awwlatin.560&work_title=De+Los+Santos%2C+Lita. Richard Gonzales, "Latino War Vets Changed World at Home, Abroad," *National Public Radio* Weekend Edition—Sunday, http://www.npr.org/templates/story/story.php?storyId=14579935. "World War II: Mexican Air Force Helped Liberate the Philippines," Historynet.com, http://www.historynet.com/world-war-ii-mexican-air-force-helped-liberate-the-philippines.htm. "Untold stories of Mexican-American WWII veterans," *San Gabriel Valley Tribune*, http://www.sgvtribune.com/mexicanveterans.

23 Gary Y. Okihiro, Lionel C. Bascom, James E. Seelye Jr., Emily Moberg Robinson, Guadalupe Compeán, eds. The Great American Mosaic: An Exploration of Diversity in Primary Documents, Vol. I.) New York: Greenwood, 2014), pp. 243–244.

24 Figueroa, "G.I. José," 20. Joyce Valdez, "Stories Hispanic WWII Veterans Discuss Today's War Against Terrorism," *Hispanic Magazine* (March 3, 2002): 20–22. Joanne R. Sánchez, "Lifetime of Caring: War Nurse, Rafaela Muñiz Esquivel," *U.S. Latinos and Latinas & World War II* 3, No. 1 (Fall 2001), University of Texas at Austin; available at http://lib.utexas.edu/ww2latinos/template-stories-indiv.html?work_urn=urn%3Autlol%3Awwlatin.029&work_title=Esquivel%2C+Rafaela+Muniz. Roseanna Aytes, "Women Changed Wartime Work Patterns," *Borderlands*, El Paso Community College, http://epcc.libguides.com/content.php?pid=309255&sid=2621863. Chris Marín, "Arizona Men and Women in Military," *BarrioZona*, http://www.barriozona.com/Mexican-American_Men_and_Women_in_WWII.html.

25 Cecilia Rasmussen, "A Teenager's Courage Remembered," *Los Angeles Times,* Ventura County Edition (April 7, 1998). Janice Harumi Yen, "Who Was Ralph Lazo?" Nikkei for Civil Rights & Redress Education Committee, http://www.ncrr-la.org/news/7_6_03/2.html. "NCRR and Visual Communications to premiered Stand Up for Justice at Day of Remembrance 2004," http://www.ncrr-la.org/news/stand_up_for_justice.html. "Intersections: Hispanic and Japanese American History," Densho Blog, September 23, 2015. https://densho.org/intersections-hispanic-andjapanese-american-history/

26 Ryan Reft. "Segregation in the City of Angels: A 1939 Map of Housing Inequality in L.A.," KCET, November 14, 2017, https://www.kcet.org/shows/lost-la/segregation-in-the-city-of-angels-a-1939-map-of-housing-inequality-in-la. Philip J. Ethington, William H. Frey, and Dowell Myers, "The Racial Resegregation of Los Angeles County, 1940–2000," *Public Research Report*, No. 2001-04, A University of Southern California and University of Michigan Collaborative Project, May 12, 2001, http://popdynamics.usc.edu/pdf/2001_Ethington-Frey-Myers_Racial-Resegregation.pdf.

27 Octavio Paz, The Labyrinth of Solitude: Life and Thought in Mexico. (New York: Grove Press/Evergreen, 1961), 13–14.

28 Javier Durán. "Nation and Translation: The "Pachuco" in Mexican Popular Culture: Germán Valdéz's Tin Tan," The Journal of the Midwest Modern Language Association, Vol. 35, No. 2, Translating in and across Cultures (Autumn, 2002), pp. 41–49.

29 Jim Willard. "'Dead End Kids' found new life as 'Bowery Boys'," Home Trivially Speaking Story, Reporter Herald, Jul 7, 2018. http://www.reporterherald.com/columnists/trivially-speaking/ci_31989481/dead-end-kids-found-new-life-bowery-boys.

30 See Joan W. Moore, *Homeboys: Gangs, Drugs, and Prison in the Barrios of Los Angeles* (Philadelphia, PA: Temple University Press, 1978), 64. James Diego Vigil, *Barrio Gangs: Street Life and Identity in Southern California* (Austin: University of Texas Press, 1988), 9,

22, 33, 67, 93. Edward J. Escobar, *Race, Police, and the Making of a Political Identity: Mexican Americans and the Los Angeles Police Department, 1900–1945* (Berkeley: University of California Press, 1999), 181–82.

31. Catherine Sue Ramírez, "The Pachuca in Chicana/o Art, Literature and History: Reexamining Nation, Cultural Nationalism and Resistance" (PhD Dissertation, University of California, Berkeley, 2000), 50, 96. Catherine Sue Ramírez, *The Woman in the Zoot Suit: Gender, Nationalism, and the Cultural Politics of Memory* (Durham, NC: Duke University Press, 2009). Elizabeth Rachel Escobedo, "Mexican American Home Front: The Politics of Gender, Culture, and Community in World War II Los Angeles" (PhD Dissertation, University of Washington, 2004), 65, 71–72, 85, 97.

32. "Sleepy Lagoon," words and music by Jack Lawrence and Eric Coates, recorded by Harry James, 1940, http://www.youtube.com/watch?v=I1yQLPhEGGY&feature=related. Ismael Dieppa, "The Zoot-Suit Riots Revisited: The Role of Private Philanthropy in Youth Problems of Mexican-Americans" (DSW Dissertation, University of Southern California, 1973), 14. Carey McWilliams Papers, Special Collections Library, University of California at Los Angeles. Ramírez, "The Pachuca in Chicana/o Art," 15–20. Escobedo, "Mexican American Home Front," 67–68.

33. Sheila Marie Contreras, *Blood Lines: Myth, Indigenism and Chicana/o Literature* (Austin: University of Texas Press, 2008), 75–76. Carey McWilliams, *North from Mexico* (New York: Greenwood Press, 1968), 233–35. Interestingly, Deputy Sheriff Ed Durán Ayres was also an amateur historian who wrote a series of articles for the *Civic Center Sun* (Los Angeles) on "The Background of the History of California." Some of these articles appeared in the April 18, April 25, May 16, May 30, June 6, July 4, and August 1, 1940, issues of the paper. The content of the articles seriously questions whether Ayres wrote the Grand Jury Report. According to Guy Endore, the report was developed by the sheriffs, who signed Ayres's name. Kevin Allen Leonard, *The Battle for Los Angeles: Racial Ideology and World War II* (Albuquerque: University of New Mexico Press, 2006), 91–107. Luis Váldez's *Zoot Suit* (1982) should be seen on DVD. Video On Demand, Amazon.com.

34. George J. Sánchez, *Becoming Mexican American: Ethnicity, Culture and Identity in Chicano Los Angeles, 1900–1945* (New York: Oxford University Press, 1993), 251. "Alice McGrath (1917–2009)," *American Experience*, PBS, http://www.pbs.org/wgbh/amex/zoot/eng_peopleevents/p_mcgrath.html. Oxnard New Film, "Alice McGrath interview," http://www.youtube.com/watch?v=96N-Y8RKYiE. "Dear Alice Interview with Alice McGrath," Blip, http://blip.tv/el-teatro-campesino/dear-alice-an-interview-with-alice-mcgrath-3093765.

35. Mari Jo Buhle, Paul Buhle, and Dan Georgakas, eds., *Encyclopedia of the American Left* (Urbana: University of Illinois Press, 1992), 684–86. "The Sleepy Lagoon Case," Prepared by the Sleepy Lagoon Defense Committee (Formerly The Citizens' Committee for the Defense of Mexican-American Youth) (Los Angeles, CA: The Sleepy Lagoon Defense Committee, 1943), http://content.cdlib.org/view?docId=hb7779p4zc&brand=calisphere&doc.view=entire_text.

36. Conversations with Lupe Leyvas, sister of Henry Leyvas, over the past 10 years. Confirmed in an interview on October 10, 1998. Her story, that of her family, and that of the other defendants' families remain untold. Anthony Quinn, *The Original Sin: A Self-Portrait by Anthony Quinn* (New York: Little, Brown & Company, 1972), 81–85. Scott, "The Mexican American," 223, 225. Citizens' Committee for the Defense of Mexican-American Youth, *The Sleepy Lagoon Case* (Los Angeles, 1942), 21. McWilliams, *North from Mexico*, 228–33. Mario García, *Mexican Americans, Leadership, Ideology, & Identity, 1930–1960* (New York: Yale University Press, 1989), 165–70. J. Sánchez, "Lifetime of Caring," 249. "Pachuco Crimes," Report of Joint Fact-Finding Committee on Un-American Activities in California, Senate Journal of April 16, 1945, 161–62, 171, 173–75, 181–83, in Rodolfo F. Acuña and Guadalupe Compeán, eds., *Voices of the U.S. Latino Experience*, 3 Vols. (Westport, CN: Greenwood Press, 2008), 694–99.

37. *The People, v. Gus Zammora et al.*, 66 Cal. Ap. 2d 166; 152 2d 180; 1944 Cal. Ap. LEXIS 1170; October 4, 1944. "From Sleepy Lagoon to Zoot Suit: The Irreverent Path of Alice McGrath," video, 32 minutes (Santa Cruz, CA: Giges Productions, 1996). Alice McGrath was a CIO organizer who became executive secretary of the Sleepy Lagoon Defense Committee. One of the main characters in the play and movie *Zoot Suit* was patterned after her. Carlos Lozano, "Alice McGrath: 50 Years on the Front Lines," *Los Angeles Times*, Ventura County Edition (February 22, 1998). Escobedo, "Mexican American Home Front," 67–68, 93–94. Ramírez, "The Pachuca in Chicana/o Art," 24–40. Nash, *American West*, 111–20.

38. Joseph Tovares, "American Experience: Zoot Suit Riots," KCET-TV, Los Angeles, February 10, 2002. "Zoot Suit Documentary," http://www.pbs.org/wgbh/amex/zoot/eng_sfeature/sf_zoot_mx.html. McWilliams, *North from Mexico*, 244–54. Dieppa, "Zoot-Suit Riots," 9, 22–23. *Los Angeles Times* (June 7, 1943). *Time Magazine* (June 21, 1943). *PM* (June 10, 1943). S. I. Hayakawa, "Second Thoughts: The Zoot Suit War," *The Chicago Defender* (June 26, 1943), 15; this article appeared in a progressive African

American newspaper. Hayakawa during the 1960s would become an ultra-conservative.

39. FBI Report, "Racial Conditions (Spanish-Mexican Activities in Los Angeles Field Division)," (Los Angeles, January 14, 1944). The *Eastside Journal* (Los Angeles, June 9, 1943) wrote an editorial defending the zoot-suiters; it pointed out that 112 had been hospitalized, 150 hurt, and 12 treated in the hospitals as outpatients. See also McWilliams, *North from Mexico*, 250–51. Ed Robbins, *PM* (June 9, 1943).

40. *Senate Journal* of April 16, 1945, containing Report of the Joint Fact-Finding Committee on Un-American Activities in California. State Senate of California, 161–62, 171, 173–75, 181–83. Acuña and Compeán, eds., *Voices of the U.S. Latino Experience*, 693–98. *Los Angeles Times* (June 10, 1943 and July 10, 1943). McGucken Report, California Legislature, Report and Recommendations of Citizens Committee on Civil Disturbances in Los Angeles (June 12, 1943), 1. Mauricio Mazón, *The Zoot-Suit Riots: The Psychology of Symbolic Annihilation* (Austin: University of Texas Press, 1988), 67–77. Guide to the Robert Walker Kenny Papers, 1920-1947 BANC MSS .C-B 510, Online Archive of California, Revised 2018. https://oac.cdlib.org/findaid/ark:/13030/tf2r29n6db/entire_text/. Patricia Trujillo, "The lasting impact of the Zoot Suit Riots", Santa Fe New Mexican, Jun 16, 2018. http://www.santafenewmexican.com/opinion/commentary/the-lasting-impact-of-the-zoot-suit-riots/article_54a376cd-56ea-5335-992a-93f918eac122.html.

41. Julie A. Campbell, "*Madres y Esposas*: Tucson's Spanish-American Mothers and Wives Association," *Journal of Arizona History* 31, No. 2 (Summer 1990), 161–82. Christine Marin, "La Asociacion Hispano-Americana de Madres y Esposas: Tucson's Mexican American Women in World War II," http://www.eric.ed.gov/ERICWebPortal/custom/portlets/recordDetails/detailmini.jsp?_nfpb=true&_&ERICExtSearch_SearchValue_0=ED315253&ERICExtSearch_SearchType_0=no&accno=ED315253. Chris Lukinbeal, Daniel D. Arreola, and D. Drew Lucio, "Mexican Urban Colonias in the Salt River Valley of Arizona," *The Geographical Review* (January 2012).

42. Escobedo, "Mexican American Home Front," 9, 11, 33, 93–94, 103.

43. *Andrea D. Perez et al.*, Petitioners, *v. W. G. Sharp*, as County Clerk, etc., Respondent. [L.A. No. 20305]. *Perez v. Sharp* 32 Cal.2d 711, 198 P.2d 17 (1948), http://www.multiracial.com/government/perez-v-sharp.html. The case would be cited in *Brown v. the Board of Education* (1954), http://sshl.ucsd.edu/brown/perez.htm. Derrick Z. Jackson, "Court's Ruling Opens New Era in Civil Rights," *Boston Globe* (November 21, 2003), http://www.commondreams.org/views03/1121-01.htm. Peggy Pascoe, "Miscegenation Law, Court Cases, and Ideologies of Race in Twentieth-Century America," in Werner Sollors, ed., *Interracialism: Black-White Intermarriage in American History, Literature, and Law* (Cambridge: Oxford University Press, 2000), 196–202.

44. "*Rosie the Riveter*: Real Women Workers in World War II," Journeys & Crossings, Library of Congress, http://www.loc.gov/rr/program/journey/rosie.html or http://www.youtube.com/watch?v=04VNBM1PqR8.

45. Carlos G. Vélez-Ibáñez, *Border Visions: Mexican Cultures of the Southwest United States* (Tucson: University of Arizona Press, 1996), 19. Hedda Garza, *Latinas: Hispanic Women in the United States* (New York: Franklin Watts, 1994), 74. Monica Rivera, "Josephine Kelly Ledesma Walker: A Woman Ahead of Her Time," *U.S. Latinos and Latinas & World War II* 3, No. 1 (Fall 2001), University of Texas at Austin; available at http://www.lib.utexas.edu/ww2latinos/template-stories-indiv.html?work_urn=urn%3Autlol%3Awwlatin.058&work_title=Ledesma+Walker%2C+Josephine+. Sherri Fauver, "Henrietta López Rivas—Kelly Air Force Base Her Proving Ground," *U.S. Latinos and Latinas & World War II* 1, No. 2 (Spring 2000); available at http://www.lib.utexas.edu/ww2latinos/template-stories-indiv.html?work_urn=urn%3Autlol%3Awwlatin.089&work_title=Rivas%2C+Henrietta++Lopez. Cheryl Smith, "Elisa Rodriguez: Wartime Civil Servant," *U.S. Latinos and Latinas & World War II* 1, No. 1 (Fall 1999); available at http://www.lib.utexas.edu/ww2latinos/template-stories-indiv.html?work_urn=urn%3Autlol%3Awwlatin.093&work_title=Rodriguez%2C+Maria+Elisa+Reyes. Richard Santillán, "Rosita and the Riveter: Midwest Mexican American Women During World War II, 1941–1945," *Perspectives in Mexican American Studies* 2 (1989), 115–46.

46. Carlos E. Castañeda, "Discrimination Against Mexican Americans in War Industries," Mexican American Voices, *Digital History*, University of Houston. Richard Griswold del Castillo, ed., *World War II and Mexican American Civil Rights* (Austin: University of Texas Press, 2008), 75–78. Robert Garland Landolt, *The Mexican-American Workers of San Antonio, Texas* (New York: Arno Press, 1976), 76–77, 88–117; Pauline R. Kibbe, *Latin Americans in Texas* (New York: Arno Press, 1974), 161–62. Charles Loomis and Nellie Loomis, "Skilled Spanish-American War Industry Workers from New Mexico," *Applied Anthropology* 2 (October–December 1942): 33.

47. Clete Daniel, *Chicano Workers and the Politics of Fairness: The FEPC in the Southwest, 1941–1945* (Austin: University of Texas Press, 1991), 8–9. Manuel Ruiz, Jr., "Closing Remarks," Making Public Employment A Model of Equal Opportunity: A Report of the

Proceedings of Regional Civil Rights Conference II. Sponsored by the U.S. Commission on Civil Rights in Boston, Massachusetts, September 22–24, 1974, 34–35, http://www.law.umaryland.edu/marshall/usccr/documents/cr12an72.pdf. Guide to the Manuel Ruiz Papers, 1931-1986, Department of Special Collections and University Archives Stanford University Libraries, Stanford, California, 1998, https://oac.cdlib.org/findaid/ark:/13030/tf9199p0dg/entire_text/.

48 David Montejano, *Anglos and Mexicans in the Making of Texas, 1836–1986* (Austin: University of Texas Press, 1987), 270. Carlos E. Castañeda, September 8, 1944, on Bill 2048 to Prohibit Discrimination Because of Race, Creed, Color, National Origin or Ancestry, Fair Employment Practices Act Hearings, quote in Perales, ed., *Are We Good Neighbors?*, 92–104.

49 Vélez-Ibáñez, *Border Visions*, 117. Daniel, *Chicano Workers and the Politics of Fairness*, 77–105, 115. Matthew Gritter, New School for Social Research, "Good Neighbors and Good Citizens: People of Mexican Origin and the FEPC1," (Under Review at *Journal of Policy History*), http://www.newschool.edu/uploadedFiles/NSSR/Departments_and_Faculty/Political_Science/Recent_Placements/GritterSample.pdf. Gritter, "Shaping Incorporation: People of Mexican Origin and Anti-Discrimination Policy" (Dissertation, New School for Social Research, New York, NY, 2010).

50 Statement of Frank Paz, President of the Spanish-Speaking People's Council of Chicago, quoted in Perales, ed., *Are We Good Neighbors?*, 111–14.

51 Perales, *Are we Good Neighbors?*, 93, 94, 112–13, 117, 121. Daniel, *Chicano Workers and the Politics of Fairness*, 1, 4–5, 42, 52–76, 64, 115. Emilio Zamora, "The Failed Promise of Wartime Opportunity for Mexicans in the Texas Oil Industry," *Southwestern Historical Quarterly* 95, No. 3 (January 1, 1992), 323–50, critiques the work of the FEPC in the booming oil industry in Texas.

52 FBI, "Racial Conditions (Spanish-Mexican Activities in Los Angeles Field Division)," A confidential report, January 14, 1944; available at Acuña Archives, CSUN Library.

53 Escobedo, "Mexican American Home Front," 14, 18, 125–36, 139, 153, 155.

54 "The Postwar Economy: 1945–1960," *American History*, http://www.let.rug.nl/usa/outlines/history-1994/postwar-america/the-postwar-economy-1945-1960.php.

55 Gary McLauchlan, "World War II and the Transformation of the U.S. State: The Wartime Foundations of U.S. Hegemony," *Sociological Inquiry* 67, No. 1 (Winter 1997), 1–2, 22.

56 "The Postwar Economy: 1945–1960," Ibid. Barry Rundquist; Jeong-Hwa Lee, Jungho Rhee, "Distributive Politics of Cold War Defense Spending: Some State Level Evidence," *Legislative Studies Quarterly*, 1 May 1996, Vol. 21(2), 265–281.

57 "Taft–Hartley Act—1947," http://www.historycentral.com/Documents/Tafthatley.html. John Wojcik, "After 64 years, still paying the price for Taft-Hartley," *People's World*, April 5, 2011, http://www.peoplesworld.org/article/after-64-years-still-paying-the-price-for-taft-hartley/. Charles J. Morris, "How The National Labor Relations Act Was Stolen and How It Can Be Recovered: Taft-Hartley Revisionism and the National Labor Relations Board's Appointment Process," *Berkeley Journal of Employment and Labor Law*, 1 January 2012, Vol. 33(1), 1–71.

58 Timothy Noah, "The Great Divergence and the Death of Organized Labor," *Slate*, Sept 12, 2010, https://slate.com/news-and-politics/2010/09/the-great-divergence-and-the-death-of-organized-labor.html.

59 Luisa Moreno, http://www.youtube.com/watch?v=7upHqNX6654. Luisa Moreno Labor Studies Collection at Southern California Library, Allen Kerri, "The Legacy of Luisa Moreno," *The Hispanic Outlook in Higher Education*, Paramus 14, No. 18 (June 14, 2004), 22. G. Sánchez, *Becoming Mexican American*, 244–45, 249, 252.

60 Vicki L. Ruiz, *Cannery Women, Cannery Lives: Mexican Women, Unionization, and California Food Processing Industry, 1930–1950* (Albuquerque: University of New Mexico Press, 1987), 78–79, 83, 110–14. Patricia Zavella, *Women's Work & Chicano Families: Cannery Workers of the Santa Clara Valley* (Ithaca, NY: Cornell University, 1987), 49. Garza, *Latinas*, 79. David G. Gutiérrez, *Walls and Mirrors: Mexican Americans, Mexican Immigrants, and the Politics of Ethnicity* (Berkeley: University of California, 1995), 110–11. "The Roots of the HUAC Committee," HistoryBlogger, http://thehistoryblogger.blogspot.com/2007/08/roots-of-huac-committee.html.

61 García, *Mexican Americans*, 145–74. Dolores Hayden, *The Power of Place: Urban Landscapes as Public History* (Boston: M.I.T. Press, 1997), 196–99. Francisco A. Rosales, *Chicano! The History of the Mexican American Civil Rights Movement*, 2nd Revised ed. (Houston, TX: Arte Público Press, 1997), 123–24. Matt S. Meier and Margo Gutiérrez, *Encyclopedia of the Mexican American Civil Rights Movement* (Westport, CT: Greenwood Press, 2000), 82. Jeffrey M. Garcilazo, "McCarthyism, Mexican Americans, and the Los Angeles Committee for Protection of the Foreign-Born," *The Western Historical Quarterly* 32, No. 3 (Autumn 2001), 278. Paul Buhle and Dave Wagner, *Radical Hollywood: The Untold Story Behind America's Favorite Movies* (The New Press, 2002), 91. "Spanish Congress Hits War Job Discrimination," *Los Angeles Times* (May 24, 1942), A1. "Influences Behind Gang Wars Here to Be Studied," *Los Angeles Times* (December 14, 1942), A8. Escobedo, "Mexican American Home Front," 116. "Josefina Fierro de

Bright, 1920–1998," http://www.mhschool.com/ss/ca/eng/g4/u4/g4u4_bio2.html.

62 Enrique M. Buelna, *The Mexican Question: Mexican Americans in the Communist Party, 1940–1957*, Center for Research on Latinos in a Global Society (UC Irvine: Center for Research on Latinos in a Global Society, 1999); Retrieved from: http://www.escholarship.org/uc/item/9mk997k1.

63 José Angel Gutiérrez, "Under Surveillance," *The Texas Observer Magazine* (January 9, 1987), 8–13. FBI Report (Los Angeles, June 16, 1943). FBI Report, "Racial Conditions" (January 14, 1944).

64 Enrique M. Buelna, "Resistance from the margins: Mexican American radical activism in Los Angeles, 1930–1970" (PhD Dissertation: University of California, Irvine, 2007). Rodolfo F. Acuña, *A Community Under Siege: A Chronicle of Chicanos East of the Los Angeles River, 1945–1975* (Los Angeles: Chicano Studies Research Center Publications, 1984), 21–106, 275–94, 407–50.

65 David E. Hayes-Bautista, Werner O. Schink, and Jorge Chapa, *The Burden of Support: Young Latinos in an Aging Society* (Stanford, CA: Stanford University Press, 1988), 15, 18–21. Mario García, *Memories of Chicano History: The Life and Narrative of Bert Corona* (Berkeley: University of California Press, 1994), 161–63. Katherine Underwood, "Pioneering Minority Representation: Edward Roybal and the Los Angeles City Council, 1949–1962," *Pacific Historical Review* 66, No. 3 (August 1, 1997), 399–425. John R. Chávez, *The Lost Land: The Chicano Image of the Southwest* (Albuquerque: University of New Mexico, 1984), 107–27.

66 Grebler et al., *The Mexican-American People*, 150, 154. Thomas E. Sheridan, *Los Tucsonenses: The Mexican Community in Tucson, 1854–1941* (Tucson: University of Arizona Press, 1986), 235–36. David A. Badillo, "From West San Antonio to East L.A.: Chicano Community Leadership Compare," Working Paper Series, No. 24. (April, 1989), Stanford Center for Chicano Research.

67 U.S. Immigration and Naturalization Service, Historical Statistics of the United States, Part 1 (1975), U.S. Bureau of the Census, 1980 and 1990, and March Current Population Survey, 1995 and 1996. (1)These figures are based on CPS data that are adjusted for undercount and thus are not comparable to census figures. (2) Mexican-origin population calculated as a sum of the Mexican-born population and natives of Mexican parentage. See George J. Borjas and Lawrence F. Katz, "The Evolution of the Mexican-Born Workforce in the United States," Harvard University and National Bureau of Economic Research (April 2005), http://www.aeaweb.org/assa/2006/0108_1015_0302.pdf. Jeffrey Passel and D'Vera Cohn, "How Many Hispanics? Comparing Census Counts and Census Estimates," Pew Hispanic Center (March 15, 2011). One of the most accurate surveyors.

68 "The 60th Anniversary of Mendez vs. Westminster," http://uprisingradio.org/home/?p=1896. "Mendez v Westminster," http://mendezvwestminster.com/_wsn/page3.html.

69 "Delgado v. Bastrop ISD," *Handbook of Texas Online*, http://www.tshaonline.org/handbook/online/articles/DD/jrd1.html.

70 Kibbe, *Latin Americans in Texas*, 212, 214–15. "First Regional Conference on the Education of Spanish-Speaking people in the Southwest—A Report" (March 1946). *Image* (Federation of Employed Latin American Descendants [FELAD], Vallejo, California), May 1976. J. Sánchez, "Lifetime of Caring," 9–11. Vélez-Ibáñez, *Border Visions*, 129. Gilbert G. González, *Labor and Community: Mexican Citrus Worker Villages in a Southern California County, 1900–1950* (Urbana: University of Illinois Press, 1994), 172–77. Steven H. Wilson, "Brown over Other White: Mexican Americans' Legal Arguments and Litigation Strategy in School Desegregation Lawsuits," *Law and History Review* 21, No.1 (Spring 2003), 145–194, http://www.historycooperative.org/journals/lhr/21.1/forum_wilson.html.

71 Henry A. J. Ramos, *The American G.I. Forum: In Pursuit of the Dream, 1948–983* (Houston, TX: Arte Público Press, 1998), 23. Patrick J Carroll, *Felix Longoria's Wake: Bereavement, Racism, and the Rise of Mexican American Activism* (Austin: University of Texas, 2003). "American G.I. Forum," http://www.pbs.org/kpbs/theborder/history/timeline/19.html. "A Class Apart," WGBH American Experience, http://www.pbs.org/wgbh/americanexperience/class/photoGallery/. "Felix Z. Longoria: Private, United States Army," http://www.arlingtoncemetery.net/longoria.htm.

72 Rosales, *Chicano!*, 97.

73 Ramos, *The American G.I. Forum*, 23.

74 "Mexican American Movement," Urban Archives, California State University at Northridge, http://library.csun.edu/Collections/SCA/UAC/SCMAM. Rosales, *Chicano!*, 99–102. G. Sánchez, *Becoming Mexican American*, 206–7, 257–61. Carlos Muñoz, *Youth, Identity, Power: The Chicano Movement*, Revised ed. (London: Verso, 2007), 35–44. Ohio Citizen Action, "The Organizer's Tale," http://www.ohiocitizen.org/about/training/chavez.html. Saul Alinsky, "Community organizing and rules for radicals," http://www.infed.org/thinkers/alinsky.htm. Cynthia Orozco, *No Mexicans, women, or dogs allowed: The rise of the Mexican American civil rights movement* (Austin, Tex.: University of Texas Press, 2009).

75 "Lester Tate joins the Los Angeles Civil Rights Congress," January 1950, Los Angeles, University of Southern California Digital Collection, http://digarc.usc.edu/search/controller/view/scl-m0316.html. Gerald Horne, *Fire This Time: The Watts Uprising and the 1960s* (Charlottesville: University Press of Virginia, 1995), 7–9. Enrique Meza Buelna, "Resistance from the Margins: Mexican American Radical Activism in Los Angeles, 1930–1970" (PhD Dissertation, University of California Irvine, 2007), 125, 132, 135, 190–91; Mexican Americans like Celia Rodríguez were very much involved in the Congress, which was a radical Black organization with ties to the Communist Party. It attracted activists such as Ralph Cuarón, who opened a storefront in Boyle Heights. In 1947, an affiliate was formed, the Mexican Civil Rights Committee, which became the Mexican American Civil Rights Congress. This organization was involved in the Salcido case. Simultaneously, many of the activists were involved with the organizing committee of the Independent Progressive Party in 1947.

76 Acuña, *A Community Under Siege*, 25, 418–19. Meza Buelna, "Resistance from the Margins," 105. John Sides, "'You Understand My Condition': The Civil Rights Congress in the Los Angeles African-American Community, 1946–1952," *Pacific Historical Review* 67, No. 2 (May 1998), 233–57. Tony Castro, *Chicano Power: The Emergence of Mexican-Americans* (New York: Saturday Review Press, 1974), 188. Miguel Tirado, "The Mexican-American Minority's Participation in Voluntary Political Associations" (PhD Dissertation, Claremont Graduate School and University Center, 1970), 65. Luis Arroyo, "Chicano Participation in Organized Labor: The CIO in Los Angeles, 1938–1950, An Extended Research Note," *Aztlán* 6, No. 2 (Summer 1975), 297. *Eastside Sun* (Boyle Heights) (April 2, 1948). Keyes had shot four people in 18 months. See also Guy Endore, *Justice for Salcido* (Los Angeles: Civil Rights Congress of Los Angeles, 1948), 5–9, 13. Salcido was hit four times—in the head from ear to ear, twice in the back of the head, and in the arm.

77 Buelna, "Resistance from the Margins," 106, bases much of his dissertation on extensive interviews with Ralph Cuarón, one of the premier activists of the post–World War II era and the 1960s. Like so many other activists, Cuarón's parents were originally from Chihuahua, settling for a time in the mining town of Morenci, Arizona, scene of many bitter copper strikes. Deeply touched by the Great Depression, Cuarón joined the Communist Party. Ralph Cuarón was a descendant of Abráan Salcido, the leader of the 1903 Clifton-Morenci Strike. Ralph's daughter Margarita Cuarón is a well-known artist in the LA area.

78 See Rodolfo Acuña, *Occupied America: A History of Chicanos*, 2nd and 3rd eds. (New York: Harper & Row, 1981 and 1988). *Eastside Sun* (April 9, 1948 and August 22, 1947). The Progressive Citizens of America, along with Councilman Christensen of the 9th Councilmanic District and Ed Elliot of the 44th Assembly District, requested the suspension of Keyes; *Eastside Sun* (April 23, 1948). The American Jewish Congress protested the admitted shooting of an unarmed Mexican. "AJC Requests Action in Salcido Killing," *Eastside Sun* (July 23, 1948). Endore, *Justice for Salcido*, 17, 19–21, 24, 29–30. "Community Teachers Support Civil Rights Congress," an article in the *Eastside Sun* (April 30, 1948), criticized the *Times* editorial, stating that Mexicans historically suffered police brutality. Grebler et al., *The Mexican-American People*, 533. Laura L. Cummings, "Cloth-Wrapped People, Trouble, and Power: Pachuco Culture in the Greater Southwest," *Journal of the Southwest* 45, No. 3 (Autumn 2003), 329–48. Arturo Madrid Barela, "In Search of the Authentic Pachuco—An Interpretive Essay, Part I," *Aztlan* 4, No. 1 (1973), 34–35.

79 Meza Buelna, "Resistance from the Margins," 83, 105, 132, 135. "Amigos de Wallace" rally, 1948, Lincoln Park Stadium(?), Los Angeles, University of Southern California, Digital Archive, http://digarc.usc.edu/search/controller/view/scl-m0276. Selected Works of Henry A. Wallace, New Deal Network, Franklin and Eleanor Roosevelt Institute, http://newdeal.feri.org/wallace/index.htm.

80 Perales, *Are We Good Neighbors?*, 81, 165–66, 166–67, 173–74, 178–79, 283–96.

81 Bill Dredge, "Machines and Men Bringing in Cotton," *Los Angeles Times* (November 18, 1948). W. K. Barger and Ernesto M. Reza, *The Farm Labor Movement in the Midwest: Social Change and Adaptation Among Migrant Farmworkers* (Austin: University of Texas Press, 1994), 21, map of migrant streams, http://www.illinoismigrant.org/farmwrk1.html. José Alamillo, *El Otro Norte: Latinos and Latinas in the Pacific Northwest: The Latinization of the Pacific Northwest*, Latinos in Northwest Project, http://www.josealamillo.com/latinos%20northwest.htm. "Mexican Americans in the Columbia Basin, Railroad and Migrant Workers," http://www.vancouver.wsu.edu/crbeha/ma/ma.htm#rail. Dennis Nodín Valdes, *Al Norte: Agricultural Workers in the Great Lakes Region, 1917 to 1970* (Austin: University of Texas Press, 1991).

82 Dennis Nodín Valdes, "Machine Politics in California Agriculture, 1945–1990s," *Pacific Historical Review* 63, No. 2 (May 1, 1994), 205. Ernesto Galarza, *Spiders in the House and Workers in the Field* (Notre Dame, IN: University of Notre Dame Press, 1970), 23–27, 35, 40–48, 64–66, 88, 153, 231–47, 288–97. John Phillip Carney, "Postwar Mexican Migration, 1945–1955,

with Particular Reference to the Policies and Practices of the United States Concerning Its Control" (PhD Dissertation, University of Southern California, 1957), 157. Ernesto Galarza, *Farmworkers and Agribusiness in California, 1947–1960* (Notre Dame: University of Notre Dame Press, 1977), 99, 100, 103. National Advisory Committee on Farm Labor, *Farm Labor Organizing, 1905–1967: A Brief History* (New York: National Advisory Committee on Farm Labor, 1967), 37. Sam Kushner, *Long Road to Delano* (New York: International Publishers, 1975), 82. D. Gutiérrez, *Walls and Mirrors*, 155–60. Rosales, *Chicano!*, 119–20. Ernesto Galarza Commemorative Lectures, Stanford University, http://www.stanford.edu/dept/csre/PUBL_galarza.htm.

83. Javier Flores Carrera y Jorge Alejandro Sosa Hernández, Alianza Nacional de Braceros, Centro de Tabajadores Agricolas, El Paso, Texas, Bracero 1 De 7 Documental Programa Bracero, a seven part series in Spanish. Excellent, http://www.youtube.com/watch?v=6l5fuTEpOeQ&feature=PlayList&p=D5DCDF858D4E313E&index=6. Ramón Rentería, "UTEP Works to Recover History of Braceros: Workers Helped Fill Void During WWII," *El Paso Times* (January 28, 2003). Braceros Resources in the OSU [Oregon State University] Libraries Collections, Photograph Collection, http://digitalcollections.library.oregonstate.edu/cdm4/client/bracero/related.php.

84. George O. Coalson, *The Development of the Migratory Farm Labor System in Texas: 1900–1954* (San Francisco, CA: R&E Research Associates, 1977), 67, 82, 94. Mark Reisler, *By the Sweat of Their Brow: Mexican Immigration to the United States, 1900–1940* (Westport, CT: Greenwood Press, 1976), 260. Ernesto Galarza, *Merchants of Labor* (Santa Barbara, CA: McNally & Lottin, 1964), 47. Richard B. Craig, *The Bracero Program* (Austin: University of Texas Press, 1971), 36, 54, 58–59, 104, 107, 109, 112, 119, 198. D. Gutiérrez, *Walls and Mirrors*, 143; according to D. Gutiérrez, 154–55, LULAC was among the foremost opponents of the *bracero* program and the use of undocumented labor. Henry Anderson, *The Bracero Program in California* (Berkeley: School of Public Health, University of California, July 1961), 146. Erasmo Gamboa, "Under the Thumb of Agriculture: Bracero and Mexican American Workers in the Pacific Northwest" (PhD Dissertation, University of Washington, 1984), 24–26. Patricia Morgan, *Shame of a Nation* (Los Angeles: Committee for the Protection of Foreign Born, 1954), 28. Ernesto Galarza, *Tragedy at Chualar: El Crucero de las Treinta y dos Cruces* (Santa Barbara, CA: McNally & Loftin, 1977). The American Committee for the Protection of the Foreign Born, *Our Badge of Infamy*, A Petition to the United Nations on the Treatment of the Mexican Immigrant (April 1959), 24. Lily Rothman. "Long-Lost Photos Reveal Life of Mexican Migrant Workers in 1950s America," *Time*, Apr. 11, 2017, http://time.com/4711867/bracero-program-sid-avery/.

85. Nodín Valdes, *Al Norte*. 89–117, quote on 116.
86. Erasmo Gamboa, *Mexican Labor and World War II: Braceros in the Pacific Northwest, 1942–1947* (Seattle: University of Washington Press, 1999), viii.
87. Gregory W. Hill, *Texas-Mexican Migratory Agricultural Workers in Wisconsin*, Agricultural Experimental Station Stencil Bulletin 6 (Madison: University of Wisconsin, 1948), 5–6, 15–16, 18–20. Coalson, *The Development of the Migratory Farm Labor*, 110. Kibbe, *Latin Americans in Texas*, 199–200. Richard W. Slatta, "Chicanos in the Pacific Northwest: An Historical Overview of Chicanos," *Aztlán* 6, No. 3 (Fall 1975), 327. Erasmo Gamboa, "Chicanos in the Northwest: An Historical Perspective," *El Grito* 7, No. 4 (Summer 1973), 61–63. Everett Ross Clinchy, Jr., *Equality of Opportunity for Latin-Americans in Texas* (New York: Arno Press, 1974), 87.
88. Douglas E. Foley, Clarice Mota, Donald E. Post, and Ignacio Lozano, *From Peons to Politicos: Ethnic Relations in a South Texas Town, 1900–1977* (Austin: University of Texas, Center for Mexican American Studies, 1977), 75, 85–86, 89. Kibbe, *Latin Americans in Texas*, 153, 160–63, 169. Landolt, *The Mexican-American Workers*, 117. Coalson, *The Development of the Migratory Farm Labor*, 87–88, 100–02, 107.
89. Victoria-María MacDonald, "Demanding their Rights: The Latino Struggle for Educational Access and Equity," National Park Service, https://www.nps.gov/heritageinitiatives/latino/latinothemestudy/education.htm.
90. Chapter 10, "Education - Census Bureau," U.S. Census Bureau, https://www.census.gov/population/www/cen2000/censusatlas/pdf/10_Education.pdf. Barbara Schneider, Sylvia Martinez, and Ann Owens, "Barriers to Educational Opportunities for Hispanics in the United States," *Hispanics and the Future of America* (Washington, DC: The National Academies Press, 2006), https://www.ncbi.nlm.nih.gov/books/NBK19909/.
91. Rodolfo F. Acuña, *The Making of Chicana/o Studies: In the Trenches of Academe* (New Brunswick, NJ: Rutgers University Press, 2011), 10.

Chapter 12
"Happy Days": Mexican American Communities under Siege

Learning Objectives

12.1 Describe how the 1950s resembled the 1920s.

12.2 Explain how American obsession to control the world social order impacted Mexican Americans through domestic policies and the Korean War.

12.3 Analyze how the interventionist policies and domestic attacks on Mexican American communities are inter-related.

12.4 Analyze the relationship between education and political empowerment for Mexican Americans and other people of color in the 1950s.

12.5 Contextualize the Mexican American struggle for civil rights in the 1950s in relation to the growing numbers of Mexicans and slight improvements in education.

12.6 Evaluate the impact of suburbanization and urban renewal on housing and education.

12.7 Explain why the successful launch of *Sputnik* shook U.S. education.

In the first edition of *Occupied America* (1972) I wrote,

> The 1950s presented an enigma. Many Anglo-Americans tend to associate the decade with President Dwight D. Eisenhower and, therefore, have concluded that it was a period of stability during which nothing much happened. To Chicanos, the 1950s represented a "decade of defense," a decade in which the proponents of reaction attempted to crush the rising aspirations for liberation by overtly intimidating them.[1]

For years, the statement that the 1950s was a "decade of defense"—a decade when not much happened—stuck in my throat. I was wrong and I could not defend it. To test the hypothesis, I microfilmed the articles in the *Eastside Sun* and the *Belvedere Citizen* that serviced the unincorporated area of East Los Angeles year by year from 1933 to 1975.[2] I then synthesized the articles on 5×8 cards, and lined them up using a timeline and asked, "What were the causes and effects?" From this exercise, I learned that the decade of the 1950s was extremely important and eventful: just like the 1920s, it was a decade when American corporations sought to take control of government and expanded their Empire.

On January 17, 1961 President Dwight Eisenhower after playing the policeman of the world, left office and in his farewell address warned the nation of the growing "military–industrial–congressional complex."[3] Through lobbyists, the military and industrial sectors were buying off congressional representatives. By exploiting the growing number of lobbyists, Republicans under the cover of getting rid the country of subversives targeted the social network of the New Deal.

During the decade, government funded transportation and housing and promoted the bulldozing and destruction of minority communities making huge profits for developers. The "economic royalists," as Franklin Roosevelt called them, used racism, nativism, the shrewdness of Sen. Joseph McCarthy, and the Cold War to obfuscate class interests to quietly favor the rich. Their surrogates in Congress led the attacks on New Deal programs using anti-Communism as a smoke screen. The times were a period of relative calm compared to the 1940s or '60s. The Korean War (1950–1953) also heightened the Red Scare, and many white Americans became unnerved and wanted to rid the United States of an enemy from within. The leader of the anti-Communist propaganda was Senator McCarthy from Wisconsin. In February 1950, Senaator McCarthy and his Senate Committee presented an alleged list of Communist Party members or Communist dupes working in the State Department that attracted considerable press.

The 1950s saw the advent of a new global economy led by the United States Developed market economies grew between 1950 and 1973, averaging an annual real GDP growth of around 5 percent. "World War II left the United States in a uniquely powerful position." Europe and Asia experienced extensive destruction and loss of life. The United States was left untouched with factories ready to lead the new global economy and make huge profits.[4]

Globalization contributed to dramatic changes in the workforce as American corporation prepared to out source industrial jobs and bank to invest in foreign producers. Domestically more service and light industry workers became essential to the workplace. The United States transitioned from a manufacturing economy to a service economy. By 1956 a majority of workers held white-collar employment that included professional, managerial, and administrative jobs. Automation played a role but so did government policy and corporate priorities. This marked the beginning of the end of a manufacturing-based economy to a industrial service economy. It brought an end to the promise of well-paying union jobs that had benefitted European immigrants. Advanced education was at a premium. Training for the new economy required at least a high school education from which Mexicans and other minorities were excluded because of racism and other factors.[5]

During the decade, Mexican migration to the United States began with increased vigor. Like in the past U.S. policy and the needs of American enterprises managed the migration. In 1956, the rate of incoming undocumented entrants rose from 6,372 in 1951 to over 65,000 annually. In the 1950s almost 293,500 entered the United States. These figures do not tell the entire story, for many thousands of *braceros* and mojados [pejorative term meaning "wetbacks"] lived in the United States. The *braceros* were farm laborers who worked under a contract for a short period (i.e., one season) and the return to Mexico. The mojados as they pejoratively undocumented entrants some stereotyped as having swam the Rio Grande to enter the United States.

Meanwhile, by the early 1950s, the Black Civil Rights movement picked up steam. The Black numbers and the Black churches and culture refreshed the memory of many Americans. This energy contributed to a political maturity among Mexican Americans. Out of 179,323,175 Americans, Blacks accounted for 18,871,831 over 10 percent. Moreover, large numbers of Blacks were now in big cities with the concentration adding to a sense of power. Black Americans felt that their day had come.

Mexican Americans

12.1 Describe how the 1950s resembled the 1920s.

Mexicans and Mexican Americans continued to live primarily in the five southwestern states of Texas, New Mexico, Colorado, Arizona, and California in 1950. Officially, fewer than three million Spanish-surname residents lived in the region, about 11 percent of all south westerners. Over two-thirds of Mexican Americans lived in cities. In California, three-quarters of the Mexican-origin population lived in cities, and in Texas, slightly more than two-thirds.[6] The major urban centers were Los Angeles, El Paso, and San Antonio; however, large concentrations also lived in the Lower Rio Grande Valley, the Salt and Gila Valleys of Arizona, and Fresno County, California. Most Mexicans were young with a median age of 20.6, versus 31.6 for whites and 27.3 for non-whites.[7]

The median years of schooling of Mexican Americans in the Southwest was 5.2, compared with 11.3 for white Americans and 7.8 for non-whites. In Texas, the median was 3.5; in Arizona, 6.0; in California, 7.8; in Colorado, 6.5; and in New Mexico, 6.1. The median was higher in the cities: for example, in Tucson the education median was 6.5 years; Los Angeles, 8.2; and Albuquerque, 7.7. In El Paso, it was 5.2 and in Lubbock, Texas, only 1.7. A rule of thumb was that the lower the median age, the more segregated the schools were and the poorer the community.

The first- and second-generation Mexicans comprised a large percentage of the total Spanish-speaking population. According to the 1950 U.S. Census, less than 83 percent of the Spanish-speaking population was native-born, with some 17 percent of all Spanish-surname persons born in Mexico or Latin America. Again, the figures varied from state to state, with New Mexico and Colorado having the highest native-born populations—87.2 percent and 83.2 percent, respectively—as well as the smallest Mexico-born population—3.9 and 4.2 percent, respectively. Throughout the decade, the birth rate among Mexican-origin people was 4.1 percent, versus 3.1 percent for white Americans and 3.3 for the total population.

Mexican Americans were a people on the move. Between 1955 and 1960, close to 60 percent of the interstate movers went to California; 17 percent went to Texas. During the 1950s, the percentage of Mexicans in Texas fell sharply from 45 percent to 36 percent; in California it went up from 34 to 42 percent. Arizona's and New Mexico's Mexican population declined slightly, whereas in Illinois the population of Mexican immigrants grew—nearly all in the Chicago area. Mexicans developed regional differences: Tejanos, for example, wore boots and cowboy hats and spoke English with a Texas twang, saying "Y'all" and calling men "Sir!" Everyone seemed to want to move out of Texas during that time—the state was the principal exporter of Mexican workers to other regions. Still, many Mexican Americans who lived in the Midwest yearned for the sounds of the accordion or the warmth of the sun. In Chicago, Mexicans lived in brownstone houses that had no front lawns and always seemed cold. Perhaps because of their isolation, Midwestern Mexican Americans appeared to be more Mexican than Mexicans elsewhere. In New Mexico,

New Mexicans protested that they were not Mexicans, but "Spanish Americans," and lived under the illusion that *they* were the founders of the state. Since Californians did not have a set identity, Californian Mexicans seemed.

A layering of Mexican American generations was apparent with an increased growth of the second generation. There was less use of Spanish and the growth of *pochos*—who did not speak Spanish well and were more assimilated than earlier generations. Pocho was a pejorative term that meant discolored or faded, or a fruit that never ripens. They were brown gringos to some Mexicans. It was divisive, however, there were exceptions, and whether Mexican Americans spoke fluent Spanish depended on where people lived what generation they were.[8]

The Cold War

12.2 Explain how American obsession to control the world social order impacted Mexican Americans through domestic policies and the Korean War.

By the end of 1949, reversals in the Cold War intensified American angst, and Communism became the country's Number One fear. Consequently, the 1950s saw the rise of McCarthyism and the escalation of the Cold War, at home and abroad. Cold War anxieties agitated a Red Scare that peaked from 1946 to 1952. Red hunters such as FBI director J. Edgar Hoover exaggerated the danger of a monolithic, worldwide conspiracy directed from Moscow. The presidential Loyalty Review Board encouraged purges of "reds" in the unions, universities, and entertainment industry. The Korean War saw the revival of the military draft, and the war became a justification for the battle against Communism. The Alien Registration Act (the Smith Act) in June 1940 required all adult non-citizens to register with the U.S. government and made it criminal offense for anyone to advocate, abet, or teach the desirability of overthrowing the government, or to be a member of a group devoted to such advocacy.[9] Using the Smith Act, the federal government prosecuted Communist Party and the Socialist Workers Party leaders, most of whom did not support violence. By the early 1950s, Republican politicians such as Richard Nixon and Joseph McCarthy and Democrats such as white nationalist Senator Pat McCarran played on this hysteria to boost their careers and advance their economic imperialist ideology.[10]

The Korean War: Historical Amnesia

It is inaccurate to call the Korean War the "Forgotten War." Some 33,665 U.S. military personnel were killed in action and 3,275 died from non-hostile causes. Some 92,134 were wounded in action, and from June 25, 1950, to July 27, 1953, 1,789,000 served in the Korean theater. The Korean conflict began in June 1950 between the Democratic People's Republic of Korea (North Korea) and the Republic of Korea (South Korea). An estimated three million people lost their lives in this war, which was not officially called a war in the United States but a "conflict." The United States joined the war on the side of the South Koreans. The People's Republic of China (PRC), which had been established just two years earlier, eventually came to Communist North Korea's aid.

The North Korean forces overwhelmed the South Korean army; the latter rushed four ill-equipped and ill-trained United Nations (UN) divisions into the battle. The UN forces were driven southward. Reinforcements led by General Douglas MacArthur turned the tide for the South Koreans. As the Allied forces advanced northward to the 38th parallel, which was the dividing line between North Korea and South Korea, China warned of retaliatory action, fearing that the presence of UN forces in North Korea would be a threat to the security of China. The UN forces, however, ignored the warnings and crossed the 38th parallel into North Korea with the expressed purpose of "unifying" North and South Korea.

In November 1950, China entered the war and approximately 180,000 Chinese troops drove the Allied troops southward. For the next two and a half years, both sides fought a bloody trench-and-guerrilla war. Many people feared the possibility of a global conflict. The heavy casualties and reports of South Korean atrocities made the war unpopular back home in the United States. Opposition to the war started slowly and then expanded, much like with the more recent war in Iraq. The war ended in July 1953, when the United States declared an armistice. The importance of the war globally was that it established a precedent for U.S. intervention to contain the so-called Communist expansion.

Six Mexican Americans won Medals of Honor during "this conflict." Eugene A. Obregón, 20, from Los Angeles, enlisted in the Marine Corps at the age of 17. Obregón was killed while saving a fellow marine's life. Joseph C. Rodríguez from San Bernardino, California and Rodolfo P. Hernández, from nearby Colton, California, were awarded Medals of Honor. Edward Gómez, 19, from Omaha, Nebraska, Ambrosio Guillén, 24, from La Junta, Colorado, and Benito Martínez from Hancock, Texas, were posthumously awarded Medals of Honor.

According to anthropologist Carlos Vélez-Ibáñez, a Korean War veteran, "The disproportion of Mexicans fighting and dying in wars continued through Korea and Vietnam." Company E of the 13th Infantry Battalion, U.S. Marine Corps Reserve of Tucson, Arizona, for example, was composed of 237 men, 80 percent of them Mexicans, when the Company was called to active duty on July 31, 1950. Two months later, Company E landed as part of an invasion force in Inchon, Korea. The U.S. Marines shipped these young Mexicans and others overseas with a scant two to three weeks of training, teaching them how to fire M-1 rifles and machine guns aboard ship and giving them only another two weeks of basic training in Japan. Ten of the 231 *Tucsonense* Mexican Americans who fought in Korea lost their lives.[11]

The draft maintained the armed forces throughout the Cold War. College deferments were available during most of the Korean War and sometimes led to draft avoidance. These deferments were beyond the reach of most Mexican Americans. The Educational Testing Service of Princeton, New Jersey, developed a nationwide Selective Service College Qualification Test for deferring draftees based on test scores. The Testing Service administered the test to college students and potential college students in the spring of 1951. It sent test scores to the students' local draft board along with their class standing. The Selective Service System drafted 1.5 million men during the Korean War; 1.3 million volunteered—mostly in the Navy and Air Force. Again, education was a litmus test for admission into the "safer" military branches. It was a vicious circle: U.S.-born Mexicans had to go into the army because of a lack of education and then they could not take advantage of the education stipends of the G.I. Bill, again because of a lack of education.[12]

The Empire Strikes

12.3 Analyze how the interventionist policies and domestic attacks on Mexican American communities are inter-related.

During the Cold War, it was common for the United States to talk about satellite countries within the Soviet Union's "sphere of influence," meaning that they were subsidiary states that were de facto Soviet colonies. In reality, all superpowers have spheres of influence and setting the altruistic rhetoric aside, the United States was no better than other colonial powers.

During the 1950s, U.S. foreign policy was more aggressive worldwide and the United States acted in its self-interest, which was allegedly based on national "security strategy." The government justified its aggression by claiming that it was saving the world from the horrors of Communism. Its true, overwhelming motivation was to neutralize the Russians and the Chinese as competing superpowers. In this pursuit, in August 1953, the CIA participated in the overthrow of democratically elected Premier Mohammed Mosaddeq and reinstated the Shah of Iran. It supported the Iranian military with financial assistance, and for the rest of the Cold War Iran was a U.S. client state.[13] The motive for the support was oil.

The next year, in 1954, the CIA overthrew Guatemalan President Jacobo Árbenz based on ideological grounds. Another factor was pressure from the United Fruit Company, which held monopoly over banana, on Allen Dulles, who was the director of the CIA and a board member of United Fruit. Allen Dulles was the brother of Secretary of State John Foster Dulles.[14] The United Fruit Company owned 42 percent of the land in Guatemala and was exempt from all taxes and duties on both imports and exports. Fifty-seven years after the coup, Guatemalan President Alvaro Colom apologized to Árbenz's son for what he called a "great crime." The admission awakened Latin Americans and put the Western Hemisphere on notice that the Colossus of the North lived, and the resolve of Latin American societies to break their dependence on the United States.

Hostilities toward Guatemalan plans to redistribute land intensified American Cold War politics. President Harry S. Truman sought to contain Communism, whereas President Dwight Eisenhower took direct action in Latin America. His policies went from containment of Communism to active intervention supposedly to defend American interests abroad. The overthrow of Árbenz and imposition of dictator Armas sent a clear warning to Russia that America would not tolerate the spread of Communism in the Western Hemisphere, and invoked the Monroe Doctrine. The leader of the military coup, Carlos Castillo Armas, promoted American interests in Guatemala and launched a reign of terror in the nation and in Central America, setting the stage for further U.S. intervention in in Central America through covert operations.[15]

Keeping America White

Post–World War II saw the Cold War that fueled a racist nativism, declare another kind of war on the foreign-born. History tells us that every time conservatives did not get their way or if something goes wrong they create a diversion and blamed non-white people and radicals or Labor activists. In 1933, Roger Baldwin of the ACLU and others organized the American Committee for Protection of Foreign Born (ACPFB) to defend the constitutional rights of the foreign-born. When the government accused labor activists such as Harry Bridges, later president of the International Longshoremen's and Warehousemen's Union, of being a Communist and tried to deport him in 1939, 1941, 1948 and again in 1953, the ACPFB successfully defended him.[16] After World War II, the ACPFB, along with the United Electrical, Radio, and Machine Workers Union continued the struggle for the defense of the foreign-born. Super patriots renewed their attacked on the ACPFB and trade unions, accusing them of being Communist-front organizations.[17]

The Los Angeles Committee for Protection of Foreign Born (LACPFB) defended Mexican Americans against deportations in the late 1940s and 1950s.[18] Within the Mexican American community, the Civil Rights Congress (CRC), the Independent Progressive Party (IPP), the *Asociación Nacional México-Americana* (ANMA), and the Community Service Organization (CSO)[19] also participated in the defense of the foreign-born throughout the 1950s.

ACPFB leader Isabel González of Denver spoke against injustices Mexican Americans suffered. In the mid-1940s, she defended the rights of Mexican sugar beet workers, and later she served as ANMA's vice president. In Denver, González was executive secretary of the Committee to Organize the Mexican People. She presented her epic paper "Step Children of a Nation" at the 1947 Convention of the Committee for the Protection of the Foreign Born in Cleveland Ohio; it was published that same year. Aside from reporting on the oppression of U.S. Mexicans, she described the efforts of the Committee on behalf of Refugio Ramón Martínez of the United Packing Workers of America,[20] and Nicaraguan-born Humberto Silex of El Paso, former regional director of the International Union of Mine, Mill, and Smelter Workers of America.[21] They had entered the country legally and had U.S.-born children, yet deportation proceedings were brought against both—based on political grounds.[22] Because Luisa Moreno refused to cooperate with the House Un-American Activities Committee, her application for citizenship was denied and she was later deported.[23]

By the late 1940s, the plight of World War II refugees and displaced persons encouraged many liberals to consider scrapping immigration quotas based on national origins. However, Democratic Senator Patrick A. McCarran of Nevada, who fashioned himself as the protector of the nation's racial purity, saw the admission of any number of foreigners as a threat. He therefore sponsored the Internal Security Act of 1950, also known as the Subversive Activities Control Act of 1950 or the McCarran Act that gave government broad powers, with which they could harass and deport foreign-born union activists joined McCarran and co-sponsored the Act to tighten immigration laws and to arbitrarily exclude the "subversive elements".[24] The bill required "communist front" organizations to register with the Justice Department. President Harry Truman vetoed the bill, but Congress overrode Truman's veto.

McCarran–Walter Act was passed in 1952 during the heat of the Korean War. It upheld the national origins quota system established by the Immigration Act of 1924, and also from immigrating to the United States ended the exclusion of Asians. It gave government broad discretionary powers, with which it could harass and deport foreign-born union activists.

Title I of the McCarran Act established a Subversive Activities Control Board to investigate subversion in the United States. The Act was known as the government built six internment camps Title II authorized construction of concentration camps to intern suspected subversives without a trial or hearing if either the president or Congress declared a national emergency. In 1952, the government designated future sites for six internment camps. Despite the draconian nature of the law, few groups protested it, and it was largely through the efforts of the Japanese American Citizens League that the courts abolished Title II in the 1970s.

The 1952 McCarran-Walter Act made some reforms that included a long list of grounds for the deportation or exclusion of aliens; for example, it allowed the denaturalization of naturalized citizens. It gave the Immigration and Naturalization Service (INS) the authority to interrogate so-called aliens suspected of being in the country "illegally." The immigration service could search boats, trains, cars, trucks, or planes and enter and search private lands within 25 miles of the border. President Harry S. Truman opined that the law created a group of second-class citizens; it distinguished between native and naturalized citizens. Truman also objected to the revocation of the citizenship of naturalized citizens for political reasons.

The 1952 Act eliminated the statutes of limitation for foreigners who had been members of a so-called subversive organization, and gave government the authority to deport foreigners even for minor technical infractions. The Commission on Immigration and Naturalization, appointed by President Truman in 1952, criticized the Act as unconstitutional because foreigners could be convicted of crimes—actions that were not crimes at the time of their occurrence. Indeed, the Internal Security and the McCarran–Walter Acts led to gross violations of human rights. The purpose was transparent—to bust unions and intimidate activists.

For example Humberto Silex faced deportation in 1946 and in 1952 deportation proceedings were brought against him. Silex had entered the country legally and served in the armed forces. He organized Local 509 of the United Mine, Mill, and Smelter Workers Union of El Paso at American Smelting and Refining Company in 1938. In 1945, Silex got into a fistfight for which he was arrested and fined $35; the following year, Silex faced deportation proceedings on grounds of "moral turpitude." Although Silex won the case, the court banned him from union organizing.

In 1954, the LACPFB reported that, of the Mexican Americans it defended on deportation charges, seven had lived in the country for more than seven years, three for more than 20 years, and three others for more than 30 years; 17 had U.S.-born children and grandchildren; and 22 were trade unionists. Tobias Navarrete entered the United States in 1927. Married and with eight U.S.-born children, he had served in the armed forces. From 1936 to 1938, he was a member of the Workers Alliance. The INS alleged that he was a member of the Communist Party. A paid informant who faced deportation testified that he saw Navarrete at two Communist Party meetings and a rally. After a long battle, Navarrete won his case and continued to work in Boyle Heights as a jeweler and watch repairer. He died in April 1964.

Victims of the McCarran–Walter Act waited years for final resolution of their cases. After seven years, in a 5–4 decision, the U.S. Supreme Court absolved José Gastélum in 1963 of charges that would have deported him. The LACPFB defended Gastélum. Organizations such as the American Civil Liberties Union (ACLU) committed resources to fighting these violations of human rights, and the Community Service Organization (CSO) in Los Angeles extended free legal services to anyone whose human rights were violated by immigration policies.[25]

Militarization of the Immigration and Naturalization Service

Several factors during the 1940s and 1950s contributed to the mass migration of Mexicans to the north. Improved transportation eased flow from the interior. In 1940, all-weather roads covered about 2,000 miles; by 1950, the figure increased to nearly 15,000 miles. In addition, there were 15,000 miles of railroad lines. The population of Mexico grew by 2.7 percent per annum between 1940 and 1950, and by 3.1 percent per annum between 1950 and 1960. In 1950 there were 27 million Mexicans in Mexico; 10 years later, 35 million. Cotton production on the Mexican side of the border, especially around Matamoros, gave employment to workers from the interior. Like their counterparts in the United States, Mexican growers advertised for more workers than they needed; thus, many who had migrated from the interior but were unable to find employment continued their journey northward across the border to find work in the cotton fields of the Rio Grande Valley of Texas.

Furthermore, the INS intentionally left the border open at the direction of growers. It rarely rounded up undocumented workers during harvest time, and instructed its agents to stop searches and deportations until after the picking season. When sufficient numbers of *braceros* or domestic laborers worked cheaply, agents enforced the laws; when a labor shortage occurred, they opened the border's doors, disregarding both international and moral law. Finally, recessions such as that of 1949 resulted in massive roundups of undocumented workers. When the Korean War caused a labor shortage, the U.S. unilaterally opened the border; during the 1953–1955 recession that followed the war, the U.S. unilaterally closed it. Newspapers called for the exclusion of the undocumented workers, whom they portrayed as dangerous, malicious, and subversive. Even liberal Democrats supported the border patrol, calling for fines on employers who hired these workers, as did the Mexican government and most Mexican American organizations. This erratic U.S. policy brought hundreds of thousands of *braceros* into the country annually, then kicked them out when the economy slowed, turning the border into a revolving door.[26]

President Dwight Eisenhower's attorney general, Herbert Brownell, initially opposed additional appropriations for the border patrol. However, pressured by Ike, Brownell toured the border, after which he reconsidered and called for increased appropriations for the border patrol and for tougher laws. At the urging of Eisenhower, Brownell became a hawk. His rhetoric, couched in military terms, grew hotter. He wanted to use the army to stem the "tide" by sending soldiers to the border, but army brass was cool to the idea. Ike then appointed Lieutenant General Joseph M. Swing to head the INS. His qualifications? He was a classmate of President Eisenhower at West Point, and was on General John Pershing's punitive expedition against Pancho Villa in 1916. Swing upgraded the border patrol with new equipment and smart, forest-green uniforms. He then launched "Operation Wetback," a military-style campaign to kick the Mexicans out. He requested millions of dollars to build a 150-mile-long fence, and set a deportation quota for each target area.

According to its press releases, from 1953 to 1955, the INS deported more than a million Mexicans annually. Through newspapers and the heavy presence of INS officers in the *barrios*, it spread terror. Most mainstream Mexican American organizations favored controlling undocumented immigration. They justified their excesses in the name of national security. University of Barcelona Professor Avi Astor made the point:

> Hispanic civic groups also partook in the use of securitizing rhetoric linking Mexican immigration to threats to internal security. The tenuousness of the relationship between Mexican Americans and Mexican immigrants has roots dating back to the nineteenth century. Up until the rise of the Chicano Movement and the civil rights struggles that took place during the 1960s and 1970s, the main strategy of Hispanic civic organizations was assimilationist. The goal was to become "white," rather than to gain acceptance as a national minority. Mexican Americans and long-term Mexican residents in the United States perceived the entry of poor Mexican peasants into the Southwest not only as a source of job competition, but also as a barrier to their full assimilation and acceptance in American society, as they were often poor, illiterate and unfamiliar with the cultural and linguistic norms of the United States.[27]

Mexican American organizations set the ideological tone for anti-immigrant campaigns of the 1950s.[28] At the same time, many on the left in the community were offended by the racist INS propaganda and the agency's violation of human rights. On October 15, 1953, Ralph Guzmán, a Mexican American activist, wrote, "A few weeks ago Herbert Brownell, the U.S. Attorney General, wanted to shoot wetbacks crossing into the U.S., but farmers, fearing the loss of a cheap labor market because of G.I. bullets, complained bitterly and Brownell changes [sic] his mind." Guzmán's charge was substantiated. In May 1954 William P. Allen, publisher of the *Laredo Times*, wrote to Eisenhower that Brownell asked for the support of labor leaders at a May 11 dinner if he shot the "wetbacks" down in cold blood.

ANMA was closely associated with progressive trade unions such as the Mine, Mill, and Smelter Workers and cooperated with the IPP and the ACPFB, and continuously criticized the INS raids. Meanwhile, Operation Wetback an immigration law enforcement initiative, spread fear that supposedly ended the immigration flow. ANMA laid the foundation for today's pro-immigration movement. Meanwhile, improvements in the U.S. economy accelerated the northward movement of Mexicans.[29]

The abuse of human rights of the foreign-born was so blatant that on April 17, 1959, a group of progressive organizations and individuals presented a petition to the United Nations, charging violations of the Universal Declaration of Human Rights. It was adopted in 1948; the U.S. government was censored for the mistreatment of Mexican immigrants. San Antonio Archbishop Robert E. Lucey in the preface to the petition wrote, "And so the poor bracero, compelled by force and fear, will endure any kind of injustice and exploitation to gain a few dollars that he needs so desperately." The report recalled the military-style sweeps of the mid-1950s that kept Mexicans in "a state of permanent insecurity," subjecting them to "raids, arrests, and deportation drives."[30]

The Diaspora: An American Odyssey

As the Mexican centers of population in the Southwest swelled, they fanned out to the north, west, and east in search of other opportunities. White Americans considered Mexican Americans, especially migrants, to be foreigners—even though 90 percent of the children were born in the United States. In the case of New Mexico and Colorado migrants, U.S. nativity went as far back as their great-grandparents. The story of the Gallegos family is typical. Originally, from the New Mexican highlands, the family moved in the 1930s to the valley called Amalia, part of the Sangre de Cristo land grant of the 1870s. The family tried farming, working in sugar beets, but were nudged out by farm barons.

During the 1950s, the Gallegos family worked on farms from Colorado to Washington. Mechanization hit the crops that needed the least care in handling, such as sugar beets and potatoes, and other crops in which Mexicans and Mexican Americans were concentrated. The Gallegos family travelled from place to place on recommendations of friends, finally settling in the Yakima Valley in Washington, one of the 10 most productive valleys in the United States.

The Gallegos family continually suffered discrimination. In Odessa, Texas, Mexicans were not allowed in motels, and restaurants denied them service. In Prosser in the Yakima Valley, proprietors allowed Mexicans into the theater only on Sundays. During the week, cops harassed Mexicans in the town. As other Mexican families poured into the area from Colorado, the Midwest, and Texas, a sense of community began to form in the Yakima, although many still longed for home. This homesickness would change with the birth of offspring in the Yakima.[31]

Texas played a central role in dispersing Mexicans throughout the United States. Some call the migration the accordion trail. Frequently students throughout the Midwest where I was often a guest speaker would ask me to recommend a Chicano band. After I would give them names of some of my favorites they would apologetically ask, "Do they have an accordion?"

The migrant stream began annually from South Texas. Following the crops the migrants would drop off for the winter in places like Madison, Wisconsin, Chicago, and other cities. Some found permanent employment and build colonias. A good portion returned to Texas to visit friends and relatives. In this way, they renewed their culture. Music was one of the experiences that Mexican and Tex Mex music anything with an accordion the stream along transported to cafes, mom and dad stores and cantinas. Nostalgia often gripped the migrants who filled coffee cans with *Yerba buena* and geranium plants.

This stream was extremely important in the forming of a national Chicana/o community and provided militant leaders and ideas. The migrant stream played a huge role in maintaining unity between Texas and the Midwest and North during the 1960s.

The Cities The 1950 U.S. Census still had a difficult time saying "Mexican-origin." Some 83 percent of Mexicans were native-born or naturalized American citizens. Some 16 percent were not born in the United States. Yet 55 percent still had one or both parents born in Mexico. A large portion of U.S. Mexicans lived outside the evolving *barrios* of El Paso, San Antonio, Los Angeles, and Chicago. Large numbers resided in Brownsville, Corpus Christi, Laredo, Albuquerque, Phoenix, San Diego, and San Francisco. Outside this Southwest belt, they resided in sizable numbers in Kansas City, Detroit, and Milwaukee. By 1960, the vast migrations from Texas gave Illinois a Mexican population larger than Colorado's and New Mexico's combined.[32]

EL PASO: IN SEARCH OF A HOME By the 1950s, El Paso Mexicans no longer lived exclusively in Chihuahuita or its neighboring El Segundo Barrio, the oldest *barrios* in the city. The Alamito housing projects warehoused 2.3 percent of the Southside neighborhood's housing. Landlords fought the construction of more public housing because federal grants brought stricter oversight in the form of more rigid housing codes. The El Segundo Barrio, or the "Second Ward," home to the poorest of the poor, deteriorated to the point that the military brass at Fort Bliss complained.[33]

The lack of decent housing continued to be a major problem. Only 5 percent of the families had showers; 3 percent had tubs. The average number of people per toilet was 71. A 1948 survey of South El Paso reported a population of 23,000. The area housed slightly more than 19 percent of the city's population, yet it registered just over 88 percent of its juvenile crime, 51 percent of its adult crime, and two-thirds of its infant mortality. Not surprisingly, poverty pushed up street crime. The El Paso press meanwhile blamed the victims and depicted Mexicans as murderers, drug users, and rapists. Conditions became so bad that, without the intervention of church agencies and local Mexican American organizations, the Second Ward would have self-destructed.

Between World War II and the Korean War, availability of low-interest federal housing loans to veterans accelerated their movement to the suburbs. Federal funding also expedited highway construction. The Paisano Drive highway (1947), intended to improve transportation to the central city business district, displaced 750 families—6,000 residents of the Second Ward. The highway further isolated South El Paso, causing a "shanty" boom—with *jacales* (shacks) made of plywood, sheet metal, and cardboard replacing former homes.[34]

San Antonio   The 1950 U.S. Census showed that San Antonio Mexicans continued to suffer from a lack of education; less than half had gone beyond the fifth grade. Less than 10 percent finished high school, and less than 1 percent completed college. Their limited education checked the Mexicans' upward mobility during a time of prosperity for most white Americans. The state's right-to-work law also hindered the Mexicans' advance in occupational status. Mexicans mostly belonged to pick-and-shovel unions—for instance, Mexicans comprised almost 100 percent of the hod carriers and 90 percent of the plasterers. They made up 6 percent of the electricians and just over 10 percent of the cement masons. And San Antonio unions were weak; thus, wages were lower than in California.

Many Mexicans lived in floorless shacks without plumbing, sewage connections, or electricity. Open shallow wells—sources of water used for drinking and washing—were next to outside toilets. During World War II, San Antonio had the distinction of having the highest tuberculosis death rate of any large city in the country—a distinction that San Antonio undoubtedly kept into the postwar era. After the war, with the return of thousands of Mexican American veterans, the conditions of overcrowded housing and unpaved streets and sidewalks only worsened.

The rapid economic growth brought about by the war and increased government spending in San Antonio attracted South Texans to the Alamo City. Highly segregated, Mexicans lived mostly on the West Side. (Blacks resided on the East, lower- and middle-class whites on the South, and middle- and upper-class whites on the North Side.) Movement out of the *barrio* was infrequent. The lack of unionization and the size of the reserve labor pool further worsened conditions. By design, San Antonio attracted light industry, keeping heavy industry and unions out of the city. During the 1940s, civilian jobs at the military installations helped the population grow from 253,854 to just fewer than 410,000. As in other U.S. cities, some San Antonians moved to the suburbs; the building of highways displaced the poorest residents. In turn, however, new housing meant jobs, as did the upswing in highway and airport construction.

The San Antonio Mexican population climbed from 160,420 in 1950 to 243,627 (out of a total of 587,718) by the end of the decade. In 1959, San Antonio ranked second only to Los Angeles in the number of Mexicans. Its first and second generations increased from 30,299 to 75,590 during this span. Over a quarter of the Mexican women worked outside the home, primarily in garment and electronic factories and as domestics and civil servants. Mexican employment in the military installations tripled during World War II, and by the 1950s, a small core of Mexicans moved into supervisory and technical positions. Access to jobs was often gained through the intervention of sympathetic elected officials.[35]

Los Angeles   California's Mexican population of 760,453 in 1950 trailed that of Texas, which numbered over a million. Californian Mexicans were the most urbanized in the Southwest, making Los Angeles their favorite destination in California. Los Angeles differed structurally from San Antonio. The majority of Mexicans did not live in one *barrio*; instead, enclaves dotted the entire Los Angeles basin.

The G.I. Bill encouraged the suburbanization of the Mexican American middle class. Like other Angeleños, Mexicans followed the freeways. Much of the internal migration was toward the east from East Los Angeles, following Interstate 10 (the San Bernardino Freeway) to new communities like Pico-Rivera, La Puente, and Covina. Many Mexicans remained in outlying localities such as Wilmington, San Pedro, Venice, San Fernando, and Pacoima, many of which were once agricultural colonias. Overall, Mexicans were not as isolated in Los Angeles as they were in Texas. Mexican neighborhoods such as Boyle Heights were more polyglot ethnically and racially, with Japanese, Jews, Armenians, and others living close to each other. Intermarriage also increased dramatically after the war.[36]

Politically, Mexican Americans in Los Angeles predominantly voted for Democrats and the party took them for granted. Politicos gerrymandered their districts, not so much to keep Mexicans powerless as to maintain their incumbents in office. Liberal incumbents benefited from this manipulation of electoral districts. Unlike the San Antonio elite, the Los Angeles ruling class did not need a traditional political machine to stay in office. It was white power all the way, and this group made huge profits by promoting the development of West Los Angeles and the San Fernando Valley.

From 1940 to 1960, the freeway system expanded dramatically, accelerating suburbanization and degrading city centers in the process. To revive the downtown area, the power elite formed Greater Los Angeles Plans, Inc., which set three goals—to build a convention center, a sports arena, and a music center. This decision brought far-reaching consequences for minorities and the poor, since these projects encroached on living space. Until 1958, the downtown elite were entirely Republican; then the group expanded and supported "responsible" Democrats. Over the next few years, a committee of 25, based within the Chamber of Commerce, informally planned and controlled the future of Los Angeles. Few elites even bothered to think about the Mexican communities that would be displaced by "urban renewal."

Meanwhile, an important change took place in East Los Angeles that would impact succeeding generations of Mexican Americans. In January 1948, the new East Los Angeles College campus opened near Atlantic Boulevard and Floral Avenue; and in 1956, the Los Angeles State College campus opened on Los Angeles's East Side. The proximity of the two new campuses made higher education easier for working-class students. Unlike UCLA, the new campuses were more accessible to working students, and student fees were less than $10 a semester.[37]

Chicago   The repatriation of the 1930s reduced the official number of Mexicans in Chicago from 20,000 to 16,000. World War II revived the movement of Mexicans to Chicago From 1943 to 1945, the railroads imported some 15,000 *braceros*. During the decade, the Mexican population grew from 16,000 to 20,000 in the city and from 21,000 to 35,000 in the metropolitan area. By 1953, the INS estimated that about 100,000 Mexicans lived in Chicago, of whom 15,000 were, in the words of the INS, "wetbacks."

Several Mexican *barrios* were located close to places of employment, in small pockets throughout the Chicago area. Until the 1960s, many Mexicans lived in Back of the Yards; where the meatpackers' union helped them assimilate. Work in the stockyards was stable, and wages were higher than in other industries. As early as 1939, social activist Saul Alinsky organized the Back of the Yards Neighborhood Council that was made up of a network of Catholic Church groups.

South Chicago was on the south shore of Lake Michigan and was untouched by urban renewal. As the number of Mexican steelworkers increased during the 1950s, they formed the Mexican Community Committee, which focused on local issues. South Chicago Mexicans thrived economically in comparison to Mexican Americans in other sections of the city.

By the 1950s, the Mexican immigrant colonials in the communities of South Deering and South Chicago attracted new immigrants. Living near Serbian, Polish, Croatian, and other neighborhoods, Mexicans comprised roughly 24 percent of Deering's foreign-born population. A 1950s Chicago Commission on Human Relations report, recognizing the existence of inequality, stated that Mexicans "carry the badge of color which places them as a minority group." Mexicans were largely unwelcome in the Southside. In order to be accepted some Mexicans living in South Deering resisted the entry of African Americans. During the Trumbull Park Race Riots of 1953–1954, some Mexicans felt vulnerable and fought back while others refused to join the riots.[38]

By the end of the decade, Mexicans formed enclaves in other parts of Chicago as bulldozers uprooted older *barrios*. Urban renewal also displaced Mexicans in the Near Westside *barrio* of La Taylor during the decade, pushing them into the nearby Pilsen district.[39]

Education a National Mexican American Priority

In the 1950s, the Mexican American community had very few elected officials. Most were born and died Democrats. The memories of Franklin D. Roosevelt and the Civil Rights legislation of Harry Truman were still fresh in the 1950s. Soon, however, a radical postwar "turn to the right" dashed the high hopes of the New Deal and Fair Deal Organizations like LULAC and the American G.I. Forum tried to maintain non-partisan postures; however, most of its leadership and rank and file voted Democrat and they lacked national visibility and clout.[40]

It was not as if the "Sleeping Giant" suddenly awakened in the post–World War II era. Numbers mattered and Mexicans had not reached the point that they could disrupt. In each of the states, there were small associations that lobbied for quality education for Mexicans. Arizona and New Mexico both had rich histories of struggle for education reform. Since the 1910s, *La Alianza Hispano Americana* and *La Liga Protectora* lobbied for education reform and made proposals for bilingual education. In 1925, Mexican Americans filed a desegregation case against the Tempe School District. Adolfo Romo, whose four children attended the Eighth Street School, sued on the basis of race-based segregation. The district practiced de facto segregation, requiring all Mexican-origin children to attend the Eighth Street School "regardless of their educational attainment or ability to speak English" and white children to attend the Tenth Street School. The Maricopa County Superior Court found for Romo: The school district failed to meet the separate-but-equal test of *Plessy v. Ferguson*. Romo children qualified as members of the Caucasian race who had been unfairly segregated based on blood, descent, and nationality. It was the earliest known legal challenge to Mexican American educational segregation in the Southwest.[41]

In the 1930s a number of Mexican American youth were involved in the Mexican American Movement (MAM) that held conferences and advocated education for the community. The movement had strong ties with the Protestant community. A contingent attended Arizona State Teachers' College where, in 1937, Josephine and Rebecca Muñoz were among those forming Los Conquistadores, the first Mexican American club at ASU.

Most of the civil rights cases were filed in Texas. As early as 1910, parents in San Angelo, Texas boycotted the schools because of segregated facilities; in September of the following year, Tejanos convened El Primer Congreso Mexicanista, a conference that addressed educational reform. After World War II, awareness of educational reform increased and with the formation of LULAC, the Mexican-origin community sued local schools districts. This activity continued into the 1950s. Led by Mexican American attorney Gus García, they appeared before the U.S. Supreme Court. In 1947, the Ninth

Circuit Court of Appeals in the *ruling* of Mendez v. Westminster was the first ruling to hold that school segregation itself is unconstitutional and violates the Fourteenth Amendment.[42]

In the first seven years of the 1950s, Mexican Americans filed 15 school desegregation cases. Guadalupe San Miguel makes the point that the litigation strategy was implemented by an expanding Mexican American middle class that was conscious of its duty to protect the civil rights of the entire community. Education was foremost on their agenda as a strategy for this transformation. A priority was to end the policy of separate and unequal schools.[43]

Dr. George I. Sánchez collaborated in most of the cases. The professor, along with Texas attorney Gustavo C. García, worked with progressives such as Robert C. Eckhardt of Austin and A. L. Wirin of the Los Angeles Civil Liberties Union. García filed *Delgado v. Bastrop ISD* (1948), the decision of which made illegal the segregation of children of Mexican descent in Texas. García played a leading role in revising the 1949 LULAC Constitution to permit non–Mexican Americans to become members. He was also active in the Felix Longoria case and advocated fair treatment for the *bracero*.[44]

Sánchez also worked with "Robert Marshall Civil Liberties Trust of the American Civil Liberties Union (ACLU) . . . the Marshall Trust [was] designed for Spanish speakers of the Southwest, and in 1951 [it] appointed Sanchez, through the new organization Sanchez founded—the American Council of Spanish-Speaking People (ACSSP)—to administer block grants for the funding of civil rights lawsuits.[45]" Sánchez used part of this money to defend the rights of Mexican immigrants. In April 1955, Mexican Americans sued the schools of Carrizo Springs and Kingsville, Texas. Austin Elementary had been segregated since 1914; it was known as the "Mexican Ward School," with a 100 percent Mexican student population.

In the early 1960s bilingual education was a cornerstone of the struggle for equal educational opportunity. Research on bilingual education had been conducted since the 1920s in response to race-based studies on intelligence. According to Carlos K. Blanton, "By the 1960s, leading psychologists, linguists and educators increasingly reasoned that bilingualism actually benefited intelligence."[46] Sánchez was a main actor in shifting the paradigm.

New Mexico: The Illusion of Being Political Players

12.4 **Analyze the relationship between education and political empowerment for Mexican Americans and other people of color in the 1950s.**

New Mexico had the largest population of native-born Mexicans. Most adult New Mexicans were eligible to vote and, as they comprised almost half the state, these numbers gave them the illusion that they were power players. They elected U.S. Senator Dennis Chávez, Jr., a liberal who supported the New Deal and the Fair Deal. Despite having more Mexican American elected officials than other states, New Mexico suffered from what Texas political scientist Rodolfo Rosales has called the "illusion of inclusion."

Drought, depression, and World War II almost ended the New Mexican way of life. From 1940 to 1960, the government spent enormous sums of money to accelerate the industrialization of the state. Chain stores, national corporations, and large-scale finance institutions displaced merchant houses and speculative capital. In 1949, there were 1,362 farms operating in Taos; 10 years later, only 674 farms remained. Throughout the 1950s, the rural population declined. In 1947, the median per capita income in the seven northern counties was only $452.26, compared with $870.04 in the seven white American counties.

Why were New Mexicans still marginalized after 100 years of U.S. occupation? New Mexicans lived in a "Third World" environment? By 1950, Mexican Americans comprised about half the population of New Mexico; just over 87 percent were U.S.-born. Mexican Americans lived in seven northern counties, while white Americans controlled eastern and southern New Mexico. Racism worsened after World War II when large numbers of white Texans arrived to work in the oil fields. "Little Texas" in the eastern half of the state harbored discrimination against Mexicans, barring them from the "better" barbershops, restaurants, hotels, and amusement centers. Mexicans attended separate schools and churches, and Mexican American war veterans could not even join the local American Legion Post.

New Mexicans lacked education, a necessity in the new labor market. The illiteracy rate was 16.6 percent for Mexicans compared with 3.1 percent for others. Teachers in Mexican counties had less-than-adequate training: 46.2 percent held BAs, compared with 82.2 percent in the white American counties. According to the 1950 U.S. Census, the median education for Mexicans was 6.1 years, compared with 11.8 for white Americans. Ten years later, the figures climbed to 7.4 and 12.2 years, respectively. In 1965, New Mexico had the highest percentage of draftees failing the intelligence exam of any southwestern state—25.4 percent. This was a population that was hardly prepared to compete in a technologically advanced society.[47]

Los Angeles Politics

From 1949 to 1962, Edward R. Roybal dominated the political history of Mexican Americans in Los Angeles. Roybal's rise is linked to the emergence of the Community Service Organization (CSO), California's most important Mexican American association. CSO differed from LULAC in employing more strident tactics. The CSO used the strategies of the Industrial Areas Foundation (IAF) and its founder, Saul Alinsky. Many CSO leaders were middle class, but unlike LULAC professionals, they did not monopolize the leadership; leaders frequently came out of the labor movement. "By 1963 the CSO had established thirty-four chapters across the Southwest (primarily in California), with over 10,000 paid members."[48]

The origins of the CSO were in the small towns beyond East Los Angeles—in Chino, Ontario, and Pomona, where Ignacio López organized civic or unity leagues. In 1946, he formed the Pomona Unity League, and soon unity leagues sprang up in Chino, Ontario, and Redlands. Fred Ross of the American Council on Race Relations joined López. The leagues emphasized mass action, bloc voting, and neighborhood protests. Organizers held meetings in homes, churches, and public buildings. Their first order of business was to encourage Mexican Americans to run for political office, and get them elected to city councils.

Soon after, López established unity leagues in San Bernardino and Riverside, California, where school discrimination was a primary issue. The leagues in turn influenced the IAF in the Back of the Yards area of South Chicago in the late 1940s. The IAF planned to work with Mexicans in the Los Angeles area. A group known as the Community Political Organization (CPO) formed in East Los Angeles about the same time. Not wanting to be confused with the Communist Party or with partisan politics, the CPO changed its name in 1947 to the Community Service Organization (CSO). The organization evolved from Mexican American steelworkers and volunteers in Roybal's unsuccessful bid for a Los Angeles City Council seat in 1947. There the IAF merged efforts with the CSO.[49]

Although the CSO was supposedly not political, it registered 12,000 new voters. This increase in registered Mexican American voters helped elect Roybal to the Los Angeles City Council in 1949—the first person of Mexican descent to serve on that body since 1881. After Roybal's victory, the CSO did not directly support another candidate for office. Instead, it concentrated on fighting housing discrimination, police brutality, and school segregation. In 1950 the CSO fielded 112 volunteer deputy registrars; within three months, 32,000 new Latino voters were registered. The CSO grew to 800 members in two years. By the early 1960s, it had 34 chapters with 10,000 dues-paying members. The CSO promoted understanding of local governance among taxpayers and urged them to press for better public services.

As a member of the City Council, Roybal confronted the Los Angeles power elite in defense of principle. The 1950 Census showed that the Los Angeles population was 81 percent white, 9 percent Black, and 8 percent Latino/a. Roybal fought for a strong Fair Employment Practices Commission (FEPC) ordinance, opposed the registration of Communists, supported rent controls and public housing, and campaigned against urban renewal. He also criticized police brutality. However, Roybal had few allies on the City Council, where most of the members supported growth at the expense of minority areas. There was considerable bias on the council; on Roybal's first day on the job, the council president introduced him as the "Mexican Council member, elected by the Mexican people of his District."[50]

Roybal's popularity went beyond the Mexican American community. His own council manic district in 1950 was 34 percent Mexican American and 45 percent African American. Only some 16,000 registered voters out of 87,000 were Mexican Americans. In 1954, Roybal lost a campaign for lieutenant governor. Four years later, he ran for county supervisor, and won the election on the first ballot, only to lose after three dubitable recounts.

Many political observers still believe that what cost Roybal the election was his threatening the interests of the county's downtown power structure by exposing the Chávez Ravine giveaway to the Dodgers and the forced removal of the Bunker Hill residents (the area directly west of the Civic Center). Roybal submitted affidavits to the grand jury showing that supporters of his opponent had intimidated minority voters. Grace Montañez Davis, a volunteer campaign worker in the Roybal camp, sent 98 affidavits to the FBI, the state FEPC, and the U.S. Civil Rights Commission.[51]

That same year, 1958, Hank López ran for lieutenant governor of California. Although the party swept the statewide elections, Lopéz lost. During the campaign, many Democrats refused to share the same platform with López.[52]

More coordinating councils—the G.I. Forum, LULAC, and the Council for Mexican American Affairs (CMAA)—emerged in Los Angeles. The CMAA, made up of select professionals, wanted to unify the various groups to coordinate Mexican American political action. Mexican American groups expressed optimism, predicting the community's awakening and their achievement of political power. Nevertheless, Mexicans won a few victories. They celebrated the appointment of Carlos Terán to the municipal court in 1958 with all the grandeur of a coronation.[53]

San Antonio

In Texas, the poll tax continued to drive down voter registration drives. The leading Mexican American politician was Henry B. González, whose parents were political refugees from Durango, Mexico, where they owned a mine. González was born in 1916; he graduated from St. Mary's Law School and then worked for a time as a juvenile officer. He was involved in civic affairs and ran unsuccessfully for state representative in 1950; a year later, he won a City Council seat. González, who did not belong to the LULAC clique, put together a grassroots campaign.

González often clashed with the Good Government League (GGL), established in the early 1950s, which ran the city of San Antonio. Like Edward Roybal in Los Angeles, González championed civil rights causes. In 1956, he ran for the State Senate, winning by 282 votes. The campaign of Albert Peña, Jr., for county commissioner greatly helped González.

The race issue resurfaced, with opponents frequently accusing González of being a leftist. In the State Senate, González championed liberal causes. In 1958, he unsuccessfully ran for governor.

Segregated schools continued throughout Texas: in east Texas, state legislators introduced a dozen bills in the 1956–1957 session to withhold funds from integrated schools and prohibit interracial sporting events. Nonetheless, some changes took place during the 1950s that altered the political landscape in the late 1970s: an increasing number of legislative districts changed from rural to urban—which favored those in cities. Mexican Americans by this time were concentrated in cities where they developed a growing political awareness.[54] Veterans' organizations such as the Loyal American Democrats, the West Side Voters League, the Alamo Democrats, the School Improvement League, and the American G.I. Forum (AGIF) would challenge the old machines. The names of the new organizations were mostly in English, suggesting feelings of patriotism and a desire to assimilate. However, another explanation is that the political environment in Texas and the impact of McCarthyism might have coerced many Mexican Americans to adopt this sort of expression of Americanism to defuse racism and red-baiting, which were prevalent there.

El Paso

As in other cities, El Paso Mexican Americans were politically more active during this decade. The illusion was that Mexicans could win if they ran politicos whom white people would accept. In 1957 Raymond Telles, a Mexican American and a retired Korean War Air Force lieutenant colonel ran for mayor of El Paso. The city elite opposed Telles though he took every opportunity to assure voters of his Americanism. Members of the El Paso business establishment openly said they did not believe that a Mexican was qualified to be mayor. Conservatives billed Telles's white opponent as the "candidate for all El Paso." Telles's victory shattered the myth that Mexicans would not turn out to vote—90 percent of eligible Mexicans voted.

Telles in many ways symbolized the times: He had "made it." Telles went to Catholic schools, and was a World War II veteran. El Pasoans elected Telles as city clerk in 1948, and LULAC supported him throughout his career. Though he was well qualified to run for mayor in any case, one factor promoting his candidacy was his light skin. Given the logic of the times, this was rational, since most white Americans and many Mexican Americans interpreted qualification as being white. To get Telles elected, LULAC and other organizations mobilized the voter base, which was the Mexican American community. Telles won by 2,754 votes—18,688 to 15,934. Voters reelected Telles in 1959, and he served four years as mayor. Despite generating high hopes, Telles's election brought little change. The 1960 Census showed little improvement in living conditions for Mexican Americans; 70 percent of the Southside housing remained deteriorated or dilapidated.[55]

Civil Rights

12.5 Contextualize the Mexican American struggle for civil rights in the 1950s in relation to the growing numbers of Mexicans and slight improvements in education.

Organizationally, a growing number of Mexican Americans became angrier at injustices directed at them and had the ability to fight back. This moral outrage was necessary to respond collectively. As the optimistic illusions of many Mexican Americans turned into skepticism, a sense of moral outrage and militancy increased. Inequality became more obvious to many as real wages fell 5 percent and corporate profits rose 69 percent during the so-called "Happy Days" of the 1950s. The gap between white people and people of color widened. This was in spite of the tax rate for the top bracket, those earning over $400,000, being 91 percent. (In 2003 it fell to 35 percent.)[56]

In California, in 1950, a Latino male earned 69.5 percent of the wages of a white American male counterpart; Latinas, correspondingly, earned 37.4 percent. Ten years later Latino males still earned 69.5 percent, and the rate for Latinas had fallen further to only 34.1 percent.[57] The power of labor declined as rightist pressure cleaned out the left. Tragically, some of the expelled members were the strongest advocates for increasing labor's inclusion of minorities. By mid-1950s, the CIO once again merged with the AFL, curtailing many of the CIO's community-oriented projects and reducing the admission of minorities. Still, a cadre of politicized Mexican Americans had developed within the middle and working classes despite efforts to repress them.

The "Salt of the Earth"

The "Salt of the Earth" strike pitted 1,400 members (90 percent Mexican) of Local 890, International Union of Mine, Mill, and Smelter Workers, against Empire Zinc and Grant County—inspired a classic film of the same name that received worldwide acclaim but was banned in the United States. The film depicts the strike and focuses on the role of women in stopping production. The strike lasted 15 months, from October 1950 to January 1952; it was the longest strike in New Mexico's history. Some leaders were admittedly Communists, the rank and file however, were more concerned about abusive working and living conditions than about ideology.[58]

The McCarthy hysteria intimidated organized labor. The CIO buckled under political pressure and asked its union officers to sign affidavits that they were not Communists. Government refused to consider that the

Communist Party's appeal to workers of color was a product of American racism; instead, it rationalized that Communists were seducing Mexicans. Meanwhile, the Empire Zinc workers suffered indignities such as separate payroll lines, toilet facilities, and housing in the company town. Owners limited Mexicans to backbreaking mucking and underground mining jobs, while assigning whites to surface and craft jobs. Local 890 demanded payment for collar-to-collar work (i.e., compensation for all the time the miners spent underground), holiday pay, and the elimination of the no-strike clause in their contract. The miners did not consider these demands out of line, and were surprised when Empire Zinc refused to negotiate. It is obvious that the management wanted to break the union.

Mexican Americans comprised 50 percent of Grant County. When the strike began, the county authorities demanded that the governor send the National Guard to the area. The strike itself was a typical management–labor dispute until a local judge issued an injunction that the workers stop picketing the mine. At that point, the women's auxiliary, formed in 1948, took over the lines because the injunction did not cover the women. A dramatic confrontation took place between the women and the deputies. At one point, deputies jailed 45 women, 17 children, and a 6-month-old baby. This event caught the attention of other unions and women's groups, who supported the auxiliary. Efforts to suppress the women led to frequent clashes between the women, the scabs, and the sheriff's deputies.

The governor intervened, siding with the management, and sent in state troopers, who enforced the injunction and prohibited the blocking of the road leading to the mine. The governor's action thwarted the use of women on the picket line, since the state penitentiary could house all the picketers. The strike halted, with the workers winning minimal gains. Empire Zinc was eager to settle because of wartime profits, but refused to drop charges against union leaders, many of whom eventually spent three months in jail and paid thousands of dollars in fines.[59]

Toward Equality

In 1952, Tempe, Arizona, attorney Ralph Estrada, on behalf of the *Alianza Hispano Americana* filed a desegregation suit against the Tolleson School District, for violating the Fourteenth Amendment of the U.S. Constitution. School officials claimed that the separation was based on "language barriers" not race. In 1955, the judge ruled the separation unconstitutional, which set off more cases against Arizona school districts.[60] All of these activities produced a measure of moral outrage—each victory, and even each defeat, politicized larger numbers of Mexican Americans.

A main tactic of civil rights organizations involved high-profile court cases that challenged the legality of public agencies, such as schools and police de facto discrimination. A giant of these times was Texas attorney Gustavo C. García. Born in Laredo, García moved to San Antonio and graduated with a law degree from the University of Texas. During World War II, he served with the Judge Advocate Corps. In April 1947, he filed suit against school authorities in Cuero, Texas to force closure of the Mexican school there. Aided by Robert C. Eckhardt of Austin and A. L. Wirin of the Los Angeles Civil Liberties Union, García filed *Delgado v. Bastrop ISD* (1948). The case decision made illegal the segregation of children of Mexican descent in Texas. García played a leading role in revising the 1949 LULAC Constitution to permit non–Mexican Americans become members. As legal advisor to the American G.I. Forum, he worked to pass a general anti-discrimination bill in Texas and served on the first board of directors of the American Council of Spanish-Speaking People and the Texas Council on Human Relations. García was an attorney in the *Hernandez v. State of Texas* case, which he argued before the Supreme Court. García died alone and homeless on a park bench in San Antonio in 1964.[61]

Texas Mexican Americans applauded the landmark *Brown v. Board of Education* school desegregation decision.[62] A 1954 poll showed that Mexicans approved of integration in larger numbers than did African Americans or whites: Although 77 percent of all Mexicans surveyed supported integration of African Americans, only 62 percent of African Americans themselves supported integration. In April 1955, Mexican Americans sued the schools of Carrizo Springs and Kingsville, Texas. In Kingsville, Austin Elementary had been segregated since 1914; it was known as the "Mexican Ward School," with a 100 percent Mexican student population. Of the 31 Mexican teachers in Kingsville, all but four taught in the all-Mexican school.

The Texas G.I. Forum also filed police brutality cases. On June 20, 1953, in Mercedes, the Forum brought enough pressure to force the resignation of Darrill F. Holmes, a policeman who intimidated George Sáenz and his wife at their grocery store; as a result of the police abuse, Sáenz was treated for a nervous condition. The Forum was also involved in the Jesse Ledesma case. On the afternoon of June 22, 1953, Austin police officer Bill Crow stopped Ledesma, who was suffering from insulin shock. Crow claimed Ledesma looked drunk and beat him up, inflicting a one-inch cut on the right side of his head and bruises on his legs, back, and shoulders.[63]

On September 16, 1953, in Fort Worth, Texas, Officer Vernon Johnson shot Ernest L. García in the chest while Johnson was delivering a court order for custody of a child in the García home. Johnson threatened members of the García family when they asked him if he had a warrant; the officer pulled a gun and pressed it against García's chest. Johnson claimed that he shot Ernest because he was afraid the García family would mob him. The Forum lawyers handled the case and got Johnson indicted for aggravated assault.[64]

On May 3, 1954, the U.S. Supreme Court unanimously decision, banned discrimination in jury selection. In Edna, Texas, an all-white jury found Peter Hernández guilty of murdering Joe Espínosa and sentenced him to life imprisonment. The Court of Criminal Appeals turned down this case because, according to the court, Mexicans were white and therefore was not a class apart from the white population. Hernández appealed, and the U.S. Supreme Court found that for 25 years the Court of Criminal Appeals had treated Mexicans as a class apart, and that out of 6,000 citizens considered for jury duty, the panel had never selected a Mexican juror. The lower court again tried Peter Hernández; this time he pled guilty and the court sentenced him to 20 years.[65]

The *Hernández* case is a landmark civil rights case. While the Civil Rights Act of 1875 guaranteed Black Americans the right to serve on juries, Mexican Americans did not have this constitutional protection. The courts held that the Fourteenth Amendment did not guarantee this right to Mexican Americans since they were legally white. Mexican American attorneys argued that Mexican Americans were "a class apart"; they did not fit into the Black–white Americans paradigm. The Supreme Court upheld the argument and ruled that as a "class apart" Mexican Americans had suffered historic discrimination, and were entitled to the protections of the Fourteenth Amendment.

California

In February 1950, Los Angeles County sheriffs raided a baby shower at the home of Natalia Gonzáles. Sheriffs had given the occupants three minutes to evacuate the premise. They arrested some 50 guests for charges ranging from disturbing the peace to resisting arrest. The Maravilla Chapter of the ANMA petitioned the county supervisors for relief. But the supervisors refused to intervene. Lieutenant Fimbres of the sheriff's foreign relations bureau whitewashed the incident. Virginia Ruiz, along with the ANMA, then formed the Maravilla Defense Committee.

On May 26, 1951, police raided a baptismal party at the home of Simon Fuentes. Officers received a call complaining that the music was too loud. Police broke into the house without a warrant and assaulted the guests. They pushed an eight-months-pregnant woman and a disabled man to the floor. Police broke Frank Rodríguez's leg when he went to the aid of the disabled man. ANMA played an active role in this case as well. In the "Bloody Christmas" case, on December 24, 1951, approximately 50 Los Angeles police took seven young Mexicans out of their cells at the Lincoln Heights jail and brutally beat them. Police mauled Danny Rodella so badly that jailers had to send him to Los Angeles County General Hospital. Public outcries from the white, Black, and brown communities forced the district attorney's office to bring charges against the officers. The courts indicted some of the officers and sentenced them to jail. According to historian Edward Escobar, "[Chief William] Parker and his allies in city government stifled external investigations into department matters, vilified LAPD critics, and even ignored perjury by officers. They thus helped create an organizational culture that valued LAPD independence above the rule of law and led to the LAPD's estrangement from Mexican American and other minority communities."[66]

On May 8, 1953, Los Angeles deputy sheriffs Lester Moll and Kenneth Stiler beat David Hidalgo, age 15; other deputies looked on as Hidalgo pleaded for mercy. Hidalgo's stepfather, Manuel Domínguez, pressed a civil suit against the Los Angeles County sheriff's department. *La Alianza Hispano-Americana* supported his lawsuit. Two years later, the court awarded Domínguez damages of $1,000.

The *Alianza* handled the appeals in the murder and conspiracy conviction of Manuel Mata, Robert Márquez, and Ricardo Venegas, whom the state found guilty of murdering William D. Cluff in a fight in Los Angeles on December 6, 1953; Cluff intervened in a fight involving the three defendants and a marine. The defense introduced expert medical testimony that Cluff died of an enlarged heart, advanced arteriosclerosis of cerebral blood vessels, and arterial heart disease; he had not died of injuries inflicted during the fight. Los Angeles newspapers inflamed public rage, and the court convicted the three Mexican Americans. After a series of appeals, the defendants received a new trial.[67]

The CSO, along with the ACLU, took the leadership in police brutality cases in East Los Angeles. Mexican American activist Ralph Guzmán wrote in the *Eastside Sun* on September 24, 1953, "It is no secret that for years law and order in the Eastside of Los Angeles County has been maintained through fear and brutal treatment." Los Angeles newspapers whipped up hysteria against Mexicans. Guzmán, again in the *Eastside Sun*, wrote on January 7, 1954, "It is becoming more and more difficult to walk through the streets of Los Angeles—and look Mexican!" On January 14, 1954, he continued, "Basically, Eugene Biscailuz's idea to curb kid gangs is the evening roundup, a well-known western drive." Biscailuz was the longtime LA County Sheriff who was a member of an old Californio family and rarely identified with the working-class community. The white community loved him and cheered him as he rode his horse at the head of civic parades. Guzmán, through Biscailuz, vehemently castigated the Los Angeles press for irresponsibly promoting a Fantasy History.

National Spanish-Speaking Council

Middle-class Mexican American organizations remained active during this period. Most preferred to follow the path set by the civil rights tradition, and to work within the mainstream. On May 18–19, 1951, leaders of many of these associations met in El Paso for the founding convention of the American Council of Spanish-Speaking People. George I. Sánchez chaired the convention. The *Alianza Hispano-Americana*, CSO, LULAC, the Texas G.I. Forum, and the Community Service Club of Colorado composed the core group. Leaders such as Gus García, Tony Rios, Ignacio López, José Estrada, and Dennis Chávez, Jr., U.S. senator from New Mexico attended the convention.

Tibo J. Chávez, the lieutenant governor of New Mexico, was elected president of the council, and George I. Sánchez served as its executive director. In 1952, the organization received a grant from the Robert Marshall Foundation to be used in promoting the civil rights of Mexican Americans. The council worked closely with the *Alianza* in desegregation cases. In 1952, for instance, in Arizona, these groups made challenges in Glendale, Douglas, Miami, and Winslow. In the case against Glendale and the Arizona Board of Education, the council challenged school segregation. The Glendale board refused to go to court, knowing that they would be forced to integrate.

In 1954, the *Alianza* filed a suit against Winslow, Arizona, to open its swimming pool to Mexicans. Winslow officials settled the suit out of court. In 1955, the *Alianza* established a Civil Rights department and named Ralph Guzmán its director. In a desegregation case in El Centro, California, it collaborated with the NAACP. The El Centro School Board had assigned only Black teachers to the two elementary schools that were predominantly Mexican and African American. El Centro had avoided desegregation by allowing white students to transfer to an adjoining district that was already overcrowded. A federal judge ruled that the plaintiffs must exhaust state courts before a federal court could hear the case. The Court of Appeals for the Ninth Circuit, however, reversed the lower court decision, holding that El Centro practiced segregation of students and staff. This was significant cooperation between the *Alianza* and the NAACP. On the downside the *Alianza* excluded African Americans.[68]

The American Council of Spanish-Speaking People remained active for years, but like many other organizations, it perished when continued funding did not materialize. At that juncture in history, the Mexican American middle class was not large or prosperous enough to support such an ambitious project, and white American foundations did not recognize the need. Older Mexican American associations continued to support Mexican Americans in support of their civil rights through their legal-aid programs.

The Struggle to Preserve the *Barrios*

12.6 Evaluate the impact of suburbanization and urban renewal on housing and education.

Government transportation policy and federal loans accelerated the decay of the inner city as the game of Monopoly picked up speed. Thousands of miles of highways or freeways integrated the nation. At the same time, these programs segregated the United States, ingraining housing patterns that exist today in U.S. metropolitan areas Federal loan policy allowed federal administrators and the housing industry to work hand in hand with developers, separating the suburbs and inner cities. The highway policy gave the states hundreds of millions of dollars to accelerate white middle-class workers movement to the suburbs: white flight was not an accident or the invisible workings of the market. Depression and industrialization accelerated the Mexicans' move to the city, and housing and urban redevelopment policies enacted during the New Deal and postwar years encouraged the abandonment of inner cities by those who could afford to leave, reinforcing separation based on race and class.

The FHA Mortgage Guarantee and the G.I. Bill

The Federal Housing Administration's (FHA) mortgage-loan guarantees, established by the National Housing Act of 1934, and the Veterans Administration's (VA) loan guarantees of the Servicemen's Readjustment Act of 1944 (the G.I. Bill) created the suburban building boom that further encouraged segregation. The FHA set housing policy. Between 1935 and 1974, the agency insured close to 11.5 million home mortgages. The money went mostly to mortgage insurance that backed the construction of new suburban housing. In this way, the FHA propelled the unprecedented flight of millions of white Americans, who left the cities for the suburbs. In all, the FHA and VA programs insured about one-third of all homes purchased. Unfortunately, government administrators shared the real estate industry's view that racial segregation was closely linked to stability of neighborhoods and housing values. When the FHA issued its Underwriting Manual to banks in 1938, one of its guidelines for loan officers instructed them not to integrate new tracts. "A change in social or racial occupancy generally contributes to instability and a decline in values." Thus, government policy encouraged discrimination against Mexican Americans and African Americans by limiting their options as to where they could buy.[69]

Urban Renewal: The Day of the Bulldozer

The 1949 Housing Act tied urban renewal to public housing, so that the worst slums were to be bulldozed for "a decent home and suitable living environment for every American family."[70] Politicians built their political careers on urban renewal, favoring clearance projects that protected downtown business districts from the slums. Urban development perpetuated racial tension and shaped contemporary racist attitudes and stereotypes. Federally financed expressways ripped the urban core and furthered suburbanization. Minorities were prevented from buying homes in the suburbs, which created today's "underclass." Overall, the gap between people of color and white Americans widened as low-cost housing gave homeowners tax breaks and inflation built home equity.

During the 1950s, urban renewal menaced Mexican Americans and other poor people. By 1963, 609,000 people were uprooted nationwide, two-thirds of whom were minority group members. For Mexicans, Los Angeles was the prototype, and other cities mirrored their experiences. In Los Angeles, the Eastside *barrio* came under attack by urban-land grabbers engaged in freeway building, business enterprises, and urban renewal. Like other poor people throughout the United States, Mexicans had settled in the older sections near the center of the town. When freeway plans were proposed, planners considered poorer neighborhoods expendable. Government used the power of eminent domain to dislocate Mexican Americans so that money interests could reap large profits.

In the 1950s, the low-income housing stock decreased by 90 percent. By the fall of 1953, the San Bernardino, Santa Ana, and Long Beach freeways already scarred Mexican neighborhoods, and Mexicans protested the projected building of still another freeway through East Los Angeles. However, unlike the residents of Beverly Hills, Mexicans were not able to stop the bulldozers, and the $32 million Golden State Freeway wiped out another Mexican sector. In 1957, the Pomona Freeway displaced thousands of Mexicans in the Hollenbeck area. The history of freeways in Los Angeles is one of plunder, fraud, and utter disregard for the lives and welfare of people. Land developers knew just why and where they planned the routes; they conveniently bypassed the property of powerful corporate interests, such as the large Sears Roebuck store and the *Los Angeles Times* facilities. Developers and politicians made millions.

The outcome was the erosion of the city's tax base and the diversion of revenues to the suburbs. As a consequence, downtown developers and other elites pressured the federal government for relief, which they received through the Federal Housing Act of 1949. Over the years, the scope of the Act broadened: Under the public housing legislation of the New Deal, government could force a homeowner to sell their land under the power of eminent domain for public purposes, and the land could also be taken for private use and to profit developers. Under the guise of public housing program, municipalities bought and cleared the land and then sold it to developers at a loss. The federal government made up two-thirds of the loss. It was developer friendly since developers bought the redeveloped property at 30 percent of cost.[71]

The Dodgers and Chávez Ravine

Because of the renewal process, Mexican neighborhoods were kept in a state of flux throughout the 1950s, as they became the targets of developers. In October 1957, the city removed Mexican homeowners from the Chávez Ravine neighborhood, near the center of Los Angeles, giving more than 300 acres of private land to Walter O'Malley, owner of the Dodgers baseball team. The Dodgers deal angered many Angeleños and the residents of Chávez Ravine, who resisted physically. In one instance in 1959, the county sheriff's department forcibly removed the Aréchiga family. Councilman Ed Roybal condemned the action: "The eviction is the kind of thing you might expect in Nazi Germany or during the Spanish Inquisition." Supporters of the Aréchigas protested to the City Council. Victoria Augustian, a witness, pointed a finger at Council Member Rosalind Wyman, who, with Mayor Norris Poulson, supported the giveaway. Poulson was a puppet of the Chandler family, who owned the *Los Angeles Times*, which backed the land handover.[72]

Joseph Eli Kovner, publisher and editor of the *Eastside Sun*, exposed connections between the mayor's office and capitalist interests in Los Angeles, and urban renewal proposals in Watts, Pacoima, Canoga Park, Bunker Hill, and Boyle Heights (Watts was a Black community and the other four are predominantly Mexican). Kovner cited a memo from the Sears Corporation to its executives, instructing them to support urban renewal because the company had an economic interest in protecting its investment. According to the memo, the presence of too many minorities depressed land values and merchants were deprived of white middle-class customers. Urban renewal ensured construction of business sites and higher-rent apartments that inflated property values. On July 31, 1958, the *Eastside Sun* exposed the Boyle Heights Urban Renewal Committee's plot to remove 480 homes north of Brooklyn between McDonnell and Mednick and to displace more than 4,000 people.

Actions of the neo-robber barons became so outlandish that De Witt McCann, an aide to Mayor Poulson's Urban Renewal Committee, resigned, stating, "I don't want to be responsible for taking one man's private property through the use of eminent domain and giving it over to another private individual for his private gain." Poulson and his associates displaced thousands of poor, white senior citizens and Mexicans in Bunker Hill and turned over prime land in the downtown section of the city to private developers. Citizens of Bunker Hill lost their battle, but progressives derailed the scheme that eventually would have handed all of Boyle Heights, City Terrace, and Belvedere to private developers. Mayor Norris Poulson responded to the critics of urban renewal: "If you are not prepared to be part of this greatness, if you want Los Angeles to revert to pueblo status . . . then my best advice to you is to prepare to resettle elsewhere."[73]

The mayor and the city officials were guilty of criminal negligence. The Los Angeles Community Redevelopment Administration's board of directors ordered Gilbert Morris, superintendent of building and safety, not to enforce safety regulations in the Bunker Hill area. Improvements would raise the value of property and the officials wanted to keep costs down. Poulson also instructed the commissioner of the Board of Building and Safety not to issue building permits. Consequently, existing buildings deteriorated.

The inevitable occurred when a four-story apartment building collapsed; fortunately, firefighters were able to save the 200 occupants. Councilman Ed Roybal accused Poulson of playing politics with human lives.[74]

Urban Removal in the Midwest

Urban renewal followed a similar pattern in most cities in which Mexicans lived. The renewal process dispersed Mexicans throughout Detroit; many moved to the suburbs. As in other cities, a pattern of uprooting by speculators, industrialists, and land developers emerged, disrupting the phenomenon of community building that had been crucial to the security of Mexican Americans for so long. For instance, in the 1960s redevelopment plans wiped out and moved the Bagley Avenue Mexican business district to Vernor. The G.I. Forum in Detroit defended the civil rights of displaced residents and lobbied to gain access for Mexicans to public institutions. Detroit Mexicans, fed up with the reactionary Catholic hierarchy's silence on these issues, refused to rebuild Nuestra Señora de Guadalupe Church and discouraged the formation of new Mexican Catholic groups.

In Chicago, freeways, the expansion of the university campus, and other renewal programs wiped out the Near West Side *barrio*. In 1947, the city organized the Chicago Land Commission to supervise slum clearance and urban "removal." The flight of white families and industries from the city to the suburbs had begun and it cost city jobs. This loss of employment would greatly affect Mexican Americans.

Neighborhoods around the University of Chicago were cleared and rebuilt during the late 1950s, as was a big part of the Lincoln Park neighborhood along North Avenue.[75] Later, the federal interstate highway program funded construction of five expressways that displaced 50,000 city dwellers. The civil rights movement of the late 1960s prevented most of the rest of Chicago from being gentrified. The targeted African Americans and other ethnics joined with white ethnic neighborhoods, like Taylor Street's Italian area, to revolt against urban renewal. In the early 1960s, however, developers bulldozed more than 800 houses and 200 businesses—most owned by citizens of Italian, Mexican, and Greek ancestry—to make way for what was then called the University of Illinois Chicago Circle Campus.

The aftershock of urban renewal would be felt in the 1960s, when accelerated redevelopment caused a major disruption of the dominant social order. It transformed downtowns and surrounding areas, contributing greatly to the decentralization of the city while centralizing commercial and political power in the hands of a few elites. The most obvious disruption for the poor was the destruction of sound, affordable housing without adequate replacement. Conditions in the inner city worsened as housing and services became overburdened. Unemployment and inflation resulted, and poverty increased—as did crime and neighborhood gang activity. Urban renewal, essentially, also killed public housing, which was labeled socialistic.[76]

The Sputnik Moment

12.7 Explain why the successful launch of *Sputnik* shook U.S. education.

The 1950s closed with another challenge to U.S. world dominance as the Russians beat them into space accelerating the arms war. The launch of *Sputnik* in October 1957 led to cries for educational reform in the United States. The United States reacted by spending billions of dollars into reforming the teaching of math and science, and a substantial amount went into funding of the humanities and the social sciences. For a time, government grants to higher education stimulated interest in reforming language teaching methods. However, Mexican Americans and other minorities benefitted very little from this massive expenditure due to the cumulative effect of poverty and poor education.

The Sputnik era was important because Americans focused on education in their efforts to prove their superiority over the Soviet Union, and not to bring about equality. It influenced me and others since it gave us the opportunity to experiment with ideas. But once the money dried up, so did the interest in higher education. Unfortunately, even Schools of Education abandoned experimentation once the money was gone.

Conclusion: A New Generation

In 1959, the Cuban Revolution overthrew the U.S.-backed dictator Fulgencio Batista y Zaldívar; Fidel Castro became the symbol of Latin American resistance to American colonialism, and he dethroned a dictator that the United States put in power during the 1930s. For many younger Mexican Americans attending universities, the study of Latin American history created an awareness of U.S. imperialism in Latin America and at home.

At home, an excellent study prepared by the Historic Preservation Office of the City of Phoenix, Arizona, articulates what it calls the acculturation of Mexican Americans in the post–World War II years. It makes the point that World War II greatly impacted the Mexican community. Almost a half-million Mexican-origin people served in the armed forces, with several millions of family members suffering vicariously with them. The soldiers fought not only as Americans but also as Mexicans—a fact they could not escape. Their deaths had a ripple effect on the family members. When the servicemen returned, their expectations were not met. The numbers grew as did their numbers. Their leadership base was expanded with leadership old-time activists as they joined mainstream and radical organizations. Older *barrios* saw a sudden expansion and many moved to new neighborhoods—but they were acculturated, not assimilated.

Dramatic changes occurred during World War II and the Korean War. Case study about the City of Phoenix tells of Amadeo Suárez, a World War II veteran and professor at the American Institute of Foreign Trade, who in 1947 sought to buy a home in the white part of town but was prevented "due to the race restrictive deed, which stated, 'No lot or tract, or any part thereof, shall be leased, let, occupied, sold or transferred to anyone other than to members of the white or Caucasian race except those of Mexican or Spanish Ancestry.'"[77]

During World War II a critical mass of Mexican American women worked in white-collar and blue-collar jobs and attended college. They began to take advocacy roles. For example, Graciela Gil Olivárez became a radio disc jockey and a community leader, and, later, worked in an important government post in Washington, D.C. Born in 1928 in Phoenix and raised in the mining community of Barcelona, Arizona, she worked her way up, starting as a stenographer and translator at KIFN Spanish-language radio; by 1952 she was Phoenix's first female disc jockey. She was involved in women's issues and soon went into counseling for the "Careers for Youth" program in Phoenix. During the 1960s, Olivárez became State Director of the Office of Economic Opportunity for Arizona. She enrolled in the Notre Dame School of Law, and, in 1970, became the first woman to graduate from this school. In 1977, President Jimmy Carter appointed her Director of the Community Service Administration in Washington, D.C. Meanwhile, generational change was taking place in the Mexican American community.

Notes

1 Rodolfo Acuña, *Occupied America: The Chicano's Struggle Toward Liberation* (San Francisco, CA: Canfield Press, 1972), 210.

2 Rodolfo F. Acuña, *A Community Under Siege: A Chronicle of Chicanos East of the Los Angeles River, 1945–1975* (Los Angeles: Chicano Studies Research Center Publications, University of California Los Angeles, 1984).

3 WashingtonsBlog, "What Eisenhower REALLY Said About the "Military Industrial Complex," October 10, 2015. http://www.washingtonsblog.com/2015/10/what-eisenhower-really-said-about-the-military-indutrial-complex.html. Robert Reich, "How to Disrupt the Military-Industrial-Congressional Complex," July 3, 2015. http://robertreich.org/post/123138820185. Rodolfo F. Acuña Collection, 1857–2006. Special Collections, California State Northridge Library.

4 Geoffrey Jones, "Restoring a Global Economy, 1950–1980," Working Knowledge Harvard Business School, Aug. 22, 2005, https://hbswk.hbs.edu/item/restoring-a-global-economy-19501980.

5 Enrico Beltramini, "Changes in Business Organization, Integration in American Workplace in the early 1970s," in Knud Andresen, Stefan Müller, eds., *Contesting Deregulation: Debates, Practices and Developments in the West since the 1970s*, (Oxford: Berghahn Books, 2017), 90–91.

6 John P. Schmal, "The Tejano Struggle for Representation," The Hispanic Experience, Houston Institute for Culture, http://www.houstonculture.org/hispanic/tejano1.html. Also see http://www.houstonculture.org/hispanic/tejano2.html. Because of the size of the Mexican American population in Texas, and its longevity, it had a stronger organizational base at this time than California did.

7 An epic film on 1950s racism toward Mexican Americans in Texas is *Giant* (1956), director George Stevens's adaptation of the Edna Ferber novel about a great cattle ranch family in Texas starring Rock Hudson, James Dean, and Elizabeth Taylor, http://www.tcm.com/mediaroom/video/240954/Giant-Movie-Clip-Sarge-s-Place.html. Your school or public library should have a free copy. Another epic book on the subject is Beatrice Griffith, *American Me* (Boston: Houghton Mifflin Co., 1948).

8 Leo Grebler, Joan W. Moore, and Ralph C. Guzman, *The Mexican-American People: The Nation's Second Largest Minority* (Glencoe, IL: Free Press, 1971), 105, 107, 112–13, 119, 121, 150, 154. Jorge Durand, Douglas Massey, and Chiara Capoferro, "The New Geography of Mexican Immigration," in Víctor Zúñiga and Rubén Hernández-León, eds., *New Destinations: Mexican Immigration in the United States* (New York: Russell Sage Foundation, 2005), 8.

9 Michal R. Belknap, *Cold war political justice: The Smith Act, the Communist Party, and American civil liberties* (Contributions in American History; No. 66), (Westport, Conn.: Greenwood Press, 1977). Messer-Kruse, T. Smith Act, in *The Oxford Companion to United States History* (Oxford: The Oxford Companion to United States History, 1977). Mario T. García,

Mexican Americans: Leadership, Ideology, and Identity, 1930–1960 (Yale University Press, 1991), 210.

10 Enrique Meza Buelna, "Resistance From the Margins: Mexican American Radical Activism in Los Angeles, 1930–1970" (PhD Dissertation, University of California, Irvine, 2007), 128, makes the succinct point that California State Senator "Tenney was vehemently opposed to any legislation that attempted to outlaw discrimination, denouncing them as deliberate interference with employer rights and the free flow of trade." "Senator Joseph McCarthy," Spartacus Educational, http://www.spartacus.schoolnet.co.uk/USAmccarthy.htm. "Smith Act of 1940," http://en.wikipedia.org/wiki/Smith_Act. Smith Act Trials, http://www.english.illinois.edu/maps/poets/g_l/jerome/smithact.htm. Rick Kelly, "Anticommunism Run Amok: The Life of Senator Pat McCarran" (December 18, 2004), The World Socialist Web Site, http://www.wsws.org/articles/2004/dec2004/mcca-d18.shtml.

11 Carlos G. Vélez-Ibáñez, *Border Visions: Mexican Cultures of the Southwest United States* (Tucson: University of Arizona Press, 1996), 203–4. "Roles Of Mexican Americans In Korean War," History Rocket, http://www.historyrocket.com/American-History/timeline/1950-1999/korean-war/Roles-Of-Mexican-Americans-In-Korean-War.html. Gregg Barrios, "A 'Platoon' Without Latinos: Mexican-Americans Are Being Denied Their Place in History," *Los Angeles Times*, April 19, 1987, http://articles.latimes.com/1987-04-19/entertainment/ca-1681_1_latino-characters. Jennifer Vo and John P. Schmal, "Mexican Americans Defending the United States, " *LatinoLA*, April 16, 2007, http://latinola.com/story.php?story=4062.

12 Vélez-Ibáñez, *Border Visions*, 203–4. Carlos G. Vélez-Ibáñez, "Los Chavalones of E-Company: Extraordinary Men in Extraordinary Events," Address to the 40th Reunion of E Company, Tucson, Arizona (July 28, 1990). "Selective Service/College Deferment," Korean War Educator, http://www.koreanwar-educator.org/topics/homefront/p_selective_service.htm. Hugh Deane, "Korea, China, and the United States: A Look Back," *Monthly Review* 46, No. 9 (February 1995), 20ff. Raúl Morín, *Among the Valiant: Mexican Americans in WWII and Korea* (Alhambra, CA: Borden Publishing, 1966), 259–76. Kathy Gill, "Military Conscription, Recruiting and the Draft," *U.S. Politics: Current Events* (June 27, 2005), http://uspolitics.about.com/od/electionissues/a/draft_2.htm. Rodolfo Acuña, "Today's Hawks Conveniently Avoided Combat," *Miami Herald* (November 1, 2002). Daniel Y. Kim, "The Borderlands of the Korean War and the Fiction of Rolando Hinojosa," positions (2015) 23 (4): 665–694.

13 Saeed Kamali Dehghan and Richard Norton-Taylor, "CIA admits role in 1953 Iranian coup," *The Guardian*, Aug. 19, 2013, https://www.theguardian.com/world/2013/aug/19/cia-admits-role-1953-iranian-coup.

14 Jim Schrider, "CIA coup files include assassination manual," *National Catholic Reporter*, 07/18/97, Vol. 33, Issue 34, 10. Central Intelligence Agency Document on Guatemala, 1954, Document 1, "CIA and Guatemala Assassination Proposals, 1952–1954," *CIA and Assassinations: The Guatemala 1954 Documents*, by Kate Doyle and Peter Kornbluh, National Security Archive Electronic Briefing Book No. 4, http://www.whale.to/b/doyle.html.

15 Elisabeth Malkin, "An Apology for a Guatemalan Coup, 57 Years Later" *New York Times*, Oct. 20, 2011, http://www.nytimes.com/2011/10/21/world/americas/an-apology-for-a-guatemalan-coup-57-years-later.html?_r=0. "Guatemala 1954," The Cold War Museum, http://www.coldwar.org/articles/50s/guatemala.asp. Max Holland, "Operation PBHISTORY: The Aftermath of SUCCESS," *International Journal of Intelligence and Counterintelligence*, Vol. 17, Issue 2, 2004, 300–332, http://www.tandfonline.com/doi/full/10.1080/08850600490274935.

16 "Harry Bridges: Life and Legacy," Waterfront Workers History Project, Harry Bridges Center for Labor Studies, University of Washington, http://depts.washington.edu/dock/Harry_Bridges_intro.shtml. Edited by Harvey Schwartz, Curator, "Harry Bridges: An Oral History About Longshoring, The Origins of the ILWU and the 1934 Strike," ILWU Oral History Collection, https://www.ilwu.org/oral-history-of-harry-bridges/.

17 K. Mason/K. Stallard, E. Uhl, 1983–1984, "Finding Aid for American Committee for Protection of Foreign Born," Records, 1926–1980s, Special Collections Library, Labadie Collection, University of Michigan, http://quod.lib.umich.edu/s/sclead/umich-scl-acpfb?rgn=main;view=text.

18 Processed by Patricia Martinez and Nina Chang, Southern California Library for Social Studies and Research, Los Angeles Committee for Protection of Foreign Born Records, 1938–1973, Online Archive of California, http://content.cdlib.org/view?docId=kt067nb6v8&chunk.id=scopecontent-1.7.4&brand=oac. Guide compiled by Martin Schipper, "Records of the Subversive Activities Control Board, 1950–1972," Part I: Communist Party USA, Part II: Communist-Action and Communist-Front Organizations (A microfilm project of University Publications of America, 1988), http://cisupa.proquest.com/ksc_assets/catalog/10837.pdf. Patricia Litwin, "How could a woman . . . not even five feet

tall, change the world?" Rose Chernin and the Los Angeles Committee for the Protection of the Foreign Born (Master of Arts Degree, Sarah Lawrence College, May 18, 2007).

19 Wendy Plotkin, Community Service Organization (CSO) History Project, http://comm-org.wisc.edu/papers96/alinsky/cso.html. Community Service Organization (CSO), California, Wayne State Labor Archives, http://www.reuther.wayne.edu/node/300. The Southern California Library: The People's Library, http://www.socallib.org/, is the most complete library of progressive documents of Los Angeles.

20 U.S. Supreme Court, *American Committee v. SACB*, 380 U.S. 503 (1965), argued December 9, 1964, decided April 26, 1965, http://supreme.justia.com/us/380/503/case.html.

21 Evelyn Barker, "Labor Activism During the Cold War: The Case of Humberto Silex," University of Texas at Arlington Library, http://www.uta.edu/library/k12/lessons/labor-files/labor-activism.pdf.

22 John W. Sherman, *A Communist Front at Mid-Century: The American Committee for Protection of Foreign Born, 1933–1959* (Westport, CT: Praeger Publishers, 2001). Jeffrey M. Garcilazo, "McCarthyism, Mexican Americans, and the Los Angeles Committee for Protection of the Foreign-born, 1950–1954," *Western Historical Quarterly* 32, No. 3 (Autumn 2001), 273–95. "President Lauds Tolerance Here; Foreign-born Group Urged to Be Vigilant Against Injustices," *Los Angeles Times* (March 3, 1940). Carey McWilliams, *North from Mexico: The Spanish-Speaking People of the United States*, New edition with Matt Meier (New York: Praeger, 1990), 23. Isabel González, *Step-Children of a Nation: The Status of Mexican-Americans* (New York: American Committee for Protection of Foreign Born, 1947). Rachel Ida Buff, "The Deportation Terror," *American Quarterly* 60, No. 3 (September 2008), 523–51. Nicolás Kanellos, Kenya Dworkin y Méndez, and Alejandra Balestra, *Herencia: Anthology of Hispanic Literature in the United States* (New York: Oxford University Press, 2002), 162.

23 Garcilazo, "McCarthyism," 274.

24 "McCarran Act or Internal Security Act of 1950," http://www.writing.upenn.edu/~afilreis/50s/mccarran-act-intro.html. "1952 Immigration and Nationality Act," a.k.a. the McCarran–Walter Act, U.S. immigration legislation online, University of Washington Bothell, http://library.uwb.edu/guides/USimmigration/1952_immigration_and_nationality_act.html.

25 Patricia Morgan, *Shame of a Nation* (Los Angeles Committee for Protection of Foreign Born, September 1954), 4, 39–47. Jethro K. Lieberman, *Are Americans Extinct?* (New York: Walter, 1968), 106, 109. Rodolfo F. Acuña, *A Community Under Siege*, 40. Steven R. Shapiro, "Commentary: Ideological Exclusions: Closing the Border to Political Dissidents," *Harvard Law Review* 100, No. 930 (February 1987). David G. Gutiérrez, *Walls and Mirrors: Mexican Americans, Mexican Immigrants, and the Politics of Ethnicity* (Berkeley: University of California Press, 1995), 172–78. U.S. President's Commission on Immigration and Naturalization, *Whom We Shall Welcome* (New York: Da Capo Press, 1970), 196–98. See also Robert K. Murray, *Red Scare* (Minneapolis: University of Minnesota Press, 1955), 65. Grebler et al., *Mexican-American People*, 519. "Hope Mendoza Gets Immigration Job Appointment," *Eastside Sun* (Boyle Heights, June 4, 1953). Ralph Guzmán, "Front Line G.I. Faces Deportation," *Eastside Sun* (June 30, 1953). Louie Gilot, "Former ASARCO Labor Leader Dies at 99," *El Paso Times* (March 18, 2002). "Our Badge of Infamy, A Petition to the United Nations on the Treatment of the Mexican Immigrant," American Committee for the Protection of the Foreign Born (April 1959), 13–14, 36–38. "Nacional-Mexico Americano[sic] Fights Deportation Move," *Eastside Sun* (Boyle Heights, March 13, 1952). Joseph Eli Kovner, "The Tobias Navarrette Case," *Eastside Sun* (July 25, 1957). *Eastside Sun* (August 8 and August 29, 1957). George Mount, "Tobias Navarrette, E.L.A. Humanitarian, Is Dead," *Eastside Sun* (September 6, 1964). One of the best studies is Ralph Guzmán, *Roots Without Rights* (Los Angeles, CA: American Civil Liberties Union, Los Angeles Chapter, 1958). John F. Méndez, Editorial, *Eastside Sun* (May 2, 1957). Juan Ramón García, *Operation Wetback: The Mass Deportation of Mexican Undocumented Workers in 1954* (Westport, CT: Greenwood Press, 1980), 173–74. "Jose Gastelum Free of Mexico Deportation," *Eastside Sun* (Boyle Heights, June 20, 1963). "Deportation Is Meeting Topic," *Eastside Sun* (March 28, 1957).

26 John Dillin, "How Eisenhower Solved Illegal Border Crossings from Mexico," *Christian Science Monitor* (July 6, 2006), http://www.csmonitor.com/2006/0706/p09s01-coop.html. Pierre Tristam, "Operation Wetback: Illegal Immigration's Golden-Crisp Myth," *Daytona Beach News-Journal* (April 5, 2007). "The Braceros," The Oregon Experience, Oregon Public Broadcasting, http://www.opb.org/programs/oregonexperiencearchive/braceros/.

27 Avi Astor, "Unauthorized Immigration, Securitization and the Making of Operation Wetback," *Latino Studies* 7, No. 1 (Spring 2009), 5–29; a link between immigration and Communism was made. Ronald L. Mize, Jr., "Mexican Contract Workers and the U.S. Capitalist Agriculture Labor Process: The Formative Era, 1942–1964," *Rural Sociology* 71, No. 1 (2006), 85–108.

28 Carlos Kevin Blanton, "The Citizenship Sacrifice: Mexican Americans, the Saunders-Leonard Report,

and the Politics of Immigration, 1951–1952," *Western Historical Quarterly* 40, No. 3 (Autumn 2009), 301. Garcilazo, "McCarthyism," 276–77.

29 Buelna, "Resistance from the Margins," 210. Kelly Lytle Hernández, "The Crimes and Consequences of Illegal Immigration: A Cross-Border Examination of Operation Wetback, 1943 to 1954," *Western Historical Quarterly* 37, No. 4 (Winter 2006), 430–34. Good account of deportees.

30 Saul Edmund Bronder, "Robert E. Lucey: A Texas Paradox" (PhD Dissertation, Columbia University, New York, 1979), 138, 175. John Phillip Carney, "Postwar Mexican Migration: 1945–1955, with Particular Reference to the Policies and Practices of the United States Concerning Its Control" (PhD Dissertation, University of Southern California, 1957), 20, 48, 127. Lyle Saunders and Olen E. Leonard, "The Wetback in the Lower Rio Grande Valley of Texas," reprinted in Carlos E. Cortés, ed., *Mexican Migration to the United States* (New York: Arno Press, 1976), 165. Art Liebson, "The Wetback Invasion," *Common Ground* 10 (Autumn 1949): 11–19. E. Idar, Jr., and Andrew C. McLellan, *What Price Wetbacks* (Austin: American G.I. Forum of Texas, Texas State Federation of Labor [AFL]), reprinted in Cortés, ed., *Mexican Migration*, 28–29. J. R. García, *Operation Wetback*, 172–74, 188–89, 192, 199, 206, 212, 225, 227–32, 235. Morgan, *Shame of a Nation*, 3. Lamar Babington Jones, "Mexican American Labor Problems in Texas" (PhD Dissertation, University of Texas, 1965), 25–26. Acuña, *A Community Under Siege*, 30–36, 40–43, and accompanying *Belvedere Citizen* and *Eastside Sun* references. Gutiérrez, *Walls and Mirrors*, 155. John Dillin, "Clinton Promise to Curb Illegal Immigration Recalls Eisenhower's Border Crackdowns," *Christian Science Monitor* (August 25, 1993). Ralph Guzmán, "Ojinaga, Chihuahua and Wetbacks," *Eastside Sun* (October 15, 1953). "Our Badge of Infamy," iii–v.

31 Sarah Deutsch, *No Separate Refuge: Culture, Class, and Gender on an Anglo-Hispanic Frontier in the American Southwest, 1880–1940* (New York: Oxford University Press, 1987). Bruce Johansen and Roberto Maestas, *El Pueblo: The Gallegos Family's American Journey, 1503–1980* (New York: Monthly Review Press, 1983). Pauline R. Kibbe, *Latin Americans in Texas* (Albuquerque: University of New Mexico Press, 1946), 19, 91.

32 Gutiérrez, *Walls and Mirrors*, 162. Grebler et al., *The Mexican-American People*, 122.

33 "Paso del Sur," http://www.pasodelsur.com/historia/Intro.html. Chihuahuita began forming in the early 1800s as people from Ciudad Juárez moved across the river to build their homes. As the Mexican colonia expanded, El Segundo Barrio formed as a distinct neighborhood, which eventually became the largest Mexican *barrio* in El Paso. There is an ongoing battle over the preservation of Segundo Barrio. I always wondered how it got the name El Segundo Barrio until an old-timer told me recently, "Well, the first barrio is Juárez": it made sense. Eileen Welsome, "Eminent Disaster: A Cabal of Politicians and Profiteers Targets an El Paso Barrio," *The Texas Observer* (May 4, 2007), http://www.texasobserver.org/article.php?aid=2483.

34 Celeste Delgado, "Teens Rebel Against Authority," *Borderlands*, El Paso Community College, http://epcc.libguides.com/content.php?pid=309255&sid=2629727. Benjamín Márquez, "Power and Politics in a Chicano Barrio" (PhD Dissertation, University of Wisconsin-Madison, 1983), 45–110.

35 Rodolfo Rosales, *The Illusion of Inclusion: The Untold Political Story of San Antonio* (Austin: University of Texas Press, 2000), 51. Everett Ross Clinchey, "Equality of Opportunity for Latin-Americans in Texas: A Study of the Economic, Social, and Educational Discrimination Against Latin-Americans in Texas, and the Efforts of the State Government on Their Behalf" (PhD Dissertation, Columbia University, 1954). Robert Garland Landolt, "The Mexican American Workers of San Antonio, Texas" (PhD Dissertation, University of Texas, Austin, 1965), 191–92. Edwin L. Dickens, "The Political Role of Mexican-Americans in San Antonio, Texas" (PhD Dissertation, Texas Tech University, 1969), 44, 87–93, 140. Frances Jerome Woods, *Mexican Ethnic Leadership in San Antonio* (Washington, DC: Catholic University Press, 1949), 31–36. David R. Johnson, John A. Booth, and Richard J. Harris, eds., *The Politics of San Antonio: Community, Progress, and Power* (Lincoln: University of Nebraska Press, 1983), 19–23. Eugene Rodríguez, Jr., *Henry B. González: A Political Profile* (New York: Arno Press, 1976), 9. Grebler et al., *The Mexican-American People*, 54. Center for American History unveils Henry B. González Collection and website, University of Texas Austin (October 27, 2006), http://www.utexas.edu/news/2006/10/27/cah/.

36 Leland M. Roth, *American Architecture: A History*, 2d ed. (Boulder, CO: Westview Press, 2003), 460–61; in 1946, 2.15 million cars were built; by 1955, 7.5 million were being built annually; and 10 years later 9.3 million. White Americans wanted to emulate the German autobahn system, and after the war the U.S. economy spurred by industry promoted this. In 1920, General Motors, Firestone Tire, Standard Oil of California, Phillips Petroleum, Mack, and the Federal Engineering Corporation organized a holding company, and bought more than 100 electric transit systems in 45 cities. Then the fossil fuel cabal lobbied that cars, buses and trucks were more efficient and they had local and state governments destroy rail transportation, So they destroyed rail transportation

and then lobbied for more freeways. Los Angeles had two electric car systems, which were destroyed. Meanwhile, Los Angeles became a web of freeways that displaced tens of thousands of people. Federal funds were used to finance the system at a nine to one ratio. This was the plot of the motion picture *Who Framed Roger Rabbit?* Touchtone Films, 1988, http://www.youtube.com/watch?v=Smzs_0ZoheE&feature=related. The movie is about urban renewal and freeways in Los Angeles. The Mexicans are the toons—they work for peanuts.

37 Acuña, *A Community Under Siege*, 21–121. Jerry Gonzalez, "'A Place in the Sun': Mexican Americans, Race, and the Suburbanization of Los Angeles 1940–1980" (PhD Dissertation, University of Southern California, Los Angeles, 2009).

38 Peter T. Alter. "Mexicans and Serbs in Southeast Chicago: Racial Group Formation during the Twentieth Century," Journal of the Illinois State Historical Society (1998–) Vol. 94, No. 4 (Winter, 2001/2002), pp. 403–419.

39 Louise Año Nuevo Kerr, "The Chicano Experience in Chicago: 1920–1970" (PhD Dissertation, University of Illinois at Chicago Circle, 1976), 116–210. Also see Howard Zinn, *A People's History of the United States* (New York: Colophon Books, 1980), 428. Richard O. Boyer and Herbert M. Morais, *Labor's Untold Story*, 3rd ed. (New York: United Electrical, Radio and Machine Workers of America, 1974), 340. Peter T Alter, "Mexicans and Serbs in Southeast Chicago: Racial Group Formation during the Twentieth Century," *Journal of the Illinois State Historical Society* (Winter 2001/2002), http://dig.lib.niu.edu/ISHS/ishs-2001winter/ishs-2001winter403.pdf.

40 Nicholas J. O'Shaughnessy, *Politics and Propaganda: Weapons of Mass Seduction* (Ann Arbor: University of Michigan Press, 2004). Gutiérrez, *Walls and Mirrors*, 162–67. Ellen Wight, "Making Mexican-ness in Pilsen: Perspectives on the Meaning of Cultural Production in City Space" (All Academic Research, January 17, 2006); can be downloaded at http://citation.allacademic.com/meta/p_mla_apa_research_citation/1/0/3/8/9/pages103892/p103892-3.php.

41 Laura Munoz, "Romo v. Laird: Mexican American Segregation and the Modern Pedagogy of the Tempe Normal School," *Paper presented at the annual meeting of the American Studies Association Annual Meeting*, Renaissance Hotel, Washington D.C., 2014-11-28. Rodolfo F. Acuña, *The Making of Chicana/o Studies: In the Trenches of Academe* (New Brunswick: Rutgers University Press, 2011), 31.

42 Segregation in Schools as a Violation of the XIVth Amendment (*Mendez, et al v. Westminster School District of Orange County* 1946), (1947), *Columbia Law Review*, 47(2), 325–327. "Mendez v. Westminster: School desegregation and Mexican-American rights," Choice Reviews Online (2010), 48(04), 48: 2367.

43 Acuña, *Making of Chicano Studies*, p. 12.

44 Lonn Taylor, "A tale of two Garcias and the fight against discrimination," *The Big Bend Now*, February 24, 2011. Henry A. J. Ramos, *The American G.I. Forum: In Pursuit of the Dream, 1948–1983* (Houston, TX: Arte Público Press, 1998), 23. Patrick J Carroll, *Felix Longoria's Wake: Bereavement, Racism, and the Rise of Mexican American Activism* (Austin: University of Texas, 2003). American G.I. Forum, http://www.pbs.org/kpbs/theborder/history/timeline/19.html (November 5, 2009). "A Class Apart," WGBH American Experience, http://www.pbs.org/wgbh/americanexperience/class/photoGallery/ (accessed November 5, 2009).

45 Acuña, ibid.

46 Quoted in Carlos K. Blanton, "George I. Sanchez, ideology, and whiteness in the making of the Mexican American civil rights movement, 1930-1960," *Journal of Southern History* (August 1, 2006), 569ff.

47 E. B. Fincher, *Spanish-Americans as a Factor in New Mexico* (New York: Arno Press, 1974), 27–49, 67–73, 94, 150–58. Rosales, *Illusion of Inclusion*. Grebler et al., *The Mexican-American People*, 150.

48 Carlos Conde, "Latino Kaleidoscope; Edward R. Roybal: The Angry Mexican-American," *Hispanic Outlook in Higher Education* 16, No. 8 (January 30, 2006), 8. I knew Roybal for the better part of 40 years. Shana Bernstein, "Interracial Activism in the Los Angeles Community Service Organization: Linking the World War II and Civil Rights Eras," *Pacific Historical Review* 80, No. 2 (May 2011), 231.

49 "Community Service Organization CSO Papers," Urban Archives, California State University Northridge, http://digital-library.csun.edu/cdm/singleitem/collection/LatinoArchives/id/236.

50 Soc 105 Ch. 12 Flashcards | Quizlet, https://quizlet.com/290216045/soc-105-ch-12-flash-cards/.

51 Frank Javier Garcia Berumen, *Edward R. Roybal: The Mexican American Struggle for Political Empowerment* (Los Angeles: Bilingual Educational Services, inc, 2015)

52 "Enrique Hank Lopez," *New York Times* (October 25, 1985), http://www.nytimes.com/1985/10/25/arts/enrique-hank-lopez.html.

53 Fincher, *Spanish-Americans as a Factor in New Mexico*, 27–49. Grebler et al., *The Mexican-American People*, 150. Mario T. García, *Mexican Americans: Leadership, Ideology, and Identity, 1930–1960* (New Haven, CT: Yale University Press, 1991), 88–112, 221, claims that Bert Corona insisted that CSO was formed to prevent "radicals" and "Communists" from organizing the Mexican communities. Mario T. García, *Memories of Chicano History: The Life and Narrative of Bert Corona* (Berkeley: University of California Press, 1995), 162–68. Acuña, *A Community Under Siege*, 27–29.

Also see Raphael J. Sonenshein, *Politics in Black and White: Race and Power in Los Angeles* (Princeton, NJ: Princeton University Press, 1993), 31, 38, 41, 65. Kay Lyon Briegel, "Alianza Hispano-Americana, 1894–1965: A Mexican Fraternal Insurance Society" (PhD Dissertation, University of Southern California, 1974), 175. George J. Sánchez, "Concerning Segregation of Spanish-Speaking Children in the Public Schools," *Inter-American Education Papers* (Austin: University of Texas, 1951), 13–19. Robin Fitzgerald Scott, "The Mexican American in the Los Angeles Area, 1920–1950: From Acquiescence to Activity" (PhD Dissertation, University of Southern California, 1971), 293. Ralph C. Guzmán, *The Political Socialization of the Mexican American People* (New York: Arno Press, 1976), 138–39, 140, 141, 142. Katherine Underwood, "Pioneering Minority Representation: Edward Roybal and the Los Angeles City Council, 1949–1962," *Pacific Historical Review* 66, No. 3 (August 1, 1997), 399, 401, 403, 406, 415.

54 David Montejano, *Anglos and Mexicans in the Making of Texas, 1836–1986* (Austin: University of Texas Press, 1987), 276, 278. Rosales, *Illusion of Inclusion*, 13, 29, 42–43. Interview with Albert Peña, Jr., by José Angel Gutiérrez, July 2, 1996, Tejano Voices, University of Texas Arlington, http://library.uta.edu/tejanovoices/xml/CMAS_015.xml.

55 M. García, *Mexican Americans*, 113–41. Also see Mario T. García, *The Making of a Mexican American Mayor: Raymond L. Telles of El Paso* (El Paso: Texas Western, 1998). Márquez, "Power and Politics," 55–57, 72, 120–32. After the election, Democratic Party leaders abolished the primary for mayor. The party would now name its candidate, supposedly for saving the cost of running a primary. Telles, who had been chosen in a primary, supported the change because he incorrectly predicted that it would improve the Mexican community's chances of electing a mayor.

56 "Are the Rich Really Different?" Economist.com, April 11, 2009, http://www.economist.com/blogs/freeexchange/2007/04/11/are-the-rich-really-different. This is significant because the rich argue that taxation stunts productivity.

57 David E. Hayes-Bautista, Werner O. Schrink, and Jorge Chapa, *The Burden of Support: Young Latinos in an Aging Society* (Stanford, CA: Stanford University Press, 1988), 58.

58 *Salt of the Earth*—Herbert Biberman (1954), [the entire movie] http://www.youtube.com/watch?v=aXTcDUxu22A. Michael Wilson, *Salt of the Earth*, Screenplay (New York: The Feminist Press at the City University of New York, 1977). Ellen R Baker, "'Salt of the Earth': Women, the Mine, Mill and Smelter Workers' Union, and the Hollywood Blacklist in Grant County, New Mexico, 1941–1953" (PhD Dissertation, University of Wisconsin-Madison, 1999), 179.

59 George J. Sánchez, *Becoming Mexican American: Ethnicity, Culture and Identity in Chicano Los Angeles, 1900–1945* (New York: Oxford University Press, 1993), 251. Jack Cargill, "Empire and Opposition: The 'Salt of the Earth' Strike," in Robert Kern, ed., *Labor in New Mexico: Unions, Strikes and Social History Since 1881* (Albuquerque: University of New Mexico Press, 1983), 179–240.

60 *Joe R. Romero et al.* (plaintiffs) *v. Guy Weakley et al.* (defendants) and *R. J. Burleigh et al.* (plaintiffs) *v. Guy Weakley et al.* (defendants), Defendants. Nos. 1712-SD, 1713-SD. United States District Court for the Southern District of California, Southern Division. 131 F. Supp. 818; 1955 U.S. Dist. May 5, 1955. http://sshl.ucsd.edu/brown/romero.htm.

61 Best series on the *Hernandez v. State of Texas* case, *A Class Apart*, PBS Series, http://www.pbs.org/wgbh/americanexperience/films/class/player/. Best book on the case: Ignacio M. Garcia, *White But Not Equal: Mexican Americans, Jury Discrimination, and the Supreme Court* (Tucson: University of Arizona Press, 2008). Raul A. Reyes, "Remembering Gus Garcia, Mexican-American Civil Rights Pioneer," NBCNews, July 27, 2017. https://www.nbcnews.com/news/latino/remembering-gus-garcia-mexican-american-civil-rights-pioneer-n786391.

62 On May 17, 1954, the U.S. Supreme Court ruled unanimously that racial segregation in public schools violated the Fourteenth Amendment's equal protection clause, thus overturning *Plessy v. Ferguson* (1896) that permitted "separate but equal" public facilities. Meyer Weinberg, *Minority Students: Research Appraisal* (Washington, DC: U.S. Department of Health, Education and Welfare, 1977), 286–87. *G.I. Forum News Bulletin* (December 1953). "Edgar Taken to Federal Court on Segregation," *G.I. Forum News Bulletin* (April 1955). Carla M. McCullough, "*Brown v. Board of Education* (1954): An Analysis of Policy Implementation, Outcomes, and Unintended Consequences" (Ed.D. dissertation: Loyola Marymount University, 2012).

63 Henry A. J. Ramos, *The American GI Forum: In Pursuit of the Dream, 1948–1983* (Houstin: Arte Publico Press, 1998), 76.

64 *G.I. Forum News Bulletin* (January 1955). "Mercedes Policeman Who Menaced Family Resigns as Result of G.I. Forum Pressure," *G.I. Forum News Bulletin* (June 1953, September 1953, December 1953, May 1954, and February–March 1956). The G.I. Forum published numerous articles on police abuse throughout the Southwest.

65 *Hernandez v. Texas*, Civil Rights Story, http://forchicanachicanostudies.wikispaces.com/Reviews. "A Class Apart," Documentary on the

Hernandez Case, http://www.pbs.org/wgbh/americanexperience/class/. Ignacio M. García, *White but Not Equal: Mexican Americans, Jury Discrimination, and the Supreme Court* (Tucson: University of Arizona Press, 2008). Clare Sheridan, "'Another White Race': Mexican Americans and the Paradox of Whiteness in Jury Selection," *Law and History Review* 21, No. 1 (Spring 2003), http://www.historycooperative.org/journals/lhr/21.1/forum_sheridan.html.

66 Edward J. Escobar, "Bloody Christmas and the Irony of Police Professionalism: The Los Angeles Police Department, Mexican Americans, and Police Reform in the 1950s," *Pacific Historical Review* 72, No. 2 (May 2003), 171.

67 Briegel, *Alianza Hispano-Americana,* 183, 184. Armando Morales, "A Study of Mexican American Perceptions of Law Enforcement Policies and Practices in East Los Angeles" (DSW Dissertation, University of Southern California, 1972), 41, 77. In August 1949, a "Committee of 21" was created in the Hollenbeck area to improve police–community relations. It held two meetings and then faded away (Morales, "A Study," 83–84). See also *Eastside Sun* (Boyle Heights, March 9, April 13, 20, 1951). "El Sereno Defense Group to Give Dance," *Eastside Sun* (July 12, 1951). Ralph Guzmán, *Eastside Sun* (December 29, 1953). *Eastside Sun* (Boyle Heights, September 17, 1953). *G.I. Forum News Bulletin* (February–March 1956).

68 Fincher, *Spanish-Americans as a Factor in New Mexico,* 95–97. *Eastside Sun* (Boyle Heights, February 16, April 20, July 20, 1950; August 7, September 4, 1952). "New Spanish Speaking Group Formed in Texas," *Eastside Sun* (May 31, 1951). See also *Eastside Sun* (August 11, November 29, 1951, September 11, 1952). Briegel, *Alianza Hispano-Americana,* 179–83. *Eastside Sun* (Boyle Heights, February 10, 1955).

69 Dennis R. Judd, "Segregation Forever? Housing Discrimination," *The Nation* 253, No. 20 (December 9, 1991), 740 ff.

70 The reader is encouraged to analyze the coding in this quote. Was housing policy predicated on the goal of "a decent home and suitable living environment for every American family" or was this a pretext to spend hundreds of millions of dollars to satisfy the middle class and subsidize bankers and the construction industry?

71 Jacqueline Leavitt, "Urban Renewal Is Minority Renewal; Public Housing: Razing Units in Boyle Heights Reflects an Old Agenda," *Los Angeles Times* (October 11, 1996).

72 The History of Chávez Ravine, Independent Lens, PBS, http://www.pbs.org/independentlens/chavezravine/cr.html. Don Normark, *Chavez Ravine: 1949: A Los Angeles Story* (San Francisco, CA: Chronicle Books, 2003); wonderful photographs. Chavez Ravine & Segundo Barrio: Film Discussion, http://www.youtube.com/watch?v=MX1PDITprFA. Lawrence Bouett, "Were the Chávez Ravine Evictions Racist?" Chavez Ravine, Oct 2, 2015, https://www.chavezravine.org/blog/were-the-chavez-ravine-evictions-racist.

73 Mitchum Huehls, "Private Property as Story: Helena Viramontes' Their Dogs Came with Them," *Arizona Quarterly: A Journal of American Literature, Culture, and Theory*, Vol. 68, No. 4 (Johns Hopkins University Press, Winter, 2012), 155–182.

74 Acuña, *A Community Under Siege,* 58–61, 66–78; also accompanying references to the *Eastside Sun* and the *Belvedere Citizen*. Ronald William López, "The Battle for Chavez Ravine: Public Policy and Chicano Community Resistance in Post–War Los Angeles, 1945–1962" (PhD Dissertation, University of California, Berkeley, Fall 1999). Joseph Eli Kovner, "Route Would Slash Through Residential and Business Districts; Protests Mount," *Eastside Sun* (Boyle Heights, October 1, 1953). See also *Eastside Sun* (March 10, 1955; October 3, 17, and 24, 1957; February 27, December 30, 1958) and Joseph Eli Kovner, "The Arechiga Family Bodily Evicted from Home in Chavez Ravine," *Eastside Sun* (May 14, 1959). And see the Joseph Eli Kovner articles in the *Eastside Sun* (April 10, 17, 24; May 1, 8, 15; June 6, 12; July 3, 17, 24, 31, 1958). Joseph Eli Kovner, "Aide Quits in Bunker Hill Row," *Eastside Sun* (Boyle Heights October 9, 1958). *Eastside Sun* (December 4, 30, 1958). Joseph Eli Kovner, "'Resettle Elsewhere,' Says Mayor, 'If You Don't Want Urban Renewal,'" *Eastside Sun* (January 8, 1959). Joseph Eli Kovner, "Brazen Politics Endangers Lives to Lower Property Taxes," *Eastside Sun* (Boyle Heights, March 12, 1959). Bunker Hill cost the taxpayers $30 million to profit private individuals.

75 "Demographics of Chicago," http://en.wikipedia.org/wiki/Demographics_of_Chicago; follow the link and click on "1950 Ethnic Map of Chicago."

76 John McCarron, "Memory of Early Days Leaves Urban Renewal with Cross to Bear," *Chicago Tribune* (August 29, 1988). This section draws heavily from Dennis Nodín Valdes, *El Pueblo Mexicano en Detroit y Michigan: A Social History* (Detroit, MI: Wayne State University, 1982). Also see Manuel Castells, *The Urban Question: A Marxist Approach* (Cambridge, MA: MIT Press, 1979), 393–95. Lalo Guerrero: "Barrio Viejo," Cerritos College (1999), http://www.youtube.com/watch?v=vj-odkXy7hA, a nostalgic song on the destruction of Tucson's oldest *barrios*.

77 David R. Dean and Jean A. Reynolds, "Acculturation and the Roots of Social Change: 1940–1956," Hispanic Historic Property Survey, Historic Preservation Office, City of Phoenix (Athenaeum Public History Group, 2006), 73–75, 79–80, 85–86, 101–2, http://phoenix.gov/webcms/groups/internet/@inter/@dept/@dsd/documents/web_content/pdd_hp_pdf_00043.pdf.

Chapter 13
Goodbye America: The Chicana/o in the 1960s

 Learning Objectives

13.1 Characterize Mexican Americans based on the demographic profile at the start of the 1960s.

13.2 Discuss the influence of Civil Rights and the Vietnam War on Mexican American political activity in the 1960s.

13.3 Evaluate the relationship between GI Generation and Mexican American activists.

13.4 Explain how the War on Poverty motivated political involvement.

13.5 Analyze the transition from the GI Generation to the Chicano Generation.

13.6 Contextualize the impact of the 1965 Immigration Act on the priorities of the Chicana/o Movement.

13.7 Analyze the 1960s Chicana/o movement and the role of youth.

13.8 Describe the challenges and the results of the Chicana/o Youth Movement.

13.9 Explain how the government subversion disrupted the Chicano movement.

From 1946 to 1964, 76 million babies were born in the United States. The sheer magnitude of this group profoundly affected the economy, politics, fashions, and music of the 1960s as well as their relations with Chicanos, who as a community were younger than other groups.[1] A significant number of this rock-and-roll generation supported integration and opposed the Vietnam War. Youth played a role in the "leveling" of society. They were more receptive to the Black Civil Rights and Radical activists than the previous generation and became involved in the national dialogue on social and political justice.[2]

World War II also shaped the consciousness of a critical people in the colonies who internalized the promise of making the world safe for democracy. The idea of self-determination drove these aspirations and brought about the breakup of colonial empires built during the previous three centuries. They hoped to decolonize their countries and end their dependency on industrialized nations. The Western powers resisted this challenge to the world order, fearing that many of the new free nations would be vulnerable to Communist control or influence and, hence, opposed the liberation of non-white people. The Vietnam War was the result of failure of Western nations to live up to the promise of World War II—democracy for all—which made the movement to liberate the Third World inevitable and necessary. In turn, these liberation movements affected the Black Civil Rights movement and influenced liberal-minded people in the United States.[3]

World War II also heightened an awareness of civil rights and liberties among minorities. Social movements were and are driven by inequality and moral outrage about the at the lack of fairness in the system. Organizations such as the National Association for the Advancement of Colored People (NAACP), the League of United Latin American Citizens (LULAC), and the *Alianza Hispano-Americana* were active in obtaining these rights before World War II. During and after the war, "civil rights" took on a new meaning.[4]

Like the Civil Rights movement, the rock and roll began in the African American community influenced by blues tunes, gospel music, and jazz-influenced vocal music. It was adopted by the baby boomers of all colors, and set the rhythm for the Decade of Protest and innovation. Rock and roll was a form of rebellion that pulled together youth of all races—often as a vehicle for political and cultural rebellion.[5]

The Early 1960s

13.1 Characterize Mexican Americans based on the demographic profile at the start of the 1960s.

Between 1950 and 1960 the Spanish-surnamed population of the Southwest increased by 51 percent. Immigration from Mexico accounted for some of this growth, but more credit must given to fertility rate among U.S. Mexican women. According to the 1960 Census, an African American population of 18.9 million outnumbered the Mexican American population by almost five to one, and Latinos as a whole just less than four to one. U.S. Mexicans were also concentrated geographically, with Texas and California housing 82 percent of its population.[6]

The revolt of the youth challenged the control of the middle class and ruling elite. The Civil Rights, antiwar, and youth movements forged space for Chicanos and other Latinos within this opposition to the old order. Increasingly, urban Chicanos would be influenced by the political language and expressions, for example, of African Americans—especially their emphasis on identity politics and the call for power.

In Denial: Proving Poverty

Statistics are vital in proving the obvious—poverty and its causes. In the 1960s, the Ford Foundation funded a million dollar grant to University of California economist Leo Grebler to study Mexican Americans in the 1960 Census.[7] The Census counted 3,464,999 Spanish-surnamed persons in the Southwest with a per capita income of $968, compared with $2,047 for white Americans and $1,044 for nonwhites. Of the Spanish-surnamed population, 29.7 percent lived in deteriorated housing versus 7.5 percent of Americans and 27.1 percent of other non-whites. The Census further showed that the average size of the Spanish-surnamed family was 4.77, compared with 3.39 for Americans and 4.54 for other non-whites. Unemployment, too, was higher among Chicanos than among whites. The median school grade in the Southwest for Spanish-surnamed persons over 14 years of age was 8.1, versus 12.0 for Americans and 9.7 for other non-whites. Significantly, the median school grade attained by Spanish-surnamed in Texas was 4.8. Although Chicanos were not as strictly segregated as African Americans, most of them lived apart from the white community. Strict social segregation still existed, and in places like Texas and eastern Oregon, "No Mexicans Allowed" signs were common.[8]

THE EYES OF TEXAS: POVERTY IN SAN ANTONIO San Antonio, the second-largest Mexican American city, had a Mexican population of 243,627—17.2 percent of the 1,417,810 Mexicanos in state. Some 30,299 were first generation; 75,950, second generation; and 137,738, third or later generations. As in El Paso and Corpus Christi, a substantial number of Mexicans in San Antonio worked as migrants. Unemployment among Spanish-surnamed males was 7.7 percent, compared with 5.1 percent for males of all races; the unemployment rate of Mexican American females was 7.9 percent, versus 4.7 percent for all other females. Only 1.4 percent of the Chicanos had a college degree, and over three-quarters of Chicano high school students were enrolled in vocational classes.

The average annual income of Mexican Americans was about $2,000 less than whites. Some 42 percent of Spanish-surnamed families earned wages below the poverty line of $3,000 per year, compared with 16.2 percent for American families. In 1960, only Corpus Christi Mexicans had a lower median annual family income than San Antonio Mexicans—$2,974—who had a median of 4.5 years of education. In Houston, the Mexican families' median income was $4,339, with 6.4 school years. In South Texas, Mexicans lived in even more depressing conditions.

In San Antonio, less than 10 percent of the workforce belonged to trade unions. Few Mexicans were able to participate in the city's craft union apprenticeship programs; thus only a few could rise above the lowest ranks and become skilled tradesmen, who were in high demand and were better paid. Mexican were concentrated in pick-and-shovel occupations; for example, 85.4 percent of the hod carriers and 90 percent of cement workers were Mexican. They made up 59.5 percent of the city's 12 housing projects' residents. Only 49.7 percent of Mexicans population lived in homes with plumbing, in comparison to 94 percent for the whites.[9]

EL PASO, THE GATEWAY CITY El Paso has historically been a port of entry—the home of the historic El Segundo Barrio.[10] In 1960, the median family income for El Paso Mexicans was $3,857, and their median education was 6.5 years. Mexicans had spread throughout the city, with older colonias such as Ysleta making up the core of the expanded *barrios*. El Segundo Barrio (the Second Ward) continued to house the poorest of the poor in dilapidated housing. In 1967, three children in El Paso—Ismael, 8; Orlando, 7; and Leticia Rosales, 4—were burned to death in a fire caused by faulty electricity. Moral outrages resulted from the tragedy and Mexican community pressured the city for more programs, especially juvenile delinquency programs, It brought together young people who formed the Mexican American Youth Association (MAYA), the most active Chicano organization in El Paso during the 1960s. Renters also formed tenant unions to press for public housing. Militancy carried over to the University of Texas at El Paso, where, by the end of the decade, Chicano students demanded the admission of more Chicanos and a Chicano studies program.[11]

CITY OF THE ANGELS By 1960 Los Angeles housed the largest Mexican American community in the United States with its own cultural markers.[12] It was no accident that like San Antonio Los Angeles. would become one of the major centers of the Chicana/o movement. Los Angeles County's Mexican population mushroomed during the 1960s, going from 576,716 to 1,228,593—an increase of 113 percent. The white population decreased from 4,877,150 to 4,777,909—a 2 percent drop. In 1966, 76,619 white babies were born in Los Angeles, compared with 24,533 Latinos and 17,461 Blacks. Eight years later, 41,940 white babies, 45,113 Latino babies, and 16,173 Black babies were born in Los Angeles. Toward the end of the decade, the San Francisco–Oakland area experienced a similar growth, as the Latino population increased to 362,900. This population growth, however, differed from that of Los Angeles; it included larger numbers of Central and South Americans and Puerto Ricans. Unemployment and poverty among Mexican Americans were high throughout the first half of the 1960s.

As residential segregation increased, schools became more segregated. Mexicans made up more than 80 percent of the Boyle Heights–East Los Angeles area. Eastside schools had overcrowded classrooms, double sessions, a lack of Mexican American teachers, and a high pushout (dropout) rate.[13] Local leaders, along with the press, complained about the rise in juvenile delinquency and crime. By contrast, the San Fernando Valley, then a suburb where the white baby boomers went to school, received the bulk of the city's education and building funds. Even in the Valley Mexicans were segregated and lived in doughnut enclaves.[14]

CHICAGO: REIGN OF THE BULLDOZERS The first wave of Mexican migration to Chicago began in the mid to late 1910s. Much of it consisted of Mexican migrant workers stranded in the Midwest during the winter. Chicago is a city of immigrants a place known for its urban renewal programs. Mayor Richard Daley, land speculators, and developers who made a bundle of money bulldozing neighborhoods. During the 1950s and 1960s, expressways, the expansion of the Medical Center, and the University of Illinois at Chicago displaced many Mexicans, who moved a few blocks south and settled on *La Dieciocho* (Eighteenth Street, Pilsen *barrio*). Pilsen was a major manufacturing center, where the 1886 strike at the McCormick Reaper took place. The last wave of ethnics to occupy the Pilsen, consisted of Mexicans, many of whom were newcomers from Guanajuato, Jalisco, Michoacán, and Durango. The Mexican community was fractured along lines of citizenship, language, and documentation or lack of it. The median age in the Pilsen district—22—was lower than in Back of the Yards and South Chicago: 24.5 and 26 years, respectively. The most stable Chicana/o community was the South Side where Mexicans shared the area with other groups, including a significant number of Puerto Ricans.[15]

From 1950 to 1960, Chicago's Mexican population grew nearly fivefold—from 24,000 to 108,000—and congestion in the *barrios* worsened. Increasingly, new residents bypassed Texas and came directly from Mexico. From 1940 to 1960, approximately 401,000 whites fled the city. In the 1950s, the white population in the south suburbs nearly doubled and segregation became even more acute for the ghetto poor of the inner city. More than a third of Mexicans lived in overcrowded housing, paying abnormally high rent.[16]

Harvest of Shame: The Forgotten People

On November 25, 1960—the night after Thanksgiving—a Edward R. Murrow narrated a one-hour television documentary "Harvest of Shame". Murrow began, "These are the forgotten people, the under protected, the undereducated, the under clothed, and the underfed."[17] The documentary went on to tell the miserable plight of migrant workers, showing families working in blistering heat and living in rundown housing, enduring misery so an affluent nation could eat. Unlike their urban counterparts, migrants did not even receive Social Security benefits, since the government had exempted growers from paying into the fund. Over three-quarters of the children lived below the poverty line.[18]

The largest migrant stream of Mexican Americans was mostly from South Texas and included entire families. Some would travel only within the state, but many went into the Rocky Mountain, Great Plains, and Great Lakes states; the Northwest; and Florida. According to the documentary, "Along the routes, the Anglos are usually employed in tree crops, the Mexican Americans in stoop labor."[19]

In 1960, 16 percent of Spanish-surnamed males in the Southwest were farm laborers, compared to 2.1 percent of whites. In 1968, three-quarters of the Texas migrants worked in family units. In South Texas, the average Mexican American family consisted 6.5 members. In the 1960s (and even today), whole families—with small children often younger than 12 years of age—worked in the fields. The long work hours interfered with the education of the child workers, and few received more than a primary education.

Another migrant stream composed mostly of Mexican Americans traveled within California and along the Pacific Coast, often intersecting with Tejano migrants. Wages had changed little since 1956, when the average daily wage for a migrant was $5.14 in Texas. In that same year, a single migrant averaged $781 per year, and family income (i.e., with small children working at stoop labor) approximated $2,240 annually.[20] Most migrants got no paid holidays, sick days, or overtime, and no retirement or disability plans, or medical coverage.[21]

Delusions of the Awakening of the Sleeping Giant

13.2 Discuss the influence of Civil Rights and the Vietnam War on Mexican American political activity in the 1960s.

In January 1961, North Americans had high hopes that President John Fitzgerald Kennedy would "get the country moving again." No group was more optimistic than Mexican Americans who had played an active role in Kennedy's narrow victory in 1960. Without their vote, Kennedy would have lost Texas and the election.[22]

Officially, the U.S. Census counted nearly 4 million Mexican Americans: 87 percent lived in the Southwest, and 85 percent were born in the United States. This number was up 2 percent from 1950. The feeling among many Mexican Americans was that they achieved the critical mass to force the society to close the gaps in socioeconomic and political inequality through the ballot box. "Viva Kennedy" clubs almost gave JFK a victory in California and furnished a narrow win in Texas. Hence, the Mexican Americans felt that their vote was crucial to Kennedy's election; this gave them the illusion of power and acceptance in the world of gringo politics.[23] The sleeping giant was awake.[24]

San Antonio and Texas Politics

The Good Government League (GGL) controlled San Antonio politics and consisted of a downtown elite of bankers, developers, merchants, and real estate brokers. Members of the GGL also filled the San Antonio utility boards, and planning and zoning commissions with white representatives. As a matter of policy, the city government made few civic improvements on the West Side. Mayor W. W. McAllister, hostile to civic improvements in minority areas, promoted private development efforts, such as the Hemisfair, the South Texas Medical Center, the University of Texas at San Antonio, and new industry. Taxes were kept low by depriving minority communities of public services.

LULAC and the G.I. Forum remained active in San Antonio and South Texas and challenged the GGL. The leaders in both LULAC and the Forum had strong ties to the Democratic Party establishment. Most Mexican Americans were Catholic and Democrats, and supported President Lyndon Baines Johnson, who funneled patronage through the major Chicano organizations, when he succeeded to the presidency following JFK's assassination in 1963.

Many Mexicans joined a liberal faction led by George I. Sánchez and Mexican American labor leaders. They supported Ralph Yarborough's 1963 bid for governor, against LBJ's choice. The LBJ faction was composed of the old rural conservative Mexican American leadership. Johnson periodically nurtured his Mexican ties by referring to the Longoria case, his stint as a teacher in a Mexican school, his patronage to Mexicans, and his friendship with Mexican American leaders. In the late 1950s, he actively courted LULAC and the Forum during his unsuccessful 1960 bid for the presidency. However, most Mexican Americans supported JFK, with liberals criticizing LBJ's anti–civil rights record. In 1960, the Viva Kennedy clubs and the election of President John F. Kennedy stimulated political activity. Henry B. González was elected to the San Antonio City Council in 1951; by 1961 he was a congressman.[25] County Commissioner Albert Peña, Jr., and his aide Albert Fuentes organized Viva Kennedy clubs throughout Texas.[26] The clubs played a key role in electing Kennedy and in the formation of the Political Association of Spanish-speaking Organizations (PASO)[27] in 1961, which became an all-Texas affair. Peña and the Teamsters supported the Mexican American efforts to gain proportional representation on Crystal City Council in 1963, with temporary success.[28]

PASO split into liberal and conservative factions. Peña led liberals; the G.I. Forum's Dr. Hector García, along with LULAC's Bonilla brothers, William and Tony, headed the conservatives. García and the Bonillas criticized PASO's role in the 1963 Crystal City takeover, claiming that the Teamsters had gained control of PASO. Dr. García and members of the LULAC walked out of PASO's 1963 convention. García, a staunch supporter of LBJ and Texas Governor John Connally, feared Mexican involvement with more liberal Democrats. Shortly afterward, LULAC and the Forum entered the poverty program network. The Crystal City takeover lasted only two years. Personality conflicts and factionalism tore the coalition apart. Meanwhile, Mexican Americans were upset when Kennedy did not give them representation in office. They criticized the selection of conservative Reynaldo Garza, an old friend of LBJ, to the federal court.

Meanwhile, PASO chose Crystal City, Texas—a small town of 10,000 in the Winter Garden region of southwest Texas—the majority were Mexican people. It was chosen by PASO as a test site for a get-out-the-Mexican-vote drive. PASO's slate of city council candidates for the city council was successful, electing Juan Cornejo, a local Teamsters Union business agent, along with four other Mexican Americans. Though the electoral coup only lasted two years, it lit a spark for later successes and was a training ground for leaders such as José Angel Gutiérrez, founder of the Mexican American Youth Organization (MAYO) in 1967 and *La Raza Unida* Party in 1969. *Time* magazine ran an article declaring that the sleeping giant had awakened, predicting that Mexican Americans going to become a national power group. It described how the Texas Rangers stood by in case of trouble. The article went on:

> In a way, the Crystal City Mexicans did stir up trouble for themselves. They control the town's government, but the Anglos control its economy. One council-seat winner

got fired from his job in a hardware store. Another found his wages cut in half by his Anglo employer. But, mindful that Mexicans outnumber Anglos in South Texas, PASO looks upon the Crystal City election as a momentous triumph. Says Albert Fuentes, the PASO official who led the campaign: "We have done the impossible. If we can do it in Crystal City, we can do it all over Texas. We can awake the sleeping giant." On Election Day, the Mexicans have learned, all South Texans are equal.[29]

In 1964, Mexican Americans elected Eligio (Kika) de la Garza to Congress.[30] Slowly, the playing field became less bumpy, and in 1966, the 24th Amendment abolished the poll tax. It renewed hope as Mexican Americans increasingly ran for office. In Mathis, in San Patricio County near Corpus Christi, Mexicans formed the Action Party in 1965, taking control of the municipal government. Their goal was to improve municipal services for Mexicans. In 1967, the Action Party won reelection.[31]

Los Angeles Politics

California did not have an organizational network comparable to that of Texas. The Mexican American Political Association (MAPA) was formed in 1959, but like most Mexican American organizations, its membership was low. Many MAPA members were active in the liberal California Democratic Council (CDC) that supported the Civil Rights movement and promoted representation for African Americans—but ignored Mexicans. Party leaders rationalized that gerrymandering Mexican districts would be beneficial for that community. Incumbents blatantly gerrymandered Mexican *barrios* throughout California. Reapportionments of 1961, 1965, and 1967 purposely split the Mexican American population, for example, in East Los Angeles, where the 40th, 45th, 48th, 50th, and 51st Assembly Districts cut into the area to pick up 20 to 30 percent of the Mexican American districts; the 52nd, 53rd, 65th, and 66th took smaller bites. The purpose was to create of Democratic district.[32]

In 1962, John Moreno and Phil Soto were elected to the California State Assembly. Moreno failed to get reelected two years later, and Soto was voted out in 1966.[33] The election of Edward R. Roybal to the U.S. Congress, also in 1962, also left a void in local politics. The Los Angeles City Council, despite community protests, appointed an African American—Gilbert Lindsay—to replace Roybal. The council reapportioned the districts, making the election of three Blacks probable but a victory for a Mexican American impossible. Without local leadership, the Mexican community was vulnerable to the schemes of opportunistic politicians such as Councilwoman Rosalind Wyman who was an advocate of urban renewal and one of the main players in bringing the Dodgers to Los Angeles (wiping out the Mexican community of Chavez Ravine. The Wymans were also known to support the interests of the Westside at the expense of the Eastside.

Los Angeles highly influenced California politics. Although its Mexican population was the largest in the United States, Mexican Americans held few political offices. The Democratic Party purposely allowed the voting registration of Mexican Americans to lapse. The only place Mexican Americans could win was in small compact districts in judicial races. In 1963, Los Angeles Municipal Court Judge Leopold Sánchez noted that out of 5,000 judicial appointments made by Governor Edmund G. Brown, Sr., fewer than 30 were Chicanos. Mexican Americans were incensed when Brown implied a lack of qualified persons to choose from them.[34]

Political Organizing in Chicago

The type of political involvement Mexicans engaged in depended on where they lived in Chicago. For example, in South Chicago second-generation steelworkers took part in union affairs and local politics. They formed the Tenth Ward Spanish-Speaking Democratic Organization. With the support of this Tenth Ward Organization and that of the steelworkers' union, John Chico, was a community activist, openly challenged the Daley machine. Chico lost the election, and Daley retaliated; he withheld patronage, gerrymandering the Tenth into two separate wards to dilute Mexican voting power.[35]

During the decade, Pilsen, the largest Mexican *barrio*, developed a strong identity. Within Pilsen, neighborhood organizations evolved to defend the space against gentrification. The new residents were poor and were plagued with problems such as gangs, crime, and high rates of school dropouts—yet there was a growing awareness of place among Chicanos. Increasingly, they began identifying with the Chicano movement.

During the 1960s, the Little Village community (26th Street) integrated into the Pilsen (18th Street). Little Village Mexicans/Latinos were on the average economically better off than the Pilsen residents. Both these communities suffered from inability to adjust to the change in a Mexican neighborhood. At that time, schools, the churches, and the Daley machine responded to older ethnics than to the new majority (whiter ethnics). By the end of the 1960s, however, Mexican institutions and agencies emerged in greater numbers: *El Centro de La Causa,* BASTA (Brotherhood Against Slavery to Addiction), Mexican American Mental Health, the Mexican American Council on Education, the Brown Berets, and the Organization of Latin American Students. In response to this growing Mexican nationalism, Howell House changed its name to Casa Aztlán, the home of the Benito Juárez Health Clinic. Chicanos in Chicago readily adopted the nationalist symbols of their southwestern counterparts.[36]

The Building of a Civil Rights Coalition

13.3 Evaluate the relationship between GI Generation and Mexican American activists.

John Kennedy, moved by huge civil rights demonstrations and urban and campus unrest, appealed to liberals and minorities by announcing his "New Frontier" initiative. It was more a statement of aspirations than a program. The assassination of Kennedy in November 1963. As a consequence, President Lyndon B. Johnson skillfully pushed major civil rights legislation through Congress and launch his Great Society (the so-called War on Poverty). Like Kennedy and Franklin Roosevelt, Johnson relied heavily on eastern intellectuals to plan his national program, part of which was intended to placate the growing militancy among African Americans.[37]

Viva Johnson

Johnson's 1964 election campaign immediately built a "Viva Johnson" network. Dr. Hector García headed the Texas operation, and Bert Corona managed the California campaign. Johnson brought back Vicente Ximenes, the ambassador to Ecuador, to head the national effort to garner the Mexican American vote. Ximenes actively recruited Mexican American women as volunteers and staff, calling them the "best source of grassroots campaign work."[38] However, only a few found their way into the higher levels of the organization. Some of these women, such as Polly Baca (Colorado), head of the G.I. Forum Ladies Auxiliary; Fran Flores (California); and Cleotilde García (Texas). Although the roles of the two women were minimized they played crucial roles. García, for instance, headed the Viva Johnson campaign in Nueces County. organizing rallied and spearheading registration drives.

Not all Mexican American organizations operated under the Viva Johnson campaign. Labor leader César Chávez and the farmworkers worked independently to support Johnson. Herman Gallegos and the Community Service Organization (CSO) operated through the California State Democratic Committee. After the election, the Democratic Party again showed its lack of loyalty by dismantling the Viva Johnson network, much as it done four years ago in dismantling Viva Kennedy.[39]

Building the Great Society

In 1964, LBJ went beyond JFK's New Frontier, declaring a "War on Poverty," and proposing the Economic Opportunity Act of 1964. The Act laid the framework for the planning and coordination of the war on poverty through the Office of Economic Opportunity (OEO).[40] Johnson's plan, labeled "The Great Society," dramatically escalated job-training programs, which were initiated by the Manpower Development and Training Act (MDTA) of 1962. New programs such as the Job Corps, Head Start, Upward Bound, and Volunteers in Service to America (VISTA) fell under the OEO. Congress allocated $1.6 billion annually to eliminate poverty—an amount, considering that 30–40 million poor living in the United States, did not go very far.[41]

The War on Poverty strengthened LBJ's patronage network, and the G.I. Forum and LULAC were first in line for patronage funds. Congressman Henry B. González received his share of the patronage. Though Johnson practiced more inclusion of Mexican American males, Mexicanas did not fare well with him personally. According to historian Julie Leininger Prycior, supporters knew Johnson was antagonistic toward women; he refused to include them in meetings, and would say, "Get those women out of here!" Nevertheless, there were exceptions such as Cleotilde García who established nursing programs with OEO seed money in South Texas; María Urquides of Arizona served on the National Advisory Council on Extension and Continuing Education; and Californian Henrietta Villaescusa acted as a liaison between the Department of Health, Education, and Welfare and local community groups.[42] Graciela Olivárez of Arizona worked her way up the OEO bureaucracy to become Arizona's acting OEO director, but was bypassed for the permanent position. Olivárez was the first Chicana to organize on a national scale when Johnson appointed her to the Equal Employment Opportunity Commission (EEOC).[43] As a consequence of the Civil Rights movement, President Johnson was able to push through the Voting Rights Act of 1965 which became his signature legislation.[44]

The Albuquerque, New Mexico, Walkout

On March 28, 1966, the federal Equal Employment Opportunity Commission (EEOC) held a meeting in Albuquerque, New Mexico, to investigate Chicana/o employment problems. Fifty Chicanos, including Graciela Olivárez, walked out because, although the commission advocated equal employment, the EEOC did not have a single Mexican on staff. When asked for a reason, EEOC Executive Director Herman Edelman blamed the disorganization of Mexican American organizations, stating that only 12 of the 300 complaints since 1965 had came from Mexican Americans. The dissidents formed the Mexican American Ad Hoc Committee in Equal Employment Opportunity. President Johnson met with *selected* MAPA, G.I. Forum, and LULAC leaders at the White House on May 26, 1966. Johnson pacified the invited guests by promising them a White House conference. In June 1967 he appointed Vicente Ximenes to the EEOC. Shortly afterward, LBJ named Ximenes head of the newly created Interagency Committee on Mexican American Affairs. This office mollified some middle-class activists whose primary goal was affirmative action.

LBJ did not keep his promise of holding a White House conference. The president feared that Chicanas/os would walk out and embarrass him politically. Instead, in October 1967 Johnson held cabinet committee hearings at El Paso, Texas. Johnson did not bother inviting the leading activists—César Chávez, Reies López Tijerina, or Rodolfo "Corky" Gonzales. The conference coincided with the celebration of the signing of the Chamizal Treaty, a disputed section of land on the Mexico–Texas border. (The Rio Grande had shifted over the years, leaving land formerly belonging to Mexico on the U.S. side. The treaty gave this disputed land back to Mexico). The Chamizal Treaty displaced 5,595 residents, mostly Mexican American, who had to move to the U.S. side. At El Paso, Johnson bused *his* Mexicans to join the celebrations of the return of the Chamizal people to Mexico.

LULAC and the G.I. Forum were the largest Mexican American organizations represented at the cabinet committee hearings. Meanwhile, dissident activists boycotted and picketed the hearings. They called their group *La Raza Unida* (the United Race or People); Ernesto Galarza of San José, Corky Gonzales, and Reies López Tijerina played leading roles in this opposition. Representatives of 50 Chicano organizations met at San Antonio and pledged support to the idea of *La Raza Unida*; about 1,200 people attended.[45]

Bilingual Education

13.4 Explain how the War on Poverty motivated political involvement.

According to Congressman Edward R. Roybal, a California Democrat, Johnson pushed the notion of bilingual education. During a flight in Air Force One, LBJ recalled his teaching experience in a Mexican school describing how smart the children were but did not know how to speak English. Mexican children therefore lost valuable time learning to speak English. Bilingual education in the early days was a simple concept that studying in both languages would make Mexican American child bilingual -bicultural. It was never meant to be for remediation, as Dr. George I. Sánchez so aptly put it. In Sánchez's view, it also included the teaching of Spanish language to Mexican Americans.[46]

In reality, the initiative for the first bilingual bill came from U.S. Senator Ralph Yarborough from Texas. Lupe Anguiano, who joined the Department of Health, Education and Welfare after the preplanning conference for the El Paso Hearings, and others also lobbied for bilingual education.[47] Anguiano became an advocate after witnessing the great number of schools in California that labeled students "mentally retarded" because they did not know how to speak English. Schools throughout the Southwest banned the speaking of Spanish on school grounds. Anguiano and others prepped sponsors on the bill, which was introduced on January 17, 1967.

Meanwhile, the Office of Education offered Armando Rodríguez the opportunity to head its Mexican American unit; it involved working with White House staffers to draw up a bilingual education bill. Up to this point Lupe Anguiano organized strategy in the House of Representatives, and she lobbied for a Mexican American to head the newly formed unit. However, Anguiano and Rodríguez clashed over policy, and by the end of 1967, Anguiano rejoined César Chávez.

Rodríguez departed from Dr. Sánchez's insistence on teaching Spanish; he emphasized pedagogical methods to teach Mexican students to speak both in English and Spanish. At this point there was consensus among Rodríguez, Anguiano, and Roybal that the bilingual education bill should not be included in the poverty bill; they feared that the program would be stigmatized. The bill passed 12 months later, with little support from White House aides. Much of the funding for the first bilingual program came from the Hearst Corporation.[48]

The Black–White Syndrome

As a result of the War on Poverty, African Americans and other minorities competed for resources. Many Chicanas/os at the time believed that federal and state bureaucrats played off the two groups against each other—seeing life as black and white. Undoubtedly, the intensity of the African American struggle and the size of its population forced Washington to pay more attention to their demands. By the mid-1960s, the Black community exploded. Urban renewal in the 1950s reduced the supply of low-rent housing, thus dislocating thousands of poor people. Northern cities became tinderboxes. Los Angeles's Black population was small before World War II but it zoomed in the postwar years. Freeways isolated that community, hiding poverty behind concrete walls. In places like Watts, the infrastructure was grossly inadequate to absorb newcomers. Unemployment hovered around 30 percent.

In August 1965, the African Americans in Watts rebelled, leaving 35 dead and causing property damage of $200 million. The governor sent 14,000 members of the National Guard to occupy Watts.[49] Two years later, another rebellion hit Newark, New Jersey, leaving 26 dead. In 1969, 43 died in a rebellion in Detroit, where 8,000 guardsmen and 4,700 paratroopers occupied the battle zone. Because these incidents heightened middle-class fears, Congress passed legislation to control the political threat by keeping the rebellious African Americans in tow.

Substandard economic and social conditions similar to those of African Americans plagued Mexican *barrios* throughout the United States. The *barrios* did not explode with the same force as the Black ghettos did. In the mid-1960s, some Mexican Americans offered naïve cultural explanations about why Mexicans did not riot; they pictured themselves as more peaceful than African Americans. According to Lorena Oropeza, the tendency of many established Mexican American leaders was to represent their community as worthy of society's attention "based upon the Mexican Americans' commendable behavior on the battlefield, but also—indicating increasing political participation—at the polls."[50] One explanation for the difference in the responses of the two communities to oppression is that institutions of social control were stronger in the Mexican *barrios* than in ghettos like Watts. Mexicans had lived in colonias such as San Antonio for generations. In Los Angeles, Mexican communities, despite continuous population shifts, were more stable than the Black areas. The Mexican family remained much more intact than families in Watts. A common language and a similar cultural background kept intact at least the facade of a Mexican American community. Homeownership was also higher in Mexican American areas than in Watts.

The absence of a militant response from the Mexican American community made African Americans believe that Chicanos were not making the same level of sacrifice as Blacks were. Given the overwhelming presence of African Americans, Mexican Americans and other minorities had a difficult time convincing people that they too belonged to the Civil Rights movement. When the United Civil Rights Coalition was formed in Los Angeles in 1963, it refused to admit Mexican Americans. They had to wait until the *Cisneros v. Corpus Christi Independent School District* decision (1970) for the courts to classify Mexican Americans as an "identifiable ethnic minority with a pattern of discrimination."[51]

A Second Coming

This was changing. When Carey McWilliams wrote *North from Mexico* in 1948 there was little interest in the history of the Mexican Americans. In 1950 Mexican Americans were about 3,231,409 Mexicans in the United States 2.1% of the total U.S. population. By the 1960s a change took place with a growth in the Mexican American numbers. This growth drove a demand for the reprint of North From Mexico.

Along with the growth of the Mexican American community, political activist and a growing militancy the was more coverage on the group. Los Angeles being a media center helped. Carey McWilliams attributed the growing presence of Mexican Americans to the 1960 presidential election, *"This was the first time that the Spanish-speaking vote figured prominently in a Presidential election. It was this vote, enlarged by an active registration campaign that probably saved Texas for the Kennedy-Johnson Ticket."* Carey McWilliams, in a reprint edition in 1969, acknowledges this new burst of interest, wrote that it *". . . in large part, has come about as a result of activities and developments for which they (the Mexican Americans) themselves are responsible."*[52]

The Disillusion

13.5 **Analyze transition from the GI Generation to the Chicano Generation.**

Almost from the beginning, the War on Poverty ran into difficulties. City bosses viewed community action programs that supposedly organized the poor as subversive and promoting rebellion. These political machines responded by making the moves gain local control of the federally administered poverty programs and their budgets. The War on Poverty also lacked funds because the Johnson administration had siphoned off money to finance the Vietnam War. The country could not afford two wars. Space, missile, and armament programs took precedence over people. North American society did not consider the ending of poverty a worthwhile goal. White Americans increasingly wanted the poor to just go away. According to U.S. Senator Barry Goldwater, "The fact is that most people who have no skill have no education for the same reason—low intelligence or low ambition."[53]

Bureaucratic conflicts also weakened the War on Poverty. The Department of Labor refused to cooperate with OEO; social workers perceived it as a threat to the welfare bureaucracy and their hegemony among the poor. Local politicians claimed that OEO programs "fostered class struggle." Meanwhile, as government officials and others quickly gained control of the programs, the participation of the poor declined. By 1966, President Johnson began dismantling the OEO, with Head Start going to Health, Education, and Welfare, and the Job Corps to the Department of Labor. He then substituted the "Model Cities" program for OEO. Johnson, faced with opposition within his own party over the war in Vietnam, announced that he would not seek reelection. The assassination of Robert Kennedy during the California primary also dealt a blow to Mexican American hope. The election of Richard Nixon in 1968 put the proverbial final nail in the coffin.

Impact of the War on Poverty

The impact of the War on Poverty on Mexican Americans was huge. A study of 60 OEO advisory boards in East Los Angeles–Boyle Heights–South Lincoln Heights, for instance—showed that 1,520 individuals, 71 percent of whom lived in these communities, served on the boards; two-thirds were women. Many Mexican American activists of the 1960s developed a sense of political consciousness as a result of poverty programs, which advertised the demands and grievances of the poor and created an ideology that legitimized protest. Many minorities realized that they had the right to work in government and to petition it. Legal aid programs and Head Start, a public preschool system, also proved invaluable to the poor. The number of poor fell dramatically between 1965 and 1970 as Social Security, health, and welfare payments more than doubled. When the federal government cut the last of the War on Poverty programs in the 1980s, poverty escalated.[54]

Magnetization of the Border

13.6 Contextualize the impact of the 1965 Immigration Act on the priorities of the Chicana/o Movement.

A population boom in Mexico tossed millions into Mexico's labor pool, thus intensifying push factors. In 1950, Mexico had a population of 25.8 million; it jumped to 34.9 million 10 years later and was rushing toward 50 million by the end of the 1960s. Driving this increase was the fertility rate of Mexican women, which increased from 1.75 percent in 1922–1939 to 2.25 percent in 1939–1946 to 6.9 percent in the late 1950s. The data are based on the percentage of growth for a particular year or years.[55] During these years, Mexico had the fastest-growing gross national product (GNP) in Latin America, but this did not offset this dramatic population increase.

The termination of the *bracero* (guest worker) program in 1964 worsened Mexico's plight drastically cutting remittances sent by migrant workers to their families at home. Mexico's economy simply could not absorb its increasing population. Matters worsened with a decline of ruralism, caused in part by mechanization and the growing commercialization of Mexican farms, which displaced small farmers. Simultaneously, the United States was going through good times, attracting underemployed and unemployed Mexican workers. The wartime economy, the Civil Rights movement, and the youth culture temporarily distracted white citizens from the heavy migration of undocumented workers. The nation's racist, nativist tendencies remained dormant.

American growers pressured the border patrol to keep the border porous, ensuring a continuous flood of workers. Meanwhile, the phenomenon known as "runaway shop" took form. Simply said, Mexico became a favorite destination for North American multinational businesses to enjoy special privileges and exploit loopholes provided by the U.S. law. The Customs Simplification Act of 1956 allowed the processing abroad of metal goods, which would be returned to the United States for finishing. Congress broadened this provision in 1963 to include items such as apparel and toys. These runaway shops were located along the border to cut down on transportation and labor costs. Understandably, U.S. labor opposed these loopholes, but it lacked sufficient power to stop the flow of jobs out of the United States.

Mexico agreed to the Border Industrialization Program (BIP), which entailed waiving duties and regulations on the import of raw materials, and relaxing restrictions on foreign capital within 12.5 miles of the border (this area has continuously been expanded); 100 percent of the finished products were to be exported out of the country and 90 percent of the labor force was to consist of Mexicans. In 1966, 20 BIP plants operated along the border; this number increased to 120 in 1970 and to 476 in 1976. The so-called *maquiladoras* (assembly plants) did create jobs (20,327 in 1970) but this did not relieve Mexico's unemployment problems. More than 70 percent of the BIP workforce were women who earned the minimum Mexican wage. North American employers offered no job security, and the *maquiladoras* could move at the owners' whim. Furthermore, the BIP left relatively little capital in Mexico. Like the *bracero* program, the border program increased Mexican dependence on the United States.[56]

The Immigration Act of 1965

Journalist Theodore White said that the 1965 Amendment to the Immigration Act "was noble, revolutionary—and probably the most thoughtless of the many acts of the Great Society."[57] The Act changed immigration policy: The basis for admitting immigrants shifted from national origin to family preference; those already having family in the United States were given higher quota preferences. At the time, legislators expected Europeans to be the main applicants; thus, there was no problem.[58]

The national-origin system of immigration of the 1920s shielded the United States from against the fresh immigration of Poles, Italians, Slavs, and Eastern European Jews. The laws were intentionally racist and from 1930 to 1960, about 80 percent of U.S. immigrants came from Western Europe or Canada. The 1965 Act opened the country to other races and ethnic peoples, specifically Asians. (Improved conditions in Western Europe made the United States less of an attraction to Europeans, and few applied.) During the first years of the Act, most white Americans were not concerned, because those applying were highly educated Latin Americans and Asians. Liberals such as Senator Edward Kennedy sponsored the legislation because they wanted to correct the past injustice of excluding Asians from legal entry. Before the Act there had been no quota for Latin Americans; however, the trade-off for taking the exclusion of Asians off the books was the placing of Latin Americans and Canadians on a quota system. The law specified that 170,000 immigrants from the Eastern Hemisphere and 120,000 from the Western could enter annually. Until the 1965 Act, Mexico had been the principal source of Latin American immigration; the new law put a cap of 40,000 from any one nation.[59]

Mexican American Reaction to Nativism

During the 1950s Mexican American organizations supported restricting undocumented workers and encouraged the government to exclude undocumented Mexicans. Organizations such as the American G.I. Forum and LULAC gave the federal government almost unconditional support. Trade unions supported this restrictive policy and rationalized that the exclusion of Mexican nationals was necessary to cut unfair labor competition between Mexican American and other U.S. based workers. Even so, Mexican American organizations were concerned about gross human rights violations, and pro-foreign-born groups concerned with human rights flourished among Latinos. Immigration, however, was not a priority among Mexican Americans in 1965.

Yet, the cumulative experiences and collective memories of old-time activists alerted them to a probable renewal of racist nativism. *La Hermandad Mexicana Nacional* (the Mexican National Brotherhood), based out of the San Diego area and established in 1951, reflected the tradition of the American Committee for Protection of Foreign Born. During the 1960s, Hermandad joined Bert Corona, then the driving force behind MAPA. Corona correctly deduced that the passage of the 1965 Immigration Act would renew the nativism of the 1950s. With Soledad "Chole" Alatorre, an Los Angeles labor organizer, Juan Mariscal, and Estella García, among others, Corona opened a Hermandad office in Los Angeles to protect the constitutional rights of workers without papers. Hermandad functioned like a *mutualista*, offering self-help services. It then opened additional centers known as *Centro de Acción Social Autónoma* (CASA). At the height of its influence, CASA had 4,000 members. Both Corona and Alatorre were also very active in other aspects of Mexican American political life of the time, and their influence would be felt through the next three decades. In fact, CASA created the progressive template for the protection of the foreign-born.[60]

The Road to Delano

For many, César Chávez began the Chicano movement. Chávez and the farmworkers gave Mexican Americans a cause, symbols, and a national space to claim their presence in the country's Civil Rights movement.[61] On September 8, 1965, the Filipinos in the Agricultural Workers Organizing Committee (AWOC) struck the grape growers of the Delano area in the San Joaquín Valley for higher wages. The Di Giorgio Corporation led the growers. On September 16, the National Farm Workers Association (NFWA) voted to join the Filipinos. The end of the *bracero* program in late 1964 significantly strengthened the union's position. The strike itself dragged on for years, during which time its dramatic events and the brutality of many of the growers attracted millions of non–Chicano supporters. Chávez's strategy was to maintain the union's moral authority by employing civil disobedience and fasts to call attention to the *causa* (cause), following the example of Mohandas Gandhi and the Rev. Martin Luther King, Jr. The strategy of civil disobedience was to call attention to injustices by refusing to obey unjust laws and injunctions. César frequently went to jail and would fast in order to rally his supporters.[62]

Born in Yuma, Arizona, in 1927, César Chávez spent his childhood as a migrant worker. In the 1940s, he moved to San José, California, where he married Helen Fabela. In San José, Chávez met Father Donald McDonnell, who tutored him in *Rerum Novarum*, Pope Leo XIII's encyclical supporting labor unions and social justice. Chávez met Fred Ross of the CSO and became an organizer for the CSO, learning grassroots organizing methods. He went on to become the general director of the national CSO, but in 1962, he resigned and moved to Delano, where he organized the NFWA.[63]

Chávez carefully selected a loyal cadre of proven organizers, such as Dolores Huerta and Gil Padilla, whom he had met in the CSO. Huerta was born Dolores Fernández in a mining town in New Mexico in 1930. She was a third-generation Mexican American, and her father was a miner and seasonal sugar beet worker. When her parents divorced, Huerta's mother and siblings moved to Stockton, California, where her mother worked night shift in a cannery. Eventually, Huerta became a CSO organizer; it was there she met César Chávez, whom she joined in forming the NFWA.[64]

By the middle of 1964, the NFWA was self-supporting; a year later, the union had some 1,700 members. Volunteers, fresh from civil rights activities in the South, joined the NFWA at Delano. Protestant groups inspired by the Civil Rights movement championed the workers' cause. A minority of Catholic priests influenced by the Second Vatican Council joined Chávez.[65] American labor belatedly joined the cause. In Chávez's favor was the growing number of Chicano workers living in the United States, many of whom were in trade unions. The changing times allowed Chávez to make the farmworkers' movement a crusade.

The most successful strategy was the boycott. The NFWA urged supporters not to buy Schenley products or Di Giorgio grapes. The first breakthrough came in 1966 when the Schenley Corporation signed a contract with the union. The next opponent was the Di Giorgio Corporation, one of the largest grape growers in the Central Valley. In April 1966, owner Robert Di Giorgio unexpectedly announced that he would allow his workers at Sierra Vista to vote on whether the farmworkers wanted a union. However, Di Giorgio did not act in good faith, and his agents set out to intimidate the workers.

Di Giorgio invited the Teamsters to compete with and thus break the NFWA. Di Giorgio held a series of fraudulent elections certifying the Teamsters as the bargaining agent. The NFWA pressured Governor Edmund G. Brown, Sr., to investigate the elections. Brown needed the Chicano vote, as well as that of liberals who were committed to the farmworkers. The governor's investigator recommended a new election, and the date was set for August 30, 1966. Di Giorgio red-baited the union and carried on an active campaign that drained the union's financial resources. This forced Chávez to reluctantly apply for affiliation in the American Federation of Labor and form the United Farm Workers Organizing Committee (UFWOC), which won the election—573 votes to the Teamsters' 425. Field workers voted 530 to 331 in favor of the UFWOC.

In 1967, the UFWOC targeted the Giumarra Vineyards Corporation (the largest producer of table grapes in the United States), boycotting all California table grapes. The result was a significant decline in grape sales. In June 1970, when the strike was approaching its fifth year, a group of Coachella Valley growers agreed to sign contracts. Victories in the San Joaquín Valley and other areas followed.

After the grape industry victory, the union turned to the lettuce fields of the Salinas Valley; growers of the area were among the most powerful in the state. During July 1970, the Growers–Shippers Association and 29 of the largest growers in the valley entered into negotiations with the Teamsters. Agreements signed with the truckers' union in Salinas were worse than sweetheart contracts. (A sweetheart contract is one made through collusion between management and labor representatives containing terms beneficial to management and detrimental to union workers.) The contracts provided no job security, no seniority rights, no hiring hall, and no protection against pesticides.

By August 1970, many workers refused to abide by the Teamster contracts, and 5,000 workers walked off the lettuce fields. The growers launched a campaign of violence. Thugs beat Jerry Cohen, a farmworker lawyer, into unconsciousness. On December 4, 1970, Judge Gordon Campbell of Monterey County jailed Chávez for refusing to obey an injunction and held him without bail. This arbitrary action gave the boycott the needed publicity; dignitaries visited Chávez in jail. On the face of mounting pressure, authorities released him on Christmas Eve. By the spring of 1971, Chávez and the Teamsters signed an agreement that gave the UFWOC sole jurisdiction.[66]

La Casita Farms Corporation Strike of 1966 and the Aftershocks

Texas remained a union organizer's nightmare. South Texas's long border ensured growers' access to a constant and abundant supply of cheap labor. The Texas Rangers, the local courts, and right-to-work laws gave growers almost an insurmountable advantage. The Chávez movement in California and the growing militancy after the 1963 Crystal City takeover influenced the Texas farmworkers, resulting 1966–1967 strikes. Eugene Nelson (who had been with Chávez in California), Margil Sánchez, and Lucio Galván formed the Independent Workers Association (IWA) in May 1966. In June, IWA members voted to affiliate with the NFWA and the UFWOC. More than 400 workers voted to strike the melon growers of Starr County on June 1, 1966. From the beginning, it was a violent strike, with the Texas Rangers under Captain A. Y. Allee, Jr., spreading a reign of terror.[67]

In the concluding days of June 1967, strikers began a march from Rio Grande City to Austin that ended on Labor Day. Over 15,000 people joined the march in its final days, with thousands more greeting the marchers as they made their way to Corpus Christi, to San Antonio, and then to Austin, the capital of Texas. Not wanting to meet the marchers in the state capital, Governor John Connally, Speaker of the House Ben Barnes, and Attorney General Waggoner Carr met the marchers in New Braunfels in August. Connally, who favored agribusiness, tried unsuccessfully to dissuade the marchers from entering Austin. Tens of thousands of supporters converged on the Texas state capitol. César Chávez and U.S. Senator Ralph Yarborough participated in the march.[68]

After this, the marchers wound their way through Starr and Hidalgo Counties. At the Roma Bridge in Starr County, they tried to take control of the bridge to stop the recruitment of undocumented workers to break the strike. Texas Rangers made mass arrests. On September 30, 1967, a hurricane destroyed the citrus crop, depressing labor conditions and ending all hope of success. Chávez pulled back, saying that the strike was premature in Texas, where Chávez did not have the liberal support that the farmworkers had in California.[69] Moreover, Texas growers were not as vulnerable to a secondary boycott. Chávez left Antonio Orendain, 37, in charge of membership and placement services in Texas. The strike was supported by Archbishop Robert Lucey of San Antonio, and the congressional hearings drew attention to the Third World–like conditions in the Valley. Throughout the strike, the Rangers and the state bureaucratic establishment favored the growers.

Inspired by the California *campesino* (farmworker) movement, and more directly by the events in Texas such as the takeover of Crystal City in 1963, Chicano activism increased in the Midwest during the second half of the 1960s. Twenty-two-year-old Jesús Salas, a native of Crystal City, Texas, led Texas-Mexican cucumber workers in Wisconsin. In January 1967, Salas organized an independent farmworkers' union called *Obreros Unidos* (United Workers) of Wisconsin. The organization remained active throughout that year and the next and published *La Voz del Pueblo*.

Financial difficulties and the loss of support of the AFL–CIO led to the end of *Obreros Unidos* in 1970.[70] (The Midwest Chicano student and Labor Movement was motivated by the 1963 Chicano takeover of Crystal City. The leadership was originally from Texas. Leaders such as Salas, for instance, joined the migrant stream and in Texas and took memories with them as they confronted racism.)[71]

Michigan employed more migrant workers than any other northern state. Led by Rubén Alfaro—a barber from Lansing—migrants, labor, and students from Michigan State marched on to Governor George Romney, hoping to get a commitment from him to support their crusade and veto any legislation that would "take away the human dignity of the migrant workers. . . ." Michigan attracted more than 100,000 migrants during the harvest season. Romney refused to take a stand. The migrants were supported by the AFL–CIO "in their crusade for better pay, housing, medical care and education for the migrants' children." Alfaro garnered the support of César Chávez and the United Farm Workers (UFW), and of U.S. Senator Robert F. Kennedy sent a telegram to Céxzr that signed off with the words *Viva La Causa!* They marched from Saginaw to Lansing, announcing, "Governor, our feet are sore . . . Some of us have walked more than 70 miles to tell you about our problems," and handed the lieutenant governor their petition. A news reporter described the scene:

> They held American and Mexican flags, and banners depicting the Virgin of Guadalupe—revered saint of Mexico. Hand-lettered signs carried such slogans as "Viva La Causa," "Human Dignity for Migrant Workers" and "Chicken Coops are for the Bird."[72]

In 1967 in Ohio, Mexican farmworkers demanded better wages and enforcement of health and housing codes. Some 18,000–20,000 Mexicans worked in Wallace County, Ohio, and throughout the tomato belt that encircled northwest Ohio, southern Michigan, and northern Indiana. Hunt, Campbell Soup, Libby, McNeil, Vlasic, and Heinz controlled production. Baldemar Velásquez, 21, and his father organized a march in 1968 from Leipsic, Ohio, to the Libby tomato plant and a later march to the Campbell Soup plant. They established a newspaper, *Nuestra Lucha* (Our Struggle), and a weekly radio program. In 1968, the Farm Labor Organizing Committee (FLOC) signed 22 contracts with small growers.[73]

Meanwhile, in the Pacific Northwest, *La Raza* was mobilizing against economic injustices. During the peak of the harvesting season, as many as 25,000 migrant Mexicans resided in the state of Washington. Migrant children attended only 21 weeks of school, and the Washington Citizens for Migrant Affairs pointed out that the migrant family had a median of five years of education. The heart of the migrant community was in the agriculturally rich Yakima Valley, where in 1965 the Yakima Valley Council for Community Action (YVCCA) was organized to coordinate War on Poverty programs. The next year, Tomás Villanueva and Guadalupe Gamboa from Yakima Valley College traveled to California where they met with César Chávez. Subsequently, in 1967 Villanueva helped organize the first Chicano activist organization in Washington. The Mexican American Federation was organized that year in Yakima, to advocate for community development and political empowerment in the Yakima Valley. In May 1967, Big Bend Community College raised expectations by receiving a $500,000 grant for the basic education of 200 migrants.[74]

The Road to Brown Power

13.7 Analyze the 1960s Chicana/o movement and the role of youth.

The median age of Mexican-origin people at the end of the 1960s was about 21. They were very compatible with the baby boomers who dominated the decade, sharing their music and many of their values while at the same time, because of their isolation, sharing the culture of the *barrios* they lived in. A sizeable number were of military draft age and some filtered into colleges, while some joined the Anti-Vietnam War movement. A growing number understood the issues better than their parents. In the 1960s many were not as confined to Mexican spaces as in previous generations. They were young, nationalistic and idealistic, and wanted to retain their native language. They were no longer primarily rural. In 1970, out of 4.5 to 5 million Mexican Americans, fewer than a million were Mexican immigrants living in the United States.[75]

In 1968, 91 percent of the students enrolled in U.S. institutions of higher learning were white, 6 percent were African American, and just under 2 percent were Latinos; probably fewer than half that number were of Mexican origin. Chicanos were identifiable as a group. They did not begin to enroll in college in significant numbers until after 1968 following the school walkouts in California and Texas. What set them apart from other students was that most were from working-class families and first-generation college students. The Chicana/o student revolt beginning in that year challenged and rattled the tactics of middle-class Mexican American organizations.

The first challenge to the old guard by Chicana/o students came from Texas, where students organized in Kingsville at Texas A&I University in 1964. José Angel Gutiérrez, Ambriocio Meléndez, and Gabriel Tafoya, among others, formed the Texas A&I student group, focusing on the usual issues of admission discrimination, segregated dorms, and poor housing. Organizers emphasized forging a Mexican student community in order to develop broader political power among the Mexican community as a whole. In 1964, Texas A&I Mexican students attended the PASO state convention, where they met with other Mexican students from Austin who had similar goals. The students successfully lowered the eligibility age for PASO membership from 21 to 18.[76]

Meanwhile, in 1967 Tejano students formed MAYO at St. Mary's College in San Antonio. PASO's 1963 Crystal City takeover energized them. It was PASO's involvement in La Casita Farms Corporation strike of 1966 in the Rio Grande Valley that Tejano historian David Montejano calls the catalyst for the Chicano Movement in Texas—especially for Mexican American students from Texas A&I and future MAYO leaders throughout the state. It was in the heat of the Casitas strike in the spring of 1967 that MAYO was formed. The organizers included José Angel Gutiérrez, Nacho Pérez, Mario Compeán, and Willie Velásquez. Most of the founders were graduate students at St. Mary's College; they were well aware of the Student Nonviolent Coordinating Committee (SNCC), the strategies of its leader Stokely Carmichael, the Students for a Democratic Society (SDS), and the Port Huron statement. MAYO played a pivotal role in bringing about civil rights for Mexican Americans and developed a master plan to take over boards of education and city councils throughout South Texas. Soon after its formation, other university and high school students started MAYO chapters, mostly as a result of planned high school walkouts beginning in the spring of 1968 and extending into the 1970s. The strategy was to build a cadre of organizers using charismatic leaders from the various school districts and establish beachheads in the campaign to seize political control. More than three dozen school walkouts rocked Texas. MAYO formed local chapters, which attracted Chicanas such as Choco Meza, Rosie Castro, Juanita Bustamante, Viviana Santiago, and Luz Bazán Gutiérrez who played leadership roles and helped build consensus in MAYO and later in *La Raza Unida* Party.[77]

MAYO differed from California Mexican American student organizations. By the mid-1960s there were few Chicano college students in California and elsewhere in the Southwest, whereas in Texas, comparatively speaking, had a larger number of second-, third-, and fourth-generation students attending college. In 1964, there were about 1,030 Chicana/o students, or 25 percent of the total student body, at Texas A&I—not a significant number, but in relation to California or Colorado, for example, substantial. By contrast, at San Fernando Valley State (now California State University at Northridge) fewer than three dozen Chicanos attended. Rampant discrimination and enforced social constraints unified Chicanos at Texas A&I. Though not ideologically united, they socialized together, eventually forming informal networks. This pattern was also evident at other colleges and universities, where racism encouraged group organizing. By marked contrast, California institutions favored a dispersion of Mexican students until about 1967.[78]

The next challenge came from California, where Mexican American youth were the most urbanized in the Southwest and thus were subject to fewer institutional and social constraints. When California youth entered the Chicano movement, they did not have to deal with large entrenched organizations such as the American G.I. Forum or LULAC. However, the Black and white radical student movements as well as the farmworker movements around them politicized California students. They listened to radio broadcasts teeming with music of social protest. By the mid-1960s, youth in California had become more politically aware—partly because of the national youth revolution and partly because the Mexican American movement itself pushed educational issues to the forefront.

By 1967, more students of Mexican origin filtered into the colleges. That year, students at East Los Angeles Community College formed the Mexican American Student Association (MASA) and on May 13, 1967, Chicano students met at Loyola University (Los Angeles) and founded the United Mexican American Students (UMAS). Most were first-generation college students; most were the children of immigrants.[79] On December 16–17, 1967, the second general UMAS conference was held at the University of Southern California campus.

Majority of Chicana/o students identified with the UFW; its successes and tribulations became their own. On campus, they joined with the Black student movement and the SDS. By the spring of 1969, Chicano college student organizations were beginning to spread throughout California. Priority issues included public education, access to universities, Mexican American studies programs, and the Vietnam War. Speakers such as Corky Gonzales[80] and Reies López Tijerina[81] added to the momentum.

Simultaneously, Chicana/o student associations formed throughout the country—in places like Tucson, Phoenix, Seattle, and the Midwest—in large part motivated by the UFW boycott and the alienation on campus.[82] In 1968, Alfredo Gutiérrez, who had been with the grape boycott since 1965, was a student at Arizona State University at Tempe. He along with graduate student Miguel Montiel took over Liga Pan Americana, and changed the name of the organization to the Mexican American Student Organization (MASO). Early members included María Rose Garrido and Christine Marín. MASO developed strong ties with Gustavo Gutiérrez and the Arizona Farm Workers. In 1967, in Tucson, Arizona, Salomón Baldenegro, a student with a strong sense of justice and identification with the Civil Rights, antiwar, and labor movements, organized the Mexican American Liberation Committee at the University of Arizona, where he recruited Raúl Grijalva, Isabel García, and Guadalupe Castillo, who were high school students; the committee advocated bilingual and Mexican culture classes. This organization evolved into the Mexican American Student Association (MASA).[83]

In New Mexico, students at Highlands University organized to demand the end of the suppression of Spanish, history classes that reflected the Mexican American experience, more Mexican American teachers, and school counseling programs. By 1968, protests were taking place against the schools at Albuquerque, Las Vegas, Española, Portales, Roswell, and Santa Fé. That year the Brown Berets and the Black Berets began operating in Albuquerque. The same year in the northern part of the state, *El Grito del Norte* began publication[84] and MAYA (later the Chicano Youth Association) began to appear on campuses. Meanwhile, small numbers of Chicano students began filtering into the colleges of the Pacific Northwest and Midwest.

The Making of a Movement

In California and elsewhere the Educational Opportunity Program (EOP) gave Chicanas and Chicanos a tremendous boost; as mentioned, before 1968 colleges could count the number of Chicano students in the dozens. For the first time, many received financial aid and were recruited to go to college—much the same way as athletes were. The added presence of Chicano youth on campuses nurtured the considerable discontent festering in the *barrios* themselves. On the campuses and in the *barrios*, the injustice of the Vietnam War took on an added air of urgency. At the universities, many white and Black students were from middle-class backgrounds and thus were very much involved with the Civil Rights and antiwar movements. Many of the white student radicals were red diaper babies, that is, their parents had been involved in radical politics; many African American students had been involved through their churches. The political involvement of Chicano students was new.

The Vietnam War split many Mexican American organizations, with those opposing the war being accused of unpatriotic motives and even cowardliness. In California in 1966, largely through the work of peace activists, the MAPA executive board passed a resolution condemning the war in Vietnam. In Texas, by 1967, Chicano public leaders such as Commissioner Albert Peña, Jr., State Senator Joe Bernal, Representative Henry B. González, and Archbishop Robert Lucey opposed the war, although Hector García of the G.I. Forum continued to support LBJ, sending representatives to the airport to greet the coffins of dead Mexican Americans.

As with the movement as a whole, the 1960s' *veteranos/veteranas* worked alongside recent converts and aided the socialization process. In California, Dolores Huerta became vice president of the UFW, while East Los Angeles Chicana activists like Julia Luna Mount and her sister Celia Luna de Rodríguez, active since the 1930s, continued working for social change. Luna de Rodríguez, a key organizer in the Barrio Defense Committee, spoke out against police abuse.

Julia Luna Mount, active in the 40th Assembly District chapter of MAPA, often criticized MAPA leadership. Julia was a driving force in the antiwar movement even before the mid-1960s. She unsuccessfully ran for the Los Angeles School Board in 1967, and was a founding member of the Peace and Freedom Party. Her daughter Tanya was a leader in the 1968 East LA school walkouts.[85]

The Formation of Core Groups

Beginning in 1963, the Los Angeles County Human Relations Commission—staffed by Richard Villalobos, Mike Durán, and others—sponsored annual Chicano junior high and high school student conferences, which pushed identity politics. The commission conducted seminars and invited speakers to motivate student leaders. At these sessions, students not only discussed identity but also compared the grievances they had against their schools. For example, the dropout rate of Chicanas/os in high schools was of over 50 percent: 53.8 percent dropped out at Garfield and 47.5 at Roosevelt. Many of the seminar participants later became leaders in the 1968 student walkouts. High school students such as Vicki Castro, Jorge Licón, John Ortiz, David Sánchez, Rachel Ochoa, and Moctesuma Esparza attended the 1966 conference at Camp Hess Kramer, sponsored by the County Human Relations Commission. These students formed the Young Citizens for Community Action (YCCA) in May 1966. In 1967, the Young Citizens worked for the election of Julian Nava to the Los Angeles School Board.

Student leader David Sánchez was recruited to go to Father John B. Luce's Social Action Training Center at the Church of the Epiphany (Episcopal) in Lincoln Heights. The center was associated with the CSO. Luce introduced Sánchez to Richard Alatorre, a staff member of the Los Angeles Community Services Program, who helped him get an appointment to the Mayor's Youth Council. Moctesuma Esparza, another Hess Kramer conference veteran, was also a member of the Youth Council. Meanwhile, other members of the YC became more politicized by the Training Center, and by meeting people like César Chávez. This transition is reflected in the name change of their organization to the Young Chicanos for Community Action.

The Church of the Epiphany helped organize *La Raza* (The Race, or The People) newspaper, under the direction of Eleazar Risco, a Cuban national. Risco arrived in Los Angeles in 1967 to help organize a grape boycott and soon afterward formed the Barrio Communications Project. Risco also helped publish the farmworker newspaper *El Malcriado*. *La Raza* focused on *barrio* issues.[86] Meanwhile, Father Luce's Social Action Training Center attracted other activists, such as Lincoln Heights Teen Post director Carlos Montes.

The East LA Walkout

By the 1968–1969 academic year, Chicana/o students in East Los Angeles made up 96 percent of Garfield High School, 83 percent of Roosevelt, 89 percent of Lincoln, 76 percent of Wilson, and 59 percent of Belmont. Sal Castro, a teacher at Lincoln High School who was well known among students, helped them articulate their discontent. As early as September 1967, Castro addressed students at the Piranya Coffee House about the failure of the schools to provide quality education, access to the latest college prep courses, or counseling. By early 1968, the group formed the Brown Berets, led by David Sánchez. Their goal was to put an end to the discrimination and other injustices suffered by Chicana/o students. Meanwhile, the Los Angeles sheriff's department harassed them; in response, the Berets led demonstrations against the police. Sánchez was arrested at a February 20, 1968 demonstration, following which he spent 60 days at Wayside Maximum Security facility.

Meanwhile, high school and college students held strategy sessions on the blowout (walkout). As a result of Castro's involvement, the students articulated clear demands. Castro, during the planning stages of the blowouts, worked very closely with UMAS students, who functioned as bridge to the high school students.

Castro had been in trouble at Belmont High in 1963, when he encouraged Mexican-origin students to form a slate and run for student government. When the slate won, administrators accused Castro of being divisive for telling the students to say a couple of words in Spanish—as John F. Kennedy had done at Olvera Street during his presidential campaign. The transfer of Castro from Belmont to Lincoln High caused community uproar. School officials thought that Castro and not the schools were the problem, and with time the controversy would pass.[87]

In March 1968, nearly 10,000 Chicano students walked out of five Los Angeles high schools—Lincoln, Roosevelt, Garfield, Wilson, and Belmont. Following their example, students at Jefferson, a predominantly Black school, also walked out. Tanya Luna Mount, a student organizer at Roosevelt High School and a junior, encouraged her fellow students to boycott; she witnessed and wrote about the senseless overreaction of police. Paula Cristóstomo, a senior at Lincoln High who had previously attended the Camp Hess Kramer Youth Conference, and Margarita Mita Cuarón, a sophomore at Garfield High School, urged students to walk out. Police targeted the Brown Berets using them as a pretext to brutally suppress the walkout participants. (One of the leaders, Moctesuma Esparza, produced a film, *Walkout* (2006), memorializing the events.)[88]

Although high school students formed the core of the walkouts, Chicana college students like Vicki Castro from California State University, Los Angeles, and Rosalinda Méndez (later González) from Occidental College, as well as the leaders of UMAS chapters, also provided leadership.

Prior to the walkout, the school system pushed out more than 50 percent of the Chicano high school students, through either expulsion or transfers to other schools. Eastside schools were overcrowded and run down compared with American and Black schools. The students demanded that racist teachers be removed, charging that school authorities had implemented a curriculum that purposely obscured the Chicanos' culture and programed students to be content with low-skilled jobs. In 1967, only 3 percent of the teachers and 1.3 percent of administrators had Spanish surnames, and many of these were white women married to Latinos. Whites made up 78 percent of the teachers, 91.4 percent of the administrators, and 54 percent of the students—more than 20 percent of the students were Latinos. Chicano community leaders and supporters formed the Educational Issues Coordinating Committee (EICC) to defend the students and to follow up on their demands.

It was clear that sheriffs' deputies and police overreacted and treated the protests as insurrections. Police authorities wanted to make an example of Mexican Americans and control and subjugate them. Many activists were caught by surprise; however, moderates began to question the fairness of the justice system and were radicalized by the events. They were moved by Sal Castro, who said he had walked out with his students because in good conscience he could not remain inside the school knowing that the demands of his students were legitimate.[89]

On June 2, 1968, a Los Angeles grand jury indicted Castro and other activists on several charges that included conspiracy to commit misdemeanors. (After two years of appeals, the courts found the counts unconstitutional.)[90] The California Department of Education attempted to revoke Castro's credentials, and he was subjected to frequent and arbitrary administrative transfers. Meanwhile, on September 1968, several thousand protesters, led by the EICC, marched in front of Lincoln High School, demanding Castro's reinstatement to Lincoln. During these confrontations, unexpected help came from the presidential campaign of Robert Kennedy, who met with Chicano leaders. Kennedy hired enlightened Chicanas such as Lupe Anguiano and Polly Baca on his campaign staff, and he was one of the few politicos of any race to reach out to youth.[91]

Chicana/o Student Militancy Spreads

The Los Angeles walkouts, because of the size of the blowouts and the location, called national attention to the plight of Chicanas/os in education, and encouraged other walkouts throughout the Southwest and the Midwest. On March 20, 1968, students walked out of classes at Denver's

West Side High School. They made demands for Mexican teachers, counselors, and courses, as well as for better facilities. Twenty-five people were arrested, including Corky Gonzales.

The perfect storm hit Texas as more than 50 separate walkouts of students occurred. As mentioned, MAYO agitated throughout Texas from the spring of 1968 through the early 1970s. The first walkout in Texas occurred at Lanier High School in San Antonio on April 9, 1968. The student council elections triggered the strike when teachers did not approve the nominees and suspended student council member Elida Aguilar for insubordination. MAYO organizer Willie Velásquez persuaded the students to form a coordinating committee and to incorporate larger concerns into their demands. Seven hundred students walked out demanding more academic courses, the right to speak Spanish, and more democracy. More pungent was the students' demand for Mexican American history and culture classes. The importance of the walkouts was that it generated considerable community support. Among early supporters were the Neighborhood Youth Corps, the Bishops' Committee for the Spanish Speaking, State Senator Joe Bernal, County Commissioner Alberto Peña, and Councilman Felix Treviño.[92] Peña received a standing ovation when he said "We're handicapped because we have an educational system that doesn't understand bilingual students."[93]

On May 16, students rose once again against racist administrators. A young Willie Velásquez—then a graduate student at St. Mary's University, and later an activist who would earn a national reputation—exhorted the students.

With the education you get at Edgewood, most of you are going to wind up either in Vietnam or as a ditch digger . . . At Jefferson, Alamo Heights or Lee, there is a chance that you'll go to college. But 85 per cent of you will not go—$80 a week is the most you will earn the rest of your life . . . . Tell Stemhauser this is the problem.[94]

The walkout was 80 percent effective. The students ended the boycott on Sunday, May 19, to show that they were not walking out on education.[95] Fundamental to the strike was the district's inability to attract qualified teachers. The all-Mexican Edgewood High spent $356 per student annually versus $594 at Alamo Heights, which was predominantly white. On June 30, Demetro Rodríguez, Martin Cantú, Reynaldo Castañono, and Alberta Snid filed a suit against San Antonio in the federal district court citing the inequality in funding.[96]

Meanwhile, MAYO based its campaign on a brand of Tejano nationalism calculated to take political control of South Texas. Tejano nationalism was based on the Texas experience: a blend of Mexican history, family values, Tejano music, and the Spanish language.[97] The next stepping stone was at Edcouch-Elsa High (and Middle) School in Hidalgo County, a town of fewer than 10,000. This was the first student strike in the rural Rio Grande Valley.[98] Chicana/o students there suffered numerous indignities. By mid-October 1968, students and parents began informal meetings, with a few MAYO members, VISTA volunteers, and PASO members in attendance. The chair was Jesús Ramírez, a MAYO member. It was supported by State Senator Joe Bernal, and Dr. Hector García, the founder of the G.I. Forum, was present. On November 13, the students rose from their desks and walked out. The school officials bypassed the local police and reported the walkout to county sheriffs, who arrested the walkout leaders. Meanwhile, the superintendent suspended 168 students for three days.[99] Here again students objected to the "No Spanish" rule and wanted classes on Mexican American contributions to Texas history. The students demanded courses and counseling that would prepare them for college. They demanded an end to discrimination.[100] When the students were expelled, the recently organized Mexican American Legal Defense and Education Fund (MALDEF) filed a suit, and board policy was ruled unconstitutional.[101]

According to José Angel Gutiérrez, MAYO led or participated in at least 50 walkouts before the December 1969 Crystal City walkout. Beachheads were established at these venues with local MAYO members leading walkouts in communities where they grew up. The walkouts hit a common nerve that many of the adults identified with. They demanded the right to speak Spanish, the right to learn about Mexican American history, the right to get a quality education, and schools that were free of discrimination. The walkouts made the movement—they brought to the surface the community's moral outrage.

On May 5, 1970, Chicana/o students walked out of Delano Joint Union High School in the San Joaquín Valley of California. Protest was centered on the denial of a Chicano speaker at an assembly. On May 7, police encircled the school. The walkout lasted till the end of the school year. Police arrested the strikers when they attempted to enter graduation ceremonies; protesters were beaten up and dragged into padded wagons.[102] The perfect storm, which spread throughout the Southwest, had a tremendous impact on the participants; many of the students remained activists and went on to receive higher education.

Brown Berets and White Angst

Law enforcement authorities actually believed that the Brown Berets were capable of overthrowing the government—or perhaps they used it as an excuse. The Los Angeles police and sheriff's departments harassed, intimidated, and persecuted the Brown Berets, a treatment that few Chicano organizations have experienced in recent times. Police and sheriff's deputies raided the Berets, infiltrated, libeled and slandered them, and even encouraged counter groups to attack members. The objective was to destroy the Berets and to invalidate them in the public eye.

The police and sheriff's department made Brown Berets scapegoats, and branded members as outside agitators while playing down the legitimate grievances of Chicano students. A grand jury later indicted 13 Chicanos on conspiracy charges stemming from the walkouts; seven were Brown Berets. The defendants appealed, and the appellate court ruled the case unconstitutional, but only after years of legal harassment.

Law enforcement informers and special agents infiltrated the Berets in order to entrap the members by encouraging acts of violence. Police purposely subverted the Berets, keeping them in a state of flux and preventing the organization from solidifying. Meanwhile, the Berets dealt with the immediate needs of the *barrios*—food, housing, employment, and education. The political struggle and the street molded their ideology. On May 23, 1969, the Berets published a monthly newspaper called *La Causa* (The Cause) to attract new members. Chicanas, such as Gloria Arellanes, the Brown Berets' Minister of Finance and Correspondence, played key roles in the establishment and operation of *La Causa*. Arellanes, along with Andrea Sánchez, also organized a free medical clinic managed by Chicana members of the Berets. Other Beret chapters also established free clinics and free breakfast programs. The clinic raised issues of gender equality that strained relations between Sánchez and other women, eventually leading to a schism; these women left the Berets.[103]

Brown Berets chapters spread through the Mexican *barrios* of San Antonio, Albuquerque, El Paso, Denver, Seattle, and San Diego—no one yet knows how many *barrios* had chapters, only that the chapters were small.[104] However, to white America they were the symbols of Brown Power and terrorism. It is unimaginable how reasonable people could see young men and women wearing their brown berets and khaki uniforms and be struck with so much terror and exaggerate their numbers. Texas A&M graduate student Jennifer G. Correa obtained 1,200 pages of FBI Surveillance Files, focusing on East Los Angeles, under the Freedom of Information Act.[105] The documents reveal, among other information, that in 1968 FBI Director J. Edgar Hoover had decided to fully investigate the Brown Berets in order to find out if they were a "threat to national security of the United States," admonishing agents in Sacramento and San Diego for not gathering enough information on the Berets. Agents responded that the Berets were under "continuous and aggressive investigative attention." Considering the small numbers of Berets, the FBI reaction can only be labeled as delusional, and their actions as an abuse of authority, since they were directed at spying and controlling a movement.

This abuse mirrored the fears of American society. As late as July 1, 1976, the *Syracuse Herald-Journal* in New York carried headlines such as "Brown Beret Alert Cancelled: Police Playing Down Border Terrorist Warning." The *Herald-Journal* warned its readers about the Brown Berets, a little-known, but according to the newspaper, a heavily armed radical group that reportedly vowed "to kill a cop." Brown Berets were allegedly driving around the East Coast in broad daylight in vans. According to the article, the New York state troopers were in touch with the FBI concerning the Berets and their possible threat to the Montreal Olympics.[106]

Tlatelolco, Mexico

On October 2, 1968, in the Tlatelolco (once an Azteca stronghold) district of Mexico City—just 10 days before the opening of the XIX Olympiad—a massacre occurred, which reinforced the Chicanos' emotional bonds with Mexico. Soldiers and riot police opened fire on a demonstration held by thousands of citizens, killing hundreds, if not thousands, of Mexicans, most of them students. The Mexican government tried to play down the slaughter, claiming that "only" a dozen or so were killed; but most conservative estimates put the figure at more than 500 dead or missing.

Student activists exposed the atrocities in documentaries such as *The Frozen Revolution*, which were played in classrooms and halls throughout the United States. *La matanza* (the massacre) led to movements such as that of Rosario Ibarra, who demanded to know the fate of the more than 500 *desaparecidos* (the disappeared), including her son. Chicano youth supported the Mexicans' struggle, and students hung posters reviving memories of Tlatelolco and, even farther back, the Mexican Revolution. Tlatelolco added to the anger and experiences of Chicano youth, who identified with the Mexican youth.[107]

"Wild Tribes of . . . the Inner Mountains of Mexico"

On January 27, 1960, Los Angeles Police Chief William Parker testified before the U.S. Civil Rights Commission: "Some of these people [Mexicans] were here before we were but some are not far removed from the wild tribes of the district of the inner mountains of Mexico."[108] It caused an uproar, but Police Commissioner R. J. Carreón, Jr., said that he had heard Parker's story and ordered the Mexican American community to drop the controversy. Local newspapers excused Parker, and they even went as far as to censure Edward R. Roybal for demanding an apology and/or Parker's resignation, accusing Roybal of demagoguery.

Parker's racist attitude was replicated in many instances of police brutality that came about in succeeding years. In 1966, for example, the Los Angeles police called for a backup team after an angry crowd assembled as police attempted to make an arrest. Police fired two warning shots into the crowd. In July, the Happy Valley Parents Association organized a monitoring of police. In September of that year, the American Civil Liberties Union (ACLU), in cooperation with the CSO, opened a center in East Los Angeles. (From September 1966 to July 1968, the ACLU investigated 205 police abuse complaints; 152 were filed by Chicanos.)[109]

In the summer of 1967 about 300 Chicanas/os attended a conference on police–community relations at Camp Hess Kramer. Police–community relations in Los Angeles reached a new low, and the participants asked the federal government to intervene. The government's failure to protect the rights of the community worsened the situation. Meanwhile, political consciousness increased throughout California. Older activists of MAPA, CSO, LULAC, and the American G.I. Forum, as well as youth, professionals, and poverty workers, criticized the schools and the government's treatment of Mexican Americans. Many new organizations such as the Association of Mexican American Educators (AMEA, 1965) and UMAS (1967) expressed the community's frustrations. Mexican Americans expressed concerns about lack of gains made by them in comparison to African Americans, and they insisted that more attention be paid to their needs.[110]

Meanwhile, tensions rose higher as the Vietnam War sabotaged Lyndon Johnson's "Great Society" programs. By 1966, the government's commitment to ending poverty was sliding; it spent $22 billion on the war in Southeast Asia compared with about $1.5 billion to fight poverty. Nevertheless, as late as 1967, Hector P. García assured LBJ that, "As far as I know, the majority, if not the total Mexican American people, approve of your present course of action in Vietnam."[111]

Gringos and Tejanos

On March 30, 1969, some 2,000 Chicanos assembled at San Felipe Del Rio (about 160 miles west of San Antonio) to protest Governor Preston Smith's cancellation of a VISTA program. Smith had canceled the program because VISTA workers participated in a demonstration against the police beatings of Uvalde resident Natividad Fuentes and his wife. The G.I. Forum, LULAC, and other organizations supported the mass rally.

José Angel Gutiérrez, 24, a MAYO speaker at Del Rio, demanded reinstatement of the VISTA program and protested inequality, poverty, and police brutality throughout Texas. At the rally Gutiérrez said, "We are fed up. We are going to move to do away with the injustices to the Chicano and if the 'gringo' doesn't get out of our way, we will stampede over him." Gutiérrez angrily attacked the gringo establishment at a press conference and called upon Chicanos to "Kill the gringo," by which he meant that the white rule of Mexicans should end, and not literally killing the white people. Nevertheless, Representative Henry B. González from San Antonio called for a grand jury investigation of MAYO, attacked Gutiérrez.[112]

Gutiérrez was a product of Texas culture—a Confederate state with a tradition of southern racism and historical exclusion of Mexican Americans. White Texans had never come to grips with the fact that Mexicans won at the Alamo. Texas also is home to national leaders of the Ku Klux Klan and the White Citizens Council. In the 1960s, whites could still count on the Texas Rangers to keep Mexicans in their place in South Texas, one of the most deprived regions of the country. Gutiérrez and the "we've had enough" rhetoric appealed to many Chicanas/os whom the society had marginalized. Ranger Joaquín Jackson, a long-time adversary, says of Gutiérrez, "He radiated cunning, resourcefulness, intelligence, and charisma. A tireless worker and a gifted, passionate speaker, he was further armed with the conviction that he was right." In his book, Jackson also acknowledges the merit of the Chicana/o grievances against the system.[113]

Tex-Mexicans lived in a string of dusty, neglected towns on the "wrong side of the tracks." Mexican Americans resented their status and poverty. The intensity of racism fostered nationalism among them, causing resentment at the moderate way older organizations such as LULAC and the G.I. Forum dealt with the gringo establishment. Many Chicano students was tired of being docile; they knew what Black militancy had achieved, and they were influenced not only by the Black literature of the time but also by a handful of progressive white professors. José Angel Gutiérrez was one of the leaders who expressed the frustrations of the MAYO generation. His contribution to the Chicana/o cause was indispensable; it influenced Chicanos throughout the country.[114]

On June 20, 1969, Luz Bazán Gutiérrez,[115] José Angel Gutiérrez, and several young volunteers moved to Angel's hometown of Crystal City (population 8,500), Texas, to organize politically and launch the Winter Garden Project (WGP), which was oriented toward community control and committed to the decolonization of South Texas. Although Chicanos composed over 85 percent of the Winter Garden area, a white minority, who owned 95 percent of the land, controlled the city's politics. The agribusiness income in Dummit, La Salle, and Zavala Counties totaled about $31 million; yet, in Zavala County, the median family income was $1,754 a year. The median years of education were 2.3 grades for Chicanos. School authorities vigorously enforced a "no-Spanish" rule and more than 70 percent of Chicano students dropped out of Crystal City High School. Few Mexicans held offices or were professionals; those who received an education moved away. Americans considered themselves racially and culturally superior to Chicanos. The Texas Rangers patrolled the area, terrorizing Mexicans. Adding to the plight of the Chicana/o, a substantial number of them were migrants who had to follow the crops. Many Mexicans routinely left the Winter Garden area in late spring and did not return until the fall. Small hamlets of the region became ghost towns during this period.

A school crisis at Crystal City in November 1969 gave the young volunteers the ideal issue with which to confront the gringo. Although Chicanas/os students comprised the majority in the system, school policy excluded them from participating much of the extracurricular activities. When students complained, the school board ignored them, refusing to even discuss their grievances. Left with no other recourse, parents and students organized a school boycott in December. Student leader Severita Lara published and distributed leaflets and agitated the students. Polemics played a role in agitating parents, and MAYO and the Gutiérrezes were an indispensable part of this discourse in building a political vocabulary. Over 1,700 Chicana/o students participated in the walkout; the students and their parents formed a citizens' organization that intended to take over the school board in the spring election of 1970.[116]

Meanwhile, during the first quarter of 1970, *La Raza Unida* Party (LRUP) emerged from the citizen action group. Intensive mobilization took place, and in April 1970, LRUP won four of the seven seats on the Crystal City Board of Education; all the Chicana/o city council candidates in Carrizo Springs, Cotula, and Crystal City were elected. Cotula elected its first Chicano mayor. Chicanos in the Winter Garden area elected 15 candidates along with two new mayors, two school board majorities, and two city council majorities. Only one gringo won the election. The *Cristal* (Crystal City) victory used the MAYO Plan for Aztlán as a template. They intended to use Cristal as the linchpin across the "Accordion Trail"—the migrants' trail from Texas throughout the Midwest and Northwest—to spread their political revolt.[117]

No Place for Mexicans

The history of land grant i rooted in the past and memorialized by Spanish law, which in New Mexico institutionalized common land usage. The holding of land and the peasant farmers' place in the society were was central to their identification and social status. The *ejido* (communal land) functioned alongside private grants to individuals, with villages holding common lands such as forests or pastures. The community of peasants collectively owned the common land. The *ejido* is romanticized in Mexican history on both sides of the border, with historical figures such as Emiliano Zapata immortalized for calling for the breakup and redistribution of *latifundio* (a large plantation) lands to the peasants. New Mexicans also idealized the collective ownership of communal lands and lamented the loss of ancestral acreage.

The U.S. conquest marked an end to this way of life, as private developers took control of the water, common lands, and finally the villagers' farms. Memories of the past remained strong in the minds of many New Mexicans, who alleged that the gringo had taken the land from them in violation of the Treaty of Guadalupe Hidalgo (1848). Emotions run high to this day.

In 1963, local activist Reies López Tijerina formed *La Alianza Federal de Mercedes* (The Federal Alliance of Land Grants), invoking the Treaty of Guadalupe in the struggle to hold on to common lands. The *Alianza*'s membership jumped from 6,000 in 1964 to 14,000 one year later. A basic premise of the *Alianza*'s demands was that people don't "give away" their lands or rights in treaties. For them, forcing a defeated nation to "sell" territory under duress was intrinsically unjust.

Reies López Tijerina was born in 1926, in Fall City, Texas, where his family lived a marginal existence. Tijerina became a preacher and wandered into northern New Mexico, where he witnessed the poverty of the people. *El Tigre* (the Tiger), as Tijerina was called, became interested in the land-grant question. He studied the Treaty of Guadalupe Hidalgo and became convinced that the national forest in Tierra Amarilla belonged to the Pueblo de San Joaquín de Chama. *Ejido* land belonged to the people in common and could not be sold. Villagers had the right to graze their animals and cut and gather timber in these forestlands.[118]

The Forest Service through the early 1960s rigorously restricted the number of cattle permitted to graze in forestlands. For dryland ranchers, having a permit was a matter of life and death. During the first part of the decade, *Alianza* members staged protests, petitioned government, appealed to public opinion, and sought alliances with African Americans and Native Americans among others. The *Alianza* raised the cry of *Tierra y Libertad!* (Land and Liberty!)

On October 15, 1966, Tijerina and 350 *Alianza* members occupied the Echo Amphitheater in the national forest campground, claiming the *ejido* rights of the Pueblo de San Joaquín de Chama. On October 22, *Alianza* members made a citizen's arrest and detained two Rangers for trespassing and being a public nuisance. The *Alianza* court found them guilty but suspended the sentence.

Tijerina was charged with illegal trespassing on national forest land and other crimes, 20 *Alianza* members entered Tierra Amarilla to make a citizen's arrest of District Attorney Alfonso Sánchez, also for trespassing. In doing so, the members wounded a jailer. The government sent 200 military vehicles (including tanks), almost 400 soldiers, and scores of police and lawmen to hunt down Tijerina. On November 6, 1967, Tijerina stood trial. A jury convicted him of two counts of assault, and the judge sentenced him to two years in a state penitentiary. Tijerina immediately appealed the verdict.

In May and June of 1968, Tijerina participated in the Poor People's Campaign, threatening to pull the Chicano contingent out if Black organizers did not treat them as equals. In the fall, he ran for governor of New Mexico on the People's Constitutional Party ticket. In mid-February 1969, the Court of Appeals for the Tenth Circuit upheld the Amphitheater conviction; Tijerina's lawyer immediately appealed to the Supreme Court.[119] In June, *El Tigre* again attempted to occupy the Kit Carson National Forest at the

Coyote Campsite. Tijerina stood trial in late 1968 for the Tierra Amarilla raid at which Tijerina acted in his own defense. Much of the trial centered on the right to make a citizen's arrest. Tijerina proved his point, and the jury entered a verdict of not guilty.

The higher court denied Tijerina's appeal on the Amphitheater case, and Tijerina went to prison. For seven months, prison authorities kept him in isolation. Tijerina became a symbol, convicted of political crimes rather than "crimes against society." Authorities released him in the summer of 1971.

The Crusade for Justice

Rodolfo "Corky" Gonzales symbolized the struggle for control of the urban *barrios*. Born in Denver on June 18, 1928, the son of migrant sugar beet workers, Gonzales grew up the hard way—using his fists. A Golden Gloves champion who turned professional, he was a featherweight contender from 1947 to 1955. He later established a bail bonds business and opened an auto insurance agency. During the 1960s, Gonzales became increasingly critical of the system. In 1963, he organized *Los Voluntarios* (The Volunteers), who protested against police brutality. Two years later he became a director of Denver's War on Poverty youth programs, but was fired for his involvement in the Albuquerque EEOC walkout. He published his own newspaper, *El Gallo: La Voz de la Justicia* (The Rooster: The Voice of Justice).

Gonzales's epic poem, *I Am Joaquín*, was the most influential piece of Chicano movement literature written in the 1960s. Luis Valdez of the Teatro Campesino made the poem into a film documentary. Conditions differed in *barrios* such as Denver and Los Angeles, where an identity crisis had developed after World War II. Corky Gonzales understood and summed up this identity crisis in his poem.

Gonzales formed the Crusade for Justice; it operated a school, a curio shop, a bookstore, and a social center. The Denver school, named *Tlatelolco: La Plaza de las Tres Culturas* (Tlatelolco: The Plaza of the Three Cultures), enrolled about 200 students, from preschool to college age. On June 29, 1968, the Crusade led a march on Denver police headquarters to protest an officer-related killing of 15-year-old Joseph Archuleta. In 1969, the Crusade participated in a walkout at West Side High School, with parents in support. That same year, the Crusade organized the First Annual Chicano Youth Conference at Denver, adopting *El Plan Espiritual de Aztlán*—a revolutionary plan that publicized the term *Chicano* as a symbol of resistance.[120]

Every political movement is driven by moral outrage and symbols that inspire unity. Alurista (Alberto Baltazar Urista Heredia), a poet and activist, wrote the *Plan* using the symbol of *Aztlán* as confrontational, saying to white America, "we were here first, so if you don't like it go back to where you came from!"[108] *Aztlán* was the mythical or legendary homeland of the Aztecas. It is significant to point out that the Disturnell Map (1847), considered the most authoritative map of its time, was used as the official map to designate the boundary between the United States and Mexico; it noted the Antigua Residencia de los Aztecas, which it placed north of the Hopi Indians, so this was hardly Alurista's invention.[121] (The Chicano movement was adept at using symbols which some would label nationalistic. One of the most interesting collectives was based in Sacramento, California, and called itself the Royal Chicano Air Force [RCAF]. It was comprised of artists and poets; the most prominent was José Montoya, a poet, artist, and musician. Even the name of the group was a slap in society's face.)[122]

Meanwhile, the Crusade worked with Native American organizations such as the American Indian Movement (AIM), supporting AIM during the Native Warriors' "Era of Indian Power." It maintained close ties with AIM cofounder Dennis Banks and supported AIM in 1972 as it launched its Trail of Broken Treaties caravan, calling attention to the plight of Native Americans. The Crusade perceived Mexicans as Native Peoples—pointing out that 60 percent of Mexicans were mestizos and another 30 percent were full-blooded Native American. (Fewer than 1 percent of Americans have Native American blood.) The Crusade also strongly supported Black activist and scholar Angela Davis. Gonzales and the Crusade assisted in establishing the Colorado branch of LRUP, which ran candidates for state and local offices on November 4, 1970.[123]

El Grito del Norte

The Chicano movement attracted activists such as Elizabeth "Betita" Martínez from the Civil Rights movement. Martínez brought in experiences that helped define oppression of Chicano/as in the context of multinational struggle. In the late 1950s, Martínez worked for the United Nations as a researcher on colonialism. In the 1960s, she participated in the Student Nonviolent Coordinating Committee (SNCC) in Mississippi and became coordinator of SNCC's New York office. Martínez played a key role in this movement, editing and discussing the works of major civil rights activists. She also worked with the Black Panthers. In 1968, she moved to New Mexico, where she cofounded and published *El Grito del Norte* (The Call of the North) for five years, while working on various *barrio* projects. *El Grito del Norte* was the first internationalist and nationalist Chicano newspaper published and almost totally staffed and run by women. The newspaper was based in Española, New Mexico, which is significant in view of the historic independence of women in this region. New Mexico was a natural starting place, since it was a classic colony. Among other books, Martínez coauthored *Viva la Raza: The Struggle of the Mexican American People* with Enriqueta Vásquez. A theme in Martínez's works is a critique of capitalism and the effects of exploitation.[124]

Enriqueta Longeaux y Vásquez was a New Mexican activist, who coedited *El Grito del Norte*. Vásquez, born in Colorado of farmworker parents, had been involved with Denver activist Corky Gonzales and the Crusade for Justice.[125] Her passionate columns denounced capitalism, the military, the Catholic Church, and "gringo" society. Vásquez wrote vigorously about women's issues, highlighting that women's liberation was possible within the Chicano movement. Some Chicanas later criticized her writing on feminist issues as "loyalist," alleging that she was loyal to male networks of power. However, others point out that Vásquez was working within the Chicano movement at the time, attempting to change it, and that she was one of the first Chicanas to publicly take on the issue of Chicana oppression in the mainstream press as well as in the alternative press. In her column ¡*Despierten Hermanos!* Vásquez encouraged the total liberation of men and women and drew the connection between racism and capitalism.[126]

Rubén Salazar: The Schools Failed Us

In the 1960s, American public schools had written the Mexican Americans off as failures, blaming their lack of progress on their culture—labeling them culturally deprived and culturally disadvantaged. Mexican American journalist Rubén Salazar, killed by Los Angeles Sheriff deputies while covering the Chicano Moratorium of August 29, 1970, capsulized the reaction of Mexican American educators to the term "culturally deprived," writing in 1963: "Presumably they want to save these poor people [of this] terrible void by giving them culture . . . What they don't seem to realize is that Mexican-Americans have a culture . . . ."[127]

Two years later the National Education Association (NEA) came out with *The Invisible Minority*, basing many of its findings on a survey of the Tucson schools. Aside from the teaching of bilingual education, the report recommended the building of pride in Mexican American students.

The report quotes a 13-year-old eighth grade Chicana's essay:

> "To begin with, I am a Mexican. That sentence has a scent of bitterness as it is written. I feel if it weren't for my nationality I would accomplish more. My being a Mexican has brought about my lack of initiative. No matter what I attempt to do, my dark skin always makes me feel that I will fail. Another thing that 'gripes' me is that I am such a coward. I absolutely will not fight for something even if I know I'm right. I do not have the vocabulary that it would take to express myself strongly enough."[128]

Salazar's death on August 29, 1970 was a blow to the Chicana/o Community. His op-ed pieces in the *Los Angeles Times* educated an entire generation of Chicana/o activists and Angeleños on obstacles Mexican Americans faced. The NEA asked, "Is there something inherent in our system of public schooling that impedes the education of the Mexican-American child—that indeed drives him to drop out?" The NEA report found the schools complicit; Mexican Americans were schooled to fit a stereotype. In the process, it embedded a negative self-image that produced the haunting words "I feel if it weren't for my nationality I would accomplish more."[129]

Other Movement Voices

Discussing all the varied voices of the time would be impossible. There were literally scores of newspapers, magazines, and independently published poems and essays. Further, there were *conjuntos* (small musical groups) that played and composed movement songs. Visual artists like Malaquías Montoya produced politically inspired posters that have become classics. One of the best-known cultural artists was Luis Váldez of the *Teatro Campesino*, who contributed greatly to the growth of the new consciousness and to the formation of other *teatros* (theaters). Starting as a farmworker group, the *Teatro Campesino* publicized as the struggles of the farmworkers and Chicanas/os in one-act plays. It played *corridos* that popularized the Chicanos' struggle for liberation in the United States.[130] Also important was the publication of *El Grito: A Journal of Contemporary Mexican American Thought*, which began in the fall of 1967. It was published by Octavio Romano, a professor at the University of California at Berkeley, who organized *Quito Sol*, a publishing collective. *El Grito* published, in addition to poetry and art, scholarly articles challenging U.S. scholarship and criticizing its effect on Chicanos. Its critique of Chicano art helped shape the discourse of the times.[131]

There was a plethora of local activist magazines and newspapers. Francisca Flores, an activist for all of her life, worked on the Sleepy Lagoon case, consulted with Carey McWilliams on *North from Mexico*, and edited *Carta Editorial* in the early and mid-1960s. She was a leader in *la Asociación México Americana* and a critic of Senator Joseph McCarthy. During the 1960s she opposed the Vietnam War and founded *Regeneración*, named after the *Partido Liberal Mexicano*'s newspaper. Francisca played an important role in pushing the progressive agenda of Chicanos during the 1960s and into the 1970s. Based on her experience she brought a clear vision of societal problems and what was to be done. She was at the vanguard of feminist expressions of the time.[132]

Arts flourished during this period, heavily influenced by the artists of the Mexican Revolution. Chicana/o artists wanted to paint murals with strong political messages; they were also influenced by public murals painted under the auspices of the Works Progress Administration in the 1930s. The art was often raw with strong political messages attached to the UFW and political currents such as the Crusade for Justice and *La Raza Unida*. Frequent themes were *la Virgen de Guadalupe*, Ché Guevara, Zapata, *las Adelitas*, and Pancho Villa. The Mural Movement took off in the early 1970s when it entered a semiprofessional stage. More attention has to be paid to murals painted in the late 1960s, like that of Sergio Hernández at San Fernando Valley State, which were painted over. (Sergio also authored a comic strip with *Con Safos*, a *barrio* literary magazine.) Guillermo Bejarano was also an early muralist who worked with the Mexican master Siqueiros. In Texas there were *Festival de Flor y Canto* and *Canto al Pueblo,* as well as many young artists. No one locale had a monopoly on this artistic production that remains one of the most significant footprints of the Chicano movement.[133]

The Chicano Youth Movement Gains Steam

13.8 Describe the challenges and the results of the Chicana/o Youth Movement.

In March 1969, Chicano students from throughout the Southwest and Midwest met in Denver and held the First National Chicano Youth Liberation Conference. The conference adopted *El Plan Espiritual de Aztlán*, setting the goals of nationalism and self-determination for the Chicano Youth Movement. At this conference, the students also adopted the label "Chicano," partly in response to the Black Power Movement, which had changed its identification from "Negro" to "Black." The adoption of "Chicano" was an attempt to dedicate the movement to the most exploited sector of the U.S. Mexican community, those whom traditional Mexicans and Mexican Americans pejoratively called "Chicanos."

Shortly after the Denver Conference, the newly formed Chicano Council on Higher Education (CCHE) that was mostly based in California invited college and university students, faculty, staff, and community activists at the University of California at Santa Barbara to draw up a plan of action for higher education, called *El Plan de Santa Bárbara*. During the conference, Mexican American student organizations changed their name to *El Movimiento Estudiantil Chicano de Aztlán* (MEChA: the Chicano Student Movement of Aztlán).[134] The students' militancy reinforced attitudes already expressed in the community and their mass entry into the movement electrified events. At the 1970 Denver Youth Conference, Gonzales pushed for active antiwar involvement.[135] Meanwhile, MEChA was at the forefront of the establishment of Chicano studies in California and throughout the nation.

Where Is God?

In 1969, 65 percent of the Catholics in the Southwest were Mexicans; yet there were fewer than 180 priests of Mexican extraction, and none were bishops. In Los Angeles, Cardinal James Francis McIntyre, with support from the diocese's Catholic elites, censured priests participating in civil rights activities. The attitude of the powerful Monsignor Benjamin G. Hawkes was, "The rich have souls, too."

In November 1969, Ricardo Cruz, a young law student from Loyola University (Los Angeles), formed *Católicos Por La Raza* (CPLR). Its members were infuriated over the closing of Our Lady Queen of Angels Girls' High School, a predominantly Mexican school, allegedly owing to lack of funds. Cardinal McIntyre had just spent $4 million to build St. Basil's Church in the exclusive Wilshire district of Los Angeles. On Christmas Eve 1969, members of CPLR protested in front of St. Basil's Church. The picketing was peaceful and orderly. When the mass began, demonstrators attempted to enter the church, but sheriffs' deputies posing as ushers locked them out. When a few did gain entry, armed deputies expelled them. Police units arrested 21 demonstrators, 20 of whom stood trial for disturbing the peace and assaulting police officers. The so-called "people" convicted Ricardo Cruz of a misdemeanor, and on May 8, 1972, he began serving a 120-day sentence for his conviction.[136]

Simultaneously, changes were taking place within the Chicano clergy itself. Because of the heated discourse surrounding the unequal treatment of Mexicans by the Catholic Church, Mexican American priests in San Antonio formed the group PADRES (*Padres Asociados para los Derechos Religiosos, Educativos, y Sociales*), and in October 1969, 50 Spanish-speaking clergy developed the agenda for a national meeting. Diocesan priests Ralph Ruiz and Henry Casso, Francisco Manuel Martínez, and Jesuit Edmundo Rodríguez were among the leaders. PADRES held its first convention on February 2–5, 1970, in Tucson, Arizona. It successfully lobbied the Church for the appointment of Father Patricio Fernández Flores as the first Chicano bishop in the United States. The group also played a role in resolving labor disputes and establishing various grassroots organizations—among them the Mexican American Cultural Center in San Antonio, founded by Father Virgilio Elizondo, who was a major influence in PADRES.[137]

Las Hermanas was founded in 1970 in Houston by Gloria Gallardo, SHG, and Gregoria Ortega, OLVM (the initials are for religious orders). Both sisters were heavily involved in community work. In the spring of 1971, they sent out a call to other nuns to join them in Houston for their first organizational meeting. Their primary objective was to raise awareness of the needs of the community and to work for social change. Its first national meeting was held in Santa Fé, New Mexico, in November of that year. Liberation Theology and the Vatican Reform inspired them to form *comunidades de base*—small communities to empower the people, and they also worked closely with the United Farm Workers.[138]

The nuns, while recognizing that racism existed in their orders, were more concerned with serving the poor. The Hermanas organization furnished them with a network to expand their world vision; some sisters studied liberation theology in Quito, Ecuador, where they forged religious and intellectual bonds with Latin American nuns and clergy. The new awareness led to even more involvement with the poor, and many nuns became advocates for the people. *Las Hermanas* were among the founders of the Mexican American Cultural Center in San Antonio in 1972, which sensitized priests and nuns throughout the country to the needs of Mexican Americans. Many members of *Las Hermanas* became involved in Communities Organized for Public Service (COPS) in San Antonio, established in 1974 by Ernesto Cortés, a native of San Antonio, and others. The nuns' involvement in social issues represented a new sense of identity among Chicano/as, which fueled activism. However, the nuns in the Church were especially vulnerable since at that time the Church did not pay into Social Security, and many were expelled from their respective order because of their activism, and lacked a safety net.

Gender and homophobia

Chicanas participated in all phases of the Chicana/o movement. Yet they were invisible to those on the outside. The cultures of the times, partly ignorance and a reluctance to accept gender equality, combined to blur the women's role. A dialogue on gender was advanced only after a bitter struggle not only within the Chicana/o movement but also in the Black Civil Rights movement; homophobia was intense and it tragically continues to this day.

As late as 1970 most right-wing and even some Marxist organizations attributed homosexuality to decadent capitalism. However, a minority of left organizations such as the Socialist Workers Party and Maoist groups forced a reasoned debate. Looking back, the anti-homosexual rhetoric was an injustice. Credit must be given to the gay community taking the issue out of the closet and launching a movement for LGBT Rights.

LGBT scholars such as Gloria E. Anzaldúa furthered awareness of the Chicana/o LGBT community in the United States. Anzaldúa was a scholar of cultural theory, feminist theory, and queer theory. She born in Harlingen, Texas, and died in her early 60s. Her master work is *Borderlands/La Frontera: The New Mestiza*; Borderlands; It crosses over; it is not only Chicana work but an American masterpiece. *La frontera* is rooted Anzaldúa's experience as a Chicana, a lesbian, an activist, and a writer. The work challenges the identity that was at the core of the Chicana/o movement. It is a story of resistance. Anzaldua's use of symbols concept of borders, geographical and folklore is rooted to a theoretical framework.[139] For me, Anzaldúa more than any other Chicana/o author explained the identity of Queer People as well as Chicanas/os.

Inspiration also comes from the white queer community. The Stonewall Riots of 1969 in New York City were historic. Although the 1969 rebellion was not the first rebellion, it launched the Gay rights movement. The Stonewall Inn was located in the heart of Manhattan's Greenwich Village; the New York Police brutally attacked gay patrons. Although Stonewall was not the first confrontation between police and the gay community. However, the LGBT community made the riots a symbol of the growing oppression and the community's determination to fight for equality. They sent the message that they would not suffer discrimination in silence.

During this period, increasing numbers of gay Latinos staked out their identities and demanded respect. Urban Planner James Rojas writes,

> "Times have changed. Same-sex marriage is now legal across the United States, and gay hubs are emerging in once-unthinkable places like Salt Lake City. The ticky-tacky 'out' architecture of establishments like the French Market may seem irrelevant to a younger generation, but it will always remain an important part of the history of L.A.'s LGBTQ community."[140]

Violence at Home

Judge Gerald S. Chargin of Santa Clara County (California) Juvenile Court on September 2, 1969, called a 17-year-old Chicano—who had allegedly committed incest—an animal and ordered that he should be sent back to Mexico. The judge concluded: "Maybe Hitler was right. The animals in our society probably ought to be destroyed because they have no right to live among human beings."[141] Throughout the Southwest, Mexicans were deprived of defense counsels and representation on juries. In the County of Los Angeles, where the Chicana/o population numbered about one million, only four Mexicans served on a grand jury in 12 years (grand jurors were nominated by judges). In adjacent Orange County, with more than 44,000 Mexicans, there had been only one Chicano on the grand jury panel in 12 years. No Chicano had served on the grand jury of Monterey County from 1938 through 1968.

The Mexican American community lacked a legal framework to take on these issues. Tejanos formed the Mexican American Legal Defense and Education Fund (MALDEF) in 1968. In the late 1960s, the federal government funded a program called California Rural Legal Assistance (CRLA). Although the CRLA did not handle criminal cases, it represented the poor in various other matters. In Kings County, for example, growers received $10,179,917 from the government in the form of farm subsidies *not* to grow certain crops, but Kings County spent less than $6,000 on food for the poor. The CRLA sued the county on behalf of the poor, charging that it was violating federal statutes. As complaints mounted against the CRLA by reactionary elements such as the California growers, Governor Ronald Reagan became more incensed about the federal government's support of an agency that sued private enterprise.

In December 1970, Reagan vetoed the federal appropriation to CRLA, and the work of the agency was curtailed.[142]

Chicanas/os under Siege

The universities played a major role in spreading the antiwar message and transforming public opinion about the Vietnam War. Lea Ybarra, later a professor of Chicana/o Studies at Fresno State and Johns Hopkins, was active on the Berkeley campus with her friends Nina Genera and María Elena Ramírez, performing *actos* (one-act plays) that criticized the war. The women offered draft counseling through the American Friends Committee, publishing and distributing an anti-draft pamphlet. Betita Martínez was another early voice in comparing the plight of the Vietnamese people to the Chicano experience. Ideas spread like wildfire. Moral outrage against the war in Southeast Asia spread among Chicanas/os, boosting militancy in the *barrios*. The anti–Vietnam War movement united Mexicans and moved even the middle-class and flag-waving groups like the Forum to the left. In Los Angeles, the Congress of Mexican American Unity (CMAU), consisting of some 300 Los Angeles organizations, supported the antiwar effort.

Chicana/o activists began organizing protests against the war. Rosalio Muñoz, a former student body president at the University of California at Los Angeles (UCLA); Sal Baldenegro of the University of Arizona; Ernesto Vigil of the Crusade for Justice in Denver; and Manuel Gómez, a former member of MASA at Hayward State College, refused military induction. Muñoz had initially set out to organize protests against the draft, not the war. Ramsés Noriega, a fellow student at UCLA and an artist, accompanied Muñoz.

The Brown Berets formed the National Chicano Moratorium Committee that held its first demonstration drew over a 1000 demonstrators on December 20, 1969. Rosalio Muñoz joined as cochairperson with David Sánchez. On February 28, 1970, the group staged another protest, in which 6,000 Chicanos participated, braving the pouring rain.

Simultaneously, mobilizations took place outside Los Angeles. In March, the Second Annual Chicano Youth Conference was held in Denver. A series of Chicano moratoria, climaxing with a national moratorium in Los Angeles on August 29, was planned. Meanwhile, police–community tension increased. On July 4, 1970, a demonstration held at the East Los Angeles sheriff's substation, protesting the death of six Mexican American inmates in the preceding five months, clashed with police. Windows of buildings along Whittier Boulevard were broken and a youth was shot by the police. Twenty-two arrests were made before the rebellion was quelled by 250 deputies and members of the California Highway Patrol. Tension increased as the date of the moratorium approached.

Organizational work gathered momentum during the days preceding the August 29 moratorium. According to Rosalio Muñoz, the women of the Brown Berets were especially dedicated. In different locations, mini-moratorium groups were formed to organize the bases; campuses became centers of activity. Chicanas like Irene Tovar, who ran San Fernando Valley College's Community Center, worked relentlessly. Irene had been active in community organization since her teen years. She was a cofounder of the Latin American Civic Association in 1961 and was part of a vast personal network of friends and leaders of organizations. A long-time advocate for quality education for Mexican American children, she testified on behalf of bilingual education throughout the 1960s. It was this credibility of the leaders that drew many from the San Fernando Valley to the protest—this scenario was replicated up and down the state of California.

On the morning of August 29, contingents from all over the United States started arriving in East Los Angeles. By noon, participants' number swelled to just below 30,000. *Conjuntos* blared out *corridos*; *Vivas* and other shouts filled the air; placards read: *Raza sí, guerra no!* and *Aztlán: Love it or Leave it!* The march ended peaceably and the parade turned into Laguna Park. A minor incident at a liquor store a block away from Laguna Park, where teenagers pilfered some soft drinks, sparked a major confrontation. The police, instead of isolating this incident, rushed squad cars to the park, and armed officers prepared to enter the park area. Their hostile behavior caused a reaction, and a few marchers angrily threw objects at the police. Authorities saw that conference monitors had restrained the few protesters. However, police had found a pretext to break up the demonstration.[143]

Deputies rushed into the park, trapping men, women, and children, and causing considerable panic. Wielding clubs, they trampled spectators, hitting those who did not move fast enough. In the main section of the park, the crowd was caught unaware by the police. Numbering more than 500, the deputies moved in military formation, sweeping the park. Wreckage could be seen everywhere: The stampede trampled baby strollers into the ground; four deputies beat up a man in his 1960s; tear gas filled the air. The number of police escalated to more than 1,200. Mass arrests followed and sheriffs kept prisoners, chained together in fours, in two buses at the East Los Angeles substation. Sheriffs' deputies did not allow them to drink water or go to the bathroom for about four hours. Deputies killed a 15-year-old boy at Laguna Park and deputies manhandles a pregnant girl.

Late in the afternoon Rubén Salazar and two coworkers from KMEX-TV, the Spanish-language television station, stopped at the nearby Silver Dollar Bar for a beer. Problems for television journalist Rubén Salazar had begun on July 16, 1970, when five Los Angeles detectives and two San Leandro police officers burst into a hotel room in downtown

Los Angeles, shooting and killing two Mexican nationals—Guillermo Sánchez, 22, and Beltrán Sánchez, 23, who came to be known as the Sánchez cousins. Police claimed it was a case of "mistaken identity." In the weeks to follow, Rubén Salazar exposed inconsistencies in the police reports. Law enforcement officials called on Salazar and ordered him to tone down his television coverage, alleging that he was inciting the people to violence. A federal grand jury issued an indictment against the officers involved in the Sánchez shootings for violating the civil rights of the two men. When the city of Los Angeles paid for the defense of three of the police officers, a storm of protest arose. A federal court later acquitted the officers.

A month after his exposé of the police brutality issue, Salazar inadvertently found himself caught in the crossfire, this time literally. Deputies surrounded the bar, allegedly looking for a man with a rifle. When some occupants of the Silver Dollar attempted to leave, police forced them back into the premises. Police claimed that deputies broadcast warnings for all occupants to come out; witnesses testified that they heard no such warning. Sheriffs shot a 10-inch tear-gas projectile into the bar. The missile could pierce 7-inch-thick plywood at 100 yards, and it struck Salazar in the head. Another shot filled the bar with gas. Customers made their way out of the establishment. About 5:30 p.m., two of Salazar's colleagues frantically informed deputies that Salazr was still in the bar. Deputies refused to listen, and it was not until two hours later that Salazar's body was discovered.

On September 10, 1970, a coroner's inquest probed the circumstances surrounding Rubén Salazar's death. Officers testified as to the Chicano community's riotous nature. Testimony showing the malfeasance of the deputies was suppressed. *La Raza* magazine reporters, eyewitnesses to the events at the Silver Dollar Bar, contradicted the deputies' testimony. For example, deputies claimed that they did not force the customers of the Silver Dollar to return to the bar. *La Raza* produced a photo showing that they had. Shortly afterward, *La Raza* published a special issue featuring the photos taken on August 29. The *Los Angeles Times* obtained permission from the *barrio* publication to reprint many of the photos.[144]

Four inquest jurors found "death at the hands of another"; the three remaining jurors decided "death by accident." After their verdicts, the jurors questioned the officers' recklessness and wondered if they would have acted in the same manner in Beverly Hills. Los Angeles District Attorney Evelle J. Younger announced on October 14, 1970, that he would not prosecute, and there was clearly a cover-up. Many Chicanas/os posited that Younger decided not to try the officers responsible for Salazar's death out of political opportunism. A candidate for California State Attorney General (he was elected), Younger knew the law-and-order mentality of Californians who demanded this response. As usual, the *Los Angeles Times* supported Younger.

On September 16, 1970, a peaceful Mexican Independence Day parade ended in violence when police attacked the crowd as marchers reached the end of the parade route. TV newscasters Baxter Ward and George Putnam made inflammatory statements against the demonstrators. Then, on January 9, 1971, Chicanos protested against police brutality, marching to the Parker Center, the LAPD Headquarters. Police incited a riot and arrested 32 people. Chief Davis blamed "swimming pool Communists" and the Brown Berets for the riot.

Numerous minor incidents followed; the last major confrontation took place on January 31, 1971. Contingents arrived at Belvedere Park in East Los Angeles from the four major *barrios* in Los Angeles. The demonstration was peaceful, and as the rally ended, Rosalio Muñoz told supporters, numbering around 5,000, to disperse. Some, however, marched to the sheriff's substation on Third Street and staged a rally. A confrontation ensued, which left one man dead and 19 people wounded by buckshot, two with stab wounds, and numerous people with broken bones. Property damage was estimated at more than $200,000.[145]

The Provocateurs

13.9 Explain how the government subversion disrupted the Chicano movement.

In October 1971 Louis Tackwood, a Black informer, stunned the Los Angeles public by testifying that the Criminal Conspiracy Section (CCS) of the Los Angeles Police Department paid him to spy on militants. The LAPD assigned Tackwood to a group of officers who, in cooperation with the FBI, planned to provoke a disruption of the 1972 Republican convention in San Diego by militants; they planned to kill minor officials to force President Richard Nixon to use his powers to break the militant movement. Tackwood named Dan Mahoney (CCS) and Ed Birch (FBI) as the supervisors of the operation. In private conversations he also described how the police used drug pushers as informers in return for protection from prosecution.

Officer Fernando Sumaya worked as an undercover agent for the LAPD. In the fall semester of 1968 he attempted to infiltrate the UMAS chapter at San Fernando Valley State College (now California State University at Northridge) during campus protests there. He was ousted from the group because he was unknown and because he came on too strong. Sumaya then moved to East Los Angeles, where he infiltrated the Brown Berets. In the spring of 1969 he was involved in the Biltmore Hotel affair, where Chicanos were accused of disrupting a speech by Governor Ronald Reagan at a Nuevas Vistas Education Conference, sponsored by the California Department of Education and the reactionary California Superintendent of Schools, Max Rafferty. Thirteen Chicanos were arrested on the charge of disturbing the peace; 10 of the 13 were charged with conspiracy to commit arson. After two years of appeals the defendants were tried. The key witness for the prosecution was Sumaya. The defendants all denied any involvement with the fires. Some charged that Sumaya set the fires. The jury found the defendants not guilty. Meanwhile, Carlos Montes, a Brown Beret, and his wife, Olivia Montes, had left the area, so he was not tried. The Monteses remained at large until the mid-1970s. The LAPD destroyed records documenting Sumaya's role in the Biltmore fires. After relentless hounding, the Montes family was caught, and Carlos was tried. In November 1979, a jury found Montes not guilty—evidently the jury questioned Sumaya's and the LAPD's suspect role. Also questioned by the Berets' *La Causa* was the suspect role of Sergeant Abel Armas in the Special Operation Conspiracy of the LAPD. Freedom of information documents obtained by Professor Ernesto Chávez reveal that the FBI was extremely active in investigating the Berets.[146]

At a press conference on January 31, 1972, Eustacio (Frank) Martínez, 23, revealed that since July 1969 he had infiltrated Chicano groups. A federal agent for the Alcohol, Tobacco, and Firearms Division (ATF) of the Internal Revenue Service recruited Martínez, who, in return for not being prosecuted for a federal firearms violation, agreed to work as an informant and agent provocateur. He infiltrated the MAYO and the Brown Berets in Houston and Kingsville, Texas. He admitted that he committed acts of violence to provoke others. From September 1969 to October 1970 Martínez participated in many protest marches. During the one in Alice, Texas, he tried to provoke trouble "by jumping on a car and trying to cave its top in." He attempted to entice militants to buy guns and to provoke police. MAYO members rebuked him.[147]

In October 1970 ATF agents sent Martínez to Los Angeles, where he worked for agents Fernando Ramos and Jim Riggs. Martínez began spreading rumors against Rosalio Muñoz, accusing him of being too soft, and in November 1970 Martínez ousted Muñoz and became chair of the Chicano Moratorium Committee. Martínez later named officers Valencia, Armas, Savillos, and Domínguez of the CCS as contacts. To put it plainly, when Martínez took part in the Los Angeles rebellions on January 9 and 31, 1971, the Los Angeles police knew of his involvement. He continued in this capacity until March 1971, when he returned to Texas. There Martínez became a member of the Brown Berets and, according to informants, went around waving a carbine and advocating violent tactics.

Upon his return from Texas Martínez was instructed by Ramos and Riggs to infiltrate *La Casa de Carnalismo* in order to learn about the Chicano Liberation Front (CLF) that had been allegedly involved in numerous bombings. Martínez reported that the main functions of *Carnalismo* were to eliminate narcotics, to sponsor English classes, and to dispense food to the needy; he could no links with CLF. The officers told him that his "information was a bunch of bullshit." He was to find evidence by any means necessary. They then instructed him to use his influence to get a heroin addict by the name of "Nacho" to infiltrate *Carnalismo*. Martínez refused to take part in the frame-up. He finally became disillusioned when, on the first anniversary of the Chicano National Moratorium, agents told him to plead guilty to charges of inciting a riot. He had been promised protection from prosecution.[148]

Although some reporters questioned the reliability of Martínez's disclosures, they did not call for congressional investigations into the provocateur activities of federal and local agencies. Louis Tackwood and Frank Martínez were admitted provocateurs. The latter's revelations cast a shadow on the actions of the police in the Los Angeles Chicano rebellions.

Whatever were their roles, they lie buried in the secret files of the different branches of the federal and local police agencies. Such aspects of history remain closed to historians. The ACLU, in a suit settled in the early 1980s, uncovered extensive police-spying on progressive white, Black, and Chicano communities.

Conclusion: The Chicana/o Legacy

For Mexican Americans and Latinos, numbers mattered. Socially defined as non-white, in 1965 they were 4 percent of the nation's population; up from 3.6 in 1960. In 1960 California was

> Only 20 percent of the state's Latino population was foreign-born, and the median age of the foreign-born was 42; only 5 percent were school-age children and immigrants constituted two-thirds of the aged. The second generation was one-third of the total Latino population, but nearly half of those [were] in their prime working years, 25–44; it was the core of working-age adults. Nearly half of all California Latinos were native-of-native, overwhelmingly third-generation in California; but they were mostly children and constituted two-thirds of all Latinos under the age of 16.[149]

Conclusion: These statistics shifted dramatically, affecting future generations.

The 1960s reached the perfect storm in the mobilization of Chicano/a youth. Many were second-generation survivors of the massive deportations of the 1930s and 50s. The children of GI veterans were not as vulnerable as immigrant generations. Their interests dovetailed with the interests of progressives in the GI generation. Youth collectively benefitted from the impatience of decade. They called themselves Chicanos, a choice that was in keeping with the identity politics of the times. In a sense they joined other groups in coming out of the closet and took pride in being Chicano.

What is amazing is that a relatively small number of Chicana/o youth succeeded in mobilizing the largest proportion of the community thus far in the history of Mexican Americans in the United States. In part, the success of this mobilization was due to the large number of young people in the Chicana/o community in Texas, California and elsewhere who listened and nurtured a hope that they could change society. They integrated with other youth through music; listening to rock 'n' roll bound many together. The Vietnam War tapped an energy that generated anger—anger at the war, anger at society, anger at seeing the unequal treatment of people at home and abroad.

The Chicano movement left legacies, not least of which was a community much more aware of its human rights. As a consequence, many more persons of Mexican extraction got involved in trying to ensure civil rights guarantees for Chicanos and the Spanish-speaking people in the United States. A larger sector joined student organizations such as MEChA and MAYO and mobilized community groups to fight for their rights. Youth activists furthered the Mexican American civil rights tradition of the past, and every subsequent generation of immigrants coming into the country would benefit from this legacy.[150]

Notes

1. "Baby Boomers," Ohio History Central, http://www.ohiohistorycentral.org/entry.php?rec=1699.
2. "Civil Rights Struggle of the 1960s," http://www.youtube.com/watch?v=EYqsJizN4gI. Today, for example, youth are less homophobic than were the older generation; more youth than those over 55 voted for a Black president.
3. "Hearts and Minds," Top Documentary Films, http://topdocumentaryfilms.com/hearts-and-minds/. Ibid, http://www.youtube.com/watch?v=1d2ml82lc7s.
4. "America in Ferment: The Tumultuous 1960s," Viva la Raza! 1960s, *Digital History*, http://www.digitalhistory.uh.edu/era.cfm?eraID=17&smtID=2.
5. Paul Friedländer, *Rock and Roll* (Boulder, CO: Westview Press, 1996), 287. Barbara Ehrenreich, "The Rock Rebellion," http://spiritlink.com/rock-rebellion.html.
6. "Facts on U.S. Immigrants, 2016. Statistical portrait of the foreign-born population in the United States," Pew Research Center, September 14, 2018. http://www.pewhispanic.org/2018/09/14/facts-on-u-s-immigrants-trend-data/. Luis R. Fraga, et al., "Redefining America: Findings from the 2006 Latino National Survey," http://www.washington.edu/diversity/files/2013/05/HouseDemsSlidesFinalD_2.14.07.pdf Lisa Wade, "U.S. Racial/Ethnic Demographics: 1960, Today, and 2050," Sociological Images, November 14, 2012. https://thesocietypages.org/socimages/2012/11/14/u-s-racialethnic-demographics-1960-today-and-2050/comment-page-1/.
7. Leo Grebler, Joan W. Moore, and Ralph C. Guzmán, *The Mexican American People: The Nation's Second Largest Minority* (New York: Free Press, 1970).
8. Grebler et al., *Mexican American People*, 106, 126, 143, 150, 185, 236, 251. Richard W. Slatta, "Chicanos in the Pacific Northwest: An Historical Overview of Oregon's Chicanos," *Aztlán* 6, No. 3 (Fall 1975), 335. Mexicans in the Columbia Basin, http://www.vancouver.wsu.edu/crbeha/ma/ma.htm. "No dogs or Mexicans allowed (No Mexicans or dogs allowed)", The Big Apple, http://www.barrypopik.com/index.php/new_york_city/entry/no_dogs_or_mexicans_allowed_no_mexicans_or_dogs_allowed/.
9. Robert Coles and Harry Huge, "Thorns on the Yellow Rose of Texas," *New Republic* (April 19, 1969): 13–17. Robert Garland Landolt, *The Mexican American Workers of San Antonio, Texas* (New York: Arno Press, 1976), 320, 326.
10. Today, Segundo Barrio is fighting for survival. Dr. Lydia R. Otero, Paso Del Sur Group, http://pasodelsur.com/news/plea.html (accessed November 8, 2009). Joe Olvera, "El Segundo Barrio, Cradle of the Chicano Movement," News Paper Tree, http://newspapertree.com/opinion/1007-el-segundo-barrio-cradle-of-the-chicano-movement. "Cultural Life of el Segundo Barrio," http://pasodelsur.com/historia/Culturallife.html.
11. Benjamin Márquez, "Power and Politics in a Chicano Barrio" (PhD Dissertation, University of Wisconsin, Madison, 1983), chs 4 and 5. Barry J. Kaplan, "Houston: The Golden Buckle of the Sunbelt," in Richard M. Bernard and Bradley R. Rice, eds.,

Sunbelt Cities: Politics and Growth Since World War II (Austin: University of Texas Press, 1983), 196–212.

12 Because of the size of the Mexican *barrios*, Los Angeles fostered Chicano sounds. Anthony Macias, *Mexican American Mojo: Popular Music, Dance, and Urban Culture in Los Angeles, 1935–1968* (Durham, NC: Duke University Press, 2008). Steve Loza, *Barrio Rhythm: Mexican American Music in Los Angeles* (Champaign: University of Illinois Press, 1993).

13 Marcos de León, "Statements of Philosophy and Policy as They Pertain to the Acculturation and Education of the Mexican-American" (Unpublished manuscript, 1964) in Rodolfo F. Acuña and Guadalupe Compeán, eds., *Voices of the U.S. Latino Experience*, 3 Vols. (Westport, CT: Greenwood, 2008), 807–9.

14 *Los Angeles Times* (March 8, 1972). Ray Hebert, "L.A. County Latin Population Grows 113 Percent," *Los Angeles Times* (August 18, 1972). *Forumeer* (February 1970). Mike Davis, *City of Quartz: Excavating the Future in Los Angeles* (London:Verso, 1990), 164. Henry Joseph Gutiérrez, "The Chicano Education Rights Movement and School Segregation, Los Angeles, 1962–1970" (PhD Dissertation, University of California, Irving, 1990), 35.

15 Rita Arias Jirasek and Carlos Tortolero, *Mexican Chicago* (Chicago, IL: Arcadia Publishing, 2001), 53, 63. The Chicago Mexican community was part of a circuit of Mexican musical events, and they enjoyed traditional music from both Mexico and Texas.

16 Anthony Baker, "The Social Production of Space of Two Chicago Neighborhoods: Pilsen and Lincoln Park" (PhD Dissertation, University of Illinois at Chicago Circle, 1995), 30, 42. Louise Año Nuevo Kerr, *The Chicano Experience in Chicago: 1920–1970* (Chicago: University of Illinois at Chicago Circle, 1976), 171–76. Peter T. Alter, "Mexicans and Serbs in Southeast Chicago: Racial Group Formation During the Twentieth Century," *Journal of the Illinois State Historical Society* (January 2001), http://dig.lib.niu.edu/ISHS/ishs-2001winter/ishs-2001winter403.pdf. "Mexicans," *The Electronic Encyclopedia of Chicago* (Chicago: Chicago Historical Society, 2005), http://www.encyclopedia.chicagohistory.org/pages/824.html. Rob Paral and Michael Norkewicz, *The Metro Chicago Immigration Fact Book* (Institute for Metropolitan Affairs, Roosevelt University, June 2003), http://www.robparal.com/downloads/chicagoimmfactbook_2003_06.pdf.

17 David K. Shipler, *The Working Poor: Invisible In America* (New York: Vintage Books, 2005), 96.

18 1960: "Harvest of Shame," http://www.youtube.com/watch?v=yJTVF_dya7E.

19 Ibid. Edward Bliss, *Now the News: The Story of Broadcast Journalism* (New York: Columbia University Press, 1992), 391–93. Robert Niemi, *History in the Media: Film and Television* (Santa Barbara, CA: ABC-CLIO, 2006), 323–24.

20 "Stoop Farm Labor 1959," http://www.youtube.com/watch?v=BiMjKmuva0I.

21 Grebler et al., *Mexican American People*, 209. Anne Brunton, "The Chicano Migrants," in Livie Isaudro Durán and H. Russell Bernard, eds., *Introduction to Chicano Studies*, 2nd ed. (New York: Macmillan, 1982), 260–71. Sara Hoffman Jurand, "Human Rights Group Reports Poor Working Conditions for Child Farmworkers," *Trial* 36, No. 9 (September 2000), 98. Meg Grant, "Still a Harvest of Shame: The Exploitation of Migrant Farm Workers Shocked the Nation 30 Years Ago—But Their Pain Continues," *People Weekly* 34, No. 21 (November 26, 1990), 44–50.

22 B. Drummond Ayres Jr. "KENNEDY COURTING MEXICAN-AMERICANS," *New York Times* (1923–Current file), May 1, 1980, LATINO VOICES, "John F. Kennedy's Complex Relationship With The Mexican American Community" HuffPost, Nov. 22, 2013 01:18 pm ET Updated Jan 25, 2014. https://www.huffingtonpost.com/2013/11/22/john-f-kennedy-mexican-am_n_4324888.html

23 George Mowry and Blaine A. Brownell, *The Urban Nation 1920–1980,* rev. ed. (New York: Hill and Wang, 1981), 211–12. Ignacio M. García, *Viva Kennedy: Mexican Americans in Search of Camelot* (College Station: Texas A&M University Press, 2000), 5, 33, 73, 110.

24 Melinda S. Jackson, "Priming the Sleeping Giant: The Dynamics of Latino Political Identity and Vote Choice," *Political Psychology*, Vol. 32, No. 4 (August 2011), pp. 691–716. "We, the American Hispanics," U.S. Census Bureau, https://www.census.gov/prod/cen1990/wepeople/we-2r.pdf.

25 Patrick L. Cox, *Ralph W. Yarborough, the People's Senator* (Austin: University of Texas Press, 2002), 233–34. Jan Jarboe Russell, "Henry B. González," *Texas Monthly* 29, No. 1 (January 2001), 204.

26 Interview by José Angel Gutiérrez, Voices Tejanas, Albert Peña, Jr., Tejano Voices, University of Texas Arlington, http://library.uta.edu/tejanovoices/xml/CMAS_015.xml. José Angel Gutiérrez, Albert A. Peña Jr.: Dean of Chicano Politics (East Lansing, MI: Michigan State University Press, 2017), 117–40.

27 "Political Association of Spanish-Speaking Organizations," *Handbook of Texas Online*, http://www.tshaonline.org/handbook/online/articles/PP/vep1.html.

28 See award winning biography, José Ángel Gutiérrez, Albert A. Peña Jr.: Dean of Chicano Politics (East Lansing: Michican State University, 2017).

29 "Revolt of the Mexicans," *Time* (April 12, 1963), http://www.time.com/time/magazine/

article/0,9171,828075,00.html. Rodolfo F. Acuña, *The Making of Chicana/o Studies: In the Trenches of Academe* (New Brunswick: Rutgers University Press, 2011), 22–25.

30. "Eligio 'Kika' De La Garza II," http://www.loc.gov/rr/hispanic/congress/delagarza.html.

31. Julie Leininger Pycior, *LBJ & Mexican Americans: The Paradox of Power* (Austin: University of Texas Press, 1997), 49, 60, 98, 100, 113, 123, 134. Lorena Oropeza, "La Batalla Esta Aqui! Chicanos Oppose the War in Vietnam" (PhD Dissertation, Cornell University, 1996), 105. Charles Ray Chandler, "The Mexican American Protest Movement in Texas" (PhD Dissertation, Tulane University, 1968), 157–60, 173–90. Louise Ann Fish, *All Rise: Reynaldo G. Garza, the First Mexican American Federal Judge* (College Station: Texas A&M University Press, 1996), 88–122. "Revolt of the Masses," *Time* (April 12, 1963). Tony Castro, *Chicano Power: The Emergence of Mexican Americans* (New York: Saturday Review Press, 1974), 28. Edwin Larry Dickens, "The Political Role of Mexican Americans in San Antonio" (PhD Dissertation, Texas Tech University, 1969), 169.

32. Heather Rose Parker, "The Elusive Coalition: African American and Chicano Political Organization and Interaction in Los Angeles, 1960–1973" (PhD Dissertation, University of California, Los Angeles, 1996). Rodolfo F. Acuña, *A Community Under Siege: A Chronicle of Chicanos East of the Los Angeles River 1945–1975* (Los Angeles, CA: Chicano Studies Research Center Publications, 1984), 85. Acuña, *Anything but Mexican: Chicanos in Contemporary Los Angeles* (London: Verso, 1996).

33. California Latino Caucus, "Historical Overview of the Latino Caucus," http://www2.legislature.ca.gov/latinocaucus/History.asp.

34. Raphael J. Sonenshein, *Politics in Black and White: Race and Power in Los Angeles* (Princeton, NJ: Princeton University Press, 1993), 55–84. Larry N. George, "Red Wind: Anticommunism and Conservative Hegemony in Cold War Los Angeles," in Gerry Riposa and Carolyn Dersch, eds., *City of Angels* (Dubuque, IA: Kendall/Hunt, 1992), 1–14. Davis, *City of Quartz*, 125–28. *G.I. Forum News Bulletin* (March 1963 and September 1964).

35. Pilsen Art Tours, http://www.ppat.space/.

36. Kerr, "Chicano Experience," 183–84. William Kornblum, *Blue Collar Community* (Chicago: University of Chicago Press, 1974), 161–87. Baker, "The Social Production of Space," 155, 158, 160.

37. Mowry and Brownell, *Urban Nation*, 213–14. Pycior, *LBJ*, 148–51.

38. Rodolfo F. Acuña, The Making of Chicana/o Studies: In the Trenches of Academe (New Brunswick: Rutgers Uni-versity Press, 2011), p. 26.

39. Pycior, *LBJ*, 149, 151.

40. Maris A. Vinovskis, *The Birth of Head Start: Preschool Education Policies in the Kennedy and Johnson Administrations* (Chicago: University of Chicago, 2005), 59–68.

41. "LBJ State of Union War on Poverty," http://www.youtube.com/watch?v=qfT03Ihtlds. Timothy Werner, "T. The War on Poverty and the Racialization of "Hillbilly" Poverty: Implications for Poverty Research," *Journal of Poverty*, 19(3) (2015)., 1-1. Biliana C. S Ambrecht, *Politicizing the poor: the legacy of the war on poverty in a Mexican-American community* (New York: Praeger, 1976)

42. *The Invisible Minority*, Report of the NEA–Tucson Survey on the Teaching of Spanish to the Spanish Speaking, Department of Rural Education, National Education Association, Washington, D.C., 1966. Ernesto Galarza, *La Mula No Nacio Arisca*, *Center Diary* (September–October 1966), 26–32, reprinted in Acuña and Compeán, *Voices of the U.S. Latino*, 813–18.

43. Graciela Gil Olivárez, Arizona Women's Heritage Trail, http://www.womensheritagetrail.org/women/GracielaGilOlivarez.php. Mowry and Brownell, *Urban Nation*, 221–22. Biliana María Ambrecht, "Politicization as a Legacy of the War on Poverty: A Study of Advisory Council Members in a Mexican American Community" (PhD Dissertation, University of California at Los Angeles, 1973). V. Kurtz, "Politics, Ethnicity, Integration: Mexican Americans in the War on Poverty" (PhD Dissertation, University of California, Davis, 1970). This section draws specifically from Greg Coronado, "Spanish-Speaking Organizations in Utah," in Paul Morgan and Vince Mayer, eds., *Working Papers Toward a History of the Spanish Speaking in Utah* (Salt Lake City: American West Center, Mexican American Documentation Project, University of Utah, 1973), 121. Vernon M. Briggs, Jr., Walter Fogel, and Fred H. Schmidt, *The Chicano Worker* (Austin: University of Texas Press, 1977), 38. *Forumeer* (March 1967) states that the Forum almost dropped sponsorship of SER because LBJ was hedging on the White House conference. Pycior, *LBJ*, 152–53, 159, 161.

44. Voting Rights Act, 1965, United States Department of Justice, Civil Rights Division, http://www.justice.gov/crt/about/vot/intro/intro_b.php. Mexican Americans were not initially entitled under the Act.

45. Pycior, *LBJ*, 164, 170, 178–82. Carey McWilliams, *North from Mexico* (New York: Greenwood Press, 1968), 17. *Forumeer* (October 1967). The Forum supported the conference. John Hart Lane, Jr., "Voluntary Associations Among Mexican Americans in San Antonio, Texas: Organization and Leadership Characteristics" (PhD Dissertation, University of Texas,

1968), 2. Richard Gardner, *Grito! Reies Tijerina and the New Mexico Land Grant War of 1967* (New York: Bobbs-Merrill, 1970), 231–32. Craig A. Kaplowitz, *LULAC, Mexican Americans, and National Policy* (College Station: Texas A&M University Press, 2005), 98–104.

46 David Nieto, "A Brief History of Bilingual Education in the United States," *Perspectives on Urban Education* (Spring 2009), 61–72.

47 Anguiano, a former nun, had been a national organizer for the United Farm Workers. She later founded, along with Gloria Steinem and Bella Abzug, the National Women's Political Caucus (1971). Jasmin K. Williams, "Lupe Anguiano—A Tireless Warrior Woman," *New York Post* (March 12, 2007).

48 Prycior, *LBJ*, 183–87.

49 "Watts Riots Project," https://www.youtube.com/watch?v=aJUS9aa0Yms.

50 Oropeza, "La Batalla," 95, 100–1.

51 Davis, *City of Quartz*, 101–6. Gerald Horne, *Fire This Time: The Watts Uprising and the 1960s* (New York: Da Capo Press, 1997), an excellent presentation of the causes of the uprisings. Meyer Weinberg, *A Chance to Learn: A History of Race and Education in the United States* (Cambridge, England: Cambridge University Press, 1977), 174.

52 Carey McWilliams, *North from Mexico: The Spanish-Speaking People of the United States*, 3rd Edition (ABC-CLIO, 2016), xix.

53 Quoted in James T. Patterson, *America's Struggle Against Poverty 1900–1980* (Cambridge, MA: Harvard University Press, 1981), 145–46. Kaplowitz, *LULAC*, 98, 108, 125, 220.

54 Acuña, *Community Under Siege*, 145. Patterson, *America's Struggle*, 148.

55 Morris Singer, *Growth, Equality and the Mexican Experience* (Austin: University of Texas Press, 1969), 31.

56 Ibid., 31. María Fernández-Kelly, *For We Are Sold, I and My People: Women and Industry in Mexico's Frontier* (Albany: State University of New York Press, 1983), 24, 132, 134. Lamar Babington Jones, "Mexican American Labor Problems in Texas" (PhD Dissertation, University of Texas, 1965), 33, 35–37.

57 Theodore White, *America in Search of Itself* (New York: Harper Collins, 1984), 363.

58 Emily Cadei, "Fifty Years Later, the Immigration Bill That Changed America; The 1965 immigration reform act, now 50 years old, wasn't supposed to encourage Mexican immigration," *Newsweek*, Sept. 25, 2015, Vol.165(11)

59 "The Immigration Act of 1965: Intended and Unintended Consequences of the 20th Century," http://iipdigital.usembassy.gov/st/english/publication/2008/04/20080423214226eaifas0.9637982.html#axzz2BynJjSpp.

60 James Fallows, "Immigration: How It's Affecting Us," *The Atlantic*, 252, No. 5 (November 1983), 45–68. Acuña, *Anything but Mexican*, 114. Mario T. García, *Memories of Chicano History: The Life and Narrative of Bert Corona* (Berkeley: University of California, 1994), 290–300. David G. Gutiérrez, "Sin Fronteras? Chicanos, Mexican Americans, and the Emergence of the Contemporary Immigration Debate, 1968–1978," in David Gutiérrez, ed., *Between Two Worlds: Mexican Immigrants in the United States* (Wilmington, DE: Scholarly Resources, 1996), 175–209. Miriam J. Wells, *Strawberry Fields: Politics, Class, and Work in California Agriculture* (Ithaca, NY: Cornell University Press, 1996), 63.

61 Chávez was a civil rights leader much on par with the Rev. Martin Luther King, Jr., and he used movement symbols to attract a wider constituency. Farmworker Movement, https://libraries.ucsd.edu/farmworkermovement/.

62 National Farm Workers Association Collection, Records, 1960–1967, Walter P. Reuther Library of Labor and Urban Affairs, http://microformguides.gale.com/Data/Download/9177000C.pdf.

63 Richard W. Etulain, ed., *César Chávez: A Brief Biography with Documents* (New York: Palgrave Macmillan, 2002), 8–10. "The Fight in the Fields, Cesar Chávez and the Farmworkers' Struggle," PBS. http://www.pbs.org/itvs/fightfields/cesarchavez.html. Richard Steven Street, "Poverty in the Valley of Plenty: The National Farm Labor Union, Di Giorgio Farms, and Suppression of Documentary Photography in California, 1947–66," *Labor History* 48 (February 2007): 25–48.

64 Dolores Huerta: Labor Leader and Social Activist, http://latino.si.edu/virtualgallery/OJOS/bios/bios_Huerta.htm.

65 "Vatican II—Urgent & Essential," http://www.vatican2voice.org/default.htm.

66 Peter Matthiessen, *Sal Si Puedes: César Chávez and the New American Revolution* (New York: Random House, 1969), 41, 50–51, 333–34. Joan London and Henry Anderson, *So Shall Ye Reap* (New York: Crowell, 1971), 146–49. Mark Day, *Forty Acres: César Chávez and the Farm Workers* (New York: Praeger, 1971), 42, 54, 55. Hedda Garza, *Latinas: Hispanic Women in the United States* (New York: Franklin Watts, 1994), 11–13, 114. Vickie Ruiz, *From Out of the Shadows: Mexican Women in Twentieth-Century America* (New York: Oxford University Press, 1998), 134–35. Margaret Rose, "From the Fields to the Picket Line: Huelga Women and the Boycott, 1965–1975," *Labor History* 31, No. 3 (Summer 1990), 272. Samuel R. Berger, *Dollar Harvest: The Story*

of the Farm Bureau (Lexington, MA: Heath, 1971), 161–63. *Forumeer* (May 1966). Gregory Dunne, *Delano* (New York: Farrar, Straus & Giroux, 1967), 51, 144–45, 147–48. Ronald B. Taylor, *Chávez and the Farm Workers* (Boston: Beacon Press, 1975), 157, 251, 259, 261–69, 287. Sam Kushner, *Long Road to Delano* (New York: International Publishers, 1975), 173.

67 The affiliation with the NFWA was not popular among all the Texans; Sánchez and Galván bolted, forming the Texas Independent Workers Association. Robert M. Utley, *Lone Star Lawmen: The Second Century of the Texas Rangers* (Cambridge, MA: Oxford University Press, 2007), 238–45. "Farmworkers ask help against 'terror campaign,'" Texas Farm Workers Support Committee, http://chavez.cde.ca.gov/ResearchCenter/DocumentDisplayRC.aspx?rpg=/chdocuments/documentdisplay.jsp&doc=56d6ce%3Aeae63c6e4f%3A-7e83&searchhit=yes. Sons of Zapata: A Brief Photographic History of Farm Workers' Strike in Texas, http://www.farmworkermovement.us/ufwarchives/elmalcriado/Frankel/Strike.pdf. Acuña, *Making of Chicana/o Studies*, 36–38.

68 David Montejano, *Anglos and Mexicans in the Making of Texas, 1836–1986* (Austin: University of Texas Press, 1987), 284. Charles Cotrel interviewed by José Angel Gutiérrez (Tejano Voices, University of Texas, Arlington, San Antonio, July 2, 1992), 4, 6, 9, 16, http://library.uta.edu/tejanovoices/xml/CMAS_020.xml. "Priests Active in Valley Strike," *San Antonio Express* (July 7, 1966).

69 Gilbert Padilla 1962–1980, Interview, 2, http://www.farmworkermovement.us/essays/essays/005%20Padilla_Gilbert.pdf. "U.S. Senate Sub-Committee hearings," *San Antonio Express/News* (July 1, 1966). La Casita Farms strike was called a complete failure. "Farm Strike Could Turn into Social Movement," *Big Spring Herald* (Texas, July 17, 1966). José Angel Gutiérrez, *The Making of a Chicano Militant: Lessons from Crystal* (Madison: University of Wisconsin, 1999), 105. "Melon Packers Did Cross Picket Line," *Brownsville Herald* (July 13, 1967). Timothy Paul Bowman, "What About Texas? The Forgotten Cause of Antonio Orendain and the Rio Grande Valley Farm Workers, 1966–1982" (Master's Thesis, University of Texas, Arlington, 2005), 7–10, 45–55. "Orendain Sparks UFWOC Organizing Drive in Texas," *El Malciado*, 3, No. 11 (August 15–September 15, 1969), 13. http://www.farmworkermovement.org/ufwarchives/elmalcriado/1969/August%2015%20-%20Sept%2015,%201969%20No%2011_PDF.pdf.

70 Mark Erenberg, "*Obreros Unidos* in Wisconsin," U.S. Bureau of Labor Statistics, *Monthly Labor Review* 91 (June 1968), 20–23. National Advisory Committee on Farm Labor, *Farm Labor Organizing, 1905–1967: A Brief History* (New York: National Advisory Committee on Farm Labor, 1967), 59. Dennis Nodín Valdés, *Al Norte: Agricultural Workers in the Great Lakes Region, 1917–1970* (Austin: University of Texas, 1991), 189–92. James Maraniss, "Wautoma: New Season, Same Woes," *The Capital Times* (July 31, 1967). *The Post-Crescent* (Appleton, Wisconsin, January 8, 1967). *Oshkosh Daily Northwestern* (August 15, 1966). *The Post-Crescent* (Appleton, Wisconsin, January 8, 1967).

71 Acuña, *Making of Chicana/o Studies*, 29–31. Marc Simon Rodriguez, "Obreros Unidos: Migration, Migrant Farm Worker Activism, and the Chicano Movement in Wisconsin and Texas, 1950–1980" (PhD Dissertation, University of Illinois, Evanston, 2000). Marc Simon Rodriguez, *The Tejano Diaspora: Mexican Americanism and Ethnic Politics in Texas and Wisconsin* (Chapel Hill: University of North Carolina Press, 2011).

72 Hob Voces, "Long March Converges on Capitol Steps," *The News-Palladium* (Benton Harbor, Michigan, March 27, 1967). "Migrant Unit Gets Hearing with Romney," *Record Eagle* (Traverse City, Michigan, April 5, 1967). "Romney Aide Works with Migrants," *The Holland* (Michigan, Evening Sentinel, April 5, 1967). "Migrants to Ask Romney to Intervene," *The Holland*, (Michigan, Evening Sentinel April 13, 1967). Acuña, *Making of Chicana/o Studies*, 31–32.

73 National Advisory Committee on Farm Labor, 60. Barbara Jane Macklin, *Structural Stability and Cultural Change in a Mexican American Community* (New York: Arno Press, 1976), vi. Farm Labor Organizing Committee AFL–CIO, http://www.floc.com/.

74 "Governor to Get Report on Migrant Workers," *Walla Walla Union-Bulletin* (May 11, 1967). "Timeline: Movimiento from 1960–1985," Seattle Civil Rights and Labor History Project, http://depts.washington.edu/civilr/mecha_timeline.htm.

75 Ana Gonzalez-Barrera and Mark Hugo Lopez, "A Demographic Portrait of Mexican-Origin Hispanics in the United States," Pew Research Center, May 1, 2013, http://www.pewhispanic.org/2013/05/01/a-demographic-portrait-of-mexican-origin-hispanics-in-the-united-states/. Betsy Guzmán, "Hispanic Population," U.S. Census Bureau, U.S. Department of Commerce, May 2001, https://www.westchestergov.com/planning/research/Census2000/Oct03Updates/Briefs/hispanic.pdf.

76 "Dr. José Angel Gutiérrez," Tejano Voices, http://library.uta.edu/tejanovoices/gutierrez.php. Acuña, *Making of Chicana/o Studies*, 56–57.

77 Viviana Santiago Cavada, Interview, Tejano Voices, https://library.uta.edu/tejanovoices/xml/CMAS_066.xml. Acuña, *Making of Chicana/o Studies*, 56–58.

78 Armando Navarro, *Mexican American Youth Organization: Avant-Garde of the Chicano Movement in Texas* (Austin: University of Texas Press, 1995), 80–97. J. Gutiérrez, *The Making of a Chicano Militant*, 79.

79 United Mexican-American Students Symposium—UCLA February 1968, Pacifica Radio Archive, http://www.archive.org/details/UnitedMexican-americanStudentsSymposium-UclaFeburary1968. Acuña, *Making of Chicana/o Studies*, 41–42.

80 Rodolfo Corky Gonzales, "I Am Joaquin," http://www.latinamericanstudies.org/latinos/joaquin.htm.

81 "Chicano—Quest for a Homeland," Part 1 in 6 parts, http://www.youtube.com/watch?v=RHQ4XS-DrqM.

82 Rosales, *Chicano!*, 211–13. Pedro Acevez, MEChA de UW, Interview, Seattle Civil Rights and Labor Project, http://depts.washington.edu/civilr/acevez.htm. Erasmo Gamboa MEChA; UFW Grape Boycott; Historian; UW Professor, Seattle Civil Rights and Labor Project, http://depts.washington.edu/civilr/Erasmo_Gamboa.htm. Roberto Maestas, El Centro de la Raza, Seattle Civil Rights and Labor Project, http://depts.washington.edu/civilr/maestas.htm. Yolanda Alaniz, MEChA de UW, Radical Women, Freedom Socialist Party, http://depts.washington.edu/civilr/alaniz.htm.

83 Rosales, *Chicano!*, 211–13. Francisco A. Rosales, ed., *Testimonio: A Documentary History of the Mexican American Struggle for Civil Rights* (Houston, TX: Arte Público Press, 2000), 126–27. Dan Pavillard, "Minorities Like Taste of Honey—Huerta Says," *Tucson Daily Citizen* (October 20, 1967). Maritza De La Trinidad, "Collective Outrage: Mexican American Activism and the Quest for Educational Equality and Reform: 1950–1990" (Tucson: PhD Dissertation, University of Arizona, 2008), 150, 162, 183. Acuña, *Making of Chicana/o Studies*, 55–56.

84 Enriqueta Vásquez (Author), Dionne Espínoza (Editor), Lorena Oropeza (Editor), *Enriqueta Vasquez and the Chicano Movement: Writings from El Grito del Norte* (Houston, TX: Arte Público Press, 2006).

85 Navarro, *Mexican American Youth*, 55–66. Juan Gómez-Quiñones, *Mexican Students por La Raza: The Chicano Student Movement in Southern California 1967–1977* (Santa Barbara, CA: Editorial La Causa, 1978), 17–18, 22–23. Gerald Paul Rosen, "Political Ideology and the Chicano Movement: A Study of the Political Ideology of Activists in the Chicano Movement" (PhD Dissertation, University of California at Los Angeles, 1972), 248. In Los Angeles, Francisca Flores, a veteran activist, and Ramona Morín (women's auxiliary of the Forum) cofounded the California League of Mexican American Women. Flores published and edited *La Carta Editorial*, which reported on political activism in the mid-1960s, and published *Regeneración*, an activist magazine focusing on women's issues.

86 H. Gutiérrez, "Chicano Education Rights," 53. Gómez-Quiñones, *Mexican Students Por La Raza*, 17. Rosales, *Chicano!*, 186–88.

87 Mario T. Garcia and Sal Castro, *Blowout!: Sal Castro and the Chicano Struggle for Educational Justice* (Chapel Hill: University of North Carolina Press, 2011).

88 "Walkouts," HBOFilms, http://store.hbo.com/walk-out-dvd/detail.php?p=100589. "Walkout: The True Story of the Historic 1968 Chicano Student Walkout in East L.A.," Democracy Now, http://www.democracynow.org/2006/3/29/walkout_the_true_story_of_the. Acuña, *Making of Chicana/o Studies*, 38–42.

89 Blowout Panel 3, http://www.youtube.com/watch?v=hXt8IJZhTM4.

90 *Salvatore B. Castro et al. v. The Superior Court of Los Angeles County*, 9 Cal. App. 3d 675; 88 Cal. Rptr. 500; 1970 Cal. App. LEXIS 1985, July 17, 1970.

91 Dolores Delgado Bernal, "Chicana School Resistance and Grassroots Leadership: Providing an Alternative History of the 1968 East Los Angeles Blowouts" (PhD Dissertation, University of California, Los Angeles, 1997), 84–85. Ernesto Chávez, "Creating Aztlán: The Chicano Movement in Los Angeles, 1966–1978" (PhD Dissertation, University of California, Los Angeles, 1994), 65, 73. Carlos Muñoz, Jr., *Youth, Identity, Power: The Chicano Movement* (London: Verso, 1989), 64, 68, 132. Rosales, *Chicano!*, 190, 191, 192–94. Sánchez was Prime Minister of the Brown Berets; Carlos Montes, Minister of Information of the Berets; and Cruz Olmeda, Minister of Discipline of the Berets. They had approximately 30 members by mid-1968. H. Gutiérrez, "Chicano Education," 4–5, 56 on the EICC. Along with Castro, the others indicted were Eleazear Risco, editor of *La Raza* newspaper; Joe Razo, coeditor; Patricio Sánez, community activist; Moctezuma Esparza of UCLA UMAS; David Sánchez and Carlos Montes of the Berets; Ralph Ramírez, minister of defense of the Berets, Fred López of the Berets; and Richard Vigil, Gilberto C. Olmeda, and Henry Gómez. Pycior, *LBJ*, 220–21. Oropeza, "La Batalla," 94.

92 Juan A. Sepúlveda, *Life and Times of Willie Velásquez: Su Voto Es Su Voz* (Houston, TX: Arte Público Press, 2005), 69–72. Doris Wright, "Lanier High Students Get Civic Leader Support," *San Antonio Express* (April 11, 1968).

93 Rodolfo F. Acuña, *The Making of Chicana/o Studies: In the Trenches of Academe* (New Brunswick: Rutgers University Press, 2011), 38

94 Ron White, "3,000 Ask Reforms in Walkout," *San Antonio Light* (May 16, 1968). "School Chief Insists

It's Classes as Usual v. Meet Demands," *San Antonio Light* (May 17, 1968).

95 Ron White, "Edgewood Rally Held," *San Antonio Light* (May 21, 1968). "Edgewood Hearing in Recess," *San Antonio Light* (May 24, 1968). Frank Trejo, "Board Promises Solution to Grievances," *San Antonio Light* (May 24, 1968). Frank Trejo, "School to Act on Grievances," *San Antonio Light* (May 28, 1968).

96 Baldemar James Barrera, "'We Want Better Education!' The Chicano Student Movement for Educational Reform in South Texas, 1968–1970" (PhD Dissertation, University of New Mexico, Albuquerque, 2007), 102. Richard R. Valencia, *Chicano Students and the Courts: The Mexican American Legal Struggle for Educational Equality* (New York: New York University Press, 2008), 92–103. Acuña, *Making of Chicana/o Studies*, 37–41.

97 Elaine Ayala, "The Year Latino Students Stood Up, Walked Out," *San Antonio Express News* (May 7, 2008). On March 21, 1973, the Supreme Court in a five-to-four decision ruled against Rodríguez, stating that the system of school finance did not violate the federal constitution. Texas should resolve the issue.

98 David Robles, "Walking Out: The Success of the Edcouch-Elsa Student Walkout of 1968 through the Media," (Master's, University of Texas-Pan American, 2012), 2, 18, makes the valid point that the Edcouch-Elsa walkouts of 1968 "commenced public discourse within the community about the educational practices as well as racism occurring in schools, and opinions over whether or not these students were in the right." Barrera, "'We Want Better Education!,'" is an excellent background to the walkouts.

99 "Valley School Hit by Boycott," *Odessa American* (November 14, 1968), blames the MAYO movement. "Five Arrested in School Boycott," *Galveston Daily News* (November 16, 1968) reported those arrested as Mirtala Villarreal, Homer Trevino, Freddie Sainz, Arnulfo Sustaita, and Xavier Ramírez. Nolene Hodges, "Edcouch-Elsa Students in Class Revolt," *Brownsville Herald* (November 14, 1968). Norma R. Cuellar, "The Edcouch-Elsa Walkout," Mexican-American History 2363, Dr. Rodolfo Rocha (June 29, 1984), 1, http://www.aaperales.com/school/files/walkout/eewalkout.doc. Robles, "Walking Out," 20–22, copy of demands.

100 Cuellar, "The Edcouch-Elsa Walkout," 3.

101 "Refuses Boycotting Pupils," *Big Spring Herald* (Texas, November 19, 1968). Gary Garrison, "Return to School Sought," *Corpus Christi Times* (November 19, 1968). "Edcouch-Elsa Board Hears Each Student," *Brownsville Herald* (November 20, 1968). "Edcouch Student Hearings Scheduled for Wednesday," *Brownsville Herald* (November 26, 1968). "Valley Students Stage Walkout," *Big Spring Herald* (Texas, November 14, 1968). Kenneth Clark, "VISTAs Tied to Boycott," *Brownsville Herald* (November 25, 1968). Cuellar, "The Edcouch-Elsa Walkout," 6–8.

102 Oscar Acosta, "The East L.A. 13 vs. the Superior Court," *El Grito* 3, No. 2 (Winter 1970), 14. London and Anderson, *So Shall Ye Reap*, 25. William Parker Frisbie, "Militancy Among Mexican Americans: A Study of High School Students" (PhD Dissertation, University of North Carolina at Chapel Hill, 1972), 4, 143. *Forumeer* (October, December 1968). Eugene Acosta Marín, "The Mexican American Community and Leadership of the Dominant Society in Arizona: A Study of Their Mutual Attitudes and Perceptions" (PhD Dissertation, U.S. International University, 1973), 12. Ian F. Haney-López, *Racism on Trial: The Chicano Fight for Justice* (Cambridge, MA: Belknap Press of Harvard University Press, 2004).

103 David Sánchez, *Expedition Through Aztlán* (La Puente, CA: Perspectiva Press, 1978). Rona M. Fields and Charles J. Fox, "Viva La Raza: The Saga of the Brown Berets" (unpublished manuscript). See also G. Rosen, "Political Ideology." David Sánchez himself remained anti-Communist throughout his career. Other factions such as La Junta adopted a revolutionary focus. Marguerite Marín, *Social Protest in an Urban Barrio: A Study of the Chicano Movement, 1966–1974* (Lanham, MD: University Press of America, 1991).

104 David Montejano, *Quixote's Soldiers: A Local History of the Chicano Movement, 1966–1981* (Austin: University of Texas Press, 2010).

105 Jennifer G Correa, "The Targeting of the East Los Angeles Brown Berets by a Racial Patriarchal Capitalist State: Merging Intersectionality and Social Movement Research," *Critical Sociology*, January 2011, Vol. 37(1), 83–101.

106 Jennifer G. Correa, "Chicano Nationalism: The Brown Berets and Legal Social Control," (Master's Thesis, Texas A&M University, Kingsville, Texas, 2006), 79–97, quoted FBI File #105-178715: March 27, 1968. FBI File #157-2163: March 7, 1968 reported on the ELA Walkouts. Correa also quoted FBI File #105-178715: February 25, 1969.

107 Patrick J. McDonnell, "1968 Massacre in Mexico Still Echoes Across Nation; Activism: Killing of Students Just Before Olympics Radically Changed Country and Questions Continue," *Los Angeles Times* (October 2, 1993). Kate Doyle, "The Tlatelolco Massacre: U.S. Documents on Mexico and the Events of 1968," Posted October 10, 2003, National Security Archive, http://www.gwu.edu/~nsarchiv/NSAEBB/NSAEBB99/. William Kelly, "Nothing Has Happened Here: Memory and the Tlatelolco

Massacre, 1968–2008" (PhD Dissertation, Texas Christian University, 2010), 35–52. J. Scherer García, C. Monsiváis, and M. García Barragán, *Parte de guerra, Tlatelolco 1968: Documentos del general Marcelino García Barragán: Los hechos y la historia* (1st ed., Nuevo siglo). Col. del Valle, México, D.F.: Nuevo Siglo/Aguilar, 1999.

108 L.A. Police Chief William Parker before the U.S. Civil Rights Commission in January 27, 1960.

109 Armando Morales, "A Study of Mexican American Perceptions of Law Enforcement Policies and Practices in East Los Angeles" (DSW Dissertation, University of Southern California, 1972), 87, 89, 90. *New York Times* (October 25, 1971). Christopher Rand, *Los Angeles: The Ultimate City* (New York: Oxford University Press, 1967), 131. Joan W. Moore, *Mexican Americans*, 2nd ed. (Englewood Cliffs, NJ: Prentice-Hall, 1976), 93. *G.I. Forum News Bulletin* (March–April 1960). *Eastside Sun* (Los Angeles, February 4, 1960). *Eastside Sun* (February 4 and 11, 1960). See Martin J. Siesl, "Behind the Badge: The Police and Social Discontent in Los Angeles Since 1950," in Norman M. Klein and Martin J. Siesl, *20th Century Los Angeles: Power, Promotion and Social Conflict* (Claremont, CA: Regina Books, 1990), 153–94. *Eastside Sun* (February 11, 1960). "Roybal Comments on Crime Reports of East Los Angeles," *Eastside Sun* (March 10, 1960). "Police Maltreatment Subject at Conference at Biltmore Hotel," *Eastside Sun* (June 16, 1960). Edward J. Escobar, "Bloody Christmas and the Irony of Police Professionalism: The Los Angeles Police Department, Mexican Americans, and Police Reform in the 1950s," *Pacific Historical Review* 72, No. 2 (May 2003), 171–73.

110 Morales, "Mexican American Perceptions," 89, 90. *New York Times* (October 25, 1971).

111 Oropeza, "La Batalla," 109, 113.

112 Congressman Henry B. González's Congressional Speech of April 22, 1969, *Congressional Record*, 91st Cong., 1st Sess. (April 22, 1969). Josh Gottheimer, ed., *Ripples of Hope: Great American Civil Rights Speeches* (New York: Basic Civitas Books, 2003), 331–39.

113 H. Joaquín Jackson and David Marion Wilkinson, *One Ranger: A Memoir* (Austin: University of Texas Press, 2005), 46, 63–75. Acuña, *Making of Chicana/o Studies*, 126–27.

114 José Angel Gutiérrez, *Tejano Voices*, Oral History Collection, University of Texas Arlington, and The José Angel Gutiérrez Papers, 1959–1991, at University of Texas at San Antonio; A Guide to the Jose Angel Gutierrez Papers, 1959–1991, http://www.lib.utexas.edu/taro/utsa/00002/utsa-00002.html; these are priceless for Chicano research.

115 Vicki Ruiz and Virginia Sánchez Korrol, eds., *Latinas in the United States: A Historical Encyclopedia* (Indiana University Press, 2006), 305.

116 "Severita Lara, Crystal City Walkout Leader," http://www.youtube.com/watch?v=sQIcz_2HgkE&feature=related. MAYO document, "José Angel Gutiérrez files, Crystal City, Texas," in Rosales, ed., *Testimonio*, 387–88.

117 Jackson and Wilkinson, *One Ranger*, 69. David G. Gutiérrez, *Walls and Mirrors: Mexican Americans, Mexican Immigrants, and the Politics of Ethnicity* (Berkeley: University of California Press, 1995), 186–87. Navarro, *Mexican American Youth*, 100. J. Gutiérrez, *The Making of a Chicano Militant*, 103. *Forumeer* (February, May 1969). Castro, *Chicano Power*, 156–57. José Angel Gutiérrez, "*Aztlán*: Chicano Revolt in the Winter Garden," *La Raza* 1, No. 4 (1971), 34–35, 37, 39–40. John Staples Shockley, *Chicano Revolt in a Texas Town* (South Bend, IN: University of Notre Dame Press, 1974), 119–21. José Angel Gutiérrez's speech at a meeting in San Antonio, on May 4, 1970, "Mexicanos Need to Control Their Own Destinies," www.clnet.ucla.edu/research/docs/razaunida/control.htm.

118 "The Tierra Amarilla Courthouse Raid," http://www.youtube.com/watch?v=phF376VK3ek&feature=related. Reies Tijerina, Jose Angel Gutierrez, *They Called Me "King Tiger": My Struggle for the Land and Our Rights* (Houston: Arte Público Press, 2000).

119 Malcolm Ebright, *Land Grants & Lawsuits in Northern New Mexico* (Albuquerque: University of New Mexico Press), 11, 14. Fred Rosen, "The Fate of the *Ejido* (threats to existence of system of communal ownership of agricultural land)," *NACLA Report on the Americas* 26, No. 5 (May 1993), 3ff. Gardner, *Tijerina*, 66–84, 129–30, 208, 265–79. Peter Nabokov, *Tijerina and the Courthouse Raid* (Albuquerque: University of New Mexico Press, 1969), 19, 28, 30, 250–66. Clark Knowlton, "Guerrillas of Rio Arriba: The New Mexico Land Wars," in F. Chris García, ed., *La Causa Politica: A Chicano Politics Reader* (Notre Dame, IN: University of Notre Dame Press, 1974), 333. Reies López Tijerina, "A Letter from the Santa Fe Jail," Reies López Tijerina Collection, University of New Mexico, Albuquerque.

120 *El Plan Espiritual de Aztlán*, http://www.utpa.edu/orgs/mecha/aztlan.html.

121 Aztlan Exploration 2000, http://ttzlibrary.yuku.com/topic/617/Aztec-origins#.UKD2i4bs9nU. "San Ce Tojuan: We Are One: Documentary screening and art exhibit focuses on origins of Uto-Nahuatl people, March 12," LatinoLA: February 24, 2005, http://latinola.com/story.php?story=2442.

122 "Guide to the Montoya, José Papers 1969–2001," http://www.oac.cdlib.org/findaid/ark:/13030/kt1m3nf0sm/entire_text/.

123 Stan Steiner, *La Raza: The Mexican Americans* (New York: Harper & Row, 1969), 378–92. Christine Marín, *A Spokesman of the Mexican American Movement: Rodolfo "Corky" Gonzales and the Fight for Chicano Liberation, 1966–1972* (San Francisco: R&E Research Associates, 1977), 1–3, 5. *Forumeer* (November 1965, June 1966). *The Militant* (December 4, 1970). The best book on the Crusade is Ernesto B. Vigil, *The Crusade for Justice: Chicano Militancy and the Government's War on Dissent* (Madison: University of Wisconsin Press, 1999).

124 Elizabeth Martinez, "500 Years of Chicana Women's History Parts 1–3," http://www.youtube.com/watch?v=JzYISUV_Sc8. "Activist Elizabeth 'Betita' Martínez Speaks at Michigan State," http://www.vimeo.com/1211392.

125 Haney-López, *Racism on Trial*, 225.

126 Naomi Helena Quiñonez, "*Hijas de la Maline* (Malinche's Daughters): The Development of Social Agency Among Mexican American Women and the Emergence of First Wave Chicana Cultural Production" (PhD Dissertation, Claremont Graduate School, Claremont, California, 1997), 153. Elizabeth Martínez, "'On Time' in Mississippi: 1964–1994: Confronting Immoral Power with Moral Power," *Z Magazine* (September 1994), 37–40. Elizabeth Martínez, *De Colores Means All of US: Latina Views for a Multi-Colored Century* (Cambridge, MA: South End Press, 1998). Dionne Elaine Espinoza, "Pedagogies of Nationalism and Gender: Cultural Resistance in Selected Representational Practices of Chicana/o Movement Activists, 1967–1972" (PhD Dissertation, Cornell University, 1996), 147–201.

127 Rodolfo F. Acuña, "Mexicans Are Not Dumb, the Schools Fail," Reader Supported News, June 24, 2010. Ruben Salazar & Mario T, García, M. Border correspondent: Selected writings, 1955-1970 (Berkeley: University of California, 1998).

128 Eric Ed017222: "The Invisible Minority." Report of the NEA-Tucson Survey on The Teaching of Spanish to the Spanish-Speaking, Publication date 1966.

129 Rodolfo F. Acuña, "Mexicans Are Not Dumb, the Schools Fail," Reader Supported News. June 2, 2010. https://readersupportednews.org/opinion/124-124/2280-mexicans-are-not-dumb-the-schools-fail

130 "Luis Valdez Profile," http://www.youtube.com/watch?v=C1Yy-lqDIjo. "El Teatro Campesino 2008 Actos Promo," http://www.youtube.com/watch?v=8Sr4P6woodk.

131 Felipe de Ortego y Gasca, "Octavio Romano and the Chicano Literary Renaissance," *Chicano Literature Latino Literature—Pluma Fronteriza*, November 6, 2006,

132 Bill Flores, "Francisca Flores: 1913–1996," http://clnet.ucla.edu/research/francisca.html. Marissa Harrington-Verb, "Francisca Flores, a Dissenter from the Inside," Jewish Women's Archive, February 7, 2014, https://jwa.org/blog/risingvoices/francisca-flores-dissenter-from-inside.

133 María Cardalliaguet Gómez-Málaga, "The Mexican and Chicano Mural Movements," Yale-New Haven Teachers Institute, http://www.yale.edu/ynhti/curriculum/units/2006/2/06.02.01.x.html. The Chicano Park Historical Documentation Project, http://www.chicanoparksandiego.com/intro.html. "Malaquías Montoya," http://www.metroactive.com/papers/metro/08.07.97/art-9732.html. Boyle Heights-Murals-Brooklyn Ave-Footage, http://www.youtube.com/watch?v=f5f9gCGRjvg. "Tucson: the City of Murals," http://www.youtube.com/watch?v=j7ksyDL37QI.

134 *El Plan de Santa Barbara*, MEChA, Pan American University, http://www.panam.edu/orgs/MEChA/st_barbara.html.

135 Oropeza, "La Batalla," 115–18, 232–33. The LA Spanish-language newspaper *La Opinion* also supported the antiwar effort. Delfino Varela, "The Making of Captain Medina," *Regeneración* 1, No. 1 (1970), 8–13. Navarro, *Mexican American Youth*, 41–42, 66–70.

136 Albert L Pulido, "Are You an Emissary of Jesus Christ? Justice, the Catholic Church, and the Chicano Movement," *Explorations in Ethnic Studies*, 14, No. 1 (January 1991), 17–34. Acuña, *Anything but Mexican*, 35. *Los Angeles Times* (September 23, 1985). Interviews and conversations with Ricardo Cruz; Cruz passed the California bar, but had to fight to be certified because of his conviction. "Law Students Seek Signatures; Petition Protests Denial of Certification by Bar for Chicanos Active in Barrios," *Belvedere Citizen* (Los Angeles, March 16, 1972).

137 Richard Edward Martínez, *PADRES: The National Chicano Priest Movement* (Austin: University of Texas Press, 2005), 55. Jay Dolan and Allan Figueroa Deck, S. J., eds., *Hispanic Catholic Culture in the U.S.: Issues and Concerns* (Notre Dame, IN: University of Notre Dame Press, 1994), 224–26. Anthony M. Stevens-Arroyo, "The Emergence of a Sacred Identity Among Latino Catholics: An Appraisal," in Dolan and Deck, eds., *Hispanic Catholic Culture*, has a different take. Martin McMurtrey, *Mariachi Bishop: The Life Story of Patrick Flores* (San Antonio, TX: Corona, 1987). Juan Romero, "Charisma and Power: An Essay on the History of PADRES," *U.S. Catholic Historian* 9 (Spring 1990).

138 Lara Medina, "The Challenges and Consequences of Being Latina, Catholic and Political," in Gaston Espinosa, Virgilio Elizondo, and Jesse Miranda, eds., *Latino Religions and Civic Activism in the United States* (New York: Oxford University Press, 2005), 97–108. Lara Medina, *Las Hermanas: Chicana/Latina Religious-Political Activism in the U.S. Catholic Church* (Philadelphia, PA: Temple University Press, 2004). "Las Hermanas," *Handbook of Texas Online*, http://www.tshaonline.org/handbook/online/articles/LL/ixl3.html. Ana María Díaz-Stevens, "The Saving Grace: The Matriarchal Core of Latino Catholicism," *Latino Studies Journal* 4, No. 3 (September 1993), 60–78.

139 Gloria Anzaldúa, *Borderlands / La Frontera: The New Mestiza* 2nd edition (San Francisco: Aunt Lute Books, 1999).

140 James Rojas, "Is L.A. Losing Its Outrageous Past? The Birth of Gay Urbanism in 1970s West Hollywood," KCET, February 26, 2016. https://www.kcet.org/shows/lost-la/is-la-losing-its-outrageous-past-the-birth-of-gay-urbanism-in-1970s-west-

141 Quoted in Morales, "Mexican American Perceptions," 43. Rubén Salazar, "State Calls for Probe of Judge in Latin Slurs," *Los Angeles Times* (October 3, 1969), 3.

142 See previous editions of this book where the treatment of this topic is considerably longer. Morales, "Mexican American Perceptions," 43, 103–7. U.S. Commission on Civil Rights, *Mexican Americans and the Administration of Justice in the Southwest* (Washington, DC: Government Printing Office, 1970), 4–5, 37–38, 40. *La Raza* 1, No. 2 (1970), 18–19. *Forumeer* (October 1968). On September 1, 1968, Jess Domínguez, 41, was beaten by at least 15 officers and charged with assaulting an officer. On November 9, 1968, Salvador Barba, 13, was beaten by Los Angeles police and received a head wound requiring 40 stitches. On May 5, 1969, Frank Gonzales, 14, of Los Angeles was skipping school and was shot and killed by Officer Thomas Parkham. On September 8, 1968, in Fairfield, California, Sergeant David Huff shot and killed José Alvarado. *Forumeer* (January 19, 1970; March 1970). "Roybal Demands Removal of San Jose Judge," *Belvedere Citizen* (October 16, 1969). "Judge's Intemperate Outburst Against Mexicans Investigated," *Eastside Sun* (October 9, 1969). *Ideal* (February 12–15, 1970). *Los Angeles Times* (February 7, 1972). *Justicia O* 1, No. 3 (January 1971). Gerard J. De Groot, "Ronald Reagan and Student Unrest in California, 1966–1970," *Pacific Historical Review*, LXV, No. 1 (February 1996), 107–29.

143 Quoted in Oropeza, "La Batalla," 133–36, 171–72, 175, 180, 212–16, 221, 226, 228. Mario T. García, ed., *Ruben Salazar, Border Correspondent: Selected Writings, 1955–1970* (Berkeley: University of California Press, 1995). *Los Angeles Times* (July 17, 1970). Gene Blake and Howard Hertel, "Court Won't Drop Case Against Officers in 'Mistake' Slayings," *Los Angeles Times* (April 27, 1971). Letter from Manuel Ruiz, a member of the U.S. Commission on Civil Rights, to Herman Sillas, chairperson of the California State Advisory Committee to the Commission, September 14, 1970, in "A Report of the California State Advisory Committee to the U.S. Commission on Civil Rights: Police-Community Relations in East Los Angeles, California" (October 1970). *Los Angeles Times* (December 18, 1971). Ralph Guzmán, "Mexican American Casualties in Vietnam," *La Raza* 1, No. 1 (1971), 12. *Forumeer* (November 1969). In "Population Control—Weeding Out Chicanos in Vietnam War?," *Forumeer* (April 1970). In the Southwest, out of 2,189 casualties, 316 were Chicanos. *Forumeer* (July 1970). Ralph Guzmán, "Mexican Americans Have Highest Vietnam Death Rate," *Belvedere Citizen* (October 16, 1969). Information about the moratorium is also drawn from the *Belvedere Citizen* (July 9, 1970) and my role as a participant observer.

144 "Ruben Salazar," http://www.youtube.com/watch?v=qh7YQtjP4uo. Chicano Moratorium, http://www.youtube.com/watch?v=famNeiosTVk. Enrique Hank López, "Overkill at the Silver Dollar," *The Nation* (October 19, 1970), 365–68.

145 *La Raza*, 3 (Special Issue 1970) features a photo essay of the moratorium, documenting police repression. Armando Morales, *Ando Sangrando! I Am Bleeding* (Los Angeles: Congress of Mexican American Unity, 1971), 105, 117. Chávez, "Aztlán," 118–19, 124. Putnam's transcript on file. "Police Chief Davis Claims Latin Youths Being Used by Reds," *Belvedere Citizen* (January 21, 1971). *Eastside Sun* (February 4, 1971).

146 Chávez, "Aztlán," 82–91. Those arrested were Chris Augustine, Luis Arroyo, Jaime Cervantes, Adelaida R. Del Castillo, Ernest Eichwald, Moctesuma Esparza, Reynaldo Macias, Francisco Martínez, Rene Nuñez, Frank Sándoval, Victor Resendez, James Vigil, Thomas Varela, and Petra Valdez. The 10 indicted were Anthony Salamanca, Esmeralda Bernal, Carlos Montes, Ralph Ramírez, Thomas Varela, Rene Nuñez, Ernest Eichwald Cebeda, Juan Robles, Moctezuma Esparza, and Willie Méndoza. Aside from Sumaya, Abel Armas and Robert Avila were listed as infiltrators. Others were Sergio Robledo and Frank Martínez. *Carlos Montes et al. v. The Superior Court of Los Angeles County*, 10 Cal. App. 3d 343; 88 Cal. Rptr. 736; 1970 Cal. App. LEXIS 1845 August 7, 1970.

147 *Los Angeles Times* (July 27, August 18, 1971). *Valley News* (Van Nuys, California, November 27, 1979). Frank

Del Olmo, "Provoked. Trouble for Lawmen, Chicano Informer Claims," *Los Angeles Times* (February 1, 1972). *Los Angeles Free Press* (February 4–10, 1972).

148 *Los Angeles Free Press* (February 4–10, 1972). "Chicano Liberation Front Group Claims Bombing Credit," *Belvedere Citizen* (August 19, 1971). "Officials Probe, Seek Links in East LA Bombings," *Belvedere Citizen* (May 6, 1971). "Roosevelt High Bombings Linked to Series of Explosions in Area," *Belvedere Citizen* (June 10, 1971).

149 Ana Gonzalez-Barrera, Mark Hugo Lopez, "Statistical Profile A Demographic Portrait of Mexican-Origin His-panics in the United States," Pew Hispanic Research Center, May 1, 2013, http://www.pewhispanic.org/files/2013/05/2013-04_Demographic-Portrait-of-Mexicans-in-the-US.pdf.

150 Briggs, Fogel, and Schmidt, *The Chicano Worker*, 5, 34, 36–38, 44, 53–54, 59–60, 68. Moore, *Mexican Americans*, 60. *Los Desarraigados* (Winter 1976–1977), 6. Castro, *Chicano Power*, 210–11. D. Gutiérrez, *Walls and Mirrors*, 183. Yen Le Espiritu, "Immigration and the Peopling of Los Angeles," in Riposa and Dersch, *City of Angels*, 75.?

Chapter 14
The 1970s: The Resurgence of White Nationalism

Learning Objectives

14.1 Analyze the social and political struggle of Mexican Americans from 1960 to 1980.

14.2 Describe the sociopolitical normalization of racism in the 1970s

14.3 Discuss the success and failures of *La Raza Unida* in the context of the existing social order

14.4 Evaluate how activists addressed prejudice within and outside of the Chicana/o movement.

14.5 Discuss how the growth of immigration impacted the priorities in the issues of the Chicana/o Movement.

14.6 Discuss how the Immigration Reform Act of 1965 accelerated xenophobia and white nationalism during the 1970s

14.7 Summarize how the Bakke decision was an expression of the growing white nationalism

14.8 Outline the anti-immigrant legislation during the 1970s.

14.8 Contextualize the growing desperation of the American Empire from Salvador Allende to Anastasio Somoza

In 1971, Lewis Powell distributed a political manifesto that called corporate America to action. The Powell memo called for class unity and the maintenance of a corporate social order. The memo laid out a "winner take all" strategy to perpetuate the illusions of America's oligarchs. It was simple: The Empire would remain strong by avoiding taxes and taking control of history, much the same as when the Robber Barons did after the Gilded Age when they took back their version of history and christened themselves "Captains of Industry." According to the plan, they would create institutions through which they would create non-foundations.

Over the next few years, Corporate America founded the Heritage Foundation (1973), the Manhattan Institute (1978), the Cato Institute (courtesy of the Charles Koch Foundation in 1974), Citizens for a Sound Economy (1984), Accuracy in Academe, and other powerful organizations. Corporations immediately moved to control communication and lead the charge against reformers who, according to them, were out to destroy their America. By the 1980s, right-wing foundations were playing on the fears of aging whites—a war was declared on trade unions and immigrants.[1] William E. Simon, Secretary of Treasury of the United States for three years under Richard Nixon and Gerald Ford, in his 1977 book *Time for the Truth*, laid out a blueprint for conservatives to build tax-free philanthropic foundations to literally control the nation's ideology from birth to the grave.[2] The Powell Memo and Simon's book set the tone for decades of birth to the American exceptionalism.

The Baby Boomers Retire

14.1 Analyze the social and political struggle of Mexican Americans from 1960 to 1980.

The 1960s, the Vietnam War, the youth rebellion, and the Civil Rights movement contributed to the backlash of the seventies and questioned Powell's vision. The school walkouts of 1968 politicized thousands of Chicana/o students throughout the country; it had led to their involvement in the anti-Vietnam War protests and Civil Rights movement. Because of the sacrifices of Chicana/o and Mexican American earlier generations, more Chicanos and Chicanas entered college than at any time in history. The expectations of the community increased as more people began thinking in terms of constitutional rights and taking control over their own lives.

What is remarkable is that in 1970 fewer than one million 20 percent were Chicana/os in 1968. Beginning in the 1970s and taking off in the 1980s, By 2016 about one-third, or 17.9 million, of the nation's "Hispanic" population is younger than 18, and about a quarter, or 14.6 million, of all Hispanics are Millennials (ages 18 to 33 in 2014).[3] (The percentage of Chicas/os would be higher since they were younger than the so-called Latino population.) "Altogether, nearly six-in-ten Hispanics are Millennials or younger."[4] This is mentioned at this point to dramatize the dramatic change in the political landscape.

Demands for human and constitutional rights and the 1965 Immigration Reform Act produced a backlash among President Richard Nixon's white silent majority. As the white establishment resisted reform, Chicanas/os and other minorities pushed back. Within this struggle an awareness of race, gender, and economic issues competed with the Vietnam War for attention and challenged Powell's America.[5]

Some Chicanas/os organized along national lines, believing that change was possible through the identity politics of the 1960s. *La Raza Unida* Party (LRUP), founded in 1970, was formed to end the marginalization of the Chicana/o community and the tyranny perpetuated by the two major parties: Democrats and Republicans elected white candidates and kept minorities powerless. It was a complex but exciting movement with some Chicanas/os seeking to build revolutionary cells, while others preferring to work within the system.

In order to get a sense of how immigration became a priority we must consider the numbers. In 1970, Mexican immigrants made up 7.9 percent of the foreign-born population of the United States. Ten years later Mexican immigrants grew to 15.6 percent; and by 2006 30.7 percent. In 1970, fewer than one million Mexican immigrants lived in the United States. They only comprised about a fifth of the Mexican American population. In 1970, most Mexican Americans were second or third generations. In the 1960s, education and political representation were the more pressing issues. By the 1980s, immigration population grew significantly and Mexican American organizations and the media took notice. During the seventies, Mexican immigrants entered the United States in larger numbers and benefited from the entitlements won by earlier Mexican American and Chicana/o generations. Chicanas/os also benefitted from the entry of a significant number into the colleges. Place like Los Angeles, San Antonio, Houston, and Chicago obviously benefited because of critical masses of Mexican Americans living there. This pull was facilitated by the sharp slowdown in the number of whites entering college as a result of a decline in their birth rate. The entry of more Chicanas and Chicanos into college, and their graduation, brought about an expansion of the Chicana/o middle class.[6] This swift climb into the middle class was subsidized by the entry of Chicanas into the workforce. One paycheck did not make a person middle class; with two paychecks some were on the way. By the end of the 1970s, more Chicanos were getting elected to political office, or at least tinkering with electoral politics. Meanwhile, between 1970 and 1980, the number of Chicanas/os nearly doubled; the same thing occurred by 1990, dramatically increasing their electoral potential.[7] As mentioned the amendments to the 1965 Immigration Act radically changed the racial and ethnic mix of the nation. In the 1950s, 53 percent of immigrants were from Europe, 25 percent from Latin America, and 6 percent from Asia. By the 1980s, only 11 percent of immigrants were from Europe, whereas 42 percent from Latin America, and 42 percent from Asia.[8] The bulk of Latin American immigration was from Mexico—a result of Mexico's high birth rate, the modernization of agriculture, and a decline of ruralism. In 1970, the Mexican birth rate in Mexico was 6.8 children per female, which was down from 7.3 children per female in 1960. Mexico was a young country; the median age in 1970 was 17.[9]

More Mexicans would have migrated to the United States but for Mexico's economic growth in the late 1970s that was based on the illusion of an "Oil Boom." The presence of large numbers of foreign-born people, especially darker-skinned ones, triggered an increase in U.S. nativism, as politicos and journalists took cheap shots at and criminalized Mexican immigrants. The Immigration and Naturalization Service (INS) became more aggressive. In 1980, the Mexican-origin population climbed to 8.8 million, up from about five million in 1970.[10] The Mexican foreign-born population grew to 2.2 million by1980.[11] These subtle changes brought a shift in the priorities of Chicanas/os with immigration eclipsing farmworkers as the number one priority of Mexican Americans. Immigration also spotlighted the fear in many white Americans that they were losing their country to immigrants. Instead of competing for jobs and increasing productivity, they blamed darker-skinned people for their failures and those of the American system.

Using the broadest terms, white Americans from 1790 and 1980 comprised 80 to 90 percent of the U.S. population. By the year 2000, the decline of the white race was noticeable:

> In the total population, 211.5 million people, or 75.1 percent, reported only White. An additional 5.5 million people reported White and at least one other race. In just ten years in 2010, white people were only fifty-three percent of nation's young people; in 1990, they were nearly 70 percent. Meanwhile, Mexican/Latinos rose from twelve percent to percent of young Americans.[12]

Numbers and immigration brought about a redefinition of the Chicana/o identity. The Census Bureau in 1960 lumped the "white population of Spanish surname in five Southwestern States--Arizona, California, Colorado, New Mexico, and

Texas."[13] Government, the Census Bureau, and the media lumped Spanish speakers under the grouping of Hispanic, and then Latino. Large waves of immigrants during the 1970s and 1980s rejected the term *Chicano* that was viewed as pejorative among first-generation immigrants. Among the second generation and youth, the term *Chicano* remained popular, largely because of the collective memory of youth who more and more saw how the system was failing them.[14]

Not much changed since the Navy Riots of 1943. Instead of addressing the grievances of youth, the media portrayed them as malcontents who wanted to destroy society. This historical distortion allowed for a redefinition of the 1960s; the death of Rubén Salazar was thus interpreted as an unfortunate accident. The lack of a coherent historical memory gains of the 1960s led to a lessening of identity politics of the Chicana/o community. By July 25, 1983, a *Los Angeles Times* poll showed that 25 percent of Chicanas/os preferred the identity "Mexican"; 23 percent, "Mexican American"; 18 percent, "Latino"; and 14 percent, "Hispanic." The reversal followed a decade of unrelenting propaganda that blurred the term *Chicano* or even *Mexican*.[15]

After World War II, American oligarchs exaggerated the Communist threat and labeled the New and Fair Deal programs as socialistic and a threat to American democracy. Social programs such as the War on Poverty, according to the ruling elite, were expensive and in order to lessen taxes on corporation. Soon after the 1960s, the right wing attacked the Great Society's civil rights legislation and its commitment to equality and justice. The American public distorted the meaning of words such as *racism* and *victim*. Corporate America intentionally changed, twisted, and exaggerated the truth to make it appear different from reality: "If the poor are poor, it is because the poor do not want to work."[16]

In the 1970s, white homeowners and big business shifted the burden of funding social programs to the middle class, thus eliminating many social and educational programs. The recessions of the 1970s bred corporate and homeowner taxpayer discontent. In 1978, California's Proposition 13 limited taxation to 1 percent of the full value of the property at the 1975 assessment or the assessment after ownership changed, giving tax advantages to property owners who had purchased before the initiative was passed. Proposition 13 gave windfall profits to commercial, industrial, and landlord interests; it cut services to the majority and shifted the property tax burden to renters and those buying homes after 1978. Consequently, Proposition 13 weakened the public school systems where Latino students were in the majority.[17]

The *Bakke v. University of California* case (1978) represented another major victory for white America. Conservatives launched a well-funded campaign to manipulate public opinion. They saturated the airways with the message that the poor were poor because they wanted to be poor, adding a new twist: It was an insult to call anyone a victim because it implied that the poor were passive. These logic conservatives deduced falsely that racism was no longer a problem; the problem was programs designed to end racism: These programs discriminated against white males and promoted mediocrity. It used clichés such as "reverse racism." Thus, conservatives encouraged the formation of a white nationalist mindset.

Distorting Racism

14.2 Describe the sociopolitical normalization of racism in the 1970s.

During the 1960s, *racism* was a dirty six-letter word, and for a brief time to be called a racist was offensive. In the 1970s, popular culture watered down the term *racism*. Symbolic of this change is the television character Archie Bunker in *All in the Family* that premiered in January 1971.[18] Norman Lear, a man of impeccable liberal credentials and intentions, produced the series, during the twilight of the Vietnam War protests. Archie Bunker, a lower-middle-class hard hat, hated African Americans, Latinos, and Jews, and harbored a strong antipathy toward social and political reform. Lear intended Archie's son-in-law, Michael, and daughter, Gloria, to ridicule Archie's outlandish prejudices and make the audience laugh at Archie's racism. In retrospect, just the opposite occurred as Archie gave bigotry respectability. Archie became so popular that spin-offs and copycat sitcoms such as *Maude*, *The Jeffersons*, and *Sanford and Son* became hits. All except *Maude* featured African American bigots.[19]

During this decade, Mexican Americans became sensitive to racial stereotyping, and protested against them. They demanded more Mexican Americans and Latinos in the media.[20] However, Chicanas/os lacked the success of African Americans because their numbers were lower and they lacked the moral authority that the Civil Rights movement gave Blacks. Mexicans by many were considered foreigners and a regional minority. In 1970, the African American population numbered 22.6 million, about 11 percent of the total U.S. population. That year, the Mexican-origin population numbered just under 4.5 million, a fifth of the Black population, and thus lacked sufficient national presence to force politicos to do the right thing.[21]

Government Legitimizes Racism

In the summer of 1969, presidential advisor Arthur Burns defined *poverty* as an "intellectual concept" or notion; Nixon later appointed Burns to head the Federal Reserve. The Supreme Court also altered its approach, with the Warren Burger Court became less interested. During the 1970s, the courts took the teeth out of the *Brown v. Board of Education* case (1954) decision and sought to criminalize undocumented workers. Initially, Mexicans and Latinos fared well in voting rights and bilingual education, but by the 1990s, these laws and safeguards were neutered.[22]

In the courts, Mexican Americans continued the strategy of classifying themselves as white; mistakenly believing that this would entitle them to the protections of the U.S. Constitution and the Treaty of Guadalupe-Hidalgo. No matter that, they were not considered white. Out of convenience, the courts accepted the subterfuge that Mexicans were separate because of language deficiency. After World War II, Mexican Americans adopted the legal strategy of being "other white." Then in the 1950s, the Court accepted that Mexican Americans as "a class apart"; consequently, succeeding cases did not include Mexican Americans under the protections of *Brown v. Board of Education* (1954).[23]

This mess was somewhat straightened out after 1968 when José Cisneros and other Chicana/o parents filed suit against the Corpus Christi Independent School District. Attorney James de Anda abandoned the "other white" strategy and argued that Mexican Americans were an identifiable minority group and that the Corpus Christi Schools segregated Mexicans, denying them equal protection under the 14th Amendment of the U.S. Constitution. The court found for the plaintiffs: Mexican Americans were an identifiable minority based on physical, cultural, religious, and linguistic distinctions, with a history of discrimination against them. *Cisneros v. Corpus Christi Independent School District* was the first case to entitle Mexican Americans under the *Brown* decision. It replaced the "other white" findings of *Hernández v. State of Texas*.[24]

A Politics of Cynicism: Nixon's Hispanic Strategy

14.3 Discuss the success and failures of *La Raza Unida* in the context of the existing social order.

The 1968 Election was important because it gave the "silent majority" – white Americans wings. Hubert Humphrey in that election received 90 percent of the Mexican vote. However, if Nixon had received 5 percent more of the Chicana/o votes in Texas, he would have carried the Lone Star State. As a result, Nixon embarked on a "Hispanic" strategy to court brown middle-class Mexican Americans by giving them high-level appointments and more government jobs.[25]

Next year, President Nixon replaced the Inter-Agency Committee on Mexican American Affairs with the Cabinet Committee on Opportunities for the Spanish-speaking People, broadening the target group from Chicanos to Hispanics. Nixon appointed Martín Castillo the head of the Cabinet Committee. In 1970, Nixon helped form the National Economic Development Association (NEDA), a national organization funded by state and federal agencies to promote private development in low-income areas. By 1972, Nixon had appointed 50 Chicanas/os to high federal posts. Among them was Romana Bañuelos, a Los Angeles food manufacturer, to serve as the Treasurer of the United States (1971–1974).[26]

The "brown mafia," a network of community leaders, was led by Alex Armendaris of South Bend, Indiana. It played a key role in the Committee to Re-Elect the President (CREEP). Nixon was expected to get at least 20 percent of the Latino vote. The Republicans made it clear to the brown mafia that if they did not reach this goal, the administration would cut federal appointments and stop federal funding to Latinos. Nixon received 31 percent of the Mexican vote nationally. Yet the president dismantled the War on Poverty program.[27]

In 1973, Nixon appointed Ann Armstrong, a white woman, to the post of White House Aide on domestic Latino affairs. According to Nixon, Armstrong was qualified because her husband owned a large ranch that employed Mexicans. Patronage was funneled through Latino Republicans, especially Cuban American Republicans who became the new power brokers. From 1972 to 1980, the Republican National Hispanic Assembly raised $400,000 to register Republican voters. Nixon then promoted programs benefiting the managerial, professional, and business sectors of the Latino community. After reelection in 1972, Nixon launched his New Federalism with renewed vigor. New Federalism was a euphemism for decentralizing social programs, returning tax moneys to the municipalities and the states, and relying on the city bosses' good faith to care for the poor.[28]

Dismantling the War on Poverty

Nixon substituted block grants in the place of the War on Poverty to municipalities to spend as they wished. In 1973, Congress passed the Comprehensive Employment and Training Act (CETA), which changed job-training policy. Previous programs targeted low-skilled, unemployed, non-white workers; CETA targeted mostly better-off white males. CETA and other government programs reduced services to the disadvantaged, giving more control to local politicians and to the private sector. This policy shift devastated Chicanas/os as a whole; poverty, inflation, and a sharp rise in the cost of living worsened their plight, and the number of poor and unemployed increased throughout the 1970s and into the 1980s.[29]

La Raza Unida Party

On March 30, 1970, activist Corky Gonzales announced the formation of the Colorado RUP.[30] At the 1970 Second Annual Youth Liberation Conference in Denver, the 2,500 activists attending endorsed the notion of a Chicano party. The Crusade for Justice Leadership intended to form the *Congreso de Aztlán* and build a Chicano nation. In May, LRUP held a state convention in Pueblo, where they endorsed candidates for statewide office. Although police authorities continuously harassed the RUP slate, the party was able to run candidates, albeit without success, at all levels of government. LRUP's purpose was not so much to win but to raise the political consciousness of the Mexican-origin people. By 1971, the stress of police harassment took its toll; only 500 attended the Third Annual Chicano Liberation Conference.[31]

In Texas José Angel Gutiérrez raised the notion of LRUP at a Mexican American Youth Organization (MAYO) meeting in 1968; the executive board rejected it. Meanwhile, MAYO implemented the Winter Garden Project, a blueprint to take over South Texas, which was 80 percent Mexican American. It led to Chicana/o electoral victories in Crystal City, Cotula, and Carrizo Springs. Buoyed by the success, Tejanos moved to form a third party. The linchpin to the Chicano revolt was the takeover of the Crystal City School Board. In December 1969, at a national MAYO meeting, Chicano activists endorsed the formation of a third party. In 1971, LRUP went statewide as 300 activists gathered in San Antonio on October 31 and formally launched the party.[32]

The Gutiérrezes, José Angel and Luz, argued that a strong community power base had to be developed before the party went statewide. However, Mario Compeán, a founder of MAYO, supported by University of Texas professor Armando Gutiérrez, pushed for an immediate statewide party. The Texas LRUP tasted some initial success as it registered 22,388 voters in 1972.[33]

Tejanas were more visible in LRUP than were Chicanas elsewhere, forming *Las Mujeres por la Raza Unida* (Women for the Raza Unida Party) that supported the Equal Rights Amendment. They were led by Marta Cotera, Alma Canales, Rosie Castro, Evey Chapa, and Virginia Múzquiz. The LRUP platform advocated community control of schools, bilingual education, and women's and workers' rights. In 1972, Alma Canales unsuccessfully ran as RUP candidate for Texas lieutenant governor; Cotera unsuccessfully ran for the Texas State Board of Education; and Viviana Santiago successfully ran for the Crystal City Independent School District Board of Trustees. Statewide, attorney Ramsey Muñiz, 29, a former Baylor University football star, ran for governor on the LRUP ticket, accumulating 214,118 votes (6.28 percent). Republicans won the governorship by 100,000 votes.[34]

The California LRUP was divided into northern and southern California. Although LRUP registered close to 23,000 voters and ran candidates statewide, the party was never a force in California. As mentioned, Leftist organizations were training grounds for Chicana/o labor organizers.[35] They began the conversation and their activism formed the answers. Many Chicanas/os grew disillusioned with LRUP's attempt at electoral politics and gravitated to other groups such as the Labor Committee of LRUP that became the core of the August 29th Movement (ATM), a Marxist cell. The ATM later became the League of Revolutionary Struggle (LRS) that was active into the 1990s.[36] Others joined the *Centro de Acción Social Autónoma* (CASA; Autonomous Center for Social Action)[37] that, like the LRS, became an important trainer of union organizers and future politicos in California.

The City Terrace chapter of the RUP ran a candidate for the 48th Assembly District who polled 7.93 percent (2,778) of the votes. However, the chapter denied Democratic Party candidate Richard Alatorre the victory. The Republican margin of victory was 46.71 percent (16,346 votes) to 42.17 percent (14,759 votes). Alatorre won the next election, in which LRUP did not field a candidate. The City Terrace LRUP campaign was controversial because the LA Central Committee wanted the LRUP to be known more for its principles rather than a vehicle for defeating Democrats, and with the local LRUP central committee criticized the City Terrace chapter for the lack of consultation with other Los Angeles County chapters.[38]

The Last Days of *La Raza Unida*

In September 1972, LRUP held its national convention in El Paso. Tragedy marked the event when a white bigot shot and killed Richard Falcón at Orogrande, New Mexico, who was on his way to the convention. Most Chicano leaders except César Chávez participated (predictably, Chávez, whose union was part of the AFL-CIO, endorsed George McGovern rather than Richard Nixon). A split occurred when José Angel Gutiérrez defeated Corky Gonzales for national chair of LRUP. Texas dominated the vote, largely because Tejanos had settled in states as they traveled along the migrant stream. They settled in places like Michigan, Wisconsin and elsewhere in the Midwest. Although a symbolic show of unity followed, the division was irreversible; and within two years, the Colorado RUP left the national organization.[39]

The Texas RUP split into camps. Many looked to Muñiz, a relative newcomer, to lead the party, while others considered Mario Compeán, a founder of MAYO from San Antonio as the logical choice. After Muñiz's unsuccessful run, tension developed between the Compeán and Muñiz camps. Documents obtained by Gutiérrez under the Freedom of Information Act show Central Intelligence Agency (CIA) surveillance of LRUP. Additionally, local police provocateurs ran campaigns to destroy the party. The popularity of LRUP was based on the loyalty of young nationalists whose fervor turned off many Mexican American voters. The party's appeal and success was mostly in Texas, where in small towns they forged community-based organizations. In the end, Gutiérrez's rural strategy was correct.[40]

As mentioned, Texas had the largest percentage of second-generation eligible Mexican American voters, but it lacked a financial base to successfully launch candidacies. Additionally, many old-line Mexican American organizations were beholden to the Democratic Party, as in New Mexico, where progressive and popular Democrats such as Tiny Martínez in Las Vegas, New Mexico, made launching a third party difficult. California on the other hand inexperienced cadres and lacked experienced political leadership.[41]

By 1974, LRUP began to implode. In Crystal City, the RUP's success led to disunity and by 1977 the party lost its control. The emergence of the Southwest Voter Registration and Education Project (founded by Willie Velásquez, a former MAYO activist) encouraged the defection of some RUP members to the Mexican American Democrats (MAD). The arrest of Ramsey Muñiz on drug charges was a mortal blow. Nevertheless, a large core of Texas RUP activists remained in the political arena.[42]

Inequality from Within: Never Letting Go

14.4 Evaluate how activists addressed prejudice within and outside of the Chicana/o movement.

When talking about gender, sexism, homophobia, or other forms of discrimination, the discussion must be prefaced with the clear statement that discrimination was and is wrong. A failure to put discrimination into historical context led to unnecessary conflict and retarded a resolution. In 1970, for example, sexism was a proof of inequality. Nevertheless prior to the fall of 1972, universities did not give gender, racial, or ethnic diversity much thought. In 1970, there were few white women at the leading law and medical schools and even fewer minorities. Affirmative action encouraged the admission of more women to professional schools. The number of women radically changed the gender composition in universities and workforce. There was resistance to students of color, largely because of their race and economic class. The assumption was that they came from inferior schools and were unqualified.

As a rule, more middle-class women attend college than males. This trend began by 1870. By 1920, over 60 percent of high school graduates were women. This trend slowed down after World War II, when males on the G.I. Bill entered college in large numbers. Minorities were excluded because of lower education attainment or other factors. However, college enrollment among all women climbed steadily during the 1970s and 1980s. By 1992, women earned 54.2 percent of bachelor's degrees, 58.9 percent of two-year degrees, 51.5 percent of Master of Arts and professional degrees, and 37.3 percent of PhDs.[43] Nevertheless, it took affirmative action to integrate women into the professional class. By 1992, 53 percent of U.S. college students were women, but only 31 percent were faculty members. In Cuba, 55 percent of students were females and 47 percent were faculty members.[44]

The question of gender inequality fractured the Chicana/o movement because many Chicanas/os resisted the call for equality of sexes. Changes took place because of intensive discourse that ferreted out contradictions and decolonized both males and females. Credit is due to a small group of women activists who did not let the question of inequality die. Some, like Martha Cotera, criticized LRUP but worked within the structure to change it. Others, like Magdalena Mora, a committed student activist and union organizer who died of cancer in 1981 at age 29, chose to work within CASA and worked as a columnist for its newspaper, *Sin Fronteras*, and later for *El Foro de Pueblo*, speaking out against sexism while campaigning for workers' rights. Still others stressed the importance of developing autonomous feminist organizations.

Major credit must be given to Chicana lesbians who during uncomfortable times kept these issues at the forefront. These activists included intellectuals such as Emma Perez, author of *The Decolonial Imaginary: Writing Chicanas into History*,[45] Deena González, and a cadre of women who pressed for a conversation of the women's question at the National Association for Chicana/o Studies and other venues. Meanwhile, Gloria Evangelina Anzaldúa broke new ground with her writings.[46] In retrospect, one can see that feminists were right and the majority was wrong.

Strategies changed, and even when they did not, there were inevitable personality clashes and bruised egos that were difficult to untangle. In general, the more to the left the organization, the more inclusive it became of women's and LGBT issues. To its credit, *The Militant*, published by the Socialist Workers Party, was at the cutting edge of the question of feminism and sexual preference.[47] By contrast, most leftist groups, while generally progressive in offering lip service to feminist issues, were in the Stone Age when it came to sexual preferences; homophobia was rampant during the 1970s and into the late 1980s.

Chicana Voices

An important Chicana and Chicano voice was *El Grito del Norte*, a newspaper published by Enriqueta Longeaux y Vásquez and Elizabeth "Betita" Martínez. Vásquez, in her featured column asked the U.S. Mexican people to "'stand up' and rethink the social order," including U.S. militarism, interventions in Vietnam and Latin America, the Catholic Church, gringo society, and sexism—forcing many readers to rethink their positions on these issues. Vásquez's work is one of the early feminist voices that chose to work from within the nationalist majority. To call Vásquez a loyalist (an apologist for male domination) is a distortion. Vásquez was attempting to reconcile her own evolving political positions with the reality and the political vocabulary of the community at that time. The challenge for Vásquez was how to obtain women's liberation and transform the entire nuclear family, leading to the question of how to change those organizations and the people in them.

Like Marxism and nationalism, feminism has contradictions. Critics claim Vásquez's declaration that she was a *Chicana primero* meant that race should take precedence over gender in analyzing oppression. Within the heat of the debate, myths often emerge especially among the true believers. Take, for example, an event at the First National Chicano Youth Conference in Denver, Colorado, in May 1969. When the time came to report on the resolutions formulated at the workshop on the Chicana, Enriqueta Vásquez was shocked at the wording of the resolution that stated that the Chicana woman did not want to be liberated. She understood the tremendous pressure by the men in the hall, although she did not agree with the statement, she did not make an issue of it. Vásquez raised the possibility that the proclamation meant that Chicanas did not want white women to liberate them.[48] What was important was the Learning Curve.

The Learning Curve

Whether we like it or not even when we are in opposition to the ideas of a system, we assimilated many falsehoods. While the Chicana/o movement changed those who participated and even those who did not listen, it also did not correct many contradictions. This was true in the decolonization of racism, sexism, and homophobia. Most of us also go through a process of assimilation that distinguishes us from prior generations. UCLA study titled "Generations of Exclusion: Mexican Americans, Assimilation, and Race," conducted in the 2000s suggests that while speaking English and listening to American music even and becoming Protestants and voting Republican, Mexicans are not assimilating as quickly as European immigrants, Mexican Americans even by the third and fourth generations were not fully integrated or incorporated.[49] The study asks what were the barriers to Mexican integration. Could it be color? Are there other factors?

Patterns of assimilation and incorporation of Mexicans differ from those of Europeans: only 10 percent of Mexican immigrants and 17 percent of second-generation Mexicans were married to non-Latinos. One explanation may be that Mexicans communities were at the time more segregated. A probable answer is that they lived in cohesive *barrios* that incubated them for a longer period of time.[50] The study went on to point out that only 10 percent identified as "American," a pattern that continued into the fourth generation. The *barrios* remained remarkably ideologically similar.

In discussing the effects of gender or any other cultural or institutional barriers on changing attitudes such as religion, gender, and homophobia these obstacles must be discussed. For instance, values such as homophobia and patriarchy are passed on generationally. In 1969, I do not remember having a single student, including myself, that came from a college-educated household. Racism and living in isolation reinforced and perpetuated cultural nationalism.[51] By the 1970s this was changing, as more Mexican Americans went to college and gentrification was destroying *barrios* (communities). No longer were the *barrios* incubators and the likelihood of their retaining their ability to grow and maintaining their cultural identity became increasingly unlikely.

Many ideas taken for granted today were new in 1970, when feminism was considered by some to be a white women's concern, and even some leftists considered homosexuality to be part of decadent capitalism. This wrongheaded thinking and resistance to change caused numerous clashes. A series of conferences on the Chicana question took place in the early 1970s. Chicanas formed women's caucuses within the Mexican American Political Association (MAPA) and other organizations.

In 1970, Chicanas sponsored a workshop on women at the Mexican American National Issues Conference in Sacramento. The latter begot *La Comisión Femenil Mexicana* (The Mexican Feminist Commission), a group that was important in generating Chicana community programs through government grants; Francisca Flores and Grace Montañez Davis were among its leaders.[52] Flores edited *Regeneración*, a magazine that published articles on *la mujer*. That year, local Chicana forums became more popular—for instance, at California State University at Los Angeles, a Chicana forum honored María Cristina de Penichet, Mexico's first woman brain surgeon, and Celia Luna Rodríguez, leader of the Barrio Defense Committee and before that of the Mexican Civil Rights Congress.

In May 1971, over 600 Chicanas from 23 states attended *La Conferencia de Mujeres por La Raza* (the Women's Conference for the Latino People), sponsored by the YWCA in Houston. Some 40 percent of the attendees (300 women)—mostly Tejanas—walked out of the conference and held their own conference in a park. The dissenters, largely consisting of the Houston Mexican community, objected to the lack of Chicanos/as on staff at the YWCA. They alleged that the YWCA was racist and its staff was white, elitist, and bureaucratic. Those participants who remained inside the conference claimed that the dissenters were anti-feminist, loyalists, and cultural nationalists. Despite the disagreement, most attendees overall agreed on fundamental issues such as abortion, but disagreed on tactics and the role of the YWCA.[53]

Increasingly, Chicana groups focused on the special problems of Mexican women. They discussed male chauvinism, abortion, childcare, and sexism within the Chicana/o and the white women's movement. Debates over the gender question were very intense within MEChA (*Movimiento Estudiantil Chicano/a de Aztlán*) and within the community. At the universities, because of the formation of Chicano Studies programs, there was a network for the production and consumption of ideas regarding social change. A problem has been that a large body of works has not been produced within the area of Chicana/o Studies. In 1973, Chicanas spearheaded the opposition to the Talmadge Amendment to the Social Security Act that required mothers on public assistance with children over six years of age to register with the state employment office and to report every two weeks until they found work.

As early as 1971, Dorinda Moreno published a journal, *Las Cucarachas* (The Cockroaches). In 1973, she published an anthology, *La Mujer—En Pie de Lucha* (The Woman in Struggle). Moreno also published the newspaper *La Razón Mestiza* (Mestizo Reason) in the San Francisco area in 1974. A recurrent theme in her works was the unequal status of women.[54] By the late 1970s, a broader participation of middle-class Chicanas took place, with Chicana professionals and activists attending the International Women's Year Conference in Mexico City in 1975 and the National Women's Conference in Houston two years later.

There were personal stories: Rosa Salazar Rosales was denied entrance to college after high school, but was able to attend after becoming a mother, and graduated from the University of Michigan. She returned to San Antonio in the late 1970s and became a union organizer. She formed strong networks of women and pushed feminist issues within the Chicana community and the population at large.[55] From 2002–2010, she was the 45th national president of the League of United Latin American Citizens.

The role of Leftist newspapers in spreading feminist thought and exposing homophobic ideas was essential in promoting understanding of these issues. These newspapers far outnumbered nationalist newspapers in circulation. Although tension existed among leftist and nationalist groups due partly to party building, such news sources had a positive impact on the Chicana/o community. They were very critical and were at the forefront of the campaign against the *Bakke* decision.

The Birth of Chicana/o Studies

Chicana/o Studies is one of the few academic programs that was not born within academe. Chicana/o Studies has courses in sociology that examine the Chicana/o Studies corpus of knowledge but it does not belong to the field of sociology. If it were strictly sociology, it could be reduced to one or two courses on race. Chicana/o Studies is a strategy that incorporates multiple disciplines.[56] The pedagogical approach emerged in 1968 as Chicano school walkouts hit California and Texas, and spread throughout the Southwest, Midwest, and Pacific Northwest.[57] Most Chicana/o Studies Departments were first established at California State Colleges where in the spring of 1969, fewer than 1,000 Chicana/o students were enrolled systemwide. This was an appropriate starting point because the state colleges were teaching institutions, unlike the universities that were research institutions.

California was at the forefront of Chicana/o Studies. The first wave of Chicana/o students matriculated to CSC in the fall of 1968 as part of the Educational Opportunity Program and over its lifetime, EOP was responsible for graduating no fewer than 250,000 minority students.[58]

On the CSU campuses, Chicana/o students caught the tailwinds of the Black student movement, the farmworker struggle, and the Vietnam War. By the spring of 1969 the small cores of Chicana/o students were integrated into the National Chicano Student Movement, which, after the Denver Chicano Youth Conference, sponsored a conference at Santa Barbara, California, to formulate the *Plan of Santa Barbara* (*El Plan de Santa Bárbara*; see Chapter 13) that contextualized the disparate efforts on California campuses. For example, California State Colleges at Los Angeles, San Fernando, Long Beach, San Diego, and Fresno had already formulated programs, as had the Universities of California and many junior colleges, where professors such as Gracia Molina de Pick of San Diego Mesa College pioneered Chicana/o Studies.[59] Research institutions formed research centers and state colleges created departments. *The Plan of Santa Barbara* incorporated the disparate movements that spread throughout the Southwest, Pacific Northwest, and Midwest with varying degrees of success.

Research centers were established in California, Texas, Arizona, and New Mexico. Chicanos elsewhere lobbied for Mexican American programs. Anywhere Mexicans matriculated, the demand for Chicana/o Studies followed, with varying degrees of success; the most notable efforts were the community colleges. In the Lone Star State, at the University of Texas, El Paso, there was a militant but unsuccessful drive for a Chicano Studies department that originated in *el Segundo Barrio* after the burning deaths of the three children of Miguel Rosales on January 4, 1967.[60]

What made the formation of Chicana/o Studies extraordinary was that initially it involved so few students and that they were overwhelmingly first-generation college students. Unlike Mexicans in Mexico, they did not have a tradition of seeing Mexicans in positions of authority. Blacks had a history of Black churches, colleges, and Black intellectualism. As Dr. Warren Furumoto pointed out in the documentary *Unrest*, Mexican American students lacked this background—they were street kids and few of their leaders had political interaction with other groups.[61] Unlike the Black Studies and Women's Studies programs, Chicanas/os did not have a large middle-class college student constituency. They were children of immigrants and in every Southwestern state, with the exception of New Mexico, they comprised less than 5 percent of the state's students; in the Pacific Northwest and Midwest they were less than 1 percent.[62] A Ford Foundation Study in 1973 reported that fewer than 3,000 Blacks and probably no more than 200 Chicanos, Puerto Ricans, and Native Americans held doctorates out of 300,000 PhDs nationally.[63] They did not have long-standing contacts with philanthropic foundations, and received little outside help.

On campuses the programs became central to Chicana/o student activism and were a training ground for future Chicana/o leaders and cultural workers within the community. Indeed, in the 1980s and 1990s many elected officials and labor and community organizers came out of the

Chicano student movement, as did most artists and musicians. The campuses were laboratories where Chicano and Chicana ideas evolved from a largely nationalist perspective to a more universal school of thought. It was there that sexist and homophobic notions were challenged and in some cases changed. Chicano Studies continuously advocated for the admission of more students of Latino origin, more Chicana/o Studies programs, appointment of more Chicana/o professors, and financial aid, as well as progressive social causes.

Sterilization: Saving Taxpayers' Money

During the 1970s, the issue of sterilization became a cause of major concern in the United States with the sterilization of Latinas, Native Americans, and Blacks. Sterilization is rooted in the eugenics movement of social Darwinism in the early twentieth century when American eugenicists believed that people could be categorized according to intelligence.[64] They believed that it was possible to genetically engineer the U.S.'s racial composition. The justification was that those sterilized had inferior genes. This notion was popular into the 1960s. There is evidence that even the members of President John F. Kennedy's Peace Corps, established in 1961, sponsored sterilization programs in Latin America. Such programs were common in Puerto Rico, and were used as a policy to reduce alleged overpopulation of nonwhites.[65] From 1973 to 1976, medical authorities sterilized one-third of the women of childbearing age in Puerto Rico and more than 3,000 Native Americans in the United States.

At the USC/Los Angeles County Hospital (a.k.a. General Hospital), serving the largest Mexican population in the United States, doctors routinely performed involuntary sterilizations during the early 1970s. According to Dr. Bernard Rosenfeld—who strongly opposed the practice as reminiscent of Nazi experimentation with Jews, gypsies, and the mentally retarded—doctors developed the attitude that by sterilizing the breeders the hospital saved the taxpayers millions of dollars in welfare payments.

Los Angeles General Hospital was in the business of training doctors. To gain practice, physicians often persuaded teenagers to authorize tubal ligations and hysterectomies, even rationalizing this malpractice: "I want to ask every one of these girls if they want their tubes tied. I don't care how old they are. . . . Remember, every one you get to get her tubes tied now means less work for some son of a bitch next time."[66] Some doctors claimed that they waited until the anesthesia wore off to seek permission to perform the operations. Often, the doctors gave English-language forms to patients who spoke only Spanish. Sterilization of poor minority women became a national issue when two Black girls, ages 12 and 14, were sterilized in Montgomery, Alabama. Chicanas who spearheaded a suit against General Hospital passionately opposed this practice.

Meanwhile, the issue of abortion split the community. Many Mexican Americans were Catholic, and they followed the Church teachings that abortion was a sin. Feminists and many activists considered abortion a personal choice in which women should have full control of their bodies. Many Chicanas supported *Roe v. Wade* (1973), the U.S. Supreme Court decision legalizing abortion; however, on the matter of sterilization, activists pointed out that poor women did not have a personal physician and did not speak English, and thus were not given a choice.

The Road to Delano

14.5 Discuss how the growth of immigration impacted the priorities in the issues of the Chicana/o Movement.

Pete Beltrán an auto worker from nearby Pacoima who was also a union activist became president of Local 645/GM Van Nuys, which championed the farmworker cause. UAW Unite Auto Workers supported the UFW because many of the rank and file were Mexican American. In 1972, the growers proposed Proposition 22, an initiative to outlaw boycotting and limit secret ballot elections to full-time nonseasonal farmworkers. The United Auto Workers (UAW) supported the United Farm Workers (UFW) and Prop 22 lost. Meanwhile, the Schenley Corporation refused to renegotiate with the UFW on these issues, sparking a strike in which police arrested 269 strikers. The Nixon administration pressured the Teamsters and the growers to break the strike. In the spring of 1973, the Teamsters' Agricultural Workers Organizing Committee declared war on the UFW in the Imperial Valley. The Seafarers Union offered Chávez help to get rid of the thugs, but Chávez, committed to nonviolence, refused. Teamsters brutally attacked farmworkers.

Governor Edmund G. Brown, Jr., helped form the Agricultural Labor Relations Board (ALRB) in 1975 to supervise elections and resolve appeals. The board allowed secondary boycotts only if employers refused to negotiate. After Brown left office, the ALRB became a tool of the growers and the Republican-controlled legislature constantly harassed the UFW, intervening on the side of the growers.

In Ohio, the Farm Labor Organizing Committee (FLOC) organized Mexicans in the fields of Ohio and Indiana and sensitized Midwesterners to INS abuses. FLOC, with the Ohio Council of Churches, sponsored a conference on immigration in 1977. The Catholic bishops supported FLOC and called a nationwide boycott of Campbell's Soup products. This boycott lasted until the spring of 1986, when FLOC signed a contract with Campbell's.

The UFW was unsuccessful at unionizing Texas farmworkers in the 1960s. Although Chávez wanted to expand operations there, difficulties in securing his California base distracted him. For a time UFW left Antonio Orendian in Texas to organize farmworkers. A split developed and Orendian left the UFW to organize the Texas Farm Workers (TFW). However, as times worsened the TFW became less effective.[67]

The Farah Strike: The Breaking of Labor

Willie Farah operated textile plants in Texas and New Mexico. At his largest facility and headquarters in El Paso, Farah employed some 9,500 workers—85 percent were female, mostly Chicanas. The Amalgamated Clothing Workers Union of America (ACWUA) began organizing workers at Farah's San Antonio plant in the late 1960s. In October 1970, in an NLRB-supervised election, the cutting department voted to affiliate with the union. Willie Farah refused to bargain in good faith and resorted to reprisals such as firing union loyalists or making them sweep floors and perform other menial labor. Willie erected barbed-wire fences around his five facilities.

By 1972, 4,000 Farah employees in El Paso, San Antonio, Victoria, and Las Cruces, New Mexico, were striking Farah. In July, the union called for a nationwide boycott of Farah that lasted for two years and took a tremendous personal toll on the strikers and their families. The backbone of the strike were the women, who created a group called *Unidad Para Siempre* (Unity Forever). In 1974, Farah signed a contract with the union but continued to harass union activists. By 1976, he closed his San Antonio factory and moved his operations across the border. Slowly the workers' support of the union eroded. Part of the problem was that the union failed to develop leadership and did not continue the political education of the workers. The International office of the ACWUA never fully appreciated or encouraged local Chicana workers.[68]

Sin Fronteras

14.6 Discuss how the Immigration Reform Act of 1965 accelerated xenophobia and white nationalism during the 1970s.

The Border Industrialization Program (BIP) reduced Mexico to the equivalent of an underdeveloped nation. Since the *maquiladoras* (assembly factories) imported 98 percent of their raw materials from the United States and Japan, they did little to stimulate other domestic industries. By the end of the decade, Mexico gained the reputation of paying even lower wages than the four "Asian Tigers," while having lower energy costs than in the Far East. The "Asian Tigers," "Four Asian Dragons," or "Four Little Dragons," are the economies of Hong Kong, Singapore, South Korea, and Taiwan, which underwent rapid industrialization and maintained exceptionally high growth rates between the early 1960s and 1990s.

In 1974, 476 *maquiladoras* operated in Mexico. During the recession of 1973–1975, the number of *maquiladoras* dramatically declined. As worker militancy grew, transnational managers, through the American Chamber of Commerce in Mexico, pressured Mexican President Luis Echeverría to intervene on the side of capital investors or lose the *maquiladoras*. Mexico was almost bankrupt. The International Monetary Fund (IMF) and the World Bank refinanced Mexico's loans, on condition that Mexico agrees to austerity measures and to reduce the number of public jobs, produce more oil, and devalue the peso. Devaluation cut wages in half and revived the *maquiladoras* by doubling their profits.

Meanwhile, there was an increased migration of workers from Mexico's interior to the border areas, initially, so workers could seek work in the *maquilas*. However, hunger forced workers to cross the border to seek employment in the United States. The migration furnished U.S. electrical and garment factories with a surplus of cheap labor. Simultaneously in the United States, factories in closed-shop union states moved to right-to-work states, which weakened the political and economic power of Chicano-dominated locals.[69]

Nativism Is White

The recession of 1973–1974 revived the America First "Greek chorus," that blamed immigrants for their failures and those of the American marketplace. By the mid-1970s, the anti-immigrant hysteria was in full swing. The country had come full circle since the nineteenth century, when Americans stereotyped Mexicans as bandits to justify keeping military forts open so that merchants could make a profit from government contracts. In the 1970s, Mexicans again became bandits, blamed for stealing jobs. Criminalization served multiple purposes: It justified paying undocumented immigrants less than other workers. Next it justified increasing budget allocation for the INS that was the source of much of the distorted misinformation about immigrants. It also distracted the media from the failures of the system, playing on American fear and ignorance of the "other." Unfortunately, many poor and middle-class Chicanas/os "believed" that undocumented immigrants, like aliens from another planet, were invading their land and taking their jobs.

Centro de Acción Social Autónoma–Hermandad General de Trabajadores

Bert Corona, founder of the *Centro de Acción Social Autónoma–Hermandad General de Trabajadores* (CASA-HGT), led the movement to protect the foreign-born, first in California and then nationally. Corona, born in El Paso in 1918, was active in trade unions and civic and political groups since the

1930s. By the late 1960s, Corona built a massive organization supported by large segments of the Mexican and progressive population to defend the rights of undocumented workers.

CASA established chapters in San Diego, San José, San Antonio, Colorado, and Chicago, and claimed a membership of 2,000 undocumented workers. Along with the charismatic Soledad "Chole" Alatorre, Corona organized undocumented immigrants and educated others to their plight. Indeed, undocumented immigrants were merely scapegoats for failures in the country's unregulated economic structure.

In 1973, under the leadership of *barrio* lawyer Antonio Rodríguez, head of *Casa Carnalismo*, the Committee to Free *Los Tres* (a national committee formed after the arrest of three *Casa Carnalismo* members for allegedly killing an undercover agent whom they suspected of selling drugs), joined by *Comité Estudiantil del Pueblo* (CEP), became part of CASA. By the mid-1970s, the young cadre took over the organization, and transformed CASA from a mass movement organization to a vanguard Marxist group. At this point, Corona and Alatorre left CASA, and merged their supporters into *La Hermandad Mexicana Nacional* (Mexican National Brotherhood) that was formed in the San Diego area in 1951 to protect the rights of the foreign-born.

With the change in leadership, CASA members devoted less energy to organizing workers and more to movement-building operations in Chicano communities, forming alliances with North American and Mexican radicals. More time was spent in Marxist study and publishing of the newspaper *Sin Fronteras*, whose editorial staff included Isabel Rodríguez Chávez (who became a civil rights attorney) and Chicana activist Magdalena Mora. CASA trained leaders, some Marxists and some not, and gave Chicanos a global view of society. Importantly, CASA politicized a broad cadre of Chicana/o activists who became labor organizers and politicos in California.[70]

Criminalization of Mexicans

In a repetition of the 1920s, 1930s, and 1950s, xenophobia became a characteristic of the 1970s. The Republican Party and nativists were at the forefront of this anti-Mexican movement. In the 1960s, education and political representation were the more pressing issues. The growth of the immigration population and the vehemence of what later became white nationalism and their attack on immigrants changed the priorities of the Mexican American community, organizations, and the media.

In order to divert attention from the growing inequality and the shifting of the costs America's continuing wars, ultra-conservative foundations financed nativist laws. They initiated a culture war between nativist and civil rights proponents that rages to this day. In 1971, California passed the Dixon–Arnett Act, fining employers who hired undocumented workers. (The State Supreme Court declared the act unconstitutional because it infringed on federal powers.) The next year, U.S. Representative Peter Rodino (D–New Jersey) introduced a bill making it a felony to knowingly employ undocumented workers and specified penalties ranging from warnings for first-time offenders to heavy fines and jail terms for repeat offenders. Senator Edward Kennedy introduced a similar bill that additionally granted amnesty to all aliens living in the country for at least three years. Chicanas/os opposed the Rodino and Kennedy bills. Senator James O. Eastland (D–Mississippi), chair of the Senate Judiciary Committee and a large grower, killed the Rodino bill in committee.

By 1976, Representative Joshua Eilberg (D–Pennsylvania) successfully sponsored a bill lowering the annual number of immigrants entering from any one country from 40,000 to 20,000. Eilberg's bill was a slap in the face to Mexico because at that time, it was the only Latin American country sending more than 40,000 immigrants. The law further granted preferences to professionals and scientists, encouraging a brain drain from Latin America. Lastly, the law made the parents of U.S.-born children ineligible for immigration. Children had the option of being deported and returning when they reached legal age, or becoming wards of the court.

INS commissioner Leonard Chapman, Jr., manufactured statistics to support his propaganda claims of a Mexican invasion to hide the improprieties uncovered during "Operation Clean Sweep." The INS apprehended 348,178 undocumented workers in 1971, 430,213 in 1972, and 609,573 in 1973. News reporters and scholars attribute this stepped-up activity, in part, to the U.S. border patrol's effort to divert attention from internal problems, including rapes, prostitution, bribery, and the running of concentration camp–like detention facilities. At the same time, there were scholars on the payrolls of nativist research foundations: even respected public foundations like the National Endowment for the Humanities funded anti-immigrant research. The federal government gave Mexican specialist Arthur Corwin a grant to conduct a so-called definitive border study, even though Corwin was not a border expert.[71]

Hidden behind the veil of pure research, Corwin launched an attack on Chicana/o scholars for questioning the role of the INS. On July 16, 1975, he sent Henry Kissinger a letter demanding action and control of migration from Latin America. According to Corwin, the United States was becoming a "welfare reservation," and if the trend were to continue, the Southwest would become a Mexican "Quebec." Corwin recommended that the Army be mobilized and that Congress appropriate $1 billion to the INS, so that the agency could hire 50,000 additional border officers. Corwin also advocated the building of an electrified fence. Fortunately, the Corwin letter fell into the hands of the Mexican press, who discredited him.

Scholars F. Ray Marshall, an economics professor at the University of Texas and secretary of labor under Jimmy Carter, and University of Texas Professor Vernon M. Briggs, Jr., who previously worked with César Chávez, favored restricting undocumented workers.[72] Expressing concern that undocumented workers took jobs from Chicanos, Marshall and Briggs called for fining employers in order to discourage migration.[73]

The Media Sell Racist Nativism

The media's anti-immigrant rhetoric sensationalized immigration and gave credence to the myth of a "Mexican invasion."[74] It uncritically reported INS propaganda and nativist "scholarship," and promoted the notion that undocumented workers caused poverty, were criminals, and took jobs away from North Americans. On May 2, 1977, *Time* magazine ran two articles: "Getting Their Share of Paradise" and "On the Track of the Invader." They quoted INS sources saying that the "invaders came by land, sea, and air," adding that U.S. taxpayers spent $13 billion annually on social services for aliens, who sent another $13 billion out of the country annually. Thus, employers could buy their labor power at ever-lower rates and could deny living wages to these stateless workers.[75]

Getting Away with Terror

In October 1972, border patrol officer Kenneth Cook raped Martha López, 26, and threatened to harm her two children. In the summer of 1976, George Hanigan, a Douglas, Arizona rancher and Dairy Queen Owner, and his two sons, Patrick, 22, and Thomas, 17, kidnapped three undocumented workers looking for work. They "stripped, stabbed, burned [them] with hot pokers and dragged [them] across the desert."[76] The Hanigans held a mock hanging for one of the Mexicans and shot another with buckshot. Judge Anthony Deddens, a friend of the Hanigans, refused to issue arrest warrants. Later, an all-white jury acquitted the Hanigans. Activists on both sides of the border protested the verdict and pressured U.S. Attorney General Griffin Bell to indict them. The Hanigan case went to a federal grand jury that in 1979 indicted the Hanigans for violating the Hobbs Act, involving interference in interstate commerce (obviously the civil rights of the undocumented workers were not at issue). Another all-white jury was deadlocked in a first trial. At the second trial in 1981, the jury found the Hanigan brothers guilty (the father had died by that time).[77]

In Defense of the Foreign Born

In the spring of 1976, the INS broke into the Tucson office of *Concilio Manzo*, an organization that offered free counseling and legal services to undocumented workers and their families. The INS confiscated files and arrested Margo Cowan, Sister Gabriel Marcaisq, Margarita Ramírez, and Cathy Montano. INS authorities accused the *Manzo* workers of not reporting "aliens" to the INS. The court, after an extended period and the expenditure of funds and time, dismissed the case.

Throughout the 1970s, Chicano organizations mobilized their constituencies in defense of undocumented workers. Support came from every sector of the Chicano community, crossing party and class lines. In 1976, Carter received 81 percent of the Latino vote, with a 205,800-vote plurality in Texas. Consequently, the Carter White House appointed more Latinos than previous administrations. Although the Latino population's growth was a determining factor in these appointments, the appointees were accountable to those who signed their paychecks. The Special Assistant for Hispanic Affairs, a post held first by José Aragón and then by Estebán Torres, both from Los Angeles, had limited power—the power to select the lobbyists who had access to the president.

The wave of xenophobia did not stop with the election of Jimmy Carter. In retrospect, Carter tried to placate everyone. On August 4, Carter sent Congress a four-point package: 1) to revise the Rodino bill with civil penalties for employers who "knowingly hire illegal aliens"; 2) to provide for more military equipment and border patrol personnel to stop immigration; 3) to give limited amnesty to undocumented immigrants already in the country; and 4) to give multilateral aid to Mexico and other sending countries to create jobs. Although he nominated Ray Marshall, Secretary of Labor, and Leone J. Castillo to head the INS, the plan came under immediate attack from the left and right.

The Carter Plan mobilized Republican nativist organizations as well as the Ku Klux Klan whose attack on the Carter Administration plan claimed that it "would include amnesty for hundreds of thousands, perhaps millions, of foreigners, mostly Mexicans, who are living in the United States illegally."[78] With the Greek Chorus sounding the drums and the Ku Klux Klan leading the assault, Chicano and other progressive organizations took to the streets.

In San Diego, in fall 1977, in response to Jimmy Carter's attempted immigration reform legislation, more than a thousand activists, led by Herman Baca, Rodolfo "Corky" Gonzales, and Bert Corona, marched against the Ku Klux Klan. In December of that same year, Armando Navarro of the San Bernardino–Riverside area assembled 1,200 community folk for a conference on immigration. Meanwhile, Chicano organizations, CASA, and the National Coalition for Fair Immigration Laws became increasingly critical of Chávez because he wanted to stem the flow of undocumented workers. The coalition, made up of the G.I. Forum, LULAC, and the Comisión Femenil, pressured Chávez for a statement criticizing anti-immigrant policies. Forced to respond, Chávez went on record saying that the UFW was supportive of progressive legislation to protect the rights of undocumented workers—adding that if there were no undocumented workers, "we could win those strikes overnight."

In October 1977, José Angel Gutiérrez and LRUP held a conference in San Antonio attended by 2,600 Chicano activists from all over the country. Mexican American organizations across the board such as the League of United Latin American Citizens (LULAC) and the G.I. Forum criticized anti-immigrant legislation. To this day Republicans have opposed the issue of amnesty or, for that matter, immigration reform.

Chicanas/os For Sale

The growth of the Mexican American population and the expansion of the middle class was a market bonanza. Beer companies distributed calendars with photos of "Hispanics," celebrating them as role models for the community. The term *Hispanic* appealed to many marketers; it packaged the Mexican American, the Puerto Rican, the Cuban, and other Latin Americans in one innocuous wrapper. Most of the new heroes and heroines were not activists but business executives, politicians, and political appointees—both Democrat and Republican. Newly formed Chicano and Chicana groups followed this pattern of celebrating the success of persons selected by the system. The term *Hispanic* also appealed to this new wave of middle-class Mexican Americans, and this identity was much more in line with their class biases and aspirations.

This change of identity laid the foundation for the Colorado-based Coors Brewing Company deal of October 1984, when Hispanic organizations called off a boycott initiated by the Chicano community in 1966 to protest owner Joseph Coors's labor and race policies. The Coors family actively supported and funded conservative politicians, organizations, and causes. Over the years, both the American G.I. Forum and LULAC had negotiated with the beer company, trying to reach an accord and end the boycott. In 1975, the Forum reached an agreement with Coors, but Forum members rejected it because of a recently called AFL–CIO strike against Coors.

In October 1984, the G.I. Forum, the Cuban National Planning Committee, the National Council of La Raza, the National Puerto Rican Coalition, and the U.S. Hispanic Chamber of Commerce signed a contract with Coors, ending the boycott. The agreement supposedly made Coors a "good corporate citizen."[79] The pact pledged that Coors, from 1985 to 1990, would return $350 million to the community in the form of advertisements in Hispanic media, investments in Hispanic businesses, grants to selected community organizations, and some scholarships. Coors tied the amount it would donate to the organizations to how much beer the "Hispanic" community drank.

Chicanas/os/Mexican Americans were the largest sector in the pseudo-Hispanic community, and were expected to drink the largest share of beer. LULAC's leadership at first refused to ratify the agreement that linked how much money the programs received for beer consumption. Coors, according to LULAC, did not insist on the beer-drinking clause when it funded other non-Latino organizations—such as the arch-reactionary Heritage Foundation. Meanwhile, activists and trade unions such as the UFW continued with the Coors boycott.[80]

A Redefinition of the Political Middle

A downside of the LRUP and much of the Chicana/o left abandoning traditional Chicano organizations was the redefinition of the political middle. Without the left, the former right-of-center became the center, and the far right became the right-of-center. Without a leftist voice, conservatives gained control of established organizations such as LULAC and the American G.I. Forum, and in the process, Republicans gained new respectability. During the Lyndon Johnson presidency, these organizations became dependent on patronage. This arrangement continued in the 1970s under Nixon and then Gerald Ford. The only thing that changed was the political brokers shifted between the organizations and the party in power.

In 1964, LULAC and the Forum began managing the Service, Employment, and Redevelopment (SER) agency. By the end of the 1970s, SER supervised 184 projects in 104 cities with an annual budget of $50 million. LULAC and the Forum received these grants because of their Washington connections. With Republicans in control of the Executive Branch for most of the 1970s and all of the 1980s, Latino Republicans monopolized government liaisons. This facilitated the Republican penetration of the Forum and LULAC and other organizations. By the mid-1970s, the media and the public- and private-sector bureaucracies looked almost exclusively to middle-class Hispanics to represent the Chicano community's interests.[81]

Meanwhile, concerned about the growing influence of Republicans, LULAC President Rubén Bonilla broke with the Brown Republicans and criticized U.S. immigration policy and Washington's intervention in Central America.

Political Gains

By the grace of the Voting Rights Act, the Chicana/o movement, and the population boom, changes took place in the early 1970s, not because of, but despite the dismal record of Chicana/o elected officials. In Los Angeles, Chicanas/os remained unrepresented on the City Council and Board of Supervisors. The situation was the same throughout the Southwest. Just getting people elected was not enough. For example, in 1974, both Eligio (Kika) de la Garza and Henry B. González voted against extending the benefits of the Voting Rights Act to Chicanas/os. Arizona Governor Raúl

Castro, elected in 1974, spent most of his time supporting the state's right-to-work law and placating Arizona's conservatives. In 1977, Castro resigned under a cloud of suspicion of mismanagement and became U.S. ambassador to Argentina.

In 1975, Representative Edward R. Roybal organized the National Association of Latino Elected Officials (NALEO).[82] Its goals were to lobby, coordinate voter registration, and get out the vote. By 1980, NALEO had 2,500 members, with a potential of 5,000. In addition, in the mid-1970s, the four Latino congressional members formed the so-called Hispanic Caucus; by 1984, the caucus had 11 members. The Hispanic Caucus did not have the muscle or the ideological clarity of the Black Caucus, partly because of the ultra-conservative Cuban American cabal.[83]

Education: The Stairway to the American Dream

14.7 Summarize how the Bakke decision was an expression of the growing white nationalism.

In 1968, Congress set the framework for bilingual instruction and passed the Bilingual Education Act, Title VII. In *Lau v. Nichols* (1974), the U.S. Supreme Court unanimously ruled that the school district had the duty to meet the linguistic needs of students who had a limited grasp of English. If the district did not, it deprived the children of equal protection under the Civil Rights Act of 1964.

By the mid-1970s, Mexican Americans were under the impression that bilingual education was the law of the land. However, many nativist teachers saw bilingual education as a threat to U.S. institutions. They believed in the supremacy of the English language race and culture; they were concerned that they would become obsolete. Their basic argument was simple: Spanish-speaking students lived in the United States, and held the burden of learning English; teachers had no such duty to learn Spanish.

Some 50 percent of Mexican Americans students dropped out of school, and more than three-quarters of 12th graders fell into the bottom quartile of reading level. Traditional education failed because less than 3 percent of Mexican students in the Southwest had access to the new bilingual education, and less than 5.5 percent had access to English as a Second Language (ESL) classes. Many conservative critics attempted to make bilingual education itself the scapegoat for the failure of the schools, rather than the inadequate implementation of these programs.

In the early 1970s, the U.S. Civil Rights Commission found school districts still enforced the no-Spanish rule. In California, 13.5 percent of elementary schools discouraged the use of any Spanish; in Texas, it was 66.4 percent.

According to the Commission, 40 percent of the Chicana/o students in developmentally disabled classes did not speak English. School districts often mislabeled Spanish-speaking children and put them in developmentally disabled classes.

Resistance to bilingual education increased during the Reagan years. Federal appropriations reached $171 million in the 1980s. Reagan, who at one time supported bilingual education, appointed opponents of it to the National Advisory and Coordinating Council on Bilingual Education. Consequently, the Bilingual Education Act of 1984 lowered its appropriation to $139 million despite the fact that community support remained high. In San Antonio, 65 percent of the Mexican population surveyed believed that the federal government and local schools spent too little on bilingual education; only 6 percent believed that the schools spent too much. In East Los Angeles, 55 percent said the schools spent too little, and only 9 percent disagreed. A survey showed that 89 percent of Chicana/o leaders favored spending more money, while 2 percent did not. The report found that 93 percent of Mexicans favored bilingual education in San Antonio; in East Los Angeles, 87 percent; and among Chicana/o leaders it was 96 percent.[84]

The Lack Educational Equity

From 1968 to 1974, U.S. Mexicans made gains in education; after this point, they slipped backward. The dropout rate again began to climb. In 1974–1975, the high school dropout rate for Chicanos/as was 38.7 for 20- and 21-year-olds; the number rose to 44.1 percent in 1977–1978. In Texas, the state tied funding to teacher and professional salaries. Thus, Mexican schools received about three-fifths the appropriations of white schools.

In *Serrano v. Priest*, John Serrano, Jr., sued the California Department of Education in 1968,[85] claiming that because schools in East Los Angeles were financed by local property taxes, his son had received an inferior education. Serrano alleged that poor districts received less funding than did the wealthier ones, and consequently, the children received unequal treatment. In 1971, the California Supreme Court held that financing primarily through local property taxes failed to provide equal protection under the law and a district's wealth determined the quality of its schools. Therefore, if equal educational opportunity was a right, the rich and the poor must be funded equally. The U.S. Supreme Court (1976) upheld the California Supreme Court's ruling in *Serrano*, but limited its decision to California, holding that the financing system violated the state constitution's equal protection clause by denying equal access to education.[86]

In *San Antonio School District v. Rodríguez* (1968), the Supreme Court had found that the U.S. Constitution did not include equal education as a fundamental right. San Antonio housed multiple school districts that were segregated along race and class lines. The poorest, Edgewood, was Chicana/o; the richest, Alamo Heights, was mostly white. Edgewood parents sued under the equal protection clause of the Fourteenth Amendment.

During the 1970–1971 academic year, the state allocated Alamo Heights $492 per child and Edgewood, $356. In 1971, the 162 poorest districts paid higher taxes than did the 203 richest districts. The poor spent $130 a year in property taxes for education on a $20,000 home, while the rich paid $46 a year on the same type of home. In 1973, the Warren Burger Court overturned a court of appeals ruling that found in favor of the Edgewood parents. The Burger Court found that the Texas method of funding was imperfect but rational. It refused to consider the question of race discrimination. Thus, the Edgewood school district continued to have fewer counselors, fewer library books, and fewer course offerings—all because of unequal funding.[87]

In 1970–1971, Latinos in the Los Angeles Unified Schools made up more than 20 percent of the student population; by the end of the decade, they approached a majority. In San Antonio *Serrano* made few changes; the wealthier districts still had better facilities and more experienced and better-educated teachers. Latino and Black schools continued to be overcrowded, and year-round schools in the 1980s were found almost exclusively in Latino areas. (Year-round schools often split families who had children on different tracks.) Mexican school buildings were older; they housed more students per square foot and offered smaller recreational areas. Thirty years after the *Brown* case (1954), schools remained separate, unequal, and segregated.[88]

The "Pochoization" of the Political Vocabulary

The evolving student political ideology can be compared to the enrichment of vocabulary. The Spanish vocabulary of many Chicanos, for example, remains at a third-grade level owing to the lack of use of Spanish and the lack of reading in the language. Similarly, student activists often fail to enrich their political vocabulary because they do not continue their involvement. Their political vocabulary stagnates once they leave the campus. Often new students who are not involved neither possess nor acquire the basic vocabulary to understand history or societal inequality. They neither know nor learn about the sacrifices made by earlier generations of Chicanas/os and Mexican Americans to gain them access to opportunities. Most take college admission for granted.

The Myth of a Color-Blind Society

Armed with billions of dollars from right-wing foundations xenophobes took their prejudices to the courts. In *Regents of the University of California v. Bakke*, 438 U.S. 265 (1978) the U.S. Supreme Court ruled that race could not be used as a criterion for the admission of minorities. During 1973–1974, Alan Bakke, a 34-year-old engineer, applied to 13 medical schools, all of which rejected him because of his age. A white administrator at the University of California at Davis encouraged Bakke to sue, since allegedly "less-qualified minorities" were admitted. Bakke challenged the Davis special admission program, initiated in 1970 that set aside 16 out of 100 slots for disadvantaged students. Before this plan began, only three minority students had ever been admitted to Davis's medical school. A lower court found for Bakke, as did the California Supreme Court, which flatly stated that race could not be used as a criterion for admission.

On June 28, 1978, the U.S. Supreme Court, in a 5–4 decision, upheld *Bakke*. It based its decision on the 1964 Civil Rights Act, holding that using race as the sole criterion for admission was unconstitutional. Justice Thurgood Marshall dissented, stating that the Court had come "full circle" in returning to the post–Civil War era when the courts stopped congressional initiatives to give former slaves full citizenship. Justice Marshall's dissent was prophetic. The *Bakke* decision gave racist faculties and administrators an excuse for excluding minorities. *Bakke* became the law of the land, and it signaled an assault on affirmative action that continued into the late 1990s. *Bakke* was part of a "culture war" funded by right-wing extremists opposed to the idea of equity in education.

The need for minority doctors and other professionals speaks for itself. In California in 1975, one American lawyer practiced for every 530 Americans; for Asians, the ratio was 1:1,750; for African Americans, 1:3,441; for Latinos, 1:9,842; and for Native Americans, 1:50,000. In primary-care medicine, one white doctor practiced for every 990 whites; the ratio for Blacks was 1:4,028; for Native Americans, 1:7,539; and for Latinos, 1:21,245. *Bakke* supporters argued that overall there was an oversupply of professionals and that services did not depend on the professional's ethnic or racial background. Admittedly, little research has gone into this latter area. However, Dr. Stephen Keith of the Charles Drew Post Graduate School in Los Angeles conducted a study, and his findings suggested that the probability that African American and Latino professionals would work with poor and minority clients was much higher than that for their white counterparts.[89]

William Raspberry, a Pulitzer Prize-winning columnist, wrote that the:

> The assumption is that large numbers of highly qualified whites are being shunted aside in order to make room for marginal blacks, and that the only defensible approach is now to re-turn to a system where admissions decisions are based solely on relative merit. ... The truth is that such a system has never existed. Admissions preferences are the rule, not the exception. Sons and daughters of alumni usually are given preference in admissions.[90]

Legacy Admits

The debate over preferential treatment of minorities continues even today with some whites claiming "reverse racism." Critics of *Bakke* point out that groups, such as veterans, the children of alumni, the children of donors to the university, or those over 65 years of age, receive preferential treatment. Today society has handicap ramps, which some people would call preferential treatment. According to Alex Liebman, the overall acceptance rate for Princeton's class of 2001 was 13 percent; the statistic for "legacy admits" (children of alumni) was 41 percent; and that for minorities (which includes Asians) was 26 percent. There seemed to be an assumption that Latinos and African Americans were not qualified if they were special admits and that the legacy admits were qualified. At Harvard University during the 1990s, the children of alumni were almost four times more likely to be admitted than other applicants. Harvard University admitted about 40 percent of its entering class using the criterion that the student was the son or daughter of an alumnus or donor. In the same period, 66 percent of children-of-alumni applicants were accepted by the University of Pennsylvania, whereas the overall acceptance rate was 11 percent. Admissions officers saved 25 percent of Notre Dame's first-year class openings for the children of alumni.[91] The preferential treatment given to legacy admits exposes the hypocrisy and racial bias of those who challenge affirmative action.

Why Progressive Organizations Fail

14.8 Outline the anti-immigrant legislation during the 1970s.

Documents obtained under the Freedom of Information Act suggest the extent of federal monitoring of progressive political organizations. José Angel Gutiérrez and Ernesto Vigil are among a number of Chicano scholars doing research in the field. However, almost no evidence is available on local police spying. An exception was a suit filed by the American Civil Liberties Union (ACLU) in 1978: *CAPA (Committee Against Police Abuse) v. Los Angeles Police Department*. Some 141 plaintiffs, individuals and groups, went to court in an attempt to restrain police infiltration of political organizations.

Suing the police is an almost impossible task because of the deep pockets of big cities. For example, *CAPA v. LAPD* almost bankrupted the ACLU, which paid out nearly $1 million in legal costs before the LAPD settled. The plaintiffs argued that responsibility for spying went all the way to Chief Daryl Gates, and that further discovery would yield even more evidence of police spying. The plaintiffs voted to settle because they did not have the money to go on. The negotiated settlement included extensive guidelines calling for outside monitoring of the LAPD. Further, the court set up an independent committee to conduct the audit of the agency, and for the first time, the court ordered the police department not to investigate private individuals or groups without reasonable and articulated suspicion. "For first time, an LA court investigated the police department for surveillance of private individuals and groups and forced a settlement of a million dollars compensating the ACLU for costs."[92]

The Swagger Stick: The Unraveling of the Empire

14.9 Contextualize the growing desperation of the American Empire from Salvador Allende to Anastasio Somoza.

The swagger stick represents power. It was used as a symbol of authority by colonial armies. To this day it adorns the uniform of the occupiers. It is distinct—shorter than a cane, often used as a riding crop. The custom goes back to the Roman centurions. "In 1952 an order was promulgated permitting Marines in the grade of staff sergeant and above including officers – to carry a swagger stick."[93] Like armies of occupation, police wear uniforms and carry swagger sticks called batons. There is a relationship in how we treat non-white people at home and abroad—prodding them with the swagger stick.

In the 1970s, Americans began to feel the withdrawal pains of the war. Many came to grips that they lost the war to a tiny developing nation. The Vietnam War cost "$173 billion (equivalent to $770 billion in 2003 dollars). Veterans' benefits and interest would add another $250 billion ($1 trillion in 2003 dollars). But the real cost of the war was its impact on the economy, including agriculture."[94] About 58,000 American soldiers lost their lives and another 304,000 were wounded. This is not counting the loss of Vietnamese lives.[95] American planes dropped more than twice as many bombs as U.S. forces used during World War II (1939–1945). The war marked the decline of the American Empire that although had lost its swagger stick, still wagged its stick—the Vietnamese forced them to live off a credit card.

The Oil Embargo of 1973–1974 was the first aftershock. As a result of the 1973 Arab–Israeli War (Yom Kippur War) in reprisal for the U.S. decision to continue supplying the Israeli military and supporting it in the post war peace negotiations, Arab members of the Organization of Petroleum Exporting Countries (OPEC) imposed an embargo against the United States and other countries supporting

Israel.[96] The embargo had short- and long-term effects on global politics and the global economy.

> The 1973 Oil Embargo acutely strained a U.S. economy that had grown increasingly dependent on foreign oil. The efforts of President Richard M. Nixon's administration to end the embargo signaled a complex shift in the global financial balance of power to oil-producing states and triggered a slew of U.S. attempts to address the foreign policy challenges emanating from long-term dependence on foreign oil.[97]

The attitude in the United States was that OPEC was taking or stealing American oil. The long gas lines and American insecurities fed the growing xenophobia.

As in the 1950s, the United States continued its interventions in Latin America. On September 11, 1973, the CIA-sponsored military overthrow of constitutionally elected Chilean President Salvador Allende brought Chilean refugees to the United States.[98] General Augusto Pinochet, in league with the CIA, led a military coup assassinating Allende. It unleashed a reign of terror that in the first year saw conservatively over 11,000 people murdered. By 1982 neoliberal wunderkind Milton Friedman declared that dictator Pinochet *supported a fully free-market economy as a matter of principle. Chile is an economic miracle.*[99] Pinochet, in partnership with "the Chicago Boys"—free-market economists—set out to convert Chile into a free market, reducing the role of the state and cutting back inflation. According to Pinochet, Chile would become "a nation of entrepreneurs."

Pinochet sought to convert Chilean education into a *mercado*. As a result, Chilean education became among the most expensive in the world, for example, Chile's primary school system ranked 119th of 144 countries. Students could not afford "to graduate, and even those who attain degrees seldom earn enough to pay off their debt."[100] Public education received limited public funding. In 2006 students took to the streets in what became known as the Penguin Revolution[101]—the students wore black and white uniforms, carrying signs reading, *education is a human right*. Not seduced by minor victories, they continued to fight for free education.

The CIA's overthrow of President Salvador Allende in 1973 more than a million Chileans left the country between 1973 and 1990; a minority of these political refugees migrated to the United States. Many Chileans returned to Chile after military dictator Augusto Pinochet left office, leaving about 69,000 Chileans living in the United States.

In 1979, the overthrow of dictator Anastasio Somoza Debayle by Nicaraguans set off a series of revolutions in Central America. The wars pushed political refugees from El Salvador and Guatemala as well as other Central American countries into the United States. In the 1980s the world saw increased military repression and rural counterinsurgency warfare programs supported by the United States. The result was numerous massacres; forced displacement; assassinations of political, religious, labor, student, and peasant leaders; and the disappearance of thousands.

In 1979 the Islamic Revolution resulted in the overthrow of the Shah of Iran, the U.S.'s number one ally in the Middle East. It saw the rise of the Ayatollah Ruhollah Khomeini. President Jimmy Carter announced: "[The Shah is] now in Egypt, and he will later come to our own country. But we would anticipate, and would certainly hope, that our good relationships with Iran will continue in the future."[102]

The Ayatollah Khomeini became a symbol of the Islamic Revolution. The State Department evacuated 1,350 Americans on the day of the Ayatollah's return. The Iran hostage crisis was a diplomatic standoff between Iran and the United States. Fifty-two American diplomats and citizens were held hostage for 444 days from November 4, 1979, to January 20, 1981.

Central America was shaken by the overthrow of the most reliable puppet of the United States whose family had ruled Nicaragua since the 1930s. Debayle's or junior as he was called (His father Anastasio Somoza García) had been put in power in the 1930s put there by a coup... Junior's overthrow did not come overnight. In 1972, a giant earthquake devastated Managua—leaving 6,000 dead and 20,000 injured. Matters worsened when it was learned that junior embezzled temporarily reaffirmed from international relief funds. Martial law was declared; and junior was temporarily reaffirmed Chief Executive of the Nicaraguan government. U.S. marines were sent to Nicaragua to prop up Somoza's regime.

In 1978, an economic slowdown fanned discontent. Joaquín Chamorro, editor of the anti-Somoza newspaper, *La Prensa*, was assassinated and Somoza was blamed. The Sandinista National Liberation Front (FSLN), an anti-Somoza guerrilla force, launched a military uprising against Somoza. On July 17, Somoza fled and on July 20, Sandinista forces took Managua, beginning a domino effect throughout Central America.[103]

Conclusion: The Final Year

Historically there has been a pattern of irrational white American angst that someone was taking America away from white Americans. The paranois got worse during times of uncertainty; the media and popular culture fanned the fear. Similar go horror movies like *Friday the thirteenth* nativists exploited this fear; they played the terrors and emotions of white people especially the old and the vulnerable. In the case of white suburban women, the fear was that the inner city would catch up to them and dark men would stalk them. These irrational fears conditioned reactions toward unauthorized immigrants. They were going to take away their jobs, marry their daughters and steal their "American Dream." Many Americans refused to listen to the evidence that California, for instance, has benefited from immigration. In 1984, the Urban Institute of Washington estimated that 645,000 jobs were created in Los Angeles County since 1970; immigrants took about one-third of the jobs. Without immigrants, LA factories employing Angeleños would have left the area, resulting in the flight of higher-paying jobs. The final year of the 1970s was eventful. Eighty percent of Mexican Americans lived in metropolitan areas. Because of poverty and segregation there was a higher incidence of crime and violence among them. In Los Angeles, Mexican Americans and Latinos were 2.3 times more likely than Americans to become homicide victims. The largest increase in crime statistics—over 166.7 percent—occurred among Chicanos and Latinos; murders went from 11.1 per 100,000 in 1970 to 29.6 per 100,000 in 1979.[104] In the years to come, 1979 would have far-reaching implications for the Mexican-origin population. During the 1970s, the growing foreign-born population was already impacting the Chicana/o community. This crisis was one of several factors that brought to power a succession of ultra-conservative administrations during the 1980s.[105]

Notes

1. "The Powell Memo" (also known as the "Powell Manifesto"). The Powell Memo was first published on August 23, 1971. Confidential Memorandum: Attack of American Free Enterprise System, August 23, 1971, TO: Mr. Eugene B. Sydnor, Jr., Chairman, Education Committee, U.S. Chamber of Commerce; FROM: Lewis F. Powell, Jr., in "Reclaim Democracy," http://reclaimdemocracy.org/powell_memo_lewis/. Lewis was later appointed to the Supreme Court. Jean Stefanic and Richard Delgado, *No Mercy: How Conservative Think Tanks and Foundations Changed America's Social Agenda* (Philadelphia, PA: Temple University Press, 1996). Bill Moyers, "The Powell Memo: A Call-to-Arms for Corporations," Moyers & Co, September 14, 2012, http://billmoyers.com/content/the-powell-memo-a-call-to-arms-for-corporations/.
2. Deborah McCarthy and Daniel Faber (eds.), *Foundations for Social Change: Critical Perspectives on Philanthropy and Popular Movements* (Boulder: Rowman & Littlefield, 2005), 90. Heather Boushey and Adam S. Hersh "The American Middle Class, Income Inequality, and the Strength of Our Economy: New Evidence in Economics," Center for American Progress, May 2012, https://cdn.americanprogress.org/wp-content/uploads/2012/05/93905594-The-American-Middle-Class-Income-Inequality-and-the-Strength-of-Our-Economy.pdf.
3. "The Nation's Latino Population Is Defined by Its Youth," Pew Reseach Center, April 20, 2016, http://www.pewhispanic.org/2016/04/20/the-nations-latino-population-is-defined-by-its-youth/.
4. Ibid
5. Che Guevara Internet Archive, http://www.marxists.org/archive/guevara/index.htm.
6. Jody Agius Vallejo, "The Mexican Origin Middle Class in Los Angeles." CSII Publications, December 2009, https://dornsife.usc.edu/csii/agius-mexican-middle-class/.
7. "We the American . . . Hispanics," U.S. Department of Commerce, Bureau of Census, September 1993, 2, https://www.census.gov/prod/cen1990/wepeople/we-2r.pdf. The U.S. Census contributed to the confusion as to the identity of the individual Latino groups. It was a major chore to learn specific data on individual groups and to track history. Each group has a unique history that is hidden. For example, Mexicans died at the Alamo, not Ecuadorans. The lack of preciseness has led to Italians and Spaniards being included as Latinos and Hispanics that epistemologically is false—or as it is said today, fake.
8. David Reimers, "An Unintended Reform: The 1965 Immigration Act and Third World Immigration to the United States," *Journal of American Ethnic History* 3, No. 1 (1983), 9–28.
9. In 1970 the Mexican birth rate in Mexico was 6.8 children per female. "Fertility rate, total (births per woman)," The World Bank, https://data.worldbank.org/indicator/SP.DYN.TFRT.IN. Jeffrey S. Passel, D'Vera Cohn and Ana Gonzalez-Barrera, "Net Migration from Mexico Falls to Zero—and Perhaps Less V. Mexico, by the Numbers," Pew Research Center, April 23, 2012, http://www.pewhispanic.org/2012/04/23/v-mexico-by-the-numbers/.
10. Gustavo López, "Hispanics of Mexican Origin in the United States, 2013," Pew Research Center, September 15, 2015, http://www.pewhispanic.org/2015/09/15/hispanics-of-mexican-origin-in-the-united-states-2013/.
11. Lopez, Ibid.

12 Eileen Patten," The Nation's Latino Population Is Defined by Its Youth." Pew Research Center, April 20, 2016. http://www.pewhispanic.org/2016/04/20/the-nations-latino-population-is-defined-by-its-youth/.

13 1960 Census: Subject Reports, Persons of Spanish Surname: Social and Economic Data for White Persons of Spanish Surname in Five Southwestern States, U.S. Census, 1965, https://www.census.gov/library/publications/1965/dec/population-pc-2-1b.html.

14 Marjorie Heins, *Strictly Ghetto Property: The Story of Los Siete de La Raza* (Berkeley, CA: Ramparts Press, 1972), 11–12, 49–51, 203–6. In 1969, Central American youth from the Mission District of San Francisco were approached by two plainclothes policemen while moving furniture. An altercation resulted and an officer died from a gunshot wound. Swarms of officers hit the building and fired automatic rifles and flooded the building with tear gas. Seven youths were arrested in Santa Cruz for murder and attempted murder in the case. Gary Lescallett, Daniel Melendez, Jose Rios, Rudolpho Martinez, Jose Martinez, and Danillo Melendez were acquitted; they included four Salvadorans, one Nicaraguan, and one Honduran. The seventh defendant, George López, was never apprehended. They had been involved in a youth group, the Mission Rebels. The Mission District was a mixed Latino *barrio* held together by La Raza. At trial the stories conflicted and the defendants insisted that the police had drawn their guns. They were in plain clothes. The trial lasted a year and a half, and the seven were acquitted. "Los Siete" Defense Committee helped raise the consciousness of youth.

15 "The Word Chicana/o," Chicana Chicano Public Scholar, http://forchicanachicanostudies.wikispaces.com/Chicana+Chicano+Public+Scholar.

16 Otto Santa Ana, *Brown Tide Rising: Metaphors of Latinos in Contemporary American Public Discourse* (Austin: University of Texas Press, 2002).

17 Isaac William Martin, "Proposition 13 Fever: How California's Tax Limitation Spread," *California Journal of Politics and Policy*, 1, No. 1 (2009), Art. 17, 1–17. California Chief Justice Rose Bird Loses Election, http://www.youtube.com/watch?v=Kd162US36to.

18 Richard Adler, ed., *All in the Family: A Critical Appraisal* (New York: Praeger, 1979).

19 You can view episodes of these sitcoms. See "All in the Family—Archie Bunker Meets Sammy Davis," http://www.youtube.com/watch?v=O_UBgkFHm8o.

20 "Culture Clash Show—Lalo Sings No Chicanos on TV," http://www.youtube.com/watch?v=JZt6lZ6RDAU.

21 Rocio Rivadeneyra, "The Influence of Television on Stereotype Threat among Adolescents of Mexican Descent" (PhD Dissertation, Ann Arbor: University of Michigan, 2001). Frito Bandito 1, http://www.youtube.com/watch?v=fOUilxJWm24. The statistics as to the number of Mexican Americans were and are spotty.

22 Michael Harrington, *The Other America: Poverty in the United States* (Baltimore, MD: Penguin Books, 1963), x. George Mowry and Blaine A. Brownell, *The Urban Nation 1920–1980*, rev. ed. (New York: Hill and Wang, 1981), 311. "All in the Family—Archie's Civil Rights 3-3," http://www.youtube.com/watch?v=ZDuZQabywjw.

23 Carlos Sandoval and Peter Miller, " A Class Apart: A Mexican American Civil Rights Story, " http://aclassapartmovie.com/about-synopsis.php.

24 *Jose Cisneros et al., Plaintiffs-Appellees, v. Corpus Christi Independent School District et al., Defendants-Appellants,* United States Court of Appeals for the Fifth Circuit August 2, 1972, 467 F.2d 142, http://law.justia.com/cases/federal/appellate-courts/F2/467/142/154342/. Neil Foley, "Straddling the Color Line," in Nancy Foner and George M. Fredrickson, eds., *Not Just Black and White: Historical and Contemporary Perspectives on Immigration, Race, and Ethnicity in the United States* (New York: Russell Sage Foundation, 2004), 351–54.

25 Joan Hoff, *Nixon Reconsidered* (New York: Basic Books, 1995), 97–98. Peter Leyden and Simon Rosenberg, "The 50-Year Strategy," *Mother Jones* (November–December 2007), http://www.motherjones.com/politics/2007/10/50-year-strategy-new-progressive-era-no-really. Deirdre Martínez, *Who Speaks for Hispanics? Hispanic Interest Groups in Washington* (Albany: State University of New York Press, 2009), 32–33.

26 Tony Castro, *Chicano Power: The Emergence of Mexican Americans* (New York: Saturday Review Press, 1974), 103, 199–201; Richard A. Santillán, *La Raza Unida* (Los Angeles, CA: Tlaquila, 1973), 80–81.

27 Frank Del Olmo, "Watergate Panel Calls 4 Mexican Americans," *Los Angeles Times* (June 5, 1974). Report of the Senate Select Committee on Presidential Activities, *The Senate Watergate Reports*, Vol. 1 (New York: Dell, 1974), 345–72. Castro, *Chicano Power*, 7–8, 202–3, 210. See also "La Raza Platform Prohibits Support of Non-Chicanos," *Los Angeles Times* (July 4, 1972). Cindy Parmenter, "La Raza Unida Plans Outlined," *Denver Post* (June 20, 1974). Jim Wood,

"La Raza Sought Nixon Cash," *San Antonio Express* (November 18, 1973).

28 "Top Woman Aide Gets U.S. Latin Position," *Los Angeles Times* (March 8, 1977). "Spanish-Speaking Aide Hits Cutbacks," *Santa Fe New Mexican* (March 26, 1973). Julia Moran, "The GOP Wants Us," *Nuestro* (August 1980), 26. Joe Holley, "Leading Texas Republican Anne Armstrong," *Washington Post* (July 31, 2008), http://www.washingtonpost.com/wp-dyn/content/article/2008/07/30/AR2008073002605.html. David Binder, "Charles (Bebe) Rebozo, 85; Longtime Nixon Confidant," *New York Times* (May 9, 1998).

29 Moran, "The GOP Wants Us," 26. Grace A. Franklin and Randall B. Ripley, *C.E.T.A.: Politics and Policy, 1973–1982* (Knoxville: University of Tennessee Press, 1984), 12, 67, 120.

30 Christine Marín, *A Spokesman of the Mexican American Movement: Rodolfo "Corky" Gonzales and the Fight for Chicano Liberation, 1966–1972* (San Francisco, CA: R&E Research Associates, 1977), 17. Kelly Simpson, "Defining 'Chicanismo' Since the 1969 Denver Youth Conference," KCET, March 24, 2016. https://www.kcet.org/history-society/defining-chicanismo-since-the-1969-denver-youth-conference "Corky" Gónzales and the National Chicano Youth Liberation Conference, Religious Left Law, March 27, 2017. http://www.religiousleftlaw.com/2017/03/corky-gonz%C3%A1les-and-the-national-chicano-youth-liberation-conference.html.

31 Armando Navarro, *La Raza Unida Party: A Chicano Challenge to the U.S. Two-Party Dictatorship* (Philadelphia, PA: Temple University Press, 2000), 95.

32 Armando Navarro, *La Raza Unida Party* (Philadelphia: Temple University Press, 2000), 42.

33 Ibid., 41–48, 153–56.

34 Ibid., 70. Naomi Helena Quiñonez, "Hijas De La Malinche (Malinche's Daughters): The Development of Social Agency Among Mexican American Women and the Emergence of First Wave Chicana Cultural Production" (PhD Dissertation, Claremont Graduate School, 1997), 175. Armando Navarro, *Mexican American Youth Organization: Avant-Garde of the Chicano Movement in Texas* (Austin: University of Texas Press, 1995), 75–83. Ignacio M. García, *United We Win: The Rise and Fall of La Raza Unida Party* (Tucson: Mexican American Studies & Research Center, University of Arizona, 1989). Evey Chapa, "Mujeres Por La Raza Unida," in A. García, ed., *Chicana Feminist Thought*, 178–79. "Early FBI File References to the 1970 LA Moratorium" (Ernesto Vigil FOIA FBI Documents Collection), https://library.ucsd.edu/dc/object/bb91481315/_1.pdf.

35 "Marta (Martha) Cotera," http://www.umich.edu/~ac213/student_projects05/cf/interview.html. Martha P. Cotera, *Diosa y Hembra: The History and Heritage of Chicanas in the U.S.* (Austin, TX: Information Systems Development, 1976). "Remembering a Revolutionary Mujer: Compañera Magdalena Mora," *¡La Verdad!*, http://uniondelbarrio.org/lvp/newspapers/97/janmay97/pg01.html. Rosaura Sánchez and Rosa Martínez, eds., *Essays on La Mujer* (Los Angeles: University of California Los Angeles Chicano Studies Research Center, 1977). Adelaida R. Del Castillo and Rosa M. Martinez, eds., *Mexican Women in the United States: Struggles Past and Present* (Los Angeles: University of California Los Angeles Chicano Studies Research Center, 1980). The latter two citations are among the first academic contributions on Chicana feminism.

36 Paul Saba (Transcription, Editing, and Markup), in the pamphlet, "Statements on the Founding of the League of Revolutionary Struggle (Marxist-Leninist)," *Encyclopedia of Anti-Revisionism On-Line*, 1978, https://www.marxists.org/history/erol/ncm-1a/atm-history.htm.

37 Guide to the Centro de Accion Social Autonomo Papers, 1963–1978, Special Collections M0325, Collection location Stanford University: Manuscripts Division, Online Archive of California, http://www.oac.cdlib.org/findaid/ark:/13030/tf587004hp/. Arnoldo Garcia, "Toward a Left without Borders: The Story of the Center for Autonomous Social Action," General Brotherhood of Workers, *Monthly Review*, July/August 2002, https://solidarity-us.org/pdfs/cadreschool/fws.garcia.pdf.

38 Castro, *Chicano Power*, 202. Ernesto Chávez, "Creating Aztlán: The Chicano Movement in Los Angeles, 1966–1978" (PhD Dissertation, University of California, Los Angeles, 1994), 152–53, 170–71. Mario T. García, *Memories of Chicano History: The Life and Narrative of Bert Corona* (Berkeley: University of California Press, 1994), 266–69; for Corona's story of what happened, see 308–15. Santillán, *La Raza Unida*, 84–86. Navarro, *La Raza Unida Party*, 46–49, 141–44. Carlos Muñoz, *Youth, Identity, Power: The Chicano Movement* (London: Verso, 1989) 108.

39 Navarro, *La Raza Unida Party*, 236–37. Jose Angel Gutierrez, *The Making of a Chicano Militant: Lessons from Cristal* (Madison: University of Wisconsin Press, 1999), important documents in Appendix, 215–240.

40 Gutierrez, *Making Militant*, 309–315.

41 Ibid., 41, 46–48. "Oral History Interview of Richard A. Santillán," 1989, by Carlos Vásquez, UCLA Special Collections. Chávez, in "Creating Aztlán," says that Santillán concluded that the Republicans funded

42. "William C. Velásquez: 1944–1988," Willie Velásquez Institute, http://www.wcvi.org/wcvbio.htm. Juan A. Sepúlveda, *Life and Times of Willie Velásquez: Su Voto Es Su Voz* (Houston, TX: Arte Público Press, 2005). Navarro, *La Raza Unida Party*, 70–71, 79.
43. Acuña, Rodolfo F. "Getting It Right," in *The Making of Chicana/o Studies: In the Trenches of Academe* (New Brunswick: Rutgers University Press, 2011), 143–63, http://www.jstor.org/stable/j.ctt5hj8kr.14.
44. Rodolfo F. Acuña, *The Making of Chicana/o Studies: In the Trenches of Academe* (New Brunswick: Rutgers University Press, 2011), 143–144. Tamar Lewin, "At Colleges, Women Are Leaving Men in the Dust," *New York Times*, July 9, 2006, https://www.nytimes.com/2006/07/09/education/09college.html. "New Report Looks at the Status of Women in Higher Education," *American Council on Education*, January 15, 2016. https://www.acenet.edu/news-room/Pages/New-Report-Looks-at-the-Status-of-Women-in-Higher-Education.aspx.
45. Emma Perez, *The Decolonial Imaginary: Writing Chicanas into History* (Indiana University Press, 1999).
46. Gloria Anzaldua, *Borderlands/La Frontera: The New Mestiza*, 4th Ed. (Aunt Lute Books, 2012).
47. The [Puerto Rican] Young Lords Party, Position Paper on Women (May 1971), *Palante*, 11–14, http://younglords.info/resources/position_paper_on_women.pdf. Young Lords Party, Position on Women's Liberation, *Palante* (May 1971), 16–17, http://younglords.info/resources/position_on_womens_liberation_may1971.pdf.
48. Enriqueta Vásquez, *Enriqueta Vásquez and the Chicano Movement: Writings from El Grito del Norte* (Houston, TX: Arte Público, 2006). Alma M. García, "The Development of Chicana Feminist Discourse, 1970–1980," *Gender & Society* 3, No. 2 (June 1989), 174, 218, 224, 232. Dionne Elaine Espinosa, "Pedagogies of Nationalism and Gender: Cultural Resistance in Selected Representational Practices of Chicana/o Movement Activists, 1967–1972" (PhD Dissertation, Cornell University, 1996), 149, 150, 152, 155. Enriqueta Vásquez, "The Woman of La Raza," *El Grito del Norte* (July 6, 1969). F. Arturo Rosales, *Chicano! The History of the Mexican American Civil Rights Movement* (Houston, TX: Arte Público Press, 1996), 183.
49. Letisia Marquez, "Mexican American integration slow, education stalled, study finds UCLA report charts Chicano experience over four decades," UCLA Newsroom, March 20, 2008. http://newsroom.ucla.edu/releases/ucla-study-of-four-generations-46372. Edward M. Telles and Vilma Ortiz, *Generations of Exclusion: Mexican-Americans, Assimilation, and Race* (Russell Sage Foundation, 2009), 176.
50. Telles, Ortiz, Ibid.
51. Ibid.
52. Maylei Blackwell, "Contested Histories: Las Hijas de Cuauhtémoc, Chicana Feminisms, and Print Culture in the Chicano Movement, 1968–1973," in Gabriela F. Arredondo, Aida Hurtado, Norma Klahn, Olga Nájera-Ramírez, and Patricia Zavella, eds., *Chicana Feminisms: A Critical Reader* (Duke University Press, 2003), 77–78.
53. "Lucy R. Moreno Collection, 1971–1997," University of Texas Austin, http://www.lib.utexas.edu/taro/utlac/00103/lac-00103.html. Vicki L. Ruiz, *From Out of the Shadows: Mexican Women in Twentieth-Century America* (New York: Oxford University Press, 1999), 108–9. Marta Cotera, "La Conferencia De Mujeres Por La Raza, Houston, Texas, 1971," in A. Garcia, ed., *Chicana Feminist Thought*, 155–57.
54. *Dictionary of Literary Biography* on Dorinda Moreno, *Book Rags*, http://www.bookrags.com/biography/dorinda-moreno-dlb/. "Flor Y Canto," University of Southern California 1973, http://readraza.com/florycanto/index.htm.
55. "Rosa Rosales, Interview by José Angel Gutiérrez," University of Texas Arlington, Tejano Voices, http://library.uta.edu/tejanovoices/xml/CMAS_045.xml. Key profiles, Bios & Links Blog, http://key-profiles.blogspot.com/2006/10/profile-rosa-rosales-lulac-national.html. President of LULAC on Homies Nation TV, http://www.youtube.com/watch?v=2JB63EseIJ4.
56. Rodolfo Acuña "Mexican American Studies: A Pedagogy Not Sociology," *Counterpunch*, June 15, 2012, https://www.counterpunch.org/2012/06/15/mexican-american-studies-a-pedagogy-not-sociology/.
57. Fabio Rojas, *From Black Power to Black Studies: How a Radical Social Movement Became an Academic Discipline* (Baltimore, MD: Johns Hopkins University Press, 2007), 79. SF State Third World Student Strike, http://www.youtube.com/watch?v=7ar2i-G5O-0&feature=related.
58. CSUN student political activism 1960s/70s "The Storm at Valley State," http://www.youtube.com/watch?v=NB3s_3RDEIc. On the Formation of Chicano Studies at Northridge see Miguel Durán, "Unrest," Documentary: Full Movie, http://www.youtube.com/watch?v=erf3j3UOmWE. Rodolfo F. Acuña, *The Making of Chicana/o Studies: In the Trenches of Academe* (New Brunswick: Rutgers University Press, 2011). Tlanavision, "Unrest," Documentary: Full Movie, https://www.youtube.com/watch?v=erf3j3UOmWE.

59 Javier Rangel, "The Educational Legacy of El Plan de Santa Barbara: An Interview with Reynaldo Macías," *Journal of Latinos and Education*, 6, No. 2 (2007), 192. Ruben Salazar, "Chicanos Set Their Goals in Education," *Los Angeles Times* (May 4, 1969), G8. *El Plan De Santa Bárbara: A Chicano Plan for Higher Education*, Analyses and Positions by the Chicano Coordinating Council on Higher Education (Oakland, CA: La Causa Publications, October 1969).

60 Acuña, *The Making of Chicana/o Studies*.

61 "Unrest" Documentary: Full Movie, https://www.youtube.com/watch?v=erf3j3UOmWE.

62 Adapted from Urban Education Inc., Office for Civil Rights Data, p. 130, Office of Civil Rights, Racial and Ethnic Enrollment Data from Institutions of Higher Education, Fall 1972, OCR-74-12 (U.S. Department of Heath, Education, and Welfare, 1974), 79–80, in Ronald W. López, Arturo Madrid-Barela, and Reynaldo Flores Macias, eds., *Chicanos in Higher Education: Status and Issues*. The National Commission on Higher Education, Monograph No. 7 (Los Angeles: Chicano Studies Center Publications, University of California, Los Angeles, 1976), 63–64, 67–68.

63 *Four Minorities and the Ph.D.: Ford Foundation Graduate Fellowships for Blacks, Chicanos, Puerto Ricans, and American Indians* (New York: Ford Foundation, October 1973), 3, 5.

64 Hilary N. Weaver, "The Colonial Context of Violence: Reflections on Violence in the Lives of Native American Women," *Journal of Interpersonal Violence*, September 3, 2008, https://doi.org/10.1177/0886260508323665.

65 "Cabinet Meeting Decisions" (Puerto Rico), October 6, 1960, Women in World History, http://chnm.gmu.edu/wwh/modules/lesson16/lesson16.php?menu=1&s=12. Harriet B. Presser, "Puerto Rico: The Role of Sterilization in Controlling Fertility," *Studies in Family Planning*, 1, No. 45 (September 1969), 8.

66 Norma Solis, "Do Doctors Abuse Low-Income Women?" *Chicano Times* (April 15–29, 1977). "Doctor Raps Sterilization of Indian Women," *Los Angeles Times* (May 22, 1977). "Puerto Rican Doctor Denounces Sterilization," *Sin Fronteras* (May 1976). Dr. Helen Rodrigues, head of pediatrics at Lincoln Hospital in San Francisco, said that by 1968, 35 percent of the women in Puerto Rico had been sterilized. See also Bernard Rosenfeld, Sidney M. Wolfe, and Robert E. McGarrah, Jr., *A Health Research Group Study on Surgical Sterilization: Present Abuses and Proposed Regulation* (Washington, DC: Public Citizens, 1973), 1, 7. Robert Kistler, "Women 'Pushed' into Sterilization, Doctor Charges," *Los Angeles Times* (December 2, 1974). See also Robert Kistler, "Many U.S. Rules on Sterilization Abuses Ignored Here," *Los Angeles Times* (December 3, 1974). Georgina Torres Rizk, "Sterilization Abuses Against Chicanos in Los Angeles" (Los Angeles Center for Law and Justice, December 2, 1976). Richard Siggins, "Coerced Sterilization: A National Civil Conspiracy to Commit Genocide upon the Poor?" (Chicago, IL: Loyola University School of Law, January 15, 1977), 12. Forced Sterilizations of American Indian Women, http://www.youtube.com/watch?v=WadjMamG4eQ. Reproductive Justice for Latinas: Coerced, Forced, and Involuntary Sterilization, http://www.youtube.com/watch?v=tShnkBmoe3Y.

67 Ronald B. Taylor, *Chávez and the Farm Workers* (Boston: Beacon Press, 1975), 278, 289. "A Boost for Chavez," *Newsweek* (May 26, 1975). "California Compromise," *Time* (May 19, 1975). "Chavez vs. the Teamsters: Farm Workers' Historic Vote," *U.S. News & World Report* (September 22, 1975), 82–83. American Friends Service Committee, *A Report of Research on the Wages of Migrant Farm Workers in Northwest Ohio* (July, August 1976), 1–9. Baldemar Velásquez, interview by Rodolfo Acuña, Toledo, Ohio, August 8, 1977. "Statement of Problem," *Farm Labor Organizing Committee Newsletter* (January 1977). "FLOC: Both a Union and a Movement," *Worker's Power* (May 9, 1977). Thomas Ruge, "Indiana Farm Workers, Legislative Coalition Fights H.B. 1306," *OLA* (April 1977). Jim Wasserman, "FLOC Goal Is Power Base for Migrants," *Fort Wayne Journal-Gazette* (September 14, 1976). Fran Leeper Buss, ed., *Forged Under the Sun/Forjada bajo el sol: The Life of Maria Elena Lucas* (Ann Arbor: University of Michigan Press, 1993). Anon., *The Struggle of the Texas Farm Workers' Union* (Chicago, IL: Vanguard Press, 1977), 4, 14–15. Ignacio M. García, "The Many Battles of Antonio Orendian," *Nuestro* (November 1979), 25–29.

68 Irene Ledesma, "Texas Newspapers and Chicana Worker's Activism, 1919–1974," *Western Historical Quarterly* 26, No. 3 (Fall 1995), 327 Laurie Coyle, Gail Hershatter, and Emily Honig, *Women at Farah: An Unfinished Story* (El Paso, TX: Reforma, 1979). Bill Finger, "Victoria Sobre Farah," *Southern Exposure* 4, Nos. 1–2 (1976), 5, 46, 47–49. Numerous articles ran in *San Antonio Express* and *El Paso Times* during 1972 and 1973 on the Farah strike, the boycott, and the closing of the plant. "Fury Stands Pat on Farah," *San Antonio Express* (December 14, 1973), is a solid article that lays out reasons for the bishops' support of the boycott. Laura E. Arroyo, "Industrial and Occupational Distribution of Chicana Workers," *Aztlán* 4, No. 2 (1973), 358–59. Philip Shabecoff,

"Farah Strike Has Become War of Attrition; The Worst Part," *New York Times* (June 16, 1973).

69 Peter Wiley and Robert Gottlieb, *Empires in the Sun* (Tucson: University of Arizona Press, 1982), 257, 265. Gay Young, "Gender Identification and Working-Class Solidarity Among Maquila Workers," in *Ciudad Juarez: Stereotypes and Realities*, in Vicki L. Ruiz and Susan Tiano, eds., *Women on the U.S.–Mexico Border: Responses to Change* (Boston: Allen & Unwin, 1987), 105–28. Devon Peña, "Tortuosiadad: Shop Floor Struggles of Female Maquiladoras Workers," in Ruiz and Tiano, *Responses to Change*, 129–54.

70 Chávez, "Creating Aztlán," 179–86, 199, 200–01. David G. Gutiérrez, *Walls and Mirrors: Mexican Americans, Mexican Immigrants, and the Politics of Ethnicity* (Berkeley: University of California Press, 1995), 191. David G. Gutiérrez, "Sin Fronteras? Chicanos, Mexican Americans, and the Emergence of the Contemporary Mexican Immigration Debate, 1968–1978," in David G. Gutiérrez, ed., *Between Two Worlds: Mexican Immigrants in the United States* (Wilmington, DE: Scholarly Resources, 1996), 175–209. M. García, *Bert Corona*, 290–95. Carlos Muñoz, Jr., *Youth, Identity, Power: The Chicano Movement* (London: Verso, 2007), 92–94. See Juan Gómez-Quiñones, *Chicano Politics: Reality and Promise 1940–1990* (Albuquerque: University of New Mexico Press, 1990). Gómez-Quiñones, *Mexican Students For La Raza: The Chicano Student Movement in Southern California 1967–1977* (Santa Barbara, CA: Editorial La Causa, 1978).

71 Jerry Kammer, " The Career of Vernon Briggs, Jr.: A Liberal Economist's Struggle to Reduce Immigration," *Center for Immigration Studies*, September 9, 2012, https://cis.org/Career-Vernon-Briggs-Jr.

72 Arthur F. Corwin, "Mexican-American History: An Assessment," *Pacific Historical Review* Vol. 42, No. 3 (Aug., 1973), pp. 269–308

73 Rodolfo F. Acuña, *Occupied America: A History of Chicanos*, 2nd ed. (New York: Harper & Row, 1981), 168–71. Vernon M. Briggs, "Labor Market Aspects of Mexican Migration to the United States," in Stanley R. Ross, ed., *Views Across the Border* (Albuquerque: University of New Mexico Press, 1979), 21, 211, 221. Ronald Bonaparte, "The Rodino Bill: An Example of Prejudice Toward Mexican Immigration to the United States," *Chicano Law Review* 2 (Summer 1975), 40–50. Frank Del Olmo, "Softer Penalties in Alien Cases Urged," *Los Angeles Times* (April 20, 1977). Arthur F. Corwin, *Letter to Henry Kissinger* (July 16, 1975), 2–3, 20, 21, 39; photocopy in possession of Professor Jorge Bustamante, University of Notre Dame, Indiana.

74 Stuart Hall, "Racist Ideologies and the Media," In Paul Marris, Sue Thornham, Caroline Basset, *Media Studies: A Reader* (New York: New York University Press, 2002), pp. 271–282.

75 David S. North and Marion Houston, "Illegal Aliens: Their Characteristics and Role in the U.S. Labor Market," study conducted for the U.S. Department of Labor by Linton and Co. (November 17, 1975). Vic Villalpando, "Abstract: A Study of the Impact of Illegal Aliens in the County of San Diego on Specific Socioeconomic Areas," in Antonio José Ríos-Bustamante, ed., *Immigration and Public Policy: Human Rights for Undocumented Workers and Their Families*, Chicano Studies Center Document No. 5 (Los Angeles: Chicano Studies Center Publications, University of California Los Angeles, 1977), 223–31. Jorge Bustamante, "The Impact of the Undocumented Immigration from Mexico on the U.S.–Mexican Economics: Preliminary Findings and Suggestions for Bilateral Cooperation," Forty-sixth Annual Meeting of the Southern Economic Association, Atlanta, Georgia, November 1976.

76 Rodolfo f. Acuña, "A Tolerance of Violence On the Border," *Znet*, June 20, 2005, http://rudyacuna.net/rodolfo-f-acuna-a-tolerance-of-violence-on-the-border-znet-june-20-2005/. Bill Curry, "Alien-Torture Case Ends in Mistrial for 2 Ranchers," *Los Angeles Times* (July 30, 1980). "Border Patrol under scrutiny for deadly force," *USA Today*, Nov. 14, 2012, https://www.usatoday.com/story/news/nation/2012/11/14/border-patrol-probe/1705737/.

77 Bill Curry, "Alien-Torture Case Ends in Mistrial for 2 Ranchers," *Los Angeles Times* (July 30, 1980). "The Nation; Judge Sets 3rd Trial in Alien Torture Case," *Los Angeles Times* (September 3, 1980). Tom Miller, *On the Border* (New York: Ace Books, 1981), 158–79. *Arizona Republic*, "Third Trial to Begin in Beating of Aliens: Two Arizona Ranchers Have Been Acquitted Once and a 2d Jury Could Not Reach a Verdict," *New York Times* (January 20, 1981). "Rancher in Plea to High Court in Case of Tortured Mexicans," *New York Times* (December 5, 1982). *United States of America, Plaintiff-Appellee, v. Patrick W. Hanigan, Defendant-Appellant*, No. 81-1262. 681 F2d 1127 (1982), http://openjurist.org/681/f2d/1127/united-states-v-w-hanigan.

78 James P. Sterba, "Carter Plan Would Give Amnesty To Illegal Aliens Already in U.S.," *New York Times*, April 18, 1977, https://www.nytimes.com/1977/04/18/archives/carter-plan-would-give-amnesty-to-illegal-aliens-already-in-us.html.

79 Rodolfo Acuña, *Anything But Mexican: Chicanos in Contemporary Los Angeles* (London: Verso, 1996), 31.

80 Gutiérrez, *Walls and Mirrors*, 199. David Reyes, "In Pursuit of the Latino American Dream," *Los Angeles Times* (July 24, 1983), Orange County section. Armando Navarro, *Mexicano Political Experience in Occupied Aztlán: Struggles and Change* (Lanham, MD: Altamira Press, 2005), 519. Jay Mathews, "Coors Campaign Splits Hispanics," *Washington Post*, November 16, 1984, https://www.washingtonpost.com/archive/business/1984/11/16/coors-campaign-splits-hispanics/b7f26da6-765e-48be-9c09-922b0594dc5a/?noredirect=on&utm_term=.bf52a07abee6.

81 Juan Gómez Quiñones, *Chicano Politics: Reality & Promise 1940–1990* (Albuquerque: University of New Mexico Press, 1990), 166. Moises Sándoval, "The Struggle Within LULAC," *Nuestro* (September 1979), 30. Navarro, *Mexicano Political Experience*, 519–22. Craig A. Kaplowitz, *Lulac, Mexican Americans, and National Policy* (College Station: Texas A&M University Press, 2005), 153, 194.

82 NALEO Education Fund, http://www.naleo.org/.

83 Congressional Hispanic Caucus Institute, http://www.chci.org/.

84 Keith J. Henderson, "Bilingual Education Programs Spawning Flood of Questions," *Albuquerque Journal* (June 11, 1978). Meyer Weinberg, *Minority Students: A Research Appraisal* (Washington, DC: U.S. Department of Health, Education and Welfare, 1977), 287. U.S. Commission on Civil Rights, *The Excluded Student: Educational Practices Affecting Mexican Americans in the Southwest*, Mexican American Education Study, Report iii (Washington, DC: Government Printing Office, 1972); bilingual education reached only 2.7 percent of the entire Chicano population. Rosalie Pedalino Porter, "The Case Against Bilingual Education: Why even Latino parents are rejecting a program designed for their children's benefit," *The Atlantic*, May 1998, https://www.theatlantic.com/magazine/archive/1998/05/the-case-against-bilingual-education/305426/

85 *Serrano v. Priest*, "Separate And Unequal: Serrano Played an Important Role in Development of School-District Policy," Find Law, http://corporate.findlaw.com/law-library/separate-and-unequal-serrano-played-an-important-role-in.html

86 *Serrano v. Priest*, 5 Cal. 3d 584; 96 Cal. Rptr. 601; 487 P.2d 1241 (1971). David C. Long, "Litigation Concerning Educational Finance," in Clifford P. Hooker, ed., *The Courts and Education* (Chicago, IL: University of Chicago, 1978), 221–29.

87 *San Antonio Independent School District v. Rodriguez*, 411 U.S. 1 (1973), Appeal from the United States District Court for the Western District of Texas, No. 71-1332 Argued: October 12, 1972—Decided: March 21, 1973. "Rodríguez v. San Antonio ISD," *Handbook of Texas Online*, http://www.tshaonline.org/handbook/online/articles/RR/jrrht.html.

88 Alexander W. Astin, *Minorities in American Higher Education* (San Francisco, CA: Jossey-Bass, 1982), 29. Meyer Weinberg, *A Chance to Learn: A History of Race and Education in the United States* (Cambridge, UK: Cambridge University Press, 1977), 164, 340–45. Thomas Carter and Roberto D. Segura, *Mexican Americans in School* (New York: College Examination Board, 1979), 233–35.

89 Rodolfo F. Acuña, *Sometimes There Is No Other Side: Chicanos and the Myth of Equality* (Notre Dame, IN: University of Notre Dame Press, 1998), 21–32. Minority Admissions Summer Project, sponsored by the National Lawyers Guild and the National Congress of Black Lawyers, *Affirmative Action in Crisis: A Handbook for Activists* (Detroit, 1977); hereafter referred to as *Minority Admissions*. Celeste Durant, "California Bar Exam—Pain and Trauma Twice a Year," *Los Angeles Times* (August 27, 1978). Robert Montoya, "Minority Health Professional Development: An Issue of Freedom of Choice for Young Anglo Health Professionals" (Paper presented at the Annual Convention of the American Medical Student Association, Atlanta, Georgia, March 4, 1978). *Regents of the University of California v. Bakke*, 438 U.S. 265 (1978); No. 76–811.

90 William Raspberry, "Minorities Have No Access," *Los Angeles Times* July 24, 1977; pg. I5. Thomas Muller, *California's Newest Immigrants: A Summary* (Washington, D.C.: Urban Insti-tute Press, 1984), ix–x, 7, 13, 28.

91 Stephen N. Keith, R. M. Bell, A. G. Swanson, and A. Williams, "Effects of Affirmative Action in Medical Schools: A Study of the Class of 1975," *New England Journal of Medicine* 313 (1985), 1519–25. Rodolfo F. Acuña, *U.S. Latinos Issues* (Westport, CT: Greenwood Press, 2004), Chapter 5 on affirmative action. Alex Liebman, "How'd That Guy Get In, Anyway?" *Argos* 1, No. 2 (Summer 1998); hyperlink no longer available. Delano R. Franklin and Samuel W. Zwickel, "Legacy Admit Rate Five Times That of Non-Legacies, Court Docs Show," *The Crimson*, June 20, 2018. https://www.thecrimson.com/article/2018/6/20/admissions-docs-legacy/

92 See Furillo, Andy, "Police Officials Won't Be Disciplined in Spying Case," *Los Angeles Times* (Jan. 11, 1985). Welkos, Robert, "L.A. Panel Votes to Open Some Police Files to Public," *Los Angeles Times* (1923–Current File); Los Angeles, Calif. [Los Angeles, Calif] May 10, 1983. I was a plaintiff in the suit and privy to discovery documents that

92 were sealed. José Angel Gutiérrez, *The Eagle Has Eyes: The FBI Surveillance of César Estrada Chávez of the United Farm Workers* (East Lansing: Michigan State University Press, 2019). Max Felker-Kantor, Groundbreaking work. *Policing Los Angeles: Race, Resistance, and the Rise of the LAPD* (Chapel Hill: University of North Carolina Press, 2018.

93 Jack T. Paxton, "An Old Gunny Remembers... The Swagger Stick," *Marine Corp*, Mar. 5, 2014, https://www.mca-marines.org/mcaf-blog/2014/02/28/old-gunny-remembers-swagger-stick.

94 "The Vietnam War," Wessels's Farming in the 60s & 70s, https://livinghistoryfarm.org/farminginthe50s/life_08.html.

95 Marc Jason Gilbert, *Why the North won the Vietnam War*, 1st ed. (New York: Palgrave, 2002). "Economic Consequences of War on the U.S. Economy," The Institute for Economics & Peace, http://economicsandpeace.org/wp-content/uploads/2015/06/The-Economic-Consequences-of-War-on-US-Economy_0.pdf.

96 "Oil Embargo, 1973–1974," Office of the Historian, https://history.state.gov/milestones/1969-1976/oil-embargo.

97 Ibid.

98 Classified U.S. State Department Documents on the Overthrow of Chilean President Salvador Allende, 1973, Peter Kornbluh, Chile and the United States: Declassified Documents Relating to the Military Coup, National Security Archive, New Declassified Details on Repression and U.S. Support for Military Dictatorship, http://www.gwu.edu/~nsarchiv/NSAEBB/NSAEBB185/index.htm. "New Kissinger, 'Telcons' Reveal Chile Plotting at Highest Levels of U.S. Government," National Security Archive Electronic Briefing Book No. 255, http://www.gwu.edu/~nsarchiv/NSAEBB/NSAEBB255/index.htm.

99 Rodolfo Acuña, "Impaction, What Goes Around Comes Around," rudyacuna.net, Feb. 15, 2015, http://rudyacuna.net/impaction-what-goes-around-comes-around/. Mark Provost, "Economy. Chile Is Doing Something Huge For Its Students That We Wish America Would Do," *Attn.*, Feb 10. 2015, http://www.attn.com/stories/836/chile-makes-college-tuition-free?utm_source=social&utm_medium=social&utm_campaign=usu. Milton Friedman, "Free Markets and the Generals," *Newsweek* (January 25, 1982), 59, http://0055d26.netsolhost.com/friedman/pdfs/newsweek/NW.01.25.1982.pdf.

100 Mark Provost, "Economy. Chile Is Doing Something Huge For Its Students That We Wish America Would Do," *Attn.*, Feb. 10, 2015, http://www.attn.com/stories/836/chile-makes-college-tuition-free?utm_source=social&utm_medium=social&utm_campaign=usu.

101 Jorge Fábrega, "Education: Three Years After Chile's Penguin Revolution," *Quarterly Las Américas*; from issue: *The Environment*, Fall 2009, http://www.americasquarterly.org/node/982/. "La Rebelion de los Pinguinos" (1/3), YouTube, https://www.youtube.com/watch?v=7oDTQlR1ZwE.

102 Jimmy Carter, "The President's News Conference," The American Presidency Project, UCSB January 17, 1979, http://www.presidency.ucsb.edu/ws/index.php?pid=32324.

103 "S. O. B.," http://www.youtube.com/watch?v=odRqoMZRm_Y. Anthony Lake, *Somoza Falling* (Boston: Houghton Mifflin, 1989), 94, 186, 260, 273. "Anastasio Somoza Debayle," http://www.youtube.com/watch?v=TDRWSFroSbk&feature=related. Bob Woodward. Veil: *The secret wars of the CIA, 1981–1987*. New York: Simon and Schuster, 1987.

104 Thomas Muller, *California's Newest Immigrants: A Summary* (Washington, D.C.: Urban Institute Press, 1984), ix–x, 7, 13, 28.

105 Homicide-Los Angeles, 1970–1979, *Morbidity and Mortality Weekly Report* 35, No. 5 (February 7, 1986), 61–65, http://www.cdc.gov/mmwr/preview/mmwrhtml/00000841.htm. "S. O. B.," http://www.youtube.com/watch?v=odRqoMZRm_Y. Anthony Lake, *Somoza Falling* (Boston: Houghton Mifflin, 1989), 94, 186, 260, 273. Anastasio Somoza Debayle, http://www.youtube.com/watch?v=TDRWSFroSbk&feature=related.

106 "People and Events: The Iranian Hostage Crisis, November 1979–January 1981," http://www.pbs.org/wgbh/amex/carter/peopleevents/e_hostage.html. U.S. Interventions: 1945–2000, http://www.metacafe.com/watch/1181268/u_s_interventions_1945_2000/.

Chapter 15
Blade Runner: Replicants are Illegal

 Learning Objectives

15.1 Summarize the circumstances that led to increased Mexican immigration and U.S xenophobia in the latter decades of the twentieth century.

15.2 Describe the impact of Reagan-era neoliberalism on U.S. inequality.

15.3 Analyze how government domestic and foreign policies changed immigration and immigrant experiences.

15.4 Compare U.S. attitudes to the Berlin Wall and the wall on the Mexican border.

15.5 Contextualize the struggles of Chicana/o organized labor in the 1980s and 1990s.

15.6 Describe Chicana/o movements for political representation in the 1980s and 1990s.

15.7 Characterize the struggles of Mexican women in the last decades of the twentieth century.

15.8 Differentiate Chicano/o experiences by U.S. region.

15.9 Explain how the debate over the preservation of Olvera Street reflected concerns about privatization.

The 1980s ushered in the presidency of Ronald Reagan and the ascension of Prime Minister Margaret Thatcher. The duo apostles of neoliberalism heralded the coming of a new global order. As in the game of *Monopoly*, any thinking person should have predicated the outcome. A single player ends up with all of the assets. Neoliberalism also recalled the 1920s that led to the collapse of the American Economy as the result of this game. Monopoly historically has led to financial meltdowns, and environmental disasters putting societies on the brink of collapse. Neoliberalism was the capitalist dream that societies would be managed by an oligarchy that would promoted a deregulated global market. Popularized in the 1980s and 1990s, it justified inequality among nations and the haves and the have-nots. Elizabeth Martinez and Arnoldo García predicted that the "effects of neo-liberalism" are that "the rich grow richer and the poor grow poorer."[1] The term itself is not new and refers to the strategy defined in the nineteenth-century by French philosopher Auguste Comte (1798–1857). In the nineteenth century religious and economic liberty meaning changed and it became a justification of exploitation.

When it was reintroduced in the 1980s, critics predicted the outcome. It was ahistorical; it had already failed in nineteenth-century Mexico as well as during the U.S. Gilded Age of the post–Civil War era and the 1920s. Moreover, anyone who has ever played the game *Monopoly* knows how it ends "Winner Take All." It is no wonder that the latest neoliberalism is resulting in a growing stratification leading to growing homeless brought about by gentrification. Neoliberalism does not close the gaps between owner and renter; rather, just like *Monopoly*, it widens them. This inequality hit close to home when a student recently told me, "I will never be able to return to my *barrio*, I cannot afford it."

I looked around and saw that society had entered the Blade Runner stage.[2] Americans are obsessed with movies. They base their collective fears and their collective history on movies. *Blade Runner* (1982) is a science fiction movie about Los Angeles in 2019. It is a city that is falling apart—it is in complete disarray. A feeling of homelessness overshadows the film. Satirist Guillermo Gómez Peña says that "A sense of community rapidly shrinks, so does your sense of belonging to a city that no longer seems to like you. You begin to feel like a foreigner and internal exile: freaky Alice in techno-Wonderlandia; the Alien Caterpillar who inhaled . . . You become an orphan."[3] The gentrification of San Francisco is the movie *Blade Runner* set in words. According to Gómez-Peña, the invaders are the "zombie techies who make well over $200 grand a year, but behave not unlike obnoxious teenage frat boys" intent on driving out the alien replicants.[4]

Blade Runner is a nightmare about ethnic cleansing; according to Peña, San Francisco is in "the post-gentrification era." A special police force, called ICE, like the Blade Runners, run down and eliminate replicants—fictionalized, humanoid robots who are illegal. It does not take too much imagination to distinguish who the replicants are in real life.

A new version of the old game, "Monopoly for Millennials," has the tagline: "Forget real estate. You can't afford it anyway."[5] Anyone playing the neoliberal game in the 1980s could predict the end with the oligarchs winning everything and the so-called players "Going to Jail" or becoming homeless.

The Replicants in 1980

15.1 Summarize the circumstances that led to increased Mexican immigration and U.S xenophobia in the latter decades of the twentieth century.

The 1980 Census reported fewer than nine million Mexican Americans living in the United States The number grew to 12.6 million by 1989; and to 20.6 million by 2000. The population further increased from 22.4 million in 1990 to 35.3 million in 2000.[6] The growth underscores what Argentine Juan Bautista Alberdi said in 1853: that *Gobernar es poblar* (to govern is to populate). Alberdi called for liberal immigration policies;[7] immigration meant power. In Argentina, as in the United States, immigrants built a new nation on the graves of the Indigenous nations and built by the sweat of immigrants. In the United States,

> The decade of the 1970s ended a long period of economic growth based on a development model applied widely in the years after World War II. The fundamental aim of this model was to create and sustain internal markets that could serve as springboards for broader economic growth. In industrial nations, governments employed regulation, spending, and monetary policies to generate consumer demand capable of supporting mass production and sustained growth.[8]

Mexico attempted to emulate the U.S.'s post–World War II industrialization model that by the 1970s was coming apart. Mexico did not have a sufficient internal market or capital to sustain industrial growth. Thus, it abandoned the old model "in favor of a new economic model based on international trade." The reliance on foreign markets was bound to fail; the United States controlled these markets and the capital and manufacturing was being maintained on a global scale.[9] Mexico simply could not compete.

In the 1980s, Mexican immigration to the United States increased because of the collapse of the Mexican economy. At the same time, Central American civil wars, political instability, and economic hardship drove large numbers of Central Americans northward. The Central American population in the United States tripled to over a million people.[10] Almost instantly, immigrants became the public enemies of well-funded xenophobic organizations and a rabid press that criminalized Mexican and Central American immigrants.

From 1965 to 2000, 4.3 million persons of Mexican origin immigrated to the United States (undocumented immigrants numbered around 8.5 million). Violence and instability brought close to a million Central Americans to the United States during the 1980s, mostly from Guatemala, El Salvador, and Honduras. Many Central Americans benefited from Public Law 99-603 (Immigration Act of 1986), passed to control and deter undocumented immigration to the United States. It legalized undocumented persons who had been continuously unlawfully present since 1982, giving preference to agricultural workers, placing sanctions on employers who knowingly hired undocumented workers, and calling for increased enforcement at U.S. borders.

By the 1980s the lives of Mexican Americans as well as Latinos changed. Before this decade, the social mobility of Mexican Americans was based on jobs in heavy industry and government. In Los Angeles, plants operated included the Van Nuys General Motors Plant, South Gate General Motors, the Pinto Car Factory in Pico Rivera, Lockheed, Boeing Rocketdyne plants throughout the San Fernando Valley as well as shipyards in the Long Beach–San Pedro area.

Steel mills with a heavy Mexican/Latino workforce closed in places like South Chicago and Indiana. The 1980s saw many of these plants move abroad. The loss of good union paying jobs that paid double and triple the minimum wage was devastating. Jobs in light industry and the service sector replaced jobs in heavy industry. These were jobs that few American citizens took, with immigrant labor subsidizing light industry.

The expansion of farm employment and the growth of small industries during the 1980s attracted immigrants. These sectors paid minimum wages, and they generally did not provide health benefits. What was disturbing to many Americans was the skin color of many of the new immigrants. The speaking of Spanish and commercial signs in a foreign language sent the message that the body snatchers had arrived!

The Immigration Act of 1965 also allowed more political refugees to enter the country. As a result, the foreign-born population increased from 9.6 million in 1970 to 22.8 million in 1994—a jump of 137 percent. In 1988, 43 percent of authorized immigrants were from Latin America, 41 percent from Asia, and only 10 percent from Europe. By 2015, there were 43.2 million immigrants, making up 13.4 percent of the United States Increased numbers of darker-skinned people who spoke foreign languages triggered xenophobia that right-wing think tanks and foundations as well as fanatics and conservative extremists exploited to make a lot of money.[11]

The Decade of the Hispanic

15.2 Describe the impact of Reagan-era neoliberalism on U.S. inequality.

The National Council of La Raza President Raul Yzaguirre christened the 1980s "the Decade of the Hispanic," suggesting that Mexican Americans would reap the fruits of their struggle for equality based on the logic that they were too big to fail. Congressional Representative Edward R. Roybal[12] at the G.I. Forum Convention immediately debunked the Yzaguirre forecast:

> We have been told over and over that the 1980s will be the Decade of the Hispanics. But, we all remember we were told the same thing at the start of the 1970s. The real answer, my friends, is that we have no clout.[13]

The theme of the G.I. Forum conference was, appropriately, "Merchandising the Mexican American Market in the United States."[14] California elected one Mexican American congressman, and in Los Angeles, the second-largest Mexican city in the world, at the beginning of the decade there was no Mexican representation at the city or county levels.

In reality, the growth of the Mexican American community carried baggage. The Decade of the Hispanic became the advertising logo for many Mexican/Latino elected officials and organizational leaders. They resembled a Greek chorus, they knew that the media paid attention to numbers, and actively exploited their inflated numbers to benefit their own brands. Often Hispanic Power was more an impression than a reality. The good was that political expectations raised issues about inequality.

Meanwhile, the election of Ronald Reagan ushered in neoliberalism, an era of privatization and conservatism; it intensified the war on the poor, immigrants, and unions. "Neoliberalism sees competition as the defining characteristic of human relations. It redefines citizens as consumers, whose democratic choices are best exercised by buying and selling, a process that rewards merit and punishes inefficiency. It maintains that 'the market' delivers benefits that could never be 'achieved by planning.'"[15] It was a return to the nineteenth-century survival of the fittest and it widened inequality in America.

Former Secretary of Labor under Bill Clinton, Robert B. Reich, underscores the growing wage inequality and the structural problems generated by inequality.[16] Reich blames the problems on the concentration of wealth in the hands of a small percentage of Americans. The wealthy, according to Reich, reaped inordinate benefits from a growing economy and middle-class wages stopped climbing. Meanwhile, the rich spent only a fraction of their fortunes to grow the economy. The federal government, instead of restructuring and narrowing the wage gap, deregulated, privatized, and mythicized the powers of a free market. Americans compensated by working longer hours, sent more women to work, and borrowed more to make ends meet. They used their home as collateral, if they had one. The increased pressure made people angry and they looked for scapegoats. The irony was that they chose victims that, like women, subsidized the economy.

Mexican American leaders were too busy trying to get elected to shed much light on structural flaws of the economy. The deindustrialization of the economy, specifically the downsizing of heavy manufacturing, was a blow to the working class.[17] Factories historically provided stepping stones to the middle class. Mexican Americans and Latinos subsidized a new light industry economy that competed globally. Education became a target for neoliberalism—the source of enormous profits. Meanwhile, immigrant children school attendance kept schools open from kindergarten through college.[18]

> The debt when Reagan entered office was just over $900 billion, not historically high in constant dollars or as a percent of GDP, but by the time Reagan left office it had almost tripled in nominal terms, and in percent of GDP it had gone from 33.4 percent to 51.9 percent. At the end of his term, the debt stood at $2.6 trillion, with a substantial portion of it contributed by Reagan's own policies: a mountain over 160 miles high in loose or tight bricks.[19]

Republicans abandoned their priority of a balanced budget by spiking tax cuts for the rich while conflating them with tax cuts for the middle class, providing a rationalization that "allowed them to go against opinion polls [that] had shown strong and consistent opposition to deficits."[20] Neoliberalism dramatically accelerated inequality by cutting wages, benefits, and extending the age of retirement for wage earners in order to cut taxes for the rich.[21]

Reagan's policies of privatization and deregulation set a template for nearly 40 years of limiting and in many cases dismantling access to the professions, not only for minorities but also for whites. The costs for production were shifted to the middle class and poor in the form of increased tuition fees, privatized government services, profit-based education, and the loss of jobs as government became part of the marketplace.[22] "The privatisation or marketisation of public services such as energy, water, trains, health, education, roads and prisons has enabled corporations to set up tollbooths in front of essential assets and charge rent, either to citizens or to government, for their use."[23]

Immigrants Keep the Economy Going

15.3 Analyze how government domestic and foreign policies changed immigration and immigrant experiences.

The Immigration Act of 1965 opened the door for non-white groups. The preferred destinations of 70 percent of these immigrants were just seven states—California, New York, Florida, Texas, New Jersey, Illinois, and Massachusetts. As mentioned, the new immigrants were in larger numbers darker-skinned people. Immediately there was rise in xenophobia Right-wing think tanks and foundations, as well as politicians running for office appealed to hate. They built their organizations careers on fear—and made a lot of money in the process.[24]

The Central American Wave

Prior to the Central American civil wars, there was a population explosion in Central America. From 1950 to 1990, the region swelled from just over nine million to almost 29 million. The populations of El Salvador and Guatemala went from 5.3 million to 9.1 million in 1990. The population explosion led to a flight to the cities, as farming became nearly impossible owing to monopolization of the land by elite families and foreign coffee and banana conglomerates. For example, U.S. corporations owned 400,000 acres in Honduras—land obtained free in deals with friendly dictators at the beginning of the twentieth century. Owing to the lack of a manufacturing infrastructure, the cities could not absorb displaced Salvadorans and Guatemalans. Inequality produced unrest and civil wars. In Salvador, an estimated 5–20 percent of the total population fled to the United States.[25]

U.S. interventionist policy was a major cause of the diaspora. As mentioned, the fall of U.S.-anointed Nicaraguan dictator Anastasio Somoza in 1979 set off civil wars throughout Central America. The Somoza overthrow weakened North American hegemony, and set off a domino effect in Central America.

El Salvador was in a state of flux. In 1932, Farabundo Martí, supported by the Communist Party, led a revolt that the Salvadoran military sadistically suppressed. More than 12,000 peasants, mostly Indigenous, died and Martí was murdered. During the 1960s, under the influence of Liberation Theology,[26] Catholic clergy and lay persons formed base, grassroots biblical communities that questioned inequality; many peasants were politicized by these communities. Elite groups reacted negatively, and in the early 1970s, the ruling elite held elections and supported the rise of Roberto D'Aubuisson, a neo-Nazi, who led death squads in a campaign of terror.[27] In 1977, D'Aubuisson's White Warriors machine-gunned Jesuit Father Rutilio Grande and ordered all Jesuits out of the country. Archbishop Oscar Romero spoke out against injustice, and in 1980, he was murdered while celebrating mass. That year, the Salvadoran National Guard tortured, raped, and killed four North American churchwomen.[28]

In 1980, a coalition of Christian Democrats, Social Democrats, minor parties, trade unions, students, and others formed the *Frente Democrático Revolucionario* (FDR) and joined hands with the *Farabundo Martí Liberación Nacional* (FMLN). To appease these groups and give the government an air of legitimacy, a centrist party won the national presidential elections. Meanwhile, the ultra-right controlled the legislature. The United States financed military operations against the FMLN. Some 50,000 Salvadorans—mostly civilians—were killed. Unable to find peace at home, hundreds of thousands of Salvadorans fled north.

The U.S. government sent the Salvadoran military $4.2 billion to conduct the war, destroying any semblance of a free market. The military, through the Arena Party, controlled a large bloc of votes during the 1991 elections—which it won by committing gross fraud. The warring factions signed peace accords that year.[29]

In Nicaragua, the Sandinista National Liberation Front (*Frente Sandinista de Liberación Nacional*, or FSLN) successfully set up a revolutionary government.[30] The United States labeled it a Communist state and a threat to the United States, and supported the Counterrevolutionaries (Nicaragua numbered 2.4 million people. The United States numbered 226.6 million people in 1980). The United States intensified the war, stating that Nicaragua was a threat to the security of the United States and that it was supplying arms to El Salvador. Ronald Reagan's 1980 election escalated the war against the Sandinistas. Reagan stationed 2,000 troops in Honduras, where the CIA and the Contras (the ultra-right opposition)—led military operations against the Nicaraguan government. The CIA violated the Boland Amendment that prohibited the use of U.S. funds to overthrow a foreign government.[31]

Reagan insisted that Soviet and Cuban influence in Nicaragua threatened U.S. security. As they did in Guatemala (1954), the Dominican Republic (1963–1965), and Chile (September 11, 1973), the United States attempted to overthrow the Nicaraguan government. In 1984, the Sandinistas held elections. Western European and Latin American nations praised the elections as being open;

Reagan labeled them a sham. Reagan and then George H. W. Bush isolated Nicaragua, and in 1990, the Nicaraguan people, weary of war, voted for the United Nicaraguan Opposition.

The Sandinistas gave up power peacefully, ending the dirty little war that led to an indictment of Ronald Reagan's former Defense Secretary Caspar W. Weinberger on charges that he lied to Congress, claiming no knowledge of U.S. arms sales to Iran or enlisting other countries to help underwrite the Nicaraguan War. The CIA was accused of allowing the Contras to ship illegal drugs to the United States to be sold and the proceeds used by Contra leaders to buy arms. President George H. W. Bush pardoned Weinberger and five others, preventing an adjudication of evidence that Bush, while he was Reagan's vice president, was involved in the conspiracy. The media called this unconstitutional operation *Iran Contra*.[32]

During 1966–1968, President Lyndon Johnson sent Green Berets to Guatemala, to train government forces against insurgents. Government troops crushed the revolution that resurged in the 1980s. Knowing the peasants supported the rebels, the military burned Indigenous villages, enclosing the natives into key cities. A secret army unit, U.S.-financed and -trained, operated in the countryside, kidnapping, torturing, and executing Guatemalans suspected of subversion. This was the longest and bloodiest butchery in Central America, killing more than 200,000 people. Over 50,000 disappeared in a nation of 11 million. The war displaced about a million and a half Guatemalan peasants during this "permanent counterinsurgency" against the nation's five million Maya.[33]

The Invasion of the Body Snatchers

Neoliberalism transformed the Mexican and world economies that were in the midst of this change. After decades of a Keynesian compromise, the goals of full employment, education, and healthcare were suffocated by the policy of stopping the spread of Communism.[34] Mexico was unprepared, caught in the middle and unable to cope with this transformation, resulting in the collapse of local economies. Neoliberalism changed the old rules, which were set aside much like old monopoly rules, substituting a new set of values that changed real estate to finance and local markets to international (global) enterprises.

Attending an immigration conference in Guanajuato in the early 1980s to which a Mexican academic invited me, I had breakfast at El Presidente Hotel, which was noted for its buffet. Waiting for my friend to arrive, I was surprised when he walked in with an entourage: his wife, two children, and his sister-in-law and her two children. I later asked him who was paying for all of these frills. I was surprised when he answered that the Mexican government was: It was not costing it a cent because it was borrowing money that would inflate and by the time the note came due the repayment would be 50 cents on the dollar.

"Between 1975 and 1995, the nation [Mexico] experienced recurrent currency, debt and banking crises with devastating effects on real economic activity."[35] An international crisis devastated Mexico's economy in 1982. Outgoing President José López Portillo dramatically stated in 1981, "Defenderé el peso como un perro!" ("I will defend the peso like a dog!")[36] The devalued peso plunged from 12.5 pesos to the dollar to more than 700 pesos to the dollar in the next three years. The reason for the devaluation was supposedly to stop the flight of dollars from Mexico.

The country's external debt, both private and public, climbed to $85 billion. Mexico needed dollars to pay its 1986 debts, which approached $100 billion. In 1978 the minimum wage in Ciudad Juárez was 125 pesos ($5.30) a day. Three years later 600 *maquiladoras* (assembly plants) operated south of the border; 90 percent were along the border. They employed 130,000 workers, 75–90 percent of them women, 70 percent of whom were single. The system employed 80,000 workers in Juárez and another 5,000 white-collar jobs in El Paso. Mexican *maquila* wages averaged $2 an hour in 1982 before the devaluation; by 1987, Mexican workers averaged $0.67 an hour, lower than Asian wages. The year before a *maquiladora* tsunami hit Juárez. Corporations like General Motors assembled wire harnesses, maintaining large operations all along the border. Low wages and cheap transportation to American markets made the *maquilas* highly profitable.

In order to pay off its debts to the World Bank and International Monetary Fund, Mexico borrowed heavily even before the crash. By 1986, Mexico defaulted on the loans and declared a repayment moratorium. Meanwhile, Mexico's domestic situation worsened—and soon it could no longer comply with the International Monetary Fund (IMF) demands without facing severe internal consequences. The situation seemed hopeless after a nearly 50 percent plunge in the price of oil that amounted to 70 percent of Mexico's export exchange and 50 percent of government revenues.[37] The crisis pushed Mexicans north and it was not uncommon to find Mexican medical doctors working in the United States as busboys. This was the intended result as labor was reduced to the status of a machine.

Films like *The Invasion of the Body Snatchers* were produced in the 1980s worsening America's historical anxiety. It was similar to watching the Zombie movies of the 1950s. In the the last 1970s and 1980s, over two hundred slasher movies were produced and among them *Halloween* (1978) and *Friday the 13th* (1980) that seemed intent on scaring people and bringing about "a general national anxiety toward radiation and conformity, both communist and anticommunist." These movies came at a time of change: a rise in anti-Communism and the movement of minorities to the suburbs. The analogy could be extended to immigrants. In the case of immigrants, the film *Get Out* (2017) produced much the same effect on white Americans.[38] The audiences' fear reached its climax during anticipated scary situations.[39] In the case of white suburban women, the manufactured fear was that the inner city would swallow them up and dark men would stalk them. The fear is as irrational as the fear that unauthorized immigrants were taking "white" jobs or that immigrants wanted to steal their "American Dream." This fear led them to accept propaganda as news and reject facts such as the 1984 Urban Institute of Washington's report that 645,000 jobs were created in Los Angeles County since 1970; that immigrants took about one-third of the jobs. Forgotten is that without immigrants, the factories hiring them would have shut down and left the area, resulting in the loss of higher-paying jobs.[40]

Nativists, oblivious to their own mediocrity and how American economic policies had necessitated immigration, became more strident in 1986, as Californians passed the "English Is the Official Language" Proposition 63 by a 3 to 1 margin. The campaign to pass Prop 63 was based on half-truths, lies, and hate. Within a year, seven other states passed similar measures, and 31 more considered English-Only measures. Yeshiva University Psychology professor Joshua Fishman questioned the good faith and concern for the "functional protection of English." He asked how English was endangered in a country where 97 percent of the population spoke the language. Fishman raised the possibility of a "hidden agenda."[41]

Congress passed the Immigration Reform and Control Act (IRCA), a compromise that included employer sanctions as well as amnesty for unauthorized immigrants who were residents since January 1, 1981, or could prove they had done farm work for 90 days, from May 1, 1985, to May 1, 1986. By January 1989, some 2.96 million applied for amnesty (about 70 percent of them were Mexican). IRCA allocated $1 billion a year for four years to fund English, U.S. history, and government classes to be administered by the State Legislation Impact Assistance Grant. The classes were mandatory for all amnesty applicants, and organizations such as *Hermandad Mexicana Nacional* and One-Stop Immigration hoped to use the funds to teach the new immigrants English and assimilate them into the social and political life of Mexican Americans. The anti-amnesty forces were led by foundations such as the American Immigration Control Foundation (AICF) and the Federation for American Immigration Reform (FAIR) whose opposition was ideological rather than rational. The Center for New Community reported:

> Much of the AICF leadership crosses the thin ideological line separating xenophobic nativism and outright white nationalism. Former AICF board chair Sam Francis (1992–1995), for example, is well-known for his racist and biological determinist positions. Longtime AICF board member Brent Nelson is on the Editorial Advisory Board of the *Citizens Informer*, the flagship publication of the white nationalist Council of Conservative Citizens (C of CC) and often pens articles for this publication, as does AICF President and Immigration Watch editor John Vinson. Moreover AICF has received strong financial support from the Pioneer Fund, a foundation which has been linked to eugenics and other "racial" research.[42]

Elected officials, like parasites, pecked down: They had nothing to lose and a lot to gain by spreading panic. Their plan was to attract big funds from right-wing foundations and small donations from frightened white individuals. Dallas Mayor Pro Tem Jim Hart broadcast that aliens had "no moral values," and that they were destroying Dallas neighborhoods and threatening the security of the city. California Congressman Elton Gallegly (R–Simi Valley) proposed a constitutional amendment to deny citizenship to U.S.-born children of undocumented immigrants. California Representative Anthony Bielenson (D–San Fernando Valley), considered a liberal Democrat, raised the bogus prospect of a Mexican invasion.[43] This tension emboldened far-right racists. A hate campaign was conducted to dump California Supreme Court Justice Rose Bird and Associate Justices Joseph Grodin and Cruz Reynoso, a highly respected Chicano jurist with a long history of involvement in public interest law. Nativists lied about the justices' votes against the death penalty. They intentionally increased public angst and hatred. *Los Angeles Times* columnist Frank de Olmo said of the campaign to remove Reynoso:

> The campaign against Reynoso and his colleagues, including Chief Justice Rose Elizabeth Bird, is being pushed by law-and-order advocates who claim that the "liberal" justices are lenient on crime. It has been waged for several years and has been analyzed more than any other issue on the state ballot—except for a troubling undercurrent that Californians have become too polite to discuss openly: racism.
>
> I don't mean the ugly racism that motivates some people to burn crosses. The campaign against Reynoso is more subtle. It indirectly suggests that because Reynoso came from a large family of farm workers he is not quite as capable as judges with a different (that is, "better") social background. And it slyly hints that a Mexican-American judge can't analyze cases affecting poor people dispassionately.[44]

The Backlash

15.4 Compare U.S. attitudes to the Berlin Wall and the wall on the Mexican border.

In July 1978, CIA Director William Colby was asked, what the "greatest threat to America was today?" Reporters anticipated that Colby would respond China, the USSR, or a similar rival. Instead, Colby said "the most obvious threat is . . . that there are sixty million Mexicans today [and there will be] one-hundred-twenty million [at] the end of the century [and] there are seven to eight million . . . In the

United States today." Colby added, "[The Border Patrol] will not have enough bullets to stop them."[45]

By the 1990s, there was growing militancy among immigrant students whose undocumented parents had brought them to the United States. They, however, were brought up in the United States under the illusion that it was a democracy. Until the 1990s, California colleges and universities allowed undocumented immigrant students to attend as if they were citizens if they could show residence for a year and a day when they applied and declare that they intended to make California their residence. An outcome was the successful lawsuit *Leticia A. v. Board of Regents* (1985), brought against the University of California and the California State University Systems, for the right of undocumented students to attend as residents.

Immediately the xenophobes began circling and a UCLA employee named David Paul Bradford sued the University of California, alleging that he was coerced to quit because he would not implement the *Leticia A.* ruling. By 1991 the courts found in favor of Bradford; many *Leticia A.* supporters justifiably claimed that the UC system folded under intense right-wing pressure. The University of California said that after June of 1991 it would classify undocumented students as non-residents. In 1992, the California Student Aid Commission followed Bradford's led and stopped awarding Cal Grants to undocumented students. The California Community Colleges (CCCs) adopted the UC policy although they were not mentioned in the Bradford ruling. The CSU appealed the decision but lost, and in 1995 began implementing it. Many *Leticia A.* supporters believed that all was lost with the passage of California Proposition 187 in 1994. However, a nucleus of activism was growing daily that did not give up hope or abandon its dreams.

La Zorra Nunca Se Ve Su Cola (The Fox Tail Never Sees His Own Tail)

The Berlin Wall, separating East and West Germany, came down in 1989. A year later, the U.S. Defense Department built an 11-mile fence in the San Diego area, allegedly as part of its War on Drugs. Two years later, the Army Corps of Engineers announced plans to place floodlights along a 13-mile strip of border near San Diego to "deter drug smugglers and illegal aliens." A 1992 *Atlantic* piece wrote, "It would not require much killing: the Soviets sealed their borders for decades without an excessive expenditure of ammunition," adding that a systematic policy of shooting illegal immigrants would deter most Mexicans, but "adopting such a policy is not a choice most Americans would make. Of course, there would be no question of free trade."[46]

The Berlin Wall (Berliner Mauer) was symbolic of America's walled society, on which construction began in 1961. The Berlin Wall was guarded by towers and armed men. Those building the wall claimed that it was built to keep the people from fascist elements in West Germany from infiltrating East Germany. In fact, it was built to stop the massive out-emigration and defection that caused a massive brain drain from East Germany. The capitalist world condemned the Berlin Wall and referred to it as the "Wall of Shame." Over time it came to symbolize the "Iron Curtain" separating the Western and Eastern Blocs.

Critics saw the Iron Curtain for what it was, but viewed the walls to keep Mexicans out differently. Instead of a wall, they called it a border fence. They rationalized that it was necessary to check the flow of "illegal Immigrants" into the United States, forgetting that in the summer of 1963, President John F. Kennedy visited Berlin and told the world, "Let Them Come to Berlin":

> There are many people in the world who really don't understand, or say they don't, what is the great issue between the free world and the Communist world. Let them come to Berlin. There are some who say that communism is the wave of the future. Let them come to Berlin. And there are some who say in Europe and elsewhere we can work with the Communists. Let them come to Berlin. And there are even a few who say that it is true that communism is an evil system, but it permits us to make economic progress. Lass'sie nach Berlin kommen. Let them come to Berlin.[47]

The Berlin Wall became a symbol of the free movement of people. On May 18, 1987 President Ronald Reagan shouted at General Secretary Gorbachev, "if you seek peace, if you seek prosperity for the Soviet Union and eastern Europe, if you seek liberalization, come here to this gate. Mr. Gorbachev, open this gate. Mr. Gorbachev, Mr. Gorbachev, tear down this wall!"[48]

Many Americans lack a historical memory, forgetting that an estimated 171 people were killed or died attempting to escape the Berlin Wall between August 13, 1961 and November 9, 1989.[49] The hypocrisy did not escape former Mexican President Felipe Calderón (2006–2012), who compared the proposed U.S. border to the Berlin Wall. From 2010–2011, 183 Mexicans died on the Arizona border corridor; in 2009–2010, 253 died; and in 2004–2005, 282 perished. "The number of migrant deaths tallied at the border jumped 17% from 204 in the first seven months of 2016 to 232 migrant fatalities in 2017."[50]

President Bill Clinton, mindful of his 1980 defeat in the Arkansas gubernatorial election because he allegedly did not act quickly enough to put down a riot of Cuban inmates at Fort Chaffee, Arkansas, played Mr. Tough Guy and followed the policies of Reagan and George H. W. Bush. Like other presidents, Clinton manufactured a war against undocumented immigrants, ordering Attorney General Janet Reno to build blockades and conduct roundups in the El Paso and San Diego areas. By the end of the Clinton administration, San Diego was Ground Zero in the anti-immigrant war. The Clinton administration called it

"Operation Gatekeeper" (1995), sealing the border in western San Diego County and forcing undocumented immigrants to cross the deadly desert to the east. The government increasingly commingled crackdowns on immigrants and the war against drugs—falsely equating immigration and drug smuggling and thus further criminalizing the immigrant. However, immigration hysteria lessened considerably by 1998—partially because of improved economic conditions, but in good part because of the backlash within the Mexican American and other Latino communities.[51]

Mexican American Labor

15.5 Contextualize the struggles of Chicana/o organized labor in the 1980s and 1990s.

The poverty rate climbed throughout the late 1970s and 1980s and reached a 27-year high in 1991, with 35.7 million people living below the poverty line—the highest rate since 1964. Frequent economic recessions during the 1980s and early 1990s especially hurt women, most of whom had few job skills. From 1973 to 1990, the median salary of female heads-of-households under the age of 30 fell 32 percent in real dollars—over 50 percent of Mexicanas earned less than $10,000 annually. Close to 50 percent (47.7 percent) of Mexican households with an absent father lived in poverty; and close to 40 percent (37.3 percent) of Mexican-origin workers who did not have a high school education lived in poverty, versus 16.7 percent in the non-Latino community.

While the white population increased its college enrollment from 31.8 to 39.4 percent during the 1980s, and African American enrollment went from 27.6 to 33 percent, the Latino enrollment fell from 29.8 to 29 percent. Latino segregation, unlike Black school segregation that fluctuated within a narrow range over 25 years, kept increasing. In 1970, Black students attended schools that, on average, were 32 percent white; by 1994, it was 33.9 percent. At schools attended by Latino students, white enrollment went down—from 43.8 to 30.6 percent. The harshness of the new economy and the growing gap between the rich and poor did not escape Archbishop Roger Mahoney, who in 1985 said, "we cannot evaluate our economy primarily by the extraordinary opportunities it offers a few."[52]

History does not repeat itself; we forget the truth. During the 1950s, Republicans sought to dismantle the safety net built by the New Deal, though the memory of the Great Depression was still fresh. By the 1980s, the memories faded or were suppressed. Historical amnesia gave Reagan the opportunity that reactionaries had awaited for 40 years—to dismantle the safety nets to make the country "business friendly" again. In 1982 Reagan signed the Garn–St. Germain Depository Institutions Act, which lessened regulations on savings and loans and banks. According to Reagan, "This bill is the most important legislation for financial institutions in the last 50 years. It provides a long-term solution for troubled thrift institutions. . . . All in all, I think we hit the jackpot."[53]

Just a year before, in 1981, Reagan declared an all-out war on organized labor and fired 11,400 air traffic controllers, decertifying the Professional Air Traffic Controllers Organization (PATCO), and replacing them with scabs. As a result, labor was paralyzed. During 1980–1987, strike activity fell some 50 percent in certain unions, and the number of strikers replaced by scabs jumped 300 percent. The number of strikes "plummeted very sharply and employer willingness to hire permanent striker replacements seriously hampered cooperation between labor and management."[54] Union membership declined nationally, with overall union participation in the private sector falling below 15 percent. In the face of this, the trade union movement became more submissive, reluctant to strike or fight back.[55]

In eastern Arizona, the cradle of the Chicana/o labor movement, in July 1983, 13 unions, led by the Steelworkers' Local 616 at Clifton-Morenci, Arizona, struck the workers' old nemesis Phelps Dodge.[56] A confrontation followed as Phelps Dodge imported scabs to break the strike. The Reagan National Labor Relations Board (NLRB) sided with management, conducting a poll on whether to hold elections to certify or decertify the miners' union, and allowing only scabs to vote; it was no surprise when the outcome of the vote was to decertify the union. In August 1983 liberal Arizona Democratic Governor Bruce Babbitt sent the state National Guard to Morenci-Clifton to break a strike. The invasion included tanks and helicopters.

Babbitt busted the miners' union. The majority of miners were Mexican; the intervention shifted the union's majority to white. Greenlee County was historically Democrat, and now it became Republican. The mineworkers solicited support from outside the area. A ladies' auxiliary led by activists such as Jessie Téllez toured the Southwest, talking to Chicana/o and labor groups. Despite insurmountable odds, the miners continued to strike, facing eviction and harassment. However, by 1987, the Morenci strike that had been led by the union's president, Angel Rodríguez, was dead. Barbara Kingsolver, in her book *Holding the Line: Women in the Great Arizona Mine Strike of 1983*, captures the feelings of women who struggled for their space in the movement.[57]

The Return of the Sleeping Giant:

In the 1960s and 1970s, it was common for Mexican Americans to talk about the awakening of the Sleeping Giant. In the 1980s and 1990s, the term "Sleeping Giant" took on a broader and deeper significance. Bill Clinton's Housing and Urban Development Secretary Henry Cisneros commented in 2009 on the probability of a Latino president: "I don't know if he or she's in elementary school or in law school or is already elected . . . to public office, but I believe that that person is already alive and we're 20 years or less away from having a Latino or Latina president."[58] These changes point to the emergence of Latinos/Mexicans as a permanent part of American society, which is probably the greatest fear of white nationalists.

By 1980, the Mexican-origin population numbered 8.8 million. Internally, the foreign-born population of Mexican origin doubled during the 1970s. These numbers did not tell the entire story and the focus on immigrants often detracted from what was happening to the U.S.-born population. The growth of the Latino population cannot be attributed only to immigration. A major factor is high rates of Latina fertility that roughly half of all growth.[59]

> Once considered a sleeping giant, the Latino population has not only grown tremendously but also now constitutes a significant presence throughout most of the United States. Once confined to a small number of states, the Latino population has migrated to new regions, including much of the South, moved into new sectors of the economy, and become an important voting bloc in many states. Its impact is heightened by the fact that it is considerably younger than an aging non-Latino America, making its potential impact on America's future all the greater.[60]

Latino births increased in the 1980s and 1990s, from 44 percent of all growth to 52 percent.[61] This growth along with generational changes had far-reaching effects, especially since, at fertility rate among whites fell to the "lowest-low" in the United States and Europe.

The growth of Mexican/Latino, immigration and continued fertility, contributed to a youthful age structure that is important to an aging America. It predicts stability within a sizeable portion of the Latino and especially the Mexican American community that suggests a sizeable third generation. On average, Mexican Americans were and are younger than other major racial and ethnic groups. Mexican immigrant women ages 40 to 44 gave birth to an estimated one-third more children than the typical U.S.-born Mexican-American of the same age—2.7 versus 2.1.[62]

Structural changes brought about different needs and a prophesy of the future. This large influx of immigrants brought new memories that enriched the Mexican American community culturally. More communicated in Spanish and took cultural pride in not only foods but the arts and history. The biggest change was that people who often identified as Spanish in 1980 were increasing identifying as Indigenous. Because of the Chicana/o movement, more wanted to go to college and more went, although their numbers lagged behind white and other Americans.

Latin America Population and distance to the United States

A rough synthesis of where future Latin American immigration will come from depends on the country's size and distance from the United States. Below is a rough synthesis of the population of Latin America. Numbers and distance are important to a student of immigration. The statistics are from the CIA *World Factbook*, which despite its sponsors is accurate.[63]

United States	318,892,103	Distance
Brazil	202,656,788	4552 miles
Mexico	125,000,000	
Argentina	43,024,374	5610 miles
Colombia	46,245,297	2627 miles
Canada	34,834,841	0
Peru	30,147,935	3471 miles
Venezuela	28,868,486	2804 miles
Chile	17,363,894	5267 miles
Ecuador	15,654,411	2918 miles
Guatemala	14,647,083	1512 miles
Cuba	11,047,251	1521 miles
Dominican Republic	10,349,741	2001 miles
Honduras	8,598,561	1622 miles
Paraguay	6,703,860	4840 miles
El Salvador	6,125,512	1665 miles
Nicaragua	5,848,641	1797 miles
Costa Rica	4,755,234	2034 miles
Puerto Rico	3,620,897	2195 miles
Uruguay	3,332,972	5462 miles
Jamaica	2,930,050	1725 miles
U.S. Mexican origin	35,000,000	

Why Mexican Americans Fail to Organize

Recent studies by Ernesto Vigil and José Angel Gutiérrez on FBI and police surveillance are just hitting the tip of the iceberg.[64] An untouched aspect of this surveillance and disruption is that of local police agencies that are more difficult to monitor. At Cal State Northridge, their presence was noticeable from the late 1960s increasing as more minorities entered CSUN. Miguel Valenzuela was a brilliant person who had a sickness; he was addicted to drugs and had come to the college to turn his life around. Miko was a student assistant in Carlos Arce's *Language of the Barrio* class; his *retórica*, the use of *chuco*, was poetic. In another life Miko would have been a linguist, a university professor. One day, he looked despondent, so I asked him why. He confessed that he had done a terrible thing, according to him. The Devonshire police took him in and, in his words, "sweat me." They knew he had a monkey on his back and wanted him to tell them about me and the department. He said that he played loose with the truth because he wanted his fix. A week later, Miko overdosed in a Pacoima gas station restroom.[65]

On November 11, 1972, Chicana/o students caught Lt. Don Yelverton, a Black campus police officer, wiretapping a statewide MEChA conference at San Fernando Valley State. The campus police did it at the request of the Devonshire Division. CSUN President James Cleary denied the incident happened—he said it was a misunderstanding. According to Cleary, "Yelverton's actions Nov. 11 were within the scope of his authority."[66] The college chapter of the American Federation of Teachers hired Howard Berman to represent MEChA but he dropped the case to run for the California Assembly.

The American Civil Liberties Union sued the Los Angeles Police Department and uncovered widespread surveillance of activists and organizations.[67] MEChA and several Cal State Northridge professors were plaintiffs and were given access to documents yielded in discovery. The LAPD's Public Disorder Intelligence Department (PDID) unlawfully gathered intelligence in association with right-wing groups. LAPD Chief Daryl Gates knew about the agency malfeasance but was part of the cover-up. When it became evident to the public that the unit was operating beyond the restraints of the law, PDID officers illegally hid documents in cars and in private garages, and in many instances handed over documents to rings of right-wing cohorts. Because of the ACLU suit, the spy unit was disbanded and a new unit was formed that would only investigate *terrorists*.[68]

According to the *LA Times*, three officers spied on CSUN MEChA and the BSU from 1974 to 1979; the discovery documents that were not open to the public were read by the plaintiffs and suggest that there were at least six undercover officers taking Chicano Studies classes. The officers lived in the campus dorms. PDID officer Donald Rochon spied on the BSU and officers Augustine "Augie" Moreno and Joe Ramirez infiltrated MEChA and *La Raza Unida* Party. They attended MEChA meetings from 1976 through 1978.[69]

As a plaintiff, I reviewed the discovery documents and ran across an item filed by Rochon. According to his report, a meeting took place at a Jack in the Box restaurant near the campus on Reseda Blvd. Black and brown students attended the meeting. Rochon named members of the League of Revolutionary Struggle—he knew them, they were friends. According to Rochon, they talked about assassinating me. The plaintiffs were not supposed to discuss the reports other than with other plaintiffs. However, knowing some of these people since they were teens, I confronted one of the LRS members. He confirmed that there was a meeting and that there was criticism of me; however, he denied any talk of assassinating me or doing me bodily harm. After about two hours of discussion, I calmed down. We continued to talk, and that individual today is one of the most positive forces in the movement.[70]

As for me, I believed him—it was Rochon who to the last was planting a story to cause dissension. Moreover, if the alleged conspiracy took place, why hadn't the police informed me or campus authorities? Not to do so would have endangered not only my life but that of students and faculty. The story does not end there.

The last incident in the 1990s involved LA County Sheriff Lee Baca. I was caught off guard when I saw him at a fundraiser in Arcadia held by attorney Rees Lloyd, whose "Robin Hood Foundation in Glendale delights in dragging the rich and powerful into court on behalf of poor workers."[71] Rees was a character; he started the foundation to sue anyone who would stereotype the Welsh as being cheap and use stereotypes such as "he Welshed Out."' Rees was Welsh and Robin Hood was from Wales. He also sued on behalf of the farmworkers and César Chávez and helped me in my discrimination case against the University of California at Santa Barbara. He would saunter into court wearing a leather jack, helmet, and motorcycle boots.

I was surprised when I saw Sheriff Lee Baca at the event and he gave me a warm *abrazo* (hug). He was spying on the Chicano Movement and said he had been assigned to keep tabs on me. Baca said in retrospect, although there was no cause, the culture of the police at the time justified it. I concluded that if it happened at Northridge, there was a strong probability that it happened at Cal State LA, San Diego, El Paso, and at other Chicana/o Studies programs.

The New Breed

The 1980s were the beneficiary of the previous two decades. A new leadership emerged with many participating in student groups such as MEChA (Movimiento Estudiantil Chicanos de Aztlán) and MAYO (Mexican American Youth Organization). Many if not most activists were college educated. Moreover, because of their altruism, they transitioned from proponents of farmworkers' rights and protesting the war into supporting pro-immigrant rights—a transition that was intellectual as well as ethnic focused. Much of the new leadership were first-generation college students—the children of immigrants or immigrants themselves. They were key to changing the liberal attitude toward immigrants.

The new organizers were a natural fit for the growing militancy of immigrant workers. Products of the 1960s, they communicated with whites and African Americans. Many were students and came out of the Chicana/o student movement of the 1960s and 1970s. Hotel and restaurant labor had a core of Chicana/o activists. María Elena Durazo's parents were immigrants. Her interest in the protection of the foreign-born began when she was a student at St. Mary's College and member of CASA (Center for Autonomous Social Action). Durazo worked alongside Magdalena Mora, a dedicated UC Berkeley student from Mexico who died young of cancer. After working for the

International Ladies Garment Workers Union (ILGWU), Local 11, the Hotel Employees and Restaurant Employees Union (HERE) hired Durazo in 1983 as a worker representative. Four years later Durazo won the presidency of the local. The international organization put the local into receivership. In 1989, Durazo was again reelected president. Under her leadership, HERE took on business giants such as the Hyatt Hotel chain. The union returned to militant unionism, picketing and courting arrest to call attention to the plight of the workers. Local 11 relentlessly pressured politicos to support the union.[72]

Cleaning service sector immigrant workers were among the most vulnerable workforces. In the 1980s the union organized across the country. They fought for decent wages and medical health coverage. Membership in Los Angeles Local 399, Justice for Janitors, plunged 77 percent in the 1980s, and by 1987, only 1,500 janitors remained under contract. With the assistance of white and Mexican college graduates, the workers began to rebuild. Among the standout organizers were Salvadoran Ana Navarette and Chicana Patricia Recino. Navarette was active in the Salvadoran liberation struggle and Recino was a product of the Chicano student movement and social justice organizations since her teens.

Fearing permanent replacement, Local 399 adopted the strategy of going directly to the streets—making it financially dangerous for subcontractors to get in the union's way. Among the targets were Century City and the International Service System, Inc. (ISS), the world's largest commercial cleaning contractor. On May 15, 1990, 150 armed LAPD officers attacked janitors and their supporters. The officers gave the order to picketers to disperse—in English only. A police riot ensued, resulting in 40 arrests and 16 injuries, and two women had miscarriages after being beaten. The janitors sued the LAPD, and in September 1993 they settled for $2.35 million.[73]

Confrontational tactics sensationalized the injustices and helped union organizers in recruiting low-paid minority workers. The percentage of union janitors working in major Los Angeles commercial buildings rose from 10 percent in 1987 to 90 percent in the mid-1990s. However, tensions between the members and the union leadership surfaced. In June, a 21-member dissident slate called "Multiracial Alliance" won control of the union's executive board. Once in power, the dissident slate "cleaned house." Regretfully, it fired many leaders who contributed to the success of the union. The new Latino officers (Salvadoran, Guatemalan, and Mexican) accused the former leadership of paternalism and racism.

The international headquarters of the janitors' union responded by placing the local union in receivership and naming Mike García (a CSUN graduate)[74] of San Jose as the interim head. Most of the so-called dissidents left the union, because they won a fair election only to be overturned by the headquarters of the janitors' union. The old guard, in turn, believed that nationalism caused the rupture. In reality, the labor movement was largely to blame for this and other ruptures, for its failure to employ adequate resources to expand membership among immigrants and Mexicans/Latinos.[75]

In the 1970s, Los Angeles, once known as the Detroit of the West, employed 15,000 autoworkers producing a half million cars annually. Automakers suddenly began to dismantle their California operations; the Ford Pinto factory in Pico Rivera geared down, as did the General Motors plant in South Gate. By 1982, Van Nuys workers saw the handwriting on the wall. They knew it was only a matter of time before GM would shut down that plant.

Led by the United Auto Local 645 president, Pete Beltrán, the workers, and the community built a coalition that threatened a boycott if the GM plant was closed. Although the labor/community strategy bore fruit, the UAW International capitulated and sold workers on the notion that if they cooperated, the plant would remain open. In the summer of 1991, General Motors announced the shutdown of the Van Nuys plant. Some GM workers, forced to sell their houses, moved to other states where GM employed them, but others collected severance pay for a year while the community inherited a worsening economic situation as more businesses closed down.

Despite the closing, the "Keep G.M. Van Nuys" campaign was instrumental in forming the Labor/Community Strategy Center under the leadership of Eric Mann, who spearheaded the campaign to keep the plant open.[76] The center did outstanding environmental work. In 1992, the Strategy Center initiated a transportation policy group. Two years later, the group organized "Billions for Buses" campaign to confront the racism reflected in the policies of the Metropolitan Transportation Authority of Los Angeles (MTA). Membership in the Bus Riders Union grew to more than 3,000 dues-paying members and 50,000 self-identified members on the buses. Most of the riders were Latinos and women.[77]

Tear Off the Label

To repeat, undocumented immigrants saved agriculture as well as light industry in many large American cities. Many new arrivals from Mexico and Central America refused to go along with exploitive wages and conditions and they organized unions. As late as the 1980s, labor federations such as the Los Angeles County Federation of Labor lobbied to crack down on undocumented labor. However, the waves of immigrants changed this as many gained legal status. The new immigrants did what European immigrants did before and joined and formed trade unions. Moreover, a new class of organizers came on the scene; many were active in the 1960s.

In San Antonio, Texas, Levi Strauss, the world's largest apparel manufacturer, closed its plant in 1990, resulting in 1,100 layoffs. The plant, acquired in 1981, was the main domestic facility for the Dockers line of casual pants, which required twice the labor needed for jeans. The company produced $70 million worth of Dockers and Officers Corp jeans. The San Antonio plant earned record profits in 1989 when it was Levi's largest factory. To cut costs, Levi transferred work previously done in San Antonio to independent contractors in the Caribbean and Costa Rica, where wages ranged from 30 cents to $1 an hour, compared with $6–$7 per hour in the United States. The company notified workers 90 days before closing the plant, 30 days more than is required by law. Levi Strauss laid off 10,400 workers between 1981 and 1990, and it shut down 26 plants nationwide from 1985 to 1993. The city of San Antonio lost 10,000 jobs in 1990 alone.[78]

Virginia Castillo, a sewing machine operator at Levi Strauss, was still bitter four years after the San Antonio plant closed. The shutdown ended Castillo's employment of 16 years and began the unraveling of her life as a factory worker. She had limited job and language skills. Her health deteriorated owing to nerve damage to her back and wrists caused by factory work. Her marriage failed. Yet her experiences made Castillo a labor activist. She moved to San Francisco to take on Levi Strauss and to tell the world that, despite its socially conscious image and record of philanthropy, the company continued to exploit workers in the United States and abroad.

Castillo belonged to *Fuerza Unida* (United Strength), a 480-member group of former San Antonio Levi Strauss workers. *Hispanic* magazine voted Levi Strauss as one of the 100 best companies in the United States for Hispanic workers, and *Vista* magazine placed it among the top 50 companies for Latina women. The fact was that Levi Strauss did not act in a socially responsible manner toward the San Antonio workers. Most of the women lacked education. Paid on a piece rate, they worked extremely fast and hard. The shutdown caused vast unemployment. The women lost their homes and cars.[79]

Fuerza Unida claimed that Levi Strauss cheated the former employees of severance pay, profit sharing, and other compensation from pensions, vacation time, holiday overtime, and a $500 Christmas bonus promised to each employee the December before the layoffs. In total, the company owed the workers about $4 million. Levi Strauss responded that it compensated its former employees, and a federal lawsuit by *Fuerza Unida* was dismissed in 1993. Levi Strauss continued restructuring. In November 1997, Levi Strauss shut down 11 plants in the United States and laid off another 6,395 workers—one-third of its U.S. manufacturing force. According to former San Antonio workers, the 1997 shutdowns saved Levi Strauss $200 million. Even before the 1997 shutdowns, Levi made profits of $357 million on nearly $5 billion in sales in 1991. Closing their plant was not an economic necessity, the former workers say, but a tactic to earn more profits. Meanwhile, under the leadership of Chicanas, *Fuerza Unida* continued their fight-back campaign.[80]

Sabotaging Labor

A 1985 poll showed that 53 percent of the American public held a favorable opinion of César Chávez, and only 21 percent opposed him. Chávez's organizational problems were related to the length and intensity of the struggle. Personality clashes occurred over leadership and the direction of the union. Some wanted to deal solely with trade union issues while others wanted to become move involves with political issues. Others wanted to use more militant tactics. Compounding the UFW's woes, California Governor George Deukmejian, heavily indebted to agribusiness, torpedoed the Agricultural Labor Relations Board (ALRB) by appointing David Stirling, a hatchet man for the growers, as general counsel to the board. Under Stirling only 10 percent of the cases filed reached the ALRB, compared with 35 percent under the appointees of Governor Edmund G. Brown, Jr. Deukmejian cut the ALRB's budget by one-third; by 1986 the board became inoperative when it came totally under the growers' control because of the governor's appointees. Government and industrial growers conspired against the UFW.

President Reagan contributed to sabotaging the union and appointing John R. Norton—head of J. R. Norton Company, one of the largest lettuce producers of the world—as the U.S. deputy secretary of agriculture. Republican–grower complicity continued at the state and national levels throughout the administrations of California Governor Pete Wilson and President George H. W. Bush.

In 1985, 4,000 farmworkers walked out of the fields in the Imperial Valley. The growers hired armed guards and attack dogs that injured many strikers. A grower's car struck Isauro López and permanently crippled him. Thugs hired by growers shot Rufino Contreras through the head and killed him. Judge William Lehnhardt refused to disqualify himself, even though his wife had worked as a strikebreaker. Lehnhardt ruled the union was responsible for the violence and crop loss and did not prosecute growers' agents for murder. The union, on the other hand, raised $3.3 million to appeal this perversion of justice and waited for years to get its day in court. The UFW continued to struggle against enormous odds to organize workers.[81] Meanwhile, the success in organizing workers greatly depended on state regulation with right-to-work states such as Texas frustrating efforts to organize workers.

Adding to the challenge of organizing farmworkers was that the Mexican American community was not the same as in 1970. Other issues competed for resolutions.

Saint Ronald: The Seduction of the Political Game

15.6 Describe Chicana/o movements for political representation in the 1980s and 1990s.

The Reagan administration rigorously enforced the 1965 Voting Rights Act because it hurt Democrats and helped Republicans, not because he loved downtrodden minorities. He signed the 1982 amendment to the Act and his justice department vigorously enforced the law. Mexican Americans took full advantage of the 1965 Voting Rights Act and its amendments. As with labor leadership, Mexican/Latino candidates emerged from the activist core of the 1960s and 1970s.

The Southwest Voter Registration and Education Project (SVREP) and the Mexican American Legal Defense and Education Fund (MALDEF) were major players. The former registered Chicanos to vote, and the latter used court challenges to give them a fighting chance to exercise their franchise. MALDEF sued the city of Los Angeles for violations of the Voting Rights Acts in its redistricting plans; two Latino-friendly council districts resulted. Meanwhile, SVREP increased Mexican American registration from 488,000 in 1976 to over 1 million by 1985. The project published reports and analyses of Chicano voting potential and trends. Along with MALDEF and sympathetic lawyers, the SVREP challenged reapportionment and at-large voting practices that diluted the electoral strength of Latinos. Meanwhile, amendments to the Voting Rights Act in 1975 and 1982 made it easier for SVREP and MALDEF to persuade local municipalities to restructure their electoral units, *por las buenas o las malas* (literally, "the easy way or the hard way").[82]

By 1981, 19 Chicano candidates were elected to local offices in Salinas and the San Joaquín Valley. Latino population increased in 16 districts. The following year, Mario Obledo, former California Secretary of Health and Welfare and cofounder of MALDEF, with considerable credibility within the mainstream Mexican American community, decided to enter the Democratic Party primary for governor. Liberals criticized Obledo for running against Los Angeles Mayor Tom Bradley. The unsuccessful campaign mobilized Mexican American activists throughout the state, increasing political aspirations. Unfortunately, the new awareness and the success of redistricting led to political infighting in East Los Angeles, as elected officials attempted to forge a political machine. An early defector was Gloria Molina, who ran successfully for the State Assembly in 1982.[83]

Assemblyman Art Torres raised eyebrows by successfully challenging State Senator Alex García for his senate seat. Although criticized at the time, Assemblyman Richard Alatorre, as chair of the Assembly Elections and Reapportionment Committee, managed to add a new congressional seat. Another congressional seat became vacant when the incumbent retired. Former White House aides Esteban Torres and Matthew Marty Martínez ran successfully for the open congressional seats in 1982.[84]

The prize was the Los Angeles City Council seat held by Art Snyder for a decade and a half. His political base scared off most Latino challengers. However, in 1983 a relatively unknown urban planner, Steve Rodríguez, challenged Snyder and almost beat him. (The Los Angeles political establishment did not support Rodríguez because he was once a member of *La Raza Unida* Party.) The closeness of the race raised expectations—especially when Larry González, 27, beat ultraconservative Richard Ferraro for an LA Unified Board seat. Consequently, in 1986, Richard Alatorre was elected to the Council, replacing Snyder, making him potentially the most powerful Chicana/o politico in California.[85]

Chicanas/os pressured the Justice Department to file a suit against the city of Los Angeles—*U.S. v. City of Los Angeles* (1985)—alleging that the city violated civil and voting rights guarantees of Latinos' equal protection under the Fourteenth and Fifteenth Constitutional Amendments and the Voting Rights Acts of 1965, 1975, and 1982. The suit forced the Los Angeles City Council to resubmit a districting plan to the court in 1986. A compromise was reached whereby another Chicano district was formed, opening the possibility of yet another seat in the San Fernando Valley.

Redistricting made the election of Gloria Molina to the Council possible—it added a second Mexican American seat. Statewide, other patterns emerged: The Latino population of the San Gabriel Valley, east of East Los Angeles, and small cities along the San Bernardino Freeway, grew by almost 50 percent. This area was more middle class than the Los Angeles Eastside and was a base of funding Chicana/o politicos.[86] The 1920 Census reported just over 21,000 people were in the valley. A huge shift in racial demographics took place from 1980 to 2004. The valley's population numbered 940,000 in 1980 and the white population declined to about 780,000 in 2004. At this point the Mexican/Latino population began to climb, and reached 770,000 in 2004. This changed institutions such as California State University Northridge that by 2010 was 42 percent Latino. The white population was only 41 percent.[87] These statistics go a long way in explaining why California State University Northridge has the largest Chicana/o Studies Department in the nation. Numbers Matter!

In 1986, Texas led the nation in the number of Latino elected officials: 1,466, compared with 588 in New Mexico and 450 in California. Tejanos in the Lone Star State made up one-fifth of the voting-age population that year. They were 12.9 percent of the electorate in November 1988, but only 5.6 percent of the Texas City council members. In 1986,

Tejanos comprised 50 percent of the state's first graders; only 6.6 percent of Texas school board members were of Mexican origin.

In 1976 Texas-Mexicans received a big boost from the Justice Department when the department halted San Antonio annexations of surrounding areas. The white power elite used annexation as a device to dilute the voting power of minorities. Texas municipalities annexed surrounding neighborhoods to include more whites, deliberately absorbing white areas to neutralize the Mexican and Black population increases. The rise of the Communities Organized for Public Service (COPS) countered these efforts by politicizing and registering Mexican voters.

During the 1980s and 1990s, Henry Cisneros was the best-known Chicano politico in terms of offices held as well as his national visibility.[88] Mexican-dominated San Antonio elected Cisneros to the San Antonio City Council in 1975. He was a crossover candidate favored by the American elite and their Good Government League (GGL). That year, Mexicans comprised 51.8 percent of the city, but only 37 percent of the registered voters; whites made up 39 percent of the population and almost 56 percent of the registered voters. The Cisneros victory generated more Tejano political participation, and two years later Chicanas/os and African Americans took over the San Antonio City Council.

Henry Cisneros was the first Mexican American mayor of San Antonio in 1981, and in the 1990s, Cisneros became Secretary of Housing and Urban Development in President Bill Clinton's cabinet. Born in San Antonio, Cisneros attended Central Catholic High and graduated from Texas A&M. An urban planner, Cisneros received his doctorate from George Washington University and returned in 1974 to San Antonio, where he solicited GGL sponsorship. Cisneros's father, a retired Army Reserve colonel, worked at Fort Sam Houston; his mother, Elvira Mungía Cisneros, was from an elite family who fled Mexico during the revolution. Cisneros's maternal grandfather, Henry Romulo Mungía, ran a print shop and shared ties with other exile families that included a surprising number of the present generation of San Antonio's Mexican American leaders. Cisneros was ideologically more Republican than Democrat. He was one of the few politicos who did not have roots in the 1960s era. Cisneros emphasized economic growth, participation in the technological revolution, and the necessity for attracting high-tech business to San Antonio. Cisneros appealed to middle-class Mexican Americans, who were becoming a larger proportion of the community.[89]

In regard to Cisneros and the politics of the 1980s professor Rodolfo Rosales asked:

> Did the change in the structure of political representation create political inclusion for the Chicano community, or did it create an illusion, simply setting the stage for individualistic politicians to serve as brokers for the business community? Stated in another manner, can politicians in this system be held accountable to the needs of the community? The other side of the question is: Can the community electorally advance an agenda that is geared to its social and economic needs in a political system that is geared to economic development?[90]

Rosales's question became the title of his book on San Antonian politics known as *The Illusion of Inclusion*.[91]

By the mid-1980s, Texas elected three Tejanos to Congress, four state senators, and 21 state representatives. By 1986, Texas led in the number of Chicanas elected to public office. As for electoral politics, Texas had a higher percentage of native-born Mexican Americans than any state outside of New Mexico. In 1980, 83 percent of the Latino population of San Antonio was born in the United States, in contrast to 43 percent of the Latino population in Los Angeles. One hundred and fifty years of housing segregation resulted in residential bonding.[92]

Much of the Tejanos' electoral strength came from the leadership development of the Mexican American Youth Organization and the political successes of *La Raza Unida* Party that pressured the Democratic Party to open its doors. In addition, Texas developed an organizational network; the League of United Latin American Citizens (LULAC), the American G.I. Forum, RUP, SVREP, MALDEF, and followers of Saul Alinsky—who founded the Industrial Areas Foundation (IAF) in Chicago and trained community organizers for organizations such as COPS—all originated in Texas. COPS was part of the IAF network that had organizations throughout the Southwest. In the Latino community, the IAF organizations were heavily involved in Catholic Church networks. Ernesto Cortez, head of the IAF, was a major power, negotiating with state politicos to end the "legacy of neglect." Cortez organized in the *barrios* of the Rio Grande Valley, Houston, San Antonio, and El Paso.[93]

Chicago

By the 1980s Chicago ranked second in the United States in terms of a Mexican-origin population. It had a unique history, and Chicago Chicanas/os functioned within a well-defined "patronage system." Its wards defined the boundaries of the city's ethnic neighborhoods. By 1986, Chicago's Latino population approximated 540,000—19 percent of the city's total population; They comprised about 60 percent of the Latino group as a whole. In 1983, they helped elect Harold Washington, an African American, mayor of Chicago, in a coalition with Puerto Ricans, African Americans, and progressive whites. The Pilsen district remained the principal port of entry for Latinos, and housed the greatest concentration of Mexicans. The South Side *barrios* of Pilsen, Little Village, and South Chicago numbered more Mexicans than other Latinos. A Mexican minority also lived in the North Side, where they shared space with Puerto Ricans and other Latino groups. Although a large percentage of the Mexican population was foreign-born, in the mid-1980s the Latino Institute found that 83 percent of the Latino youth were born in the United States.[94]

In 1981, not a single Latino served on the Chicago City Council; council members gerrymandered the districts, making the future election of a Latino impossible. The following year, MALDEF sued the Chicago City Council under the 1965 Voters Rights Act as amended in 1982. The remapping of the districts, according to MALDEF, diluted Latino voting strength. Four years later, the court issued a judicial order that created four Latino wards—the 22nd, 25th, 26th, and 31st; the 22nd and 25th were predominantly Chicana/o. A special election took place in March, in which Jesús García and Juan Solíz were elected from the 22nd and 25th Wards, respectively. The creation of the Latino wards was crucial to the growing power of Chicanos and Latinos in Chicago.[95]

Back to the Milagro Beanfield War

In 1982, Mexican Americans along with organized labor elected Toney Anaya governor of New Mexico. Anaya, the former state attorney general, received 85 percent of the *manito* (New Mexican) vote. Anaya was an energetic governor who took strong and controversial stands opposing the death penalty. He declared New Mexico a sanctuary for Central American political refugees, and was pro–foreign-born, condemning racist nativism. He was criticized for bold steps that focused on Latino issues. For instance, he appointed *manitos* to key posts to protect their interests. Anaya appointed John Páez to the University of New Mexico's Board of Regents in 1983, giving Latinos a majority for the first time. The next year he appointed Jerry Apodaca and Robert Sánchez to the Board of Regents.

New Mexico was also the home to newcomer Representative Bill Richardson, elected in 1980 to Congress two years after he arrived in the state. He made friends with the New Mexican power brokers, who supported his rise. A Democrat, he was elected to the House of Representatives from New Mexico in 1982 and reelected seven times. Richardson's mother was Mexican, and his American father was born in Nicaragua, grew up in Boston, and worked for Citibank as an executive in Mexico. Richardson was raised in Mexico City, but moved to Massachusetts at age 13 to attend a Boston-area high school. Richardson, under Clinton, was named U.S. ambassador to the United Nations and Energy Secretary in 1998.

Mexicans/Latinos in New Mexico rivaled Mississippi as the state with the highest percentage of children living below the poverty line. San Miguel County rivaled the Rio Grande Valley in claiming the worst poverty. How could this be? Nativists could not blame it on the immigrants, as they did in California. The tragedy was that the old *patrón* politics of the nineteenth century still infected New Mexican politics.

They largely voted according to personal and family loyalties rather than for issues. Sadly, by the 1980s, outsiders—primarily elderly Americans—were migrating into the state, and the ability to make substantive changes was slipping away.[96]

Not as nationalistic as Texas, Colorado was divided into north and south, with the latter being more like New Mexico than Denver and the north. Federico Peña, Denver's first Mexican American mayor, was a Texas transplant. Born in Laredo in 1947 and raised in Brownsville, Texas, Peña attended St. Joseph's Academy and received his law degree from the University of Texas in 1971. After law school, he moved to Denver, where he was first elected as state representative in 1978 and then as mayor in 1982—79,200 votes to 74,700. At this time, Mexicans made up only 18 percent of the city's population and 12 percent of its voters.

Peña, a young, upwardly mobile urban Latino, migrated to Denver from Texas and built a rapport with the young building developers, who supported economic development. No doubt Peña, a world apart from the Crusade for Justice Chicanos of the 1960s, was a welcome relief to the white establishment. Peña also enjoyed the support of unions and construction companies because he promoted the expansion of Denver's infrastructure, which to them meant contracts and jobs. Although Peña benefited from being Mexican American, he played down his ethnicity. Peña did not promote a Mexican agenda, stating, "I am not an Hispanic candidate. I just happen to be Hispanic." Still, Peña's success encouraged other Latinos nationwide. Peña went on to become secretary of transportation under Clinton.[97]

Can You Smell the Refried Beans?

The 1990s was a decade in which Mexican American and Latino candidates made significant electoral gains. The exuberance was expressed by Xavier Hermosillo, a Mexican American Republican from California who said, "We're taking it back, house by house, block by block. . . . We have a little saying here: 'If you're in California, speak Spanish.' . . . People ought to wake up and smell the refried beans: Not only are we the majority of the population, but we're not going anywhere."[98] Because of the growth in population of Mexican-origin people and the enlargement of the Central American population, there was a dramatic increase in the voting power of Latinos.

Numbers count in politics. A presidential candidate needs 270 electoral votes to win an election. Eighty-three percent of Latinos were concentrated in eight states that alone accounted for 187 electoral votes: Arizona held 8 electoral votes; California, 54; Colorado, 8; Florida, 25; Illinois, 22; New Mexico, 5; New York, 33; and Texas, 32. Of these eight states, Latino population was the highest in three—California, Illinois, and Texas.

The growth in Latino population did not immediately translate into elected officials at the national level. There were no Latinos in the 100-member U.S. Senate in 1999, and only 18 Latinos of 435 voting members in the House of Representatives. Eleven of them were from Texas and California. African Americans, on the other hand, with only a slightly greater population, had 39 seats. Nevertheless, Latino visibility was increasing. As already mentioned, in 1993, Transportation Secretary (later Energy Secretary) Federico Peña and Housing and Urban Development Secretary Henry Cisneros served on the Clinton cabinet. Clinton later appointed UN Ambassador Bill Richardson as Energy Secretary.[99]

The Glass Ceiling

15.7 Characterize the struggles of Mexican women in the last decades of the twentieth century.

Some scholars characterized Mexican American/Latinas as invisible in politics, which was often true—and often not—before the 1980s. For example, Olga Peña, wife of Bexar County Supervisor Albert Peña, Jr., during his initial run for supervisor, is generally credited with putting together Peña's political machine and getting him elected.[100] By the 1980s, larger numbers of Mexican American women attended universities or were working outside the household. Their voices grew louder and more persistent in pursuing their interests. Chicanas were developing a profile quite distinct from that of their male counterparts: In Texas and California, for instance, Mexican American women were less likely than Mexican American men to identify with the Republican Party, a trend that continued through the end of the century. Studies in the 1990s showed that there was an 18-percentage-point gender gap in party identification among Latino voters: 69 percent of Latinas claimed Democratic Party affiliation compared with 51 percent of Latino men. In 1986, the number of Latino elected officials grew to 3,314, and the number of Latino women in office jumped to 592—a 20 percent increase in one year. Women accounted for 18 percent of all elected Latino officials.[101]

By 1980, 51 percent of Latinas were either unemployed or underemployed; Latinas earned 49¢ to every dollar made by white males, versus 58¢ for white women and 54¢ for Black women. Half completed less than 8.8 years of education. Some 67 percent of households were headed by women with children under 18 and they lived below the poverty line. This statistical profile did not change much in the next two decades.

Just over 18 percent of Latinas, and 16 percent of Mexican-origin females, were professionals. More than 50 percent were white-collar workers. Between 1980 and 1990, the percentage of Latinas with BA degrees increased from 7.7 to 10. However, not all the statistics were rosy; only a fraction of 1 percent of all PhDs at the University of California were awarded to Latinas in the late 1970s, and universities nationwide awarded Latinas barely 0.4 percent of the doctorates. The achievements were small, but they represented an important avenue for the change of traditional female roles as well as attracting commercial notice as an identifiable market segment. By the mid-1980s, even Chicana Republicans claimed space in the "Hispanic women's movement."[102]

Conscious of the disparities, Chicanas challenged inequalities. In 1982, Gloria Molina ran successfully against Richard Polanco in the Democratic primary race for the California Assembly. Chicano politicos tried to dissuade her from contesting against Polanco, warning that a woman could not win in East Los Angeles, that she was not tough enough to negotiate with the heavyweights, and that she could not raise sufficient funds without their support. Molina was a field representative to Assemblyman Art Torres and had participated in the founding of the national *Comisión Femenil* (Feminist Commission).

The issue that catapulted Molina into local prominence was her opposition to building a prison in downtown Los Angeles. This issue pitted Molina against recently elected Assemblyman Richard Polanco, who had promised that he would vote against the prison but broke his promise. Molina's leadership in the struggle against the prison attracted a constituency of grassroots activists. Among them were the Mothers of East Los Angeles, a lay Catholic group from Resurrection Parish headed by Father John Moretta, and St. Isabel Parish, whose women members were led by Juana Gutiérrez. During the summers of 1986 and 1987, these groups attracted 1,500–3,000 protesters at their weekly marches.[103]

The coalition fought Governor George Deukmejian for six years, enlisting the support of Archbishop Roger Mahoney for the "Stop the Prison in East Los Angeles" effort. The prison issue provided a springboard for Molina, who in the fall of 1986 announced her candidacy for the newly created First Council District. Molina registered a landslide victory in the contested race in February 1987. In February 1991, Molina was elected to the Los Angeles County Board of Supervisors. At 48, Molina represented 1.9 million people and became one of five people overseeing a $13 billion budget. Molina developed her own network, surrounding herself with women such as Antonia Hernández, the chief council of MALDEF; Mónica Lozano, publisher of *La Opinión*, perhaps the largest Spanish-language newspaper in the country; and Vilma Martínez, a prominent attorney and former chief counsel of MALDEF.

The election of Molina was aided by the prolonged struggle of the Mothers of East Los Angeles with the Department of Corrections. They methodically exposed flaws in the Environmental Impact Report (EIR). The EIR revealed a total lack of common sense. "Not one of them thought to consider the symbolism of a 70-foot-high prison located in an area, easily visible from the freeway, where the tallest buildings are 35 feet. But maybe L.A.'s proposed Statue of Liberty West should be a prison."[104] The Environmental Impact Report ignored the impact that the prison would have on the city's sewage system and how it would delay the construction of housing units.[105] Finally, after six years The Mothers of East Los Angeles won its battle against the state and the prison plan was killed in 1992.[106]

The Mothers of East Los Angeles tackled environmental racism, opposing the installation of a gas pipeline in their community that ran from Santa Barbara to San Pedro. They also marched against a planned toxic waste incinerator in Vernon. The Mothers of East Los Angeles joined the Concerned Citizens of South Central Los Angeles, a largely African American group, in drawing attention to environmental racism. In the San Fernando Valley, Latinos together with Blacks and whites protested the expansion and efforts to extend the life of the Lopez Canyon landfill for another five years after 1996.[107]

Immigrant Women Workers

A lack of education and the absence of skill development programs for immigrant women stacked the odds against their achieving success. Clearly, deindustrialization affected Latinas, as did their defined class roles. Female immigrants provided a large, motivated, inexpensive, and specialized workforce for service and manufacturing sectors, which supported the expanding export-oriented economies of places like Los Angeles, San Antonio, and Chicago. In 1980, only 8 percent of recently arrived European females worked in blue-collar occupations, compared with 62 percent of Mexican female immigrants. Seventy-five percent of the Mexican female immigrants were employed in part-time occupations and were paid extremely low wages. They had little education and a limited ability to speak English, and their situation did not improve over time.[108]

By 1980, the mean years of schooling among Chicanas was 11.3, compared with 8.3 years among established immigrant women and 6.8 for recently arrived immigrants. Some 36.3 percent of Chicanas did not have a high school diploma, compared with 64.5 percent of established immigrants and 83.8 percent of recently arrived Mexican female immigrants. Of the Chicanas, 4.8 percent held college degrees, compared with 2 percent of the established immigrant women and 1.7 percent of those recently arrived. The only advantage of age was that the older female workers were more likely to organize. Younger workers were generally more passive and naïve, probably not yet realizing they would be subject to the glass ceiling that would limit their opportunities.

Not all immigrant Latina workers were Mexican. In the 1980s, an estimated 500,000 men and women migrated from El Salvador alone. In 1985, 32.4 percent of the Salvadoran population in the United States was under 10 years of age and 57.3 percent was under the age of 20. More than 89 percent of Salvadoran refugees and 95 percent of the immigrants (those arriving before 1980) lived in family-based households. Labor force participation among Salvadoran males was 74 percent for refugees in 1988. For Salvadoran females, it was 66.7 percent, which was higher than the 52 percent for other Latinas. Salvadoran female refugees had the highest unemployment at 16.7 percent. Median age was 27.7 for females and 25.6 for males. In addition to economic deprivation, these refugees suffered from the experiences of civil war, oppression, and trauma.

Latinas of all nationalities engaged in self-help. Libertad Rivera, 28, from Tepic, Nayarit, in Mexico, worked for the Coalition for Humane Immigration Rights of Los Angeles (CHIRLA), educating and uniting domestic servants. Women also worked in AIDS programs. As of the late 1980s, 18 percent of all teenagers infected with HIV were Latinos. In Los Angeles, 38 percent of the babies and children infected with AIDS are Latino—more than double the Latino share of adult AIDS cases. At least 40 percent of Latinas with AIDS contracted it through their husbands or boyfriends. Fear of deportation kept many undocumented Latinas away from healthcare systems and other support services.[109]

By the end of the decade, Raúl Yzaguirre, president of the National Council of La Raza, sang another tune: "I can't look at any institution, I can't look at any aspect of America, and say, 'This is where we've made progress.'"[110]

Regional Differences

15.8 Differentiate Chicana/o experiences by U.S. region.

Texas differed from California and other states. For one thing, the RUP had a much greater impact on Chicanas/os in Texas than in California, and Tejanas were more quickly integrated into mainstream politics. The 1970s saw the rise of grassroots political activists such as San Antonian Rosie Castro, who in 1971 was one of the first candidates for city council when she ran on a slate with Gloria Cabrerra and two Tejano males. Castro was very active, demanding equality and forging political space for Chicanas in the process. Another activist was María Antonietta Berriozábal, who successfully ran for the San Antonio City Council in 1981, supported by a grassroots network of Chicanas. This victory led to the election of Yolanda Vera to the council in 1985. Berriozábal's procommunity stances put her at odds with the rest of the council, who tended to favor business interests. In 1991, Berriozábal ran for mayor and came close to becoming the first Chicana mayor of a major city.[111]

In San Antonio, Chicanas enjoyed a measure of success in politics, the success was, however, limited. Outside San Antonio, the problem of exclusion was even more marked. For example, in Texas the most powerful elected position within local government is the county judge. In 1998, Texas had 254 county judges, of whom 23 were white women and 7 were Chicano. Only one, Norma Villarreal of Zapata

County, was a Tejana. An obvious impediment was that the election for county judge ran countywide, not only making the race expensive but also diluting the Mexican American voting numbers.

In 1986 in Crystal City, Texas, Severita Lara ran against an incumbent county judge. On the first count, she won by one vote. On a recount, she lost by two votes. Although there was foul play, Lara did not have the funds to challenge the verdict of the electoral panel, which the incumbent heavily influenced. Lara ended up $7,000 in debt, an amount she had to pay from her pocket. Unlike Molina, she did not have access to funding from feminist groups. Lara was later elected to the Crystal City Council and then served as mayor.[112]

Alicia Chacón from El Paso and Enriqueta Díaz from Eagle Pass won races for county judge in the early 1990s; however, both were defeated in reelection. One impediment was that they never became part of the old-boys' network and did not conduct politics in the usual way, which was to go down to the local bar for informal sessions. Chacón was later elected to the City Council.[113]

Norma Villarreal Ramírez made a successful bid for county judge of Zapata County in 1994. Armed with a $20,000 loan from her father, she challenged the county's count in an election, which she lost by 40 votes. The courts found fraud and ordered a recount, which Villarreal won by several hundred votes. However, once she took office, few people came forward to help Villarreal. "The collegial arrangements between male members from the same political affiliation and/or ethnic group do not extend to women either. The men simply do not want the women in charge."[114]

By the 1980s, a critical mass of Chicanas entered politics. Fewer belonged to the generation that was active in *La Raza Unida* or the 1960s and more to the generation that benefited from those earlier struggles. They cut their teeth in more traditional political routes working in campaigns of others before running themselves. Many, such as Elvira Reyna, learned their politics under the tutelage of white politicos. (Reyna later became a state representative.) What they shared with the previous generation were their life experiences, which in Texas were formed more by the Confederate culture of the state. The socialization of this generation was different; racism was different—you could choose where you would live and what you would join. Elvira was raised in Dallas, picked cotton, but became a Republican. She was married with two children before she went to college. She began working part time for law-and-order State Representative Bill Blackwood. Elvira first ran for office, as a Republican, in 1993. This experience was much different from that of a Rosie Castro or Severita Lara, who formed their worldviews through activism.[115]

Other changes took place: In San Antonio, Texas, *Casa Esperanza* fought for freedom from "domination and inequality—[for] women, people of color, lesbians and gay men, the working class and poor. We believe in creating bridges between people by exchanging ideas and educating and empowering each other. We believe it is vital to share our visions of hope . . . we are *esperanza* [hope]."[116]

In 1987 a group of queer and straight Chicanas organized *Esperanza*; they wanted a place where community-based organizers, activists, and cultural artists could meet and engage in dialogue against all forms of social, political, and economic oppression.

> The organization has been active in women's reproductive choice, human rights, and the rights of Spanish-speaking workers. Esperanza has organized antiwar protests, low-cost housing actions, and demonstrations against the Klu [sic] Klux Klan. Esperanza has presented the work of hundreds of artists and cultural workers, particularly those who have been ignored or silenced in mainstream arenas. Individually, the women and men of Esperanza have done the work at home. They have talked, challenged, and learned with their own families and with neighborhood friends. With great courage, they have strived to live the changes they advocate and to empower the people they love.[117]

By the mid-1990s, *Esperanza* threatened the establishment by advocating a broader definition of diversity. Responding to the pressure of the religious right and homophobes, the city of San Antonio cut funding for its cultural arts programs in 1997. San Antonio then tried to isolate *Esperanza* by threatening the funding of other gay/lesbian, Latino, and African American groups. Although San Antonio had a Confederate mentality, it also built a network of progressives—many of them women like those in *Fuerza Unida*, who organized the Levi Strauss boycott. Meanwhile, *Esperanza* was reluctant to sue because to do so would threaten the funding for other worthy programs; however, it was now or never.

The organization began a *Todos Somos Esperanza* dialogue that "brought the issues of cultural diversity and public funding for cultural arts to discussions throughout the city." It then brought a suit in federal court against the city, which went to trial in 2001. At the trial,

> Esperanza Executive Director Graciela Sánchez identified herself as a lesbian and a woman who had grown up working class in San Antonio's Westside barrio. Graciela used numerous Spanish words as she testified about the work of Esperanza, speaking in a bilingual weave that is familiar among Chicanos in San Antonio. Judge Garcia listened closely, and the courtroom filled with the power of Spanish spoken openly, without translation, in the formal atmosphere of federal court. The audience was completely silent in recognition of the moment. Sánchez testified to the judge and to her family, friends, and allies. The determined, engaged presence of community members was essential as a testament to that moment.[118]

Federal Judge Orlando García found in *Esperanza*'s favor.

Gold Fever: The Erasure of History

15.9 Explain how the debate over the preservation of Olvera Street reflected concerns about privatization.

Olvera Street for years was a tourist attraction that no self-respecting Chicana/o would frequent. Frank Villalobos of Barrio Planners, who was involved in the struggle of the Mothers of East Los Angeles to prevent the building of a prison in ELA, shared his plans, commissioned by the merchants association, to develop the street.[119] In the summer of 1987, *The Herald-Examiner* published a piece:

> The fate of Olvera Street, Los Angeles's oldest, is up for grabs. Earthquake laws, historical preservation, the pimping of Mexican culture and a political power struggle over who will control El Pueblo de Los Angeles Historic Park, all are playing a role.
>
> During the 1880s, Olvera Street was part of a larger Mexican barrio—encompassing today's Chinatown—called Sonora Town. Although they competed with newcomers to Los Angeles to live there, Mexicans made up a majority of its residents at the turn of the century.
>
> But by the mid-1920s, Sonora Town, now reduced to Olvera Street, was in its last urban cycle. Its residential character was gone, its buildings occupied by commercial enterprises. When light industry moved in, almost everyone expected Olvera to be bulldozed. Enter Mrs. Christine Sterling, who wanted to save the Avilla house, as well as other buildings, and preserve a bit of "Old Mexico."[120]

It was intended to be a tourist attraction and showplace of Los Angeles's Mexican heritage. During the Great Depression, a mural critical of American capitalism—"America Tropical" by David Siquieros, the great Mexican muralist—was whitewashed. In 1953 California established El Pueblo Park and Olvera's merchants, mostly small vendors, had great expectations. These hopes were short-lived. The argument was not that Olvera had to be preserved; the question was how? State bureaucrats made the restoration of the street's buildings their priority—but they focused on the Italians, Chinese, and other ethnics. At this time, although every major ethnic group had a museum, Mexicans did not have a place in the city or Southern California that marked that they, after the Yang Na People, had the longest presence there.[121]

How to preserve Olvera Street got caught up in the ambitions of Councilpersons Gloria Molina and Richard Alatorre. The city at this time was promoting a "Fantasy Heritage" and like Old Town San Diego, many wanted to reconstruct a history of Los Angeles that resembled MacDonald's and other franchises—it wanted white people dressed in Mexican costumes. The Olvera Street vendors and their families worked their concessions for 50 years in some cases. The leader of the Olvera Street vendors was Vivian Bonzo, 34, the owner of La Golindrina Restaurant.[122]

By 1989 the battle over Olvera Street raged and the committee to preserve the street was called the Mexican Conservancy. It met almost nightly. Minnie Fergusson and Marcos Aguilar joined the group. Meanwhile, large Latino developers jockeyed for a piece of the street, supported by Richard Riordan, then head of the Los Angeles Parks Commission, and Alatorre. In what almost became a physical confrontation I questioned Riordan whether he wanted Olvera Street to become a MacDonald's and he answered yes. He wanted the street privatized and everything else in LA privatized. The big prize would be the schools.[123]

Jean Poole, the curator of the museum, who even her supporters admitted was paternalistic, was intent on neutralizing the Mexican presence on the street, and enlisted the support of the Italians and the Chinese by promising them a piece of "Old Mexico."

> For 12 years, Poole and her gaggle of Anglo historians have been plotting to impose their Mexican-less vision of Olvera Street. Their opportunity for success came when administration of El Pueblo Park passed from state to the city Recreation and Parks Commission. Eager to renovate, the commissioners put together a proposal. Since they and the Recreation and Parks Dept. lack the expertise to make historical recommendations, Peter Snell, an architectural historian, was paid to make some. Snell is a close friend of Poole and has acted as a consultant for El Pueblo Park.[124]

The Mexican Conservancy and the supporters of Olvera Street marched on City Hall and marched on City Hall and packed the Recreation and Parks Commission meeting which took "a 4-0 vote [that was supposed] . . . to have ended the emotional wrangling that has stalled the request for competitive bids for several months." Five hundred spectators jammed the Los Angeles City Council chambers, and stamped their feet and clapped their hands over assertions that the commission had authority over Olvera Street. Riordan did not show up to the meeting. After three hours of debate, the city council authorized the restoration of a community hall and museum for Italian Americans. "This is simply not acceptable," screamed Vivien Bonzo, president of the Olvera Street Merchants Association. Rodolfo Acuña added "We're not anti-Italian. We have a Chinese museum (approved recently by the commission) at one end and now we have an Italian museum on the other . . . Who is going to stand up for us?" Filmmaker Luis Váldez told the commissioners that the proposal was full of "little tricks that are meant to bring in the McDonald's . . . to bring in Taco Bell."[125] Historian Gloria Ricci Lothrop said the Italians wanted to take back important historic sites—sites they had built after they uprooted the Mexicans, who had occupied the space before and after the Italian occupation.[126] Eventually, Councilpersons Alatorre and Molina agreed to support a seven-member "authority" to oversee El Pueblo Park that housed Olvera Street. This ended the street's oversight by the city's parks commission.[127] Slowly the Mexican American community lost space on the street with their historical past bartered away by white and brown politicians who supported Italian, Chinese, and other interests at the expense of Mexicans. Privatization was alive and well in Los Angeles, where land is gold.

Conclusion: The End Industrial Labor and Upward Mobility

At the beginning of the 1980s, National Council of La Raza President Raul Yzaguirre christened the 1980s "the Decade of the Hispanic." By the end of the 1980s, the prediction seemed like a bad joke. Neoliberalism swallowed Mexico and Latin America and in the United States ended the American Dream of union jobs with benefits such as health care. Neoliberalism like a plague cut opportunities for workers; debtor nations like Mexico, that were pressured to take out loans from the World Bank and the International Monetary Fund or to go bankrupt Mexico assumed massive debts. As a condition for getting the loans, the international banking giants forced Mexico to eliminate or reduce large numbers of its public sector employment.

These austerity programs put thousands of Mexicans out of work. Large numbers of laborers and their families were forced to migrate north. Because immigration law tightened and criminalized the immigration process, Mexican migration was no longer circular. Laborers did not migrate to the U.S. and return to the families after working in the U.S. temporarily. Mexican workers were forced to migrate with their families.

As mentioned, young single males at the time worked a few short years before returning to Mexico or other homelands. Now, they were forced to remain in the country or be deported. It proved to be no solution. It was dangerous to enter the US without documents, so married workers brought their families and stayed for longer periods of time. Instead of stopping undocumented immigration, these new laws increased the numbers of people who had never migrated in large numbers: they now included women and children.

Worse, in militarizing the border places like Juárez/El Paso, Nogales and Tijuana/San Diego, immigrants were forced to enter through isolated rural areas of Texas and Arizona's blazing deserts. Thousands died. Few Americans would openly admit that racism was a major factor driving immigration policy. White Americans feared the browning of the USA. Finally, immigration law encouraged vigilantism.

Mexican poverty benefited the United States. The undocumented immigrants saved agriculture as well as light industry in a large number of American cities. Light industry was important in keeping Los Angeles solvent softening the flight of heavy industry from the City of the Angels. America's Imperialist Wars in Central America drove Central Americans to the United States.

Meanwhile, in 1986 Reagan and the Democrats struck a bargain and passed the Immigration Reform and Control Act that became law on November 6, 1986. The purpose of this legislation was to amend, revise, and reform/re-assess the status of unauthorized immigrants outlined in the Immigration and Nationality Act. However, by this time Nativist Republicans and Democrats formed a coalition against amnesty for undocumented workers. Progressives opposed IRCA because it strengthened the border patrol and favored a bracero program.

Many new arrivals from Mexico and Central America refused to go along with exploitive wages and conditions and they organized unions. As late as the 1980s, labor federations such as the Los Angeles County Federation of Labor lobbied to crack down on undocumented labor. Despite opposition, IRCA passed as immigrants gained legal status they participated in civil society. The new immigrant did what immigrants did before them and joined and formed trade unions. At the same time, a new class of organizers came on the scene; many were trained in the 1960s. For example, in 1983 Local 11 of the Hotel Employees and Restaurant Employees Union (HERE) hired María Elena Durazo, the daughter of immigrants, as an organizer. Four years later Durazo won the presidency of the local. Durazo was elected Executive Secretary/Treasurer of the Los Angeles Federation of Labor in 2005, one of the most powerful positions in California Labor. Organized labor had once been the undocumented workers greatest critics. Under Durazo labor and the immigrant community LA became a union town.

The growth of the Mexican American population pressured and threatened elected officials. Many of their districts had large Latino voting constituencies. This led to changes in California where term limits made long time incumbents vulnerable, leading to the election of a plurality of Mexican/Latino office holders. This in turn caused a backlash. IRCA and increased Latino representation angered anti-immigrant foundations that sought to limit Latino student access to higher education. They used this to stir outrage and fear among donors and to increase contributions.

During the 1980s, the Mexican immigrant population jumped from 2.2 to 4.3 million. U.S. financed Civil Wars pushed Central Americans whose U.S. population jumped from 354,000 in 1980 to 1,134, 000 in 1990. In turn white Americans were told that they were being invaded.

Notes

1. Elizabeth Martinez and Arnoldo Garcia, " What is Neoliberalism? A Brief Definition for Activists," National Network for Immigrant and Refugee Rights, CorpWatch, January 1, 1997, https://corpwatch.org/article/what-neoliberalism. "Neoliberalism: origins, theory, definition," http://web.inter.nl.net/users/Paul.Treanor/neoliberalism.html.
2. Gale Holland, "L.A.'s homelessness surged 75% in six years. Here's why the crisis has been decades in the making," *Los Angeles Times* (Feb. 1, 2018), http://www.latimes.com/local/lanow/la-me-homeless-how-we-got-here-20180201-story.html.
3. Rodolfo F. Acuña, "Gracias a la Vida!," *Mexmigration*, July 31, 2015, http://mexmigration.blogspot.com/2015/07/acuna-on-guillermo-gomez-pena.html.
4. Guillermo Gómez-Peña, "Notes From Technotopia 3.0: On The 'Creative City' Gone Wrong: An anti-gentrification philosophical tantrum," *Art Change US*, 2012–2016, https://artsinachangingamerica.org/notes-technotopia-3-0-guillermo-gomez-pena/.
5. Ben Tobin, "'Monopoly for Millennials' reminds players that 'adulting is hard'," *USA Today* (Nov. 14, 2018), https://www.usatoday.com/story/money/2018/11/14/monopoly-millennials/2003129002/.
6. Betsy Guzmán, "The Hispanic Population: Census 2000 Brief," May 2001, http://www.census.gov/prod/2001pubs/c2kbr01-3.pdf.
7. Janet Burke and Ted Humphrey (eds.), *Nineteenth-Century Nation Building and the Latin American Intellectual Tradition* (Indianapolis: Hackett Publishing Company, 2007). William H Katra, *The Argentine generation of 1837: Echeverría, Alberdi, Sarmiento, Mitre* (London: Fairleigh Dickinson University Press. 1996). Sam Schulman, "Juan Bautista Alberdi and His Influence on Immigration Policy in the Argentine Constitution of 1853," *The Americas*, Vol. 5, No. 1 (Jul., 1948), 3.
8. Jorge Durand, Douglas S. Massey, Emilio A. Parrado, "The new era of Mexican migration to the United States: Rethinking History and the Nation-State: Mexico and the United States," *Journal of American History*, Sept, 1999, Vol. 86(2), 518(27). Also see http://archive.oah.org/special-issues/mexico/jdurand.html.
9. Durand, Massey, Parrado Ibid., 519–20.
10. Gabriel Lesser and Jeanne Batalova, "Central American Immigrants in the United States," Migration Policy Institute, April 5, 2017, https://www.migrationpolicy.org/article/central-american-immigrants-united-states.
11. Gustavo López and Jynnah Radford, "Facts on U.S. Immigrants, 2015: Statistical portrait of the foreign-born population in the United States," Pew Research Center, May 3, 2017, http://www.pewhispanic.org/2017/05/03/facts-on-u-s-immigrants-cur-rent-data/.
12. Edward R. Roybal, "Hispanic Americans in Congress, 1822–1995," http://www.loc.gov/rr/hispanic/congress/roybal.html.
13. David Reyes, "GI Forum Address," *Los Angeles Times* (August 7, 1980).
14. Ibid.
15. George Monbiot, "Neoliberalism – the ideology at the root of all our problems," *The Guardian* (Apr. 15, 2016), https://www.theguardian.com/books/2016/apr/15/neoliberalism-ideology-problem-george-monbiot.
16. Robert B. Reich, *Aftershock: The Next Economy and America's Future* (New York: Knopf, September 21, 2010), 32–35, 42–48. Robert B. Reich, "Aftershock: The Next Economy and America's Future," https://www.youtube.com/watch?v=f4ZTwPsmpnc
17. Deindustrialization is the reduction of heavy industry and manufacturing within the country's borders and sending the production abroad. Paul L. Street, *Racial Oppression in the Global Metropolis: A Living Black Chicago History* (Lanham, MD: Rowman & Littlefield Publishers, Inc., 2007), 132. Joan Moore, "Latina/o Studies: The Continuing Need for New Paradigms," Occasional Paper No. 29, Julian Samora Research Institute, December 1997, http://www.jsri.msu.edu/pdfs/ops/oc29.pdf.
18. Monica Prasad, "The Popular Origins of Neoliberalism in the Reagan Tax Cut of 1981," *Journal of Policy History*, 2012, Vol. 24(3), 351–383.
19. Monica Prasad Ibid., 351.
20. Monica Prasad Ibid., 352–53.
21. David Jacobs and Lindsey Myers, "Union Strength, Neoliberalism, and Inequality," *American Sociological Review*, 2014, Vol. 79(4), 754. Rachel Martin, "How Reagan's Tax Cuts Fared," NPR, December 8, 2017, https://www.npr.org/2017/12/08/569345901/how-reagans-tax-cuts-fared.
22. Jacobs and Myers, Ibid., 752–774.
23. Monbiot, "Neoliberalism."
24. Jorge Chapa, "The Burden of Interdependence: Demographic, Economic, and Social Prospects for Latinos in the Reconfigured U.S. Economy," in Frank Bonilla, Edwin Meléndez, Rebecca Morales, and María de los Angeles Torres, eds., *Borderless Borders: U.S. Latinos, Latin Americans and the Paradox of Interdependence* (Philadelphia, PA: Temple University Press, 1998), 71–82. Stefanic and Delgado, *No Mercy*. Ben J. Wattenberg, "Immigrants and 'comparative advantage'; they help vitalize the American economy and maintain our traditions of hard work and patriotism," *The Wall Street Journal Eastern Edition*, August 9, 2012.

25. Robert W. Fox, "Neighbors' Problems, Our Problems: Population Growth in Central America," Negative Population Growth (NPG) Forum Series, http://www.npg.org/forum_series/BalancingHumansInTheBiosphere.pdf. Thomas F. O'Brien, *The Revolutionary Mission: American Enterprise in Latin America, 1900–1945* (Cambridge, UK: Cambridge University Press, 1999), 51–53. Charles D. Brockett, *Land, Power and Poverty: Agrarian Transformation and Political Conflict in Central America* (Boulder, CO: Westview Press, 1990), 70–76.

26. Phillip Berryman, *Liberation Theology: Essential facts about the revolutionary movement in Latin America–and beyond* (Philadelphia: Temple University Press, 1987). Stephen Keating, "A Brief History of Latin American Liberation Theology," An und für sich, May 3, 2013, https://itself.blog/2013/05/03/a-brief-history-of-latin-american-liberation-theology/.

27. El Salvador in the 1980s, http://www.youtube.com/watch?v=1bEpEK7uKzE&feature=related. David Kirsch, "Death Squads in El Salvador: A Pattern of U.S. Complicity," *Covert Action Quarterly*, Summer 1990, http://www.thirdworldtraveler.com/; US_ThirdWorld/deathsquads_ElSal.html. "El Salvador: Civil War," PBS, http://www.pbs.org/itvs/enemiesofwar/elsalvador2.html. Ron Rhodes, "Christian Revolution in Latin America: The Changing Face of Liberation Theology," Part One in a Three-Part Series on Liberation Theology, Reasoning from the Scriptures Ministries, http://home.earthlink.net/~ronrhodes/Liberation.html. Roberto D'Abussion [*sic*] interview (1984), http://www.youtube.com/watch?v=0e-jnwAwIKE&feature=related.

28. "Massacre in El Salvador During Oscar Romero's Funeral," http://www.youtube.com/watch?v=EN6LWdqcyuc&feature=related. Karen Zraick, "Oscar Romero, Archbishop Killed While Saying Mass, Will Be Named a Saint on Sunday," *The New York Times* (Oct. 14, 2018).

29. I was in El Salvador in the spring of 1991 before the peace accords. Rodolfo F. Acuña, "Column Left; Latin Generals Count on the Wages of War," *Los Angeles Times* (April 1, 1991). Tom Gibb, "US Role in Salvador's Brutal War," *BBC News/America* (March 24, 2002), http://news.bbc.co.uk/2/hi/americas/1891145.stm.

30. "Nicaraguan Sandinistas," Latin American Studies, http://www.latinamericanstudies.org/sandinistas.htm.

31. "Boland Amendment—Definition and Overview," WorldIQ.com, http://www.wordiq.com/definition/Boland_Amendment. "Secrets of The CIA—Nicaragua," http://www.youtube.com/watch?v=zKXZfwG43pU. Scharfen, J. (1985). The 1984 Boland Amendment, Digital National Security Archive—DNSA: Document Records: Edwin Meese, With Reagan: The inside story (Washington, D.C., Lanham, MD: Regnery Gateway, 1992).

32. Lawrence E. Walsh, Independent Counsel, "Final Report of the Independent Counsel for Iran/Contra Matters," in *Volume I: Investigations and Prosecutions*, August 4, 1993 (Washington, DC, United States Court of Appeals for the District of Columbia Circuit Division for the Purpose of Appointing Independent Counsel, Division No. 86–6), http://www.fas.org/irp/offdocs/walsh/. "Iran Contra Coverup : Part 1" (All eight can be found on YouTube), http://www.youtube.com/watch?v=35KcYgMPiIM. "CIA, Guns, Drugs, Fraud, Iran Contra," http://www.youtube.com/watch?v=bbt9PsaSUiI. Sewall Menzel, *Dictators, Drugs & Revolution: Cold War Campaigning in Latin America 1965–1989* (Bloomington, IN: AuthorHouse, 2006).

33. Ginger Thompson and Mireya Navarro, "Rights Groups Say Logbook Lists Executions by Guatemalan Army," *New York Times* (May 20, 1999). Rachel Cobb, "Guatemala's New Evangelists," *Natural History* 107, No. 4 (May 1998), 32ff. "Guatemala Civil War 1960–1996," GlobalSecurity.org, http://www.globalsecurity.org/military/world/war/guatemala.htm.

34. Gérard Duménil, Dominique Lévy, *Capital Resurgent: Roots of the Neoliberal Revolution* (Cambridge: Harvard University Press, 2004), pp. 1–3.

35. Erwan Quintin and José Joaquín López, "Mexico's Financial Vulnerability: Then and Now." Vol. 1, No. 6, June 2006, Economic Letter, https://www.dallasfed.org/~/media/documents/research/eclett/2006/el0606.pdf.

36. "Defenderé el peso como un perro," *El Debate*, March 21, 2015, https://www.debate.com.mx/mexico/Hace-34-anos-Defendere-el-peso-como-un-perro-20150321-0164.html.

37. "Maquiladoras," *Handbook of Texas Online*, http://www.tshaonline.org/handbook/online/articles/MM/dzm2.html. María Patricia Fernández-Kelly, *For We Are Sold. I and My People: Women and Industry in Mexico's Frontier* (Albany: State University of New York Press, 1983), 45–84. Devon G. Peña, *The Terror of the Machine: Technology, Work, Gender, & Ecology on the U.S.–Mexico Border* (Austin: CMAS Book, University of Texas Press, 1997). James M. Cypher, "Mexico: Financial Fragility or Structural Crisis?" *Journal of Economic Issues* 30, No. 2 (June 1996), 454–55.

38. *Get Out* (2017), http://www.imdb.com/title/tt5052448/.

39. Katrina Mann, "'You're Next!': Postwar Hegemony Besieged in Invasion of the Body Snatchers (1956)," *Cinema Journal*, 44, No. 1 (Fall 2004), 49–68. This article is an interesting take.

40. Thomas Muller, *California's Newest Immigrants: A Summary* (Washington, DC: Urban Institute Press, 1984), ix–x, 7, 13, 28.

41 James Crawford, "California Vote Gives Boost to 'English-Only' Movement," *Education Weekly* (April 1, 1987), http://www.edweek.org/ew/articles/1987/04/01/27useng.h06.html. There was also the reality that 50 percent of the supporters spoke functionally illiterate English.

42 Leo R. Chávez, "The Power of the Imagined Community: The Settlement of Undocumented Mexicans and Central Americans in the United States," *American Anthropologist* 96, No. 1 (1994), 52–73. Margo De Ley, "Taking from Latinos to Assist Soviet Immigrants—an Affront to Fairness," *Los Angeles Times* (March 19, 1989). "A Look at the Forces Behind the Anti-Immigrant Movement," Democracy Now! May 2, 2007, http://www.democracynow.org/2007/5/2/a_look_at_the_forces_behind.

43 Terry Maxon, "Hart Angers Hispanics with Letter on Aliens," *Dallas Morning News* (February 5, 1985). Stephen Moore, "A Pro-Family, Pro-growth Legal Immigration Policy for America," *Backgrounder* No. 735, The Heritage Foundation (November 6, 1989), 1–7. Elton Gallegly, "Just How Many Aliens Are Here Illegally?" *Los Angeles Times* (March 13, 1994).

44 "California Chief Justice Rose Bird Loses Election," http://www.youtube.com/watch?v=Kd162US36to. "Cruz Reynoso Honored for Civil Rights Commitments," http://www.youtube.com/watch?v=wViKbfS_Gds&feature=related. Frank del Olmo, "Ugly or Polite, It's Racism," *Los Angeles Times* (October 30, 1986).

45 Justin Akers Chacón, "War on immigrants," *International Socialist Review*, Issue 47, May–June 2006, http://www.isreview.org/issues/47/waronimmigrants.shtml. Rodolfo F. Acuña, U.S. Latino Issues, 2nd Edition (Santa Barbara: Greenwood, 2017), 112.

46 William Langwiesche, "The Border," *Atlantic Monthly* (May 1992), 69. Sebastian Rotella, "Border Abuses Continue 2 Years, Study Says," *Los Angeles Times* (February 26, 1992). Sebastian Rotella, "INS Agents Abuse Immigrants, Study Says," *Los Angeles Times* (May 31, 1992). "Undocumented Immigrant Students: A Very Brief Overview of Access to Higher Education In California," http://tcla.gseis.ucla.edu/reportcard/features/5-6/ab540/pdf/undocimmigstud.pdf. Larry Gordon, "Cal State Held to In-State Fees for Immigrants: Education: Superior Court judge's decision contradicts similar California cases on whether undocumented students must pay higher non-resident rate," *Los Angeles Times* (May 21, 1992), http://articles.latimes.com/1992-05-21/news/mn-334_1_cal-state.

47 Thomas Putnam, "The Real Meaning of Ich Bin ein Berliner," *The Atlantic*, Fall 2013, https://www.theatlantic.com/magazine/archive/2013/08/the-real-meaning-of-ich-bin-ein-berliner/309500/.

48 Ronald Reagan, "Tear Down This Wall," The History Place, June 12, 1987, http://www.historyplace.com/speeches/reagan-tear-down.htm.

49 "The Cold War," Doc Side, https://documents.tips/documents/the-cold-war-56c13c59bca96.html.

50 Amanda Holpuch, "Migrant deaths at US-Mexico border increase 17% this year, UN figures show," Aug. 5, 1017, https://www.theguardian.com/us-news/2017/aug/05/migrants-us-mexico-border-deaths-figures.

51 Stuart Silverstein, "Years Later, Many Scoff at Immigration Act," *Los Angeles Times* (August 29, 1993). Dan Freedman, "U.S. to Boost Border Patrols," *Los Angeles Daily News* (February 3, 1994). "Southern Exposure—Perspective," *California Journal* (May 1, 1998). "U.S. Border Patrol in S. California Developing Deadly But Ineffective Operation Gatekeeper," *In Motion Magazine*, http://www.inmotionmagazine.com/rm99.html.

52 Robert R. Brischetto and Paul A. Leonard, "Falling Through the Safety Net: Latinos and the Declining Effectiveness of Anti-Poverty Programs in the 1980s," *Public Policy Report* 1, Southwest Voter Research Institute, 1988. Rebecca Morales and Frank Bonilla, "Restructuring and the New Inequality," in Rebecca Morales and Frank Bonilla, eds., *Latinos in a Changing U.S. Economy: Comparative Perspectives on Growing Inequality* (Newbury Park, CA: Sage Publications, 1993), 11–12. Roger M. Mahoney, "Democracy's Obligated to the Poor," *Los Angeles Times* (October 23, 1985). Jason DeParle, "Poverty Rate Rose Sharply Last Year as Incomes Slipped," *Los Angeles Times* (September 27, 1991). James Risen, "History May Judge Reaganomics Very Harshly," *Los Angeles Times* (November 8, 1992). Harry Bernstein, "Closing the Wage Gap: Job Equality," *Los Angeles Times* (April 8, 1993).

53 Paul Krugman, "Reagan Did It," *New York Times* (June 1, 2009).

54 Michael H. LeRoy, "Lockouts Involving Replacement Workers: An Empirical Public Policy Analysis and Proposal to Balance Economic Weapons Under the NLRA, 74 Wash. U. L. Q. 981 (1996), 984–987, https://openscholarship.wustl.edu/cgi/viewcontent.cgi?referer=https://www.google.com/&httpsredir=1&article=1629&context=law_lawreview.

55 Harry Bernstein, "Put Teeth Back in Worker's Right to Strike," *Los Angeles Times* (July 5, 1993). "Patco: Ex-Controllers Regret Striking in 1981," *Los Angeles Times* (July 17, 1991). Bob Baker, "Workers Fear Losing Jobs to Replacement in Strikes," *Los Angeles Times* (June 7, 1990). Jane Slaughter, "What Went Wrong at Caterpillar?" *Labor Notes* (May 1991). Bob Baker, "Union Buster Turns to 'A Labor of Love,'" *Los Angeles Times* (September 5, 1993). G. William Domhoff, "The Rise

and Fall of Labor Unions in the U.S.: From the 1830s until 2012 (but mostly the 1930s–1980s)," Who Rules America? http://www2.ucsc.edu/whorulesamerica/power/history_of_labor_unions.html.

56 Rodolfo F. Acuña, *Corridors of Migration: The Odyssey of Mexican Laborers, 1600–1933* (Tucson: University of Arizona Press, 2007).

57 Robert B. Reich, "Business Dynamism Gone Overboard," *Los Angeles Times* (November 17, 1985). Barbara Kingsolver, *Holding the Line: Women in the Great Arizona Mine Strike of 1983* (Ithaca, NY: ILR Press, Cornell University, 1996). Jonathan D. Rosenblum, *Copper Crucible: How the Arizona Miners Strike of 1983 Recast Labor-Management Relations in America* (Ithaca, NY: ILR Press, Cornell University, 1995) 4, No. 2 (Summer 1988), 251–68.

58 Elaine Ayala, "Cisneros: First Latino president already has been born," mySA, January 28, 2009, http://blog.mysanantonio.com/latinlife/2009/01/cisneros-first-latino-president-already-has-been-born/.

59 Jorge Durand, Edward Telles, and Jennifer Flashman, "The Demographic Foundations of the Latino Population," in Marta Tienda and Faith Mitchell, eds., *Hispanics and the Future of America* (Washington, D.C.: The National Academies Press, 2006), 66–80, https://www.ncbi.nlm.nih.gov/books/NBK19905/pdf/Bookshelf_NBK19905.pdf.

60 Durand, Telles, and Flashman, Ibid., 66.

61 Durand, Telles, and Flashman, Ibid.

62 Ibid., 68.

63 CIA Factbook, https://www.cia.gov/library/publications/the-world-factbook/rankorder/2119rank.html, http://www.distancefromto.net/distance-from/United+States/to/.

64 José Angel Gutiérrez, *The Eagle Has Eyes: The FBI Surveillance of César Estrada Chávez of the United Farm Workers* (East Lansing: Michigan State University, 2019).

65 Rodolfo F. Acuña, *The Making of Chicano Studies: The Trenches of Academe* (New Brunswick: Rutgers University Press, 2011), Chapter 6.

66 Richard Knee, "Professors' Union Considers Filling Suit Over Bugging at CSUN," *The Valley News*, Nov. 30, 1972.

67 *Committee Against Police Abuse (CAPA) v PDID*.

68 Victor Merina, "Reiner Defends PDID Blast," *Los Angeles Times* (Jan. 20, 1983), C1. Joel Sappell, "New LAPD Unit for Intelligence Asked," *Los Angeles Times* (Mar. 4, 1983), D1. In one case, a PDID officer lived with a white female plaintiff for seven years, and they even had a daughter, while he was spying on her friends.

69 Michael Seiler, "LAPD Accused of Spying at University," *Los Angeles Times* (June 11, 1982), D5.

70 I did not mention the individual's name because it would serve no purpose. He is a good friend who has made substantial contributions to the community. I would say this even if he had been involved in a plot to assassinate me. It is the police who had the duty to protect me.

71 John Johnson, "The Guerrilla Lawyer: Justice: With his one-man Robin Hood Foundation, attorney Rees Lloyd crusades in court for the rights of poor workers," *Los Angeles Times* (November 30, 1991), http://articles.latimes.com/keyword/rees-lloyd.

72 Marita Hernandez, "Latina Leads Takeover of Union from Anglo Male," *Los Angeles Times* (May 6, 1989). *Raiz Fuerte que no se arranca*," pamphlet paying homage to Magdalena Mora (Los Angeles, CA: Editorial Prensa Sembradora, 1981). Steve Proffitt, "María Elena Durazo," *Los Angeles Times* (September 27, 1992). Bob Baker, "Union, Hyatt Hotels Still at Odds," *Los Angeles Times* (July 23, 1991). See Rodolfo F. Acuña, *Anything but Mexican: Chicanos in Contemporary Los Angeles* (London: Verso, 1996). Patrick J. McDonnell, "Hotel Boycott Is a High-Stakes Battle for Union," *Los Angeles Times* (February 3, 1996). Maria Elena Durazo was elected to the California State Senate, representing District 24 November 6, 2018, https://ballotpedia.org/Maria_Elena_Durazo.

73 "Justice for Janitors actions (1990 through 2006)," http://www.youtube.com/watch?v=WKfQgUn7UNg. "Stronger Colorado/Justice for Janitors Denver Rally," http://www.youtube.com/watch?v=WV_1vb0JDHg. "NOW 'Janitor Justice'?"; PBS (October 26, 2007), http://www.youtube.com/watch?v=kdK7Chg7Dm4&feature=related.

74 "Remembering One of Labor's Great Organizers - PBF Remembers Mike Garcia," Peggy Browning Fund, March 31, 2017, https://www.peggybrowningfund.org/news/item/719-remembering-one-of-labor-s-great-organizers-pbf-remembers-mike-garcia. Ruth Milkman, *L.A. Story: Immigrant Workers and the Future of the U.S. Labor Movement* (Russell Sage Foundation, 2006), 160–162.

75 Sonia Nazario, "Janitors Settle Suit, Involving Clash in 1990," *Los Angeles Times* (September 4, 1990). Rodolfo F. Acuña, "America Retreats on Labor Laws," *Los Angeles Times* (July 16, 1990). Bob Baker, "Tentative Accord Ok'd to End Janitor's Strike," *Los Angeles Times* (June 26, 1990). Sonia Nazario, "For Militant Union, It's a War," *Los Angeles Times* (August 19, 1993). Harry Bernstein, "It's a Fine Line Between Profit and Greed," *Los Angeles Times* (January 2, 1994).

76 Labor Community Strategy Center, http://www.thestrategycenter.org/project/bus-riders-union.

77 Bob Baker, "L.A.'s Booming Auto Industry Now a Memory," *Los Angeles Times* (July 20, 1991). Henry Weinstein, "Boycott by UAW of GM Threatened,"

Los Angeles Times (May 15, 1983). Eric Mann, *Taking on General Motors: A Case Study of the UAW Campaign to Keep GM Van Nuys Open* (Los Angeles: Center for Labor Research and Education, Institute of Industrial Relations, University of California Los Angeles, 1987), 7–9, 219–50. James F. Peltz, "General Motors Plant in Van Nuys to Close," *Los Angeles Times* (July 2, 1991).

78 Hector Figueroa, "Unions Doing Significant Organizing Among Latino Workers," Tweet, NACLA, https://nacla.org/article/unions-doing-significant-organizing-among-latino-workers.

79 "The Women of 'Fuerza Unida'," http://www.youtube.com/watch?v=TlIODcghnHk. Christopher Bonastia, "The Historical Trajectory of Civil Rights Enforcement in Health Care." *Journal of Policy History*, Cambridge University Press, Vol. 18, No. 3, 2006, 362—386.

80 "Texas Plant Closure Still Haunting Levi's" (November 1, 1992). Reese Erlich, "Former Levi Strauss Workers Protest Texas Plant Closing," *Christian Science Monitor* (November 9, 1992). Alexander Cockburn, "Merciless Cruelties of Bottom Line," *Arizona Republic* (Phoenix, May 23, 1993). Suzanne Espinosa Solis, "Rare Shadow on Company's Image: Ex-Workers Take on Levi Strauss," *San Francisco Chronicle* (July 18, 1994). "Fuerza Unida, http://fuerzaunida.freeservers.com/. Leslie Kaufman, "Levi Is Closing 11 Factories; 5,900 Jobs Cut," *New York Times*, Feb. 23, 1999. http://www.nytimes.com/1999/02/23/business/levi-is-closing-11-factories-5900-jobs-cut.html. "Levi Strauss & Co.," Independent Lens, PBS, http://www.pbs.org/independentlens/chinablue/levis.html.

81 Harry Bernstein, "Farm Workers Still Mired in Poverty," *Los Angeles Times* (July 25, 1985). Harry Bernstein, "The Boycott: Chávez Gets a Slow Start," *Los Angeles Times* (July 25, 1985). Harry Bernstein, "Growers Still Addicted to Foreign Workers," *Los Angeles Times* (October 2, 1985). Harry Bernstein, "Ruling May Devastate Chávez's Union," *Los Angeles Times* (February 25, 1987). Union organizing among Mexicans was fertile in the 1980s and 1990s and up to the present. Indeed, the material could fill a book. Denisse Roca-Servat, "Justice for Roofers," *Labor Studies Journal*, Sep. 2010, Vol. 35(3), 343–363. Ruth Milkman, ed., *Organizing immigrants: The challenge for unions in contemporary California* (Ithaca, N.Y.: ILR Press, 2000).

82 Rochelle L. Stanfield, "Reagan Courting Women, Minorities, But It May Be Too Late to Win Them," *National Journal* 15, No. 22 (May 28, 1983), 1118ff. *Dallas Morning News* (October 19, 1984). Juan Vásquez, "Watch out for Willie Velásquez," *Nuestro* (March 1979), 20.

83 Robert Gnaizda, "Mario Obledo, Latino Vote: The 'Sleeping Giant' Stirs," *Los Angeles Times* (November 13, 1983). Gloria Molina interviewed by Carlos Vásquez (1944), Courtesy of the Department of Special Collections/UCLA Library, Calisphere (1990), http://content.cdlib.org/xtf/view?docId=hb8b69p65d&chunk.id=div00011&brand=calisphere&doc.view=entire_text.

84 Chip Jacobs, "Return of the Native," *Los Angeles City Beat* (April 7, 2005), http://chipjacobs.com/articles/profiles/return-of-the-native/. John P. Schmal, "Chicano Representation: Coming into their own (1975–1984)," HispanicVista.com, http://www.hispanicvista.com/HVC/Columnist/jschmal/071805jpschmal1.htm. Acuña, *Anything but Mexican*, 56, 74, 98.

85 Frank del Olmo, "Snyder's Narrow Victory Gives Latino Political Activists a Rude Awakening," *Los Angeles Times* (April 28, 1983). Janet Clayton, "Snyder's Decision Throws Eastside Seat Up for Grabs," *Los Angeles Times* (January 3, 1985). Frank del Olmo, "Alatorre Vs. Snyder," *Los Angeles Times* (January 31, 1985).

86 Douglas Johnson, "Latinos and Redistricting: 'Californios for Fair Representation' and California Redistricting in the 1980s," The Rose Institute of State and Local Government, Claremont McKenna College, July 1991.

87 KRISTA DALY, "The Demographics of the San Fernando Valley," *El Nuevo Sol* (May 5, 2011), http://elnuevosol.net/2011/05/the-demographics-of-the-san-fernando-valley/.

88 Douglas Johnson, "Latinos and Redistricting: 'Californios for Fair Representation' and California Redistricting in the 1980s," The Rose Institute of State and Local Government Claremont McKenna College, July 1991. Henry Cisneros Interview: Charlie Rose: July 26, 1996, no longer available on Internet.

89 Henry Cisneros, *Regionalism: The New Geography of Opportunity* (Washington DC: The Urban Institute, 1995). Rodolfo Rosales, "Personality and Style in San Antonio Politics, Henry Cisneros and Bernardo Eureste, 1975–1985," in David Montejano, ed., *Chicano Politics and Society in the Late Twentieth Century* (Austin: University of Texas Press, 1999), 3–30.

90 Rodolfo Rosales, *The Illusion of Inclusion: The Untold Political Story of San Antonio* (Austin: University of Texas Press, 2000), p. 4.

91 Rosales, Ibid.

92 Kemper Diehl and Jan Jarboe, *Henry Cisneros: Portrait of a New American* (San Antonio, TX: Corona Publishing, 1985). Rodolfo F. Acuña, *Occupied America: A History of Chicanos*, 3rd ed. (New York: Harper & Row, 1988), 430–37. Marshall Ingersol, "San Antonio's Mayor Is Simply 'Henry' to

Everyone," *Christian Science Monitor* (March 24, 1984). James García, "Cisneros Fall Wasn't a Tragedy," *Dallas Morning News* (January 4, 1998).

93 "Where Minority Mayors Ride High," *U.S. News & World Report* (April 22, 1985), 12. Peter Skerry, "Neighborhood COPS; The Resurrection of Saul Alinsky," *New Republic* (February 6, 1984), 27. Peter Skerry, *Mexican Americans: The Ambivalent Minority* (New York: Free Press, 1993), 66. Robert Reinhold, "Mexican-Americans in Texas Move into Political Mainstream," *New York Times* (September 15, 1985).

94 Teresa Cordova, "Harold Washington and the Rise of Latino Electoral Politics in Chicago, 1982–1987," in Montejano. Ibid., pp. 31–57.

95 Rita Arias Jirasek and Carlos Tortolero, *Mexican Chicago* (Chicago, IL: Arcadia Publishing, 2001), 135–45. Ray Hutchison, "Historiography of Chicago's Mexican Community," Urban and Regional Studies University of Wisconsin-Green Bay, April 1999, http://tigger.uic.edu/~marczim/mlac/papers/hutchison.htm. Chicago Activist Voices Opinion on Immigration, Online News Hour, PBS, http://www.pbs.org/newshour/bb/social_issues/july-dec06/immigration_08-18.html. Karen Mary Davalos, "Ethnic Identity Among Mexican and Mexican American Women in Chicago, 1920–1991" (PhD Dissertation, Yale University, 1993). Latino Institute, *Al Filo/At the Cutting Edge: The Empowerment of Chicago's Latino Electorate* (Chicago, IL: Latino Institute, 1986), 1–6, 11, 14–15, 18–19, 24–26.

96 "New Mexico Offers a Preview of Mobilization," *New York Times* (September 1, 1983); interview with nine academicians within the state. Ted Robbins, "1980 Race Set Tone for Richardson's Political Future," NPR, September 13, 2007, http://www.npr.org/templates/story/story.php?storyId=14361319.

97 Chip Martínez, "Federico Peña: Denver's First Hispanic Mayor," *Nuestro* (August 1983), 14–17. Steve Padilla, "In Search of Hispanic Voters," *Nuestro* (August 1983), 20. "A Mile High: Denver Buys Peña's Dream," *Time* (July 4, 1983), 22. Kenneth T. Walsh, "Minority Mayors on Fast Track," *U.S. News & World Report* (April 7, 1986), 31–32.

98 Bill Boyarsky, "Battle Over Hermosillo: It's Just the Start," *Los Angeles Times*, August 25, 1993.

99 Acuña, *Anything but Mexican*, 152–53. Mark Z. Barabak, "Latinos Struggle for Role in National Leadership, Politics," *Los Angeles Times* (July 7, 1998).

100 José Angel Gutiérrez, *Albert A. Peña Jr.: Dean of Chicano Politics* (East Lansing: Michigan State University Press; 2017).

101 Rodolfo F. Acuña, *Sometimes There Is No Other Side: Chicanos and the Myth of Equality* (Notre Dame, IN: University of Notre Dame Press, 1998), 66. Lisa J. Montoya, Carol Hardy-Fanta, and Sonia Garcia, "Latina Politics: Gender, Participation, and Leadership," *PS: Political Science & Politics* 33, No. 3 (September 2000), 555–61. Mary Benanti, "Hispanic Officeholders 'Barometer' of Progress," *USA Today* (September 18, 1987).

102 Sarah Deutsch, "Gender, Labor History, and Chicano/a Ethnic Identity," *Frontiers* 14, No. 2 (1994), 1–9. Virginia Escalante, Nancy Rivera, and Victor Valle, "Inside the World of Latinas," *Los Angeles Times* (August 7, 1983). "For Business: Making Full Use of the Nation's Human Capital. Fact-Finding Report of the Federal Glass Ceiling Commission Release by the Department of Labor," March 1995, Washington, DC, http://digitalcommons.ilr.cornell.edu/cgi/viewcontent.cgi?article=1118&context=key_workplace.

103 Mary Pardo, *Mexican American Women Activists: Identity and Resistance in Two Los Angeles Communities* (Philadelphia, PA: Temple University Press, 1998). Rodolfo F. Acuña's *Herald-Examiner* articles on the Mothers of East Los Angeles are in his collection at the California State Northridge Library.

104 Rodolfo F. Acuña, "In fighting East L.A. prison, Molina and Roybal-Allard challenge male politicos," *Los Angeles Herald Examiner* (August 5, 1988).

105 Rodolfo F. Acuña, Ibid.

106 Matea Gold, "The Mothers' Saga: How a Movement Split in Two: Activism: A plan for a prison near Boyle Heights spurred a group of women to action. Along the way, a bitter division occurred, and it endures to this day," *Los Angeles Times* (August 29, 1999).

107 Marilyn Martinez, "Legacy of a Mother's Dedication: Juana Gutierrez, a Beacon for East L.A., Wins National Award," *Los Angeles Times* (September 7, 1995).

108 Rebecca Morales and Paul Ong, "Immigrant Women in Los Angeles," *Economic and Industrial Democracy* 12, No. 1 (February 1991), 65–81. Benjamin Mark Cole, "Do Immigrants Underpin L.A. Business World?" *Los Angeles Business Journal* (May 27, 1991). Elaine M. Allensworth, "Earnings Mobility of First and '1.5' Generation Mexican-Origin Women and Men: A Comparison with U.S.-Born Mexican Americans and Non-Hispanic Whites," *Internal Migration Review* 31, No. 2 (Summer 1997), 386–410. Elizabeth Martínez and Ed McCaughan, "Chicanas and Mexicanas within a Transnational Working Class," in Adelaida R. Del Castillo, ed., *Between Borders: Essays on Mexicana/Chicana History* (Los Angeles, CA: Floricanto Press, 1990), 31–52. Pierrette Hondagneu-Sotelo, *Gendered Transition: Mexican Experiences of Immigration* (Berkeley: University of California Press, 1994). Rebecca Morales and Paul M. Ong, "The Illusion of Progress," in Morales and Bonilla, eds., *Latinos*, 69–70.

109 Morales and Ong, "The Illusion of Progress," 64–77. Claudia Dorrington, "Central American Refugees in Los Angeles: Adjustment of Children and Families," in Ruth E. Zambrana, ed., *Understanding Latino Families: Scholarship, Policy, and Practice* (Thousand Oaks, CA: Sage, 1995), 111. Claire Spiegel, "Prenatal Care in L.A. Worsening, Report Concludes," *Los Angeles Times* (July 12, 1988). Jill L. Sherer, "Neighbor to Neighbor: Community Health Workers Educate Their Own," *Hospitals & Health Networks* 68, No. 20 (October 20, 1994), 52. Leo R. Chaves, Estebán T. Flores, and Marta López-Garza, "Undocumented Latin American Immigrants and U.S. Health Services: An Approach to a Political Economy of Utilization," *Medical Anthropology Quarterly* 6, No. 1 (March 1, 1992),: 6–26. David James Rose, "Coming Out, Standing Out: Hispanic American Gays and Lesbians," *Hispanic* (June 1994), 44ff.

110 Knight-Ridder Newspapers, "Lost Ground In '80s, Hispanics Say," *Chicago Tribune*, December 17, 1989, http://articles.chicagotribune.com/1989-12-17/news/8903180827_1_non-hispanic-whites-household-poverty.

111 José Angel Gutiérrez, Michelle Meléndez, and Sonia Adriana Noyola, *Chicanas in Charge: Texas Women in the Public Arena* (Lanham, MD: Rowman & Littlefield, 2007), 106–12. "María Antonietta Berriozabal," Tejano Voices, http://library.uta.edu/tejanovoices/interview.php?cmasno=033.

112 "Severita Lara," Tejano Voices, UT Arlington, http://library.uta.edu/tejanovoices/interview.php?cmasno=013. Gutiérrez et al., *Chicanas in Charge*, 113, 121.

113 "Alicia Chacón," Tejano Voices, UT Arlington, http://library.uta.edu/tejanovoices/interview.php?cmasno=002. Gutiérrez et al., *Chicanas in Charge*, 47–55.

114 "Norma Villarreal Ramírez," Tejano Voices, http://library.uta.edu/tejanovoices/interview.php?cmasno=007. José Angel Gutiérrez, "Experiences of Chicana County Judges in Texas Politics: In Their Own Words," *Frontiers* 20, No. IL (July–August 1999), 181ff. See Tejano Voices, http://library.uta.edu/tejanovoices/gallery.php.

115 Gutiérrez et al., *Chicanas in Charge*, 131–35, 144.

116 Esperanza Peace and Justice Center, http://www.esperanzacenter.org/.

117 Amy Hilsman Kastely, "Esperanza v. City of San Antonio: Politics, Power, and Culture," *Frontiers: A Journal of Women Studies* 24, Nos. 2 & 3 (2003), 189, 190. *Esperanza Peace and Justice Center, a Non-Profit Corporation, The San Antonio Lesbian & Gay Media Project, an Unincorporated Association, and VAN, an Unincorporated Association, Plaintiffs, v. City of San Antonio, and Howard Eak, in his official capacity as Mayor of the City of San Antonio, Defendants*. Cause No. Sa-98-ca-0696-og United States District Court for the Western District of Texas, San Antonio Division 316 F. Supp. 2d 433; 2001 U.S. Dist. Lexis 6259 May 15, 2001, Decided.

118 Kastely, "Esperanza v. City of San Antonio," 195.

119 Rodolfo F. Acuña, ""The less redevelopment on the East Side, the better," *Los Angeles Herald Examiner* (July 10, 1987).

120 Rodolfo Acuña, "Olvera Street faces wholesale changes," *Los Angeles Herald Examiner* (August 7, 1987). These articles were also published in *La Opinión* in Spanish.

121 Rodolfo Acuña, "Power grabbers threaten dream of Latino museum," *Los Angeles Herald Examiner* (January 29, 1988). Rodolfo F. Acuña, "Shut Out by Historical Amnesia—Latinos: Denied their past, these original Californians have become our political underclass," *Los Angeles Times* (Feb. 25, 1990), 5. Gloria L Charnes, "LA's Olvera Street Paved With History," *Orlando Sentinel* (Feb. 19, 1989), H.3.

122 Rodolfo Acuña, "Our 'fantasy heritage' gets royal touch," *Los Angeles Herald Examiner* (October 9, 1987).

123 George Ramos, "*Olvera Street* Political Battle Waged Over Plan to Upgrade Tattered Tourist Spot," *Los Angeles Times* (Feb. 3, 1989), 1.

124 Rodolfo F. Acuña, "History Is People, Not Bricks; Olvera Street: Mexicans were here long before the gringo. A multi-ethnic museum would trample that heritage," *Los Angeles Times* (Apr. 2, 1990), 5.

125 George Ramos, "Olvera Street Revival Wins Approval of Commission Cultural: But merchants loudly decry the action, saying it could threaten the area's Mexican heritage," *Los Angeles Times* (June 12, 1990), 1.

126 Gloria Ricci Lothrop, "Italians Have a Legitimate Los Angeles History, Too; Olvera Street: Given the legitimacy and limited scope of the museum proposal, the argument against it is a red herring," *Los Angeles Times* (June 19, 1990), 7. Len Pitt, "Olvera Street: One Person's Fantasy Becomes Los Angeles Realpolitik Restoration: Proving the past can be what you perceive it, a crime-ridden, rat-infested service road was transformed into a Mexican marketplace," *Los Angeles Times* (July 1, 1990), 5.

127 George Ramos, "Plan to Put Eatery in Pico House Draws Fire Development: Chicano activists and Olvera Street merchants say $15-million project that includes restaurant will disrupt the Mexican flavor of El Pueblo de Los Angeles park," *Los Angeles Times* (Oct. 12, 1990), 3.

Chapter 16
The Millennium

Learning Objectives

16.1 Determine the roles of construction and erasure in creating social illusions in the United States.

16.2 Relate demographic and voting rights changes to Latina/o political representation in the 1990s.

16.3 Analyze how Mexicans fought neoliberal institutions and policies initiated through NAFTA.

16.4 Analyze the relationship between Central Americans and the United States during the 1990s.

16.5 Compare Chicana/o responses to police brutality in California and Washington in the 1990s.

16.6 Explain how Chicana/o students decolonized history through engagement with Indigenous art and identity.

16.7 Contextualize the fight for academic freedom and Chicana/o identities on college campuses in the 1990s.

16.8 Describe the Chicana/o response to California's attempts to annihilate their history and identity through racist-nativist Propositions in the 1990s.

16.9 Compare regional changes in migration in the 1990s.

16.10 Explain how the War on Drugs led to the destabilization of Mexico and Chicana/o communities.

16.11 Describe how U.S. neoliberal values influenced the Mexican elite.

The 1990s saw the emergence of dozens of Millenarian Movements. Throughout Christian history, the year 2000 marked the 2000-year anniversary of the birth of Christ. In 1990, believers believed that the millennium would bring about the Christian prophecy of the second coming of Christ and the creation of the perfect society. The 2000-year age would end and a "golden age of peace, justice, and prosperity" would begin. The 1990s were a time of general unrest but they failed to bring peace, justice, and prosperity.

The Millennial Era of the 1990s were also years of change. The Y2K (Year 2000) problem was cultural because of American angst that computers would fail when their clocks would update to January 1, 2000. Because computers were programmed to automatically assume the date began with "19" as in "1977" and "1988," people feared that when the time turned from December 31, 1999, to January 1, 2000, computers would be so confused that they would shut down completely."[1] This caused panic the computer bugs or the aliens would take over much like the body snatchers.

It was a decade of fear for Americans. In turn, Mexicans/Latinos entered in school in greater numbers. The millennial as they called them had a greater sense of history and human rights. More and more of them questioned whether the last three wars had been fought for democracy. There parents had lived through the 1968 LA and MAYO School Walkouts and participated in college groups such as the Movimiento Estudiantil Chicanas/os de Aztlan (MEChA). Their communitarian network was larger and feelings of collectivity was stronger among larger numbers of them. The millennials also grew up in a world where the United States was not the greatest country in the world.

The Chickens Come Home to Roost

16.1 Determine the roles of construction and erasure in creating social illusions in the United States.

During the 1980s, the Mexican immigrant population jumped from 2.2 to 4.3 million. U.S.-financed civil wars uprooted Central Americans, whose population in the United States jumped from 354,000 in 1980 to 1,134,000 in 1990.[2] The chickens come home to roost is an old saying meaning that curses always return home to roost. In other words, offensive words or actions rebound: "What goes around comes around." Geoffrey Chaucer in "The Parson's Tale" (ca. 1390), wrote that curses are like "a bird that returns again to his own nest." The saying is key to understanding the worldwide migration of people that is today taking place.

Like climate change, migration is human-made. It is caused by inequality and a history of colonialism and exploitation by European and American occupations that short-circuited the dreams and the identity of many civilizations that were evolving at the time the destroyers arrived. In order to control colonized people, the occupiers stole their history and identity. American and European imperialism brought about the great migrations taking place today; they are the consequence of inequality and a global caste system based on race. The American and other Empires created the illusion that the colonized were part of the grandeur of America and European empires.

The American Dream is like the lottery constructed to create false dreams. Fashion magazines, the media, motion pictures, and the lottery (a green card) keep these dreams alive. The aura of American Empire kindles the illusions of Empire. Since the early nineteenth century Americans and others have believed that the United States had the material trappings that most of the rest of the world lacked.[3] According to the Word Watch Institute, "As many as 2.8 billion people on the planet struggle to survive on less than $2 a day, and more than one billion people lack reasonable access to safe drinking water." At the same time, "The United States, with less than 5% of the global population, uses about a quarter of the world's fossil fuel resources—burning up nearly 25% of the coal, 26% of the oil, and 27% of the world's natural gas."[4]

By the beginning of the millennium, this illusion of invincibility began to evaporate as people in the rest of the world sensed America's decline. Failed wars in Korea, Vietnam, and Central America pierced the aura of superiority. Walls could not keep people out. It was like when people grow old, and those around them can see and feel the decline. By the end of the 1990s, Americans and others could feel the degeneration, and the world around America reacted differently to it than after World War II.

The Erasure of Memory

The value of history is the creation of a collective historical memory that forms a counternarrative to the official story.[5] "Memory is a product of ideological construction that can be used as a key element in the elaboration of collective identity."[6] It gives political and social significance to events and it links them to a community and creates an awareness of a collective past such as the walkouts and the present injustices in the treatment of immigrants. A collective memory triggers the question, why? And in whose interest?[7] Collective memory is like touching a hot iron and may evoke a collective response, so it was in the interest of the colonizers to erase it.

By the 1990s, fewer Americans were under the illusion that the American Dream included them. Social scientists such as Claude Lévi-Strauss exposed how national and local ruling elites use misconceptions and misunderstandings to erase truth. This erasure keeps the structure intact, allowing the socialization of individuals within minority communities to accept the belief that if they don't make it is their fault.[8] Although some minority individuals are the beneficiaries of past community struggles, some support politicians who clearly oppose their social and economic interests. Simone de Beauvoir, in her book *The Ethics of Ambiguity*, wrote, "the oppressor would not be so strong if he did not have accomplices among the oppressed themselves; mystification is one of the forms of oppression."[9] Thus it is no surprise to find the unconscious and conscious collaboration of the colonized with the deception.

Toward the Millennium

16.2 Relate demographic and voting rights changes to Latina/o political representation in the 1990s.

Numbers matter:

> "During the 1990s, the Latino population marked its dominance as the ethnic group most responsible for population growth in the United States. The Latino population expanded from 22.4 million in 1990 to 35.3 million in 2000, a growth rate of 58 percent."[10]

The 1990 Census showed that 25 percent of California's 29,760,021 inhabitants (an undercount) were Latinos, an increase from 4,544,331 (19 percent) in 1980 to 7,687,938 (almost 26 percent) 10 years later. This population was heavily concentrated in 10 assembly districts, yet Mexicans/Latinos represented only four of the districts. (The California Assembly had a total of 80 seats.) At stake in redistricting were seats in both houses of the state legislature and in Congress. The basic problem was that Chicana/os and Latinos did not always vote, for various reasons: Many were not citizens, and a substantial number were under 18, or were 18- to 35-year-olds, which made up a large proportion of the Latino population. That demographic overall had lower registration and turnout rates. In 1990, only 844,000 Latinos voted out of a population of 4,739,000 who were 18 or older. Some 2,301,000 adults were citizens, 1,218,000 of whom were registered to vote. Another problem was incumbency: White politicos stayed in office for years, and it took substantial efforts to win their seats. As always, Democrats in the California legislature protected their own. Meanwhile, Governor Pete Wilson vetoed three proposed redistricting bills, claiming that the Democratic majority was seeking an "unfair partisan advantage."

Because the legislature and the governor could not agree on a plan, the Chief Justice of the California Supreme Court appointed a panel of three jurists. They remapped districts for the state legislature and Congress. Court-devised maps made it possible for Latinos to increase their representation by 40 percent in the state legislature. The 1992 elections made room for gains in the Assembly, where seven Latinos won election. Latinos did not do as well in Congress and gained only one additional seat. The Mexican American community believed that with proper redistricting it could have gained an addition congressional seat. In 1992, Assemblywoman Lucille Roybal-Allard, the daughter of retiring Congressman Edward R. Roybal, was elected to Congress. Nationwide, that same year 17 Latinos were elected to Congress. In California alone, an estimated one million Latinos voted. The following spring, Latinos won some 60 city council elections in Los Angeles County alone.[11]

Up to this point, population growth and the Voting Rights Act of 1965 and its amendments drove Chicano political victories. In Texas, population clusters made it almost impossible to prevent Mexican Americans getting elected. However, in California in 1990 it was almost impossible for Latino candidates to dislodge incumbents who would literally die in office. In 1990, by a margin of 52 percent to 48 percent, California voters passed Proposition 140 that put term limits on most state offices. Pushed by Republicans in the days when the Democrats held sway over the California legislature, the proposition reflected the mood of Californians, who trusted neither themselves nor politicos to govern. In their usual self-righteous way, California voters thought that by passing an initiative they would empower themselves merely by forcing incumbents out of office.

Term limits opened the floodgates for more Latinos to enter politics. The proposition led to the election of Cruz Bustamante as the first Mexican American speaker of the California Assembly, and term limits forced him to seek higher office. He was later elected California Lieutenant Governor in 1998—a first in the twentieth century. The 1998 elections increased the number of Latina/o elected officials in the state legislature to 24, including a historic high of four Latino Republicans. That year Antonio Villaraigosa was elected speaker of the Assembly. Cruz Bustamante became lieutenant governor. The engineer of this growth was State Senator Richard Polanco, who was chair of the Latino Caucus. However, these gains did not come without pain.[12]

During the 1990s, the population of Texas grew by 23 percent, compared to 13 percent nationwide. The number of Latinos rose from 4.3 million in 1990 to almost 6.7 million in 2000, a 53 percent rise—one of every three Texans identified as a Latino/a. The white population grew by only 6 percent. Latinos became the largest ethnic group in Houston, Dallas, San Antonio, and El Paso. Seven Tejanos sat in the state legislature in 1960, 6 in 1965, 15 in 1974, 19 in 1983, and 25 in 1992. Elected women officials among Mexican Americans outnumbered women officials from other groups. The first Chicana elected to the Texas state legislature was Irma Rangel from Kingsville in 1976, and the first elected to the state senate was Judith Zaffirini from Laredo in 1984. Other changes took place, such as most *La Raza Unida* activists joining Mexican American Democrats (MAD). "[By] 1990 more than 1,000 Mexican Americans (not all MAD members) attended the state convention."[13]

The number of Tejano elected officials increased to 2,030 in 1993, more than in any other state. It is estimated that 40 percent of all Latino elected officials in the country were from Texas. Latinos, mostly Mexican Americans, made up a quarter of the state's 17 million residents. Some 2,684,000 Latinos were eligible to vote in Texas; 40 percent (1,073,600) were registered. In 1994 the Texas congressional delegation included five Mexican Americans, all members of the House. However, the question remained: Do numbers automatically translate into political power?

Most pundits assume that Mexican Americans vote for the Democratic Party as a matter of course. Yet in the 1994 national congressional elections, Latino support for the Democratic Party dropped from 72 percent in 1992 to 61 percent in 1994. There was a spillover to state legislative races; of 140 Latino incumbents in nine states, four lost their seats. Nonetheless, as a group, they were effective and brought about some reforms.[14]

Outside California and Texas, it was difficult to get Mexican/Latinos elected to office. For instance, in Iowa the population of Mexican/Latinos grew 153 percent during the 1990s. They aspired to be represented in the famed Iowa Caucus since that would have been an indicator of the power of the Latino vote. Their numbers were not large enough, however, for representation. Latinos—especially

Mexican Americans—were young, with almost 40 percent of the nation's Latinos not yet of voting age. Another relevant fact was that many Mexican/Latinos were not yet U.S. citizens.

How important are numbers then? University of Maryland political science professor James G. Gimpel shows that as of 2004, 70.2 percent of U.S. House campaign contributions came from outside the candidates' districts. It is no wonder then that as much as 90 percent of campaign contributions in Los Angeles City Council are estimated to come from outside the city council districts.[15]

The North American Free Trade Agreement

16.3 Analyze how Mexicans fought neoliberal institutions and policies initiated through NAFTA.

Because of the history of racism toward Mexicans and as a justification for the occupation of Mexico's former territories, Mexico has been historically demonized. In 1990 Mexico had a population of 85,609,404 people. By 2000 it reached 103 million and 15 years later around 130 million. It was the 10th largest nation in the world, larger than Canada, and that alone made it an important market. Therefore its inclusion as a trading partner and a source of labor made it vital to American interests.[16]

In 1991 President George Herbert Walker Bush proposed the North American Free Trade Agreement (NAFTA). Bush then pressured Congress to put the negotiations on the "fast track"—ensuring that congressional debate and criticism of the treaty would be minimal. Mexican President Carlos Salinas de Gortari hyped the treaty as the key to Mexico's future. NAFTA's advocates dismissed questions about its effects on the environment, human rights, political reform, Mexican workers, and Indigenous populations. The most controversial feature was a change in Article 27 of the Mexican Constitution, pertaining to the nation's *ejidos* (communal lands): NAFTA made it possible for *ejido* farmers to sell or mortgage their land. It was a clear attack on the reforms of the Mexican Revolution as Gortari launched his neoliberal policies and plans to privatize Mexico's land and resources.[17]

Mexico was demoralized by the crash of the early 1980s and austerity programs of the World Bank and the International Monetary Fund. Mexico turned to neoliberalism that was sweeping Latin America and a program of privatization, turning away from the "aging nationalism" that had gripped the nation since the Mexican Revolution.[18] Under Salinas de Gortari, a new generation of U.S.-trained economists and policymakers implemented market-oriented strategies that the United States promoted in Eastern Europe and the Soviet Union. It laid the groundwork for NAFTA.

American universities played a role similar to the U.S. Army's center at Fort Benning, Ga., the School of the Americas that trained 60,000 South and Central American soldiers. The privatization of state enterprises accelerated under Harvard-trained Salinas de Gortari who made it the cornerstone of his structural adjustment program. By 1993, Salinas sold a total of 390 state enterprises—63 percent of the firms held by Mexico in 1988. Among the American-trained technocrats: President Ernesto Zedillo (Yale, PhD, '78), Carlos Salinas de Gortari (Harvard, PhD, '78) and Miguel de la Madrid (Harvard, Master's, '65) as well as finance secretaries Jaime Serra Puche (Yale, PhD, '79) and Guillermo Ortiz Martinez (Stanford, PhD, '77). The Mexican alumni admired and emulated their mentors and professors at elite U.S. Management Schools.[19]

As a result of NAFTA, the Mexican standard for progress became the number of billionaires neoliberalism produced. Mexico, where 50 percent of the people lived in poverty, had 11 billionaires by 2012. A leading beneficiary of privatization was Carlos Slim Helú, who became the richest man in the world — a Mexican business magnate, investor, and philanthropist. As of December 2013, his corporate holdings amounted to U.S. $71.2 billion. Slim made his money in communications, technology, retailing, and finance.[20]

The debate over NAFTA split Latinos into ideological camps. Union activists, environmentalists, and human rights groups campaigned against NAFTA. They argued that NAFTA would take U.S. jobs away, threaten environmental laws, and hurt Mexican farmers and workers by privatizing the Mexican economy. Their campaigns, for the most part, were ineffective and often bordered on racism. U.S. labor in general was mainly concerned about job loss and depressed wages. Meanwhile, Bill Clinton became president and brought reluctant Mexican/Latino organizations into line through aggressive use of patronage. On November 18, 1993, the U.S. House passed NAFTA by 234–200 votes, 16 more than the needed 218; 102 Democrats voted for and 156 voted against it.[21] As expected, the Senate voted for the accord. The Latino vote in the House of Representatives (which was essentially Chicano) included two Chicanos against it—Henry B. González and Marty Martínez.

On January 1, 1994, the day that NAFTA went into effect, the *Ejercito Zapatista de Liberación Nacional* (EZLN; Zapatista National Liberation Army) rebelled in the southern Mexican state of Chiapas, citing the passage of NAFTA and the changes in Article 27 of the Constitution. NAFTA would encourage the influx of cheap corn into Mexico, underselling the small farmer. The Indigenous People argued that the privatization of land would lead to the death of their culture and way of life.[22]

Tensions in Mexico rose as fears of NAFTA rallied Indigenous Villagers in defense of their traditional lands and way of life. The Zapatistas knew that NAFTA would increase their removal from the land and eliminate their *ejidos*. Mexico's post-NAFTA policies wiped out thousands of Mexican rural farms and increased rural poverty and lawlessness. In the United States, many youth and activists supported the Zapatistas.[23]

The Zapatistas raised the "Land and Liberty" banner of Emiliano Zapata. The Zapatistas were supported by Monsignor Samuel Ruiz García.[24] In 1974, Ruiz convened an Indigenous Congress to call attention to the plight of Mexico's Indigenous People. In 1989, Ruiz García founded the Fray Bartolomé Human Rights Center to investigate human rights violations and conflicts over land and religion. García joined the movement after he read the NAFTA agreement; he saw it as the final straw in the systematic destruction of Indigenous communities. For his work, Ruiz was labeled a subversive and he became the target of assassination attempts. Fr. García died at the age 86 in 2011.[25]

On December 22, 1997, with the concurrence of Mexican government officials the Acteal massacre occurred. Masked gunmen from a paramilitary group murdered 45 unarmed Tzotzil who sought refuge in a camp on the road to the village of Acteal, some 20 miles north of San Cristobal. Children, women, and old people were massacred while praying and fasting for peace in the chapel of Acteal. The murdered villagers belonged to the Abejas, who were sympathetic to the Zapatistas. The Mexican government did not negotiate in good faith with the Zapatistas. Thus a stalemate resulted that continues to this day. Because of world opinion, the Mexican government so far has not mobilized the army for fear of worldwide reprisals. Meanwhile, the Zapatistas engaged in "low-intensity warfare" to preserve the land and culture. They pursued, as much as possible, a non-violent struggle.[26]

Demoralization and skepticism spread among Mexicans. Shortly before President Carlos Salinas de Gortari left office, drug scandals broke out involving his family and his brother Raul was implicated. Carlos's brother Raul Salinas placed more than $120 million in foreign banks.[27] Just as NAFTA was in the hands of Euro-American capitalists, most people in Mexico were aware of who controlled of the drug trade: They were dependent on the U.S. market and U.S. bankers.

"Don't Mourn, Organize!"

César Chávez died in his sleep in 1993, while on union business in Arizona. More than 40,000 mourners attended Chávez's funeral in Delano, California. Chávez followed a Franciscan regimen: He exercised regularly; he ate healthy, vegetarian, pesticide-free food; and he often fasted. However, he died of exhaustion, having pushed his body to its limits. César told his son-in-law the night before his death, "I'm tired . . . I'm really very tired."[28] His death marked the passing of a generation hovered between the Baby Boomers and the millennials. Chávez's son-in-law, Arturo Rodríguez, assumed the UFW presidency. The union immediately stepped up activity in the fields, launching a major campaign to organize farmworkers in California; the struggle was often bitter. The UFW relied heavily on its vast network of boycott volunteers. The workers, mostly poor Mexican Americans, earned an average of only $8,500 a season for up to 12-hour days with no overtime or benefits. Growers continually sprayed fields with a cancer-causing pesticide. The first target was California's strawberry industry, producing 80 percent of all berries eaten in the United States and grossing more than $550 million. More than 10,000 workers were concentrated in the Watsonville–Salinas area alone.[29] Four times more Mexican Americans lived in the United States than in 1970. "The 1990 Census included 4.3 million immigrants from Mexico. By 2000, this population more than doubled to 9.2 million with a further increase to 9.8 million in 2002."[30]

During the 1990s the number of Mexican immigrants living in the United States rose by nearly five million people. The number of working-age Mexican immigrants were recorded in the 2000 Census by year of arrival.

> At the time of the census, Mexican immigrants represented 4.1 percent of the working-age population, nearly double their proportion in 1990. The surge in arrivals from Mexico was accompanied by a remarkable shift in their residence patterns. In previous decades, nearly 80 percent of Mexican immigrants settled in either California or Texas. Over the 1990s, however, this fraction fell rapidly . . . 6.1, less than one-half of the most recent Mexican immigrants were living in California or Texas in 2000.[31]

The Brown Wave was clearly spreading.

Haciendo Patria (Creating the Homeland)

16.4 Analyze the relationship between Central Americans and the United States during the 1990s.

"Over half of all Central Americans resided in California, Texas, and Florida." This growth was mostly from immigrants from El Salvador and Guatemala.[32] Central Americans were notable in that they did not fully rely on established networks and founded organizations such as the Central American Resource Center (CARECEN), *El Rescate* (the Rescue), the Oscar Romero Health Clinic, and the Coalition for Humane Immigrant Rights of Los Angeles (CHIRLA), among others. Many Central Americans were engaged in street vending, day labor, and domestic work, and were often exploited by employers. CHIRLA instructed the workers about the laws that govern all businesses, including individual homeowners who routinely hired them for odd jobs.

Apart from a cluster in Los Angeles, Central Americans were spread throughout the United States. Salvadorans were among the most organized, and in the early 1980s the FMLN had sent organizers without documents to Washington, D.C., to lobby Congress and organize information centers. After the end of hostilities in 1991, most of them stayed and lobbied for domestic programs. That year, riots broke out in the Mt. Pleasant neighborhood of Washington, D.C., a *barrio* comprised mostly of Salvadorans and Dominicans. A confrontation between residents and the police ensued when police shot an immigrant in a *barrio* street. Several days of rebellion followed; it led to confrontations between Latinos and African Americans. This happened a year before the South Central Los Angeles uprisings.

Central American women played key roles. In the Langley Park area of Washington, D.C., Salvadoran women pushed grocery carts loaded with home cooking, selling to immigrant laborers who live in the area. Langley Park's "pupusa ladies" fed their tired, hungry neighbors for a dollar a dish. Most of the women were unwilling to put a sign on their chest begging for work. Many of them came to the United States during and after the war, leaving children behind with grandparents and other relatives, and sent money back to give them a better life. Guilt about being separated from their children and fear that they might never see them again consumed them.[33]

Making the Caravans Inevitable: Exporting Gangs

On March 3, 1991 riots broke out in South Central Los Angeles when a video was shown on television showing Los Angeles Police Department officers brutally beating Rodney King, a Black man, following a high-speed car chase. The South Central Black community rioted against the injustice. Four LAPD officers were indicted on charges of assault with a deadly weapon and excessive use of force by a police officer.

"The American Civil Liberties Union, in a report scheduled for release today, has concluded that 83.1% of Los Angeles police officers live outside the city limits, a finding that department critics say bolsters the longstanding characterization of the LAPD as an occupying army whose officers have little connection to the communities they serve."[34] The report showed that " . . . a total of 293 LAPD officers live in Simi Valley, while fewer than 200 live in the area covered by the department's Central Bureau."[35] The trial of the officers was moved from Los Angeles County to a white bedroom community in the Simi Valley of Ventura County. After a three-month trial, three of the officers were acquitted of all charges, deadlocking on one charge of excessive force against one officer. Enraged by the injustice, the African American community rebelled. "The violence was responsible for more than 50 deaths and $1 billion in property damage."[36]

During the Rodney King Rebellions following the verdict, the INS detained thousands of Mexicans and Latinos, and deported almost 800 of them. The INS also launched its Violent Gang Task Force, and in the fall of 1992 a wave of anti-immigrant sentiment infected the 1992 presidential elections.[37] This encouraged xenophobic legislation, and in 1996 new laws took effect that aimed to accelerate the deportation of illegal aliens and legal immigrants who committed crimes.

> The transfer of gang culture to El Salvador is emblematic of a problem that affects countries throughout Central America and the Caribbean. El Salvador's 12-year civil war alone drove more than a million refugees from the country; many of them made their way illegally to Southern California. But in the 1980s, Congress pressed the INS to improve its record of deporting illegal aliens. In the riots that followed the Rodney King verdict in 1992, the Los Angeles Times reported, thousands of Latinos were detained, and the INS deported almost 800 of them. The INS also launched its Violent Gang Task Force, and that fall a wave of anti-immigrant sentiment swept through electoral politics.[38]

For all intents and purposes the gang members were American made and their deportation added to the problems of countries ravaged by wars that were also made in the United States.[39] The war-weary Central American nations were not equipped to cope with this bombardment that along with the War on Drugs destroyed their civil societies.

> Congress passed the Immigration Act of 1990 that established TPS (Temporary protected status) that extended temporary protection first to Salvadorans and later to Hondurans. It was vaunted as a 90. It's a humanitarian program "whose basic principle is that the United States should suspend deportations to countries that have been destabilized by war or catastrophe." The emphasis is on temporary and the recipients are generally in limbo. The recipients are eligible for work authorization and a driver's license, but the TPS "is subject to U.S. government review" that can be "extended for up to 18 months."[40]

Meanwhile, the TPS Program is subject to review and holds nations such as El Salvador hostage. "Foreign nationals with TPS protections are generally able to obtain work authorization and a driver's license, but the TPS designation is subject to U.S. government review and can only be extended for up to 18 months. Salvadorans are by far the largest group of TPS holders."[41]

All along the Executive Branch and Congress gave ultra-right refugees preferential treatment in immigrating to the United States. Congress passed the 1997 Nicaraguan Adjustment and Central American Relief Act (NACARA) to protect Nicaraguans and Cubans from deportation if they could prove they fled Communism. By contrast, U.S. government policy excluded thousands of Salvadorans and Guatemalans from entering the United States without documents. These refugees routinely applied for political asylum and were routinely denied. Eventually, Salvadorans and Guatemalans, through Temporary Protected Status (TPS), won the right to go before an immigration judge to prove, on a case-by-case basis, that returning to their countries would cause them to suffer "extreme hardship." Under new rules, the U.S. government presumed that returning refugees to their countries of origin would in itself pose an extreme hardship for them. An INS official would hear the cases rather than a judge.

Racism is based on color: Police Brutality

16.5 Compare Chicana/o responses to police brutality in California and Washington in the 1990s.

In 1995 in Sun Valley, California, a suburb of Los Angeles, William Masters II, 35, killed an 18-year-old tagger (graffiti artist) named César Rene Arce and wounded his friend, David Hillo, 20. Both taggers were unarmed. Many Americans applauded Masters, while the Chicana/o community remained largely indifferent. In the end, the district attorney did not indict Masters for the murder; and still the community led by Latino elected officials remained silent.[42]

According to Lisa García Bedolla,

> These events reflect a system hostile to Latinos on a number of levels. First, Masters shot the youths because of racial assumptions he made about them, yet this crime was not conceptualized nor was it prosecuted as a hate crime. Second, the criminal justice system treated Hillo and Masters very differently. Though Hillo was wounded, police interrogated him for six hours and told him, falsely, that a security guard had witnessed the shooting. Masters's story was never questioned in depth, and when he gave his statement, the police rarely interrupted him.[43]

In other words, Masters was assumed innocent and the taggers guilty.

In 1999, the Los Angeles Police Department's (LAPD) Rampart scandal became public when Officer Rafael Pérez, a Rampart Community Resources Against Street Hoodlums (CRASH) anti-gang officer, negotiated a plea bargain for having stolen drugs from LAPD evidence lockers—in return for providing evidence of widespread corruption and brutality committed against gang members by the Rampart CRASH unit. Dozens of police were implicated in waging a systematic war against youth in the Pico-Union neighborhood. Despite the severity of the violations only a few Chicanos and Central Americans protested this gross violation of human rights; many Latino elected officials sided with the police.[44]

In Bellevue, a suburb of Seattle, Washington, police killed Nelson Martínez Méndez, 24, an unarmed Guatemalan accused of domestic violence against a cousin. Seattle Police shot him when he reached for his wallet. *El Centro de la Raza* of Seattle, led by Roberto Maestas, organized protests against the injustice. In January 2002, an inquest jury ruled it justifiable homicide, and the district attorney refused to prosecute the officer.[45] "The city of Bellevue... reached a $75,000 settlement with the family of a Guatemalan immigrant shot and killed by a police officer in 2001."[46]

Chicana/o Studies is a Pedagogy

16.6 Explain how Chicana/o students decolonized history through engagement with Indigenous art and identity.

By 1990 the Mexican American college student population saw a dramatic increase. This new generation did not come of age in the 1960s and did not necessarily call themselves Chicanas/os. Mostly children of immigrants, they entered the country or were born there during and after the 1960s. They often did not know about the sacrifices made by earlier generations that got them on campus. Neither the schools nor the history books gave them that sense of history. The escalating costs of education forced them to drop out of campus political activities. Along with many Mexican-origin people, a growing number of Central Americans called themselves Hispanics while others sought out their own specific national origins. Generational change and the other factors brought about a reduction of the number of activists on campus, and MEChA as an organization shrank as more Mexican Americans joined sororities and fraternities and "passed."

Meanwhile, Indigenous images in Chicana/o Literature and culture contributed to the formation of an Indigenous Chicana/o cultural politics.[47] Strands of cultural studies, identity, feminism, and nationalism formed a new narrative. In the early 1970s, student and community mariachis were common, as was Chicana/o art. Folklorico groups multiplied during the decade and Danzantes became popular; by 1979 numerous groups banded together held a Danzantes Unidos Festival at UCLA.[48] Groups such as the

Mexica Movement, built on Mexicans' Indigenous identity, produced solid research and materials; they raised questions about Mexican identity. The study of Nahuatl and Mayan was incorporated into many Chicana/o studies programs and breakthroughs were made in the area of education; identity was the key to motivating students to learn. More important was Indigenism's role in decolonizing students and helping them peel the onion and work through the erasure of history and the construction conflicting identities such as mestizo, Hispanic, and Latino. Increasingly, many students of Chicana/o studies called for a decolonization of its history.

The Mexican Bandito and the Mexican Whore

16.7 Contextualize the fight for academic freedom and Chicana/o identities on college campuses in the 1990s.

By the late 1980s, college campuses once more became battlegrounds. Groups such as the National Association of Scholars (NAS) and other conservative academic organizations waged war on minorities. With funding from conservative think tanks, they formed groups dedicated to keeping America white. The Massachusetts Association of Scholars, a 150-member affiliate of the NAS, in 1984 released an 80-page study that condemned affirmative action and diversity seminars: "For example, the NAS has conducted an incessant and well-funded campaign against multiculturalism, ethnic studies and affirmative action calling them un-American and anti-western civilization."[49]

The NAS alleged that academic freedom and American institutions were under siege by "tenured radicals" who wanted to impose political correctness ("PC") and to assault academic freedom. According to the NAS, a conspiracy of liberals, Latinos, African Americans, radicals, and homosexual professors intended to take over the Academy (universities).[50] According to the NAS, it was the tenured radicals' demands for greater diversity that was politicizing the university.[51]

The extremism of NAS and other right-wing groups emboldened fraternities and their assault on civility. Theme parties that featured racial stereotypes became common. These stereotypes singled out Mexicans and Blacks, depicting them in racist ways and signaling the return of the image of Mexicans as bandits, thieves, and whores. One of the most outrageous examples was the production of a student film at the University of California, Los Angeles, called Animal Attraction, showing a Mexican woman having sex with a donkey.[52]

Another racist incident occurred in 1992. A song to "Lupe" was found in the Theta Xi education manual for new members by a UCLA student, who turned it over to the Chicana/o student newspaper *La Gente*, which in turn published it. After reading the song, Chicanas/os were furious over verses such as these about an eight-year-old Mexican girl:

> 'Twas down in Cunt Valley, where Red Rivers flow
> Where cocksuckers flourish, and maidenheads grow,
> 'Twas there I met Lupe, the girl I adore
> My hot fucking, cocksucking Mexican whore
> She'd fuck you, she'd suck you, she'd tickle your nuts
> And if you're not careful, she'd suck out your guts,
> She'd wrap her legs round you, till you think you'll die
> I'd rather eat Lupe than sweet cherry pie[53]

The Theta Xi chapter president responded that the song had absolutely "no effect on my view of women. We teach etiquette here. We teach respect for women."[54] Ana Rojas, coordinator of UCLA *La Raza* women, replied, "These are college men. The politicians, the lawyers, the doctors and the teachers of our future. They don't acknowledge women ... we're all whores."[54]

In November 1991, the UCLA student government sanctioned Theta Xi members for painting sexist slogans such as "cheap chicks for sale" on Winnebagos bound for a football game at Stanford. Members were required to take gender-related workshops, observe a five-week suspension of social activities, and perform community service. Chancellor Charles Young was reluctant to discipline fraternities because many powerful alumni protected them.

The Lupe affair found its way to California State University, Northridge, inciting a conflict between Chicanas/os on campus and the Zeta Beta Tau fraternity. The ZBT got clearance to hold a party dedicated to "Lupe." The campus administration admonished the fraternity but ZBT officers responded that it was their First Amendment right to call the party anything they wanted, and to express their "solidarity with their brothers at UCLA."[55] They held the party.

On 27 October 1992, more than 200 members of MEChA—Mechistas—packed an Associated Student Government meeting, supported by the Black Student Union president, Strong Queers United in Stopping Heterosexism, and others, urging that the ZBT be disciplined. That weekend over 500 Chicana/o students marched on the ZBT house.[56] The fraternity was suspended for 14 months. In spring 1993, ZBT was reinstated at CSUN after it filed a lawsuit against the university. Almost immediately the administration folded, claiming that it would lose ZBT lawsuit based on the First Amendment.

Meanwhile, *Los Angeles Times* reporter Sam Enriquez revealed that CSUN agreed to pay for all ZBT's legal expenses and to pay for its full-page ads in the *Sundial*, apologizing to the Chicana/o community for the incident. MEChA was never supposed to be told about the secret deal, nor were Chicana/o students supposed to learn about conservative activist David Horowitz's involvement in the case. According to *Times* reporter Sharon Bernstein, Horowitz recruited a national network of right-wing lawyers to his Individual Rights Project to defend fraternities and other campus conservatives. Horowitz had intervened at Occidental College in favor of Alpha Tau Omega, forcing the college to drop a disciplinary action against fraternities. Horowitz ran the Los Angeles-based $700,000-a-year Center for the Study of Popular Culture, funded by the conservative Olin and Bradley Foundations and the Scaife Trusts.

Who Am I? The Fight for Identity

The UCLA Hunger Strike of 1993 led to the foundation of the Chicana/o Studies Department (the César Chávez Center) at the University of California Los Angeles (UCLA). Marcos Aguilar and Minnie Fergusson, who led the strike, had worked for four years to get a Chicana/o Studies Department. In a seemingly impossible journey, they braved the opposition of Chancellor Charles Young, Associate Vice-Chancellor Raymundo Paredes, and the institution itself. With the exception of Juan Gómez-Quiñonez and later Leo Estrada, most of the Chicana/o faculty members were divided and did not push for a department.

In the years preceding the hunger strike, Minnie and Marcos were involved in the Olvera Street struggle to preserve Olvera Street as Mexican cultural space. They won community support, studied curriculum, and held conferences on campus to help organize the United Community and Labor Alliance that was also involved in the Olvera Street campaign.[57] Marcos was so adamant about creating a department that after four years he was kicked out of MEChA; its members became increasingly concerned about polarizing faculty members and students, and reducing its membership and influence.

After three years of disagreement and nit-picking, Chancellor Young on April 28, 1993 announce, that Chicano studies "will not be elevated to an independent department at the Westwood campus."[58] For Marcos and Minnie it became a now-or-never moment. Young announced his decision on the eve of the funeral of César Chávez—a slap in the face of the Chicano community.

Without internal support, Marcos and Minnie went on the offensive and formed Conscious Students of Color, a multiracial group of students, most of whom had never been active in campus politics. A rally began at noon on May 11 that attracted about 200 participants. According to the *Los Angeles Times*, "When they were denied entrance to the faculty center, some of the demonstrators broke windows with hammers, chairs and backpacks and about 80 began a sit-in inside."[59] Two hundred LAPD officers assisted UC campus police in arresting 89 students on felony charges. On the second day, a rally drew a crowd of 1,000 people to the front of Royce Hall, and, seeing their friends arrested, some Mechistas returned to the fold. Because the quarter end was fast approaching, most observers, myself included, speculated that the drive to get a department was over, and that Marcos and Minnie would be blamed.[60]

Pushed to the edge by an intransigent administration, on May 25, Marcos, Minnie, sisters Cindy and Norma Montañez, Balvina Collazo, and María Lara—along with Jorge Mancillas, an assistant professor of medical biology, and two other students—began a hunger strike that lasted 14 days.[61] The strike attracted the support of thousands of Chicana/o and Latino students in surrounding high schools and universities citywide, who spontaneously walked out of school. Tensions mounted as a 20-mile support march made its way from Olvera Street to UCLA on the 12th day to pressure UCLA administration to meet with the hunger strikers. The march garnered considerable community support, as a 1,000 supporters converged on the UCLA campus. The strike was settled two days later, and UCLA got the César Chávez Center for Interdisciplinary Instruction in Chicano/Chicana Studies. It functioned as a department but was not given full departmental status—Chancellor Young and Paredes were vengeful to the last.[62]

The success of the UCLA strike inspired hunger strikes at the University of California at Santa Barbara, Columbia, and Princeton, the Claremont Colleges, the University of Texas at Austin, the University of California at Berkeley, and other schools. In tandem with the UCLA Hunger Strike, Chicana/o activists—labor leaders, politicos, and students—began to oppose the imminent siege on the foreign-born. The question of immigration eclipsed other issues. Racists in politics and the media, such as California Governor Pete Wilson, Glenn Spencer's *American Patrol* website, CNN's *Lou Dobbs*, and Fox's *O'Reilly Factor*, took every opportunity to label MEChA and other Chicano organizations terrorist. By the turn of the century, the rabid right-wing reaction exceeded the McCarthy witch hunts of the 1950s. These hate groups were anti-immigrant, anti–affirmative action, and pro-racist. Their campaigns took their toll on Chicana/o student activists.

Fight for the Truth

Simultaneous with the struggle for Chicana/o Studies, Rodolfo F. Acuña sued the University of California system for discrimination. In 1990, Acuña was invited to apply for a professorship in the Chicano Studies Department at the University of California, Santa Barbara. Although the department submitted Acuña's name as the sole candidate for the position, he was not offered the position because a campus-wide committee overruled the department, using racist statements. In 1992, Acuña filed suit against UCSB for racial, political, and age discrimination. From the beginning, UC used the court system to frustrate Acuña's case, preventing it from being tried in Los Angeles. Federal Court

Judge Audrey Collins, a UCLA alumni and student of the former UCSB vice-chancellor, finally heard the case even after motions for her to recuse herself. Judge Collins rejected the claims of ethnic and political bias, but the case was tried on the grounds of age discrimination, though the standards of proof were the same as for political discrimination. The UC spent over $5 million in legal fees. On October 30, 1995 a jury unanimously found for Acuña[63].

The suit probably would have never gone forward but for the racist attack by all white faculty review committee. Jeffrey Russell, the chair of the Committee on Academic Personnel, testified that the role of the scholar is the search for truth, but that "absolute truth is whatever would exist in the mind of God, to which we have no access ... we cannot even hope to get close to it [absolute truth]."[64] In a March 7, 1991 lecture, Russell said, "The purpose of the University is to proclaim the intricate mystery and glory of God ... " In reviewing Acuña's scholarship he claimed that it was Marxist because Acuña used terms such as "hegemony" and "subjugated people." The court documents showed Russell attempted to appoint Otis Graham, Jr., a founder of the Federation of American Immigration Reform (FAIR), to chair the ad hoc (secret) committee that reviewed Acuña's academic credentials.

A 1986 textbook written by Robert Kelley, a member of the committee, Kelley made frequent references to Mexican immigrants as "wetbacks." Kelley throughout the process referred to himself as a friend of Mexicans and an expert on Chicanos. Kelley testified that *Occupied America* "lied," first because of the title and second because the book said that the United States invaded Mexico. Another reviewer, and a member of the ad hoc committee, Wallace Chafe, supposedly a renowned linguist, an expert in Native American languages, and a former Central Intelligence Agency member, testified that Noam Chomsky was a charlatan.

The suit was brought to defend the truth. The chances of winning were slim; the UC system had deep pockets while the plaintiff relied on pro bono attorneys and fundraisers. Acuña was represented by 15 attorneys who had never tried a discrimination case and were working for nothing. They only got paid after the suit was won. The 9th Circuit awarded the lawyers more than a million dollars in attorney fees. Acuña was awarded $300,000 for lost pay after UC refused to hire him because, according to the defendants, if hired he would control all the Mexicans and instigate a revolution in Santa Barbara. He established a foundation to defend Chicana/o professors and provide scholarships to Mexican/Latino students.

The Renaissance in Chicana/Chicano Thought and Arts

The impact of Chicana/o Studies went beyond the formation or lack of formation of Chicana/o Studies programs or their influence on the campuses. A large number of the murals, paintings, literature, and music in the communities owe their geneses to Chicana/o Studies. *El Centro De La Raza* in Seattle, the murals on the walls of Chicano park in San Diego, the National Mexican Art Museum in Chicago's Pilsen District, mariachi and Mexican Folk dance groups and Danzantes throughout the country, as well as many theater groups, were nourished by Chicana/o Studies. It drove the demand for Chicana/o literature of all forms. These programs were a source of support for progressive causes such as the Zapatistas and the movement to protect the foreign-born. Chicana/o Studies went beyond the walls of academe. They were instrumental in the formation of a collective historical memory.[65]

The curricula of Chicana/o Studies changed over time. In the late 1960s and 1970s, the symbol of the farmworker's eagle and the face of César were ubiquitous. Although initially it was an almost all-male club, since the 1990s the main current has been a greater visibility for Chicanas and Chicana/o LGBT students. In 1991, a cursory survey of Proquest's 72 dissertations and a smattering of theses in Chicana/o Studies revealed that 49 were written by women. In 2008, out of 94 dissertations and MA theses, 70 were written by women; this suggests who will be teaching in those programs in the future. Dissertations are important in synthesizing the existing fund of knowledge.

Historian Emma Pérez, the author of *The Decolonial Imaginary: Writing Chicanas into History*, intertwines modernist and postmodernist theory. Pérez analyzes the self-colonization and institutionalization that internalizes the colonization Chicanas internalize. A Chicana lesbian, Pérez writes in a restless style reminiscent of African American writers such as Langston Hughes.[66] Noteworthy are the essays, poetry, and playwriting of Cherríe Moraga. She teaches Creative Writing, Chicano/Latino literature, Xicana-Indigenous Performance, Indigenous Identity in Diaspora in the Arts, and Playwriting at Stanford and other universities. She was a founding member of La Red Xicana Indígena, "a network of Xicanas organizing in the area of social change through international exchange, Indigenous political education, spiritual practice, and grass roots organizing." Moraga's use of symbols enriches her writing with brilliant colors not frequently found in Euro-American society.[67] It would be easy to draw up a shopping list of cutting-edge Chicana scholars, among them Yolanda Broyles-González of the University of Arizona and historian Antonia Castañeda.[68]

Gloria Anzaldúa (1942–2004) was a product of the border; she blended this reality with history. A postmodernist, a feminist, and a lesbian, she was a major force in Chicana cultural theory and queer theory. Anzaldúa collaborated with writers such as Moraga. Her *New Mestiza* calls for an awareness of conflicting and meshing identities; her point of conflict is the border. Many feminists see her "new mestiza" as a way to understand postcolonial feminism. Anzaldúa talked about consciousness and boldly trespasses into space thought to be reserved for Indigenistas. Anzaldúa was spiritual in a field that was once dominated by materialists, thus resolving the past with the present. She is one of the few Chicana/o scholars to win universal appeal.[69]

Follow the Money

16.8 Describe the Chicana/o response to California's attempts to annihilate their history and identity through racist-nativist Propositions in the 1990s.

The growth in the Mexican American population pressured and threatened elected officials. Many of their districts had large Latino voting constituencies. The passage of Immigration Reform and Control Act of 1986 led to changes in California where along with term limits, led to the election of a plurality of Mexican/Latino office holders. This in turn caused a backlash. IRCA and increased Latino representation angered anti-immigrant foundations that sought to limit Latino student access to higher education and limit the rights of immigrants. They used this fear as a fundraising strategy to stir moral outrage and fear among donors and to increase contributions. This fear ultimately led to the passage of Proposition 187.

Racist-nativist anti-immigration groups spent millions of dollars in framing the immigrant debate—repeating incessantly and irresponsibly raising threats of the "illegal alien." These organizations received unlimited funds through conservative think tanks that were financed by reactionaries such as Richard Mellon Scaife, Cordelia Scaife May, Charles and David Koch, and Joseph Coors, among other billionaires.[70] Taxpayers paid for the hate campaigns, since the donations to the think tanks are tax deductible. They financed the English-Only political campaigns; Cordelia Scaife May donated $650,000 to U.S. English. She used the severe recession of the early 1990s to fan an anti-immigrant hysteria—politicos and racist nativists played on the fears of "Americans." Meanwhile, supporters contributed hundreds of millions of dollars to hate groups that subsidized the research of right-wing scholars. For example, the Heritage Foundation helped fund *The Bell Curve: Intelligence and Class Structure in American Life* (1994) by Richard Herrnstein and Charles Murray, a book that argues that inherited intelligence is the determinant of success or failure in society. The authors tied the question of intelligence to race and concluded that African Americans were unsuccessful not because society did not invest in them, but because they lacked intelligence.[71]

These and other foundations poisoned public opinion toward affirmative action, immigration, and bilingual education by funding vicious campaigns. The tactics of this program resembled the spreading of distorted news during the 2016 presidential campaign. The Hoover Institution at Stanford sponsored the work of John Bunzell, an intellectual godfather of the anti-affirmative action movement.

Republican President Herbert Hoover founded The Hoover Institution in 1919 as the Hoover Institution Library and Archives; it has grown to be a major right-wing think tank with major contributors and close ties to George H. W. Bush, Ronald Reagan, British Prime Minister Margaret Thatcher, and neoliberal fellow travelers. The Hoover Institution held ties with the National Association of Scholars (NAS), a right-wing professional organization founded with a gift of $100,000 from the Smith Richardson Foundation. The Center for Individual Rights, founded in 1989, also had close ties to the NAS; it led the fight in *Hopwood v. Texas* (1996), a case filed against the University of Texas Law School in 1992, which resulted in a decision that severely limited affirmative action programs nationally. The U.S. Court of Appeals for the Fifth Circuit found that the University of Texas Law School violated the equal protection clause of the Fourteenth Amendment by denying admission to Cheryl Hopwood, a white woman, and three white men while admitting African American and Mexican American students with lower grade-point averages and test scores. The court held that race could not be used as a "factor in deciding which applicants to admit."[72]

The number 187 is a police code for Murder or Death, referring to the California Penal Code section for *Murder* or *Homicide*. It became an insider joke among the supporters of Proposition 187. The Proposition 63 campaign in 1986 ("English Is the Official Language") laid the groundwork for Proposition 187; more than $1 million was spent on the Prop 63 campaign—$500,000 of it from U.S. English, the largest English-first organization in the country. From that point on, the anti-immigrant movement picked up speed with "angst dollars" pouring in from small contributors. FAIR and extremist groups such as Voices of Citizens Together (VCT) spun statistics manufactured by the INS and the think tanks. Internet fundraising was also a bonanza for many immigrant hate groups that collected tax-deductible donations.

Its supporters called it "The SOS (Save Our State) Initiative." Proposition 187 appeared on the November 1994 California ballot. It proposed denying health and educational services to undocumented immigrants. Governor Pete Wilson immediately supported the proposition. Supporters of the breakup of the Los Angeles Unified School District, the voucher campaign, and the "3 strikes and you're out" proposition joined him. Even Democratic candidates opposed to 187 took potshots: in July, U.S. Senate candidate Diane Feinstein ran an ad claiming that 3,000 "illegals" crossed the border each night. "I'm Diane Feinstein and I've just begun to fight for California."

Chicana/o organizations and individuals in Los Angeles, led by 60s activists, responded to anti-immigrant hate crimes by going to the streets. In February 1994, a pro-immigrant march in Los Angeles drew 6,000 demonstrators. On May 28, another march attracted about 18,000 people who trekked up Broadway to City Hall. On October 16, more than 150,000 protesters marched down Avenida César Chávez to City Hall. Some Latino leaders feared that the large number of Mexican flags would turn off white voters and hurt the Democratic Party. Some Latino politicos, having become members of Team Clinton, opposed the demonstrations.

Despite this opposition, school walkouts took place at Huntington Park, Bell, South Gate, Los Angeles, Marshall, and Fremont High Schools, and throughout the San Fernando Valley. Police were called in Van Nuys where students took to the main street; 200 officers were put on tactical alert. News sources estimated that 10,000 students walked out of 39 schools—an estimate that was probably on the low side.

A September 1994 *Los Angeles Times* poll showed that 52 percent of Latinos supported Proposition 187. However, Latinos were increasingly alarmed by the racist tone of the anti-immigrant rhetoric, and a field poll about a month before the election showed Latinos in California sharply divided over Proposition 187: Latinos opposed the measure by a slight margin of 48 to 44 percent, and white voters favored it by 60 to 17 percent. White support for 187 remained constant; another *Los Angeles Times* poll showed that Californian whites favored 187 by 65 to 35 percent, and Latinos by 52 to 48 percent. As expected, on November 8 California overwhelmingly passed 187. Only the San Francisco Bay voted against 187.

Before the election, Cardinal Mahoney said that the measure would undermine "clear moral principles"—stopping just shy of calling it a mortal sin. The victory of 187 was a blow to the moral authority of the Catholic Church. White Catholics voted 58 to 42 percent for 187. Catholic bishops did not deny the sacraments to those voting for 187, as they did in the case of the abortion. Most Protestant churches remained silent.[73]

On November 5, 1996, California voters passed Proposition 209, which had been placed on the ballot by the California Association of Scholars. It said that "preferential treatment" because of race, sex, ethnicity, or national origin was forbidden. In effect, Proposition 209 mooted anti-discrimination laws. Institutions were not required to recruit or enroll minorities; consequently, there were no damages if they discriminated. Proponents of 209 argued that affirmative action went too far and now was resulting in discrimination against whites who were better qualified. The United States was supposedly a color-blind society.

African Americans voted against Proposition 209 by 73 percent and Latinos by 70 percent. Asian Americans also voted against it, although by only 56 percent. Whites made up three-fourths of the voters; white males voted for 209 by a 66 percent margin and white females by 58 percent. The death of an idea such as social justice does not happen by accident. Indeed, it is difficult to reverse public policy and change basic commitments to ideals such as civil rights.

The mean-spirited and extremist organizations and people who supported Proposition 209 ranged from opportunists such as the VCT, led by Glenn Spencer, who ranted and raved about the Mexican invasion of the United States, to the California Association of Scholars, an affiliate of the NAS that conducted a well-funded, well-thought-out campaign designed to change the definition of *fairness*. The message was, "We live in a classless society; there is equal opportunity for all; work hard enough and you'll make it to the middle-class heaven."

Unfortunately, the Latino community did not organize marches of any size against Proposition 209. Latinos, however, held a march in Washington, D.C., in October 1996. More than 50,000 people marched through the capital in support of Latino and immigrant rights. Although it was successful, the march in Washington was criticized. Many politicians and their minions felt that a march in Los Angeles to protest Proposition 209 would embarrass President Clinton. It was not until the end of the presidential campaign in California, when Clinton was certain to win by a landslide, that the Democratic Party took a more visible profile.[74]

In June 1998, Californians overwhelmingly approved Proposition 227, insidiously called the "English for the Children" initiative. Californians based their vote not so much on the merits of bilingual education, but on numerous untested assumptions that bilingual education was a failure.

Ron Unz, the man behind Proposition 227, was a Silicon Valley millionaire with dreams of running for governor. He had opposed 187 and knew that the core constituency of anti-immigrant, anti-minority voters in California was still very much alive. Unz did nothing to silence it. Unz was also a contributor to the *Heritage Foundation Policy Review*. (Ironically, the Heritage Foundation, while against most progressive agendas, favored the family reunification immigration policy.)

Proposition 227 did not enjoy the near-unanimous Republican support that 187 and 209 had. First, nativism subsided due to the improving economy and there were defections from the party among Republicans running for statewide offices or in districts with a sizable Latino constituency. Republican candidates were becoming aware of the backlash in the Chicano/Latino community in the aftermath of Propositions 187 and 209. Their nativism was tempered by the realization that they were losing Latino voters, who once marginally supported them.

Exit polls for Proposition 227 indicated that Latinos opposed it—some 63 percent of the Latino electorate voted against Proposition 227. Because of the perception that the proposition was racist, some Republican candidates began to distance themselves from the anti-immigrant, anti–affirmative action, and anti–bilingual education sentiments of their party. Attorney General Dan Lungren, aware of the growing antipathy of Chicanos and Latinos toward Republicans, came out against Proposition 227 to try to stem the loss of their support.

Spanish-language media were crucial to informing the public about 187 and 227. Reporters identified with the issues. In the Greater Los Angeles area, 9.74 million radio listeners divided their attention among 81 stations, 12 of which broadcast in Spanish. Two of the 10 TV broadcast channels were in Spanish in the "designated market area" of Los Angeles County; all of Orange, San Bernardino, and Ventura Counties; and parts of Kern, Riverside, and San Diego Counties. Los Angeles–based Univision KMEX Channel boasted higher ratings for its 6 p.m. and 11 p.m. newscasts than its English-language competitors could.[75]

From the Heart of Texas: The Migrant Stream

16.9 Compare regional changes in migration in the 1990s.

Texas played a central role in the spread of Mexicans throughout the United States. Some call the migration the accordion trail.

By the 1980s, migration patterns in Mexico to the United States were changing. Mexico has 31 states and a federal district that are as distinct as separate countries. All of the links are important because they form social networks and work specializations. U.S. labor recruiters know their individual characteristics and target Mexicans facilitated taking them up through the stream that in recent times has been complicated by independents seeking employment. The work, while heavily in agriculture, is not exclusively farm work.[76]

According to Douglas S. Massey, Jacob S. Rugh, and Karen A. Pren,

> "After 1980, new regions of out-migration arose in Mexico's central region (comprising the Distrito Federal, Guerrero, Hidalgo, México, Morelos, Oaxaca, Puebla, Querétaro, and Tlaxcala), along with the southeastern portion of the country (Campeche, Chiapas, Quintana Roo, Tabasco, Veracruz, and Yucatán) and the border region (Baja California, Chihuahua, Coahuila, Nuevo León, Sinaloa, Sonora, and Tamaulipas)."[77]

Contrary to popular belief, by the year 2000 the Mexican border region was not a major contributor to the immigrant stream. The border states of California, Arizona, New Mexico, and Texas, and the industrial hub of Illinois remained favorite destinations. After 1986, the Immigration Reform and Control Act began to harden. In 1993, the U.S. Border Patrol began military operations in places such as the El Paso sector (Operation Blockade) and San Diego (Operation Gatekeeper) in 1994, both during the Clinton administration.

As late as 1990, 63 percent of Mexican immigrants went to California, 14 percent went to Texas, and 6 percent went to Illinois. By 2005, however, 33 percent went to California, 15 percent to Texas and 5 percent to Illinois. After 1990, those traveling to a state other than Illinois and four border states rose from about 13 percent to 40 percent in 2005.[78] The overwhelming majority were from Mexico's central region. Established patterns were developing among undocumented Mexicans. For instance, during the 1990s Mexico's southeastern states emerged as a significant sending region, with migrants flowing into Florida, Georgia, and North Carolina as well as to the Chicago region and the border states. American immigration policy—or the lack of one—was a major factor in the destabilization of immigration patterns.[79]

The Northwest, once largely populated by migrants coming from the Lone Star State, by 2000 included more of a mix of Texans and immigrants. According to the 1980 Census, the Latino population in Washington grew to 118,432, which was 3 percent of the state's total population to approximately 123,000; by the end of the decade this number nearly doubled. The 2000 Census showed it increased to 441,509. Similarly, neighboring Oregon grew to 450,062 by 2012, which was 11.7 percent of the total population, up from 8 percent in 2000.[80] Latinos are a community in transition, with the Latino population doubling every decade. Although Mexican-origin people make up approximately 80 percent of the Latino population, other Latinos are growing in numbers. The changes taking place are interesting. For example, the number of Mexican *tortillerías* have sprung up in places like the Yakima Valley of Washington amazes the outsider. Indeed, Latino-owned companies in Washington grew 64 percent between 1992 and 1997, employing 18,830 persons by 1997. The number of Latino farmers there also grew from 378 in 1992 to 625 four years later. Two-thirds of the farmers owned and operated their own farms, 120 were part-time owners, and only 79 were tenants. No longer is the region a stopping-off place for migrants; established communities were formed.

Looking at the Mexican-origin population in the Pacific Northwest, from the vantage point of numbers, the population is growing dramatically, and this is made more significant by the fact that the percentage of the white population is declining. In 1990 just over 380,000 Latinos, of whom over 80 percent were of Mexican origin, lived in Washington, Oregon, and Idaho (they were 4.4 percent of the total population). Ten years later the Mexican portion grew to

623,000. Unlike in many regions of the country, the growth is in agricultural communities.

In 1980, whites were 90.2 percent of Washington's population. Just two decades later the percentage dipped to 76.2. It was not so much that the white population was falling but that the Latino population, which remained overwhelmingly of Mexican origin, was skyrocketing. Asian and Latino immigration played a huge role, too. In 1980, 5.8 percent of Washingtonians were foreign-born; it would double in the next two decades. By 2000, 67.2 percent of Washington's Asian population and 45.6 percent of Latinos were foreign-born. The 2000 Census indicated 88.64 percent of all Latinos were classified as white.

The Yakima Valley continued and continues to be a major entry port for Mexican migrants. For instance, the town of Wapato, according to the 2000 Census, numbered 4,572, of which 76 percent were Latino—and this is not counting undocumented residents.[81] Whites call it "Mexican Town." Mexican residency goes back to World War II when undocumented workers, *braceros*, and Tejanos and Mexican sugar beet workers came to pick crops. In the 1970s, cold-storage facilities in Wapato and Union Gap opened new opportunities and made possible year-round employment. In the 1980s Mexican immigrants displaced Chicana/o migrants as the primary farm workforce. The landscape took on more diversity as local restaurants, cantinas, and tortilla plants run by Mexican immigrants and Chicanas/os multiplied. Some Mexicans own farms, but agriculture is still dominated by white Americans.[82]

The largest state in the Pacific Northwest is Washington. In 2000, its total population was 5,894,121—of which 441,509 (or 7.5 percent) were Latinos. Mexicans made up 329,934 or just fewer than 75 percent of the Latino population. Puerto Ricans were the next largest group (16,140), followed by Central Americans (12,126). As with other states, the Mexican/Latino population of Washington doubled during the 1990s. Some 40 percent were under 18, making it the youngest ethnic group. Adams and Franklin Counties in eastern Washington were 50 percent Latino, and Yakima County was 35 percent Latino. Central Americans became more numerous as Guatemalans moved into Shelton and Salvadorans into Aberdeen.

Besides this resident population, 100,000 migrants arrive in Washington annually. Another trend is the in-migration of Indigenous Mexicans who know little Spanish or English. The Spanish-speaking residents are bound together by a chain of Spanish-language radio stations playing Spanish music. Despite some economic progress, the low educational attainment, and low incomes, have contributed to low rates of home ownership in comparison with other groups. The big banana in Washington is Seattle, home of Microsoft. It is a white city, ranking last in terms of percentage of minorities among the 25 most populous cities. "The U.S. Census reports that in 2017 only 15.3 percent of Seattleites were under 18 with whites alone 65 percent of the population."[83] Sixty-eight percent of Seattle's population is white. It ranked second in the Pacific Northwest behind Portland, Oregon.

In 2000, Latinos made up at least 20 percent of the school enrollment in 26 Oregon towns—and 65 percent in Woodburn, Oregon. The Latino population of Oregon was expected to grow to 500,000 by 2025. Nevertheless, Latinos lacked political representation.[84] The town of Salem, Oregon, experienced dramatic growth in the Mexican-origin population since the 1970s. As in other places in the Pacific Northwest, the roots of the Mexican population extend back into the nineteenth century—but up until recently their numbers have not been significant. World War II was a turning point, with significant numbers of migrants and *braceros* finding their way into Oregon.

By the 1970s, immigrants arrived from Michoacán and Oaxaca to work in tree farms and canneries. A similar growth occurred in surrounding areas, and, by the beginning of the twentieth century, 55,000 Latinos lived in Marion and Polk Counties and over 100,000 lived in Clackamas, Multnomah, and Washington Counties alone.[85] By the beginning of the twenty-first century, the proportion of whites in the population was declining and the Latino population was increasing. As in the Southwest and Midwest, the Mexican and Latino communities were increasingly divided into those with green cards and those without. On one hand, more Mexican American students attended universities; on the other hand, like California, Oregon attracted thousands of Mixtec and other Mexican migrants coming to work in the fields. They differentiate themselves from other Latinos, and many do not speak Spanish or English and are the victims of exploitation, living in fear.[86]

As in Oregon and Washington, Mexicans migrated to Idaho for agricultural work.[87] The sugar beet companies recruited Mexicans during World War I as Central European labor was restricted. Mexicans also worked on the railroads. During World War II, *braceros* entered the state, as did Mexican American migrants. The Mexican population changed in the 1960s, 70s, and 80s, and the existing Mexican American population settled in as the state's economy diversified. Mexican American and Latino businesses became more common, and ethnic communities formed. These communities were more conscious of their rights. Migrant workers continued in Idaho, where as many as 100,000 arrived in the summer months. Tejanos continued to be a significant part of the workforce. By 1991, the Idaho Migrant Council estimated that the Mexican-origin population had reached more than 58,000 in the southern Snake River Valley.[88]

War on Drugs

16.10 Explain how the War on Drugs led to the destabilization of Mexico and Chicana/o communities.

In a February 2015 speech in Mexico City, Bill Clinton apologized to Mexicans:

> "I wish you had no narco-trafficking, but it's not really your fault," Clinton told an audience of students and business leaders at the recent Laureate Summit on Youth and Productivity. "Basically, we did too good of a job of taking the transportation out of the air and water, and so we ran it over land. I apologize for that."[89]

Clinton was referring to the U.S. drug enforcement policy toward Mexico that began under Richard Nixon and was expanded by Ronald Reagan and George H. W. Bush. The United States shut down the Caribbean Sea trafficking route between the United States and South and Central America and forced the transport through Mexico, begetting smuggling in Mexico and giving rise to the drug cartels and the destruction of civil society in Mexico.[90]

Clinton's apology was quaint but as my mother used to say, *Palo dado, ni Dios lo quita* (not even God can undo beatings or wrongs).

As mentioned, the War on Drugs refers to a government-led initiative that aimed to stop illegal drug use, distribution, and trade by increasing and enforcing penalties for offenders and shifting the blame for the drug trade from the consumers to Mexico. The United States gave Mexico almost a billion dollars annually to stop the flow of drugs into the United States—money that went into the pockets of corrupt politicians, the Mexican military, and the cartels. Over the years, people have had mixed reactions to the campaign and blame it for the arming of Mexico. Most reached the conclusion that the so-called War on Drugs was racist and dramatically increased violence.

> On the one side is neoliberalism, with all its repressive power and its machinery of death; on the other side is the human being. There are those who resign themselves to being one more number in the huge exchange of power . . . But there are those who do not resign themselves . . . In any place in the world, anytime, any man or woman rebels to the point of tearing off the clothes resignation has woven for them and cynicism has died grey. Any man or woman, of whatever color, in whatever tongue, speaks and says to himself or to herself: Enough is enough! Ya basta! —Subcomandante Marcos[91]

As he did with NAFTA, Clinton pushed the War on Drugs and neoliberalism in the United States and Latin America. The process was synthesized in 1998 Michael Meeropol's *How the Clinton Administration Completed the Reagan Revolution*.[92] This occurred two years after Bill Clinton was reelected on November 5, 1996 to a second term as president of the United States, and the Republicans took control of the two houses of Congress. According to Michael Meeropol, everyone got caught up in campaigns that obscured the difference between the parties.[93] Democrats sent the message that they were protecting working Americans while Republicans promised to defend traditional American values. Both did neither, but they protected capitalism and the "[re]distribution of income to the nonelderly [was] no longer a federal responsibility."[94] In sum, there was consensus between the two parties.

In 1997 both parties put limits on Medicare spending that was against the interests of the elderly and the poor.[95] At the time, former Reagan Republicans focused on cutting the budget. They claimed the economy was unhealthy because the government spent too much on social programs. Their solution was to cut government employment and social programs. According to conservatives, rising incomes and the lifestyle of the middle class was proof that the American Dream was healthy, and according to them, Americans owed their "success" to business.[96] To insure the illusion continued, conservatives resurrected French philosopher Auguste Comte's doctrine of positivism and Herbert Spencer's Social Darwinism and renamed them neoliberalism. Privatization and deregulation were neoliberalism's feet.

President Clinton's welfare, budget, and tax bills from 1995–1997 "signaled surrender: the Reagan revolution was going to achieve its major goals."[97] "The Reagan neoliberal program of small government, tax cuts, deregulation, free trade, and monetarist financial policies was more than just consolidated"[98] during this period. It became the norm and was carried over into the Bush I and Clinton presidencies. During Clinton's last days as president, Congress and Clinton deregulated the market in a manner that was reminiscent of what Republicans did in 1928. In 1999, Clinton signed the Gramm-Leach-Bliley Act of 1999 that gutted the Glass–Steagall Act of 1932, which had been passed during the Great Depression to prevent commercial banks from trading securities with their clients' deposits. Deregulation was a boon to Chase Manhattan Bank and Wall Street as well as a major cause of the 2008 financial collapse. In the span of 15 years, neoliberals took over higher education, Congress, and the Supreme Court.[99]

The U.S. War on Drugs was part of U.S. foreign policy since the time of the administration of Richard Nixon. It did not address the problem that the American demand for drugs drove the drug trade. John Ehrlichman, Nixon's chief domestic advisor during Watergate, recalls that Nixon announced the "war on drugs" in 1971, citing the high death toll and the negative social impacts of drugs to justify expanding federal drug control agencies. According to Ehrlichman :

> The Nixon campaign in 1968, and the Nixon White House after that, had two enemies: the antiwar left and black

people. You understand what I'm saying? We knew we couldn't make it illegal to be either against the war or black, but by getting the public to associate the hippies with marijuana and blacks with heroin, and then criminalizing both heavily, we could disrupt those communities. We could arrest their leaders, raid their homes, break up their meetings, and vilify them night after night on the evening news. Did we know we were lying about the drugs? Of course we did.[100]

Arrests on minor drug charges led to incarceration, which was devastating to the Mexican/Latino and Black communities. Not only did it distinguish the United States as the nation with the highest rate of incarceration and largest prison population in the world, it was inequitably applied.[101] It would double the Latino adult male prison population in the next 20 years and have a devastating impact on Mexican/Latino families. At the same time, it was a graduate school in crime.

It did not go unnoticed that neoliberalism accelerated the privatization of prisons that had begun during the Reagan Years. The process worked, according to Mother Jones, like " . . . you just sell it like you were selling cars, or real estate, or hamburgers . . . ."[102]

Meanwhile, the War on Drugs ravaged Mexico to the point that it destroyed its civil society. The War on Drugs had been initiated by President Richard Nixon in 1969 when drugs were was declared public enemy No. 1. The major market was the United States and during the 1970s they were shipped or flown into the United States by the Medellin cartel. By the 1980s, because of Drug Task Forces, cocaine trafficking was channeled through Panama and Central America and Mexico, giving rise to new drug cartels and precipitating drug wars. In order to divert attention, the United States gave aid to the Mexican government to the tune of a billion dollars annually. As mentioned, the money flowed into the pockets of corrupt government officials, cartels, and the buying of arms. These wars and corruption contributed to destruction of Mexico's infrastructure, resulting in Mexicans pursuing extralegal activities in the underworld to survive. Today, for example, Mexico is a leading source of porn to the United States. In 2011 there were 27,213 homicides in Mexico.[103]

The Clintons used the notion of personal responsibility to shame poor Blacks for their economic predicament. Indeed, Bill Clinton titled his notorious welfare to work legislation as the "The Personal Responsibility and Work Opportunity Reconciliation Act of 1996."[104] This act and the mass incarceration policies passed under Bill Clinton's administration furthered racial inequality. With the Clintons at the helm, the "New Democrats" pushed strident anti-crime policies and other attacks on the poor, like their assault on welfare. Meanwhile, Mexican/Latinos were making gains in electoral politics and voted more Mexican/Latinos to office. Once on the Clinton team, they did not want to rock the boat or endanger their positions and instead put their efforts toward cheerleading. After all, don't criticize the game.

The Mexican Billionaires

16.11 Describe how U.S. neoliberal values influenced the Mexican elite.

By the grace of Carlos Salinas de Gortari and neoliberalism, Carlos "Slim" Helú became one of richest men in the world not because he earned it but because the Mexican government gave him land and resources belonging to the Mexican people. A Mexican business magnate, investor, and philanthropist. Slim was a war profiteer of sorts; he bought on the cheap and sold high using his political connections. Money was sequestered in banks in any place but Mexico. In concert with France's Télécom and Southwestern Bell Corporation, Slim bought the landline telephone company Telmex in the 1990s from the Mexican government. By 2006, Telmex operated 90 percent of the telephone lines in Mexico. His subsidiary Telcel operated almost 80 percent of Mexico's cellphones. His godfather and benefactor was President Carlos Salinas de Gortari.[105]

In contrast, some 50 percent of Mexicans lived below the poverty line; 17 percent lived in poverty. Critics charge that Slim's monopoly frustrated the growth of smaller companies, and his monopolistic practices resulted in a shortage of paying jobs, contributing to migration to the United States.

How did neoliberalism spread so fast in Mexico? There have been always been strong ties between American and Mexican elites. In 1988, U.S. involvement in Mexican economic policy became more apparent. Salinas de Gortari's U.S.-trained economists and policymakers implemented strategies that led directly the North American Free Trade Agreement (NAFTA)—a free trade agreement with the United States and Canada, reducing the role of the public sector and eliminating social legislation. The agreement was sold under the myth of job creation and job stability.[106]

Meanwhile, the American education system worked as a conduit to spread American ideas and values. The Mexican elites accepted their status as members of a client state. Since the mid-1980s, every Mexican Secretary of Economy (*Secretario de Economía*) and Finance (*Secretario de Hacienda y Crédito Público*) earned a PhD from U.S. Ivy League Universities. For instance, Mexico's Secretario de Hacienda, Luis Videgarray (2012–2016), who successfully pushed for the privatization of PEMEX, the national gasoline company, earned his PhD from MIT. The outcome was that privatization eliminated more than 400,000 jobs between 1983 and 1993.

During 1995, Zedillo awarded five concessions to joint ventures between Mexican and foreign companies to operate ventures that included long-distance telecommunications and the privatization of the secondary petrochemicals operation Petróleos Mexicanos–Pemex, but the steamroller met opposition.[107]

Mexicans Become a National Minority

The 1990s began a mass movement of immigrants outside the Southwest, Midwest, and Northwest. Mexican/Latino numbers grew, making them a national population. Previously their presence was largely regional. An example was New York City, where a large Mexican community thrived in the Bronx and settled along 138 Street, East Harlem or Spanish Harlem, Queens, and Brooklyn. Unlike the migration into the Southwest that was from northern Mexico and Jalisco, Mexicans in New York came from southern Mexico places like Puebla, Oaxaca, and Chiapas. It came from southern Mexico where NAFTA dispossessed village farmers of their *ejidos* and worsened unemployment. Some estimate the New York population numbered as high as a million, which appears on the high side. What is certain is that Mexican-born population in the United States was larger than the total populations of all but seven U.S. states: California, Texas, New York, Florida, Illinois, Pennsylvania, and Ohio.

An anti-Mexican/Latino backlash was picking up steam. Instead of going underground, immigrants fought back, especially youth. Millions of Mexican and Central American youth were brought to the United States in their infancy. They had never seen their home countries and were Americans for all intents and purposes. Despite all odds, many found their way to college buying into the illusion of the American Dream. In places like California, opportunities to go to college were blocked in the 1990s. Taking inspiration from the Civil Rights movement, students began to organize.

Conclusion: The Problem of Becoming the Nation's Largest Minority

Not only had the Mexican population grown dramatically, but it could no longer be assumed that Latinos were a homogeneous population—there were Mexicans, there were Puerto Ricans, and, to a lesser extent, there were Cuban Americans. Nor did these different people live in isolated pockets—all Mexicans did not live in the Southwest; nor Puerto Ricans in New York; nor Cubans in Florida. By 2000, most Latino groups were scattered throughout the country, with the most dramatic shift taking place in the South. A report of the Pew Hispanic Center wrote:

> The Hispanic population is growing faster in much of the South than anywhere else in the United States. Across a broad swath of the region stretching westward from North Carolina on the Atlantic seaboard to Arkansas across the Mississippi River and south to Alabama on the Gulf of Mexico, sizeable Hispanic populations have emerged suddenly in communities where Latinos were a sparse presence just a decade or two ago.[108]

The new settlements differed from California, Texas, and New York, where migrants joined well-established Latino communities with networks of organizations. The changed demographic posed new challenges to national Latino organizations, a majority of which were still Mexican American. There would also be the challenge of how the member communities of this amorphous group called "Latinos" would relate to each other and how they could find unity and the consensus to develop a common agenda.

Notes

1. Jennifer Rosenberg. "The Y2K Problem: A Computer Glitch That Scared the World," ThoughtCo., Updated August 29, 2017, https://www.thoughtco.com/the-y2k-bug-1779442.
2. Gabriel Lesser and Jeanne Batalova, "Central American Immigrants in the United States," *Migration Policy Institute*, Apr. 5, 2017, https://www.migrationpolicy.org/article/central-american-immigrants-united-states.
3. Rodolfo F. Acuña, "The American Dream," mexmigration, February 4, 2013, http://mexmigration.blogspot.com/2013/02/acuna-on-american-dream-as-nightmare.html. Rodolfo F. Acuña, *Assault on Mexican American Collective Memory, 2010–2015: Swimming with Sharks* (Lanham: Rowman & Littlefield, 2017.)
4. "The State of Consumption Today," *World Watch Institute*, November 30, 2018. http://www.worldwatch.org/node/810

5. Wilhelm, Ron W. "Chapter 4: Remembering together: reflections on the value of collective historical memory." Curriculum and Teaching Dialogue 11.1–2 (2009): 23+. Expanded Academic ASAP. Web. 5 Feb. 2016.
6. Ines Gabel, "Historical memory and collective identity: West Bank settlers reconstruct the past," *Media Culture Society*, March 2013 Vol. 35 No. 2 250–259.
7. MULLER, FELIPE. HIRST, WILLIAM, "Resistance to the influences of others: Limits to the formation of a collective memory through conversational remembering," *Applied Cognitive Psychology*, July 2010, Vol. 24 Issue 5, 608–625.
8. Albert Doja, "Claude Lévi-Strauss at His Centennial: Toward a Future Anthropology," Theory, Culture & Society 2008 (SAGE, Los Angeles, London, New Delhi, and Singapore), Vol. 25(7–8): 321–340. William Mishler and Richard Rose, "Trust, Distrust and Skepticism: Popular Evaluations of Civil and Political Institutions in Post-Communist Societies," *The Journal of Politics*, Vol. 59, No. 2 (May, 1997), 418–451
9. Simone de Beauvoir, III The Positive Aspect of Ambiguity in The Ethics of Ambiguity, 1947, https://www.marxists.org/reference/subject/ethics/de-beauvoir/ambiguity/ch03.htm. de Beauvoir, *The Ethics of Ambiguity* (Philosophical Library, 1947), E-Book.
10. Rogelio Saenz, "Latinos and the Changing Face of America," Population Reference Bureau, http://www.prb.org/Publications/Articles/2004/LatinosandtheChangingFaceofAmerica.aspx.
11. Marita Hernandez, "Gloria Molina," *Los Angeles Times* (February 13, 1989). Virginia Escalante, Nancy Rivera, and Victor Valle, "Inside the World of Latinas," in Southern California's Latino Community. A Series of Articles Reprinted from the *Los Angeles Times* (Los Angeles, CA: Los Angeles Times, 1983), 82–91. Daniel M. Weintraub, "Remap Bills Are Vetoed by Wilson," *Los Angeles Times* (September 24, 1991). "Proposed Redistricting in Los Angeles County," *Los Angeles Times* (January 3, 1992). Frederick Muir, "Reapportionment Shuffles the Political Deck," *Los Angeles Times* (January 3, 1992). "Latino Voters in California," *Nuestro Tiempo* (April 30, 1992).
12. "World Politics and Current Affairs," *The Economist* (September 29, 1990). Madeleine May Kunin, "Give Everyone a Turn at the Game; Term Limits," *Los Angeles Times* (September 13, 1991).
13. Britney Jeffrey, "Rangel, Irma Lerma," *Handbook of Texas Online*, http://www.tshaonline.org/handbook/online/articles/fra85, accessed December 5, 2013. Cynthia Orozco, "Mexican American Democrats," *Handbook of Texas Online*, http://www.tshaonline.org/handbook/online/articles/wmm02.
14. José Angel Gutiérrez and Rebecca E. Deen, "Chicanas in Texas Politics" (Occasional Paper No. 66, Julian Samora Research Institute, October 2000). Roberto R. Calderón, "Tejano Politics," *Handbook of Texas Online*, http://www.tshaonline.org/handbook/online/articles/TT/wmtkn.html. Guillermo X. García, "Texas Surpasses N.Y. as Second Most Populous State," *USA Today* (March 13, 2001).
15. Lee Drutman, "The Rise of the Political Donor Class," Miller-McCune (August 28, 2008), http://www.psmag.com/politics/the-rise-of-the-political-donor-class-4305 http://www.miller-mccune.com/politics/the-rise-of-the-political-donor-class-562.
16. John W. Warnock, *The other Mexico: the North American triangle completed* (Montreal: Black Rose books, 1995). Julián Castro-Rea, "From Revolutionary Nationalism to Orthodox Neoliberalism: How NAFTA Contributed to Push Mexico into the Right-Wing Stranglehold," *Nuevo mundo mundos nuevos*, Feb 13, 2014. Rodolfo F. Acuña, *Anything But Mexican: Chicanos in Contemporary Los Angeles* (London: Verso Books, 1996). Acuña, *Swimming with Sharks*.
17. Rodolfo F, Acuña, "Remembering Ruben Jaramillo: A Recent History of Privatization," WordPress, July 5, 2015, http://rudyacuna.net/remembering-ruben-jaramillo/.
18. Ibid., 4. Rodolfo F. Acuña, "Our Politicos Have sold us Out Selling Public Space: The Chickens will Come Home to Roost," mexmigration, May 24, 2014, http://mexmigration.blogspot.com/.
19. Rodolfo F. Acuña, "Remembering Ruben Jaramillo: A Recent History of Privatization," *Hecho en Aztlan*, July 5, 2015, http://www.notesfromaztlan.com/2015/07/05/remembering-ruben-jaramillo-a-recent-history-of-privatization/.
20. Rodolfo F. Acuña, "The Age of the Billionaires," *Counterpunch*, December 27, 2013, https://www.counterpunch.org/2013/12/27/the-age-of-the-billionaires/.
21. Marie Claire Acosta, "The Democratization Process in Mexico: A Human Rights Issue," *Resist* (January 1991), 3–6. Bob Howard, "U.S. Latinos Speak up on Free Trade Accord," *Nuestro Tiempo* (November 7, 1991). "The U.S. and Mexico: A Close Look at Costs of Free Trade," *Business Week* (May 4, 1992), 22. Joel D. Nicholson, John Lust, Aljeandro Ardila Manzanera, and Javier Arroyo Rico, "Mexican-U.S. Attitudes Toward the NAFTA," *International Trade Journal 8*, No. 1 (1994), 93–115. Acuña, *Anything but Mexican*, 231–49.
22. North American Free Trade Agreement (NAFTA), Public Citizen, http://www.citizen.org/trade/nafta/. "1994—60 Minutes—Subcomandante

Marcos," Part 1 of 2, http://www.youtube.com/watch?v=AIi_88YoUFk. Denise Bedell, "Revisiting Nafta," *Global Finance*, 23, No. 3 (2009), 22–24. Garrett Zehr, "On NAFTA," *This*, 42, No. 2 (2008), 20–21.

23 Rodolfo F. Acuña, "On the Bacon Trail: Exposing Historical Myopia," WordPress, August 20, 2015, http://rudyacuna.net/on-the-bacon-trail/.

24 David Agren, "Bishop Samuel Ruiz Garcia, 86, champion of indigenous, dies in Mexico," *Catholic News Service*, http://www.catholicnews.com/data/stories/cns/1100290.htm.

25 Victor Hugo López, "Chiapas Human Rights Center Celebrates 25 Years," Chiapas Support Committee, March 29, 2014, https://chiapas-support.org/2014/03/29/chiapas-human-rights-center-celebrates-25-years/. Julia Prestonjan, "Bishop Samuel Ruiz García, Defender of Mexico's Mayans, Dies at 86," *New York Times* (Jan 26, 2011), www.nytimes.com/2011/01/27/world/americas/27ruiz.html.

26 José Johnston, "Pedagogical Guerrillas, Armed Democrats, and Revolutionary Counterpublics: Examining Paradox in the Zapatista Uprising in Chiapas Mexico," *Theory and Society*, Vol. 29, No. 4 (Aug., 2000), 463–505.

27 Denise Dresser, "A Painful Jolt for the Body Politic," *Los Angeles Times* (January 12, 1994). Juanita Darling, "With Chiapas Cease Fire, Political Fallout Begins," *Los Angeles Times* (January 14, 1994). Michael Lowy, "Sources and Resources of Zapatism," *Monthly Review* 49, No. 10 (March 1998), 1ff. Catherine Capellaro, "My Visit with the Bishop of Chiapas; Bishop Samuel Ruíz García; Interview," *Progressive* (November 1998), 26ff. J. C. Seymour, "Two-Hearted in Chiapas: After the Massacre; Relations between Indians of Chiapas, Mexico, and the Mexican Government," *Christian Century* (April 1, 1998), 333ff. James D. Cockcroft, *Mexico's Hope: An Encounter with Politics and History* (New York: Monthly Review Press, 1998), 221–22, 336. Andy Gutierrez, "Codifying the Past, Erasing the Future: NAFTA and the Zapatista Uprising of 1994," *West-Northwest Journal of Environmental Law & Policy* 14 (2008), 883–1703.

28 "A History of Hispanic Achievement in America," Cesar Chavez, Cesar Chavez Foundation, http://www.chavezfoundation.org/_cms.php?mode=view&b_code=001013000000000&b_no=472&page=4&field=&key=&n=11.

29 Miriam J. Wells, *Strawberry Fields: Politics, Class, and Work in California Agriculture* (Ithaca, NY: Cornell University Press, 1996). David Bacon, "Fruits of Their Labor: In Steinbeck Country, the United Farm Workers Are Battling the Strawberry Growers in the Fields and in the Suites," *LA Weekly* (August 8, 1997).

30 Jeffrey Passel, "Mexican Immigration to the U.S.: The Latest Estimates," *Migration Policy Institute*, March 1, 2004, https://www.migrationpolicy.org/article/mexican-immigration-us-latest-estimates.

31 David Card and Ethan G. Lewis, "The Diffusion of Mexican Immigrants during the 1990s: Explanations and Impacts," National Bureau of Economic Research, May 2007, 193, https://www.nber.org/chapters/c0095.pdf.

32 Aaron Terrazas, "Central American Immigrants in the United States," *Migration Policy Institute*, January 10, 2011, https://www.migrationpolicy.org/article/central-american-immigrants-united-states-0.

33 Little Central America LA—Pico Union/Salvadoran Culture, http://www.youtube.com/watch?v=ylAxy8xYXa0. "Salvadoran Riots 1991 Mount Pleason [sic] Washington, D.C. Riots," http://www.youtube.com/watch?v=-gpjiUSRA38. José Cardenas, "State Official Tells Day Laborers How Laws Can Work for Them; Jobs: Exploitation All Too Common, Labor Commissioner José Millan Says in Outreach Program Held to Educate Workers," *Los Angeles Times* (June 30, 1998). Pamela Constable, "Central Americans Protest Uncertain Future Under Refugee Amnesty Program," *Washington Post* (October 23, 1994). Philip Pan, "Honorable Work or Illegal Activity? In Langley Park, It's 'Pupusa Ladies' vs. County Agencies, with Latino Officers Caught in Middle," *Washington Post* (August 24, 1997). Lisa Leff, "Sacrifice Through Separation; Salvadoran Women Grieve for Children They Left Behind," *Washington Post* (March 31, 1994). Making pupusas at Chicago's Pupuseria Las Delicias, http://www.youtube.com/watch?v=qe96acRppe0&feature=related. Ana Patricia Rodríguez, *Dividing the Isthmus: Central American Transnational Histories, Literatures, and Cultures* (Austin: University of Texas Press, 2009), 184–85.

34 Jim Newton, "ACLU Says 83% of Police Live Outside L.A.: LAPD: Study is first of its kind. It says the results support contention that officers have little connection to areas they serve. Police Protective League disputes that conclusion," *Los Angeles Times* (March 29, 1994), http://articles.latimes.com/1994-03-29/local/me-39666_1_los-angeles-police-protective-league.

35 Ibid.

36 CNN Wire Staff, "Rodney King dead at 47," CNN, June 18, 2012, http://www.cnn.com/2012/06/17/us/obit-rodney-king/index.html.

37 Fen Montaigne, "Deporting America's Gang Culture," *Mother Jones*, July/August 1999 Issue, http://www.motherjones.com/politics/2013/04/deporting-americas-gang-culture-el-salvador/.

38 Ibid.

39 Tim Johnson, "U.S. export: Central America's gang problem began in Los Angeles," McClatchy DC Bureau, August 5, 2014, http://www.mcclatchydc.com/news/nation-world/world/article24771469.html. Daniel Denvir, "Deporting people made Central America's gangs. More deportation won't help," *Washington Post* (July 20, 2017).

40 Nick Miroff, "What is TPS, and what will happen to the 200,000 Salvadorans whose status is revoked?" *Washington Post* (January 9, 2018), https://www.washingtonpost.com/news/worldviews/wp/2018/01/09/what-is-tps-and-what-will-happen-to-the-200000-salvadorans-whose-status-is-revoked/?noredirect=on&utm_term=.e512c1b8039f.

41 Ibid.

42 Julie Tamaki, Jeannette DeSantis, and Nicholas Riccardi, "Prosecutors Won't Charge Tagger's Killer," *Los Angeles Times* (February 03, 1995), http://articles.latimes.com/1995-02-03/news/mn-27794_1_tagger-masters.

43 Lisa García Bedolla, Fluid Borders: *Latino power, identity, and politics in Los Angeles* (Berkeley: University of California Press, 2005), 32–33, https://epdf.tips/fluid-borders-latino-power-identity-and-politics-in-los-angeles35876.html.

44 Kevin Gaines, "Rampart Scandal Timeline," PBS, March 18, 1997, https://www.pbs.org/wgbh/pages/frontline/shows/lapd/scandal/cron.html. Laurie L. Levenson, "Symposium: The Rampart Scandal: Policing The Criminal Justice System: Unnerving The Judges: Judicial Responsibility For The Rampart Scandal," *L.A.L. Rev.*, Vol. 34, 787–1567. Paul J. Kaplan, "Looking Through the Gaps: A Critical Approach to the LAPD's Rampart Scandal," *Social Justice*, 1, January 2009, Vol. 36(1 (115), 61–81.

45 Margaret Taus, "Officer is silent, so others tell of slaying. Inquest jury given more details of Bellevue incident from police side," *Seattle Pi* (November 7, 2001), http://www.seattlepi.com/seattlenews/article/Officer-is-silent-so-others-tell-of-slaying-1071102.php.

46 Ashley Bach, "Bellevue settles deadly force case for $75,000," *Seattle Times Eastside*, December 16, 2005, http://old.seattletimes.com/html/eastsidenews/2002686636_hetle16e.html.

47 Sheila Marie Contreras, *Blood Lines: Myth, Indigenism, and Chicana/o Literature* (Austin: University of Texas Press, 2009).

48 Juan Gómez-Quiñones, Irene Vásquez, *Making Aztlán: Ideology and Culture of the Chicana and Chicano Movement* (Albuquerque: University of New Mexico Press, 2014), 265.

49 William H. Young, "Multiculturalism and Western Civilization," *National Association of Scholars* (Aug. 25, 2011), https://www.nas.org/articles/Multiculturalism_and_Western_Civilization; PBS, "The Latin-Americanization of the Universities," *National Review* (May 24, 1993), 18.

50 The NAS received money from the Heritage, Smith-Richardson, and Olin Foundations, among others. Louis Menand, "English at Queens College Grad Center of CCNY," *Harper's* (Dec. 1991), 47–56.

51 See Carol Iannone, "PC with a Human Face," *Commentary*, Vol. 95, No. 6, 44. Iannone incorrectly labels the PCers members of the hard Left. Conor Friedersdorf, "The Lessons of Bygone Free-Speech Fights," *The Atlantic*, Dec. 10, 2015, https://www.theatlantic.com/politics/archive/2015/12/what-student-activists-can-learn-from-bygone-free-speech-fights/419178/.

52 Nina Golgowski, "University of Texas fraternity under investigation for alleged racist 'border patrol' party. There were ponchos, sombreros, construction outfits and a giant bottle of tequila at the Saturday night event, but the president of the Phi Gamma Delta chapter defended it as 'Western'—not 'border patrol'—themed. A university spokesman said it received at least 9 complaints," *New York Daily News* (February 10, 2015), http://www.nydailynews.com/news/national/texas-frat-accused-throwing-racist-border-patrol-party-article-1.2109867. Rheana Murray, "Penn State sorority girls busted for offensive photo at Mexican-themed party," *New York Daily News* (December 5, 2012), http://www.nydailynews.com/news/national/sorority-girls-busted-mexican-themed-pic-article-1.1213746.

53 *Theta Xi Songbook*, quoted in Kelly Besser and Heather Skinazi, "A Theta Xi Education," *together*, 28 Sept. 1992, 3.

54 Al Martinez, "'Lupe' and the Guys," *Los Angeles Times* (November 12, 1992).

55 Thomas E. Piernack, Director, Office of Campus Activities, to Dave Wagner, President, Zeta Beta Tau, 12 October 1992: "The blatant insensitivity on your fraternity's part and the ignorance of your leadership as to why this is a serious issue astounded me. Your actions merit serious sanctions from the University and National organization as well as public apology to women, the Chicana/o community, and to your fellow fraternities who will unfortunately share in the questions of organizational character." Piernack went on: "At one point your Vice President Harris Barton challenged me on two issues other than your right to be in 'solidarity' with Theta Xi at UCLA." Considering this and other communications to ZBT, it cannot be doubted that they intended to insult, and knew what the issues were.

56 Sam Enriquez, "CSUN Official May Suspend Fraternity on Racism Issue," *Los Angeles Times* (October 22, 1992). Mary Ballesteros, "MEChA se enfrenta a uno

grupo que hizo un presunta ofensa a la mujer mexicana," *La Opinion* (22 Oct. 1992).

57. George Ramos, "UCLA Cuts in Chicano Studies Hit Education: Protests Have Spread off Campus to Involve Latino Leaders," *Los Angeles Times* (January 9, 1991), 1. Chancellor Young told *LA Times* editor Frank del Olmo that there would never be a department as long as he was chancellor.

58. Larry Gordon, "UCLA Resists Forming Chicano Studies Department," *Los Angeles Times* (April 29, 1993), B1.

59. Larry Gordon and Marina Dundjerski, "Protesters Attack UCLA Faculty Center: Education: Up to $50,000 in vandalism follows the university's refusal to elevate Chicano studies program to departmental status. Police arrest 90," *Los Angeles Times* (May 12, 1993), http://articles.latimes.com/1993-05-12/local/me-34320_1_chicano-studies.

60. Larry Gordon and Marina Dundjerski, "Protesters Attack UCLA Faculty Center," 1. Larry Gordon and Marina Dundjerski, "UCLA Has 2nd Day of Protest over Program," *Los Angeles Times* (May 13, 1993), B1. "UCLA Students Demand Chicano Studies Department," *San Francisco Chronicle* (May 13, 1993), A7. "Reassessment, Please, in UCLA Controversy: Rethinking Chicano Studies Issue in Wake of Protest," *Los Angeles Times* (May 13, 1993), 6. Rodolfo F. Acuña, *The Making of Chicana/o Studies: In the Trenches of Academe* (New Brunswick: Rutgers University Press, 2011), 179–187.

61. "Chicano Studies Activists Begin Hunger Strike at UCLA," *Los Angeles Times* (May 26, 1993), 4. Mary Anne Perez, "A Hunger for Change Protest: Students from the Central City Join the Fight for Chicano Studies Department," *Los Angeles Times* (June 6, 1993). Raymundo Paredes, "Chicano Studies at UCLA: A Controversy with National Implications," *Hispanic Outlook in Higher Education* 2, No. 3 (November 30, 1991), 10.

62. "A hunger strike ends, a center is born," UCLA History Project, June 7, 1993, http://www.uclahistoryproject.ucla.edu/Fun/ThisMonth_JunTent.asp. Semillas Community Schools, Winter 2008, http://www.dignidad.org/index.php?option=com_content&view=article&id=81&Itemid=55. Acuña, *Anything but Mexican*, chap. 12. Robert A. Rhoads, "'Immigrants in Our Own Land': The Chicano Studies Movement at UCLA," in *Freedom's Web: Student Activism in an Age of Cultural Diversity* (Baltimore, MD: Johns Hopkins Press, 1998), 61–94, http://orion.neiu.edu/~tbarnett/102/race.htm. Marcos Aguilar and Minnie Fergusson interviewed by Rodolfo F. Acuña (August 12, 2009) in El Sereno, California.

63. Rodolfo F. Acuña, "Forty Years of Chicana/o Studies: When the Myth Becomes a Legend," http://forchicanachicanostudies.wikispaces.com/Chicana+Chicano+Studies.

64. Ibid.

65. "El Centro de La Raza," Transcript: El Centro de la Raza, *NOW*, PBS, http://www.pbs.org/now/transcript/transcript_laraza.html. "The History of Chicano Park, San Diego, California," http://www.chicanoparksandiego.com/. "Mexican Art in the Pilsen District of Chicago," http://artpilsen.blogspot.com/. Harry Gamboa, "Chicano Art," http://www.harrygamboajr.com/.

66. Emma Pérez, *The Decolonial Imaginary: Writing Chicanas into History* (Bloomington: Indiana University Press, July 1, 1999), 20. Emma Pérez, "Queering the Borderlands: The Challenges of Excavating the Invisible and Unheard," *Frontiers: A Journal of Women Studies* 24, Nos. 2 & 3 (2003), 122–31.

67. "About Cherríe Moraga," http://www.cherriemoraga.com/index.php?option=com_content&view=section&layout=blog&id=5&Itemid=53.

68. The title "the Great" is used sparingly, as in the case of La Gran Lola Beltrán.

69. "Borderlands/La Frontera," http://www.youtube.com/watch?v=c2jvSN_-JS4. Gloria Anzaldúa, *Borderlands/La Frontera, The New Mestiza*, 3rd ed. (San Francisco, CA: Aunt Lute Books, 2007). "Gloria Anzaldúa" http://almalopez.com/projects/ChicanasLatinas/anzalduagloria5.html.

70. "Who is Richard Mellon Scaife?" http://www.youtube.com/watch?v=km_yDCfDNn0. "Behind The Veil: America's Anti-Immigration Network," http://www.youtube.com/watch?v=qpiq1nAK4a0. Bamn, http://www.bamn.com/boycott-coors/. "Codewords of Hate," http://www.youtube.com/watch?v=5kCpoXbCpqQ&feature=related. J. Stefancic and R. Delgado, *No mercy: How conservative think tanks and foundations changed America's social agenda* (Philadelphia, PA: Temple University Press, 1996), names most of the early benefactors.

71. "A Look at the Forces Behind the Anti-Immigrant Movement," *Democracy Now*, http://www.democracynow.org/2007/5/2/a_look_at_the_forces_behind. Excerpt from James Crawford, "Hispanophobia," Chapter 6, in *Hold Your Tongue: Bilingualism and the Politics of "English Only"* (Reading, MA: Addison Wesley, 1993), http://www.languagepolicy.net/archives/HYTCH6.htm. An important work in understanding the extent of the new-rights' financing of the "culture war" is Stefancic and Delgado's *No Mercy*. Alexander Cockburn, "In Honor of Charlatans and Racists," *Los Angeles Times* (November 3, 1994). Nina J. Easton, "Linking Low IQ

to Race, Poverty Sparks Debate," *Los Angeles Times* (October 30, 1994). Richard Herrnstein and Charles Murray, *The Bell Curve: Intelligence and Class Structure in American Life* (New York: Free Press, 1994).

72 Laura C. Scanlan, "Hopwood v. Texas: A Backward Look at Affirmative Action in Education," *New York University Law Review*, 71, No. 6 (1996), 1580–1633.

73 "Wilson's Re-Election Ads on Illegal Immigration," http://www.youtube.com/watch?v=o0f1PE8Kzng&feature=related. Barbara Sellgren, "California's Proposition 187: A Painful History Repeats Itself," *U.C. Davis Journal of International Law & Policy*, 1 (1995), 153–331. Richard D. Lamm and Robert Hardway, "Pro 187 Opposition Has Origins in Racism," *Daily News* (November 22, 1994). Patrick J. McDonnell, "March Just 1st Step, Latino Leaders Vow," *Los Angeles Times* (June 4, 1994). Ed Mendel, "Voters Still Favor Pro 187 but Field Poll Finds Latinos Split on Issue," *San Diego Union-Tribune* (September 27, 1994). Paul Feldman, "Times Poll: Pro 187 Is Still Favored Almost 2 to 1," *Los Angeles Times* (October 15, 1994). Howard Breuer, "Voters Approve Pro 187, Lawsuits to Follow," *Los Angeles Daily News* (November 9, 1994). John Dart, "187 Shows Clergy's Weak Influence on Electorate," *Los Angeles Times* (November 19, 1994).

74 Acuña, *Sometimes There Is No Other Side*, Chapter 1. Juan González, "In Washington, Latino Chorus Lifts Its Voice," *New York Daily News* (October 15, 1996). Amy Pyle, Patrick J. McDonnell, and Hector Tobar, "Latino Voter Participation Doubled Since '94 Primary," *Los Angeles Times* (June 4, 1998). Patrick J. McDonnell and George Ramos, "Latino Voters Had Key Role in Some States," *Dallas Morning News* (November 10, 1996). Linda O. Valenty and Ronald D. Sylvia, "Thresholds for Tolerance: The Impact of Racial and Ethnic Population Composition on the Vote for California Propositions 187 and 209," *Social Science Journal* 41, No. 3 (2004), 433–46.

75 Pyle et al., "Latino Voter Participation." McDonnell and Ramos, "Latino Voters." Dave Lesher and Mark Z. Barabak, "Gubernatorial Hopefuls Hold Landmark Forum," *Los Angeles Times* (May 24, 1998). Jeffrey L. Rabin, "Elusive Univision Chairman Spreads Wealth Around in Gubernatorial Race," *Los Angeles Times* (March 2, 2001); the chair of Univision was A. Jerrold Perenchio, an Italian American. He donated $1.5 million to defeat 227. However, he also donated $1,040,000 in support of vouchers for private schools, and $425,000 to support school board members for the Los Angeles. school districts who were on a slate supported by L.A.'s former Republican mayor, Richard Riordan. "A Proposition 227 Story," http://www.youtube.com/watch?v=TQwKrz_6dRY.

76 Rubén Martínez, *Crossing Over: A Mexican Family on the Migrant Trail* (New York: Picador, 2013). Douglas S. Massey, Jacob S. Rugh, and Karen A. Pren, "The Geography of Undocumented Mexican Migration," *Mex Studies* (Winter 2010), 26(1), 129–152, https://www.ncbi.nlm.nih.gov/pmc/articles/PMC2931355/.

77 Massey et al, Ibid.

78 Massey et al, Ibid.

79 Roberto Suro, "Attitudes about Immigration and Major Demographic Characteristics," Part One, Pew Hispanic Research Center, March 2, 2005, http://www.pewhispanic.org/files/reports/41.pdf.

80 Jerry Garcia, "History of Latinos in the Northwest," https://www.k12.wa.us/CISL/pubdocs/History-LatinoPacificNorthwest.pdf. Nikole Hannah-Jones, "Oregon's 2010 Census Shows Striking Latino and Asian Gains," *The Oregonian* (February 23, 2011), http://www.oregonlive.com/pacific-northwest-news/index.ssf/2011/02/2010_census.html.

81 "Washington County Selection Map," U.S. Census Bureau, http://quickfacts.census.gov/qfd/maps/washington_map.html.

82 Carlos Arnaldo Schwantes, *The Pacific Northwest: An Interpretive History*, Revised and Enlarged ed., (Lincoln: University of Nebraska Press, 1996), 6, 450. Gonzalo Guzmán, "Wapato—Its History and Hispanic Heritage," HistoryLink.org 7937, September 16, 2006, http://www.historylink.org/index.cfm?DisplayPage=output.cfm&file_id=7937. "Mexican Americans in the Columbia Basin," Washington State University, http://www.vancouver.wsu.edu/crbeha/ma/ma.htm. "Chicano/Latino Archive," Evergreen State College Library, http://chicanolatino.evergreen.edu/introduction_en.php.

83 Matthew Caruchet, "Who Really Pays: An analysis of the tax structures in 15 cities throughout Washington State," *Economic Opportunity Institute*, April 2018, http://www.opportunityinstitute.org/_v1/wp-content/uploads/2018-EOI-Income-Tax-Brief.pdf.

84 QuickFacts, Seattle city, Washington, https://www.census.gov/quickfacts/fact/table/seattlecitywashington/EDU685216.

85 Oregon County Selection Map, http://quickfacts.census.gov/qfd/maps/oregon_map.html.

86 "Latinos in Salem," http://www.salemhistory.net/people/latinos.htm. "Modern Society in the Pacific Northwest: The Second World War as Turning Point," http://www.washington.edu/uwired/outreach/cspn/Website/Classroom%20Materials/Pacific%20Northwest%20History/Lessons/Lesson%2020/20.html. Oregon State University, "Bracero Collection," http://library.state.or.us/repository/2008/200805231544055. Gosia

Wozniacka, "Hispanic Surge Is Reshaping Oregon," *Oregonian* (May 13, 2009), OregonLive.com, http://www.oregonlive.com/washingtoncounty/index.ssf/2009/05/2008_census_estimates_hispanic.html. Robert Bussel, ed., *Understanding the Immigrant Experience in Oregon: Research, Analysis, and Recommendations from University of Oregon Scholars* (Eugene: University of Oregon, 2008), http://library.state.or.us/repository/2008/200805231544055/index.pdf. Lynn Stephen, "Globalization, the State, and the Creation of Flexible Indigenous Workers: Mixtec Farmworkers in Oregon," The Center for Comparative Immigration Studies, University of California, San Diego, Working Paper 36, April 2001, http://escholarship.org/uc/item/4wd691zw.

87. Idaho County Selection Map, http://quickfacts.census.gov/qfd/maps/idaho_map.html.
88. Errol D. Jones, "Invisible People: Mexicans in Idaho History," http://web1.boisestate.edu/research/history/issuesonline/fall2005_issues/1f_mexicans.html. "Mexicans figured in Idaho events of Frontier Days," Idaho Digital Resources, http://idahodocs.cdmhost.com/cdm/singleitem/collection/p4012coll2/id/103. Amando Alvarez, "The Mexican Experience in Idaho," http://www.angelfire.com/journal2/luz/cuentos04.htm. "Idaho History," Raices, http://raices2.obiki.org/approach/cluster_sites/idaho.html.
89. Ryan Grim and Matt Ferner, "Bill Clinton Apologizes To Mexico For War On Drugs," *Huffingtonpost*, Feb. 13, 2015, https://www.huffingtonpost.com/2015/02/13/bill-clinton-apology-drug-war-mexico_n_6680412.html.
90. Ibid.
91. Rodolfo F. Acuña, "The Chickens will Come Home to Roost," *Dos Centavos*, May 23, 2014, https://doscentavos.net/tag/rodolfo-acuna/.
92. Michael Meeropol, *Surrender: How the Clinton Administration Completed the Reagan Revolution* (Ann Arbor: University of Michigan Press, 1998), 1–5.
93. Ibid., p. 1.
94. Ibid.
95. Ibid., p. 3.
96. Ibid., p. 28.
97. Gregory Albom, "Neoliberalism from Reagan to Clinton," *Monthly Review*, Vol. 52, Issue 11 (April 2001), https://monthlyreview.org/2001/04/01/neoliberalism-from-reagan-to-clinton/.
98. Ibid.
99. Edward Morris, "Why Bernie's Right About Glass-Steagall," *Moyers & Company*, April 4, 2016, http://billmoyers.com/story/why-bernies-right-about-glass-steagall/.
100. Hilary Hanson, "Nixon Aide Reportedly Admitted Drug War Was Meant To Target Black People," *HuffPost*, https://www.huffingtonpost.com/entry/nixon-drug-war-racist_us_56f16a0ae4b03a640a6bbda1.
101. "How Mass Incarceration Underdevelops Latino Communities," *Criminal Law And Criminology* (Oct. 7, 2015), https://lawexplores.com/how-mass-incarceration-underdevelops-latino-communities/.
102. Madison Pauly, "A Brief History of America's Private Prison Industry," *Mother Jones*, July/August 2016, http://www.motherjones.com/politics/2016/06/history-of-americas-private-prison-industry-timeline/.
103. Eli Meixler, "With Over 29,000 Homicides, 2017 Was Mexico's Most Violent Year on Record," *Time* (Jan. 21, 2018), http://time.com/5111972/mexico-murder-rate/.
104. Jordan Weissmann, "The Failure of Welfare Reform: How Bill Clinton's signature legislative achievement tore America's safety net," *Slate* (June 1, 2016), https://slate.com/news-and-politics/2016/06/how-welfare-reform-failed.html.
105. Rodolfo Acuña, "The Age of the Billionaires," *Counterpunch*, December 27, 2013, https://www.counterpunch.org/2013/12/27/the-age-of-the-billionaires/.
106. Rodolfo F. Acuña, "Remembering Ruben Jaramillo" A Recent History of Privatization," Word Press, July 5, 2015.
107. Acuña, "Remembering Ruben Jaramillo," Ibid.
108. Rakesh Kochhar, Roberto Suro, and Sonya Tafoya, "The New Latino South: The Context and Consequences of Rapid Population Growth," Pew Hispanic Center (July 26, 2005), http://pewhispanic.org/reports/report.php?ReportID=50. "U.S.-Born Hispanics Increasingly Drive Population Developments," Pew Hispanic Center, http://pewhispanic.org/files/factsheets/2.pdf.

Chapter 17
The Decline of the American Empire

Learning Objectives

17.1 Characterize the U.S. and Latina/o social and political life in the early 2000s.

17.2 Compare Chicana/o political experiences locally and nationally in the early 2000s.

17.3 Summarize demographic changes in New York during the 2000s.

17.4 Relate changing U.S. demographics to racist and anti-racist movements.

17.5 Describe the fight for ethnic studies and public schooling versus racist opposition.

17.6 Characterize the millennial generation and its political challenges.

The Empire is Broken

17.1 Characterize the U.S. and Latina/o social and political life in the early 2000s.

[Empires]regularly unravel with unholy speed: just a year for Portugal, two years for the Soviet Union, eight years for France, 11 years for the Ottomans, 17 years for Great Britain, and, in all likelihood, 22 years for the United States, counting from the crucial year 2003.[1]

This sort of speculation about the unraveling has become common since the end of the Vietnam War. Some Americans expected the decline to be a free fall as in the case of the Soviet Union that went over the cliff after the fall of the Berlin Wall on November 9, 1989. The crumbling of an Empire, however, does not normally work that way. Empires, as mentioned in Chapter 16, are like decaying fruit: Everyone knows it is happening, but avoid speaking about the inevitable conclusion until the stench sets in. In the case of the Soviet Union it disintegrated in 1989 because its people lost faith in the system and it imploded within two years.

The American Century as a world power began after World War II, and in less than 70 years it finds itself rivaled by other nations. The United States is no longer the world's preeminent economic power; China is close on its heels economically. Technologically, India is gaining ground and will rival or surpass the United States. The current supply of brilliant American scientists and engineers are ready to retire and the nation's younger generation is ill-educated largely because of a decaying education system.[2] Another indication of the decline is that America is also falling behind China and the European Union in exports. "After leading the world for decades in 25- to 34-year-olds with university degrees, the country sank to 12th place in 2010. The World Economic Forum ranked the United States at a mediocre 52nd among 139 nations in the quality of its university math and science instruction in 2010."[3] While the United States is overreliant on oil, Germany and China are becoming energy self-sufficient.[4]

Power has limits and the United States has become a debtor nation. Failed American wars in Korea, Vietnam, and the Middle East have accelerated this decay. According to Chinese billionaire Jack Ma, "the U.S. has wasted over $14 trillion in fighting wars over the past 30 years rather than investing in infrastructure at home" in which the only winners were American multinational companies. They have made trillions in past 30 years.[5] Americans are oblivious or in denial that colonial wars such as the Afghanistan and Iraq Wars were fought on credit and that the bills are due.

Meanwhile, its major competitors spend a fraction of their budgets on their military. "In fiscal year 2015, military spending [was] projected to account for 54 percent of all federal discretionary spending, a total of $598.5 billion"[6] The government spent $70 billion on education and $66 billion on Medicare and Health.) The United States and its allies no longer have "unimpeded access to air, sea, space, cyberspace, and the electromagnetic spectrum in order to underwrite their security and prosperity."[7] Americans are old and no longer the hardworking factory workers of the 1950s.

Into the Twenty-first Century: No More Babies

By the year 2000, the decline of the American white race was unmistakable:

> In the total population, 211.5 million people, or 75.1 percent, reported only White. An additional 5.5 million people reported White and at least one other race. In just ten years in 2010, white people were only fifty-three percent of nation's young people; in 1990 they were nearly 70 percent.[8]

Meanwhile, Mexican/Latinos rose from 12 percent of young Americans: "About one-third, or 17.9 million, of the nation's Hispanic population is younger than 18, and about a quarter, or 14.6 million, of all Hispanics are Millennials (ages 18 to 33 in 2014)."[9] The 2000 Census suggested the importance of Mexican/Latino millennials and their growth of a sense of place and inclusion. (In reality, Americans were white in name only. If the clock were set back to 1920 most who call themselves white would be considered otherwise.)

The Death of Democracy

The Supreme Court's *Gore v. Bush* decision (2000) stole the election from Al Gore and gave George W. Bush the presidency. For many Americans it showed that the Court and the presidency were in the pocket of corporate interests.[10] The blatant power grab recalled Calvin Coolidge's speech in which he said, "The business of America is business," sending the message that government did not give a damn about ordinary citizens.[11] *Gore v. Bush* further exploded the myth that America held clean and honest elections and that the courts were impartial. According to CNN, "Taken as a whole, the recount studies show Bush would have most likely won the Florida statewide hand recount of all undervotes. Undervotes are ballots that did not register a vote in the presidential race."[12] The bottom line was that the Court "exercised power that belonged to Congress, the legislature of Florida, Florida's courts and administrators, and, most importantly, the people of the state."[13]

A Florida recount would have given Al Gore the presidency. The U.S. Supreme Court stopped the recount. The motivation of the justices was suspicious and was partisan rather than judicial. That George W. Bush's brother Jeb was governor of Florida did not help this impression.[14] Because of apparent corruption "four in ten Americans had doubts about whether Bush had legitimately won the election".[15]

After this political heist the floodgates opened and rigged elections became commonplace.

The loss of moral authority of the Supreme Court is huge and similar to a loss of religious faith. White Americans after World War II believed in their institutions' fairness. (Most did not know the history of the Court.[16]) This faith was gradually shaken. Images of voter registrars looking for chads on voting ballots and the Court's stopping the recount, handing the election to George W. Bush, shocked many of them. There was an overwhelming feeling that the election was rigged.

The Bankrupting of the Empire

On September 11, 2001, 19 al-Qaeda operatives hijacked four commercial passenger airliners and crashed two of them into the Twin Towers of the World Trade Center in New York City. Both towers collapsed within two hours. The third airliner crashed into the Pentagon in Arlington, Virginia, and the fourth plane into a field in rural Somerset County, Pennsylvania. The attacks claimed 2,974 lives in addition to the lives of the 19 hijackers. The United States retaliated by launching a "War on Terrorism."

On October 7, 2001, the United States and a handful of NATO nations that included the United Kingdom and Australia invaded Afghanistan, launching Operation Enduring Freedom. The mission was allegedly to capture Osama bin Laden, the leader of al-Qaeda. In March 2003, the United States and its allies invaded Iraq under the pretext that Iraq possessed weapons of mass destruction and that al-Qaeda and Iraqi leader Saddam Hussein were cohorts— this was proven to be untrue. The lie that the United States faced a danger from terrorists and rogue states seeking to use these weapons was spread to garner support from the American public for the Middle East Wars. From 2003 to 2012, the wars in Iraq, Afghanistan, and Pakistan cost $3.2 to $4 trillion in direct and indirect costs. This was more than enough money to support quality education and health systems. The wars impacted Latinos who made up 27 percent of all Marine fatalities in Iraq, although they were only 14 percent of the Corps. California contributed nearly one of every three green card soldiers. In some Los Angeles neighborhoods, Army and Marine recruiters estimated that 50 percent of the enlistee pool were non citizens.[17] (Many of these undocumented veterans were later deported after serving in the Middle East.)[18]

The trillions of dollars spent on the wars diverted funding from needed projects such as education and the rebuilding of a crumbling national infrastructure and an economy that was dependent on Chinese loans. Programs such as Bush's "No Child Left Behind" mandated reforms, but lacked proper funding. The wars also suppressed a reasonable discussion of issues such as immigration.

Initially the all-volunteer army consisted mostly of men and women who joined the armed forces or the National Guard in peacetime. The draft was not implemented because lawmakers feared that Americans would not tolerate another Vietnam. Minorities comprised about 30 percent of the U.S. population and 35 percent of the armed forces. To fight sustained wars, larger numbers of Mexican/Latinos were recruited.[19] This was logical since the U.S. Census in 2000 reported the median age of Latinos was 25.9 years, and that of the Mexican-origin population was 24.3 years.[20] "The 2010 census indicated that the median age for whites was 42 years. For Asians, it was 35.4. For Hispanics, it was 27.3, and for Blacks it was 32.4."[21]

> After increasing to 30 in 1950, the median age [of Americans] fell, as a result of the baby boom, to 28 in 1970 ... Beginning in the 1970s, lower fertility combined with the aging of the baby boom generation (the oldest turned age 30 in 1976), pushed the median age sharply higher. It reached 30 in 1980—the same median age as in 1950—and continued to increase to a record high of 35 in 2000.[22]

By 2006, Latinos were 11 percent of enlisted men; Latinas were 12 percent of enlisted women; they constituted 4.8 percent and 5.3 percent respectively of the commissioned officers. They made up 15 percent of the Marine Corps and 6 percent of the Air Force. Statistics are deceiving, though: Latinos excluding immigrants, made up 16 percent of the workforce—they comprised 8.2 percent of the qualified civilian workforce.

Since the 1980s a tightening took place in internal political controls as army recruiters competed for more college-eligible Mexicans and Latinos. This caused a resistance in the high schools; many teachers and administrators did not want to pander to the war machine. In 1996, the Republican-led Congress passed the Solomon Amendment that withheld federal funding from schools not providing adequate access to military recruiters.[23] The Solomon Amendment was considered an assault on the autonomy of institutions of higher education. In 1999, the Congress set up the Student and Exchange Visitor Program to manage foreign students and exchange visitors in the United States. After 9/11, the Homeland Security on Research and Education Act further curtailed civil liberties—often in secret. Through government funding, universities were whipped into line, thus becoming part of the military–industrial complex. Finally many accused the Bush administration of McCarthyism. In this atmosphere, some government representatives raised the prospect of security clearance for university administrators and professors.

On January 8, 2002, Congress passed Section 9528 of the No Child Left Behind Act, which included a section titled "Armed Forces Recruiter Access to Students and Student Recruiting Information," stating that "each local educational agency receiving assistance under this Act shall provide," upon request of military recruiters, access to the high school students' names, addresses, and telephone listings.[24]

The Patriot Act was signed into law on October 26, 2001. Under the guise of Homeland Security the Latino community was invaded. Even in normal circumstances, the Mexican-origin community suffered from the excesses of the border patrol. The Homeland Security Act of 2002 authorized the U.S. Immigration and Customs Enforcement (ICE) agency, supposedly to protect the United States and uphold public safety. The agency identified and investigated possible violations of 400 federal statutes within the United States and by attachés to major U.S. embassies overseas. Besides criminal investigation, protection of federal buildings within the United States also came under ICE's purview.

Census 2000

Politically, numbers matter. That is why the various racial and ethnic groups are absorbed with the accuracy of the national Census that occurs at the beginning of each decade. Resources and representations are allocated according to the numbers. They determine how many presidential electoral votes each state gets, how many congressional seats, the budget, and more. The 2000 Census showed that three of four U.S. Latinos lived in California, Texas, New York, Florida, Illinois, Arizona, and New Jersey.[25] Half of the nation's Latinos lived in California or Texas, whose populations were heavily Mexican in origin. Although the largest concentration of Mexicans lived in Los Angeles, Chicago, Houston, San Antonio, and Phoenix, many Mexicans and Latinos lived in small hamlets throughout the Southwest, Midwest, and Northwest. With the increasing numbers Mexican/Latinos' voting strength was growing, although at a snail's pace compared to their numbers.

Youth and citizenship remained obstacles to political power, though the Latino population grew overall, from Oregon to the rural South, which by 2000 was 12 percent Mexican. Nationally, the U.S. Mexican population increased by 53 percent, with the number of registered Mexican/Latino voters increasing from 5.5 million in 1994 to less than 8 million in 2000. Three states California, Texas, and Illinois had 108 of the 270 electoral votes needed to elect the president.

Mexicans/Latinos cast 1.61 million votes in the 2000 election—15.2 percent of the total votes cast in California. They turned out at a rate of 70.4 percent, far higher than the national average of 51 percent.[26] According to the

William C. Velásquez Institute, California Latino registration numbered 2.3 million in October 10, 2000. It estimated that U.S. Latino registration hovered between 7.2 million and 7.7 million. The juggernaut was the city of Los Angeles whose population was larger than 42 states. The city was 46 percent Latino, 30 percent white, 11 percent African American, and 10 percent Asian. California as a whole had a total population of 33,871,648 people, of whom 10,966,556 were Mexican/Latino and 8,455,926 were of Mexican origin.

Chicago mirrored the rest of the country in the growth of its Latino numbers. It had 175,793 Latino registered voters. As in Los Angeles, even when they were a majority in a ward, a white minority outvoted them. A large number of Mexicans were either too young or not citizens and could not vote. There was also increasing competition with Black voters. Despite these numbers, the chance of Mexicans/Latinos winning in wards where they were in the minority was highly improbable.[27]

WHO ARE LATINOS? WHERE DO THEY LIVE? Based on my experiences and countless Chicana/o scholars I have interviewed, the Census Bureau, the media, and institutions seemed to generalize anyone with brown hair and brown eyes or whose name ends in a vowel as Latino.[28] They are often confused as Mexicans although they are Central or South Americans. This causes tensions because Central Americans have a strong sense of national identity. This generalization is similar to that of Asians who are generalized as Chinese. Even Mexican Americans refer to Koreans, for example, as "chinos."[29] Each group has its own nationality, history, identity, and personality. In 2000, 32.8 million Latinos resided in the United States, representing 12 percent of the total U.S. population.[30] The 2010 Census registered about 33 million Mexican-origin residents (approximately 64.9 percent of Latinos which count was in all probability closer to 70 percent); mainland Puerto Ricans numbered 4.7 million (9.2 percent); Cuban Americans, 1.9 million (3.7 percent); Salvadorans, 1.8 million (3.6 percent); Dominicans, 1.5 million (3 percent); Guatemalans, 1.1 million (2.2 percent); Colombians, 972,000 (1.9 percent); Hondurans, 731,000 (1.4 percent); Ecuadorans, 665,000 (1.3 percent); and Peruvians, 609,000 (1.2 percent). By 2012, the number climbed to 53 million Latinos, comprising 17 percent of the total U.S. population.[31]

> A majority (51%) say they most often identify themselves by their family's country of origin; just 24% say they prefer a pan-ethnic label ... by a ratio of more than two-to-one (69% versus 29%), survey respondents say that the more than 50 million Latinos in the U.S. have many different cultures rather than a common culture. Respondents do, however, express a strong, shared connection to the Spanish language. More than eight-in-ten (82%) Latino adults say they speak Spanish, and nearly all (95%) say it is important for future generations to continue to do so.[32]

The Migration Institute Report in March 2012 reported that 11.1 million unauthorized immigrants resided in the United States. In 2012, just over 37.1 percent of Mexican/Latinos were foreign-born; 36 percent of Mexicans, 59 percent of Cubans, 57 percent of Dominicans, and 62 percent of Salvadorans were foreign-born—suggesting strong ties with their mother countries.[33]

California with 11.8 million Mexican/Latinos was followed by Texas with 8.4 million Mexicans. These two states accounted for 61 percent of the total Mexican American population.[34] The Census Bureau reported that over one in five Latinos lived in just four counties: Mexicans/Latinos comprise comprised 48.1 percent of Los Angeles County's 9.9 million people; 64.5 percent of 2.5 million people in Miami-Dade, Florida; 41.9 percent of 4.2 million people in Harris County, Texas, which includes Houston; and 16.2 percent of 12.9 million people in Cook County, Illinois, which includes Chicago. U.S. Mexicans were the overwhelming majority of Latinos in three of these four counties.[35]

Individually, Latino groups shared characteristics such as language, but each was different. For example, except for Cubans, most Latinos were much younger than white Americans. The median age of Latinos nationally was 27 years, 10 years younger the national median of 37. The median age for Mexicans nationwide was 25 years; Puerto Ricans, 27 years; Salvadorans, 29; Dominicans, 29; and Cubans, 40. The age of Mexicanas contributed to a higher birth rate. Based on this internal growth, demographers project that by the year 2030, Latinos will comprise half of Texas. "The majority of babies now being born in California are of Hispanic descent, forecasting Latinos will be a majority sometime in the future."[36] Though the numbers of U.S. Mexicans are overwhelming, other U.S. Latino groups have a strong and unique presence and naturally want to preserve their individuality. Significant for future elections is that "[The Latino] median age is 27 years—and just 18 years among native-born Hispanics—compared with 42 years for that of white non-Hispanics."[37]

The Latino population doubled from 2000 to 2010. "Among the 10 states with the highest rapid growth in the Latino population [in 2000], the percentage increases ranged from a low of 155 percent in Nebraska to 394 percent in North Carolina. This growth was primarily ... associated with the restructuring of the meat-processing industry and the expansion of low-wage jobs in the South and the Midwest, primarily in nonmetropolitan areas."[38] Although Mexican/Latinos remained concentrated in the West, and were an urban population, since the 1990s the population spread nationally, largely in search of employment. Most Mexican/Latinos continued to live in nine states: Arizona, California, Colorado, Florida, Illinois, New Mexico, New Jersey, New York, and Texas. However, the population shifted (2000–2010), moving beyond city borders. The top five fastest-growing Latino counties in the country were Luzerne, Pennsylvania (479 percent change); Henry, Georgia (339 percent change); Kendall, Illinois (338 percent change); Douglas, Georgia (321 percent change); and Shelby, Alabama (297 percent change). Moreover, Latinos are now in Arkansas, Kentucky, Maryland, Mississippi, North Carolina, South Carolina, Tennessee, and South Dakota. Most of these are conservative, former Confederate states.[39]

Mexican/Latino Population 2010 Census	
Latino	50,730,000
Mexican	32,916,000
Puerto Ricans	4,683,000
Cubans	1,884,000
Salvadorans	1,827,000
Dominicans	1,509,000
Guatemalans	1,108,000
Colombians	972,000
Hondurans	731,000
Ecuadorans	665,000
Peruvians	609,000

SOURCE: Adapted Research Center[40]

In studying these numbers, it must be kept in mind that Mexico is the 10th largest nation in the world, that it shares a 2,000-mile border with the United States and that the Southwest belonged to Mexico before 1848.

Political Roundup: 2000

In 2000, Antonio Villaraigosa lost the election for mayor of Los Angeles partially due to personal reasons. Then Assemblyman Tony Cárdenas, Los Angeles City Councilman Alex Padilla, and Congressman Xavier Becerra supported Jim Hahn because Villaraigosa supported a white liberal to replace him as Speaker of the Assembly. This schism gave many white liberals and African Americans an excuse to support Hahn, who ran racist ads associating Villaraigosa with gang members and drug dealers.

California Latinos as a whole entered a new era. Electoral politics brought out the worst in most aspirants. To run successfully for city council or mayor required more money than the Mexican/Latino community could raise independently. To attract huge sums of money, compromises were made with the business community, whose interests did not always match those of Mexican Americans and other Latinos. Term limits, personal ambitions, and the need to raise campaign funds changed the direction of Chicana/o politics.

In the years past, nationalists such as Richard Alatorre disciplined politicians. However, times changed, and by 2000, Mexican Americans and Latinos wanted to believe that they were players. Reading through an extensive number of news clippings, few can be found of Latinos criticizing the big dog (Clinton). This is despite the fact that "Hispanics remain underrepresented in the Federal workforce: they make up only 6.4 percent of the Federal civilian workforce, roughly half of their total representation in the civilian labor force."[41]

The redistricting processes in 1980 and 1990 had been contentious. In 2000, the Mexican American community assumed that it was part of the establishment, given its new power in Sacramento. Latinos were now incumbents, and incumbents in both parties worked out a bipartisan redistricting plan that protected them. It kept intact 13 seats (7 state senators; 6 members of Congress) currently held by Latinos. The legislature would also create a new Chicano congressional district in Los Angeles County. The Mexican American Legal Defense and Education Fund (MALDEF) challenged the plan. Considering the growth and size of the Latino population, many felt that it was reasonably entitled to more.

MALDEF sued California over new election boundaries that were drawn to protect incumbents. The new boundaries were supported by 23 of California's 26 Latino lawmakers—the deal that strengthened their election prospects because their districts were padded. Although this worked against the election of more Latinos, they defended their vote, calling MALDEF racially divisive and claiming that elections were no longer about race. State Senators Marta Escutia and Gloria Romero criticized MALDEF, defending the deal in the name of multiracial cooperation. The Chicana senators failed to acknowledge the undemocratic outcome of the redistricting.[42] MALDEF President Thomas A. Saenz responded that he was "obviously disappointed" by the criticism but that it's not the first time MALDEF has found itself at odds with Latino elected officials." Saenz said "MALDEF is representing the interests of the Latino community, while Latino lawmakers are trying to "protect themselves."[43]

According to Chicana/o elected officials, the benefits of multiracial coalitions were huge. However, this came at the cost of ethnic solidarity. During the 2001 reapportionment, MALDEF filed a lawsuit challenging the redrawn boundaries for congressional and state Senate seats. MALDEF objected to a bipartisan redistricting plan that, while it protected the rights of minorities, made a deal to protect incumbents. Latinos held 13 assembly seats and seven state senators; they had six members of Congress. According to the Census, they were entitled to two more congressional seats. However, a deal was made and the Latino leadership agreed to only one in Los Angeles County. *Los Angeles Times* associate editor Frank Del Omo called it "blatant gerrymandering."[44] MALDEF complained that Howard Berman's Valley congressional seat should have a higher percentage of Latinos in order to give them a shot at representation. However, Berman was a Democratic Party power broker who was obviously protected. In an editorial, State Senators Martha Escutia and Gloria Romero defended the backroom deal as progressive, writing, "In the era of term limits, Latinos need not limit themselves to only seeking office in 'safe' Latino districts. We should not relegate ourselves to only a few court-imposed *barrios*."[45] (Later Romero broke with the Democratic Party and she joined the Charter School Movement at more than twice her previous salary.)

By 2002, there were 26 Latino legislators. In June of the same year, the Ninth Circuit Court found that the redistricting plan—a blatant deal—was not unreasonable. In effect, it held that rules protecting minorities were no longer necessary because of the dramatic political progress Latinos made in California in recent years—such as winning dozens of seats in Congress and the California legislature and nearly electing a Latino mayor in Los Angeles. This decision was significant since it came from the court's most liberal judges. In the space of just under three decades, society returned to the era of legal gerrymandering.[46]

In Texas, the success of George W. Bush was due to his cultivating Latino voters to form his base there. Latinos were not a factor in California where Gore was the overwhelming favorite. They were much more of a factor in places such as New York. Nationally, the U.S. Latino community took a huge leap during the 1990s. In 2000 they were 58 percent, or 35.3 million people; 12.5 percent of the national population there constituted 7 percent of all voters. However, in some cases numbers did not result in Latino representation. For example, according to the 2000 Census 30 percent of citizens in Fort Worth, Texas were Latino. Yet, there were no Latinos on the City Council. They did better on the Fort Worth school board where they held three of the nine seats. It was estimated that Latinos needed at least a 60 percent majority to elect a candidate.[47] This was a pattern nationwide.

The Death Penalty: A Symptom of Inequality or Racism

At one time, the manufacture of weapons was for national defense. By the advent of the wars in the Middle East, it became a major American business. Despite the decline in military spending, the business of remains a good one. The *Huffington Post* points out: "Worldwide military expenditure shrunk in 2013 for the second consecutive year, falling by 1.9% to $1.75 trillion. The 100 largest arms-producers sold a combined $402 billion worth of arms and military services in 2013, also down — for the third consecutive year."[48]

The 100 largest arms producers and military services contractors recorded $395 billion in arms sales in 2012. Lockheed Martin, the largest arms seller, accounted for $36 billion in such sales during 2012. Based on figures compiled by the Stockholm International Peace Research Institute (SIPRI), 24/7 Wall St. examined the 10 companies profiting most from war.[49]

Under neoliberalism, the industrial–military complex promoted sales through fear and lobbying. Similar scenarios are true of anti-immigration, and the specter of crime is a big money maker. The prison system was at one time for punishment and supposedly rehabilitation. By the year 2000 it was a for-profit industry whose main motivation was making money from prisoners of color, who the public demanded be warehoused or annihilated. Fear has led to cries for the death penalty where the passions of the mob are satisfied. Mexicans and Latinos along with Blacks became sacrificial lambs:

> Hispanics constituted almost 20% of the new admissions to death row in 2009 (18 new inmates). Half of the new Hispanic death row inmates were from California, bringing their total to 157 Hispanic inmates, the most in the country. Hispanics now represent 13.5% of the U.S. death row population. In 2000, they made up 11% of death row. Of the executions carried out in 2009, 13% (7 out of 52, correcting earlier number) were of Hispanic inmates. All of the executions of Hispanics occurred in the South.[50]

As of January 1, 2009, 376 Latinos sat on death row, with the greatest number in California and Texas. In the Golden State, 148 of the 678 prisoners on death row were Latinos; in Texas, 104 of 358. It surprises many people to learn that this is one of the longest-standing civil rights controversies between Mexicans and the law. Studies suggest that the race of the victim is a determining factor in a decision to sentence a defendant either to death or to life in prison. Realizing this and the fallibility of the court system, New Mexico Governor Bill Richardson signed a law abolishing the death penalty in 2009. Supreme Court Justice John Paul Stevens, who was among the Justices when the Supreme Court reinstated the death penalty in 1976, in 2008 called it "anachronistic." But the truth is that the death penalty plays a role similar to that of horror films in white suburbia— it alleviates society's fears of the inner city. According to Amnesty International, in 1999, the United States—along with China, Congo, Iran, and Saudi Arabia—accounted for 85 percent of the world's executions. Because a disproportionate number of Latinos are poor and young, the death penalty also disproportionately affects them. Occasionally, a defendant can successfully challenge the system, as in the case of Manuel Salazar, a young Chicano on death row in Illinois, whose sentence for the 1984 murder of a white Joliet police officer was overturned. A new jury found Salazar guilty of involuntary manslaughter in the case, and he was freed because he had served more than twice the sentence for that charge.[51]

In January 2000, Republican Governor of Illinois George Ryan declared a moratorium on executions. Illinois had exonerated 13 death-row inmates since 1976, which shook the conservative governor's faith in the fairness of the system. A case that weighed in his decision was that of Rolando Cruz, freed after 12 years on Illinois's death row for the 1983 murder and rape of a 10-year-old girl. Cruz and Alejandro Hernández were charged with the murder of the small girl—although police had arrested a repeat sex offender and murderer named Brian Dugan, who confessed to the crime. DNA testing linked Dugan to the crime. At Cruz's first trial, an expert claimed that she could tell a person's class and race by shoe imprints identifying Cruz. At the third trial in 1995, a police officer admitted that he had lied when he testified that Cruz had confessed to a "vision" about the girl's murder. The judge declared Cruz not guilty. An investigation led to criminal charges against the authorities that prosecuted Cruz, and resulted in the identification of the actual killer.[52]

Texas and Virginia accounted for almost half of all executions in the United States. During his term as governor of Texas, George W. Bush, the "compassionate conservative," refused to grant stays of execution in death penalty cases even when they were riddled with evidence of racial bias. When the Republican presidential candidate was asked how he could be so certain that in all of the executions the defendants were guilty, he replied that nothing like what happened in Illinois had happened on his watch: "I'm confident of the guilt of the person who committed the crime." (Bush presided over more than 135 executions, a record for any governor in U.S. history.) The *Chicago Tribune* cast doubt on Bush's statement, and its investigative reporters found that of the 131 death-row executions in Texas under Governor George W. Bush, 43 resulted from trials using defense attorneys who were publicly sanctioned for misconduct, either before or after their work on the cases. Forty of the executions involved trials in which the defense attorneys presented no evidence or only one witness during the sentencing phase. Twenty-nine cases included testimony by psychiatrists whom the American Psychiatric Association categorized as unethical and untrustworthy. Twenty-three included jailhouse informants, who were considered among the least credible of witnesses. Twenty-three included visual hair analysis, which has consistently been proved unreliable. Incidentally, Texas ranked 40th among states in money spent for indigent defense.[53]

Between 1992 and 1997, 47 states passed laws making it easier to try children as adults. Of the 38 states that authorize death penalty, 19 sanction the execution of 16- and 17-year-olds and 4 permit the execution of those aged 17 and older. In 1988, the U.S. Supreme Court held that executing children under the age of 16 violated the Eighth Amendment's ban against "cruel and unusual punishment." This ruling has recently been challenged. Former Governor Pete Wilson, the architect of California's Proposition 21, which passed in 2000, said that the age for the death penalty should be lowered to 14; Texas legislator Jim Pitts proposed lowering the age to 11. The Bureau of Justice Statistics reports that the number of youths under the age of 17 committed to adult prisons more than doubled, rising from 3,400 in 1985 to 7,400 in 1997. Two-thirds of the youths in the juvenile system nationally are minorities; African American youth make up 62 percent, although they comprise only 17 percent of U.S. youths.[54] In 2009, the Bureau of Justice Statistics reported that approximately 2,778 youth under age 18 were held in adult state prisons.[55] However, by 2007, national opinion was shifting, and the U.S. Supreme Court, in a 5–4 ruling, abolished the execution of anyone convicted of murder that was 17 years or younger when the crime was committed. In that year more than 70 people sat on death row for committing capital crimes when they were 16 or 17.

In this climate of fear, Wall Street speculators and bankers financed the rise of the Corrections Corporation of America (CCA) and other companies profiting billions from the detention and imprisonment of undocumented immigrants and other workers. This has given rise to private for-profit prison and detention sector.[56] The media strengthens the relationship between government and corporations, reducing undocumented immigrants to a commodity. The media abetted the criminalization and allowed corporations to get away with writing hateful, anti-immigrant laws, such as SB 1070 in Arizona. These types of laws are supported by bed quotas that the government established in 2009.

By law, Immigration Custom Enforcement requires an average of 34,000 people in detention every day. This benefits the corporations who own private prisons that make $200 per inmate a day. In the early 2010s, this added up to five billion dollar in profits that private prisons make in one year. Overall, undocumented immigrants are an asset to these corporations that work hard to increase the xenophobia among the American citizens. These types of laws and quotas influence the maltreatment of immigrant people, instilling fear among the community to keep them invisible and quiet.[57]

By the year 2018, Juan Sánchez through his Southwest Key Corporation built a billion-dollar business incarcerating undocumented immigrants. That same year he purchased an old Walmart warehouse where he housed Central America refugees from a caravan that President Donald Trump said was invading the United States.[58] Sánchez's Southwest Key, of which he is president and chief executive, on the Texas border have made a fortune:

> Southwest Key has collected $1.7 billion in federal grants in the past decade, including $626 million in the past year alone. But as it has grown, tripling its revenue in three years, the organization has left a record of sloppy management and possible financial improprieties, according to dozens of interviews and an examination of documents. It has stockpiled tens of millions of taxpayer dollars with little government oversight and possibly engaged in self-dealing with top executives.[59]

Southwest Key had a capacity to warehouse 5,000 children in its 24 shelters. This type of privatization and exploitation is in line with how other public institutions are viewed. Along with Sánchez, the Prison Guard Unions formed a powerful lobby and private foundations collecting fear money from the elderly. Hate makes money in the United States.

California Electoral Politics

17.2 Compare Chicana/o political experiences locally and nationally in the early 2000s.

The pattern and practices of the privatization of society carried over into politics. Numbers became increasingly important and all Latinos whether large or small benefitted from the surge in the Mexican/Latino population. Throughout California voters elected Latinos, mostly Mexicans, to city governments and school boards; this trend had accelerated in the 1990s when Mexicans/Latinos elected a critical mass in the state legislature and Senate. The year 2000 triggered another census and a reapportionment of electoral districts.

Additional splits occurred when Mexican American office holders supported white candidates to further their own career interests. In a few instances, the deals were logical—either the white or Black candidate was the best choice. Term limits opened local and state offices to Mexican/Latinos, African Americans, and Asians, but office holding quickly became a game of musical chairs. Previously, incumbents remained in office for life, and they were maintained by corporate sponsors who contributed to their campaigns. The positive thing in this model was that incumbents learned their craft. Mexican American politicos were very skilled. After term limits were instated, politicos were swept in and out of office every eight years, so they spent the second half of their incumbency looking for a new office and donors. Money talks; the election to a Los Angeles School Board seat costs over $200,000. For statewide elections, the stakes were higher, and building a constituency outside the Latino base often involved trading selling out the interests of Latinos.[60]

In 2003, Lieutenant Governor Cruz M. Bustamante made an unsuccessful bid for governor of California after the recall of Governor Gray Davis. Bustamante grew up south of Fresno, California. He dropped out of college and worked as a butcher. Along the way, he became an intern to the local congressman; returning to Fresno, he enrolled in the local state college and was active in MEChA, which advocated the recruitment of Latinos to the campus. During the campaign, although he was to the right of moderate, his opponents distorted his affiliation with the Chicano student organization and red-baited him. To his credit, he did not disavow the past as some of his Latino colleagues did. After a vicious campaign, he lost to Republican Arnold Schwarzenegger.

After a second try, Antonio Villaraigosa was elected mayor of Los Angeles in 2005. Villaraigosa was the first Latino mayor of Los Angeles since 1872. The city had a total population of 3,845,541, nearly half of whom were Latinos. Los Angeles's sphere included a metropolitan area twice its size. Villaraigosa was from the radical left. Since his college years, he was a member of MEChA and CASA Hermandad Mexicana, an organization for the protection of the foreign-born. There was a world of difference between him and his opponent, James Hahn, who was conservative and was not above engaging in race-baiting. Villaraigosa won handily. When Hahn refused to retain Los Angeles Chief of Police Bernard Parks, an African American, he lost the support of African Americans who had supported Hahn in the previous election.

The Eyes of Texas Are Upon You

In 2017, the prestigious magazine the *New Yorker* ran an article "America's Future Is Texas." At the time, it appeared to be more of an illusion than real for Mexican Americans. What struck me was that Texas in 2017 seemed to be a private political game between white Republicans and Democrats. Mexicans were not part of the equation. Texas was a solid Red State.

Tex-Mexicans up to this point never reached their full potential. It had more second-generation eligible voters than any other state but they never seemed motivated to vote. Like in other states many Mexicans were either too young to vote or not citizens. "32 percent of the 2016 eligible Hispanic voters in Texas were between the ages of 18 and 29. The great migration of undocumented immigrants from Mexico to Texas occurred before the year 2000."[61] Its population swelled. Although Chicanas/os had never reached their political potential, as in other places it dreamt of the Awakening of their Sleeping Giant.

Los Angeles Times columnist Frank del Olmo wrote in 2002:

> Recently, former state Atty. Gen. Dan Morales, of San Antonio, and Tony Sanchez, a Laredo oilman and rancher, faced off in televised debates with a uniquely Tejano twist. The first hour was in English, the second in Spanish.[62]

That spring, Texas Republican Congressman Tony Bonilla ran unopposed in the Republican primary; former Texas Secretary of State Henry Cuellar never stood a chance in the November election.

In November 2002, Texas Republican Governor Rick Perry beat Democrat Tony Sánchez by 18 points. Sánchez spent $60 million of his personal fortune, estimated to be $600 million at the time of the election, in this unsuccessful race. Amid controversy surrounding Sánchez's loss it was speculated that Sánchez did not excite Latino voters. Perry received about 35 percent of the Latino vote; the Southwest Voter Registration Education Project disagreed with this statistic, claiming Perry received only 12 percent of the Mexican/Latino vote. The truth is that many factors contributed to confusion among Mexican/Latino voters. Many Latinos considered Sánchez more Republican than a Democrat; many Chicano Democrats resented that he contributed to George W. Bush's candidacy; and some Latinos and Texas liberals did not like him because of his business dealings—including those with Enron. However, the fact remains that more than 70 percent of white voters voted against Sánchez. The banker/oilman was the first Mexican American gubernatorial candidate in Texas.[63] Meanwhile, "The Lone Star State's population swelled to 25,145,561 [in 2010], a 20.6 percent increase since 2000." By 2011, 38.1 percent of Texas's population was Latino; it had 34 electoral votes, a growth of 2 percent since 2000. The historical memory of disaffected *Raza Unida* members and the new generation were growing tired of the Eyes of Texas.[64] Similar changes were occurring elsewhere.

The Sleeping Giant

Since the before the election of John F. Kennedy in 1960, Mexican Americans spoke of their political potential and used phrases such as the "Sleeping Giant" to describe this prospect. This worldview was, however, local. It widened with the growth and spread of the community. Although New Mexico from the beginning of the occupation had a sizeable Mexican-origin population, it had been eclipsed by American colonials. This changed with additional numbers of Mexican migrants and the internal growth of the *manitos* (New Mexicans).

In New Mexico in 2002, Bill Richardson, a former ambassador to the United Nations, who served on Bill Clinton's cabinet as secretary of energy, ran successfully for governor of New Mexico. Richardson served for 15 years in the U.S. Congress before joining the Clinton administration. (In 2008, he ran unsuccessfully for President.) Neighboring Colorado elected Ken Salazar as the junior senator in January 2005. Salazar, a former state attorney general, was considered a moderate. President Barack Obama appointed him to the cabinet post of secretary of interior.[65]

In neighboring Arizona, Mexicans/Latinos comprised a quarter of the state's 5.5 million residents. The National Association of Latino Elected and Appointed Officials (NALEO) reported that there were 369 Latinos serving in elected offices in Arizona, which included school boards, city councils, boards of supervisors, the state legislature, and the U.S. Congress. In 2003, Raúl M. Grijalva went to Washington to represent Arizona's seventh congressional district. Grijalva was active in Tucson politics since his youth, serving on the local school board and as a consistent voice for educational reform. Grijalva's parents were farmworkers who migrated to southern Arizona as *braceros*. As a congressman, nativists accused him of having been a member of MEChA and blamed him for "terrorists" coming into the country.

Meanwhile, Mexican/Latino numbers climbed in the state of Washington; in 2002 the Latino population numbered 490,448, by 2011 it rose to 11.6 percent out of 6,830,038 residents. In the early part of the century, Antonio Ginatta, executive director of the Washington State Commission on Hispanic Affairs in Olympia, predicted, "It's just a matter of time before the Latino groups organize to exercise their political power." In 2012, it was reported that while the Latino vote grew in importance, representation remained at mid-1990 levels.[66] The rise in Mexican/Latino numbers revived a "dying South" where the young were moving out, leaving an aging population behind. The growth in population increased the region's national representation and allowed it to retain representation.

Mapping Mexican Americans

In the struggle between Texas and Colorado for control of *La Raza Unida* Party, many believed that Colorado would win because of the attraction of Corky Gonzales and the Crusade for Justice in urban areas. What people forgot was that many if not most Mexican Americans who lived in the Midwest and Northwest had either passed through or were originally from Texas. At this point these ties were reinforced by familial contacts. A century-old history of transnational Latino labor networks developed that was consolidated in the twenty-first century with growing populations. The migrant trails extended into the Old South where Mexicans picked cotton, cultivated agricultural products, and worked in the growing poultry industry as many Blacks migrated to the East and Midwest.[67]

Between 2000 and 2010, there was a growth of 9.8 to 19.3 percent. As mentioned, Mexican/Latino population drove much of this growth. The percentage of the Mexican growth in Georgia rose 16.8 percent from 2000 to 2002, and by 2011 9.1 percent of the state was Latino. A similar rise occurred in North Carolina (8.6 percent Latino), Kentucky (3.2 percent), South Carolina (5.3 percent), Virginia (8.2 percent), and Alabama (4.0 percent). Other states such as Mississippi benefited from heavy seasonal migration into the state.

Permanency brought families and youth together who began to fight for their rights; they refused to be invisible. University of Southern California historian George Sánchez wrote:

> A year ago, on Wednesday March 29th, 2006, two thousand Latinos marched to the state capitol in Nashville, Tennessee to protest the role of Senator Bill Frist, the then-US Senate majority leader, in trying to criminalize the undocumented in the United States in pending legislation before Congress, as well as protesting the abolition of a driving certificate program for undocumented workers sponsored by that state.[68]

For many of the protestors, this was the first time they participated in a protest march. Similar actions occurred throughout the South: 5,000 in Charlotte, North Carolina and 150 in Birmingham, Alabama. In Atlanta they decided not to march but boycotted work and shopping. Despite these actions, however, they were unable to stop the Georgia legislature from passing a bill curtailing government benefits to illegal immigrants. Protests and rallies were also organized in Mississippi, Alabama, and South Carolina in April 2006 to support the growing immigrant rights movement. In South Carolina, this effort was led by the Coalition for New South Carolinians. While the size of these protests was dwarfed by the half million that marched in Los Angeles on March 25 or the 200,000 that marched in Chicago, the very public act of protest itself was critical in these new southern communities without a long history and with many in undocumented status.[69]

Latinos were the fastest-growing population in Oklahoma, where from 2000 to 2004 the total increased by 24.4 percent; by 2011 Mexicans/Latinos made up 9.2 percent of Oklahoma. There were few Latino political successes in these states considering the population, and a "super majority" to elect Latinos was required.[70] An economy cannot be built by an aging population.

Another significant phenomenon was occurring. The Mexican American population continued to grow rapidly, "with births accounting for 63% of the 11.2 million increases from 2000 to 2010." At 31.8 million in 2010, Mexican Americans comprise comprised 63 percent of the U.S. Hispanic population and 10 percent of the total U.S. population. U.S.-born Mexican population could outgrow all other Latino immigrant arrivals through a natural population growth alone.[71] During the previous two decades the number of new immigrants either matched or exceeded the number of U.S. births. This means that no matter who the president of United States is the Mexican/Latino electorate will continue to grow.

The 2007 Immigration Bill

Senator Arlen Specter's Comprehensive Immigration Reform Act of 2006 (S. 2611) passed in the Senate in May 2006; it failed to make it through the House of Representatives. Its full name was the Secure Borders, Economic Opportunity and Immigration Reform Act of 2007 (S. 1348). Senators Ted Kennedy, D–Mass., John McCain, R–Ariz., and others, had tried to put a bipartisan bill through the Democrat-controlled Congress. Kennedy and McCain had tried in 2005 and 2006 to put through a similar bill. George W. Bush was in support. Hillary Clinton and center-left Democrats were also in support of what they called an effort to pass a comprehensive immigration reform bill based on tough rhetoric on border security and immigration enforcement. The left and progressive Democrats wanted to balance border security and the human rights of immigrants.

Republicans automatically opposed amnesty; the bill provided a pathway to legalization for existing immigrants. Democrats in 2007 regained control of the House. Deals were made with several moderate and even conservative Republicans. Most of the left was skeptical and turned off by Hillary Clinton's rhetoric of sending undocumented children back to the border. Not everyone saw merit in Kennedy's balancing act approach and pointed to his disastrous compromise in the 1965 Immigration Act that placed Mexicans and Latinos on immigration quotas.

Labor was split. The Service Employees International Union supported a deal. The AFL-CIO leadership opposed guest worker programs intended to entice Big Business and GOP support. Pro-immigration groups largely opposed the deals. Leftist critics accused the Democrats of not prioritizing immigration reform and of posturing to get Mexican/Latino electoral support. Republicans were aware of the sizeable support Latinos had given George W. Bush. Some speculated that "There may have been some factor there in which Democratic members thought that they'd rather do this under a Democratic administration."

At the time, there were approximately 12 million undocumented immigrants in the United States who would have been provided legal status and a path to citizenship. The bill was portrayed as a compromise between providing a path to citizenship for "illegal aliens" and increased border enforcement: It included funding for 300 miles (480 km) of vehicle barriers, 105 camera and radar towers, and 20,000 more Border Patrol agents, while simultaneously restructuring visa criteria to favor high-skilled workers. The bill also received heated criticism from both sides of the immigration debate. The bill was introduced in the Senate on May 9, 2007, but was never voted on, though a series of votes on amendments and cloture took place. The last vote on cloture, on June 7, 2007, failed 34–61, effectively ending the bill's chances. A related bill, S. 1639, also failed, 46–53, on June 28, 2007.[72]

A weakness in the bill was that it contained multiple compromises: S.1639 would have created a new class of visa, the "Z visa" would allow everyone into the United States without a valid visa, and after eight years would make the holder of this visa eligible for a green card once they had paid a $2,000 fine and back taxes for some of the period in which they worked. S.1639 would have required undocumented immigrants to be in their home country when applying for a green card. S.1639 would have also ended family reunification. It eliminated the employer-sponsored immigration system and replaced it with a point-based "merit" system that discriminated against working-class applicants. It was based on a guest worker program. "Y visa" would have been created to let temporary guest workers stay in the country for two years, after which they would have to return home.

The bill would increased enforcement have on the U.S.–Mexico border. It added 20,000 Border Patrol agents and expanded 370 miles (600 km) of fencing. It would have added the "Employment Eligibility Verification System," a central database holding immigrant-status information on all workers living in the United States. All employers would have been mandated to assemble this information and to update it. Almost immediately Republicans pushed for additional fencing.

In sum, the right and left wings clashed. Conservatives attacked a path to citizenship for undocumented immigrants; liberals criticized the points-based system and provisions limiting family reunification. Labor unions, human rights, and Mexican and Latino organizations attacked the guest worker program, "claiming that it would create a group of underclass workers with no benefits." Hope of any type of immigration reform ended in 2010 with the Republicans taking control of the Senate and the House.[73]

The Presidential Election of 2004

The election showed that the Brown Wave was spreading throughout the country. According to the William C. Velásquez Institute (WCVI), over 7.6 million Latinos went to the polls in 2004, up 1.6 million from the 2000 presidential election. Between 2000 and 2004, the U.S. Latino population accounted for half of the population growth in the United States, increasing by 5.7 million. Exit polls conducted by the Associated Press and television networks found that Bush in 2004 won 44 percent of the Latino vote, up from 35 percent in 2000. Kerry won 53 percent of Latinos, down from 62 percent against for Al Gore four years earlier. One-third of "Hispanics" self-identified as born-again Christians, and nearly 20 percent of them listed moral values as their top priority, suggesting areas they had more in common with Republicans than with Democrats. By more than a 3-to-1 margin, these religious conservatives supported Bush.[74]

Mexico continued as the main source of undocumented immigration. "The 1990 Census included 4.3 million immigrants from Mexico. By 2000, this population more than doubled to 9.2 million with a further increase to 9.8 million in 2002. The undocumented population from Mexico increased from two million in 1990 to 4.8 million in 2000 and to 5.3 million in 2002."[75] At the same time, between 1990 and 2002, the documented Mexican population doubled with the total undocumented population growing by 165 percent.

Not everything was political in 2004, as Mexicans moved at the whim of the economy. In the 1980s and 1990s, work in light industry and the service sector allowed many Mexicans to stay one place. By the turn of the century these jobs were scarcer and undocumented immigrants were squeezed into the south and east coast, to find jobs or to escape immigration authorities. Some, like Ernestina Miranda who migrated from Mexico in 1979 in the trunk of a car, became disillusioned and noted the changes:

> "My American dream has turned into a nightmare," she said, over a glass of strawberry Kool-Aid in her listing trailer. Until recently, she had made a life on $7.50 an hour. She has become a temporary worker in a plastics plant that used to be based in Michigan, earning minimum wage, no benefits, no security. Her husband, Miguel, is unemployed. The mortgage on the slapdash home is in peril.[76]

With aging, the Mexican/Latino voting population increased dramatically. In general they supported Democrats by 63.0 percent to 33.2 percent: Mexicans/Latinos preferred Democratic congressional candidates.[77] Chicago was the second-largest Mexican American city. However, cities such as Dallas, Houston, and New York rivaled this growth. Because of the growing presence of non-Mexican Latinos, it became increasingly difficult to ferret out clear statistical data. Puerto Ricans, for example, resided in Chicago in large numbers. Central Americans were also becoming more visible. The number of Latinos reached 1,722,843 residents by the mid-2010s and the Mexican-origin population was 1,357,353 or 78.79 percent of the Latino total. Puerto Ricans were next at 153,206 (8.9 percent). Much of the Mexican growth was in the Chicago suburbs.[78]

The Big Apple

17.3 Summarize demographic changes in New York during the 2000s.

> "In New York, the growth in Mexican immigration has been recent and abrupt. According to 'The Newest New Yorkers,' a study of foreign-born residents compiled by the city in 2013, the city's Mexican population has grown by a factor of almost six since 1990—from the 17th largest to the third largest migrant population in the city."[79]

Meanwhile, the Mexican/Latino population jumped 2.5 percent between 2006 and 2007, totaling 2.3 million. Puerto Ricans were the largest Latino group, comprising about a third of the total. Dominicans were next at 602,093, or a quarter of the total, followed by Mexicans at 289,755. The Mexican population was the fastest-growing national group in New York, increasing by 9.8 percent between 2006 and 2007 and by 57.7 percent since 2000. Most studies attributed the dramatic growth of the Mexican-origin population to high fertility rates; this may be one factor, but more compelling arguments are the proximity of the United States to Mexico, cheaper land transportation, the historic corridors of scores of years of migration, and the fact that Mexico has a much higher population than most other Latin American nations.[80]

> "By some estimates, there are 4.3 million Mexican immigrants in the New York metropolitan area, and according to a 2015 Migration Policy Institute study, they are the most disadvantaged immigrant group in the United States."[81]

While this figure appears high, "Nearly half of Mexican children in New York City are growing up poor," which should be of concern.[82]

The Building of a Collective Historical Memory: Solidarity

17.4 Relate changing U.S. demographics to racist and anti-racist movements.

In a conversation with Eric Mann, a former weatherman, labor organizer, author, and intellectual, he talked about how his adrenaline would shoot up when he along with several thousand auto workers would pour into the parking lot after his last shift. It gave him a sense of power. Over the 60 years of teaching I can see the adrenaline of students rise with the increase in their numbers. Along with this was an increase in the students' fund of knowledge. Many more were reaching a state that Marx called a "praxis": the process where a theory, lesson, or skill is enacted. In other words, they are engaging, applying, exercising, realizing, or practicing ideas. This praxis has been greatly influenced by education which includes marches and walkouts—a collective reaction to racism. The feeling is similar to what Mann felt in being part of something.

A timeline can be traced from the school walkouts of 1968 that took place in Los Angeles, spreading to Texas and the rest of the nation. By the 1990s they spread as the immigrant movement spread. The farmworker movement had been important but protection of the foreign-born was less abstract since many youth were immigrants or the children of immigrants. This affinity took the identification with the foreign-born to the heart of the urban community. The walkouts of 1994, 96, and 98 were training grounds. The backlash to the amnesty of 1986 made it clear to many activists and students that the time had come to fight back. Thus they formed the Leticia A. Network (See Chapter 15). For all intents and purposes, they lost with the Passage of Prop 187. However, this did not kill the movement.

It was evident that by 2006 Mexican/Latino immigrants were losing their fear. Unlike in the first half of the twentieth century, they did not foster illusions that the Mexican government would or could protect their human rights. Mexicanas/Latinas spoke out and sought support from legal aid agencies and from battered women's shelters for domestic abuse. Homosexuals demanded space as members of society and they formed groups and demanded space in the larger community.

Reviewing history, in 1970 Mexican immigrants made up 7.9 percent of the foreign-born population of the United States. Ten years later Mexican immigrants were 15.6 percent; and by 2006, 30.7 percent. In 1970, there were fewer than one million Mexican immigrants living in the United States, about a fifth of the Mexican American population. Because most Mexican Americans were second or third generations in 1970, education and political representation were the more pressing issues. As mentioned, with the growth of the immigrant population, nationally Mexican American organizations and the media increasingly covered this population. The attack on the foreign-born affected the entire Mexican/Latino community since most were themselves or were the children of immigrants.

In 2005, Wisconsin Republican Jim Sensenbrenner introduced the Border Protection, Anti-terrorism, and Illegal Immigration Control Act of 2005; it was passed by the U.S. House of Representatives on December 16, 2005 by a vote of 239 to 182. The bill touched off the 2006 U.S. immigration reform protests. This was the first legislation passed by Congress in the U.S. immigration debate. Especially inflammatory was that it would be a crime to assist an illegal immigrant to "remain in the United States... knowing or in reckless disregard of the fact that such person is an alien who lacks lawful authority to reside in or remain in the United States." Furthermore, the prison term applicable to a removed alien would also be applicable to anyone who knowingly "aids or assists that alien to reenter the United States."[83] Current laws already prohibited "aiding and abetting" illegal immigrants.

Chicago struck first on March 10, 2006; an estimated 100,000 took to the streets. Marches followed throughout the country. On March 25, 2006 in downtown Los Angeles, police estimated more than 500,000 people marched in what was called "La Gran Marcha" ("The Great March"). Many observers estimated the crowd at a million. On April 10, 2006, millions of people, mostly immigrants, took to the streets of 140 cities across the nation. They were tired of being afraid, intimidated by ICE and by bullies who called themselves "minutemen." The protestors yelled no to U.S. House of Representatives Bill (H.R.) 4437: They were not criminals, they were not felons, and they were workers. They marched in Los Angeles, in Dallas, and in Chicago. Despite provocation, the marches were peaceful.[84]

Prior to these marches, thousands of students walked out of schools to protest H.R. 4437. Key Chicana/o activists supported the organization of events throughout the country. However, the protests were organized largely by a network of immigrant resources. Spanish-language radio and other media supported the marches. There was a backlash with the right-wing media claiming that many of the marchers waved Mexican and Salvadoran flags instead of *American* flags—ironically, nativists did not complain when other groups did the same. In April 2006, 900,000 people marched through the streets of the Dallas and thousands more students left their classes to protest the proposed anti-immigrant legislation; on May 1, 700,000 participated in a march in Chicago. Los Angeles was divided as politicos, labor, and the Catholic Church called an alternative march. Yet thousands marched, and a confrontation broke out in MacArthur Park; Los Angeles police overreacted and beat up the protestors.[85]

The marches built solidarity, a sense of community, not only in the Latina/o communities, but among progressives throughout the country. The protection of the foreign-born became part of the human rights agenda. More important was the transformation that took place in people who barely survived economically, had no papers, and were constantly harassed by ICE and threatened by racists. Yet they walked out of their jobs, often at the risk of losing those jobs, to fight back. Economic bad times sapped much of this energy, but the protests sent the message that if pushed too far, the community would fight back.[86]

Democrats Never Learn: Presidential Elections 2008

The 2008 presidential election in many ways reminds observers of the political strategies of the Gore (2000) and Kerry (2004) electoral races: Candidates professed to love Latinos but campaigned only in the larger electoral states, focusing on them only where they represented the swing vote. The general election was between Arizona Senator John McCain and Illinois Senator Barack Obama. In the primaries, the Mexican/Latino vote was contested and split by Senator Hillary Clinton and Obama. Support varied according to age group. In the November 2008 elections, 76.3 percent of the total 131 million people who voted were white, versus 12.1 percent Black, 7.4 percent Latinos, and 2.5 percent Asians. Latinos supported Obama and Joe Biden over Republicans John McCain and Sarah Palin by more than two to one. Latinos voted 56–41 percent for Obama even in McCain's home state of Arizona. In Illinois, Obama's home state, the Latino vote was 72–27 percent in favor of Obama. In battleground states, the Mexican/Latino votes favoring Obama were: Colorado 61–39 percent, Florida 57–42, Michigan 65–33, Nevada 76–22, Pennsylvania 72–28, and Virginia 65–34. In the non-battleground states, Obama's Latino vote percentages were just as dramatic: California 74–23, New Mexico 69–30, New Jersey 78–21, Illinois 72–27, and Texas 63–35. Even Latino evangelicals supported Obama 57–43 percent.[87]

As a consequence of Obama's election, in 2009 Congresswoman Hilda Solis (D–CA) was appointed Secretary of Labor by Obama, and an election to replace her followed in Los Angeles's 32nd Congressional District. It was a dividing moment. The 32nd was a Latino district—drawn in 1982 as a result of pressure from the Latino community, which sued under the Civil Rights Voting Act. At least 62 percent of the population was Latino, and 18 percent Asian; of the 126,000 registered voters, 53 percent were Latino and 17 percent Asian. The 32nd includes parts of East Los Angeles and has a large immigrant base. State Senator Gilbert Cedillo, a longtime activist since his youth, who had worked in the pro-immigrant rights and labor movements, ran for the office. It was a dirty campaign with opponents of Cedillo running multiple Spanish-surnamed candidates. On May 19, 2009, Cedillo lost and so did immigrant rights.[88]

According to the Pew Research Center's exit polls, "Latinos voted for President Barack Obama over Republican Mitt Romney by 71% to 27%" in 2012. According to exit polls, a record 11.2 million Latinos voted; nevertheless, the number was still lower than other groups.[89] A key to the Obama strategy was to form coalitions with single women, African Americans, Asian Americans, and Latinos. Although Latinos were critical of Obama's deportation policies and his failure to put through a meaningful immigration reform, the alternative was Republican Mitt Romney, who said undocumented people should self-deport themselves.

The Crash of 2008

Ronald Reagan introduced a neoliberal agenda when he was governor of California in the late 1960s. As president, he joined forces with British Prime Minister Margaret Thatcher and converted neoliberalism into a global venture. The ideology spread throughout Latin America and the rest of the world. In theory it favored free trade, privatization, minimal government intervention in business (deregulation), reduced public expenditure for social services, and cuts in public employment. It sold the illusion that the private sector could do it cheaper and better and that everyone would benefit. It boiled down to austerity for the worker while increasing profits for corporations and banks. Neoliberalism profoundly influenced Mexico and led to the diminishing role of agriculture.

As a consequence of the economic recession after the 2008 election, Obama became the scapegoat for the fall of the economy. The recession had been expected since Clinton's repeal of Franklin Roosevelt's 1930's Glass–Steagall Act that regulated greedy commercial bank involvement in stock market investment. Plainly capital could not regulate itself and the bust was inevitable. Obama's presidency came at a time when Americans could no longer say "I will have it better than my parents." Homeownership was out of the reach of most as wages declined and real estate was more completely commodified.[90]

In real wages most Americans had not received a raise for 35 years. Wage inequality was the widest in U.S. history. The incomes of workers in the bottom 60 percent dropped. The economy grew because of the entrance of substantial numbers of women into the workforce who subsidized the economy and by men and women working more hours. It was a period in which corporations reaped high profits and CEO salaries zoomed. These wage gaps were widest among minorities and females and worsened inequality.

Hatred and fear diverted American attention from the systemic abuse of the system. Instead, the spotlight was put on the immigrant and social issues that had nothing to do with corporate greed. Immigrants had nothing to do with the lack of jobs and the lack of education of the average American. They did not wage costly wars. Immigrants did not defraud the public and cause the implosion of the American economy in 2008.

What was questionable about Obama's policies was that he bailed out Wall Street, the main culprit. Instead of going after those who caused the fall, Obama pushed the passage of the American Recovery and Reinvestment Act of 2009, in which Wall Street was bailed out at a huge cost to taxpayers— a $700 billion bailout. Instead of the bailout going directly to average Americans in form of funding for education and healthcare, the gap in wealth between the rich and the poor was widened.

It had a tremendous impact on marginalized communities such as Mexican Americans. Despite their economic disadvantages individual families would pool their money and buy a house. The 2008 Recession in great part was about the bursting of the housing bubble that came about as a result of bad loans and government overspending during the Afghanistan and Iraq Wars. Bill Clinton and George Bush's neoliberal policies of deregulation of banks and financial institutions led to graft and corruption. They led to the crash of many banks that over speculated. The crash had nothing to do with Obama but was created by Ronald Reagan, Gorge Bush I, Bill Clinton, and George Bush II—but Obama did nothing about Wall Street buying up loans and putting the cost of housing out of the reach of most working people.

The Dreamers

The Dreamers were immigrant youth just being Americans and pursuing the August 28, 1963 speech of Martin Luther King "I Have A Dream" in which King spoke of the gap between the American dream and reality. Beginning in the 1990s, many of these youth who were nurtured on American history began to fight back and demanded acceptance. Many politicians were openly sympathetic since these youth were college bound or already college students. The Dream Act was first introduced to Congress in 2001 to create a pathway to citizenship for young people who were brought to the United States as children without documentation. In 2001, the bill was introduced to the Senate by Senators Dick Durbin (D–Illinois) and Orrin Hatch (R–Utah). It failed and immigrant youth continued to lobby for a Dreamer bill that would lead to a permanent status. Supporters would often travel to state capitals such as Sacramento, Phoenix, Austin, and Washington, D.C., at their personal risk and expense.[91]

They had no choice but to fight because conditions in their home counties in Latin America, Asia, and Africa were made worse by the United States. In the case of Mexico and Central America, the U.S. War on Drugs and political interventions destroyed their home countries' civil society. The U.S. drug market and policies destroyed Mexico's economy and neoliberalism destroyed its economic infrastructure. So there was no question of returning to a home country that they had never seen.[92]

Surprisingly, on June 15, 2012 Obama issued an executive order creating a new policy calling for deferred action for selected undocumented young people who came to the United States as children. The Deferred Action for Childhood Arrivals ("DACA") allowed undocumented immigrants who entered the country before their 16th birthday and before June 2007 to receive a renewable two-year work permit and exemption from deportation. The program potentially would solve many problems. It was a no-brainer; it added skilled and assimilated technicians to the American economy. Nevertheless, there was public and political opposition to DACA that was based more on the color of the Dreamers' skin than logic. Racism played a huge part. A sizeable number of Americans believed that America was a white nation and that it was being overrun by immigrants. These white nationalists voted and controlled many politicos. Further, the U.S. political system protects many of the smaller states where xenophobia infects the political ambience. The popular vote means little and it is only relevant in the election of the House of Representatives. The president and senators are elected by a system that is weighted in favor of smaller states. California, for instance, has a population of 31 million, larger than 42 states. It has two senators while Arkansas, with one million, has the same number of senators. Additionally, the California population has a much higher educational median than the so-called Red States.[93]

The Pew Research Center estimated that up to 1.7 million students were eligible for DACA and as of June 2014, about 581,000 individuals were issued permits.[94] DACA offered wins all around. Students attended U.S. schools for a dozen years. The cost of their education to the state amounted to hundreds of thousands of dollars for each student. Deportations would throw this investment away. These immigrant students represented the best in American society. Studies show that an aging population prevents the growth and prosperity of a nation, and the United States was assimilating and acculturating this youth population.[95] Another plus was that the Democrats would benefit from this policy change because it was very popular among the Latino population, where 23.4 million were eligible to vote.

In all, Obama's immigration record was disappointing. Many progressives called him the "Deporter in Chief." He removed more than 2.5 million people through immigration orders. This does not include those who "self-deported" or who U.S. Customs and Border Protection (CBP) turned away. DACA saved his legacy as a champion of immigrants. In part it was the result of tireless work by the Dreamers themselves. No doubt he implemented DACA because of the size of the Mexican/Latino voting bloc.

The Killing Fields: Words have consequences

Hate and fear are money makers in America.[96] In 2005, the media went wild. Nightly, CNN's Lou Dobbs—who was married to a Mexican woman—told horror stories of a Mexican invasion. Dobbs was carried on Fox News, a station that actively campaigned against immigrants and minorities. The mainstream media also made outrageous statements; on November 28, for example, *U.S. News & World Report* carried a cover with the headlines, "Border Wars." The cover story was titled, "Border wars: More illegal immigrants. More violence. More death." These inflammatory statements emboldened vigilantes to run around with guns, trying to pick off brown people who were entering the country to survive. Adding to the hysteria, ex-California Governor Arnold Schwarzenegger cheered on the "Minutemen." By December 2005, Republican Congressmen were proposing a constitutional amendment to deprive children of undocumented parents of their citizenship.[97] They used the racist expression "anchor babies" to refer to children conceived by undocumented women. Their hyperbole encouraged violence. That same year, an LAPD SWAT team killed 19-month-old Susie López Peña in an exchange of gunfire with her father, who was holding her. Police fired over 60 shots at the father, with numerous bullets hitting and killing Susie. Not one politico challenged Police Chief William J. Bratton, who defended his officers.[98]

On May 30, 2009, in Arizona, Minutemen burst into the Flores home, nine-year-old Brisenia Flores "was sleeping with her puppy." The invaders identified themselves as law enforcement. After shooting the father, one of the intruders shot Brisenia as she pleaded, "Please don't shoot me!" The Minutemen assassinated the nine-year-old, twice shooting her point-blank in the head. For two years there was very little coverage in the press about this outrage.[99]

In 2017 it was reported "[Their remains] make up a fraction of the death toll along the border in Texas. In just one county, the bodies and remains of more than 500 migrants have been found since 2009."[100] Arizona was an overcrowded graveyard. In 2016, a ministry of the Unitarian Universalist Church of Tucson worked with volunteers from, *La Coalición de Derechos Humanos*, on a 34-page report titled "No More Deaths." It drew on a survey of 58 border crossers and 544 cases from the Missing Migrant Crisis Line. Tens of thousands have gone missing since the 1990s, including 1,200 in 2015.[101]

Communitarianism: Helping the family!

Other than military aid, the United States has given Latin America relatedly little foreign aid. Countries such as Mexico would have experienced severe turmoil if it had not been for family members living in the United States with or without documents. In the absence of this aid poverty would have increased and many Mexicans would have been forced to join the underground economy or starve. As it is, cartel leaders such Joaquín Archivaldo Guzmán (El Chapo) have often given more informal aid to the villagers than Mexico or the United States. Relatives in the United States send remittances, monies to Mexican relatives. These gifts do not cost the American taxpayer a penny.

In 2003, Mexico received nearly $13.3 billion in workers' remittances, an amount equivalent to about 140 percent of direct foreign investment and 71 percent of oil exports. During this same period, remittances from Salvadorans in the United States reached an all-time high of $2.5 billion in 2004—approximately 17.1 percent of El Salvador's gross domestic product (GDP). During the 2008 Depression, "the money Mexican migrants sent home fell for the first time in history . . . from $26 billion to $25 billion."[102] Remittances are the second-largest source of foreign income in Mexico after oil. But as things got bad in 2008, Latinos sent less money home, more than seven in ten reported they sent less back in 2008 than in the previous year. This money somewhat stabilized the economy of Mexico and was entirely earned by tax-paying workers. It was sent back by people like María, 33, who migrated to Milwaukee in 2005; "she worked two jobs and sent as much as $2,000 to Mexico every two months."[103] Without remittances, the Mexican and Central American economies would have collapsed.

Border Towns

The border places are towns like Juarez/El Paso, Nogales and Tijuana/San Diego. They are places that would not have been in decay if there was no border. As it is, they seem to exist solely to make Americans feel better than Mexicans living there. They serve no other purpose than being "fun towns" for other forms of corruption. Historically, they furnish labor. They are poor.

Because of rampant inequality, corruption and violence are tolerated that would not be accepted elsewhere. Many Mexicans go there because border towns are ports of entry where money can be made. The U.S. drug market and the concentration of *maquiladoras* attract people. Because they are border towns, drug wars spill into places such as Laredo, Juárez, and Nogales where "respectable" U.S. bankers get rich from activities such as money laundering. Violence ebbs and flows there.

As mentioned, border towns are near North American transportation networks and profits are high. There are few regulations or restrictions. They don't have to worry about polluting or sexual harassment. In Juárez, women regularly disappear. At least 370 women, 24 per year on average, succumbed to violence from 1993 through January 2004. Police authorities ignored these homicides/disappearances until women's activist groups pressured them for some kind of action. The annual female disappearance and homicide rates were higher than for the entire United States and 38 times the total homicide rates for all of the Canadian provinces combined. Many critics speculated that the motives behind these crimes were sexual or related to serial murders, drug crimes, or slavery, or they were killed for body parts.[104] No one seems to care; it is a border town. No one asks about the dead women disappeared or why they were killed—for sex or dismembered for their body parts.[105]

The Consequences of a Lack of a Firewall

History is always moving—it marches on. While other factors affect the treatment of immigrants in the United States, distance from the mother country has a lot to do with how Americans treat them. The Italians were discriminated against and would have been deported in larger numbers if it not been for an ocean that served as a firewall. The cost of sending them back was prohibitive. So why haven't Mexicans been deported in larger numbers?

One factor that prevented a repetition of the mass terrorism of the 1930s repatriations is the population numbers. By the 1980s the numbers of Mexican Americans and their political participation prevented mass deportations. Simply too many undocumented Mexicans and Latin Americans lived in the United States. Moreover, their status changed and today there are more Mexican-origin people born in the United States than there are immigrants with or without papers. By the year 2000 there were also more Mexican/Latino elected office holders. This presents a serious dilemma to white supremacists since a growing number of Mexican Americans are citizens and can vote. Thus Mexicans have created a firewall and most will remain in the United States, absent a genocide.

In 2012, Republican candidate for governor of California Meg Whitman spent more than $141.5 million of her own money in an unsuccessful bid to defeat Democrat Jerry Brown. Brown won 64 percent of California's Mexican/Latino vote while Republican Whitman won 31 percent.[106] Republican Carly Fiorina, the former CEO of Hewlett Packard, also unsuccessfully challenged U.S. Senator Barbara Boxer. Democrat Boxer won 65 percent of the Latino vote while Fiorina won 29 percent. Fiorina and Whitman paid for the anti-immigrant rhetoric they had engaged in during their party primaries. Because of the firewall, Republicans have not been elected statewide in California since Proposition 187 in 1994, and the name Pete Wilson has gone down in infamy.

Arizona did not have a firewall or political buffer similar to that of California. Mexican elected officials as a group were weak, and could not or would not pressure the Barack Obama administration to enforce their Constitutional protections. Since the 1970s Tucson has been under a court order to desegregate, which it avoided. Xenophobia and anti-Mexican hysteria were out of control since the late 1960s. In 2010 Arizona legislators passed Senate Bill (SB) 1070, an anti-immigrant law, and Arizona House Bill (HB) 2281 that made the teaching of ethnic studies and Mexican studies in particular unlawful. It said that that Mexican American Studies divided races and was subversive.[107] The Tucson Unified School District banned books including *Occupied America* and William Shakespeare's *The Tempest*.[108] By 2015, it was projected that Arizona's population would increase by more than 30 percent to 7.9 million. The migration to Arizona brought retired white people who knew only what they saw in the movies about Mexicans. From 1990 to 2000, the Arizona Mexican/Latino population grew 88 percent (from about 700,000 to 1.3 million). From 2000 to 2004, it grew 22 percent (to 1.5 million), which alarmed white nationalists.[109]

Part of the threat to white Americans was the growing number of Latinos in the state. The Arizona Mexican population was young, with a median age of 24 versus 38 for white residents (some figures say 24 and 44). These statistics frightened many colonials who knew that in time Mexican/Latinos would outvote them and that Americans would become dependent on their labor. By 2013–2014, Mexicans were expected to represent more than 40 percent of all public high school graduates. Although the Mexican/Latino community doubled from 1990 to 2004, Mexicans/Latinos with bachelor's degrees grew by 3 percent.[110]

Corporate predators such as the Koch brothers and ALEC—the American Legislative Exchange Council—took advantage of white fears and invaded Arizona. The latter controlled over 50 state legislators and wrote SB 1070. In league with the prison industry, ALEC spearheaded the privatization of prisons reaping a bonanza from incarcerating undocumented and other Latinos. The Koch brothers funded the Tea Party that agitated racial hatred within the state. In the process they seized control of the Republican Party, and silenced Democrats who were prominent in the ranks of the Blue Dogs (Democrats who voted with Republicans). The Mexican American Studies Program was labeled subversive, unpatriotic, and racially divisive by state Superintendent of Schools John Huppenthal and state Attorney General Tom Horne.[111]

Up until the 2012 election, Democrats showed little interest in defending the civil rights of Mexican Americans who comprised over two-thirds of the Latino bloc. Behind the scenes more Mexican American leaders outside Arizona became critical of the national government and Arizona Latino politicos for not constructing a political buffer to protect the rights of the foreign-born and the Latino community.[112]

Squeezed out of the American Dream

In 2008, tuition reached $8,000 at most University of California campuses and half of that amount at California State Universities—and the rates were projected to increase by more than 30 percent annually! This was a far cry from the 1960s when students paid $50 a semester. Today students often graduate with $100,000 in debt!

In this environment of shrinking opportunities, Supreme Court Justice Sonia Sotomayor said, "I would hope that a wise Latina woman with the richness of her experiences would more often than not reach a better conclusion than a white male who hasn't lived that life."[113] Life experiences are important in forming identity. The fact that most Supreme Court justices are from upper-middle-class families and attended Harvard, Yale, or other Ivy League law schools makes a difference in how they see things. The bottom line is that not all Americans have the same economic and political interests, just as they don't share similar life experiences. There are differences of class, ethnicity, gender, and sexuality. Identity goes beyond a surname or color; the past shaped us.[114] For this reason it is important to examine the life experiences and interests of politicians such as Marco Rubio, Ted Cruz, or Miguel Estrada—ethnicity has nothing to do with it.

The Death of the Salesman

Citizens United is important because it dramatically changed the regulatory environment of campaign finance in the United States. "Since 2010, the judiciary has decided that corporations and labor unions may freely spend in American elections, and that so-called 'Super PACs (Political Action Committees)' can accept unlimited contributions from private citizens for the purpose of buying election advertising."[115] This is not the first time the courts have favored corporations and intervened on their side. During the Gilded Age in the nineteenth century, the Supreme Court ruled that corporations were persons entitled to the protections of the Fourteenth Amendment. In *Citizens United*, corporations are people entitled to First Amendment protections.

In effect it deregulated contributions, dramatically altering the rules of engagement. It made it difficult to follow the money and learn where Super PACs got "their money." It made it difficult to learn who controlled the Super PAC. American elections are no longer about one person, one vote, because the so-called "Super PACs" are free to accept unlimited contributions from private citizens for the purpose of buying election advertising.

The ruling encouraged unlimited contributions to political campaigns. In a 5–4 decision the Court rule that the government "may not ban political spending by corporations in candidate elections." According to the Court majority, such a limitation violated the First Amendment's most basic free speech principle. It ruled that the government was regulating political speech. The dissenting opinion countered that this case licensed corporate money to flood the political marketplace.

Citizens United seriously altered the political playing field. It allowed conservative groups such as Americans for Prosperity, founded by billionaires Charles and David Koch, to spend $122 million during the 2012 electoral campaign. The Koch brothers' political network spent over $400 million during this same campaign, more than double the total spent by the top 10 labor unions combined. It encouraged the bribing of elected office holders to reduce regulation and taxes for the super-rich. The Kochs also financed groups such as the Tea Party, as mentioned, to create a climate of political chaos and to push tax breaks and deregulation.[116]

Citizens United paved the way for the rise of Donald Trump and gross corruption in both houses of the U.S. Congress. According to Justice Ruth Bader Ginsburg, *Citizens United* was the worst of the court's rulings.[117] "The notion that we have all the democracy that money can buy strays so far from what our democracy is supposed to be."[118] The ruling encouraged the expansion of PACs, who could now raise unlimited funds from individuals, corporations, unions, and others "without any legal limit on donation size."[119] *Citizens United* "defined the modern federal campaign finance system."[120] In fact, it changed lobbying by enhancing it. It also lifted the ban on political spending by foreign interests. It gave rise to excesses such as those of the pharmaceutical industry that employed about two lobbyists for each member of Congress. In 2016 it spent $152 million to influence federal and state legislation. More than $20 million went directly to political campaigns.[121]

A Changing Community

Cities such as Los Angeles, San Antonio, Chicago, and New York have well-established organizational infrastructures because of money and the presence of large human rights organizations and trade unions; smaller cities and those living on the periphery of urban areas have fewer resources for basic needs such as medical care or to fight racism.[122] This lack of an organizational infrastructure makes it hard for those on the periphery to organize and to tap into networks. The absence of a defense complex has worked to the detriment of places such as Arizona and those in the south. Thus outside money from special interests often overwhelms local Mexican/Latino organizations.

An example of corporate influence is Arizona SB 1070. It was written by the corporate-funded American Legislative Exchange Council (ALEC) that has contacts with right-wing extremists such as David Horowitz.[123] In Arizona, ALEC targeted Latino undocumented workers and their families. A cabal of nativist organizations also spearheaded HB 2281 that dismantled the Tucson Unified School District's Mexican American Studies department.[124]

Arizona State Senator Russell Pearce, a political lackey of ALEC, sponsored Arizona SB 1070. It became known as the "show me your papers" immigration law.[125] The Support Our Law Enforcement and Safe Neighborhoods Act was the broadest and strictest anti-illegal immigration measure passed at the time. It targeted undocumented Latinos and had a money-making component built in to subsidize the incarceration of undocumented people.[126]

The law created a new misdemeanor offense for a non-citizen who failed to complete and carry immigrant registration documents. The Supreme Court later struck down three of the four provisions. It retained two clauses known as the "show me your papers" allowing police to check the immigration status and requires police to check immigration status "if they have reasonable suspicion to believe someone is here illegally." Those clauses were largely symbolic victory for the Arizona politicians. Section 2(b) required law enforcement officers to make a "reasonable attempt" to determine the immigration status of people stopped for other reasons if "reasonable suspicion exists that the person is an alien and is unlawfully present in the United States."[127]

It came down to profit: Many of Arizona's public services and resources were privatized. "Private prisons in Arizona have housed DUI offenders and other low- and medium-security inmates since the early 1990s."[128] By the late part of the first decade of this century, state legislators were privatizing maximum security prisons. The profits from warehousing inmates and controlling employee pension funds were huge.[129] SB 1070 ensured a bonanza by providing additional prison inmates.

> The Corrections Corporation of America, one of the largest private prison corporations in the US, earned over $1.7 billion in revenue in 2009, 40% of which came from ICE, the US Marshalls Office and Federal Bureau of Prisons. In Arizona specifically, the Governor's office proposed a budget that set aside $98 million for private prison corporations alone, mostly to accommodate the influx of undocumented immigrants with new private and state prison beds, according to the Arizona Education Network.[130]

Corruption led to abuses such as those committed by Maricopa County Sherriff Joe Arpaio.

> ICE has relied on local police, like Sheriff Joe Arpaio, to meet its goal to detain hundreds of thousands of immigrants. This has led to the detention of more than 380,000 people in FY 2009 in unsafe and inhumane conditions with no meaningful access to lawyers or hope for a fair day in court. It has also resulted in the deportation of 387,000 people, tearing apart countless families. SB 1070 will be effective at one thing: continuing to fill Arpaio's jails and driving the growth of the detention industry across the country.[131]

SB 1070 and poor schools guaranteed that Mexican and Latino inmates filled the jails.

There is a contrast between the media's coverage of border patrol shootings of immigrants and the shooting of border patrol agents. The media ignored the plight of the immigrants. *The Guardian* reported, "For six long years the family of José Antonio Elena Rodríguez have been caught in a legal saga seeking justice for the 16-year-old who was killed by a US border patrol agent who fired 16 times from Arizona into Mexico."[132] More often the media jumped to unfounded conclusions when reporting the shooting of border patrol officers. Hatred blinded white Arizonans who ignored the corporate takeover of their state. Many injustices were committed by the Tea Partiers and Minutemen that ran wild, holstering guns and intimidating progressives and minorities. These groups were financed the Koch brothers, third-richest who also funded Tea Party through front organizations such as Americans for Prosperity, Freedom Works, and Citizens for a Sound Economy ($12 million).[133] The chaos helped make the National Rifle Association and gun dealers rich. Many of the drug cartels shopped in Arizona where gun dealers did not have to register guns or ammunition. U.S. banks laundered the profits.[134]

Education Under Attack: Fight Back

17.5 Describe the fight for ethnic studies and public schooling versus racist opposition.

The fear machine kept charter schools stocked with white students as rumors of violence exaggerated racial tensions. Mexicans and other minorities, according to charter school advocates, diminished the quality of education. Charter schools in Arizona in effect nullified desegregation. Meanwhile, xenophobic and anti-Mexican elected officials subverted bilingual education and educational reform.[135]

The Tucson Mexican American Studies program was established in the late 1990s as part of a desegregation order. It was highly successful and praised by educators because it stemmed the high dropout rate and dramatically improved the rates of students going to college. In the midst of efforts to disband the program, Arizona Superintendent of Instruction John Huppenthal ordered the Cambium study that cost the taxpayers at least $112,000 (initial reports said $170,000). According to Huppenthal, the report was supposed to prove that the TUSD Mexican American Studies program was un-American, racist, promoted the overthrow of the government, and ineffective. Most feared the worst because the study was commissioned by Huppenthal and his predecessor Attorney General Tom Horne. According to the findings of the Cambium report: " . . . students taking MAS classes were more likely to pass reading and writing portions of the standardized tests. Consequently, high school seniors enrolled in a MASD course are more likely to graduate than their peers."[136]

It took The Defense of Ethnic Studies seven years to resolve the Tucson Case at a huge personal and economic sacrifice by the plaintiffs. The director, Sean Arce, lost his job, home, and wife. Arce was forced to leave Tucson to support his children. The case that split the community and opposition from within was more personal than substantive.

The plaintiffs lacked financial backing, and many of them constantly traveled to raise funds. The political harassment and lies about the program and its teachers was defended by Tom Horne and John Huppenthal. Huppenthal used state funds and resources in an attempt to bankrupt the plaintiffs. Horne and Huppenthal knew little about the Tucson programs that cut the school dropout rate and dramatically improved the number of Mexican students going to college.[137] In 2013, U.S. Circuit Judge A. Wallace Tashima made the decision to uphold disparate treatment of Mexican Americans, and affirm the constitutionality of HB 2281 that had been specifically passed to ban ethnic studies in general at the same session that 1070 had been passed.

The year 2015 opened with the plaintiffs waiting for the ruling Judge Tashima's ruling on HB 2281. Many supporters tired and moved on to other issues. Sean Arce concentrated on completing his dissertation and along with other plaintiffs formed. The Institute for Teaching and Organizing. Meanwhile, the Mexican American Legal Defense and Education Fund filed desegregation suits lumbered through the courts.

On January 12 of that year, dozens of ethnic studies supporters "packed a [San Francisco] courtroom at the 9th U.S. Circuit Court of Appeals, where a three-judge panel's questions suggested skepticism of Arizona's claim that a state law banning a Mexican-American curriculum wasn't intended to discriminate." Erwin Chemerinsky, the founding Dean and Distinguished Professor of Law, and Raymond Pryke, Professor of First Amendment Law at the University of California, Irvine School of Law, represented the plaintiffs. They challenged the constitutionality of Arizona's 2010 ethnic studies law. Chemerinsky argued the law was too vague, limited the free speech of teachers and students, and discriminated against Mexican Americans in violation of the Constitution's equal protection clause in the Fourteenth Amendment. As a result of the ruling of the Ninth Circuit panel, the case was remanded as *Maya Arce, et al. v. John Huppenthal, et al*, to Tashima for a 10-day trial.[138]

In August Tashima ruled:

"[The] plaintiffs have proven their First Amendment claim by proving that no legitimate pedagogical objective motivated the enactment and enforcement of A.R.S. § 15-112 against the MAS program. First, defendants had no legitimate basis for believing that the MAS program was promoting racism such that eliminating it would reduce racism," the judge ruled.[139]

The case was a major civil rights victory for supporters, the attorneys and Richard Martínez, the lead attorney, as well as a community victory that came at great personal sacrifice.

The Tucson ruling encouraged campaigns in California, Texas, and elsewhere to make ethnic studies required for graduation.[140] Across California from San Diego to Sacramento millennials led by community activists packed boards of education demanding ethnic studies. They were fighting back!

Keeping the Masses in Tow

17.6 Characterize the millennial generation and its political challenges.

In Los Angeles, attorney Richard Riordan made a fortune by speculating in municipal and county properties and downtown Los Angeles real estate. He became mayor in 1993, and moved to privatize everything he could, even making an unsuccessful move to privatize the main city library. Riordan, along with billionaire Eli Broad, controlled a host of politicos including the Los Angeles mayor and most of City Schools Board of Education.

In 2012, neoliberals in California worked against Proposition 30 and for Proposition 32.[141] The assault on Prop 30 was to avoid a $6 billion tax, primarily on the rich, to repair California's embattled and decaying public schools. The opposition to Proposition 30 wanted to destroy teacher unions by making sure that the public school system went off the fiscal cliff. Proposition 32 was meant to destroy trade unions; it was a power grab designed to empower the super-rich to take over California as they had taken Arizona. It denied unions the right to contribute to elections, thus giving corporations the power to attack worker and teacher rights. Not surprisingly, money flowed from Arizona to help fund Proposition 32 and other corporate-friendly California propositions. This is a historical struggle dating back to the passage of the Taft–Hartley Act of 1948 that weakened unions by purging militants from labor.

The passage of California Proposition 13 (1978) underfunded K–12 and higher education in California. It dismantled a premier educational system, resulting in California joining Mississippi and Arizona in low levels of school funding. In the absence of strong teacher unions, the cost of funding schools was transferred from wealthy home and commercial property owners to the poor. No longer did municipalities fund education through property taxes; this responsibility was shifted to the state's General Fund. The Koch brothers joined California neoliberals such as former Los Angeles City Mayor Richard Riordan and billionaire Charles Munger, Jr. These forces aimed to affect a corporate takeover of California. The loss of Proposition 32 showed strength and presence of Latino elected officials.

Conclusion: Politics Begin At Home: The Rise of the Millennials

Roberto Suro wrote in 2016,

> As their population in the United States surged from 35 million in 2000 to nearly 57 million, Latinos became the subjects of a feel-good political story that bathed a marginalized minority in the glow of demographic triumphalism. Acting as a cohesive political force, Latinos were supposed to power Democratic majorities for decades and enshrine the welcoming immigration policies they overwhelmingly favor.[142]

Tongue in cheek, Suro asked what happened to the cries of "Today we march. Tomorrow we vote" that brought millions of Latinos to the streets in 2006 but failed to produce its major goal of immigration reform, despite the fact that the Latino population grew from 35 million in 2000 to nearly 57 million in 2016. He criticized it as a "feel-good political story that bathed a marginalized minority in the glow of demographic triumphalism."

Reporter Dennis Romero wrote in 2018, "The signposts of a Chicano renaissance are everywhere. On streets and college campuses, in fashion and in art, there's renewed energy around a term associated with 1960s civil rights and farm worker activism."[143] Romero went on: "The recharged movement is a metaphorical safe space for young Mexican-Americans and Latinos who feel battered not only by President Donald Trump's policies and rhetoric regarding south-of-the-border immigrants but also by a far right emboldened by his rhetoric. In San Diego's Chicano Park, demonstrators twice stood up to far-right protesters who targeted the National Historic Landmark's flag, which includes the slogan, 'This is my land.'"[144] Romero continued, "The term and the movement seemed to hit a low point in the 1980s and 90s when assimilation and economic mobility became a goal for many middle-class Mexican-Americans. Many people with Mexican roots adopted the terms Hispanic and Latino, joining forces with Central Americans, Puerto Ricans, Cuban-Americans, Dominicans and South Americans."[145]

The millennials' change in attitude is bound to affect the Mexican American community that is seven times larger today than in the 1960s. As mentioned, according to the Pew Research Center, "Between 2006 and 2010 alone, more than half (53%) of all Mexican-American births were to Mexican immigrant parents. As a group, these immigrants are more likely than U.S.-born Americans to be in their prime childbearing years. They also have much higher fertility."[146] What this means is the second generation will continue to grow. However, they are different from the 1960s generation that was largely second generation. They have developed a collective memory that includes events such as the ELA and Texas walkouts and the struggle to protect the foreign-born.

Educationally the millennials are the best-educated Mexican American generation. Less drop out of school and more attend college. Their collective memory offers them a way of correcting past mistakes. It is undeniable that the Tucson SES Committee and its young and inexperienced organizers made mistakes. The attorney and leaders could not overcome these liabilities. Over a 40-year span, the state avoided compliance with the most fundamental right, the right to equal protection under the law. The lesson learned was especially evident in the San Diego area where a pro-immigrant movement thrived in South San Diego where, from his print shop, Herman Baca launched the Committee on Chicano Rights in the early 1970s. In 1977, Baca helped organize a 10,000 person protest at the border against the KKK.[147]

From this nucleus the *Unión del Barrio* developed. According to the Union webpage, "*Unión del Barrio* was formed in 1981 by a half-dozen activists as a San Diego *barrio*-based organization, and has over time transformed itself into a revolutionary nationalist formation with members in Los Angeles, Oxnard, Riverside, and San Jose California, El Paso Texas, Phoenix Arizona, New York City, as well as other locations." The founding core of Union organizers were Young Turks active in the Committee on Chicano Rights (CCR), an organization active in the South Bay and throughout California under the leadership of Herman Baca. For a time, CCR was one of the largest and most active of the pro-Mexican immigration organizations. There was not a march on the Tijuana border that did not go through CCR.

A Union del Barrio founder and part of the CCR Turks was Ernesto Bustillos (1952–2012). In 1987 Bustillos created *Somos Raza Magazine*, in 1989 re-established ¡*La Verdad!*, and authored and coauthored several books. Over the 30 years, the Union matured and filled a void left by the demise of other leftist groups after 1969. During this period, the Union intellectually matured and became much more proficient in the use of electronic media and political vocabulary. It no longer shouted but organized, and it built an impressive membership comprised of waves of younger students from middle school to beyond college.

In the 1980s and 1990s, the Union engaged in useless ideological competition with other organizations that resented the Union's aggressive party building. With time, its members became much more political in their arguments. At CSUN, we have had a dozen or more Union members both as undergraduates and graduates and they are noteworthy because they are political and remain active. Today, its membership often reaches back through several generations and religiously return to Chicago Park Day every year.

The Union begot the Association of Raza Educators (A.R.E) in the 1990s. A.R.E. is a mass organization. As in the case of the Union, A.R.E. went through a maturation period beginning in 1994 with the passage of Proposition 187.

Its primary mission is to organize educators and students around issues of quality education, historical memory, and the militarization of the schools. It sponsors education conferences and other events for youth and has attracted a wide following among non-Latino and non-minority educators. A.R.E. has chapters in San Diego, Los Angeles, Sacramento, and Oakland. Both the Union and A.R.E. saw the danger of an assault on the MAS and organized around the issue of Chicana/o Studies.

Members recognized the need to take the campaign to the public schools where the bulk of the Chicana/o and Latinos were and where the preservation and protection of a community memory was desperately needed. Its members launched the unsuccessful campaign for Ron Gochez for Los Angeles City Council District 9 in South Central Los Angeles. Gochez was active organizing a campaign in Los Angeles to defend street vendors from the LAPD/Sheriffs. Gochez attracted an impressive group of middle and high school students to his campaign and they militantly brought attention to the issue.

A major thrust to get ethnic studies as a requirement for high school graduation was from la Union. The campaign was spearheaded by Jose Lara, a high school history teacher and dean at Santee High School in South Central Los Angeles. A member the Unión del Barrio, he also sat on the Board of Directors of the United Teachers of Los Angeles, representing teachers as Area Chair of South Central Los Angeles. Lara also was elected to the Governing Board of the El Rancho Unified School District (Pico Rivera, CA). Lara is also the student advisor for MEChA at Santee as well as the Gay-Straight Alliance advisor. Lara was married with three children, his son Jose Jr., 14, his daughter Maya, 3, and his 1-year-old nephew Diego. He was involved in organizing and fundraising for undocumented students' rights and fought the privatization of education. He became the coordinator for the Ethnic Studies Now! committee (ESN) and led the statewide campaign to expand Ethnic Studies programs across the state of California with the ultimate goal of making Ethnic Studies a universal graduation requirement.

In less than one year, ESN built a network that included El Rancho, Los Angeles, Montebello, Woodland, Basset, and El Monte. The Sacramento City School Districts passed resolutions to make Ethnic Studies a graduation requirement, inspiring districts such as San Francisco, Santa Ana, San Diego, Lynwood, Garden Grove, Anaheim, and San Juan (Carmichael) to establish or expand Ethnic Studies programs. Union and A.R.E. facilitated this growth. Lara's home district El Rancho was a flagship and El Rancho Unified was the first district to fully implement Ethnic Studies as a graduation requirement in 2016. All incoming freshmen are required to take at least one Ethnic Studies class. This had been in the making for over 30 years and now the time had come. The lessons of Arizona are paying dividends, and similar movements are taking place in Texas and wherever there is a critical number of Latino youth. The future of Chicana/o Studies is in the hands of Chicanas who compose three-quarters of the programs and departments on many campuses.

Many of the Mexican/Latino millennials supported Bernie Sanders in 2016 and welcomed him as a homeboy, adding, "I am voting for the Jewish guy." Their placards read "Honduras," "Palestine," "Standing Rock," "No one is Illegal," and some denouncing neoliberalism and gentrification. Millennials had an established oppositional narrative learned in the protests and activism. The future is with the millennials, "The median age of Mexican Americans is 25; the median for Non-Hispanic whites is 42.3." [148]

Notes

1. Alfred W. McCoy, "The Decline and Fall of the American Empire," *The Nation*, December 6, 2010, https://www.thenation.com/article/decline-and-fall-american-empire/.
2. Matthew Reisz, "Engineering graduate numbers 'triple in Mexico'," The World University Rankings, September 23, 2016, https://www.timeshighereducation.com/news/engineering-graduate-numbers-triple-mexico. William Booth, "Mexico is now a top producer of engineers, but where are jobs?" *Washington Post* (October 28, 2012), https://www.washingtonpost.com/world/the_americas/mexico-is-now-a-top-producer-of-engineers-but-where-are-jobs/2012/10/28/902db93a-1e47-11e2-8817-41b9a7aaabc7_story.html?utm_term=.c72c4f41135f.
3. John Farrell, "U.S. Science Education: Standards of Mediocrity?" *Forbes*, Dec. 7, 2010, https://www.forbes.com/sites/johnfarrell/2010/12/07/u-s-science-education-standards-of-mediocrity/#7f7e807e4406.
4. Richard Anderson, "How American energy independence could change the world," BBC News, April 3, 2014, http://www.bbc.com/news/business-23151813.
5. Jay Yarow, "Chinese billionaire Jack Ma says the US wasted trillions on warfare instead of investing in infrastructure," CNBC, Jan. 8, 2017, https://www.cnbc.com/2017/01/18/chinese-billionaire-jack-ma-says-the-us-wasted-trillions-on-warfare-instead-of-investing-in-infrastructure.html.

6 "Military Spending in the United States," National Priorities Project, https://www.nationalpriorities.org/campaigns/military-spending-united-states/.

7 Nigel Hamilton, "From FDR to Donald Trump – the decline of the American empire," *Statesman*, September 4, 2017, https://www.newstatesman.com/world/north-america/2017/09/fdr-donald-trump-decline-american-empire. Nafeez Ahmed, "Pentagon study declares American empire is 'collapsing'," *Surge Intelligence*, July 17, 2017, https://medium.com/insurge-intelligence/pentagon-study-declares-american-empire-is-collapsing-746754cdaebf.

8 Elizabeth M. Grieco, "The White Population: 2000 Census 2000 Brief," U.S. Department of Commerce Economics and Statistics Administration U.S. Census Bureau, August 2001, https://www.census.gov/prod/2001pubs/c2kbr01-4.pdf.

9 Eileen Patten, "The Nation's Latino Population Is Defined by Its Youth," Pew Research Center, April 20, 2016, http://www.pewhispanic.org/2016/04/20/the-nations-latino-population-is-defined-by-its-youth/.

10 Andrew Gumbel, "The history of 'rigged' US elections: from Bush v Gore to Trump v Clinton," *The Guardian*, Oct. 25, 2016, https://www.theguardian.com/us-news/2016/oct/25/donald-trump-rigged-election-bush-gore-florida-voter-fraud.

11 Arthur F. Fleser, *A Rhetorical Study of the Speaking of Calvin Coolidge* (Lewiston, NY: Edwin Mellen Press, 1990), 103.

12 Wade Payson-Denney, "So, who really won? What the Bush v. Gore studies showed," CNN, October 31, 2015, https://www.cnn.com/2015/10/31/politics/bush-gore-2000-election-results-studies/index.html. B. Ackerman, *Bush v. Gore: The question of legitimacy* (New Haven: Yale University Press, 2002).

13 Richard Friedman, " 'Bush' v. Gore'," *Commonweathl*, Jan. 12, 2001, Vol. 128(1), 11.

14 Jared Thompson, "A Supremely Bad Decision: The Majority Ruling in Bush v. Gore," Swarthmore, 2005, https://www.swarthmore.edu/writing/a-supremely-bad-decision-majority-ruling-bush-v-gore

15 Elspeth Reeve, "Just How Bad Was Bush v. Gore? Jeffrey Toobin says that it was very, very bad," *The Atlantic*, Nov. 29, 2010, https://www.theatlantic.com/politics/archive/2010/11/just-how-bad-was-bush-v-gore/343247/.

16 Jonathan H. Adler, "In election years, a (spotty) history of confirming court nominees," *Washington Post* (February 17, 2016), https://www.washingtonpost.com/news/volokh-conspiracy/wp/2016/02/17/in-election-years-a-spotty-history-of-confirming-court-nominees/?noredirect=on&utm_term=.e518d4d04450. Charles M. Cameron and Jeffrey A. Segal, "The Politics of Scandals: The Case of Supreme Court Nominations, 1877–1994," http://citeseerx.ist.psu.edu/viewdoc/download?doi=10.1.1.199.9301&rep=rep1&type=pdf.

17 "Cost of War," National Priorities Project, http://costofwar.com/. Deborah White, "Iraq War Facts, Results & Statistics at January 31, 2012," *U.S. Liberal Politics*, http://usliberals.about.com/od/homelandsecurit1/a/IraqNumbers.htm; 4,487 US Soldiers Killed, 32,223 Seriously Wounded.

18 Kristine Phillips, "The story behind this powerful photo of deported military veterans saluting the U.S. flag," *Washington Post* (November 16, 2017), https://www.washingtonpost.com/news/checkpoint/wp/2017/11/16/the-story-behind-this-powerful-photo-of-deported-military-veterans-saluting-the-american-flag/?noredirect=on&utm_term=.5aac02f63feb. Theresa Waldrop, "US Army veteran who served two tours in Afghanistan has been deported to Mexico," CNN, March 26, 2018, https://www.cnn.com/2018/03/25/us/us-veteran-deported-to-mexico/index.html.

19 It is difficult to ferret out statistics on Mexicans and Central American nationalities.

20 "Hispanics in the Military," The Pew Hispanic Center (March 27, 2003), http://pewhispanic.org/files/reports/17.pdf. "Median Age for Hispanics is Lower Than Median Age for Total U.S. Population," The Pew Hispanic Center (July 2, 2012), http://www.pewresearch.org/daily-number/median-age-for-hispanics-is-lower-than-median-age-for-total-u-s-population/.

21 William H. Frey, "Five Charts That Show Why a Post-White America Is Already Here," *New Republic*, November 21, 2014, https://newrepublic.com/article/120370/five-graphics-show-why-post-white-america-already-here.

22 Hobbs, Frank and Nicole Stoops, U.S. Census Bureau, Census 2000 Special Reports, Series CENSR-4, Demographic Trends in the 20th Century, U.S. Government Printing Office, Washington, DC, 2002. pp. 57 and 77, https://www.census.gov/prod/2002pubs/censr-4.pdf

23 Solomon Amendment, http://www.yalerotc.org/Solomon.html.

24 No Child Left Behind Act (Public Law 107-110), Sec. 9528; Armed Forces Recruiter Access to Students and Student Recruiting Information, http://prhome.defense.gov/rfm/MPP/ACCESSION%20POLICY/docs/no_child_act.pdf. "What Are Some Criticisms of No Child Left Behind?" Wise Geek, http://www.wisegeek.com/what-are-some-criticisms-of-no-child-left-behind.htm. Linda Darling-Hammond,

"Evaluating 'No Child Left Behind'," *The Nation* (May 21, 2007), http://www.thenation.com/article/evaluating-no-child-left-behind.

25 *Again, although the statistics are reported as Hispanic or Latino,* they are made up of various Latino groups. Because of the size of Mexico, proximity to the United States and long history of contact with it, they comprise two-thirds of the 70 percent of U.S. Latinos. At the same time, more affluent Latinos who do not share interests with Mexicans, Puerto Ricans, and Central Americans are included in the count.

26 Matt A. Barreto, Ricardo Ramírez, Luis R. Fraga, Fernando Guerra, "Why California Matters: How California Latinos Influence the Presidential Election," In Rodolfo O. de la Garza, Louis DeSipio and David Leal (Eds.) *Beyond the Barrio: Latinos in the 2004 Elections.* South Bend, ID: University of Notre Dame Press, 2009. http://mattbarreto.com/papers/ca04_chapter.pdf

27 Dan Mihalopoulos and Evan Osnos, "Chicago a hub for Mexicans," *Chicago Tribune* (May 10, 2001). http://www.chicagotribune.com/news/ct-xpm-2001-05-10-0105100211-story.html.

28 This happened in 1971 at San Fernando State College. When we pressed the college for a list of Mexican professors we got a long list of Italians and the name of Warren Furumoto, a Japanese American biologist. Middle Eastern students are often mistakenly taken for Mexican. Brian Gratton and Emily Klancher Merchant, "La Raza: Mexicans in the United States Census," *The Journal of Policy History*, Vol. 28, No. 4, 2016, https://neukom.dartmouth.edu/docs/16_gratton_la_raza_merchant.pdf. José Hernández, Leo Estrada And David Alvírez, "Census Data and the Problem of Conceptually Defining the Mexican American Population," *Social Science Quarterly*, 1 March 1973, Vol. 53(4), 671–687.

29 Rodolfo F. Acuña, "La china has a name," WordPress, February 16, 2018, http://rudyacuna.net/la-china-has-a-name/.

30 The estimated numbers often vary slightly. Melissa Therrien and Roberto R. Rami, "The Hispanic Population in the United States Population Characteristics," March 2000, https://www.census.gov/population/socdemo/hispanic/p20-535/p20-535.pdf.

31 Seth Motel and Eileen Patten, "The 10 Largest Hispanic Origin Groups: Characteristics, Rankings, Top Ten Counties," Pew Hispanic Center (Updated: July 12, 2012).

32 Paul Taylor, Mark Hugo Lopez, Jessica Hamar Martínez and Gabriel Velasco, "When Labels Don't Fit: Hispanics and Their Views of Identity," Pew Hispanic Center (April 4, 2012).

33 "Latinos in America: A Demographic Overview," Immigration Policy Center (April 2012), http://www.immigrationpolicy.org/sites/default/files/docs/latinos_in_america_-_a_demographic_overview_042612.pdf.

34 Seth Motel and Eileen Patten, "The 10 Largest Hispanic Origin Groups."

35 "State & County QuickFacts," U.S. Census Bureau, http://quickfacts.census.gov/qfd/states/17000.html.

36 Carol Morello and Ted Mellnik, "Census: Minority babies are now majority in United States," *Washington Post* (May 17, 2012), https://www.washingtonpost.com/local/census-minority-babies-are-now-majority-in-united-states/2012/05/16/gIQA1WY8UU_story.html?utm_term=.727b53ddf098.

37 Ibid. "Median Age for Hispanics is Lower Than Median Age for Total U.S. Population," Pew Hispanic Center (December 7, 2012), http://pewresearch.org/databank/dailynumber/?NumberID=1533. Paul Taylor, Ana Gonzalez-Barrera, Jeffrey Passel, and Mark Hugo Lopez, "An Awakened Giant: The Hispanic Electorate Is Likely to Double by 2030," Pew Hispanic Center (November 14, 2012), http://www.pewhispanic.org/2012/11/14/an-awakened-giant-the-hispanic-electorate-is-likely-to-double-by-2030/. For demographics on Mexicans I rely heavily on Pew Research Center, Migration Policy Institute, and U.S. Census. Variations exist. For example, the Census tends to undercount.

38 Rogelio Saenz, "Latinos and the Changing Face of America," Population Reference Bureau, http://www.prb.org/Publications/Articles/2004/LatinosandtheChangingFaceofAmerica.aspx.

39 Sam Stein, "Hispanic Population, Rising Faster Than Anticipated, A 'Huge Weapon' For Obama," *Huffington Post*, July 3, 2011, http://www.huffingtonpost.com/2011/05/31/hispanic-population-rising-faster-than-anticipated_n_869209.html. Jeffrey Passel, D'Vera Cohn, and Mark Hugo Lopez, "Census 2010: 50 Million Latinos: Hispanics Account for More than Half of Nation's Growth in Past Decade," Pew Hispanic Center (March 24, 2011).

40 Seth Motel and Eileen Patten, "The 10 Largest Hispanic Origin Groups: Characteristics, Rankings, Top Counties," Pew Research Center, June 27, 2012, http://www.pewhispanic.org/2012/06/27/the-10-largest-hispanic-origin-groups-characteristics-rankings-top-counties/.

41 William J. Clinton, Tweet Executive Order 13171—Hispanic Employment in the Federal Government, American Presidency Project, UCSB, October 12, 2000, http://www.presidency.ucsb.edu/ws/?pid=61688.

42. Karin Mac Donald. "Adventures in Redistricting: A Look at the California Redistricting Commission," *Election Law Journal: Rules, Politics, and Policy* 11, No. 4 (December 2012): 472–89, doi:10.1089/elj.2012.1148. Antonio Olivo, "Special Report: They Have Opened Up Legislative Seats, But Also Created Some Bitter Political Rivalries, Making Term Limits a Mixed Blessing for Latinos," *Los Angeles Times* (July 2, 2000). Marta Escutia and Gloria Romero, "MALDEF's Lawsuit Is Racially Divisive," *Los Angeles Times* (November 1, 2001).

43. Laura Mecoy, "MALDEF ripped over remap fight," *Sacramento Bee* (November 16, 2001), http://www.laprensa-sandiego.org/archieve/november16/MALDEF.HTM.

44. Frank del Olmo, "Getting Away With a Blatant Gerrymander," *Los Angeles Times* (June 16, 2002).

45. Martha Escutia and Gloria Romero, "MALDEF's Lawsuit Is Racially Divisive," *Los Angeles Times* (November 1, 2001), http://articles.latimes.com/2001/nov/01/local/me-64038.

46. David Rosenzweig, "Judges Asked to Postpone Voting in 4 House Districts," *Los Angeles Times* (November 1, 2001). Thomas B. Edsall, "A Political Fight to Define the Future; Latinos at Odds over California's Two New Democratic Congressional Districts," *Washington Post* (October 31, 2001). Carl Ingram, "Davis OKs Redistricting That Keeps Status Quo," *Los Angeles Times* (September 28, 2001). Frank del Olmo, "Getting away with a Blatant Gerrymander for the Record," *Los Angeles Times* (June 16, 2002).

47. Ambika Kapur, "Encouraging the Latino Vote," *Carnegie Reporter* 1, No. 3 (Fall 2001), http://carnegie.org/publications/carnegie-reporter/single/view/article/item/38/. Richard Gonzales, "Where Are the Latino Office Holders?" *Fort Worth Star-Telegram* (December 9, 2001).

48. 24/7 Wall St., "Companies Profiting The Most From War," *Huffington Post*, Mar. 23, 2015, https://www.huffingtonpost.com/2015/03/22/companies-profiting-from-war_n_6919292.html.

49. Vince Calio and Alexander E.M. Hess, "Here Are the 5 Companies Making a Killing Off Wars Around the World," *Time Magazine*, March 14, 2014, http://time.com/24735/here-are-the-5-companies-making-a-killing-off-wars-around-the-world/.

50. Death Penalty Information Center (Bureau of Justice Statistics), "Capital Punishment 2009," U.S. Department of Justice, 2010, https://deathpenaltyinfo.org/new-resources-hispanics-and-death-penalty.

51. National Statistics on the Death Penalty and Race, Race of Death Row Inmates Executed Since 1976, Death Penalty Information Center, http://www.deathpenaltyinfo.org/race-death-row-inmates-executed-1976%23defend. "Citing Race and Regional Bias, Latino Leaders Join Call for Halt to Federal Executions," ACLU, June 13, 2001, http://www.aclu.org/capital/unequal/10570prs20010613.html. James Oliphant, "In a Reversal, Justice Stevens Calls the Death Penalty 'Anachronistic,'" *Los Angeles Times* (April 17, 2008).

52. Governor George Ryan's Clemency Speech, http://www.youtube.com/watch?v=Cv75EcK1arI. Steve Mills and John Chase, "Rolando Cruz Seeks Pardon: Petition Criticizes Ryan on Nicarico," *Chicago Tribune* (September 19, 2002).

53. Alexander Cockburn, "George W. Bush: The Death Penalty Governor," *San Jose Mercury News* (February 9, 2000). "Death Penalty in America, Executions in America," *Chicago Tribune* Special Issue (2012), http://www.chicagotribune.com/news/nationworld/chi-dpdpamerica-special,0,4453522.special.

54. "Juvenile Justice," Children's Defense Fund, State of America's Children (2011), http://www.childrensdefense.org/child-research-data-publications/state-of-americas-children-2011/pdfs/jj.pdf, J-2.

55. Ibid., J-9.

56. Devon G. Peña, "mexmigration: History and Politics of Mexican Immigration." May 13, 2011, http://mexmigration.blogspot.com/2011/05/immigrants-for-sale-prison-detention.html.

57. Richard Delgado, "Rodrigo's Portent: California and the Coming Neocolonial Order," 87 *Wash. U. L. Rev.* 1293 (2010), Available at http://openscholarship.wustl.edu/law_lawreview/vol87/iss6/2. There are numerous articles on the privatization of prisons often with slightly varying stats.

58. Camila Domonoske, "A Latino Nonprofit Is Holding Separated Kids. Is That Care Or Complicity Or Both?" NPR, June 22, 2018, https://www.npr.org/2018/06/22/622186779/a-latino-nonprofit-is-holding-separated-kids-is-that-care-or-complicity-or-both.

59. Michael E. Miller, Emma Brown and Aaron C. Davis, "Inside Casa Padre, the converted Walmart where the U.S. is holding nearly 1,500 immigrant children," *Washington Post* (June 14, 2018), https://www.washingtonpost.com/local/inside-casa-padre-the-converted-walmart-where-the-us-is-holding-nearly-1500-immigrant-children/2018/06/14/0cd65ce4-6eba-11e8-bd50-b80389a4e569_story.html?utm_term=.ef4577bcc279. Manny Fernandez and Katie Benner, "The Billion-Dollar Business of Operating Shelters for Migrant Children," *New York Times* (June 21, 2018), https://www.nytimes.com/2018/06/21/us/migrant-shelters-border-crossing.html.

60. Laura Mecoy, "MALDEF Ripped over Remap Fight," *La Prensa San Diego* (November 16, 2001), http://www.laprensa-sandiego.org/archieve/november16/MALDEF.HTM. Leo F. Estrada, "Redistricting 2000:

A Lost Opportunity for Latinos," *La Prensa San Diego* (June 7, 2002), http://www.laprensa-sandiego.org/archieve/june07-02/lost.htm.

61 R.G. Ratcliffe. "Latinos Won't Turn Texas Blue Anytime Soon," *Texas Monthly*, Feb. 21, 2017, https://www.texasmonthly.com/burka-blog/latinos-wont-turn-texas-blue-anytime-soon/.

62 Frank del Olmo, "Commentary; The Lucha Libre That Is Latino Politics," *Los Angeles Times* (March 10, 2002): M5.

63 "Articles about Tony Sanchez," *New York Times*, http://topics.nytimes.com/topics/reference/timestopics/people/s/tony_sanchez/index.html.

64 Alexa Ura and Ryan Murphy, "Why is Texas voter turnout so low? Demographics play a big role," *The Texas Tribune* (Feb. 23, 2018,) https://www.texastribune.org/2018/02/23/texas-voter-turnout-electorate-explainer/.

65 "Governor Bill Richardson," http://www.billrichardson.com/about-bill/biography. Kenneth Salazar, "U.S. Congress Votes Base," *Washington Post*, http://projects.washingtonpost.com/congress/members/s001163/.

66 Regina Graham, "Washington State's Latinos Find 'Politics Has Not Changed with the Population'," *Guardian (UK)*, (October 7, 2012). "Washington," State & County QuickFacts, U.S. (2012) Census, http://quickfacts.census.gov/qfd/states/53000.html. "Hispanic Population Jumps 10 Percent in Washington," *RedOrbit* (September 18, 2003), http://www.redorbit.com/news/science/10835/hispanic_population_jumps_10_percent_in_washington/. Manuel Valdes, "Lack of Diversity in New Wash. Legislature," *Seattle Times* (November 24, 2012).

67 George Sánchez, "Latinos, the American South, and the Future of US Race Relations," *Southern Spaces*, April 26, 2007, https://southernspaces.org/2007/latinos-american-south-and-future-us-race-relations.

68 George Sánchez, Ibid.

69 George Sánchez, Ibid.

70 Campbell, "Texas' Population Reaches 25.1 Million." "Hispanic Population Fastest Growing in State of Oklahoma," *RedOrbit* (August 11, 2005). Halimah Abdullah, "Hispanic Population Growth Could Realign South's Politics," *McClatchy Newspapers* (April 22, 2011). Tony Pugh, "New 2010 Census Data Alter Balance of Power in Congress," *McClatchy Newspapers* (December 21, 2010), http://www.mcclatchydc.com/2010/12/21/105625/us-population-grows-at-slowest.html.

71 "The Mexican-American Boom: Births Overtake Immigration," Pew Research Center, July 14, 2011, http://www.pewhispanic.org/2011/07/14/the-mexican-american-boom-brbirths-overtake-immigration/.

72 Jeb Bush and Ken Mehlman, "A Good Immigration Bill," *Wall Street Journal* (May 31, 2007), A15. Miriam Jordan, "U.S. News: Immigration Bill Slow to Stir Foes' Passion—Fierce Backlash That Derailed 2007 Overhaul Bid Has Yet to Materialize, Though Opponents Vow to Intensify Campaign," *Wall Street Journal* (May 29, 2013), A4. Fawn Johnson, "Lessons From 2007's Failed Immigration Reform Bill," *National Journal*, Dec 13, 2012.

73 Immigrant Policy, Comprehensive Immigration Reform Act of 2006 S.2611. NCSL, http://www.ncsl.org/research/immigration/comprehensive-immigrationreform-act-of-2006-summ.aspx.

74 C. J. Karamargin, "Bush Owes 'Gracias' to Latino Voters," *Arizona Daily Star* (November 8, 2004). Dee Allsop, "Election Results and Implications for Regional Stewardship," *Wirthlin Worldwide* (November 12, 2004). "More Than 7.6 Million Latinos Vote in Presidential Race," Press Release, William C. Velásquez Institute, November 4, 2004, http://wcvi.org/press_room/press_releases/2004/us/nat_to_110404.html.

75 Jeffrey Passel, "Mexican Immigration to the U.S.: The Latest Estimates," *Migration Policy Institute*, March 1, 2004, https://www.migrationpolicy.org/article/mexican-immigration-us-latest-estimates.

76 Charlie Leduffoct, "Mexicans Who Came North Struggle as Jobs Head South," *New York Times* (Oct. 13, 2004), https://www.nytimes.com/2004/10/13/us/mexicans-who-came-north-struggle-as-jobs-head-south.html.

77 "Latino Voters Show Strong Democratic Support in Congressional Races, Split Democratic Support in Governor's Race," Press Release, WCVI, November 9, 2006, http://wcvi.org/press_room/press_releases/2006/exitpoll_TX2006.htm.

78 Esther J. Cepeda, "Chicago's Latino Landscape 2008: A Statistical Portrait of Chi-Town Hispanics," *Huffington Post* (March 20, 2009), http://www.huffingtonpost.com/esther-j-cepeda/chicagos-latino-landscape_b_177169.html. "City of Chicago," Institute for Latino Studies, Notre Dame University, http://www.nd.edu/~chifacts/chicago.html.

79 Tyler J. Kelley, "In New York, Mexico's richest immigrants lend hand to their countrymen," *Christian Science Monitor*, October 26, 2015, https://www.csmonitor.com/USA/Society/2015/1026/In-New-York-Mexico-s-richest-immigrants-lend-hand-to-their-countrymen.

80 Laura Limonic, *The Latino Population of New York City, 2007*, Center for Latin American, Caribbean & Latino Studies, Latino Data Project—Report 20—(December 2008), 3, http://web.gc.cuny.edu/lastudies/latinodataprojectreports/The%20Latino%20Population%20of%20New%20York%20City%202007.pdf. "Mexican

Population Distribution," City of New York Queens Community Board 3 East Elmhurst—Jackson Heights—North Corona, http://www.cb3qn.nyc.gov/page/54812/.

81. Tyler J. Kelley, "In New York, Mexico's richest immigrants lend hand to their countrymen," *Christian Science Monitor* (Oct. 26, 2015), https://www.csmonitor.com/USA/Society/2015/1026/In-New-York-Mexico-s-richest-immigrants-lend-hand-to-their-countrymen.

82. Lazar Treschan and Apurva Mehrotra "Policy Brief: young Mexican-Americans in New York City: Working more, learning and earning less," *Community Service Society*, March 2013, https://www.db.com/usa/docs/CSS_Report_Young_Mexican_Americans.pdf.

83. H.R.4437—Border Protection, Antiterrorism, and Illegal Immigration Control Act of 2005 109th Congress (2005-2006). https://www.congress.gov/bill/109th-congress/house-bill/4437.

84. "Pro-Immigrant Marches Surging Nationwide," *The Nation* (April 10, 2006), http://www.thenation.com/blog/pro-immigrant-marches-surging-nationwide. Jennifer Ludden, "Hundreds of Thousands March for Immigrant Rights," National Public Radio, https://www.npr.org/templates/story/story.php?storyId=5333768.

85. "Ku Klux Klan Rebounds with New Focus on Immigration, ADL Reports," *PR Newswire* (February 6, 2007). Cynthia Leonor Garza, "Immigration Debate Reached the Point of Protests, Walkouts," *Houston Chronicle* (December 31, 2006), 1. Leslie Fulbright, "Huge Crowd Marches Through L.A.," *San Francisco Chronicle* (May 2, 2006), A8. Gong Lin II and Arin Gencer, "The Immigration Debate; Gearing Up, and Girding for, Protests; Around the U.S., Cities Brace for Marches. In L.A., a Huge Crowd Is Expected Along Wilshire," *Los Angeles Times* (May 1, 2006), A1. Kevin Roderick, "Police Fighting with Protestors," *LA Observed* (May 1, 2006).

86. Immigration March in Dallas, CBS, April 20, 2006, http://www.cbsnews.com/video/watch/?id=1483046n. "Police Shooting Mexican Protest Chief Bratton Riot," http://www.youtube.com/watch?v=CLfWLp4C8e0. Immigrants March NYC (May 1, 2006), http://www.youtube.com/watch?v=oTHoA-0TjYg. "César Chávez and Immigrants' Rights (March 2006), Sacramento," http://www.youtube.com/watch?v=-3mkPF0WTH8. Immigration March in Seattle (May 1, 2006), http://www.youtube.com/watch?v=g2km0cyWQnQ. [LA] Immigration March, http://www.youtube.com/watch?v=4markP8B4Vg. "Dallas Mega-March Movie, April 9, 2006" (producer Bill Millet), http://www.youtube.com/watch?v=U0PiTtZdvAM. "Second Day of North Texas Student Walkouts," http://www.youtube.com/watch?v=ucL_mARah2I&feature=related.

87. Mark Hugo López and Paul Taylor, "Dissecting the 2008 Electorate: Most Diverse in U.S. History," Pew Hispanic Research Center (April 30, 2009), http://pewhispanic.org/reports/report.php?ReportID=108. James G. Gimpel, "Latino Voting in the 2008 Election: Part of a Broader Electoral Movement," Center for Immigration Studies (January 2009), http://www.cis.org/latinovoting.

88. Javier Rodriguez, "Gil Cedillo, The Activist Politician and the Latino Wars to Replace Hilda Solis" (May 19, 2009), http://forchicanachicanostudies.wikispaces.com/News+Items. Immigrant Student Adjustment/DREAM Act, National Immigration Law Center, http://www.nilc.org/econ_bens_dream&stdnt_adjst_0205.html. "CA Democrats shelve driver's licenses for illegal aliens," http://24ahead.com/blog/archives/005448.html. Hecubus, WordPress, "Morons Want to Reward Illegal Immigrants . . . Again" (August 23, 2006), http://hecubus.wordpress.com/2006/08/23/morons-want-to-reward-illegal-immigrants-again/.

89. Mark Hugo Lopez and Paul Taylor, "Latino Voters in the 2012 Election," Pew Research Center, November 7, 2012. http://www.pewhispanic.org/2012/11/07/latino-voters-in-the-2012-election/.

90. Rodolfo F. Acuña, "Gentrification The Struggle for Affordable Housing," WordPress, April 11, 2015, http://rudyacuna.net/gnetrification-no-time-for-renters/.

91. "Growing Activism: Undocumented Students/DREAM Act," University of California Television, http://www.uctv.tv/search-details.aspx?showID=12488.

92. "War on drugs and Mexico's demise," http://www.youtube.com/watch?v=Yj7LKauVzro. "Mexico Drug War," http://www.youtube.com/watch?v=pLlrbAZv9Do. "DREAM Act: President Obama Reaffirms Unwavering Support for DREAM Act at Univision's Latino Forum," *Washington Times* (September 21, 2012).

93. Jay Willis, "The Case for Abolishing the Senate," *GQ*, October 16, 2018, https://www.gq.com/story/the-case-for-abolishing-the-senate. Noah Feldman, "Revamping the Senate Is a Fantasy," *Bloomberg*, October 10, 2018, https://www.bloomberg.com/opinion/articles/2018-10-10/u-s-senate-is-undemocratic-but-there-s-no-way-to-change-it.

94. "Immigration Equality," http://www.immigrationequality.org/get-legal-help/our-legal-resources/path-to-status-in-the-u-s/daca-deferred-action-for-childhood-arrivals/. "DACA (Deferred Action for Childhood Arrivals)," Immigration Equality, http://

www.immigrationequality.org/get-legal-help/our-legal-resources/path-to-status-in-the-u-s/daca-deferred-action-for-childhood-arrivals/. Jens Manuel Krogstad and Jeffrey S. Passel, "Those from Mexico will benefit most from Obama's executive action," Pew Research Center, Retrieved November 21, 2014, http://www.pewresearch.org/fact-tank/2014/11/20/those-from-mexico-will-benefit-most-from-obamas-executive-action/. DREAM Act: Questions and Answers about President.

95 "Like the rest of the world, the US is an ageing society. This will place substantial additional pressure on publicly-funded health, long-term and income support programmes for older people. This paper analyses the demographic changes that the US faces and how they will affect those programmes, concentrating on the factors that may affect the economic burden that these programs impose." Joshua M Wiener and Jane Tilly, "Population ageing in the United States of America: implications for public programmes," *International Journal of Epidemiology*, Vol. 31, Issue 4, 776–781, http://ije.oxfordjournals.org/content/31/4/776.full.

96 Mexican Immigrants in the United States, 2008, "Fact Sheet," Pew Hispanic Center, April 15, 2009, 1, http://pewhispanic.org/files/factsheets/47.pdf. Rakesh Kochhar, Ana Gonzalez-Barrera, and Daniel Dockterman, "Through Boom and Bust: Minorities, Immigrants and Homeownership," Pew Hispanic Center, May 12, 2009, http://pewhispanic.org/reports/report.php?ReportID=109.

97 Warren Vieth, "GOP Faction Wants to Change 'Birthright Citizenship' Policy," *Los Angeles Times* (December 10, 2005). Ronald Brownstein, "Immigration May Again Drive a Wedge Between GOP, Latinos," *Los Angeles Times* (December 16, 2005). Marc Cooper, "The 15-Second Men," *Los Angeles Times* (May 1, 2005). "Rick Sanchez vs Lou Dobbs on immigration," http://www.youtube.com/watch?v=cG_vHkm-C9E. "Lou Dobbs - National Council of La Raza (The Race)," http://www.youtube.com/watch?v=7kmTLk2Fgas&feature=related.

98 Stuart Eskenazi, "150 Years of Seattle History: Familiar Landscape Lured Scandinavians," *Seattle Times* (November 4, 2001). Robin Fields and Ray Herndon, "Segregation of a New Sort Takes Shape; Census: In a Majority of Cities, Asians and Latinos Have Become More Isolated from Other Racial Groups," *Los Angeles Times* (July 5, 2001). Gordy Holt, "Hetle Again Spurns Shooting Review; But Bellevue Officer Meets Arbitrator on Another Matter," *Seattle Post-Intelligencer* (January 11, 2002).

99 Raul A. Reyes, "Brisenia Flores Was a Victim of Border Vigilantes and Media Indifference," *Huffington Post* (March 8, 2011), http://www.huffingtonpost.com/raul-a-reyes/brisenia-flores-was-a-vic_b_832416.html. Vanessa Williamson, Theda Skocpol, and John Coggin, "The Tea Party and the Remaking of Republican Conservatism," *Perspectives on Politics* 9, No. 1 (March 2011), 28–43, http://scholar.harvard.edu/files/williamson/files/tea_party_pop.pdf.

100 Manny Fernandez, "Marked by More and More Bodies," *New York Times*, May 4, 2017, https://www.nytimes.com/interactive/2017/05/04/us/texas-border-migrants-dead-bodies.html.

101 Rory Carroll, "US Border Patrol uses desert as 'weapon' to kill thousands of migrants, report says," *The Guardian*, Dec. 7, 2016, https://www.theguardian.com/us-news/2016/dec/07/report-us-border-patrol-desert-weapon-immigrants-mexico.

102 Nurith Aizenman, "Mexicans In The U.S. Are Sending Home More Money Than Ever," NPR, February 10, 2017, https://www.npr.org/sections/goatsandsoda/2017/02/10/514172676/mexicans-in-the-u-s-are-sending-home-more-money-than-ever. Patrick Gillespie, "Mexicans in U.S. send cash home in record numbers," CNN Money, January 3, 2018, https://money.cnn.com/2018/01/02/news/economy/mexico-remittances/index.html.

103 Richard S. Lefrak and A. Gary Shilling, "Immigrants Can Help Fix the Housing Bubble," juantornoe.blogs, March 17, 2009, https://juantornoe.blogs.com/hispanictrending/hispanic_business/page/119/.

104 "Resolution on Violence Against Women in Ciudad Juárez," Washington Office on Latin America, http://www.wola.org/es/node/383. John Burnett, "Explosive Theory on Killings of Juarez Women: Journalist Hints Wealthy Drug Lords Behind Scores of Murders," NPR (February 22, 2003), http://www.npr.org/templates/story/story.php?storyId=1532607. "Bordertown—Jennifer Lopez," http://www.youtube.com/watch?v=NvZrbLjJowA. "The Dead of Juarez," http://www.youtube.com/watch?v=2jvvk7AKKq4. "Stop the Killing of the Women of Juarez," National Organization of Women, http://www.now.org/issues/global/juarez/.

105 Damien Cave, "Wave of Women's Killings Confounds Juarez," *New York Times* (June 23, 2012), https://www.nytimes.com/2012/06/24/world/americas/wave-of-violence-swallows-more-women-in-juarez-mexico.html.

106 Mark Hugo Lopez, "The Latino Vote in the 2010 Elections," Pew Hispanic Center (November 2, 2010).

107 Rodolfo F. Acuña, *Assault on Mexican American Collective Memory, 2010–2015: Swimming with Sharks* (Lanham, Maryland: Lexington Books, 2017). "Outlawing

Shakespeare: The Battle for the Tucson Mind," The Nonprofit Network, Video, Posted: Nov. 16, 2012, http://newamericamedia.org/2012/11/outlawing-shakespeare-the-battle-for-the-tucson-mind.php.

108 Jeff Biggers, "Yes, Virginia, They Still Ban Books in Tucson, Arizona," *Huffington Post* (September 28, 2012), http://www.huffingtonpost.com/jeff-biggers/yes-virginia-they-still-b_b_1923928.html. Mari Herreras, "TUSD Banning Books? Well Yes, and No, and Yes," (January 17, 2012), http://www.tucsonweekly.com/TheRange/archives/2012/01/17/tusd-banning-book-well-yes-and-no-and-yes.

109 Rodolfo Acuña, "The Identity Crisis of Mexican Americans," *Counterpunch*, October 25, 2013, https://www.counterpunch.org/2013/10/25/the-identity-crisis-of-mexican-americans/.

110 "Arizona's Human Capital: Latino Students and their Families" January 21, 2019, www.edexcelencia.org/system/files/AZ-ACHE-FINAL.pdf. "Demographic Profile of Hispanics in Arizona, 2010," Pew Hispanic Center (2012), http://www.pewhispanic.org/states/state/az/. Teresa Wiltz, "Expanding Age Gap Between Whites and Minorities May Increase U.S. Racial Divide," *America's Wire*, http://americaswire.org/drupal7/?q=content/expanding-age-gap-between-whites-and-minorities-may-increase-us-racial-divide. America's *Wire* states, "In Arizona, the median age for whites is 43 compared with 25 for Latinos, who comprise 31 percent of the state's population. On per-pupil spending for education, census data show that Arizona ranks 49th among the states and the District of Columbia. In terms of spending on transportation, the state is in the bottom quarter of all states, according to Dominique Apollon, research director at the Applied Research Center, which has offices in New York, Chicago and Oakland."

111 "Curriculum Audit of the Mexican American Studies Department Tucson Unified School District," Cambium Learning, Inc., May 2, 2011, https://www.tucsonweekly.com/images/blogimages/2011/06/16/1308282079-az_masd_audit_final_1_.pdf. Rodolfo F. Acuña, "Giving Hypocrisy a Bad Name: Censorship in Tucson," *Counterpunch* (February 7, 2012). I have written several dozen articles on the situation in Tucson, which can be found in *Counterpunch* and *ThreeSonorans*.com. Also see Jeff Biggers, *State Out of the Union: Arizona and the Final Showdown Over the American Dream* (New York: Nation Books, 2012). Cambium Report, May 2, 2011, http://saveethnicstudies.org/assets/docs/state_audit/Cambium_Audit.pdf. Nolan L. Cabrera, Ph.D., Jeffrey F. Milem, Ph.D., Ronald W. Marx, Ph.D., "An Empirical Analysis of the Effects of Mexican American Studies Participation on Student Achievement within Tucson Unified School District," Report Submitted June 20, 2012, to Willis D. Hawley, Ph.D., Special Master for the Tucson Unified School District Desegregation Case. The Special Master found for the program. However, the question is what the implementation of the decision will be like.

112 Rodolfo F. Acuña, "The Illusive Race Question & Class: A Bacteria That Constantly Mutates," Occasional Paper No. 59, *Latino Studies Series*, Julian Samora Center, November 2005, https://jsri.msu.edu/upload/occasional-papers/oc59.pdf.

113 Charlie Savage, "A Judge's View of Judging Is on the Record," *New York Times* (May 14, 2009), http://www.nytimes.com/2009/05/15/us/15judge.html.

114 James Clifford, "Taking Identity Politics Seriously: 'The Contradictory, Stony Ground . . . .'" in Paul Gilroy, Lawrence Grossberg, and Angela McRobbie, eds., *Without Guarantees: Essays in Honour of Stuart Hall* (London: Verso, 2000), 94–112. "The Word Chicana/o," http://forchicanachicanostudies.wikispaces.com/Chicana+Chicano+Public+Scholar.

115 Conor M. Dowling, Super PAC!: money, elections, and voters after citizens united (New York: Routledge, 2014).

116 Rodolfo F. Acuña, "Catch-22: The Protection of the American Way," meximigration, March 13, 2011, http://mexmigration.blogspot.com/2011/03/guest-blog-rodolfo-acuna-on-delusions.html.

117 Michael Hiltzik, "Five years after Citizens United ruling, big money reigns," *Los Angeles Times* (Jan. 24, 2015).

118 Elaine Godfrey, "Why So Many Democratic Candidates Are Dissing Corporate PACs," *Atlantic*, Aug. 23, 2018, https://www.theatlantic.com/politics/archive/2018/08/why-so-many-democratic-candidates-are-ditching-corporate-pacs/568267/.

119 Chris McGreal, "How big pharma's money – and its politicians – feed the US opioid crisis," *The Guardian* (Oct. 19, 2017), https://www.theguardian.com/us-news/2017/oct/19/big-pharma-money-lobbying-us-opioid-crisis.

120 Ibid.

121 Ibid.

122 Richard Fausset, "New Latino South," *Los Angeles Times* (The series began on December 30, 2011), http://www.latimes.com/news/nationworld/nation/new-latino-south,0,565070.storygallery; "The Latino population in the South has grown dramatically over the last decade. The *Times*'s occasional series chronicles the lives of Latinos in a changing region."

123 "ALEC Exposed," Center for Media and Democracy, https://www.alecexposed.org/wiki/ALEC_Exposed.

124 Brendan DeMelle, "Study Confirms Tea Party Was Created by Big Tobacco and Billionaire Koch

Brothers," *Huffington Post*, The Blog (February 11, 2012).

125 Rodolfo F, Acuña, "Is the Glass Half Full or Half Empty? A Stupid Question," mexmigration, June 28, 2012, http://mexmigration.blogspot.com/2012/06/acuna-on-sb1070-ruling.html#!/2012/06/acuna-on-sb1070-ruling.html.

126 "Arizona SB 1070," https://ballotpedia.org/Arizona_SB_1070.

127 Michael Kiefer, "Arizona settles final issues of SB 1070 legal fight," *The Republic*, Sept. 15, 2016, https://www.azcentral.com/story/news/politics/immigration/2016/09/15/arizona-settlement-sb-1070-lawsuit-aclu-immigration/90424942/.

128 Leonard Gilroy, "Future of Private Prisons in Arizona Corrections," Morrison Institute for Public Policy State of Our State Conference, November 20, 2015, https://morrisoninstitute.asu.edu/sites/default/files/content/products/Private%20Prisons%20-%20The%20Costs.pdf. Jennifer Steinhauer, "Arizona May Put State Prisons in Private Hands," *New York Times* (Oct. 23, 2009), http://www.nytimes.com/2009/10/24/us/24prison.html.

129 Jeremy Duda, "Privatization Proposal for Maximum Security Prisons Raises Concerns," *AzCapitolTimes* (June 18, 2009), http://azcapitoltimes.com/news/2009/06/18/privatization-proposal-for-maximum-security-prisons-raises-concerns/#ixzz2EUGOrbaY. "Gender and the Prison Industrial Complex (2012)," Arizona Prison Watch: A community resource for monitoring, navigating, surviving, and dismantling the prison industrial complex in Arizona, http://arizonaprisonwatch.blogspot.com/. Beau Hodai, "Private Prison Companies Behind the Scenes of Arizona's Immigration Law," *Prison Legal News* (December 2012), https://www.prisonlegalnews.org/displayArticle.aspx?articleid=22734&AspxAutoDetectCookieSupport=1.

130 Seth Hoy, "Prisonomics 101: How ALEC and the Prison Industry Got Arizona's SB1070 onto Gov. Jan Brewer's Desk," *LA Progressive* (no date), http://www.laprogressive.com/sb1070-gov-jan-brewers-desk/#sthash.jW9xqAfK.dpuf.

131 "Detention and Deportation Consequences of Arizona Immigration Law (SB 1070): Why Is Arizona SB 1070 a Problem?" *Detention Watch Network* (no date), http://detentionwatchnetwork.org/SB1070_Talking_Points. Carlos Galindo, "The Business Side of SB1070," *Tucson Citizen* (June 26, 2012), http://tucsoncitizen.com/arizona-unapologetic-liberal/2012/06/26/the-business-side-of-sb1070/.

132 Sarah Macaraeg, "Fatal encounters: 97 deaths point to pattern of border agent violence across America," *The Guardian*, May 2, 2018, https://www.theguardian.com/us-news/2018/may/02/fatal-encounters-97-deaths-point-to-pattern-of-border-agent-violence-across-america. Nicole Chavez, "Border Patrol agent acquitted in fatal shooting of Mexican teen," CNN, November 22, 2018, https://www.cnn.com/2018/11/22/us/border-patrol-agent-acquitted-mexican-teen-killing/index.html.

133 Peter Fenn, "Tea Party Funding Koch Brothers Emerge from Anonymity," *USNews & World Report* (February 2, 2011), http://www.usnews.com/opinion/blogs/Peter-Fenn/2011/02/02/tea-party-funding-koch-brothers-emerge-from-anonymity.

134 Jeremy Pelofsky, "Gun Lobby Fights Mexico Border Rifle Sale Control," *Reuters* (August 3, 2011), http://www.reuters.com/article/2011/08/03/us-usa-mexico-guns-idUSTRE7725DB20110803. David Neiwert, "Mexican drug cartels go shopping for their guns in Arizona," *Crooks and Liars* (January 27, 2011), http://crooksandliars.com/david-neiwert/mexican-drug-cartels-go-shopping-the.

135 Rodolfo F. Acuña, *Swimming with Sharks*.

136 Rodolfo Acuña, "The Vindication of Mexican-American Studies," *Counterpunch*, November 15, 2012, https://www.counterpunch.org/2012/11/15/the-vindication-of-mexican-american-studies/.

137 Cambium Report, Ibid.

138 Soyenixe Lopez, "Court orders new hearing for Tucson schools' Mexican-American studies program," Cronkite News, July 7, 2015, https://cronkitenews.azpbs.org/2015/07/07/court-orders-new-hearing-for-tucson-schools-mexican-american-studies-program/.

139 Dylan Smith, "Judge: Law barring TUSD's ethnic studies unconstitutional, motivated by racism; Ruling: 2010 Arizona statute violates 1st & 14th amendments," *Tucson Sentinel* (Aug. 22, 2017), http://www.tucsonsentinel.com/local/report/082217_tusd_mas/judge-law-barring-tusds-ethnic-studies-unconstitutional-motivated-by-racism/.

140 Annie Gilbertson, "LAUSD requiring ethnic studies for graduation," KPCC, November 19, 2014. https://www.scpr.org/blogs/education/2014/11/19/17582/lausd-requiring-ethnic-studies-for-graduation/.

141 "Take a Stand—Yes on Prop. 30," http://www.youtube.com/watch?v=RtO1xsnWsw4. "Progressive Caucus on Prop. 32—California, November 2012," http://www.youtube.com/watch?v=CwgVTPSyQzo.

142 Roberto Suro, "Whatever Happened to Latino Political Power?" *New York Times* (Jan. 2, 2016), https://www.nytimes.com/2016/01/03/opinion/sunday/whatever-happened-to-latino-political-power.html?mtrref=www.google.com&assetType=opinion.

143 Dennis Romero, "A Chicano renaissance? A new Mexican-American generation embraces the term," ABC, July 15, 2018, https://www.nbcnews.com/news/latino/chicano-renaissance-new-mexican-american-generation-embraces-term-n869846.
144 Romero, Ibid.
145 Ibid.
146 "The Mexican-American Boom: Births Overtake Immigration," Pew Research Center, July 14, 2011, http://www.pewhispanic.org/2011/07/14/the-mexican-american-boom-brbirths-overtake-immigration/.
147 "Herman Baca, Chicano Rights Activist," South Bay Compass, n.d., http://southbaycompass.com/hermanbaca/.
148 Rodolfo F. Acuña, "Latinos and the Fracturing Democratic Coalition," *Verso*, November 21, 2016, https://www.versobooks.com/blogs/2957-latinos-and-the-fracturing-democratic-coalition.

Epilogue: Peeling the Onion

In 2017, as Donald Trump assumed the office of the presidency. Because of the similarities between Trump and George Orwell's Big Brother in the latter's novel *1984*, about a dystopian future where critical thought is suppressed under a totalitarian regime, book sales surged, quickly rising to the top of the Amazon best-seller list.[1] Both Trump and Big Brother lied, repeated the lie, and "his listeners either cower in fear, stammer in disbelief, or try to see how they can turn the lie to their own benefit."[2] There is no doubt, that, Trump's Invasion of America touched a cord. Trump and his staff issued a barrage of false claims starting with describing the size of the inaugural ceremony as the "largest audience ever to witness an inauguration." Sean Spicer, the White House press secretary and other staffers defended Trump's hyperbole. Staffer Kellyanne Conway justified Spicer's lie calling it "alternative facts"—drawing an obvious comparison with Orwell's 1984's doublespeak. Like in the movies fiction became fact as "unreality that is propagated as reality."[3]

Doublespeak cannot be entirely laid at the feet of Donald Trump. U.S. history is replete with similar distortions. But truth is important; it exposes injustices and contradictions in a system and thus never welcome by unjust rulers. Frantz Fanon wrote that "By definition, colonies produce fragmented societies that are haunted by fear and suspicion. As such they remain divided and their culture, increasingly rigid."[4] Take the case of the Tucson Mexican American Studies: It was about the truth and attempts to erase Mexican American history and the memory of injustices. (See Chapter 17.) In order to maintain a social caste system people live a lie. Right-wing foundations and individuals spend hundreds of millions of dollars to obfuscate the truth.

Today, doublespeak has developed into a science. For example, the documentary *Waiting for Superman* (2010) was explicitly produced to create an alternative narrative about the privatization of education in the United States and Mexico. "Superman" premiered on the 24-floor offices of the World Bank rather than in movie theaters. Bill Gates, who donated billions to privatize public schools, promoted *Waiting for Superman*.[5] It raised eyebrows when it premiered at the national PTA (Parent-Teachers Association) convention. "Some have wondered if . . . [the PTA's] decision to promote the film has anything to do with its receipt of a $1 million donation from the Gates Foundation."[6] Gates's solution to the budget crisis was not to raise taxes on the rich but for school districts to cut pension payments for retired teachers and to privatize public schools.

Waiting for Superman was directed by Davis Guggenheim. It won high praise from President Obama, Bill Clinton, and Obama's former neoliberal Secretary of Education, Arne Duncan among others.[7] *Waiting for Superman* has two intertwining narratives. It is a masterpiece in the art of détournement—the art of "rerouting, hijacking" and reinventing the truth.[8] Well financed by right-wing foundations and pushed by billionaires such as Bill Gates, *Waiting for Superman* is a running commercial for charter schools. The heroes are the charter school advocates versus the enemies the greedy teachers.

The supermen include the controversial Michelle Rhee, the chancellor of Washington, D.C.'s public schools during Rhee's three-year tenure. Rhee became a polarizing yet popular figure, appearing in *Time Magazine*, celebrated for her reform efforts in a feature story. Along with Bill Gates of Microsoft fortune, the supermen included David Levin and Michael Feinberg, the founders of the KIPP (Knowledge Is Power Program) schools, and former Milwaukee Superintendent Howard Fuller, a proponent of school vouchers. The villains were the tenured teachers. According to the counternarrative, unions were "blocking genuine educational reform by militating against the charter school movement". In Tucson, détournement was key in the war against Mexicans as it is today against immigrants. It offered a means "of restructuring culture and experience."[9]

Deny, Deny, Deny!

Those in power have the choice of telling the truth, finding the truth, or denying it. The reader has the choice of accepting fairy tales or finding solutions through critical thinking. A major hurdle to achieving peace at home, preventing crime, and ensuring a healthy society is to know how to solve critical thinking problems something that is almost impossible in a society where the oligarchs control the common sense.

During the last 50 years, the average wealth in the United States increased, yet not everyone shared equally. The gap between white and Black widened since 1963 when the average wealth of white families was $121,000 higher than the average wealth of non-white families. "By 2016, the average wealth of white families ($919,000) was over $700,000 higher than the average wealth of black families ($140,000) and of Hispanic families ($192,000)."[10] Inequality was not the result of the increased productivity of whites but the stacking of the deck of cards. Corporations and the wealthy, through large donations controlled elected representatives, rewrote the rules of the game to favor themselves. The truth is that workers today are more productive but get paid less.[11]

As mentioned *Waiting for Superman* blamed trade unions for inequality. In turn, many white workers blamed the immigrants and we live the lie that America is the home of opportunity. The truth is, America is no longer the leader of Western Civilization we live a lie:

> The economic engine of the EU, Germany single-handedly saved the Eurozone from collapse in 2012. At the same time, German workers enjoy unparalleled worker protections and shorter working hours than most of their global counterparts. How can a country that works an average of 35 hours per week (with an average 24 paid vacation days to boot) maintain such a high level of productivity?[12]

The average American earns an annual salary of $34,645 compared to $40,223 for German workers. So why is this important?

The difference between the American and the German economy is that Germany has strong labor comprehensive unions. Workers sit on corporate boards. Germans collect paid medical insurance and have a strong social network. In America, American capitalists decimated worker benefits. Meanwhile, American CEOs earn twice as much as German executives. Why?

The Disintegration of Civil Society

Driving down Los Angeles's skid row, one sees a decaying industrial sector to the east. It is like seeing the movie "Blade Runner"[13] become a reality. Homeless people live in makeshift tents with people sleeping under bridges or the cement sidewalks. Society is a disintegrating. Further to the east is the community of Bole Heights. It is about 80 percent Mexican with the rest Latinos; about three-quarters are renters (and in Los Angeles that means that it is time for the developers and hipsters to move in).[14]

You get the feeling that Boyle Heights is the present and Skid Row the future. The satirist Guillermo Gómez Peña points out in "Notes From Technotopia: On The Cruelty Of Indifference: An anti-gentrification philosophical tantrum, 2015":

> Imagine that during the reconstruction process, the rent—your rent—increases by two or three hundred percent overnight. The artists and the working class at large can no longer pay it. You are being forced to leave, at best to a nearby city, at worst back to your original hometown. The more intimate history you have with the old city, the more painful it is to accept this displacement. You have no choice.[15]

According to Gómez Peña gentrification is the last stage before the disintegration of a community.

Part of forming a collective historical memory involves collectively recognizing the truth. A student the other day commented that she could not return to her *barrio* because she could not afford the rent. It was once the dream of many Mexicans to buy a home. When I was as old as my students, I bought my first home. They were cheap—cost $8,000 to $10,000—no money down. You could become a peasant landlord and buy a second house; and you knew your children would have the same opportunities that you had. Housing markets would periodically collapse and housing prices would correct for inflation. However, today is different and the truth is that rentals are scarcer.[16]

A slight rise in housing costs occurred during the 1950s, with a correction a correction taking place in the 1960s and 1970s. By the 1980s, a hosing boom again made buying that extra home almost impossible. In the 1990s, before leaving office, William Jefferson Clinton ended the regulatory acts of the 1930s, which ended the ability of the housing market to recuperate, making the housing bubbles of the first decade of the twenty-first century inevitable. Meanwhile, Presidents George Bush and Barack Obama gave bailouts to Wall Street and the banks. Instead of disciplining them, Bush and Obama rewarded Wall Street speculators. The family housing market became the property of the super-rich. The Obama administration enabled Wall Street to monopolize the buying of government foreclosures.[17] The largest bankers and hedge-fund operators seized control of Fannie and Freddie Mae, grabbing half the nation's mortgages and some 200,000 homes.[18] Speculators and government colluded; the Obama administration sold off tax liens to the former super-rich.

Land speculation is part of the fabric of the Cities of the Angels and Chicago. It is a disease that has spread to almost every major city. It pits developers against homeowners and landlords against renters. Billions if not trillions of dollars were made bulldozing people. In Los Angeles, gentrification took it to a higher level, impacting communities such as Highland Park, Silver Lake, Echo Park, Boyle Heights, and South Central Los Angeles. It spread to East Hollywood, North Hollywood, and the entire East San Fernando Valley. Following the transit lines is like following the money.

Meanwhile, small operators with capital bought fixer-uppers and flipped them at higher prices to hipsters and middle-class buyers from the suburbs. The process drove up not only the prices of homes but apartments as well.

Renters saw their rents zoom from $800/$1000 a month to $2000/$3000. The developers and the flippers have become Public Enemy Number 1. Many activists targeted art galleries and businesses not indigenous to the area. However, the culprits are the elected officials who are in league with the developers and the flippers. They profit from the change in the form of higher taxes because of increased property reassessment.

These communities share a history of exploitation. Unwanted facilities such as prisons and toxic waste dumps have invaded their space. After World War II, freeways crisscrossed the Los Angeles's Eastside, displacing about 10,000 living units. "When plans for freeways were proposed, these sections [east of the Los Angeles River] were considered expendable . . . . . Freeways ultimately displaced ten percent of the area's inhabitants."[19]

Affluent middle-class whites and Latinos displaced lower-income minority residents. This displacement is not a natural phenomenon and it takes significant public or non-profit redevelopment investment. The result is that prices escalate and the new homeowners develop a lower tolerance for social service facilities such as public housing that they see as undesirable. Their obsession is protecting their investment.

> Lydia Avila-Hernández writes that improvements "will cause the in-migration of whites which will further spread the misperception that the neighborhood will get better as the number of white people increase."[20]

Gentrification is not about cultural integration, and it is not about racial or social integration. In order to stop the siege, its effects cannot be trivialized. The next step is *Blade Runner*.

Kill Zapata!

Who would have thought 40 years ago that salsa would become the number one condiment in the United States? Mexican friends always marvel at how México Lindo in the Southwest remains so Mexican. The truth is that although it is next door, most Mexicans in the United States rarely visit it. México Lindo is a dream. It comes as a shock to many that México Lindo today is a "Mass Grave." Before the 1980s, visitors could travel throughout Mexico. Civil society then began to disintegrate. NAFTA, the spread of neoliberalism, the War on Drugs, and inequality eroded social control. During the late 1980s the cartels grew and Mexico could not control them and was unable to provide jobs for its citizens.

In 2014, 43 Normalistas (normal school trainees) from the Ayotzinapa Rural Teachers' College traveled to Iguala, Guerrero. Historically the Normalistas, rural school teachers, were the custodians and scientists of the poor *ejido* villages. They kept alive memories such as the 1968 Tlatelolco student massacre.[21]

Mexicans know the Normalistas' history of self-sacrifice; the idealistic teachers who were wanted to build a new society. The rural school movement began as a result of the Mexican Revolution (1910–1921). Mexican youth went into the countryside to teach rural Mexicans to read and write. The Ayotzinapa Normal School was founded in 1926 in the aftermath of the Mexican Revolution as a teachers' boarding school. The Normalistas of Ayotzinapa took this tradition seriously and participated in the progressive struggles of the nation. Meanwhile, tensions in Mexico grew after the signing of the North American Free Trade Agreement in 1994. The majority of the 43 disappeared Normalistas grew up in rural Guerrero farm villages devastated by Mexico's post-NAFTA economy; the privatization of the Mexican economy wiped out Mexican rural farms and increased rural poverty and lawlessness. They were traveling to the state capital to raise funds when they were stopped by the police and disappeared.

The disappearance of the 43 Ayotzinapa Normalistas killed the odds of regaining any moral authority that the Mexican state had of creating an alternative political party that would make a difference.

According to Lorena Ojeda, Ayotzinapa case shows "the deterioration of Mexico's political and social spheres. The missing normalistas are poor, indigenous or mestizo (mixed-race), and brown-skinned." They were campesinos. Many with Indigenous surnames with intonations peculiar to rural Mexican folk. Ojeda added "Simply put, they are Mexicans." They joined the country's seemingly infinite number of mass graves. For the parents there is "heartrending pain" their sons are missing. Experienced by the parents whose sons are missing."[22]

Some Chicanas/os were at first reluctant to criticize Mexico, lest they encourage Mexico-bashing or be considered unpatriotic. However, a growing number of Mexican Americans were becoming disillusioned.

Mexican President Carlos Salinas de Gortari (1988–1994) proceeded to implement his neoliberal program for resolving Mexico's acute economic problems that bore a chilling resemblance to the "positivism" of dictator Porfirio Díaz. Foreign investment was part of Salinas's vision, along with attempts to bring back capital that fled the country in the early 1980s. Salinas moved toward deregulation of the economy and privatization of state-owned enterprises, thus abandoning any pretense of loyalty to the objectives of the Mexican Revolution. Conditions improved for the rich, the number of Mexican billionaires jumped from four to twenty-four, while the gap broadened between rich and poor.[23] Nevertheless, many U.S. Latinos believed Salinas was smart and was doing a good job. A *Los Angeles Times* poll in 1991 showed 51 percent of those polled approved of Salinas's performance in office.[24]

After the 1982 economic crisis, the Mexican government increasingly aligned its foreign and economic policies with the United States. It showed a willingness to condemn Manuel Noriega even before President H. W. Bush's invasion of Panama (1989); Mexico offered to increase oil exports to the United States during "Operation Desert Storm" (Aug. 2, 1990–Feb. 28, 1991). At the request of U.S. officials, in 1993 Mexico deported 658 Chinese immigrants on ships off the coast of Baja California, helping to prevent them from reaching U.S. shores. Such actions, and the high cost of economic growth, troubled many Mexicans in the United States. Supporters of the Democratic Revolutionary Party (PRD) and human rights activists frequently picketed the Mexican Consulate. Mexican American involvement in political issues affecting Mexico accelerated as the debate over the North American Free Trade Agreement heated up.[25]

NAFTA accelerated the privatization of Mexico's education. According to Bacon:

> "A network of large corporations and banks extends throughout Latin America, financed and guided in part from the United States, pushing the same formula: standardized tests, linking teachers' jobs and pay to test results, and bending the curriculum to employers' needs while eliminating social critique. In both countries, there was grassroots opposition—from parents and teachers. In Seattle, teachers at Garfield High refused to give the tests. In Michoacán, in central Mexico, sixteen teachers went to jail because they also refused."[26]

The Mexican government accused teacher unions of leading opposition to charter schools. Partnership for Educational Revitalization in the Americas (PREAL), established by the Inter-American Dialogue in Washington, D.C. and the Corporation for Development Research in Santiago, Chilein 1995, set the neoliberal agenda for Latin America. PREAL's mission was to build a broad and active constituency "for education reform." Supporting PREAL were the Ford Foundation and the World Bank and powerful financial interests.[27] Notable was the support of the U.S. Agency for International Development that among many Latin Americanist is considered a CIA (Central Intelligence Agency) clone.

Ten days after Mexican President Enrique Peña Nieto took office in December 2012, he sent constitutional changes regarding education to Mexico's Congress. This marked the death of Article 3 of the Mexican Constitution that secularized public education and paved the way for attacks on José Vasconcelos's idealistic education system. Ten days later, the Mexican Congress ratified the so-called reforms with no discussion with teachers, consultation with education experts, or public debate. *The New York Times* was part of the conspiracy to keep information on what was happening from the Mexican public.[28] The parallels between President Ronald Reagan and Peña Nieto are startling — both were figureheads for Wall Street.

Under Peña Nieto, the Mexican government fast-tracked the molting of Mexico—stripping the people of the constitutional guarantees of the Mexican Constitution of 1917 and privatizing Mexico's public resources. The Mexican Constitution of 1917 was the first Constitution in the world that protected social rights. Article 3 forbade censorship of prohibited books, and guaranteed free, mandatory, and lay education. Article 27 vested the nation in the direct ownership of all natural resources, that is, all minerals and water. Only Mexicans had the right to own land, water, and minerals or to acquire concessions for their exploitation. Article 28 prohibited monopolies of any kind. Article 123 empowered the labor sector. By 2017, Articles 3, 27, and 28 were under siege. The reforms allowed the Mexican government to grant licenses and share oil profits with multinational corporations such as Exxon and Chevron. These so-called reforms would rolled back President Lazaro Cardenas's historic nationalization of the oil industry in 1938.[29]

The Aftermath of NAFTA[30]

As mentioned, former president Clinton apologized for the War on Drugs. The Mexican newspaper *Sin Embargo* ran a story titled, *Clinton pide perdón a México por la guerra contra el narco que se desató en su mandato*—roughly translated, it means, "Clinton says he is sorry to Mexico for the War on Drugs that began on his watch!" Clinton spoke in Mexico City on February 6, 2015 at a "Juventud y Productividad" conference (see Chapter 16).[31]

A memo written by an analyst for Chase Manhattan Bank, on January 13, 1995 barely a year after the Zapatista rebellion began, "revealed a direct link between multinational banks in the North and state repression in the South . . . ," according to *Gloves Off* the memo stated, "While Chiapas, in our opinion, does not pose a fundamental threat to Mexican political stability, it was perceived to be so by many in the investment community. The government would need to eliminate the Zapatistas to demonstrate their effective control of the national territory and of security policy."[32] Many Mexicans charge that the so-called War on Drugs was used to strengthen the hegemony of the billionaires and hid other policies that created more billionaires.

The United States and Mexico frightened people into supporting threats to basic freedoms. As a reminder, the United States spent hundreds of million dollars to shut down ocean drug corridors, from Colombia to Miami, diverting them through Central America and Mexico. The drug trade corrupted their governments and their civil societies. The new corridors took migrants to Texas, New Mexico, Arizona, and California. The American government purposely channeled them through the deserts of Sonora and Arizona, cynically reasoning that if the border patrol did not get them, the deserts would.

What drives the drug trade is the U.S. drug market's huge demand. By deporting thousands of gang members to their homelands, the United States compounded worsened the conditions in the Central American. Most deportees were raised in the United States and introduced to crime in U.S. prison system. The enormous profits in drugs spawned cartels and caused wars among the cartels and with local, state, and federal authorities. From January 2007 to November 2, 2009, 9,903 Mexicans were killed as a result of this war.[33]

Make America Great Again

A lie is a lie, and the statement that America is a nation of immigrants is a lie. Madison Grant, in *The Passing of the Great Race: Or, The Racial Basis of European History* (1916), warned that intermarriage would lead to "racial suicide." The eugenicist called for "the balances of superior and inferior peoples" and warned that intermarriage would eventually lead to the disappearance of white civilization.[34] Grant influenced the social and racial engineering of the 1920s immigration acts.[35] Neither Grant nor Donald Trump invented white racism. American ideas of race and racism date back to colonialism and slavery. They were used to justify the genocide of Indigenous Peoples. The importance of eugenics, according to progressive author Michelle Chen, was that it "fostered a new scientific field of race nationalism—one that rebranded old assumptions of the superiority of Northern European whiteness with a veneer of intellectual legitimacy."[36] It gave racists a pseudo-scientific justification for their racism.

From the beginning, Americans have tried to annihilate Indigenous People, Mexicans, and anyone whose ethnic origins were outside of Northwestern Europe. The 1920s immigration laws discriminated against Italians, southern and eastern Europeans, and those whom they considered "unclean." The 1921 and 1924 Immigration Acts limited immigration from many European Union member states favoring those from Northwestern Europe. Regulations relating to resident permits and family reunification rights, however, were implemented that in recent years have been whittled away and Mexicans and Latinos have replaced Italians as the most undesirable aliens. As of January 2019, two small children died in what charitably could be called concentration camps.

Eugenic policies are not harmless; witness their influence on sterilization laws implemented in the United States. The first eugenic sterilization laws targeted Native Americans in Indiana in 1907 and were sanctioned by the Supreme Court in 1927 (*Buck v. Bell*).[37] The sterilization laws mainly targeted Black, Native American, and Latino people. The Virginia Sterilization Act was passed in 1924:

> In total, 7325 individuals were sterilized in Virginia under its sterilization law. Of those sterilized about half were deemed "mentally ill" and the other half deemed "mentally deficient." Approximately 62% of total individuals sterilized were female. Some estimate the total number of sterilizatios as high as 8,300 individuals."[38]

Eugenics was "spread by social workers, preachers, social activists, mental health workers and school book authors"[39] who sought to pass racism off as a science. It fostered the notion that "'the poorer and the less developed races', the 'weaker gender', the 'weaker classes' and the 'weaker Races' were blamed for their own misery: they were not thought to be genetically as evolved as white, heterosexual and wealthy men."[40]

Foundations support eugenics research, such as *The Bell Curve: Intelligence and Class Structure in American Life* (1994) by Richard J. Herrnstein and Charles Murray.[41] It argues that IQ differences are genetic. The message is that society can put all of the money it wants into educating African Americans and Latinos but genetically they are just not equal to the rigors of education. The Pioneer Fund, with ties to far right-wing funders, seeded Murray's early "research." Ishmael Reed wrote in *Counterpunch*, "Using Murray's 'theories' which were embraced by the New Aryans at Commentary, the New Republic and the New York Times Book Review, black kids are uneducable."[42] So why waste money on educating them?

The current white nationalism retains the urgency and hyperbole of Madison Grant's theme of "racial suicide." Most of today's white nationalists are not intellectuals and the majority could not you who Madison Grant was. Most know little about the Civil War, believing that the Confederacy won the war, not knowing that their ancestors probably either fought on the side of the Union, or were not considered white at the time of their arrival. The current racist climate seems to be based on discontent, with people blaming affirmative action for their own failures.

Some of the white nationalists belonged to groups such as the Ku Klux Klan, neo-Confederate, neo-Nazi, racist skinhead, and Christian Identity organizations. They range from non-violent to vulgar provocateurs. They are often violent, either provoking violence or killing innocent people. In 2017, they murdered 28 people; double that of the year before.[43] "In the past decade, right-wing extremism made up 71 percent of extremist-related murders, compared with 26 percent of murders by Islamic extremists."[44]

The election of Donald Trump in 2016 became a major rallying point for white nationalists. It was not a new notion, it was American as apple pie. President Trump by design appealed to their prejudices throughout the primary, on campaign rallies, and incessant tweets. He "relentlessly" attacked Mexicans and other minorities. These assaults fell on fertile ground and appealed to the white Americans through the drumbeat of "be proud to be white." Trump enlisted populist radio talk-show, Fox News, and neo-fascists such as Richard Spencer, who has been billed as "the voice of the new, embattled white minority." Spencer, like other white nationalists, has foundations that, according to him, protect freedom of speech, religion, and equality before the law. They declared total war "to further the interests of our people." They were at rallies in Charlottesville, Virginia and Knoxville, Tennessee, and reportedly were armed.[45] Although white nationalist James A. Fields deliberately rammed a car into a crowd of counter protesters, killing 32-year-old counter protester Heather Heyer, President Trump waffled in condemning the right, saying there were "Some very fine people on both sides."[46]

Although he enabled racists, President Trump did not invent the scapegoating. *The New Yorker* recently wrote: "Over the years, Trump honed a performer's ear for the needs of his audience." Trump "recycled from Ronald Reagan's 1980 motto for the White House—"Make America Great Again!"[47]

On June 16, 2016, President Trump announced his candidacy; he vowed to build a 2000-mile-long wall to stop Mexico from "sending people that have lots of problems." He said, "They're bringing drugs. They're bringing crime. They're rapists. And some, I assume, are good people."[48] It did not matter that it was not the truth; it mattered that it was what many Americans wanted to hear. The rise of Trump was paved by the Tea Party that received heavy funding from the Koch Brothers and other right-wing philanthropists, as well as foundations that paid for research such as *The Bell Curve* distorts the study of race.[49] It could be asked how privileged white students fall behind minority students from poor families that suffer racism can claim that minorities have received preferential treatment.[50]

While many right-wing fringe groups form the Trump phalanx, many are out of the south and rural areas. Many political pundits have come to the conclusion that "Education, Not Income, Predicted Who Would Vote For Trump."[51] The base is made up of evangelicals and disaffected whites for whom the American Dream is dead. Many want to bring on Armageddon to save America through the second coming of Jesus Christ.

In 2016, Hillary Clinton's candidacy surged in the nation's more educated counties and cities but collapsed in the least educated, where people were more apt to believe Trump's lies about undocumented immigrants and to fear them. For example, they believed that Honduras, a nation of 9 million people, was poised to invade the United States. It was as absurd as it was to claim that undocumented Mexicans were taking jobs away from white Americans when thousands of empty jobs remain unfilled. It becomes all the more absurd when one considers that Trump employs undocumented immigrants to make his bed.[52]

The real dilemma is that Americans are growing old and they can't come to grips with old age. *Time Magazine* recently ran an article titled, "More White People Are Dying than Are Being Born in 17 States."[53] An often-quoted fact is that by the year 2025, one out of two children born in the United States will be Latino. Whites fret over this but who is blame for their not having children? The fact that the median age of Mexican American women is 10 years lower than white women plays a role in decreasing fertility among whites due to aging. In addition to white America's shrinking birth rate, there is also a decrease in their mortality rate, and a higher life expectancy.

"An estimated seventy percent of adults turning sixty-five next year will eventually need some level of long-term care and support services." If white Americans want a Scrooge moment they should visit an old age home or visit people tended by home care and see who will care for them. The truth is told, they cannot afford to eliminate immigrants.[54]

Illusions and Delusions

In 1997 the movie *Wag the Dog* premiered. The storyline was about an American president who, weeks before reelection, is caught in the middle of a sex scandal. The president's handlers enlist a spin doctor to distract the voters; they hire a Hollywood producer to fabricate a mythical war in Albania. The media becomes so focused on the war that they and the voters ignore the presidential scandal. The "wagging of the dog" expression refers to the diverting attention from the truth. It is similar to what Michael Harrington wrote in *The Other America* (1962): "Beauty can be a mask for ugliness," referring to rural poverty in Appalachia where the beauty of the landscape hid the poverty.[55] According to Harrington, "America has the best-dressed poverty in the world," allowing poor whites to go unnoticed and giving the illusion of equality.

Camouflaging of the truth is not an American invention and it does not happen by accident. "Panem et circenses" ("Bread and circuses") were promoted by Roman oligarchs; it was "a superficial means of appeasement," diverting and distracting attention from the ugliness of war, racism, and inequality. Powerless, the masses became part of a Roman mob. "Bread and circuses" hid the detestable corruption and dulled compassion. Imperial expansion and domestic policing were perceived as justified. Violent military interventions were clothed in humanitarian terms.

As the illusion of "one man one vote" vanished and equality before the law eroded, the "bread and circuses" have become more necessary. Sports are part of the modern "panem et circenses." Few plebeians can afford the Colosseum, so they watch games on TV under the illusion is perpetuated that they are equal to the wealthy ticket holders.

The Mexican government regularly manipulates the truth. Mexican reporter Francisco Goldman wrote that on "the verge of monumental decisions," Mexican politicos scheduled legislative sessions to precisely coincide with the World Cup or on December 12, the Feast of the Virgin of Guadalupe and the start of the Christmas holiday season. As for the United States it is the puppet master, benefiting from the lack of unity in the Americas.[56]

Trump and the Last Days of the Empire

It is difficult to evaluate the impact of the Trump Years. As of January 2019 it appears that he will be indicted for multiple felonies as a result of Special Counsel for the Department of Justice Robert Mueller's investigation that began in May 2017. In arriving at the truth there are many layers of the onion that have to be peeled. The conviction of Trump would not cure the lie or lies. For example, there was great concern about the Russian influence on the American elections. Personally, I am not too concerned because other nations have spied and tried to influence the United States namely Israel and Saudi Arabia. We regularly attempt to subvert other nations, such as Honduras, Chile, Venezuela, and Mexico. And this is something we would not acknowledge or remedy. So as long as the lie remains is not peeled off the core of the onion will remain rotten.

What is criminal about Trump is the corruption. It was and is wrong for a president or any other elected official to take bribes or personally profit from ventures with foreign governments. Trump's immorality does not greatly concern me because John F, Kennedy, Lyndon Johnson, and Bill Clinton were not models of chastity. Trump, however, goes beyond what is normal behavior. So to cure the lie I want to put it into proper context to prevent future abuses of power. The government letting him get away with tax fraud is unforgivable. The extent of fraud shows that some people are above the law.[57] To cure the lie, peel it like an onion, layer by layer. The truth cannot be selectively applied.

I am concerned about the lies about immigration and immigrants. These lies are malicious and like sticks and stones, they harm people. Immigrants benefit society. I recently had a conversation on the question of who is to blame. Who is to blame for the crops rotting in the fields? The conversation, if you can call it that, was with a white man, who shouted at me that they are going to get robots to pick the crops and then would not need the damn Mexicans. The shallowness of the argument reminded me of the story of Henry Ford II who was touring an automated plant with Walter Reuther, the head of the United Auto Workers. Suddenly Ford asked Reuther, "Walter, how are you going to get those robots to pay your union dues? Reuther quickly responded, "How are you going to get them to buy your cars?" The moral is that you need people not only to work but to buy, and the truth is few people are buying American today. I don't see too many American cars on the road.[58] Immigrants are not only workers but consumers with a population of 170 million people in the United States and Mexico.

The Blue Wave

Essential to the question of decolonization is the correction of the lies we live with. I hope that this and other books can be part of the peeling of the onion. Reading history is part of the correction process. A correction of the Mexicans' colonial history is at the heart of Mexican American identity. Knowing who they are is essential to the identity that Spanish and American colonialism have distorted. As we close the writing of 9/e of *Occupied America*, the nation stands at the crossroads. A Blue Wave hit the country in the midterm elections of 2018, further polarizing the country. The Democrats took back the House of Representatives and the Republicans retained control of the Senate. Republicans no longer control the three branches of government. In real terms, the House of Representatives is more indicative of the popular vote. The Senate, however, controls appointments to the Supreme Court.

A general feeling one gets from the elections is that they were rigged.[59] As the investigation of special counsel Robert Mueller winds down. The indictment of Trump assistants suggests that they acted at the "direction of the president." There are varying opinions as what should be done. If the president obtained the office by fraud should he be charged? Not only does the presidency have be cleaned up, but the system itself needs a cleaning.[60] The truth is America has morally never been great. A lie is a lie, and for the oligarchs, "Ignorance is strength."[61]

Meanwhile, Mexican Americans and Latinos must continue to peel the onion. As Frantz Fanon argued it is not enough to remain silent and signal acceptance of the colonial administration. This only signals complicity— resistance is necessary to bring about change. That change can only mature by peeling off 500 years of American and European colonialism at the heart of our wrongheaded beliefs. At the core of the onion is a Eurocentric view of ourselves and the world. We have a choice and can exercise freedom of thought, choice, and action. But in order to do this we must learn who we are and know how colonialism has disfigured us. Like psychoanalysis decolonization is a long and tedious process and the peeling of the onion is a search for the truth which is colonialism has annihilated our past.

Notes

1. Kimiko de Freytas-Tamura, "George Orwell's '1984' Is Suddenly a Best-Seller," *New York Times* (Jan. 25, 201), https://www.nytimes.com/2017/01/25/books/1984-george-orwell-donald-trump.html.
2. Adam Gopnik, "Orwell's "1984" and Trump's America." The new Yorker, January 27, 2017. https://www.newyorker.com/news/daily-comment/orwells-1984-and-trumps-america.
3. Ibid.
4. Nigel Gibson, "Fanon and the politics of truth and lying in a colonial society," The Coversation, September 10, 2018. http://theconversation.com/fanon-and-the-politics-of-truth-and-lying-in-a-colonial-society-102594
5. Peter Dreier, "Why Is Public Television Against Public Schools?" *Huffington Post*, Apr. 11, 2014, http://www.huffingtonpost.com/peter-dreier/public-television-education_b_5130372.html.
6. Peter Dreier, "Go Public" – Finally, A Film That Celebrates Public Schools," Truthout:Alternet, July 16, 2013.
7. Perry Bacon Jr., "How Arne Duncan Reshaped American Education and Made Enemies Along the Way," *New York Times* (Jan. 2 2016), http://www.nbcnews.com/meet-the-press/how-arne-duncan-reshaped-american-education-made-enemies-along-way-n480506.
8. James Trier, "Challenging 'Waiting for Superman' through detournement. (Critical essay)," *Journal of Popular Film & Television*, 2013 Vol. 41 Issue 2, 68–77. Amy Elias, 2010. "Psychogeography, Détournement, Cyberspace," *New Literary History*, 41, No. 4: 821–845.
9. James Trier (ed.), *Detournement as Pedagogical Praxis* (Chapel Hill: University of North Carolina Press, 2014), 16.
10. "Nine Charts about Wealth Inequality in America," Urban Institute, http://apps.urban.org/features/wealth-inequality-charts/.
11. Elise Gould, "Wage inequality continued its 35-year rise in 2015," *Economic Policy Institute*, March 10, 2016, http://www.epi.org/publication/wage-inequality-continued-its-35-year-rise-in-2015/.
12. Amol Sarva, "Why Germans Work Fewer Hours But Produce More: A Study In Culture," *HuffPost*, Dec. 6, 2017, https://www.huffingtonpost.com/amol-sarva/why-germans-work-fewer-ho_b_6172262.html.
13. Daniel Valencia, "Blade Runner and the Cybermexic Organism: the erasure of Mexicans in science fiction film," 2009, CSUN Solar, http://scholarworks.csun.edu/handle/10211.3/144004.
14. Carl Abbott, "'Blade Runner' and the Dystopic Los Angeles," *City Lab*, Oct. 3, 2017, https://www.citylab.com/design/2017/10/blade-runner-and-the-dystopic-los-angeles/539574/.
15. Guillermo Gómez-Peña, "Notes From Technotopia: On The Cruelty Of Indifference: An anti-gentrification philosophical tantrum," 2015. https://docs.google.com/document/d/1v-nwi3b0OC0CAfHMbBpp8soGQ8M_HefUKrjz6DsyFYU/edit
16. Rodolfo Acuña, "Hedge Funds and the Death of the Peasant Landowner," *Counterpunch*, June 10, 2013, http://www.counterpunch.org/2013/06/07/hedge-funds-and-the-death-of-the-peasant-landowner/.
17. Rodolfo F, Acuña, "Gentrification: The Struggle for Affordable Housing," El BeiSMan, April 4,,2015. http://www.elbeisman.com/article.php?action=read&id=663
18. " Government Takes Control of Fannie, Freddie," Reuters, Sept. 7, 2008, 5 Aug 2010, https://www.cnbc.com/id/26590793. Dave Ransom, "Big Capital is Moving into Single-family Housing Investments," *Tribuno del Pueblo*, February | March 2013, http://www.tribunodelpueblo.org/2013/02/big-capital-is-moving-into-single-family-housing-investments/.
19. Acuña, *Occupied America*, 3/e. Jimmy Centeno, "The Gentrification of LA: Fight on Boyle Heights," *Counterpunch*, August 21, 2017, https://www.counterpunch.org/2017/08/21/the-gentrification-of-la-fight-on-boyle-heights/.
20. Lydia Avila-Hernández, "Grassroots Community Action and Accountable Development," Urban Environmental Policy, Occidental Colleges, 2007.
21. Rodolfo F. Acuña, "Political Graffiti Part IV Historical Truth Matters Normalistas: 'Mexico Is a Mass Grave'" *WordPress*, November 1, 2014, http://rudyacuna.net/political-graffiti-part-iv-historical-truth-matters-normalistas-mexico-is-a-mass-grave-by-rodolfo-f-acuna/.
22. Lorena Ojeda, "Not everyone mourns for Ayotzinapa's students," *The Berkeley Blog*, Nov. 4, 2014, http://blogs.berkeley.edu/2014/11/04/not-everyone-mourns-for-ayotzinapas-students/. Rodolfo Acuña, "'There will be no change': Debunking the Illusion," *WordPress*, Nov. 19, 2014, http://rudyacuna.net/there-will-be-no-change-debunking-the-illusion-by-rodolfo-acuna-11-19-14.
23. Berry, *Mexico*, 79; Reimundo Reynoso, "Mexico anuncia medida para protegar a mexicanos que viven en

24 Estados Unidos," *La Opinion*, Feb. 22, 1992; Jorge G. Castafieda, "Again, People Are Mexico's No. 1 Export," *Los Angeles Times* (March 24, 1992).
24 Richard Boudreaux, "Mexicans Favor Trade Pact," *Los Angeles Times* (Oct. 22, 1991). Berry, *Mexico*, 96: one-sixth of Mexicans in poverty are concentrated in the states of Hidalgo, Oaxaca, Chiapas, and Guerrero.
25 Sebastian Rotella, "Mexico to Send Back Chinese Held at Sea1," *Los Angeles Times* (July 15, 1993). "Oposicion mexicana acusa al Gobiemo de ceder ante EU1," *La Opinion*, June 20, 1992. After the NAFTA negotiations got underway, accusations were made by Central Americans that the Mexican government was cracking down on refugees, a charge denied by Mexican officials. In 1993, some 130,000 Central Americans were ejected from Mexico. Many of them had been stranded on their way to the United States and were reduced to working in brothels in border towns such as Tecun Uman.
26 David Bacon, "US-Style School Reform Goes South," *The Nation*, March 12, 2013, http://www.thenation.com/article/us-style-school-reform-goes-south/.
27 Guillermo Ferrer, *Educational Assessment Systems in Latin America:Current Practice and Future Challenges* (Washington, DC: PREAL, 2006). http://siteresources.worldbank.org/INTINDIA/4371432-1194542322423/21542197/LatinAmericanAssessmentSystems.pdf The acknowledgements: "generous support of the U.S. Agency for International Development, the Inter-American Development Bank, the Tinker Foundation, the International Association for the Evaluation of Educational Achievement, the World Bank, the GE Foundation, and others."
28 "Mexico's President Pena Nieto defends education reform," BBC, September 2, 2013, http://www.bbc.com/news/world-latin-america-23937171.
29 Rodolfo F. Acuña, "¡Tierra y Libertad! Does History Matter?" *LA Progressive*, November 30, 2013, https://www.laprogressive.com/history-of-privatization-in-america/. "Why do Mexicans get so worked up about their oil?" *The Economist*, Nov. 28, 2013, http://www.economist.com/node/21590776/comments. David Agren, "Mexico opens up petroleum business to private and foreign companies," *USA Today* (Dec. 20, 2013), https://www.usatoday.com/story/news/world/2013/12/20/mexico-petroleum-oil-foreign/4152521/.
30 NAFTA has been renegotiated. It is too early to tell what the outcome will be.
31 "Clinton pide perdón a México por la guerra contra el narco que se desató en su mandato," *Sin Embargo*, February 6, 2015, http://www.sinembargo.mx/06-02-2015/1242709. Rodolfo F. Acuña, "The Zapatistas were right! The Silence of the Lambs," *LA Progressive*, Feb. 8, 2015, https://www.laprogressive.com/zapatistas-protest/.
32 Mexico Political Update, January 13, 1995, Chase Manhattan's Emerging Markets Group Memo, by Riordan Roett in "The Financial Connection," National Commission for Democracy in Mexico, http://www.criscenzo.com/jaguarsun/chiapas/corp1.html. "In the Belly of the Beast—Part III NAFTA and the Zapatista Uprising [the early and mid 1990s]," *Gloves Off*, http://www.glovesoff.org/features/gjamerica_3.html.
33 "Mexico Under Siege: The Drug War at Our Door Steps," *Los Angeles Times*, http://projects.latimes.com/mexico-drug-war/#/its-a-war. "The 'War on Drugs' is a joke (part 1)," http://www.youtube.com/watch?v=4cefoV_A878. The Global Addiction—40 minutes documentary, http://www.youtube.com/watch?v=6SOvTdpQJwo&feature=related. "War on drugs and Mexico's demise," http://www.youtube.com/watch?v=Yj7LKauVzro.
34 Chen, Michelle, "Fit for Citizenship?: The Eugenics Movement and Immigration Policy," *Dissent*, 2015, Vol.62(2), 74. Paul Lombardo,, "Eugenic Laws Against Race Mixing," *Eugenics Archives*, https://www.google.com/search?q=madison+grant+intermarriage&ie=utf-8&oe=utf-8&client=firefox-b-1.
35 "European history has been written in terms of nationality and of language, but never before in terms of race; yet race has played a far larger part than either language or nationality in molding the destinies of men; race implies heredity and heredity implies all the moral, social and intellectual characteristics and traits which are the springs of politics and government," Madison Grant, *The Passing of the Great Race: or The Racial Basis of European History* 4th ed., (New York: Charles Scribner's Sons, 1936), vii.
36 Chen, Ibid., p. 73.
37 Eugenics Archives, *Buck vs. Bell* Trial, http://www.eugenicsarchive.org/html/eugenics/static/themes/39.html. Jarmila Rajas, "Disciplining the human rights of immigrants: market veridiction and the echoes of eugenics in contemporary EU immigration policies," *Journal Third World Quarterly*, Vol. 36, 2015, 1131. "Virginia," Eugenics Archives, https://www.uvm.edu/~lkaelber/eugenics/VA/VA.html.
38 Gregory M. Dorr, "Defective or Disabled? Race, Medicine, and Eugenics in Progressive Era Virginia and Alabama," *Journal of the Gilded Age and Progressive Era* 5, 4 (2006), 384.
39 Rajas, Ibid., p. 1137.
40 Rajas, Ibid., pp. 1138–141.

41 Richard J. Herrnstein, Charles Murray, *The Bell Curve: Intelligence and Class Structure in American Life* (New York: Free Press, 1996).

42 Ishmael Reed, "2013: My Top Stories," *Counterpunch*, February 7, 2014, https://www.vox.com/2018/4/30/17302140/caravan-border-illegal-asylum-trump.

43 Beatrice Dupuy, "White Supremacists Killed 18 People in 2017, Double the Number From 2016, New Report Finds," *Newsweek*, Jan. 17, 2018. http://www.newsweek.com/white-supremacists-killed-2017-extremist-783638.

44 Ibid.

45 Ibid.

46 Rosie Gray, "Trump Defends White-Nationalist Protesters: 'Some Very Fine People on Both Sides'," *The Atlantic*, Aug. 15, 2017, https://www.theatlantic.com/politics/archive/2017/08/trump-defends-white-nationalist-protesters-some-very-fine-people-on-both-sides/537012/.

47 Evan Osnos, "The Fearful and the Frustrated Donald Trump's nationalist coalition takes shape—for now," *New Yorker*, August 31, 2015, https://www.newyorker.com/magazine/2015/08/31/the-fearful-and-the-frustrated.

48 Washington Post Staff. "Full text: Donald Trump announces a presidential bid," *Washington Post*, June 16, 2015, https://www.washingtonpost.com/news/post-politics/wp/2015/06/16/full-text-donald-trump-announces-a-presidential-bid/?utm_term=.24bd59890db2.

49 Richard J. Herrnstein (Author), Charles Murray, *The Bell Curve: Intelligence and Class Structure in American Life* (New York: Free Press, 1996).

50 Eric Turkheimer, Kathryn Paige Harden, and Richard E. Nisbett, "There's still no good reason to believe black-white IQ differences are due to genes," *Vox*, June 17, 2017, https://www.vox.com/the-big-idea/2017/6/15/15797120/race-black-white-iq-response-critics.

51 Nate Silver, "Education, Not Income, Predicted Who Would Vote For Trump," ABC, Nov. 22, 2016, https://fivethirtyeight.com/features/education-not-income-predicted-who-would-vote-for-trump/?fbclid=IwAR0Lc2KnMuBLtdfou68QjJXCj9A2THldXnzsxdn7f9RLhLPdbgDfE6Or5Ek.

52 Dominique Mosbergen, "Undocumented Housekeeper At Trump Golf Course Says She Does Not Regret Going Public," *HuffPost*, Dec. 9, 2018, https://www.huffingtonpost.com/entry/victorina-morales-trump-golf-club-undocumented_us_5c0d2f72e4b035a7bf5c0e27.

53 Josh Sanburn, "More White People Are Dying Than Are Being Born in 17 States," *Time*, November 29, 2016.

54 Mellissa Hellmann, "U.S. Health Care Ranked Worst in the Developed World 2014," *Time Magazine*, June 17, 2014, http://time.com/2888403/u-s-health-care-ranked-worst-in-the-developed-world. Josh Sanburn, "More White People Are Dying Than Are Being Born in 17 States," *Time*, November 29, 2016.

55 Excerpt from: Michael Harrington, *The Other America* (1962), http://www-personal.umd.umich.edu/~ppennock/doc-OtherAmerica.htm.

56 Rodolfo Acuña, "Bread and Circuses: On the Inequality of Sports," *Counterpunch*, August 10, 2015, https://www.counterpunch.org/2015/08/10/bread-and-circuses-on-the-inequality-of-sports/. Francisco Goldman, "Fooling Mexican Fans," *New York Times*, June 22, 2014, https://www.nytimes.com/2014/06/23/opinion/fooling-mexican-fans.html.

57 David Barstow, Susanne Craig, and Russ Buettner, "Trump Engaged in Suspect Tax Schemes as He Reaped Riches From His Father," *New York Times* (Oct. 2, 2018), https://www.nytimes.com/interactive/2018/10/02/us/politics/donald-trump-tax-schemes-fred-trump.html. Russ Buettner and Susanne Craig, "As the Trumps Dodged Taxes, Their Tenants Paid a Price," *New York Times*, Dec. 15, 2018. https://www.nytimes.com/2018/12/15/us/politics/trump-tenants-taxes.html

58 George Zarkadakis, "Will a Robot Replace You?," *HuffPost*, Nov. 8, 2016, https://www.huffingtonpost.com/george-zarkadakis/will-a-robot-replace-you_b_8506324.html.

59 Joel Bleifuss, "Yes, Voter Suppression Is Real. But Young Voters May Bridge the Gap," *In These Times*, October 29, 2018. Sam Levine, "More Evidence Of Illegal Activity Emerges In North Carolina Congressional Race," *HuffPost*, Dec. 7, 2018, https://www.huffingtonpost.com/entry/north-carolina-election-investigation_us_5c0aff86e4b0a606a9a8bb49?fbclid=IwAR0IE4jBXqr6NGyqn3Tmm-mhL1Fadc0HVos4gmf3E1Efx2W4R3jOZnzhe0M.

60 Ramsey Touchberry, "If Trump Obtained Presidency by Fraud he Should be Treated as he Treats Illegal Immigrants, Former Prosecutor Says." *Newsweek*, Dec. 12, 2018, https://www.newsweek.com/trump-possibly-procured-presidency-fraud-prosecutor-1250940?fbclid=IwAR3ljX-5DQcMkWZpM21HiYiS6z17o-gdPZBOxkcTAMkdQDJuUpY-mEoolp8.

61 Seaton et al., Ibid.

Index

A

Aboites, Luis, 164
Abortion, 211, 334, 336
Acosta, Salvador, 117
ACPFB. *See* American Committee for Protection of Foreign-Born (ACPFB)
Act for Government and Protection of Indians (California), 135
Acuña, Rodolfo F., 388–389
Adams, John Quincy, 46
Adams-Onís Treaty (1819), 46
Adams, Sam, 46, 47
Affirmative action, 333, 342, 343
AFL. *See* American Federation of Labor (AFL)
African Americans, 80, 281
  Black–White syndrome, 297–298
  in California, 170, 246
  civil rights movement, 291
  competition with Mexicans, 73
  fugitive slaves, 70
  lynching of, 71
Afromestizos, 114
Agribusiness, in California, 162, 195, 212, 254–255
Agricultural Labor Relations Board (ALRB), 336, 364
Agricultural Workers Industrial League (AWIL), 214, 219
Agricultural Workers Organizing Committee (AWOC), 300, 336
Agricultural Workers Union (AWU), 220
Agriculture. *See also* Cotton growers
  in Arizona, 123–124, 213
  of Aztecs, 9
  of Corn People, 3
  El Monte strike, 215
  farm workers' revolts, 214
  Great Depression and, 212
  of Hohokams, 11
  industrialization of, 162
  of Mayans, 4, 6
  in Midwest, 257
  in New Mexico, 95, 103
  sugar-beet industry, 100, 161, 163, 166, 171, 193–194, 219–220
  in Texas, 73, 79, 80
  undocumented immigrants, 363
  unions, 195–197
La Agrupación Protectora Mexicana (Mexican Protective Association), 167
Aguilar, Marcos, 371, 388
Aguírre, Lauro, 81, 82, 159, 161
AIDS programs, 369
Alamillo, José, 209
Alamo myth, 48, 69
Alatorre, Richard, 304, 407
Alatorre, Soledad "Cole," 300
Alberdi, Juan Bautista, 354
Albert, Margo, 254
Albuquerque Walkout (New Mexico, 1966), 296–697
Alemany, Joseph Sadoc, 144
Alexander, Pope VI (1493), 240–241
Alfaro, Rubén, 302
La Alianza Federal de Mercedes, 309
La Alianza Hispano Americana (Hispanic American Alliance), 103, 122, 167, 194, 279, 280, 291
Alien Labor Law, 168, 208
Alinsky, Saul, 253, 275, 276
Allende, Salvador, 344
All in the Family (TV series), 330
Almonte, Juan H., 47
al-Qaeda, 404
Alta California, 12, 34–35, 131
Alvarado, Juan Bautista, 138
Alvárez, Manuel, 92
Amabisca, Felipe, 117
Amalgamated Clothing Workers Union of America (ACWUA), 337
Amat, Taddeus, 144
"Amazons" protest (Carmelita Torres story), 169
American Civil Liberties Union (ACLU), 270, 271, 276, 280, 343, 362, 385
American Committee for Protection of Foreign-Born (ACPFB), 270, 300
American Council of Spanish-Speaking People, 276, 279–281
American Council of Spanish-Speaking People (ACSSP), 276
American Dream, 74, 102, 341, 358, 381, 418–419. *See also* Dream Act
American Empire, 403–423
American Farm Bureau Federation, 196
American Federation of Labor (AFL), 218, 223, 251. *See also* Congress of Industrial Organizations
  deportations (1930s), 211
  Oxnard strike (1903), 163
  racism in, 171
  United Farm Workers Organizing Committee (UFWOC), 301
American G.I. Forum, 252–253, 275, 278, 279, 294, 296, 297, 300, 303, 340, 366
American Immigration Control Foundation (AICF), 358
American Indian Movement (AIM), 310
Americanization, 185–187
  American Peace Society, 53
  vs. nationalism, 186–187
  Protestant churches and, 186, 226
  in Tucson, 117–118
American Protective Association, 122

American Recovery and Reinvestment Act of 2009, 416
The American Southwest (Perrigo), 56
Among the Valiant (Morín), 241, 242
Anasazi civilization, 11
Anders, Evan, 79
Angels with Dirty Faces (film, 1938), 245
Anguiano, Lupe, 297, 305
ANMA. *See Asociación Nacional México-Americana* (ANMA)
Anzaldúa, Gloria, 389
Apache people, 12, 69, 81, 90, 91, 115
  enslavement of, 114
  wars, in Arizona, 118
Arab–Israeli War, 343
Árbenz, Jacobo, 270
Archuleta, Diego, 92
Archuleta, Guadalupe, 101
Are We Good Neighbors? (Perales), 254
Arizona (invasion of Sonora)
  agriculture in, 213
  conquest
    border conflicts, 120
    filibustering expeditions, 115–116
    race war, 116–117
  economics
    adobe to copper, 119–120
    emergence of trade unions, 123
    mining industry, 115, 119–121, 160–161, 168–169, 224, 249
    mutual aid societies, 122
    railroad, impact on, 118, 120, 121, 123
    transformation, 119–120
    water resources, 123–124
  Mexican population in, 158
  socialization
    Americanization in Tucson, 117–118
    intermarriage, 117–118
    middle class society (Mexicans), 122
  USS St. Mary, 115
  war against Apache, 118
Arizona Cotton Growers Association (ACGA), 193

Arizona Rangers, 123, 161
Armed forces, Latinos in
  World War I, 170
  World War II, 241–244
Armendaris, Alex, 331
Armijo, Manuel, 92
Asian peoples, 183, 299
Asociación Nacional México-Americana (ANMA), 254, 270–272, 280
Association of the Brotherhood for the Protection of the Rights and Privileges of the People of New Mexico, 101
Astor, Avi, 272
Austin, Moses, 46
Austin, Stephen, 46, 47
Avila, Leo, 243
Avila, Modesta, 145
Avitia, Manuel, 224
AWOC. *See* Agricultural Workers Organizing Committee (AWOC)
Axtell, Samuel B., 97
Ayres, Ed Durán, 245–246
Azteca, 8–10, 13

B

Baby boomers, 251–252, 291, 293, 328–330
Baca, Cruz, 159
Baca, Herman, 339
Baca, Onofrio, 74
Baca, Polly, 305
Bailey, Cleveland M., 255
Bakke v. University of California (1976), 330
Bakunin, Mikhail, 159
Bancroft, Hubert Howe, 93, 115
Bandini, Arcadia, 138
Banking, 121, 134
Bankrupting, 404–405
Barela, Francisco "Chico," 77
Barker, Eugene C., 47, 48
Barkley, David, 187
Barrera, John, 78
Barrera, Juan de la, 55
Barrio clubs (gangs), 210–211, 244, 246–248
Barrios (Mexican neighborhoods), 143, 192, 210–211, 228, 273, 274, 295, 297–298
  struggle to preserve, 281–283, 293

Barry, R. C., 138
Bartlett, John Russell, 94
Bass, Carlotta, 246
Batista y Zaldívar, Fulgencio, 283
Bear Flag, of California, 133–134
Beaubien, Charles, 96
Beauvoir, Simone de, 381
Beers, George A., 142
Belden, Sam, 70
The Bell Curve: Intelligence and Class Structure in American Life (1994), 390
Bell, Horace, 137, 142
Beltrán, Pete, 336
Benavides, José Luis, 139, 141
Bent, Charles, 91, 92
Bernal, Joe, 304, 306
Berreyesa, Encarnación, 140
Berreyesa, José S., 140
Berriozábal, María Antonietta, 369
Betancourt, Sóstenes, 145
Biden, Joe, 415
Bilingual education, 167, 276, 297–298, 341
Bilingual Education Act, 341
Billy the Kid (William Bonnie), 97
BIP. *See* Border Industrialization Program (BIP)
Bird, Rose, 358
Bisbee Daily Review (newspaper), 160, 161
Black Civil Rights, 291
Blade Runner (science fiction film, 1982), 354
Blanton, Carlos K., 276
Bliss, George R., 208
Bloody Christmas case, 280
Bonanzas, mining, 120, 160
Bonilla brothers, 294
Bonilla, Rubén, 340
Bonilla, Tony, 410
Bonzo, Vivian, 371
Border Industrialization Program (BIP), 299, 337. *See also Maquiladoras* (assembly plants)
Border militarization, 164, 165
Border Protection, Anti-terrorism, and Illegal Immigration Control Act of 2005, 414

Borrajo, Antonio, 77
Boss Rule in South Texas (Anders), 79
Botiller v. Dominguez (1889), 144
Boundary Commission, 74
Bouvier, Virginia Marie, 133
The Bowery Boys, 245
Bowie, James, 48
Bowron, Fletcher, 247
Boxer, Barbara, 418
Box, John Calvin, 184, 211
Braceros (guest workers), 250, 255–257, 275, 299, 393
Bradford, David Paul, 359
Brahan, R. W., Jr., 76
Brent, Joseph Lancaster, 138
Brichta, Bernábe, 167
Bridges, Harry, 270
Briggs, Vernon M., Jr., 339
Briones de Miranda, Juana, 133
Brooks, Homer, 222
Brown Berets, 304–307, 314–316
Brown, Edmund G., 295, 301, 364
Brownell, Herbert, 272
Brown, Jerry, 418
Brown mafia, Nixon and, 331
Brown power, 302–312
Brownrig, Cora, 136
Brownsville, Texas, 70, 71
Brown v. Board of Education (1954), 252, 279, 342
Broyles-González, Yolanda, 389
Buchanan, James, 55, 72, 115
Bunker, Archie *(All in the Family)*, 330
Burns, Hugh M., 255
Bush, George H. W., 357, 364, 390, 394, 404, 408, 409, 416
Bustamante, Cruz M., 382, 410
Butler, Anthony, 47

C

Cabajal, José Maria, 74
Cabrera, Tomás, 72
Caddo confederacies, 12, 49
Cáhita people, 13
Calhoun, James S., 93
Calhoun, John C., 52
California
  Alien Labor Law (1931), 208
  ballot propositions, 336
  conquest
    acquisition of land, 136–139, 142
    U.S. invasion (Bear Flag), 133–134
  economics
    agribusiness in, 162, 195, 212
    foreign miners' tax (legalized theft), 135–136
    Gold Rush, 134–136
    political demographic data, 145
    railroad, impact on, 137, 143
    taxation without representation, 137–138
    violence (legitimization), 137–138
  electoral politics, 409–413
  Indian tribes, 131, 135, 144
  Indigenas tribes, 35
  interracial marriage, 248
  regional differences, 360–370
  resistance
    Clamor Público (newspaper), 139–140
    farmworker activism, 214, 301
    Oxnard protests (1903), 163
    social banditry, 141–143
    unions, 196, 255
  socialization
    class divisions, 132–133, 140–141
    intermarriage, 133
    Mexican, 143–145
    missions, 35, 130–131
  Treaty of Cahuenga, 134
  U.S. attitudes *vs.* Berlin Wall/Mexican border, 358–360
California Community Colleges (CCCs), 359
California Congressman Elton Gallegly (R–Simi Valley), 358
California Department of Education, 305, 341
California Federation of Labor (CFL), 255
California Gold Rush and, 134
California Land Act of 1851, 136
California Representative Anthony Bielenson (D–San Fernando Valley), 358
California Rural Legal Assistance (CRLA), 313
Californios, 131, 135–141, 143, 144
Callaghan, Bryan V., Jr., 78
Calvillo, Ignacio, 122
Camino Real, 91
Campa, Arthur L., 225, 226, 258
Campbell, Julie A., 248
Campbell, Tom, 167
Campos, Francisco, 159
Campos, Victor, 224
Canales, J. T., 79, 167, 188
Cannery and Agricultural Workers Industrial Union (C&AWIU), 215, 217
Cannibalism, 114
Cannon, Fred, 138
Cantúa, Gabriela, 161
Cantú, Antonia, 187
Cantwell, John J., 186
CAPA (Committee Against Police Abuse), 343
Capitalism, industrial, 79, 121
CARCEN. *See* Central American Resource Center (CARCEN)
Cárdenas, Juan, 74
Cárdenas Martínez, León, 164
Cardis, Louis, 77
Carranza, Venustiano, 170
Carrigan, William D., 71, 116, 134, 136
Carrillo, Jesús, 120
Carrillo, José A., 135
Carter, Jimmy, 284, 339, 344
CASA. *See Centro de Acción Social Autónoma*
Casa Carnalismo, 338
Casas Grandes, 12
La Casita Farms Corporation strike, 301–303
Castañeda, Antonia I., 35, 133, 389
Castañeda, Carlos E., 46, 47, 225, 249–250
Castellón, Aureliano, 81
Castillo, Virginia, 364
Castro, Fidel, 283
Castro, Raúl, 340–341
Castro, Rosie, 303
Castro, Sal, 305
Catalán, Magín, 145

Catholic Church, 192, 222, 300
  abortion and, 336
  American, 98
  Americanization of, 186
  in California, 144
  Chicano movement and, 312–315
  cristero revolt (1920s), 193
  and Great Depression, 209, 211
  Holy Brotherhood of Penitentes, 98
  interracial marriage, 248
  Liberation Theology and, 312
  military intervention (Mexican Revolution), 165
  in New Mexico, 94, 98
Catholic Youth Organization (CYO), 209, 226
Católicos Por La Raza (CPLR), 312
Catron, Thomas B., 96, 97
Cattle ranching, 79, 94, 96, 97, 119, 136, 143
La Causa (newspaper), 307
Cavazos family, 70
C&AWIU. *See* Cannery and Agricultural Workers Industrial Union (C&AWIU)
Cedillo, Gilbert, 415
Census. *See* U.S. Census
Central American Resource Center (CARCEN), 384
Central Americans, 14, 57
Central Intelligence Agency (CIA), 270, 332
Central Labor Union, 171
Centro de Acción Social Autónoma (CASA), 300, 339, 362
  Hermandad Mexicana, 338
Centro de Acción Social Autónoma–Hermandad General de Trabajadores (CASA-HGT), 337–338
Cerda, Ramón De La, 75
Chacón, Alicia, 370
Chamberlain, Samuel E., 54
Chambers, Pat, 215, 217
Chamizal Treaty (1967), 297
Chaucer, Geoffrey, 381
Chávez, César, 296, 297, 300–302, 304, 336, 339, 362, 364, 384
Chávez, Dennis, 227, 249, 276, 281

Chávez, Isabel Rodríguez, 338
Chávez Ravine, 277, 282–283
Chávez, Tibo J., 281
Chemerinsky, Erwin, 421
Chiapas, 3, 4, 7
Chicago
  abuses (post-World War II effects), 183
  Congress of Industrial Organizations (CIO), 218
  gentrification, 295
  Haymarket Square Riot, 159
  Industrial Areas Foundation (IAF), 276
  Mexican-origin population, 366–367
  Mexicans in, 191–193, 195, 223–224, 228, 268, 275
  railroad laborers, 195
  steel strike (1937), 223
Chicana/o Studies, 334–336, 386–387
  fight for identity, 388
  fight for truth, 388–389
  renaissance in thought and arts, 389–390
  war on drugs, 394–395
Chicano Council on Higher Education (CCHE), 312
Chicano Liberation Front (CLF), 316
Chicano Manifesto (Rendón), 56
Chicano movement, 225, 300, 333, 362. *See also* Chicano Youth Movement
  gender inequality, 333
  labor unions, 336
  Marxism in, 335
  middle class and, 335, 340
  political power, 340–341
Chicanos
  in Chicago, 228
  fighting segregation, 227
Chicano Youth Movement, 312–316, 335
  Brown Berets, 304–307, 314–316
  Catholic clergy and, 312
  school walkouts, 305–306, 335
  under siege, 314–315
Chichimeca, 8
Chinampas (Aztec agriculture), 9

Chinese Exclusion Act of 1882, 144, 145, 158
Chinese laborers, 144, 157
CHIRLA. *See* Coalition for Humane Immigrant Rights of Los Angeles (CHIRLA)
Chisum, John H., 97
Chumash Indians, 131
CIA. *See* Central Intelligence Agency (CIA)
CIO. *See* Congress of Industrial Organizations (CIO)
Cisneros, Henry, 366
Cisneros v. Corpus Christi Independent School District (1970), 298
Civilian Conservation Corps, 207
Civilization. *See also* Mayan civilization
  Azteca, 8–10
  Corn People, 2–3
  Los Norteños, 10–13
  Olmeca (1500–500 bc), 3–4
  Tarasco, 8
  Teotihuacán, 6–7
  Tolteca, 7
  trade and urbanism, 6–7
  Zapoteca, 7–8
Civil Practice Act of 1850, 137
Civil rights, 278–281, 298
  agenda (World War II), 252, 291
  coalition building, 296–297
  in education, 279
  organizations of (Mexican American), 188
  Salt of the Earth strike, 278–279
  toward equality, 278–279
Civil Rights Act of 1964, 341, 342
Civil Rights Commission, 341
Civil Rights Congress, 270
Civil Rights Voting Act, 415
Civil War, 72–73
  in Arizona, 116
  in New Mexico, 95, 99
  in Texas, 69
El Clamor Público (newspaper), 139–141
Clark, Mark, 242, 243
Clark, Victor, 162

Class divisions. *See also* Middle class
  in Azteca society, 9
  in California, 132–133, 140–141
  in Mayan society, 6
  in Mexican American community, 187
Clifton-Morenci-Metcalf mining camps, 160, 161, 169
Clinton, Bill, 355, 383, 391, 394, 395
Clinton, Hillary, 412, 416
Cluff, William D., 280
Coalition for Humane Immigrant Rights of Los Angeles (CHIRLA), 369, 384–385
Coffee, John Donelson, Jr., 76
Colby, William, 358
Cold War, 250–251, 269–270
  Immigration and Naturalization Service (INS), 271, 272
Colombo, Frank, 160, 161
Colonization of New Mexico
  conquest
    the American invasion, 92–94
    gringo go home, 92
    racial attitudes of New Mexicans, 93–94
  economics
    growth of industrial mining, 102–103
    mining industry (Colorado), 100
    railroad, impact on, 99
    trade policies, 89, 94
    transition, 94
  political control
    decline of Santa Fe Ring, 102–103
    federal encroachment, 103
    Gringos and Ricos, 95
    Santa Fe Ring and land grab, 95
  resistance
    land grabbers, and fencing, 100–101
    Lincoln County War, 97
    village defense strategies, 101–102
  socialization
    American, Catholic Church, 98
    New Mexican diaspora, 99
    women in marketplace, 99
Colonization of Texas, 33–34
  conquest
    between 1836 and 1845, 68–69
    "Cheno" Cortina, 71–72, 74, 75
    Civil War, 71–73
    controlling Northwest border, 69–70
    Mexican corridor, 70–73
    Mexicans in Texas, 79–80
    trade wars, 71
  economics
    commercialization of agriculture, 79, 80
    El Paso del Norte, 33–34
    military and U.S. merchants, 73
    racist nativism, 80–81
    railroad, impact on, 79
  political control
    gender discrimination, 76
    post-Civil War period, 78
    racism, 74, 76
    Ranger's activities, 74, 75, 77–79
    United States, 69, 71, 74
  resistance
    anti-Díaz movement, 82
    Gregorio Cortez (social bandit), 77–78
    people's revolt, 77
    San Antonio, importance of, 34
    Tlaxcala and castas, 34
Colorado
  American Federation of Labor (AFL), 196
  Community Service Club, 281
  Coors Brewing company, 340
  Gonzales, Isabel (activist), 228
  immigrants, 158, 273
  Ludlow Massacre (1913), 168
  Manitos, 219–220
  Maxwell land grant, 97
  Mexicans and Mexican Americans, 194
  mining, 99, 100, 102, 157
  racial divide, 120
  sugar-beet companies, 100, 103, 193–194, 219–220
  worker societies, 103, 193
Committee Against Police Abuse (CAPA) v. LAPD, 343
Communism, 224, 246, 250, 251, 269, 270, 357
Communist Party, 214, 217, 219, 222, 224, 226, 267, 269, 271, 277, 279, 356
Communitarianism, 417
Communities Organized for Public Service (COPS), 366
Community, forging, 189
Community Service Organization (CSO), 252–254, 270, 271, 276, 277, 296, 300
Company E (All-Mexican unit), 242–243, 269
Comprehensive Employment and Training Act (CETA), 331
Comprehensive Immigration Reform Act of 2006, 412
Concilio Manzo, 339
Confederación de Uniónes de Campesinos y Obreros Mexicanos (CUCOM), 196, 218
Confederación de Uniónes Mexicanas, 218
Confederación Regional Orbrera Mexicana (CROM), 196
El Congreso de los Pueblos de Habla Expañol, 226–227
El Congreso del Pueblo de Habla Española, 251
Congress of Industrial Organizations (CIO), 218, 221, 223, 250, 251
Connally, John, 294, 301
Contreras, Antonio, 117
Coolidge, Calvin, 183, 211
Cooperative Society of Unemployed Mexican Ladies, 210
Coors, Joseph, 390
Copper mines, 119, 121, 160–161, 164, 168–169, 224
COPS. *See* Communities Organized for Public Service (COPS)
Cordena, José María, 74

Córdova, Vicente, 69, 70
Corn People
　GMOs and, 3
　history of origin, 2–3
　Los Norteños, 11
Corona, Bert, 223, 296, 300, 339
Coronel, Antonio, 138
El Correo Mexicano (newspaper), 192
Corridos (ballads), 75, 209
Cortes, Hernán, 5
Cortés, Manuel, 93
Cortez, Frank, 214
Cortez, Gregorio, 77–78, 167
Cortina, Juan "Cheno," 71–72, 74, 75, 78, 82
Corwin, Arthur, 338
Corwin, Tom, 52
Cossley-Batt, Jill L., 141–142
Cota Robles, Amado, 167
Cotton growers
　Arizona, 123, 172, 193, 218
　California, 254
　Mexico (Matamoros), 272
　San Joaquin Valley Cotton Strike, 216–217
　Texas, 47, 72, 73, 79–80, 172, 213, 257
Council for Mexican American Affairs, 277
Council of Conservative Citizens, 358
Crabb, Henry, 115
Crescion Rejon, Manuel, 56
Criminalization (undocumented worker), 338–339
La Crisis. *See* Great Depression (1930s)
Crockett, Davy, 48, 49
La CrÓnica (newspaper), 139, 166
Cruz, A. C., 161
La Cruz Azul (Blue Cross), 194, 210
Cruz, Guillermo, 69
CSO. *See* Community Service Organization (CSO)
Cuba
　Platt Amendment and, 155
　Revolution in, 283
CUCOM. *See* Confederación de Uniónes de Campesinos y Obreros Mexicanos (CUCOM)

Cuenca, Laura Méndez de, 160
Culture
　in Aztec civilization, 9, 10
　in Mayan civilization, 4, 7
　popular, in 1930s, 209, 210
Cycles of Conquest (Spicer), 12

D

Daley, Richard, 293, 295
Daniel, Pancho, 140
D'Avila, Defino, 217
Davis, Grace Montañez, 277
Davis, Gray, 410
Davis, James J., 184
Davis, Sylvester, 248
The Dead End (film, 1937), 245
Decker, Caroline, 217
The Decolonial Imaginary: Writing Chicanas into History, 389
Decolonization, 387
De la Guerra, José Noriega, 144
Delgado, Antonio, 71
Delgado, Manuel, 254
Delgado v. Bastrop ISD (1948), 252, 276, 279
Democracy, 404
Democratic Party, 79, 141, 272, 274, 294, 295, 365, 366, 368, 382
Denver Post (newspaper), 183
de Olmo, Frank, 358
Deportation, 183, 193, 196, 251, 271, 369
　fate of deportee in Mexico, 212–213
　Great Depression and, 211–213, 219, 241, 248
　Mexican-quota bill, 211
Desert Land Act (1887), 119
Detroit, Michigan, 193, 273, 283
Deukmejian, George, 368
Deutsch, Sarah, 95, 183
Diaspora
　American Odyssey, 273–275
　Mexican, 162
　New Mexican, 99
Díaz, Enriqueta, 370
Díaz, José, 245, 246
Díaz, Porfirio
　dictatorship of, 81, 158
　feminist critiques of, 159
　Mexican resistance, 81, 158–159, 161
　supporters of, 165, 167

Diego, San, 359
Di Giorgio Corporation, 254–255, 300, 301
Di Giorgio, Joseph, 255
Di Giorgio, Robert, 300
Dingley Tariff of 1897, 100, 162
Disease
　decline, Mayan civilization, 6
　detention cause, 212
　in early California, 131–132, 143
　in Los Angeles, 191
　Teresa García Coronado's story, 209
　tuberculosis, 208, 211, 274
Dixon-Arnett Act (1971), 338
Doak, William N., 212
Dodgers (baseball team), 277, 282
Doniphan, Alexander W., 54, 92
Dos Amades, 54
Dream Act, 416
Drug trade, 394
DuBois, W. E. B., 188
Duerler, Gustave, 221
Dulles, John Foster, 270
Dunbar-Ortiz, Roxanne, 33
Dunn, W. M., 77
Durazo, María Elena, 362–363, 372
Durbin, Dick, 416

E

East Los Angeles
　educational equity in, 341
　school walkouts, 305
Economic Opportunity Act, 296
Economic Opportunity and Immigration Reform Act of 2007, 412
Economics
　Gold Rush, 94
　Santa Fe Trail, 91
　trade policies, 91, 94
Education, 268, 341–342
　Americanization of, 185, 210
　in Arizona, 116, 167
　bilingual, 167, 297–298, 341
　Catholic Church, 94, 98
　in Chicago, 223, 228
　civil rights agenda, 252
　cost of higher (public schools), 275

draft deferments, 270
elite resistance to (New Mexico), 103–104
equity in, 341–342
escuelas de burro, 211
escuelitas, 186
fighting for, 257–258
Literacy Act (1917), 207
Mexicans, 419–421
post-World War II opportunities, 251–252
in San Antonio, 274
U.S. Census, 276, 292
walkouts, 296–297, 305–306, 335
Educational Opportunity Program (EOP), 304, 335, 341
Edwards, Hayden, 46
Ehrenberg, Herman, 115
Eilberg, Joshua, 338
Eisenhower, Dwight, 267, 272
Ejercito Zapatista de Liberación Nacional (EZLN), 383–384
Elías, Arturo, 161
Elías, Eulalia, 118
Elkins, John T., 97
Elkins, Stephen B., 96, 97
Ellsworth, Luther E., 158
El Monte gang, 140
El Monte strike (1933), 215
El Paso, 91
  bilingual education, 297
  Brown Berets chapters, 307
  colonization of Texas, 33–34
  Company E, 242
  demographic data (Latinos), 228
  Gateway city, 292
  housing issues, 273
  Johnson cabinet hearings, 297
  LRUP convention, 331
  Mexican women in, 171
  Mexican worker strike in, 163, 337
  middle class in, 228
El Paso Evening Tribune (newspaper), 81
El Primer Congreso Mexicanista (First Mexican Congress), 166–167
El Salvador, 384, 417
"El Soldado Razo" (song), 242, 243

Emergency Quota Act of 1921, 183
Emerson, Ralph Waldo, 52
Environmental Impact Report (EIR), 368
EOP. *See* Educational Opportunity Program (EOP)
Equal Employment Opportunity Commission (EEOC), 296
Equia y Leronbe, Joseph Manuel, 114
Ernst, W. H., 221
Escobar, Edward, 280
Escobedo, Elizabeth Rachel, 248, 250
Escutia, Martha, 408
Esparza, Moctesuma, 304, 305
Espinosa, Fermina, 133
Esquivel, Rafaela Muñoz, 243
Estrada, Ralph, 279
The Ethics of Ambiguity (Beauvoir), 381
Eugenics, 211, 336
La Evolución (newspaper), 188
Ewell, R. S., 115

F
Fair Employment Practices Act, 252
Fair Employment Practices Commission (FEPC), 249–250, 277
Fair Labor Standards Act (1938), 222
Farabundo Martí Liberación Nacional (FMLN), 385
Farah strike (1972), 337
Farming. *See* Agriculture
Farm Labor Organizing Committee (FLOC), 302, 336
Farm Security Administration, 207, 255
Farm workers' revolts, 214–220, 301–302
FBI (Federal Bureau of Investigation), 246, 250, 251, 269, 277
Federal Housing Administration (FHA), 281
Federal Reclamation Act, 123

Federation for American Immigration Reform (FAIR), 358, 389
Federation of Mexican Societies, 196
Federation of Spanish-Speaking Voters, 225–226
FEPC. *See* Fair Employment Practices Commission (FEPC)
Fergusson, Minnie, 388
Fergusson, Minnie, 371
Ferraro, Richard, 365
Fierro de Bright, Josefina, 226, 251, 254
Filibustering, 115–116, 139
  in Texas, 46, 48, 50, 69
First Regional Conference on Education of the Spanish-Speaking People in the Southwest (1945), 258
Fishman, Joshua, 358
FLOC. *See* Farm Labor Organizing Committee (FLOC)
Flora Chapa, Manuel, 82
Flores, Feliciano G., 188
Flores, Juan, 140
Florida, Spanish colonization of, 46
Foley, Neil, 68
Food, Tobacco, Agricultural, and Allied Workers of America, 251
Ford, Rip, 72, 74, 75
Foreign born, defense of, 167, 270, 271, 338
Foreign Miners' Tax (California), 135–136, 138
Foster, Stephen C., 137
Fountain, Albert J., 77
Francis, Sam, 358
Franklin, Benjamin, 44
Free Workers' Society, 194, 223
Fremont, John C., 133–134
El Frente Popular (Popular Front), 223
Frente Sandinista de Liberación Nacional (FSLN), 356
Fricke, Charles W., 246
Friday the 13th (film, 1980), 357
Frieselle, S. Parker, 184
Frontier Protection Act of 1874, 74

Frost, Max, 96
Fuentes, Albert, 294, 295

G

Gabaldón, Guy, 242
La Gaceta (newspaper), 139
Gadsden, James, 115
Gadsden Treaty (1853), 94, 115
Gaines, Edmund Pendleton, 50
Galarza, Ernesto, 225, 226, 297
Gallegos family, 273
Gallegos, Guillermo, 254
Gallegos, Herman, 296
Gallegos, José Manuel, 94
Galván, Jeremiah, 72
Galván, Lucio, 301
Gamboa, Erasmo, 257
Gándara, Francisco, 116
García, Alex, 365
García, Arnoldo, 353
García, Cleotilde, 296
García Conde, Pedro, 94
García Coronado, Teresa, 209
García de Lama, Pedro, 82
García, Ernest L., 279
García, Estella, 300
García, Gustavo C., 276, 279
García, Hector, 294, 296, 304, 306, 308
García, Jesús, 367
García, Juan R., 210
García, Macario, 243
García, Mateo, 116
García, Mike, 363
García, Orlando, 370
García, Samuel Ruiz, 384
García, Valente, 81
Garment industry (women and girls), 171, 220–221
Garn–St. Germain Depository Institutions Act (1982), 360
Garrison, Homer, Jr., 254
Garza, Ben, 79
Garza, Catarino, 82, 159
Garza, Eligio de la "Kika," 340
Garza, María Luisa, 189
Garza, Reynaldo, 295
Gastélum, José, 271
Gates, Daryl, 362
Gender gap, 9, 221. *See also* Women
 race, in Texas, 76
General Motors (GM), 222

Genetically modified organisms (GMOs), 3
La Gente (newspaper), 387
Gentrification, in Chicago, 295
Gentrification, in San Francisco, 354
GGL. *See* Good Government League (GGL)
G.I. Bill, 258, 270, 274, 281
G.I. Forum. *See* American G.I. Forum
Gillespie, Archibald H., 133
Gillett, Charles L., 214
Gimpel, James G., 383
Glass–Steagall Act of 1932, 394, 415
Glavecke, Adolphus, 71
GMOs (genetically modified organisms), 3
Gold Rush, 94, 134–136
Goldwater, Barry, 298
Gómez, Laura, 93
Gompers, Samuel, 163, 169, 171, 172, 184
Gonzales, Corky, 331
Gonzales, Deena, 91, 95, 98
Gonzales, Isabel Malagram, 228, 270
Gonzales, Luisa M. De, 98
Gonzales, Mary Ann, 210
Gonzales, Nancie, 93
Gonzales, Rodolfo "Corky," 297, 303, 306, 339
Gonzales, Trinidad, 82
González, Henry B., 277, 294, 296, 304, 340, 383
González, Isabel (activist), 270–271
González, Manuel, 79
Good Government League (GGL), 277, 294, 366
Gore, Al, 404, 413
Gore v. Bush, 404
Gorras Blancas (White Caps), 101–102
Gortari, Carlos Salinas de, 383, 384, 395
Gramm-Leach-Bliley Act of 1999, 394
El Gran Círculo de Obreros de México, 159
Grant Camp Massacre (1871), 118

Grant, Ulysses S., 45, 51, 53
Gray, Paul Bryan, 141
Greaser Act (1855), 137
Great Depression (1930s), 241
 Arizona farms, 213
 California farms, 213–214
 El Monte strike, 215
 farmworkers' revolt, 214–220
 fate of deportees (in Mexico), 212–213
 Imperial valley during, 214, 217
 labor contractors, 214
 La Crisis, 208–209
 life during the great depression, 209–211
 Mexican strikes (1935), 218
 nativist deportations, 211–213
 New Deal, 207, 213, 250
 popular culture, 209
 repatriation (Texas-style), 212
 rural workers (Texas), 213, 219
 San Antonio and, 211
 San Joaquin valley cotton strike, 216–217
 Tagus Ranch, 215
 trading securities, 394
Great Society, 296, 299, 330
Grebler, Leo, 292
Green, Jerome T., 208
Green, Thomas Jefferson, 135
Gregg, Josiah, 91
Grijalva, Raúl M., 411
Griswold del Castillo, Richard, 137
El Grito Del Norte (newspaper), 310–311, 333
Grodin, Joseph, 358
Guadalupe Hidalgo Treaty (1848), 55–56, 80, 94, 99, 113
 California law and, 136–139, 208
Guatemala, 3, 4, 270, 384
Guerra family, 79
Guerra, Manuel, 79
Guerra, Ramón, 71
Guerrero, Práxedis, 161
Guerrero, Vicente, 45
Gutiérrez, Alfredo, 303
Gutiérrez, David G., 187, 218
Gutiérrez, José Angel, 251, 294, 302, 306, 340, 343, 361

Gutiérrez, Ramón, 32
Gutiérrez, Rita Cetina, 159
Guzmán, Joaquín Archivaldo, 417
Guzmán, Ralph, 272, 281
Gwinn, William, 136

H
Haas, Lisbeth, 132
Haciendas (estates), 90, 91
Halloween (film, 1978), 357
Hancock, Stanley, 217
Hanigan family, 339
Haro, Francisco, 134
Haro, Ramón de, 134
Harvard University, 343
Harvest of Shame (TV documentary), 293
Hatch, Orrin, 416
Hayes-Bautista, David, 143
Healy, Dorothy Ray, 217
Hell's Kitchen (film, 1939), 245
Helú, Carlos Slim, 383
Heritage Foundation, 340
Las Hermanas (Catholic organization), 313
La Hermandad Mexicana Nacional (Mexican National Brotherhood), 300, 338
Hermandad Mexicana Nacional organization, 358
Hermosillo, Xavier, 367
Hernández, Alejandro, 409
Hernández de Sánchez, Angeles, 212
Hernández, Dolores, 217
Hernández v. Texas (1954), 252, 279
Herrera, Juan José, 101, 102
Herrera, Pablo, 102
Herrnstein, Richard, 390
Hidalgo y Costilla, Miguel, 45
Hieroglyphs, in Mesoamerica, 4, 7
Las Hijas de Anáhuac, 159
Hijos de México (Sons of Mexico), 188
Hijos de Texas (Sons of Texas), 188
Hinojosa, Gilberto, 34
Hispanic (magazine), 364
Hispanic, as term, 340, 413
Hispanic Caucus, 341
Hobsbawm, E. J., 76–77

Hobson, J. A., 241
Hohokam civilization, 12, 114
Holladay Damico, Denise, 91, 99
Holy Brotherhood of Penitentes, 98
Homestead Act of 1862, 118, 137
Hoover, Herbert, 211, 390
Hoover, J. Edgar, 269
Hopwood v. Texas (1996), 390
Horne, Tom, 418, 420, 421
Horowitz, David, 419
Hotel Employees and Restaurant Employees Union (HERE), 363, 372
Housing Act (1949), 281
Houston, Sam, 46, 47, 49, 50, 115
Howard, Charles, 77
Hubbard, Richard B., 77
Huerta, Carmen, 159, 170
Huerta, Dolores, 300, 304
Huerta, Victoriano, 164, 165, 170
Hughes, John, Bishop, 144
Hull House (Chicago), 192, 228
Human rights violations, 271, 272, 384
Huntington, Henry E., 163
Huppenthal, John, 421

I
Idaho, Mexicans in, 194
Idar, Clemente N., 196
Idar, Jovita, 167
Idar, Nicasio, 166
ILGWU. *See* International Ladies Garment Workers Union (ILGWU)
Illegal alien, as term, 211
Illegal aliens, 385, 390
Illinois, death penalty in, 408
The Illusion of Inclusion, 366
IMF. *See* International Monetary Fund (IMF)
Immigration Act of 1924, 183, 184
Immigration Act of 1965, 299, 355, 356
Immigration Act of 1990, 385
Immigration and Naturalization Service (INS), 256, 271, 337, 385
  militarization of, 272–273
  Operation Clean Sweep, 338
Immigration Custom Enforcement, 409

Immigration reform, 412–413
Immigration Reform and Control Act (IRCA), 358, 372, 390, 392
el Imperio español, 22
Independent Progressive Party (IPP), 252, 270
Independent Workers Association, 301
Industrial Areas Foundation (IAF), 276, 366
Industrialization
  in Arizona, 120–123
  in California, 143
  of farms, 162
  Mexican labor (1920s), 193
  movement to cities, 281
  in New Mexico, 276
  societal changes, 103
  in Texas, 79
  U.S. Civil War impact on, 160
  World War I, 171
  World War II, 249
Industrial Workers of the World (IWW), 163, 168, 194, 196, 218
  National Miners Union, 224
Inequality, 279–280. *See also* Civil rights
  in education, 342
  gender, 333
  racism, 408–410
  in 1960s, 291–293
Internal Security Act of 1950, 271
International Ladies Garment Workers Union (ILGWU), 220–221, 363
International Longshore and Warehouse Union (ILWU), 223
International Monetary Fund (IMF), 337, 357
International Service System, Inc. (ISS), 363
The Invasion of the Body Snatchers (film), 357–358
IPP. *See* Independent Progressive Party (IPP)
IQ testing, 185, 225
Iran Contra (unconstitutional operation), 357
Irving, John "Red,", 139

Irving, Leonard, 255
Iturbide, Agustin de, 45
IWW. *See* Industrial Workers of the World (IWW)
Izábal, Rafael, 161

J

Jackson, Andrew, 47, 51
Jackson, Helen Hunt, 131
Japanese-Americans, internment of, 244
Japanese-Mexican Labor Association, 163
Jefferson, Thomas, 44
Jenkins, William W., 140
Johnson, Albert, 184
Johnson, Lyndon Baines (LBJ), 253, 357
   bilingual education and, 296
   campaign, 296
   Chicano's support, 294, 296, 304
   Voting Rights Act, 296
   War on Poverty, 296, 298
Johnson, Vernon, 279
Jones–Costigan Act of 1934, 219
Jones, John B., 77
José, Nicolás, 131
J. R. Norton Company, 364
Juárez, Ciudad, 357
Juntas Patrióticas, 143

K

Kearny, Stephen Watts, 92, 134
Kenedy, Mifflin, 70, 71, 73–76, 79
Kennedy, Edward "Ted," 299, 338
Kennedy, John F., 336, 411
Kennedy, John Fitzgerald, 294, 305
Kennedy, Robert F., 298, 302, 305
Kennedy, Ted, 412
Kennerly, F. M., 212
Kerble, Fred, 74
Kerner, Charles, 77
Kerr, Louise, 228
Keyes, William, 253–254
Kilday, Owen, 221, 222
King, John H., 77
King, Martin Luther, 416
The King Ranch (Lea), 71
King, Richard, 70, 71, 74, 76
King, Rodney, 385

Knights of Labor, 101
Koch, David, 390
Korean War, 267, 269–270
Kovner, Joseph Eli, 282
Ku Klux Klan, 78, 171, 187, 194, 220, 339

L

Lady Kanal-Ikal, 5
Lady Zac-Kuk, 5
Lamar, Mirabeau Buonaparte, 69
Lamy, Fray J. B., 98
Landa, Diego de, 5
Land grants, 95–97, 99, 100, 103, 118, 136
   communal, 35, 94, 95, 102, 309
Land ownership
   in California, 136–139
   in Texas, 69, 70
Land privatization, 383
La Nueva Vida Club, 226
La Opinión (newspaper), 190
LAPD. *See* Los Angeles Police Department
Lara, Severita, 370
La Raza Unida Party (LRUP), 294, 297, 303, 340, 382, 411
Laredo colony, 34
Larkin, Thomas O., 133
Larrazolo, Octaviano A., 104
Las Adelitas, 164
Las Vegas, New Mexico, 92, 100, 101
Latin American immigration, 361
Latino electorate
   California assembly, 332
   electoral politics, 407
   Johnson, Viva (1964), 296
   Kennedy's victory (1960), 294
   Los Angeles politics, 295
   1976, 339
   Nixon, Richard, 331
   People's Party (1890), 102
Laustaunau, Weneslado H., 161
Lau v. Nichols (1974), 341
Law enforcement authorities, 253. *See also* Police brutality; Texas Rangers
   Brown Berets, 307
Lazo, Ralph, 243

League of Revolutionary Struggle (LRS), 332
League of United Latin American Citizens (LULAC), 188–189, 222, 225, 251, 253, 254, 275–280, 291. 294, 300, 339–340, 366
Lea, Tom, 71
Ledesma, Jesse, 279
Ledesma, Josephine, 248–249
Lee, Robert E., 72
Leticia A. v. Board of Regents (1985), 359
Levi Strauss (apparel manufacturer), 364
Lévi-Strauss, Claude, 381
Leyvas, Henry, 246, 253
Leyvas, Lupe, 253
La Liga Femenil Mexicanista (Mexican Feminist League), 166–167
La Liga Obrera de Habla Española (League of Spanish-Speaking Workers), 227
La Liga Pro-Mexicana, 189
La Liga Protectora Latina, 167, 193
Lincoln, Abraham, 45, 52, 53
Lincoln County War (New Mexico), 97
Literacy Act of 1917, 172
Little, James, 116
Livermore, Abiel Abbot, 53
Loaiza, Manuel José, 138
Long, James, 46
Longoria, Felix, 253
López, Felipe, 102
López, Fernando, 74
López, Francisco, 134
López, Ignacio, 227, 277, 281
López, José M., 241
López, Lorenzo, 101
López Tijerina, Reies, 297
Lord, Walter, 48
Lorente, José Antonio, 23
Lorenzana, Apolinaria, 133
Los Angeles, 132, 138, 215, 297, 305, 336
   automakers, 363
   Blade Runner (fiction), 354
   Committee for Protection of Foreign Born, 270, 271
   freeway system in, 274, 282

gang *(pachuco)* violence in, 244–247
Mexican community in, 225–226
Mexican immigrants in, 171, 172, 190–191, 209, 210, 212
Olvera Street, 371–372
plant operation, 354
politics in (1947–1962), 276–277
segregation in, 143, 244, 293
union activism in, 220–223
urban renewal in, 281–282
Los Angeles Police Department (LAPD), 280, 343, 385, 386
Criminal Conspiracy Section (CCS), 315–316
Los Angeles Times (newspaper), 165, 169, 172, 190, 228, 245, 247, 254, 358, 385, 387, 388, 391, 407, 410
Louisiana Purchase, 44, 46
Love, Harry, 141
Lozano, Ignacio, 190
Lozano, Toribio, 77
LRUP. *See* La Raza Unida Party (LRUP)
Luce, John B., 304
Lucey, Robert E., 186, 273, 301, 304
Luckingham, Bradford, 123
Ludlow (Colorado) Massacre (1913), 168
Lugo brothers, 138
Lugo, Don Antonio María, 137
LULAC. *See* League of United Latin American Citizens (LULAC)
Luna, Andrés de, 79
Luna de Rodríguez, Celia, 304
Luna Mont, Julia, 304
Lungren, Dan, 392
Lynchings
in colonization of Texas, 69, 71, 74, 81
in New Mexico, 96, 101

M

MacArthur, General Douglas, 269
Madden, Martin, 184
Madero, Francisco, 164
Madrid, Miguel de la, 383

Magliari, Michael, 135
Magoffin, James W., 92
Magón, Ricardo Flores, 159, 160, 164, 166, 169, 170, 226
Mahoney, Cardinal, 391
Mahoney, Roger, 360
MALDEF. *See* Mexican American Legal Defense and Education Fund (MALDEF)
MAM. *See* Mexican American Movement (MAM)
Mandin, Constant, 161
Maney, Mitch, 97
Manifest Destiny, 52
Manitos, 93, 219–220, 227–228
Mann, Eric, 414
Manteana, Murgía, 160
Manuel, H. T., 225
Manzanar internment camp, 244
Maquiladoras (assembly plants), 299, 337
Mariscal, Juan, 300
Márquez, Robert, 280
Marriage, 8
anti-miscegenation law and, 248
in Arizona, 117–118
in Azteca Empire, 10
intermarriage, 8, 13, 76, 98, 117, 133, 190
in Texas, 76
Marshall, F. Ray, 339
Marten, James, 70, 72
Martínez, Andrés, 74
Martinez, Elizabeth, 353
Martínez, Elizabeth "Betita," 314, 333
Martínez, Fray Antonio José, 92, 96, 98
Martinez, Guillermo Ortiz, 383
Martínez, Ignacio, 82
Martínez, Marty, 383
Martínez, Ramón, 250
Martínez, Refugio Ramón, 223, 271
Martínez, Vicente, 78
Marvin, George, 170
Massey, Douglas S., 392
Mata, Manuel, 280
Maxey, Thomas, 81
Maxwell Land Grant, 96, 97, 103
Maxwell, Lucien, 96

MAYA. *See* Mexican American Youth Association (MAYA)
Maya Arce v. John Huppenthal, 421
Mayan civilization, 4–6, 13
ball game, 4
calendars, 4
decline, 5–6
human sacrifice in, 7
society, 5
May, Cordelia Scaife, 390
MAYO. *See* Mexican American Youth Organization (MAYO)
McAllister, W. W., 294
McCain, John, 412, 415
McCann, De Witt, 282
McCarran–Walter Act of 1952, 271
McCarthyism, 405
McCarthy, Joseph, 269, 278, 311
McCluskey, H. S., 172
McCormick, LaRue, 246
McCormick, Paul J., 252
McDonnell, Donald, 300
McDowell, Mary, 228
McGrath, Alice, 246
McGroarty, John Steven, 131
McKelvey, William, 145
McLean, Robert N., 186
McLeod, Hugh, 92
McNeeley, Matthew M., 184
McNeely, Leander, 74
McWilliams, Carey, 131, 212, 213, 246
Meade, George Gordon, 53
MEChA. *See* Movimiento Estudiantil Chicano/a de Aztlán (MEChA)
Media, 339. *See also* Newspapers; Spanish language publications
Meeropol, Michael, 394
Meléndez, Ambriocio, 302
Mena, Antonia, 211
Mena, Ramón, 159
Menchaca, Antonio, 69
Menchaca, Martha, 57
Méndez, Felicitas, 252
Méndez v. Westminster School District (1946), 252
Mendiola, Enrique, 75
Méndoza, Juana Gutíerrez, 160

Mesoamerica
  calendars in, 3, 4
  early villages, 3
  hieroglyphic writing, 4–5
  homosexuality, 4
  human sacrifice in, 7, 10
  Los Norteños, 10–13
  mathematics in prehistory, 4, 5
  Mayans, 4–6, 13
  migration to and from, 2
  Mixteca civilization, 8, 13
  Oaxaca core zone, 3, 7
  Oco civilization, 3
  Olmeca civilization, 3–4
  Tarasco, 8, 13
  Teotihuacán, 6–7
  trade in, 3, 6–7, 14
  world system (1519), 13–14
  writing, 4, 8
Mestizos, 33, 36, 131, 228
Metropolitan Transportation Authority of Los Angeles (MTA), 363
Mexican(s)
  Americanization of (*See* Americanization)
  in California (*See* Californios)
  in colonization of Texas, 75–76
  in early Arizona, 116–117, 120
  education, 419–421
  immigrant quotas, 183–184
  immigrants, 414
  maquiladoras (factories), 299, 337
  migration to U.S., 157–158, 162
  mining strikes by, in Arizona, 160–161
Mexican American Democrats (MAD), 333, 382
Mexican American Legal Defense and Education Fund (MALDEF), 306, 365–368, 407
Mexican American Movement (MAM), 186, 226, 253, 275
Mexican American Political Association (MAPA), 295, 304, 334
Mexican Americans, 411–412. *See also* Mexican American workers
  in California, 190–191, 268
  in Colorado, 268
  Decade of the Hispanic, 355–356
  discrimination against, 245
  immigration impact on economy, 356–358
  maquila wages, 357
  Mexicans and, 187
  middle class, 187, 274, 280
  nativism and, 300
  in New Mexico, 268
  in Northwest, 302
  population in 1940, 241
  population in 1950s, 268, 299
  regional tensions and, 209
  replicants in 1980s, 354–355
  return of "Sleeping Giant," 360–361
  as scapegoats, 244–245
  scholars characterized, 368–369
  seduction of political game, 365–368
  struggles of Chicana/o organized labor, 360–364
  in Texas, 268
  voting power of, 367–368
  World War I, 187–189
  World War II, 241–242
Mexican American Student Association (MASA), 303
Mexican–American War, 51–52
  American aggression, 51–52
  history as propaganda, 52–53
  invasion of Mexico, 51–52
  manufactured war, 51
  Mexican women in, 54
  San Patricio Battalion (Irish immigrant), 53–54
  treaty ending (*See* Guadalupe Hidalgo Treaty)
  war crimes in, 54
Mexican American workers
  Los Angeles, 190, 220–221
  in Ludlow Massacre (1913), 168
  in Midwest, 195
  in Northwest, 194
  San Antonio's West Side, 189
  strikes, 163, 224
Mexican American Youth Association (MAYA), 292, 294, 295, 304
Mexican American Youth Organization (MAYO), 332, 333, 362
Mexican Colonization Act, 96
Mexican diaspora, 162
Mexican National Brotherhood, 300, 338
Mexican Revolution, 161, 164–167, 169, 188
  Mexicans in, 228
Mexican Ward School, 276
Mexican War of Independence, 35–36
Mexican Youth Party, 228
Mexico. *See also* Mesoamerica; Mexican(s)
  academic freedom, 387–390
  Azteca, 8–10, 13
  Chicana/o identities, 387–390
  corn civilization, 3
  death penalty in, 408
  image and reality loss, California, 131–134
  immigrants, 384
  independence of, 45
  Mayans, 3–5
  NAFTA, 383–384, 395
  1970–1980, 328, 337
  population (1810), 36
  population (1960s), 299
  repatriates, in Depression (1930s), 207, 212–213
  U.S. border issues, 167, 299
  war on drugs, 394–395
  wetbacks, 389
  World War I effects on, 182
Mexico City
  Tlatelolco massacre, 307
  U.S. occupation of, 54, 55
Meyer, Michael, 164–165
Michigan Field Crops, Inc., 257
Michigan, migrant activism in, 302
Middle class
  Chicano, 335, 340
  Mexican American, 187, 228, 274, 280
  Mexican, in Arizona, 122, 167
  Mexican, in Texas, 80, 225, 228
Migration Policy Institute (MPI), 384
Milagro Beanfield War, 367
Milhiser v. Padilla, 100–101
Militarization
  Chicana/o students, 305–306
  of immigration and naturalization, 272–273
  U.S.–Mexican border, 165

Mills, Charles E., 162
Mills, W. W., 77
Mining
 in Arizona, 117–118, 160–161, 169, 196, 249
 bonanzas, 120, 160
 in California, 144
 in Colorado, 99, 100, 102, 157
 copper, 119, 121, 160, 161, 168, 169, 224
 Gold Rush and, 134–136
 Mexican American miners' revolt, 224
 in New Mexico, 103–104
 racial segregation in, 144, 162
 strikes, 159, 196
 unions, 167, 169, 171
Miranda, Guadalupe, 96
Mission Memories (McGroarty), 130
Missions
 Americanization, 186
 in California, 35, 130–131, 133
 Protestant churches, 186
 secularization of, 132–133
Mixteca civilization, 8, 13
Moffatt, Stanley, 254
Mogollon people, 12
Molina de Pick, Gracia, 335
Molina, Gloria, 368
Monopoly (game), 353
Monroe Doctrine, 46
Montalvo, A. L., 80
Montejano, David, 72, 303
Montoya, Nestor, 102
Montoya, Pablo, 92
Moore, Joan W., 210, 245
Moraga, Cherríe, 389
Moralez brothers, 243
Morelos y Pavón, José María, 45
Moreno, Dorinda, 335
Moreno, John, 295
Moreno, Luisa, 218, 226, 227, 251, 254, 271
Morín, Raúl, 241–243
Morris, W. T. "Brack," 78
Morton, Thurston B., 255
Mothers of East Los Angeles, 369
Movimiento Estudiantil Chicano/a de Aztlán (MEChA), 334, 362
Mowry, Sylvester, 115
Moya family, 74

La Mujer Mexicana (magazine), 160
Multiracial Alliance, 363
Munguía, Dora, 210
Murieta, Joaquin, 141–142, 145
Murieta, Mariana, 145
Murphy, Laurence Gustave, 97
Murray, Charles, 390
Murrow, Edward R., 293
Mutualistas (mutual aid societies), 80, 81, 103, 122, 160, 161, 167, 191, 194, 196, 214
 status of women in, 189
 urbanization and, 159, 191, 223
My Confessions (Chamberlain), 54

N

NAACP. *See* National Association for the Advancement of Colored People (NAACP)
Nacogdoches, 69
NAFTA (North American Free Trade Agreement), 57, 383–384, 395
NAS (National Association of Scholars), 387
Nash, June, 10
National Association for the Advancement of Colored People (NAACP), 188, 252, 281, 291
National Association of Latino Elected and Appointed Officials (NALEO), 341, 411
National Association of Scholars (NAS), 387, 390
National Chicano Youth Conference, 334
National Education Association (NEA), 311
National Farm Labor Union (NFLU), 255
National Farm Workers Association (NFWA), 300, 301
National Guard, 165, 168, 279, 297
National Housing Act (1949), 281

Nationalism
 vs. Americanization, 186–187
 Chicano, 333, 336
 Mexican, 143–145
 Tejano, 306
National Labor Relations Act (1935), 218, 226, 254
National Labor Relations Board (NLRB), 224, 250–251, 337, 360
National Miners Union, 224
National Origins Act of 1924, 183
National Recovery Act (NRA), 220, 221
National Spanish-Speaking Council, 280–281
Nativism, 182, 186, 194, 338
 in Arizona, 122
 in Chicago, 223–224
 deportations, 172, 211–213
 Mexican American reaction to, 300
 racist, 80–81, 158, 208, 337
 in Texas, 81
Navarette, Gabriel, 242
Navarrete, Tobias, 271
Navarro, Angel, 70
Navarro, Diego, 140
Navarro, José Antonio, 70, 78
Nelson, Eugene, 301
Neoliberalism, 353, 355–357, 372
New Mexico. *See also* Colonization of New Mexico
 Gallegos family, 273
 inclusion, 94–95, 276
 labor migration from, 219–220
 Mexican population in, 158
 miners' revolt (1930s), 224
 Pueblo Revolt of 1680, 90
 "Salt of the Earth" strike in, 278–279
 Santa Fe Expedition, 69
 student protests in, 303
 workers from, in Colorado, 194
Newspapers, 141, 333, 335. *See also* Spanish language publications; *specific newspapers*
New York Times, 119
Nicaragua, 344

Nicaraguan Adjustment and Central American Relief Act (NACARA), 386
Nieto, A. N., 163
Los Niños Heroes, 55
Nixon, Richard, 255, 269, 298, 332, 394, 395
  Hispanic strategy, 331
NLRB. *See* National Labor Relations Board (NLRB)
No Pasarán (communist organization), 226
Norma Villarreal Ramírez, 370
Norris, Edwin, 92
North American Free Trade Agreement (NAFTA), 57, 383–384, 395
Northwest, Mexicans in, 194, 302
Norton, John R., 364
Nuevo Santander, 34
NWFA. *See* National Farm Workers Association (NFWA)

O

Obama, Barack, 411, 415, 418
Obregón, Alvaro, 183, 191
Obregón, Eugene A., 269
El Obrero (magazine), 159
Obreros Unidos (United Workers), 302
Ochoa, Estevan, 117
Ochoa, Juan, 224
Ochoa, Victor L., 81, 159
Oco civilization, 3
O'Donnell, James, 70
Office of Economic Opportunity (OEO), 296, 298
Ohio, farmworkers in, 302, 336
Olazábal, María, 210
Olbés, Ramón, 131
Olivárez, Graciela Gil, 284, 296
Olivas, B. H., 217
Oliver, Thomas, 116
Olmeca civilization, 3–4
Olmsted, Frederick Law, 69
Olvera Street Merchants Association, 371
Olympiad–XIX, Tlateloco massacre, 307
Operation Blockade, 392
Operation Clean Sweep, 338
Operation Gatekeeper, 360, 392
Operation Wetback, 272
Orden de Caballeros, 188
Orendain, Antonio, 301, 337
Orenstein, Dara, 137
Organization of Petroleum Exporting Countries (OPEC), 343–344
Origins of the War with Mexico (Price), 52
Oropeza, Lorena, 298
Ortiz Equivel, José, 192
Ortiz, Juan Felipe, 92
Ortiz, Rosa, 118
Ortiz, Roxanne Dunbar, 91
Ortiz, Tomás, 91
Ortiz y Pino, Concha, 227
Otero, Miguel A., 94, 98, 101, 103

P

Pacal (Mayan ruler), 5
Padilla, Gil, 300
PADRES (*Padres Asociades para los Derechos Religiosos, Educativos y Sociales*), 312
Palin, Sarah, 415
Pallares, Jesús, 227
Palomares, Frank J., 217
Pan American Conference (1918), 172
Papal Bulls, 240, 241
Paquime (Casas Grandes), 12
Paramount Dress Company strike, 220
Paredes, Américo, 75
Paredes, Mariano, 51
The Parson's Tale (Chaucer), 381
Partido Liberal Mexicano (PLM), 159–161, 165, 166, 169, 172
La Pasionaria (Emma Tenayuca), 221
PASO. *See* Political Association of Spanish-Speaking Organizations (PASO)
Patriarchy, 27–28
  in Arizona, 122–123
Patrón, Juan, 97
Paul, David, 359
Pax, Frank, 228
Paz, Frank, 250
Pearl Harbor (World War II), 240
Pecan Shellers' Strike, 221–222
Pels, M. P., 96
Peña, Albert, Jr., 277, 294, 304, 306, 368
Peña, Federico, 367
Peña, Juan, 224
Peña, Manuel de la, 55
Peña, Olga, 368
Peoples' Party, 80, 102
People's Revolt, 77
People v. Hall (1854), 137
Perales, Alonso S., 79, 188, 249, 251, 254, 258
Peralta, Domingo, 136
Pérez, Andrea, 248
Pérez, Emma, 389
Pérez, Eulalia, 133
Pérez García, Hector, 253
Perrigo, Lynn J., 56
Perry, Rick, 410
Pershing, John J. "Black Jack," 165, 272
Personal Responsibility and Work Opportunity Reconciliation Act of 1996, 395
Peso devaluation, 337
Pesotta, Rose, 220
Pesqueira, Ignacio, 115
Phelps Dodge Mining Company, 121, 162, 167, 224, 249
Phoenix, Arizona, 116, 119
Pico, Andrés, 140, 141
Pico, Pío de Jesús, 132, 141
Pierce, Franklin, 115
Pima Indians, 12, 112, 114, 116–119, 123, 124
Pitt, Leonard, 140
Pizaña, Ancieta, 170
Plan of Iguala, 45
Plan of Santa Barbara, 312, 335
PLM. *See* Partido Liberal Mexicano (PLM)
Pluma Roja (magazine), 160
Polaco, Rafael, 116
Polanco, Richard, 382
Police brutality
  Bloody Christmas case, 280
  Chicana/o responses to, 386
  LAPD, 280
  Leyvas, Lupe, 253
  Reyna, Juan, 191
  Salcido, Agustino, shooting, 253–254
  strikes and, 217
  Texas G.I. Forum and, 279–280

Political Association of Spanish-Speaking Organizations (PASO), 294–295, 302–303
Political discrimination, 389
Politics (1949–1962)
 Chicago, 275, 295
 El Paso, 278
 Los Angeles, 276–277, 295
 New Mexico, 276
 San Antonio, 277–278, 294–295
Polk, James K., 51–53, 55, 56, 133
Pomeroy, John L., 208
Pompa, Aurelio, 191
Pools, segregation of, 227, 281
Population. *See also* U.S. Census
 in Mexico (1840s–1910), 157
Porfiriato, 158, 159, 164, 166. *See also* Díaz, Porfirio
Porter, William, 115
Postclassic period, 2
Poston, Charles, 115
Poulson, Norris, 282
Poverty, 292–293. *See also* War on Poverty
 Chicago, 293
 El Paso, 292
 Los Angeles, 293
 San Antonio, 292
Poverty in the Land of Plenty (film), 255
Powderly, Terence, 101
Powers, Stephen, 78
Pren, Karen A., 392
La Prensa (newspaper), 188, 189, 222
Presidential Elections
 2004, 413
 2008, 415
Price, Glenn W., 52
Price, Sterling, 92
Primitive Rebels (Hobsbawm), 76
Prince, Le Baron Bradford, 96, 101
Privatization, 372
Prize, Pulitzer, 240
Professional Air Traffic Controllers Organization (PATCO), 360
Proposition 13, 330, 421
Proposition 22, 336
Proposition 30, 421
Proposition 32, 421
Proposition 63, 390

Proposition 187 (Save Our State), 390, 391
Proposition 209, 391
Proposition 227, 391, 392
Protestant churches, 94, 98, 192, 209, 211, 300
 Americanization and, 186, 226
Proudhon, Joseph, 159
Prycior, Julie Leininger, 296
Pryke, Raymond, 421
Public Disorder Intelligence Department (PDID), 362
Public Law 99-603 (Immigration Act of 1986), 354
Puche, Jaime Serra, 383
Pueblo people, 12, 92, 95
 revolt by (1680), 90
Puerto Rico, 336

Q

Quevedo, Eduardo, 226, 251
Quicksilver Mining Company, 144
Quintana, Andrés, 131

R

Race/racism, 57, 96. *See also* Racist nativism
 in Arizona, 116–117
 categories in New Spain, 35–36
 death penalty and, 408–410
 education and, 186
 eugenics and, 211, 336
 inventing whiteness, 93–94, 137
 in Los Angeles, 138, 247
 in Marines, 242
 media and, 339
 Mexican Revolution and, 164
 in Midwest, 195
 police brutality, 386
 purity of blood (*limpieza de sangre*), 114, 132
 real estate sales, 284
 skin color and, 68, 76, 93–94
 in Texas, 74, 76, 79, 80, 168, 256
 xenophobia and, 157, 164
Racist nativism, 80–81, 208, 337, 390. *See also* Nativism
Railroads, 79, 97, 99, 137, 143, 157–159, 170, 195, 223, 248
 in Arizona, 118, 120, 121, 123, 208
 bracero program and, 250

Ramírez, Catherine Sue, 245
Ramírez, Francisco, 139–141
Ramírez, Sara Estela, 160
Ramona (Jackson), 131
Ramos, Basilio, 170
Rampart Community Resources Against Street Hoodlums (CRASH), 386
Raza Unida Party. *See* La Raza Unida Party (LRUP)
Reagan, Ronald, 341, 353, 355, 390, 394, 415, 416
Recessions
 1920–1921, 183, 195, 206
 1949, 272
 1953–1955, 272
 1958, 257
 1973–1974, 337
 1973–1975, 337
Reed, Charles, 116
Regeneración (newspaper), 159, 166, 169, 170
Reich, Robert B., 355
Religion. *See also* Catholic Church; Missions; Protestant churches
 in Azteca civilization, 10
 in Great Depression, 209, 211
 intermarriage and, 78
 in Mayan society, 5
 in Tolteca civilization, 7
 in Zapoteca civilization, 8
Rendón, Armando, 56
Repartimiento, 193
Report of the Immigrant Commission, 162, 164
Reyes Berreyesa, José de los, 134
Reyna, Juan, 191
Reynoso, Cruz, 358
Rhodes, Thaddeus, 74
Rican, Puerto, 252
Richardson, Bill, 367, 408
Ringgold, Jeanne Parks, 160
Rio Abajo, 33, 90
Rio Arriba area, 91, 94, 99
Rio Bravo, 51, 164
Rio Grande, 51, 55, 68, 91, 95
Rio Grande Valley, 162, 209, 212, 219, 268
Riordan, Richard, 421
Risco, Eleazar, 304
Rivas, Henrietta López, 249
Rivera, Columba, 160
Rivera, Librado, 159

Roberto Alvarez v. Board of Trustees of the Lemon Grove School District, 208
Robledo, Refugia, 78
Rock and roll generation, 291
Rodino, Peter, 338
Rodríguez, Antonio, 164
Rodríguez, Armando, 297
Rodríguez, Elisa, 248
Rodríguez, Ramón, 78
Rodríguez, Steve, 365
Roe v. Wade (1973), 336
Romero, Gloria, 408
Romero, Tomasito, 92
Romney, Mitt, 415
Romo, Adolpho "Babe," Sr., 186
Romo, Reginaldo, 254
Ronquillo, Rosalio, 248
Ronstadt, Féderico José María, 122
Roosevelt, Eleanor, 247
Roosevelt, Franklin D., 207, 221, 244, 249, 267, 275, 296
Rosales, Rodolfo, 366
Rosenfeld, Bernard, 336
Ross, Fred, 252, 253, 277, 300
Roybal, Edward R., 276–277, 295, 297, 341, 355
Rubio Goldsmith, Raquel, 119
Rugh, Jacob S., 392
Ruiz, Alejo, 78
Ruiz, Antonio, 140
Ruiz, Dennis, 249
Ruiz, Virginia, 280
Ryan, George, 408

S

Sáenz, J. Luz, 170, 187
Saenz, Thomas A., 407
Salas, Jesús, 301
Salazar Rosales, Rosa, 335
Sálaz, Rubén, 94
Salcido, Abraham, 160, 161
Salcido, Agustino, 253, 254
Salt of the Earth strike, 278–279
Salt War, 77
Salyer, Clarence "Cockeye," 217
Samaniego, M. G., 117, 118
San Antonio, 71, 79, 303, 335
  Canary Islanders in, 72
  Farah strike, 337
  machine politics in, 78
  Mexican population in, 172, 274
  mutualistas in, 191
  Pecan Shellers' Strike, 221–222
  poverty in (1960s), 292
  Rio Bravo links, 34
  school segregation in, 225
  school walkout in, 306
  Tejano elite, 68
  Texas politics and, 277–278, 294–295
  West Side, 189–190, 211, 274
  women workers' strikes, 221
San Antonio School District v. Rodriguez (1968), 341
Sánchez, Agustín, 189
Sánchez brothers, 243
Sánchez, David, 304, 305
Sánchez, E. R., 253, 254
Sánchez, George I., 185, 190, 225–227, 251, 258, 276, 280, 281, 294, 297
Sánchez, Graciela, 370
Sánchez, José María, 169
Sánchez, Juan, 409, 411
Sánchez, Margil, 301
Sánchez, Tomás, 34, 138
Sánchez, Tony, 410
San Francisco, Fray Garcia de, 33
San Jacinto, battle of, 51
San Joaquin valley cotton strike, 216–217
  La Crisis, 208
  Tagus Ranch, 215
San Joaquín valley cotton strike, 216–217
San Román, José, 72
Santa Anna, Antonio López de, 45, 47–49
La Santa de Cabora. See Urrea, Teresa
Santa Fe, 69, 98
  New Mexican (newspaper), 96
  Santa Fe Ring, 96–97
Santa Fe Trail, 91–92
Santistevan, Jacinto, 96
Santos Benavides, Colonel, 73
Scaife, Richard Mellon, 390
Schools. *See* Education
Schwarzenegger, Arnold, 417
Scott, Robin, 190, 241
Scott, Winfield, 55
Sebree, Victor, 81
Segovia, Josefa (Juanita), 138
Segregation, 246
  Americanization programs and, 185, 208
  in education, 185, 279
  fighting against, 194, 227
  in Los Angeles, 143, 244, 293
  LULAC and, 225
  Menchaca citing, 57
  of Mexican children, 163, 185, 208
  in mining, 144
  Tolleson school district suit, 279
  white flight and, 281
  white population and, 293
Seguin, Juan, 68
Selective Service System, 270
Sensenbrenner, Jim, 414
Serna, Marcelino, 171
Serra, Junípero, 35, 131
Serrano v. Priest (1968), 341
Servicemen's Readjustment Act (1944), 258, 281
Seward, William, 70
Sharecropping, 73, 213, 219
Sheep raising, 77, 91, 94, 97, 119
Sheep Shearers Union (SSU), 219
Sheridan, Thomas, 118, 209
Shirlee Frock Company, 221
La Siempreviva, 159
Silex, Humberto, 224, 271
Silver, 68, 116
Sisneros, Samuel E., 94
Skin color, 68, 76, 93–94. *See also* Race/racism
Skinning Wars, 74
Slavery
  in Arizona, 114
  in California, 135
  cannibalism and, 114
  emancipation, 73
  forced labor draft and, 132
  in New Mexico, 33, 95
  in Texas, 45, 46, 70
Sleepy Lagoon trial, 245–246
Slidell, John, 51
Sloat, John Drake, 134
Small pox, 130, 143
Smith, Justin H., 52
Smith, Persifor F., 135

Smith, Peter, 168
Snively, Jacob, 92
Social Action Training Center, 304
Social banditry, 77, 141–143
Socialist Workers Party, 333
La Sociedad de Madres Mexicanas, 191
La Sociedad de Obreros Libres (Free Workers Society), 194, 223
La Sociedad Hispanoamerica de Beneficio Mutua, 143
La Sociedad Mexicana, 82
La Sociedad Mutualista de Obreros Libres Mexicanos (Mutual Aid Society of Free Mexican Workers), 193
La Sociedad Protección Mutua de Trabajadores Unidos, 103
Solis, Hilda, 415
Solíz, Juan, 367
Somoza, Anastacio, 344
Sonora, Arizona and, 112, 113, 164
Sonora Town, 371
Sotomayor, Sonia, 419
Soto, Phil, 295
Southern Farmers Tenant Union (SFTU), 219
Southern Pacific Railroad, 120, 123, 137, 143, 167, 170, 208, 248, 250
Southwest Voter Registration and Education Project (SVREP), 365
Spain/New Spain
 colonization of Texas, 33–34
 Florida, 46
 Indios bárbados (barbaric Indians), 57
Spanish American Mothers and Wives Association, 248
Spanish–American War, 81
Spanish language
 in broadcasting, 209
 in education, 185
 See also Bilingual education
Spanish language publications, 167, 168, 187, 191, 227
 in Arizona, 118–120
 in California, 139, 226
Specter, Arlen, 412

Spell, Lota M., 51
Spencer, Glenn, 388
Speyer, Albert, 92
Spicer, Edward H., 12
Sports
 in Mayan civilization, 4
 Mexican baseball league, 209
Sputnick Moment (1957), 283
Stearns, Abel, 138
Steel Workers Organizing Committee (SWOC), 223, 224
Sterilization, 336
Stevenson, Coke, 256
Stillman, Charles, 70, 72
Stiringo, Charles A., 102
Stock Raisers Association of Western Texas, 74
Stockton, Robert F., 134
Stone, Charles P., 115
Student activism. *See* University headings; Walkouts (school)
Student Nonviolent Coordinating Committee (SNCC), 303, 310
Suárez, Amadeo, 284
Subia, Pedro, 217
Sugar-beet industry, 100, 161, 163, 166, 171, 193–194, 196, 219–220
SVREP. *See* Southwest Voter Registration and Education Project (SVREP)
Swing, General Joseph M., 272
SWOC. *See* Steel Workers Organizing Committee (SWOC)

T

Tafoya, Gabriel, 302
Taft–Hartley Act (1947), 250
Taft–Hartley Act (1948), 421
Talamantes, Armando Villarreal y, 69
Taos, New Mexico, 91
Tarasco civilization, 8
Taylor, Paul S., 195–196
Taylor, Rebecca, 221, 226
Taylor, Robert, 72
Taylor, Zachary, 51–54
Teamsters Union, 301, 336

Tejanos, colonization of Texas and, 68, 72
Telles, Raymond, 278
Téllez, Louis, 243
The Tempest (Shakespeare), 418
Temporary protected status (TPS), 385, 386
Tenayuca, Emma, 222
Tenney Committee, 246, 251, 255
Teotihuacán, 6–7
Terrorism, 307, 339, 411
Texas. *See also* Colonization of Texas
 agriculture in, 162
 cotton growers in, 47, 72, 73, 79–80, 172, 213, 257
 death penalty in, 408
 expedition into New Mexico, 92
 farmworker activism in, 301–302, 336
 G.I. Forum, 280
 Good Neighbor Commission of, 256
 invasion of, 45–51
 La Raza Unida Party, 332–333
 Mexican population in, 158, 187, 194–195
 migration in 1990s, 392–393
 repatriation program in, 212
 rural workers in, 213, 219
 Tex-Mexican organizations in, 225
 Tombstone, Arizona, 117
 U.S. annexation of, 45, 51
Texas Agriculture Organizing Committee, 219
Texas Rangers, 54, 74, 75, 77–79, 187, 219, 254, 294, 301
The Texas Rangers, The Great Plains, and *Divided We Stand* (Webb), 75
Textile industry, 159, 171, 337
Thatcher, Margaret, 353, 390, 415
The New Mexican (newspaper), 97
They Made Me a Criminal (film, 1939), 245
Thompson v. Doaksum (1886), 144

Thoreau, Henry David, 52
Tikal (Mayan city), 5
Tlaxcala people, 34
Tohono O'odhams, 12, 112, 114, 116, 118
Tolby, T. J., 96, 97
Tolteca civilization, 7
Tombstone, Arizona, 117
Torres, Carmelita, 169
Torres, Francisco, 145
Torres Vásquez, Anna, 243
Toypurina rebellion, 131
TPS (Temporary protected status), 385, 386
El Trabajo (newspaper), 192
Trade Union Unity League, 214
Tranchese, Carmelo, 211
Transcontinental Treaty (1819), 46
Travis, William Barret, 48
Treaty of Tordesillas (1494), 240
Trexler, Richard, 4
Trist, Nicholas, 55, 56
Trujillo, William, 223
Truman, Harry, 256, 270, 271, 275
Trump, Donald, 409
Tucson, 114
   Americanization in, 117–118
   middle-class Mexicans in, 167
   mob violence in, 116
   Sonoran gateway, 119, 122
Tula (Tolteca city), 7
Tunstall, John H., 97
Turner, Timothy G., 228
Twenty-first century, 404
20th century (1880–1920). *See also* World War I
   Arizona mining strikes, 160–161
   community defense, 163–164, 166–167
   cotton and Mexican workers, 172
   industrial bonanzas, 160
   Mexican American workplace, 162–163
   Mexican diaspora, 162
   Mexican Revolution, 161, 164–167, 169, 187
   Mexican workers under siege, 168–169
   racism, 161
   railroad, impact on, 157–160, 162–164, 166–168
   San Diego plan, 170
Tzintzuntzán, 8

U

UCAPAWA. *See* United Cannery, Agricultural, Packing, and Allied Workers of America
UFW. *See* United Farm Workers (UFW)
Undocumented immigrants, 363
Undocumented workers, 212, 255, 338–339
Unidad Para Siempre (Unity Forever), 337
La Unión de Repatriados Mexicanos (Union of Mexican Repatriates), 213
La Unión Federal Mexicana, 163
La Unión Protectora (Protective Union), 193
United Auto Workers (UAW), 336
United Cannery, Agricultural, Packing, and Allied Workers of America (UCAPAWA), 218, 219, 222, 226, 251
United Farm Workers (UFW), 302–304, 336, 340
United Farm Workers Organizing Committee (UFWOC), 301
United Mexican American Students (UMAS), 303, 305
United Mine Workers of America, 224
El Universal (newspaper), 183
Universities
   Chicano student activism, 303
   Chicano Studies in, 334–335
   legacy admits in, 343
University of Arizona, 303, 314, 389
University of California, 303, 311, 335, 342, 359, 388, 418
   UCLA (Los Angeles), 226, 275, 314, 334, 388, 389
University of Chicago, 223, 228, 283
University of Maryland, 383
University of New Mexico, 226
University of Texas, 248, 258, 292, 335
Urbanization
   and Mexican immigrants, 189–193
   mutualistas and, 159
   in Teotihuacán, 6
Urban renewal, 281–282
   in midwest, 283
Urquides, María, 296
Urrea, José de, 50
Urrea, Teresa, 82, 159, 161
U.S. Census
   1880 (Texas), 80
   1910, 192
   1930, 208, 210
   1940, 252
   1960, 292, 294
   2000, 405–407
   cities (1950), 273–276
   education levels, 276
   Latino population (1950), 268, 273, 274
   Latinos in, 241
   Mexican 1980, 354
   Mexican (1840s–1910), 157
   Mexicans in Chicago, 191
   political representation in 1990s, 381–382
U.S. corporations. *See* Maquiladoras (assembly plants)
U.S. Immigration and Customs Enforcement (ICE), 405
U.S. State Department, 184
U.S. v. City of Los Angeles (1985), 365
Utah, Mexicans in, 194

V

Valdés, Dennis Nodín, 257
Valenzuela, Juan, 159
Valenzuela, Miguel, 361
Vallejo, Mariano, 134, 136
Vallejo, Salvador, 136
Vásquez, Enriqueta Longeaux y, 311, 333

Vásquez, Tiburcio, 142–143
Vásquez, Tomás, 74
Vega, Cruz, 96
Velarde, Leandro, 224
Velasco, Carlos I., 122
Velasco, Treaty of (1836), 51
Velásquez, Baldemar, 302
Velásquez, Willie, 306
Vélez-Ibañez, Carlos, 11, 34, 167, 269
Venegas, Blas, 159
Venegas, Ricardo, 280
Vera Cruz, 165
Veracruz, 3, 55
Vera, Yolanda, 369
Victoria, Guadalupe, 45
Vidal, Adrián J., 73
Vidal, Petra Vela de, 76
Vietnam War, 291, 298, 304
Vigilantism, 70, 71, 74. *See also* Ku Klux Klan
 in California, 137
 White Caps, 77, 81, 101–102
Vigil, Ernesto, 361
Villaescusa, Henrietta, 296
Villa, Francisco "Pancho," 164, 165, 169, 272
Villalobos, Frank, 371
Villanueva, Tomás, 303
Villaraigosa, Antonio, 407, 410
Villareal, Antonio I., 159
Villareal, Teresa, 160
Villa, Rubén, 241
Violent Gang Task Force, 385
Virgin of Guadalupe, 54
Visel, C. P., 212
Vista (magazine), 364
Vitenam War, 242
Vogel, Clarence F., 224
Voices of Citizens Together (VCT), 390, 391
Voting Rights Act (1965), 296, 340, 365
La Voz del Pueblo (newspaper), 102, 301–302

W

Wage inequality, 415
Walker, William, 46, 139
Walkouts (school), 296–297, 305–306, 335
Wallace, Lew, 97
"Wall of Shame" (Berlin Wall), 359
Walls and Mirrors (Gutiérrez), 187
War, 74, 77. *See also* Civil War; Mexican–American War; War on Poverty; World War I; World War II
 Arab–Israeli, 343
 Azteca and, 10
 on drugs, 385, 394–395
 Spanish–American, 81
War Manpower Commission, 249
War of Independence, Mexican, 35–36
War on Poverty, 331
 bureaucratic conflict, 298
 impact on African Americans, 297–298
 impact on Mexican Americans, 298
 Johnson administration, 296–298
The War with Mexico Reviewed (Livermore), 53
The War with Mexico (Smith), 52
Washington (state), 302
Water rights, 91, 95, 123–124
Watkins, Janice Elaine, 69
Webb, Clive, 71, 116, 134, 136
Webb, Walter Prescott, 75, 170
Weber, Devra, 216
Weinberger, Caspar W., 357
Wells, James B., 78, 79
Werdel, Thomas H., 255
Western Federation of Miners (WFM), 100, 123, 163, 169
Wheatland Hop Field Riot (1913), 168
White Anglo Saxon Protestant (WASP), 183
White Caps, 77, 81, 101–102
White, Theodore, 299
Whitman, Meg, 418
Whitman, Walt, 52
William C. Velásquez Institute (WCVI), 306
Willis, Frank B., 184

Wilson, Pete, 388, 390, 418
Wilson, Woodrow, 165
Women. *See also* Gender gap; Marriage
 "Amazons" protest, 169
 Azteca, 8–10
 in California, 133
 feminism, 333
 garment workers, 171, 220–221
 Great Depression, 209–210
 immigrant workers, 369
 in *maquiladoras*, 299
 Mayan, 5
 Mexican feminists, 159
 in Midwest communities, 192–193
 in mutualistas, 189
 native, 35
 in New Mexico, 98–100, 103
 soldaderas, in Mexican-American War, 54
 supporting role, in strikes, 216–217, 279, 337
 union organizing, 251
 in War on Poverty, 296
 in World War II, 243
Women's Air Force Service Pilots (WASP), 243
Woodman, Lyman, 71
Wool trade, 27. *See also* Sheep raising
Works Progress Administration (WPA), 207
World system (1519), 13–14
World War I (effects, 1920s)
 Americanization, 185–187
 Catholic Churches, 186
 depression after (1921), 183
 industrial transformation, Mexican responses, 171
 Mexican Americans, impact, 187, 189
 Mexican union formation, 195–197
 nationalism *vs.* Americanization, 186–187
 political consciousness, 170–171
 Protestant churches, 186

World War II
  all-Mexican unit, 242–243
  begninning of, 240
  bracero program, 250, 255–257, 275
  Chicanas in military, 243
  civil rights agenda, 252, 291
  Fair Employment Practices Commission, 249–250
  gangs (barrio clubs), 244–247
  Guy Gabaldón case, 242
  industrialization model, 354
  Mexican American organizations, 248
  Mexican Americans in, 241–242, 283
  Mexicanas break barriers, 248
  mutiny (Los Angeles), 246–248
  postwar opportunities, 252–257
  profile of courage (Lazo, Ralph), 243–244
  racism at home and abroad, 243
  union activism in, 224
Wyman, Rosalind, 295

X
Ximenes, Vicente, 296

Y
Yaquí people, 13, 161
Yokut people, 35
Young Chicanos for Community Action, 304
Young Men's Christian Association (YMCA), 209, 226
Young Women's Christian Association (YWCA), 334
Ytúrria, Francisco, 72
Yturris, Rafael, 78
Yzaguirre, Raul, 355, 372

Z
Zapata, Dolores Correa de, 160
Zapata, Emiliano, 164, 384
Zapoteca civilization, 7–8, 13
Zarco, María Sandoval de, 160
Zedillo, Ernesto, 383
Zimmerman, August, 254
La Zona Libre, 71
Zoot Suiters (*pachucos*), 244, 246–247